URAL MTS.

R U S S I A

Volga

Moscow

Tallinn
ONIA

ATVIA

IA
S

BELARUS

K A Z A K H S T A N

Dnestr

Dnepr

Donets

UKRAINE

THIAN MTS.

Don

MOLDOVA
Chisinau

MANIA

de
Bucharest

Aral
Sea

Sofia
BULGARIA

kopje
ONIA

CE

CAUCASUS MTS.

Black Sea

GEORGIA
Tbilisi

Caspian
Sea

UZBEKISTAN

ARMENIA
Yerevan

Baku
AZERBAIJAN

Ankara

TURKMENISTAN

TURKEY

Ashkabad

Athens

Euphrates

Tigris

Tehran

IRAN

AFGHANISTAN

Nicosia
CYPRUS

SYRIA

Beirut
LEBANON

Damascus

Baghdad
IRAQ

a

ISRAEL
Jerusalem

Amman

JORDAN

Cairo

Kuwait
KUWAIT

PAKISTAN

EGYPT

Nile

Red
Sea

S A U D I
A R A B I A

Persian
Gulf

UNITED ARAB
EMIRATES

OMAN

QATAR

THE
WESTERN
HERITAGE

THE WESTERN HERITAGE

FIFTH EDITION

Donald Kagan
Yale University

Steven Ozment
Harvard University

Frank M. Turner
Yale University

PRENTICE HALL, *Upper Saddle River, New Jersey 07458*

Library of Congress Cataloging-in-Publication Data

Kagan, Donald.
The Western Heritage / Donald Kagan, Steven Ozment, Frank M.
Turner.—5th ed.
    p.   cm.
"Combined volume."
Includes bibliographical references and index.
ISBN 0-02-363262-3
1. Civilization, Western.   I. Ozment, Steven.   II. Turner, Frank
M. (Frank Miller).   III. Title.
CB245.K28   1995
909'.09812—dc20   94-20481
                                                        CIP

Editor: Robert Miller and Steve Dalphin
Development Editor: David Chodoff
Production Supervisor: Ann-Marie WongSam and J. Edward Neve
Production Manager: Nicholas Sklitsis
Art Director: Pat Smythe
Text Designer: Andrew Zutis
Cover Designer: Jeannette Jacobs
Cover Art: Jean Bourdichon, *The Four States of
Society: Work*, c. 1500. Manuscript illumination.
École des Beaux Arts, Paris, France.
[Giraudon/Art Resource, N.Y.]
Photo Director: Chris Migdol
Photo Researcher: Diana Gongora
Maps: Maryland Cartographics

© 1995 by Prentice-Hall, Inc.
A Simon & Schuster / A Viacom Company
Upper Saddle River, New Jersey 07458

Printed in the United States of America

10 9 8 7 6 5 4

ISBN 0-02-363262-3

Prentice-Hall International (UK) Limited, *London*
Prentice-Hall of Australia Pty. Limited, *Sydney*
Prentice-Hall Canada Inc., *Toronto*
Prentice-Hall Hispanoamericana, S.A., *Mexico*
Prentice-Hall of India Private Limited, *New Delhi*
Prentice-Hall of Japan, Inc., *Tokyo*
Simon & Schuster Asia Pte. Ltd., *Singapore*
Editora Prentice-Hall do Brasil, Ltda., *Rio de Janeiro*

Preface

The heritage of Western civilization has perhaps never been the focus of so much interest and controversy as it is today. Many commentators criticize it, many praise it, but for all it is a subject of intense discussion. *The Western Heritage,* fifth edition, is designed to allow teachers to introduce students to the subject of that discussion. It presents an overview of Western civilization, including its strengths, its weaknesses, and the controversies surrounding it.

On campus after campus, every aspect of Western civilization has become an object of scrutiny and debate. Many participants in this debate fail to recognize that such self-criticism is characteristic of Western civilization and an important part of its heritage. We welcome the debate and hope that this book can help raise its quality.

The collapse of Communism has left the people of half of Europe struggling to reorganize their political institutions and their social and economic lives. The choices they are making and the future they are forging will reflect in large measure their understanding of their heritage. To follow and participate in that process we too need to understand that heritage.

Goals of the Text

Since *The Western Heritage* first appeared, we have sought to provide our readers with a work that does justice to the richness and variety of Western civilization. Events since then have only added urgency to our purpose.

Our primary goal has been to present a strong, clear narrative account of the central developments in Western history. We have also sought to call attention to certain critical themes:

- the development of political freedom, constitutional government, and concern for the rule of law and individual rights

- the shifting relations among religion, society, and the state

- the development of science and technology and their expanding impact on thought, social institutions, and everyday life

- the major religious and intellectual currents that have shaped Western culture

We believe that these themes have been fundamental in Western civilization, shaping the past and exerting a continuing influence on the present.

BALANCED AND FLEXIBLE PRESENTATION In this edition as in past editions, our goal has been to present Western civilization fairly, accurately, and in a way that does justice to its great variety. History has many facets, no one of which alone can account for the others. Any attempt to tell the story of the West from a single overarching perspective, no matter how timely, is bound to neglect or suppress some important part of that story.

The Western Heritage, fifth edition, is designed to accommodate a variety of approaches to a course in Western civilization, allowing teachers to stress what is most important to them. Some teachers will ask students to read all the chapters. Others will select among them to reinforce assigned readings and lectures.

We do not believe that a history of the West should be limited to politics and international relations, but we share the conviction that internal and external political events have shaped the Western experience in fundamental and powerful ways. Recent events in central and eastern Europe and the former Soviet Union have strengthened that belief. We have also been told repeatedly by teachers that no matter what their own historical specialization, they believe that a political narrative gives students an effective tool to begin to organize their understanding of the past.

The Western Heritage also provides one of the richest accounts of the social history of the West available today, with strong coverage of family life, the roles of women, and the place of the family in relation to broader economic, political, and social developments. This coverage reflects the explosive growth in social historical research in the past quarter century, which has enriched virtually all areas of historical study.

Finally, no other survey text presents so full an account of the religious and intellectual development of the West. People may be political and social beings, but they are also reasoning and spiritual beings. What they think and believe are among the most important things we can know about them. Their ideas about God, society, law, gender, human nature, and the physical world have changed over the centuries and continue to change. We cannot fully grasp our own approach to the world without understanding the intellectual currents of the past and their influence on our thoughts and conceptual categories.

CLARITY AND ACCESSIBILITY Good narrative history requires clear, vigorous prose. We have paid careful attention to the quality of our writing in this edition, subjecting every paragraph to critical scrutiny and making this the most thorough revision of the text we have yet undertaken. Our goal was to make our presentation fully accessible to students without compromising vocabulary or conceptual level. We hope this effort will benefit both teachers and students.

RECENT SCHOLARSHIP As in previous editions, changes in this edition reflect our determination to incorporate the most recent developments in historical scholarship and the expanding concerns of professional historians.

Changes in the Fifth Edition

This edition of *The Western Heritage* includes several new pedagogical features, many content revisions, and a new four-color design.

NEW PEDAGOGICAL FEATURES Important new pedagogical features in this edition include part-opening comparative timelines, a list of key topics at the beginning of each chapter, chapter review questions, and questions accompanying the more than 200 source documents in the text. Each of these features is designed to make the text more accessible to students and to reinforce key concepts.

- The *part-opening timelines*, which follow the essays that open each of the six parts of the book, summarize major events in politics and government, society and economy, and religion and culture side by side.
- The *key topics* lists give a succinct overview of each chapter.
- *Questions accompanying the source documents* direct students toward important, thought-provoking issues and help them relate the documents to the material in the text. They can be used to stimulate class discussion or as topics for essays and study groups.
- *Chapter review questions* help students review the material in a chapter and relate it to broader themes. They too can be used for class discussion and essay topics.

In addition, as in the last edition, each chapter includes

- an *outline*
- *introductory* and *concluding sections*
- several *timelines* and *chronologies*
- an average of seven *primary source documents,* more than one third new to this edition, that acquaint students with the raw material of history and provide intimate contact with the people of the past and their concerns
- a *suggested readings* list updated with new titles reflecting recent scholarship

CONTENT CHANGES Over the years we have been fortunate in both the positive responses and constructive criticism we have received from readers and teachers. The major revisions in this edition reflect what we genuinely regard as the ongoing partnership between our readers and ourselves. Responding to suggestions, we have in this edition made a number of extensive changes in our coverage and organization.

- Chapter 1, "The Birth of Civilization" has been revised to reflect current scholarship on the prehistoric period and the ancient Middle East.

- New material on slavery in ancient Greece and Rome has been added to Chapter 3, "Classical and Hellenistic Greece," Chapter 4, "Rome: From Republic to Empire," and Chapter 5, "The Roman Empire."

- The coverage of Islam and the Byzantine Empire in Chapter 6, "The Early Middle Ages (476–1000)," has been further expanded.

- A new section on medieval Russia has been added to Chapter 7, "The High Middle Ages (1000–1300): The Ascendancy of the Church and the Rise of States."

- The discussion of the Hundred Years' War and the Great Schism in Chapter 9, "The Late Middle Ages (1300–1527)," has been thoroughly revised.

- Chapter 10, "Renaissance and Discovery," contains a new section on Christine de Pisan and revised material on Humanism and on the Spanish Empire in the New World.

- Chapter 11, "The Age of Reformation," has been extensively reorganized.

- Chapter 13, "Paths to Constitutionalism and Absolutism," has been wholly rewritten for clarity and to bring it up to date with current scholarship.

- Chapter 14, "New Directions in Thought and Culture in The Sixteenth and Seventeenth Centuries," has been reorganized and now includes the section on witchcraft previously in Chapter 12.

- Chapter 16, "Society and Economy Under the Old Regime in The Eighteenth Century," has been substantially reorganized and includes a new section on the emergence of a consumer economy.

- New material on women in the Enlightenment and the emergence of a print culture has been added to Chapter 18, "The Age of Enlightenment."

- New material on women in the French Revolution has been added to Chapter 19, "The French Revolution."

- Chapter 21, "Restoration, Reaction, and Reform (1815–1832)," has been substantially revised and contains a new section on the character of nationalism.

- New material on late nineteenth- and early twentieth-century women's history has been added to Chapter 24, "The Building of European Supremacy."

- Chapter 25, "The Birth of Modern European Thought," has new sections on modernism and on women and modern thought.

- Chapter 27, "Political Experiments of the 1920s," has been reorganized.

- Chapter 31, "Toward a New Europe and the Twenty-first Century," has been substantially reworked with comprehensive new material on post-World War II social history and the most extensive coverage of recent events in eastern Europe to be found in any western history textbook.

MAPS AND ILLUSTRATIONS Probably the most striking change for readers familiar with previous editions of *The Western Heritage* is the introduction of color throughout the text. The benefits of this change are most apparent in maps and illustrations. The skillful use of color in the maps greatly improves their clarity and pedagogical usefulness. All 90 maps in the text have been carefully edited for accuracy and redrafted to take advantage of the new four-color design. The text also contains almost 500 color and black and white illustrations.

Ancillary Instructional Materials

The Western Heritage, fifth edition, comes with an extensive package of ancillary materials.

- **Instructor's Manual** with test items prepared by Perry M. Rogers of Ohio State University. This includes chapter summaries, key points and vital concepts, identification questions, multiple-choice questions, essay questions, and suggested films.

- **Map Transparencies** in full color of all maps in the text.

- **Telecourse**, *The Western Tradition*, an Annenberg/CPB project, with *Study Guides*,

Volumes I and II, and *Administrative Handbook* by Jay Boggis.

- **Study Guide** prepared by Anthony M. Brescia of Nassau Community College that includes commentary, definitions, identifications, map exercises, short-answer exercises, and essay questions.

- **Computerized Study Guide** consisting of 15 multiple-choice questions from each chapter with reinforcing feedback on correct answers and clarifying feedback on wrong answers. All answers are cross-referenced to the text.

- **Computerized Test Bank** consisting of more than 1500 multiple-choice and essay questions from the *Instructor's Manual* for IBM compatible and Macintosh systems.

Acknowledgments

We are grateful to the scholars and teachers whose thoughtful and often detailed comments helped shape this revision:

Lenard R. Berlanstein, *University of Virginia, Charlottesville*
Stephanie Christelow, *Idaho State University*
Robert L. Ervin, *San Jacinto Community College*
Victor Davis Hanson, *California State University, Fresno*
Pardaic Kenny, *University of Colorado, Boulder*
Raymond F. Kierstead, *Reed College*
Robert J. Mueller, *Hastings College*
John Nicols, *University of Oregon, Eugene*
Sandra J. Peacock, *State University of New York, Binghamton*
Robert A. Schneider, *Catholic University*
Sidney R. Sherter, *Long Island University*
Roger P. Snow, *College of Great Falls*

Finally, we would like to thank the dedicated people who helped produce this revision: our acquisitions editors, Robert Miller and Steve Dalphin; our development editor, David Chodoff; our photo director Chris Migdol and photo researcher Diana Gongora; Andy Zutis and Pat Smythe, who were responsible for the new design of this edition; John Sollami, managing editor; Ann-Marie WongSam, J. Edward Neve, and Camilla Hewitt, production supervisors; and Nick Sklitsis, production manager.

D.K.
S.O.
F.M.T.

About the Authors

Donald Kagan is Bass Professor of History and Classics and Western Civilization at Yale University, where he has taught since 1969. He received the A.B. degree in history from Brooklyn College, the M.A. in classics from Brown University, and the Ph.D. in history from Ohio State University. During 1958–1959 he studied at the American School of Classical Studies as a Fulbright Scholar. He has received three awards for undergraduate teaching at Cornell and Yale. He is the author of a history of Greek political thought, *The Great Dialogue* (1965); a four-volume history of the Peloponnesian war, *The Origins of the Peloponnesian War* (1969); *The Archidamian War* (1974); *The Peace of Nicias and the Sicilian Expedition* (1981); *The Fall of the Athenian Empire* (1987); and a biography of Pericles, *Pericles of Athens and the Birth of Democracy* (1991). With Brian Tierney and L. Pearce Williams, he is the editor of *Great Issues in Western Civilization,* a collection of readings.

Steven Ozment is McLean Professor of Ancient and Modern History at Harvard University. He has taught Western Civilization at Yale, Stanford, and Harvard. He is the author of eight books. *The Age of Reform, 1250–1550* (1980) won the Schaff Prize and was nominated for the 1981 American Book Award. *Magdalena and Balthasar: An Intimate Portrait of Life in Sixteenth Century Europe* (1986) and *Three Behaim Boys: Growing Up in Early Modern Germany* (1990) were selections of the History Book club, as is also his most recent book, *Protestants: The Birth of a Revolution,* an interpretation of the German Reformation.

Frank M. Turner is John Hay Whitney Professor of History at Yale University, where he served as University Provost from 1988 to 1992. He received his B.A. degree at the College of William and Mary and his Ph.D. from Yale. He has received the Yale College Award for Distinguished Undergraduate Teaching. He has directed a National Endowment for the Humanities Summer Institute. His scholarly research has received the support of fellowships from the National Endowment for the Humanities and the Guggenheim Foundation. He is the author of *Between Science and Religion: The Reaction to Scientific Naturalism in Late Victorian England* (1974), *The Greek Heritage in Victorian Britain* (1981), which received the British Council Prize of the Conference on British Studies and the Yale Press Governors Award, and *Contesting Cultural Authority: Essays in Victorian Intellectual Life* (1993). He has also contributed numerous articles to journals and has served on the editorial advisory boards of *The Journal of Modern History, Isis,* and *Victorian Studies.*

Brief Contents

Detailed Contents

The Foundations of Western Civilization in the Ancient World

xxxii

Europe in Transition, 1300–1750
324

Enlightenment and Revolution
646

Toward the Modern World
838

Global Conflict, Cold War, and New Directions
1066

Documents

Maps

THE
WESTERN
HERITAGE

The Foundations of Western Civilization in the Ancient World

THE ROOTS OF Western civilization may be found in the experience and culture of the Greeks. Greek civilization itself, however, was richly nourished by older, magnificent civilizations to the south and east, especially in Mesopotamia and Egypt.

Some ten thousand years ago humans first began to live in settled, agricultural villages. In the valley of the Tigris and Euphrates rivers (Mesopotamia) and soon after in the valley of the Nile in Egypt, these agricultural societies underwent another shift to a much richer and more varied organization that we call *civilization.* The use of irrigation increased agricultural productivity, and population grew. A food surplus supported nonfarming specialists—artisans, merchants, priests, and soldiers—and made possible the earliest cities. The need for organizing this new and varied activity and for keeping records led to the invention of writing. Great advances took place in the arts and the sciences, in literature, and in the development of complex religious ideas and organizations.

The earliest civilizations produced powerful, centralized governments dominated by kings. The kings' power, bolstered by religious authority, rested on control of the economy and the ability to collect taxes. In Mesopotamia, kings were considered to be representatives of the gods; in Egypt they were considered themselves to be divine. Their control over the economy permitted them to raise, train, and support armies. This concentration of political, military, economic, and religious power resulted in societies that were rigidly divided into social classes: slaves, free commoners, priests, and aristocrats, as well as the divine or semidivine monarchs.

Social mobility and individual freedom were sharply limited. Only a handful of people took part in government. As rulers vied with one another, the stronger ones forged ever larger and more powerful kingdoms and empires.

The struggle between great empires sometimes permitted smaller city-states and kingdoms to survive and flourish; two were especially important for the civilization that would some day arise in the West. The cities of Phoenicia, in what is now Lebanon, produced great sailors and traders who came into early and frequent contact with the Greeks. Through the Phoenicians, among other Eastern peoples, the Greeks learned the art of writing and were powerfully influenced by the art, technology, and mythology of the earlier cultures. Absorbed, transformed, and transmitted by the Greeks, the civilizations of Mesopotamia and Egypt became, indirectly, part of the Western heritage. Neighbors of the Phoenicians, called Hebrews or Israelites, would have a more direct influence on the civilization of the West. They conceived a religion based on belief in a single all-powerful God who ruled over all peoples and the entire universe and made strong ethical demands on human beings. This religion of the Jews, as they came to be called (from the name of one of their kingdoms, Judah) became the basis of two later religions also of great importance: Christianity and Islam.

Greek civilization arose after the destruction of the Bronze Age cultures on Crete and the Greek mainland before 1000 B.C. Based on the independent existence of hundreds of city-states called *poleis,* it developed in a sharply different pattern than its predecessors in Egypt and western Asia. The *poleis* retained their autonomy for hundreds of years before being incorporated into larger units, attaining a degree of self-government, broad political participation, and individual freedom hitherto unknown. The Greeks also introduced a new way of thinking, looking on the world as the product of natural forces that could be understood through the senses and human reason, rather than as the product of supernatural forces. The result was the invention of science and philosophy as we know them. Greek literature placed humankind at the center of its concerns, adapting and inventing a great variety of literary genres, from epic, lyric, and dramatic poetry, to history, philosophy, rhetoric, and fiction in prose. The Greeks' way of thinking, their forms of art and literature, and their commitment to self-government and political freedom became and have remained central to Western civilization.

The Greeks planted cities from Spain to the Black Sea. Ceaseless quarrels and wars among *poleis*, however, eventually so weakened the Greeks that they fell under the control of their Macedonian cousins to the north. Alexander the Great of Macedon, using Greek troops as well as his own, swiftly conquered the Persian Empire. After his death in 323 B.C. the vast territory he had come to control was divided among his successors to form the three great Hellenistic kingdoms. Anyone speaking Greek could move comfortably from city to city within these kingdoms and find a familiar and common Hellenistic culture, a culture that combined Greek elements with elements native to the peoples Alexander had conquered. In the last two centuries before the Christian era this world succumbed to Roman conquest.

The Romans were originally tough farmers who inhabited a small town on the Tiber river in west-central Italy. After deposing their king in about 500 B.C., they invented a republican constitution and a code of law that provided a solid foundation for a stable and effective political order. Constantly at war with their neighbors, the Romans achieved military discipline and skills that allowed them to fight off attacks and to gain control of most of Italy by about 270 B.C. They developed an ingenious way of organizing the lands they conquered that made the peoples of those lands allies and even fellow citizens rather than subjects. From 264 until well into the first century B.C., the Romans extended their conquests overseas until they had conquered the Carthaginians in the west and defeated all the great Hellenistic powers, dominating the shores of the Mediterranean and beyond.

The Romans were fine engineers and road builders, but in art, literature, and philosophy they had barely made a start when they came into contact with the advanced Greek civilization of the Hellenistic world. In these areas the Romans became eager students, and as the Roman poet Horace put it, "Captive Greece took Rome captive." Roman culture put its own stamp on the Greek legacy and passed it on.

Rome's conquest of most of the known world created many problems for its republican constitution, which had been designed to govern only a small collection of farmers. Competition for eminence, power, and wealth within the Roman aristocracy led to struggles and civil wars that ravaged Italy and the empire as well. Finally, Gaius Julius Caesar defeated his opponents, put an end to the republic, and established himself as dictator for life. Rumor had it that he meant to be installed as king, and he was assassinated in 44 B.C. as the result of an aristocratic plot.

His assassination, however, failed to reestablish the republic. Civil war ensued and Caesar's nephew Octavian, later called Augustus, emerged as the commander of all Rome's armed forces and as the effective ruler of the Roman Empire. His new constitution tried to conceal the death of the republic and its replacement by what was really an imperial monarchy. This disguised monarchy flourished for almost two centuries, but after the death of the emperor Marcus Aurelius in 180 A.D., Rome's decline became obvious. Pressure from barbarian tribes on the frontiers, economic troubles at home, weak and incompetent emperors, and civil wars all strained Rome's resources, human and material. By the fifth century A.D., the Roman Empire in the west had collapsed and was shared out among various Germanic tribes. The eastern portion of the empire, known to us as the Byzantine Empire, with its capital at Constantinople, was to survive for a thousand years more. Before Rome's fall the empire had abandoned paganism and had adopted Christianity as its official religion. The heritage that the ancient world passed on to its medieval successor in western Europe was a combination of cultural traditions, including those coming from Egypt, Mesopotamia, Israel, Greece, Rome, and the German tribes that destroyed the Roman Empire. ◆

1,000,000–3500 B.C.	
3500–2200 B.C.	*ca. 3100–2700 B.C.* Egyptian Early Dynastic Period; unification of Upper and Lower Egypt *ca. 2800–2340 B.C.* Sumerian city-states' early dynastic period *2700–2200 B.C.* Egyptian Old Kingdom *ca. 2370 B.C.* Sargon established Akkadian Empire
2200–1600 B.C.	*2200–2052 B.C.* Egyptian First Intermediate Period *2052–1786 B.C.* Egyptian Middle Kingdom *1792–1750 B.C.* Reign of Hammurabi; height of Old Babylonian Kingdom; publication of Code of Hammurabi *1786–1575 B.C.* Egyptian Second Intermediate Period *ca. 1700 B.C.* Hyksos' invasion of Egypt
1600–1100 B.C.	*ca. 1600 B.C.* Fall of Old Babylonian Kingdom *1575–1087 B.C.* Egyptian New Kingdom (or Empire) *ca. 1400–1200 B.C.* Height of Hittite Empire *ca. 1400–1200 B.C.* Height of Mycenaean power *1367–1350 B.C.* Reign of Amenhotep IV (Akhnaton) in Egypt *ca. 1250 B.C.* Sack of Troy (?) *1087–30 B.C.* Egyptian Post-Empire Period
1100–500 B.C.	*ca. 1000–961 B.C.* Reign of King David in Israel *ca. 961–922 B.C.* Reign of King Solomon in Israel *ca. 1100–615 B.C.* Assyrian Empire *ca.800–400 B.C.* Height of Etruscan culture in Italy *ca. 625 B.C.* Spartan constitution formed *722 B.C.* Israel (northern kingdom) falls to Assyrians *ca. 700–500 B.C.* Rise and decline of tyranny in Greece *621 B.C.* First written law code in Athens *612–539 B.C.* Neo-Babylonian (Chaldean) Empire *594 B.C.* Solon's constitutional reforms, Athens *586 B.C.* Destruction of Jerusalem; fall of Judah (southern kingdom); Babylonian Captivity *ca. 560–550 B.C.* Peloponnesian League begins *559–530 B.C.* Reign of Cyrus the Great in Persia *546 B.C.* Persia conquers Lydian Empire of Croesus, including Greek cities of Asia Minor *539 B.C.* Persia conquers Babylonia; temple at Jerusalem restored; exiles return from Babylonia *521–485 B.C.* Reign of Darius in Persia *509 B.C.* Kings expelled from Rome; Republic founded *508 B.C.* Clisthenes founds Athenian democracy
500–336 B.C.	*490 B.C.* Battle of Marathon *485–465 B.C.* Reign of Xerxes in Persia *480–479 B.C.* Xerxes invades Greece *478–477 B.C.* Delian League founded

Society and Economy	Religion and Culture
ca. 1,000,000–10,000 B.C. Paleolithic Age *ca. 8,000 B.C.* Earliest Neolithic settlements	*ca. 30,0000–6,000 B.C.* Paleolithic art
ca. 3500 B.C. Earliest Sumerian settlements *ca. 3000 B.C.* First urban settlements in Egypt and Mesopotamia; Bronze Age begins in Mesopotamia and Egypt *ca. 2900–1150 B.C.* Bronze Age Minoan society on Crete; Helladic society on Greek mainland	*ca. 3000 B.C.* Invention of writing *ca. 3000 B.C.* Temples to gods in Mesopotamia; development of ziggurat temple architecture *2700–2200 B.C.* Building of pyramids for Egyptian god–kings; development of hieroglyphic writing in Egypt
ca. 2000 B.C. Hittites arrive in Asia Minor *ca. 1900 B.C.* Amorites at Babylon	*2200–1786 B.C.* Rise of Amon-Re as chief Egyptian god *ca. 1900 B.C.* Traditional date for Hebrew patriarch Abraham
1400–1200 B.C. Hittites introduce iron-smelting *ca. 1200 B.C.* Hebrews arrive in Palestine	*1367–1350 B.C.* Religious revolution led by Akhnaton makes Aton chief Egyptian god *1347–1339 B.C.* Tutankhamen restores worship of Amon-Re
ca. 1100–750 B.C. Greek "Dark Ages" *ca. 1000 B.C.* Italic peoples enter Italy *ca. 800 B.C.* Etruscans enter Italy *ca. 750–700 B.C.* Rise of Polis in Greece *ca. 750–600 B.C.* Great age of Greek colonization *ca. 700 B.C.* Invention of hoplite phalanx *ca. 600–550 B.C.* Spartans adopt new communitarian social system *ca. 600–500 B.C.* Athens develops commerce and a mixed economy	*ca. 750 B.C.* Hebrew prophets teach monotheism *ca. 750 B.C.* Traditional date for Homer *ca. 750 B.C.* Greeks adapt Semitic script and invent the Greek alphabet *ca. 750–600 B.C.* Panhellenic shrines established at Olympia, Delphi, Corinth, and Nemea; athletic festivals attached to them *ca. 700 B.C.* Traditional date for Hesiod *ca. 675–500 B.C.* Development of Greek lyric and elegiac poetry *ca. 570 B.C.* Birth of Greek philosophy in Ionia *ca. 550 B.C.* Oracle of Apollo at Delphi grows to great influence *ca. 550 B.C.* Cult of Dionysus introduced to Athens *539 B.C.* Restoration of temple in Jerusalem; return of exiles
ca. 500–350 B.C. Spartan population shrinks *ca. 500–350 B.C.* Rapid growth in overseas trade *477–431 B.C.* Vast growth in Athenian wealth	*ca. 500–400 B.C.* Great age of Athenian tragedy *469–399 B.C.* Life of Socrates *ca. 450–400 B.C.* Great influence of Sophists in Athens

ca. 460–445 B.C. First Peloponnesian War
450–449 B.C. Laws of the Twelve Tables, Rome
431–404 B.C. Great Peloponnesian War
404–403 B.C. Thirty Tyrants rule at Athens
400–387 B.C. Spartan war against Persia
398–360 B.C. Reign of Agesilaus at Sparta
395–387 B.C. Corinthian War
392 B.C. Romans defeat Etruscans
378 B.C. Second Athenian Confederation
371 B.C. Thebans end Spartan hegemony
362 B.C. Battle of Mantinea; end of Theban hegemony
338 B.C. Philip of Macedon conquers Greece

336–31 B.C.

336–323 B.C. Reign of Alexander III (the Great)
334 B.C. Alexander invades Asia
330 B.C. Fall of Persepolis; end Achaemenid rule in Persia
323–301 B.C. Ptolemaic Kingdom (Egypt), Seleucid Kingdom
(Syria), and Antigonid Dynasty (Macedon) founded
287 B.C. Laws passed by Plebeian Assembly made binding
on all Romans; end of Struggle of the Orders
264–241 B.C. First Punic War
218–202 B.C. Second Punic War
215–168 B.C. Rome establishes rule over Hellenistic world
154–133 B.C. Roman wars in Spain
133 B.C. Tribunate of Tiberius Gracchus
123–122 B.C. Tribunate of Gaius Gracchus
82 B.C. Sulla assumes dictatorship
60 B.C. First Triumvirate
46–44 B.C. Caesar's dictatorship
43 B.C. Second Triumvirate

31 B.C.–A.D. 400

31 B.C. Octavian and Agrippa defeat Anthony at Actium
27 B.C.–A.D. 14 Reign of Augustus
A.D. 14–68 Reigns of Julio-Claudian Emperors
A.D. 69–96 Reigns of Flavian Emperors
A.D. 96–180 Reigns of "Good Emperors"
A.D. 180–192 Reign of Commodus
A.D. 284–305 Reign of Diocletian; reform and division of
Roman Empire
A.D. 306–337 Reign of Constantine
A.D. 330 Constantinople new capital of Roman Empire
A.D. 361–363 Reign of Julian the Apostate
A.D. 379–395 Reign of Theodosius
A.D. 376 Visigoths enter Roman Empire

Society and Economy	Religion and Culture
	ca. 450–385 B.C. Great age of Athenian comedy
	448–432 B.C. Periclean building program on Athenian acropolis
431–400 B.C. Peloponnesian War casualties cause decline in size of lower class in Athens, with relative increase in importance of upper and middle classes	*429–347 B.C.* Life of Plato
	ca. 425 B.C. Herodotus' history of the Persian Wars
	ca. 400 B.C. Thucydides' history of the Peloponnesian War
	ca. 400–325 B.C. Life of Diogenes the Cynic
	386 B.C. Foundation of Plato's Academy
	384–322 B.C. Life of Aristotle
	336 B.C. Foundation of Aristotle's Lyceum
	342–271 B.C. Life of Epicurus
	335–263 B.C. Life of Zeno the Stoic
ca. 300 B.C.–A.D. 150 Growth of international trade and development of large cities in Hellenistic/Roman world	*ca. 287–212 B.C.* Life of Archimedes of Syracuse
	ca. 275 B.C. Foundation of museum and library make Alexandria the center of Greek intellectual life
	ca. 250 B.C. Livius Andronicus translates the *Odyssey* into Latin
ca. 218–135 B.C. Decline of family farm in Italy; growth of tenant farming and cattle ranching	*106–43 B.C.* Life of Cicero
ca. 150 B.C. Growth of slavery as basis of economy in Roman Republic	*ca. 99–55 B.C.* Life of Lucretius
	86–35 B.C. Life of Sallust
	ca. 84–54 B.C. Life of Catullus
	70–19 B.C. Life of Vergil
	65–8 B.C. Life of Horace
	59 B.C.–A.D. 17 Life of Livy
	43 B.C.–A.D. 18 Life of Ovid
	9 B.C. Ara Pacis dedicated at Rome
	ca. 4 B.C. Birth of Jesus of Nazareth
	ca. A.D. 30 Crucifixion of Jesus
	A.D. 64 Christians persecuted by Nero
	A.D. 66–135 Romans suppress rebellions of Jews
	ca. A.D. 70–100 Gospels written
ca. A.D. 150–400 Decline of slavery and growth of tenant farming and serfdom in Roman Empire	*ca. A.D. 150* Ptolemy of Alexandria establishes canonical geocentric model of the universe
ca. A.D. 250–400 Coloni (Roman tenant farmers) increasingly tied to the land	*ca. A.D. 250–260* Severe persecutions by Decius and Valerian
A.D. 301 Edict of Maximum Prices at Rome	*A.D. 303* Persecution of Christians by Diocletian
	A.D. 311 Gallienus issues Edict of Toleration
	A.D. 312 Constantine converts to Christianity
	A.D. 325 Council of Nicaea
	A.D. 348–420 Life of St. Jerome
	A.D. 354–430 Life of St. Augustine
	A.D. 395 Christianity becomes official religion of Roman Empire

This statue is of Nefertiti, the wife of Pharaoh Amenhotep IV (1367-1350 B.C.) of the Eighteenth Dynasty of ancient Egypt. He engineered a religious revolution in Egypt, breaking from the worship of Amon-Re, changing his name to Akhnaton, and devoting himself to the worship of Aton, a god who was thought to be universal, not just an Egyptian. [Bildarchiv Preussischer Kulturbesitz]

1

The Birth of Civilization

Key Topics in This Chapter
◆ The earliest history of humanity, including the beginnings of human culture in the Paleolithic Age, the agricultural revolution and the shift from food gathering to food production, and the emergence of civilization in the great river valleys of the Near East and Asia
◆ The ancient civilizations of Mesopotamia and Egypt
◆ The Assyrians and the first great Near Eastern empires
◆ The emergence of Judaism
◆ The difference in outlook between ancient Near Eastern civilization and ancient Greek civilization

History, in its two senses—as the events of the past that make up the human experience on earth and as the written record of those events—is a subject of both interest and importance. We naturally want to know how we came to be who we are and how the world we live in came to be what it is. But beyond its intrinsic interest, history provides crucial insight into present human behavior. To understand who we are now, we need to know the record of the past and to try to understand the people and forces that shaped it.

For hundreds of thousands of years after the human species emerged, people lived by hunting, fishing, and collecting wild plants. Only some 10,000 years ago did they learn to cultivate plants, herd animals, and make airtight pottery for storage. These discoveries transformed them from gatherers to producers and allowed them to grow in number and to lead a settled life. About 5,000 years ago humans learned how to control the waters of great river valleys, making possible much richer harvests and supporting a further increase in population. The peoples of these river valley societies created the earliest civilizations. They invented writing, which, among other things, enabled them to keep inventories of food and other resources. They discovered the secret of smelting metal to make tools and weapons of bronze far superior to the stone implements of earlier times. They came together in towns and cities, where industry and commerce flourished. Complex religions took form, and social divisions increased. Kings—considered to be representatives of the gods or to be themselves divine—emerged as rulers, assisted by priests and defended by well-organized armies.

The first of these civilizations appeared among the Sumerians before 3000 B.C. in the Tigris–Euphrates Valley that we call Mesopotamia. From the Sumerians to the Assyrians, a series of peoples ruled Mesopotamia, each shaping and passing along its distinctive culture, before the region fell under the control of great foreign empires.

A second early civilization took shape in the Nile Valley around 3000 B.C. Egyptian civilization developed largely in isolation from the outside world, protected from invasion and influence by the formidable deserts and seas that surround the valley. Thus the character of the civilization, which took shape early, changed little for more than 1,000 years. The shock of invasion in the seventeenth century B.C. by a mysterious people called the Hyksos ended Egypt's isolation, bringing it in contact with neighboring states and prompting military reforms. Egyptian armies subsequently pushed into Palestine and Syria, establishing an Egyptian Empire.

By the fourteenth century B.C. several powerful empires had arisen and were vying for dominance in regions that included Egypt, Mesopotamia, and Asia Minor. Northern warrior peoples, among them the Hittites, the Kassites, and the Mitannians, conquered and ruled more civilized peoples in various areas. The Hittites dominated in Asia Minor, the Kassites in southern Mesopotamia, and the Mitannians in northern Mesopotamia. For two centuries, the Hittite and Egyptian empires struggled with each other for control of Palestine. By about 1200 B.C., however, both these empires had collapsed, to be replaced by the mighty new Assyrian Empire. The Assyrians arose in northern Mesopotamia and ultimately ruled all the fertile lands from Egypt to southern Mesopotamia. They were dominant until the seventh century B.C., when they fell to a combination of enemies. Their vast empire would soon become only a small part of the enormous empire of Persia.

Among all these great empires nestled a people called the Israelites, who maintained a small independent kingdom in the region between Egypt and Syria for several centuries. This kingdom ultimately fell to the Assyrians and later remained subject to other conquerors. The Israelites possessed little worldly power or wealth, but they created a powerful religion, Judaism, the first certain and lasting worship of a single god in a world of polytheism. Judaism was the seedbed of two other religions that have played a mighty role in the history of the world: Christianity and Islam. The great empires have collapsed, their power forgotten for millennia until the tools of archaeologists uncovered their remains, but the religion of the Israelites, in itself and through its offshoots, has endured as a powerful force.

Early Human Beings and Their Culture

Scientists estimate that the earth may be as many as six billion years old and that creatures very much like humans appeared perhaps three to five million years ago, probably in Africa. Some one to two million years ago, erect and tool-using early humans spread over much of Africa, Europe, and Asia. Our own species, *Homo sapiens*, probably emerged some 200,000 years ago, and the earliest remains of fully modern humans date to about 90,000 years ago.

Humans, unlike other animals, are cultural beings. *Culture* may be defined as the ways of living built up by a group and passed on from one generation to another. It includes behavior such as courtship or child-rearing practices; it includes material things such as tools, clothing, and shelter; and it includes ideas, institutions, and beliefs. Language, apparently a uniquely human trait, lies behind our ability to create ideas and institutions and to transmit culture from one generation to another. Our flexible and dexterous hands enable us to hold and make tools and so to create the material artifacts of culture. Because culture is learned and not inherited, it permits more rapid adaptation to changing conditions than biological evolution, making possible the spread of humanity to almost all the lands of the globe.

The Paleolithic Age

Anthropologists designate early human cultures by their tools. The earliest period—the Paleolithic (from Greek, "old stone")—dates from the earliest use of stone tools some one million years ago to about 10,000 B.C. During this immensely long period, people were hunters, fishers, and gatherers, but not producers, of food. They learned to make and use increasingly sophisticated tools of stone and of perishable materials like wood; they learned to make and control fire; and they acquired language and the ability to use it to pass on what they had learned.

These early humans, dependent on nature for food and vulnerable to wild beasts and natural disasters, may have developed responses to the world rooted in fear of the unknown—of the uncertainties of human life or the overpowering forces of nature. Religious and magical beliefs and practices may have emerged in an effort to propitiate or coerce the superhuman forces thought to animate or direct the natural world. Evidence of religious faith and practice, as well as of magic, goes as far back as archaeology can take us. Fear or awe, exultation, gratitude, and empathy with the natural world must all have figured in the cave art and in the ritual practices, such as burial, that we find evidenced at Paleolithic sites around the globe. The sense that there is more to the world than meets the eye—in other words, the religious response to the world—seems to be as old as humankind.

The style of life and the level of technology of the Paleolithic period could support only a sparsely settled society. If hunters were too numerous, game would not suffice. In Paleolithic times, people were subject to the same natural and ecological constraints that today maintain a balance between wolves and deer in Alaska.

Evidence from paleolithic art and from modern hunter–gatherer societies suggests that human life in the Paleolithic Age was probably characterized by a division of labor by sex. Men engaged in hunting, fishing, making tools and weapons, and fighting against other families, clans, and tribes. Women, less mobile because of childbearing, gathered nuts, berries, and wild grains, wove baskets, and made clothing. Women gathering food probably discovered how to plant and care for seeds. This knowledge eventually made possible the coming of the Age of Agriculture—the Neolithic revolution.

This Paleolithic cave painting of bulls and horses is found in the Dordogne valley of southern France. The animals, which were hunted by prehistoric humans, are depicted with remarkable realism. [Ancient Art and Architecture Collection/Ronald Sheridan's Photo Library]

The Neolithic Age

Only a few Paleolithic societies made the initial revolutionary shift to agriculture, and anthropologists and archaeologists disagree as to why. However it happened, some 10,000 years ago parts of what we now call the Near East began to shift from a hunter–gatherer culture to a settled agricultural one. Because the shift to agriculture coincided with advances in stone tool technology—the development of precise carving and grinding—this period is called the Neolithic Age (from Greek, "new stone"). Animals as well as food crops were domesticated. The important invention of pottery made it possible to store surplus liquids, just as the invention of baskets had earlier made it possible to store dry foods. Cloth came to be made from flax and wool. Crops required constant care from planting to harvest, and so the Neolithic people built permanent buildings, usually in clusters near the best fields.

Throughout the Paleolithic Age, the human population had been small and relatively stable.

This mound is part of the remains of the ancient city of Jericho. Located on an oasis in ancient times, it is the site of one of the earliest Neolithic settlements in the Near East. [© Zev Radovan, Jerusalem, Israel]

The shift from food gathering to food production may not have been associated with an immediate change in population, but over time in the regions where agriculture and animal husbandry appeared, the number of human beings grew at an unprecedented rate. The Neolithic revolution was a major step in human control of nature, and it was a vital precondition for the emergence of civilization. The earliest Neolithic societies appeared in the Near East about 8000 B.C., in China about 4000 B.C., and in India about 3600 B.C. The Neolithic revolution in the Near East and India was based on wheat; in China, on millet and rice; in Mesoamerica, several millennia later, it would be based on corn. The wild forebears of the plants and animals that provided the foundation for the early civilizations of the Near East were native to the foothills of the mountains north and east of the Tigris and Euphrates river valleys. It was apparently in these foothill regions that they were first domesticated, later to be carried into the river valleys.

The Bronze Age and the Birth of Civilization

Neolithic agricultural villages and herding cultures gradually replaced Paleolithic culture in much of the world. Then another major shift occurred, first in the valley of the Tigris and Euphrates Rivers in the region called Mesopotamia (modern Iraq), later in the valley of the Nile River in Egypt, and somewhat later still in the Indus Valley in India and the Yellow River basin in China. This shift was marked by the appearance of urban centers, the mastery of smelting and with it the techniques for making metal tools and weapons, and the invention of writing. These traits—urbanism, metallurgy, and writing—are defining characteristics of the form of human culture called *civilization*. At about the time the earliest civilizations were emerging, someone discovered how to smelt tin and copper to make a stronger and more useful material—bronze. The importance of this technological development is reflected in the term *Bronze Age*.

Early Civilizations to About 1000 B.C.

About 4,000 years before the Christian era, people began to move in large numbers into the river-watered lowlands of Mesopotamia and Egypt. By about 3000 B.C., when the invention of writing gave birth to history, urban life and the organization of society into centralized states was established in the valleys of the Tigris and Euphrates Rivers in Mesopotamia and of the Nile River in Egypt.

Much of the population of cities consists of people who do not grow their own food, and so urban life is possible only where farmers can produce a substantial surplus beyond their own needs. The fertile alluvial plains where civilization began made such a surplus possible. Efficient farming of alluvial plains, however, requires intelligent management of water resources for irrigation. According to one influential theory, urban life and the first centralized states, and with them civilization, arose in the great river valleys of China, India, Mesopotamia, and Egypt in response to the need for a strong authority capable of constructing irrigation and flood control systems and managing the distribution of water. This control and management, the theory goes, led to the need for record keeping and, therefore, writing as well as other important innovations of early civilizations. Recent research, however, has challenged this theory. Evidence now suggests that in Mesopotamia irrigation was controlled locally rather than by central authorities at the time of the earliest city-states, implying that water management was not crucial to their development. Water management, moreover, does not figure in the earliest written records in Mesopotamia. These tend rather to deal with the care of animals, land management, and trade. The large temple complexes that were central to Mesopotamian cities generated religious texts as well as documents to keep track of the lands they owned, the offerings they received, the services they performed, and the people they employed. As city governments became larger and more complex, they, too, had many needs for writing: to record acts of the government, laws, and different kinds of literature.

This widely varied use of writing reflects the complex culture of the urban centers in the river valleys. Commerce was important enough to support a merchant class. The great need for record keeping created a class of scribes, because the picture writing and complicated scripts of these cultures took many years to learn and could not be mastered by many. To deal with the gods, great temples were built, and many priests worked in them. The collection of all these people into cities gave the settlements an entirely new character. Unlike Neolithic villages, they were communities established for purposes other than agriculture. The city served as an administrative, religious, manufacturing, entertainment, and commercial center.

The logic of nature pointed in the direction of the unification of an entire river valley. Central control would put the river's water to the most efficient use, and the absence of central control would lead to warfare, chaos, and destruction. As a result, these civilizations produced unified kingdoms under powerful monarchs who came to be identified with divinity.

The typical king in a river valley civilization was regarded either as a god or as the delegate of a god. Around him developed a rigid class structure. Beneath the monarch was a class of hereditary military aristocrats and a powerful priesthood. Below them were several kinds of freemen, mostly peasants, and at the bottom were many slaves. The population inhabited numerous peasant villages as well as the urban centers that were the locus of administrative, commercial, religious, and military activity. Most of the land was owned or controlled by the king, the nobility, and the priests. These were traditional, conservative societies. Their cultural patterns formed early and changed only slowly and grudgingly.

Mesopotamian Civilization

The first civilization appears to have arisen in the valley of the Tigris and Euphrates Rivers, an area the later Greeks and Romans called Mesopotamia. The region is naturally divided into two ecological zones, the south (Sumer), where irrigation is vital, and the north (Assyria), where agriculture depends on rainfall and wells. The oldest Mesopotamian cities seem to have been founded by a people called the Sumerians, around 3000 B.C. Sumerian civilization is generally associated with the southern part of the Tigris and Euphrates Valleys, close to the head of the Persian Gulf, and the earliest city had long been thought to be Uruk, which lies in that region (see Map 1-1). Recent discoveries, however, have revealed Sumerian cities dating to the Uruk period in northern Syria, notably at Habuba Kabirah, suggesting that we still have much to learn about the earliest civilization of Mesopotamia.

From about 2800 to 2370 B.C., in what is called the early dynastic period, several

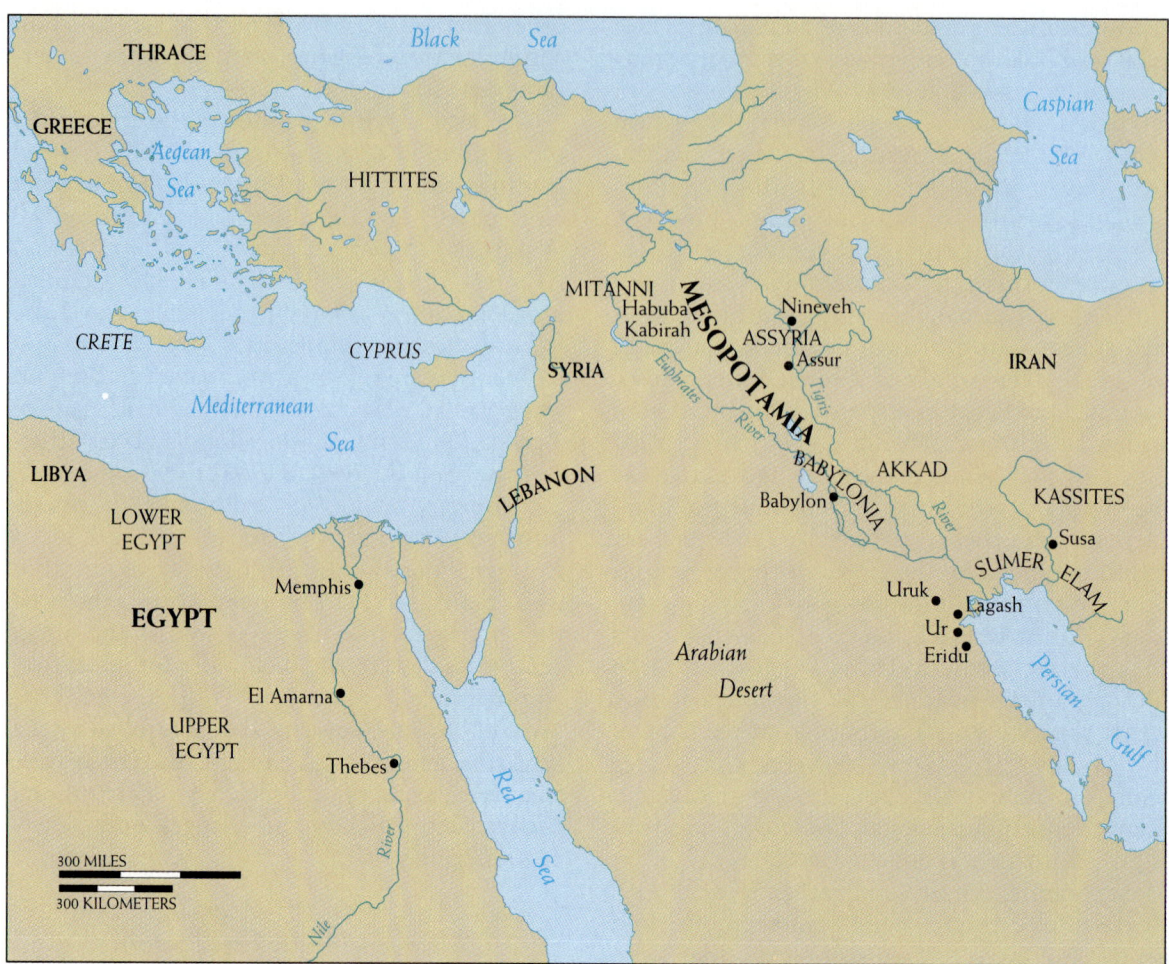

Map 1-1   The Ancient Near East   *There were two ancient river valley civilizations. While Egypt early was united into a single state, Mesopotamia was long divided into a number of city states.*

Sumerian city-states, each controlling about 100 square miles, dotted the landscape of southern Mesopotamia. Among these cities, as revealed to us by archaeologists, are Ur, Uruk, Lagash, and Eridu. Quarrels over water rights and frontiers led to incessant fighting, and in time, stronger towns conquered weaker ones and expanded to form larger units, usually kingdoms.

The region immediately upstream from the principal Sumerian city-states was occupied mostly by people who probably originally came from North Syria and who, unlike the Sumerians, spoke a Semitic language (that is, a language in the same family as Arabic and Hebrew). These people absorbed Sumerian culture and established their own kingdom, with its capital at Akkad, near the site of a later city

known to us as Babylon. Under their most famous king, Sargon, the Akkadians conquered the Sumerian cities and created an empire that extended in every direction. Sargon's name became legendary, and he is said to have conquered the "cedar forests" of Lebanon, far to the west, near the coast of the Mediterranean Sea. He ruled from about 2370 B.C. and established a family, or dynasty, of Semitic kings that ruled Sumer and Akkad for two centuries.

External attack and internal weakness destroyed Akkad. About 2125 B.C. the Sumerian city of Ur rose to dominance, and the rulers of the Third Dynasty of Ur established a large empire. About 2000 B.C., however, it was swept aside by another invasion.

The fall of the Third Dynasty of Ur put an end to Sumerian rule and to the Sumerians as

This statue of the seated King Gudea of Lagash was found in the mound of Telloh in modern Iraq, near the ancient Sumerian city of Lagash. Helping his city recover from defeat, he dedicated huge temples, expanded the irrigation system and increased foreign trade. [Giraudon/Art Resource]

This limestone disk, recovered from the region of the ancient city of Ur, is decorated with a relief carving showing Enheduanna, a daughter of Sargon. [The University Museum, University of Pennsylvania (Neg. #22090)]

an identifiable group. The Sumerian language survived only in writing, as a kind of sacred language known only to priests and scribes, preserving the cultural heritage of Sumer. For about a century after the fall of Ur, dynastic chaos reigned. Then, about 1900 B.C. a people called the Amorites gained control of the region, establishing their capital at Babylon.

The Amorite, or Old Babylonian, dynasty dominated Mesopotamia for about 300 years. Its high point was the reign of its most famous king, Hammurabi (r. ca. 1792–1750 B.C.), best known for the law code that bears his name. Codes of law existed as early as the Sumerian period, and Hammurabi's plainly owed much to earlier models. His is the fullest and best-preserved legal code we have from ancient Mesopotamia, however. The Code of

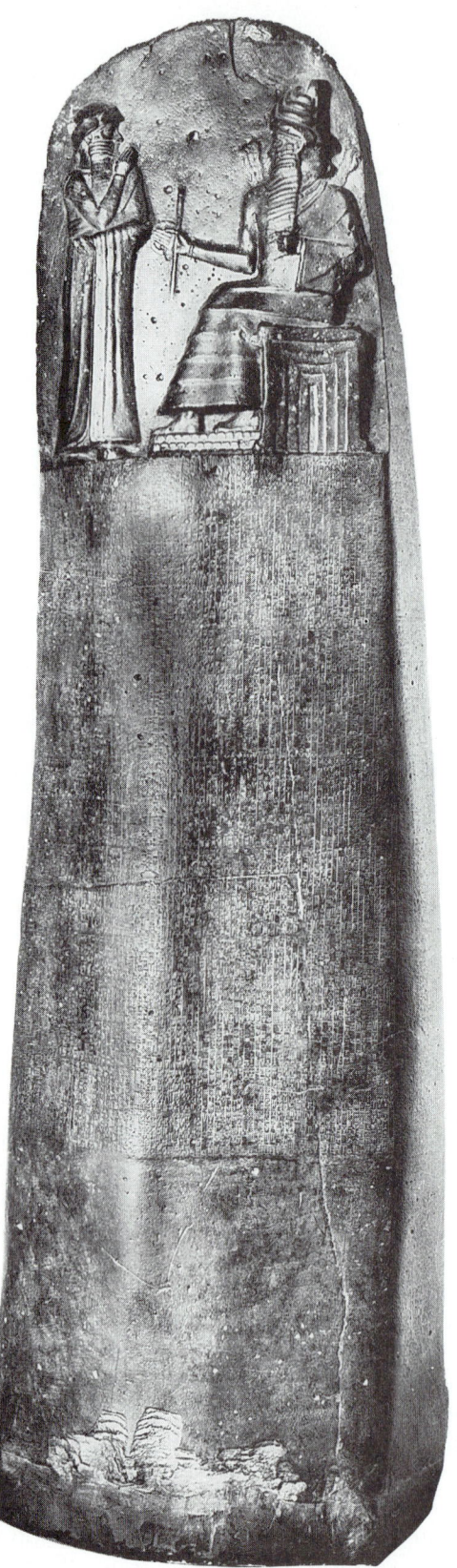

The Code of Hammurabi, the most famous ruler of the Old Babylonian Dynasty, reveals much about ancient Mesopotamian society. In the relief carving at the top of the stele on which the code is inscribed, Hammurabi receives the law from the sun god. [The Oriental Institute, University of Chicago]

Hammurabi reveals a society strictly divided by class; there were nobles, commoners, and slaves, and the law did not treat them equally. In general, punishments were harsh, based literally on the principle of "an eye for an eye, a tooth for a tooth." The prologue to the code makes it clear that law and justice came from the gods through the king.

This clay tablet from the Chaldean period (612–539 B.C.) shows a map of the world as seen by the Babylonians. The "Salt Sea" is shown as a circle. An arc inside it is labeled "Mountains." Below it is a rectangular box marked "Babylon," and to the right of the box is a small circle marked "Assyria." [Courtesy of the Trustees of the British Museum]

Epilogue to the Law Code of Hammurabi

Hammurabi was the sixth king of the Old Babylonian Dynasty. His law code is the fullest and best preserved of a series of such codes going back to Sumerian times. It provides valuable evidence of the nature of Babylonian life and society. In the prologue and the excerpt from the epilogue printed below, the king provides an explanation and justification for the code.

◆ *What reasons does Hammurabi give for people to obey the laws he has set forth? What alternatives do human societies have to a published code of law for governing social relations? What are the advantages and disadvantages of a published code?*

The righteous laws which Hammurabi the wise king established and by which he gave the land a firm support and a gracious rule. Hammurabi the perfect king am I. I was not careless nor was I neglectful of the black-headed people, whom Bel presented to me and whose care Marduk gave to me. Regions of peace I spied out for them, grievous difficulties I overcame—caused light to shine forth for them. With the powerful weapon which Zamama and Innanna intrusted to me, with the breadth of vision which Ea allotted to me, with the might which Marduk gave me, I expelled the enemy north and south; I made an end of their raids; I promoted the welfare of the land; I made the peoples to rest in habitations of security; I permitted no one to molest them. The great gods have named me and I am the guardian shepherd whose scepter is righteous; my beneficent shadow is spread over the city. In my bosom I have carried the peoples of the land of Sumer and Akkad, under my protection I brought their brethren into security; with my wisdom I covered them; that the strong might not oppress the weak, and that they should give justice to the orphan and the widow, in Babylon, the city whose head Anu and Enlil raised aloft, in Esagila, the temple whose foundations stand firm as heaven and earth, to pronounce judgments for the land, to render decisions for the land, to give justice to the oppressed, my weighty words I have written upon my monument, and in the presence of the image of me, king of righteousness, have I set it up.

Reprinted from J. M. P. Smith, The Origin and History of Hebrew Law *(Chicago, University of Chicago Press, 1931).*

About 1600 B.C. the Babylonian kingdom fell apart under the impact of invasions from the north and east by the Hittites and the Kassites. The Hittites came only as raiders, plundering what they could and then withdrawing to their home in Asia Minor. The Kassites stayed and ruled Mesopotamia for five centuries.

GOVERNMENT From the earliest historical records it is clear that the Sumerians were ruled by monarchs in some form. Some scholars have thought they could detect a "primitive democracy" in early Sumer, but the evidence, which is sketchy and hard to interpret, shows no more than a limited check on royal power even in early times. The first historical city-states had kings or priest-kings who led the army, administered the economy, and served as judges and as intermediaries between their people and the gods. At first, the kings were thought of as favorites and representatives of the gods; later, on some occasions and for relatively short periods, they instituted cults and were worshiped as divine.

This union of church and state (to use modern terminology) in the person of the king reflected the centralization of power typical of Mesopotamian life. The economy was managed from the center by the priests and the king and was planned very carefully. Each year the land was surveyed, fields were assigned to specific farmers, and the amount of seed to be used was designated. The government estimated the size of the crop and planned its distribution even before it was planted.

This process required a large and competent staff, the ability to observe and record natural phenomena, a good knowledge of mathematics, and, for all of this, a system of writing. The Sumerians invented the writing system known as *cuneiform* (from the Latin *cuneus*, "wedge") because of the wedge-shaped stylus with which they wrote on clay tablets. The writing also came to be used in beautifully cut characters in stone. The Sumerians also began the development of a sophisticated system of mathematics. The calendar they invented had twelve lunar months. To make it agree with the solar year and to make possible accurate designation of the seasons, they introduced a thirteenth month about every three years.

RELIGION The Sumerians and their successors worshiped gods with human forms, each of whom was usually identified with some natural phenomenon. They were pictured as frivolous, quarrelsome, selfish, and often childish, differing from humans only in their greater power and their immortality. They each appear to have begun as local deities. The people of Mesopotamia had a vague and gloomy picture of the afterworld. Their religion dealt with problems of this world, and they used prayer, sacrifice, and magic to achieve their ends. Expert knowledge was required to reach the perfection in wisdom and ritual needed to influence the gods, and so the priesthood flourished. A high percentage of the cuneiform writing we now have is devoted to religious texts: prayers, incantations, curses, and omens.

The Babylonians, in an effort to discover the will and intentions of the gods, cultivated several methods of divination. Seeking evidence of divine action in the movements of the heavenly bodies, they gave birth to astrology. They also sought to discover the divine will by examining

This eighth-century B.C. *alabaster relief of Gilgamesh, the godlike hero of an ancient Sumerian epic poem, was found in the ruins of the palace of the Assyrian king Sargon II and is now in the Louvre. [Giraudon/Art Resource, N.Y.]*

the entrails of sacrificial animals for abnormalities. All of this religious activity required armies of scribes to keep great quantities of records, as well as learned priests to interpret them.

Religion, in the form of myth, played a large part in the literature and art of Mesopotamia. In poetic language, the Babylonians told tales of the creation of the world, of a great flood that almost destroyed human life, of an island paradise from which the god Enki was expelled for eating forbidden plants, of a hero named Gilgamesh who performed great feats in his travels, and many more.

Religion was also the inspiration for the most interesting architectural achievement in Mesopotamia: the ziggurat. The ziggurat was an artificial stepped mound surmounted by a temple. Neighbors and successors of the Sumerians adopted the style, and the eroded remains of many of these monumental structures, some partly restored, still dot the Iraqi landscape.

SOCIETY Tens of thousands of texts from the mid-third millennium B.C. to the end of cuneiform writing give us a very full and detailed picture of the way people in ancient Mesopotamia conducted their lives and of the social conditions in which they lived. The evidence from the time of the reign of Hammurabi—including more than fifty royal letters, many business contracts, and especially the Code of Hammurabi—is particularly good. It reveals a society that was legally divided into three classes: nobles, commoners, and slaves. Punishment for crimes committed against freemen was harsher than for those against slaves, and likewise crimes committed against nobles were held to be more serious than those against commoners.

Categorizing the Code of Hammurabi according to the aspects of life with which it deals reveals much about Babylonian society. The third largest category is commerce, and the many sections of the Code devoted to such issues as debts, rates of interest, security, and default indicate the importance and sophistication of Babylonian commercial life. Sections also deal with the regulation of builders, surgeons, and other professionals. The second largest category deals with land tenure, as is not surprising in a society based so heavily on agriculture. The largest category relates to the family and its maintenance and protection.

Key Events and People in Mesopotamian History	
ca. 3500 B.C.	Earliest Sumerian settlements
ca. 2800–2370 B.C.	Sumerian city–states' early dynastic period
ca. 2370 B.C.	Sargon establishes Semitic dynasty at Akkad
ca. 2125–2027 B.C.	Third Dynasty of Ur
ca. 1900 B.C.	Amorites at Babylon, beginning of Old Babylonian dynasty
1792–1750 B.C.	Reign of Hammurabi
ca. 1600 B.C.	Invasion by Hittites and Kassites; end of Old Babylonian dynasty

Marriages were arranged by the parents, and betrothal was followed by the signing of a marriage contract. The husband-to-be made a bridal payment, and the father of the bride-to-be agreed to a dowry for his daughter. A marriage started out monogamous, but a husband whose wife was childless or ill for a long time could take a second wife. Extramarital relations between the husband and concubines, female slaves, and prostitutes were common and accepted.

The wife did not have similar privileges, but she seems to have been treated as an individual with rights protected by the law. Divorce was relatively easy and not entirely inequitable. Women divorced by their husbands without good cause received their dowry back. A woman seeking divorce could also recover her dowry if her husband could not convict her of wrongdoing. On the other hand, a woman's place was thought distinctly to be in the home. One law states that if a wife "has made up her mind to leave in order to engage in business, thus neglecting her house and humiliating her husband, he may divorce her without compensation."

For most of Mesopotamian history slavery arose from debt. Parents could sell their children into slavery or pledge themselves and their entire family as surety for a loan. In case of default, they would all become slaves of the creditor for a stated period of time. Although the practice of

The Babylonian Story of the Flood

This passage is part of the Babylonian Epic of Gilgamesh, which may have been written before 2000 B.C. Its hero, after many adventures, becomes aware of his own mortality when his friend and companion dies. Gilgamesh then seeks the secret of immortality from Utnapishtim. This man and his wife were the sole survivors of a great flood that destroyed the rest of humanity and the only two mortals known to have been granted eternal life. It is interesting to note the similarities between this tale and the biblical story of Noah, as well as the important differences between them.

✦ *How is this tale similar to the story of Noah in the Book of Genesis in the Hebrew Bible? How is it different? How does the presence of many divinities shape this story differently from the one in Genesis?*

"For six days and (seven) nights the wind blew, and the flood and the storm swept the land. But the seventh day arriving did the rainstorm subside and the flood which had heaved like a woman in travail; there quieted the sea, and the storm-wind stood still, the flood stayed her flowing. I opened a vent and the fresh air moved over my cheek-bones. And I looked at the sea; there was silence, the tideway lay flat as a roof-top—but the whole of mankind had returned unto clay. I bowed low: I sat and I wept: o'er my cheek-bones my tears kept on running.

"When I looked out again in the directions, across the expanse of the sea, mountain ranges had emerged in twelve places and on Mount Nisir the vessel had grounded. Mount Nisir held the vessel fast nor allowed any movement. For a first day and a second, fast Mount Nisir held the vessel nor allowed of any movement. For a third day and a fourth day, fast Mount Nisir held the vessel nor allowed of any movement. For a fifth day and a sixth day, held Mount Nisir fast the vessel nor allowed of any movement.

"On the seventh day's arriving, I freed a dove and did release him. Forth went the dove but came back to me: there was not yet a resting-place and he came returning. Then I set free a swallow and did release him. Forth went the swallow but came back to me: there was not yet a resting-place and he came returning. So I set free a raven and did release him. Forth went the raven—and he saw again the natural flowing of the waters, and he ate and he flew about and he croaked, and came not returning.

"So all set I free to the four winds of heaven, and I poured a libation, and scattered a food-

---

enslaving foreign war captives dates to early periods, and native Babylonians could be enslaved for certain crimes—kicking one's mother or striking an elder brother, for example—true chattel slavery did not become common until late in Mesopotamian history, in the Neo-Babylonian period (612–539 B.C.). Some slaves worked for the king and the state, others for the temple and the priests, and still others for private citizens. Their tasks varied accordingly. Most temple slaves appear to have been women, who were probably used to spin thread, weave cloth, and grind flour. Sometimes the royal slaves did the heavy work of building palaces, canals, and fortifications. Private owners used their slaves chiefly as domestic servants. Some female slaves were used as concubines.

Although laws against fugitive slaves or slaves who denied their masters were harsh, in some respects Mesopotamian slavery appears enlight-

offering, on the height of the mountain. Seven and seven did I lay the vessels, heaped into their incense-basins sweet-cane, cedarwood and myrtle. And the gods smelled the savour, the gods smelled the sweet savour, the gods gathered like flies about the priest of the offering.

"Then, as soon as the Mother-goddess arrived, she lifted up the great jewels which, (in childhood, her father) Anu had made as a plaything for her: `O ye gods here present, as I still do not forget these lapis stones of my neck, so shall I remember these days—shall not forever forget them! If it please now the gods to come here to the offering, never shall Enlil come here to the offering, for without any discrimination he brought on the deluge, even (the whole of) my people consigned to destruction.'

"But as soon as Enlil arrived, he saw only the vessel—and furious was Enlil, he was filled with anger against the (heaven) gods, the Igigi: `Has aught of livingkind escaped? Not a man should have survived the destruction!'

"Ninurta opened his mouth and spake unto warrior Enlil:

`Who except Ea could have designed such a craft? For Ea doth know every skill of invention.'

"Then Ea opened his mouth and spake unto warrior Enlil:

`O warrior, thou wisest among gods, how thus indiscriminately couldst thou bring about this deluge? (Had thou counselled): On the sinner lay his sin, on the transgressor lay his transgression: loosen (the rope) that his life be not cut off, yet pull tight (on the rope) that he do not [escape]: then instead of thy sending a Flood would that the lion had come and diminished mankind: instead of thy sending a Flood that the wolf had come and diminished mankind: instead of thy sending a Flood would that a famine had occurred and impoverished mankind: instead of thy sending a Flood would that a pestilence had come and smitten mankind. And I, since I could not oppose the decision of the great gods, did reveal unto the Exceeding-Wise a (magic) dream, and thus did he hear the gods' decision. Wherefore now take thee counsel concerning him.'

"Thereupon Enlil went up into the vessel: he took hold of my hand and made me go aboard, he bade my wife go aboard and made her kneel at my side. Standing between us, he touched our foreheads and did bless us, saying: `Hitherto Utnapishtim has been but a man; but now Utnapishtim and his wife shall be as gods like ourselves. In the Far Distance, at the mouth of the Rivers, Utnapishtim shall dwell.'

"So they took me and did make me to dwell in the Far Distance, at the mouth of the Rivers. . .."

Trans. by J. V. Kinnier Wilson in Documents from Old Testament Times, *D. Winton Thomas, ed. (London: Thomas Nelson and Sons, Ltd., 1958), lines 145–198, pp. 22–24.*

ened compared with other slave systems in history. Slaves could engage in business and, with certain restrictions, hold property. They could marry free men or women, and the resulting children would be free. A slave who acquired the necessary wealth could buy his or her freedom. Children of a slave by the master might be allowed to share his property after his death. Nevertheless, slaves were property, were subject to their master's will, and had little legal protection.

Egyptian Civilization

As Mesopotamian civilization arose in the valley of the Tigris and Euphrates, another great civilization emerged in Egypt. The center of Egyptian civilization was the Nile River. From its source in central Africa the Nile runs north some 4,000 miles to the Mediterranean, with long navigable stretches broken by several cataracts. Ancient Egypt included the 750 miles of the valley from the First Cataract to the sea and was shaped like a funnel with two distinct parts. Upper (southern) Egypt consisted of the narrow valley of the Nile. Lower (northern) Egypt consisted of the broad, triangular delta, which branches out about 150 miles along the Mediterranean coast (see Map 1-1).

The Nile alone made life possible in Egypt's almost rainless desert. Each year the river flooded and covered the land, and when it receded it left a fertile mud that could produce two crops a year. The construction and maintenance of irrigation ditches to preserve the river's water, with careful planning and organization of planting and harvesting, produced agricultural prosperity unmatched in the ancient world.

The Nile also served as a highway connecting the long, narrow country and encouraging its unification. Upper and Lower Egypt were, in fact, already united into a single kingdom at the beginning of our historical record, about 3100 B.C. Nature helped protect and isolate the ancient Egyptians from outsiders. The cataracts, the sea, and the desert made it difficult for foreigners to reach Egypt for either friendly or hostile purposes. Egypt knew far more peace and security than Mesopotamia. This security, along with the sunny, predictable climate, gave Egyptian civilization a more optimistic outlook than the civilizations of the Tigris and Euphrates, which were always in fear of assault from storm, flood, earthquake, and hostile neighbors.

The more than 3,000-year span of ancient Egyptian history is traditionally divided into thirty-one royal dynasties, from the first, founded by Menes, the unifier of Upper and Lower Egypt, to the last, established by Alexander the Great, who conquered Egypt (as we shall see in Chapter 3) in 332 B.C. The dynasties are conventionally arranged into periods (see the accompanying chronology). The unification of Egypt was vital, for more than in Mesopotamia the entire river valley benefitted from the central control of irrigation. By the time of the Third Dynasty, Egypt's kings had achieved full supremacy. Ruling from their capital at Memphis, in Upper Egypt, just above the opening of the delta, they had imposed internal peace and order, and their kingdom enjoyed great prosperity.

An Egyptian king was no mere representative of the gods but a god himself. The land was his own personal possession, and the peo-

The great pyramids of Egypt, located at Giza, near Cairo, are the colossal tombs of three pharaohs of the Fourth Dynasty (ca. 2620-2480 B.C.): Menkaure (left), Khafre (center), and Khufu (right). The smaller tombs in the foreground may have been those of the pharaohs' wives and courtiers. [Pictor/Uniphoto Picture Agency]

Periods in Ancient Egyptian History (Dynasties in Roman Numerals)	
ca. 3100–2700 B.C.	Early Dynastic Period (I–II)
2700–2200 B.C.	Old Kingdom (III–VI)
2200–2052 B.C.	First Intermediate Period (VII–X)
2052–1786 B.C.	Middle Kingdom (XI–XII)
1786–1575 B.C.	Second Intermediate Period (XIII–XVII)
ca. 1700 B.C.	Hyksos Invasion
1575–1087 B.C.	New Kingdom (or Empire) (XVII–XX)
1087–30 B.C.	Post-Empire (XXI–XXXI)

ple were his servants. Nothing better illustrates the extent of royal power than the three great pyramids built as tombs by the kings of the Fourth Dynasty. The largest, that of Khufu, was originally 481 feet high and 756 feet long on each side; it was made up of 2,300,000 stone blocks averaging 2.5 tons each. The Greek historian Herodotus, writing some 2,000 years later in history, records claims that 100,000 men spent twenty years building it. The pyramids are remarkable for the great technical skill they demonstrate, but even more for the concentration of resources they represent. They give evidence that the Egyptian kings controlled vast wealth, had the power to focus enormous human effort on a personal project, and possessed the confidence to undertake one of such a long duration. There were earlier pyramids and many were built later, but those of the Fourth Dynasty were never surpassed.

THE OLD KINGDOM (2700–2200 B.C.) In the Old Kingdom royal power was absolute. The pharaoh, as the king was later called (the term originally meant *great house* or *palace*), governed his kingdom through his family, appointing and removing officials at his pleasure. The peasants were carefully regulated, their movement was limited, and they were taxed heavily, perhaps up to as much as one fifth of what they produced. Luxury accompanied the king in life

and death, and he was raised to a remote and exalted level by his people. The Egyptians worked for the king and obeyed him because he was a living god on whom their lives, safety, and prosperity depended. He was the direct source of law and justice, and so Egypt needed no law codes.

In such a world, government was merely one aspect of religion, and religion dominated Egyptian life. The gods of Egypt had many forms: animals, humans, and natural forces. In time, Re, the sun god, came to have a special and dominant place, but for centuries there seems to have been little clarity or order in the Egyptian pantheon.

Unlike the Mesopotamians, the Egyptians had a rather clear idea of an afterlife. They took great care to bury their dead according to convention and supplied the grave with things that the departed would need for a pleasant life after death. The king and some nobles had their bodies preserved as mummies. Their tombs were beautifully decorated with paintings; food was provided at burial and even after. Some royal tombs were provided with full-sized ships for the voyage to heaven. At first, only kings were thought to achieve eternal life; then, nobles were included; finally, all Egyptians could hope for immortality. The dead had to be properly embalmed, and the proper spells had to be written and spoken.

The Egyptians developed a system of writing not much later than the Sumerians. Though the idea of writing may have come from Mesopotamia, Egyptian script developed independently. It began as picture writing and later combined pictographs with sound signs. The result was a difficult and complicated script that the Greeks later called *hieroglyph* ("sacred carvings"). Most Egyptian writing was done with pen and ink on a fine paper made from the papyrus reed found in the delta; much of what was preserved long enough to be available to us, however, is found on wall paintings and carvings. Egyptian literature was more limited in depth and imagination than that of Mesopotamia. Hymns, myths, magical formulas, tales of travel, and "wisdom literature," or bits of advice to help one get on well in the world, have been preserved. But the Egyptian world, happier and simpler than the Mesopotamian, produced nothing as

This painting from a royal Egyptian tomb shows a noble family on a boat on a trip to hunt birds in the afterlife, just as they enjoyed doing in their lives on earth. [Courtesy of the Trustees of the British Museum]

serious and probing as the Mesopotamian story of Gilgamesh.

THE MIDDLE KINGDOM (2052–1786 B.C.) The power of the kings of the Old Kingdom waned as priests and nobles gained more independence and influence. The governors of the regions of Egypt, called *nomes*, gained hereditary claim to their offices, and their families acquired large estates. About 2200 B.C. the Old Kingdom collapsed and gave way to the decentralization and disorder of the First Intermediate Period (ca. 2200–2052 B.C.). The nomarchs (governors) of Thebes in Upper Egypt eventually gained control of the country and established

the Middle Kingdom, its capital initially at Thebes, about 2052 B.C.

The rulers of the Twelfth Dynasty restored the pharaoh's power over the whole of Egypt, though they could not completely control the nobles who ruled the nomes. Still, they brought order, peace, and prosperity after the troubles of the First Intermediate Period. They encouraged trade and extended Egyptian power and influence northward toward Palestine and southward toward Ethiopia. They moved the capital from Thebes back to the more defensible site of Memphis, but gave great prominence to Amon, a god especially connected with Thebes. Amon became identified with Re, emerging as Amon-Re, the main god of Egypt.

The kings of this period seem to have emphasized their role as dispensers of justice. Statues often show them burdened with care, presumably concerned for their people. Tales of the period stress the king's interest in right and in the welfare of his people.

THE NEW KINGDOM (EMPIRE) (1575–1087 B.C.) AND AFTER The resurgent power of the local nobility and the erosion of central authority in the Thirteenth Dynasty mark the end of the Middle Kingdom and the beginning of the Second Intermediate Period (1786–1575 B.C.) About 1700 B.C., Egypt suffered an invasion. Tradition speaks of a people called the Hyksos who came from the east and conquered the Nile Delta. They seem to have been a collection of Semitic peoples from the area of Palestine and Syria at the eastern end of the Mediterranean. Egyptian nationalism reasserted itself about 1575 B.C., when a dynasty from Thebes drove out the Hyksos and reunited the kingdom, opening the New Kingdom, or Empire Period. In reaction to the humiliation of the Second Intermediate Period, the pharaohs of the Eighteenth Dynasty, the most prominent of whom was Thutmose III (r. 1490–1436 B.C.), built a powerful army, imposed an absolute government, and forged an empire that extended far beyond the Nile Valley (see Map 1-2).

From the Hyksos the Egyptians had learned new military techniques and obtained new weapons. Combining these with determination, a fighting spirit, and an increasingly militarized society, they pushed their southern frontier back a long way and extended their power into Palestine, Syria, and beyond to the upper Euphrates River. They were not checked until they came into conflict with the powerful Hittite empire of Asia Minor. The ensuing struggle between these powers weakened both. Egypt survived, but by the end of the Twentieth Dynasty, the last dynasty of the New Kingdom, its period of glory had passed. Throughout the Post-Empire period (1087–30 B.C.) it again fell victim to periodic foreign invasion and rule.

Toward the end of the Eighteenth Dynasty, after the New Kingdom empire had reached its greatest extent, Egypt witnessed an interesting religious struggle. One result of the successful imperial ventures was to increase the power of the priests of Amon, making them a threat to

This fresco painting is of Queen Nefertari of the Twentieth Dynasty, the last dynasty of the New Kingdom period. [Courtesy of the Trustees of the British Museum]

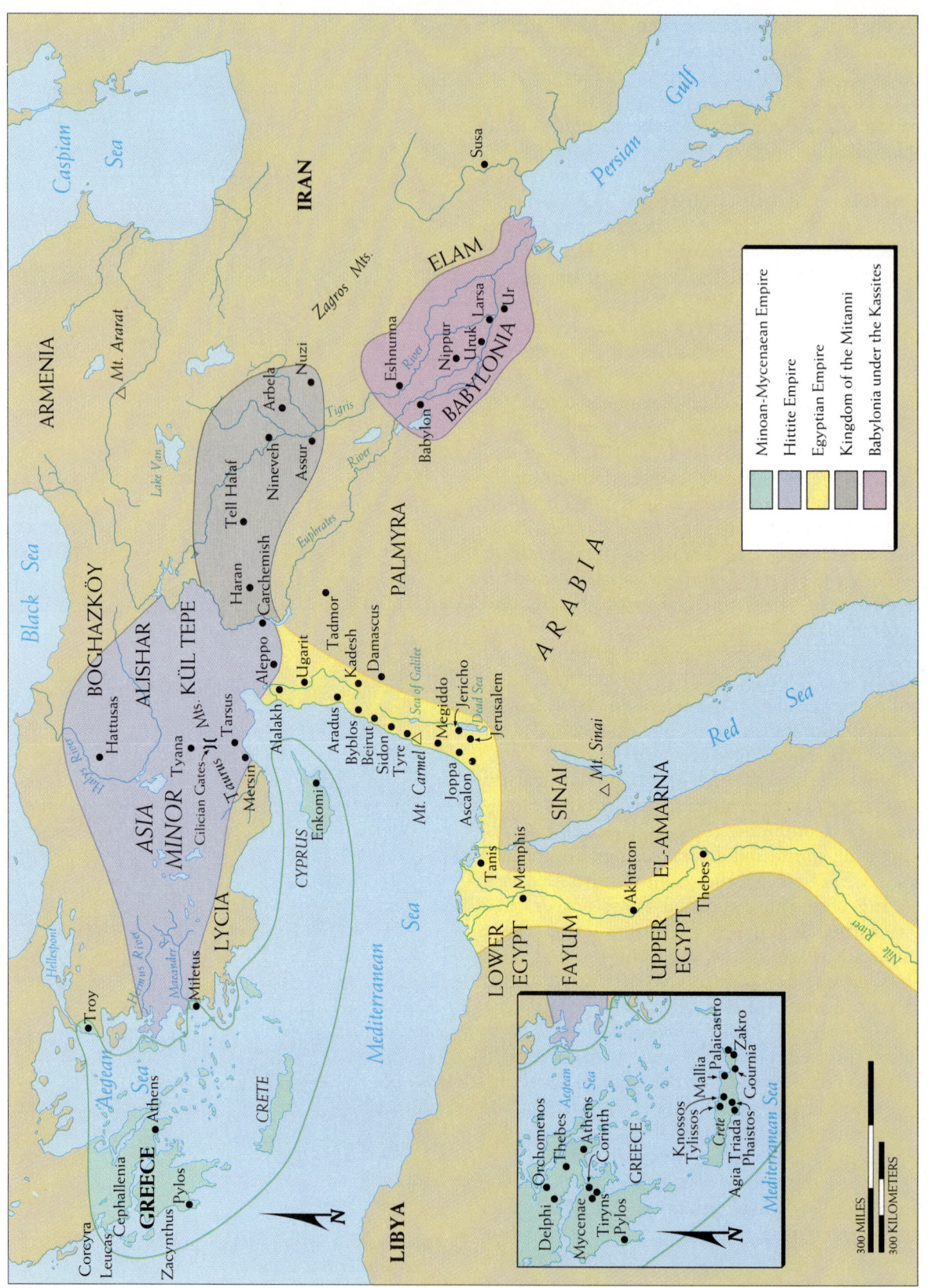

Legend

- Minoan-Mycenaean Empire
- Hittite Empire
- Egyptian Empire
- Kingdom of the Mitanni
- Babylonia under the Kassites

Caspian Sea

IRAN

Susa

ARMENIA

△ Mt. Ararat

Lake Van

ELAM

Zagros Mts.

Nuzi

Arbela

Nineveh

Assur

Tell Halaf

Tigris River

Eshnunna

Nippur

Uruk Larsa

Ur

BABYLONIA

Babylon

Haran

Carchemish

Euphrates River

Black Sea

BOGHAZKÖY

ALISHAR

KÜL TEPE

Hattusas

Halys River

ASIA MINOR

Tyana

Taurus Mts.

Clician Gates

Tarsus

Mersin

Aleppo

Ugarit

Alalakh

Tadmor

Kadesh

Damascus

PALMYRA

A R A B I A

Aradus

Byblos

Beirut

Sidon

Tyre

Mt. Carmel △

Megiddo

Jericho

Jerusalem

Sea of Galilee

Dead Sea

Joppa

Ascalon

CYPRUS

Enkomi

LYCIA

Sarus River

Pyramus River

Maeander River

Hellespont

Miletus

Troy

Mediterranean Sea

CRETE

Aegean Sea

Athens

GREECE

Corcyra

Leucas

Cephallenia

Zacynthus Pylos

LIBYA

SINAI

△ Mt. Sinai

Red Sea

Tanis

Memphis

LOWER EGYPT

FAYUM

Akhtaton

EL-AMARNA

UPPER EGYPT

Thebes

Nile River

Persian Gulf

Inset (Greece / Crete)

Delphi

Orchomenos

Thebes

Mycenae

Tiryns

Pylos

Corinth

Athens

Aegean Sea

GREECE

Knossos

Tylissos

Mallia

Palaicastro

Zakro

Gournia

Agia Triada

Phaistos

Crete

Mediterranean Sea

300 MILES

300 KILOMETERS

N

the position of the pharaoh. When young Amenhotep IV (r. 1367–1350 B.C.) came to the throne, he apparently determined to resist the priesthood of Amon. Supported by his family and advisers, he ultimately made a clean break with the worship of Amon-Re, devoting himself instead to the worship of the god Aton, the physical disk of the sun. He changed his name to Akhnaton ("it pleases Aton") and moved his capital from Thebes, the center of Amon worship, to an entirely new city—Akhtaton—about 300 miles to the north at a place now called El Amarna.

The new god was different from any that had come before him, for he was believed to be universal, not merely Egyptian. Unlike the other gods, he had no cult statue but was represented in painting and relief sculpture as the sun disk.

The universal claims for Aton led to religious intolerance of the worshipers of the other gods. Their temples were shut down, and the name of Amon-Re was chiseled from monuments on which it was carved. The old priests, of course, were deprived of their posts and privileges; the pharaoh selected new people, sometimes even foreigners, to serve him. The new religion, moreover, was more remote than the old. Only the pharaoh and his family worshiped Aton directly, and the people worshiped the pharaoh.

Akhnaton's interest in religious reform apparently led him to ignore foreign affairs, which proved disastrous. The Asian possessions of Egypt fell away, and this imperial decline and its economic consequences presumably caused further hostility to the new religion. When the king died, a strong counterrevolution swept away his life's work.

The Egyptians believed in the possibility of life after death through the god Osiris. The character of each person's life had to be tested by 42 assessor-gods before the person could be presented to Osiris. In this scene from an illustration of the Book of the Dead the deceased and his wife (on the left) watch the scales of justice weighing his heart (on the left side of the scales) against the feather of truth. The jackal-faced god Anubis also watches the scales, while the ibis-headed god Thoth keeps the record. [Courtesy of the Trustees of the British Museum]

His chosen successor was soon put aside and replaced by Tutankhamen (r. 1347–1339 B.C.), the young husband of one of the daughters of Akhnaton and his beautiful wife, Nefertiti. The new pharaoh restored the old religion and wiped out as much as he could of the memory of the worship of Aton. He restored Amon to the center of the Egyptian pantheon, abandoned El Amarna, and returned the capital to Thebes. His magnificent tomb, remarkably, survived almost fully intact until its discovery in 1922.

The end of the El Amarna age restored power to the priests of Amon and to military officers. A general named Horemhab became king (r. 1335–1308? B.C.). He restored order and recovered much of the lost empire. He referred to Akhnaton as "the criminal of Akhtaton" and erased his name from the records. Akhnaton's city and memory disappeared for over 3,000 years, to be rediscovered only by chance about a century ago.

Following Akhnaton, Egypt returned to its traditional gods and culture, but its mood had turned gloomy. *The Book of the Dead*, a product of this late period, was a collection of spells to help the dead reach the next world safely, avoiding destruction by a hideous monster. Egypt itself would soon be devoured by powerful empires no less menacing.

Ancient Near Eastern Empires

In the time of the Eighteenth Dynasty in Egypt, new groups of peoples had established themselves in the Near East: the Kassites in Babylonia, the Hittites in Asia Minor, and the Mitannians in northern Mesopotamia. The Kassites and Mitannians were warrior peoples who ruled as a minority over more civilized folk and absorbed their culture without changing it. The Hittites established a kingdom of their own and forged an empire that lasted some 200 years.

The Hittites

The Hittites arrived in Asia Minor about 2000 B.C. By about 1500 B.C. they had established a strong, centralized government with a capital at

This Neo-Hittite relief carving dates to the ninth century B.C. It comes from the citadel at Binjirli in modern Turkey and shows two banqueters. [Erich Lessing/Art Resource, N.Y.]

Hattusas (near Ankara, the capital of modern Turkey). Between 1400 and 1200 B.C. they contested Egypt's control of Palestine and Syria. By about 1265 B.C. they were strong enough to achieve a dynastic marriage with the daughter of the powerful Nineteenth Dynasty pharaoh, Ramses II. The Hittite kingdom was gone by 1200 B.C., swept away by the arrival of new, mysterious Indo-Europeans. Neo-Hittite centers flourished in Asia Minor and Mesopotamia for a few centuries longer, however.

In most respects the Hittites reflected the influence of the dominant Mesopotamian culture of the region. Their government, however, was different. Their kings did not claim to be divine or even to be the chosen representatives of the gods. In the early period the king's power was checked by a council of nobles, and the assembled army had to ratify his succession to the throne. The Hittites appear to have been responsible for a great technological advance, the smelting of iron. They also played an important role in transmitting the ancient cultures of Mesopotamia and Egypt to the Greeks, who lived on their frontiers.

The Assyrians

The fall of the Hittites was followed by the rise of the Assyrians, who established the first of a succession of powerful empires that dominated the Near East's ancient civilizations and even extended them to new areas. The homeland of the Assyrians was in the valleys and hills of northern Mesopotamia and the area east of the Tigris River. They had a series of capitals, of which the great city of Nineveh (modern Mosul, Iraq) is perhaps the best known. They spoke a Semitic language and, from early on, were culturally a part of Mesopotamia.

Akkadians, Sumerians, Amorites, and Mitannians had each in turn dominated Assyria. When the Hittites defeated the Mitannians in the fourteenth century B.C., they effectively liberated the Assyrians, allowing them to establish themselves as an independent state. After 1000 B.C. the Assyrians began a period of steady expansion, and by 665 B.C. they controlled all of Mesopotamia, much of Asia Minor, Syria, Palestine, and Egypt to its southern frontier. They succeeded thanks to a large, well-disciplined army and a society that powerfully valued the military virtues. Fierce and cruel, they boasted of their own brutality, at least in part to terrorize real and potential enemies.

Unlike earlier empires, the Assyrian Empire systematically and profitably exploited the area it held. The Assyrians used various methods of control, ranging from the mere collection of tribute to the stationing of garrisons in conquered territory to the scattering of entire populations away from their homelands, as befell the people of the kingdom of Israel. Because of their military and administrative skills, the Assyrians were able to hold vast areas even as they absorbed the teachings of the older cultures under their sway.

In addition to maintaining their empire, the Assyrians had to defend it against the incur-

A reconstruction drawing of Nimrud, one of the capitals of the Assyrian Empire. Some elements of this drawing may be fanciful, but it gives a sense of what an Assyrian city looked like. [Courtesy of the Trustees of the British Museum]

sions of barbarians on its frontiers. In the seventh century B.C. this task so drained the overextended empire that it was left vulnerable to internal rebellion. A new dynasty in Babylon threw off Assyrian rule, joined with the rising kingdom of Media to the east (in modern Iran), and defeated the Assyrians, destroying Nineveh in 612 B.C. The successor kingdoms, the Chaldean— or Neo-Babylonian—and the Median, did not last long. By 539 B.C., they were swallowed by yet another great Eastern empire, that of the Persians. We shall return to the Persians in Chapter 2.

Palestine

None of the powerful kingdoms of the ancient Near East had as much influence on the future of Western civilization as the small stretch of land between Syria and Egypt, the land called Palestine for much of its history. The three great religions of the modern world outside the Far East—Judaism, Christianity, and Islam—trace their origins, at least in part, to the people who arrived there a little before 1200 B.C. The book that recounts their experiences is the Hebrew Bible.

The Canaanites and the Phoenicians

Before the Israelites arrived in their promised land, it was inhabited by groups of people speaking a Semitic language called Canaanite. The Canaanites lived in walled cities and carried on a version of Mesopotamian culture that included the worship of many gods. The arrival of the Israelites probably forced them northward to settle among similar people who inhabited the coastal land of Phoenicia.

The Phoenicians were a people who had played an important role in commerce from a very early time. Their writing system is among the earliest decipherable examples of a nearly alphabetic script, a simplified form of writing in which the symbols represent the individual letters of a language. They founded colonies throughout the Mediterranean as far west as Spain. The most famous of these was Carthage, near modern Tunis in North Africa. Sitting astride all trade routes, the Phoenician cities were important sites for the transmission of culture and knowledge from east to west.

The Israelites

The history of the Israelites must be pieced together from various sources. They are mentioned only rarely in the records of their neighbors, and so we must rely chiefly on their own account, the Hebrew Bible. This is not a history in our sense, but a complicated collection of historical narrative, wisdom literature, poetry, law, and religious witness. Scholars of an earlier time tended to discard it as a historical source, but the most recent trend is to take it seriously while using it with caution.

According to tradition the patriarch Abraham came from Ur about 1900 B.C. and wandered west to tend his flocks in the land of the Canaanites. Some of his people settled there and others wandered into Egypt, perhaps with the Hyksos. By the thirteenth century B.C., led by Moses, they had left Egypt and wandered in the desert until they reached Canaan. They established a united kingdom that reached its peak under David and Solomon in the tenth century B.C. The sons of Solomon could not maintain the unity of the kingdom, and it split into two parts: Israel in the north and Judah, with its capital at Jerusalem, in the south (see Map 1-3 on page 31). The rise of the great empires brought disaster to the Israelites. The northern kingdom fell to the Assyrians in 722 B.C., and its people—the "ten lost tribes"—were scattered and lost forever. Only the kingdom of Judah remained. It is from this time that we may call the Israelites Jews.

A Phoenician warship. [Courtesy of the Trustees of the British Museum]

In 586 B.C. Judah was defeated by the Neo-Babylonian king Nebuchadnezzar II. He destroyed the great temple built by Solomon and took thousands of hostages off to Babylon. When the Persians defeated Babylonia, they ended this Babylonian Captivity of the Jews and allowed them to return to their homeland. After that, the area of the old kingdom of the Jews in Palestine was dominated by foreign peoples for some 2,500 years until the establishment of the State of Israel in A.D. 1948.

The Jewish Religion

The fate of this small nation of Israel would be of little interest were it not for its unique religious achievement. The great contribution of the Jews is the idea of monotheism, the existence of one universal God, the creator and ruler of the universe. This idea may be as old as Moses, as the

Jewish tradition asserts, and it certainly dates as far back as the prophets of the eighth century B.C. The Jewish God is not a natural force nor like human beings or any other creatures; He is so elevated that those who believe in Him may not picture Him in any form. The faith of the

The Israelites	
ca. 1000–961 B.C.	Reign of King David
ca. 961–922 B.C.	Reign of King Solomon
722 B.C.	Assyrian conquest of Israel (northern kingdom)
586 B.C.	Destruction of Jerusalem; fall of Judah (southern kingdom); Babylonian Captivity
539 B.C.	Restoration of temple; return of exiles

The "Israel Stele" of the Pharaoh Merenptah

These lines from a black granite stele set up about 1220 B.C. by the Pharaoh Merenptah (r. ca. 1223–1211 B.C.), son of Ramses II of the Nineteenth Egyptian dynasty, commemorate his victories over various peoples in the region. Scholars have identified Tehenu with the Libyans, Hatti with the Hittites, and Hurru with the Hurrians of northern Mesopotamia. The reference to Israel is the first outside the Bible and is generally believed to confirm the story of the Israelites' exodus from Egypt and their flight to Canaan.

◆ *Who was responsible for taking on the trouble and expense to inscribe this document on stone? What purpose or purposes was it meant to serve? How reliable is it likely to be as an accurate account of what took place?*

Great rejoicing has risen in Egypt,
  Jubilation has issued from the towns of
  To-meri;
They recount the victories
  Which Merenptah wrought in Tehenu:
"How beloved he is, the victorious ruler!
  How exalted is the king among the gods!
How fortunate he is, the master of command!
  Ah, how pleasant it is to sit when one is
  engaged in chatter!"

One may walk freely on the road,
  Without any fear in the hearts of men.
Fortresses are left to themselves;
  Wells are open, accessible to messengers;
The ramparts of the encircling wall are se-
  cure in the sunlight

Until their watchmen awake.
The Medjay are stretched out in sleep,
  The Tjukten hunt in the fields as they
  wish. . . .
The princes lie prostrate, saying, "Salaam"!
  Not one lifts his head among the Nine
  Bows.
Destruction for Tehenu! Hatti is pacified;
  Canaan is plundered with every evil;
Ashkelon is taken; Gezer is captured;
  Yanoam is made non-existent;
Israel lies desolate; its seed is no more;
  Hurru has become a widow for To-meri;
All the lands in their entirety are at peace,
  Everyone who was a nomad has been
  curbed by King Merenptah.

Trans. by R. J. Williams in Documents from Old Testament Times, *lines 33–58, p. 139.*

Jews is given special strength by their belief that God made a covenant with Abraham that his progeny would be a chosen people who would be rewarded for following God's commandments and the law He revealed to Moses.

A novelty of Jewish religious thought is the powerful ethical element it introduced. God is a severe but just judge. Ritual and sacrifice are not enough to achieve His approval. People must be righteous, and God Himself appears to be bound to act righteously. The Jewish prophetic tradition was a powerful ethical force. The prophets constantly criticized any falling away from the law and the path of righteousness. They placed God in history, blaming the misfortunes of the Jews on God's righteous and necessary intervention to punish the people for their misdeeds. The prophets also promised the redemption of the Jews if they repented, however. The prophetic tradition expected the redemption to come in the form of a Messiah who would restore the house of David. Christianity, emerging from this tradition, holds that Jesus of Nazareth was that Messiah.

Jewish religious ideas influenced the future development of the West, both directly and indirectly. The Jews' belief in an all-powerful creator (who is righteous Himself and demands right-

MAP 1-3 ANCIENT PALESTINE *The Hebrews established a unified kingdom in Palestine under Kings David and Solomon in the tenth century B.C. After the death of Solomon, however, the kingdom was divided into two parts—Israel in the north and Judah, with its capital Jerusalem, in the south. North of Israel were the great commercial cities of Phoenicia.*

eousness and obedience from humankind) and a universal God (who is the father and ruler of all peoples) is a critical part of the Western heritage.

General Outlook of Near Eastern Cultures

Our very brief account of the history of the ancient Near East so far reveals that its various peoples and cultures were different in many ways. Yet the distance between all of them and the emerging culture of the Greeks, to whom we shall turn our attention in Chapter 2, is striking. We can see this distance best by comparing the approach of the other cultures with that of the Greeks on several fundamental human problems: What is the relationship of humans to nature? To the gods? To other humans? These questions involve attitudes toward religion, philosophy, science, law, justice, politics, and government in general.

Humans and Nature

For the peoples of the Near East there was no simple separation between humans and nature or even between animate creatures and inanimate objects. Humanity was part of a natural continuum, and all things partook of life and spirit. These peoples imagined the universe to be dominated by gods more or less in the shape of humans, and the world they ruled was irregular and unpredictable, subject to divine whims. The gods were capricious because nature seemed capricious.

One Egyptian text speaks of humans as "the cattle of god." The Babylonian story of creation makes it clear that humanity's function is merely to serve the gods. The creator Marduk says:

> I will create Lullu "man" be his name,
> I will form Lullu, man.
> Let him be burdened with the toil of the gods,
> that they may freely breathe.[1]

In a world ruled by powerful deities of this kind, human existence was precarious. Even disasters that we would think human in origin the Mesopotamians saw as the product of divine will. Thus a Babylonian text depicts the destruction of the city of Ur by invading Elamites as the work of the gods, carried out by the storm god Enlil:

> Enlil called the storm.
> The people mourn.
> Exhilarating winds he took from the land.
> The people mourn.
> Good winds he took away from Sumer.
> The people mourn.

[1]Henri Frankfort et al., Before Philosophy (Baltimore: Penguin, 1949), p. 197.

He summoned evil winds.
The people mourn.
Entrusted them to Kingaluda, tender of storms.
He called the storm that will annihilate the
   land.
The people mourn.
He called disastrous winds.
The people mourn.
Enlil—choosing Gibil as his helper—
Called the (great) hurricane of heaven.
The people mourn.[2]

The helpless position of humankind in the face of irrational divine powers is clearly shown in both the Egyptian and the Babylonian versions of the story of the flood. In one Egyptian tale, Re, the god who had created humans, decided to destroy them because of some unnamed evil that the god had suffered. He sent the goddess Sekhmet to accomplish the deed, and she was in the midst of her task, enjoying the work and wading in a sea of blood, when Re changed his mind. Instead of ordering a halt, he poured 7,000 barrels of blood-colored beer in Sekhmet's path. She quickly became drunk, stopped the slaughter, and preserved humanity. In the Babylonian story, the motive for the destruction of humanity is more obvious:

In those days the world teemed, the people multiplied, the world bellowed like a wild bull, and the great god was aroused by the clamour. Enlil heard the clamour and he said to the gods in council, "The uproar of mankind is intolerable and sleep is no longer possible by reason of the babel." So the gods in their hearts were moved to let loose the deluge.[3]

The gods repented to a degree and decided to save one family, Utnapishtim and his wife, but they seem to have chosen him because he was friendly with Enki, the god of wisdom, who helped him to survive by a trick.

In such a universe humans could not hope to understand nature, much less control it. At best, they could try by magic to use some mysterious forces against others. An example of this device is provided by a Mesopotamian incantation to break a sorcerer's spell. The sufferers tried to use the magical powers inherent in ordinary salt to fight the witchcraft, addressing the salt as follows:

O Salt, created in a clean place,
For food of gods did Enlil destine thee.
Without thee no meal is set out in Ekur,
Without thee god, king, lord, and prince do not
   smell incense.
I am so-and-so, the son of so-and-so,
Held captive by enchantment,
Held in fever by bewitchment.
O Salt, break my enchantment! Loose my spell!
Take from me the bewitchment!—and as my
   Creator
I shall extol thee.[4]

Humans and the Gods, Law, and Justice

Human relationships to the gods were equally humble. There was no doubt that the gods could destroy humankind and might do so at any time for no good reason. Humans could—and, indeed, had to—try to win the gods over by prayers and sacrifices, but there was no guarantee of success. The gods were bound by no laws and no morality. The best behavior and the greatest devotion to the cult of the gods were no defense against the divine and cosmic irrationality.

In the earliest civilizations, human relations were guided by laws, often set down in written codes. The basic question about law concerned its legitimacy: Why, apart from the lawgiver's power to coerce obedience, should anyone obey the law? For the Egyptians the answer was simple: The law came from the king and the king was a god. For the Mesopotamians the answer was almost the same: They believed that the king was a representative of the gods, so that the laws he set forth were equally divine. The prologue to the most famous legal document in antiquity, the Code of Hammurabi, makes this plain:

I am the king who is preeminent among kings;
my words are choice; my ability has no equal.
By the order of Shamash, the great judge of
   heaven and earth,
may my justice prevail in the land;
by the word of Marduk, my lord,
may my statutes have no one to rescind them.[5]

The Hebrews introduced some important

---

[2]*Frankfort et al., p. 154.*
[3]*The Epic of Gilgamesh, trans. by N. K. Sandars (Baltimore: Penguin, 1960), p. 105.*

[4]*Frankfort et al., p. 143.*
[5]*James B. Pritchard, Ancient Near Eastern Texts, 2nd ed. (Princeton: Princeton University Press, 1955), pp. 164–180.*

The Second Isaiah Defines Hebrew Monotheism

The strongest statement of Hebrew monotheism is found in these words of the anonymous prophet whom we call the Second Isaiah. He wrote during the Hebrew exile in Babylonia, 597–539 B.C.

◆ In what ways is the deity in this passage different from the deities of the Mesopotamian and Egyptian societies? Are there any similarities? Many peoples have claimed that a single god was the greatest and the ruler over all others. What is there in this selection that claims a different status for the deity of the Hebrews?

42

⁵Thus says God, the LORD
  who created the heavens and stretched
    them out,
  who spread forth the earth and what
    comes from it,
  who gives breath to the people upon it
    and spirit
  to those who walk in it:
⁶"I am the Lord, I have called you in
    righteousness,
  I have taken you by the hand and kept
    you;
I have given you as a covenant to the
    people, a light to the nations,
⁷to open the eyes that are blind,
to bring out the prisoners from the dungeon,
  from the prison those who sit in darkness.
⁸I am the LORD, that is my name;
  my glory I give to no other,
  nor my praise to graven images.
⁹Behold, the former things have come to
    pass, and new things I now declare;
before they spring forth I tell you of them."

44

⁶Thus says the LORD, the King of Israel and
    his Redeemer, the LORD of hosts:
"I am the first and I am the last; besides me
    there is no god.
⁷Who is like me? Let him proclaim it,
  let him declare and set it forth before me.
Who has announced of old the things to
    come?
  Let them tell us what is yet to be.
⁸Fear not, nor be afraid;
  have I not told you from of old and
    declared it?

And you are my witnesses!
Is there a God besides me?
  There is no Rock; I know not any."

49

²²Thus says the Lord GOD:
  "Behold, I will lift up my hand to the
    nations,
  and raise my signal to the peoples;
  and they shall bring your sons in their
    bosom,
  and your daughters shall be carried on
    their shoulders
²³Kings shall be your foster fathers,
  and their queens your nursing mothers.
With their faces to the ground they shall
    bow down to you,
  and lick the dust of your feet.
Then you will know that I am the LORD;
  those who wait for me shall not be put to
    shame."
²⁴Can the prey be taken from the mighty, or
    the captives of a tyrant be rescued?
²⁵Surely, thus says the LORD:
"Even the captives of the mighty shall be
    taken,
  and the prey of the tyrant be rescued,
for I will contend with those who contend
    with you
  and I will save your children.
²⁶I will make your oppressors eat their own
    flesh,
  and they shall be drunk with their own
    blood as with wine.
Then all flesh shall know
  that I am the LORD your Savior,
  and your Redeemer, the Mighty One of
    Jacob."

Bible, Revised Standard Version *(New York: Division of Christian Education, National Council of Churches, 1952).*

new ideas. Their unique God was capable of great anger and destruction, but He was open to persuasion and subject to morality. He was therefore more predictable and comforting, for all the terror of His wrath. The biblical version of the flood story, for instance, reveals the great difference between the Hebrew God and the Babylonian deities. The Hebrew God was powerful and wrathful, but He was not arbitrary. He chose to destroy His creatures for their moral failures, for the reason that

the wickedness of man was great in the earth, and that every imagination of the thought of His heart was evil continually . . . the earth was corrupt in God's sight and the earth was filled with violence.[6]

When He repented and wanted to save someone, He chose Noah because "Noah was a righteous man, blameless in his generation."[7]

That God was bound by His own definition of righteousness is neatly shown in the biblical story of Sodom and Gomorrah. He had chosen to destroy these wicked cities but felt obliged first by His covenant to inform Abraham.[8] In this passage Abraham calls on God to abide by His own moral principles, and God sees Abraham's point.

In such a world there is the possibility of order in the universe and on this earth. There is also the possibility of justice among human beings, for the Hebrew God had provided His people with law. Through his prophet Moses, He had provided humans with regulations that would enable them to live in peace and justice. If they would abide by the law and live upright lives, they and their descendants could expect happy and prosperous lives. This idea was quite different from the uncertainty of the Babylonian view, but like it and its Egyptian partner, it left no doubt of the centrality of the divine. Cosmic order, human survival, and justice were all dependent on God.

[6]*Genesis 6:5–11.*
[7]*Genesis 6:9.*
[8]*Genesis 18:20–33.*
[9]*Benjamin Farrington,* Greek Science *(London: Penguin, 1953), p. 37.*

Toward the Greeks and Western Thought

Greek thought offered different approaches and answers to many of the concerns we have been discussing. Calling attention to some of those differences will help convey the distinctive outlook of the Greeks and the later cultures within Western civilization that have drawn heavily on Greek influence.

It is important to recognize that Greek ideas had much in common with the ideas of earlier peoples. The Greek gods had most of the characteristics of the Mesopotamian deities; magic and incantations played a part in the lives of most Greeks; and Greek law, like that of earlier peoples, was usually connected with divinity. Many, if not most, Greeks in the ancient world must have lived their lives with notions similar to those held by other peoples. The surprising thing is that some Greeks developed ideas that were strikingly different and, in so doing, set a part of humankind on an entirely new path.

As early as the sixth century B.C., some Greeks living in the Ionian cities of Asia Minor raised questions and suggested answers about the nature of the world that produced an intellectual revolution. In their speculations, they made guesses that were completely naturalistic and made no reference to supernatural powers. One historian of Greek thought, discussing the views of Thales, the first Greek philosopher, put the case particularly well:

In one of the Babylonian legends it says: "All the lands were sea . . . Marduk bound a rush mat upon the face of the waters, he made dirt and piled it beside the rush mat." What Thales did was to leave Marduk out. He, too, said that everything was once water. But he thought that earth and everything else had been formed out of water by a natural process, like the silting up of the Delta of the Nile. . . . It is an admirable beginning, the whole point of which is that it gathers into a coherent picture a number of observed facts without letting Marduk in.[9]

By putting the question of the world's origin in a naturalistic form, Thales, in the sixth century B.C., may have initiated the unreservedly rational investigation of the universe and, in so doing, initiated both philosophy and science.

The same relentlessly rational approach was

used even in regard to the gods themselves. In the same century as Thales, Xenophanes of Colophon expressed the opinion that humans think of the gods as resembling themselves, that like themselves they were born, that they wear clothes like theirs, and that they have voices and bodies like theirs. If oxen, horses, and lions had hands and could paint like humans, Xenophanes argued, they would paint gods in their own image; the oxen would draw gods like oxen and the horses like horses. Thus Africans believed in flat-nosed, black-faced gods, and the Thracians in gods with blue eyes and red hair.[10] In the fifth century B.C. Protagoras of Abdera went so far in the direction of agnosticism as to say, "About the gods I can have no knowledge either that they are or that they are not or what is their nature."[11]

This rationalistic, skeptical way of thinking carried over into practical matters as well. The school of medicine led by Hippocrates of Cos (about 400 B.C.) attempted to understand, diagnose, and cure disease without any attention to supernatural forces or beings. One of the Hippocratics wrote of the mysterious disease epilepsy:

It seems to me that the disease is no more divine than any other. It has a natural cause, just as other diseases have. Men think it divine merely because they do not understand it. But if they called everything divine which they do not understand, why, there would be no end of divine things.[12]

By the fifth century B.C. it was also possible for the historian Thucydides to analyze and explain the behavior of humans in society completely in terms of human nature and chance, leaving no place for the gods or supernatural forces.

The same absence of divine or supernatural forces characterized Greek views of law and justice. Most Greeks, of course, liked to think in a vague way that law came ultimately from the gods. In practice, however, and especially in the democratic states, they knew very well that laws were made by humans and should be obeyed because they represented the expressed consent of the citizens. Law, according to the fourth century B.C. statesman Demosthenes, is "a general covenant of the whole State, in accordance with which all men in that State ought to regulate their lives."[13]

The statement of these ideas, so different from any that came before the Greeks, opens the discussion of most of the issues that appear in the long history of Western civilization and that remain major concerns in the modern world: What is the nature of the universe, and how can it be controlled? Are there divine powers, and, if so, what is humanity's relationship to them? Are law and justice human, divine, or both? What is the place in human society of freedom, obedience, and reverence? These and many other matters were either first considered or elaborated on by the Greeks.

The Greeks' sharp departure from the thinking of earlier cultures marked the beginning of the unusual experience that we call Western civilization. Nonetheless, they built on a foundation of lore that people in the Near East had painstakingly accumulated over millennia. From ancient Mesopotamia and Egypt they borrowed important knowledge and skills in mathematics, astronomy, art, and literature. From Phoenicia they learned the art of writing. The discontinuities, however, are more striking than the continuities.

The great civilizations of the river valleys were ruled by hereditary monarchies surrounded and elevated by the aura of divinity. The rulers amassed great wealth with which they could pay large armies to dominate their own people. Powerful priesthoods presented yet another bastion of privilege that stood between the ordinary person and the knowledge and opportunity needed for freedom and autonomy. The world of the ancient Near East, in the petty kingdoms and city-states of Palestine, Phoenicia, and Syria just as in the great empires of Egypt and Mesopotamia, was dominated by religion. The secular, reasoned questioning that sought understanding of the world in which people

---

[10]*Frankfort et al., pp. 14–16.*
[11]*Hermann Diels,* Fragmente der Vorsokratiker, *5th ed., ed. by Walter Kranz (Berlin: Weidmann, 1934–38), Frg. 4.*
[12]*Diels, Frgs. 14–16.*

[13]*Demosthenes,* Against Aristogeiton, *16.*

lived, that tried to find explanations in the natural order of things rather than in the supernatural acts of the gods, was not characteristic of the older cultures. Nor would it appear in similar societies at other times in other parts of the world. The new way of looking at things was uniquely the product of the Greeks. We now need to see whether there was something special in their experience that made them raise fundamental questions in the way that they did.

Review Questions

1. How would you define "history"? What different academic disciplines do historians rely on and why is the study of history important?
2. How was life during the Paleolithic Age different from that in the Neolithic Age? What advancements in agriculture and human development had taken place by the end of the Neolithic era? Is it valid to speak of a "Neolithic Revolution"?
3. What general conclusions can you draw about the differences in the political and intellectual outlooks of the civilizations of Egypt and Mesopotamia? Compare especially Egyptian and Mesopotamian religious views. In what ways did the regional geography influence the religious outlooks of these two civilizations?
4. How did the monotheism of Akhnaton differ from that of the Hebrews? To what extent did the Hebrew faith bind the Jews politically? Why was the concept of monotheism so radical for Near Eastern civilizations?
5. Why were the Assyrians so successful in establishing their Near Eastern empire? How did their empire differ from that of the Hittites or Egyptians? In what ways did this empire benefit the civilized Middle East? Why did the Assyrian empire ultimately fail to survive?
6. In what ways did Greek thought develop along different lines from that of Near Eastern civilizations? What new questions about human society were asked as a result of Greek influence?

Suggested Readings

W. F. Albright, *From the Stone Age to Christianity* (1957). An original and interesting interpretive study.

C. Aldred, *Akhenaten, Pharaoh of Egypt: A New Study* (1968). A judicious and critical biography of the enigmatic pharaoh.

V. G. Childe, *What Happened in History* (1946). A pioneering study of human prehistory and history before the Greeks from an anthropological point of view.

R. de Vaux, *Ancient Israel: Its Life and Institutions* (1961). A fine account of social institutions.

H. Frankfort et al., *Before Philosophy* (1949). A brilliant examination of the mind of the ancients from the Stone Age to the Greeks.

A. Gardiner, *Egypt of the Pharaohs* (1961). A sound narrative history.

O. R. Gurney, *The Hittites* (1954). A good general survey.

W. W. Hallo and W. K. Simpson, *The Ancient Near East: A History* (1971). A fine survey of Egyptian and Mesopotamian history.

T. Jacobsen, *The Treasures of Darkness: A History of Mesopotamian Religion* (1976). A superb and sensitive re-creation of the spiritual life of Mesopotamian peoples from the fourth to the first millennia B.C.

D. C. Johnson and M. R. Edey, *Lucy: The Beginnings of Mankind* (1981). A study of the first human creatures based on remains found in Africa.

S. N. Kramer, *The Sumerians: Their History, Culture and Character* (1963). A readable general account of Sumerian history.

S. Lloyd, *The Archaeology of Mesopotamia*, revised edition (1984). An account of the material remains of Mesopotamia and their meaning from the Old Stone Age to the Persian Conquest.

D. Oates and J. Oates, *The Rise of Civilization*, (1976). A study of the emergence of urban life in southern Mesopotamia placed in a broad context and well illustrated with photographs.

J. Oates, *Babylon*, revised edition (1986). An introduction to the history and archaeology of Babylonia revised to make use of newly discovered evidence.

H. M. Orlinsky, *Ancient Israel* (1960). Chiefly a political survey.

J. N. Postgate, *The First Empires* (1977). A fine account of Mesopotamian history from the dawn of history to the Persian conquest.

J. N. Postgate, *Early Mesopotamia* (1992). An excellent study of Mesopotamian economy and society from the earliest times to about 1500 B.C., helpfully illustrated with drawings, pictures, and translated documents.

J. B. PRITCHARD (ed.), *Ancient Near Eastern Texts Relating to the Old Testament* (1969). A good collection of documents in translation with useful introductory material.

C. L. REDMAN, *The Rise of Civilization* (1978). An attempt to use the evidence provided by anthropology, archaeology, and the physical sciences to illuminate the development of early urban society.

W. F. SAGGS, *The Greatness That Was Babylon* (1962). An excellent narrative account of Mesopotamian history.

W. F. SAGGS, *Everyday Life in Babylonia and Assyria* (1965).

W. F. SAGGS, *The Might That Was Assyria* (1984). A history of the northern Mesopotamian empire and a worthy companion to the author's account of the Babylonian empire in the south.

N. K. SANDARS, *The Sea Peoples* (1985). A lively account of the collection of peoples who disrupted established Mediterranean civilizations in the thirteenth century B.C.

S. SANDMEL, *The Hebrew Scriptures* (1963). An examination of the Bible's value as history and literature.

K. C. SEELE, *When Egypt Ruled the East* (1965). A study of Egypt in its imperial period.

B. G. TRIGGER et al., *Ancient Egypt: A Social History* (1982).

J. A. WILSON, *Culture of Ancient Egypt* (1956). A fascinating interpretation of the civilization of ancient Egypt.

Painting of a foot race on an Athenian vase, ca. 530 B.C. Athletics were an important part of Greek culture. The gods were honored with athletic games, and physical training was part of the essential education of young men. [The Metropolitan Museum of Art, Rogers Fund, 1914 Acc. # 14.130.12]

2

The Rise of Greek Civilization

Key Topics in This Chapter
- The Bronze Age civilizations that ruled the Aegean area before the development of Hellenic civilization
- The rise, development, and expansion of the *polis*, the characteristic political unit of Hellenic Greece
- The early history of Sparta and Athens
- The wars between the Greeks and the Persians

About 2000 B.C., Greek-speaking peoples settled the lands surrounding the Aegean Sea and established a style of life and formed a set of ideas, values, and institutions that spread far beyond the Aegean corner of the Mediterranean Sea. Preserved and adapted by the Romans, Greek culture powerfully influenced the society of western Europe in the Middle Ages and dominated the Byzantine Empire in the same period. It would ultimately spread across Europe and in time cross the Atlantic to the Western Hemisphere.

At some time in their history, the Greeks of the ancient world founded cities on every shore of the Mediterranean Sea. Pushing on through the Dardanelles, they placed many settlements on the coasts of the Black Sea in southern Russia and as far east as the approaches to the Caucasus Mountains. The center of Greek life, however, has always been the Aegean Sea and the islands in and around it. This location at the eastern end of the Mediterranean very early put the Greeks in touch with the more advanced and earlier civilizations of Mesopotamia, Egypt, Asia Minor, and Syria-Palestine.

The Greeks acknowledged the influence of these predecessors. A character in one of Plato's dialogues says, "Whatever the Greeks have acquired from foreigners they have, in the end, turned into something finer."[1] This is a proud statement, but it also shows the Greeks were aware of how much they had learned from other civilizations.

The Bronze Age Minoan culture of Crete contributed to Greek civilization, and the mainland Mycenaean culture, which conquered Minoan Crete, contributed even more. Both these cultures, however, had more in common with the cultures of the Near East than with the new Hellenic culture established by the Greeks in the centuries after the end of the Bronze Age in the twelfth century B.C.

The rugged geography of the Greek peninsula and its nearby islands isolated the Greeks of the early Iron Age from their richer and more culturally advanced neighbors, shaping, in part, their way of life, and permitting them to develop that way of life on their own. The aristocratic world of the "Greek Dark Ages" (1150–750 B.C.) produced impressive artistic achievements, especially in the development of painted pottery and most magnificently in the epic poems of Homer. In the eighth century B.C., social, economic, and military changes profoundly influenced the organization of Greek political life; the Greek city-state, the polis, came into being and thereafter dominated the cultural development of the Greek people.

This change came in the midst of turmoil, for the pressure of a growing population led many Greeks to leave home and establish colonies far away. Those who remained often fell into political conflict, from which tyrannies sometimes emerged. These tyrannies, however, were in all cases transitory, and the Greek cities emerged from them as self-governing polities, usually ruled by an oligarchy, broad or narrow. The two most important states, Athens and Sparta, developed in different directions. Sparta formed a mixed constitution in which a very small part of the population dominated the vast majority and Athens developed the world's first democracy.

[1]Plato, *Epinomis*, 987 d.

The Bronze Age on Crete and on the Mainland to About 1150 B.C.

The Bronze Age civilizations in the region that the Greeks would rule arose on the island of Crete, on the islands of the Aegean, and on the mainland of Greece. Crete was the site of the earliest Bronze Age settlements, and modern scholars have called the civilization that arose there *Minoan*, after the legendary king of Crete. A later Bronze Age civilization was centered at the mainland site of Mycenae and is called *Mycenaean*.

The Minoans

With Greece to the north, Egypt to the south, and Asia to the east, Crete was a cultural bridge between the older civilizations and the new one of the Greeks. The Bronze Age came to Crete not long after 3000 B.C., and the Minoan civilization, which powerfully influenced the islands of the Aegean and the mainland of Greece, arose in the third and second millennia B.C.

Scholars have established links between stratigraphic layers at archaeological sites on Crete and specific styles of pottery and other artifacts found in the layers. On this basis they have divided the Bronze Age on Crete into three major periods—Early, Middle, and Late Minoan—with some subdivisions. Dates for Bronze Age settlements on the Greek mainland, for which the term *Helladic* is used, are derived from the same chronological scheme.

During the Middle and Late Minoan periods in the cities of eastern and central Crete, a civilization developed that was new and unique in its character and its beauty. Its most striking creations are the palaces uncovered at such sites as Phaestus, Haghia Triada, and, most important, Cnossus. Each of these palaces was built around a central court surrounded by a labyrinth of rooms. Some sections of the palace at Cnossus were as tall as four stories high. The basement contained many storage rooms for oil and grain, apparently paid as taxes to the king. The main and upper floors contained living quarters as well as workshops for making pottery and jewelry. There were sitting rooms and even bathrooms, to which water was piped through excellent plumbing. Lovely columns,

Periods of the Aegean Bronze Age	
Crete	Greece
2900–2100 B.C. Early Minoan	2900–1900 B.C. Early Helladic
2100–1575 B.C. Middle Minoan	1900–1580 B.C. Middle Helladic
1575–1150 B.C. Late Minoan	1580–1150 B.C. Late Helladic
1575–1500 B.C. Late Minoan I	1580–1500 B.C. Late Helladic I
1500–1400 B.C. Late Minoan II	1500–1425 B.C. Late Helladic II
1400–1150 B.C. Late Minoan III	1425–1150 B.C. Late Helladic III

which tapered downward, supported the ceilings, and many of the walls carried murals showing landscapes and seascapes, festivals, and sports. The palace design and the paintings show the influence of Syria, Asia Minor, and Egypt, but the style and quality are unique to Crete.

In contrast to the Mycenaean cities on the mainland of Greece, Minoan palaces and settlements lacked strong defensive walls. This evidence that the Minoans built without defense in mind has raised questions and encouraged speculation. Some scholars, pointing also to evidence that Minoan religion was more matriarchal than the patriarchal religion of the Mycenaeans and their Greek descendants, have argued that the civilizations of Crete, perhaps reflecting the importance of women, were inherently more tranquil and pacific than others. An earlier and very different explanation for the absence of fortifications was that the protection provided by the sea made them unnecessary. The evidence is not strong enough to support either explanation, and the mystery remains.

Along with palaces, paintings, pottery, jewelry, and other valuable objects, excavations have revealed clay writing tablets like those found in Mesopotamia. The tablets, preserved accidentally when a great fire that destroyed the royal palace at Cnossus hardened them, have three distinct kinds of writing on them: a kind of picture writing called hieroglyphic, and two different linear scripts called Linear A and Linear B. The languages of the other two scripts remain unknown, but Linear B proved to be an early form of Greek. The contents of the tablets, primarily inventories, reveal an organization centered on the palace and ruled by a king who was supported by an extensive bureaucracy that kept remarkably detailed records.

This sort of organization is typical of early civilizations in the Near East but, as we shall see, is nothing like that of the Greeks after the Bronze Age. Yet the inventories were written in a form of Greek. If they controlled Crete

(a)

(b)

(a) The Minoan-period Palace at Cnossus on the island of Crete. (b) A fresco painting from the east wing of the palace. The fresco shows acrobats leaping over a charging bull. It is not known whether such acrobatic displays were only for entertainment or part of some religious ritual. [(a) D.A. Harissiadis, Athens; (b) Scala/Art Resource, N.Y.]

A linear B tablet from Pylos, dated about 1200 B.C. First discovered late in the nineteenth century, Linear B was not deciphered until 1952, when a brilliant young Briton, Michael Ventris, demonstrated that it was an early Greek dialect. This tablet is part of a palace inventory. It survived because it was hardened in a fire when the palace at Pylos was destroyed by invaders. [Hirmer Verlag, Munich]

throughout the Bronze Age, why should Minoans, who were not Greek, have written in a language not their own? This question raises the larger one of what the relationship was between Crete and the Greek mainland in the Bronze Age and leads us to an examination of mainland, or Helladic, culture.

The Mycenaeans

In the third millennium B.C.—the Early Helladic Period—most of the Greek mainland, including many of the sites of later Greek cities, was settled by people who used metal, built some impressive houses, and traded with Crete and the islands of the Aegean. The names they gave to places, names that were sometimes preserved by later invaders, make it clear that they were not Greeks and that they spoke a language that was not Indo-European (the language family to which Greek belongs).

Not long after the year 2000 B.C., many of the Early Helladic sites were destroyed by fire, some were abandoned, and still others appear to have yielded peacefully to an invading people. These signs of invasion probably signal the arrival of the Greeks.

All over Greece, there was a smooth transition between the Middle and Late Helladic periods. The invaders succeeded in establishing control of the entire mainland. The shaft graves cut into the rock at the royal palace-fortress of Mycenae show that they prospered and sometimes became very rich. At Mycenae, the richest finds come from the period after 1600 B.C. The city's wealth and power reached their peak during this time, and the culture of the whole mainland during the Late Helladic Period goes by the name *Mycenaean*.

The presence of the Greek Linear B tablets at Cnossus suggests that Greek invaders also established themselves in Crete, and there is good reason to believe that at the height of Mycenaean power (1400–1200 B.C.), Crete was part of the Mycenaean world. Although their dating is still controversial, the Linear B tablets at Cnossus seem to belong to Late Minoan III, so what is called the great "palace period" at Cnossus would have followed an invasion by Mycenaeans in 1400 B.C. These Greek invaders ruled Crete until the end of the Bronze Age.

MYCENAEAN CULTURE   The excavation of Mycenae, Pylos, and other Mycenaean sites reveals a culture influenced by, but very different from, the Minoan culture. Mycenae and Pylos, like Cnossus, were built some distance from the sea. It is plain, however, that defense against attack was foremost in the minds of the founders of the Mycenaean cities. Both were built on hills in a position commanding the neighboring territory. The Mycenaean people were warriors, as their art, architecture, and weapons reveal. The success of their campaigns and the defense of their territory required strong central authority, and all available evidence shows that the kings provided it. Their palaces, in which the royal family and its retainers lived, were located within the walls; most of the population lived outside the walls. Usually paintings covered the palace walls, as on Crete; but instead of peaceful scenery and games, the Mycenaean murals depicted scenes of war and boar hunting.

About 1500 B.C. the already impressive shaft graves were abandoned in favor of *tholos* tombs. These large, beehivelike chambers were built of enormous, well-cut, and fitted stones, and approached by an unroofed passage (*dromos*) cut horizontally into the side of the hill. The lintel block alone of one of these tombs weighs over one hundred tons. Only a strong king whose wealth was great, whose power was unquestioned, and who commanded the labor of many people could undertake such a project. His wealth probably came from plundering raids, piracy, and trade. Some of this trade went westward to Italy and Sicily, but most of it was with the islands of the Aegean, the coastal towns of Asia Minor, and the cities of Syria, Egypt, and Crete. The Mycenaeans sent pottery, olive oil, and animal hides in exchange for jewels and other luxuries.

Tablets containing the Mycenaean Linear B writing have been found all over the mainland; the largest and most useful collection was found at Pylos. These tablets reveal a world very similar to the one shown by the records at Cnossus. The king, whose title was *wanax*, held a royal domain, appointed officials, commanded servants, and kept a close record of what he owned and what was owed to him. This evidence confirms all the rest; the Mycenaean world was made up of several independent, powerful, and well-organized monarchies.

THE RISE AND FALL OF MYCENAEAN POWER At the height of their power (1400–1200 B.C.), the Mycenaeans were prosperous and active. They enlarged their cities, expanded their trade, and even established commercial colonies in the East. They are mentioned in the archives of the Hittite kings of Asia Minor. They are named as marauders of the Nile Delta in Egyptian records. Sometime about 1250 B.C. they probably sacked Troy, on the coast of northwestern Asia Minor, giving rise to the epic poems of Homer, the *Iliad* and the *Odyssey* (see Map 2-1). Around 1200 B.C., however, the Mycenaean world showed signs of great trouble, and by 1100 B.C. it was gone. Its palaces were destroyed, many of its cities were abandoned, and its art, its pattern of life, and its system of writing were buried and forgotten.

What happened? Some recent scholars, noting evidence that the Aegean island of Thera (modern Santorini) suffered a massive volcanic explosion in the middle to late second millennium B.C., have suggested that this natural disaster was responsible. According to one version of this theory, the explosion occurred around 1400 B.C., blackening and poisoning the air for many miles around and sending a monstrous tidal wave that destroyed the great palace at Cnossus and, with it, Minoan culture. According to another version, the explosion took place about 1200 B.C., destroying Bronze Age culture throughout the Aegean. This second version conveniently accounts for the end of both Minoan and Mycenaean civilizations in a single blow, but the evidence does not support it. The Mycenaean towns were not destroyed all at once; many fell around 1200 B.C., but some flourished for another century, and the Athens of the period was never destroyed or abandoned. No theory of natural disaster can account for this pattern, leaving us to seek less dramatic explanations for the end of Mycenaean civilization.

THE DORIAN INVASION Some scholars have suggested that piratical sea raiders destroyed Pylos and, perhaps, other sites on the mainland. The Greeks themselves believed in a legend that told of the Dorians, a rude people from the north who spoke a Greek dialect different from that of the Mycenaean peoples. According to the legend, the Dorians joined with one of the Greek tribes, the Heraclidae, in an attack on the southern Greek peninsula of Peloponnesus, which was repulsed. One hundred years later they returned and gained full control. Recent historians have identified this legend of "the return of the Heraclidae" with a Dorian invasion.

Archaeology has not provided material evidence of a single Dorian invasion or a series of them, and it is impossible as yet to say with any certainty what happened at the end of the Bronze Age in the Aegean. The chances are good, however, that Mycenaean civilization ended gradually over the century between 1200 B.C. and 1100 B.C. Its end may have been the result of internal conflicts among the Mycenaean kings combined with continuous

MAP 2-1 THE AEGEAN AREA IN THE BRONZE AGE *The Bronze Age in the Aegean area lasted from about 1900 to about 1100 B.C. Its culture on Crete is called Minoan and was at its height about 1900–1400 B.C. Bronze Age Helladic culture on the mainland flourished from about 1600 to 1200 B.C.*

pressure from outsiders, who raided, infiltrated, and eventually dominated Greece and its neighboring islands. There is reason to believe that Mycenaean society suffered internal weaknesses due to its organization around the centralized control of military force and agricultural production. This rigid organization may have deprived it of flexibility and vitality, leaving it vulnerable to outside challengers. In any case, Cnossus, Mycenae, and Pylos were abandoned, their secrets to be kept for over 3,000 years.

The Greek "Middle Ages" to About 750 B.C.

The immediate effects of the Dorian invasion were disastrous for the inhabitants of the Mycenaean world. The palaces and the kings and bureaucrats who managed them were destroyed. The wealth and organization that had supported the artists and merchants were likewise swept away by a barbarous people who did not have the knowledge or social organization to maintain them. Many villages were abandoned and never resettled. Some of their inhabitants probably turned to a nomadic life, and many perished. The chaos resulting from the collapse of the rigidly controlled palace culture produced severe depopulation and widespread poverty that lasted for a long time.

Greek Migrations

Another result of the invasion was the spread of the Greek people eastward from the mainland to the Aegean islands and the coast of Asia Minor. The Dorians themselves, after occupying most of the Peloponnesus, swept across the Aegean to occupy the southern islands and the southern part of the Anatolian coast.

These migrations made the Aegean a Greek lake. Trade with the old civilizations of the Near East, however, was virtually ended by the fall of the advanced Minoan and Mycenaean civilizations; nor was there much internal trade among the different parts of Greece. The Greeks were forced to turn inward, and each community was left largely to its own devices. The Near East was also in disarray at this time, and no great power arose to impose its ways and its will on the helpless people who lived about the Aegean. The Greeks were allowed time to recover from their disaster and to create their unique style of life.

Our knowledge of this period in Greek history rests on very limited sources. Writing disappeared after the fall of Mycenae, and no new script appeared until after 750 B.C., so we have no contemporary author to shed light on this period. Excavation reveals no architecture, sculpture, or painting until after 750 B.C.

The Age of Homer

For a picture of society in these "dark ages," the best source is Homer. His epic poems, the *Iliad* and the *Odyssey*, emerged from a tradition of oral poetry whose roots extend into the Mycenaean Age. Through the centuries bards had sung tales of the heroes who had fought at Troy, using verse arranged in rhythmic formulas to aid the memory. In this way some very old material was preserved into the eighth century B.C., when the poems attributed to Homer were finally written down. Although the poems tell of the deeds of Mycenaean Age heroes, the world they describe clearly differs from the Mycenaean world. Homer's heroes are not buried in *tholos* tombs but are cremated; they worship gods in temples, whereas the Mycenaeans had no temples; they have chariots but do not know their proper use in warfare. Certain aspects of the

The "Trojan Horse," depicted on a seventh-century B.C. Greek vase. According to legend, the Greeks finally defeated Troy by pretending to abandon their siege of the city, leaving a giant wooden horse behind. Soldiers hidden in the horse opened the gates of the city to their compatriots after the Trojans had brought it within their walls. Note the wheels on the horse and the Greek soldiers holding weapons and armor who are hiding inside it. [Deutsche Archäologisches Institut, Athens]

society decribed in the poems appear rather to resemble the world of the tenth and ninth centuries B.C., and other aspects appear to belong to the poet's own time, when population was growing at a swift pace and prosperity was returning, thanks to important changes in Greek agriculture, society, and government.

GOVERNMENT In the Homeric poems the power of the kings is much less than that of the Mycenaean rulers. Homeric kings were limited in their ability to make important decisions by the need to consult a council of nobles. The nobles felt free to discuss matters in vigorous language and in opposition to the king's wishes. In the *Iliad*, Achilles does not hesitate to address Agamemnon, the "most kingly" commander of the Trojan expedition, in these words: "you with a dog's face and a deer's heart." Such language may have been impolite, but it was not treasonous. The king, on the other hand, was free to ignore the council's advice, but it was risky for him to do so.

The right to speak in council was limited to noblemen, but the common people could not be ignored. If a king planned a war or a major change of policy during a campaign, he would not fail to call the common soldiers to an assembly; they could listen and express their feelings by acclamation, though they could not take part in the debate. Homer shows that even in these early times the Greeks, unlike their predecessors and contemporaries, practiced some forms of limited constitutional government.

SOCIETY Homeric society, nevertheless, was sharply divided into classes, the most important division being the one between nobles and everyone else. We do not know the origin of this distinction, but we cannot doubt that at this time Greek society was aristocratic. Birth determined noble status, and wealth usually accompanied it. Below the nobles were three other classes: *thetes*, landless laborers, and slaves. We do not know whether the *thetes* owned the land they worked outright (and so were free to sell it) or worked a hereditary plot that belonged to their clan (and was therefore not theirs to dispose of as they chose).

The worst condition was that of the free but landless hired agricultural laborer. The slave, at least, was attached to a family household and so was protected and fed. In a world where membership in a settled group gave the only security, the free laborers were desperately vulnerable. Slaves were few in number and were mostly women, who served as maids and concubines. Some male slaves worked as shepherds. Few, if any, worked in agriculture, which depended on free labor throughout Greek history.

HOMERIC VALUES The Homeric poems reflect an aristocratic code of values that powerfully influenced all future Greek thought. In classical times Homer was the schoolbook of the Greeks. They memorized his texts, settled diplomatic disputes by citing passages in them, and emulated the behavior and cherished the values they found in them. Those values were physical prowess; courage; fierce protection of one's family, friends, property, and, above all, one's personal honor and reputation. Speed of foot, strength, and, most of all, excellence at fighting make a man great, and all these attributes serve to promote personal honor. The great hero of the *Iliad*, Achilles, refuses to fight in battle, allowing his fellow Greeks to be slain and almost defeated, because Agamemnon has wounded his honor by taking away his battle prize. He returns not out of a sense of duty to the army but to avenge the death of his dear friend Patroclus. Odysseus, the hero of the *Odyssey*, returning home after his wanderings, ruthlessly kills the many suitors who had, in his long absence, sought to marry his wife Penelope; they had dishonored him by consuming his wealth, wooing Penelope, and scorning his son.

The highest virtue in Homeric society was *arete*—manliness, courage in the most general sense, and the excellence proper to a hero. This quality was best revealed in a contest, or *agon*. Homeric battles are not primarily group combats, but a series of individual contests between great champions. One of the prime forms of entertainment is the athletic contest, and the funeral of Patroclus is celebrated by such a contest.

The central ethical idea in Homer can be found in the instructions that Achilles' father gives him when he sends him off to fight at Troy: "Always be the best and distinguished above others." The father of another Homeric hero has given his son exactly the same orders and has added to them the injunction: "Do not bring shame on the family of your fathers who

Kingship in Ithaca

Homer's Odyssey *tells the tale of Odysseus, king of Ithaca, who, after departing to fight at Troy, is unable to return home for twenty years. During this time his infant son Telemachus has grown to manhood and the nobles of Ithaca, thinking him dead, have paid suit to his wife Penelope, wasting his wealth and insulting his family. In this passage from the First Book of the* Odyssey, *Telemachus calls for an assembly. The ensuing debate tells us much about the peculiar nature of Homeric kingship.*

◆ *If the kingship of Ithaca belongs to Telemachus by hereditary right and Odysseus is thought to be dead, why isn't Telemachus king? What does Telemachus mean when he says there are many kings in Ithaca? What does this passage reveal about the nature of kingship in the world of Homer?*

Meanwhile in the shadowy hall the Suitors burst into uproar, and each man voiced the hope that he might share her bed.

But the wise Telemachus called them to order, 'from you who court my mother, this is sheer insolence. For the moment, let us dine and enjoy ourselves—quietly, I insist, for it is a lovely thing to listen to a minstrel such as we have here, with a voice like a god. But in the morning I propose that we all take our places in assembly, so that I can give you formal notice to quit my palace. Yes, you can feast yourselves elsewhere, and eat your own provisions in each other's homes. But if you think it a sounder scheme to destroy one man's estate and go scot-free yourselves, then eat your fill, while I pray to the immortal gods for a day of reckoning, when I can go scot-free though *I* destroy you in this house of mine.'

It amazed them all that Telemachus should have the audacity to adopt this tone, and they could only bite their lips. But at last Antinous, Eupeithes' son, spoke up in answer: 'It seems that the gods are already helping you, Telemachus, by teaching you this bold and haughty way of speaking. Being your father's son, you are heir to this island realm. Heaven grant that you may never be its king!'

But Telemachus was not at a loss. 'Antinous,' he answered, 'it may disappoint you to learn that I should gladly accept that office from the hands of Zeus. Perhaps you argue that nothing worse could happen to a man? I, on the contrary, maintain that it is no bad thing to be a king—to see one's house enriched and one's authority enhanced. However, the Achaeans are not short of princes; young and old they swarm in sea-girt Ithaca. And since the great Odysseus is dead, one of them must surely succeed him. But I intend at least to be master of my own house and the servants whom my royal father won for me in war.'

The Odyssey, *trans. by E. V. Rieu (Harmondsworth: Penguin Books, Ltd., 1946), pp. 34–35.*

were by far the best in Ephyre and in wide Lycia." Here in a nutshell we have the chief values of the aristocrats of Homer's world: to vie for individual supremacy in *arete* and to defend and increase the honor of the family. These would remain prominent aristocratic values long after Homeric society was only a memory.

The *Polis*

The characteristic Greek institution was the *polis*. The common translation of that word as "city-state" is misleading, for it says both too much and too little. All Greek *poleis* began as little more than agricultural villages or towns, and many stayed that way, so the word "city" is inappropriate. All of them were states, in the sense of being independent political units, but they were much more than that. The *polis* was thought of as a community of relatives; all its citizens, who were theoretically descended from a common ancestor, belonged to subgroups, such as fighting brotherhoods (*phratries*), clans, and tribes, and worshiped the gods in common ceremonies.

Aristotle argued that the *polis* was a natural growth and that the human being was by nature "an animal who lives in a *polis*." Humans alone have the power of speech and from it derive the ability to distinguish good from bad and right from wrong, "and the sharing of these things is what makes a household and a *polis*." Therefore, humans who are incapable of sharing these things or who are so self-sufficient that they have no need of them are not humans at all, but either wild beasts or gods. Without law and justice human beings are the worst and most dangerous of the animals. With them humans can be the best, and justice exists only in the *polis*. These high claims were made in the fourth century B.C., hundreds of years after the *polis* came into existence, but they accurately reflect an attitude that was present from the first.

Development of the *Polis*

Originally the word *polis* referred only to a citadel, an elevated, defensible rock to which the farmers of the neighboring area could retreat in case of attack. The Acropolis in Athens and the hill called Acrocorinth in Corinth are examples. For some time such high places and the adjacent farms comprised the *polis*. The towns grew gradually and without planning, as their narrow, winding, and disorderly streets show. For centuries they had no walls. Unlike the city-states of the Near East, they were not placed for commercial convenience on rivers or the sea. Nor did they grow up around a temple to serve the needs of priests and to benefit from the needs of worshipers. The availability of farmland and of a natural fortress determined their location. They were placed either well inland or far enough away from the sea to avoid piratical

raids. Only later and gradually did the *agora*—a marketplace and civic center—appear within the *polis*. The agora was to become the heart of the Greeks' remarkable social life, distinguished by conversation and argument carried on in the open air.

Some *poleis* probably came into existence early in the eighth century B.C. The institution was certainly common by the middle of the century, for all the colonies that were established by the Greeks in the years after 750 B.C. took the form of the *polis*. Once the new institution had been fully established, true monarchy disappeared. Vestigial kings survived in some places, but they were almost always only ceremonial figures without power. The original form of the *polis* was an aristocratic republic dominated by the nobility through its council of nobles and its monopoly of the magistracies.

About 750 B.C., coincident with the development of the *polis*, the Greeks borrowed a writing system from one of the Semitic scripts and added vowels to create the first true alphabet. This new Greek alphabet was easier to learn than any earlier writing system, leading to much wider literacy.

The Hoplite Phalanx

A new military technique was crucial to the development of the *polis*. In earlier times the brunt of fighting had been carried on by small troops of cavalry and individual "champions" who first threw their spears and then came to close quarters with swords. Toward the end of the eighth century B.C., however, the hoplite phalanx came into being and remained the basis of Greek warfare thereafter.

The hoplite was a heavily armed infantryman who fought with a spear and large shield. These soldiers were formed into a phalanx in close order, usually at least eight ranks deep. So long as the hoplites fought bravely and held their ground, there would be few casualties and no defeat; but if they gave way, the result was usually a rout. All depended on the discipline, strength, and courage of the individual soldier. At its best the phalanx could withstand cavalry charges and defeat infantries not as well protected or disciplined. Until defeated by the Roman legion, it was the dominant military force in the eastern Mediterranean.

The usual hoplite battle in Greece was between the armies of two *poleis* quarreling over a piece of land. One army invaded the territory of the other when the crops were almost ready for harvest. The defending army had no choice but to protect its fields. If the army was beaten, its fields were captured or destroyed and its people might starve. In every way, the phalanx was a communal effort that relied not on the extraordinary actions of the individual but on the courage of a considerable portion of the citizenry. This style of fighting produced a single decisive battle that reduced the time lost in fighting other kinds of warfare; it spared the houses, livestock, and other capital of the farmer-soldiers who made up the phalanx, and it reduced the number of casualties, as well. It perfectly suited the farmer-soldier-citizen who was the backbone of the *polis*, and, by keeping wars short and limiting their destructiveness and expense, it helped the *polis* prosper.

The phalanx and the *polis* arose together, and both heralded the decline of the kings. The phalanx, however, was not made up only of aristocrats. Most of the hoplites were farmers working small holdings. The immediate beneficiaries of the royal decline were the aristocrats, but because the existence of the *polis* depended on small farmers, their wishes could not long be wholly ignored. The rise of the hoplite phalanx created a bond between the aristocrats and the yeomen family farmers who fought in it. This bond helps explain why class conflicts were muted for some time. It also guaranteed, however, that the aristocrats, who dominated at first, would not always be unchallenged.

The Importance of the Polis

The Greeks looked to the *polis* for peace, order, prosperity, and honor in their lifetime. They counted on it to preserve their memory and to honor their descendants after death. Some of them came to see it not only as a ruler, but as the molder of its citizens. Knowing this, we can understand the pride and scorn that underlie the comparison made by the poet Phocylides between the Greek state and the capital of the great and powerful Assyrian Empire: "A little *polis* living orderly in a high place is stronger than a block-headed Nineveh."

Expansion of the Greek World

From the middle of the eighth century B.C. until well into the sixth century B.C., the Greeks vastly expanded the territory they controlled, their wealth, and their contacts with other peoples. A burst of colonizing activity placed *poleis* from Spain to the Black Sea. A century earlier a few Greeks had established trading posts in Syria. There they had learned new techniques in the arts and crafts and much more from the older civilizations of the Near East.

Magna Graecia

Syria and its neighboring territory were too strong to penetrate, and so the Greeks settled the southern coast of Macedonia and the Chalcidic peninsula (see Map 2-2). These regions were sparsely settled, and the natives were not well enough organized to resist the Greek colonists. Southern Italy and eastern Sicily were even more inviting areas. Before long there were so many Greek colonies in Italy and Sicily that the Romans called the whole region *Magna Graecia* ("Great Greece"). The Greeks also put colonies in Spain and southern France. In the seventh century B.C. Greek colonists settled the coasts of the northeastern Mediterranean, the Black Sea, and the straits connecting them. About the same time they established settlements on the eastern part of the North African coast. The Greeks now had outposts throughout the Mediterranean world.

The Greek Colony

The Greeks did not lightly leave home to join a colony. The voyage by sea was dangerous and uncomfortable, and at the end of it were uncertainty and danger. Only powerful pressures like overpopulation and land hunger drove thousands from their homes to establish new *poleis*. The colony, although sponsored by the mother city, was established for the good of the colonists rather than for the benefit of those

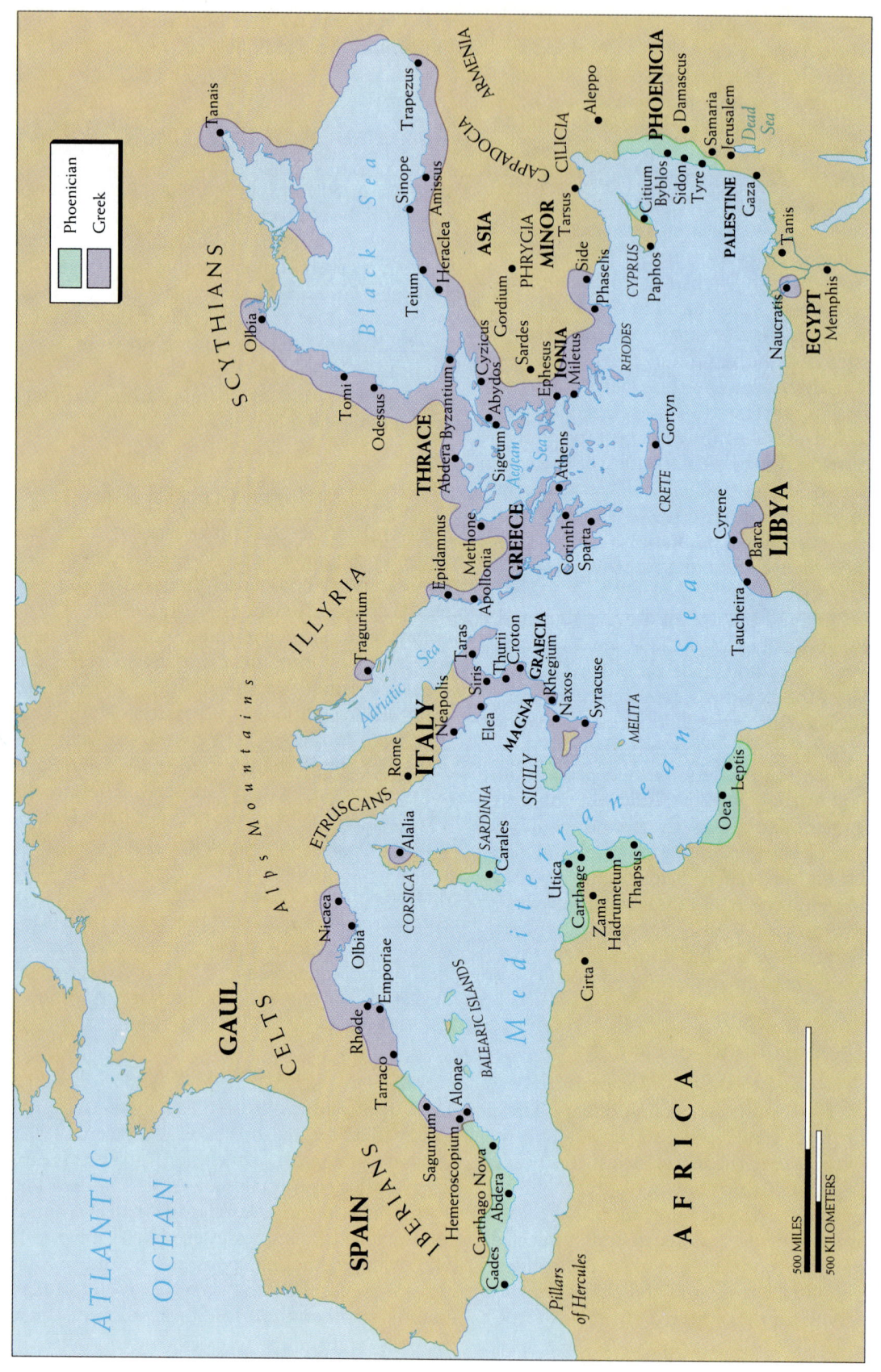

MAP 2-2 PHOENICIAN AND GREEK COLONIZATION *Most of the coastline of the Mediterranean and Black Seas was populated by Greek or Phoenician colonies. The Phoenicians were a commercial people who planted their colonies in North Africa, Spain, Sicily, and Sardinia chiefly in the ninth century B.C. The height of Greek colonization came later, between about 750 and 550 B.C.*

The temple of Hera at Paestum in southern Italy (sixth century B.C.) is considered the finest surviving example of Doric architecture. [Hirmer Verlag, Munich]

whom they left behind. The colonists tended to divide the land they settled into equal shares, reflecting an egalitarian tendency that was part of the ethical system of the yeoman farmers in the mother cities. They often copied their home constitution, worshiped the same gods as the people of the mother city at the same festivals in the same way, and carried on a busy trade with the mother city. Most colonies, though independent, were friendly with their mother cities. Each might ask the other for aid in time of trouble and expect to receive a friendly hearing, although neither was obliged to help.

Colonization had a powerful influence on Greek life. By relieving the pressure of a growing population, it provided a safety valve that allowed the *poleis* to escape civil wars. By confronting the Greeks with the differences between themselves and the new peoples they met, colonization gave them a sense of cultural identity and fostered a Panhellenic ("all-Greek") spirit that led to the establishment of a number of common religious festivals. The most important ones were at Olympia, Delphi, Corinth, and Nemea.

Colonization also encouraged trade and industry. The influx of new wealth from abroad and the increased demand for goods from the homeland stimulated a more intensive use of the land and an emphasis on crops for export, chiefly the olive and the wine grape. The manufacture of pottery, tools, weapons, and fine artistic metalwork as well as perfumed oil, the soap of the ancient Mediterranean world, was likewise encouraged. New opportunities allowed some men, sometimes outside the nobility, to become wealthy and important. The newly enriched became a troublesome element in the aristocratic *poleis*, for, although increasingly important in the life of their states, they were barred from political power, religious privileges, and social acceptance by the ruling aristocrats. These conditions soon created a crisis in many states.

The Tyrants (About 700–500 B.C.)

In some cities, perhaps only a small percentage of the more than 1,000 Greek *poleis*, the crisis produced by new economic and social conditions led to or intensified factional divisions within the ruling aristocracy. In the years between 700 and 500 B.C., the result was often the establishment of a tyranny.

THE RISE OF TYRANNY A tyrant was a monarch who had gained power in an unorthodox or unconstitutional but not necessarily wicked way and who exercised a strong one-man rule that might well be beneficent and popular.

The founding tyrant was usually a member of the ruling aristocracy who either had a personal grievance or led an unsuccessful faction. He often rose to power because of his military ability and support from the hoplites. He generally had the support of the politically powerless group of the newly wealthy and of the poor farmers. When he took power, he often expelled many of his aristocratic opponents and divided at least some of their land among his supporters. He pleased his commercial and industrial supporters by destroying the privileges of the old aristocracy and by fostering trade and colonization.

The tyrants presided over a period of population growth that saw an increase especially in the number of city dwellers. They responded with a program of public works that included the improvement of drainage systems, care for the water supply, the construction and organiza-

Tyranny at Sicyon

About 650 B.C., a man named Orthagoras established a tyranny in the city of Sicyon, not far from Corinth (where, at about the same time, Cypselus was likewise installing himself as tyrant). The following passage, which ends abruptly, provides some details about Sicyon's life and rise to prominence. The passage comes from a fragmentary papyrus found at Oxyrhynchus in the Egyptian desert that contains parts of a history written in the fourth century B.C. by an unknown author.

✦ *What is the significance of Orthagoras's birth and parentage? Of his miliary achievements? Why might the people of Sicyon have supported his tyranny?*

Being a man of the people and of low birth, he disregarded the oracle. The other sacrifices which were enjoined upon him by Delphi he rendered to the gods, but the tyranny which was fated to come about he disregarded. To Andreas was born a son, whom he raised and gave the name Orthagoras. Until adulthood he was all the time brought up and educated just as was suitable for the son of a cook and a common citizen. When his childhood was ended, he became one of the patrols guarding the land, and when war broke out between the Sicyonians and the Pelleneans, he was at all times active and accomplished. When a foray was made by the Pelleneans and they attacked unexpectedly, he went to meet them and killed some of the enemy and was by far the most distinguished of the patrol. In return for this the Sicyonians appointed him patrol commander by election. Immediately on having won this honor he conquered the enemy even more impressively, so that many of the citizens were won over and became attached to him. As time passed they elected him Polemarch [commander of the army], primarily because of his bravery and good fortune in war, and also because the majority of the citizens were well disposed to him. When he had waged war during his tenure of that office with valor and keeping the territory which was theirs secure and causing much damage to the enemy to be done, the Sicyonians once again [here the papyrus breaks off]

Adapted from Charles W. Fornara's translation of Oxyrhynchus Papyri XI 1365, *in* Archaic Times to the End of the Peloponnesian War *(Baltimore and London: Johns Hopkins University Press, 1977), pp. 12–13.*

tion of marketplaces, the building and strengthening of city walls, and the erection of temples. They introduced new local festivals and elaborated the old ones. They were active in the patronage of the arts, supporting poets and artisans with gratifying results. All this activity contributed to the tyrant's popularity, to the prosperity of his city, and to his self-esteem.

In most cases the tyrant's rule was secured by a personal bodyguard and by mercenary soldiers. An armed citizenry, necessary for an aggressive foreign policy, would have been dangerous, so the tyrants usually pursued a program of peaceful alliances with other tyrants abroad and avoided war.

THE END OF THE TYRANTS By the end of the sixth century B.C. tyranny had disappeared from the Greek states and did not return in the same form or for the same reasons. The last tyrants were universally hated for the cruelty and repression they employed. They left bitter memories in their own states and became objects of fear and hatred everywhere.

Besides the outrages committed by individual tyrants, there was something about the very concept of tyranny that was inimical to the idea of the *polis*. The notion of the *polis* as a community to which every member must be responsible, the connection of justice with that community, and the natural aristocratic hatred of monarchy all made tyranny seem alien and offensive. The rule of a tyrant, however beneficent, was arbitrary and unpredictable. Tyranny came into being in defiance of tradition and law, and the tyrant governed without either. He was not answerable in any way to his fellow citizens.

From a longer perspective, however, the tyrants made important contributions to the development of Greek civilization. They encouraged economic changes that helped secure the future prosperity of Greece. They increased communication with the rest of the Mediterranean world and cultivated the crafts and technology, as well as the arts and literature. Most important of all, they broke the grip of the aristocracy and put the productive powers of the most active and talented of its citizens fully at the service of the *polis*.

The Major States

Generalization about the *polis* becomes difficult not long after its appearance, for though the states had much in common, some of them developed in unique ways. Sparta and Athens, which became the two most powerful Greek states, had especially unusual histories.

Sparta

At first Sparta seems not to have been strikingly different from other *poleis*. About 725 B.C., however, the pressure of population and land hunger led the Spartans to launch a war of conquest against their western neighbor, Messenia. (See Map 2-3.) The First Messenian War gave the Spartans as much land as they would ever need. The reduction of the Messenians to the status of serfs, or Helots, meant that the Spartans need not even work the land that supported them.

The turning point in Spartan history came about 650 B.C., when, in the Second Messenian War, the Helots rebelled with the help of Argos and other Peloponnesian cities. The war was long and bitter and at one point threatened the

Chronology of the Rise of Greece	
ca. 2900–1150 B.C.	Minoan period
ca. 1900 B.C.	Probable date of the arrival of the Greeks on the mainland
ca. 1600–1150 B.C.	Mycenaean period
ca. 1250 B.C.	Sack of Troy (?)
ca. 1200–1150 B.C.	Destruction of Mycenaean centers in Greece
ca. 1100–750 B.C.	Dark Ages
ca. 750–500 B.C.	Major period of Greek colonization
ca. 725 B.C.	Probable date when Homer flourished
ca. 700 B.C.	Probable date when Hesiod flourished
ca. 700–500 B.C.	Major period of Greek tyranny

existence of Sparta. After the revolt had been put down, the Spartans were forced to reconsider their way of life. They could not expect to keep down the Helots, who outnumbered them perhaps ten to one, and still maintain the old free-and-easy habits typical of most Greeks. Faced with the choice of making drastic changes and sacrifices or abandoning their control of Messenia, the Spartans chose to introduce fundamental reforms that turned their city forever after into a military academy and camp.

SPARTAN SOCIETY   The new system that emerged late in the sixth century B.C. exerted control over each Spartan from birth, when officials of the state decided which infants were physically fit to survive. At the age of seven the Spartan boy was taken from his mother and turned over to young instructors. He was trained in athletics and the military arts and taught to endure privation, to bear physical pain, and to live off the country, by theft if necessary. At twenty the Spartan youth was enrolled in the army and lived in barracks with his companions until the age of thirty. Marriage was permitted, but a strange sort of marriage it was, for the Spartan male could visit his wife only infrequently and by stealth. At thirty he became a full citizen, an "equal." He took his meals at a public mess in the company of fifteen comrades. His food, a simple diet without much

meat or wine, was provided by his own plot of land, worked by Helots. Military service was required until the age of sixty; only then could the Spartan retire to his home and family.

This educational program extended to women, too, although they were not given military training. Female infants were examined for fitness to survive in the same way as males. Girls were given gymnastic training, were permitted greater freedom of movement than among other Greeks, and were equally indoctrinated with the idea of service to Sparta.

The entire system was designed to change the natural feelings of devotion to family and children into a more powerful commitment to the *polis*. Privacy, luxury, and even comfort were sacrificed to the purpose of producing soldiers whose physical powers, training, and discipline made them the best in the world. Nothing that might turn the mind away from duty was permitted. The very use of coins was forbidden lest it corrupt the desires of Spartans. Neither family nor money were allowed to interfere with the only ambition permitted to a Spartan male: to win glory and the respect of his peers by bravery in war.

SPARTAN GOVERNMENT The Spartan constitution was mixed, containing elements of monarchy, oligarchy, and democracy. There were two kings, whose power was limited by law and also by the rivalry that usually existed between the two royal houses. The origins and explanation of this unusual dual kingship are unknown, but both kings ruled together in Sparta and exercised equal powers. Their functions were chiefly religious and military. A Spartan army rarely left home without a king in command.

The oligarchic element was represented by a council of elders consisting of twenty-eight men over the age of sixty, elected for life, and the kings. These elders had important judicial functions, sitting as a court in cases involving the kings. They also were consulted before any proposal was put before the assembly of Spartan citizens. In a traditional society like Sparta's, they must have had considerable influence.

The Spartan assembly consisted of all males over thirty. Theoretically they were the final authority, but in practice, debate was carried on by magistrates, elders, and kings alone, and voting was usually by acclamation. Therefore, the assembly's real function was to ratify decisions already taken or to decide between positions favored by the leading figures. In addition, Sparta had a unique institution, the board of ephors. This consisted of five men elected annually by the assembly. Originally, they appear to have been intended to check the power of the kings, but gradually they gained other important functions. They controlled foreign policy, oversaw the generalship of the kings on campaign, presided at the assembly, and guarded against rebellions by the Helots.

The whole system was remarkable both for the way in which it combined participation by the citizenry with significant checks on its power and for its unmatched stability. Most Greeks admired the Spartan state for these qualities and also for its ability to mold citizens so thoroughly to an ideal. Many political philoso-phers, from Plato to modern times, have based utopian schemes on a version of Sparta's constitution and educational system.

THE PELOPONNESIAN LEAGUE By about 550 B.C. the Spartan system was well established, and its limitations were made plain. Suppression of the Helots required all the effort and energy that Sparta had. The Spartans could expand no further, but they could not allow unruly independent neighbors to cause unrest that might inflame the Helots.

When the Spartans defeated Tegea, their northern neighbor, they imposed an unusual peace. Instead of taking away land and subjugating the defeated state, Sparta left the Tegeans their land and their freedom. In exchange they required the Tegeans to follow the Spartan lead

MAP 2-3 THE PELOPONNESUS *Sparta's region, Laconia, was in the Peloponnesus. Nearby states were members of the Peloponnesian League under Sparta's leadership.*

The Greek and Persian Ways of War—Autocracy versus Freedom Under the Law

The Greek historian Herodotus, who wrote his account of the wars between the Greeks and Persians more than half a century after they ended, was very interested in the differences between the ways of the Greeks and other peoples of the world. In the following passage he describes a conversation between Demaratus, an exiled king of Sparta, and Xerxes, the Great King of Persia. Demaratus had come to Xerxes' court after his exile. Xerxes received him kindly and made him a royal adviser.

✦ On what does Xerxes rely for Persian military success? What is the source of Demaratus's confidence in the Spartans? Does the claim he makes hold for other Greeks as well as the Spartans? How is it possible to reconcile freedom with obedience to the laws?

How is it possible that a thousand men, or ten thousand, of fifty thousand, should stand up to an army as big as mine, especially if they were not under a single master, but all perfectly free to do as they pleased? Suppose them to have five thousand men: in that case we should be more than a thousand to one! If, like ours, their troops were subject to the control of a single man, then possibly for fear of him, in spite of the disparity in numbers, they might show some sort of factitious courage, or let themselves be whipped into battle; but, as every man is free to follow his fancy, it is not conceivable that they should do either. Indeed, my own opinion is that even on equal terms the Greeks could hardly face the Persians alone. We, too, have this thing that you were speaking of—I do not say it is common, but it does exist; for instance, amongst the Persians in my bodyguard there are men who would willingly fight with three Greeks together. But you know nothing of such things, or you could not talk such nonsense.'

'My lord,' Demaratus answered, 'I knew before I began that if I spoke the truth you would not like it. But, as you demanded the plain truth and nothing less, I told you how things are with the Spartans. Yet you are well aware that I now feel but little affection for my countrymen, who robbed me of my hereditary power and privileges and made me a fugitive without a home—whereas your father welcomed me at his court and gave me the means of livelihood and somewhere to live. Surely it is unreasonable to reject kindness; any sensible man will cherish it. Personally I do not claim to be able to fight ten men—or two; indeed I should prefer not even to fight with one. But should it be necessary—should there be some great cause to urge me on—then nothing would give me more pleasure than to stand up to one of those men of yours who claim to be a match for three Greeks. So it is with the Spartans; fighting singly, they are as good as any, but fighting together they are the best soldiers in the world. They are free—yes—but not entirely free; for they have a master, and that master is Law, which they fear much more than your subjects fear you. Whatever this master commands they do; and his command never varies: it is never to retreat in battle, however great the odds, but always to stand firm, and to conquer or die. If, my lord, you think that what I have said is nonsense—very well; I am willing henceforward to hold my tongue. This time I spoke because you forced me to speak. In any case, I pray that all may turn out as you desire.'

Xerxes burst out laughing at Demaratus' answer, and goodhumouredly let him go.

From Herodotus, The Histories, *trans. by Aubrey de Selincourt (Harmondsworth: Penguin Books, 1976), pp. 476–477.*

in foreign affairs and to supply a fixed number of soldiers to Sparta on demand. This became the model for Spartan relations with the other states in the Peloponnesus. Soon Sparta was the leader of an alliance that included every Peloponnesian state but Argos; modern scholars have named this alliance the Peloponnesian League. It provided the Spartans with the security they needed, and it also made Sparta the most powerful *polis* in Hellenic history. By 500 B.C. Sparta and the league had given the Greeks a force capable of facing mighty threats from abroad.

Athens

Athens was slow to come into prominence and to join in the new activities that were changing the more advanced states. The reasons were several. Athens was not situated on the most favored trade routes of the eighth and seventh centuries B.C., its large area (about 1,000 square miles) allowed population growth without great pressure, and the unification of the many villages and districts within this territory into a single *polis* was not completed until the seventh century B.C. (See Map 2-4.)

ARISTOCRATIC RULE In the seventh century B.C. Athens was a typical aristocratic *polis*. Its people were divided into four tribes and into several clans and brotherhoods (phratries). The aristocrats held the most land and the best land and dominated religious and political life. There was no written law, and decisions were rendered by powerful nobles on the basis of tradition and, most likely, self-interest. The state was governed by the Areopagus, a council of nobles deriving its name from the hill where it held its

MAP 2-4 ATTICA AND VICINITY *Citizens of all towns in Attica were also citizens of Athens.*

The Development of the Athenian Polis

When the Spartans invaded Attica at the beginning of the Peloponnesian War (see Chapter 3), the Athenians were forced to leave their homes in the country to seek safety behind the walls of the city of Athens. The historian Thucydides takes the opportunity to describe the development of the Athenian polis from a collection of separate towns into a single political unit. He wrote several centuries after the unification of Athens, and the details of the event are legendary, but the general outlines of what took place are credible.

✦*What kind of evidence does Thucydides give for his history of early Attica? Does it seem sufficient and reliable enough to provide an accurate account? How does he create a coherent and plausible explanation with so few facts? How does the picture given here of early kingship in Athens compare with kingship in the ancient Near East, Mycenaean Greece, and Homeric Greece?*

The Athenians . . . began to carry in their wives and children from the country, and all their household furniture, even to the woodwork of their houses which they took down. Their sheep and cattle they sent over to Euboea and the adjacent islands. But they found it hard to move, as most of them had been always used to live in the country.

From very early times this had been more the case with the Athenians than with others. Under Cecrops and the first kings, down to the reign of Theseus, Attica had always consisted of a number of independent townships, each with its own town hall and magistrates. Except in times of danger the king at Athens was not consulted; in ordinary seasons they carried on their government and settled their affairs without his interference; sometimes even they waged war against him, as in the case of the Eleusinians with Eumolpus against Erechtheus. In Theseus, however, they had a king of equal intelligence and power; and one of the chief features in his organization of the country was to abolish the council chambers and magistrates of the petty cities, and to merge them in the single council chamber and town hall of the present capital. Individuals might still enjoy their private property just as before, but they were henceforth compelled to have only one politi

cal centre, viz. Athens, which thus counted all the inhabitants of Attica among her citizens, so that when Theseus died he left a great state behind him. Indeed, from him dates the Synoecia, or Feast of Union, which is paid for by the state, and which the Athenians still keep in honour of the goddess. Before this city consisted of the present citadel and the district beneath it looking rather towards the south. This is shown by the fact that the temples of the other deities, besides that of Athene, are on the citadel; . . . Again, from their old residence in that quarter, the citadel is still known among Athenians as the *city*.

The Athenians thus long lived scattered over Attica in independent townships. Even after the centralization of Theseus, old habit still prevailed; and from the early times down to the present war most Athenians still lived in the country with their families and households, and were consequently not at all inclined to move now, especially as they had only just restored their establishments after the Median invasion. Deep was their trouble and discontent at abandoning their houses and the hereditary temples of the ancient constitution, and at having to change their habits of life and to bid farewell to what each regarded as his native city.

Thucydides, The Peloponnesian War, 2.14–16, trans. by Richard Crawley, Vol. 1, ed. by F. R. B. Godolphin, in The Greek Historians *(New York: Random House, 1942).*

sessions. Annually the council elected nine magistrates, called archons, who joined the Areopagus after their year in office. Because the archons served for only a year, were checked by their colleagues, and looked forward to a lifetime as members of the Areopagus, it is plain that the aristocratic Areopagus, not the archons, was the true master of the state.

PRESSURE FOR CHANGE   In the seventh century B.C. the peaceful life of Athens experienced some disturbances, caused in part by quarrels within the nobility and in part by the beginnings of an agrarian crisis. In 632 B.C. a nobleman named Cylon attempted a coup to establish himself as tyrant. He was thwarted, but the unrest continued.

In 621 B.C. a man named Draco was given special authority to codify and publish laws for the first time. In later years Draco's penalties were thought to be harsh; hence the saying that his laws were written in blood. (We still speak of unusually harsh penalties as Draconian.) Draco's work was probably limited to laws concerning homicide and was aimed at ending blood feuds between clans, but it set an important precedent. The publication of laws strengthened the hand of the state against the local power of the nobles.

The root of Athens' troubles was agricultural. Many Athenians worked family farms, from which they obtained most of their living. It appears that they planted wheat, the staple crop, year after year without rotating fields or using enough fertilizer. Shifting to more intensive agricultural techniques and to the planting of trees and vines required capital, leading the less successful farmers to acquire excessive debt. To survive, some farmers had to borrow from wealthy neighbors to get through the year. In return, they promised one sixth of the next year's crop. The deposit of an inscribed stone on the entailed farms marked the arrangement. As their troubles persisted, debtors had to pledge their wives, their children, and themselves as surety for new loans. Inevitably, many Athenians defaulted and were enslaved. Some were even sold abroad. Revolutionary pressures grew among the poor, who began to demand the abolition of debt and a redistribution of the land.

REFORMS OF SOLON   In the year 594 B.C., as tradition has it, the Athenians elected Solon as the only archon, with extraordinary powers to legislate and revise the constitution. Immediately, he attacked the agrarian problem by canceling current debts and forbidding future loans secured by the person of the borrower. He helped bring back many Athenians enslaved abroad and freed those in Athens enslaved for debt. This program was called the "shaking off of burdens." It did not, however, solve the fundamental economic problem, and Solon did not redistribute the land.

In the short run, therefore, he did not put an end to the economic crisis, but his other economic actions had profound success in the long run. He forbade the export of wheat and encouraged that of olive oil. This policy had the initial effect of making wheat more available in Attica and encouraging the cultivation of olive oil and wine as cash crops. By the fifth century B.C. the cultivation of cash crops had become so profitable that much Athenian land was diverted from grain production, and Athens became dependent on imported wheat. Solon also changed the Athenian standards of weights and measures to conform with those of Corinth and Euboea and the cities of the East. This change also encouraged commerce and turned Athens in the direction that would lead it to great prosperity in the fifth century. He also encouraged industry by offering citizenship to foreign artisans, and his success is reflected in the development of the outstanding Attic pottery of the sixth century.

Solon also significantly changed the constitution. Citizenship had previously been the privilege of all male adults whose fathers were citizens; to their number he added those immigrants who were tradesmen and merchants. All these Athenian citizens were divided into four classes on the basis of wealth, measured by annual agricultural production. The two highest classes alone could hold the archonship, the chief magistracy in Athens, and sit on the Areopagus.

Men of the third class were allowed to serve as hoplites. They could be elected to a council of 400 chosen by all the citizens, 100 from each tribe. Solon seems to have meant this council to serve as a check on the Areopagus and to prepare any business that needed to be put before

The Rule of the Tyrant Pisistratus

Although tyranny came to have a bad reputation, the first tyrants were often popular because they broke the unchallenged domination of the aristocrats. Their careers were sometimes remembered fondly because their achievements contrasted favorably with those of their successors. So it was with the Athenian view of the reign of their first tyrant, Pisistratus, as suggested by this passage from Aristotle's Athenian Constitution, *written two centuries after the events described.*

✦ *What were the bases of Pisistratus's power? If he was a tyrant, why is his rule portrayed as a golden age? If it was a golden age, why did the Athenians after his death pass a law against the establishment of tyranny? What was the relation between the tyranny at Athens and the rule of law?*

Such was the origin and such the vicissitudes of the tyranny of Pisistratus. His administration was temperate, as has been said before, and more like constitutional government than a tyranny. Not only was he in every respect humane and mild and ready to forgive those who offended, but, in addition, he advanced money to the poorer people to help them in their labours, so that they might make their living by agriculture. In this he had two objects, first that they might not spend their time in the city but might be scattered over all the face of the country, and secondly that, being moderately well off and occupied with their own business, they might have neither the wish nor the time to attend to public affairs. At the same time his revenues were increased by the thorough cultivation of the country, since he imposed a tax of one tenth on all the produce. For the same reasons he instituted the local justices, and often made expeditions in person into the country to inspect it and to settle disputes between individuals, that they might not come into the city and neglect their farms. It was in one of these progresses that, as the

---

the traditional assembly of all adult male citizens. The *thetes* made up the last class. They voted in the assembly for the archons and the council members and on any other business brought before them by the archons and the council. They also sat on a new popular court established by Solon. This new court was recognized as a court of appeal, and by the fifth century B.C. almost all cases came before it.

PISISTRATUS THE TYRANT Solon's efforts to avoid factional strife failed. Within a few years contention reached such a degree that no archons could be chosen. Out of this turmoil emerged the first Athenian tyranny. Pisistratus, a nobleman, faction leader, and military hero, briefly seized power in 560 B.C. and again in 556 B.C., but each time his support was inadequate and he was driven out. At last, in 546 B.C. he came back at the head of a mercenary army from abroad and established a successful tyranny. It lasted beyond his death, in 527 B.C., until the expulsion of his son Hippias in 510 B.C.

In many respects Pisistratus resembled the other Greek tyrants. His rule rested on the force provided by mercenary soldiers. He engaged in great programs of public works, urban improvement, and religious piety. Temples were built and religious centers expanded and improved. Poets and artists were supported to add cultural luster to the court of the tyrant.

Pisistratus sought to increase the power of the central government at the expense of the nobles. The newly introduced festival of Dionysus and the improved and expanded Great Panathenaic festival helped fix attention on the capital city, as did the new temples and the reconstruction of the agora as the center of pub-

story goes, Pisistratus had his adventure with the man of Hymettus, who was cultivating the spot afterwards known as "Tax-free Farm." He saw a man digging and working at a very stony piece of ground, and being surprised he sent his attendant to ask what he got out of this plot of land. "Aches and pains," said the man; "and that's what Pisistratus ought to have his tenth of." The man spoke without knowing who his questioner was; but Pisistratus was so pleased with his frank speech and his industry that he granted him exemption from all taxes. And so in matters in general he burdened the people as little as possible with his government, but always cultivated peace and kept them in all quietness. Hence the tyranny of Pisistratus was often spoken of proverbially as "the age of gold"; for when his sons succeeded him the government became much harsher. But most important of all in this respect was his popular and kindly disposition. In all things he was accustomed to observe the laws, without giving himself any exceptional privileges. Once he was summoned on a charge of homicide before the Areopagus, and he appeared in person to make his defense; but the prosecutor was afraid to present himself and abandoned the case. For these reasons he held power long, and whenever he was expelled he regained his position easily. The majority alike of the upper class and of the people were in his favour; the former he won by his social intercourse with them, the latter by the assistance which he gave to their private purses, and his nature fitted him to win the hearts of both. Moreover, the laws in reference to tyrants at that time in force at Athens were very mild, especially the one which applies more particularly to the establishment of a tyranny. The law ran as follows, "These are the ancestral statutes of the Athenians; if any persons shall make an attempt to establish a tyranny, or if any person shall join in setting up a tyranny, he shall lose his civic rights, both himself and his whole house."

Aristotle, Athenian Constitution, *16, trans. by Henry G. Dakyns, Vol. 2, ed. by F. R. B. Godolphin, in* The Greek Historians *(New York: Random House, 1942).*

lic life. Circuit judges were sent out into the country to hear cases, weakening the power of the local barons. All this time Pisistratus made no formal change in the Solonian constitution. Assembly, councils, and courts met; magistrates and councils were elected. Pisistratus merely saw to it that his supporters dominated these bodies. The intended effect was to blunt the sharp edge of tyranny with the appearance of constitutional government, and it worked. The rule of Pisistratus was remembered as popular and mild. The unintended effect was to give the Athenians more experience in the procedures of self-government and a growing taste for it.

SPARTAN INTERVENTION Pisistratus was succeeded by his oldest son, Hippias, who followed his father's ways at first. In 514 B.C., however, his brother Hipparchus was murdered as a result of a private quarrel. Hippias became nervous, suspicious, and harsh. The Alcmaeonids, one of the noble clans that Hippias and Hipparchus had exiled, won favor with the influential oracle at Delphi and used its support to persuade Sparta to attack the Athenian tyranny. Led by their ambitious king, Cleomenes I, the Spartans marched into Athenian territory in 510 B.C. and deposed Hippias, who went into exile to the Persian court. The tyranny was over.

The Spartans must have hoped to leave Athens in friendly hands, and indeed Cleomenes' friend Isagoras, a rival of the Alcmaeonids, held the leading position in Athens after the withdrawal of the Spartan army. Isagoras, however, faced competitors, chief among them Clisthenes of the restored Alcmaeonid clan. Clisthenes lost out in the initial political struggle among the noble factions.

Aristogeiton and Harmodius were Athenian aristocrats slain in 514 B.C. after assassinating Hipparchus, brother of the tyrant Hippias. After the overthrow of the Pisistratids in 510 B.C., the Athenians erected a famous statue to honor their memory. This is a Roman copy. [Scala/Art Resource, N.Y.]

Isagoras seems then to have tried to restore a version of the pre-Solonian aristocratic state. As part of his plan, he carried through a purification of the citizen lists, removing those whom Solon or Pisistratus had enfranchised and any others thought to have a doubtful claim.

Clisthenes then took an unprecedented action—he turned to the people for political support and won it with a program of great popular appeal. In response, Isagoras called in the Spartans again; Cleomenes arrived and allowed Isagoras to expel Clisthenes and many of his supporters. But the fire of Athenian political consciousness, ignited by Solon and kept alive under Pisistratus, had been fanned into flames by the popular appeal of Clisthenes. The people refused to tolerate an aristocratic restoration and drove out the Spartans and Isagoras with them. Clisthenes and his allies returned, ready to put their program into effect.

CLISTHENES, THE FOUNDER OF DEMOCRACY
A central aim of Clisthenes' reforms was to diminish the influence of traditional localities and regions in Athenian life, for these were an important source of power for the nobility and of factions in the state. He immediately restored to citizenship those Athenians who had supported him whom Isagoras had disenfranchised, and he added new citizens to the rolls. In 508 B.C. he made the *deme*, the equivalent of a small town in the country or a ward in the city, the basic unit of civic life. The *deme* was a purely political unit that elected its own officers. The distribution of *demes* in each tribe guaranteed that no region would dominate any of them. Because the tribes had common religious activities and fought as regimental units, the new organization also increased devotion to the *polis* and diminished regional divisions and personal loyalty to local barons.

A new council of 500 was invented to replace the Solonian council of 400. The council's main responsibility was to prepare legislation for discussion by the assembly, but it also had important financial duties and received foreign emissaries. Final authority in all things rested with the assembly of all adult male Athenian citizens. Debate in the assembly was free and open; any Athenian could submit legislation, offer amendments, or argue the merits of any question. In practice political leaders did most of the talking. We may imagine that in the early days the council had more authority than it did after the Athenians became more confident in their new self-government.

It is fair to call Clisthenes the father of Athenian democracy. He did not alter the property qualifications of Solon, but his enlargement of the citizen rolls, his diminution of the power of the aristocrats, and his elevation of the role of the assembly, with its effective and manageable council, all give him a firm claim to that title.

As a result of the work of Solon, Pisistratus, and Clisthenes, Athens entered the fifth century B.C. well on the way to prosperity and democracy. It was much more centralized and united than it had been, and it was ready to take its place among the major states that would lead the defense of Greece against the dangers that lay ahead.

Life in Archaic Greece

Society

As the "dark ages" ended, the features that would distinguish Greek society thereafter took shape. The roles of the artisan and the merchant grew more important as contact with the non-Hellenic world became easier. The great majority of people, however, continued to make their living from the land. Wealthy aristocrats with large estates, powerful households, families, and clans led very different lives from those of the poorer countryfolk and the independent farmers who had smaller and less fertile fields.

FARMERS Ordinary country people rarely leave a written record of their thoughts or activities, and we have no such record from ancient Greece. The poet Hesiod (ca. 700 B.C.), however, was certainly no aristocrat. He presented himself as a small farmer, and his *Works and Days* gives some idea of the life of such a farmer. The crops included grain, chiefly barley but also wheat; grapes for the making of wine; olives for food, but mainly for oil, used for cooking, lighting, and washing; green vegetables, especially the bean; and some fruit. Sheep and goats provided milk and cheese. The Homeric heroes had great herds of cattle and ate lots of meat, but by Hesiod's time land fertile enough to provide fodder for cattle was needed to grow grain. He and small farmers like him tasted meat chiefly from sacrificial animals at festivals.

These farmers worked hard to make a living. Although Hesiod had the help of oxen and mules and one or two hired helpers for occasional labor, his life was one of continuous toil. The hardest work came in October, at the start of the rainy season, the time for the first plowing. The plow was light and easily broken, and the work of forcing the iron tip into the earth

was backbreaking, even with the help of a team of oxen. For the less fortunate farmer, the cry of the crane that announced the time of year to plow "bites the heart of the man without oxen." Autumn and winter were the time for cutting wood, building wagons, and making tools. Late winter was the time to tend to the vines, May the time to harvest the grain, July to winnow and store it. Only at the height of summer's heat did Hesiod allow for rest, but when September came, it was time to harvest the grapes. No sooner was that task done than the

This terra-cotta figurine from Boeotia is a rare ancient Greek representation of the lives of ordinary people. It shows Boeotian women laundering clothes. [Louvre, Paris]

This scene on an Attic jar from late in the sixth century B.C. shows how olives, one of Athens' most important crops, were harvested. [Courtesy of the Trustees of the British Museum]

cycle started again. The work went on under the burning sun and in the freezing cold.

Hesiod wrote nothing of pleasure or entertainment, but his poetry displays an excitement and pride that reveals the new hopes of a rural population more dynamic and confident than we know of anywhere else in the ancient world. Less austere farmers than Hesiod gathered at the blacksmith's shop for warmth and companionship in winter, and even he must have taken part in religious rites and festivals that were accompanied by some kind of entertainment. Nonetheless, the lives of yeoman farmers were certainly hard and their pleasures few.

ARISTOCRATS Most aristocrats were rich enough to employ many hired laborers, sometimes sharecroppers and sometimes even slaves, to work their extensive lands. They were therefore able to enjoy leisure for other activities. The center of aristocratic social life was the drinking party, or *symposium*. This activity was not a mere drinking bout, meant to remove inhibitions and produce oblivion. The Greeks, in fact, almost always mixed their wine with water, and one of the goals of the participants was to drink as much as the others without becoming drunk.

The *symposium* was a carefully organized occasion, with a "king" chosen to set the order of events and to determine that night's mixture of wine and water. Only men took part; they ate and drank as they reclined on couches along the walls of the room. The sessions began with prayers and libations to the gods. Usually there were games, such as dice or *kottabos,* in which wine was flicked from the cups at different targets. Sometimes dancing girls or flute girls offered entertainment. Frequently the aristocratic participants provided their own amusements with songs, poetry, or even philosophical disputes. Characteristically these took the form of contests, with some kind of prize for the winner, for aristocratic values continued to emphasize competition and the need to excel, whatever the arena.

This aspect of aristocratic life appears in the athletic contests that became widespread early in the sixth century. The games included running events; the long jump; the discus and javelin throws; the *pentathlon,* which included all of these; boxing; wrestling; and the chariot race. Only the rich could afford to raise, train, and race horses, and so the chariot race was a special preserve of aristocracy. Wrestling, however, was also especially favored by the nobility, and the *palaestra* where they practiced became an important social center for the aristocracy. The contrast between the hard, drab life of the farmers and the leisured and lively one of the aristocrats could hardly have been greater.

Religion

Like most ancient peoples, the Greeks were polytheists, and religion played an important part in their lives. A great part of Greek art and literature was closely connected with religion, as was the life of the *polis* in general.

OLYMPIAN GODS The Greek pantheon consisted of the twelve gods who lived on Mount Olympus. These were

- Zeus, the father of the gods
- Hera, his wife

Hesiod's Farmer's Almanac

Hesiod was a farmer and poet who lived in a village in Greece about 700 B.C. His poem Works and Days *contains wisdom on several subjects, but its final section amounts to a farmer's almanac, taking readers through the year and advising them on just when each activity is demanded. Hesiod painted a picture of a very hard life for Greek farmers, allowing rest only in the passage that follows.*

✦ *What might be Hesiod's purposes in writing this poem? What can be learned from this passage about the character of Greek farming? How did it differ from other modes of agriculture? What are the major virtues Hesiod associates with farming? How do they compare with the virtues celebrated by Homer?*

But when House-on-Back, the snail, crawls
   from the ground up
the plants, escaping the Pleiades, it's no
   longer time for vine-digging;
time rather to put an edge to your sickles,
   and rout out your helpers.
Keep away from sitting in the shade or lying
   in bed till the sun's up
in the time of the harvest, when the sunshine
   scorches your skin dry.
This is the season to push your work and
   bring home your harvest;
get up with the first light so you'll have
   enough to live on.
Dawn takes away from work a third part of
   the work's measure.
Dawn sets a man well along on his journey,
   in his work also,
dawn, who when she shows, has numerous
   people going their ways; dawn who puts
   the yoke upon many oxen.
 But when the artichoke is in flower, and the
   clamorous cricket
sitting in his tree lets go his vociferous
   singing, that issues
from the beating of his wings, in the exhaust-

ing season of summer,
then is when goats are at their fattest, when
   the wine tastes best,
women are most lascivious, but the men's
   strength fails them
most, for the star Seirios shrivels them, knees
   and heads alike,
and the skin is all dried out in the heat; then,
   at that season,
one might have the shadow under the rock,
   and the wine of Biblis,
a curd cake, and all the milk that the goats
   can give you,
the meat of a heifer, bred in the woods, who
   has never borne a calf,
and of baby kids also. Then, too, one can sit
   in the shadow
and drink the bright-shining wine, his heart
   satiated with eating
and face turned in the direction where
   Zephyros blows briskly,
make three libations of water from a spring
   that keeps running forever
and has no mud in it; and pour wine for the
   fourth libation.

Hesiod, Works and Days, *trans. by Richmond Lattimore (Ann Arbor: University of Michigan Press, 1959), pp. 87, 89. Reprinted by permission.*

Zeus's siblings

- Poseidon, his brother, god of the seas and earthquakes
- Hestia, his sister, goddess of the hearth
- Demeter, his sister, goddess of agriculture and marriage

and his children

- Aphrodite, goddess of love and beauty
- Apollo, god of the sun, music, poetry, and prophecy
- Ares, god of war
- Artemis, goddess of the moon and the hunt

- Athena, goddess of wisdom and the arts
- Hephaestus, god of fire and metallurgy
- Hermes, messenger of the gods, connected with commerce and cunning

These gods were seen as behaving very much as mortal humans behaved, with all the foibles of humans, except that they were superhuman in these as well as in their strength and immortality. On the other hand, Zeus, at least, was seen as a source of human justice, and even the Olympians were understood to be subordinate to the Fates. Each *polis* had one of the Olympians as its guardian deity and worshiped that god in its own special way, but all the gods were Panhellenic. In the eighth and seventh centuries B.C. common shrines were established at Olympia for the worship of Zeus, at Delphi for Apollo, at the Isthmus of Corinth for Poseidon, and at Nemea once again for Zeus. Each held athletic contests in honor of its deity, to which all Greeks were invited and for which a sacred truce was declared.

IMMORTALITY AND MORALITY Besides the Olympians, the Greeks also worshiped countless lesser deities connected with local shrines. They even worshiped human heroes, real or legendary, who had accomplished great deeds and had earned immortality and divine status. The worship of these deities was not a very emotional experience. It was a matter of offering prayer, libations, and gifts in return for protection and favors from the god during the lifetime of the worshiper. There was no hope of immortality for the average human, and these devotions involved little moral teaching.

Most Greeks seem to have held to the commonsense notion that justice lay in paying one's debts. They thought that civic virtue consisted of worshiping the state deities in the traditional way, performing required public services, and fighting in defense of the state. To them, private morality meant to do good to one's friends and harm to one's enemies.

THE CULT OF DELPHIAN APOLLO In the sixth century B.C. the influence of the cult of Apollo at Delphi and of his oracle there became very great. The oracle was the most important of several that helped satisfy human craving for a clue to the future. The priests of Apollo preached moderation; their advice was exemplified in the two famous sayings identified with Apollo: "Know thyself" and "Nothing in excess." Humans needed self-control (*sophrosynē*). Its

This late-nineteenth-century painting reconstructs the sanctuary of Apollo at Delphi, which the Greeks considered the "navel of the universe." It was the site of the famous Delphic oracle. [Ecole Nationale Superieure Des Beaux Arts, Paris]

The god Dionysus dances with two female followers. The vase was painted in the sixth century B.C. [Bibliotheque Nationale, Paris]

of the twelve Olympians. Cult followers are thought to have refused to kill animals or eat their flesh and to have believed in the transmigration of souls, which offered the prospect of some form of life after death.

Poetry

The great changes sweeping through the Greek world were also reflected in the poetry of the sixth century B.C. The lyric style—poetry meant to be sung, either by a chorus or by one person—predominated. Sappho of Lesbos, Anacreon of Teos, and Simonides of Cos composed personal poetry, often relating the pleasure and agony of love. Alcaeus of Mytilene, an aristocrat driven from his city by a tyrant, wrote bitter invective.

Perhaps the most interesting poet of the century from a political point of view was Theognis

This Attic cup from the fifth century B.C. shows the two great poets from the island of Lesbos, Sappho (right) and Alcaeus. [Hirmer Verlag, Munich]

opposite was arrogance (*hubris*), brought on by excessive wealth or good fortune. Hubris led to moral blindness and finally to divine vengeance. This theme of moderation and the dire consequences of its absence was central to Greek popular morality and appears frequently in Greek literature.

THE CULT OF DIONYSUS AND THE ORPHIC CULT The somewhat cold religion of the Olympian gods and of the cult of Apollo did little to assuage human fears or satisfy human hopes and passions. For these needs the Greeks turned to other deities and rites. Of these the most popular was Dionysus, a god of nature and fertility, of the grape vine and drunkenness and sexual abandon. In some of his rites the god was followed by maenads, female devotees who cavorted by night, ate raw flesh, and were reputed to tear to pieces any creature they came across.

The Orphic cult, named after its supposed founder, the mythical poet Orpheus, provided its followers with more hope than did the worship

Sappho the Poet

Sappho was born at Mytilene on the island of Lesbos about 612 B.C. After a period of exile in Sicily, she returned and became a central figure in a thiastos, a company of revelers who sang and danced in honor of a god. Sappho's group was made up of young girls who gave honor to Aphrodite and the Muses, the goddesses of the fine arts. They lived together intimately and affectionately. Sappho wrote poems to and about them and to celebrate their marriages. Her poems were highly admired in antiquity, winning her a position among the greatest lyric poets, but they are preserved only in fragments. The following selections illustrate two types of her poetry.

◆ *How do the mood and style of the poems compare with the excerpts from Homer and Hesiod in this chapter? What aspects of Greek life do they each illuminate? Since we know little reliable information about Sappho outside the fragments of her poems, what do these selections tell us about her life and activities?*

Fragment 94

'and honestly I want to die'
—so sobbing, many times, she left me

and she said this [to me]
'My god! what awful things are happening to
    us:
Sappho, I swear I am leaving you against my
    will.'

And I replied to her in these words:
'Go with a light heart, and with memories
of me, for you know how we cherished you.

And if not, then I want to
remind you [   ]
[   ] and we had good times

For ma[ny garland]s of violets
and roses [   ] together
and [   ] you put on
    beside me

And many garlands
woven from flowers about your soft neck
[   ] fashioned
And with m[uch] myrrh
from rich flowers [   ]
and royal you rubbed your skin

And on soft beds
tender [   ]
you would satisfy desire [   ]

And there was no [   ] nothing
holy nor [   ]
from which [we] kept away

No grove [   ]
[   ] sound
[   ]'

Fragment 148

Up with the rafters high,
Ho for the wedding!
Raise them high, ye joiners,
Ho for the wedding!
The bridegroom 's as tall as Ares,
Ho for the wedding!
Far taller than a tall man,
Ho for the wedding!
Towering as the Lesbian poet
Ho for the wedding!
Over the poets of other lands,
Ho for the wedding!

Sappho, Fragment 94, trans. by Ewen Bowie, in J. Boardman, J. Griffin, and O. Murray, The Oxford History of the Classical World (Oxford and New York: Oxford University Press, n.d.), p. 104. Sappho, Fragment 148, trans. by J. M. Edmonds, in Lyra Graeca, Vol. I (Cambridge, Mass.: Harvard University Press, 1952), p. 285.

of Megara. He was an aristocrat who lived through a tyranny, an unusually chaotic and violent democracy, and an oligarchy that restored order but ended the rule of the old aristocracy. Theognis was the spokesman for the old, defeated aristocracy of birth. He divided everyone into two classes, the noble and the base; the former were the good, the latter bad. Those nobly born must associate only with others like themselves if they were to preserve their virtue; if they mingled with the base, they became base. Those born base, on the other hand, could never become noble. Only nobles could aspire to virtue, and only nobles possessed the critical moral and intellectual qualities, respect or honor and judgment. These qualities could not be taught; they were innate. Even so they had to be carefully guarded against corruption by wealth or by mingling with the base. Intermarriage between the noble and the base was especially condemned. These were the ideas of the unreconstructed nobility, whose power had been destroyed or reduced in most Greek states by this time. These ideas remained alive in aristocratic hearts throughout the next century and greatly influenced later thinkers, Plato among them.

The Persian Wars

The Greeks' period of fortunate isolation and freedom ended in the sixth century B.C. They had established colonies along most of the coast of Asia Minor from as early as the eleventh century B.C. The colonies maintained friendly relations with the mainland but developed a flourishing economic and cultural life independent of their mother cities and of their eastern neighbors. In the middle of the sixth century B.C., however, these Greek cities of Asia Minor came under the control of Lydia and its king, Croesus (ca. 560–546 B.C.). Lydian rule seems not to have been very harsh, but the Persian conquest of Lydia in 546 B.C. brought a less pleasant subjugation.

The Persian Empire

The Persian Empire had been created in a single generation by Cyrus the Great, the founder of

The Rise of Persia	
559–530 B.C.	Reign of Cyrus the Great
546 B.C.	Persians conquer Lydia
530–522 B.C.	Reign of Cambyses
522–521 B.C.	Civil war in Persia
521–485 B.C.	Reign of Darius
485–465 B.C.	Reign of Xerxes

the Achaemenid dynasty. In 559 B.C. he came to the throne of Persia, then a small kingdom well to the east of the lower Mesopotamian Valley. He unified Persia under his rule; made an alliance with Babylonia; and led a successful rebellion toward the north against the Medes, the overlords of Persia (see Map 2-5). In succeeding years he expanded his empire in all directions, in the process defeating Croesus and occupying Lydia. Most of the Greek cities of Asia Minor sided with Croesus and resisted the Persians. By about 540 B.C., however, they had all been subdued. The western part of Asia Minor was divided into three provinces, each under its own satrap, or governor.

The Ionian Rebellion

The Ionian Greeks (those living on the central part of the west coast of Asia Minor and nearby islands) had been moving toward democracy and were not pleased to find themselves under the monarchical rule of Persia. That rule, however, was not overly burdensome at first. The Persians required their subjects to pay tribute and to serve in the Persian army. They ruled the Greek cities through local individuals, who governed their cities as "tyrants." Most of the "tyrants," however, were not harsh, the Persian tribute was not excessive, and the Greeks enjoyed general prosperity. Neither the death of Cyrus fighting on a distant frontier in 530 B.C. nor the suicide of his successor Cambyses, nor the civil war that followed it in 522–521 B.C. produced any disturbance in the Greek cities. When Darius emerged as Great King (as the Persian rulers styled themselves) in 521 B.C., he found Ionia perfectly obedient.

The private troubles of the ambitious tyrant of Miletus, Aristagoras, ended this calm. He had urged a Persian expedition against the island of

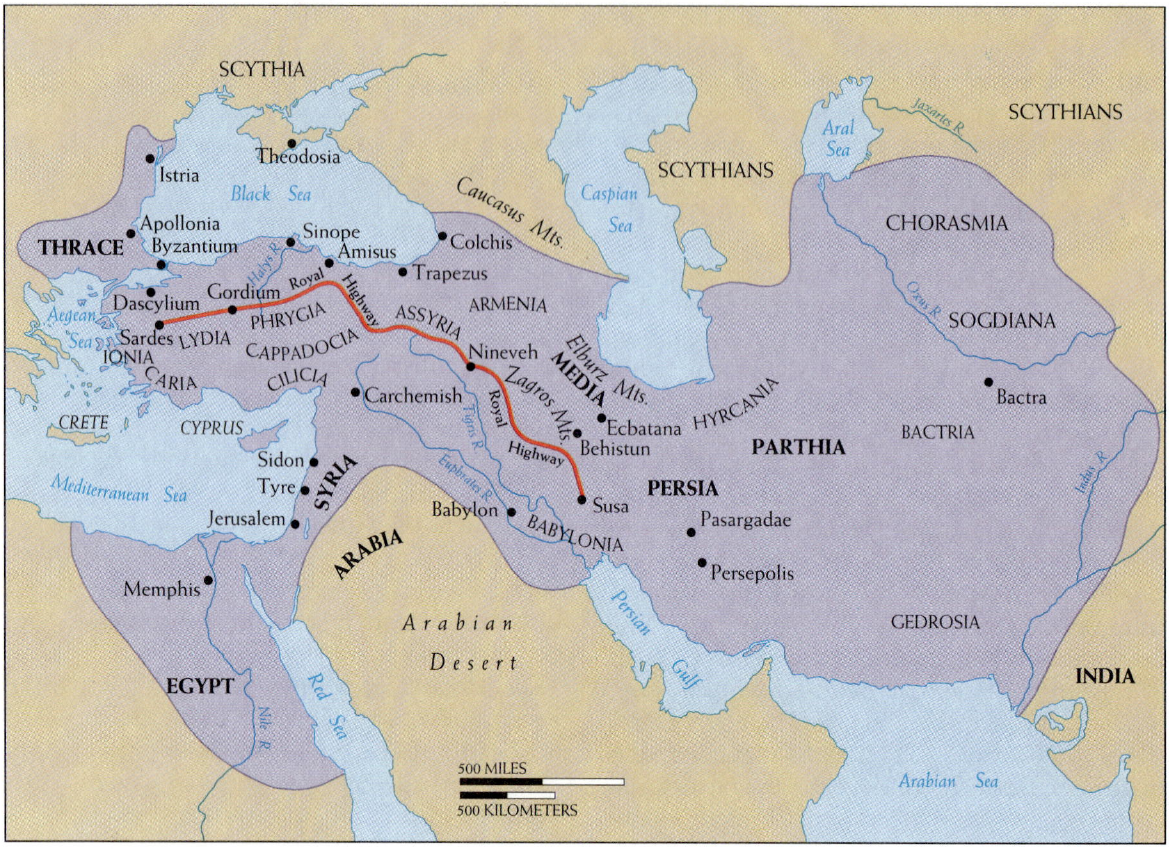

MAP 2-5   THE PERSIAN EMPIRE   *The empire created by Cyrus had reached its fullest
extent under Darius when Persia attacked Greece in 490 B.C. It extended from India to
the Aegean and even into Europe. It included the lands formerly ruled by Egyptians,
Hittites, Babylonians, and Assyrians.*

*Persian nobles pay homage to King Darius in this relief from the treasury at the Persian
capital of Persepolis. Darius is seated on the throne; his son and successor Xerxes stands
behind him. Darius and Xerxes are carved in larger scale to indicate their royal status.
[Courtesy of the Oriental Institute, the University of Chicago]*

Naxos; when it failed, he feared the consequences and organized the Ionian rebellion of 499 B.C. To gain support, he overthrew the tyrannies and proclaimed democratic constitutions. Then he turned to the mainland states for help, petitioning first Sparta, the most powerful Greek state. The Spartans, however, would have none of Aristagoras's promises of easy victory and great wealth. They had no close ties with the Ionians and no national interest in the region. Furthermore, they were terrified at the thought of leaving their homeland undefended against the Helots for a long time while their army was far off.

Aristagoras next sought help from the Athenians, who were related to the Ionians and had close ties of religion and tradition with them. Besides, Hippias, the deposed tyrant of Athens, was an honored guest at the court of Darius, and the Great King had already made it plain that he favored the tyrant's restoration. The Persians, moreover, controlled both sides of the Hellespont, the route to the grain fields beyond the Black Sea that were increasingly vital to Athens. Perhaps some Athenians already feared that a Persian attempt to conquer the Greek mainland was only a matter of time. The Athenian assembly agreed to send a fleet of twenty ships to help the rebels. The Athenian expedition was strengthened by five ships from Eretria in Euboea, which participated out of gratitude for past favors.

In 498 B.C. the Athenians and their allies made a surprise attack on Sardis, the old capital of Lydia and now the seat of the satrap, and burned it. This action caused the revolt to spread throughout the Greek cities of Asia Minor outside Ionia, but the Ionians could not follow it up. The Athenians withdrew and took no further part. Gradually the Persians reimposed their will. In 495 B.C. they defeated the Ionian fleet at Lade, and in the next year they wiped out Miletus. They killed many of the Miletan men, transported others to the Persian Gulf, and enslaved the women and children. The Ionian rebellion was over.

The War in Greece

In 490 B.C. the Persians launched an expedition directly across the Aegean to punish Eretria and Athens, to restore Hippias, and to gain control of the Aegean Sea (see Map 2-6). They landed their infantry and cavalry forces first at Naxos, destroying it for its successful resistance in 499 B.C. Then they destroyed Eretria and deported its people deep into the interior of Persia.

MARATHON Rather than submit and accept the restoration of the hated tyranny of Hippias, the Athenians chose to resist the Persian forces bearing down on them and risk the same fate that had just befallen Eretria. Miltiades, an Athenian who had fled from Persian service, led the city's army to a confrontation with the Persians at Marathon.

A Persian victory at Marathon would have destroyed Athenian freedom and led to the conquest of all the mainland Greeks. The greatest achievements of Greek culture, most of which lay in the future, would never have occurred. But the Athenians won a decisive victory, instilling them with a sense of confidence and pride in their *polis*, their unique form of government, and themselves.

THE GREAT INVASION Internal troubles prevented the Persians from taking swift revenge for their loss at Marathon. Almost ten years elapsed before Darius's successor, Xerxes, in 481 B.C., gathered an army of at least 150,000 men and a navy of more than 600 ships for the conquest of Greece. In Athens, Themistocles, who favored making Athens into a naval power, had become the leading politician. During his archonship in 493 B.C., Athens had already taken the first step in that direction by building

The Greek Wars Against Persia	
ca. 560–546 B.C.	Greek cities of Asia Minor conquered by Croesus of Lydia
546 B.C.	Cyrus of Persia conquers Lydia and gains control of Greek cities
499–494 B.C.	Greek cities rebel (Ionian rebellion)
490 B.C.	Battle of Marathon
480–479 B.C.	Xeres' invasion of Greece
480 B.C.	Battles of Thermopylae, Artemisium, and Salamis
479 B.C.	Battles of Plataea and Mycale

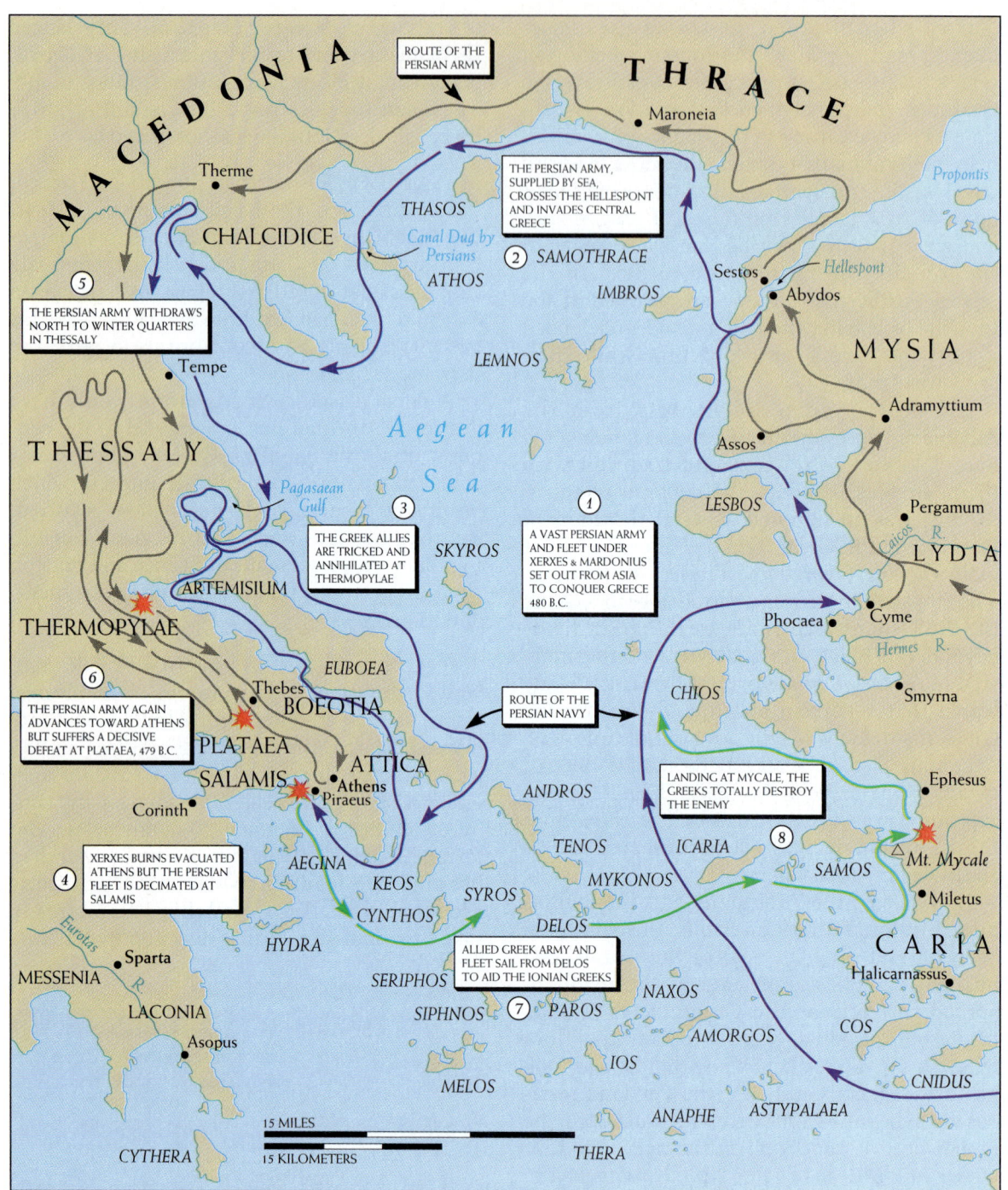

MAP 2-6 THE PERSIAN INVASION OF GREECE *This map traces the route taken by the Persian king Xerxes in his invasion of Greece in 480 B.C. The gray arrows show movements of Xerxes' army, the purple arrows show movements of his navy, and the green arrows show movements of the Greek army and navy.*

This bronze helmet was dedicated to Zeus by Miltiades to commemorate the Athenian victory over the Persians in 490 B.C. [Deutsche Archäologisches Institut, Athens]

remain in Greece long. Themistocles knew that the Aegean was subject to sudden devastating storms. His strategy was to delay the Persian army and then to bring on the kind of naval battle he might hope to win.

The Greek League, founded specifically to resist this Persian invasion, met at Corinth as the Persians were ready to cross the Hellespont. They chose Sparta as leader on land and sea and first confronted the Persians at Thermopylae (the "hot gates") on land and off Artemisium at sea. The opening between the mountains and the sea at Thermopylae was so narrow that it might be held by a smaller army against a much larger one. The Spartans sent their king, Leonidas, with 300 of their own citizens and enough allies to make a total of about 9,000.

Severe storms wrecked many Persian ships while the Greek fleet waited safely in a protected harbor. Then Xerxes attacked Thermopylae, and for two days the Greeks butchered his best troops without serious loss to themselves. On the third day, however, a traitor showed the Persians a mountain trail that permitted them to come on the Greeks from behind. Many allies escaped, but Leonidas and his 300 Spartans all died fighting. At about the same time the Greek and Persian fleets fought an indecisive battle at Artemisium. The fall of Thermopylae, however, forced the Greek navy to withdraw.

After Thermopylae, the Persian army moved into Attica and burned Athens. If an inscription discovered in 1959 is authentic (see the document on page 75), Themistocles had foreseen this possibility before Thermopylae, and the Athenians had begun to evacuate their homeland before they sent their fleet north to fight at Artemisium.

DEFEATING THE PERSIANS The fate of Greece was decided in a sea battle in the narrow waters to the east of the island of Salamis to which the Greek fleet withdrew after the battle at Artemisium. The Peloponnesians were reluctant to confront the Persian fleet at this spot, but Themistocles persuaded them to stay by threatening to remove all the Athenians from Greece and settle them anew in Italy. The Spartans knew that they and the other Greeks could not hope to win without the aid of the Athenians. Because the Greek ships were fewer, slower, and less maneuverable than those of the

a fortified port at Piraeus. A decade later the Athenians came upon a rich vein of silver in the state mines, and Themistocles persuaded them to use the profits to increase their fleet. By 480 B.C. Athens had over 200 ships, the backbone of a navy that was to defeat the Persians.

Of the hundreds of Greek states, only thirty-one—led by Sparta, Athens, Corinth, and Aegina—were willing to fight as the Persian army gathered south of the Hellespont. In the spring of 480 B.C. Xerxes launched his invasion. The Persian strategy was to march into Greece, destroy Athens, defeat the Greek army, and add the Greeks to the number of Persian subjects. The huge Persian army needed to keep in touch with the fleet for supplies. If the Greeks could defeat the Persian navy, the army could not

The Persian general Mardonius spent the winter in central Greece, and in the spring he unsuccessfully tried to win the Athenians away from the Greek League. The Spartan regent, Pausanias, then led the largest Greek army up to that time to confront Mardonius in Boeotia. At Plataea, in the summer of 479 B.C., the Persians suffered a decisive defeat. Mardonius died in battle and his army fled toward home.

Meanwhile the Ionian Greeks urged King Leotychidas, the Spartan commander of the fleet, to fight the Persian fleet at Samos. At Mycale, on the coast nearby, Leotychidas destroyed the Persian camp and its fleet offshore. The Persians fled the Aegean and Ionia. For the moment, at least, the Persian threat was gone.

◆

Hellenic civilization, that unique cultural experience at the root of Western civilization, has powerfully influenced the peoples of the modern world. It was itself influenced by the great Bronze Age civilization of Crete called Minoan, and emerged from the collapse of the Bronze Age civilization on the Greek mainland called Mycenaean. These earlier Aegean civilizations more closely resembled other early civilizations in Egypt, Mesopotamia, Palestine–Syria, and elsewhere than the Hellenic civilization that sprang from them. They had highly developed cities; a system of writing; strong, centralized monarchical systems of government with tightly organized, large bureaucracies; hierarchical social systems; professional standing armies; and a regular system of taxation supporting all this. To a greater or lesser degree, these early civilizations tended toward cultural stability—changing little over time—and uniformity—all sharing many structural features. The striking thing about the emergence of Hellenic civilization is its sharp departure from this pattern.

The collapse of the Mycenaean world produced a harsh material and cultural decline for the Greeks. Cities were swept away and replaced by small farm villages. Trade all but ended, and communication among the Greeks themselves and between them and other peoples was sharply curtailed. The art of writing was lost for more than three centuries. During

A Greek hoplite attacks a Persian soldier. The contrast between the Greek's metal body armor, large shield, and long spear and the Persian's cloth and leather garments indicates one reason the Greeks won. This Attic vase was found on Rhodes and dates from ca. 475 B.C. [The Metropolitan Museum of Art, Rogers Fund, 1906 Acc. # 06.1021.117]

Persians, the Greeks put soldiers on their ships and relied chiefly on hand-to-hand combat. In the ensuing battle the Persians lost more than half their ships and retreated to Asia with a good part of their army, but the danger was not over yet.

The Athenian Assembly Passes Themistocles' Emergency Decree

The following is a translation of a portion of the Themistocles decree. It is included in an inscription from the third century B.C. that purports to be an Athenian decree passed in 480 B.C. Some scholars are uncertain of its authenticity, but many believe it reflects a reliable tradition.

◆ *If this decree is authentic, where should it fit in the chronology of the Persian invasion? Who are the men who have been exiled for ten years? Why are they and those who have lost their citizen rights being recalled? Why are some ships being sent to Artemision [Artemisium] in Euboia [Euboea] and others to Salamis? How does this document help explain the strategies of the Greeks and Persians?*

The Gods

Resolved by the Council and the People

Themistocles, son of Neokles, of Phrearroi, made the motion:

To entrust the city to Athena the Mistress of Athens and to all the other Gods to guard and defend from the Barbarian for the sake of the land. The Athenians themselves and the foreigners who live in Athens are to send their children and women to safety to Troizen, their protector being Pittheus, the founding hero of the land. They are to send the old men and their movable possessions to safety on Salamis. The treasurers and priestesses are to remain on the acropolis guarding the property of the gods.

All the other Athenians and foreigners of military age are to embark on the 200 ships that are ready and defend against the Barbarian for the sake of their own freedom and that of the rest of the Greeks along with the Lakedaimonians, the Korinthians, the Aiginetans, and all others who wish to share the danger. . . .

When the ships have been manned, with 100 of them they are to meet the enemy at Artemision in Euboia, and with the other 100 they are to lie off Salamis and the coast of Attica and keep guard over the land. In order that all Athenians may be united in their defense against the Barbarian those who have been sent into exile for ten years are to go to Salamis and to stay there until the People come to some decision about them, while those who have been deprived of citizen rights are to have their rights restored. . . .

Trans. by M. H. Jameson, in "Waiting for the Barbarian," Greece and Rome, *Second Series, Vol. 8 (Oxford: Clarendon Press, 1961), pp. 5–18.*

this "dark age," the Greeks—poor, small in number, isolated, and illiterate—were ignored by the rest of the world and left alone to develop their own society and the matrix of Hellenic civilization.

During the three and a half centuries from about 1100 to 750 B.C. the Greeks set the foundations for their great achievements. The crucial unit in the new Greek way of life was the polis, the Hellenic city-state. There were hundreds of them, and each evoked a kind of loyalty and attachment by its citizens that made the idea of dissolving one's own polis into a larger unit unthinkable. The result was a dynamic, many-faceted, competitive, sometimes chaotic world in which rivalry for excellence and victory had the highest value. This agonal, or competitive, quality marks Greek life throughout its history. Its negative aspect was constant warfare among the states. Its positive side was an extraordinary achievement in literature and art; competition, sometimes formal and organized, spurred on poets and artists.

Kings had been swept away with the Mycenaean world and the poleis were republics. Since the Greeks were so poor, the difference in wealth among them was relatively small. Therefore, class distinctions were less marked and important than in other civilizations. The introduction of a new mode of fighting, the hoplite phalanx, had further leveling effects, for it placed the safety of the state in the hands of the average farmer. Armies were made up of citizen–soldiers, who were not paid and who returned to their farms after a campaign. As a result, political control was shared with a relatively large portion of the people, and participation in political life was highly valued. There was no bureaucracy, for there were no kings and not much economic surplus to support bureaucrats. Most states imposed no regular taxation. There was no separate caste of priests and little concern with any life after death. In this varied, dynamic, secular, and remarkably free context there arose speculative natural philosophy based on observation and reason, the root of modern natural science and philosophy.

Contact with the rest of the world increased trade and wealth and brought in valuable new information and ideas. Greek art was powerfully shaped by Egyptian and Near Eastern models that were always adapted and changed rather than copied. Changes often produced social and economic strain, leading to the overthrow of traditional aristocratic regimes by tyrants. But monarchic rule was anathema to the Greeks, and these regimes were temporary. In Athens the destruction of the tyranny brought the world's first democracy. Sparta, on the other hand, developed a uniquely stable government that avoided tyranny and impressed the other Greeks.

The Greeks' time of independent development, untroubled by external forces, ended in the sixth century, when Persia's powerful Achaemenid dynasty conquered the Greek cities of Asia Minor. When the Persian kings tried to conquer the Greek mainland, however, the leading states managed to put their quarrels aside and unite against the common enemy. Their determination to preserve their freedom carried them to victory over tremendous odds.

Review Questions

1. Describe the Minoan civilization of Crete. How did the later Bronze Age Mycenaean civilization differ from the Minoan civilization in political organization, art motifs, and military posture?
2. What are the most important historical sources for the Minoan and Mycenaean civilizations? Most particularly, what is Linear B and what problems does it raise for the reconstruction of Bronze Age history? How valuable are the Homeric epics as sources of early Greek history?
3. Define the concept of *polis*. What role did geography play in its development and why did the Greeks consider it a unique and valuable institution?
4. Compare the fundamental political, social, and economic institutions of Athens and Sparta about 500 B.C. Why did Sparta develop its unique form of government?
5. What were the main stages in the transformation of Athens from an aristocratic state to a democracy between 600 and 500 B.C.? In what ways did Draco, Solon, Pisistratus, and Clisthenes each contribute to the process?
6. Why did the Greeks and Persians go to war in 490 and 480 B.C.? What benefit could the Persians have derived from conquering Greece? Why were the Greeks able to defeat the Persians and how did they benefit from the victory?

Suggested Readings

A. ANDREWES, *The Greeks* (1967). A thoughtful general survey.

A. ANDREWES, *Greek Tyrants* (1963). A clear and concise account of tyranny in early Greece.

J. BOARDMAN, *The Greeks Overseas* (1964). A study of the relations between the Greeks and other peoples.

A. R. BURN, *The Lyric Age of Greece* (1960). A discussion of early Greece that uses the evidence of poetry and archaeology to fill out the sparse historical record.

A. R. BURN, *Persia and the Greeks,* 2nd ed. (1984). A thorough narrative and analysis of the conflict between the Persians and the Greeks down to 479 B.C.

J. B. Bury and R. Meiggs, *A History of Greece,* 4th ed. (1975). A thorough and detailed one-volume narrative history.

J. Chadwick, *The Mycenaean World* (1976). A readable account, by a man who helped decipher Mycenaean writing.

E. R. Dodds, *The Greeks and the Irrational* (1955). An excellent account of the role of the supernatural in Greek life and thought.

R. Drews, *The Coming of the Greeks* (1988). A fine study of the arrival of the Greeks as part of the movement of Indo-European peoples.

V. Ehrenberg, *The Greek State* (1964). A good handbook of constitutional history.

V. Ehrenberg, *From Solon to Socrates* (1968). An interpretive history that makes good use of Greek literature to illuminate politics.

J. V. A. Fine, *The Ancient Greeks* (1983). An excellent survey that discusses historical problems and the evidence that gives rise to them.

M. I. Finley, *World of Odysseus,* rev. ed. (1965). A fascinating attempt to reconstruct Homeric society.

W. G. Forrest, *The Emergence of Greek Democracy* (1966). A lively interpretation of Greek social and political developments in the archaic period.

W. G. Forrest, *A History of Sparta, 950–192 B.C.* (1968). A brief but shrewd account.

P. Green, *Xerxes at Salamis* (1970). A lively and stimulating history of the Persian wars.

V. D. Hanson, *The Western Way of War* (1989). A brilliant and lively discussion of the rise and character of the hoplite phalanx and its influence on Greek society.

C. Hignett, *A History of the Athenian Constitution* (1952). A scholarly account, somewhat too skeptical of the ancient sources.

C. Hignett, *Xerxes' Invasion of Greece* (1963). A valuable account, but too critical of all sources other than Herodotus.

J. M. Hurwit, *The Art and Culture of Early Greece* (1985). A fascinating study of the art of early Greece in its literary and cultural context.

S. Isager and J. E. Skydsgaard, *Ancient Greek Agriculture: An Introduction* (1993). A new study of a fundamental subject.

D. Kagan, *The Great Dialogue: A History of Greek Political Thought from Homer to Polybius* (1965). A discussion of the relationship between the Greek historical experience and political theory.

H. D. F. Kitto, *The Greeks* (1951). A personal and illuminating interpretation of Greek culture.

W. K. Lacey, *The Family in Ancient Greece* (1984).

P. B. Manville, *The Origins of Citizenship in Ancient Athens* (1990). An examination of the origins of the concept of citizenship in the time of Solon of Athens.

O. Murray, *Early Greece* (1980). A lively and imaginative account of the early history of Greece to the end of the Persian War.

A. T. Olmstead, *History of the Persian Empire* (1960). A thorough survey.

H. W. Parke, *Festivals of the Athenians* (1977). A fine discussion of the religious practices of the Athenians.

G. M. A. Richter, *Archaic Greek Art* (1949).

C. Roebuck, *Ionian Trade and Colonization* (1959). An introduction to the history of the Greeks in the East.

D. M. Schaps, *Economic Rights of Women in Ancient Greece* (1981).

B. Snell, *Discovery of the Mind* (1960). An important study of Greek intellectual development.

A. M. Snodgrass, *The Dark Age of Greece* (1972). A good examination of the archaeological evidence.

C. G. Starr, *The Economic and Social Growth of Early Greece, 800–500 B.C.* (1977).

C. G. Starr, *Origins of Greek Civilization 1100–650 B.C.* (1961). An interesting interpretation based largely on archaeology and especially on pottery styles.

E. Vermeule, *Greece in the Bronze Age* (1972). A study of the Mycenaean period.

A. G. Woodhead, *Greeks in the West* (1962). An account of the Greek settlements in Italy and Sicily.

W. J. Woodhouse, *Solon the Liberator* (1965). A discussion of the great Athenian reformer.

D. C. Young, *The Olympic Myth of Greek Athletics* (1984). A lively challenge to the orthodox view that Greek athletes were amateurs.

A boy rolling a hoop. This sport was popular in ancient Greece and remained so in many places in the world throughout history. [National Archaeological Museum, Athens]

3

Classical and Hellenistic Greece

Key Topics in This Chapter
- ◆ The Peloponnesian War and the struggle between Athens and Sparta
- ◆ Democracy and empire in fifth-century B.C. Athens
- ◆ Culture and society in Classical Greece
- ◆ The struggle for dominance in Greece after the Peloponnesian War
- ◆ The Hellenistic world

The Greeks' remarkable victory over the Persians in 480–479 B.C. won them another period of freedom and autonomy. They used this time to carry their political and cultural achievement to its height. In Athens, especially, it produced a great sense of confidence and ambition.

Spartan withdrawal from active leadership against the Persians left a vacuum that was filled by the Delian League, which soon turned into the Athenian Empire. At the same time as it tightened its hold over the Greek cities in and around the Aegean Sea, Athens developed an extraordinarily democratic constitution at home. Fears and jealousies of this new kind of state and empire created a split in the Greek world; this led to a series of major wars that impoverished Greece and left it vulnerable to conquest. In 338 B.C. Philip of Macedon conquered the Greek states, putting an end to the age of the polis.

Aftermath of Victory

The unity of the Greeks had shown strain even in the life-and-death struggle against the Persians. Within two years of the Persian retreat it gave way almost completely and yielded to a division of the Greek world into two spheres of influence, dominated by Sparta and Athens. The need of the Ionian Greeks to obtain and defend their freedom from Persia and the desire of many Greeks to gain revenge and financial reparation for the Persian attack brought on the split.

The Delian League

Sparta had led the Greeks to victory, and it was natural to look to the Spartans to continue the campaign against Persia. But Sparta was ill suited to the task, which required both a long-term commitment far from the Peloponnesus and continuous naval action.

Athens had become the leading naval power in Greece, and the same motives that led the

MAP 3-1 CLASSICAL GREECE *Greece in the classical period (ca. 480–338 B.C.) centered on the Aegean Sea. Although there were important Greek settlements in Italy, Sicily, and all around the Black Sea, the area shown in this general reference map embraced the vast majority of Greek states.*

Athenians to support the Ionian revolt prompted them to try to drive the Persians from the Aegean and the Hellespont. The Ionians were at least as eager for the Athenians to take the helm as the Athenians were to accept the responsibility and opportunity.

In the winter of 478–477 B.C. the islanders, the Greeks from the coast of Asia Minor, and from some other Greek cities on the Aegean met with the Athenians on the sacred island of Delos and swore oaths of alliance. As a symbol that the alliance was meant to be permanent, they dropped lumps of iron into the sea; the alliance was to hold until these lumps of iron rose to the surface. The aims of this new Delian League were to free those Greeks who were under Persian rule, to protect all against a Persian return, and to obtain compensation from the Persians by attacking their lands and taking booty. League policy was determined by a vote of an assembly in which each state, including Athens, had one vote. Athens, however, was clearly designated the leader.

From the first, the league was remarkably successful. The Persians were driven from Europe and the Hellespont, and the Aegean was cleared of pirates. Some states were forced into the league or were prevented from leaving. The members approved coercion because it was necessary for the common safety. In 467 B.C. a great victory over the Persians at the Eurymedon River in Asia Minor routed the Persians and added several cities to the league.

The Rise of Cimon

Cimon, son of Miltiades, the hero of Marathon, became the leading Athenian soldier and statesman soon after the war with Persia. Themistocles appears to have been driven from power by a coalition of his enemies. Ironically, the author of the Greek victory over Persia of 480 B.C. was exiled and ended his days at the court of the Persian king. Cimon, who was to dominate Athenian politics for almost two decades, pursued a policy of aggressive attacks on Persia and friendly relations with Sparta. In domestic affairs Cimon was conservative. He accepted the democratic constitution of Clisthenes, which appears to have become somewhat more limited after the Persian war. Defending this constitution and this foreign policy, Cimon led the Athenians and the Delian League to victory after victory, and his own popularity grew with success.

The First Peloponnesian War: Athens Against Sparta

The Thasian Rebellion

In 465 B.C. the island of Thasos rebelled from the league, and Cimon put it down after a siege of more than two years. The revolt of Thasos is the first recorded instance in which Athenian interests alone seemed to determine league policy, a significant step in the evolution of the Delian League into the Athenian Empire.

When Cimon returned to Athens from Thasos, he was charged with taking bribes not to conquer Macedonia, although conquering Macedonia had not been part of his assignment. He was acquitted; the trial was only a device by which his political opponents tried to reduce his influence. Their program at home was to undo the gains made by the Areopagus and to bring about further changes in the direction of democracy. In foreign policy, these enemies of Cimon wanted to break with Sparta and to contest its claim to leadership over the Greeks. They intended at least to establish the independence of Athens and its alliance. The head of this faction was Ephialtes. His supporter, and the man chosen to be the public prosecutor of Cimon, was Pericles, a member of a distinguished Athenian family. He was still a young man, and his defeat in court did not do lasting damage to his career.

The Breach with Sparta

When the Thasians began their rebellion, they asked Sparta to invade Athens the next spring, and the ephors, the annual magistrates responsible for Sparta's foreign policy, agreed. An earthquake, however, accompanied by a rebellion of the Helots that threatened the survival of Sparta, prevented the invasion. The Spartans asked their allies, the Athenians among them, for help, and Cimon persuaded the Athenians to send it.

The results of this policy were disastrous for Cimon and his faction. While Cimon was in the

Peloponnesus helping the Spartans, Ephialtes stripped the Areopagus of almost all its power. The Spartans, meanwhile, fearing "the boldness and revolutionary spirit of the Athenians," ultimately sent them home. In 462 B.C. Ephialtes was assassinated and Pericles replaced him as leader of the democratic faction. In the spring of 461 B.C. Cimon was ostracized, and Athens made an alliance with Argos, Sparta's traditional enemy. Almost overnight Cimon's domestic and foreign policies had been overturned.

The Division of Greece

The new regime at Athens, led by Pericles and the democratic faction, was confident and ambitious. When Megara, getting the worst of a border dispute with Corinth, withdrew from the Peloponnesian League, the Athenians accepted the Megarians as allies. This alliance gave Athens a great strategic advantage, for Megara barred the way from the Peloponnesus to Athens. Sparta, however, resented the defection of Megara to Athens, leading to the outbreak of the First Peloponnesian War, the first phase in a protracted struggle between Athens and Sparta. The Athenians conquered Aegina and gained control of Boeotia. At this moment Athens was supreme and apparently invulnerable, controlling the states on its borders and dominating the sea (see Map 3-2).

About 455 B.C., however, the tide turned. A disastrous defeat struck an Athenian fleet that had gone to aid an Egyptian rebellion against Persia. The great loss of men, ships, and prestige caused rebellions in the empire, forcing Athens to make a truce in Greece to subdue its

MAP 3-2 THE ATHENIAN EMPIRE ABOUT 450 B.C. *The Empire at its fullest extent shortly before 450 B.C. We see Athens and the independent states that provided manned ships for the imperial fleet but paid no tribute, dependent states that paid tribute, and states allied to but not actually in the Empire.*

allies in the Aegean. In 449 B.C. the Athenians ended the war against Persia.

In 446 B.C. the war on the Greek mainland broke out again. Rebellions in Boeotia and Megara removed Athens' land defenses and brought a Spartan invasion. Rather than fight, Pericles, the commander of the Athenian army, agreed to a peace of thirty years by the terms of which he abandoned all Athenian possessions on the Greek mainland outside of Attica. In return, the Spartans gave formal recognition to the Athenian Empire. From then on Greece was divided into two power blocs: Sparta and its alliance on the mainland and Athens ruling its empire in the Aegean.

Classical Greece

The Athenian Empire

After the Egyptian disaster the Athenians moved the Delian League's treasury to Athens and began to keep one-sixtieth of the annual revenues for themselves. Because of the peace with Persia there seemed no further reason for the allies to pay tribute, and so the Athenians were compelled to find a new justification for their empire. They called for a Panhellenic congress to meet at Athens to discuss rebuilding the temples destroyed by the Persians and to consider

how to maintain freedom of the seas. When Sparta's reluctance to participate prevented the congress, Athens felt free to continue to collect funds from the allies, both to maintain its navy and to rebuild the Athenian temples. Athenian propaganda suggested that henceforth the allies

An Athenian silver four-drachma coin (tetradrachm) from the fifth century B.C. (440–430 B.C.). On the front (a) is the profile of Athena and on the back (b) is her symbol of wisdom, the owl. The silver from which the coins were struck came chiefly from the state mines at Sunium in southern Attica. [Hirmer Verlag, Munich]

(a)

(b)

Key Events in Athenian History Between the Persian War and the Great Peloponnesian War	
478–477 B.C.	Delian League founded
ca. 474–462 B.C.	Cimon leading politician
467 B.C.	Victory over Persians at Eurymedon River
465–463 B.C.	Rebellion of Thasos
462 B.C.	Ephialtes murdered; Pericles rises to leadership
461 B.C.	Cimon ostracized
461 B.C.	Reform of Areopagus
ca. 460 B.C.	First Peloponnesian War begins
454 B.C.	Athens defeated in Egypt; crisis in the Delian League
449 B.C.	Peace with Persia
445 B.C.	Thirty Years' Peace ends First Peloponnesian War

would be treated as colonies and Athens as their mother city, the whole to be held together by good feeling and common religious observances.

There is little reason, however, to believe that the allies were taken in or were truly content with their lot. Nothing could cloak the fact that Athens was becoming the master and its allies mere subjects. By 445 B.C., when The Thirty Years' Peace gave formal recognition to an Athenian empire, only Chios, Lesbos, and Samos were autonomous and provided ships. All the other states paid tribute. The change from alliance to empire came about because of the pressure of war and rebellion and largely because the allies were unwilling to see to their own defense. Although the empire had many friends among the lower classes and the democratic politicians in the subject cities, it came to be seen more and more as a tyranny. Athenian prosperity and security, however, had come to depend on the empire, and the Athenians were determined to defend it at any cost.

Athenian Democracy

Even as the Athenians were tightening their control over their empire, they were expanding democracy at home. Under the leadership of Pericles, they evolved the freest government the world had yet seen.

DEMOCRATIC LEGISLATION Legislation was passed making the hoplite class eligible for the archonship, and in practice no one was thereafter prevented from serving in this office on the basis of property class. Pericles himself proposed a law introducing pay for jury members, opening that important duty to the poor. Circuit judges were reintroduced, a policy making swift

The Delian League Becomes the Athenian Empire

In the years after its foundation in the winter of 478–477 B.C., the Delian League gradually underwent changes that finally justified calling it the Athenian Empire. In the following selection, the historian Thucydides explains why the organization changed its character.

◆ *Why did some allies choose to pay money rather than supply ships and men? Since membership in the League was originally voluntary, why did the allies refuse to meet their obligations? Who was responsible for converting a voluntary League of allies into an Athenian Empire?*

The causes which led to the defections of the allies were of different kinds, the principal being their neglect to pay the tribute or to furnish ships, and, in some cases, failure of military service. For the Athenians were exacting and oppressive, using coercive measures towards men who were neither willing nor accustomed to work hard. And for various reasons they soon began to prove less agreeable leaders than at first. They no longer fought upon an equality with the rest of the confederates, and they had no difficulty in reducing them when they revolted. Now the allies brought all this upon themselves; for the majority of them disliked military service and absence from home, and so they agreed to contribute a regular sum of money instead of ships. Whereby the Athenian navy was proportionally increased, while they themselves were always untrained and unprepared for war when they revolted.

Thucydides, The Peloponnesian War, Vol. 2, trans. by Benjamin Jowett, in The Greek Historians, ed. by F. R. B. Godolphin (New York: Random House, 1942), p. 609.

The Acropolis was both the religious and civic center of Athens. In its final form it is the work of Pericles and his successors in the late fifth century B.C. This photograph shows the Parthenon and to its left the Erechtheum. [Meredith Pillon, Greek National Tourist Organization]

impartial justice available even to the poorest residents in the countryside.

Finally, Pericles himself introduced a bill limiting citizenship to those who had two citizen parents. From a modern perspective this measure might be seen as a step away from democracy, and, in fact, it would have barred Cimon and one of Pericles' ancestors. In Greek terms, however, it was quite natural. Democracy was defined as the privilege of those who held citizenship, making citizenship a valuable commodity. The decision to limit it would have increased its value and thus must have won a large majority. Participation in government in all the Greek states was also denied to slaves, resident aliens, and women.

How Did the Democracy Work?

Within the citizen body, the extent of Athenian democracy was remarkable. Every decision of the state had to be approved by the popular assembly—a collection of the people, not their representatives. Every judicial decision was subject to appeal to a popular court of not fewer than 51 and as many as 1,501 citizens, chosen from an annual panel of jurors widely represen-

tative of the Athenian population. Most officials were selected by lot without regard to class. The main elected officials, such as the ten generals (the generalship was an office that had both political and military significance) and the imperial treasurers, were generally nobles and almost always rich men, but the people were free to choose otherwise. All public officials were subject to scrutiny before taking office and could be called to account and removed from office during their tenure. They were held to compulsory examination and accounting at the end of their term. There was no standing army, no police force, open or secret, and no way to coerce the people.

Pericles was elected to the generalship fifteen years in a row and thirty times in all, not because he was a dictator but because he was a persuasive speaker, a skillful politician, a respected military leader, an acknowledged patriot, and a man patently incorruptible. When he lost the people's confidence, they did not hesitate to depose him from office. In 443 B.C., however, he stood at the height of his power. The defeat of the Athenian fleet in the Egyptian campaign and the failure of Athens' continental

A shoemaker's workshop, illustrated in black-figure painting on an Attic vase dating to 520–510 B.C. This type of vase is called an amphora. In black-figure painting, black pigment is used for the foreground (figure), and the red color of the fired clay for the background. [Courtesy of Museum of Fine Arts, Boston]

campaigns had persuaded him to favor a conservative policy, seeking to retain the empire in the Aegean and live at peace with the Spartans. It was in this direction that he led Athens' imperial democracy in the years after the First Peloponnesian War.

The Women of Athens—Two Views

Greek society, like most societies all over the world throughout history, was dominated by men. This was true of the democratic city of Athens in the great days of Pericles, in the fifth century B.C., no less than of other Greek cities. The actual position of women in classical Athens, however, has been the subject of much controversy.

SUBJECTION   The bulk of the evidence, coming from the law, from philosophical and moral writings, and from information about the conditions of daily life and the organization of society, shows that women were excluded from most aspects of public life. They could not vote, take part in the political assemblies, hold public office, or take any direct part in politics at all. Since Athens was one of the few places in the ancient world where male citizens of all classes had these public responsibilities and opportunities, the exclusion of women was all the more significant.

The same sources show that in the private aspects of life women were always under the control of a male guardian—a father, a husband, or, failing these, an appropriate male relative. Women married young, usually between the ages of twelve and eighteen, whereas their husbands were typically over thirty. Therefore, in a way, they were always in a relationship similar to that of a daughter to a father. Marriages were arranged; the woman normally had no choice of husband, and her dowry was controlled by a male relative. Divorce was difficult for a woman to obtain, for she needed the approval of a male relative who had to be willing to serve as her guardian after the dissolution of the marriage. In case of divorce, the dowry returned with the woman but was controlled by her father or the appropriate male relative.

The main function and responsibility of a respectable Athenian woman of a citizen family was to produce male heirs for the household (*oikos*) of her husband. If, however, her father's *oikos* lacked a male heir, the daughter became an *epikleros*, the "heiress" to the family property. In that case, she was required by law to marry a relative on her father's side in order to produce the desired male offspring. In the Athenian way of thinking, women were "lent" by one household to another for bearing and raising a male heir to continue the existence of the *oikos*.

Because the pure and legitimate lineage of the offspring was important, women were carefully segregated from men outside the family and were confined to the women's quarters in the house. Men might seek sexual gratification outside the house with prostitutes of high or low style, frequently recruited from abroad. Respectable women stayed home to raise the

Athenian Democracy: An Unfriendly View

The following selection comes from an anonymous pamphlet thought to have been written in the midst of the Peloponnesian War. Because it has come down to us among the works of Xenophon but cannot be his work, it is sometimes called "The Constitution of the Athenians" by Pseudo-Xenophon. It is also common to refer the unknown author as "The Old Oligarch"—although neither his age nor his purpose is known—because of the obviously antidemocratic tone of the work. Such opinions were common among members of the upper classes in Athens late in the fifth century and thereafter.

✦ *What are the author's objections to democracy? Does he describe the workings of the Athenian democracy accurately? How would a defender of the Athenian constitution and way of life meet his complaints? Is there any merit in his criticisms?*

Now, in discussing the Athenian constitution, I cannot commend their present method of running the state, because in choosing it they preferred that the masses should do better than the respectable citizens; this, then, is my reason for not commending it. Since, however, they have made this choice, I will demonstrate how well they preserve their constitution and handle the other affairs for which the rest of the Greeks criticise them.

Again, some people are surprised at the fact that in all fields they give more power to the masses, the poor and the common people than they do to the respectable elements of society, but it will become clear that they preserve the democracy by doing precisely this. When the poor, the ordinary people and the lower classes flourish and increase in numbers, then the power of the democracy will be increased; if, however, the rich and the respectable flourish, the democrats increase the strength of their opponents. Throughout the world the aristocracy are opposed to democracy, for they are naturally least liable to loss of self control and injustice and most meticulous in their regard for what is respectable, whereas the masses display extreme ignorance, indiscipline and wickedness, for poverty gives them a tendency towards the ignoble, and in some cases lack of money leads to their being uneducated and ignorant.

It may be objected that they ought not to grant each and every man the right of speaking in the *Ekklesia* and serving on the *Boule*, but only the ablest and best of them; however, in this also they are acting in their own best interests by allowing the mob also a voice. If none but the respectable spoke in the *Ekklesia* and the *Boule*, the result would benefit that class and harm the masses; as it is, anyone who wishes rises and speaks, and as a member of the mob he discovers what is to his own advantage and that of those like him.

But someone may say: 'How could such a man find out what was advantageous to himself and the common people?' The Athenians realise that this man, despite his ignorance and badness, brings them more advantage because he is well disposed to them than the ill-disposed respectable man would, despite his virtue and wisdom. Such practices do not produce the best city, but they are the best way of preserving democracy. For the common people do not wish to be deprived of their rights in an admirably governed city, but to be free and to rule the city; they are not disturbed by inferior laws, for the common people get their strength and freedom from what you define as inferior laws.

Aristotle and Xenophon on Democracy and Oligarchy, *trans. with introductions and commentary by J. M. Moore (Berkeley and Los Angeles: University of California Press, 1975), pp. 37-38.*

children, cook, weave cloth, and oversee the management of the household. The only public function of women—an important one—was in the various rituals and festivals of the state religion. Apart from these activities, Athenian women were expected to remain at home out of sight, quiet and unnoticed. Pericles told the widows and mothers of the Athenian men who died in the first year of the Peloponnesian War only this: "Your great glory is not to fall short of your natural character, and the greatest glory of women is to be least talked about by men, whether for good or bad."

POWER The picture of the legal status of women derived from these sources is largely accurate. It does not fit well, however, with other evidence from mythology, from pictorial art, and from the tragedies and comedies by the great Athenian dramatists. These often show women as central characters and powerful figures in both the public and the private spheres, suggesting that the role played by Athenian women may have been more complex than their

This red-figure kalyx crater, or wine bowl, was painted by the Dokimasia painter about 470–465 B.C. It shows the murder of King Agamemnon, on his return from the sack of Troy, by his wife Clytemnestra and her lover Aegisthus. In red-figure painting, the red color of the fired clay is used for the foreground (figure) and a black pigment for the background. [Museum of Fine Arts, Boston]

legal status suggests. Clytemnestra in Aeschylus' tragedy *Agamemnon*, for example, arranges the murder of her royal husband and establishes the tyranny of her lover, whom she dominates.

As a famous speech in Euripides' tragedy *Medea* makes clear, we are left with an apparent contradiction. In this speech (see the accompanying document), Medea paints a bleak picture of the subjugation of women as dictated by their legal status. Yet Medea, as depicted by Euripides, is herself a powerful and terrifying figure who negotiates with kings. She is the central figure in a tragedy bearing her name, produced at state expense before most of the Athenian population, and written by one of Athens' greatest poets and dramatists. She is a cause of terror to the audience and, at the same time, an object of their pity and sympathy as a victim of injustice. She is certainly not "least talked about by men, whether for good or for bad."

Slavery

The Greeks had some form of slavery from the earliest times, but true chattel slavery was initially rare. The most common forms of bondage were different kinds of serfdom in relatively backward areas such as Crete, Thessaly, and Sparta. As noted in Chapter 2, the Spartans conquered the natives of their region and reduced them to the status of Helots, subjects who belonged to the Spartan state and worked the land for the benefit of their Spartan masters. Another early form of bondage—involving a severe but rarely permanent loss of freedom—resulted from default in debt. In Athens, however, about 600 B.C., such bondsmen, called *hektemoroi*, were sold outside their native land as true slaves until the reforms of Solon put an end to debt-bondage entirely.

True chattel slavery began to increase about 500 B.C. and remained important to Greek society thereafter. The main sources of slaves were war captives; the captives of pirates; and those people, originally enslaved through war, piracy, or other means, sold by slave traders. Like the Chinese, Egyptians, and many other peoples, the Greeks regarded foreigners as inferior—they called them "barbarians" because they uttered words that sounded like "bar bar"—and most

Medea Bemoans the Condition of Women

In 431 B.C. Euripides (ca. 485–406 B.C.) presented his play Medea *at the Festival of Dionysus in Athens. The heroine is a foreign woman who has unusual powers. Her description of the condition of women in the speech that follows, however, appears to be an accurate representation of the condition of women in fifth-century B.C. Athens.*

✦ *Apart from participation in politics, how did the lives of men and women differ in ancient Athens? How well or badly did that aspect of Athenian society suit the needs of the Athenian people and the state in the Classical Period? Since men had a dominant position in the state and the presentation of tragedies was managed and financed by the state, how do you explain the sympathetic account of the condition of women Euripides puts into the mouth of Medea?*

Of all things which are living and can form a judgment
We women are the most unfortunate creatures.
Firstly, with an excess of wealth it is required
For us to buy a husband and take for our bodies
A master; for not to take one is even worse.
And now the question is serious whether we take
A good or bad one; for there is no easy escape
For a woman, nor can she say no to her marriage.
She arrives among new modes of behavior and manners,
And needs prophetic power, unless she has learned at home,
How best to manage him who shares the bed with her.
And if we work out all this well and carefully,
And the husband lives with us and lightly bears his yoke,
Then life is enviable. If not, I'd rather die.
A man, when he's tired of the company in his home,
Goes out of the house and puts an end to his boredom
And turns to a friend or companion of his own age.
But we are forced to keep our eyes on one alone.
What they say of us is that we have a peaceful time
Living at home, while they do the fighting in war.
How wrong they are! I would very much rather stand
Three times in the front of battle than bear one child.

Euripides, Medea, *in* Four Tragedies, *trans. by Rex Warner (Chicago: University of Chicago Press, 1955), pp. 66–67.*

slaves working for the Greeks were foreigners. Greeks sometimes enslaved Greeks, but not to serve in their home territories.

Most Greek farmers worked small holdings too poor to support more than one slave. The upper class had larger farms that were let out to free tenant farmers or were worked by slaves, generally under an overseer who was himself a slave. Large landowners generally did not have a single great estate but several smaller farms scattered about the *polis*. This arrangement did not encourage the amassing of great numbers of agricultural slaves such as those later to work the cotton and sugar plantations of the Americas.

Slaves were used in larger numbers in industry and especially mining. Nicias, a wealthy Athenian of the fifth century B.C. who was prominent during the Great Peloponnesian War, owned 1,000 slaves whom he rented to a mining contractor for profit, but this is by far the greatest number of which we know. In another instance of large slave holdings in Athens, a family of resident aliens employed about 120 slaves in their shield factory. Most manufacturing, however, was on a very small scale, with shops using one, two, or a handful of slaves. Slaves worked as artisans in most trades, and, as was true for the agricultural slaves on small farms, they worked alongside their masters. A significant proportion of slaves were domestic servants, and many were shepherds. Publicly held slaves served as police officers, prison attendants, clerks, and secretaries.

The number of slaves in ancient Greece and their importance to Greek society are the subjects of controversy arising from a shortage of reliable evidence. We have no useful figures for the absolute number of slaves or their percentage of the free population in any city except Athens. There the evidence permits estimates for the slave population in the fifth and fourth centuries B.C. that range from 20,000 to 100,000. Accepting the mean of the extremes, 60,000, and estimating the free population at its height at 40,000 households would yield a figure of fewer than two slaves per family. The distribution was unequal, with most families having one or more slaves and some having many.

Some historians have noted that in the American South during the period before the Civil War—where slaves made up less than one-third of the total population and three-fourths of free southerners had no slaves—the proportion of slaves to free citizens was similar to that of ancient Athens. Because slavery was so important to the economy of the South, these historians suggest, it may have been equally important and similarly oppressive in ancient Athens. This argument has several problems.[1] For one thing, in the American South before the Civil War a single cash crop, well suited for exploitation by large groups of slaves, dominated the economy and society, whereas in Athens the economy was mixed, the crops varied, and the land and its distribution were poorly suited to massive slavery.

Another major difference lay in the likelihood of a slave's achieving freedom. Manumission in America was relatively rare, but in Greece it was common. The most famous example is that of

the Athenian slave Pasion, who began as a bank clerk, earned his freedom, became Athens' richest banker, and was awarded Athenian citizenship. Pasion's case was certainly unusual, but the acquisition of freedom by slaves was not.

In the American South, masters were increasingly hostile to manumission and afraid of slave rebellions. In contrast, in the very different society of classical Athens, slaves walked the streets with such ease as to offend class-conscious Athenians. Plato, for example, complained that in the Athenian democracy "men and women who have been sold are no less free than their purchasers" (*Republic*, 563B).

Even more remarkable, the Athenians were on occasion willing to contemplate the liberation of all their slaves. In 406 B.C., with their city facing defeat in the Peloponnesian War, they freed all slaves of military age and granted citizenship to those who rowed the ships that won the Battle of Arginusae. Twice more at crucial moments, similar proposals were made, although without success. No such suggestion, of course, would have been conceivable in the slave societies of the Americas.

The Great Peloponnesian War

During the first decade after the Thirty Years' Peace of 445 B.C., the willingness of each side to respect the new arrangements was tested and not found wanting. About 435 B.C., however, a dispute in a remote and unimportant part of the Greek world ignited a long and disastrous war that shook the foundations of Greek civilization.

Causes

The spark that ignited the conflict was a civil war at Epidamnus, a Corcyraean colony on the Adriatic. This civil war caused a quarrel between Corcyra and her mother city and traditional enemy, Corinth, an ally of Sparta. The Corcyraean fleet was second in size only to that of Athens, and the Athenians feared that its capture by Corinth would change the balance of power at sea and seriously threaten Athenian security. As a result, they made an alliance with the previously neutral Corcyra, angering

[1] M. I. Finley, "Was Greek Civilization Based on Slave Labor?" Historia 8 (1959): 151.

Corinth and leading to a series of crises in the years 433–432 B.C. that threatened to bring the Athenian Empire into conflict with the Peloponnesian League.

In the summer of 432 B.C. the Spartans met to consider the grievances of their allies. Persuaded, chiefly by the Corinthians, that Athens was an insatiably aggressive power seeking to enslave all the Greeks, they voted for war. The treaty of 445 B.C. specifically provided that all differences be submitted to arbitration, and Athens repeatedly offered to arbitrate any question. Pericles insisted that the Athenians refuse to yield to threats or commands and that they uphold the treaty and the arbitration clause. Sparta refused to arbitrate, and in the spring of 431 B.C. its army marched into Attica, the Athenian homeland.

Strategic Stalemate

The Spartan strategy was traditional: to invade the enemy's country and threaten the crops, forcing the enemy to defend them in a hoplite battle. Such a battle the Spartans were sure to win because they had the better army and they outnumbered the Athenians at least two to one. Any ordinary *polis* would have yielded or fought and lost. Athens, however, had an enormous navy, an annual income from the empire, a vast reserve fund, and long walls that connected the fortified city with the fortified port of Piraeus.

The Athenians' strategy was to allow devastation of their own land to prove that Spartan invasions could not hurt Athens. At the same time, the Athenians launched seaborne raids on the Peloponnesian coast to show that Sparta's allies could be hurt. Pericles expected that within a year or two, three at most, the Peloponnesians would become discouraged and make peace, having learned their lesson. If the Peloponnesians held out, Athenian resources were inadequate to continue for more than four or five years without raising the tribute in the empire and running an unacceptable risk of rebellion.

The plan required restraint and the leadership only a Pericles could provide. In 429 B.C., however, in the wake of a devastating plague and a political crisis that had challenged his authority, Pericles died. After his death, no dom-inant leader emerged to hold the Athenians to a consistent policy. Two factions vied for influence: one, led by Nicias, wanted to continue the defensive policy, and the other, led by Cleon, preferred a more aggressive strategy. In 425 B.C. the aggressive faction was able to win a victory that changed the course of the war. Four hundred Spartans surrendered. Sparta offered peace at once to get them back. The great victory and the prestige it brought Athens made it safe to raise the imperial tribute, without which Athens could not continue to fight. The Athenians indeed wanted to continue, for the Spartan peace offer gave no adequate guarantee of Athenian security.

In 424 B.C. the Athenians undertook a more aggressive policy. They sought to make Athens safe by conquering Megara and Boeotia. Both attempts failed, and defeat helped discredit the aggressive policy, leading to a truce in 423 B.C. Meanwhile, Sparta's ablest general, Brasidas, took a small army to Thrace and Macedonia. He captured Amphipolis, the most important Athenian colony in the region. Thucydides was in charge of the Athenian fleet in those waters and was held responsible for the city's loss. He was exiled and was thereby given the time and opportunity to write his famous history of the Great Peloponnesian War. In 422 B.C. Cleon led an expedition to undo the work of Brasidas. At Amphipolis both he and Brasidas died in battle. The removal of these two leaders of the aggressive factions in their respective cities paved the way for the Peace of Nicias, named for its chief negotiator, which was ratified in the spring of 421 B.C.

The Fall of Athens

The peace, officially supposed to last fifty years and, with a few exceptions, guarantee the status quo, was in fact tenuous. Neither side carried out all its commitments, and several of Sparta's allies refused ratification. In 415 B.C. Alcibiades persuaded the Athenians to attack Sicily to bring it under Athenian control. This ambitious and unnecessary undertaking ended in disaster in 413 B.C. when the entire expedition was destroyed. The Athenians lost some two hundred ships, about 4,500 of their own men, and almost ten times as many allies. It shook

War and Revolution in Classical Greece

In 427 B.C., in the fifth year of the Great Peloponnesian War, a terrible civil war broke out between factions on the island of Corcyra, an important ally of the Athenians. With clinical precision and philosophical detachment, Thucydides describes and explains the causes of such events, making clear the thin and vulnerable divide between civilization and arbitrary cruelty.

✦ *In what ways does war encourage internal conflict and civil wars? Does Thucydides make moral judgments in this passage? If so, what are they? How does he portray the relationship between language and action?*

[82] So bloody was the march of the revolution, and the impression which it made was the greater as it was one of the first to occur. Later on, one may say, the whole Hellenic world was convulsed, struggles being everywhere made by the popular chiefs to bring in the Athenians, and by the oligarchs to introduce the Lacedæmonians. In peace there would have been neither the pretext nor the wish to make such an invitation; but in war, with an alliance always at the command of either faction for the hurt of their adversaries and their own corresponding advantage, opportunities for bringing in the foreigner were never wanting to the revolutionary parties. The sufferings which revolution entailed upon the cities were many and terrible, such as have occurred and always will occur, as long as the nature of mankind remains the same, though in a severer or milder form, and varying in their symptoms, according to the variety of the particular cases. In peace and prosperity states and individuals have better sentiments, because they do not find themselves suddenly confronted with imperious necessities; but war takes away the easy supply of daily wants, and so proves a rough master that brings most men's characters to a level with their fortunes. Revolution thus ran its course from city to city, and the places which it arrived at last, from having heard what had been done before, carried to a still greater excess the refinement of their inventions, as manifested in the cunning of their enterprises and the atrocity of their reprisals. Words had to change their ordinary meanings and to take those which were now given them. Reckless audacity came to be considered the courage of a loyal ally; prudent hesitation, specious cowardice; moderation was held to be a cloak for unmanliness; ability to see all sides of a question, inaptness to act on any. Frantic violence became the attribute of manliness; cautious plotting, a justifiable means of self-defence.

. . . .

The leaders in the cities, each provided with the fairest professions, on the one side with the cry of political equality of the people, on the other of a moderate aristocracy, sought prizes for themselves in those public interests which they pretended to cherish, and, recoiling from no means in their struggles for ascendancy, engaged in the direct excesses; in their acts of vengeance they went to even greater lengths, not stopping at what justice or the good of the state demanded, but making the party caprice of the moment their only standard, and invoking with equal readiness the condemnation of an unjust verdict or the authority of the strong arm to glut the animosities of the hour. Thus religion was in honour with neither party; but the use of fair phrases to arrive at guilty ends was in high reputation. Meanwhile the moderate part of the citizens perished between the two, either for not joining in the quarrel, or because envy would not suffer them to escape.

Thucydides, The Great Peloponnesian War, Book 3, Chapter 82, trans. by Richard Crowley (New York: Random House, 1951), pp. 198–200.

The Great Peloponnesian War	
435 B.C.	Civil war at Epidamnus
432 B.C.	Sparta declares war on Athens
431 B.C.	Peloponnesian invasion of Athens
421 B.C.	Peace of Nicias
415–413 B.C.	Athenian invasion of Sicily
405 B.C.	Battle of Aegospotami
404 B.C.	Athens surrenders

Athenian prestige, reduced the power of Athens, provoked rebellions, and brought the wealth and power of Persia into the war on Sparta's side.

It is remarkable that the Athenians could continue fighting in spite of the disaster. They survived a brief oligarchic coup in 411 B.C. and won several important victories at sea as the war shifted to the Aegean. Their allies rebelled, however, and were sustained by fleets paid for by Persia. The Athenians saw their financial resources shrink and finally disappear. When their fleet was caught napping and was destroyed at Aegospotami in 405 B.C., they could not build another. The Spartans, under Lysander, a clever and ambitious general who was responsible for obtaining Persian support, cut off the food supply through the Hellespont, and the Athenians were starved into submission. In 404 B.C. they surrendered unconditionally; the city walls were dismantled, Athens was permitted no fleet, and the empire was gone. The Great Peloponnesian War was over.

Competition for Leadership in the Fourth Century B.C.

The defeat of Athens did not bring domination to the Spartans. Instead, the period from 404 B.C. until the Macedonian conquest of Greece in 338 B.C. was a time of intense rivalry among the Greek cities, each seeking to achieve leadership and control over some or all of the others. Sparta, a recovered Athens, and a newly powerful Thebes were the main competitors in a struggle that ultimately weakened all the Greeks and left them vulnerable to outside influence and control.

The Hegemony of Sparta

The collapse of the Athenian Empire created a vacuum of power in the Aegean and opened the way for Spartan leadership, or hegemony. Fulfilling the contract that had brought them the funds to win the war, the Spartans handed the Greek cities of Asia Minor back to Persia. Under the leadership of Lysander, the Spartans went on to make a complete mockery of their promise to free the Greeks by stepping into the imperial role of Athens in the cities along the European coast and the islands of the Aegean. In most of the cities Lysander installed a board of ten local oligarchs loyal to him and supported them with a Spartan garrison. Tribute brought in an annual revenue almost as great as that the Athenians had collected.

Limited population, the Helot problem, and traditional conservatism all made Sparta a less than ideal state to rule a maritime empire. The increasing arrogance of Sparta's policies alienated some of its allies, especially Thebes and Corinth. In 404 B.C. Lysander installed an oligarchic government in Athens, and the outrageous behavior of its leaders earned them the title "Thirty Tyrants." Democratic exiles took refuge in Thebes and Corinth and created an army to challenge the oligarchy. Sparta's conservative king, Pausanias, replaced Lysander, arranging a peaceful settlement and ultimately the restoration of democracy. Thereafter Athenian foreign policy remained under Spartan control, but otherwise Athens was free.

In 405 B.C. Darius II of Persia died and was succeeded by Artaxerxes II. His younger brother, Cyrus, contested his rule and received Spartan help in recruiting a Greek mercenary army to help him win the throne. The Greeks marched inland as far as Mesopotamia, where they defeated the Persians at Cunaxa in 401 B.C., but Cyrus was killed in the battle. The Greeks were able to march back to the Black Sea and safety; their success revealed the potential weakness of the Persian Empire.

The Greeks of Asia Minor had supported Cyrus and were now afraid of Artaxerxes' revenge. The Spartans accepted their request for aid and sent an army into Asia, attracted by the prospect of prestige, power, and money. In 396 B.C. the command of Sparta's army was given to a new king, Agesilaus. This leader dominated

Sparta throughout its period of hegemony and until his death in 360 B.C. Some have argued that his consistent advocacy of aggressive policies that provided him with opportunities to display his bravery in battle may have been motivated by a psychological need to compensate for his physical lameness and his disputed claim to the throne.

Agesilaus collected much booty and frightened the Persians. They sent a messenger with money and promises of further support to friendly factions in all of the Greek states likely to help them against Sparta. By 395 B.C. Thebes was able to organize an alliance that included Argos, Corinth, and a resurgent Athens. The result was the Corinthian War (395–387 B.C.), which put an end to Sparta's Asian adventure. In 394 B.C. the Persian fleet destroyed Sparta's maritime empire. Meanwhile the Athenians took advantage of events to rebuild their walls, to enlarge their navy, and even to recover some of their lost empire in the Aegean. The war ended when the exhausted Greek states accepted a peace dictated by the Great King of Persia.

The Persians, frightened now by the recovery of Athens, turned the management of Greece over to Sparta. Agesilaus broke up all alliances except the Peloponnesian League. He used or threatened to use the Spartan army to interfere in other *poleis* and put friends of Sparta in power within them. Sparta reached a new level of lawless arrogance in 382 B.C., when it seized Thebes during peacetime without warning or pretext. In 379 B.C. a Spartan army made a similar attempt on Athens. That action persuaded the Athenians to join with Thebes, which had rebelled from Sparta a few months earlier, to wage war on the Spartans.

In 371 B.C. the Thebans, led by their great generals Pelopidas and Epaminondas, defeated the Spartans at Leuctra. The Thebans encouraged the Arcadian cities of the central Peloponnesus to form a league, freed the Helots, and helped them found a city of their own. They deprived Sparta of much of its farmland and of the people who worked it and hemmed it in with hostile neighbors. Sparta's population had shrunk so that it could put fewer than 2,000 men into the field at Leuctra. Sparta's aggressive policies had led to ruin. The Theban victory brought the end of Sparta as a power of the first rank.

The Hegemony of Thebes: The Second Athenian Empire

Thebes' power after the its victory at Leuctra lay in its democratic constitution, its control over Boeotia, and its two outstanding and popular generals. One of these generals, Pelopidas, died in a successful attempt to gain control of Thessaly. The other, Epaminondas, consolidated his work, making Thebes dominant over all Greece north of Athens and the Corinthian Gulf and challenging the reborn Athenian Empire in the Aegean. All this activity provoked resistance, and by 362 B.C. Thebes faced a Peloponnesian coalition as well as Athens. Epaminondas, once again leading a Boeotian army into the Peloponnesus, confronted this coalition at the Battle of Mantinea. His army was victorious, but Epaminondas himself was killed. With both its great leaders now dead, Theban dominance ended.

The Second Athenian Confederation, which Athens had organized in 378 B.C., was aimed at resisting Spartan aggression in the Aegean. Its constitution was careful to avoid the abuses of the Delian League, but the Athenians soon began to repeat them anyway. This time, however, they did not have the power to put down resistance. When the collapse of Sparta and Thebes and the restraint of Persia removed any reason for voluntary membership, Athens' allies revolted. By 355 B.C. Athens had to abandon most of the empire. After two centuries of

The Spartan and Theban Hegemonies	
404–403 B.C.	Thirty Tyrants rule at Athens
401 B.C.	Expedition of Cyrus, rebellious prince of Persia; Battle of Cunaxa
400–387 B.C.	Spartan War against Persia
398–360 B.C.	Reign of Agesilaus at Sparta
395–387 B.C.	Corinthian War
382 B.C.	Sparta seizes Thebes
378 B.C.	Second Athenian Confederation founded
371 B.C.	Thebans defeat Sparta at Leuctra; end of Spartan hegemony
362 B.C.	Battle of Mantinea; end of Theban hegemony

Xenophon Recounts How Greece Brought Itself to Chaos

Confusion in Greece in the fourth century B.C. reached a climax with the inconclusive Battle of Mantinea in 362. The Theban leader Epaminondas was killed, and no other city or person emerged to provide the needed general leadership for Greece. Xenophon, a contemporary, pointed out the resulting near chaos in Greek affairs—tempting ground for the soon-to-appear conquering Macedonians under their king Philip II.

◆ What does this passage reveal about the nature of ancient Greek warfare and the customs surrounding it? How decisive were most battles in ancient Greece? Before the Macedonian conquest of Greece in 338 B.C. why was no state able to impose its rule over the others? Why was that possible elsewhere?

The effective result of these achievements was the very opposite of that which the world at large anticipated. Here, where well-nigh the whole of Hellas was met together in one field, and the combatants stood rank against rank confronted, there was no one who doubted that, in the event of battle, the conquerors this day would rule; and that those who lost would be their subjects. But god so ordered it that both belligerents alike set up trophies as claiming victory, and neither interfered with the other in the act. Both parties alike gave back their enemy's dead under a truce, and in right of victory; both alike, in symbol of defeat, under a truce took back their dead. And though both claimed to have won the day, neither could show that he had thereby gained any accession of territory, or state, or empire, or was better situated than before the battle. Uncertainty and confusion, indeed, had gained ground, being tenfold greater throughout the length and breadth of Hellas after the battle than before.

Xenophon, Hellenica, *trans. by H. G. Dakyns, in* The Greek Historians, *ed. by F. R. B. Godolphin (New York: Random House, 1942), p. 221.*

---

almost continuous warfare, the Greeks returned to the chaotic disorganization that characterized the time before the founding of the Peloponnesian League.

The Culture of Classical Greece

The repulse of the Persian invasion released a flood of creative activity in Greece that was rarely, if ever, matched anywhere at any time. The century and a half between the Persian retreat and the conquest of Greece by Philip of Macedon (479–338 B.C.) produced achievements of such quality as to justify the designation of that era as the Classical Period. Ironically, we often use the term *classical* to suggest calm and serenity, but the word that best describes the common element present in Greek life, thought, art, and literature in this period is *tension.*

The Fifth Century B.C.

Two sources of tension contributed to the artistic outpouring of fifth-century B.C. Greece. One arose from the conflict between the Greeks' pride in their accomplishments and their concern that overreaching would bring retribution. Friction among the *poleis* intensified during this period as Athens and Sparta gathered most of them into two competing and menacing blocs.

The victory over the Persians brought a sense of exultation in the capacity of humans to accomplish great things and a sense of confidence in the divine justice that had brought low the arrogant pride of Xerxes. But the Greeks recognized that the fate that had met Xerxes awaited all those who reached too far, creating a sense of unease. The second source of tension was the conflict between the soaring hopes and achievements of individuals and the claims and limits put on them by their fellow citizens in the *polis*. These tensions were felt throughout Greece. They had the most spectacular consequences, however, in Athens in its Golden Age, the time between the Persian and the Peloponnesian wars.

ATTIC TRAGEDY Nothing reflects these concerns better than Attic tragedy, which emerged as a major form of Greek poetry in the fifth century B.C. The tragedies were presented in a contest as part of the public religious observations in honor of the god Dionysus. The festivals in which they were shown were civic occasions.

Each poet who wished to compete submitted his work to the archon. Each offered three tragedies (which might or might not have a common subject) and a satyr play (a comic choral dialogue with Dionysus) to close. The three best competitors were each awarded three actors and a chorus. The actors were paid by the state. The chorus was provided by a wealthy citizen selected by the state to perform this service as *choregos*, for the Athenians had no direct taxation to support such activities. Most of the

tragedies were performed in the theater of Dionysus on the south side of the Acropolis, and as many as 30,000 Athenians could attend. Prizes and honors were awarded to the author, the actor, and the *choregos* voted best by a jury of Athenians chosen by lot.

Attic tragedy served as a forum in which the poets raised vital issues of the day, enabling the Athenian audience to think about them in a serious yet exciting context. On rare occasions the subject of a play might be a contemporary or historic event, but almost always it was chosen from mythology. Until late in the century the tragedies always dealt solemnly with difficult questions of religion, politics, ethics, morality, or some combination of these. The plays of the dramatists Aeschylus and Sophocles, for example, follow this pattern. The plays of Euripides written toward the end of the century are less solemn and more concerned with individual psychology.

OLD COMEDY Comedy was introduced into the Dionysian festival early in the fifth century B.C. Cratinus, Eupolis, and the great master of the genre called Old Comedy, Aristophanes (ca. 450–385 B.C.), the only one from whom we have complete plays, wrote political comedies. They were filled with scathing invective and satire against such contemporary figures as Pericles, Cleon, Socrates, and Euripides.

ARCHITECTURE AND SCULPTURE The great architectural achievements of Periclean Athens, as much as Athenian tragedy, illustrate the mag-

The Theatre of Dionysus in Athens, seen from the Acropolis. It was here, in contests held in honor of Dionysus, that the great Attic tragedies and comedies were performed for the citizens of Athens. [Meredith Pillon, Greek National Tourist Organization]

The Porch of the Maidens is part of the Erechtheum on the Athenian Acropolis near the Parthenon. Built between 421 and 409 B.C., the Erechtheum housed the shrines of three different gods. In place of the usual fluted columns, the porch uses the statues of young girls taking part in a religious festival. [Meredith Pillon, Greek National Tourist Organization]

buildings were tangible proof of Pericles' claim that Athens was "the school of Hellas," that is, the intellectual center of all Greece.

PHILOSOPHY The tragic dramas, architecture, and sculpture of the fifth century B.C. are all indications of an extraordinary concern with human beings—their capacities, their limits,

The three orders of Greek architecture, Doric, Ionic, and Corinthian, have had an enduring impact on Western architecture.

Diagram of a Doric Column and Entablature:

a *Corner-Akroterion*
b *Sima with a lion's head as waterspout*
c *Geison (cornice)*
d *Tympanum*
e *Mutule with Guttae (trops)*
f *Triglyphs*
g *Metopes*
h *Regulae with guttae*
i *Architrave or Epistyle*
k *Abacus*
l *Echinus*
m *Shaft with 20 sharp-edged flutings*
n *Stylobate*
o *Krepis or Krepidoma*
p *Taenia*

Diagram of an Ionic Column and Entablature

a *Sima*
b *Geison (cornice)*
c *Tympanum*
d *Frieze*
e *Architrave or Epistyle (in three parts)*
f *Capital with Volutes*
g *Shaft with 24 flutings separated by fillets*
h *Attic Base with double Torus and a Trochilos*
i *Stylobate*
k *Krepis or Krepidoma*

Corinthian Capital

nificent results of the union and tension between religious and civic responsibilities on the one hand and the transcendent genius of the individual artist on the other. Beginning in 448 B.C. and continuing to the outbreak of the Great Peloponnesian War, Pericles undertook a great building program on the Acropolis (see Map 3-3, page 100). The funds were provided by the income from the empire. The new buildings included temples to honor the city's gods and a fitting gateway to the temples. Pericles' main purpose seems to have been to represent visually the greatness and power of Athens, but in such a way as to emphasize intellectual and artistic achievement—civilization rather than military and naval power. It was as though these

Lysistrata Ends the War

Aristophanes, the greatest of the Athenian comic poets, presented the play
Lysistrata in 411 B.C., two decades into the Great Peloponnesian War. The central
idea of the plot is that the women of Athens, led by Lysistrata, tired of the privations
imposed by the war, decide to take matters into their own hands and bring the war
to an end. The device they employ is to get the women on both sides to deny their
marital favors to their husbands, a kind of sexual strike that quickly achieves its
purpose. Before the following passage, Lysistrata has set the terms the Spartans
must accept. Next she turns to the Athenians. The play is a masterful example of
Athenian Old Comedy, which was almost always full of contemporary and histori-
cal political satirical references and sexual and erotic puns and jokes. The references
to "Peace" in the stage directions are to an actor playing the goddess Peace.

◆ To what historic event does the passage concerning "the Tyrant's days" refer?
To what does the "Promontory of Pylos" refer? What was the real role of women
in Athenian political life, and what does the play tell us about it? What is the
relationship between humor and reality in this play?

LYSISTRATA
Turning to the Athenians.
—Men of Athens, do you think I'll let *you* off?
Have you forgotten the Tyrant's days, when
    you wore
the smock of slavery, when the Spartans
    turned to the spear,
cut down the pride of Thessaly, despatched
    the friends
of tyranny, and dispossessed your oppressors?
                                        Recall:
On that great day, your only allies were
    Spartans;
your liberty came at their hands, which
    stripped away
your servile garb and clothed you again in
    Freedom!
SPARTAN
Indicating Lysistrata.

Hain't never seed no higher type of woman.
KINESIAS
Indicating Peace.
Never saw one I wanted so much to top.
LYSISTRATA
Oblivious to the byplay, addressing both
groups.
With such a history of mutual benefits con-
    ferred
and received, why are you fighting? Stop this
    wickedness!
Come to terms with each other! What pre-
    vents you?
SPARTAN
We'd a heap sight druther make Peace, if we
    was indemnified with a plumb strategic
    location.
Pointing at Peace's rear.
                            We'll take thet butte.

---

their nature, their place in the universe. The same concern is clear in the development of philosophy.

To be sure, some philosophers continued the speculation about the nature of the cosmos (as opposed to human nature) that began with Thales in the sixth century B.C. Parmenides of Elea and his pupil Zeno, in opposition to the earlier philosopher, Heraclitus, argued that

change was only an illusion of the senses. Reason and reflection showed that reality was fixed and unchanging because it seemed evident that nothing could be created out of nothingness. Empedocles of Acragas further advanced such fundamental speculations by identifying four basic elements: fire, water, earth, and air. Like Parmenides, he thought that reality was permanent, but he thought it not immobile; the

LYSISTRATA
Butte?
SPARTAN
      The Promontory of Pylos—Sparta's
     Back Door.
We've missed it fer a turrible spell.
Reaching.
               Hev to keep our
hand in.
KINESIAS
Pushing him away.
   The price is too high—you'll never take that!
LYSISTRATA
Oh, let them have it.
KINESIAS
          What room will we have left
for maneuvers?
LYSISTRATA
       Demand another spot in exchange.
KINESIAS
*Surveying Peace like a map as he addresses
   the Spartan.*
Then you hand over to us—uh, let me see—
let's try Thessaly—
Indicating the relevant portions of Peace.
        First of all, Easy Mountain . . .
then the Maniac Gulf behind it . . .
             and down to Megara
for the legs . . .
SPARTAN
      You cain't take all of thet! Yore plumb
out of yore mind!
LYSISTRATA
To Kinesias.
     Don't argue. Let the legs go.

*Kinesias nods. A pause, General smiles of
   agreement.*
KINESIAS
Doffing his cloak.
I feel an urgent desire to plow a few
   furrows.
SPARTAN
Doffing his cloak.
Hit's time to work a few loads of fertilizer in.
LYSISTRATA
Conclude the treaty and the simple life is yours.
If such is your decision, convene your councils,
and then deliberate the matter with your
   allies.
KINESIAS
Deliberate? Allies?
       We're over-extended already!
Wouldn't every ally approve of our position—
Union Now?
SPARTAN
     I know I kin speak for ourn.
KINESIAS
And I for ours.
        They're just a bunch of gigolos.
LYSISTRATA
I heartily approve.
Now first attend to your purification,
then we, the women, will welcome you to the
   Citadel
and treat you to all the delights of a home-
   cooked banquet.
Then you'll exchange your oaths and pledge
   your faith,
and every man of you will take his wife
and depart for home.

Aristophanes, Lysistrata, *trans. by Douglass Parker, in* Four Comedies by Aristophanes, *ed. by W. Arrowsmith (Ann
Arbor: University of Michigan Press, 1969), pp. 79–81.*

four elements, he contended, were moved by two primary forces, love and strife—or, as we might say, attraction and repulsion.

Empedocles' theory is clearly a step on the road to the atomic theory of Leucippus of Miletus and Democritus of Abdera. According to this theory, the world consists of innumerable tiny, solid, indivisible, and unchangeable particles—or atoms—that move about in the void.

The size of the atoms and the arrangements they form when joined produce the secondary qualities that our senses perceive, such as color and shape. These secondary qualities are merely conventional—the result of human interpretation and agreement—unlike the atoms themselves, which are natural.

Previous to the atomists, Anaxagoras of Clazomenae, an older contemporary and a

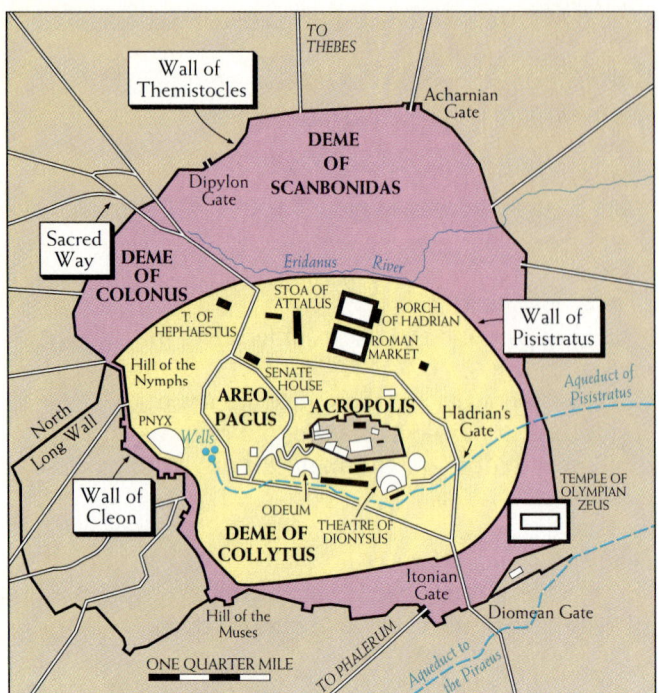

MAP 3-3 ANCIENT ATHENS *This sketch locates some of the major features of the ancient city of Athens that have been excavated and are visible today. It includes monuments ranging in age from the earliest times to the period of the Roman Empire. The geographical relation of the Acropolis to the rest of the city is apparent, as is that of the Agora, the Areopagus (where the early council of aristocrats met), and the Pnyx (site of assembly for the larger, more democratic meetings of the entire people).*

valued in democracies like Athens, where so many issues were resolved through open debate.) Some Sophists claimed to teach wisdom and even virtue. Reflecting the human focus characteristic of fifth-century thought, they refrained from speculations about the physical universe, instead applying reasoned analysis to human beliefs and institutions. In doing so they identified a central problem of human social life and the life of the *polis,* the conflict between nature and custom, or law. The more traditional among them argued that law itself was in accord with nature and of divine origin, a view that fortified the traditional beliefs of the *polis.*

Others argued, however, that laws were merely the result of convention—an agreement among people—and not in accord with nature. The laws could not pretend to be a positive moral force but merely had the negative function of preventing people from harming each other. The most extreme Sophists argued that law was contrary to nature, a trick whereby the weak control the strong. Critias, an Athenian oligarch and one of the more extreme Sophists, went so far as to say that the gods themselves had been invented by some clever person to deter people from doing what they wished. Such ideas attacked the theoretical foundations of the *polis* and helped provoke the philosophical responses of Plato and Aristotle in the next century.

HISTORY The first prose literature in the form of history was an account of the Persian war written by Herodotus. "The father of history," as he has been deservedly called, was born shortly before the outbreak of the war. His account goes far beyond all previous chronicles, genealogies, and geographical studies and attempts to explain human actions and to draw instruction from them.

Although his work was completed about 425 B.C. and shows a few traces of Sophist influence, its spirit is that of an earlier time. Herodotus accepted the evidence of legends and oracles, although not uncritically, and often explained human events in terms of divine intervention. Human arrogance and divine vengeance are key forces that help explain the defeat of Croesus by Cyrus as well as Xerxes' defeat by the Greeks. Yet the *History* is typical of its time in celebrating the crucial role of human intelligence as

friend of Pericles, had spoken of tiny fundamental particles called *seeds,* which were put together on a rational basis by a force called *nous,* or "mind." Anaxagoras was thus suggesting a distinction between matter and mind. The atomists, however, regarded "soul," or mind, as material and believed that everything was guided by purely physical laws. In these conflicting positions we have the beginning of the enduring philosophical debate between materialism and idealism.

These speculations were of interest to very few people, and in fact, most Greeks were suspicious of them. A far more influential debate was begun by a group of professional teachers who emerged in the mid-fifth century B.C. Called *Sophists,* they traveled about and received pay for teaching practical techniques of persuasion such as rhetoric. (Persuasive skills were much

This stone carving shows a doctor or priest of Asklepios, the god of healing, ministering to a patient. The woman on the right is a nurse or priestess. [Piraeus Archaeological Museum, Athens]

exemplified by Miltiades at Marathon and Themistocles at Salamis. Nor was Herodotus unaware of the importance of institutions. There is no mistaking his pride in the superiority of the Greek *polis* and the discipline it inspired in its citizen soldiers and his pride in the superiority of the Greeks' voluntary obedience to law over the Persians' fear of punishment.

Thucydides, the historian of the Peloponnesian War, was born about 460 B.C. and died a few years after the end of the Great Peloponnesian War. He was very much a product of the late fifth century B.C.. His work, which was influenced by the secular, human-centered, skeptical rationalism of the Sophists, also reflects the scientific attitude of the school of medicine named for his contemporary, Hippocrates of Cos.

The Hippocratic school, known for its pioneering work in medicine and scientific theory, placed great emphasis on an approach to the understanding, diagnosis, and treatment of disease that combined careful observation with reason. In the same way Thucydides took great pains to achieve factual accuracy and tried to use his evidence to discover meaningful patterns of human behavior. He believed that human nature was essentially unchanging, so that a wise person equipped with the understanding provided by history might accurately foresee events and thus help to guide them. He believed, however, that only a few had the ability to understand history and to put its lessons to good use. He thought that even the wisest could be foiled by the intervention of chance, which played a great role in human affairs. Thucydides focused his interest on politics, and in that area his assumptions about human nature do not seem unwarranted. His work has proved to be, as he hoped, "a possession forever." Its description of the terrible civil war between the two basic kinds of *poleis* is a final and fitting example of the tension that was the source of both the greatness and the decline of Classical Greece.

The Fourth Century B.C.

Historians often speak of the Peloponnesian War as the crisis of the *polis* and of the fourth century B.C. as the period of its decline. The war did bring powerfully important changes: the impoverishment of some Greek cities and with it an intensification of class conflict; the development of professionalism in the army; and demographic shifts that sometimes reduced the citizen population and increased the numbers of resident aliens. The Greeks of the fourth century B.C. did not know, however, that their traditional way of life was on the verge of destruction. Still, thinkers could not avoid recognizing that they lived in a time of troubles, and they responded in various ways. Some looked to the past and tried to shore up the weakened structure of the *polis*; others tended toward despair and looked for new solutions; and still others averted their gaze from the public arena altogether. All of these responses are apparent in the literature, philosophy, and art of the period.

DRAMA The tendency of some to turn away from the life of the *polis* and inward to everyday life, the family, and their own individuality is apparent in the poetry of the fourth century B.C. A new genre, called Middle Comedy, replaced the political subjects and personal invective of the Old Comedy with a comic-realistic depiction of daily life, plots of intrigue, and mild satire of domestic situations. Significantly, the role of the chorus, which in some way represented the *polis*, was very much diminished. These trends all continued and were carried even further in the New Comedy. Its leading playwright, Menander (342–291 B.C.), completely abandoned mythological subjects in favor of domestic tragicomedy. His gentle satire of the foibles of ordinary people and his tales of lovers

temporarily thwarted before a happy and proper ending would not be unfamiliar to viewers of modern situation comedies.

Tragedy faded as a robust and original form. No tragedies written in the fourth century B.C. have been preserved, and it became common to revive the great plays of the previous century. The plays of Euripides, which rarely won first prize when first produced for Dionysian festival competitions, became increasingly popular in the fourth century and after. Euripides was less interested in cosmic confrontations of conflicting principles than in the psychology and behavior of individual human beings. Some of his late plays, in fact, are less like the tragedies of Aeschylus and Sophocles than forerunners of later forms such as the New Comedy. Plays like *Helena*, *Andromeda*, and *Iphigenia in Tauris* are more like fairy tales, tales of adventure, or love stories than tragedies.

SCULPTURE The same movement away from the grand, the ideal, and the general and toward the ordinary, the real, and the individual is apparent in the development of Greek sculpture. To see these developments, one has only to compare the statue of the *Striding God of Artemisium* (ca. 460 B.C.), thought to be either Zeus on the point of releasing a thunderbolt or Poseidon about to throw his trident, or the *Doryphoros* of Polycleitus (ca. 450–440 B.C.) with the *Hermes* of Praxiteles (ca. 340–330 B.C.) or the *Apoxyomenos* attributed to Lysippus (ca. 330 B.C.).

The striding god from Artemisium is a bronze statue dating from about 460 B.C. It was found in the sea near Artemisium, the northern tip of the large Greek island of Euboea, and is now on display in the Athens archaeological museum. Exactly whom he represents is not known. Some have thought him to be Poseidon holding a trident; others believe that he is Zeus hurling a thunderbolt. In either case he is a splendid representative of the early classical period of Greek sculpture. [National Archaeological Museum, Athens]

Philosophy and the Crisis of the Polis

SOCRATES Probably the most complicated response to the crisis of the *polis* may be found in the life and teachings of Socrates (469–399 B.C.). Because he wrote nothing, our knowledge of him comes chiefly from his disciples Plato and Xenophon and from later tradition. Although as a young man he was interested in speculations about the physical world, he later turned to the investigation of ethics and morality; as Cicero put it, he brought philosophy down from the heavens. He was committed to the search for truth and for the knowledge about human affairs that he believed could be discovered by reason. His method was to go among men, particularly those reputed to know something, such as craftsmen, poets, and politicians, to question and cross-examine them.

The result was always the same. Those he questioned might have technical information and skills but seldom had any knowledge of the fundamental principles of human behavior. It is understandable that Athenians so exposed should be angry with their examiner, and it is not surprising that they thought Socrates was undermining the beliefs and values of the *polis*.

This is a Roman copy of a bronze statue made in the fifth century by the great sculptor Polycleitus. Called the Doryphoros *("the spear-bearer"), it shows a young athlete carrying a javelin. The original was made about 450–440 B.C. [Scala/Art Resource, N.Y.]*

Socrates' unconcealed contempt for democracy, which seemingly relied on ignorant amateurs to make important political decisions without any certain knowledge, created further hostility. Moreover, his insistence on the primacy of his own individualism and his determination to

This is a Roman copy of the Apoxyomenos *("the scraper") by Lysippus of Sicyon. It shows a young athlete scraping from his body the oil used for cleansing after exertion. The original was made about 330 B.C. [Robert Miller]*

pursue philosophy even against the wishes of his fellow citizens reinforced this hostility and the prejudice that went with it.

But Socrates, unlike the Sophists, did not accept pay for his teaching; he professed ignorance and denied that he taught at all. His individualism, moreover, was unlike the worldly hedonism of some of the Sophists. It was not wealth or pleasure or power that he urged people to seek, but "the greatest improvement of the soul." He differed also from the more radical Sophists in that he denied that the *polis* and its laws were merely conventional. He thought, on the contrary, that they had a legitimate claim on the citizen, and he proved it in the most convincing fashion.

In 399 B.C. he was condemned to death by an Athenian jury on the charges of bringing new gods into the city and of corrupting the youth. His dialectical inquiries had angered many important people. His criticism of democracy must have been viewed with suspicion, especially as Critias and Charmides, who were members of the Thirty Tyrants, and the traitor Alcibiades had been among his disciples. He was given a chance to escape but, as we are told in Plato's *Crito*, he refused to do so because of his veneration of the laws. Socrates' career set the stage for later responses to the travail of the *polis*. He recognized its difficulties and criticized its shortcomings, and he turned away from an active political life, but he did not abandon the idea of the *polis*. He fought as a soldier in its defense, obeyed its laws, and sought to put its values on a sound foundation by reason.

THE CYNICS One branch of Socratic thought—the concern with personal morality and one's own soul, the disdain of worldly pleasure and wealth, and the withdrawal from political life—was developed and then distorted almost beyond recognition by the Cynic school. Antisthenes (ca. 455–360 B.C.), a follower of Socrates, is said to have been its founder, but its most famous exemplar was Diogenes of Sinope (ca. 400–325 B.C.). Because Socrates disparaged wealth and worldly comfort, Diogenes wore rags and lived in a tub. He performed shameful acts in public and made his living by begging to show his rejection of convention. He believed that happiness lay in satisfying natural needs in the simplest and most direct way; because actions to this end, being natural, could not be indecent, they could and should be done publicly.

Socrates questioned the theoretical basis for popular religious beliefs; the Cynics, in contrast, ridiculed all religious observances. As Plato said, Diogenes was Socrates gone mad. Beyond that, the way of the Cynics contradicted important Socratic beliefs. Socrates, unlike traditional aristocrats such as Theognis, believed that virtue was a matter not of birth but of knowledge and that people do wrong only through ignorance of what is virtuous. The Cynics, on the other hand, believed that "virtue is an affair of deeds and does not need a store of words and learning."[2] Wisdom and happiness come from pursuing the proper style of life, not from philosophy.

They moved even further away from Socrates by abandoning the concept of the *polis* entirely. When Diogenes was asked about his citizenship, he answered that he was *kosmopolites*, a citizen of the world. The Cynics plainly had turned away from the past, and their views anticipated those of the Hellenistic Age.

PLATO Plato (429–347 B.C.) was by far the most important of Socrates' associates and is a perfect example of the pupil who becomes greater than his master. He was the first systematic philosopher and therefore the first to place political ideas in their full philosophical context. He was also a writer of genius, leaving us twenty-six philosophical discussions. Almost all are in the form of dialogues, which somehow make the examination of difficult and complicated philosophical problems seem dramatic and entertaining. Plato came from a noble Athenian family, and he looked forward to an active political career until the excesses of the Thirty Tyrants and the execution of Socrates discouraged him from that pursuit. Twice he made trips to Sicily in the hope of producing a model state at Syracuse under the tyrants Dionysius I and II, but without success.

In 386 B.C. he founded the Academy, a center of philosophical investigation and a school for training statesmen and citizens. It had a powerful impact on Greek thought and lasted until it

---

[2] *Diogenes Laertius, Life of Antisthenes, 6.11.*

was closed by the emperor Justinian in the sixth century A.D.

Like Socrates, Plato firmly believed in the *polis* and its values. Its virtues were order, harmony, and justice, and one of its main objects was to produce good people. Like his master, and unlike the radical Sophists, Plato thought that the *polis* was in accord with nature. He accepted Socrates' doctrine of the identity of virtue and knowledge. He made it plain what that knowledge was: *episteme,* science, a body of true and unchanging wisdom open to only a few philosophers, whose training, character, and intellect allowed them to see reality. Only such people were qualified to rule; they would prefer the life of pure contemplation but would accept their responsibility and take their turn as philosopher kings. The training of such men required a specialization of function and a subordination of the individual to the community even greater than that at Sparta. This specialization would lead to Plato's definition of justice: that each man should do only that one thing to which his nature is best suited.

Plato saw quite well that the *polis* of his day suffered from terrible internal stress, class struggle, and factional divisions. His solution, however, was not that of some Greeks, that is, conquest and resulting economic prosperity. For Plato the answer was in moral and political reform. The way to harmony was to destroy the causes of strife: private property, the family—anything, in short, that stood between the individual citizen and devotion to the *polis.*

Concern for the redemption of the *polis* was at the heart of Plato's system of philosophy. He began by asking the traditional questions: What is a good man, and how is he made? The goodness of a human being belonged to moral philosophy, and when goodness became a function of the state, it became political philosophy. Because goodness depended on knowledge of the good, it required a theory of knowledge and an investigation of what kind of knowledge was required for goodness. The answer must be metaphysical and so required a full examination of metaphysics. Even when the philosopher knew the good, however, the question remained how the state could bring its citizens to the necessary comprehension of that knowledge. The answer required a theory of education. Even

purely logical and metaphysical questions, therefore, were subordinate to the overriding political questions. In this way Plato's need to find a satisfactory foundation for the beleaguered *polis* contributed to the birth of systematic philosophy.

ARISTOTLE Aristotle (384–322 B.C.) was a pupil of Plato's and owed much to the thought of his master, but his very different experience and cast of mind led him in some new directions. He was born at Stagirus in the Chalcidice, the son of the court doctor of neighboring Macedon. As a young man he went to Athens to study at the Academy, where he stayed until Plato's death. Then he joined a Platonic colony at Assos in Asia Minor, and from there he moved to Mytilene. In both places he did research in marine biology, and biological interests played a large part in all his thoughts. In 342 B.C. Philip, the king of Macedon, appointed him tutor to his son, the young Alexander (see the following section).

In 336 B.C. he returned to Athens, where he founded his own school, the Lyceum, or the Peripatos, as it was also called because of the covered walk within it. In later years its members were called *Peripatetics*. On the death of Alexander in 323 B.C., the Athenians rebelled from Macedonian rule, and Aristotle found it wise to leave. He died at Chalcis in Euboea in the following year.

The Lyceum was a very different place from the Academy. Its members took little interest in mathematics and were concerned with gathering, ordering, and analyzing all human knowledge. Aristotle wrote dialogues on the Platonic model, but none survive. He and his students also prepared many collections of information to serve as the basis for scientific works. Of these only the *Constitution of the Athenians,* one of 158 constitutional treatises, remains. Almost all of what we possess is in the form of philosophical and scientific studies, whose loose organization and style suggest that they were lecture notes. The range of subjects treated is astonishing, including logic, physics, astronomy, biology, ethics, rhetoric, literary criticism, and politics.

In each field the method is the same. Aristotle began with observation of the empiri-

Plato Reports the Claims of the Sophist Protagoras

Plato (429–347 B.C.) remains to many the greatest of the ancient philosophers. Protagoras, the famous Sophist from Leontini in Sicily, came to Athens in 427 B.C. and created great excitement. In the following passage from the dialogue Protagoras, *Plato's spokesman, Socrates, introduces a young man who wishes to benefit from Protagoras' skills.*

✦ *From reading this selection why do you think Plato chose to present his philosophical ideas in the form of a dramatic dialogue? In what ways is Protagoras typical of the Sophists? In what ways is he different from Socrates? What role did the Sophists play in Athenian society? What was their importance? How would you compare the kind of education offered by Protagoras with that offered by other Sophists, by Socrates, and with your own?*

When we were all seated, Protagoras said: Now that the company are assembled, Socrates, tell me about the young man of whom you were just now speaking.

I replied: I will begin again at the same point, Protagoras, and tell you once more the purport of my visit: this is my friend Hippocrates, who is desirous of making your acquaintance; he would like to know what will happen to him if he associates with you. I have no more to say.

Protagoras answered: Young man, if you associate with me, on the very first day you will return home a better man than you came and better on the second day than on the first, and better every day than you were on the day before.

When I heard this, I said: Protagoras, I do not at all wonder at hearing you say this; even at your age, and with all your wisdom, if any one were to teach you what you did not know before, you would become better no doubt: but please to answer in a different way—I will explain how by an example. Let me suppose that Hippocrates, instead of desiring your acquaintance, wished to become acquainted with the young man Zeuxippus of Heraclea, who has lately been in Athens, and he had come to him as he has come to you, and had heard him say, as he has heard you say, that every day he would grow and become better if he associated with him: and then suppose that he were to ask him, "In what shall I become better, and in what shall I grow?" Zeuxippus would answer, "In painting." And suppose that he went to Orthagoas the Theban, and heard him say the same thing, and asked him, "In what shall I become better day by day?" he would reply, "In flute-playing." Now I want you to make the same sort of answer to this young man and to me, who am asking questions on his account. When you say that on the first day on which he associates with you he will return home a better man, and on every day will grow in like manner,—in what, Protagoras, will he be better? and about what?

When Protagoras heard me say this, he replied: You ask questions fairly, and I like to answer a question which is fairly put. If Hippocrates comes to me he will not experience the sort of drudgery with which other Sophists are in the habit of insulting their pupils; who, when they have just escaped from the arts, are taken and driven back into them by these teachers, and made to learn calculation, and astronomy, and geometry, and music (he gave a look at Hippias as he said this); but if he comes to me, he will learn that which he comes to learn. And this is prudence in affairs private as well as public; he will learn to order his own house in the best manner, and he will be able to speak and act for the best in the affairs of the state.

Plato, Protagoras, *trans. by Benjamin Jowett, in* The Dialogues of Plato, *Vol. 1 (New York: Random House, 1937), pp. 88–89.*

cal evidence, which in some cases was physical and in others was common opinion. To this body of information he applied reason and discovered inconsistencies or difficulties. To deal with these, he introduced metaphysical principles to explain the problems or to reconcile the inconsistencies.

His view on all subjects, like Plato's, was teleological; that is, both Plato and Aristotle recognized purposes apart from and greater than the will of the individual human being. Plato's purposes, however, were contained in ideas, or forms that were transcendental concepts outside the experience of most people. For Aristotle the purposes of most things were easily inferred by observation of their behavior in the world. Aristotle's most striking characteristics are his moderation and his common sense. His epistemology finds room for both reason and experience; his metaphysics gives meaning and reality to both mind and body; his ethics aims at the good life, which is the contemplative life, but recognizes the necessity for moderate wealth, comfort, and pleasure.

All these qualities are evident in Aristotle's political thought. Like Plato, he opposed the Sophists' assertion that the *polis* was contrary to nature and the result of mere convention. His response was to apply the teleology he saw in all nature to politics as well. In his view matter existed to achieve an end, and it developed until it achieved its form, which was its end. There was constant development from matter to form, from potential to actual. Therefore, human primitive instincts could be seen as the matter out of which the human's potential as a political being could be realized. The *polis* made individuals self-sufficient and allowed the full realization of their potentiality. It was therefore natural.

It was also the highest point in the evolution of the social institutions that serve the human need to continue the species—marriage, household, village, and finally, *polis*. For Aristotle the purpose of the *polis* was neither economic nor military but moral. According to Aristotle, "The end of the state is the good life" (*Politics* 1280b), the life lived "for the sake of noble actions" (1281a), a life of virtue and morality.

Characteristically, Aristotle was less interested in the best state—the utopia that required philosophers to rule it—than in the best state

practically possible, one that would combine justice with stability. The constitution for that state he called *politeia*, not the best constitution, but the next best, the one most suited to and most possible for most states. Its quality was moderation, and it naturally gave power to neither the rich nor the poor, but to the middle class, which must also be the most numerous. The middle class possessed many virtues; because of its moderate wealth it was free of the arrogance of the rich and the malice of the poor. For this reason it was the most stable class.

The stability of the constitution also came from its being a mixed constitution, blending in some way the laws of democracy and of oligarchy. Aristotle's scheme was unique because of its realism and the breadth of its vision. All the political thinkers of the fourth century B.C. recognized that the *polis* was in danger, and all hoped to save it. All recognized the economic and social troubles that threatened it. Isocrates, a contemporary of Plato and Aristotle, urged a program of imperial conquest as a cure for poverty and revolution. Plato saw the folly of solving a political and moral problem by purely economic means and resorted to the creation of utopias. Aristotle combined the practical analysis of political and economic realities with the moral and political purposes of the traditional defenders of the *polis*. The result was a passionate confidence in the virtues of moderation and of the middle class and the proposal of a constitution that would give it power. It is ironic that the ablest defense of the *polis* came soon before its demise.

The Hellenistic World

The term *Hellenistic* was coined in the nineteenth century to describe the period of three centuries during which Greek culture spread far from its homeland to Egypt and far into Asia. The new civilization formed in this expansion was a mixture of Greek and Near Eastern elements, although the degree of mixture varied from time to time and place to place. The Hellenistic world was larger than the world of Classical Greece, and its major political units were much larger than the city-states, though these persisted in different forms. The new political and cultural order had its roots in the rise to power of a Macedonian dynasty that conquered Greece and the Persian Empire in the space of two generations.

The Macedonian Conquest

The quarrels among the Greeks brought on defeat and conquest by a new power that suddenly rose to eminence in the fourth century B.C., the kingdom of Macedon. The Macedonians inhabited the land to the north of Thessaly (see Map 3-1), and through the centuries they had unknowingly served the vital purpose of protecting the Greek states from barbarian tribes further to the north.

By Greek standards Macedon was a backward, semibarbaric land. It had no *poleis* and was ruled loosely by a king in a rather Homeric fashion. He was chosen partly on the basis of descent, but the acclamation of the army gathered in assembly was required to make him legitimate. Quarrels between pretenders to the throne and even murder to secure it were not uncommon. A council of nobles checked the royal power and could reject a weak or incompetent king. Hampered by constant wars with the barbarians, internal strife, loose organization, and lack of money, Macedon played no great part in Greek affairs up to the fourth century B.C.

The Macedonians were of the same stock as the Greeks and spoke a Greek dialect, and the nobles, at least, thought of themselves as Greeks. The kings claimed descent from Heracles and the royal house of Argos. They tried to bring Greek culture into their court and won acceptance at the Olympic games. If a king could be found to unify this nation, it was bound to play a greater part in Greek affairs.

PHILIP OF MACEDON That king was Philip II (r. 359–336 B.C.), who, while still under thirty, took advantage of his appointment as regent to overthrow his infant nephew and make himself king. Like many of his predecessors, he admired Greek culture. Between 367 and 364 B.C. he had been a hostage in Thebes, where he learned much about Greek politics and warfare under the tutelage of Epaminondas. His talents for war and diplomacy and his boundless ambition made him the ablest king in Macedonian history. Using both diplomatic and military means, he was able to pacify the tribes on his frontiers and make his own hold on the throne firmer. Then he began to undermine Athenian control of the northern Aegean. He took Amphipolis, which gave him control of the Strymon Valley and of the gold and silver mines of Mount Pangaeus. The income allowed him to found new cities, to bribe politicians in foreign towns, and to reorganize his army into the finest fighting force in the world.

THE MACEDONIAN ARMY Philip put to good use what he had learned in Thebes and combined it with the advantages afforded by Macedonian society and tradition. His genius created a versatile and powerful army that was at once national and professional, unlike the amateur armies of citizen-soldiers who fought for the individual *poleis*.

The infantry was drawn from among Macedonian farmers and the frequently rebellious Macedonian hill people. In time these two elements were integrated to form a loyal and effective national force. Infantrymen were armed with thirteen-foot pikes instead of the more common nine-foot pikes and stood in a more open phalanx formation than the hoplite phalanx of the *poleis*. The effectiveness of this formation depended more on skillful use of the pike than the weight of the charge. In Macedonian tactics, the role of the phalanx was not to be the decisive force but to hold the enemy until a massed cavalry charge could strike a winning blow on the flank or into a gap. The cavalry was made up of Macedonian nobles and clan leaders, called Companions, who lived closely with the king and developed a special loyalty to him.

Philip also employed mercenaries who knew the latest tactics used by mobile light-armed Greek troops and were familiar with the most sophisticated siege machinery known to the Greeks. With these mercenaries, and with draft forces from among his allies, he could expand on his native Macedonian army of as many as 40,000 men.

THE INVASION OF GREECE So armed, Philip turned south toward central Greece. Since 355 B.C. the Phocians had been fighting against Thebes and Thessaly. Philip gladly accepted the request of the Thessalians to be their general, defeated Phocis, and treacherously took control of Thessaly. Swiftly he turned northward again to Thrace and gained domination over the northern Aegean coast and the European side of the straits to the Black Sea. This conquest threatened the vital interests of Athens, which still had a formidable fleet of 300 ships.

The Athens of 350 B.C. was not the Athens of Pericles. It had neither imperial revenue nor allies to share the burden of war on land or sea, and its own population was smaller than in the fifth century B.C. The Athenians, therefore, were reluctant to go on expeditions themselves or even to send out mercenary armies under Athenian generals, for they had to be paid out of taxes or contributions from Athenian citizens.

The leading spokesman against these tendencies and the cautious foreign policy that went with them was Demosthenes (384–322 B.C.), one of the greatest orators in Greek history. He was convinced that Philip was a dangerous enemy to Athens and the other Greeks. He spent most of his career urging the Athenians to resist Philip's encroachments. He was right, for beginning in 349 B.C. Philip attacked several cities in northern and central Greece and firmly planted Macedonian power in those regions. The king of "barbarian" Macedon was elected president of the Pythian Games at Delphi, and the Athenians were forced to concur in the election.

In these difficult times it was Athens' misfortune not to have the kind of consistent political leadership that Cimon or Pericles had offered a century earlier. Many, perhaps most, Athenians accepted Demosthenes' view of Philip, but few were willing to run the risks and make the sacrifices necessary to stop his advance. Others, like Eubulus, an outstanding financial official and conservative political leader, favored a cautious policy of cooperation with Philip in the hope that his aims were limited and no real threat to Athens.

Not all Athenians feared Philip. Isocrates (436–338 B.C.), the head of an important rhetorical and philosophical school in Athens, looked to him to provide the unity and leadership needed for a Panhellenic campaign against Persia. He and other orators had been urging such a campaign for some years. They saw the conquest of Asia Minor as the solution to the economic, social, and political problems that had brought poverty and civil war to the Greek cities ever since the Peloponnesian War. Finally, there seem to have been some Athenians who were in the pay of Philip, for he used money lavishly to win support in all the cities.

The years between 346 B.C. and 340 B.C. were spent in diplomatic maneuvering, each side trying to win strategically useful allies. At last, Philip attacked Perinthus and Byzantium, the life line of Athenian commerce; in 340 B.C. he besieged both cities and declared war. The Athenian fleet saved both, and so in the following year Philip marched into Greece. Demosthenes performed wonders in rallying the Athenians and winning Thebes over to the Athenian side. In 338 B.C., however, Philip defeated the allied forces at Chaeronea in Boeotia. The decisive blow in this great battle was a cavalry charge led by the eighteen-year-old son of Philip, Alexander.

THE MACEDONIAN GOVERNMENT OF GREECE The Macedonian settlement of Greek affairs was not as harsh as many had feared, although in some cities the friends of Macedon came to power and killed or exiled their enemies. Demosthenes remained free to engage in politics. Athens was spared from attack on the condition that it give up what was left of its empire and follow the lead of Macedon. The rest of Greece was arranged in such a way as to remove all dangers to Philip's rule. To guarantee his security, Philip placed garrisons at Thebes, Chalcis, and Corinth.

In 338 B.C. Philip called a meeting of the Greek states to form the federal League of Corinth. The constitution of the league provided for autonomy, freedom from tribute and garrisons, and suppression of piracy and civil war. The league delegates would make foreign policy in theory without consulting their home governments or Philip. All this was a facade; not only was Philip of Macedon president of the league, he was its ruler. The defeat at Chaeronea ended Greek freedom and autonomy. Although it

This sculpture of Alexander the Great, king of Macedon and conqueror of the Persian Empire, was made in the second century B.C. and found at the ancient city of Magnesia in Asia Minor. Alexander's conquests spread Greek culture far from its homeland, laying the foundation of the Hellenistic world. [Erich Lessing/Art Resource, N.Y.]

maintained its form and way of life for some time, the *polis* had lost control of its own affairs and the special conditions that had made it unique.

Philip did not choose Corinth as the seat of his new confederacy simply from convenience or by accident. It was at Corinth that the Greeks

had gathered to resist a Persian invasion almost 150 years earlier. And it was there in 337 B.C. that Philip announced his intention to invade Persia in a war of liberation and revenge as leader of the new league. In the spring of 336 B.C., however, as he prepared to begin the campaign, Philip was assassinated.

In 1977 a mound was excavated at the Macedonian village of Vergina. The structures that were revealed and the extraordinarily rich finds associated with them have led many scholars to conclude that this is the royal tomb of Philip II, and the evidence seems persuasive that they are right. Philip certainly deserved so distinguished a resting place. He found Macedon a disunited kingdom of semibarbarians, despised and exploited by the Greeks. He left it a united kingdom, master and leader of the Greeks, rich, powerful, and ready to undertake the invasion of Asia.

Alexander the Great

Philip's first son, Alexander III (356–323 B.C.), later called Alexander the Great, succeeded his father at the age of twenty. Along with the throne, the young king inherited his father's daring plans for the conquest of Persia.

THE CONQUEST OF THE PERSIAN EMPIRE
The Persian Empire was vast and its resources enormous. The usurper Cyrus and his Greek mercenaries, however, had shown it to be vulnerable when they penetrated deep into its interior in the fourth century B.C. Its size and disparate nature made it hard to control and exploit. Its rulers faced constant troubles on its far-flung frontiers and constant intrigues within the royal palace. Throughout the fourth century B.C. they had called on Greek mercenaries to suppress uprisings. At the time of Philip II's death in 336 B.C., Persia was ruled by a new and inexperienced king, Darius III. Yet with a navy that dominated the sea, a huge army, and vast wealth, it remained a formidable opponent.

In 334 B.C. Alexander crossed the Hellespont into Asia. His army consisted of about 30,000 infantry and 5,000 cavalry; he had no navy and little money. These facts determined his early strategy—he must seek quick and decisive battles to gain money and supplies from the conquered territory. He must move along the coast to neutralize the Persian navy by depriving it of ports. Memnon, the commander of the Persian navy, recommended the perfect strategy against this plan: to retreat, to scorch the earth and deprive Alexander of supplies, to avoid battles, to use guerrilla tactics, and to stir up rebellion in Greece. He was ignored. The Persians preferred to stand and fight; their pride and courage were greater than their wisdom.

Alexander met the Persian forces of Asia Minor at the Granicus River, where he won a smashing victory in characteristic style (see Map 3-4). He led a cavalry charge across the river into the teeth of the enemy on the opposite bank. He almost lost his life in the process, but he won the devotion of his soldiers. That victory left the coast of Asia Minor open. Alexander captured the coastal cities, thus denying them to the Persian fleet.

In 333 B.C. Alexander marched inland to Syria, where he met the main Persian army under King Darius at Issus. Alexander himself led the cavalry charge that broke the Persian line and sent Darius fleeing into central Asia Minor. He continued along the coast and captured previously impregnable Tyre after a long and ingenious siege, putting an end to the threat of the Persian navy. He took Egypt with little trouble and was greeted as liberator, pharaoh, and son of Re (an Egyptian god whose Greek equivalent was Zeus). At Tyre, Darius sent Alexander a peace offer, yielding his entire empire west of the Euphrates River and his daughter in exchange for an alliance and an end to the invasion. But Alexander aimed at conquering the whole empire and probably whatever lay beyond.

In the spring of 331 B.C. Alexander marched into Mesopotamia. At Gaugamela, near the ancient Assyrian city of Nineveh, he met Darius, ready for a last stand. Once again Alexander's tactical genius and personal leadership carried the day. The Persians were broken, and Darius fled once more. Alexander entered Babylon, again hailed as liberator and king.

In January of 330 B.C. he came to Persepolis, the Persian capital, which held splendid palaces and the royal treasury. This bonanza ended his financial troubles and put a vast sum of money into circulation, with economic consequences that lasted for centuries. After a stay of several months, Alexander burned Persepolis to dramatize the destruction of the native Persian dynasty and the completion of Hellenic revenge for the earlier Persian invasion of Greece.

The new regime could not be secure while Darius lived, and so Alexander pursued him eastward. Just south of the Caspian Sea, he came upon the corpse of Darius, killed by his relative Bessus. The Persian nobles around Darius had lost faith in him and had joined in the plot. The murder removed Darius from Alexander's path, but now he had to catch Bessus, who proclaimed himself successor to Darius. The pursuit of Bessus (who was soon caught), combined with his own great curiosity and longing to go to the most distant places, took Alexander to the frontier of India.

Near Samarkand, in the land of the Scythians, he founded Alexandria Eschate ("Furthest Alexandria"), one of the many cities bearing his name that he founded as he traveled. As part of his grand scheme of amalgamation and conquest, he married the Bactrian princess Roxane and enrolled 30,000 young Bactrians into his army. These were to be trained and sent back to the center of the empire for use later.

In 327 B.C. Alexander took his army through the Khyber Pass in an attempt to conquer the lands around the Indus River (modern Pakistan). He reduced its king, Porus, to vassalage but pushed on in the hope of reaching the river called Ocean that the Greeks believed encircled the world. Finally, his weary men refused to go on. By the spring of 324 B.C. the army was back at the Persian Gulf and celebrated in the Macedonian style, with a wild spree of drinking.

THE DEATH OF ALEXANDER   Alexander was filled with plans for the future: for the consolidation and organization of his empire; for geographical exploration; for building new cities, roads, and harbors; perhaps even for further conquests in the West. There is even some evidence that he asked to be deified and worshiped as a god, although we cannot be sure if he really did so or why. In June of 323 B.C., however, he was overcome by a fever and died in Babylon at the age of thirty-three. His memory has never faded, and he soon became the subject of myth,

MAP 3-4 ALEXANDER'S CAMPAIGNS *The route taken by Alexander the Great in his conquest of the Persian Empire, 334–323 B.C. Starting from the Macedonian capital at Pella,
he reached the Indus Valley before being turned back by his own restive troops. He died of*

legend, and romance. From the beginning, estimates of him have varied. Some have seen in him a man of grand and noble vision who transcended the narrow limits of Greek and Macedonian ethnocentrism and sought to realize the solidarity of humankind in a great world state. Others have seen him as a calculating despot, given to drunken brawls, brutality, and murder.

The truth is probably in between. Alexander was one of the greatest generals the world has seen; he never lost a battle or failed in a siege, and with a modest army he conquered a vast empire. He had rare organizational talents, and his plan for creating a multinational empire was the only intelligent way to consolidate his conquests. He established many new cities—seventy, according to tradition—mostly along trade routes. These cities had the effect of encouraging commerce and prosperity as well as of introducing Hellenic civilization into new areas. It is hard to know if even Alexander could have held together the vast new empire he had created, but his death proved that only he would have had a chance to succeed.

The Successors

Nobody was prepared for Alexander's sudden death in 323 B.C., and affairs were further complicated by a weak succession: Roxane's unborn child and Alexander's weak-minded half-brother. His able and loyal Macedonian generals at first hoped to preserve the empire for the Macedonian royal house, and to this end they appointed themselves governors of the various provinces of the empire. The conflicting ambitions of these strong-willed men, however, led to prolonged warfare among various combinations of them. In these conflicts three of the original number were killed, and all of the direct members of the Macedonian royal house were either executed or murdered. With the murder of Roxane and her son in 310 B.C., there was no longer any focus for the enormous empire, and in 306 and 305 B.C. the surviving governors proclaimed themselves kings of their various holdings.

Three of these Macedonian generals founded dynasties of significance in the spread of Hellenistic culture:

- Ptolemy I, 367?–283 B.C.; founder of the thirty-first dynasty in Egypt, the Ptolemies, of whom Cleopatra, who died in 30 B.C., was the last
- Seleucus I, 358?–280 B.C.; founder of the Seleucid dynasty in Mesopotamia
- Antigonus I, 382–301 B.C.; founder of the Antigonid dynasty in Asia Minor and Macedon

For the first seventy-five years or so after the death of Alexander, the world ruled by his successors enjoyed considerable prosperity. The vast sums of money that he and they put into circulation greatly increased the level of economic activity. The opportunities for service and profit in the East attracted many Greeks and relieved their native cities of some of the pressure of the poor. The opening of vast new territories to Greek trade, the increased demand for Greek products, and the new availability of desired goods, as well as the conscious policies of the Hellenistic kings, all helped the growth of commerce.

The new prosperity, however, was not evenly distributed. The urban Greeks, the Macedonians, and the Hellenized natives who made up the upper and middle classes lived in comfort and even luxury, but the rural native peasants did not. Unlike the independent men who owned and worked the relatively small and

The Rise of Macedon	
359–336 B.C.	Reign of Philip II
338 B.C.	Battle of Chaeronea; Philip conquers Greece
338 B.C.	Founding of League of Corinth
336–323 B.C.	Reign of Alexander III, the Great
334 B.C.	Alexander invades Asia
333 B.C.	Battle of Issus
331 B.C.	Battle of Gaugamela
330 B.C.	Fall of Persepolis
327 B.C.	Alexander reaches Indus Valley
323 B.C.	Death of Alexander

Arrian Speculates on Alexander's Character and Ultimate Plans

By 324 B.C. Alexander had conquered the vast Persian Empire and reached as far as the Indus Valley before turning back to the Persian Gulf. Arrian, who lived in the second century A.D., half a millennium after Alexander, wrote the fullest and most reliable account of the great Macedonian conqueror based on the works of two of the officers on his staff. In the following passage Arrian tries to guess what Alexander might have done next had he not died in 323 B.C.

✦ *What other motives might Alexander have had for his expeditions, both those he accomplished and those he planned, besides curiosity and ambition? How do Alexander's achievements compare with those of previous soldiers and rulers? How do they seem from the vantage point of more than two millennia?*

When Alexander arrived at Pasargadae and Persepolis, he was seized with an ardent desire to sail down the Euphrates and Tigris to the Persian Sea, and to see the mouths of those rivers as he had already seen those of the Indus as well as the sea into which it flows. Some authors also have stated that he was meditating a voyage round the larger portion of Arabia, the country of the Ethiopians, Libya, and Numidia beyond Mount Atlas to Gadeira, inward into our sea; thinking that after he had subdued both Libya and Carchedon, then indeed he might with justice be called king of all Asia. For he said that the kings of the Persians and Medes called themselves Great Kings without any right, since they ruled a comparatively small part of Asia. Some say that he was meditating a voyage thence into the Euxine Sea, to Scythia and the Lake Maeotis; while others assert that he intended to go to Sicily and the Iapygian Cape, for the fame of the Romans spreading far and wide was now exciting his jealousy. For my own part I cannot conjecture with any certainty what were his plans; and I do not care to guess. But this I think I can confidently affirm, that he meditated nothing small or mean; and that he would never have remained satisfied with any of the acquisitions he had made, even if he had added Europe to Asia, or the islands of the Britons to Europe; but would still have gone on seeking for some unknown land beyond those mentioned. I verily believe that if he had found no one else to strive with, he would have striven with himself.

Arrian, The Anabasis of Alexander 7.1.1–4, *trans. by Edward J. Chinnock, in* The Greek Historians, *ed. by F. R. B. Godolphin (New York: Random House, 1942).*

equal lots of the *polis* in earlier times, Hellenistic farmers were reduced to subordinate, dependent, peasant status, working on large plantations of decreasing efficiency. During prosperous times these distinctions were bearable, although even then there was tension between the two groups. After a while, however, the costs of continuing wars, inflation, and a gradual lessening of the positive effects of the introduction of Persian wealth all led to economic crisis. The kings bore down heavily on the middle classes, who were skilled at avoiding their responsibilities, however. The pressure on the peasants and the city laborers became great, too, and they responded by slowing down their work and even by striking. In Greece economic pressures brought clashes between rich and poor, demands for the abolition of debt and the redistribution of land, and even, on occasion, civil war.

These internal divisions, along with international wars, weakened the capacity of the Hellenistic kingdoms to resist outside attack. By the middle of the second century B.C. they had all, except for Egypt, succumbed to an expanding Italian power, Rome. The two centuries between Alexander and the Roman conquest, however, were of great and lasting importance. They saw the entire eastern Mediterranean coast, Greece, Egypt, Mesopotamia, and the old Persian Empire formed into a single political, economic, and cultural unit.

Hellenistic Culture

The career of Alexander the Great marked a significant turning point in the thought of the Greeks as it was represented in literature, philosophy, religion, and art. His conquests and the establishment of the successor kingdoms put an end to the central role of the *polis* in Greek life and thought. Some scholars disagree about the end of the *polis*, denying that Philip's victory at Chaeronea put an end to its existence. They point to the continuance of *poleis* throughout the Hellenistic period and even see a continuation of them in the Roman *municipia*. These were, however, only a shadow of the vital reality that had been the true *polis.*

Deprived of control of their foreign affairs, and with their important internal arrangements determined by a foreign monarch, the postclassical cities lost the kind of political freedom that was basic to the old outlook. They were cities, perhaps—in a sense, even city-states—but not *poleis.* As time passed, they changed from sovereign states to municipal towns merged in military empires. Never again in antiquity would there be either a serious attack on or a defense of the *polis,* for its importance was gone. For the most part, the Greeks after Alexander turned away from political solutions for their problems. Instead they sought personal responses to their hopes and fears, particularly in religion, philosophy, and magic. The confident, sometimes arrogant, humanism of the fifth century B.C. gave

way to a kind of resignation to fate, a recognition of helplessness before forces too great for humans to manage.

Philosophy

These developments are noticeable in the changes that overtook the established schools of philosophy as well as in the emergence of two new and influential groups of philosophers, the Epicureans and the Stoics. Athens' position as the center of philosophical studies was reinforced, for the Academy and the Lyceum continued in operation, and the new schools were also located in Athens. The Lyceum turned gradually away from the universal investigations of its founder, Aristotle, even from his scientific interests, to become a center chiefly of literary and especially historical studies.

The Academy turned even further away from its tradition. It adopted the systematic Skepticism of Pyrrho of Elis. Under the leadership of Arcesilaus and Carneades, the Skeptics of the Academy became skilled at pointing out fallacies and weaknesses in the philosophies of the rival schools. They thought that nothing could be known and so consoled themselves and their followers by suggesting that nothing mattered. It was easy for them, therefore, to accept conventional morality and the world as it was. The Cynics, of course, continued to denounce convention and to advocate the crude life in accordance with nature, which some of them practiced publicly to the shock and outrage of respectable citizens. Neither Skepticism nor Cynicism had much appeal to the middle-class city dweller of the third century B.C., who sought some basis for choosing a way of life now that the *polis* no longer provided one ready-made.

THE EPICUREANS Epicurus of Athens (342–271 B.C.) formulated a new teaching, embodied in the school he founded in his native city in 306 B.C. His philosophy conformed to the mood of the times in that its goal was not knowledge but human happiness, which he believed could be achieved if one followed a style of life based on reason. He took sense perception to be the basis of all human knowledge. The reality and reliability of sense perception rested on the acceptance of the physical universe described by the atomists, Democritus and Leucippus. The Epicureans proclaimed that atoms were continually falling through the void and giving off images that were in direct contact with the senses. These falling atoms could swerve in an arbitrary, unpredictable way to produce the combinations seen in the world.

Epicurus thereby removed an element of determinism that existed in the Democritean system. When a person died, the atoms that composed the body dispersed so that the person had no further existence or perception and therefore nothing to fear after death. Epicurus believed that the gods existed but that they took no interest in human affairs. This belief amounted to a practical atheism, and Epicureans were often thought to be atheists.

The purpose of Epicurean physics was to liberate people from their fear of death, of the gods, and of all nonmaterial or supernatural powers. Epicurean ethics were hedonistic, that is, based on the acceptance of pleasure as true happiness. But pleasure for Epicurus was chiefly negative: the absence of pain and trouble. The goal of the Epicureans was *ataraxia*, the condition of being undisturbed, without trouble, pain, or responsibility. Ideally a man should have enough means to allow him to withdraw from the world and avoid business and public life. Epicurus even advised against marriage and children. He preached a life of genteel, restrained selfishness that might appeal to intellectual men of means, but was not calculated to be widely attractive.

THE STOICS Soon after Epicurus began teaching in his garden in Athens, Zeno of Citium in Cyprus (335–263 B.C.) established the Stoic school. It derived its name from the *stoa poikile*, or painted portico, in the Athenian agora, where Zeno and his disciples walked and talked beginning about 300 B.C. From then until about the middle of the second century B.C., Zeno and his successors preached a philosophy that owed a good deal to Socrates, by way of the Cynics. It was fed also by a stream of Eastern thought. Zeno, of course, came from Phoenician Cyprus; Chrysippus, one of his successors, came from Cilicia; and other early Stoics came from such places as Carthage, Tarsus, and Babylon.

Like the Epicureans, the Stoics sought the happiness of the individual. Quite unlike them,

the Stoics proposed a philosophy almost indistinguishable from religion. They believed that humans must live in harmony within themselves and in harmony with nature; for the Stoics god and nature were the same. The guiding principle in nature was divine reason (Logos), or fire. Every human had a spark of this divinity, and after death it returned to the eternal divine spirit. From time to time the world was destroyed by fire, from which a new world arose.

The aim of humans, and the definition of human happiness, was the virtuous life: a life lived in accordance with natural law, "when all actions promote the harmony of the spirit dwelling in the individual man with the will of him who orders the universe."[3] To live such a life required the knowledge possessed only by the wise, who knew what was good, what was evil, and what was neither, but "indifferent." According to the Stoics, good and evil were dispositions of the mind or soul: prudence, justice, courage, temperance, and so on were good, whereas folly, injustice, cowardice, and the like were evil. Life, health, pleasure, beauty, strength, wealth, and so on were neutral, morally indifferent, for they did not contribute either to happiness or to misery. Human misery came from an irrational mental contraction, from passion, which was a disease of the soul. The wise sought freedom from passion (*apatheia*), because passion arose from things that were morally indifferent.

Politically the Stoics fit well into the new world. They thought of it as a single *polis* in which all people were children of the same god. Although they did not forbid political activity, and many Stoics took part in political life, withdrawal was obviously preferable because the usual subjects of political argument were indifferent. Because the Stoics strove for inner harmony of the individual, their aim was a life lived in accordance with the divine will, their attitude fatalistic, and their goal a form of apathy. They fit in well with the reality of post-Alexandrian life. In fact, the spread of Stoicism made simpler the task of creating a new political system that relied not on the active participation of the governed, but merely on their docile submission.

[3]*Diogenes Laertius*, Life of Zeno, 88.

Literature

The literature of the Hellenistic period reflects the new intellectual currents, the new conditions of literary life, and the new institutions created in that period. The center of literary production in the third and second centuries B.C. was the new city of Alexandria in Egypt. There the Ptolemies, the monarchs of Egypt during that time, founded the museum—a great research institute where royal funds supported scientists and scholars—and the library, which contained almost half a million volumes, or papyrus scrolls.

The library contained much of the great body of past Greek literature, most of which has since been lost. The Alexandrian scholars saw to it that what they judged to be the best works were copied. They edited and criticized these works from the point of view of language, form, and content and wrote biographies of the authors. Their work is responsible for the preservation of most of what remains to us of ancient literature. Much of their work proved valuable, but some of it is dry, petty, quarrelsome, and simply foolish. At its best, however, it is full of learning and perception.

The scholarly atmosphere of Alexandria naturally gave rise to work in the field of history and its ancillary discipline, chronology. Eratosthenes (ca. 275–195 B.C.) established a chronology of important events dating from the Trojan War, and others undertook similar tasks. Contemporaries of Alexander, such as Ptolemy I, Aristobulus, and Nearchus, wrote what were apparently sober and essentially factual accounts of his career. Most of the work done by Hellenistic historians is known to us only in fragments cited by later writers. It seems in general to have emphasized sensational and biographical detail over the kind of rigorous impersonal analysis that marked the work of Thucydides.

Architecture and Sculpture

The advent of the Hellenistic monarchies greatly increased the opportunities open to architects and sculptors. Money was plentiful, rulers sought outlets for conspicuous display, new cities needed to be built and beautified, and the well-to-do created an increasing demand for objects of art. The new cities were usually laid out on the grid plan introduced in the fifth century B.C. by Hippodamus of Miletus. Temples were built on the classical model, and the covered portico, or *stoa*, became a very popular addition to the agoras of the Hellenistic towns.

Reflecting the cosmopolitan nature of the Hellenistic world, leading sculptors accepted commissions wherever they were attractive. The result was a certain uniformity of style, although Alexandria, Rhodes, and the kingdom of Pergamum in Asia Minor developed their own distinctive stylistic characteristics. For the most part Hellenistic sculpture moved away from the balanced tension and idealism of the fifth century B.C. toward the sentimental, emotional, and realistic mode of the fourth century B.C. These qualities are readily apparent in the marble statue called the *Laocoon*, carved at Rhodes in the second century B.C. and afterward taken to Rome.

Mathematics and Science

Among the most spectacular and remarkable intellectual developments of the Hellenistic age were those that came in mathematics and science. The burst of activity in these subjects drew from several sources. The stimulation and organization provided by the work of Plato and Aristotle should not be ignored. To these was added the impetus provided by Alexander's interest in science, evidenced by the scientists he took with him on his expedition and the aid he gave them in collecting data.

The expansion of Greek horizons geographically and the consequent contact with the knowledge of Egypt and Babylonia were also helpful. Finally, the patronage of the Ptolemies and the opportunity for many scientists to work with one another at the museum at Alexandria provided a unique opportunity for scientific work. It is not too much to say that the work done by the Alexandrians formed the greater part of the scientific knowledge available to the Western world until the scientific revolution of the sixteenth and seventeenth centuries A.D.

Euclid's *Elements* (written early in the third century B.C.) remained the textbook of plane and solid geometry until recent times.

This is a Roman copy of one of the masterpieces of Hellenistic sculpture, the Laocoon. *According to legend, Laocoon was a priest who warned the Trojans not to take the Greek's wooden horse within their city. This sculpture depicts his punishment. Great serpents sent by the goddess Athena, who was on the side of the Greeks, devoured Laocoon and his sons before the horrified people of Troy.* [Robert Miller]

Archimedes of Syracuse (ca. 287–212 B.C.) made further progress in geometry, established the theory of the lever in mechanics, and invented hydrostatics.

These advances in mathematics, once applied to the Babylonian astronomical tables available to the Hellenistic world, spurred great progress in the field of astronomy. As early as the fourth century Heraclides of Pontus (ca. 390–310 B.C.) had argued that Mercury and Venus circulate around the sun and not the Earth. He appears to have made other suggestions leading in the

Plutarch Cites Archimedes and Hellenistic Science

Archimedes (ca. 287–211 B.C.) was one of the great mathematicians and physicists of antiquity. He was a native of Syracuse in Sicily and a friend of its king. Plutarch discusses him in the following selection and reveals much about the ancient attitude toward applied science.

◆ *Was the attitude toward science and technology attributed to Archimedes by Plutarch common in the ancient world? How can that attitude be explained? If it was common, what were the consequences? Are distinctions between the importance of pure science and applied science made in the modern world? If so, are they the same as the ancient ones? How do you explain any similarities or differences?*

Archimedes, however, in writing to King Hiero, whose friend and near relation he was, had stated that given the force, any given weight might be moved, and even boasted, we are told, relying on the strength of demonstration, that if there were another earth, by going into it he could remove this. Hiero being struck with amazement at this, and entreating him to make good this problem by actual experiment, and show some great weight moved by a small engine, he fixed accordingly upon a ship of burden out of the king's arsenal, which could not be drawn out of the dock without great labour and many men; and, loading her with many passengers and a full freight, sitting himself the while far off, with no great endeavor, but only holding the head of the pulley in his hand and drawing the cords by degrees. . . . Yet Archimedes possessed so high a spirit, so profound a soul, and such treasures of scientific knowledge, that though these inventions had now obtained him the renown of more than human sagacity, he yet would not deign to leave behind him any commentary or writing on such subjects; but, repudiating as sordid and ignoble the whole trade of engineering, and every sort of art that lends itself to mere use and profit, he placed his whole affection and ambition in those purer speculations where there can be no reference to the vulgar needs of life.

Plutarch, "Marcellus," in Lives of the Noble Grecians and Romans, *trans. by John Dryden, rev. by A. H. Clough (New York: Random House, n.d.), pp. 376–378.*

direction of a heliocentric theory of the universe. Most scholars, however, give credit for that theory to Aristarchus of Samos (ca. 310–230 B.C.), who asserted that the sun, along with the other fixed stars, did not move and that the Earth revolved around the sun in a circular orbit and rotated on its axis while doing so. The heliocentric theory ran contrary not only to the traditional view codified by Aristotle but to what seemed to be common sense.

Hellenistic technology was not up to proving the theory, and, of course, the planetary orbits are not circular. The heliocentric theory did not, therefore, take hold. Hipparchus of Nicea (b. ca. 190 B.C.) constructed a model of the universe on the geocentric theory; his ingenious and complicated model did a very good job of accounting for the movements of the sun, the moon, and the planets. Ptolemy of Alexandria (second century A.D.) adopted Hipparchus's system with a few improvements. It remained dominant until the work of Copernicus, in the sixteenth century A.D.

Hellenistic scientists made progress in mapping the earth as well as the sky. Eratosthenes of Cyrene (ca. 275–195 B.C.) was able to calculate the circumference of the earth within about 200 miles. He wrote a treatise on geography based

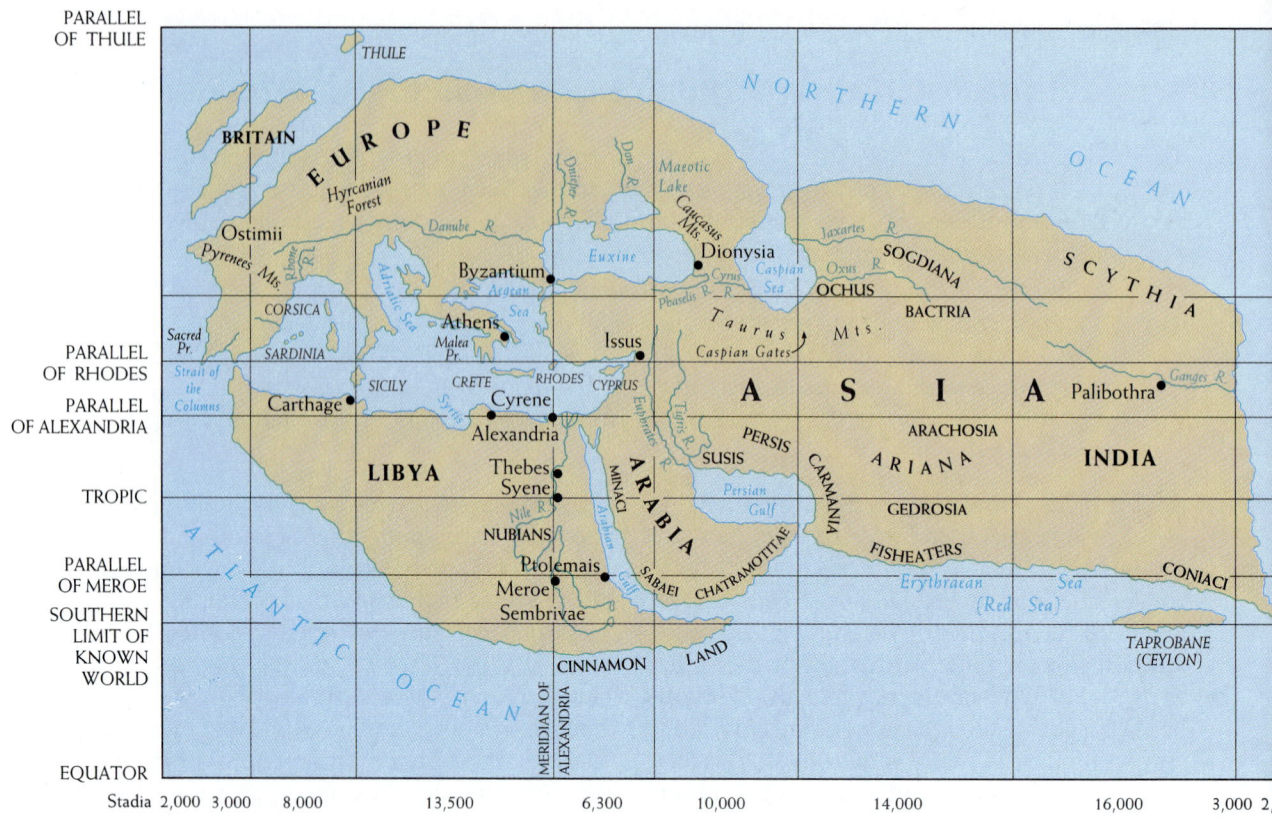

MAP 3-5 THE WORLD ACCORDING TO ERATOSTHENES *Eratosthenes of Alexandria (ca. 275–195 B.C.) was a Hellenistic geographer. His map, reconstructed here, was remarkably accurate for its time. The world was divided by lines of "latitude" and "longitude," thus anticipating our global divisions.*

on mathematical and physical reasoning and the reports of travelers. In spite of the new data that were available to later geographers, Eratosthenes' map (see Map 3-5) was in many ways more accurate than the one constructed by Ptolemy of Alexandria that became standard in the Middle Ages.

The Hellenistic Age contributed little to the life sciences, such as biology, zoology, and medicine. Even the sciences that had such impressive achievements to show in the third century B.C. made little progress thereafter. In fact, to some extent, there was a retreat from science. Astrology and magic became subjects of great interest as scientific advance lagged.

---◆---

The Classical Age of Greece was a period of unparalleled achievement. While the rest of the *world continued to be characterized by monarchical, hierarchical, command societies, in Athens democracy was carried as far as it would go before modern times. Although limited to adult males of native parentage, Athenian citizenship granted full and active participation in every decision of the state without regard to wealth or class. Democracy disappeared late in the fourth century B.C. with the end of Greek autonomy. When it returned in the modern world more than two millennia later, it was broader but shallower. Democratic citizenship did not again imply the active direct participation of every citizen in the government of the state.*

It was in this democratic imperial Athens that the greatest artistic, literary, and philosophical achievements of Classical Greece took place. Analytical, secular history, tragedy and comedy, the philosophical dialogue, an organized system of logic, and the logical philosophical treatise were among the achievements of the Classical Age. The tradition of rational, secular speculation in natural philosophy and science was carried forward, but more attention was devoted to human questions in medicine and ethical and political philosophy. A naturalistic style of art evolved that showed human beings first as they ideally might look, and then as they really looked, an approach that dominated Greek and Roman art until the late stages of the Roman Empire. This naturalistic style had a powerful effect on the Italian Renaissance and, through it, the modern world.

These Hellenic developments, it should be clear, diverge sharply from the experience of previous cultures and of contemporary ones in the rest of the world. To a great degree they sprang from the unique political experience of the Greeks, based on the independent city-states. That unique experience and the Classical period ended with the Macedonian conquest, which ultimately made the Greeks subject to or part of some great national state or empire. The Macedonian conquest introduced the Hellenistic Age.

The Hellenistic Age speaks to us less fully and vividly than that of Classical Greece, chiefly because it had no historian to compare with Herodotus and Thucydides. We lack the clear picture that a continuous, rich, lively, and meaningful narrative provides. This deficiency should not obscure the great importance of the achievements of the age. The literature, art, scholarship, and science of the period deserve attention in their own right.

The Hellenistic Age did perform a vital civilizing function. It spread Greek culture over a remarkably wide area and made a significant and lasting impression on much of it. Greek culture also adjusted to its new surroundings to a degree, unifying and simplifying its cultural cargo to make it more accessible to outsiders. The various Greek dialects gave way to a version of the Attic tongue, the *koine*, or common language.

In the same way, the scholarship of Alexandria established canons of literary excellence and the scholarly tools with which to make the great treasures of Greek culture understandable to later generations. The syn-cretism of thought and belief introduced in this period also made understanding and accord more likely among peoples who were very different. When the Romans came into contact with Hellenism, they were powerfully impressed by it. When they conquered the Hellenistic world, they became, as Horace said, captives of its culture.

Review Questions

1. How was the Delian League transformed into the Athenian empire during the fifth century B.C.? Did the empire offer any advantages to its subjects? Why was there such resistance to Athenian efforts to unify the Greek world in the fifth and fourth centuries B.C.?

2. Why did Athens and Sparta come to blows in the Great Peloponnesian War? What was each side's strategy for victory? Why did Sparta win the war?

3. Give examples from art, literature, and philosophy of the tension that characterized Greek life and thought in the Classical Period. How does Hellenistic art differ from that of the Classical Period?

4. Between 431 and 362 B.C., Athens, Sparta, and Thebes each tried to impose hegemony over the city-states of Greece, but none succeeded except for short periods of time. Why did each state fail? What does your analysis tell you about the components of successful rule?

5. How and why did Philip II conquer Greece between 359 and 338 B.C.? How was he able to turn Macedon into a formidable military and political power? Why was Athens unable to defend itself against Macedon? Where does more of the credit for Philip's success lie: in Macedon's strength, or in the weakness of the Greek city-states?

6. What were the major consequences of Alexander's death? Assess the achievement of Alexander. Was he a conscious promoter of Greek civilization, or just an egomaniac drunk with the lust of conquest?

Suggested Readings

M. Austin and P. Vidal-Naquet, *The Economic and Social History of Classical Greece* (1977). A collection of documents with commentary.

H. I. Bell, *Egypt from Alexander the Great to the Arab Conquest* (1948). A history of Hellenistic Egypt.

J. Buckler, *The Theban Hegemony, 371–362 B.C.* (1980). A study of Thebes at the height of its power.

W. Burkert, *Greek Religion* (1985). A fine general study.

P. Cartledge, *Agesilaus and the Crisis of Sparta* (1987). More than a biography of the Spartan king, it is a thorough study of Spartan society.

G. Cawkwell, *Philip of Macedon* (1978). A brief but learned account of Philip's career.

W. R. Connor, *The New Politicians of Fifth-Century Athens* (1971). A study on changes in political style and their significance for Athenian society.

J. M. Cook, *The Persian Empire* (1983). A solid history that makes good use of archaeological evidence.

J. K. Davies, *Democracy and Classical Greece* (1978). Emphasizes archaeological evidence and social history.

V. Ehrenberg, *The People of Aristophanes* (1962). A study of Athenian society as revealed by the comedies of Aristophanes.

J. R. Ellis, *Philip II and Macedonian Imperialism* (1976). A study of the career of the founder of Macedonian power.

J. Ferguson, *The Heritage of Hellenism* (1973). A good survey.

J. R. L. Fox, *Alexander the Great* (1973). An imaginative account that does more justice to the Persian side of the problem than is usual.

Y. Garlan, *Slavery in Ancient Greece* (1988). An up to date survey.

P. Green, *Alexander the Great* (1972). A lively biography.

P. Green, *From Alexander to Actium* (1990). A brilliant new synthesis of the Hellenistic period.

C. D. Hamilton, *Agesilaus and the Failure of Spartan Hegemony* (1991). An excellent biography of the king who was the central figure in Sparta during its domination in the fourth century B.C.

N. G. L. Hammond and G. T. Griffith, *A History of Macedonia, Vol. 2, 550–336 B.C.* (1979). A thorough account of Macedonian history that focuses on the careers of Philip and Alexander.

R. Just, *Women in Athenian Law and Life* (1988). A good study of the place of women in Athenian life.

D. Kagan, *The Archidamian War* (1974). A history of the first ten years of the Peloponnesian War.

D. Kagan, *The Fall of the Athenian Empire* (1987). The last period of the Peloponnesian War.

D. Kagan, *The Outbreak of the Peloponnesian War* (1969). A study of the period from the foundation of the Delian League to the coming of the Peloponnesian War that argues that war could have been avoided.

D. Kagan, *The Peace of Nicias and the Sicilian Expedition* (1981). A history of the middle period of the Peloponnesian War.

G. B. Kerferd, *The Sophistic Movement* (1981). A fine study of these worldly thinkers of the Classical period.

H. D. F. Kitto, *Greek Tragedy* (1966). A good introduction.

B. M. W. Knox, *The Heroic Temper: Studies in Sophoclean Tragedy* (1964). A brilliant analysis of tragic heroism.

J. A. O. Larsen, *Greek Federal States* (1968). Emphasis on the federal movements of the Hellenistic era.

J. Lear, *Aristotle: The Desire to Understand* (1988). A brilliant yet comprehensible introduction to the work of the philosopher.

D. M. Lewis, *Sparta and Persia* (1977). A valuable discussion of relations between Sparta and Persia in the fifth and fourth centuries B.C.

G. E. R. Lloyd, *Greek Science After Aristotle* (1974).

A. A. Long, *Hellenistic Philosophy: Stoics, Epicureans, Skeptics* (1974). A solid study.

R. Meiggs, *The Athenian Empire* (1972). A fine study of the rise and fall of the empire, making excellent use of inscriptions.

J. J. Pollitt, *Art and Experience in Classical Greece* (1972). A scholarly and entertaining study of the relationship between art and history in classical Greece, with excellent illustrations.

J. J. Pollitt, *Art in the Hellenistic Age* (1986). An extraordinary analysis that places the art in its historical and intellectual context.

M. I. Rostovtzeff, *Social and Economic History of the Hellenistic World*, 3 vols. (1941). A masterpiece of synthesis by a great historian.

B. S. Strauss, *Athens After the Peloponnesian War* (1987). An excellent discussion of Athens' recovery and of the nature of Athenian society and politics in the fourth century B.C.

W. W. Tarn, *Alexander the Great*, 2 vols. (1948). The first volume is a narrative account, the second a series of detailed studies.

W. W. Tarn and G. T. Griffith, *Hellenistic Civilization* (1961). A survey of Hellenistic history and culture.

V. Tcherikover, *Hellenistic Civilization and the Jews* (1970). A fine study of the impact of Hellenism on the Jews.

G. Vlastos, *The Philosophy of Socrates* (1971). A splendid collection of essays illuminating the problems presented by this remarkable man.

G. Vlastos, *Platonic Studies,* 2nd ed. (1981). A similar collection on the philosophy of Plato.

F. W. Walbank, *The Hellenistic World* (1981). A solid history.

A. E. Zimmern, *The Greek Commonwealth* (1961). A study of political, social, and economic conditions in fifth-century Athens.

This wall painting was found in a bedroom in a first century B.C. villa in Pompeii. It depicts a grand and fantastic imaginary villa. [The Metropolitan Museum of Art, Rogers Fund, 1903 (03.14.13)]

4

Rome: From Republic to Empire

Key Topics in This Chapter
- The emergence of the Roman Republic
- The development of the republican constitution
- Roman expansion and imperialism
- The character of Roman society in the republican era
- The fall of the republic

The achievement of the Romans was one of the most remarkable in human history. The descendants of the inhabitants of a small village in central Italy, they came eventually to rule the entire Italian peninsula, then the entire Mediterranean coastline. They conquered most of the Near East and finally much of continental Europe. They ruled this vast empire under a single government that provided considerable peace and prosperity for centuries. Never before the Romans nor since has that area been united, and rarely, if ever, has it enjoyed a stable peace. But Rome's legacy was not merely military excellence and political organization. The Romans adopted and transformed the intellectual and cultural achievements of the Greeks and combined them with their own outlook and historical experience. The resulting Graeco-Roman tradition in literature, philosophy, and art provided the core of learning for the Middle Ages and pointed the way to the new paths taken in the Renaissance. It remains at the heart of Western civilization to this day.

Prehistoric Italy

The culture of Italy developed late. Paleolithic settlements gave way to the Neolithic mode of life only about 2500 B.C. The Bronze Age came about 1500 B.C. About 1000 B.C. bands of new arrivals, warlike peoples speaking a set of closely related languages we call *Italic*, began to infiltrate Italy from across the Adriatic Sea and around its northern end. These invaders cremated their dead and put the ashes in tombs stocked with weapons and armor. Their bronzework was of a higher quality than that of the people they displaced, and they were soon making weapons, armor, and tools of iron. By 800 B.C. they had occupied the highland pastures of the Apennines and within a short time they began to challenge the earlier settlers for control of the tempting western plains. It would be the descendants of these tough mountain people—Umbrians, Sabines, Samnites, and Latins—together with others soon to arrive—Etruscans, Greeks, and Celts—who would shape the future of Italy.

The Etruscans

The Etruscans exerted the most powerful external influence on the Romans. Their civilization arose in Etruria (now Tuscany), west of the Apennines between the Arno and Tiber rivers, about 800 B.C. (see Map 4-1). Their origin is far from clear, but their tomb architecture, resembling that of Asia Minor, and their practice of divining the future by inspecting the livers of sacrificial animals point to an eastern origin.

MAP 4-1 ANCIENT ITALY *This map of ancient Italy and its neighbors before the expansion of Rome shows major cities and towns as well as several geographical regions and the locations of some of the Italic and non-Italic peoples.*

Government

The Etruscans brought civilization with them. Their settlements were self-governing, fortified city-states, of which twelve formed a loose religious confederation. At first, kings ruled these cities, but they were replaced by an aristocracy of the agrarian nobles. The latter ruled by means of a council and elected annual magistrates. The Etruscans were a military ruling class that dominated and exploited the native Italians (the predecessors of the later Italic speakers), who worked their land and mines and served as infantry in their armies. This aristocracy accumulated considerable wealth through

Much of what we know of the Etruscans comes from their funerary art. This sculpture of an Etruscan couple is part of a sarcophagus. [Erich Lessing/Art Resource, N.Y.]

agriculture, industry, piracy, and a growing commerce with the Carthaginians and the Greeks.

Religion

The Etruscans' influence on the Romans was greatest in religion. They imagined a world filled with gods and spirits, many of them evil. To deal with such demons, the Etruscans evolved complicated rituals and powerful priesthoods. Divination by sacrifice and omens in nature helped discover the divine will, and careful attention to precise rituals directed by priests helped please the gods. After a while the Etruscans, influenced by the Greeks, worshiped gods in the shape of humans and built temples for them.

Dominion

The Etruscan aristocracy remained aggressive and skillful in the use of horses and war chariots. In the seventh and sixth centuries B.C. they expanded their power in Italy and across the sea to Corsica and Elba. They conquered Latium (a region that included the small town of Rome) and Campania, where they became neighbors of the Greeks of Naples. In the north they got as far as the Po Valley. These conquests were carried out by small bands led by Etruscan chieftains who did not work in concert and would not necessarily aid one another in distress. As a result, the conquests outside Etruria were not firmly based and did not last long.

Etruscan power reached its height some time before 500 B.C. and then rapidly declined. About 400 B.C. Celtic peoples from the area the Romans called Gaul (modern France) broke into the Po Valley and drove out the Etruscans. They settled this land so firmly that the Romans thereafter called it Cisalpine Gaul (Gaul on this side of the Alps). Eventually, even the Etruscan heartland in Etruria lost its independence and was incorporated into Roman Italy. The Etruscan language was forgotten and Etruscan culture gradually became only a memory, but its influence on the Romans remained.

Royal Rome

Rome was an unimportant town in Latium until its conquest by the Etruscans, but its location—fifteen miles from the mouth of the Tiber River at the point at which the hills made further navigation impossible—gave it several advantages over its Latin neighbors. The island in the Tiber southwest of the Capitoline Hill made the river fordable, and so Rome was naturally a center for communication and trade, both east–west and north–south.

Government

In the sixth century B.C. Rome came under Etruscan control. Led by Etruscan kings, the Roman army, equipped and organized like the Greek phalanx, gained control of most of Latium. An effective political and social order that gave extraordinary power to the ruling figures in both public and private life made this success possible. To their kings the Romans gave the awesome power of *imperium*, the right to issue commands and to enforce them by fines, arrests, and corporal, or even capital, punishment. Although it tended apparently to remain in the same family, kingship was elective. The Roman Senate had to approve the candidate for the office, and a vote of the people in assembly formally granted the *imperium*. A basic characteristic of later Roman government—the granting of great power to executive officers contingent on the approval of the Senate and ultimately the people—was already apparent in this structure.

In theory and law the king was the commander of the army, the chief priest, and the supreme judge. He could make decisions in foreign affairs, call out the army, lead it in battle, and impose discipline on his troops, all by virtue of his *imperium*. In practice the royal power was much more limited.

The Senate was the second branch of the early Roman government. According to tradition, it originated when Romulus, Rome's legendary first king, chose 100 of Rome's leading men to advise him. The number of senators ultimately rose to 300, where it stayed through most of the history of the republic. Ostensibly the Senate had neither executive nor legislative power; it met only when summoned by the king and then only to advise him. In reality its authority was great, for the senators, like the king, served for life. The Senate, therefore, had continuity and experience, and it was composed of the most powerful men in the state. It could not lightly be ignored.

The third branch of government, the curiate assembly, was made up of all citizens as divided into thirty groups. (In early Rome citizenship required descent from Roman parents on both sides.) The assembly met only when summoned by the king; he determined the agenda, made proposals, and recognized other speakers, if any.

Usually, the assembly was called to listen and approve. Voting was not by head but by group; a majority within each group determined its vote, and the decisions were made by majority vote of the groups. Group voting would be typical of all future forms of Roman assembly.

The Family

The center of Roman life was the family. At its head stood the father, whose power and authority within the family resembled those of the king within the state. Over his children he held broad powers analogous to *imperium* in the state; he had the right to sell his children into slavery, and he even had the power of life and death over them. Over his wife he had less power; he could not sell or kill her. In practice his power to dispose of his children was limited by consultation with the family, by public opinion, and, most of all, by tradition. A wife could not be divorced except for stated serious offenses, and even then she had to be convicted by a court made up of her male blood relatives. The Roman woman had a respected position and the main responsibility for managing the household. The father was the chief priest of the family. He led it in daily prayers to the dead that reflected the ancestor worship central to the Roman family and state.

Clientage

Clientage was one of Rome's most important institutions. The client was "an inferior entrusted, by custom or by himself, to the protection of a stranger more powerful than he, and rendering certain services and observances in return for this protection."[1] The Romans spoke of a client as being in the *fides*, or trust, of his patron, and so the relationship always had moral implications. The patron provided his client with protection, both physical and legal. He gave him economic assistance in the form of a land grant, the opportunity to work as a tenant farmer or a laborer on the patron's land, or simply handouts. In return the client would fight for his patron, work his land, and support him politically. These mutual obligations were enforced by public opinion and tradition. When early custom was codified in the

[1]*E. Badian,* Foreign Clientelae (264–70 B.C.) *(Oxford, 1958), p. 1*

Busts of a Roman couple from the period of the Republic. Although some people have identified the individuals as Cato the Younger and his daughter Porcia, no solid evidence confirms this claim. [Scala/Art Resource, N.Y.]

mid-fifth century B.C., one of the twelve tablets of laws announced: "Let the patron who has defrauded his client be accursed."

In the early history of Rome, patrons were rich and powerful whereas clients were poor and weak, but as time passed it was not uncommon for rich and powerful members of the upper classes to become clients of even more powerful men, chiefly for political purposes. Because the client–patron relationship was hereditary and was sanctioned by religion and custom, it was to play a very important part in the life of the Roman Republic.

Patricians and Plebeians

In the royal period, Roman society was divided in two by a class distinction based on birth. The wealthy patrician upper class held a monopoly of power and influence. Its members alone could conduct state religious ceremonies, sit in the Senate, or hold office. They formed a closed caste by forbidding marriage outside their own group.

The plebeian lower class must have consisted originally of poor, dependent small farmers, laborers, and artisans, the clients of the nobility. As Rome and its population grew in various ways, families that were rich but outside the charmed circle of patricians grew wealthy. From very early times, therefore, there were rich plebeians, and incompetence and bad luck must have produced some poor patricians. The line between the classes and the monopoly of privileges remained firm, nevertheless, and the struggle of the plebeians to gain equality occupied more than two centuries of republican history.

The Republic

Roman tradition tells us that the outrageous behavior of the last kings led the noble families to revolt in 509 B.C., bringing the monarchy to a sudden close and leading to the creation of the republic.

Its Constitution

THE CONSULS The Roman constitution was an unwritten accumulation of laws and customs. The Romans were a conservative people, and so they were never willing to deprive their chief magistrates of the great powers exercised by the monarchs. They elected two patricians to the office of consul and endowed them with *imperium.* They were assisted by two financial

Lictors, pictured here, attended the chief Roman magistrates when they appeared in public. The axe carried by one of the lictors and the bound bundle of staffs carried by the others symbolize both the power of Roman magistrates to inflict corporal punishment on Roman citizens and the limits on that power. The bound staffs symbolize the right of citizens within the city of Rome not to be punished without a trial. The axe symbolizes the power of the magistrates, as commanders of the army, to put anyone to death without a trial outside the city walls. [Alinari/Art Resource, N.Y.]

officials called *quaestors,* whose number ultimately reached eight. Like the kings, the consuls led the army, had religious duties, and served as judges. They retained the visible symbols of royalty—the purple robe, the ivory chair, and the *lictors* (minor officials) who accompanied them bearing rods and axe. The power of the consuls, however, was limited legally and institutionally as well as by custom.

The power of the consulship was granted not for life but only for a year. Each consul could prevent any action by his colleague by simply saying no to his proposal, and the religious powers of the consuls were shared with others. Even the *imperium* was limited. Although the consuls had full powers of life and death while leading an army, within the sacred boundary of the city of Rome the citizens had the right to appeal to the popular assembly all cases involving capital punishment. Besides, after their one year in office, the consuls would spend the rest of their lives as members of the Senate. It was a most reckless consul who failed to ask the advice of the Senate or who failed to follow it when there was general agreement.

The many checks on consular action tended to prevent initiative, swift action, and change, but this was just what a conservative, traditional, aristocratic republic wanted. Only in the military sphere did divided counsel and a short term of office create important problems. The Romans tried to get around the difficulties by sending only one consul into the field or, when this was impossible, allowing the consuls sole command on alternate days. In really serious crises, the consuls, with the advice of the Senate, could appoint a single man, the *dictator,* to the command and could retire in his favor. The *dictator's* term of office was limited to six months, but his own *imperium* was valid both inside and outside the city without appeal.

These devices worked well enough in the early years of the republic, when Rome's battles were near home. Longer wars and more sophisticated opponents, however, revealed the system's weaknesses and required significant changes. Long campaigns prompted the invention of the proconsulship in 325 B.C., whereby the term of a consul serving in the field was extended. This innovation contained the seeds of many troubles for the constitution.

The introduction of the office of *praetor* also helped provide commanders for Rome's many campaigns. The basic function of the praetors was judicial, but they also had *imperium* and served as generals. By the end of the republic, there were eight praetors, whose annual terms, like the consuls', could be extended for military commands when necessary.

The job of identifying citizens and classifying them according to age and property was at first the responsibility of the consuls. After the middle of the fifth century B.C., it was delegated to a new office, that of *censor.* The Senate elected two censors every five years. They conducted a census and drew up the citizen rolls. Their task was not just clerical; the classification fixed taxation and status, and so the censors had to be men of reputation, former consuls. They soon acquired additional powers. By the fourth century

B.C. they compiled the roll of senators and could strike senators from that roll not only for financial but for moral reasons also. As the prestige of the office grew, it came to be considered the ultimate prize of a Roman political career.

THE SENATE AND THE ASSEMBLY

With the end of the monarchy, the Senate became the single continuous deliberative body in the Roman state, greatly increasing its influence and power. Its members were prominent patricians, often leaders of clans and patrons of many clients. The Senate soon gained control of the state's finances and of foreign policy. Its formal advice was not lightly ignored either by magistrates or by popular assemblies.

The most important assembly in the early republic was the centuriate assembly. In a sense, it was the Roman army acting in a political capacity. Its basic unit was the century, theoretically 100 fighting men classified according to their weapons, armor, and equipment. Because each man equipped himself, this meant that the organization was by classes according to wealth.

Voting was by century and proceeded in order of classification from the cavalry down. The assembly elected the consuls and several other magistrates, voted on bills put before it, made decisions of war and peace, and also served as the court of appeal against decisions of the magistrates affecting the life or property of a citizen. In theory it had final authority, but the Senate exercised great, if informal, influence.

THE STRUGGLE OF THE ORDERS

The laws and constitution of the early republic gave to the patricians almost a monopoly of power and privilege. Plebeians were barred from public office, from priesthoods, and from other public religious offices. They could not serve as judges and could not even know the law, for there was no published legal code. The only law was traditional practice, and that existed only in the minds and actions of patrician magistrates. Plebeians were subject to the *imperium* but could not exercise its power. They were not allowed to marry patricians. When Rome gained new land by conquest, patrician magistrates distributed it in a way that favored patricians. The patricians dominated the assemblies and the Senate. The plebeians undertook a campaign to achieve political, legal, and social equality, and

this attempt, which succeeded after two centuries of intermittent effort, is called the *struggle of the orders*.

The most important source of plebeian success was the need for their military service. According to tradition, the plebeians, angered by patrician resistance to their demands, withdrew from the city and camped on the Sacred Mount. There they formed a plebeian tribal assembly and elected plebeian tribunes to protect them from the arbitrary power of the magistrates. They declared the tribune inviolate and sacrosanct; anyone laying violent hands on him was accursed and liable to death without trial. By extension of his right to protect the plebeians, the tribune gained the power to veto any action of a magistrate or any bill in a Roman assembly or the Senate. The plebeian assembly voted by tribe, and a vote of the assembly was binding on plebeians. They tried to make their decisions binding on all Romans but could not do so until 287 B.C.

The next step was for the plebeians to obtain access to the laws, which they accomplished by 450 B.C. when early Roman custom in all its harshness and simplicity was codified in the Twelve Tables. In 445 B.C. plebeians gained the right to marry patricians. The main prize, the consulship, the patricians did not yield easily. Not until 367 B.C. did legislation—the Licinian-Sextian Laws—provide that at least one consul could be a plebeian. Before long plebeians held other offices, even the dictatorship and the censorship. In 300 B.C. they were admitted to the most important priesthoods, the last religious barrier to equality. In 287 B.C. the plebeians completed their triumph. They once again withdrew from the city and secured the passage of a law whereby decisions of the plebeian assembly bound all Romans and did not require the approval of the Senate.

It might seem that the Roman aristocracy had given way under the pressure of the lower class. Yet the victory of the plebeians did not bring democracy. An aristocracy based strictly on birth had given way to an aristocracy more subtle, but no less restricted, based on a combination of wealth and birth. A relatively small group of rich and powerful families, both patrician and plebeian, known as *nobiles*, attained the highest offices in the state. The significant distinction was no longer between patrician and plebeian but between the *nobiles* and everyone else.

The absence of the secret ballot in the assemblies enabled the *nobiles* to control most decisions and elections by a combination of intimidation and bribery. The leading families were in constant competition with one another for office, power, and prestige, but they often combined in marriage and less formal alliances to keep the political plums within their own group. In the century from 233 to 133 B.C., for instance, twenty-six families provided 80 percent of the consuls and only ten families accounted for almost 50 percent. These same families dominated the Senate, whose power became ever greater. Rome's success brought the Senate prestige, increased control of policy, and confidence in its capacity to rule. The end of the struggle of the orders brought domestic peace under a republican constitution dominated by a capable, if narrow, senatorial aristocracy. This outcome satisfied most Romans outside the ruling group because Rome conquered Italy and brought many benefits to its citizens.

The Conquest of Italy

Not long after the fall of the monarchy in 509 B.C., a coalition of Romans, Latins, and Italian Greeks defeated the Etruscans and drove them out of Latium for good. Throughout the fifth century B.C., the powerful Etruscan city of Veii, only twelve miles north of the Tiber River, raided Roman territory. After a hard struggle and a long siege, the Romans took it in 392 B.C., more than doubling the size of Rome.

The Rise of the Plebeians to Equality in Rome	
509 B.C.	Kings expelled; republic founded
450–449 B.C.	Laws of the Twelve Tables published
445 B.C.	Plebeians gain right of marriage with patricians
367 B.C.	Licinian–Sextian Laws open consulship to plebeians
300 B.C.	Plebeians attain chief priesthoods
287 B.C.	Laws passed by Plebeian Assembly made binding on all Romans

Roman policy toward defeated enemies used both the carrot and the stick. When they made friendly alliances with some, they gained new soldiers for their army. When they treated others more harshly by annexing their land, they achieved a similar end. Service in the Roman army was based on property, and the distribution to poor Romans of conquered land made soldiers of previously useless men. It also gave the poor a stake in Rome and reduced the pressure against its aristocratic regime. The long siege of Veii kept soldiers from their farms during the campaign. From that time on the Romans paid their soldiers, thus giving their army greater flexibility and a more professional quality.

GALLIC INVASION OF ITALY AND ROMAN REACTION   At the beginning of the fourth century B.C. a disaster struck. In 387 B.C. the Gauls, barbaric Celtic tribes from across the Alps, defeated the Roman army and captured, looted, and burned Rome. The Gauls sought plunder, not conquest, so they extorted a ransom from the Romans and returned to their homes in the north. Rome's power appeared to be wiped out.

By about 350 B.C., however, the Romans were more dominant than ever. Their success in turning back new Gallic raids added still more to their power and prestige. As the Romans tightened their grip on Latium, the Latins became resentful. In 340 B.C. they demanded independence from Rome or full equality and launched a war of independence that lasted until 338 B.C. The victorious Romans dissolved the Latin League, and their treatment of the defeated opponents provided a model for the settlement of Italy.

ROMAN POLICY TOWARD THE CONQUERED   The Romans did not destroy any of the Latin cities or their people, nor did they treat them all alike. Some near Rome received full Roman citizenship. Others farther away gained municipal status, which gave them the private rights of intermarriage and commerce with Romans but not the public rights of voting and holding office in Rome. They retained the rights of local self-government and could obtain full Roman citizenship if they moved to Rome. They followed Rome in foreign policy and provided soldiers to serve in the Roman legions.

The relief sculpture on this sarcophagus, which dates from about 225 B.C., shows a battle between Romans and Gauls. [Scala/Art Resource, N.Y.]

Still other states became allies of Rome on the basis of treaties, which differed from city to city. Some were given the private rights of intermarriage and commerce with Romans and some were not; the allied states were always forbidden to exercise these rights with one another. Some, but not all, were allowed local autonomy. Land was taken from some but not from others, nor was the percentage taken always the same. All the allies supplied troops to the army, in which they fought in auxiliary battalions under Roman officers, but they did not pay taxes to Rome.

On some of the conquered land the Romans placed colonies, permanent settlements of veteran soldiers in the territory of recently defeated enemies. The colonists retained their Roman citizenship and enjoyed home rule; in return for the land they had been given, they served as a kind of permanent garrison to deter or suppress rebellion. These colonies were usually connected to Rome by a network of military roads built as straight as possible and so durable that some are used even today. The roads guaranteed that a Roman army could swiftly reinforce an embattled colony or put down an uprising in any weather.

The Roman settlement of Latium reveals even more clearly than before the principles by which Rome was able to conquer and dominate Italy for many centuries. The excellent army and the diplomatic skill that allowed Rome to separate its enemies help to explain its conquests. The reputation for harsh punishment of

rebels—and the sure promise that such punishment would be delivered was made unmistakably clear by the presence of colonies and military roads—helps to account for the slowness to revolt. But the positive side, represented by

Original Roman pavement of the Via Appia, part of the network of military roads that tied all Italy to Rome. These roads enabled Roman legions to move swiftly to enforce their control of Italy. The Via Appia dates from the fourth century B.C. [Scala/Art Resource, N.Y.]

Rome's organization of the defeated states, is at least as important. The Romans did not regard the status given each newly conquered city as permanent. They held out to loyal allies the prospect of improving their status, even of achieving the ultimate prize, full Roman citizenship. In so doing, the Romans gave their allies a stake in Rome's future success and a sense of being colleagues, though subordinate ones, rather than subjects. The result, in general, was that most of Rome's allies remained loyal even when put to the severest test.

DEFEAT OF THE SAMNITES The next great challenge to Roman arms came in a series of wars with a tough mountain people of the southern Apennines, the Samnites. Some of Rome's allies rebelled, and soon the Etruscans and Gauls joined in the war against Rome. But most of the allies remained loyal. In 295 B.C., at Sentinum, the Romans defeated an Italian coalition, and by 280 B.C. they were masters of central Italy. Their power extended from the Po Valley south to Apulia and Lucania.

Now the Romans were in direct contact with the Greek cities of southern Italy. Roman intervention in a quarrel between Greek cities brought them face to face with Pyrrhus, king of Epirus. Pyrrhus, probably the best general of his time, commanded a well-disciplined and experienced mercenary army, which he hired out for profit, and a new weapon: twenty war elephants. He defeated the Romans twice but suffered many casualties. When one of his officers rejoiced at the victory, Pyrrhus told him, "If we win one more battle against the Romans we shall be completely ruined." This "Pyrrhic" victory led him to withdraw to Sicily in 275 B.C. The Greek cities that had hired him were forced to join the Roman confederation. By 265 B.C. Rome ruled all Italy as far north as the Po River,

---

Roman Expansion in Italy

392 B.C.	Fall of Veii; Etruscans defeated
387 B.C.	Gauls burn Rome
338 B.C.	Latin League defeated
295 B.C.	Battle of Sentinum; Samnites and allies defeated
275 B.C.	Pyrrhus driven from Italy
265 B.C.	Rome rules Italy south of the Po River

---

an area of 47,200 square miles. The year after the defeat of Pyrrhus, Ptolemy Philadelphus, king of Egypt, sent a message of congratulation to establish friendly relations with Rome. This act recognized Rome's new status as a power in the Hellenistic world.

Rome and Carthage

The conquest of southern Italy brought the Romans face to face with the great naval power of the western Mediterranean, Carthage (see Map 4-2). Late in the ninth century B.C. the Phoenician city of Tyre had planted a colony on the coast of northern Africa near modern Tunis, calling it the New City, or Carthage. In the sixth century B.C. the conquest of Phoenicia by the Assyrians and the Persians left Carthage independent and free to exploit its very advantageous situation. The city was located on a defensible site and commanded an excellent harbor that encouraged commerce. The coastal plain grew abundant grain, fruits, and vegetables. An inland plain allowed sheep herding. The Phoenician settlers conquered the native inhabitants and used them to work the land.

Beginning in the sixth century B.C. the Carthaginians expanded their domain to include the coast of northern Africa west beyond the Straits of Gibraltar and eastward into Libya. Overseas they came to control the southern part of Spain, Sardinia, Corsica, Malta, the Balearic Islands, and western Sicily. The people of these territories, though originally allies, were all reduced to subjection like the natives of the Carthaginian home territory. They all served in the Carthaginian army or navy and paid tribute. Carthage also profited greatly from the mines of Spain and from an absolute monopoly of trade imposed on the western Mediterranean.

An attack by Hiero, tyrant of Syracuse, on the Sicilian city of Messana just across from Italy first caused trouble between Rome and Carthage. Messana had been seized by a group of Italian mercenary soldiers who called themselves *Mamertines*, the sons of the war god Mars. When Hiero defeated the Mamertines, some of them called on the Carthaginians to help save their city. Carthage agreed and sent a garrison, for the Carthaginians wanted to prevent Syracuse from dominating the straits. One Mamertine faction, however, fearing that

MAP 4-2 THE WESTERN MEDITERRANEAN AREA DURING THE RISE OF ROME *This map covers the theater of conflict between the growing Roman dominions and those of Carthage in the third century B.C. The Carthaginian empire stretched westward from the city (in modern Tunisia) along the North African coast and into southern Spain.*

Carthage might take undue advantage of the opportunity, asked Rome for help.

In 264 B.C. the request came to the Senate. Because a Punic garrison (the Romans called the Carthaginians *Phoenicians*; in Latin the word is *Poeni* or *Puni*, hence the adjective *Punic*) was in place at Messana, any intervention would not be against Syracuse but against the mighty empire of Carthage. Unless Rome intervened, however, Carthage would gain control of all Sicily and the straits. The assembly voted to send an army to Messana, and expelled the Punic garrison. The First Punic War was on.

THE FIRST PUNIC WAR (264–241 B.C.)
The war in Sicily soon settled into a stalemate until the Romans built a fleet to cut off supplies to the besieged Carthaginian cities at the western end of Sicily. When Carthage sent its own fleet to raise the siege, the Romans destroyed it. In 241 B.C. Carthage signed a treaty giving up

Sicily and the islands between Italy and Sicily; it also agreed to pay a war indemnity in ten annual installments. Neither side was to attack the allies of the other. The peace was realistic and not unduly harsh; Rome had earned Sicily, and Carthage could well afford the indemnity. If it had been carried out in good faith, it might have brought lasting peace.

A rebellion, however, broke out in Carthage among the mercenaries, newly recruited from Sicily, who now demanded their pay. In 238 B.C., while Carthage was still preoccupied with the rebellion, Rome seized Sardinia and Corsica and demanded that Carthage pay an additional indemnity. This was a harsh and cynical action by the Romans; even the historian Polybius, a great champion of Rome, could find no justification for it. It undid the calming effects of the peace of 241 B.C. without preventing the Carthaginians from recovering their strength to seek vengeance in the future.

A Roman warship. Rome became a naval power late in its history, in the course of the First Punic War. Roman sailors initially lacked the skill and experience in sea warfare of their Carthaginian opponents, who could maneuver their oared ships to ram the enemy. To compensate for this disadvantage, the Romans sought to make a sea battle more like an encounter on land by devising ways to grapple enemy ships and board them with armed troops. In time, they also mastered the skillful use of the ram. This picture shows a Roman ship, propelled by oars, with both ram and soldiers, ready for either kind of fight. [Vatican Museum]

The conquest of overseas territory presented the Romans with new administrative problems. Instead of following the policy they had pursued in Italy, they made Sicily a province and Sardinia and Corsica another. It became common to extend the term of the governors of these provinces beyond a year. The governors were unchecked by colleagues and exercised full *imperium*. New magistracies, in effect, were thus created free of the limits put on the power of officials in Rome.

The new populations were neither Roman citizens nor allies; they were subjects who did not serve in the army but paid tribute instead. The old practice of extending citizenship and, with it, loyalty to Rome, thus stopped at the borders of Italy. Rome collected taxes on these subjects by "farming" them out at auction to the highest bidder. At first, the tax collectors were natives from the same province. Later they were Roman allies, and finally Roman citizens below senatorial rank who could become powerful and wealthy by squeezing the provincials hard. These innovations were the basis for Rome's imperial organization in the future. In time they strained the constitution and traditions to such a degree as to threaten the existence of the republic.

After the First Punic War, campaigns against the Gauls and across the Adriatic distracted Rome. Meanwhile Hamilcar Barca, the Carthaginian governor of Spain from 237 B.C.

until his death in 229 B.C., was leading Carthage on the road to recovery. Hamilcar sought to compensate for Carthaginian losses elsewhere by building a Punic empire in Spain. He improved the ports and the commerce conducted in them, exploited the mines, gained control of the hinterland, won over many of the conquered tribes, and built a strong and disciplined army.

Hamilcar's successor, his son-in-law Hasdrubal, pursued the same policies. His success alarmed the Romans. They imposed a treaty in which he promised not to take an army north across the Ebro River in Spain, although Punic expansion in Spain was well south of that river at the time. Though the agreement appeared to put Rome in the position of giving orders to an inferior, it benefitted both sides equally. If the Carthaginians accepted the limit of the Ebro on their expansion in Spain, the Romans would not interfere with that expansion.

THE SECOND PUNIC WAR (218–202 B.C.) On Hasdrubal's assassination in 221 B.C. the army chose as his successor Hannibal, son of Hamilcar Barca. Hannibal was at that time twenty-five years old. He quickly consolidated and extended the Punic Empire in Spain. A few years before his accession Rome had received an offer of alliance from the people of the Spanish town Saguntum (about one hundred miles south of the Ebro). The Romans accepted the friendship and the responsibilities it entailed, in the process violating at least the spirit of the Ebro treaty. At first, Hannibal was careful to avoid any action against Saguntum, but the Saguntines, confident of Rome's protection, began to interfere with some of the Spanish tribes allied with Hannibal. When the Romans sent an embassy to Hannibal warning him to let Saguntum alone and repeating the injunction not to cross the Ebro, he ignored the warning and proceeded to besiege and capture the town. The Romans sent an ultimatum to Carthage demanding the surrender of Hannibal. Carthage refused, and Rome declared war in 218 B.C.

Between the close of the First Punic War and the outbreak of the Second, Rome had repeatedly provoked Carthage, taking Sardinia in 238 B.C. and interfering in Spain, but had taken no measures to prevent Carthage from building a powerful and dangerous empire or even to prepare defenses against a Punic attack in Spain. Hannibal saw to it that the Romans paid the price for these blunders. By September of 218 B.C. he was across the Alps, in Italy and among the friendly Gauls.

The Origins of the Hannibalic War

The Second Punic War was often called the Hannibalic War after the brilliant Carthaginian general who launched it. The Roman historian Livy wrote some two centuries after the event, and his account of its origin presents what had become an orthodox Roman view.

◆ *Why does Livy think the Second Punic War was important? How did the conclusion of the First Punic War influence the outbreak of the Second? Is there any reason to doubt the story of Hannibal's oath? What difference would it make if the story were true?*

I may be permitted to premise at this division of my work, what most historians have professed at the beginning of their whole undertaking; that I am about to relate the most memorable of all wars that were ever waged: the war which the Carthaginians, under the conduct of Hannibal, maintained with the Roman people. For never did any states and nations more efficient in their resources engage in contest; nor had they themselves at any other period so great a degree of power and energy. They brought into action too no arts of war unknown to each other, but those which had been tried in the first Punic war; and so various was the fortune of the conflict, and so doubtful the victory, that they who conquered were more exposed to danger. The hatred with which they fought also was almost greater than their resources; the Romans being indignant that the conquered aggressively took up arms against their vic-tors; the Carthaginians, because they considered that in their subjection it had been lorded over them with haughtiness and avarice. There is besides a story, that Hannibal, when about nine years old, while he boyishly coaxed his father Hamilcar that he might be taken to Spain (at the time when the African war was completed, and he was employed in sacrificing previously to transporting his army thither), was conducted to the altar; and, having laid his hand on the offerings, was bound by an oath to prove himself, as soon as he could, an enemy to the Roman people. The loss of Sicily and Sardinia grieved the high spirit of Hamilcar: for he deemed that Sicily had been given up through a premature despair of their affairs; and that Sardinia, during the disturbances in Africa, had been treacherously taken by the Romans, while, in addition, the payment of a tribute had been imposed.

Livy, History of Rome 21. 1–18, trans. by D. Spiller and C. Edmonds.

Hannibal defeated the Romans at the Ticinus River and crushed the joint consular armies at the Trebia River. In 217 B.C. he outmaneuvered and trapped another army at Lake Trasimene. The key to success, however, would be defection by Rome's allies. Hannibal released Italian prisoners without harm or ransom and moved his army south of Rome to encourage rebellion. But the allies remained firm.

Sobered by their defeats, the Romans elected Quintus Fabius Maximus dictator. His strategy was to avoid battle while following and harassing Hannibal's army. He would fight only when his army had recovered and only then on favorable ground.

In 216 B.C. Hannibal marched to Cannae in Apulia to tempt the Romans, under different generals, into another open fight. They sent off an army of some 80,000 men to meet him. Almost the entire Roman army was killed or captured. It was the worst defeat in Roman history. Rome's prestige was shattered, and most of its allies in southern Italy as well as Syracuse in Sicily now went over to Hannibal. For more than a decade no Roman army would dare face Hannibal in the open field.

Hannibal, however, had neither the numbers nor the supplies to besiege walled cities, nor did he have the equipment to take them by assault. To win the war in Spain, the Romans appointed Publius Cornelius Scipio (237–183 B.C.), later called Africanus, to the command in Spain with proconsular *imperium*. Scipio was not yet twenty-five and had held no high office. But he was a general almost as talented as Hannibal. Within a few years young Scipio had conquered all Spain and had deprived Hannibal of hope of help from that region.

In 204 B.C. Scipio landed in Africa, defeated the Carthaginians, and forced them to accept a peace whose main clause was the withdrawal of Hannibal and his army from Italy. Hannibal had won every battle but lost the war, for he had not counted on the determination of Rome and the loyalty of its allies. Hannibal's return inspired Carthage to break the peace and to risk all in battle. In 202 B.C. Scipio and Hannibal faced each other at the Battle of Zama. The generalship of Scipio and the desertion of Hannibal's mercenaries gave the victory to Rome. The new peace terms reduced Carthage to the status of a dependent ally to Rome. The Second Punic War

The Punic Wars	
264–241 B.C.	First Punic War
238 B.C.	Rome seizes Sardinia and Corsica
221 B.C.	Hannibal takes command of Punic army in Spain
218–202 B.C.	Second Punic War
216 B.C.	Battle of Cannae
209 B.C.	Scipio takes New Carthage
202 B.C.	Battle of Zama
149–146 B.C.	Third Punic War
146 B.C.	Destruction of Carthage

ended the Carthaginian command of the western Mediterranean and Carthage's term as a great power. Rome ruled the seas and the entire Mediterranean coast from Italy westward.

The Republic's Conquest of the Hellenistic World

THE EAST By the middle of the third century B.C. the eastern Mediterranean had reached a condition of stability based on a balance of power among the three great Hellenistic kingdoms that allowed an established place even for lesser states. This equilibrium, however, was threatened by the activities of two aggressive monarchs, Philip V of Macedon (221–179 B.C.) and Antiochus III of the Seleucid kingdom (223–187 B.C.). Philip and Antiochus moved swiftly, the latter against Syria and Palestine, the former against cities in the Aegean, in the Hellespontine region, and on the coast of Asia Minor.

The threat that a more powerful Macedon might pose to Rome's friends and, perhaps, even to Italy was enough to persuade the Romans to intervene. Philip had already attempted to meddle in Roman affairs when he formed an alliance with Carthage during the Second Punic War, provoking a conflict known as the First Macedonian War (215–205 B.C.). In 200 B.C., in an action that began the Second Macedonian War, the Romans sent an ultimatum to Philip ordering him not to attack any Greek city and to pay reparations to Pergamum. These orders were meant to provoke, not avoid, war, and Philip refused to obey. Two years later the Romans sent out a talented young general,

Flamininus, who demanded that Philip withdraw from Greece entirely. In 197 B.C., with Greek support, Flamininus defeated Philip in the hills of Cynoscephalae in Thessaly, ending the war. The Greek cities freed from Philip were made autonomous, and in 196 B.C. Flamininus proclaimed the freedom of the Greeks.

Soon after the Romans withdrew from Greece, they came into conflict with Antiochus, who was expanding his power in Asia and on the European side of the Hellespont. On the pretext of freeing the Greeks from Roman domination, he landed an army on the Greek mainland. The Romans routed Antiochus at Thermopylae and quickly drove him from Greece. In 189 B.C. they crushed his army at Magnesia in Asia Minor. The peace of Apamia in the next year deprived Antiochus of his elephants and his navy and imposed a huge indemnity on him. Once again, the Romans took no territory for themselves and left several Greek cities in Asia free. They continued to regard Greece, and now Asia Minor, as a kind of protectorate in which they could intervene or not as they chose.

This relatively mild policy was destined to end as the stern and businesslike policies favored by the conservative censor Cato gained favor in Rome. A new harshness was to be applied to allies and bystanders as well as to defeated opponents.

In 179 B.C. Perseus succeeded Philip V as king of Macedon. He tried to gain popularity in Greece by favoring the democratic and revolutionary forces in the cities. The Romans, troubled by his threat to stability, launched the Third Macedonian War (172–168 B.C.), and in 168 B.C. Æmilius Paullus defeated Perseus at Pydna. The peace that followed this war, reflecting the changed attitude at Rome, was harsh. It divided Macedon into four separate republics, whose citizens were forbidden to intermarry or even to do business across the new national boundaries. Leaders of anti-Roman factions in the Greek cities were punished severely.

When Æmilius Paullus returned from his victory, he celebrated for three days, by parading the spoils of war, royal prisoners, and great wealth through the streets of Rome. The public treasury benefitted to such a degree that the direct property tax on Roman citizens was abolished. Part of the booty went to the general and part to his soldiers. New motives were thereby introduced into Roman foreign policy, or, perhaps, old motives were given new prominence. Foreign campaigns could bring profit to the state, rewards to the army, and wealth, fame, honor, and political power to the general.

THE WEST   Harsh as the Romans had become toward the Greeks, they were even worse in their treatment of the people of the Iberian Peninsula, whom they considered barbarians. They committed dreadful atrocities, lied, cheated, and broke treaties to exploit and pacify the natives, who fought back fiercely in guerilla style. From 154 to 133 B.C. the fighting waxed, and it became hard to recruit Roman soldiers to participate in the increasingly ugly war. At last, in 134 B.C., Scipio Aemilianus took the key city of Numantia by siege and burned it to the ground. This put an end to the war in Spain.

Roman treatment of Carthage was no better. Although Carthage lived up to its treaty with Rome faithfully and posed no threat, some Romans refused to abandon their hatred and fear of the traditional enemy. Cato is said to have ended all his speeches in the Senate with the same sentence: *Ceterum censeo delendam esse Carthaginem* ("Besides, I think that Carthage must be destroyed"). At last the Romans took advantage of a technical breach of the peace to destroy Carthage. In 146 B.C. Scipio Aemilianus took the city, plowed up its land, and put salt in the furrows as a symbol of the permanent abandonment of the site. The Romans incorporated it as the province of Africa, one of six Roman provinces, including Sicily, Sardinia–Corsica, Macedonia, Hither Spain, and Further Spain.

Roman Engagement Overseas	
215–205 B.C.	First Macedonian War
200–197 B.C.	Second Macedonian War
196 B.C.	Proclamation of Greek freedom by Flamininus at Corinth
189 B.C.	Battle of Magnesia; Antiochus defeated in Asia Minor
172–168 B.C.	Third Macedonian War
168 B.C.	Battle of Pydna
154–133 B.C.	Roman wars in Spain
134 B.C.	Numantia taken

Civilization in the Early Roman Republic

Close and continued association with the Greeks of the Hellenistic world wrought important changes in the Roman style of life and thought. The Roman attitude toward the Greeks ranged from admiration for their culture and history to contempt for their constant squabbling, their commercial practices, and their weakness. Conservatives such as Cato might speak contemptuously of the Greeks as "Greeklings" (*Graeculi*), but even he learned Greek and absorbed Greek culture.

Before long, the education of the Roman upper classes was bilingual. In addition to the Twelve Tables young Roman nobles studied Greek rhetoric, literature, and sometimes philosophy. These studies even had an effect on education and the Latin language. As early as the third century B.C. Livius Andronicus, a liberated Greek slave, translated the *Odyssey* into Latin. It became a primer for young Romans and put Latin on the road to becoming a literary language.

Religion

Roman religion was influenced by the Greeks almost from the beginning. The Romans identified their own gods with Greek equivalents and incorporated Greek mythology into their own. Mostly, however, Roman religious practice remained simple and Italian, until the third century B.C. brought important new influences from the East.

In 205 B.C. the Senate approved the public worship of Cybele, the Great Mother goddess from Phrygia. Hers was a fertility cult accompa-

Next followed young men wearing frocks with ornamented borders, who led to the sacrifice a hundred and twenty stalled oxen, with their horns gilded, and their heads adorned with ribbons and garlands; and with these were boys that carried basins for libation, of silver and gold.

After his children and their attendants came Perseus himself, clad all in black, and wearing the boots of his country, and looking like one altogether stunned and deprived of reason, through the greatness of his misfortunes. Next followed a great company of his friends and familiars, whose countenances were disfigured with grief, and who let the spectators see, by their tears and their continual looking upon Perseus, that it was his fortune they so much lamented, and that they were regardless of their own.

After these were carried four hundred crowns, all made of gold, sent from the cities by their respective deputations to Æmilius, in honour of his victory. Then he himself came, seated on a chariot magnificently adorned (a man well worthy to be looked at, even without these ensigns of power), dressed in a robe of purple, interwoven with gold, and holding a laurel branch in his right hand. All the army, in like manner, with boughs of laurel in their hands, divided into their bands and companies, followed the chariot of their commander; some singing verses, according to the usual custom, mingled with raillery; others, songs of triumph and the praise of Æmilius's deeds; who, indeed, was admired and accounted happy by all men, and unenvied by every one that was good; except so far as it seems the province of some god to lessen that happiness which is too great and inordinate, and so to mingle the affairs of human life that no one should be entirely free and exempt from calamities; but, as we read in Homer, that those should think themselves truly blessed whom fortune has given an equal share of good and evil.

Plutarch, "Aemilius Paullus," in Lives of the Noble Grecians and Romans, *trans. by John Dryden, rev. by A. H. Clough (New York: Random House, n.d.), pp. 340–341.*

nied by ecstatic, frenzied, and sensual rites that shocked and outraged conservative Romans to such a degree that they soon banned the cult. Similarly, the Senate banned the worship of Dionysus, or Bacchus, in 186 B.C. In the second century B.C. interest in Babylonian astrology also grew, and the Senate's attempt in 139 B.C. to expel the "Chaldaeans," as the astrologers were called, did not prevent the continued influence of their superstition.

Education

The education provided in the early centuries of the Roman Republic reflected the limited, conservative, and practical nature of that community of plain farmers and soldiers. Education was entirely the responsibility of the family, the father teaching his own son at home. It is not clear whether in these early times girls received any education, though they certainly did later on. The boys learned to read, write, and calculate, and they learned the skills of farming. They memorized the laws of the Twelve Tables; learned how to perform religious rites; heard stories of the great deeds of early Roman history and particularly those of their ancestors; and engaged in the physical training appropriate for potential soldiers. This course of study was practical, vocational, and moral. It aimed at making the boys moral, pious, patriotic, law-abiding, and respectful of tradition.

HELLENIZED EDUCATION In the third century B.C. the Romans came into contact with the Greeks of southern Italy, and this contact produced momentous changes in Roman education. Greek teachers introduced the study of language, literature, and philosophy, as well as

(a)

(b)

(a) The temple of Vesta at Rome was built in the first century B.C. Vesta was the Roman goddess of the hearth. Her cult included an eternal flame, which was tended by the famous Vestal Virgins. (b) A statue of a Vestal Virgin from the courthouse of the House of the Vestal Virgins. [(a) Scala/Art Resource, N.Y.; (b) Robert Miller]

the idea of a liberal education, or what the Romans called *humanitas*, the root of our concept of the humanities. The aim of education changed from the mastery of practical, vocational skills to an emphasis on broad intellectual training, critical thinking, an interest in ideas, and the development of a well-rounded person.

The new emphasis required students to learn Greek, for Rome did not yet have a literature of its own. Hereafter educated Romans were expected to be bilingual. For this purpose schools were established in which a teacher, called a *grammaticus*, taught students the Greek language and its literature, especially the poets and particularly Homer. After the completion of this elementary education, Roman boys of the upper classes studied rhetoric, the art of speaking and writing well. For the Greeks, rhetoric was a subject of less importance than philosophy. The more practical Romans took to it avidly, however, for it was of great use in legal disputes and was becoming ever more valuable in political life.

Some Romans were powerfully attracted to Greek literature and philosophy. So important and powerful a Roman aristocrat as Scipio Aemilianus, the man who finally defeated and destroyed Carthage, surrounded himself and his friends with such Greek thinkers as the historian Polybius and the philosopher Panaetius.

Equally outstanding Romans, such as Cato the Elder, were more conservative and opposed the new learning on the grounds that it would weaken Roman moral fiber. They were able on more than one occasion to pass laws expelling philosophers and teachers of rhetoric. But these attempts to go back to older ways failed. The new education suited the needs of the Romans of the second century B.C. They found themselves changing from a rural to an urban society and were being thrust into the sophisticated world of Hellenistic Greeks.

By the last century of the Roman Republic, the new Hellenized education had become dominant. Latin literature had come into being along with Latin translations of Greek poets, and these formed part of the course of study. But Roman gentlemen still were expected to be bilingual, and Greek language and literature were still central to the curriculum. Many schools were established. The number of educated people grew, extending beyond the senato-

Cato Educates His Son

Marcus Porcius Cato (234–149 B.C.) was a remarkable Roman who rose from humble origins to the highest offices in the state. He stood as the firmest defender of the old Roman traditions at a time when Hellenic ideas were strongly influential. In the following passage Plutarch tells how Cato attended to his son's education.

◆ *What was the curriculum prepared for Cato's son? Was it suitable for the kind of life he would lead? Was his education more or less helpful and appropriate in this way than that of the average American student today? Why did Cato teach his son himself? Why did he pay so much attention to Roman history? Was he wise in doing so?*

After the birth of his son, no business could be so urgent, unless it had a public character, as to prevent him from being present when his wife bathed and swaddled the babe. For the mother nursed it herself, and often gave suck also to the infants of her slaves, that so they might come to cherish a brotherly affection for her son. As soon as the boy showed signs of understanding, his father took him under his own charge and taught him to read, although he had an accomplished slave, Chilo by name, who was a school teacher, and taught many boys. Still, Cato thought it not right, as he tells us himself, that his son should be scolded by a slave, or have his ears tweaked when he was slow to learn, still less that he should be indebted to his slave for such a priceless thing as education. He was therefore himself not only the boy's reading teacher, but his tutor in law, and his athletic trainer, and he taught his son not merely to hurl the javelin and fight in armour and ride the horse, but also to box, to endure heat and cold, and to swim lustily through the eddies and billows of the Tiber. His History of Rome, as he tells us himself, he wrote out with his own hand and in large characters, that his son might have in his own home an aid to acquaintance with his country's ancient traditions.

Plutarch, Cato Major, 20, trans. by Bernadotte Perrin (London and New York: Loeb Classical Library, William Heinemann, 1914).

rial class to the equestrians and outside Rome to the cities of Italy.

In the late republic, Roman education, though still entirely private, became more formal and organized. From the ages of seven to twelve, boys went to elementary school accompanied by a Greek slave called a *paedagogus* (whence our term *pedagogue*), who looked after their physical well-being and their manners, and who improved their ability in Greek conversation. At school the boys learned to read and write, using a wax tablet and a stylus, and to do simple arithmetic with an abacus and pebbles (*calculi*). Discipline was harsh and corporal punishment frequent. From twelve to sixteen, boys went to a higher school, where the *grammaticus* undertook to provide a liberal education, using Greek and Latin literature as his subject matter. In addition, he taught dialectic, arithmetic, geometry, astronomy, and music. Sometimes he included the elements of rhetoric, especially for those boys who would not go on to a higher education.

At sixteen, some boys went on to advanced study in rhetoric. The instructors were usually Greek. They trained their charges by study of models of fine speech of the past and by having them write, memorize, and declaim speeches suitable for different occasions. Sometimes the serious student attached himself to some

This carved relief from the second century A.D. shows a schoolmaster and his pupils. The one at the right is arriving late. [Alinari/Art Resource, N.Y.]

famous public speaker and followed him about to learn what he could. Sometimes a rich and ambitious Roman would support a Greek philosopher in his own home. His son could converse with the philosopher and acquire the learning and polished thought necessary for the fully cultured gentleman. Some, like the great orator Cicero, undertook what we might call postgraduate study by traveling abroad to study with great teachers of rhetoric and philosophy in the Greek world.

One result of this whole style of education was to broaden the Romans' understanding through the careful study of a foreign language and culture. It made them a part of the older and wider culture of the Hellenistic world, a world that they had come to dominate and needed to understand.

EDUCATION FOR WOMEN Though the evidence is limited, we can be sure that girls of the upper classes received an education equivalent at least to the early stages of a boy's education. They were probably taught by tutors at home rather than going to school, as was increasingly the fashion among boys in the late republic. Young women did not study with philosophers and rhetoricians, for they were usually married by the age at which the men were pursuing their higher education. Still, some women found ways to continue their education. Some became prose writers and others poets. By the first century A.D. there were apparently enough learned women to provoke the complaints of a crotchety and conservative satirist:

Still more exasperating is the woman who begs as soon as she sits down to dinner, to discourse on poets and poetry, comparing Virgil with Homer; professors, critics, lawyers, auctioneers—even another woman—can't get a word in. She rattles on at such a rate that you'd think that all the pots and pans in the kitchen were crashing to the floor or that every bell in town was clanging. All by herself she makes as much noise as some primitive tribe chasing away an eclipse. She should learn the philosopher's lesson: "moderation is necessary even for intellectuals." And, if she still wants to appear educated and eloquent, let her dress as a man, sacrifice to men's gods and bathe in the men's baths. Wives shouldn't try to be public speakers; they shouldn't use rhetorical devices; they shouldn't read all the classics—there should be some things women don't understand. I myself cannot understand a woman who can quote the rules of grammar and never make a mistake and cites obscure, long-forgotten poets—as if men cared about such things. If she has to correct somebody let her correct her girl friends and leave her husband alone.[2]

Slavery

Like most ancient peoples, the Romans had slaves from very early in their history, but among the shepherds and family-farmers of early Rome they were relatively few. Slavery became a basic element in the Roman economy and society only during the second century B.C., after the Romans had conquered most of the lands bordering the Mediterranean. In the time

[2]*Juvenal, Satires 6.434–456, trans. by Roger Killian, Richard Lynch, Robert J. Rowland, and John Sims, cited by Sarah B. Pomeroy in* Goddesses, Whores, Wives, and Slaves *(New York: Schocken Books, 1975), p. 172.*

This wall painting from the first century B.C. comes from the villa of Publius Fannius Synistor at Pompeii and shows a woman playing a cithera. [The Metropolitan Museum of Art, Rogers Fund, 1903 (Acc. # 03.14.5)]

between the beginning of Rome's first war against Carthage (264 B.C.) and the conquest of Spain (133 B.C.), the Romans enslaved some 250,000 prisoners of war, greatly increasing the availability of slave labor and reducing its price. Many were used as domestic servants to feed the growing appetite for luxury among the Roman upper classes, whereas at the other end of the spectrum, many were put to work in the mines of Spain and Sardinia. Some worked as artisans in small factories and shops or as public clerks. Slaves were permitted to marry, and they appear to have produced sizable families that increased the slave population. As in Greece, domestic slaves and those used in crafts and commerce were permitted to earn money, to keep it, and, in some cases, to use it to purchase their own freedom. The freeing of slaves, in fact, was very common among the Romans, both upon the death of the master and during his lifetime. Rome's fire brigade at one point consisted of 7,000 former slaves. After a time a con-

A Women's Uprising in Republican Rome

In 195 B.C. Roman women staged a rare public political protest when they demanded the repeal of a law passed two decades earlier during the Second Punic War that they judged to limit their rights unfairly. Livy (59 B.C.–A.D. 17) describes the affair and the response of the traditionalist Marcus Porcius Cato (234–149 B.C.).

♦ *Of what did the women complain? How did they try to achieve their goals? Which of Cato's objections to their behavior do you think were most important? Since women did not vote or sit in assemblies, how can the outcome of the affair be explained?*

Amid the anxieties of great wars, either scarce finished or soon to come, an incident occurred, trivial to relate, but which, by reason of the passions it aroused, developed into a violent contention. Marcus Fundanius and Lucius Valerius, tribunes of the people, proposed to the assembly the abrogation of the Oppian law. The tribune Gaius Oppius had carried this law in the heat of the Punic War, in the consulship of Quintus Fabius and Tiberius Sempronius, that no woman should possess more than half an ounce of gold or wear a parti-coloured garment or ride in a carriage in the City or in a town within a mile thereof, except on the occasion of a religious festival. The tribunes Marcus and Publius Iunius Brutus were supporting the Oppian law, and averred that they would not permit its repeal; many distinguished men came forward to speak for and against it; the Capitoline was filled with crowds of supporters and opponents of the bill. The matrons could not be kept at home by advice or modesty or their husbands' orders, but blocked all the streets and approaches to the Forum, begging the men as they came down to the Forum that, in the prosperous condition of the state, when the private fortunes of all men were daily increasing, they should allow the woman too to have their former distinctions restored. The crowd of women grew larger day by day; for they were now coming in from the towns and rural districts. Soon they dared even to approach and appeal to the consuls, the praetors, and the other officials, but one consul, at least, they found adamant, Marcus Porcius Cato, who spoke thus in favour of the law whose repeal was being urged.

"If each of us, citizens, had determined to assert his rights and dignity as a husband with

siderable proportion of the Roman population included people who had been slaves themselves or whose ancestors had been slaves. It was not uncommon to see the son or grandson of a slave become wealthy as a freedman and the slave himself or his son become a Roman citizen. Because Roman slaves came from all over the Mediterranean world, one result of the growth of slavery and the high rate of manumission was the transformation of the ethnic composition of the Roman population.

But the unique development in the Roman world was the emergence of an agricultural system that employed and depended on a vast number of slaves. By the end of the republic there were between two and three million slaves in Italy, about 35 to 40 percent of the total population, most of them part of the great slave gangs that worked the vast plantations the Romans called *latifundia*. Turning from the grain that was the chief crop of the free Roman farmer, these large estates concentrated on such cash-producing products as wool, wine, and olive oil. The life of Rome's agricultural slaves appears to have been much harder than that of other Roman slaves and of slaves in other ancient societies, except possibly slaves working in mines. The owners of the *latifundia* sought

respect to his own spouse, we should have less trouble with the sex as a whole; as it is, our liberty, destroyed at home by female violence, even here in the Forum is crushed and trodden underfoot, and because we have not kept them individually under control, we dread them collectively. . . . But from no class is there not the greatest danger if you permit them meetings and gatherings and secret consultations.

. . . .

I should have said, 'What sort of practice is this, of running out into the streets and blocking the roads and speaking to other women's husbands? Could you not have made the same requests, each of your own husband, at home? Or are you more attractive outside and to other women's husbands than to your own? And yet, not even at home, if modesty would keep matrons within the limits of their proper rights, did it become you to concern yourselves with the question of what laws should be adopted in this place or repealed.' Our ancestors permitted no woman to conduct even personal business without a guardian to intervene in her behalf; they wished them to be under the control of fathers, brothers, husbands; we (Heaven help us!) allow them now even to interfere in public affairs, yes, and to visit the Forum and our informal and formal sessions. What else are they doing now on the streets and at the cor-

ners except urging the bill of the tribunes and voting for the repeal of the law? Give loose rein to their uncontrollable nature and to this untamed creature and expect that they will themselves set bounds to their licence; unless you act, this is the least of the things enjoined upon women by custom or law and to which they submit with a feeling of injustice. It is complete liberty or, rather, if we wish to speak the truth, complete licence that they desire.

"If they win in this, what will they not attempt? Review all the laws with which your forefathers restrained their licence and made them subject to their husbands; even with all these bonds you can scarcely control them. What of this? If you suffer them to seize these bonds one by one and wrench themselves free and finally to be placed on a parity with their husbands, do you think that you will be able to endure them? The moment they begin to be your equals, they will be your superiors.

. . . .

The next day an even greater crowd of women appeared in public, and all of them in a body beset the doors of those tribunes, who were vetoing their colleagues' proposal, and they did not desist until the threat of veto was withdrawn by the tribunes. After that there was no question that all the tribes would vote to repeal the law. The law was repealed twenty years after it was passed.

Livy, trans. by Evan T. Stage (Cambridge, Mass.: Harvard University Press, 1935), XXXIV, i–iii; viii, pp. 413–419, 439.

---

maximum profits and treated their slaves simply as means to that end. The slaves often worked in chains, oppressed by brutal foremen, and lived in underground prisons. Cato, for example, fed his slaves as cheaply as he could and treated them like machines, to be discarded when their usefulness ended. In this harsh treatment he was probably no different from his peers.

Such harsh treatment led to several serious slave rebellions of a kind we do not hear of in other ancient societies. A rebellion in Sicily in 134 B.C. kept the island in turmoil for more than two years, and the rebellion of the gladia-

tors led by Spartacus in 73 B.C. produced an army of 70,000 slaves that repeatedly defeated the Roman legions and overran all of southern Italy before it was crushed. The Romans executed the survivors with exemplary brutality, lining the road from Capua to Rome with 6,000 crucified slaves.

Roman Imperialism: The Late Republic

Rome's expansion in Italy and overseas was accomplished without a grand general plan (see

MAP 4-3 ROMAN DOMINIONS OF THE LATE REPUBLIC *The Roman Republic's conquest of Mediterranean lands—and beyond—until the death of Julius Caesar is shown here. Areas conquered before Tiberius Gracchus (ca. 133 B.C.) are distinguished from later ones and from client areas owing allegiance to Rome.*

Map 4-3). The new territories were gained as a result of wars that the Romans believed were either defensive or preventive. Their foreign policy was aimed at providing security for Rome on Rome's terms, but these terms were often unacceptable to other nations and led to continued conflict. Whether intended or not, Rome's expansion brought the Romans an empire and, with it, power, wealth, and responsibilities. The need to govern an empire beyond the seas would severely test the republican constitution that had served Rome well during its years as a city-state and that had been well adapted to the mastery of Italy. Roman society and the Roman character had maintained their integrity through the period of expansion in Italy. But these would be tested by the temptations and strains presented by the wealth and the complicated problems of an overseas empire.

The Aftermath of Conquest

War and expansion changed the economic, social, and political life of Italy. Before the Punic wars most Italians owned their own farms, which provided the greater part of the family's needs. Some families owned larger holdings, but their lands chiefly grew grain, and they used the labor of clients, tenants, and hired workers rather than slaves. Fourteen years of fighting in the Second Punic War did terrible damage to much Italian farmland. Many veterans returning from the wars found it impossible or unprofitable to go back to their farms. Some moved to Rome, where they could find work as occasional laborers, but most stayed in the country to work as tenant farmers or hired hands. Often the land they abandoned was gathered into large parcels by the wealthy. They converted these units, later called *latifundia,* into large plantations for growing cash crops—grain, olives, and grapes for wine—or into cattle ranches.

The upper classes had plenty of capital to stock and operate these estates because of profits from the war and from exploiting the provinces. Land was cheap, and slaves conquered in war provided cheap labor. By fair means and foul, large landholders obtained great quantities of public land and forced small farmers from it. These changes separated the people of Rome and Italy more sharply into rich and poor, landed and landless, privileged and deprived. The result was political, social, and ultimately constitutional conflict that threatened the existence of the republic.

The Gracchi

By the middle of the second century B.C. the problems caused by Rome's rapid expansion troubled perceptive Roman nobles. The fall in status of peasant farmers made it harder to recruit soldiers and came to present a political threat as well. The patron's traditional control over his clients was weakened by their flight from their land. Even those former landowners who worked on the land of their patrons as tenants or hired hands were less reliable. The introduction of the secret ballot in the 130s B.C. made them even more independent.

TIBERIUS GRACCHUS In 133 B.C Tiberius Gracchus tried to solve these problems. He became tribune for 133 B.C. on a program of land reform; some of the most powerful members of the Roman aristocracy helped him draft the bill. They meant it to be a moderate attempt at solving Rome's problems. The bill's target was public land that had been acquired and held illegally, some of it for many years. The bill allowed holders of this land to retain as many as 300 acres in clear title as private property, but the state would reclaim anything over that. The recovered land would be redistributed in small lots to the poor, who would pay a small rent to the state and could not sell what they had received.

The bill aroused great hostility. Many senators held vast estates and would be hurt by its passage. Others thought it would be a bad precedent to allow any interference with property rights, even ones so dubious as those pertaining to illegally held public land. Still others feared the political gains that Tiberius and his associates would make if the beneficiaries of their law were properly grateful to its drafters.

When Tiberius put the bill before the tribal assembly, one of the tribunes, M. Octavius, interposed his veto. Tiberius went to the Senate to discuss his proposal, but the senators continued their opposition. Tiberius now had to choose between dropping the matter and undertaking a revolutionary course. Unwilling to give up, he put his bill before the tribal assembly again. Again Octavius vetoed. So Tiberius, strongly supported by the people, had Octavius removed from office, violating the constitution. The assembly's removal of a magistrate implied a fundamental shift of power from the Senate to the people. If the assembly could pass laws opposed by the Senate and vetoed by a tribune, if they could remove magistrates, then Rome would become a democracy like Athens instead of a traditional oligarchy. At this point many of Tiberius's powerful senatorial allies deserted him.

Tiberius proposed a second bill, harsher than the first and more appealing to the people, for he had given up hope of conciliating the Senate. This bill, which passed the assembly, provided for a commission to carry it out. When King Attalus of Pergamum died and left his kingdom to Rome, Tiberius proposed to use the Pergamene revenue to finance the commission. This proposal challenged the Senate's control both of finances and of foreign affairs. Hereafter there could be no compromise. Either Tiberius or the Roman constitution must go under.

Tiberius understood the danger that he would face if he stepped down from the tribunate, and so he announced his candidacy for a second successive term, striking another blow at tradition. His opponents feared that he might go on to hold office indefinitely, to dominate Rome in what appeared to them a demagogic tyranny. They concentrated their fire on the constitutional issue, the deposition of the tribune. They appear to have had some success, for many of Tiberius's supporters did not come out to vote. At the elections a riot broke out, and a mob of senators and their clients killed Tiberius and some 300 of his followers and threw their bodies into the Tiber River. The Senate had put down the threat to its rule, but at the price of

The Ruin of the Roman Family Farm and the Gracchan Reforms

The independent family farm was the backbone both of the Greek polis *and the early Roman Republic. Rome's conquests, the long wars that kept the citizen-soldier away from his farm, and the availability of great numbers of slaves at a low price, however, badly undercut the traditional way of farming and with it the foundations of republican society. In the following passage Plutarch describes the process of agricultural change and the response to it of the reformer Tiberius Gracchus, tribune in 133 B.C.*

♦ *What were the causes of the troubles faced by Roman farmers? What were the social and political consequences of the changes in agricultural life? What solution did Tiberius Gracchus propose? Can you think of any reasons, besides selfishness and greed, that people might oppose his plan?*

Of the territory which the Romans won in war from their neighbours, a part they sold, and a part they made common land, and assigned it for occupation to the poor and indigent among the citizens, on payment of a small rent into the public treasury. And when the rich began to offer larger rents and drove out the poor, a law was enacted forbidding the holding by one person of more than five hundred acres of land. For a short time this enactment gave a check to the rapacity of the rich, and was of assistance to the poor, who remained in their places on the land which they had rented and occupied the allotment which each had held from the outset. But later on the neighbouring rich men, by means of fictitious personages, transferred these rentals to themselves, and finally held most of the land openly in their own names. Then the poor, who had been ejected from their land, no longer showed themselves eager for military service, and neglected the bringing up of children, so that soon all Italy was conscious of a dearth of freemen, and was filled with gangs of foreign slaves, by whose aid the rich cultivated their estates, from which they had driven away the free citizens.

. . . .

And it is thought that a law dealing with injustice and rapacity so great was never drawn up in milder and gentler terms. For men who ought to have been punished for their disobedience and to have surrendered with payment of a fine the land which they were illegally enjoying, these men it merely ordered to abandon their injust acquisitions upon being paid their value, and to admit into ownership of them such citizens as needed assistance. But although the rectification of the wrong was so considerate, the people were satisfied to let bygones be bygones if they could be secure from such wrong in the future; the men of wealth and substance, however, were led by their greed to hate the law, and by their wrath and contentiousness to hate the lawgiver, and tried to dissuade the people by alleging that Tiberius was introducing a re-distribution of land for the confusion of the body politic, and was stirring up a general revolution.

Plutarch, "Tiberius Gracchus," in Lives *8–9, vol. 10, trans. by Bernadotte Perrin and William Heinemann (London: G. P. Putnam's Sons, New York, 1921), pp. 159–167.*

the first internal bloodshed in Roman political history.

The tribunate of Tiberius Gracchus brought a permanent change to Roman politics.

Heretofore Roman political struggles had generally been struggles for honor and reputation between great families or coalitions of such families. Fundamental issues were rarely at stake.

The revolutionary proposals of Tiberius, however, and the senatorial resort to bloodshed created a new situation. Tiberius's use of the tribunate to challenge senatorial rule encouraged imitation in spite of his failure. From then on, Romans could pursue a political career that was not based solely on influence within the aristocracy; pressure from the people might be an effective substitute. In the last century of the republic politicians who sought such backing were called *populares,* whereas those who supported the traditional role of the Senate were called *optimates* ("the best men").

These groups were not political parties with formal programs and party discipline, but they were more than merely vehicles for the political

Sallust on Faction and the Decline of the Republic

Sallust (86–35 B.C.) was a supporter of Julius Caesar and of the political faction called populares, *translated here as "the democratic party," opponents of the* optimates, *translated here as "the nobility." In this selection from his monograph on the Jugurthine War, he tries to explain Rome's troubles in the period after the destruction of Carthage in 146 B.C.*

✦ *Why did Sallust think the destruction of Carthage marked the beginning of the decline of the Republic? Does his account of events seem fair and dispassionate? How would a member of "the nobility" have evaluated the same events? Is the existence of factions or "parties" inevitably harmful to a republic?*

The division of the Roman state into warring factions, with all its attendant vices, had originated some years before, as a result of peace and of that material prosperity which men regard as the greatest blessing. Down to the destruction of Carthage, the people and Senate shared the government peaceably and with due restraint, and the citizens did not compete for glory or power; fear of its enemies preserved the good morals of the state. But when the people were relieved of this fear, the favourite vices of prosperity—licence and pride—appeared as a natural consequence. Thus the peace and quiet which they had longed for in time of adversity proved, when they obtained it, to be even more grievous and bitter than the adversity. For the nobles started to use their position, and the people their liberty, to gratify their selfish passions, every man snatching and seizing what he could for himself. So the whole community was split into parties, and the Republic, which hitherto had been the common interest of all, was torn asunder. The nobility had the advantage of being a close-knit body, whereas the democratic party was weakened by its loose organization, its supporters being dispersed among a huge multitude. One small group of oligarchs had everything in its control alike in peace and war—the treasury, the provinces, public offices, all distinctions and triumphs. The people were burdened with military services and poverty, while the spoils of war were snatched by the generals and shared with a handful of friends. Meantime, the soldiers' parents or young children, if they happened to have a powerful neighbour, might well be driven from their homes. Thus the possession of power gave unlimited scope to ruthless greed, which violated and plundered everything, respecting nothing and holding nothing sacred, till finally it brought about its own downfall. For the day came when noblemen rose to power who preferred true glory to unjust dominion: then the state was shaken to its foundations by civil strife, as by an earthquake.

Sallust, The Jugurthine War and The Conspiracy of Catiline, The Jugurthine War *41, trans. by S. A. Handford (Baltimore and Harmondsworth: Penguin Books, 1963), pp. 77–78.*

ambitions of unorthodox politicians. Fundamental questions—such as those about land reform, the treatment of the Italian allies, the power of the assemblies versus the power of the Senate, and other problems—divided the Roman people, from the time of Tiberius Gracchus to the fall of the republic. Some popular leaders, of course, were cynical self-seekers who used the issues only for their own ambitions. Some few may have been sincere advocates of a principled position. Most, no doubt, were a mixture of the two, like most politicians in most times.

GAIUS GRACCHUS The tribunate of Gaius Gracchus (brother of Tiberius) was much more dangerous than that of Tiberius. All the tribunes of 123 B.C. were his supporters, so there could be no veto, and a recent law permitted the reelection of tribunes. Gaius developed a program of such breadth as to appeal to a variety of groups. First, he revived the agrarian commission, which had been allowed to lapse. Because there was not enough good public land left to meet the demand, he proposed to establish new colonies: two in Italy and one on the old site of Carthage. Among other popular acts, he put through a law stabilizing the price of grain in Rome, which involved building granaries to guarantee an adequate supply.

Gaius broke new ground in appealing to the equestrian order in his struggle against the Senate. The equestrians (so called because they served in the Roman cavalry) were neither peasants nor senators. A highly visible minority of them were businessmen who supplied goods and services to the Roman state and collected its taxes. Almost continuous warfare and the need for tax collection in the provinces had made many of them rich. Most of the time these wealthy men had the same outlook as the Senate; generally they used their profits to purchase land and to try to reach senatorial rank themselves. Still they had a special interest in Roman expansion and in the exploitation of the provinces. Toward the latter part of the second century B.C., they came to have a clear sense of group interest and to exert political influence.

In 129 B.C. Pergamum became the new province of Asia. Gaius put through a law turning over to the equestrian order the privilege of collecting its revenue. He also barred senators from serving as jurors on the courts that tried provincial governors charged with extortion. The combination was a wonderful gift for wealthy equestrian businessmen, who were now free to squeeze profits out of the rich province of Asia without much fear of interference from the governors. The results for Roman provincial administration were bad, but the immediate political consequences for Gaius were excellent. The equestrians were now given reality as a class; as a political unit they might be set against the Senate or be formed into a coalition to serve Gaius's purposes.

Gaius easily won reelection as tribune for 122 B.C. He aimed at giving citizenship to the Italians, both to solve the problem that their dissatisfaction presented and to add them to his political coalition. But the common people did not want to share the advantages of Roman citizenship. The Senate seized on this proposal as a way of driving a wedge between Gaius and his supporters.

The Romans did not reelect Gaius for 121 B.C., leaving him vulnerable to his enemies. A hostile consul provoked an incident that led to violence. The Senate invented an extreme decree ordering the consuls to see to it that no harm came to the republic; in effect, this decree established martial law. Gaius was hunted down and killed, and a senatorial court condemned and put to death without trial some 3,000 of his followers.

Marius and Sulla

For the moment the senatorial oligarchy had fought off the challenge to its traditional position. Before long, it faced more serious dangers arising from troubles abroad. The first grew out of a dispute over the succession to the throne of Numidia, a client kingdom of Rome's near Carthage.

MARIUS AND THE JUGURTHINE WAR The victory of Jugurtha, who became king of Numidia, and his massacre of Roman and Italian businessmen in Numidia gained Roman attention. Although the Senate was reluctant to become involved, pressure from the equestrians and the people forced the declaration of what became known as the Jugurthine War in 111 B.C.

As the war dragged on, the people, sometimes with good reason, suspected the Senate of taking bribes from Jugurtha. They elected C. Marius (157–86 B.C.) to the consulship for 107 B.C. The assembly, usurping the role of the Senate, assigned him to the province of Numidia. This action was significant in several ways. Marius was a *novus homo*, a "new man," that is, the first in the history of his family to reach the consulship. Although a wealthy equestrian, he had been born in the town of Arpinum and was outside the closed circle of the old Roman aristocracy. His earlier career had won him a reputation as an outstanding soldier and something of a political maverick.

Marius quickly defeated Jugurtha, but Jugurtha escaped and guerilla warfare continued. Finally Marius's subordinate, L. Cornelius Sulla (138–78 B.C.), trapped Jugurtha and brought the war to an end. Marius celebrated the victory, but Sulla, an ambitious but impoverished descendant of an old Roman family, resented being cheated of the credit he thought he deserved. Soon rumors circulated crediting Sulla with the victory and diminishing Marius's role. Thus were the seeds planted for a personal rivalry and a mutual hostility that would last until Marius's death.

While the Romans were fighting Jugurtha, a far greater danger threatened Rome from the north. In 105 B.C. two barbaric tribes, the Cimbri and the Teutones, had come down the Rhone Valley and crushed a Roman army at Arausio (Orange). To meet the danger, the Romans elected Marius to his second consulship when these tribes threatened again. He served five consecutive terms until 100 B.C., when the crisis was over.

While the barbarians were occupied elsewhere, Marius used the time to make important changes in the army. He began using volunteers for the army, mostly the dispossessed farmers and rural proletarians whose problems had not been solved by the Gracchi. They enlisted for a long term of service and looked on the army not as an unwelcome duty but as an opportunity and a career. They became semiprofessional clients of their general and sought guaranteed food, clothing, shelter, and booty from victories. They came to expect a piece of land as a form of mustering-out pay or veteran's bonus when they retired.

Volunteers were most likely to enlist with a man who was a capable soldier and influential enough to obtain what he needed for them. They looked to him rather than to the state for their rewards. He, on the other hand, had to obtain these favors from the Senate if he was to maintain his power and reputation. Marius's innovation created both the opportunity and the necessity for military leaders to gain enough power to challenge civilian authority. The promise of rewards won these leaders the personal loyalty of their troops, and that loyalty allowed them to frighten the Senate into granting their demands.

THE WAR AGAINST THE ITALIAN ALLIES (90–88 B.C.) For a decade Rome avoided serious troubles, but in that time the Senate took no action to deal with Italian discontent. The Italians were excluded from the land bill for Marius's veterans. Their discontent was serious enough to cause the Senate to expel all Italians from Rome in 95 B.C. Four years later the tribune M. Livius Drusus put forward a bill to enfranchise the Italians. Drusus seems to have been a sincere aristocratic reformer, but he was assassinated in 90 B.C. In frustration the Italians revolted and established a separate confederation with its own capital and its own coinage.

Employing the traditional device of divide and conquer, the Romans immediately offered citizenship to those cities that remained loyal and soon made the same offer to the rebels if they laid down their arms. Even then, hard fighting was needed to put down the uprising, but by 88 B.C. the war against the allies was over. All the Italians became Roman citizens with the protections that citizenship offered. However, they retained local self-government and a dedication to their own municipalities that made Italy flourish. The passage of time blurred the distinction between Romans and Italians and forged them into a single nation.

SULLA AND HIS DICTATORSHIP During the war against the allies Sulla had performed well. He was elected consul for 88 B.C. and was given command of the war against Mithridates, who was leading a major rebellion in Asia. At this point the seventy-year-old Marius emerged from obscurity and sought the command for himself. With popular and equestrian support, he got the assembly to transfer the command to him. Sulla, defending the rights of the Senate and his own interests, marched his army against Rome. This was the first time a Roman general had used his army against fellow citizens. Marius and his friends fled, and Sulla regained the command. No sooner had he left again for Asia than Marius joined with the consul Cinna and reconquered Rome by force. He outlawed Sulla and launched a bloody massacre of the senatorial opposition. Marius died soon after his election to a seventh consulship, for 86 B.C.

Cinna now was the chief man at Rome. Supported by Marius's men, he held the consulship from 87 to 84 B.C. His future depended on Sulla's fortunes in the East.

By 85 B.C. Sulla had driven Mithridates from Greece and had crossed over to Asia Minor. Eager to regain control of Rome, he negotiated a compromise peace. In 83 B.C. he returned to Italy and fought a civil war that lasted for more than a year. Sulla won and drove the followers of Marius from Italy. He now held all power and had himself appointed dictator, not in the traditional sense, but for the express purpose of reconstituting the state.

Sulla's first step was to wipe out the opposition. The names of those proscribed were posted in public. As outlaws they could be killed by anyone, and the killer received a reward. Sulla proscribed not only political opponents but his personal enemies and men whose only crime was having wealth and property. With the proceeds from the confiscations, Sulla rewarded his veterans, perhaps as many as 100,000 men, and thereby built a solid base of support.

Sulla had enough power and influence to make himself the permanent ruler of Rome. He was traditional enough to want a restoration of senatorial government, however, reformed so as to prevent the misfortunes of the past. To deal with the decimation of the Senate caused by the proscriptions and the civil war, he enrolled 300 new members, many of them from the equestrian order and the upper classes of the Italian cities. The office of tribune, used by the Gracchi to attack senatorial rule, was made into a political dead end.

Sulla's most valuable reforms improved the quality of the courts and the entire legal system. He created new courts to deal with specified crimes, bringing the number of courts to eight.

As both judge and jurors were senators, these courts, too, enhanced senatorial power. These actions were the most permanent of Sulla's reforms, laying the foundation for Roman criminal law.

Sulla retired to a life of ease and luxury in 79 B.C. He could not, however, undo the effect of his own example, that of a general using the loyalty of his own troops to take power and to massacre his opponents, as well as innocent men. These actions proved to be more significant than his constitutional arrangements.

Fall of the Republic

Pompey, Crassus, Caesar, and Cicero

Within a year of Sulla's death his constitution came under assault. To deal with an armed threat to its powers, the Senate violated the very procedures meant to defend them. The Senate gave the command of the army to Pompey (106–48 B.C.), who was only twenty-eight and had never been elected to a magistracy. Then, when Sertorius, a Marian general, resisted senatorial control, the Senate appointed Pompey proconsul in Spain in 77 B.C. These actions ignored Sulla's rigid rules for office holding, which had been meant to guarantee experienced, loyal, and safe commanders. In 71 B.C. Pompey returned to Rome with new glory, having put down the rebellion of Sertorius. In 73 B.C. the Senate made another extraordinary appointment to put down a great slave rebellion led by the gladiator Spartacus. Marcus Licinius Crassus, a rich and ambitious senator, received powers that gave him command of almost all Italy. Together with the newly returned Pompey, he crushed the rebellion in 71 B.C. Extraordinary commands of this sort proved to be the ruin of the republic.

Crassus and Pompey were ambitious men whom the Senate feared. Both demanded special honors and election to the consulship for the year 70 B.C. Pompey was legally ineligible because he had never gone through the strict course of offices prescribed in Sulla's constitution, and Crassus needed Pompey's help. They joined forces, though they disliked and were jealous of each other. They gained popular support by promising to restore the full powers of the tribunes, which Sulla had curtailed. And they gained equestrian backing by promising to restore equestrians to the extortion court juries. They both won election and repealed most of Sulla's constitution. This opened the way for further attacks on senatorial control and for collaboration between ambitious generals and demagogic tribunes.

In 67 B.C. a special law gave Pompey *imperium* for three years over the entire Mediterranean and fifty miles in from the coast. It also gave him the power to raise great quantities of troops and money to rid the area of pirates. The assembly passed the law over senatorial opposition, and in three months Pompey cleared the seas of piracy. Meanwhile a new war had broken out with Mithridates. In 66 B.C. the assembly transferred the command to Pompey, giving him unprecedented powers. He held *imperium* over all Asia, with the right to make war and peace at will. His *imperium* was superior to that of any proconsul in the field.

Once again Pompey justified his appointment. He defeated Mithridates and drove him to suicide. By 62 B.C. he had extended Rome's frontier to the Euphrates River and had organized the territories of Asia so well that his arrangements remained the basis of Roman rule well into the imperial period. When Pompey returned to Rome in 62 B.C., he had more power, prestige, and popular support than any Roman in history. The Senate and his personal enemies had reason to fear that he might emulate Sulla and establish his own rule.

Rome had not been quiet in Pompey's absence. Crassus was the foremost among those who had reason to fear Pompey's return. Although rich and influential, he did not have the confidence of the Senate, a firm political base of his own, or the kind of military glory needed to rival Pompey. During the 60s B.C., therefore, he allied himself with various popular leaders.

The ablest of these men was Gaius Julius Caesar (100–44 B.C.). He was a descendant of an old but politically obscure patrician family that claimed descent from the kings and even from the goddess Venus. In spite of this noble lineage, Caesar was connected to the popular party through his aunt, the wife of Marius, and through his own wife, Cornelia, the daughter of Cinna. Caesar was an ambitious and determined young politician whose daring and

Pompey the Great (106–48 B.C.) was successful in crushing rebellions against the Roman Republic. [Alinari/Art Resource, N.Y.]

rhetorical skill made him a valuable ally in winning the discontented of every class to the cause of the *populares*. Though Crassus was very much the senior partner, each needed the other to achieve what both wanted: significant military commands whereby they might build a reputation, a political following, and a military force to compete with Pompey's.

The chief opposition to Crassus's candidates for the consulship for 63 B.C. came from Cicero (106–43 B.C.), a "new man" from Marius's home town of Arpinum. He had made a spectacular name as the leading lawyer in Rome. Cicero, though he came from outside the senatorial aristocracy, was no *popularis*. His program was to preserve the republic against demagogues and ambitious generals by making the government more liberal. He wanted to unite the stable elements of the state—the Senate and the equestrians—in a harmony of the orders. This program did not appeal to the senatorial oligarchy, but the Senate preferred him to Catiline, a dangerous and popular politician thought to be linked with Crassus. Cicero and Antonius were elected consuls for 63 B.C., Catiline running third.

Cicero soon learned of a plot hatched by Catiline. Catiline had run in the previous election on a platform of cancellation of debts; this appealed to discontented elements in general but especially to the heavily indebted nobles and their many clients. Made desperate by defeat, Catiline planned to stir up rebellions around Italy, to cause confusion in the city, and to take it by force. Quick action by Cicero defeated Catiline.

Formation of the First Triumvirate

Toward the end of 62 B.C. Pompey landed at Brundisium. To general surprise, he disbanded his army, celebrated a great triumph, and returned to private life. He had delayed his return in the hope of finding Italy in such a state as to justify his keeping the army and dominating the scene. Cicero's quick suppression of Catiline prevented his plan. Pompey, therefore, had either to act illegally or to lay down his arms. Because he had not thought of monarchy or revolution but merely wanted to be recognized and treated as the greatest Roman, he chose the latter course.

Pompey had achieved amazing things for Rome and simply wanted the Senate to approve his excellent arrangements in the East and to make land allotments to his veterans. His demands were far from unreasonable, and a prudent Senate would have granted them and would have tried to employ his power in defense of the constitution. But the Senate was jealous and fearful of overmighty individuals and refused his requests. Pompey was driven to an alliance with his natural enemies, Crassus and Caesar, because all three found the Senate standing in the way of what they wanted.

In 60 B.C. Caesar returned to Rome from his governorship of Spain. He wanted the privilege of celebrating a triumph, the great victory procession that the Senate granted certain generals to honor especially great achievements, and of running for consul. The law did not allow him to do both, however, requiring him to stay outside the city with his army but demanding that he canvass for votes personally within the city. He asked for a special dispensation, but the Senate refused. Caesar then performed a political miracle. He reconciled Crassus with Pompey and gained the support of both for his own ambitions. So was born the First Triumvirate, an informal agreement among three Roman politicians, each seeking his private goals, that further undermined the future of the republic.

Julius Caesar and His Government of Rome

Though he was forced to forgo his triumph, Caesar's efforts were rewarded when he was elected to the consulship for 59 B.C. His fellow consul was M. Calpernius Bibulus, the son-in-law of Cato and a conservative hostile to Caesar and the other *populares*. Caesar did not hesitate to override his colleague. The triumvirs' program was quickly enacted. Caesar got the extraordinary command that would give him a chance to earn the glory and power with which to rival Pompey: the governorship of Illyricum and Gaul for five years. A land bill settled Pompey's veterans comfortably, and his eastern settlement was ratified. Crassus, much of whose influence came from his position as champion of the equestrians, won for them a great windfall by having the government renegotiate a tax con-

A bust of Julius Caesar. [Alinari/Art Resource, N.Y.]

Plutarch Describes How Crassus Became a Millionaire

Marcus Licinius Crassus (ca. 112–53 B.C.) was a fine general, a powerful politician, and the richest person in Rome. There is no doubt that his wealth contributed greatly to his power. In the following selection Plutarch describes how Crassus acquired his riches.

✦ *By what devices did Crassus become rich? Why is Plutarch critical of his techniques? How would they be described and evaluated in our own time? What does this passage tell us about the ways in which Roman society had changed since the days of the early republic?*

Now the Romans say that the many virtues of Crassus were obscured by his sole vice of avarice, and it seems that the one vice which became stronger than all the others in him dimmed the rest. The chief proofs of his avarice were the way in which he acquired his property and the size of it. For at first he was not worth more than 300 talents; then, during his consulship, he dedicated the tenth part of his property to Hercules, feasted the people, and gave to every citizen enough to live on for three months; still, when he made an inventory of his property before his Parthian expedition, he found it to have a value of 7,100 talents.

Most of this, if one must tell the scandalous truth, he gathered by fire and war, making the public calamities his greatest source of revenue. For when Sulla seized Rome and sold the property of those put to death by him, regarding and calling it booty, and wishing to make as many influential men as he could partners in the crime, Crassus refused neither to accept nor buy such property. Moreover, observing how natural and familiar at Rome were the burning and collapse of buildings, because of their massiveness and their closeness to one another, he bought slaves who were builders and architects. Then, when he had more than 500 of these, he would buy houses that were on fire and those adjoining the ones on fire. The owners would let them go for small sums, because of their fear and uncertainty, so that the greatest part of Rome came into his hands. But though he had so many artisans, he never built any house but the one he lived in, and used to say that those that were addicted to building would undo themselves without the help of other enemies. And though he had many silver mines, and very valuable land with laborers on it, yet one might consider all this as nothing compared with the value of his slaves, such a great number and variety did he possess—readers, amanuenses, silversmiths, stewards and table-servants. He himself directed their training, and took part in teaching them himself, accounting it, in a word, the chief duty of a master to care for his slaves as the living tools of household management.

Plutarch, Life of Crassus, trans. by N. Lewis and M. Reinhold, in Roman Civilization, *Vol. 1 (New York: Columbia University Press, 1955), pp. 458–459. Used by permission.*

tract in their favor. To guarantee themselves against any reversal of these actions, the triumvirs continued their informal but effective collaboration, arranging for the election of friendly consuls and the departure of potential opponents.

Caesar was now free to seek the military success he craved. His province included Cisalpine Gaul in the Po Valley (by now occupied by many Italian settlers as well as Gauls) and Narbonese Gaul beyond the Alps (modern Provence).

Relying first on the excellent quality of his

MAP 4-4 THE CIVIL WARS OF THE LATE ROMAN REPUBLIC *This map shows the extent of the territory controlled by Rome at the time of Caesar's death and the sites of the major battles of the civil wars of the late Republic.*

army and the experience of his officers, then on his own growing military ability, Caesar made great progress. By 56 B.C. he had conquered most of Gaul, but he had not yet consolidated his victories firmly. He therefore sought an extension of his command, but quarrels between Crassus and Pompey so weakened the Triumvirate that the Senate was prepared to order Caesar's recall.

To prevent the dissolution of his base of power, Caesar persuaded Crassus and Pompey

to meet with him at Luca in northern Italy to renew the coalition. They agreed that Caesar would get another five-year command in Gaul, and Crassus and Pompey would be consuls again in 55 B.C. After that they would each receive an army and a five-year command. Caesar was free to return to Gaul and finish the job. The capture of Alesia in 50 B.C. marked the end of the serious Gallic resistance and of Gallic liberty. For Caesar it brought the wealth, fame, and military power he wanted. He commanded thirteen loyal legions, a match for his enemies as well as for his allies.

By the time Caesar was ready to return to Rome, the Triumvirate had dissolved and a crisis was at hand. At Carrhae, in 53 B.C., Crassus died trying to conquer the Parthians, successors to the Persian Empire. His death broke one link between Pompey and Caesar. The death of Caesar's daughter Julia, who had been Pompey's wife, dissolved another.

As Caesar's star rose, Pompey became jealous and fearful. He did not leave Rome but governed his province through a subordinate. In the late 50s B.C. political rioting at Rome caused the Senate to appoint Pompey sole consul. This grant of unprecedented power and responsibility brought Pompey closer to the senatorial aristocracy in mutual fear of and hostility to Caesar. The Senate wanted to bring Caesar back to Rome as a private citizen after his proconsular command expired. He would then be open to attack for past illegalities. Caesar tried to avoid the trap by asking permission to stand for the consulship in absentia.

Early in January of 49 B.C. the more extreme faction in the Senate had its way. It ordered Pompey to defend the state and Caesar to lay down his command by a specified day. For Caesar this meant exile or death, so he ordered his legions to cross the Rubicon River, the boundary of his province (see Map 4-4). This action started a civil war. In 45 B.C. Caesar defeated the last forces of his enemies under Pompey's sons at Munda in Spain. The war was over, and Caesar, in Shakespeare's words, bestrode "the narrow world like a Colossus."

From the beginning of the civil war until his death in 44 B.C., Caesar spent less than a year and a half in Rome, and many of his actions were attempts to deal with immediate problems between campaigns. His innovations generally sought to make rational and orderly what was traditional and chaotic. An excellent example is Caesar's reform of the calendar. By 46 B.C. it was eighty days ahead of the proper season because the official year was lunar, containing only 355 days. Using the best scientific advice, Caesar instituted a new calendar. With minor changes by Pope Gregory XIII in the sixteenth century, it is the calendar in use today.

Another general tendency of his reforms in the political area was the elevation of the role of Italians and even provincials at the expense of the old Roman families, most of whom were his political enemies. He raised the number of senators to 900 and filled the Senate's depleted ranks with Italians and even Gauls. He was free with grants of Roman citizenship, giving the franchise to Cisalpine Gaul as a whole and to many individuals of various regions.

Caesar made few changes in the government of Rome. The Senate continued to play its role, in theory. But its increased size, its packing with supporters of Caesar, and his own monopoly of military power made the whole thing a sham. He treated the Senate as his creature, sometimes with disdain. His legal position rested on several powers. In 46 B.C. he was appointed dictator for ten years and in the next year for life. He also held the consulship, the immunity of a tribune (although, being a patrician, he had never been a tribune), the chief priesthood of the state, and a new position, prefect of morals, which gave him the censorial power. Usurping the elective power of the assemblies, he even named the magistrates for the next few years, because he expected to be away in the East.

The enemies of Caesar were quick to seize on every pretext to accuse Caesar of aiming at monarchy. A senatorial conspiracy gathered strength under the leadership of Gaius Cassius Longinus and Marcus Junius Brutus and included some sixty senators in all. On March 15, 44 B.C., Caesar entered the Senate, characteristically without a bodyguard, and was stabbed to death. The assassins regarded themselves as heroic tyrannicides but did not have a clear plan of action to follow the tyrant's death. No doubt they simply expected the republic to be restored in the old way, but things had gone too far for that. There followed instead thirteen more years of civil war, at the end of which the republic received its final burial.

The Second Triumvirate and the Emergence of Octavian

Caesar had had legions of followers, and he had a capable successor in Mark Antony. But the dictator had named his eighteen-year-old grandnephew, Gaius Octavius (63 B.C.–A.D. 14), as his heir and had left him three quarters of his vast wealth. To everyone's surprise, the sickly and inexperienced young man came to Rome to

Caesar Tells What Persuaded Him to Cross the Rubicon

Julius Caesar competed with Pompey for the leading position in the Roman state. Complicated maneuvers failed to produce a compromise. In the following selection Caesar gives his side of the story of the beginning of the Roman civil war. Note that Caesar writes about himself in the third person.

♦ *This selection, of course makes the case for Caesar's actions. From your reading in this book, and from any other information you have, how do you think Pompey might have replied? On constitutional and legal grounds who had the stronger case? On grounds of practical considerations and of the welfare of the Roman state, which party, if either, deserved support? If neither did, why not?*

These things being made known to Caesar, he harangued his soldiers; he reminded them "of the wrongs done to him at all times by his enemies, and complained that Pompey had been alienated from him and led astray by them through envy and a malicious opposition to his glory, though he had always favored and promoted Pompey's honor and dignity. He complained that an innovation had been introduced into the republic, that the intercession of the tribunes, which had been restored a few years before by Sulla, was branded as a crime, and suppressed by force of arms; that Sulla, who had stripped the tribunes of every other power, had, nevertheless, left the privilege of intercession unrestrained; that Pompey, who pretended to restore what they had lost, had taken away the privileges which they formerly had; that whenever the senate decreed, "that the magistrates should take care that the republic sustained no injury' (by which words and decree the Roman people were obliged to repair to arms), it was only when pernicious laws were proposed; when the tribunes attempted vio-lent measures; when the people seceded, and possessed themselves of the temples and eminences of the city; (and these instances of former times, he showed them were expiated by the fate of Saturninus and the Gracchi): that nothing of this kind was attempted now, nor even thought of: that no law was promulgated, no intrigue with the people going forward, no secession made; he exhorted them to defend from the malice of his enemies the reputation and honor of that general under whose command they had for nine years most successfully supported the state; fought many successful battles, and subdued all Gaul and Germany." The soldiers of the thirteenth legion, which was present (for in the beginning of the disturbances he had called it out, his other legions not having yet arrived), all cry out that they are ready to defend their general, and the tribunes of the commons, from all injuries.

Having made himself acquainted with the disposition of his soldiers, Caesar set off with that legion to Ariminum, and there met the tribunes, who had fled to him for protection.

Julius Caesar, Commentaries, *trans. by W. A. McDevitte and W. S. Bosh (New York: Harper and Brothers, 1887), pp. 249–250.*

claim his legacy. He gathered an army, won the support of many of Caesar's veterans, and became a figure of importance—the future Augustus.

At first, the Senate tried to use Octavius against Antony, but when the conservatives rejected his request for the consulship, Octavius broke with them. Following Sulla's grim precedent, he took his army and marched on Rome. There he finally assumed his adopted name, C. Julius Caesar Octavianus. Modern historians refer to him at this stage in his career as

Octavian, although he insisted on being called Caesar. In August of 43 B.C. he became consul and declared the assassins of Caesar outlaws. Brutus and Cassius had an army of their own, so Octavian sought help on the Caesarean side. He made a pact with Mark Antony and M. Aemilius Lepidus, a Caesarean governor of the western provinces. They took control of Rome and had themselves appointed "Triumvirs to put the republic in order," with great powers. This was the Second Triumvirate and, unlike the first, it was legally empowered to rule almost dictatorially.

The need to pay their troops, their own greed, and the passion that always emerges in civil wars led the triumvirs to start a wave of proscriptions that outdid even those of Sulla. In 42 B.C. the triumviral army defeated Brutus and Cassius at Philippi in Macedonia, and the last hope of republican restoration died with the tyrannicides. Each of the triumvirs received a command. The junior partner, Lepidus, was given Africa, Antony took the rich and inviting East, and Octavian got the West and the many troubles that went with it.

Octavian had to fight a war against Sextus, the son of Pompey, who held Sicily. He also had to settle 100,000 veterans in Italy, confiscating much property and making many enemies. Helped by his friend Agrippa, he defeated Sextus Pompey in 36 B.C. Among his close associates was Maecenas, who served him as adviser and diplomatic agent. Maecenas helped manage the delicate relations with Antony and Lepidus, but perhaps equally important was his role as a patron of the arts. Among his clients were Vergil and Horace, both of whom did important work for Octavian. They painted him as a restorer of traditional Roman values, as a man of ancient Roman lineage and of traditional Roman virtues, and as the culmination of Roman destiny. More and more he was identified with Italy and the West as well as with order, justice, and virtue.

Meanwhile Antony was in the East, chiefly at Alexandria with Cleopatra, the queen of Egypt. In 36 B.C. he attacked Parthia, with disastrous results. Octavian had promised to send troops to support Antony's Parthian campaign but never sent them. Antony was forced to depend on the East for support, and to some considerable degree this meant reliance on Cleopatra.

Octavian clearly understood the advantage of representing himself as the champion of the West, Italy, and Rome. Meanwhile he represented Antony as the man of the East, the dupe of Cleopatra, her tool in establishing Alexandria as the center of an empire and herself as its ruler. Such propaganda made it easier for Caesareans to abandon their veteran leader in favor of the

A profile of Brutus, one of Caesar's assassins, appeared on this silver coin. The reverse shows a cap of liberty between two daggers and reads "Ides of March." [H. Roger Viollet]

(a)

(b)

The Death of Cicero

In the civil war that followed the assassination of Julius Caesar, Cicero opposed the coalition of his successors, the Second Triumvirate, made up of Caesar's nephew Octavian, Marcus Lepidus, and Mark Antony. He was especially opposed to Mark Antony, whose men hunted him down and killed him. Appian tells the story.

♦ Who was responsible for Cicero's death? Why did he, or they, want him dead? Read the section on Cicero in the next chapter and see if you can think of any other motives his killers might have had. What was it about the time in which Cicero lived that made it dangerous for a Roman to engage in politics? Why would anyone pursue a political career in such times?

Cicero, who had held supreme power after Caesar's death, as much as a public speaker could, was proscribed, together with his son, his brother, and his brother's son and all his household, his faction, and his friends. He fled in a small boat, but as he could not endure the sea-sickness, he landed and went to a country place of his own near Caieta, a town of Italy, which I visited to gain knowledge of this lamentable affair, and here he remained quiet. While the searchers were approaching (for of all others Antony sought for him most eagerly and the rest did so for Antony's sake), ravens flew into his chamber and awakened him from sleep by their croaking, and pulled off his bed-covering, until his servants, divining that this was a warning from one of the gods, put him in a litter and again conveyed him toward the sea, going cautiously through a dense thicket. Many soldiers were hurrying around in squads inquiring if Cicero had been seen anywhere. Some people, moved by good-will and pity, said that he had already put to sea; but a shoemaker, a client of Clodius, who had been a most bitter enemy of Cicero, pointed out the path to Laena, the centurion, who was pursuing with a small force. The latter ran after him, and seeing slaves mustering for the defence in much larger number than the force under his own command, he called out by way of stratagem, "Centurions in the rear, to the front!"

Thereupon the slaves, thinking that more soldiers were coming, were terror-stricken, and Laena, although he had been once saved by Cicero when under trial, drew his head out of the litter and cut it off, striking it three times, or rather sawing it off by reason of his inexperience. He also cut off the hand with which Cicero had written the speeches against Antony as a tyrant, which he had entitled Philippies in imitation of those of Demosthenes. Then some of the soldiers hastened on horseback and others on shipboard to convey the good news quickly to Antony. The latter was sitting in front of the tribunal in the forum when Laena, a long distance off, shewed him the head and hand by lifting them up and shaking them. Antony was delighted beyond measure. He crowned the centurion and gave him 250,000 Attic drachmas in addition to the stipulated reward for killing the man who had been his greatest and most bitter enemy.

Appian, Civil Wars *4. 1. 2–3, trans. by Horace White (London and New York: William Heinemann and The Macmillan Company, 1913).*

young heir of Caesar. It did not help Antony's cause that he agreed to a public festival at Alexandria in 34 B.C., where he and Cleopatra sat on golden thrones. She was proclaimed "Queen of Kings," her son by Julius Caesar was named "King of Kings," and parts of the Roman Empire were doled out to her various children.

By 32 B.C. all pretense of cooperation ended.

Octavian and Antony each tried to put the best face on what was essentially a struggle for power. Lepidus had been put aside some years earlier. Antony sought senatorial support and promised to restore the republican constitution. Octavian seized and published what was alleged to be the will of Antony, revealing his gifts of provinces to the children of Cleopatra. This caused the conflict to take the form of East against West, Rome against Alexandria.

In 31 B.C.. the matter was settled at Actium in western Greece. Agrippa, Octavian's best general, cut off the enemy by land and sea, forcing and winning a naval battle. Antony and Cleopatra escaped to Egypt, but Octavian pursued them to Alexandria, where both committed suicide. The civil wars were over, and at the age of thirty-two Octavian was absolute master of the Mediterranean world. His power was enormous, but so too was the task before him. He had to restore peace, prosperity, and confidence. All of these required establishing a constitution that would reflect the new realities without offending unduly the traditional republican prejudices that still had so firm a grip on Rome and Italy.

———————◆———————

The history of the Roman Republic was almost as sharp a departure from the common experiences of ancient civilizations as that of the Greek city-states. A monarchy in its earliest-known form, Rome quite early expelled its king, abandoned the institution of monarchy, and established an aristocratic republic somewhat like the poleis *of the Greek Dark Ages. But unlike the Greeks, the Romans continued to be in touch with foreign neighbors, including the far more civilized urban monarchies of the Etruscans. Nonetheless, the Romans clung faithfully to their republican institutions. For a long time the Romans remained a nation of farmers and herdsmen, to whom trade was relatively unimportant, especially outside Italy.*

Over time the caste distinctions between patricians and plebeians became unimportant. They were replaced by distinctions based on wealth and, even more important, aristocracy, where the significant distinction was between noble families, who held the highest elected offices in the state, and those outside the nobil-

The Fall of the Roman Republic	
133 B.C.	Tribunate of Tiberius Gracchus
123–122 B.C.	Tribunate of Gaius Gracchus
111–105 B.C.	Jugurthine War
104–100 B.C.	Consecutive consulships of Marius
90–88 B.C.	War against the Italian allies
88 B.C.	Sulla's march on Rome
82 B.C.	Sulla assumes dictatorship
71 B.C.	Crassus crushes rebellion of Spartacus
71 B.C.	Pompey defeats Sertorius in Spain
70 B.C.	Consulship of Crassus and Pompey
60 B.C.	Formation of First Triumvirate
58–50 B.C.	Caesar in Gaul
53 B.C.	Crassus killed in Battle of Carrhae
49 B.C.	Caesar crosses Rubicon; Civil War begins
48 B.C.	Pompey defeated at Pharsalus; killed in Egypt
46–44 B.C.	Caesar's dictatorship
45 B.C.	End of Civil War
43 B.C.	Formation of Second Triumvirate
42 B.C.	Triumvirs defeat Brutus and Cassius at Philippi
31 B.C.	Octavian and Agrippa defeat Anthony at Actium

ity. The Roman Republic from the first found itself engaged in almost continuous warfare with its neighbors—either in defense of its own territory, in fights over disputed territory, or in defense of other cities or states who were friends and allies of Rome.

Both internally and in their foreign relations the Romans were a very legalistic people, placing great importance on traditional behavior encoded into laws. Although backed by the powerful authority of the magistrates at home and the potent Roman army abroad, the laws were based on experience, common sense, and equity. Roman law aimed at stability and fairness, and it succeeded well enough that few people who lived under it wanted to do away with it. It lived on and grew during the imperial period and beyond. During the European Middle Ages it played an important part in the revival of the West and continued to exert an influence into modern times.

The force of Roman arms, the high quality of Roman roads and bridges, and the pragmatic character of Roman law helped create something unique: an empire ruled by a republic, first a large one on land including all of Italy, later one that commanded the shores of the entire Mediterranean and quite a distance inland in many places. Rome controlled an area that bears comparison with some of the empires of the East. It acquired that territory, wealth, and power in a state managed by annual magistrates elected by the male Roman citizens and by an aristocratic Senate, which had to take notice of popular assemblies and a published, impersonal code of law. It achieved its greatness with an army of citizens and allies, without a monarchy or a regular bureaucracy.

The temptations and responsibilities of governing a vast and rich empire, however, finally proved too much for the republican constitution. Trade grew, and with it a class of merchants and financiers called equestrians that was neither aristocratic nor agricultural, but increasingly powerful. The influx of masses of slaves captured in war undermined the small farmers who had been the backbone of the Roman state and its army. As many of them were forced to leave their farms, they moved to the cities, chiefly to Rome, where they had no productive role. Conscripted armies of farmers serving relatively short terms gave way to volunteer armies of landless men serving as professionals and expecting to be rewarded for their services with gifts of land or money. The generals of these armies were not annual magistrates controlled by the Senate and the constitution but ambitious military leaders seeking glory and political advantage.

The result was civil war and the destruction of the republic. The conquest of a vast empire moved the Romans away from their unusual historical traditions toward the more familiar path of empire trodden by older rulers in Egypt and Mesopotamia.

Review Questions

1. In what ways did the institutions of family and clientage and the establishment of patrician and plebeian classes contribute to the stability of the early Roman republic? How important was education to the success of the republic? the institution of slavery?

2. What was "the struggle of the orders"? What methods did plebeians use to get what they wanted? How was Roman society different after the struggle ended?

3. Discuss Rome's expansion to 265 B.C. How was Rome able to conquer and control Italy? In their relations with Greece and Asia Minor in the second century B.C., were the Romans looking for security? wealth? power? fame?

4. Explain the clash between the Romans and the Carthaginians in the First and Second Punic wars. Could the wars have been avoided? How did Rome benefit from its victory over Carthage? What problems were created by this victory?

5. What social, economic, and political problems did Italy have in the second century B.C.? What were the main proposals of Tiberius Gaius Gracchus? What questions about Roman society did they raise? Why did the proposals fail?

6. What were the problems that plagued the Roman republic in the last century? What caused these problems and how did the Romans try to solve them? To what extent was the republic destroyed by ambitious generals who loved power more than Rome itself?

Suggested Readings

F. E. ADCOCK, *The Roman Art of War Under the Republic* (1940). A basic study of the subject.

E. BADIAN, *Foreign Clientelae* (1958). A brilliant study of the Roman idea of a client–patron relationship extended to foreign affairs.

E. BADIAN, *Roman Imperialism in the Late Republic*, 2nd ed. (1968).

A. H. BERNSTEIN, *Tiberius Sempronius Gracchus: Tradition and Apostasy* (1978). A new interpretation of Tiberius's place in Roman politics.

J. BOARDMAN, J. GRIFFIN, and O. MURRAY, *The Oxford History of the Roman World* (1990). An encyclopedic approach to the varieties of the Roman experience.

P. A. BRUNT, *Social Conflicts in the Roman Republic* (1971). A fine study by a master of the subject.

T. CORNELL and J. MATTHEWS, *Atlas of the Roman*

World (1982). Much more than the title indicates, this book presents a comprehensive view of the Roman world in its physical and cultural setting.

R. M. ERRINGTON, *The Dawn of Empire: Rome's Rise to Power* (1972). An account of Rome's conquest of the Mediterranean.

M. GELZER, *Caesar: Politician and Statesman,* trans. by P. Needham (1968). The best biography of Caesar.

E. S. GRUEN, *The Hellenistic World and the Coming of Rome* (1984). A new interpretation of Rome's conquest of the eastern Mediterranean.

E. S. GRUEN, *The Last Generation of the Roman Republic* (1973). An interesting but controversial interpretation of the fall of the republic.

W. V. HARRIS, *War and Imperialism in Republican Rome, 327–70 B.C.* (1975). An analysis of Roman attitudes and intentions concerning imperial expansion and war.

L. P. HOMO, *Primitive Italy and the Beginning of Roman Imperialism* (1967). A study of early Roman relations with the peoples of Italy.

A. KEAVENEY, *Lucullus: A Life* (1992). A biography of the famous Roman epicure.

J. F. LAZENBY, *Hannibal's War* (1978). An excellent military history of the Second Punic War.

F. B. MARSH, *A History of the Roman World from 146 to 30 B.C.,* 3rd ed., rev. by H. H. Scullard (1963). An excellent narrative account.

J. C. MEYER, *Pre-Republican Rome* (1983). A good account of early Rome.

C. NICOLET, *The World of the Citizen in Republican Rome* (1980). A valuable study of the meaning of Roman citizenship.

M. PALLOTTINO, *The Etruscans,* 6th ed. (1974). Makes especially good use of archaeological evidence.

E. T. SALMON, *The Making of Roman Italy* (1980). The story of Roman expansion on the Italian peninsula.

E. T. SALMON, *Roman Colonization Under the Republic* (1970). An account of the character and importance of the Roman colony.

H. H. SCULLARD, *A History of the Roman World 753–146 B.C,* 4th ed. (1980). An unusually fine narrative history with useful critical notes.

H. H. SCULLARD, *From the Gracchi to Nero,* 5th ed. (1982). A work of the same character and quality.

A. N. SHERWIN-WHITE, *Roman Citizenship* (1939). A useful study of the Roman franchise and its extension to other peoples.

D. STOCKTON, *Cicero: A Political Biography* (1971). A readable and interesting study.

D. STOCKTON, *The Gracchi* (1979). An interesting analytical narrative.

L. R. TAYLOR, *Party Policies in the Age of Caesar* (1949). A fascinating analysis of Roman political practices.

B. H. WARMINGTON, *Carthage* (1960). A good survey.

R. D. WEIGEL, *Lepidus: The Tarnished Triumvir* (1992). A biography of the less famous partner of Mark Antony and Augustus.

G. WILLIAMS, *The Nature of Roman Poetry* (1970). An unusually graceful and perceptive literary study.

A portrait statue of the Emperor Gallus, who ruled briefly from 251 to 253 A.D. He came from lowly ancestors and was proud of his skill as a wrestler. The intimidating pose and size of the statue (it is nearly eight feet tall) suggest a shift in the late empire away from the classical ideals of the Augustan age. [The Metropolitan Museum of Art, Rogers Fund, 1905 (05.30)]

5

The Roman Empire

Key Topics in This Chapter
- ◆ The Augustan constitution
- ◆ The organization and government of the Roman Empire
- ◆ Culture and civilization from the late republic through the imperial period
- ◆ The early history of Christianity
- ◆ The decline and fall of Rome

The victory of Augustus put an end to the deadly period of civil strife that had begun with the murder of Tiberius Gracchus. The establishment of a monarchy, at first concealed in republican forms but gradually more obvious, brought a long period of peace. Rome's unquestioned control of the entire Mediterranean permitted the growth of trade and a prosperity in the first two centuries of the Roman Empire not to be equalled for more than a millennium.

Management of the empire outside Italy became more benign and efficient. With shared citizenship, the provinces usually accepted Roman rule readily and even enthusiastically. Latin became the official language of the western part of the empire and Greek the official language in the East. This permitted the growth and spread of a common culture, today called Classical Civilization, throughout the empire. The same conditions fostered a great outburst of activity and excellence in the arts. The loss of political freedom, however, brought a decline in the vitality of the great Roman genre of rhetoric.

Christianity emerged in the first century A.D. as one of many competing Eastern cults. It continued to spread and attract converts, winning toleration and finally dominance in the fourth century. Christianity was powerfully shaped by the world of imperial Rome, absorbing and using classical culture even while fighting against it.

The third century A.D. brought serious attacks on several of Rome's frontiers, causing political and economic chaos. For a time such emperors as Diocletian (r. 284–305) and Constantine (r. 306–337) instituted heroic measures to restore order. Their solutions involved increased centralization, militarization, and attempts to control closely every aspect of life. The emperors became more exalted and remote, the people increasingly burdened with heavy taxes even as the loss of economic freedom reduced their ability to pay. At last a new wave of barbarian attacks proved irresistible, and the Roman Empire in the West ended in the second half of the fifth century.

The Augustan Principate

If the problems facing Octavian after the Battle of Actium in 31 B.C. were great, so too were his resources for addressing them. He was the master of a vast military force, the only one in the Roman world, and he had loyal and capable assistants. Of enormous importance was the rich treasury of Egypt, which Octavian treated as his personal property. He was helped by the great eagerness of the people of Italy for an end to civil war and a return to peace, order, and prosperity. In exchange for these most people were prepared to accept a considerable abandonment of republican practices and to give significant power to an able ruler. The memory of Julius Caesar's fate, however, was still fresh in Octavian's mind. Its lesson was that it was dangerous to flaunt unprecedented powers and to disregard all republican traditions.

Octavian did not create his constitutional solution at a single stroke. It developed gradually as he tried new devices to fit his perception of changing conditions. Behind all the republican

trappings and the apparent sharing of authority with the Senate, the government of Octavian, like that of his successors, was a monarchy. All real power, both civil and military, lay with the ruler—whether he was called by the unofficial title of "first citizen" (*princeps*), like Octavian, the founder of the regime, or "emperor" (*imperator*), like those who followed. During the civil war Octavian's powers came from his triumviral status, whose dubious legality and unrepublican character were an embarrassment. From 31 B.C. on, he held the consulship each year, but this circumstance was not strictly legal or very satisfactory either.

On January 13, 27 B.C., he put forward a new plan in dramatic style, coming before the Senate to give up all his powers and provinces. In what was surely a rehearsed response, the Senate begged him to reconsider. At last he agreed to accept the provinces of Spain, Gaul, and Syria with proconsular power for military command and to retain the consulship in Rome. The other provinces would be governed by the Senate as before. Because the provinces he retained were border provinces that contained twenty of Rome's twenty-six legions, his true power was undiminished. The Senate, however, responded with almost hysterical gratitude, voting him many honors. Among them was the semireligious title "Augustus," which carried implications of veneration, majesty, and holiness. From this time on, historians speak of Rome's first emperor as Augustus and of his regime as the Principate. This would have pleased him, for it helps conceal the novel, unrepublican nature of the regime and the naked power on which it rested.

In 23 B.C. Augustus resigned his consulship and held that office only rarely thereafter. Instead he was voted two powers that were to be the base of his rule thenceforth: the proconsular *imperium maius* and the tribunician power. The former made his proconsular power greater than that of any other proconsul and permitted him to exercise it even within the city of Rome. The latter gave him the right to conduct public business in the assemblies and the Senate, gave him the power of the veto, the tribunician sacrosanctity (immunity from arrest and punishment), and a connection with the Roman popular tradition. Thereafter, with only minor changes,

Augustus's powers remained those conferred by the settlement of 23 B.C.

Administration

Augustus made important changes in the government of Rome, Italy, and the provinces. Most of these had the effect of reducing inefficiency and corruption, ending the danger to peace and order from ambitious individuals, and reducing the distinction between Romans and Italians, senators and equestrians. The assemblies lost their significance as a working part of the constitution, and the Senate took on most of the functions of the assemblies. Augustus purged the old Senate of undesirable members and fixed its number at 600. He recruited its members from wealthy men of good character, who entered after serving as lesser magistrates. Augustus controlled the elections and saw to it that promising young men, whatever their origin, served the state as administrators and provincial governors. In this way equestrians and Italians who had no connection with the Roman aristocracy entered the Senate in great numbers. For all his power Augustus was careful always to treat the Senate with respect and honor.

Augustus divided Rome into regions and wards with elected local officials. He gave the city, with its rickety wooden tenements, its first public fire department and rudimentary police force. Grain distribution to the poor was carefully controlled and limited, and organizations were created for providing an adequate water supply. The Augustan period was one of great prosperity, based on the wealth brought in by the conquest of Egypt, on the great increase in commerce and industry made possible by general peace and a vast program of public works, and on a strong return to successful small farming on the part of Augustus's resettled veterans.

The union of political and military power in the hands of the *princeps* made it possible for him to install rational, efficient, and stable government in the provinces for the first time. The emperor, in effect, chose the governors, removed the incompetent or rapacious, and allowed the effective ones to keep their provinces for longer periods. Also, he provided for much greater local autonomy, giving considerable responsibility to

This statue of Emperor Augustus (r. 27 B.C.–A.D. 14), now in the Vatican, stood in the villa of Augustus's wife Livia. The figures on the elaborate breastplate are all of symbolic significance. At the top, for example, Dawn in her chariot brings in a new day under the protective mantle of the sky god; in the center, Tiberius, Augustus's future successor, accepts the return of captured Roman army standards from a barbarian prince; and at the bottom, Mother Earth offers a horn of plenty. [Charitable Foundation, Leonard von Matt]

the upper classes in the provincial cities and towns and to the tribal leaders in less civilized areas.

The Army and Defense

The main external problem facing Augustus—and one that haunted all his successors—was the northern frontier (see Map 5-1 on page 172). Rome needed to pacify the regions to the north and the northeast of Italy and to find defensible

The Powers and Titles of the Emperors

Augustus's victory in the civil war put an end to any hope for the revival of the republic. In its place he erected a monarchy cloaked in republican forms that became the system we call Imperial Rome. Over time the rulers removed the veil covering their autocracy and declared themselves emperors without embarrassment. Dio Cassius (ca. A.D. 155–230), writing when autocratic imperial rule was undisguised, describes the powers and titles acquired by the emperors.

◆ *Why did the emperors retain republican offices and their titles instead of wiping the slate clean? Which imperial titles conferred which specific powers? How were offices invented for republican government changed to serve a monarchical one? If the titles "Augustus" and "Caesar" conferred "no peculiar power," as Dio Cassius says here, why did the emperors use them?*

In this way the power of both people and senate passed entirely into the hands of Augustus, and from his time there was, strictly speaking, a monarchy. . . .

The name of monarchy, to be sure, the Romans so detested that they called their emperors neither dictators nor kings nor anything of the sort; yet since the final authority for the government devolves upon them, they must needs be kings. The offices established by the laws, it is true, are maintained even now, except that of censor; but the entire direction and administration is absolutely in accordance with the wishes of the one in power at the time. And yet, in order to preserve the appearance of having this power by virtue of the laws and not because of their own domination, the emperors have taken to themselves all the functions, including the titles, of the offices which under the republic and by the free gift of the people were powerful, with the single exception of the dictatorship. Thus, they very often became consuls, and they are always styled proconsuls whenever they are outside the pomerium [the sacred boundary of the city of Rome]. The name of *"imperator"* is held by them all for life, not only by those who have won victories in battle, but also by those who have not, in token of their independent authority, and this has displaced the titles "king" and "dictator." These last titles they have never assumed

frontiers against the recurring waves of barbarians. Augustus's plan was to push forward into central Europe to create the shortest possible defensive line. The eastern part of the plan succeeded, and the campaign in the West started well. In A.D. 9, however, a revolt broke out led by the German tribal leader Herrmann, or Arminius as the Romans called him. He ambushed and destroyed three Roman legions, and the aged Augustus abandoned the campaign, leaving a problem of border defense that caused great trouble for his successors.

Under Augustus, the armed forces achieved true professional status. Enlistment, chiefly by Italians, was for twenty years, but the pay was relatively good with occasional bonuses and the promise of a pension on retirement in the form of money or a plot of land. Together with the auxiliaries from the provinces, these forces formed a frontier army of about 300,000 men. In normal times this number was barely enough to hold the line.

The army permanently based in the provinces played a vital role in bringing Roman culture to the natives. The soldiers spread their language and customs, often marrying local women and settling down in the area of their service. They attracted merchants, who often became the nuclei of new towns and cities that became centers of Roman civilization. As time

since the time they first fell out of use in the conduct of the government, but the functions of those offices are secured to them under the appellation of *"imperator."* By virtue of the titles named they secure the right to make levies, to collect funds, declare war, make peace, rule foreigners and citizens alike everywhere and always,—even to the extent of being able to put to death both knights and senators inside the pomerium,—and all the other privileges once granted to the consuls and other officials possessing independent authority; and by virtue of holding the censorship they investigate our lives and morals as well as take the census, enrolling some in the equestrian and senatorial classes and erasing the names of others from these classes, according to their will. By virtue of being consecrated in all the priesthoods and of their right to bestow most of these positions upon others, as well as from the fact that, even if two or three persons hold the imperial office at the same time, one of them is high priest, they hold in their own hands supreme authority over all matters both profane and sacred. The tribunician power, as it is called, which used to be conferred only upon men of the greatest influence, gives them the right to nullify the effects of measures taken by any other official, in case they do not approve it, and makes them immune from scurrilous abuse; and if they appear to be wronged in even the slightest degree, not merely by deed, but even by word, they may destroy the guilty party, as one accursed, without a trial. . . .

Thus by virtue of these democratic names they have clothed themselves with all the powers of the government, to such an extent that they actually possess all the prerogatives of kings except their paltry title. For the appellation "Caesar" or "Augustus" confers upon them no peculiar power, but merely shows in the one case that they are heirs of the family to which they belong, and in the other the splendour of their official position. The term "Father" perhaps gives them a certain authority over us all—the authority which fathers once had over their children; yet it did not signify this at first, but betokened honour, and served as an admonition both to them, that they should love their subjects as they would their children, and to their subjects, that they should revere them as they would their fathers.

Dio Cassius, Roman History *53.17–19, trans. by Earnest Cary (London: Loeb Classical Library and William Heinemann, 1916).*

passed, the provincials on the frontiers became Roman citizens who helped strengthen Rome's defenses against the barbarians outside.

Religion and Morality

A century of political strife and civil war had undermined many of the foundations of traditional Roman society. Augustus thought it desirable to try to repair the damage. So he undertook a program aimed at preserving and restoring the traditional values of the family and religion in Rome and Italy. He introduced laws curbing adultery and divorce and encouraging early marriage and the procreation of legitimate children. He set an example of austere behavior in his own household and even banished his daughter, Julia, whose immoral behavior had become public knowledge.

He worked at restoring the dignity of formal Roman religion, building many temples, reviving old cults, and reorganizing and invigorating the priestly colleges. He banned the worship of newly introduced foreign gods. Writers whom he patronized, such as Vergil, pointed out his family's legendary connection with Venus. During his lifetime he did not accept divine honors, though he was deified after his death. As with Julius Caesar, a state cult was dedicated to his worship.

MAP 5-1 THE ROMAN EMPIRE, 14 A.D. *This map shows the growth of the empire under Augustus and its extent at his death.*

Civilization of the Ciceronian and Augustan Ages

The high point of Roman culture came in the last century of the republic and during the principate of Augustus. Both periods reflected the dominant influence of Greek culture, especially its Hellenistic mode. The education of Romans of the upper classes was in Greek rhetoric, philosophy, and literature, which also served as the models for Roman writers and artists. Yet in spirit and sometimes in form, the art and writing of both periods show uniquely Roman qualities, though each in different ways.

The Late Republic

CICERO   The towering literary figure of the late republic was Cicero (106–43 B.C.). He is most famous for his orations delivered in the law courts and in the Senate. Together with a considerable body of his private letters, these orations provide us with a clearer and fuller insight into his mind than into that of any other figure in antiquity. We see the political life of his period largely through his eyes. He also wrote treatises on rhetoric, ethics, and politics that put Greek philosophical ideas into Latin terminology and at the same time changed them to suit Roman conditions and values.

Cicero's own views provide support for his moderate and conservative practicality. He believed in a world governed by divine and natural law that human reason could perceive and human institutions reflect. He looked to law, custom, and tradition to produce both stability and liberty. His literary style, as well as his values and ideas, was an important legacy for the

Roman soldiers build a fort on the Danube. Along the Rhine and Danube frontier, the Roman army built many forts, which often became the nuclei of new cities. [Alinari/Art Resource, N.Y.]

Middle Ages and, reinterpreted, for the Renaissance. He was killed at the order of Mark Antony, whose political opponent he had been during the civil wars after the death of Julius Caesar.

HISTORY   The last century of the republic produced some historical writing, much of which is lost to us. Sallust (86–35 B.C.) wrote a history of the years 78–67 B.C., but only a few fragments remain to remind us of his reputation as the greatest of republican historians. His surviving work consists of two pamphlets on the Jugurthine War and on the Catilinarian conspiracy of 63 B.C. They reveal his Caesarean and antisenatorial prejudices and the stylistic influence of Thucydides.

Julius Caesar wrote important treatises on the Gallic and civil wars. They are not fully rounded historical accounts but chiefly military narratives written from Caesar's point of view and with propagandist intent. Their objective manner (Caesar always referred to himself in the third person) and their direct, simple, and vigorous style make them persuasive even today. They must have been most effective with their immediate audience.

LAW   The period from the Gracchi to the fall of the republic was important in the development of Roman law. Before that time Roman law was essentially national and had developed chiefly by juridical decisions, case by case. Contact with foreign peoples and the influence of Greek ideas, however, forced a change. From the last century of the republic on, the edicts of the praetors had increasing importance in developing the Roman legal code. They interpreted and even changed and added to existing law. Quite early the edicts of the magistrates who dealt with foreigners developed the idea of the *jus gentium,* or law of peoples, as opposed to that arising strictly from the experience of the Romans. In the first century B.C. the influence of Greek thought made the idea of *jus gentium* identical with that of the *jus naturale,* or natural law, taught by the Stoics. It was this view of a world ruled by divine reason that Cicero enshrined in his treatise on the law, *De Legibus.*

POETRY   The time of Cicero was also the period of two of Rome's greatest poets, Lucretius and Catullus, each representing a different aspect of Rome's poetic tradition. The Hellenistic poets and literary theorists saw two functions for the poet, as entertainer and as teacher. They thought the best poet combined both roles, and the Romans adopted the same view. When Naevius and Ennius wrote epics on Roman history, they combined historical and moral instruction with pleasure. Lucretius (ca. 99–55 B.C.) pursued a similar path in his epic poem *De Rerum Natura (On the Nature of the World).* In it he set forth the scientific and philosophical ideas of Epicurus and Democritus with the zeal of a missionary trying to save society from fear and superstition. He knew that his doctrine might be bitter medicine to the reader: "That is why I have tried to administer it to you in the dulcet strain of poesy, coated with the sweet honey of the Muses."[1]

Catullus (ca. 84–54 B.C.) was a thoroughly different kind of poet. He wrote poems that were personal, even autobiographical. In imitation of the Alexandrians, he wrote short poems filled with learned allusions to mythology, but he far surpassed his models in intensity of feel-

[1] *I, Lucretius,* De Rerum Natura, *lines 931ff.*

Roman Law

One of the most important achievements of Roman civilization was the establishment over a wide area of a code of law derived from experience and custom but based on principles thought to apply universally and organized according to reason. It had a powerful influence in shaping the character of Western civilization long after the fall of the empire. The following selection, from the Digest, *compiled at the order of the emperor Justinian in the sixth century A.D., quotes the* Institutes *of Ulpian, a leading jurist of the third century A.D. It discusses the fundamental issues underlying the Roman conception of law in the imperial period.*

✦ *According to this document, for what reason should a Roman citizen obey the law? How does this rationale compare with the rationale for obeying the law in the Mesopotamia of Hammurabi or in democratic Athens? What is the importance of the concept of natural law? What are the consequences of rejecting such an idea?*

Justice and Law

(Ulpian *Institutes* I) When a man means to give his attention to law, he ought first to know whence the term law (*ius*) is derived. Now it is so called from justice (*iustitia*). In fact, as Celsus neatly defines it, *ius* is the art of the good and fair. Of this art we may deservedly be called the priests; we cherish justice and profess the knowledge of the good and the fair, separating the fair from the unfair, discriminating between the permitted and the forbidden, desiring to make men good, not only by the fear of penalties, but also by the incentives of rewards, affecting, if I mistake not, a true and not a simulated philosophy.

This subject comprises two categories, public law and private law. Public law is that which reguards the constitution of the Roman state, private law that which looks to the interest of individuals; for some things are beneficial from the point of view of the state, and some with reference to private persons. Public law is concerned with sacred rites, with priests, with public officers. Private law is tripartite, being derived from the rules of natural law, or of the law of nations, or of civil law. Natural law is that which all animals have been taught by nature; this law is not peculiar to the human race, but is common to all animals which are produced on land or sea, and to the birds as well. From it comes the union of male and female, which we call matrimony, and the procreation and rearing of children; we find in fact that animals in general, even the wild beasts, are marked by acquaintance with this law. The law of nations is that which the various peoples of mankind observe. It is easy to see that it falls short of natural law, because the latter is common to all living creatures, whereas the former is common only to human beings in their mutual relations—

Justinian, Digest *I, i. iii–iv, trans. by Naphtali Lewis and Meyer Reinhold, in* Roman Civilization, *Vol. 2 (New York: Columbia University Press, 1955), p. 534.*

ing. He wrote of the joys and pains of love, he hurled invective at important contemporaries like Julius Caesar, and he amused himself in witty poetic exchanges with others. He offered no moral lessons and was not interested in Rome's glorious history and in contemporary politics. In a sense he is an example of the proud, independent, pleasure-seeking nobleman who characterized part of the aristocracy at the end of the republic.

The Age of Augustus

The spirit of the Augustan Age, the Golden Age of Roman literature, was quite different, reflecting the new conditions of society. The old aristocratic order, with its system of independent nobles following their own particular interests, was gone. So was the world of poets of the lower orders, receiving patronage from any of a number of individual aristocrats. Augustus replaced the complexity of republican patronage with a simple scheme in which all patronage flowed from the *princeps,* usually through his chief cultural adviser, Maecenas.

The major poets of this time, Vergil and Horace, had lost their property during the civil wars. The patronage of the *princeps* allowed them the leisure and the security to write poetry; at the same time it made them dependent on him and limited their freedom of expression. They wrote on subjects that were useful for his policies and that glorified him and his family. These poets were not mere propagandists, however. It seems clear that mostly they were persuaded of the virtues of Augustus and his reign and sang its praises with some degree of sincerity. Because they were poets of genius, they were also able to maintain a measure of independence in their work.

VERGIL   Vergil (70–19 B.C.) was the most important of the Augustan poets. His first important works, the *Eclogues* or *Bucolics,* are pastoral idylls in a somewhat artificial mode. The subject of the *Georgics,* however, was suggested to Vergil by Maecenas. The model here was the early Greek poet Hesiod's *Works and Days,* but the mood and purpose of Vergil's poem are far different. It pays homage to the heroic human effort to forge order and social complexity out of an ever hostile and sometimes brutal natural environment. It was also a hymn to the cults, traditions, and greatness of Italy.

All this served the purpose of glorifying Augustus's resettlement of the veterans of the civil wars on Italian farms and his elevation of Italy to special status in the empire. Vergil's greatest work is the *Aeneid,* a long national epic that succeeded in placing the history of Rome in the great tradition of the Greeks and the Trojan War. Its hero, the Trojan warrior Aeneas, personifies the ideal Roman qualities of duty, responsibility, serious purpose, and patriotism. As the

Romans' equivalent of Homer, Vergil glorified not the personal honor and excellence of the Greek epic heroes but the civic greatness represented by Augustus and the peace and prosperity that he and the Julian family had given to imperial Rome.

HORACE   Horace (65–8 B.C.) was the son of a freedman and fought on the republican side until its defeat at Philippi. He was won over to the Augustan cause by the patronage of Maecenas and by the attractions of the Augustan reforms. His *Satires* are genial and humorous. His great skills as a lyric poet are best revealed in his *Odes,* which are ingenious in their adaptation of Greek meters to the requirements of Latin verse. Two of the *Odes* are directly in praise of Augustus, and many of them glorify the new Augustan order, the imperial family, and the empire.

OVID   The career of Ovid (43 B.C.–A.D. 18) reveals the darker side of Augustan influence on the arts. He wrote light and entertaining love elegies that reveal the sophistication and the loose sexual code of a notorious sector of the Roman aristocracy. Their values and way of life were contrary to the seriousness and family-centered life Augustus was trying to foster. Ovid's *Ars Amatoria,* a poetic textbook on the art of seduction, angered Augustus and was partly responsible for the poet's exile in A.D. 8. Ovid tried to recover favor, especially with his *Fasti,* a poetic treatment of Roman religious festivals, but to no avail. His most popular work is the *Metamorphoses,* a kind of mythological epic that turns Greek myths into charming stories in a graceful and lively style. Ovid's fame did not fade with his exile and death, but his fate was an effective warning to later poets.

HISTORY   The achievements of Augustus, his emphasis on tradition, and the continuity of his regime with the glorious history of Rome encouraged both historical and antiquarian prose works. Some Augustan writers wrote scholarly treatises on history and geography in Greek. By far the most important and influential prose writer of the time, however, was Livy (59 B.C.–A.D. 17), an Italian from Padua. His *History of Rome* was written in Latin and treated the period from the legendary origins of Rome until 9 B.C. Only a fourth of his work is

Ruins of the Roman Forum. From the earliest days of the city, the Forum was the center of Roman life. Augustus had it rebuilt, and it was frequently rebuilt and refurbished by his successors, so most of the surviving buildings date to the imperial period. [The Bettmann Archive]

extant; of the rest we have only pitifully brief summaries. He based his history on earlier accounts and made no effort at original research. His great achievement was in telling the story of Rome in a continuous and impressive narrative. Its purpose was moral, and he set up historical models as examples of good and bad behavior, and, above all, patriotism. He glorified Rome's greatness and connected it with Rome's past, as Augustus tried to do.

ARCHITECTURE AND SCULPTURE Augustus was the great patron of the visual arts as he was of literature. He embarked on a building program that beautified Rome, glorified his reign, and contributed to the general prosperity and his own popularity. He filled the Campus Martius with beautiful new buildings, theaters, baths, and basilicas; the Roman Forum was rebuilt; and Augustus built a forum of his own. At its heart was the temple of Mars the Avenger,

A panel from the Ara Pacis *(Altar of Peace). The altar was dedicated in 9 B.C. It was part of a propaganda campaign—involving poetry, architecture, myth, and history—that Augustus undertook to promote himself as the savior of Rome and the restorer of peace. This panel shows the goddess Earth and her children with cattle, sheep, and other symbols of agricultural wealth. [Nimatallah/Art Resource, N.Y.]*

which commemorated Augustus's victory and the greatness of his ancestors. On Rome's Palatine Hill he built a splendid temple to his patron god, Apollo, in pursuit of his religious policy.

Most of the building was influenced by the Greek classical style, which aimed at serenity and the ideal type. The same features were visible in the portrait sculpture of Augustus and his family. The greatest monument of the age is the Altar of Peace (*Ara Pacis*) dedicated in 9 B.C. Set originally in an open space in the Campus Martius, its walls still carry a relief. Part of it shows a procession in which Augustus and his family appear to move forward, followed in order by the magistrates, the Senate, and the people of Rome. There is no better symbol of the new order.

Imperial Rome A.D. 14–180

The central problem for Augustus's successors was the position of the ruler and his relationship to the ruled. Augustus tried to cloak the monarchical nature of his government, but his successors soon abandoned all pretense. The ruler came to be called *imperator*—from which comes our word *emperor*—as well as *Caesar*. The latter title signified connection with the imperial house, and the former indicated the military power on which everything was based.

The Emperors

Because Augustus was ostensibly only the "first citizen" of a restored republic and his powers were theoretically voted him by the Senate and the people, he could not legally name his successor. In fact, he plainly designated his heirs by lavishing favors on them and by giving them a share in the imperial power and responsibility. Tiberius (r. A.D. 14–37),[2] his immediate successor, was at first embarrassed by the ambiguity of his new role, but soon the monarchical and hereditary nature of the regime became patent. Gaius (Caligula, r. A.D. 37–41), Claudius (r. A.D. 41–54), and Nero (r. A.D. 54–68) were all descended from either Augustus or his wife, Livia, and all were elevated because of that fact.

[2]*Dates for emperors give the years of each reign.*

This cameo shows profiles of the Emperor Claudius and his wife, Agrippina the younger, superimposed over profiles of Germanicus, the nephew of the Emperor Tiberius, and his wife Agrippina the elder, mother of the wife of Claudius. [Kunsthistorisches Museum, Vienna]

In A.D. 41 the naked military basis of imperial rule was revealed when the Praetorian Guard dragged the lame, stammering, and frightened Claudius from behind a curtain and made him emperor. In A.D. 68 the frontier legions learned what the historian Tacitus called "the secret of Empire . . . that an emperor could be made elsewhere than at Rome." Nero's incompetence and unpopularity, and especially his inability to control his armies, led to a serious rebellion in Gaul in A.D. 68. The year 69 saw four different emperors assume power in quick succession as different Roman armies took turns placing their commanders on the throne.

Vespasian (r. A.D. 69–79) emerged victorious from the chaos, and his sons, Titus (r. A.D. 79–81) and Domitian (r. A.D. 81–96), carried forward his line, the Flavian dynasty. Vespasian was the first emperor who did not come from the old Roman nobility. He was a tough soldier who came from the Italian middle class. A good administrator and a hard-headed realist of rough wit, he resisted all attempts by flatterers to find noble ancestors for him. On his deathbed he is said to have ridiculed the practice of deifying emperors by saying, "Alas, I think I am becoming a god."

The assassination of Domitian put an end to the Flavian dynasty. Because Domitian had no close relative who had been designated as successor, the Senate put Nerva (r. A.D. 96–98) on the throne to avoid chaos. He was the first of the five "good emperors," who included Trajan (r. A.D. 98–117), Hadrian (r. A.D. 117–138), Antoninus Pius (r. A.D. 138–161), and Marcus Aurelius (r. A.D. 161–180). Until Marcus Aurelius none of these emperors had sons, and so they each followed the example set by Nerva of adopting an able senator and establishing him as successor. This rare solution to the problem of monarchical succession was, therefore, only a historical accident. The result, nonetheless, was almost a century of peaceful succession and competent rule, which ended when Marcus Aurelius allowed his incompetent son, Commodus (r. A.D. 180–192), to succeed him, with unfortunate results.

The genius of the Augustan settlement lay in its capacity to enlist the active cooperation of the upper classes and their effective organ, the Senate. The election of magistrates was taken from the assemblies and given to the Senate.

The Senate became the major center for legislation and it exercised important judicial functions. This semblance of power persuaded some contemporaries and even some modern scholars that Augustus had established a "dyarchy," a system of joint rule by *princeps* and Senate. This was never true.

The hollowness of the senatorial role became more apparent as time passed. Some emperors, like Vespasian, took pains to maintain, increase, and display the prestige and dignity of the Senate. Others, like Caligula, Nero, and Domitian, degraded the Senate and paraded their own despotic power. But from the first the Senate's powers were illusory. Magisterial elections were, in fact, controlled by the emperors, and the Senate's legislative function quickly degenerated into mere assent to what the emperor or his representatives put before it. The true function of the Senate was to be a legislative and administrative extension of the emperor's rule.

There was, of course, some real opposition to the imperial rule. It sometimes took the form of plots against the life of the emperor. Plots and the suspicion of plots led to repression, the use of spies and paid informers, book burning, and executions. The opposition consisted chiefly of senators who looked back to republican liberty for their class and who found justification in the

Rulers of the Early Empire	
27 B.C.–A.D. 14	Augustus
The Julio-Claudian Dynasty	
A.D. 14–37	Tiberius
A.D. 37–41	Gaius (Caligula)
A.D. 41–54	Claudius
A.D. 54–68	Nero
A.D. 69	Year of the Four Emperors
The Flavian Dynasty	
A.D. 69–79	Vespasian
A.D. 79–81	Titus
A.D. 81–96	Domitian
The "Good Emperors"	
A.D. 96–98	Nerva
A.D. 98–117	Trajan
A.D. 117–138	Hadrian
A.D. 138–161	Antoninus Pius
A.D. 161–180	Marcus Aurelius

Greek and Roman traditions of tyrannicide as well as in the precepts of Stoicism. Plots and repression were most common under Nero and Domitian. From Nerva to Marcus Aurelius, however, the emperors, without yielding any power, again learned to enlist the cooperation of the upper class by courteous and modest deportment.

The Administration of the Empire

The provinces flourished economically and generally accepted Roman rule easily (see Map 5-2). In the eastern provinces the emperor was worshiped as a god; even in Italy most emperors were deified after their death as long as the imperial cult established by Augustus continued. Imperial policy usually combined an attempt to unify the empire and its various peoples with a respect for local customs and differences. Roman citizenship was spread ever more widely, and by A.D. 212 almost every inhabitant of the empire was a citizen. Latin became the language of the western provinces. Although the East remained essentially Greek in language and culture, even it adopted many aspects of Roman

life. The spread of *Romanitis,* or Roman-ness, was more than nominal, for senators and even emperors began to be drawn from provincial families.

LOCAL MUNICIPALITIES From an administrative and cultural standpoint the empire was a collection of cities and towns and had little to do with the countryside. Roman policy during the Principate was to raise urban centers to the status of Roman municipalities with the rights and privileges attached to them. A typical municipal charter left much responsibility in the hands of local councils and magistrates elected from the local aristocracy. Moreover, the holding of a magistracy, and later a seat on the council, carried Roman citizenship with it. Therefore, the Romans enlisted the upper classes of the provinces in their own government, spread Roman law and culture, and won the loyalty of the influential people.

There were exceptions to this picture of success. The Jews found their religion incompatible with Roman demands and were savagely repressed when they rebelled in A.D. 66–70, 115–117, and 132–135. In Egypt the Romans exploited the peasants with exceptional ruth-

Spoils from the temple in Jerusalem were carried in triumphal procession by Roman troops. This relief from Titus's arch of victory in the Roman Forum celebrates his capture of Jerusalem after a two-year siege. The Jews found it difficult to reconcile their religion with Roman rule and frequently rebelled. [Scala/Art Resource, N.Y.]

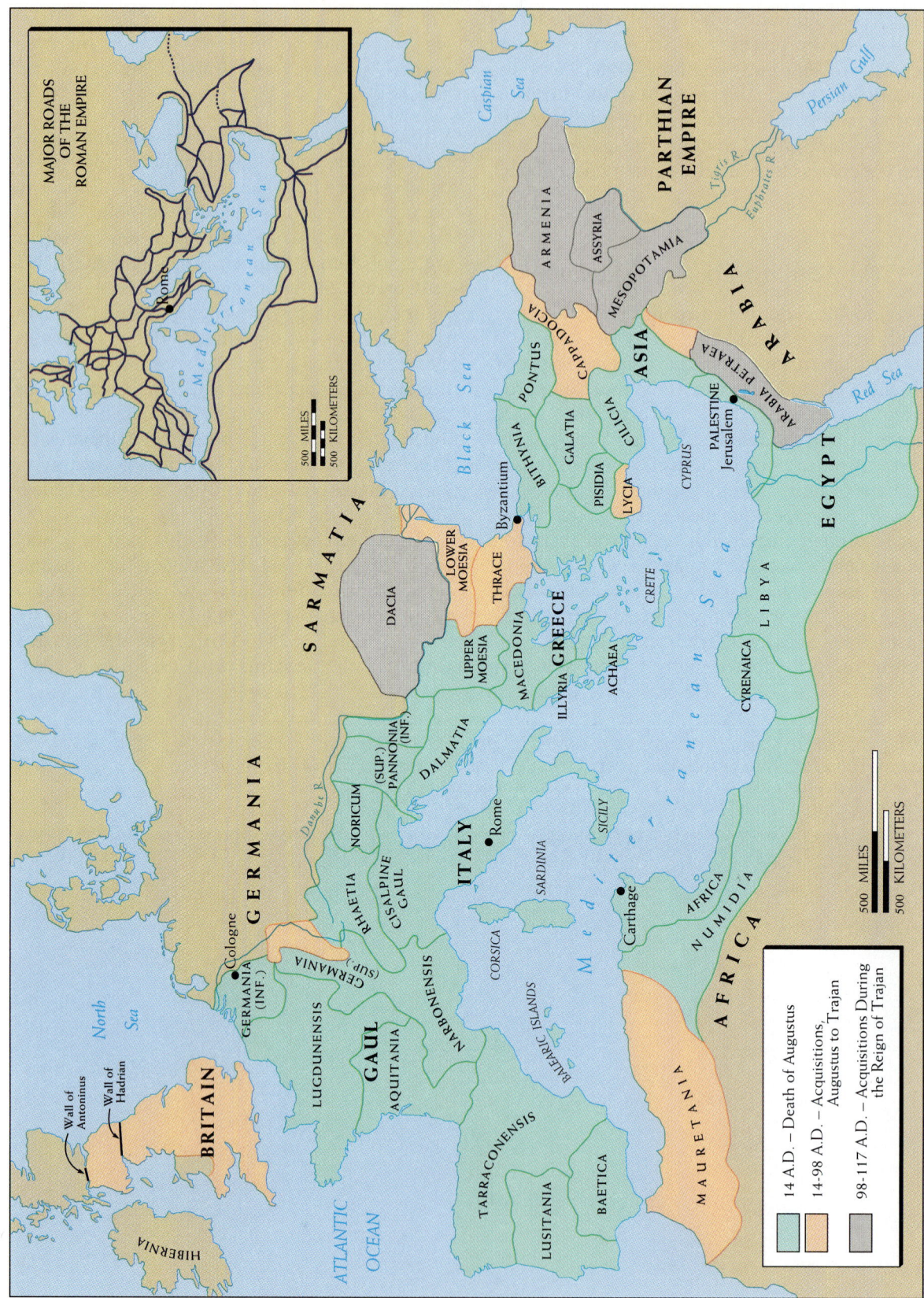

MAP 5-2 PROVINCES OF THE ROMAN EMPIRE TO A.D. 117 The growth of the empire to its greatest extent is here shown in three stages—at the death of Augustus in A.D. 14, at the

Legend:
- 14 A.D. – Death of Augustus
- 14-98 A.D. – Acquisitions, Augustus to Trajan
- 98-117 A.D. – Acquisitions During the Reign of Trajan

Daily Life in a Roman Provincial Town: Graffiti from Pompeii

On the walls of the houses of Pompeii, buried and preserved by the eruption of Mount Vesuvius in A.D. 79, are many scribblings that give us an idea of what the life of ordinary people was like.

◆ *How do these graffiti differ from those one sees in a modern American city? What do they reveal about the similarities and differences between the ordinary people of ancient Rome and the people of today? How would you account for the differences?*

I

Twenty pairs of gladiators of Decimus Lucretius Satrius Valens, lifetime *flamen* of Nero son of Caesar Augustus, and ten pairs of gladiators of Decimus Lucretius Valens, his son, will fight at Pompeii on April 8, 9, 10, 11, 12. There will be a full card of wild beast combats, and awnings [for the spectators]. Aemilius Celer [painted this sign], all alone in the moonlight.

II

Market days: Saturday in Pompeii, Sunday in Nuceria, Monday in Atella, Tuesday in Nola, Wednesday in Cumae, Thursday in Puteoli, Friday in Rome.

III

Pleasure says: "You can get a drink here for an *as* [a few cents], a better drink for two, Falernian for four."

IV

A copper pot is missing from this shop. 65 sesterces reward if anybody brings it back, 20 sesterces if he reveals the thief so we can get our property back.

V

The weaver Successus loves the innkeeper's slave girl, Iris by name. She doesn't care for him, but he begs her to take pity on him. Written by his rival. So long.

[Answer by the rival:] Just because you're bursting with envy, don't pick on a handsomer man, a lady-killer and a gallant.

[Answer by the first writer:] There's nothing more to say or write. You love Iris, who doesn't care for you.

VI

Take your lewd looks and flirting eyes off another man's wife, and show some decency on your face!

VII

Anybody in love, come here. I want to break Venus' ribs with a club and cripple the goddess' loins. If she can pierce my tender breast, why can't I break her head with a club?

VIII

I write at Love's dictation and Cupid's instruction;

But damn it! I don't want to be a god without you.

IX

[A prostitute's sign:] I am yours for 2 *asses* cash.

N. Lewis and M. Reinhold, Roman Civilization, *Vol. 2 (New York: Columbia University Press, 1955), pp. 359–360.*

The Bar-Kochba Rebellion: The Final Jewish Uprising Against Rome

Unlike most conquered peoples the Jews found accommodation to Roman rule difficult. Their first rebellion was crushed by Vespasian's son, the future Emperor Titus, in A.D. 70. At that time the Temple in Jerusalem was destroyed. A second revolt was put down in A.D. 117. Finally, when Hadrian ordered a Roman colony placed on the site of Jerusalem, a final uprising was led by Simon, called Bar Kochba (Son of the Star), from 132 to 135. Dio Cassius describes the brutality of its suppression.

✦ *Did the Romans treat the Jews differently from other people under their control? What special problems did the Roman conquest pose to the Jews? What problems did the Jews present to the Romans?*

At Jerusalem Hadrian founded a city in place of the one which had been razed to the ground, naming it Aelia Capitolina, and on the site of the temple of the god he raised a new temple to Jupiter. This brought on a war of no slight importance nor of brief duration, for the Jews deemed it intolerable that foreign peoples should be settled in their city and foreign rites planted there. . . .

At first the Romans took no account of them. Soon, however, all Judaea had been stirred up, and the Jews everywhere were showing signs of disturbance, were gathering together, and giving evidence of great hostility to the Romans, partly by secret and partly by overt acts; many outside peoples, too, were joining them through eagerness for gain, and the whole world, one might almost say, was being stirred up over the matter. Then, indeed, Hadrian sent his best generals against them. Foremost among these was Julius Severus, who was dispatched against the Jews from Britain, where he was governor. . . . [In Judaea] he was able, rather slowly . . . but with comparatively little danger, to crush, exhaust, and exterminate them. Very few of them in fact survived. Fifty of their most important strongholds and 985 of their most famous villages were razed to the ground; 580,000 men were slain in the various raids and battles, and the number of those that perished by famine, disease, and fire was past finding out.

Dio Cassius, Roman History 59.12–14, trans. by Earnest Cary (London: Loeb Classical Library and William Heinemann, 1916).

---

lessness and did not pursue a policy of urbanization.

As the efficiency of the bureaucracy grew, so did the number and scope of its functions and therefore its size. The emperors came to take a broader view of their responsibilities for the welfare of their subjects than before. Nerva conceived and Trajan introduced the *alimenta*, a program of public assistance for the children of indigent parents. More and more the emperors intervened when municipalities got into difficulties, usually financial, sending imperial troubleshooters to deal with problems. The impor-

tance and autonomy of the municipalities shrank as the central administration took a greater part in local affairs. The provincial aristocracy came to regard public service in their own cities as a burden rather than an opportunity. The price paid for the increased efficiency offered by centralized control was the loss of the vitality of the cities throughout the empire.

The success of Roman civilization also came at great cost to the farmers who lived outside Italy. Taxes, rents, mandatory gifts, and military service drew capital away from the countryside to the cities on a scale not previously seen in the Graeco-Roman world. More and more the rich life of the urban elite came at the expense of millions of previously stable farmers.

FOREIGN POLICY Augustus's successors, for the most part, accepted his conservative and defensive foreign policy. Trajan was the first emperor to take the offensive in a sustained way. Between A.D. 101 and 106 he crossed the Danube and, after hard fighting, established the new province of Dacia between the Danube and the Carpathian Mountains. He was tempted, no doubt, by its important gold mines, but he probably was also pursuing a new general strategy: to defend the empire more aggressively by driving wedges into the territory of threatening barbarians. The same strategy dictated the invasion of the Parthian Empire in the East (A.D. 113–117). Trajan's early success was astonishing, and he established three new provinces in Armenia, Assyria, and Mesopotamia. But his lines were overextended. Rebellions sprang up, and the campaign crumbled. Trajan was forced to retreat and died before getting back to Rome.

Hadrian's reign marked an important shift in Rome's frontier policy. Heretofore, even under the successors of Augustus, Rome had been on the offensive against the barbarians. Although the Romans rarely gained new territory, they launched frequent attacks to chastise and pacify troublesome tribes. Hadrian hardened the Roman defenses, building a stone wall in the south of Scotland and a wooden one across the Rhine–Danube triangle.

The Roman defense became rigid, and initiative passed to the barbarians. Marcus Aurelius was compelled to spend most of his reign resisting dangerous attacks in the East and on the Danube frontier.

AGRICULTURE: THE DECLINE OF SLAVE LABOR AND THE RISE OF *COLONI* The defense of its frontiers put enormous pressure on the human and financial resources of the empire, but the effect of these pressures was not immediately felt. The empire generally experienced considerable economic growth well into the reigns of "good emperors." Internal peace and efficient administration benefitted agriculture as well as trade and industry. Farming and trade developed together as political conditions made it easier to sell farm products at a distance.

Trajan's Column was erected at Rome about 110 A.D. to celebrate the Emperor Trajan's (r. 98–117) victory over the Dacians beyond the Danube. Trajan pushed the boundaries of the Roman Empire to their farthest limits, defeating the Parthians in the east as well as the Dacians in the north. Carved in a spiraling relief, the column shows more than a thousand figures, accurately depicting people, buildings, flowers, animals, implements, and weapons. [Robert Miller]

Small farms continued to exist, but the large estate, managed by an absentee owner and growing cash crops, became the dominant form of agriculture. At first, as in the republican period, these estates were worked chiefly by slaves, but in the first century this began to change. Economic pressures on the free lower classes forced many of them to become tenant farmers, or *coloni*, and eventually these *coloni* replaced slaves as the mainstay of agricultural labor. Typically, these sharecroppers paid rent in labor or in kind, though sometimes they made cash payments. Eventually, their movement was restricted, and they were tied to the land they worked, much as were the manorial serfs of the

Middle Ages. Whatever its social costs, the system was economically efficient, however, and contributed to the general prosperity.

Although the economic importance of slavery began to decline in the second century with the rise of *coloni* labor, the institution was never abolished nor did it disappear so long as the Roman Empire lasted. Pockets of slave labor remained as late as the time of Charlemagne (see Chapter 6).

Life in Imperial Rome: The Apartment House

The civilization of the Roman Empire depended on the vitality of its cities. The typical city had about 20,000 inhabitants and perhaps only three or four had a population of more than 75,000. The population of Rome, however, was certainly greater than 500,000, perhaps more than a million. People coming to Rome for the first time found it overwhelming and were either thrilled or horrified by its size, bustle, and noise. The rich lived in elegant homes called *domūs*. These were single-storied houses with plenty of space, an open central courtyard, and several rooms designed for specific and different purposes, such as dining, sitting, or sleeping, in privacy and relative quiet. Though only a small portion of Rome's population lived in them, these houses took up as much as a third of the city's space. Public space for temples, markets, baths, gymnasiums, theaters, forums, and governmental buildings took up another quarter of Rome's territory.

This left less than half of Rome's area to house the mass of its inhabitants, who were squeezed into multiple dwellings that grew increasingly tall. Most Romans during the imperial period lived in apartment buildings called *insulae* ("islands") that rose to a height of five or six stories and sometimes even more. The most famous of them, the Insula of Febiala, seems to have "towered above the Rome of the Antonines like a skyscraper."[3]

These buildings were divided into separate apartments (*cenicula*) of undifferentiated rooms, the same plan on each floor. The apartments were cramped and uncomfortable. They had neither central heating nor an open fireplace; heat and fire for cooking came from small, portable stoves. The apartments were hot in summer, cold in winter, and stuffy and smoky when the stoves were lit. There was no plumb-

[3] *J. Carcopino,* Daily Life in Ancient Rome *(New Haven, Conn.: Yale University Press 1940), p. 26.*

This is a reconstruction of a typical Roman apartment house found at Ostia, Rome's port. The ground floor contained shops, and the stories above it held many apartments. [Scala/Art Resource, N.Y.]

ing, so tenants needed to go into the streets to wells or fountains for water and to public baths and latrines, or to less well-regulated places. The higher up one lived, the more difficult these trips, and so chamber pots and commodes were kept in the rooms. These receptacles were emptied into vats on the staircase landings or in the alleys outside; on occasion, the contents, and even the containers, were tossed out the window. Roman satirists complained of the discomforts and dangers of walking the streets beneath such windows. Roman law tried to find ways to assign responsibilities for the injuries done to dignity and person.

In spite of these difficulties, the attractions of the city and the shortage of space caused rents to rise, making life in these buildings expensive as well as uncomfortable. It was also dangerous. The houses were lightly built of concrete and brick, far too high for the limited area of their foundations, and so they often collapsed. Laws limiting the height of buildings were not always obeyed and did not, in any case, always prevent disaster. The satirist Juvenal did not exaggerate much when he wrote, "We inhabit a city held up chiefly by slats, for that is how the landlord patches up the cracks in the old wall, telling the tenants to sleep peacefully under the ruin that hangs over their heads."

Even more serious was the threat of fire. Wooden beams supported the floors, and the rooms were lit by torches, candles, and oil lamps and heated by braziers. Fires broke out easily and, without running water, were not easily put out; once started, they usually led to disaster.

When we consider the character of these apartments and compare them with the attractive public places in the city, we can easily understand why the people of Rome spent most of their time out of doors.

The Culture of the Early Empire

The years from A.D. 14 to 180 were a time of general prosperity and a flourishing material and artistic culture, but one not so brilliant and original as in the Age of Augustus.

LITERATURE In Latin literature the years between the death of Augustus and the time of Marcus Aurelius are known as the Silver Age.

As the name implies, this age produced work of high quality although probably not of so high a quality as in the Augustan era. In contrast to the hopeful, positive optimists of the Augustans, the writers of the Silver Age were gloomy, negative, and pessimistic. In the works of the former period, praise of the emperor, his achievements, and the world abounds; in the latter, criticism and satire lurk everywhere. Some of the most important writers of the Silver Age came from the Stoic opposition and reflected its hostility to the growing power and personal excesses of the emperors.

The writers of the second century A.D. appear to have turned away from contemporary affairs and even recent history. Historical writing was about remote periods so that there was less danger of irritating imperial sensibilities. Scholarship was encouraged, but we hear little of poetry, especially any dealings with dangerous subjects. In the third century A.D. romances written in Greek became popular and provide further evidence of the tendency of writers of the time to seek and provide escape from contemporary realities.

ARCHITECTURE The main contribution of the Romans lay in two new kinds of buildings—the great public bath and a new, free-standing kind of amphitheater—and in the advances in engineering that made these large structures possible. While keeping the basic post-and-lintel construction used by the Greeks, the Romans added to it the principle of the semicircular arch, borrowed from the Etruscans. They also made good use of concrete, a building material first used by the Hellenistic Greeks and fully developed by the Romans. The arch, combined with the post and lintel, produced the great Colosseum built by the Flavian emperors. When used internally in the form of vaults and domes, the arch permitted great buildings like the baths, of which the most famous and best preserved are those of the later emperors Caracalla and Diocletian.

One of Rome's most famous buildings, the Pantheon, begun by Augustus's friend Agrippa and rebuilt by Hadrian, combined all these elements (see Map 5-3 on page 188). Its portico of Corinthian columns is of Greek origin, but its rotunda of brick-faced concrete with its domed ceiling and relieving arches is thoroughly Roman. The new engineering also made possible the

Juvenal on Life in Rome

The satirical poet Juvenal lived and worked in Rome in the late first and early second centuries A.D. His poems present a vivid picture of the material and cultural world of the Romans of his time. In the following passages, he tells of the discomforts and dangers of life in the city, both indoors and out.

◆ *According to Juvenal what dangers awaited pedestrians in the Rome of his day? Who had responsibility for the condition of Rome? If the situation was as bad as he says, why was nothing done about it? Why did people choose to live in Rome at all and especially in the conditions he describes?*

Who, in Praeneste's cool, or the wooded
    Volsinian uplands,

Who, on Tivoli's heights, or a small town like
    Gabii, say,

Fears the collapse of his house? But Rome is
    supported on pipestems,

Matchsticks; it's cheaper, so, for the landlord
    to shore up his ruins,

Patch up the old cracked walls, and notify all
    the tenants

They can sleep secure, though the beams are
    in ruins above them.

No, the place to live is out there, where no
    cry of *Fire!*

Sounds the alarm of the night, with a neigh-
    bor yelling for water,

Moving his chattels and goods, and the whole
    third story is smoking.

This you'll never know: for if the ground floor
    is scared first,

You are the last to burn, up there where the
    eaves of the attic

Keep off the rain, and the doves are brooding
    over their nest eggs.

. . . .

Look at other things, the various dangers of
    nighttime.

How high it is to the cornice that breaks, and
    a chunk beats my brains out,

Or some slob heaves a jar, broken or cracked,
    from a window.

Bang! It comes down with a crash and proves
    its weight on the sidewalk.

You are a thoughtless fool, unmindful of sud-
    den disaster,

If you don't make your will before you go out
    to have dinner.

There are as many deaths in the night as
    there are open windows

Where you pass by; if you're wise, you will
    pray, in your wretched devotions,

People may be content with no more than
    emptying slop jars.

Juvenal, The Satires of Juvenal, trans. by Rolfe Humphries (Bloomington: Indiana University Press, 1958), pp. 40, 43.

construction of more mundane but useful structures like bridges and aqueducts.

SOCIETY Seen from the harsh perspective of human history, the first two centuries of the Roman Empire deserve their reputation of a "golden age." But by the second century A.D., troubles had arisen, troubles that foreshadowed the difficult times ahead. The literary efforts of the time reveal a flight from the present, from reality, and from the public realm to the past, to romance, and to private pursuits. Some of the same aspects may be seen in the more prosaic world of everyday life, especially in the decline of vitality in local government.

In the first century A.D. members of the upper classes vied with one another for election to municipal office and for the honor of doing service to their communities. By the second century A.D. it became necessary for the emperors to intervene to correct abuses in local affairs and even to force unwilling members of the ruling classes to accept public office. Magistrates and council members were held personally and collectively responsible for the revenues due. There were even some instances of magistrates

Dinner at Trimalchio's: A Satire on the Newly Rich at Rome

The following selection is from Trimalchio's Feast, *part of a fragmentary satire called* The Satyricon, *by Petronius, a writer of the first century A.D. The speaker is a guest at a lavish dinner given by Trimalchio, a former slave risen to great wealth at Rome. Included among the jibes and sneers is some useful information about life in this period.*

✦ *What is the source of Trimalchio's wealth? What sources of wealth were available at the time? What does this selection reveal about social mobility in the first century? What of the range of commerce? How do you explain the tone of the narrator?*

"As for old Trimalchio, that man's got more farms than a kite could flap over. And there's more silver plate stuffed in his porter's lodge than another man's got in his safe. As for slaves, whoosh! So help me, I'll bet not one in ten has ever seen his master. Your ordinary rich man is just peanuts compared to him; he could knock them all under a cabbage and you'd never know they were gone.

"And buy things? Not him. No sir, he raises everything right on his own estate. Wool, citron, pepper, you name it. By god, you'd find hen's milk if you looked around. Now take his wool. The home-grown strain wasn't good enough. So you know what he did? Imported rams from Tarentum, bred them into the herd. Attic honey he raises at home. Ordered the bees special from Athens. And the local bees are better for being crossbred too. And, you know, just the other day he sent off to India for some mushroom spawn. Every mule he owns had a wild ass for a daddy. And you see those pillows there? Every last one is stuffed with purple or scarlet wool. That boy's loaded!

"And don't sneer at his friends. They're all ex-slaves, but every one of them's rich. You see that guy down there on the the next to last couch? He's worth a cool half-million. Came up from nowhere. Used to tote wood on his back. People say, but I don't know, he stole a cap off a hobgoblin's head and found a treasure. He's the god's fair-haired boy. That's luck for you, but I don't begrudge him. Not so long ago he was just a slave. Yes sir, he's doing all right.

Petronius, The Satyricon, *trans. by William Arrowsmith (Ann Arbor: University of Michigan Press, 1959), pp. 35–36.*

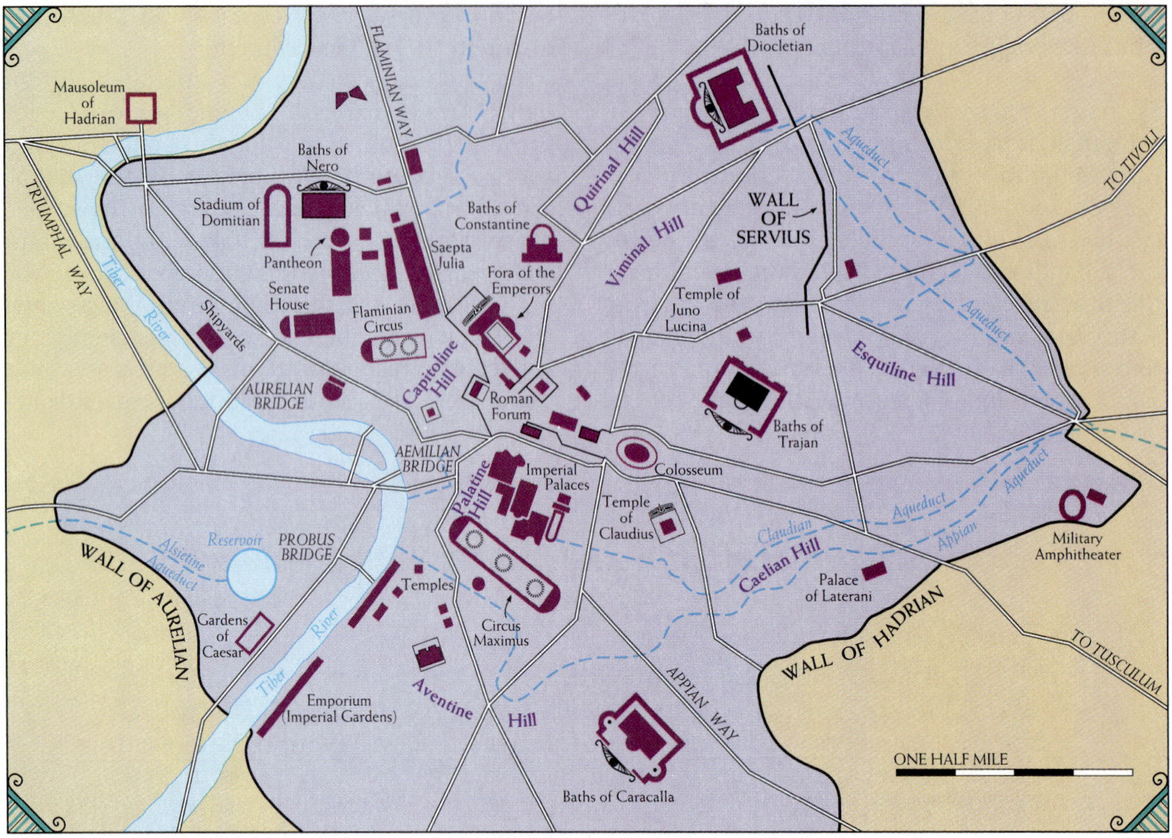

MAP 5-3 ANCIENT ROME *This map of Rome during the late empire shows the seven hills on and around which the city was built, and the major walls, bridges, and other public sites and buildings.*

These are the remains of the Baths built by the Emperor Caracalla in Rome in the third century A.D. Public baths were found throughout the cities of the empire, serving as vast community centers for social life and recreation. [Scala/Art Resource, N.Y.]

fleeing to avoid their office, a practice that became widespread in later centuries.

These difficulties reflected more basic problems. The prosperity brought by the end of civil war and the influx of wealth from the East could not sustain itself beyond the first half of the second century A.D. There also appears to have been a decline in population for reasons that remain mysterious. The cost of government kept rising. The emperors were required to maintain a standing army, minimal in size but costly, to keep the people in Rome happy with "bread and circuses," to pay for an increasingly numerous bureaucracy, and to wage expensive wars to defend the frontiers against dangerous and determined barbarian enemies. The ever-increasing need for money compelled the emperors to raise taxes, to press hard on their subjects, and to bring on inflation by debasing the coinage. These elements brought on the desperate crises that ultimately destroyed the empire.

The Rise of Christianity

Christianity emerged, spread, survived, and ultimately conquered the Roman Empire in spite of its origin among poor people from an unimportant and remote province of the empire. Christianity faced the hostility of the established religious institutions of its native Judaea. It also had to compete against the official cults of Rome and the highly sophisticated philosophies of the educated classes and against other "mystery" religions like the cults of Mithra, Isis, and Osiris. In addition to all this, the Christians faced the opposition of the imperial government and formal persecution. Yet Christianity

This early Christian art shows Christ arrested by soldiers on the night before his crucifixion. Note that Christ is portrayed clean-shaven and dressed in the toga of a Roman aristocrat. [Hirmer Verlag, Munich]

achieved toleration and finally exclusive command as the official religion of the empire.

Jesus of Nazareth

An attempt to understand this amazing outcome must begin with the story of Jesus of Nazareth. The most important evidence about his life is in the Gospel accounts, all of them written well after his death. The earliest, by Mark, is dated about A.D. 70, and the latest, by John, about A.D. 100. They are not, moreover, attempts at simply describing the life of Jesus with historical accuracy. Rather they are statements of faith by true believers. The authors of the Gospels believed that Jesus was the son of God and that he had come into the world to redeem humanity and to bring immortality to those who believed in him and followed his way. To the Gospel writers, Jesus' resurrection was striking proof of his teachings. At the same time, the Gospels regard Jesus as a figure in history, and they recount events in his life as well as his sayings.

There is no reason to doubt that Jesus was born in the province of Judaea in the time of Augustus and that he was a most effective teacher in the tradition of the prophets. This tradition promised the coming of a Messiah (in Greek, *christos*—so *Jesus Christ* means "Jesus the Messiah"), the redeemer who would make Israel triumph over its enemies and establish the kingdom of God on earth. In fact, Jesus seems to have insisted that the Messiah would not establish an earthly kingdom but would bring an end to the world as human beings knew it at the Day of Judgment. On that day God would reward the righteous with immortality and happiness in heaven and condemn the wicked to eternal suffering in hell. Until that day (which his followers believed would come very soon), Jesus taught the faithful to abandon sin and worldly concerns; to follow him and his way; to follow the moral code described in the Sermon on the Mount, which preached love, charity, and humility; and to believe in him and his divine mission.

Jesus won a considerable following, especially among the poor, which caused great suspicion among the upper classes. His novel message and his criticism of the religious practices connected with the temple at Jerusalem and its priests provoked the hostility of the religious establishment. A misunderstanding of the movement made it easy to convince the Roman governor that Jesus and his followers might be dangerous revolutionaries. He was put to death in Jerusalem by the cruel and degrading device of crucifixion, probably in A.D. 30. His followers believed that he was resurrected on the third day after his death, and that belief became a critical element in the religion that they propagated throughout the Roman Empire and beyond.

The new belief spread quickly to the Jewish communities of Syria and Asia Minor. There is reason to believe, however, that it might have had only a short life as a despised Jewish heresy were it not for the conversion and career of Saint Paul.

Paul of Tarsus

Paul was born Saul, a citizen of the Cilician city of Tarsus in Asia Minor. He had been trained in Hellenistic culture and was a Roman citizen. But he was also a zealous member of the Jewish sect known as the Pharisees, the group that was most strict in its insistence on adherence to the Jewish law. He took a vigorous part in the persecution of the early Christians until his own conversion outside Damascus about A.D. 35.

The great problem facing the early Christians was to resolve their relationship to Judaism. If the new faith was a version of Judaism, then it must adhere to the Jewish law and seek converts only among Jews. James, called the brother of Jesus, was a conservative who held to that view, whereas the Hellenist Jews tended to see Christianity as a new and universal religion. To force all converts to follow Jewish law would have been fatal to the growth of the new sect. Jewish law's many technicalities and dietary prohibitions were strange to gentiles, and the necessity of circumcision—a frightening, painful, and dangerous operation for adults—would have been a tremendous deterrent to conversion. Paul, converted and with his new name, supported the position of the Hellenists and soon won many converts among the gentiles. After some conflict within the sect, Paul won out. Consequently, the "apostle to the gentiles" deserves recognition as a crucial contributor to the success of Christianity.

Mark Describes the Resurrection of Jesus

Belief that Jesus rose from the dead after his Crucifixion (about A.D. 30) was and is central to traditional Christian doctrine. The record of the Resurrection in the Gospel of Mark, written a generation later (toward A.D. 70), is the earliest we have. The significance to most Christian groups revolves about the assurance given them that death and the grave are not final and that, instead, salvation for a future life is possible. The appeal of these views was to be nearly universal in the West during the Middle Ages. The Church was commonly thought to be the means of implementing the promise of salvation; hence the enormous importance of the Church's sacramental system, its rules, and its clergy.

✦ *Why are the stories of miracles such as the one described here important for the growth of Christianity? What is special and important about this miracle? Why is it important in the story that days passed between the death of Jesus and the opening of the tomb? Why might the early Christians believe this story? Why was belief in the resurrection important for Christianity in the centuries immediately after the life of Jesus? Is it still important today?*

And when evening had come, since it was the day of Preparation, that is, the day before the sabbath, Joseph of Arimathea, a respected member of the council, who was also himself looking for the kingdom of God, took courage and went to Pilate, and asked for the body of Jesus. And Pilate wondered if he were already dead; and summoning the centurion, he asked him whether he was already dead. And when he learned from the centurion that he was dead, he granted the body to Joseph. And he bought a linen shroud, and taking him down, wrapped him in the linen shroud, and laid him in a tomb which had been hewn out of the rock; and he rolled a stone against the door of the tomb. Mary Magdalene and Mary the mother of Jesus saw where he was laid.

And when the sabbath was past, Mary Magdalene, and Mary the mother of James, and Salome, bought spices, so that they might go and anoint him. And very early on the first day of the week they went to the tomb when the sun had risen. And they were saying to one another, "Who will roll away the stone for us from the door of the tomb?" And looking up, they saw that the stone was rolled back; for it was very large. And entering the tomb, they saw a young man sitting on the right side, dressed in a white robe; and they were amazed. And he said to them, "Do not be amazed; you seek Jesus of Nazareth, who was crucified. He has risen, he is not here, see the place where they laid him. But go, tell his disciples and Peter that he is going before you to Galilee; there you will see him, as he told you." And they went out and fled from the tomb; for trembling and astonishment had come upon them; and they said nothing to any one, for they were afraid.

Gospel of Mark 15:42–47; 16:1–8, Revised Standard Version of the Bible (New York: Thomas Nelson and Sons, 1946, 1952).

Paul believed it important that the followers of Jesus be evangelists (messengers), to spread the gospel ("good news") of God's gracious gift. He taught that Jesus would soon return for the Day of Judgment, and it was important that all who would should believe in him and accept his way. Faith in Jesus as the Christ was necessary but not sufficient for salvation, nor could good deeds alone achieve it. That final blessing of salvation was a gift of God's grace that would be granted to some but not to all.

Organization

Paul and the other apostles did their work well. The new religion spread throughout the Roman Empire and even beyond its borders. It had its greatest success in the cities and mostly among the poor and uneducated. The rites of the early communities appear to have been simple and few. Baptism by water removed original sin and permitted participation in the community and its activities. The central ritual was a common meal called the *agape* ("love feast"), followed by the ceremony of the *Eucharist* ("thanksgiving"), a celebration of the Lord's Supper in which unleavened bread was eaten and unfermented wine was drunk. There were also prayers, hymns, and readings from the Gospels.

Not all the early Christians were poor, and it became customary for the rich to provide for the poor at the common meals. The sense of common love fostered in these ways focused the community's attention on the needs of the weak, the sick, the unfortunate, and the unprotected. This concern gave the early Christian communities a warmth and a human appeal that stood in marked contrast to the coldness and impersonality of the pagan cults. No less attractive were the promise of salvation, the importance to God of each human soul, and the spiritual equality of all in the new faith. As Paul put it, "There is neither Jew nor Greek, there is neither slave nor free, there is neither male nor female; for you are all one in Christ Jesus."[4]

The future of Christianity depended on its communities' finding an organization that would preserve unity within the group and help protect it against enemies outside. At first, the churches had little formal organization. Soon, it appears, affairs were placed in the hands of boards of *presbyters* ("elders") and *deacons* ("those who serve"). By the second century A.D., as their numbers grew, the Christians of each city tended to accept the authority and leadership of bishops (*episkopoi*, or "overseers"). Bishops were elected by the congregation to lead them in worship and to supervise funds. As time passed, the bishops extended their authority over the Christian communities in outlying towns and the countryside. The power and almost monarchical authority of the bishops were soon enhanced by the doctrine of Apostolic Succession, which asserted that the powers that Jesus had given his original disciples were passed on from bishop to bishop by ordination.

The bishops kept in touch with one another, maintained communications between different Christian communities, and prevented doctrinal and sectarian splintering, which would have destroyed Christian unity. They maintained internal discipline and dealt with the civil authorities. After a time they began the practice of coming together in councils to settle difficult questions, to establish orthodox opinion, and even to expel as heretics those who would not accept it. It is unlikely that Christianity could have survived the travails of its early years without such strong internal organization and government.

The Persecution of Christians

The new faith soon incurred the distrust of the pagan world and of the imperial government. At first Christians were thought of as a Jewish sect and were therefore protected by Roman law. It soon became clear, however, that they were quite different, seeming both mysterious and dangerous. They denied the existence of the pagan gods and so were accused of atheism. Their refusal to worship the emperor was judged to be treason. Because they kept mostly to themselves, took no part in civic affairs, engaged in secret rites, and had an organized network of local associations, they were misunderstood and suspected. The love feasts were erroneously reported to be scenes of sexual scandal. The alarming doctrine of the actual presence of Jesus' body in the Eucharist was distorted into an accusation of cannibalism.

The privacy and secrecy of Christian life and worship ran counter to a traditional Roman dislike of any private association, especially any of a religious nature. Christians thus earned the reputation of being "haters of humanity." Claudius expelled them from Rome, and Nero tried to make them scapegoats for the great fire that struck the city in A.D. 64. By the end of the first century "the name alone"—that is, simple membership in the Christian community—was a crime.

But, mostly, the Roman government did not take the initiative in attacking Christians in the first two centuries. When one governor sought

[4]*Galatians 3:28*. Revised Standard Version of the Bible.

instructions for dealing with the Christians, the emperor Trajan urged moderation. Christians were not to be sought out, anonymous accusations were to be disregarded, and anyone denounced could be acquitted merely by renouncing Christ and sacrificing to the emperor. Unfortunately, no true Christian could meet the conditions, and so there were some martyrdoms.

Most persecutions in this period, however, were started not by the government but by mob action. Though they lived quiet, inoffensive lives, some Christians must have seemed unbearably smug and self-righteous. Unlike the tolerant, easygoing pagans, who were generally willing to accept the new gods of foreign people and add them to the pantheon, the Christians denied the reality of the pagan gods. They proclaimed the unique rightness of their own way and looked forward to their own salvation and the damnation of nonbelievers. It is not surprising, therefore, that pagans disliked these strange and unsocial people, tended to blame misfortunes on them, and, in extreme cases, turned to violence. But even this adversity had its uses. It weeded out the weaklings among the Christians, and brought greater unity to those who remained faithful. It also provided the Church with martyrs around whom legends could grow that would inspire still greater devotion and dedication.

The Emergence of Catholicism

Division within the Christian church may have been an even greater threat to its existence than persecution from outside. The great majority of Christians never accepted complex, intellectualized opinions but held to what even then were traditional, simple, conservative beliefs. This body of majority opinion and the Church that enshrined it came to be called *Catholic,* which means "universal." Its doctrines were deemed orthodox, that is, "holding the right opinions," whereas those holding contrary opinions were heretics.

The need to combat heretics, however, compelled the orthodox to formulate their own views more clearly and firmly. By the end of the second century A.D., an orthodox canon had been shaped that included the Old Testament, the Gospels, and the Epistles of Paul, among

This is the Catacomb of the Jordani in Rome. The early Christians built miles of tunnels, called catacombs, in Rome. They were used as underground cemeteries and as refuges from persecution. [Charitable Foundation, Leonard von Matt]

other writings. The process of creating a standard set of holy books was not completed for at least two more centuries, but a vitally important start had been made. The orthodox declared the Church itself to be the depository of Christian teaching and the bishops to be its receivers. They also drew up creeds, brief statements of faith to which true Christians should adhere.

In the first century all that was required of one to be a Christian was to be baptized, to partake of the Eucharist, and to call Jesus the Lord. By the end of the second century an orthodox Christian—that is, a member of the Catholic church—was required to accept its creed, its canon of holy writings, and the authority of the bishops. The loose structure of the apostolic Church had given way to an organized body with recognized leaders able to define its faith and to exclude those who did not accept it. Whatever the shortcomings of this development, there can be little doubt that it provided the clarity, unity, and discipline needed for survival.

Rome as a Center of the Early Church

During this same period the Church in Rome came to have special prominence. As the center of communications and the capital of the empire, Rome had natural advantages. After the Roman destruction of Jerusalem in 135 A.D., no other city had any convincing claim to primacy in the Church. Besides having the largest single congregation of Christians, Rome also benefitted from the tradition that both Jesus' apostles Peter and Paul were martyred there.

Peter, moreover, was thought to be the first bishop of Rome. The Gospel of Matthew (16:18) reported Jesus' statement to Peter: "Thou art Peter [in Greek, *Petros*] and upon this rock [in Greek, *petra*] I will build my church." Eastern Christians might later point out that Peter had been leader of the Christian community at Antioch before he went to Rome. But in the second century the church at Antioch, along with the other Christian churches of Asia Minor, was fading in influence, and by 200 A.D. Rome was the most important center of Christianity. Because of the city's early influence and because of the Petrine doctrine derived from the Gospel of Matthew, later bishops of Rome claimed supremacy in the Catholic church. But as the era of the "good emperors" came to a close, this controversy was far in the future.

The Crisis of the Third Century

Dio Cassius, a historian of the third century A.D., described the Roman Empire after the death of Marcus Aurelius as declining from "a kingdom of gold into one of iron and rust." Although we have seen that the gold contained more than a little impurity, there is no reason to quarrel with Dio's assessment of his own time.

Commodus (r. A.D. 180–192), the son of Marcus Aurelius, proved the wisdom of the "good emperors" in selecting their successors for their talents rather than for family ties. Commodus was incompetent and autocratic. He reduced the respect in which the imperial office was held, and his assassination brought the return of civil war.

Barbarian Invasions

The pressure on Rome's frontiers, already serious in the time of Marcus Aurelius, reached massive proportions in the third century. In the East a new power arising in the old Persian Empire threatened the frontiers. In the third century B.C. the Parthians had made the Iranians independent of the Hellenistic kings and had established an empire of their own on the old foundations of the Persian Empire. Several Roman attempts to conquer them had failed, but as late as A.D. 198 the Romans could reach and destroy the Parthian capital and bring at least northern Mesopotamia under their rule.

In A.D. 224, however, a new Iranian dynasty, the Sassanians, seized control from the Parthians and brought new vitality to Persia. They soon recovered Mesopotamia and made raids deep into Roman provinces. In A.D. 260 they humiliated the Romans by actually taking the emperor Valerian prisoner; he died in captivity.

On the western and northern frontiers the pressure came not from a well-organized rival empire but from an ever-increasing number of German tribes. Though they had been in contact with the Romans at least since the second century B.C., they had not been much affected by civilization. The men did no agricultural work, but confined their activities to hunting, drinking, and fighting. They were organized on a family basis by clans, hundreds, and tribes. They were led by chiefs, usually from a royal family, elected by the assembly of fighting men. The king was surrounded by a collection of warriors, whom the Romans called his *comitatus*. Always eager for plunder, these tough barbarians were attracted by the civilized delights they knew existed beyond the frontier of the Rhine and Danube rivers.

The most aggressive of the Germans in the third century A.D. were the Goths. Centuries earlier they had wandered from their ancestral home near the Baltic Sea into the area of southern Russia. In the 220s and 230s A.D. they began to put pressure on the Danube frontier. By about A.D. 250 they were able to penetrate the empire and overrun the Balkan provinces. The need to meet this threat and the one posed by the Persian Sassanids in the East made the Romans weaken their western frontiers, and other Germanic peoples—the Franks and the Alemanni—broke through in those regions. There was considerable danger that Rome would be unable to meet this challenge.

Rome's perils were caused, no doubt, by the unprecedentedly numerous and simultaneous attacks, but its internal weakness encouraged these attacks. The Roman army was not what it had been in its best days. By the second century A.D. it was made up mostly of romanized provincials. The pressure on the frontiers and epidemics of plague in the time of Marcus Aurelius forced the emperor to resort to the conscription of slaves, gladiators, barbarians, and brigands. The training and discipline with which the Romans had conquered the Mediterranean world had declined. The Romans also failed to respond to the new conditions of constant pressure on all the frontiers. A strong, mobile reserve that could meet a threat in one place without causing a weakness elsewhere might have helped, but no such unit was created.

Septimius Severus (r. A.D. 193–211) and his successors played a crucial role in the transformation of the character of the Roman army. Septimius was a military usurper who owed everything to the support of his soldiers. He meant to establish a family dynasty, in contrast to the policy of the "good emperors" of the second century. He was prepared to make Rome into an undisguised military monarchy. Septimius drew recruits for the army increasingly from peasants of the less civilized provinces.

Economic Difficulties

These changes were a response to the great financial needs caused by the barbarian attacks. Inflation had forced Commodus to raise the soldiers' pay. Yet the Severan emperors had to double it to keep up with prices, which increased the imperial budget by as much as 25 percent.

To raise money, the emperors resorted to inventing new taxes, debasing the coinage, and even to selling the palace furniture. Even then it was hard to recruit troops. The new style of military life introduced by Septimius—with its laxer discipline, more pleasant duties, and greater opportunity for advancement, not only in the army but in Roman society—was needed to attract men into the army. The policy proved effective for a short time but could not prevent the chaos of the late third century.

The same forces that caused problems for the army did great damage to society at large. The shortage of workers for the large farms, which had all but wiped out the independent family farm, reduced agricultural production. As external threats distracted the emperors, they were less able to preserve domestic peace. Piracy, brigandage, and the neglect of roads and harbors all hampered trade. So, too, did the debasement of the coinage and the inflation in general. Imperial taxation and confiscations of the property of the rich removed badly needed capital from productive use.

More and more the government was required to demand services that had been given gladly in the past. Because the empire lived hand-to-mouth, with no significant reserve fund and no system of credit financing, the emperors were led to compel the people to provide food, supplies, money, and labor. The upper classes in the cities were made to serve as administrators without pay and to meet deficits in revenue out of their own pockets. Sometimes these demands caused provincial rebellions, as in Egypt and Gaul. More typically they caused peasants and even town administrators to flee to escape their burdens. The result of all these difficulties was a weakening of Rome's economic strength when it was most needed.

The Social Order

The new conditions caused important changes in the social order. Direct attacks from hostile emperors and economic losses decimated the Senate and the traditional ruling class. Their ranks were filled by men coming up through the army. The whole state began to take on an increasingly military appearance. Distinctions among the classes by dress had been traditional since the republic; in the third and fourth cen-

This relief shows Roman tax collectors. The economic, military, and social problems of the third century forced the emperors to increase the burden of taxation, which fell with increasing severity on the middle and upper classes of the provinces. [Trier Museum]

A mosaic from Carthage illustrating aspects of life on the manorial estate of a certain Julian in the province of Africa. His housing, provisions, and entertainment appear to have been opulent. Social boundaries hardened in the late empire, and large fortified estates like this increasingly dominated social and economic life. [Photothèque du Musèe du Bardo]

turies A.D. the people's everyday clothing had become a kind of uniform that precisely revealed status. Titles were assigned to ranks in society as to ranks in the army. The most important distinction was the one formally established by Septimius Severus, which drew a sharp line between the *honestiores* (senators, equestrians, the municipal aristocracy, and the soldiers) and the lower classes, or *humiliores*. Septimius gave the *honestiores* a privileged position before the law. They were given lighter punishments, could not be tortured, and alone had the right of appeal to the emperor.

As time passed, it became more difficult to move from the lower order to the higher, another example of the growing rigidity of the late Roman Empire. Peasants were tied to their lands, artisans to their crafts, soldiers to the army, merchants and shipowners to the needs of the state, and citizens of the municipal upper class to the collection and payment of increasingly burdensome taxes. Freedom and private initiative gave way before the needs of the state and its ever-expanding control of its citizens.

Civil Disorder

Commodus was killed on the last day of A.D. 192. The succeeding year was like the year 69. Three emperors ruled in swift succession, Septimius Severus emerging, as we have seen, to establish firm rule and a dynasty. The death of Alexander Severus, the last of the dynasty, in A.D. 235 brought on a half century of internal anarchy and foreign invasion.

The empire seemed on the point of collapse. Then the two conspirators who overthrew and succeeded the emperor Gallienus proved to be able soldiers. Claudius II Gothicus (A.D. 268–270) and Aurelian (A.D. 270–275) drove back the barbarians and stamped out internal disorder. The soldiers who followed Aurelian on the throne were good fighters who made significant changes in Rome's system of defense. Around Rome, Athens, and other cities they built heavy walls that could resist barbarian attack. They drew back their best troops from the frontiers, relying chiefly on a newly organized heavy cavalry and a mobile army near the emperor's own residence.

Hereafter the army was composed largely of mercenaries who came from among the least civilized provincials and even from among the Germans. The officers gave personal loyalty to the emperor rather than to the empire. These officers became a foreign, hereditary caste of aristocrats that increasingly supplied high administrators and even emperors. In effect, the Roman people hired an army of mercenaries, who were only technically Roman, to protect them.

This ivory relief, carved a little after 395 A.D. shows a Vandal warrior, Stilicho, who rose to prominence in the Roman army. From the third century onward, the Roman army was composed increasingly of foreign mercenaries. [Monza Cathedral, Italy/Alinari/Art Resource, N.Y.]

The Late Empire

During the fourth and fifth centuries the Romans strove to meet the many challenges, internal and external, that threatened the survival of their empire. Growing pressure from barbarian tribes pushing against its frontier intensified the empire's tendency to smother individuality, freedom, and initiative, in favor of an increasingly intrusive and autocratic centralized monarchy. Economic and military weakness increased, and it became even harder to keep the vast empire together. Hard and dangerous times may well have helped the rise of Christianity, encouraging people to turn away from the troubles and dangers of this world to concern about the next.

The Fourth Century and Imperial Reorganization

The period from Diocletian (r. A.D. 284–305) to Constantine (r. A.D. 306–337) was one of reconstruction and reorganization after a time of civil war and turmoil. Diocletian was from Illyria (the former Yugoslavia). He was a man of undistinguished birth who rose to the throne through the ranks of the army. He knew that he was not a great general and that the job of defending and governing the entire empire was too great for one man.

Diocletian therefore decreed the introduction of the tetrarchy, the rule of the empire by four men with power divided territorially (see Map 5-4). He allotted the provinces of Thrace, Asia, and Egypt to himself. His coemperor, Maximian, shared with him the title of Augustus and governed Italy, Africa, and Spain. In addition, two men were given the subordinate title of Caesar: Galerius, who was in charge of the Danube frontier and the Balkans, and Constantius, who governed Britain and Gaul. This arrangement not only provided a good solution to the military problem but also provided for a peaceful succession.

Diocletian was recognized as the senior Augustus, but each tetrarch was supreme in his own sphere. The Caesars were recognized as successors to each half of the empire, and their loyalty was enhanced by marriages to daughters of the Augusti. It was a return, in a way, to the precedent of the "good emperors," A.D. 96–180, who chose their successors from the ranks of the ablest men. It seemed to promise orderly and peaceful transitions instead of assassinations, chaos, and civil war.

Each man established his residence and capital at a place convenient for frontier defense, and none chose Rome. The effective capital of Italy became the northern city of Milan. Diocletian beautified Rome by constructing his monumental baths, but he visited the city only once and made his own capital at Nicomedia in Bithynia. This was another step in the long leveling process that had reduced the eminence of Rome and Italy. It was also evidence of the growing importance of the East.

In 305 Diocletian retired and compelled his coemperor to do the same. But his plan for a smooth succession failed completely. In 310 there were five Augusti and no Caesars. Out of this chaos Constantine, son of Constantius, produced order. In 324 he defeated his last opponent and made himself sole emperor, uniting the empire once again; he reigned until 337. Mostly, Constantine carried forward the policies of Diocletian. He supported Christianity, however, which Diocletian had tried to suppress.

DEVELOPMENT OF AUTOCRACY The development of the imperial office toward autocracy was carried to the extreme by Diocletian and Constantine. The emperor ruled by decree, consulting only a few high officials, whom he himself appointed. The Senate had no role whatever, and its dignity was further diminished by the elimination of all distinctions between senator and equestrian.

The emperor was a remote figure surrounded by carefully chosen high officials. He lived in a great palace and was almost unapproachable. Those admitted to his presence had to prostrate themselves before him and kiss the hem of his robe, which was purple and had golden threads going through it. The emperor was addressed as *dominus* ("lord"), and his right to rule was not derived from the Roman people but from heaven. All this remoteness and ceremony had a double purpose: to enhance the dignity of the emperor and to safeguard him against assassination.

Constantine erected the new city of Constantinople on the site of ancient

MAP 5-4 DIVISIONS OF THE ROMAN EMPIRE UNDER DIOCLETIAN *Diocletian divided the sprawling empire into four prefectures for more effective government and defense. The inset map shows their boundaries, and the larger map gives some details of regions and provinces. The major division between East and West was along the line running south between Pannonia and Moesia.*

Byzantium on the Bosporus, which leads to both the Aegean and Black seas. He made it the new capital of the empire. Its strategic location was excellent for protecting the eastern and Danubian frontiers, and, surrounded on three sides by water, it was easily defended. This location also made it easier to carry forward the policies that fostered autocracy and Christianity. Rome was full of tradition, the center of senatorial and even republican memories and of pagan worship. Constantinople was free from both, and its dedication in A.D. 330 marked the beginning of a new era. Until its fall to the Turks in 1453, it served as a bastion of civilization, the preserver of classical culture, a bulwark against barbarian attack, and the greatest city in Christendom.

The autocratic rule of the emperors was carried out by a civilian bureaucracy, carefully separated from the military to reduce the chances of rebellion by anyone combining the two kinds of power. Below the emperor's court the most important officials were the praetorian prefects, each of whom administered one of the four major areas into which the empire was divided: Gaul, Italy, Illyricum, and the Orient. The four prefectures were subdivided into twelve territorial units called *dioceses,* each under a vicar who

The Arch of Constantine, built in 315 A.D., represents a transition between classical and medieval, pagan and Christian. Many of the sculptures incorporated in it were taken from earlier works dating to the first and second centuries. Others, contemporary with the arch, reflect a new, less refined style. [Robert Miller]

was subordinate to the prefect. The dioceses were further divided into almost a hundred provinces, each under a provincial governor.

The operation of the entire system was supervised by a vast system of spies and secret police, without whom the increasingly rigid organization could not be trusted to perform. In spite of these efforts, the system was corrupt and inefficient.

The cost of maintaining a 400,000-man army as well as the vast civilian bureaucracy, the expensive imperial court, and the imperial taste for splendid buildings put a great strain on an already weak economy. Diocletian's attempts to establish a uniform and reliable currency failed, leading instead to increased inflation. To deal with it, he resorted to price control with his Edict of Maximum Prices in A.D. 301. For each product and each kind of labor, a maximum price was set, and violations were punishable by death. The edict failed despite the harshness of its provisions.

Peasants unable to pay their taxes and officials unable to collect them tried to escape. Diocletian resorted to stern regimentation to keep all in their places and at the service of the government. The terror of the third century forced many peasants to seek protection in the *villa* ("country estate") of a large and powerful landowner and to become tenant farming *coloni*. As social boundaries hardened, they and their descendants became increasingly tied to these estates.

DIVISION OF THE EMPIRE The peace and unity established by Constantine did not last long. His death was followed by a struggle for succession that was won by Constantius II (r. A.D. 337–361), whose death, in turn, left the empire to his young cousin Julian (r. A.D. 361–363). Julian was called "the Apostate" by the Christians because of his attempt to stamp out Christianity and restore paganism. Julian undertook a campaign against Persia with the aim of putting a Roman on the throne of the Sassanids and ending the Persian menace once and for all. He penetrated deep into Persia but was killed in battle. His death put an end to the expedition and to the pagan revival.

The Germans in the West took advantage of the eastern campaign to attack along the Rhine and upper Danube rivers. And even greater trouble was brewing along the middle and upper Danube (see Map 5-5). That territory was occupied by the eastern Goths, known as the Ostrogoths. They were being pushed hard by their western cousins, the Visigoths, who in turn had been driven from their home in the Ukraine by the fierce Huns, a nomadic people from central Asia.

The emperor Valentinian (r. A.D. 364–375) saw that he could not defend the empire alone

MAP 5-5 THE EMPIRE'S NEIGHBORS *In the fourth century the Roman Empire was nearly surrounded by ever more threatening neighbors. The map shows who these so-called barbarians were and where they lived before their armed contact with the Romans.*

and appointed his brother Valens (r. A.D. 364–378) as coruler. Valentinian made his own headquarters at Milan and spent the rest of his life fighting successfully against the Franks and the Alemanni in the West. Valens was given control of the East. The empire was once again divided in two. The two emperors maintained their own courts, and the halves of the empire became increasingly separate and different. Latin was the language of the West and Greek of the East.

In 376 the hard-pressed Visigoths asked and received permission to enter the empire to escape the Huns. Contrary to the bargain, the Goths kept their weapons and began to plunder the Balkan provinces, but the Romans did not keep their side of the bargain either, treating the Goths harshly and forcing them to trade their children for dogs to eat. Valens attacked the Goths and died, along with most of his army, at

Adrianople in Thrace in 378. Theodosius (r. A.D. 379–395), an able and experienced general, was named coruler in the East. By a combination of military and diplomatic skills Theodosius pacified the Goths, giving them land and a high degree of autonomy and enrolling many of them in his army. He made important military reforms, putting greater emphasis on the cavalry. Theodosius tried to unify the empire again, but his death in 395 left it divided and weak.

THE RURAL WEST The two parts of the empire went their separate and different ways. The West became increasingly rural as barbarian invasions continued and grew in intensity. The *villa*, a fortified country estate, became the basic unit of life. There, *coloni* gave their services to the local magnate in return for economic assistance and protection from both barbarians and imperial officials. Many cities shrank to no more than tiny walled fortresses ruled by military commanders and bishops. The upper classes moved to the country and asserted ever greater independence of imperial authority. The failure of the central authority to maintain the roads and the constant danger from robber bands sharply curtailed trade and communications, forcing greater self-reliance and a more primitive style of life.

The new world emerging in the West by the fifth century and after was increasingly made up of isolated units of rural aristocrats and their dependent laborers. The only institution providing a high degree of unity was the Christian church. The pattern for the early Middle Ages in the West was already formed.

THE BYZANTINE EAST In the East the situation was quite different. Constantinople became the center of a vital and flourishing culture that we call *Byzantine* and that lasted until the fifteenth century. Because of its defensible location, the skill of its emperors, and the firmness and strength of its base in Asia Minor, it could deflect and repulse barbarian attacks. A strong navy allowed commerce to flourish in the eastern Mediterranean and, in good times, far beyond. Cities continued to prosper and the emperors made their will good over the nobles in the countryside. The civilization of the Byzantine Empire was a unique combination of classical culture, the Christian religion, Roman law, and eastern artistic influences.

While the West was being overrun by barbarians, the Roman Empire, in altered form, persisted in the East. While Rome shrank to an insignificant ecclesiastical town, Constantinople flourished as the seat of empire, the "New Rome." The Byzantines called themselves "Romans." When we contemplate the decline and fall of the Roman Empire in the fourth and fifth centuries, we are speaking only of the West. A form of classical culture persisted in the Byzantine East for a thousand years more.

The Triumph of Christianity

The rise of Christianity to dominance in the empire was closely connected with the political and cultural experience of the third and fourth centuries. Political chaos and decentralization had religious and cultural consequences.

RELIGIOUS CURRENTS IN THE EMPIRE In some of the provinces, native languages replaced Latin and Greek, sometimes even for official purposes. The classical tradition that had been the basis of imperial life became the exclusive possession of a small, educated aristocracy. In religion the public cults had grown up in an urban environment and were largely political in character. As the importance of the cities diminished, so did the significance of their gods. People might still take comfort in the worship of the friendly, intimate deities of family, field, hearth, storehouse, and craft, but these gods were too petty to serve their needs in a confused and frightening world. The only universal worship was of the emperor, but he was far off, and obeisance to his cult was more a political than a religious act.

In the troubled times of the fourth and fifth centuries people sought powerful, personal deities who would bring them safety and prosperity in this world and immortality in the next. Paganism was open and tolerant. It was by no means unusual for people to worship new deities alongside the old and even to intertwine elements of several to form a new amalgam by the device called *syncretism*.

Manichaeism was an especially potent rival of Christianity. Named for its founder, Mani, a Persian who lived in the third century A.D., it

Reigns of Selected Late Empire Rulers (All dates are A.D.)	
180–192	Commodus
193–211	Septimius Severus
222–235	Alexander Severus
249–251	Decius
253–260	Valerian
253–268	Gallienus
268–270	Claudius II Gothicus
270–275	Aurelian
284–305	Diocletian
306–337	Constantine
324–337	Constantine sole emperor
337–361	Constantius II
361–363	Julian the Apostate
364–375	Valentinian
364–378	Valens
379–395	Theodosius

contained aspects of various religious traditions, including Zoroastrianism from Persia and both Judaism and Christianity. The Manichaeans pictured a world in which light and darkness, good and evil, were constantly at war. Good was spiritual and evil was material. Because human beings were made of matter, their bodies were a prison of evil and darkness, but they also contained an element of light and good. The "Father of Goodness" had sent Mani, among other prophets, to free humanity and gain its salvation. To achieve salvation, humans must want to reach the realm of light and to abandon all physical desires. Manichaeans led an ascetic life and practiced a simple worship guided by a well-organized Church. The movement reached its greatest strength in the fourth and fifth centuries, and some of its central ideas persisted into the Middle Ages.

Christianity had something in common with these cults and answered many of the same needs felt by their devotees. None of them, however, attained Christianity's universality, and none appears to have given the early Christians and their leaders as much competition as the ancient philosophies or the state religion.

IMPERIAL PERSECUTION   By the third century Christianity had taken firm hold in the eastern provinces and in Italy. It had not made much headway in the West, however (see Map 5-6). Christian apologists pointed out that Christians were good citizens who differed from others only in not worshiping the public gods. Until the middle of the third century, the emperors tacitly accepted this view, without granting official toleration. As times became bad and the Christians became more numerous and visible, that policy changed. Popular opinion blamed disasters, natural and military, on the Christians.

About 250 the emperor Decius (r. A.D. 249–251) invoked the aid of the gods in his war against the Goths and required that all citizens worship the state gods publicly. True Christians could not obey, and Decius started a major persecution. Many Christians, even some bishops, yielded to threats and torture, but others held out and were killed. Valerian (r. A.D. 253–260) resumed the persecutions, partly to confiscate the wealth of rich Christians. His successors, however, found other matters more pressing,

and the persecution lapsed until the end of the century.

By the time of Diocletian the number of Christians had grown still greater and included some high state officials. At the same time hostility to the Christians grew on every level. Diocletian was not generous toward unorthodox intellectual or religious movements. His own effort to bolster imperial power with the aura of divinity boded ill for the Church, and in 303, he launched the most serious persecution inflicted on the Christians in the Roman Empire. He issued a series of edicts confiscating Church property and destroying churches and their sacred books. He deprived upper-class Christians of public office and judicial rights, imprisoned clergy, and enslaved Christians of the lower classes. He placed heavy fines on anyone refusing to sacrifice to the public gods. A final decree required public sacrifices and libations. The persecution horrified many pagans, and the plight and the demeanor of the martyrs often aroused pity and sympathy.

Ancient states could not carry out a program of terror with the thoroughness of modern totalitarian governments, and so the Christians and their Church survived to enjoy what they must have considered a miraculous change of fortune. In 311 Galerius, who had been one of the most vigorous persecutors, was influenced, perhaps by his Christian wife, to issue an edict of toleration permitting Christian worship.

The victory of Constantine and his emergence as sole ruler of the empire changed the condition of Christianity from a precariously tolerated sect to the religion favored by the emperor. This put it on the path to becoming the official and only legal religion in the empire.

EMERGENCE OF CHRISTIANITY AS THE STATE RELIGION   The sons of Constantine continued to favor the new religion, but the succession of Julian the Apostate posed a new threat. He was a devotee of traditional classical pagan culture and, as a believer in Neoplatonism, an opponent of Christianity. Neoplatonism was a religious philosophy, or a philosophical religion, whose connection with Platonic teachings was distant. Its chief formulator was Plotinus (A.D. 205–270), who tried to combine classical and rational philosophical speculation with the mystical spirit of his time. Plotinus's successors

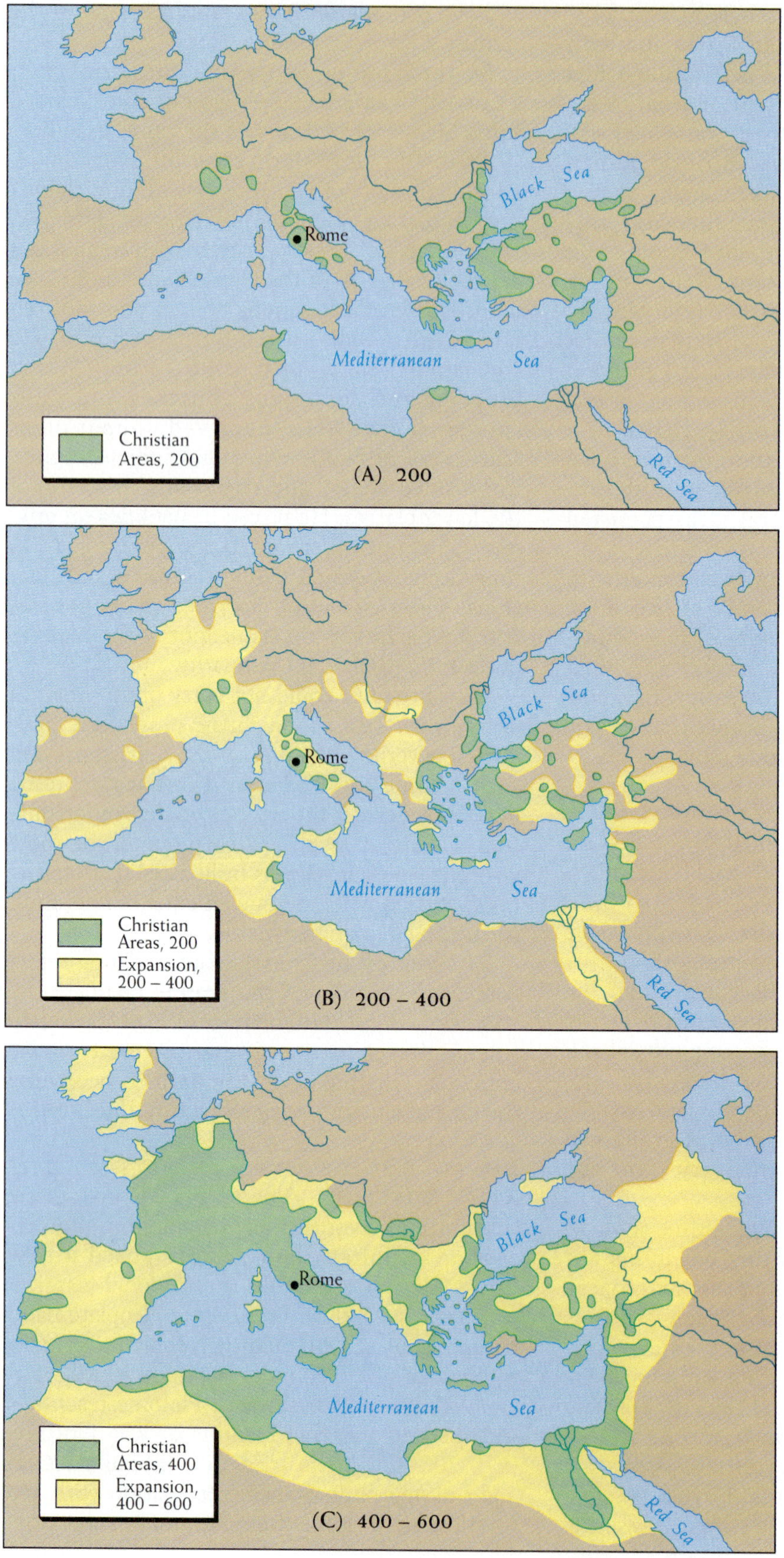

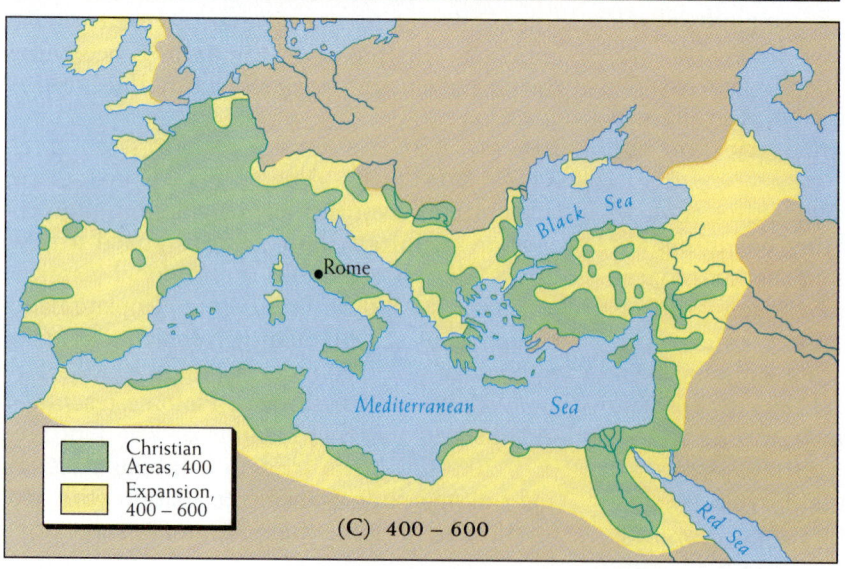

MAP 5-6 THE SPREAD OF CHRISTIANITY *Christianity grew swiftly in the third, fourth, fifth, and sixth centuries—especially after the conversion of the emperors in the fourth century. By 600, on the eve of the birth of the new religion of Islam, Christianity was dominant throughout the Mediterranean world and most of western Europe.*

On the three maps:

(A) 200
Christian Areas, 200

(B) 200–400
Christian Areas, 200
Expansion, 200–400

(C) 400–600
Christian Areas, 400
Expansion, 400–600

A Hostile View of Christianity

In its long struggle to victory in the Roman Empire, Christianity had to fight against ignorant prejudice, sincere rejection, and hostile propaganda. The following selection is from "Octavius," an invented dialogue written by the third-century writer Minucius Felix, between a Christian and a polytheist in which the latter repeats widespread complaints against the Christians.

♦ From your reading in this book and from your own knowledge of Christianity, how would you assess these charges? Which might be true, which caused by misunderstanding, and which entirely false? To what extent is the criticism based on the difference between the morality of pagan Rome and that of Christianity? In what ways were these ethical systems different? Were they the same in any respects?

Is it not deplorable that a faction . . . of abandoned, hopeless outlaws makes attacks against the gods? They gather together ignorant persons from the lowest dregs, and credulous women, easily deceived as their sex is, and organize a rabble of unholy conspirators, leagued together in nocturnal associations and by ritual fasts and barbarous foods, not for the purpose of some sacred rite but for the sake of sacrilege—a secret tribe that shuns the light, silent in public but talkative in secret places. They despise the temples as if they were tombs, they spit upon the gods, they ridicule our sacred rites. Pitiable themselves, they pity . . . our priests; half-naked themselves, they despise offices and offical robes. What amazing folly! What incredible arrogance! They despise present tortures yet dread uncertain future ones; while they fear to die after death, they have no fear of it in the meantime; deceptive hope soothes away their terror with the solace of a life to come.

. . . .

What is told of the initiation of neophytes is as detestable as it is notorious. An infant covered with spelt to deceive the unsuspecting is set before the one to be initiated in the rites. The neophyte is induced to strike what seem to be harmless blows on the surface of the spelt, and this infant is killed by his random and unsuspecting blows. Its blood—oh, shocking!—they greedily lap up; the limbs they eagerly distribute; and by this victim they league themselves, and by this complicity in crime they pledge themselves to mutual silence. . . . Their form of banqueting is notorious; everywhere all talk of it. . . . On an appointed day they assemble at a feast with all their children, sisters, and mothers, people of both sexes and every age. There, after much feasting, when the banquet has become heated and intoxication has inflamed the drunken passions of incestuous lust, a dog which has been tied to a lamp is incited to rush and leap forward after a morsel thrown beyond the range of the cord by which it was tied. The telltale light is upset and extinguished, and in the shameless dark they exchange embraces indiscriminately, and all, if not actually, yet by complicity are equally involved in incest. . . .

Furthermore, they threaten the whole world and the universe itself and its stars with fire, and work for its destruction. . . . Not content with this insane notion, they add to and weave old wives' tales: they say that they are reborn after death from the cinders and ashes, and with unaccountable confidence believe in one another's lies. . . .

But you [Christians] meanwhile in anxious doubt abstain from wholesome pleasures; you do not attend the shows; you take no part in the processions; fight shy of public banquets; abhor the sacred games, meats from the sacrificial victims, drinks poured in libation on the altars.

Minucius Felic, Octavius, viii, 3–xii.6 (abridged), *trans. by N. Lewis and M. Reinhold, in* Roman Civilization, *Vol. 2 (New York: Columbia University Press, 1955), pp. 584–586.*

A bust of the Alexandrian philosopher Plotinus, who lived ca. 205–270 A.D. [Giraudon, Art Resource, N.Y.]

created new ones and complicated some old ones. The favored position of the Church attracted converts for the wrong reasons and diluted the moral excellence and spiritual fervor of its adherents. The problem of the relationship between Church and state arose, presenting the possibility that religion would become subordinate to the state, as it had been in the classical world and in earlier civilizations. In the East that is what happened to a considerable degree.

In the West the weakness of the emperors prevented such a development and permitted Church leaders to exercise remarkable independence. In 390 Ambrose, bishop of Milan, excommunicated Theodosius for a massacre he had carried out, and the emperor did humble penance. This act provided an important precedent for future assertions of the Church's autonomy and authority, but it did not put an end to secular interference and influence in the Church.

ARIANISM AND THE COUNCIL OF NICAEA Internal divisions proved to be even more troubling as new heresies emerged. Because they threatened the unity of an empire that was now Christian, they took on a political character and inevitably involved the emperor and the powers of the state. Before long, the world would view Christians persecuting other Christians with a zeal at least as great as had been displayed against them by the most fanatical pagans.

Among the many controversial views that arose, the most important and the most threatening was Arianism. It was founded by a priest named Arius of Alexandria (ca. A.D. 280–336) in the fourth century. The issue creating difficulty was the relation of God the Father and God the Son. Arius argued that Jesus was a created being, unlike God the Father. He was, therefore, not made of the substance of God and was not eternal. "The Son has a beginning," he said, "but God is without beginning." For Arius, Jesus was neither fully man nor fully God but something in between. Arius's view did away with the mysterious concept of the Trinity, the difficult doctrine that holds that God is three persons (the Father, the Son, and the Holy Spirit) and also one in substance and essence.

were bitter critics of Christianity, and their views influenced Julian. Though he refrained from persecution, he tried to undo the work of Constantine by withdrawing the privileges of the Church, removing Christians from high offices, and attempting to introduce a new form of pagan worship. His reign, however, was short, and his work did not last.

In 394 Theodosius forbade the celebration of pagan cults and abolished the pagan religious calendar. At his death Christianity was the official religion of the Roman Empire.

The establishment of Christianity as the state religion did not put an end to the troubles of the Christians and their Church; instead it

The Arian concept had the advantage of appearing to be simple, rational, and philosophically acceptable. To its ablest opponent, Athanasius, however, it had serious shortcomings. Athanasius (ca. A.D. 293–373), later bishop of Alexandria, saw the Arian view as an impediment to any acceptable theory of salvation, to him the most important religious question. He adhered to the old Greek idea of salvation as involving the change of sinful mortality into divine immortality through the gift of "life." Only if Jesus were both fully human and fully God could the transformation of humanity to divinity have taken place in him and be transmitted by him to his disciples. "Christ was made man," he said, "that we might be made divine."

To deal with the growing controversy, Constantine called a council of Christian bishops at Nicaea, not far from Constantinople, in 325. For the emperor the question was essentially political, but for the disputants salvation was at stake. At Nicaea the view expounded by Athanasius won out, became orthodox, and was embodied in the Nicene Creed. But Arianism persisted and spread. Some later emperors were either Arians or sympathetic to that view. Some of the most successful missionaries to the barbarians were Arians; as a result, many of the German tribes that overran the empire were Arians. The Christian emperors hoped to bring unity to their increasingly decentralized realms by imposing the single religion. Over time it did prove to be a unifying force, but it also introduced divisions where none had existed before.

Arts and Letters in the Late Empire

The art and literature of the late empire reflect the confluence of pagan and Christian ideas and traditions as well as the conflict between them. Much of the literature is of a polemical nature and much of the art is propaganda.

The salvation of the empire from the chaos of the third century was accomplished by a military revolution based on and led by provincials whose origins were in the lower classes. They brought with them the fresh winds of cultural change, which blew out not only the dust of classical culture but much of its substance as well. Yet the new ruling class was not interested

The Triumph of Christianity	
ca. 4 B.C.	Jesus of Nazareth born
ca. A.D. 30	Crucifixion of Jesus
64	Fire at Rome—Persecution by Nero
ca. 70–100	Gospels written
ca. 250–260	Major persecutions by Decius and Valerian
303	Persecution by Diocletian
311	Galerius issues Edict of Toleration
312	Battle of Milvian Bridge—Conversion of Constantine to Christianity
325	Council of Nicaea
395	Christianity becomes official religion of Roman Empire

in leveling; it wanted instead to establish itself as a new aristocracy. It thought of itself as effecting a great restoration rather than a revolution and sought to restore classical culture and absorb it. The confusion and uncertainty of the times were tempered in part, of course, by the comfort of Christianity. But the new ruling class sought order and stability—ethical, literary, and artistic—in the classical tradition as well.

THE PRESERVATION OF CLASSICAL CULTURE One of the main needs and accomplishments of this period was the preservation of classical culture. Ways were discovered to make it available and useful to the newly arrived ruling class. Works of the great classical authors were reproduced in many copies and were transferred from perishable and inconvenient papyrus rolls to sturdier codices, bound volumes that were as easy to use as modern books. Scholars also digested long works like Livy's *History of Rome* into shorter versions and wrote learned commentaries and compiled grammars. Original works by pagan writers of the late empire were neither numerous nor especially distinguished.

CHRISTIAN WRITERS On the other hand, the late empire saw a great outpouring of Christian writings. There were many examples of Christian apologetics in poetry as well as in prose, and there were sermons, hymns, and biblical commentaries. Christianity could also boast important scholars. Jerome (A.D. 348–420), thoroughly trained in both the East and the West in classical Latin literature and rhetoric, produced a revised version of the Bible in Latin. Commonly called the Vulgate, it became the Bible used by the Catholic church. Probably the most important eastern scholar was Eusebius of Caesarea (ca. A.D. 260–340). He wrote apologetics, an idealized biography of Constantine, and a valuable attempt to reconstruct the chronology of important events in the past. His most important contribution, however, was his *Ecclesiastical History,* an attempt to set forth the Christian view of history. He saw all of history as the working out of God's will. All of history, therefore, had a purpose and a direction, and Constantine's victory and the subsequent unity of empire and Church were its culmination.

The closeness and also the complexity of the relationship between classical pagan culture and that of the Christianity of the late empire are nowhere better displayed than in the career and writings of Augustine (A.D. 354–430), bishop of Hippo in North Africa. He was born at Carthage and was trained as a teacher of rhetoric. His father was a pagan, but his mother was a Christian and hers was ultimately the stronger influence. He passed through several intellectual way stations, skepticism and Neoplatonism among others, before his conversion to Christianity. His training and skill in pagan rhetoric and philosophy made him peerless among his contemporaries as a defender of Christianity and as a theologian.

His greatest works are his *Confessions,* an autobiography describing the road to his conversion, and *The City of God.* The latter was a response to the pagan charge that Rome's sack by the Goths in 410 was caused by the abandonment of the old gods and the advent of Christianity. The optimistic view held by some Christians that God's will worked its way in history and was easily comprehensible needed further support in the face of this disaster. Augustine sought to separate the fate of Christianity from that of the Roman Empire. He contrasted the secular world, the City of Man, with the spiritual, the City of God. The former was selfish, the latter unselfish; the former evil, the latter good.

Augustine argued that history was moving forward, in the spiritual sense, to the Day of Judgment but there was no reason to expect improvement before then in the secular sphere. The fall of Rome was neither surprising nor important. All states, even a Christian Rome, were part of the City of Man and were therefore corrupt and mortal. Only the City of God was immortal, and it, consisting of all the saints on earth and in heaven, was untouched by earthly calamities.

Though the *Confessions* and *The City of God* are Augustine's most famous works, they emphasize only a part of his thought. His treatises *On the Trinity* and *On Christian Education* reveal the great skill with which he supported Christian belief with the learning, logic, and philosophy of the pagan classics. Augustine believed that faith is essential and primary (a thoroughly Christian view), but it is not a substitute for reason (the foundation of classical thought). Instead, faith is the starting point for and liberator of human reason, which continues to be the means by which people can understand what faith reveals. His writings constantly reveal the presence of both Christian faith and pagan reason, as well as the tension between them, a legacy he left to the Middle Ages.

Problem of the Decline and Fall of the Empire in the West

Whether important to Augustine or not, the massive barbarian invasions of the fifth century put an end to effective imperial government in the West. For centuries people have speculated about the causes of the collapse of the ancient world. Every kind of reason has been put forward, and some suggestions seem to have nothing to do with reason at all. Soil exhaustion, plague, climatic change, and even poisoning caused by lead water pipes have been suggested as reasons for Rome's decline in population, vigor, and the capacity to defend itself. Some blame the institution of slavery and a resulting failure to make advances in science and technology. Others blame excessive government interference in the economic life of the empire, and still others the destruction of the urban middle class, the carrier of classical culture.

Perhaps a simpler and more obvious explanation can be found. It might begin with the observation that the growth of so mighty an empire as Rome's was by no means inevitable. Rome's greatness had come from conquests that provided the Romans with the means to expand still further, until there were not enough Romans to conquer and govern any more peoples and territory. When pressure from outsiders grew, the Romans lacked the resources to advance and defeat the enemy as in the past. The tenacity and success of their resistance for so long were remarkable. Without new conquests to provide the immense wealth needed for the defense and maintenance of internal prosperity, the Romans finally yielded to unprecedented onslaughts by fierce and numerous attackers.

To blame the ancients and the institution of slavery for the failure to produce an industrial and economic revolution like that of the later Western world (one capable of producing wealth without taking it from another) is to stand the problem on its head. No one yet has a satisfactory explanation for those revolutions. So it is improper to blame any institution or society for not achieving what has been achieved only once in human history. Perhaps we would do well to think of the problem as Gibbon did:

The decline of Rome was the natural and inevitable effect of immoderate greatness. Prosperity ripened the principle of decay; the cause of the destruction multiplied with the extent of conquest; and, as soon as time or accident had removed the artificial supports, the stupendous fabric yielded to the pressure of its own weight. The story of the ruin is simple and obvious; and instead of inquiring why the Roman Empire was destroyed, we should rather be surprised that it had subsisted so long.[5]

◆

Out of the civil wars and chaos that brought down the republic, Augustus brought unity, peace, order, and prosperity. As a result he was regarded with almost religious awe and attained more military and political power than any Roman before him. He ruled firmly but with moderation. He tried to limit military adventures and the costs they incurred. Augustus supported public works that encouraged trade and communication in the empire. He tried to restore and invigorate the old civic pride, and in this he had considerable success. He was less successful in promoting private morality based on family values. He patronized the arts so as to beautify Rome and glorify his reign. On his death Augustus was able to pass on the regime to his family, the Julio-Claudians.

For almost two hundred years, with a few brief interruptions, the empire was generally prosperous, peaceful, and well run. But problems were growing. Management of the many responsibilities assumed by the government required the growth of a large bureaucracy that placed a heavy and increasing burden on the treasury, required higher taxes, and stifled both civic spirit and private enterprise. Pressure from barbarian tribes on the frontiers required a large standing army, which was also very costly and led to further rises in taxation.

In the late empire Rome's rulers resorted to many devices for dealing with their problems. Policies came to include putting down internal military rebellions led by generals from different parts of the empire. More and more, the emperors' rule and their safety depended on the loyalty of the army, and so they courted the soldiers' favor with gifts of various kinds. This only increased the burden of taxes; the rich and powerful found ways to avoid their obligations, making the load on everyone else all the heavier. The government's control over the lives of its people became ever greater and the society more rigid as people tried to flee to escape the crushing load of taxes. Expedients were tried, including inflating the currency, fixing farmers to the soil as serfs (coloni), building walls to keep the barbarians out, and bribing barbarian tribes to fight for Rome against other barbarians. Ultimately, all these measures failed. The Roman Empire in the West fell, leaving disunity, insecurity, disorder, and poverty. Like similar empires in the ancient world, it had been unable to sustain its "immoderate greatness."

Review Questions

1. Discuss the Augustan constitution and government. What solutions did Augustus pro-

[5]*Edward Gibbon*, Decline and Fall of the Roman Empire, 2nd ed., Vol. 4, ed. by J. B. Bury (London, 1909), pp. 173–174.

vide for the problems that had plagued the Roman republic? Why was the Roman population willing to accept Augustus as head of the state?

2. How was the Roman empire organized and why did it function smoothly? What role did the emperor play in the maintenance of political stability?

3. How did the literature in the Golden Age of Augustus differ from that of the Silver Age during the first and second centuries A.D.? How did the poetry of Vergil and Horace contribute to the stability of Augustus's rule?

4. In spite of unpromising beginnings, Christianity was enormously popular by the fourth century A.D. Why were Christians persecuted by Roman authorities? What were the more important reasons for Christianity's success?

5. What were the political, social, and economic problems that beset Rome in the third and fourth centuries A.D.? How did Diocletian and Constantine deal with them? Were they effective in stemming the tide of decline and disintegration in the Roman empire? What problems were they unable to solve?

6. Discuss three theories that scholars have advanced to explain the decline and fall of the Roman empire. What are the difficulties involved in explaining the fall? What explanation would you give?

Suggested Readings

J. P. V. D. BALSDON, *Roman Women* (1962). A standard treatment.

T. BARNES, *The New Empire of Diocletian and Constantine* (1982). A study of the character of the late empire.

P. BROWN, *Augustine of Hippo* (1967). A splendid biography.

P. BROWN, *The World of Late Antiquity, A.D. 150–750* (1971). A brilliant and readable essay.

J. BURCKHARDT, *The Age of Constantine the Great* (1956). A classic work by the Swiss cultural historian.

C. M. COCHRANE, *Christianity and Classical Culture* (1957). A study of intellectual change in the late empire.

S. DILL, *Roman Society in the Last Century of the Western Empire* (1958). A classic social history.

E. R. DODDS, *Pagan and Christian in an Age of Anxiety* (1965). An original and perceptive study.

A. FERRILL, *The Fall of the Roman Empire, The Military Explanation* (1986). An interpretation that emphasizes the decline in the quality of the Roman army.

A. FERRILL, *Caligula: Emperor of Rome* (1991). A biography of the monstrous young emperor.

E. GIBBON, *The History of the Decline and Fall of the Roman Empire*, 7 vols., ed. by J. B. Bury, 2nd ed. (1909–1914). One of the masterworks of the English language.

M. GRANT, *The Fall of the Roman Empire* (1990). A lively, well-written account.

T. R. HOLMES, *Architect of the Roman Empire*, 2 vols. (1928–1931). An account of Augustus's career in detail.

A. H. M. JONES, *The Later Roman Empire*, 3 vols. (1964). A comprehensive study of the period.

D. KAGAN, ed., *The End of the Roman Empire: Decline or Transformation?* 3rd. ed. (1992). A collection of essays discussing the problem of the decline and fall of the Roman Empire.

M. L. W. LAISTNER, *The Greater Roman Historians* (1963). Essays on the major Roman historical writers.

J. LEBRETON and J. ZEILLER, *History of the Primitive Church*, 3 vols. (1962). The Catholic viewpoint.

H. LIETZMANN, *History of the Early Church*, 2 vols. (1961). From the Protestant viewpoint.

E. N. LUTTWAK, *The Grand Strategy of the Roman Empire* (1976). An original and fascinating analysis by a keen student of modern strategy.

R. MACMULLEN, *Enemies of the Roman Order* (1966). An original and revealing examination of opposition to the emperors.

R. MACMULLEN, *Roman Social Relations, 50 B.C. to A.D. 284* (1981). An interesting study of social developments.

R. MACMULLEN, *Corruption and the Decline of Rome* (1988). A study that examines the importance of changes in ethical ideas and behavior.

R. W. MATHISON, *Roman Aristocrats in Barbarian Gaul: Strategies for Survival* (1993). An unusual slant on the late empire.

F. G. B. MILLAR, *The Roman Empire and Its Neighbors* (1968). An analysis of Roman foreign relations in the imperial period.

F. G. B. MILLAR, *The Emperor in the Roman World, 31 B.C.–A.D. 337* (1977). A study of Roman imperial government.

A. MOMIGLIANO, ed., *The Conflict Between Paganism and Christianity* (1963). A valuable collection of essays.

H. M. D. Parker, *A History of the Roman World from A.D. 138 to 337* (1969). A good survey.

M. I. Rostovtzeff, *Social and Economic History of the Roman Empire*, 2nd. ed. (1957). A masterpiece whose main thesis has been much disputed.

V. Rudich, *Political Dissidence Under Nero, The Price of Dissimulation* (1993). A brilliant exposition of the lives and thoughts of political dissidents in the early empire.

E. T. Salmon, *A History of the Roman World, 30 B.C. to A.C. 138* (1968). A good survey.

C. G. Starr, *Civilization and the Caesars* (1965). A study of Roman culture in the Augustan period.

G. E. M. de Ste. Croix, *The Class Struggle in the Ancient World* (1981). An ambitious interpretation of all of classical civilization from an idiosyncratic Marxist perspective.

R. Syme, *The Roman Revolution* (1960). A brilliant study of Augustus, his supporters, and their rise to power.

L. R. Taylor, *The Divinity of the Roman Empire* (1931). A study of the imperial cult.

The Middle Ages, 476–1300

DURING the eight centuries between the fall of Rome and the beginning of the Renaissance, the major institutions of western European civilization acquired a definite shape. These same centuries saw Eastern or Byzantine civilization peak and Islamic civilization rise and crest; both were militarily and culturally superior to the West. The many formative outside influences that had come upon the West from the Byzantine Empire, the migrating Germanic tribes, and the Islamic world during the early Middle Ages were folded into a distinctive western civilization.

The Middle Ages saw the division of Christendom into two very different and opposed Christian churches: the Western Church centered in Rome, and the Byzantine Church centered in Constantinople. The Roman Catholic church emerged from the chaos of the Roman Empire's collapse as a major custodian of Western culture. Firmly based in the cities and directed by the pope from Rome, its broad network of loyal clergy made it the only Western institution capable of extending its influence over many diverse regions.

The Carolingian rulers came to power in the seventh century and, with the assistance of the church, brought a modest revival of Western imperial pretensions. Particularly during the long reign of Charlemagne, Christian bishops and clergy became important allies in the organization of the Carolingian Empire, both in the countryside and in the towns.

New developments in farming increased the productivity of the rural manors, where 95 percent of the population lived. By Charlemagne's time a better harness for oxen and ploughs that could cut deeply into the soil, furrowing it, improved crop yields. Rotation of crops among three fields kept land fertile and productive. These new techniques stimulated population growth and cultural development.

In the twelfth and thirteenth centuries, thanks to a great rise in mercantile activity, towns and urban culture grew rapidly. A new merchant class emerged in the towns and took its place alongside the nobility and the clergy. Rulers increasingly drew on this class for servants and administrators. This group formed a loyal bureaucracy and brain trust that allowed rulers to challenge both the nobility and the Church successfully. The alliance between rulers and towns was an important factor in the rise of Europe's new secular monarchies and the creation of Europe's major nation-states.

In the twelfth and thirteenth centuries in England and France, the foundations of Western monarchies were laid. Parliaments and popular assemblies also formed to represent the growing power of the privileged classes (that is, the nobility, the clergy, and property-owning townspeople). Western capitalism was at this time in the birthing chair. The new wealth created by trade and conquest made possible the creation of universities, which multiplied to twenty in Catholic Europe by 1300.

Emperors and kings clashed repeatedly with popes during the twelfth and thirteenth centuries, when the Roman Catholic church was still a formidable political power. At the end of the Investiture Controversy in the twelfth century, a clear distinction was drawn between the spheres of ecclesiastical and secular authority. After 1300, monarchs progressively limited the Church's influence over their political and economic affairs, restricting the Church to the important but less threatening spiritual and cultural sphere of influence.

The Crusades to the Holy Land attested to the Church's continuing popularity in the high Middle Ages, even though these ventures had acquired a mercenary character by the thirteenth century. In an increasingly materialistic age, the rise of the Dominican and Franciscan friars signaled a new spiritual revival among the clergy that also attracted large numbers of pious laity. Until the Reformation, church reformers rallied under the banner of apostolic poverty. ◆

300–500	*315* Constantinople becomes new capital of Roman Empire *410* Visigoths sack Rome *451–453* Attila the Hun invades Italy *455* Vandals overrun Rome *476* Odovacer deposes the last Western emperor *489–493* Theodoric's Ostrogoth kingdom established in Italy
500–700	*527–565* Reign of Justinian *568* Lombard invasion of Italy *632–733* Muslim expansion and conquests
700–900	*734* Charles Martel defeats Muslims at Poitiers *768–814* Reign of Charlemagne *843* Treaty of Verdun partitions Carolingian empire
900–1100	*918* Saxon Henry I becomes first non-Frankish king, as Saxons succeed Carolingians in Germany *987* Capetians succeed Carolingians in France *1066* Battle of Hastings (Norman Conquest of England) *1071* Seljuk Turks defeat Byzantine armies at Manzikert *1099* Jerusalem falls to Crusaders
1100–1300	*1152* Frederick I Barbarossa first Hohenstaufen emperor *1187* Saladin reconquers Jerusalem from West *1204* Fourth Crusade captures Constantinople *1214* Philip II Augustus defeats English and German armies at Bouvines *1215* Magna Carta *1240* Mongols dominate Russia *1250* Death of Frederick II (end of Hohenstaufen dynasty) *1257* German princes establish electoral college to elect emperor

Society and Economy	Religion and Culture
	312 Constantine embraces Christianity
	325 Council of Nicaea
400 Cities and trade begin to decline in the West; Germanic (barbarian) tribes settle in the West	380 Christianity becomes the official religion of the Roman empire
	413–426 St. Augustine writes *City of God*
	451 Council of Chalcedon
	496 The Franks embrace Christianity
533–534 *Corpus Juris civilis* compiled by Justinian	529 St. Benedict founds monastery at Monte Cassino
	537 Byzantine Church of Hagia Sophia completed
632–733 Muslims disrupt western Mediterranean trade	590–604 Pope Gregory the Great
	622 Muhammad's flight from Mecca (Hegira)
700 Agrarian society centered around the manor predominates in the West	
700–800 Moldboard plow and three field system in use	725–787 Iconoclastic Controversy in East
	ca. 775 Donation of Constantine
700 Islam enters its Golden Age	782 Alcuin of York runs Charlemagne's palace school
800 Byzantium enters its Golden Age	800 Pope Leo crowns Charlemagne emperor
800 Introduction of collar harness	
850 Muslims occupy parts of Spain	
880s Vikings penetrate central Europe	
900 Introduction of the horseshoe	910 Benedictine monastery of Cluny founded
900–1100 Rise of towns, guilds, and urban culture in West	980s Orthodox Christianity penetrates Russia
1086 Domesday Book	1054 Schism between Eastern and Western churches
	1075 Pope Gregory VII condemns lay investiture
	1095 Pope Urban II preaches the First Crusade
1130 Gothic architecture begins to displace Romanesque	1122 Concordat of Worms ends Investiture Controversy
	1158 First European university founded in Bologna
1200 Shift from dues to rent tenancy on manors	1210 Franciscan Order founded
	1216 Dominican Order founded
	1265 Thomas Aquinas' *Summa Theologica* begun
	ca. 1275 Romance of the Rose

An early Byzantine portrayal of the Virgin and Jesus, flanked by the martyred Christian saints Theodore and George, with guardian angels behind them keeping watch. This icon dates from the sixth century. [Ronald Sheridan/Ancient Art & Architecture Collection]

6

The Early Middle Ages (476–1000): The Birth of Europe

Key Topics in This Chapter
◆ How the fusion of Germanic and Roman culture laid the foundation for a distinctively European society after the collapse of the Western Roman Empire
◆ The Byzantine and Islamic empires and their impact on the West
◆ The role of the Church in Western society during the early Middle Ages
◆ The political and economic features of Europe under the Franks
◆ The characteristics of feudal society

The early Middle Ages mark the birth of Europe. This period of recovery from the collapse of Roman civilization gave rise to forced experimentation with new ideas and institutions. Greco-Roman culture combined with the new Germanic culture and an evolving Christianity *to create distinctive political and cultural forms within what had been the northern and western provinces of the Roman Empire. In government, religion, and language, as well as geography, these regions grew separate from the eastern Byzantine world and the Islamic Arab world that extended across North Africa from Spain to the eastern Mediterranean.*

The early Middle Ages have been called, not with complete fairness, a "dark age," because during these centuries western Europe lost touch with classical, especially Greek, learning and science. People the Romans somewhat arrogantly called "barbarians"—because their origins were rural and they knew no Latin—intruded on the region from the north and east. German tribes that had been settling peacefully around the empire since the first century B.C. began to migrate directly into it by the fourth century. During the fifth century, these tribes turned fiercely against their Roman hosts, largely because the Romans treated them so cruelly. To the south, Arab dominance transformed the Mediterranean into an often inhospitable "Islamic lake," greatly reducing (although by no means completely severing) western trade with the East and isolating western people more than they had been before. Thus surrounded and assailed from north, east, and south, Europe understandably became somewhat insular and even stagnant.

On the other hand, being forced to manage by themselves, western Europeans also learned to develop their native resources. The reign of Charlemagne saw a modest renaissance of antiquity. And the peculiar social and political forms that emerged during this period—manorialism and feudalism—not only were successful at coping with unprecedented chaos on local levels but also proved to be fertile seedbeds for the growth of distinctive Western institutions.

On the Eve of the Frankish Ascendancy

As we have already seen, by the late third century the Roman Empire had become too large for a single sovereign to govern and was failing in many respects. The Emperor Diocletian (284–305) tried to strengthen the empire by dividing it between himself and a co-emperor, Maximian. The result was a dual empire with an eastern and a western half, each with its own emperor and, eventually, imperial bureaucracy. A critical shift of the empire's resources and orientation to the east accompanied these changes.

In 284 Diocletian moved to Nicomedia (in modern Turkey), where he remained until the last two years of his reign. As imperial rule weakened in the West and strengthened in the East, it also became increasingly autocratic.

In an attempt to end the factional strife that followed Diocletian's reign and to position himself better to meet the empire's new eastern enemies, Constantine the Great (r. 306–337) briefly reunited the empire by conquest (it would be redivided by his three sons and subsequent successors) and ruled as sole emperor of the East and the West after 324. In that year he moved the capital of the empire from Rome to Byzantium, an ancient city that stood at the crossroads of the major sea and land routes between Europe and Asia Minor. On the site of this ancient city, Constantine built the new city of Constantinople, dedicated in 330. Serving as the imperial residence and the new administrative center of the empire, Constantinople gradually became a "new Rome." The "old" Rome, suffering from internal political quarrels and geographically distant from new military fronts in Syria and along the Danube River, declined in importance. The city and the western empire were actually on the wane in the late third and fourth centuries, well before the barbarian invasions in the West began. Milan had replaced Rome as the imperial residence in 286; in 402 the seat of western government would be moved yet again, to Ravenna. When the barbarian invasions began in the late fourth century, the West was in political disarray, and imperial power and prestige had shifted decisively to Constantinople and the East.

Germanic Migrations

The German tribes did not burst in on the West all of a sudden. They were at first a token and benign presence on the fringes of the empire and even within it. Before the massive migrations from the north and the east, Roman and Germanic cultures had commingled peacefully for centuries. The Romans had "imported" barbarians as domestics, slaves, and soldiers. Barbarian soldiers rose to positions of high leadership and fame in Roman legions.

Beginning in 376 with a great influx of Visigoths (west Goths) into the empire, this peaceful coexistence ended. The Visigoths, accomplished horsemen and fierce warriors, were themselves pushed into the empire by the emergence of a notoriously violent people, the Huns, from the region of modern Mongolia. The Visigoths ultimately reached southern Gaul and Spain. Soon to be Christianized, they won rights of settlement and material assistance within the empire from the eastern emperor Valens (364–378) in exchange for defending the eastern frontier as *foederati,* or special allies of the emperor.

A Contemporary Description of Attila the Hun

In 448 a Roman envoy, Priscus, visited the home of Attila in a Scythian village at the base of the Danube River, three years before Attila's famous invasion of Italy. Knowing Attila's reputation for savagery, he was surprised to find him a simple and cultured man.

✦ *How would you account for the discrepancy between this portrait of Attila and his reputation? Has history falsely portrayed this fiercest of warriors? What does it say about the Huns' system of justice that Attila dispensed judgments on the street as he walked?*

Attila's residence . . . was made of polished boards, and surrounded with wooden enclosures, designed not so much for protection as for appearance's sake. . . . I entered the enclosure of Attila's palace, bearing gifts to his wife, whose name was Kreka. . . . Having been admitted by the barbarians at the door, I found her reclining on a soft couch. The floor of the room was covered with woolen mats for walking on. . . . Having approached, saluted her, and presented the gifts, I went out and walked to the other houses. . . . Attila came forth from [one of] the house[s] with a dignified strut, looking round on this side and on that. . . . Many persons who had lawsuits with one another came up and received his judgment. Then he returned into the house and received ambassadors of barbarous peoples. . . .

[We were invited to a banquet with Attila at three o'clock.] The cupbearers gave us a cup, according to the national custom, that we might pray before we sat down. Having tasted the cup, we proceeded to take our seats, all the chairs being ranged along the walls of the room on either side. Attila sat in the middle on a couch; a second couch was set behind him, and from it steps led up to his bed, which was covered with linen sheets and wrought coverlets for ornament, such as Greeks and Romans used to deck bridal beds. The places on the right of Attila were held chief in honor; those on the left, where we sat, were only second. . . .

The attendant of Attila first entered with a dish full of meat, and behind him came the other attendants with bread and viands [plates of food], which they laid on the tables. A luxurious meal, served on silver plate, had been made ready for us and the barbarian guests, but Attila ate nothing but meat on a wooden trencher [a wooden plate]. In everything else, too, he showed himself temperate; his cup was of wood, while to the guests were given goblets of gold and silver. His dress, too, was quite simple, affecting only to be clean. The sword he carried at his side, the latchets of his . . . shoes, the bridle of his horse were not adorned with gold or gems or anything costly . . . like those of the other Scythians.

[After two courses were eaten and] evening fell, torches were lit and two barbarians, coming forward in front of Attila, sang songs they had composed, celebrating his victories and deeds of valor in war.

James Harvey Robinson, ed., Readings in European History, *Vol. 1 (Boston: Athenaeum, 1904), pp. 47–48.*

Instead of the promised assistance, however, the Visigoths received harsh treatment from their new allies. They had arrived in the empire an impoverished people fleeing the Huns. So bad off were they that they traded their own children to the Romans for dogs to eat. The Romans, showing no mercy, charged them one child per dog. After repeated conflicts, the Visigoths rebelled and handily defeated Roman armies under Valens at the Battle of Adrianople in 378.

After Adrianople, the Romans passively permitted the settlement of barbarians within the very heart of western empire. The Vandals crossed the Rhine in 406 and within three decades gained control of Northwest Africa and a sizable portion of the Mediterranean. The Burgundians, who came on the heels of the Vandals, settled in Gaul. Most important for subsequent Western history were the Franks, who settled northern and central Gaul, some along the sea coast (the Salian Franks) and others along the Rhine, Seine, and Loire Rivers (the Ripuarian Franks).

Why was there so little Roman resistance to these Germanic tribes, whose numbers—at most 100,000 people in the largest of them—were comparatively very small? The invaders were successful because they had come upon a badly overextended western empire divided politically by ambitious military commanders and physically weakened by decades of famine, pestilence, and overtaxation. By the second half of the fourth century, Roman frontiers had become too vast to manage. Efforts to do so by "barbarizing" the Roman army, that is, by recruiting many peasants into it and by making the Germanic tribes key Roman allies, only weakened it further. The eastern empire retained enough wealth and vitality to field new armies or to buy off the invaders. The western empire, in contrast, succumbed not only because of moral decay and materialism, but also because of a combination of military rivalry, political mismanagement, disease, and sheer poverty.

Fall of the Roman Empire

In the early fifth century, Italy and the "eternal city" of Rome suffered a series of devastating blows. In 410, the Visigoths, under Alaric (ca. 370–410), revolted and sacked Rome. In 452, the Huns, led by Attila—known to contemporaries as the "scourge of God"—invaded Italy. And in 455 Rome was overrun yet again, this time by the Vandals.

By the mid-fifth century, power in western Europe had passed decisively from the hands of the Roman emperors to those of barbarian chieftains. In 476, the traditional date given for the fall of the Roman Empire, the barbarian Odovacer (ca. 434–493) deposed and replaced the western emperor Romulus Augustulus. The eastern emperor, Zeno (r. 474–491), recognized Odovacer's authority in the West, and Odovacer acknowledged Zeno as sole emperor, contenting himself to serve as Zeno's western viceroy. In a later coup in 493 manipulated by Zeno, Theodoric (ca. 454–526), king of the Ostrogoths (east Goths), replaced Odovacer. At least until the last part of his reign, Theodoric governed with the full acceptance of the Roman people and the Christian church.

By the end of the fifth century, barbarians had thoroughly overrun the western empire. The Ostrogoths settled in Italy, the Franks in northern Gaul, the Burgundians in Provence, the Visigoths in southern Gaul and Spain, the Vandals in Africa and the western Mediterranean, and the Angles and Saxons in England (see Map 6-1).

Western Europe, however, was not transformed into a savage land. Its new masters were willing to learn from the people they had conquered; barbarian military victories did not result in a great defeat of Roman culture. Except in Britain and northern Gaul, Roman language, law, and government coexisted with the new Germanic institutions. In Italy under Theodoric, Roman law gradually replaced tribal custom. Only the Vandals and the Anglo-Saxons—and, after 466, the Visigoths—refused to profess at least titular obedience to the emperor in Constantinople.

That the Visigoths, the Ostrogoths, and the Vandals entered the West as Christianized people contributed to this accommodation of cultures. They were followers, however, of the Arian creed, considered heretical in the West. Arian Christians believed that Jesus Christ was not one identical being with God the Father—a point of view the Council of Nicea had condemned in 325 (see Chapter 5).

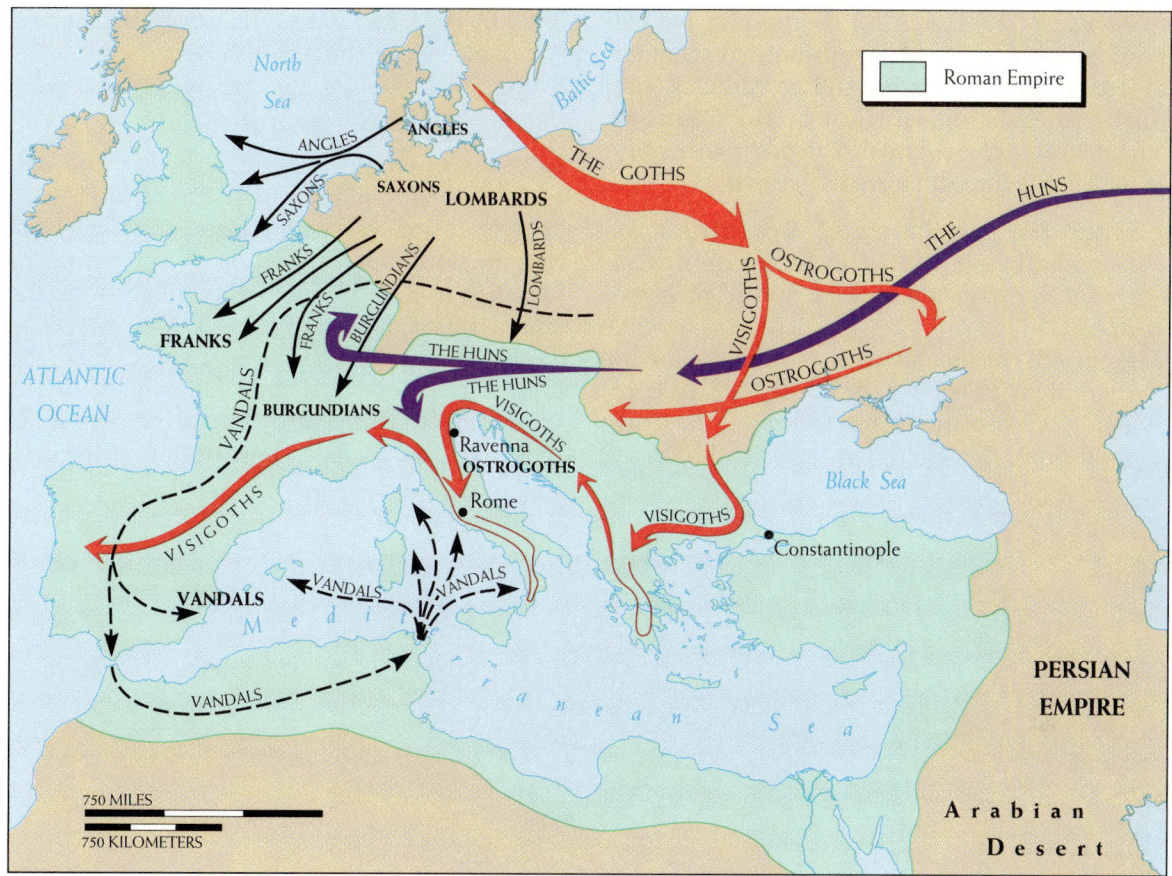

MAP 6-1 BARBARIAN MIGRATIONS INTO THE WEST IN FOURTH AND FIFTH CENTURIES *The forceful intrusion of Germanic and non-Germanic barbarians into the Roman Empire from the last quarter of the fourth century through the fifth century made for a constantly changing pattern of movement and relations. The map shows the major routes taken by the usually unwelcome newcomers and the areas most deeply affected by main groups.*

In spite of the hostility their Arian Christianity provoked, the Germans themselves admired Roman culture and had no desire to destroy it, although their rural lifestyle further weakened its urban foundations. Later, around 500, the Franks, under their strong king, Clovis, converted to the orthodox, or "Catholic," form of Christianity supported by the bishops of Rome. Then, as Roman Christians, the Franks helped conquer and convert the Goths and other barbarians in western Europe.

All things considered, rapprochement and a gradual interpenetration of two strong cultures—a creative tension—marked the period of the Germanic migrations. The stronger culture was the Roman, and it became dominant in a later fusion. Despite western military defeat, the Goths and the Franks became far more romanized than the Romans were germanized. Latin language, Nicene Christianity, and eventually Roman law and government were to triumph in the West during the Middle Ages.

The Byzantine Empire

As western Europe succumbed to the Germanic invasions, imperial power shifted to the Byzantine Empire, that is, the eastern part of the Roman Empire. Emperor Constantine the Great began the rebuilding of Byzantium in 324, renaming the city Constantinople and dedicating it in 330. Constantinople became the sole capital of the empire and remained so until the successful revival of the western empire in the eighth century by Charlemagne.

Between 324 and 1453 the empire passed from an early period of expansion and splendor to a time of contraction and splintering and finally to catastrophic defeat by the Ottoman Turks. Historians commonly divide the history of the empire into three distinct periods:

1. From the rebuilding of Byzantium as Constantinople in 324 to the beginning of the Arab expansion and the spread of Islam in 632,
2. From 632 to the conquest of Asia Minor by the Seljuk Turks after the fall of Manzikert in 1071, or, as some prefer, to the fall of Constantinople to western Crusaders in 1204,
3. From 1071 or 1204 to the defeat of Constantinople by the Turks in 1453.

The Reign of Justinian

In terms of territory, political power, and culture, the first period of Byzantine history (324–632) was by far its greatest. The height of this period was the reign of the emperor Justinian (r. 527–565) and his brilliant wife, the empress Theodora (d. 548) (see Map 6-2). The daughter of a bear trainer in the circus, the empress in her youth had fallen prey to the seedy side of sixth-century circus life. Her activities may have included prostitution, if the con-

A sixth-century ivory panel depicting the Byzantine emperor Justinian as the champion of the Christian faith. From 500 to 1100, the Byzantine empire was the center of Christian civilization. [Giraudon/Art Resource, N.Y.]

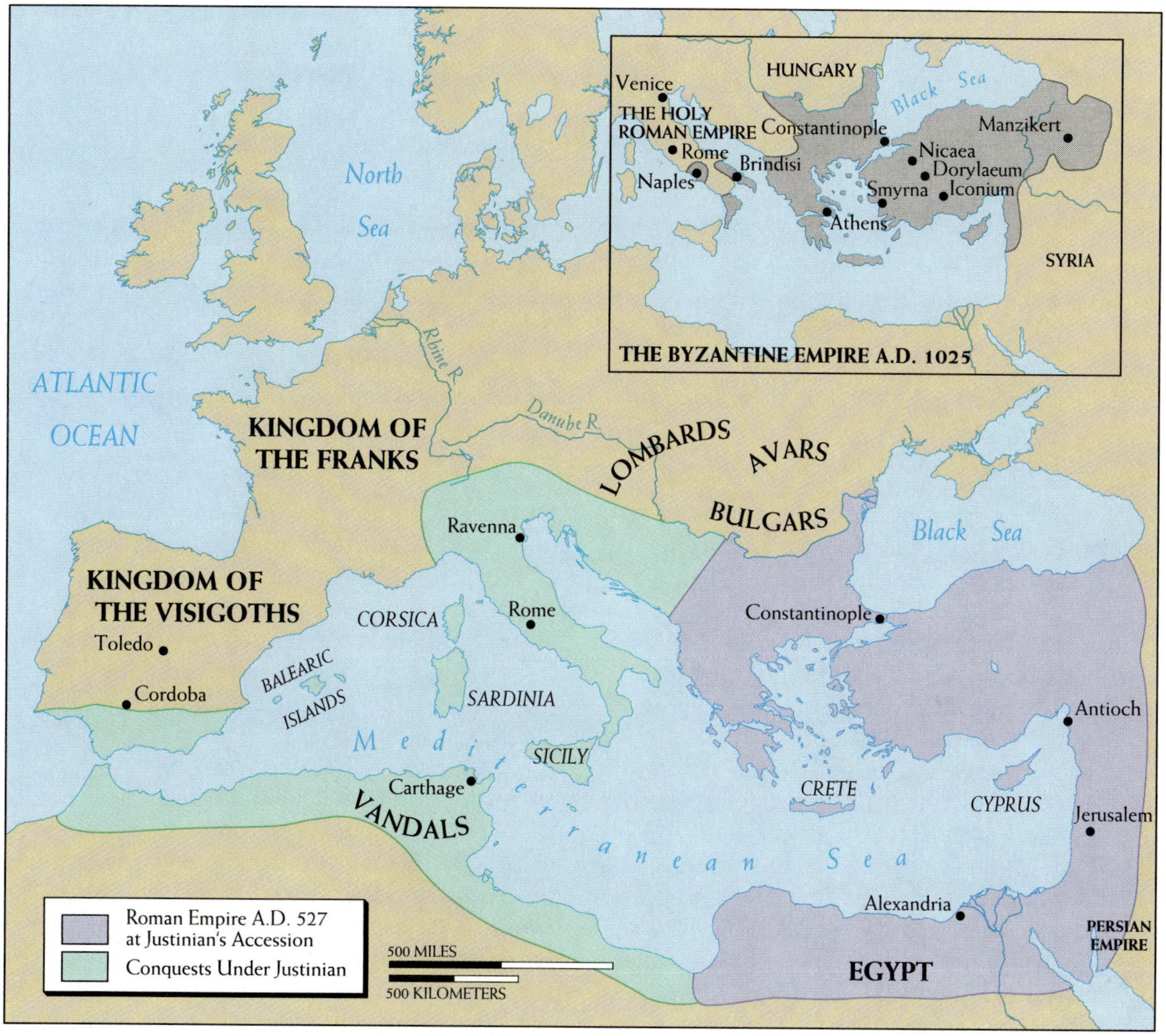

HUNGARY
Black Sea
Venice
THE HOLY ROMAN EMPIRE
Constantinople
Manzikert
Rome
Nicaea
Brindisi
Dorylaeum
Naples
Smyrna
Iconium
Athens
SYRIA
THE BYZANTINE EMPIRE A.D. 1025
North Sea
Rhine R.
ATLANTIC OCEAN
KINGDOM OF THE FRANKS
Danube R.
LOMBARDS
AVARS
BULGARS
Black Sea
Ravenna
KINGDOM OF THE VISIGOTHS
CORSICA
Rome
Constantinople
Toledo
BALEARIC ISLANDS
Cordoba
SARDINIA
Antioch
Mediterranean Sea
SICILY
Carthage
CRETE
CYPRUS
VANDALS
Jerusalem
Alexandria
Roman Empire A.D. 527 at Justinian's Accession
Conquests Under Justinian
500 MILES
500 KILOMETERS
EGYPT
PERSIAN EMPIRE

Map 6-2 The Byzantine Empire at the Death of Justinian

troversial *Secret History* by Justinian's court historian, Procopius, is to be believed. Her background may have given her a toughness that fully matched and even exceeded that of her husband.

An influential counselor, Theodora became a major figure in imperial government. In 532, Justinian contemplated abdication following riots against his rule that left much of Constantinople in ruins and thousands dead. Theodora stiffened his resolve, reportedly insisting that he crack down ruthlessly on the rioters and firmly reestablish his authority, which he most decisively did. In doctrinal matters, the empress clearly had a mind and will of her own. Whereas Justinian remained strictly orthodox in his Christian beliefs, Theodora lent her support to a Christian heresy known as Monophysitism, which taught that Jesus had only one nature, a composite divine–human one, not a fully human and fully divine dual nature, as orthodox doctrine taught. In the sixth century the Monophysites formed a separate church that had a very strong influence in the eastern provinces of the empire. The imperial government persecuted them as heretics after Theodora's death, a policy that cost the empire dearly when, in the seventh century, Persian and Arab armies besieged its eastern frontiers. Bitter over their treatment, the Monophysites offered little resistance to the invaders.

The Character and "Innovations" of Justinian and Theodora

According to their court historian and biographer, Procopius, the emperor and his wife were tyrants, pure and simple. His Secret History *(sixth century), which some historians distrust as a source, had only criticism and condemnation for the two rulers. Procopius especially resented Theodora, and he did not believe that the rule of law was respected at the royal court.*

◆ *Is Procopius being fair to Justinian and Theodora? Is the* Secret History *an ancient tabloid? How does one know when a source is biased and self-serving and when it is telling the truth? What does Procopius most dislike about the queen? Was Theodora the last woman ruler to receive such criticism?*

Formerly, when the senate approached the Emperor, it paid homage in the following manner. Every patrician kissed him on the right breast; the Emperor [then] kissed the patrician on the head, and he was dismissed. Then the rest bent their right knee to the Emperor and withdrew. It was not customary to pay homage to the Queen.

But those who were admitted [in]to the presence of Justinian and Theodora, whether they were patricians or otherwise, fell on their faces on the floor, stretching their hands and feet out wide, kissed first one foot and then the other of the Augustus [i.e., the emperor], and then retired. Nor did Theodora refuse this honor; and she even received the ambassadors of the Persians and other barbarians and gave them presents, as if she were in command of the Roman Empire: a thing that had never happened in all previous time.

And formerly intimates of the Emperor called him Emperor and the Empress, Empress.... But if anybody addressed either of these two as Emperor or Empress without adding "Your Majesty" or "Your Highness," or forgot to call himself their slave, he was considered either ignorant or insolent, and was dismissed in disgrace as if he had done some awful crime or committed some unpardonable sin.

And [whereas] before, only a few were sometimes admitted to the palace ... when these two came to power, the magistrates and everybody else had no trouble in fairly living in the palace. This was because the magistrates of old had administered justice and the laws according to their conscience ... but these two, taking control of everything to the misfortune of their subjects, forced everyone to come to them and beg like slaves. And almost any day one could see the law courts nearly deserted, while in the hall of the Emperor there was a jostling and pushing crowd that resembled nothing so much as a mob of slaves.

Procopius, Secret History, *in The Early Middle Ages 500–1000, ed. by Robert Brentano (New York: Free Press, 1964), pp. 70–71.*

LAW   The imperial goal in the East—as reflected in the policy "one God, one empire, one religion"—was to centralize government and impose legal and doctrinal conformity. To this end, Justinian collated and revised Roman law. This codification had become a pressing matter because of the enormous number of often contradictory legal decrees that had piled up since the mid-second century as the empire grew increasingly Christian and imperial rule increasingly autocratic.

Justinian's *Corpus Juris civilis* (body of civil law) was a fourfold compilation undertaken by a learned committee of lawyers. The first compilation, known as the *Code,* appeared in 533. It revised imperial edicts issued since the reign of

Empress Theodora and her attendants. The union of political and spiritual authority in the person of the empress is shown by the depiction on Theodora's mantle of three magi carrying gifts to the Virgin and Jesus. [Scala/Art Resource, N.Y.]

Hadrian (r. 117–138). A second compilation, the *Novellae* ("new things"), contained the decrees issued by Justinian and his immediate successors after 534. The third compilation, the *Digest*, was a summary of the major opinions of the old legal experts. The fourth compilation, the *Institutes*, was a textbook for young scholars that drew its lessons from the *Code* and the *Digest*. These works had little immediate effect on medieval common law, but, beginning with the Renaissance, they provided the foundation for most subsequent European law down to the nineteenth century. They especially served well those rulers who aspired to centralize their states.

RELIGION Religion as well as law served imperial centralization. Since the fifth century, the patriarch of Constantinople had crowned emperors in Constantinople. This practice reflected the close ties between rulers and the Church. In 380 Christianity had been proclaimed the official religion of the eastern empire. All other religions and sects were denounced as "demented and insane."[1] Between

the fourth and sixth centuries the patriarchs of Constantinople, Alexandria, Antioch, and Jerusalem acquired enormous wealth in the form of land and gold. The Church, in turn, acted as the state's welfare agency, drawing on its generous endowments from pious rich donors to aid the poor and needy. The prestige and comfort of the clergy swelled the clerical ranks of the Eastern church.

Orthodox Christianity was not, however, the only religion within the empire with a significant following. Nor did the rulers view religion as merely a political tool. At one time or another the Christian heresies of Arianism, Monophysitism, and Iconoclasm also received imperial support. Persecution and absorption into popular Christianity served to curtail many pagan religious practices.

The empire was also home, although at times a less than hospitable one, to large numbers of Jews. Romans who were not Christian considered Jews in comparison with Christians to be narrow, dogmatic, and intolerant people, and they had little love for them. Under Roman law Jews had legal protection so long as they did not proselytize among Christians, build new synagogues, or try to enter sensitive public offices or professions. Justinian (the emperor most intent on religious conformity within the empire)

---

[1]*Cyril Mango,* Byzantium: The Empire of New Rome *(New York: Charles Scribner's Sons, 1980), p. 88.*

(a)

(b)

(a) The great church of Hagia Sophia (Holy Wisdom). Built in Constantinople (now Istanbul, Turkey) by the emperor Justinian between 532 and 537, this church was one of the most influential achievements of Byzantine art and architecture. This interior view shows part of the great dome of the church (107 feet in diameter) and its rich decoration of marbles and mosaics. [Giraudon/Art Resource, N.Y.] (b) The exterior of Hagia Sophia is plain and ordinary compared with the interior—a reflection of the priority the Byzantines attached to the inner life. The four towering minarets were among additions made by the Turkish Muslims after they conquered Constantinople in 1453 and transformed the building into a mosque. Since 1935, it has been a national museum. [Giraudon/Art Resource, N.Y.]

adopted a policy of encouraging Jews to convert voluntarily. Later emperors ordered all Jews to be baptized and granted tax breaks to those who voluntarily complied. But neither persuasion nor coercion succeeded in converting the empire's Jews.

CITIES During Justinian's reign the empire's strength was its more than 1,500 cities. The largest, with perhaps 350,000 inhabitants, was Constantinople, the cultural crossroads of the Asian and European civilizations. The large provincial cities had populations of 50,000. Between the fourth and fifth centuries, councils of about 200 members, all of whom were local wealthy landowners known as *decurions*, governed the cities. Decurions were the intellectual and economic elite of the empire. They were also heavily taxed, and for this reason they were not always the emperor's most docile or loyal servants. By the sixth century, special governors and bishops, appointed from the landholding classes, replaced the decurion councils and proved to be more reliable instruments of the emperor's will.

A fifth-century statistical record gives us some sense of the size and splendor of Constantinople at its peak. It lists 5 imperial and 9 princely palaces; 8 public and 153 private baths; 4 public fora; 5 granaries; 2 theaters; a hippodrome; 322 streets; 4,388 substantial houses; 52 porticoes; 20 public and 120 private bakers; and 14 churches.[2] The most popular entertainments were the theater, frequently denounced by the clergy for nudity and immorality, and the races at the hippodrome. Many public taverns existed as well.

Eastern Influences

During the reign of Heraclius (r. 610–641) the empire took a decidedly Eastern, as opposed to Roman, direction. Heraclius spoke Greek, not Latin. He spent his entire reign resisting Persian and Islamic invasions, the former successfully, the latter in vain. Islamic armies progressively overran the empire after 632, directly attacking Constantinople for the first time in 677. Not until the reign of Leo III of the Isaurian dynasty (r. 717–740) were the Islamic armies repulsed and most of Asia Minor regained by the Byzantines.

Leo, however, offended western Christians when he forbade the use of images in Eastern churches and tried to enforce the ban also in the West. This was an affront to western Christianity, which had carefully nurtured the adoration of Jesus, Mary, and the saints in images and icons. Historians have speculated that Leo and his immediate successors pursued this policy under the influence of Islam, which condemned image veneration, perhaps hoping to placate the Muslims by joining them on this point of doctrine. Be that as it may, the banning of images was a major expression of eastern Caesaro-papism—the direct involvement of the emperor in religious dogma and practice as if he were both secular ruler and the head of the Church—which, as we will see, the Western church always resisted. In addition to creating a new division within Christendom, the ban on images led to the destruction of much religious art until it was reversed in the late eighth century.

In 1071, the Byzantine Empire suffered a major defeat at the hands of the Muslim Seljuk Turks. Successful over Byzantine armies at Manzikert, the Turks rapidly overran the eastern provinces of the empire. This defeat was the beginning of the end of the empire, although the actual end—at the hands of the Seljuks' cousins, the Ottoman Turks—still lay centuries ahead. After two decades of steady Turkish advance, the eastern emperor Alexius I Comnenus (r. 1081–1118) invoked western aid in 1092. Three years later the West launched the first of the Crusades. A century later (1204) the Crusaders would inflict far more damage on Constantinople and eastern Christendom than all previous non-Christian invaders had done.

Throughout the early Middle Ages, the Byzantine Empire remained a protective barrier between western Europe and hostile Persian, Arab, and Turkish armies. The Byzantines were also a major conduit of classical learning and science into the West down to the Renaissance. While western Europeans were fumbling to create a culture of their own, the cities of the Byzantine Empire provided them a model of a civilized society.

[2]*Mango, p. 76.*

Islam and the Islamic World

A new drama began to unfold in the sixth century with the awakening of a rival far more dangerous to the West than the German tribes: the new faith of Islam. By the time of Muhammad's death (632), Islamic armies absorbed the attention and the resources of the emperors in Constantinople and rulers in the West.

At first, the Muslims were both open and cautious. They borrowed and integrated elements of Persian and Greek culture into their own. The new religion of Islam adopted elements of Christian, Jewish, and native pagan religious beliefs and practices. Muslims tolerated religious minorities within the territories they conquered so long as these minorities recognized Islamic political rule, refrained from proselytizing among Muslims, and paid their taxes. Nonetheless, the Muslims were keen to protect the purity and integrity of Islamic religion, language, and law from any corrupting foreign influence. With the passage of time, and increased conflict with eastern and western Christians, this protective tendency grew stronger. Despite significant contacts and exchanges, Islamic culture would not penetrate the West as creatively as Germanic culture did, but would remain largely strange and threatening to westerners.

Muhammad's Religion

Muhammad (570–632), an orphan, was raised by a family of modest means. As a youth, he worked as a merchant's assistant, traveling the major trade routes. When he was twenty-five, he married a wealthy Meccan widow. Thereafter, himself a wealthy man, he became a kind of social activist, criticizing Meccan materialism, paganism, and unjust treatment of the poor and needy. When he was about forty a deep religious experience heightened his commitment to reform and transformed his life. He began to receive revelations from the angel Gabriel, who recited God's word to him at irregular intervals. These revelations grew into the Qur'ān (literally, a "reciting"), which his followers compiled between 650 and 651. The basic message Muhammad received was a summons to all Arabs to submit to God's will. Followers of Muhammad's religion came to be called *Muslim* ("submissive" or "surrendering"); the name applied to the religion itself, *Islam*, has the same derivation and means "submission."

The message was not a new one. It had been reiterated by a long line of Jewish prophets going back to Noah. According to Muslims, however, this line ended with Muhammad, who, as the last of God's chosen prophets, became "the Prophet." The Qur'ān also recognized Jesus Christ as a prophet, but did not view him as God's coeternal and coequal son. Like Judaism, Islam was a monotheistic and theocentric religion, not a Trinitarian one like Christianity.

Mecca was a major pagan pilgrimage site (the Ka'ba—a black meteorite that became Islam's holiest shrine—was originally a pagan object of worship). Muhammad's attacks on idolatry and immorality threatened the trade that flowed from the pilgrims, enraging the merchants of the city. Persecuted for their attacks on traditional religion, Muhammad and his followers fled in 622 to Medina, 240 miles to the north. This event came to be known as the Hegira and marks the beginning of the Islamic calendar.

In Medina, Muhammad organized his forces and drew throngs of devoted followers. He raided caravans going back and forth to Mecca. Also at this time he had his first conflicts with Medinan Jews, who were involved in Meccan trade. By 624 his army was powerful enough to conquer Mecca and make it the center of the new religion.

During these years the basic rules of Islamic practice evolved. True Muslims were expected (1) to be honest and modest in all their dealings and behavior; (2) to be unquestionably loyal to the Islamic community; (3) to abstain from pork and alcohol at all times; (4) to wash and pray facing Mecca five times a day; (5) to contribute to the support of the poor and needy; (6) to fast during daylight hours for one month each year; and (7) to make a pilgrimage to Mecca and visit the Ka'ba at least once in a lifetime. The last requirement reflects the degree to which Islam was an assimilationist religion; here it "Islamicized" a major pagan religious practice.

In another distinctive feature, Islam permitted Muslim men to have up to four wives—provided they treated them all justly and gave each equal attention—and as many concubines as they wished. A man could divorce a wife with a simple declaration, whereas a wife, to divorce her husband, had to have a very good reason and go before an official. A wife was expected to be totally loyal and devoted to her husband. She was allowed to show her face to no man but him.

In contrast to Christianity, Islam drew no rigid distinction between the clergy and the laity. A lay scholarly elite developed, however, that held moral authority within Islamic society and formed a kind of magisterium in moral and religious matters. This elite, known as the *ulema* (persons with correct knowledge), served a social function similar to that of a professional priesthood or rabbinate. Its members were men of great piety and obvious learning whose opinions came to have the force of law in Muslim society. They also kept a critical eye on Muslim rulers, seeing that they adhered to the letter of the Qur'ān.

Islamic Diversity

The success of Islam lay in its ability to unify and inspire tribal Arabs and other non-Jewish and non-Christian people. In a world where Christianity and Judaism had reigned supreme among religions, Islam must also have appealed to Arab pride, for it made Muhammad history's major religious figure and his followers God's chosen people.

As early as the seventh century, however, disputes arose among Muslims over the shape of Islamic society that left permanent divisions within it. Disagreement over the true line of succession to Muhammad—the caliphate—was one source of discord. Another, tied to the first, was disagreement on doctrinal issues involving the extent to which Islam was meant to be an inclusive religion, open to the weak as well as to the strong. Several groups emerged from these disputes. The most radical was the Kharijites, whose leaders seceded from the camp of the caliph Ali (656–661) because Ali compromised with his enemies on a matter of principle. Righteous and judgmental, the Kharijites wanted to exclude all but rigorously virtuous Muslims from the community of the faithful. In 661 one of their members assassinated Ali.

Another, more influential, group was the Shi'a, or "partisans of Ali" *(Shi'at Ali)*. The Shi'a looked on Ali and his descendants as the rightful successors of Muhammad not only by virtue

Muslims are enjoined to live by the divine law, or Shari'a, *and have a right to have disputes settled by an arbiter of the* Shari'a. *Here we see a husband complaining about his wife before the state-appointed judge, or* qadi. *The wife, backed up by two other women, points an accusing finger at the husband. In such cases, the first duty of the* qadi, *who should be a learned person of faith, is to try to effect a reconciliation before the husband divorces his wife, or the wife herself seeks a divorce.* [Bibliothèque Nationale, Paris]

of kinship, but also by the expressed will of the Prophet himself. To the Shi'a, Ali's assassination revealed the most basic truth of a devout Muslim life: a true *imam* or ruler must expect to suffer unjustly even unto death in the world, and so too must his followers. A distinctive theology of martyrdom has ever since been a mark of Shi'a teaching. And the Shi'a, until modern times, have been an embattled minority within mainstream Islamic society.

A third group, which has been dominant for most of Islamic history, was the majority centrist Sunnis (followers of *sunna*, or tradition). Sunnis have always put loyalty to the community of Islam above all else and have spurned the

MAP 6-3 MUSLIM CONQUESTS AND DOMINATION OF THE MEDITERRANEAN TO ABOUT 750
*Islam spread rapidly (both its religion and military-political power). From the West's view-
point, the important fact was that in the 125 years after Muhammad's rise Muslims came
to dominate Spain and all areas south and east of the Mediterranean.*

exclusivism and purism of the Kharijites and
the Shi'a.

Islamic Empires

Under Muhammad's first three successors—the
caliphs Abu Bakr (632–634), Umar (634–644),
and Uthman (644–656)—Islam expanded by
conquest throughout the southern and eastern
Mediterranean, territories mostly still held
today by Islamic states. In the eighth century
Muslim armies occupied parts of Spain in the
West and India in the East, producing a truly
vast empire. (See Map 6-3.) The capital of this
empire moved from Mecca to Damascus, and
then, in 750, to Baghdad after a civil war in
which the Abbasid dynasty replaced the
Umayyad dynasty in the caliphate. Thereafter,
the huge Muslim empire broke up into separate states, each with its own line of caliphs,
each claiming to be the true successor of
Muhammad.

These conquests would not have been so
rapid and thorough had the contemporary
Byzantine and Persian empires not been
exhausted after a long period of war. The
Muslims struck at both empires shortly after
the Byzantine emperor Heraclius (r. 610–641)
had recovered Egypt, Palestine, Syria, and Asia
Minor from the Persians. Before Heraclius died
in 641, however, Arab armies had conquered
Egypt, Palestine, and Syria and by 643 had overrun most of the Persian Empire. Byzantine territory in North Africa fell by the end of the seventh century. Most of the inhabitants in the
territory Heraclius had reconquered from the
Persians, although Christian, were, like the
Arabs, Semitic. Any religious unity they felt
with the Byzantine Greeks may have been offset
by hatred of the Byzantine Greek army of occupation. The Christian community was in any
case badly divided. Heraclius's efforts to impose
Greek "orthodox" beliefs on the monophysitic
churches of Egypt and Syria only increased the

One of the reasons the Byzantines were able to repulse the Arab attack on Constantinople in 717–718 was a secret weapon: Greek fire, a highly flammable mixture of petroleum, sulphur, and pitch that would burn even on water. In this fourteenth-century manuscript, the Byzantine navy is spraying Greek fire from a copper tube onto an enemy vessel. [Amplicaciones y Reproducciones Mas (ARXIU MAS)]

enmity between Greek and Semitic Christians. As a result, many Egyptian and Syrian Christians, hoping for deliverance from Byzantine oppression, may have welcomed the Islamic conquerors.

Although Islam gained Christian converts in North Africa and Spain, its efforts to invade the heart of Christendom were in the end successfully rebuffed. In the West the ruler of the Franks, Charles Martel, defeated a raiding party of Arabs on the western frontier of Europe at Poitiers (today in central France) in 732. This victory ended any possible Arab effort to expand into western Europe by way of Spain. Beginning with Emperor Leo III (r. 717–740), the Isaurian dynasty of Byzantine rulers successfully defended Asia Minor from Islamic aggression. So effective were they that the subsequent Macedonian dynasty of Byzantine rulers (867–1057) expanded militarily and commercially into Arab lands. Muslim disunity after the tenth century greatly aided Byzantine success. The Byzantine Empire would ultimately fall to the Ottoman Turks, who would continue to strike terror in Christian hearts well into the sixteenth century, but after the Seljuk Turks took the Islamic capital of Baghdad in 1055 and the Christian crusaders captured Jerusalem in 1099, the Muslims never again posed a serious threat to western Christendom.

The Western Debt to Islamic Culture

Despite the hostility of the Christian West to the Islamic world, there was nonetheless much creative interchange between these two very different cultures, and the West greatly profited from it. The more advanced Arab civilization, which was enjoying its golden age during the West's early Middle Ages, taught western farmers how to irrigate fields and western artisans how to tan leather and refine silk. The West also gained from its contacts with Islamic scholars. Thanks to Arabic translators, major Greek works in astronomy, mathematics, and medicine became available to scholars in much of the West for the first time in Latin translation. And down to the sixteenth century, after the works of the famous ancient physicians Hippocrates and Galen, the basic gynecological and childcare manuals followed by western midwives and physicians were compilations by the famed

Baghdad physician Al-Razi (Rhazes), the philosopher and physician ibn-Sina (Avicenna) (980–1037), and Averröes (1126–1198), Islam's greatest authority on Aristotle. Jewish scholars also thrived amid the intellectual culture Islamic scholars created. The famed Spanish Jewish scholar, Moses Maimonides (1135–1204), wrote in Arabic as well as Hebrew.

Western Society and the Developing Christian Church

Facing barbarian invasions from the north and east and a strong Islamic presence in the Mediterranean, the West found itself in decline during the fifth and sixth centuries. As trade waned, cities rapidly fell on hard times, depriving the West of centers for the exchange of goods and ideas that would enable it to look and live beyond itself.

In the seventh century, the Byzantine emperors, their hands full with the Islamic threat in the East, were unable to assert themselves in the West, leaving most of the region in the control of the Franks and the Lombards (a Germanic tribe that invaded Italy in the sixth century and settled in the Po Valley). Islamic dominance of the Mediterranean likewise closed the West to much trade or cultural influence from the East. As a result, western Europeans were forced to rely on their own resources and develop their Germanic and Greco-Roman heritage into their own distinctive culture.

As western shipping declined in the Mediterranean, populations that would otherwise have been engaged in trade-related work in the cities moved in great numbers into interior regions. There they found the employment and protection they sought on the farms of the great landholders. The landholders, for their part, needed laborers and welcomed the new emigrants.

Peasants made up ninety percent of the population. Those who owned their own land were free peasants. Some peasants became "serfs" by surrendering their land to a more powerful landholder in exchange for assistance in time of dire need, like prolonged crop failure or foreign invasion. Basically serfdom was a status of servitude to an economically and politically stronger person. Powerful landholders, after seizing all the agricultural land they could control, essentially reallocated it to the people who supplied labor and goods, offering them protection in return.

As the demand for agricultural products diminished in the great urban centers and as traffic between town and country declined, the farming belts became regionally insular and self-contained. Production and travel adjusted to local needs. There was little incentive for bold experimentation and exploration. The domains of the great landholders became the basic social and political units of society, and local barter economies sprang up within them. In these developments were sown the seeds of what would later come to be known as manorial and feudal society (which we will discuss in more detail). Manorial society involved a division of land and labor among lords, serfs, and other peasants for the profit of the lords and the protection of all. Feudal society involved the emergence of a special class of aristocratic warrior knights as guarantors of order.

While all of this was going on, one institution remained firmly entrenched within the cities: the Christian church. The Church had long modeled its own structure on that of the imperial Roman administration. Like the imperial government, Church government was centralized and hierarchical. Strategically placed "generals" (bishops) in European cities looked for spiritual direction to their leader, the bishop of Rome. As the western empire crumbled, Roman governors withdrew, and populations emigrated to the countryside, local bishops and cathedral chapters filled the resulting vacuum of authority. The local cathedral became the center of urban life and the local bishop the highest authority for those who remained in the cities. In Rome, on a larger and more fateful scale, the pope took control of the city as the western emperors gradually departed and died out. Left to its own devices, western Europe soon discovered that the Christian church was its best repository of Roman administrative skills and classical culture.

The Christian church had been graced with special privileges, great lands, and wealth by Emperor Constantine and his successors. In the first half of the fourth century, Christians gained legal standing and a favored status within the empire. In 391 Emperor Theodosius I (r. ca. 379–395) raised Christianity to the official religion of the empire. Both Theodosius and his predecessors acted as much for political effect as out of religious conviction. In 313 Christians made up about one fifth of the population of the empire and Christianity was unquestionably the strongest of the competing religions. Its main rivals were Mithraism, the religion popular among army officers and restricted to males, and the Egyptian cults of Isis and Serapis.

Challenged by Rome's decline to become a major political force, the Church survived the period of Germanic and Islamic invasions a somewhat spiritually weakened and compromised institution. Yet it remained a potent civilizing and unifying force. It had a religious message of providential purpose and individual worth that could give solace and meaning to life at its worst. It had a ritual of baptism and a creedal confession that united people beyond the traditional barriers of social class, education, and gender. And alone in the West, the Church retained an effective hierarchical administration, scattered throughout the old empire, staffed by the best-educated minds in Europe, and centered in emperorless Rome.

Writing after the fall of Rome but before the emergence of Islam, Augustine (354–430) eloquently elaborated the Christian message and the force of its appeal in his chaotic times. In his *City of God*, he defended Christianity against those who held it responsible for the collapse of Roman civilization, allegedly because it rejected the Roman gods and because its message of love and forgiveness fostered weakness. He pointed out the empire's internal weaknesses and the constructive nature of Christian teaching, which he deemed superior to the ancient philosophies. He stressed in particular the discipline of the Church and the power of its sacraments to heal and unite humankind in a new spiritual empire. The book became a favorite of the Frankish king Charlemagne nearly 400 years later.

Monastic Culture

The Church enjoyed the services of growing numbers of monks, who were not only loyal to its mission but also objects of great popular respect. Monastic culture proved again and again to be the peculiar strength of the Church during the Middle Ages.

The first monks were hermits who withdrew from society to pursue a more perfect way of life. They were inspired by the Christian ideal of a life of complete self-denial in imitation of Christ. The popularity of monasticism began to grow as Roman persecution of Christians waned and Christianity became the favored religion of the empire during the fourth century. Monasticism replaced martyrdom as the most perfect way to imitate Christ and to confess one's faith.

Christians came to view monastic life—embracing, as it did, the biblical "counsels of perfection" (chastity, poverty, and obedience)—as the purest form of religious practice, going beyond the baptism and creedal confession that identified ordinary believers. This view evolved during the Middle Ages into a belief in the general superiority of the clergy and the mission of the Church over the laity and the state. This belief served the papacy in later confrontations with secular rulers.

Anthony of Egypt (ca. 251–356), the father of hermit monasticism, was inspired by Jesus' command to the rich young ruler: "If you will be perfect, sell all that you have, give it to the poor, and follow me" (Matthew 19:21). Anthony went into the desert to pray and work, setting an example followed by hundreds in Egypt, Syria, and Palestine in the fourth and fifth centuries.

This hermit monasticism was soon joined by the development of communal monasticism. In the first quarter of the fourth century, Pachomius (ca. 286–346) organized monks in southern Egypt into a highly regimented community in which hundreds shared a life of labor, order, and discipline enforced by a strict penal code. Such monastic communities grew to contain a thousand or more inhabitants. They were little "cities of God," trying to separate themselves from the collapsing Roman and the nominal Christian world. Basil the Great (329–379) popularized communal monasticism throughout the East, providing a rule that lessened the asceticism of Pachomius and directed monks beyond their segregated enclaves of perfection into such social worldly services as caring for orphans, widows, and the infirm in surrounding communities.

Athanasius (ca. 293–373) and Martin of Tours (ca. 315–399) introduced monasticism to the West. The teachings of John Cassian (ca. 360–435) and Jerome (ca. 340–420) then helped shape the basic values and practices of western monasticism. The great organizer of western monasticism, however, was Benedict of Nursia (ca. 480–547). In 529 he established a monastery at Monte Cassino, in Italy, founding the form of monasticism—Benedictine—that bears his name and that quickly came to dominate in the West. It eventually replaced an Irish, non-Benedictine monasticism that was common until the 600s in the British Isles and Gaul.

Benedict wrote *Rule for Monasteries*, a sophisticated and comprehensive plan for every activity of the monks, even detailing the manner in which they were to sleep. His *Rule* opposed the severities of earlier monasticism that tortured the body and anguished the mind. Benedict insisted on good food and even some wine, adequate clothing, and proper amounts of sleep and relaxation. Periods of devotion (about four hours each day) were set aside for the "work of God." That is, regular prayers, liturgical activities, and study alternated with manual labor (farming). This program permitted not a moment's idleness and carefully nurtured the religious, intellectual, and physical well-being of the cloistered monks. The monastery was directed by an abbot, whose command had to be obeyed unquestioningly.

Individual Benedictine monasteries remained autonomous until the later Middle Ages, when the Benedictines became a unified order of the Church. During the early Middle Ages Benedictine missionaries Christianized both England and Germany. Their disciplined organization and devotion to hard work made the Benedictines an economic and political power as well as a spiritual force wherever they settled.

The Doctrine of Papal Primacy

Constantine and his successors, especially the eastern emperors, ruled religious life with an iron hand and consistently looked on the Church as little more than a department of the state. Such political assumption of spiritual power involved the emperor directly in the Church's affairs, even to the point of playing the theologian and imposing conciliar solutions on its doctrinal quarrels. State control of religion was the original church-state relation in the West. The bishops of Rome, however, never accepted such intervention and opposed it in every way they could. In the fifth and sixth centuries, taking advantage of imperial weakness and distraction, they developed for their own defense the weaponry of the doctrine of papal primacy. This doctrine raised the Roman pontiff to an unassailable supremacy within the Church when it came to defining all other Church doctrine. It also put him in a position to

Saint Gregory the Great, shown in a monastic scriptorium, or study, receiving the divine word from a dove perched on his shoulder. Below him three monks are writing. The middle monk holds an inkwell in his left hand. [Kunsthistorisches Museum, Vienna]

The Benedictine Order Sets Its Requirements for Entrance

Much was demanded of the new monk, both during and after his probationary period, described herein. Benedict tried to improve the quality of cloistered life. His Rule *is a balanced blend of religious, physical, and intellectual activities within a secure and well-structured community.*

✦ *Why did the religious life have such a great appeal at this time in history? Were there materialistic as well as spiritual reasons for entering a cloister? What are Benedict's reasons for not allowing a monk to change his mind and leave the cloister once vows have been taken?*

When anyone is newly come for the reformation of his life, let him not be granted an easy entrance; but, as the Apostle says, "Test the spirits to see whether they are from God." If the newcomer, therefore, perseveres in his knocking, and if it is seen after four or five days that he bears patiently the harsh treatment offered him and the difficulty of admission, and that he persists in his petition, then let entrance be granted him, and let him stay in the guest house for a few days.

After that let him live in the novitiate, where the novices study, eat, and sleep. A senior shall be assigned to them who is skilled in winning souls, to watch over them with the utmost care. Let him examine whether the novice is truly seeking God, and whether he is zealous for the Work of God, for obedience and for humiliations. Let the novice be told all the hard and rugged ways by which the journey to God is made.

If he promises stability and perseverance, then at the end of two months let this Rule be read through to him, and let him be addressed thus: "Here is the law under which you wish to fight. If you can observe it, enter; if you cannot, you are free to depart." If he still stands firm, let him be taken to the above-mentioned novitiate and again tested in all patience. And after the lapse of six months let the Rule be read to him, that he may know on what he is entering. And if he still remains firm, after four months let the same Rule be read to him again.

Then, having deliberated with himself, if he promises to keep it in its entirety and to observe everything that is commanded him, let him be received into the community. But let him understand that, according to the law of the Rule, from that day forward he may not leave the monastery nor withdraw his neck from under the yoke of the Rule which he was free to refuse or to accept during that prolonged deliberation.

St. Benedict's Rule for Monasteries, *trans. by Leonard J. Doyle (Collegeville, Minn.: Liturgical Press, 1948), pp. 79–80.*

make important secular claims, leading to repeated conflicts between Church and state, pope and emperor, throughout the Middle Ages.

Papal primacy was first asserted as a response to the decline of imperial Rome that accompanied the shift of the imperial residence in the West to Milan and, later, Ravenna. It was also a response to the concurrent claims of the patriarchs of the Eastern church, who, after imperial power was transferred to Constantinople, looked on the bishop of Rome as a peer, not as a superior. In 381 the ecumenical Council of Constantinople declared the bishop of Constantinople to be of first rank after the bishop of Rome "because Constantinople is the new Rome." In 451 the ecumenical Council of Chalcedon recognized Constantinople as having the same religious primacy in the East as Rome had traditionally possessed in the West. By the mid-sixth century the bishop of Constantinople regularly described himself in correspondence as a "universal" patriarch.

Roman pontiffs, understandably jealous of such claims and resentful of the ecclesiastical interference of eastern emperors, launched a counteroffensive. Pope Damasus I (366–384)[3] took the first of several major steps in the rise of the Roman church when he declared a Roman "apostolic" primacy. Pointing to Jesus' words to Peter in the Gospel of Matthew (16:18) ("Thou art Peter, and upon this rock I will build my church"), he claimed himself and all other popes to be Peter's direct successors as the unique "rock" on which the Christian church was built. Pope Leo I (440–461) took still another fateful step by assuming the title *pontifex maximus*—"supreme priest." He further proclaimed himself to be endowed with a "plentitude of power," thereby establishing the supremacy of the bishop of Rome over all other bishops in the Church. During Leo's reign an imperial decree recognized his exclusive jurisdiction over the Western church. At the end of the fifth century, Pope Gelasius I (492–496) proclaimed the authority of the clergy to be "more weighty" than the power of kings because priests had charge of divine affairs and the means of salvation.

Events as well as ideology favored the papacy. The Germanic and Islamic invasions, just as they had isolated the West by diverting the attention of the eastern empire, also prevented either emperors or eastern patriarchs from interfering in the affairs of the Western church. Islam may even be said to have "saved" the Western church from eastern domination. At the same time, the emergent Lombards and Franks provided the Church with new political allies. Eastern episcopal competition with Rome ended as bishopric after bishopric fell to Islamic armies in the East. The power of the exarch of Ravenna—the Byzantine emperor's viceroy in the West—was eclipsed by invading Lombards, who, thanks to Frankish prodding, became Nicene Christians loyal to Rome and increasingly a counterweight to eastern power and influence in the West. In an unprecedented act, Pope Gregory I, "the Great" (590–604), negotiated an independent peace treaty with the Lombards,

---

³*Papal dates give the years of each reign.*

completely ignoring the eastern emperor and the imperial authorities in Ravenna, who were too weak to resist.

The Division of Christendom

As the events just discussed suggest, the division of Christendom into Eastern (Byzantine) and Western (Roman Catholic) churches has its roots in the early Middle Ages. The division was due in part to linguistic and cultural differences between the Greek East and the Roman, Latin-speaking West. A novel combination of Greek, Roman, and Asian elements shaped Byzantine culture, giving eastern Christianity more of a mystical orientation than western Christianity. Compared with their western counterparts, eastern Christians seemed to attribute less importance to life in this world and to be more concerned about questions affecting their eternal destiny. This strong mystical orientation toward the next world may also have permitted the eastern patriarchs to submit more passively than western popes could ever do to royal intervention in Church affairs.

As in the West, Eastern church organization closely followed that of the secular state. A patriarch ruled over metropolitans and archbishops in the cities and provinces; and they, in turn, ruled over bishops, who stood as authorities over the local clergy. Except for the patriarch Michael Cerularius, who tried unsuccessfully in the eleventh century to free the Church from its traditional tight state control, the patriarchs were normally carefully regulated by the emperor.

Contrary to the evolving western tradition of universal clerical celibacy (which western monastic culture encouraged), the Eastern church permitted the marriage of parish priests (but not monks), while strictly forbidding bishops to marry. The Eastern church also used leavened bread in the Eucharist, contrary to the western custom of using unleavened bread, and rejected the western doctrine of purgatory. Unlike the Roman church, the Eastern church accommodated the laity by recognizing divorce and by using vernacular liturgies. The Roman church also objected to the tendency of the Eastern church to compromise doctrinally with the politically powerful Arian and Monophysite Christians. Finally, in the background, the

Eastern and Western churches both laid claim to jurisdiction over the newly converted areas in the North Balkans.

Beyond these issues, three major factors lay behind the religious break between East and West. The first revolved around questions of doctrinal authority. The Eastern church put more stress on the authority of the Bible and the ecumenical councils of the Church in the definition of Christian doctrine than on the counsel and decrees of the bishop of Rome. The claims of Roman popes to a special primacy of authority on the basis of the apostle Peter's commission from Jesus in the Gospel of Matthew were unacceptable to the East. In the East the independence and autonomy of national churches held sway. As Steven Runciman summarized, "The Byzantine ideal was a series of autocephalous state churches, linked by intercommunion and the faith of seven councils."[4] This basic issue of authority in matters of faith lay behind the mutual excommunication of Pope Nicholas I and Patriarch Photius in the ninth century and that of Pope Leo IX (through his ambassador to Constantinople, Cardinal Humbert) and Patriarch Michael Cerularius in 1054.

A second major factor in the separation of the two churches was the western addition of the *filioque* clause to the Nicene-Constantinopolitan Creed. According to this anti-Arian clause, the Holy Spirit proceeds "also from the Son" *(filioque)* as well as from the Father. This addition made clear the western belief that Christ was "fully substantial with God the Father" and not a lesser being.

The third factor dividing the Eastern and Western churches was the iconoclastic controversy of the first half of the eighth century. As noted in the discussion of the Byzantine Empire, after 725 the eastern emperor, Leo III, banned the use of images in Eastern churches and attempted to enforce the ban in the West also. Images were greatly cherished in the West, and his actions met fierce official and popular resistance there. To punish the West for this disobedience, Leo confiscated papal lands in Sicily and Calabria (in southern Italy) and placed them under the jurisdiction of the subservient patri-

[4]*Steven Runciman,* Byzantine Civilization *(London: A. and C. Black, 1933), p. 128.*

A ninth-century Byzantine manuscript shows an iconoclast whiting out an image of Christ. The iconoclastic controversy was an important factor in the division of Christendom into separate Latin and Greek branches. [State Historical Museum, Moscow]

arch of Constantinople. Because these territories provided essential papal revenues, the Western church could not but view the emperor's action as a declaration of war. (Later the empress Irene made peace with the Roman church on this issue and restored the use of images at the ecumenical Council of Nicea in 787.)

The emperor Leo's direct challenge of the pope coincided with a renewed threat to Rome and the Western church from the Lombards of northern Italy. Assailed on two fronts, the Roman papacy seemed surely doomed. There has not, however, been a more resilient and enterprising institution in Western history than the papacy. Since Gregory the Great, who 150

Major Political and Religious Developments of the Early Middle Ages	
313	Emperor Constantine issues the Edict of Milan
325	Council of Nicaea defines Christian doctrine
410	Rome invaded by Visigoths under Alaric
413–426	St. Augustine writes *The City of God*
451	Council of Chalcedon further defines Christian doctrine
451–453	Europe invaded by the Huns under Attila
476	Barbarian Odovacer deposes western emperor and rules as king of the Romans
489–493	Theodoric establishes kingdom of Ostrogths in Italy
529	Saint Benedict founds monastery at Monte Cassino
533	Justinian codifies Roman law
622	Muhammad's flight form Mecca (*Hegira*)
732	Charles Martel defeats Muslims at Poitiers
754	Pope Stephen II and Pepin III ally

years earlier had negotiated a treaty with the Lombards, popes had recognized the Franks of northern Gaul as Europe's ascendant power and seen in them their surest protectors. In 754, Pope Stephen II (752–757), initiating the most fruitful political alliance of the Middle Ages, enlisted the Franks and their ruler, Pepin III, to defend the Church against the Lombards and as a western counterweight to the eastern emperor. This marriage of religion and politics created a new Western church and empire; it also determined much of the course of Western history into our time.

The Kingdom of the Franks

Merovingians and Carolingians: From Clovis to Charlemagne

A warrior chieftain, Clovis (ca. 466–511), who converted to orthodox Christianity around 496, founded the first Frankish dynasty, the

Merovingians, named for Merovich, an early leader of one branch of the Franks. Clovis and his successors united the Salian and Ripuarian Franks, subdued the Arian Burgundians and Visigoths, and established the kingdom of the Franks within ancient Gaul, making the Franks and the Merovingian kings a significant force in western Europe. The Franks themselves occupied a broad belt of territory that extended throughout modern France, Belgium, the Netherlands, and western Germany, and their loyalties remained strictly tribal and local.

GOVERNING THE FRANKS In attempting to govern this sprawling kingdom, the Merovingians encountered what proved to be the most persistent problem of medieval political history—the competing claims of the "one" and the "many." On the one hand, the king struggled for a centralized government and transregional loyalty, and on the other, powerful local magnates strove to preserve their regional autonomy and traditions.

The Merovingian kings addressed this problem by making pacts with the landed nobility and by creating the royal office of count. The counts were men without possessions to whom the king gave great lands in the expectation that they would be, as the landed aristocrats often were not, loyal officers of the kingdom. But like local aristocrats, the Merovingian counts also let their immediate self-interests gain the upper hand. Once established in office for a period of time, they too became territorial rulers in their own right, so that the Frankish kingdom progressively fragmented into independent regions and tiny principalities. This centrifugal tendency was further aided by the Frankish custom of dividing the kingdom equally among the king's legitimate male heirs.

Rather than purchasing allegiance and unity within the kingdom, the Merovingian largess simply occasioned the rise of competing magnates and petty tyrants, who became laws unto themselves within their regions. By the seventh century the Frankish king was king in title only and had no effective executive power. Real power came to be concentrated in the office of the *mayor of the palace*, spokesman at the king's court for the great landowners of the three regions into which the Frankish kingdom was divided: Neustria, Austrasia, and Burgundy.

Through this office the Carolingian dynasty rose to power.

The Carolingians controlled the office of the mayor of the palace from the ascent to that post of Pepin I of Austrasia (d. 639) until 751, when, with the enterprising connivance of the pope, they simply expropriated the Frankish crown. Pepin II (d. 714) ruled in fact if not in title over the Frankish kingdom. His illegitimate son, Charles Martel ("the Hammer," d. 741), created a great cavalry by bestowing lands known as *benefices* or *fiefs* on powerful noblemen. In return, they agreed to be ready to serve as the king's army. It was such an army that checked the Islamic probings on the western front at Poitiers in 732—an important battle that helped to secure the borders of western Europe.

The fiefs so generously bestowed by Charles Martel to create his army came in large part from landed property that he usurped from the Church. His alliance with the landed aristocracy in this grand manner permitted the Carolingians to have some measure of political success where the Merovingians had failed. The Carolingians created counts almost entirely out of the landed nobility from which the Carolingians themselves had risen. The Merovingians, in contrast, had tried to compete directly with these great aristocrats by raising landless men to power. By playing to strength rather than challenging it, the Carolingians strengthened themselves, at least for the short term. The Church, by this time dependent on the protection of the Franks against the eastern emperor and the Lombards, could only suffer in silence the usurpation of lands to which it held claim. Later, although they never returned them, the Franks partially compensated the Church for these lands.

THE FRANKISH CHURCH The Church came to play a large and enterprising role in the Frankish government. By Carolingian times monasteries were a dominant force. Their intellectual achievements made them respected centers of culture. Their religious teaching and example imposed order on surrounding populations. Their relics and rituals made them magical shrines to which pilgrims came in great numbers. And, thanks to their many gifts and internal discipline and industry, many had become very profitable farms and landed estates,

their abbots rich and powerful magnates. Already in Merovingian times the higher clergy were employed in tandem with counts as royal agents.

It was the policy of the Carolingians, perfected by Charles Martel and his successor, Pepin III ("the Short," d. 768), to use the Church to pacify conquered neighboring tribes—Frisians, Thüringians, Bavarians, and especially the Franks' archenemies, the Saxons. Conversion to Nicene Christianity became an integral part of the successful annexation of conquered lands and people. The cavalry broke their bodies, while the clergy won their hearts and minds. The Anglo-Saxon missionary Saint Boniface (born Wynfrith; 680?–754) was the most important cleric to serve Carolingian kings in this way. Christian bishops in missionary districts and elsewhere became lords, appointed by and subject to the king. In this ominous integration of secular and religious policy lay the seeds of the later Investiture Controversy of the eleventh and twelfth centuries (see Chapter 7).

The Church served more than Carolingian territorial expansion. Pope Zacharias (741–752) also sanctioned Pepin the Short's termination of the vestigial Merovingian dynasty and supported the Carolingian accession to outright kingship of the Franks. With the pope's public blessing, Pepin was proclaimed king by the nobility in council in 751, while the last of the Merovingians, the puppet king Childeric III, was hustled off to a monastery and dynastic oblivion. According to legend, Saint Boniface first anointed Pepin, thereby investing Frankish rule from the very start with a certain sacral character.

Zacharias's successor, Pope Stephen II (752–757), did not let Pepin forget the favor of his predecessor. In 753, when the Lombards besieged Rome, Pope Stephen crossed the Alps and appealed directly to Pepin to cast out the invaders and to guarantee papal claims to central Italy, largely dominated at this time by the eastern emperor. As already noted, in 754 the Franks and the Church formed an alliance against the Lombards and the eastern emperor. Carolingian kings became the protectors of the Catholic church and thereby "kings by the grace of God." Pepin gained the title *patricius Romanorum*, "patrician of the Romans," a title first borne by the ruling families of Rome and

The False Donation of Constantine

Bravado was one of the ways in which Roman churchmen fought to free the Church from political domination. One of the most ambitious assertions of its territorial and political rights was the so-called Donation of Constantine *(eighth century), a fraudulent document claiming papal succession to ownership of much of the old Roman Empire.*

◆ *Why did the Church believe that people, especially powerful kings and noblemen, would take so fraudulent a document seriously? Did the Carolingians have a better, or more legal, claim to these lands? On what terms was a ruler or a people the master(s) of a land at this time?*

The Emperor Caesar Flavius Constantinus in Christ Jesus . . . to the most Holy and blessed Father of fathers, Silvester, Bishop of the Roman city and Pope; and to all his successors, the pontiffs, who shall sit in the chair of blessed Peter to the end of time. . . . Grace, peace, love, joy, long-suffering, mercy . . . be with you all. . . . For we wish you to know . . . that we have forsaken the worship of idols . . . and have come to the pure Christian faith. . . .

To the holy apostles, my lords the most blessed Peter and Paul, and through them also to blessed Silvester, our father, supreme pontiff and universal pope of the city of Rome, and to the pontiffs, his successors, who to the end of the world shall sit in the seat of blessed Peter, we grant and by this present we convey our imperial Lateran palace, which is superior to and excels all palaces in the whole world; and further the diadem, which is the crown of our head; and the miter; as also the super-humeral, that is, the stole which usually surrounds our imperial neck; and the purple cloak and the scarlet tunic and all the imperial robes. . . .

And we decree that those most reverend men, the clergy of various orders serving the same most holy Roman Church, shall have that eminence, distinction, power and precedence, with which our illustrious senate is gloriously adorned; that is, they shall be made patricians and consuls. And we ordain that they shall also be adorned with other imperial dignities. Also we decree that the clergy of the sacred Roman Church shall be adorned as are the imperial officers. . . .

We convey to the oft-mentioned and most blessed Silvester, universal pope, both our palace, as preferment, and likewise all provinces, palaces and districts of the city of Rome and Italy and of the regions of the West; and, bequeathing them to the power and sway of him and the pontiffs, his successors, we do determine and decree that the same be placed at his disposal, and do lawfully grant it as a permanent possession to the holy Roman Church.

Henry Bettenson, ed., Documents of the Christian Church *(New York: Oxford University Press, 1961), pp. 137–141.*

heretofore applied to the representative of the eastern emperor. In 755 the Franks defeated the Lombards and gave the pope the lands surrounding Rome, creating what came to be known as the *Papal States.*

In this period a fraudulent document appeared—the *Donation of Constantine* (written between 750 and 800)—that was enterprisingly designed to remind the Franks of the Church's importance as the heir of Rome. Many believed it to be genuine until it was definitely exposed as a forgery in the fifteenth century by the humanist Lorenzo Valla.

The papacy had looked to the Franks for an ally strong enough to protect it from the eastern emperors. It is an irony of history that the Church found in the Carolingian dynasty a western imperial government that drew almost as slight a boundary between state and Church, secular and religious policy, as did eastern emperors. Although eminently preferable for the popes to eastern domination, Carolingian patronage proved in its own way to be no less constraining.

The Reign of Charlemagne (768–814)

Charlemagne, the son of Pepin the Short, continued the role of his father as papal protector in Italy and his policy of territorial conquest in the north. After decisively defeating King Desiderius and the Lombards of northern Italy in 774, Charlemagne took upon himself the title "King of the Lombards" in Pavia. He widened the frontiers of his kingdom further by subjugating surrounding pagan tribes, foremost among them the Saxons, whom the Franks brutally Christianized and dispersed in small groups throughout Frankish lands. The Muslims were chased beyond the Pyrenees and the Avars (a tribe related to the Huns) were practically annihilated, bringing the Danubian plains into the Frankish orbit. The defeat of the Avars was so complete that the expression "vanished like the Avars" came to be applied to anything that was irretrievably lost.

By the time of his death on January 28, 814, Charlemagne's kingdom embraced modern France, Belgium, Holland, Switzerland, almost the whole of western Germany, much of Italy, a portion of Spain, and the island of Corsica—an area about equal to that of the modern European Common Market (see Map 6-4).

THE NEW EMPIRE Encouraged by his ambitious advisers, Charlemagne came to harbor imperial designs. He desired to be not only king of all the Franks but a universal emperor as well. He had his sacred palace city, Aachen (in French, Aix-la-Chapelle), constructed in conscious imitation of the courts of the ancient Roman and contemporary eastern emperors. Although he permitted the Church its independence, he looked after it with a paternalism almost as great as that of any eastern emperor. He used the Church, above all, to promote social stability and hierarchical order throughout the kingdom—as an aid in the creation of a great Frankish Christian empire. Frankish

Christians were ceremoniously baptized, professed the Nicene Creed (with the *filioque* clause), and learned in church to revere Charlemagne.

The formation of a distinctive Carolingian Christendom was made clear in the 790s when Charlemagne issued the so-called *Libri Carolini*. These documents attacked the ecumenical Council of Nicea, which, in what was actually a friendly gesture to the West, had met in 787 to formulate a new, more accommodating position for the Eastern church on the use of images.

Charlemagne fulfilled his imperial pretensions on Christmas Day, 800, when Pope Leo III (795–816) crowned him emperor. This event began what would come to be known as the Holy Roman Empire, a revival of the old Roman Empire in the West, based after 870 in Germany.

In 799, Pope Leo III had been imprisoned by the Roman aristocracy but escaped to the protection of Charlemagne, who restored him as pope. The fateful coronation of Charlemagne was thus in part an effort by the pope to enhance the Church's stature and to gain some leverage over this powerful king. It was, however, no papal coup d'etat; Charlemagne's control over the Church remained as strong after as before the event. If the coronation benefitted the Church, as it certainly did, it also served Charlemagne's purposes.

Before his coronation, Charlemagne had been a minor western potentate in the eyes of eastern emperors. After the coronation, eastern emperors reluctantly recognized his new imperial dignity; and Charlemagne even found it necessary to disclaim ambitions to rule as emperor over the East.

THE NEW EMPEROR Charlemagne stood a majestic six feet three and one half inches tall—a fact confirmed when his tomb was opened and exact measurements of his remains were taken in 1861. He was restless, ever ready for a hunt. Informal and gregarious, he insisted on the presence of friends even when he bathed. He was widely known for his practical jokes, lusty good humor, and warm hospitality. Aachen was a festive palace city to which people and gifts came from all over the world. In 802 Charlemagne even received from the caliph of Baghdad, Harun-al-Rashid, a white elephant, the trans-

MAP 6-4   THE EMPIRE OF CHARLEMAGNE TO 814   *Building on the successes of his predecessors, Charlemagne greatly increased the Frankish domains. Such traditional enemies as
the Saxons and the Lombards fell under his sway.*

port of which across the Alps was as great a
wonder as the creature itself.

Charlemagne had five official wives in succession, many mistresses and concubines, and
sired numerous children. This connubial variety
created special problems. His oldest son by his
first marriage, Pepin, jealous of the attention
shown by his father to the sons of his second
wife and fearing the loss of paternal favor, joined

with noble enemies in a conspiracy against his
father. He spent the rest of his life in confine-
ment in a monastery after the plot was exposed.

PROBLEMS OF GOVERNMENT   Charlemagne
governed his kingdom through counts, of whom
there were perhaps as many as 250. They were
strategically located within the administrative
districts into which the kingdom was divided. In

Carolingian practice the count tended to be a local magnate, one who already possessed the armed might and the self-interest to enforce the will of a generous king. He had three main duties: to maintain a local army loyal to the king, to collect tribute and dues, and to administer justice throughout his district.

This last responsibility he undertook through a district law court known as the *mallus*. The mallus received testimony from witnesses familiar with the parties involved in a dispute or criminal case, much as a modern court does. Through such testimony it sought to discover the character and believability of each side. On occasion, in very difficult cases where such testimony was insufficient to determine guilt or innocence, recourse would be taken to judicial duels or to a variety of "divine" tests or ordeals. Among these was the length of time it took a defendant's hand to heal after immersion in boiling water. In another, the ordeal by water, a defendant was thrown with his hands and feet bound into a river or pond that a priest had blessed. If he floated, he was pronounced guilty, because the pure water had obviously rejected him; if, however, the water received him and he sank, he was deemed innocent.

In such ordeals God was believed to render a verdict. Once guilt had been made clear to the mallus, either by testimony or by ordeal, it assessed a monetary compensation to be paid to the injured party. This most popular way of settling grievances usually ended hostilities between individuals and families.

As in Merovingian times, many counts used their official position and new judicial powers to their own advantage and became little despots within their districts. As the strong became stronger, they also became more independent. They began to look on the land grants with which they were paid as hereditary possessions rather than generous royal donations—a development that began to fragment Charlemagne's kingdom. Charlemagne tried to oversee his overseers and improve local justice by creating special royal envoys known as *missi dominici*. These were lay and clerical agents (counts and archbishops and bishops) who made annual visits to districts other than their own. But their impact was marginal. Permanent provincial governors, bearing the title of prefect, duke, or margrave, were created in what was still another

An equestrian figure of Charlemagne (or possibly one of his sons), from the early ninth century. [Giraudon/ Art Resource, N.Y.]

attempt to supervise the counts and organize the outlying regions of the kingdom. But as these governors became established in their areas, they proved no less corruptible than the others.

Charlemagne never solved the problem of creating a loyal bureaucracy. Ecclesiastical agents proved no better than secular ones in this regard. Landowning bishops had not only the same responsibilities but also the same secular lifestyles and aspirations as the royal counts. Save for their attendance to the liturgy and to church prayers, they were largely indistinguishable from the lay nobility. Capitularies, or royal decrees, discouraged the more outrageous behavior of the clergy. But Charlemagne also sensed, rightly, as the Gregorian reform of the eleventh century would prove, that the emergence of a distinctive, reform-minded class of ecclesiastical landowners would be a danger to royal government. He purposefully treated his bishops as he treated his counts, that is, as vassals who served at the king's pleasure.

To be a Christian in this period was more a matter of ritual and doctrine (being baptized and reciting the Creed) than of following a prescription for ethical behavior and social service. Both clergy and laity were more concerned with contests over the most basic kinds of social protections than with more elevated ethical issues. An important legislative achievement of Charlemagne's reign, for example, was to give a free vassal the right to break his oath of loyalty to his lord if the lord tried to kill him, to reduce him to an unfree serf, to withhold promised protection in time of need, or to seduce his wife.

Alcuin and the Carolingian Renaissance
Charlemagne accumulated a great deal of wealth in the form of loot and land from conquered tribes. He used a substantial part of this booty to attract Europe's best scholars to Aachen, where they developed court culture and education. By making scholarship materially as well as intellectually rewarding, Charlemagne attracted such scholars as Theodulf of Orleans, Angilbert, his own biographer Einhard, and the renowned Anglo-Saxon master Alcuin of York (735–804). At almost fifty, Alcuin became director of the king's palace school in 782. He brought classical and Christian learning to Aachen in schools run by the monasteries. Alcuin was handsomely rewarded for his efforts with several monastic estates, including that of Saint Martin of Tours, the wealthiest in the kingdom.

Although Charlemagne also appreciated learning for its own sake, his grand palace school was not created simply for the love of antiquity. Charlemagne intended it to upgrade the administrative skills of the clerics and officials who staffed the royal bureaucracy. By preparing the sons of the nobility to run the religious and secular offices of the realm, court scholarship served kingdom building. The school provided basic instruction in the seven liberal arts, with special concentration on grammar, logic, rhetoric, and the basic mathematical arts. It therefore provided training in reading, writing, speaking, sound reasoning, and counting—the basic tools of bureaucracy.

Among the results of this intellectual activity was the appearance of a more accurate Latin in official documents and the development of a clear style of handwriting known as Carolingian minuscule that was far more legible than Merovingian script. By making reading both easier and more pleasurable, Carolingian minuscule helped lay the foundations of subsequent Latin scholarship. It also increased lay literacy.
A modest renaissance of antiquity occurred in the palace school as scholars collected and preserved ancient manuscripts for a more curious posterity. Alcuin worked on a correct text of the Bible and made editions of the works of Gregory the Great and the monastic *Rule* of Saint Benedict. These scholarly activities aimed at concrete reforms and served official efforts to bring uniformity to Church law and liturgy, to educate the clergy, and to improve moral life within the monasteries. Through personal correspondence and visitations, Alcuin created a genuine, if limited, community of scholars and clerics at court. He did much to infuse the highest administrative levels with a sense of comradeship and common purpose.

The Carolingian Manor The agrarian economy of the early Middle Ages was organized and controlled through village farms known as *manors*. On these, peasants labored as tenants for a lord, that is, a more powerful landowner who allotted them land and tenements in exchange for their services and a portion of their crops. The part of the land tended for the lord was the *demesne*, on average about one quarter to one third of the arable land. All crops grown there were harvested for the lord. The manor also included common meadows for grazing animals, and forests reserved exclusively for the lord to hunt in.

Peasants were treated according to their personal status and the size of their tenements. A *freeman*, that is, a peasant with his own modest allodial, or hereditary property (property free from the claims of an overlord), became a serf by surrendering his property to a greater landowner—a lord—in exchange for protection and assistance. The freeman received his land back from the lord with a clear definition of his economic and legal rights. Although the land was no longer his property, he had full possession and use of it and the number of services and amount of goods he was to supply to the lord were carefully spelled out.

Peasants who entered the service of a lord with little real property (perhaps only a few farm implements and animals) ended up as *unfree* serfs. Such serfs were much more vulnerable to the lord's demands, often spending up to three days a week working the lord's fields (see pp. 299–301). Truly impoverished peasants, those who had nothing to offer a lord except their hands, had the lowest status and were the least protected from excessive demands on their labor.

All classes of serfs were subject to various dues in kind: firewood for cutting the lord's wood, sheep for being allowed to graze their sheep on the lord's land, and the like. Thus the lord, who, for his part, furnished shacks and small plots of land from his vast domain, had at his disposal an army of servants of varying status who provided him with everything from eggs to boots. Weak serfs often fled to monasteries rather than continue their servitude. That many serfs were discontented is reflected in the high number of recorded escapes. An astrological calendar from the period even marks the days most favorable for escaping. Escaped serfs roamed the land as beggars and vagabonds, searching for new and better masters.

By the time of Charlemagne, the moldboard plow and the three-field system of land cultivation were coming into use. These developments greatly improved agricultural productivity. The older "scratch" plow had crisscrossed the field with only slight penetration and required light, well-drained soils. The moldboard plow, by contrast, cut deep into the soil and turned it to form a ridge, providing a natural drainage system and permitting the deep planting of seeds. This new type of plow made cultivation possible in the regions north of the Mediterranean, where soils were dense and waterlogged from heavy precipitation.

Unlike the earlier two-field system of crop rotation, which simply alternated fallow with planted fields each year, the three-field system increased the amount of cultivated land by leaving only one third fallow in a given year. Indeed, the third field might be reclaimed from previously passed over heavier soils now made workable by the moldboard plow, thus increasing the amount of land under cultivation in a dramatic fashion. It also better adjusted crops to seasons. In fall one field was planted with winter crops of wheat or rye and harvested in early summer. In late spring a second field was planted with summer crops of oats, barley, lentils, and legumes, which were harvested in August or September. The third field was left fallow, to be planted in its turn with winter and summer crops. The new summer crops, especially legumes, restored nitrogen to the soil and helped increase yields.

RELIGION AND THE CLERGY The lower clergy lived among and were drawn from peasant ranks. They fared hardly better than peasants in Carolingian times. As owners of the churches on their lands, the lords had the right to raise chosen serfs to the post of parish priest, placing them in charge of the churches on the lords' estates. Church law directed a lord to set a serf free before he entered the clergy. Lords, however, were reluctant to do this and risk thereby a possible later challenge to their jurisdiction over the

In this eleventh century manuscript, peasants harvest vines and plough fields behind yoked oxen. [Ardos Studio]

The Carolingian Manor

*A capitulary (or ordinance) from the reign of Charlemagne (known as "De Villis")
itemizes what the king received from his royal manors or village estates. It is a
testimony to Carolingian administrative ability and domination over the countryside.*

◆ *What gave a lord the right to absolutely everything? (Has anything been overlooked?) How did the stewards and workers share in manorial life? Was the
arrangement a good deal for them as well as for the lord?*

That each steward shall make an annual statement of all our income: an account of our lands cultivated by the oxen which our ploughmen drive and of our lands which the tenants of farms ought to plough; an account of the pigs, of the rents [a payment for the right to keep pigs in the woods], of the obligations and fines; of the game taken in our forests without our permission; of the various compositions; of the mills, of the forest, of the fields, of the bridges, and ships; of the free-men and the hundreds who are under obligations to our treasury; of markets, vineyards, and those who owe wine to us; of the hay, fire-wood, torches, planks, and other kinds of lumber; of the waste-lands; of the vegetables, millet, panic; of the wool, flax, and hemp; of the fruits of the trees, of the nut trees, larger and smaller; of the grafted trees of all kinds; of the gardens; of the turnips; of the fish-ponds; of the hides, skins, and horns; of the honey, wax; of the fat, tallow and soap; of the mulberry wine, cooked wine, mead, vinegar, beer, wine new and old; of the new grain and the old; of the hens and eggs; of the geese; the number of fishermen, smiths [workers in metal], sword-makers, and shoe-makers; of the bins and boxes; of the turners and saddlers; of the forges and mines, that is iron and other mines; of the lead mines; of the tributaries; of the colts and fillies; they shall make all these known to us, set forth separately and in order, at Christmas, in order that we may know what and how much of each thing we have.

In each of our estates our stewards are to

ecclesiastical property with which the serf, as priest, was invested. Lords preferred a "serf priest," one who not only said the Mass on Sundays and holidays but who also continued to serve his lord during the week, waiting on the lord's table and tending his steeds. Like Charlemagne with his bishops, Frankish lords cultivated a docile parish clergy.

The ordinary people looked to religion for comfort and consolation. They especially associated religion with the major Christian holidays and festivals, like Christmas and Easter. They baptized their children, attended mass, tried to learn the Lord's Prayer and the Apostles' Creed, and received the last rites from the priest as death approached. This was all probably done with more awe and simple faith than understanding. Because local priests on the manors were no better educated than their congregations, religious instruction in the meaning of Christian doctrine and practice remained at a bare minimum. The Church sponsored street dramas in accordance with the Church calendar. These were designed to impart the highlights of the Bible and Church history and to instill basic Christian moral values.

People understandably became particularly attached in this period to the more tangible veneration of saints and relics. The Virgin Mary was also widely revered, although a true cult of Mary would not develop until the eleventh and twelfth centuries. Religious devotion to saints has been compared to subjection to powerful lords in the secular world. Both the saint and the lord were protectors whose honor the serfs were bound to defend and whose favor and help

have as many cow-houses, piggeries, sheep-folds, stable for goats, as possible, and they ought never to be without these.

They must provide with the greatest care that whatever is prepared or made with the hands, that is, lard, smoked meat, salt meat, partially salted meat, wine, vinegar, mulberry wine, cooked wine, garns [a kind of fermented liquor], mustard, cheese, butter, malt, beer, mead, honey, wax, flour, all should be prepared and made with the greatest cleanliness. That each steward on each of our domains shall always have, for the sake of ornament, swans, peacocks, pheasants, ducks, pigeons, partridges, turtle-doves.

That in each of our estates, the chambers shall be provided with counterpanes, cushions, pillows, bed-clothes, coverings for the tables and benches; vessels of brass, lead, iron and wood; and irons, chains, pot-hooks, adzes, axes, augers, cutlasses and all other kinds of tools, so that it shall never be necessary to go elsewhere for them, or to borrow them. And the weapons, which are carried against the enemy, shall be well cared for, so as to keep them in good condition.

For our women's work they are to give at the proper time, as has been ordered, the materials, that is the linen, wool, woad, vermillion, madder, wool-combs, teasels, soap, grease, vessels and the other objects which are necessary.

Of the food-products other than meat, two-thirds shall be sent each year for our own use, that is of the vegetables, fish, cheese, butter, honey, mustard, vinegar, millet, panic, dried and green herbs, radishes, and in addition of the wax, soap and other small products.

That each steward shall have in his district good workmen, namely, blacksmiths, gold-smiths, silver-smiths, shoemakers, turners, carpenters, sword-makers, fishermen, foilers, soap-makers, men who know how to make beer, cider, berry, and all the other kinds of beverages, bakers to make pastry for our table, net-makers who know how to make nets for hunting, fishing and fowling, and the other who are too numerous to be designated.

Translations and reprints from the Original Sources of European History, *Vol. 3 (Philadelphia: Department of History, University of Pennsylvania, 1909), pp. 2–4.*

in time of need they hoped to receive. Veneration of saints also had strong points of contact with old tribal customs, from which the commonfolk were hardly detached. (Indeed, Charlemagne enforced laws against witchcraft, sorcery, and the ritual sacrifice of animals by monks.)

But religion also had an intrinsic appeal and special meaning to those masses of medieval men and women who found themselves burdened, fearful, and with little hope of material betterment on this side of eternity. Charlemagne shared many of the religious beliefs of his ordinary subjects. He collected and venerated relics, made pilgrimages to Rome, and frequented the Church of Saint Mary in Aachen several times a day. In his last will and testament he directed that all but a fraction of his great treasure be spent to endow masses and prayers for his departed soul.

Breakup of the Carolingian Kingdom

In the last years of his life, an ailing Charlemagne knew that his empire was ungovernable. The seeds of dissolution lay in regionalism, that is, the determination of each region, no matter how small, to look first—and often only—to its own self-interest. Despite his considerable skill and resolve, Charlemagne's realm became too fragmented among powerful regional magnates. Although they were his vassals, these same men were also landholders and lords in their own right. They knew that their sovereignty lessened as Charlemagne's increased and accordingly became reluctant royal servants. In feudal society a direct relationship existed between physical proximity to authority and loyalty to authority. Local people obeyed local lords more readily than they obeyed a glorious but distant king.

Charlemagne had been forced to recognize and even to enhance the power of regional magnates to win needed financial and military support. But as in the Merovingian kingdom, the tail came increasingly to wag the dog. Charlemagne's major attempt to enforce transregional discipline and the subordination of local interests to royal dictates was to create the institution of the *missi dominici*—royal overseers of the king's law and justice. But these new officials themselves fell prey to narrow, regional self-interest, and this effort also proved ultimately unsuccessful.

LOUIS THE PIOUS   The Carolingian kings did not give up easily, however. Charlemagne's only surviving son and successor was Louis the Pious (r. 814–840), so-called because of his close alliance with the Church and his promotion of puritanical reforms. Before his death, Charlemagne secured the imperial succession for Louis by raising him to "coemperor" in a grand public ceremony. After Charlemagne's death, Louis no longer referred to himself as king of the Franks. He bore instead the single title of emperor. The assumption of this title reflected not only Carolingian pretense to an imperial dynasty, but also Louis's determination to unify his kingdom and raise its people above mere regional and tribal loyalties.

Unfortunately Louis's own fertility joined with Salic law and Frankish custom to prevent the attainment of this high goal. Louis had three sons by his first wife. According to Salic, or Frankish, law, a ruler partitioned his kingdom equally among his surviving sons. (Salic law forbade women to inherit the throne.) Louis, who saw himself as an emperor and no mere king, recognized that a tripartite kingdom would hardly be an empire and acted early in his reign, in the year 817, to break this legal tradition. This he did by making his eldest son, Lothar (d. 855), coregent and sole imperial heir. To Lothar's brothers he gave important but much lesser appanages, or assigned hereditary lands; Pepin (d. 838) became king of Aquitaine, and Louis "the German" (d. 876) became king of Bavaria, over the eastern Franks.

In 823 Louis's second wife, Judith of Bavaria, bore him a fourth son, Charles, later called "the Bald" (d. 877). Mindful of Frankish law and custom and determined that her son should receive more than just a nominal inheritance, the queen incited the brothers Pepin and Louis against Lothar, who fled for refuge to the pope. More important, Judith was instrumental in persuading Louis to adhere to tradition and divide the kingdom equally among his four living sons. As their stepmother and the young Charles rose in their father's favor, the three brothers, fearing still further reversals, decided to act against their father. Supported by the pope, they joined forces and defeated their father in a battle near Colmar (833).

As the bestower of crowns on emperors, the pope had an important stake in the preservation of the revived western empire and the imperial title. Louis's belated agreement to an equal partition of his kingdom threatened to weaken the pope as well as the royal family. Therefore, the pope condemned Louis and restored Lothar to his original inheritance. But Lothar's regained imperial dignity only stirred anew the resentments of his brothers, including his stepbrother, Charles, who joined in renewed warfare against him.

THE TREATY OF VERDUN AND ITS AFTERMATH In 843, with the Treaty of Verdun, peace finally came to the surviving heirs of Louis the Pious (Pepin had died in 838). But this agreement also brought about the disaster that Louis had originally feared. The great Carolingian Empire was partitioned into three equal parts. Lothar received a middle section, known as Lotharingia, which embraced roughly modern Holland, Belgium, Switzerland, Alsace-Lorraine, and Italy. Charles the Bald received the western part of the kingdom, or roughly modern France. And Louis the German gained the eastern part, or roughly modern Germany (see Map 6-5).

Although Lothar retained the imperial title, the universal empire of Charlemagne and Louis the Pious ceased to exist after Verdun. Not until the sixteenth century, with the election in 1519 of Charles I of Spain as Holy Roman Emperor Charles V, would the Western world again see a kingdom so vast as Charlemagne's.

The Treaty of Verdun proved to be only the beginning of Carolingian fragmentation. When

MAP 6-5 THE TREATY OF VERDUN, 843, AND THE TREATY OF MERSEN, 870 *The Treaty of Verdun divided the kingdom of Louis the Pious among his three feuding children; Charles the Bald, Lothar, and Louis the German. After Lothar's death in 855, his lands and titles were divided among his three sons, Louis, Charles, and Lothar II. When Lothar II, who had received his father's northern kingdom, died in 870, Charles the Bald and Louis the German claimed the middle kingdom and divided it between themselves in the Treaty of Mersen.*

Lothar died in 855, his middle kingdom was divided equally among his three surviving sons, the eldest of whom, Louis II, retained Italy and the imperial title. This partition of the partition sealed the dissolution of the great empire of Charlemagne. Henceforth, western Europe saw an eastern and a western Frankish kingdom—roughly Germany and France—at war over the fractionalized middle kingdom, a contest that has continued into modern times.

In Italy the demise of the Carolingian emperors enhanced for the moment the power of the popes, who had become adept at filling vacuums. The popes were now strong enough to excommunicate weak emperors and override their wishes. In a major Church crackdown on the polygamy of the Germans, Pope Nicholas I (858–867) excommunicated Lothar II for divorcing his wife. After the death of the childless emperor Louis II (875), Pope John VIII (872–882) installed Charles the Bald as emperor against the express last wishes of Louis II.

When Charles the Bald died in 877, both the papal and the imperial thrones suffered defeat. They became pawns in the hands of powerful Italian and German magnates, respectively. Neither pope nor emperor knew dignity and power again until a new western imperial dynasty—the Saxons—attained dominance during the reign of Otto I (r. 962–973).

It is especially at this juncture in European history—the last quarter of the ninth and the first half of the tenth century—that one may speak with some justification of a "dark age." The internal political breakdown of the empire and the papacy coincided with new barbarian attacks, set off probably by overpopulation and famine in northern Europe. The late ninth and the tenth centuries saw successive waves of Normans (North-men), better known as

The tenth-century crown of the Holy Roman Emperor (the title applied to rulers who succeeded to the remains of Charlemagne's empire) reveals the close alliance between Church and throne. The crown is surmounted by a cross, and it includes panels depicting the great kings of the Bible, David and Solomon. [Kunsthistorisches Museum, Vienna]

The Carolingian Dynasty (751–987)

750–800	*Donation of Constantine* protests Frankish domination of Church
751	Pepin II "the Short" becomes king of the Franks
755	Franks protect Church against Lombards and create the Papal States
768–814	Charlemagne rules as king of the Franks
774	Charlemagne defeats Lombards in northern Italy
800	Pope Leo III crowns Charlemagne emperor
814–840	Louis the Pious succeeds Charlemagne as emperor
843	Treaty of Verdun partitions the Carolingian Empire
870	Treaty of Mersen allows eastern and western Frankish kingdoms to absorb the fragmented middle lands
962	Saxons under Otto I firmly established as successors to Carolingians in Germany
987	Capetian dynasty succeeds Carolingian in France

A Viking raid on the English coast, as imagined in this dramatic recent portrayal. Raids like these disrupted European life from Novgorod to Gibraltar in the ninth and tenth centuries. [York Archaeological Trust Historical Picture Library, England]

Vikings, from Scandinavia; Magyars, or Hungarians, the great horsemen from the eastern plains; and Muslims from the South (see Map 6-6).

For the people of western Europe, the Vikings were the more serious threat. They came in greater numbers and, thanks to their unsurpassed skills as seamen, swept over European lands from Novgorod to Gibraltar. Wherever Viking tribes settled, they brought conflict, warring among themselves when not with native peoples. In the 880s the Vikings penetrated to the imperial residence of Aachen and to Paris. Moving rapidly in ships and raiding coastal towns, they were almost impossible to defend against and kept western Europe on edge. The Franks built fortified towns and castles in strategic locations, which served as refuges. When they could, they bought off the invaders with outright grants of land (for example, Normandy) and payments of silver. In the resulting political

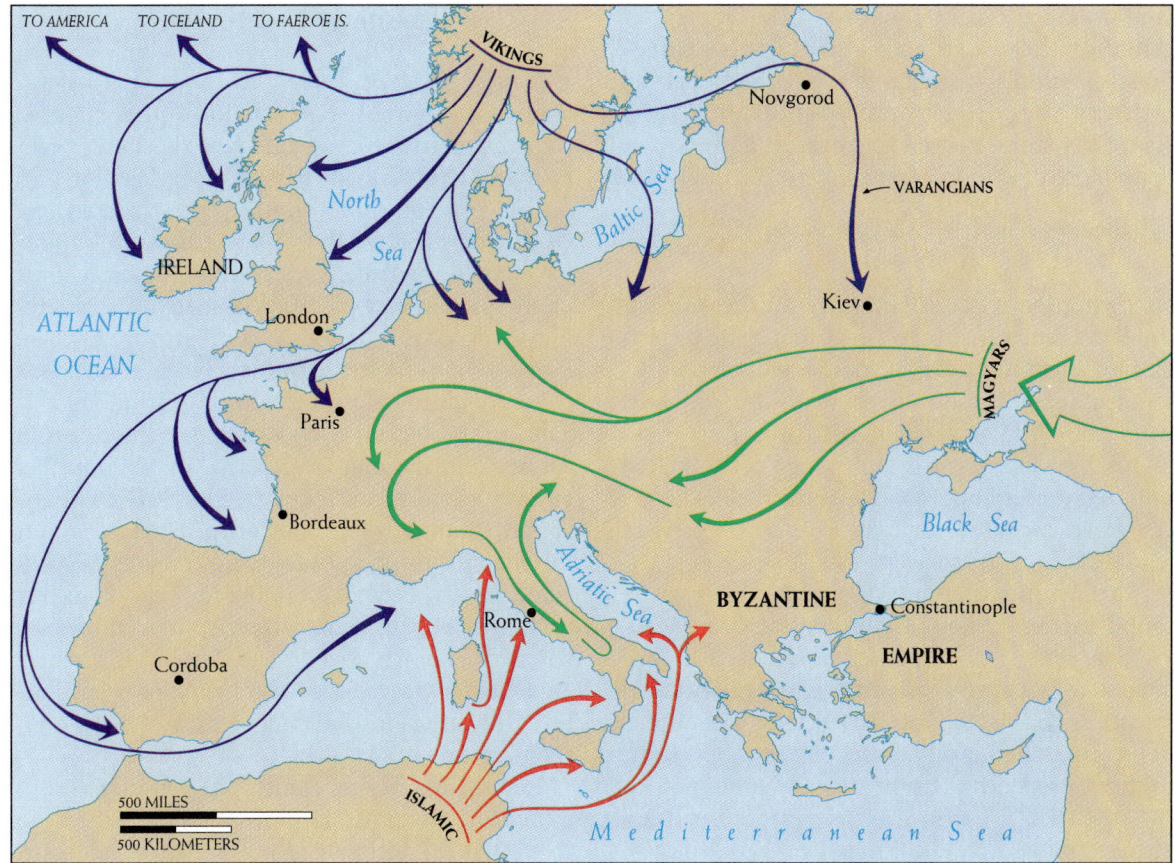

MAP 6-6 VIKING, ISLAMIC, AND MAGYAR INVASIONS TO THE ELEVENTH CENTURY *Western Europe was sorely beset by new waves of outsiders from the ninth to the eleventh century. From north, east, and south a stream of invading Vikings, Magyars, and Muslims brought the West at times to near collapse and of course gravely affected institutions within Europe.*

and social turmoil, local populations became more dependent than ever before on local strongmen for life, limb, and livelihood. This brutal reality provided the essential conditions for the maturation of feudal society in western Europe.

Feudal Society

The Middle Ages were characterized by a chronic absence of effective central government and the constant threat of famine, disease, and foreign invasion. In this state of affairs the weaker sought the protection of the stronger, and the true lords and masters became those who could guarantee immediate security from rapine and starvation. The term *feudal society* refers to the social, political, military, and economic system that emerged from these conditions.

The feudal society of the Middle Ages was a society dominated by warlords. What people needed most was the firm assurance that others could be depended on in time of dire need. Lesser men pledged themselves to powerful individuals—warlords or princes—recognizing them as personal superiors and promising them faithful service. Large warrior groups of vassals sprang up, and these developed into a prominent professional military class with its own code of knightly conduct. The result was a network of relationships based on mutual loyalty that enabled warlords to acquire armies and to rule over territory whether or not they owned land or had a legitimating royal title. The emergence of these extensive military organizations—warlords and their groups of professional military vassals—was an adaptation to the absence of strong central government and the predominance of a noncommercial, rural economy.

Origins

Following the modern authority on the subject, the late French historian Marc Bloch, historians distinguish the cruder forms of feudal government that evolved during the early Middle Ages from the sophisticated institutional arrangements by which princes and kings consolidated their territories and established royal rule during the High Middle Ages (the so-called "second feudal age").

The origins of feudal government can be found in the divisions and conflicts of Merovingian society. In the sixth and seventh centuries it became customary for individual freemen who did not already belong to families or groups that could protect them to place themselves under the protection of more powerful freemen. In this way the latter built up armies and became local magnates, and the former solved the problem of simple survival. Freemen who so entrusted themselves to others were known as *ingenui in obsequio* ("freemen in a contractual relation of dependence"). Those who so gave themselves to the king were called *antrustiones*. All men of this type came to be described collectively as *vassi* ("those who serve"), from which evolved the term *vassalage*, meaning the placement of oneself in the personal service of another who promises protection in return.

Landed nobles, like kings, tried to acquire as many such vassals as they could, because military strength in the early Middle Ages lay in numbers. Because it proved impossible to maintain these growing armies within the lord's own household (as was the original custom) or to support them by special monetary payments, the practice evolved of simply granting them land as a "tenement." Such land came to be known as a *benefice* or a *fief*; vassals were expected to dwell on it and maintain their horses and other accouterments of war in good order. Originally vassals, therefore, were little more than gangs-in-waiting.

Vassalage and the Fief

Vassalage involved "fealty" to the lord. To swear fealty was to promise to refrain from any action that might in any way threaten the lord's well-being and to perform personal services for him on his request. Chief among the expected services was military duty as a mounted knight. This could involve a variety of activities: a short or long military expedition, escort duty, standing castle guard, or the placement of one's own fortress at the lord's disposal, if the vassal was of such stature as to have one. Continuous bargaining and bickering occurred over the terms of service. Limitations were placed on the number of days a lord could require services from a vassal. In France in the eleventh century, about forty days of service a year were considered sufficient. It also became possible for vassals to buy their way out of military service by a monetary payment, known as *scutage*. The lord, in turn, applied this payment to the hiring of mercenaries, who often proved more efficient than contract-conscious vassals.

Beyond his military duty, the vassal was also expected to give the lord advice when he requested it and to sit as a member of his court when the latter was in session. The vassal also owed his lord financial assistance when his lord was in obvious need or distress, for example, when he had been captured by his enemies and needed to be ransomed, or when he was outfitting himself for a crusade or a major military campaign. And gifts of money might also be expected when the lord's daughters married and his sons became knights.

Beginning with the reign of Louis the Pious (814–840), bishops and abbots swore fealty to the king and received their offices from him as a benefice. The king formally "invested" these clerics in their offices during a special ceremony in which he presented them with a ring and a staff, the symbols of high spiritual office. Louis's predecessors had earlier confiscated Church lands with only modest and belated compensation to the Church in the form of a tithe required of all Frankish inhabitants. Long a sore point with the Church, the presumptuous practice of the lay investiture of the clergy provoked a serious confrontation of Church and state in the late tenth and eleventh centuries. At that time reform-minded clergy rebelled against what they then believed to be a kind of involuntary clerical vassalage. Even reform-minded clerics, however, welcomed the king's grants of land and power to the clergy.

The lord's obligations to his vassals were very specific. First, he was obligated to protect the vassal from physical harm and to stand as his advocate in public court. After fealty was sworn and homage paid, the lord provided for the vassal's physical maintenance by the bestowal of a benefice, or fief. The fief was simply the physical or material wherewithal to meet the vassal's military and other obligations. It could take the form of liquid wealth as well as the more common grant of real property. There were so-called money fiefs, which empowered a vassal to receive regular payments from the lord's treasury. Such fiefs created potential conflicts because they made it possible for a nobleman in one land to acquire vassals among the nobility in another. Normally the fief consisted of a landed estate of anywhere from a few to several thousand acres. But it could also take the form of a castle.

In Carolingian times a benefice, or fief, varied in size from one or more small villas to several *mansi*, agricultural holdings of twenty-five to forty-eight acres. The king's vassals are known to have received benefices of at least 30 and as many as 200 such *mansi*, truly a vast estate. Royal vassalage with a benefice understandably came to be widely sought by the highest classes of Carolingian society. As a royal policy, however, it ultimately proved deadly to the king. Although Carolingian kings jealously guarded their rights over property granted in benefice to vassals, resident vassals were still free to dispose of their benefices as they pleased. Vassals of the king, strengthened by his donations, in turn created their own vassals. These, in turn, created still further vassals of their own—vassals of vassals of vassals—in a pyramiding effect that had fragmented land and authority from the highest to the lowest levels by the late ninth century.

Fragmentation and Divided Loyalty

In addition to the fragmentation brought about by the multiplication of vassalage, effective occupation of land led gradually to claims of hereditary possession. Hereditary possession became a legally recognized principle in the ninth century and laid the basis for claims to real ownership. Fiefs given as royal donations became hereditary possessions and, with the passage of time, in some instances even the real property of the possessor.

Further, vassal engagements came to be multiplied in still another way as enterprising freemen sought to accumulate as much land as possible. One man could become a vassal to several different lords. This development led in the ninth century to the "liege lord"—that one master whom the vassal must obey even to the harm of his other masters, should a direct conflict arise among them.

The problem of loyalty was reflected not only in the literature of the period, with its praise of the virtues of honor and fidelity, but also in the ceremonial development of the very act of "commendation" by which a freeman became a vassal. In the mid-eighth century an "oath of fealty" highlighted the ceremony. A vassal reinforced his promise of fidelity to the lord by swearing a special oath with his hand on a sacred relic or the Bible. In the tenth and eleventh centuries paying homage to the lord involved not only the swearing of such an oath but also the placement of the vassal's hands between the lord's and the sealing of the ceremony with a kiss.

As the centuries passed, personal loyalty and service became quite secondary to the acquisition of property. In developments that signaled the waning of feudal society in the tenth century, the fief came to overshadow fealty, the benefice became more important than vassalage, and freemen proved themselves prepared to swear allegiance to the highest bidder.

Feudal arrangements nonetheless provided stability throughout the early Middle Ages and aided the difficult process of political centralization during the High Middle Ages. The genius of feudal government lay in its adaptability. Contracts of different kinds could be made with almost anybody, as circumstances required. The process embraced a wide spectrum of people, from the king at the top to the lowliest vassal in the remotest part of the kingdom. The foundations of the modern nation state would emerge in France and England from the fine tuning of essentially feudal arrangements as kings sought to adapt their goal of centralized government to the reality of local power and control.

———————————◆———————————

The centuries between 476 and 1000 saw both the decline of classical civilization and the birth of a new European civilization in the regions of what had been the Western Roman Empire. Beginning in the fifth century, barbarian invasions separated western Europe culturally from much of its classical past. Although some important works and concepts survived from antiquity and the Christian church preserved major features of Roman government, the West would be recovering its classical heritage for centuries in "renaissances" that stretched into the sixteenth century. Out of the mixture of barbarian and surviving (or recovered) classical culture, a distinct Western culture was born. Aided and abetted by the Christian church, the Franks created a new imperial tradition and shaped basic Western political and social institutions for centuries to come.

The early Middle Ages also saw the emergence of a rift in Christendom between the Eastern church and the Western church. Evolving from the initial division of the Roman Empire into eastern and western parts, this rift widened, resulting in bitter conflict between popes and patriarchs.

During this period, the capital of the Byzantine Empire, Constantinople, far exceeded in population and culture any city of the West. Serving as both a buffer against Persian, Arab, and Turkish invasions of the West, and as a major repository of classical learning and science for western scholars, the Byzantine Empire did much to make possible the development of western Europe as a distinctive political and cultural entity. Another cultural and religious rival of the West, Islam, also saw its golden age during these same centuries. Like the Byzantine world, the Muslim world also preserved ancient scholarship, and, especially through Muslim Spain, provided a conduit for retransmitting it to the West. But despite examples of coexistence and even friendship, the cultures of the Western and Muslim worlds were too different and their people too estranged and suspicious of one another for them to become good neighbors.

The early Middle Ages were not centuries of great ambition in the West. It was a time when modest foundations were being laid. Despite a certain common religious culture, Western society remained primitive and fragmented, probably more so than anywhere else in the contemporary world. Two distinctive social institutions developed in response to these conditions: manorialism and feudalism. Manorialism ensured that all would be fed and cared for; feudalism provided protection from outside predators. Western people were concerned primarily to satisfy basic needs; great cultural ambition would come later.

Review Questions

1. Trace the history of Christianity to the coronation of the emperor Charlemagne in 800. What distinctive features characterized the early Church? What role did the Church play in the world after the fall of the Western Roman Empire?

2. Discuss the growth of the Frankish kingdom, including its relationship with the Church, through the reign of Charlemagne. What were the characteristics of Charlemagne's rule? Why did Charlemagne encourage learning at his court? How could the Carolingian renaissance have been dangerous to Charlemagne's rule? Why did his empire break apart?

3. How and why was the history of the eastern half of the Roman empire so different from the western half? How would you assess the rule of Justinian over the Byzantine empire? How would you compare Justinian to Charlemagne?

4. What were the tenets of Islam and how were the Muslims suddenly able to build an empire? Assess the importance of the Muslim invasions for the development of western Europe.

5. How and why did feudal society begin? What were the essential ingredients of feudalism? How easy do you think it would be for modern society to "slip back" into a feudal pattern?

Suggested Readings

G. Barraclough, *The Crucible of Europe: The Ninth and Tenth Centuries* (1976). Sweeping survey of political history.

R. Bartlett, *Trial by Fire and Water: The Medieval Judicial Ordeal* (1986). Makes sense of these seemingly bizarre ways of letting God decide guilt or innocence.

M. Bloch, *Feudal Society*, Vols. 1 and 2, trans. by L. A. Manyon (1971). A classic on the topic and as an example of historical study.

P. Brown, *Augustine of Hippo: A Biography* (1967). Late antiquity seen through the biography of its greatest Christian thinker.

H. Chadwick, *The Early Church* (1967). Among the best treatments of early Christianity.

R. H. C. Davis, *A History of Medieval Europe: From Constantine to St. Louis* (1972). Unsurpassed in clarity.

K. F. Drew (Ed.), *The Barbarian Invasions: Catalyst of a New Order* (1970). Collection of essays that focuses the issues.

G. Duby, *The Early Growth of the European Economy: Warriors and Peasants from the Seventh to the Twelfth Century* (1974). Readable, authoritative account of rural society.

H. Fichtenau, *The Carolingian Empire: The Age of Charlemagne*, trans. by Peter Munz (1964). Strongest on political history of the era.

J. V. A. Fine, *The Early Medieval Balkans: Sixth–Twelfth Centuries* (1983). Insight into the ethnic divisions that form the background to modern conflict in the region.

F. L. Ganshof, *Feudalism*, trans. by Philip Grierson (1964). The most profound brief analysis of the subject.

D. J. Geanakoplos, *Byzantine East and Latin West: Two Worlds of Christendom in the Middle Ages and Renaissance* (1966). Essays by the authority on eastern influence on the West.

A. F. Havighurst (Ed.), *The Pirenne Thesis: Analysis, Criticism, and Revision* (1958). Excerpts from the scholarly debate over the extent of western trade in the East during the early Middle Ages.

R. Hodges and D. Whitehouse, *Mohammed, Charlemagne and the Origins of Europe* (1982). For the social and economic history of early medieval Europe.

A. Hourani, *A History of the Arab Peoples* (1991). A comprehensive text that includes an excellent overview of the origins and early history of Islam.

D. Knowles, *Christian Monasticism* (1969). Sweeping survey with helpful photographs.

M. L. W. Laistner, *Thought and Letters in Western Europe, 500 to 900* (1957). Among the best surveys of early medieval intellectual history.

J. Leclercq, *The Love of Learning and the Desire for God: A Study of Monastic Culture*, trans. by Catherine Misrahi (1962). Lucid, delightful, absorbing account of the ideals of monks.

J. Leclercq, F. Vandenbroucke, and L. Bouyer, *The Spirituality of the Middle Ages* (1968). Perhaps the best survey of medieval Christianity, east and west, to the eve of the Protestant Reformation.

B. Lewis, *The Muslim Discovery of Europe* (1982). Authoritative account from the Muslim's perspective.

C. Mango, *Byzantium: The Empire of New Rome* (1980). Perhaps the most readable account.

M. McCormick, "Byzantium and the West, A.D. 700–900," in *The New Cambridge Medieval History*, vol. 2: *The Early Medieval West 700–900* (1993). Up-to-date framing of events and political developments.

R. McKitterick, *The Frankish Kingdoms Under the Carolingians, 751–987* (1983). The fate of Carolingian government.

P. Munz, *The Age of Charlemagne* (1971). Penetrating social history of the period.

H. Pirenne, *A History of Europe, I: From the End of the Roman World in the West to the Beginnings of the Western States*, trans. by Bernhard Maill (1958). Comprehensive survey, with now-controversial views on the demise of western trade and cities in the early Middle Ages.

S. Runciman, *Byzantine Civilization* (1970). Succinct, comprehensive account by a master.

P. Sawyer, *The Age of the Vikings* (1962). Among the best accounts.

R. W. Southern, *The Making of the Middle Ages* (1973). Originally published in 1953, but still a fresh account by an imaginative historian.

C. Stephenson, *Medieval Feudalism* (1969). Excellent short summary and introduction.

A. A. Vasiliev, *History of the Byzantine Empire 324–1453* (1952). The most comprehensive treatment in English.

W. Walther, *Woman in Islam* (1981). One hour spent with this book teaches more about the social import of Islam than days spent with others.

S. Wemple, *Women in Frankish Society: Marriage and the Cloister 500–900* (1981). What marriage and the cloister meant to women in these early centuries.

L. White, Jr., *Medieval Technology and Social Change* (1962). Often fascinating account of the way primitive technology changed life.

The "Castle of the Knights" (Krak-des-Chevaliers). It is situated in northern Syria a few miles from the Lebanese border. Its defense consisted of two massive walls, one overhanging the other, divided by a great moat. It is the most magnificient of the many crusader castles built in the Holy Land in the twelfth and thirteenth centuries; their ruins remain in modern Syria, Lebanon, and Jordan. [J. Allen Cash Ltd.]

7

The High Middle Ages (1000–1300): The Ascendancy of the Church and the Rise of States

Key Topics in This Chapter
◆ The revival of the Holy Roman Empire by a new German dynasty, the Saxons
◆ The appearance of a great reform movement in the Church and the Church's successful challenge to political domination by kings and emperors
◆ The emergence of strong, national monarchies in England and France
◆ The fragmentation of Germany in the wake of a centuries-long struggle between the emperors of the Hohenstaufen dynasty and the papacy

The High Middle Ages mark a period of political expansion and consolidation and of intellectual flowering and synthesis. The noted medievalist Joseph Strayer called it the age that saw "the full development of all the potentialities of medieval civilization."[1] Some even argue that as far as the development of Western institutions is concerned, this was a more creative period than the later Italian Renaissance and the German Reformation.

The High Middle Ages saw the borders of western Europe largely secured against foreign invaders. Although intermittent Muslim aggression continued well into the sixteenth century, fear of assault from without diminished. On the contrary, a striking change occurred in the late eleventh century and the twelfth century. Western Europe, which had for so long been the prey of foreign powers, became, through the Crusades and foreign trade, the feared hunter within both the eastern Byzantine world and the Muslim world.

During the High Middle Ages "national" monarchies emerged. Rulers in England and France successfully adapted feudal principles of government to create newly centralized political realms. At the same time, parliaments and popular assemblies emerged to secure the rights and customs of the privileged many—the nobility, the clergy, and propertied townspeople—against the desires of kings. In the process the foundations of modern European states were laid. The Holy Roman Empire, however, proved the great exception to this centralizing trend. Despite a revival of the empire under the Ottonians (Otto I, the most powerful member of the Saxon imperial dynasty, and his immediate successors, Otto II and Otto III), the events of these centuries left it weak and fragmented until modern times.

The High Middle Ages also saw the Latin, or Western, church establish itself in concept and law as a spiritual authority independent of monarchical secular government, thus sowing the seeds of the distinctive Western separation of Church and state. During the Investiture Controversy, the confrontation between popes and emperors that began in the late eleventh century and lasted through the twelfth, a reformed papacy overcame its long subservience to the Carolingian and Ottonian kings. In this struggle over the authority of rulers to designate bishops and other high clergy and to invest them with their symbols of authority, the papacy, under Gregory II and his immediate successors, won out. It did so, however, by becoming itself a monarchy among the world's emerging monarchies, preparing the way for still more dangerous confrontations between popes and emperors in the later Middle Ages. Some religious reformers later saw in the Gregorian papacy of the High Middle Ages the fall of the Church from its spiritual mission as well as a declaration of its independence from secular power.

Otto I and the Revival of the Empire

The fortunes of both the old empire and the papacy began to revive after the dark period of the late ninth century and the early tenth century. In 918 the Saxon Henry I ("the Fowler," d. 936), the strongest of the German dukes, became the first non-Frankish king of Germany.

Unifying Germany

Henry rebuilt royal power by forcibly combining the duchies of Swabia, Bavaria, Saxony, Franconia, and Lotharingia. He secured imperial borders by checking the invasions of the Hungarians and the Danes. Although much smaller than Charlemagne's empire, the German kingdom Henry created placed his son and successor Otto I (r. 936–973) in a strong territorial position.

The very able Otto maneuvered his own kin into positions of power in Bavaria, Swabia, and Franconia. He refused to recognize each duchy as an independent hereditary entity, as the nobility increasingly expected, dealing with each instead as a subordinate member of a unified kingdom. In a truly imperial gesture in 951, he invaded Italy and proclaimed himself its king. In 955 he won his most magnificent victory when he defeated the Hungarians at Lechfeld. This victory secured German borders against new barbarian attack, further unified the German duchies, and earned Otto the well-

[1] *Western History in the Middle Ages—A Short History (New York: Appleton-Century-Crofts, 1955), pp. 9, 127.*

deserved title "the Great." In defining the boundaries of the western Europe, it was comparable with Charles Martel's earlier victory over the Saracens at Poitiers in 732.

Embracing the Church

As part of a careful rebuilding program, Otto, following the example of his predecessors, enlisted the Church. Bishops and abbots—men who possessed a sense of universal empire, yet because they did not marry, could not found competitive dynasties—were made royal princes and agents of the king. Because these clergy, as royal bureaucrats, received great land holdings and immunity from local counts and dukes, they also found such vassalage to the king very attractive. The medieval Church did not become a great territorial power reluctantly. It appreciated the blessings of receiving, while teaching the blessedness of giving.

In 961 Otto, who had long aspired to the imperial crown, responded to a call for help from Pope John XII (955–964), who was then being bullied by an Italian enemy of the German king, Berengar of Friuli. In recompense for this rescue, Pope John crowned Otto emperor on February 2, 962. Otto, for his part, recognized the existence of the Papal States and proclaimed himself their special protector. The Church was now more than ever under royal control. Its bishops and abbots were Otto's appointees and bureaucrats, and the pope reigned in Rome only by the power of the emperor's sword.

Pope John, belatedly recognizing the royal web in which the Church had become entangled, joined in Italian opposition to the new emperor. This turnabout brought Otto's swift revenge. An ecclesiastical synod over which Otto presided deposed Pope John and proclaimed that henceforth no pope could take office without first swearing an oath of allegiance to the emperor. Under Otto I popes ruled at the emperor's pleasure.

As these events reflect, Otto had shifted the royal focus from Germany to Italy. His successors—Otto II (r. 973–983) and Otto III (r. 983–1002)—became so preoccupied with running the affairs of Italy that their German base began to disintegrate, sacrificed to imperial dreams. They might have learned a lesson from

Otto I presents the Magdeburg Cathedral to Christ, as the pope (holding the keys to the kingdom of heaven) watches, a testimony to Otto's guardianship of the Church. [Metropolitan Museum of Art, bequest of George Blumenthal, 1941]

the contemporary Capetian kings, the successor dynasty to the Carolingians in France. These kings, perhaps more by circumstance than by design, pursued a very different course than the Ottonians. They mended local fences and concentrated their limited resources to secure a tight grip on their immediate royal domain, never neglecting it for the sake of foreign adventure.

The Ottonians, in contrast, reached far beyond their grasp when they tried to subdue Italy. As the briefly revived empire began to crumble in the first quarter of the eleventh century, the Church, long unhappy with Carolingian and Ottonian domination, prepared to declare its independence and exact its own vengeance.

The Reviving Catholic Church

During the late ninth and early tenth centuries the clergy had become tools of kings and magnates and the papacy a toy of Italian nobles. The

Ottonians made bishops their servile princes and likewise dominated the papacy. The Church was about to gain renewed respect and authority, however, thanks not only to the failing fortunes of the overextended empire but also to a new, determined force for reform within the Church itself.

The Cluny Reform Movement

The great monastery in Cluny in east-central France gave birth to a monastic reform movement that progressively won the support of secular lords and German kings. In doing so, this

Benedictine monks at choir. The reform movement that began at the Benedictine monastery at Cluny in northern France in the tenth century spread throughout the Church and was ultimately responsible for the reassertion of papal authority. [Courtesy of the Trustees of the British Library]

movement enabled the Church to challenge its domination by royal authority at both the episcopal and papal levels.

The reformers of Cluny were aided by widespread popular respect for the Church that found expression in lay religious fervor and generous baronial patronage of religious houses. One reason so many people admired clerics and monks was that the Church was medieval society's most democratic institution as far as lay participation was concerned. In the Middle Ages any man could theoretically rise to the position of pope, who was supposed to be elected by "the people and the clergy." All people were candidates for the Church's grace and salvation. The Church promised a better life to come to the great mass of ordinary people, who found the present one brutish and without hope.

Since the fall of the Roman Empire, popular support for the Church had been especially inspired by the example set by monks. Monasteries provided an important alternative way of life for the religiously earnest in an age when most people had very few options. Monks remained the least secularized and most spiritual of the Church's clergy. Their cultural achievements were widely admired, their relics and rituals were considered magical, and their high religious ideals and sacrifices were imitated by the laity.

The tenth and eleventh centuries saw an unprecedented boom in the construction of monasteries. William the Pious, duke of Aquitaine, founded Cluny in 910. It was a Benedictine monastery devoted to the strictest observance of Saint Benedict's *Rule for Monasteries*, with a special emphasis on liturgical purity. Although the reformers who emerged at Cluny were loosely organized and their demands not always consistent, they shared a determination to maintain a spiritual Church. They absolutely rejected the subservience of the clergy, especially that of the German bishops, to royal authority. They taught that the pope in Rome was sole ruler over all the clergy.

No local secular ruler, the Cluniacs asserted, could have any control over their monasteries. They further denounced the transgression of ascetic piety by "secular" parish clergy, who maintained concubines in a relationship akin to marriage. (Later a distinction would be formalized between the *secular* clergy who lived and ministered in the world *[saeculum]* and the *regular* clergy, monks and nuns withdrawn from the world and living according to a special rule *[regula]*.)

The Cluny reformers resolved to free the clergy from both kings and "wives," to create an independent and chaste clergy. The Church alone was to be the clergy's lord and spouse. Thus, the distinctive Western separation of Church and state and the celibacy of the Catholic clergy, both of which continue today, had their definitive origins in the Cluny reform movement.

Cluny rapidly became a center from which reformers were dispatched to other monasteries throughout France and Italy. Under its aggressive abbots, especially Saint Odo (926–946), it grew to embrace almost 1,500 dependent cloisters, each devoted to monastic and Church reform. In the last half of the eleventh century, the Cluny reformers reached the summit of their influence when the papacy itself embraced their reform program.

The proclamation of a series of Church decrees called the "Peace of God" in the late ninth and early tenth centuries reflected the

A portion of the Romanesque abbey church of Cluny, reconstructed between 1080 and 1225. In the twelfth century it was Europe's largest church (555 feet long). [Adros Studio]

The Peace and the Truce of God

The proclamation of the Peace and the Truce of God at the Council of Toulouse in the mid-eleventh century provides a commentary on the violence of the age. Although designed primarily to protect the clergy and the property of the Church from the bullying of secular powers, the proclamations were also intended to protect the weak everywhere.

◆ *What does such pleading suggest about the degree to which society at this time was Christianized? Did the Church have the power to back up its threats against those who broke the peace? On whom would it rely to enforce these rules of good conduct?*

This Peace has been confirmed by the bishops, by the abbots, by the counts and viscounts and the other God-fearing nobles in this bishopric to the effect that in the future . . . no man may commit an act of violence in a church. . . . Furthermore, it is forbidden that any one attack the clergy, who do not bear arms, or the monks and religious persons, or do them any wrong; likewise it is forbidden to despoil or pillage the communities of canons, monks, and religious persons, the ecclesiastical lands . . . under the protection of the Church, or the clergy, who do not bear arms; and if any one shall do such a thing, let him pay a double composition [i.e., fine in compensation]. [Further] let no one burn or destroy the dwellings of the peasants and the clergy, the dove-cotes, and the granaries. Let no man dare to kill, to beat, or to wound a peasant or serf, or the wife of either, or to seize them and carry them off, except for misdemeanors which they have committed. . . . Let any one who has broken the peace, and has not paid his fines within a fortnight, make amends to him whom he has injured by paying a double amount. . . . The bishops . . . have [also] solemnly confirmed the Truce of God, which has been enjoined upon all Christians, from the setting of the sun of the fourth day of the week, that is to say, Wednesday, until the rising of the sun on Monday, the second day. . . . If any one during the Truce shall violate it, let him pay a double composition.

James Harvey Robinson, ed., Readings in European History, *Vol. 1 (Boston: Anthenaeum, 1904), pp. 230–231.*

influence of the Cluny movement. Emerging from a cooperative venture between the clergy and the higher nobility, these decrees tried to lessen the endemic warfare of medieval society by threatening excommunication for all who, at any time, harmed members of such vulnerable groups as women, peasants, merchants, and the clergy. The "Peace of God" was subsequently reinforced by the "Truce of God," a Church order proclaiming that all men must abstain from every form of violence and warfare during a certain part of each week (eventually from Wednesday night to Monday morning) and in all holy seasons.

Popes devoted to reforms like those urged by Cluny came to power during the reign of Emperor Henry III (r. 1039–1056). Pope Leo IX (1049–1054) promoted regional synods to oppose simony (the selling of spiritual things, such as Church offices) and clerical marriage (celibacy was not strictly enforced among the secular clergy until after the eleventh century). He also placed Cluniacs in key administrative posts in Rome. Imperial influence over the papacy, however, was still strong during Henry III's reign, and provided a counterweight to the great aristocratic families that manipulated the elections of popes for their own gain. Before Leo

IX's papacy, Henry had deposed three such popes, each a pawn of a Roman noble faction, and had installed a German bishop of his own choosing who ruled as Pope Clement II (1046–1047).

Such highhanded practices ended soon after Henry III's death. During the turbulent minority of his successor, Henry IV (r. 1056–1106), reform popes began to assert themselves more openly. Pope Stephen IX (1057–1058) reigned without imperial ratification, contrary to the earlier declaration of Otto I. To prevent local factional control of papal elections, Pope Nicholas II (1059–1061) decreed in 1059 that a body of high Church officials and advisers known as the College of Cardinals would henceforth choose the pope, establishing the procedures for papal succession that the Catholic church still follows. With this action the papacy declared its full independence from both local Italian and distant royal interference. Rulers continued nevertheless to have considerable indirect influence on the election of popes.

Pope Nicholas II also embraced Cluny's strictures against simony and clerical concubinage and even struck his own political alliances with the Normans in Sicily and with France and Tuscany. His successor, Pope Alexander II (1061–1073), was elected solely by the College of Cardinals, although not without a struggle.

The Investiture Struggle: Gregory VII and Henry IV

Alexander's successor was Pope Gregory VII (1073–1085), a fierce advocate of Cluny's reforms who had entered the papal bureaucracy a quarter century earlier during the pontificate of Leo IX. It was he who put the Church's declaration of independence to the test. Cluniacs had repeatedly inveighed against simony, the selling of spiritual things, especially church offices. Cardinal Humbert, a prominent reformer, argued that lay investiture of the clergy—that is, the appointment of bishops and other church officials by secular officials and rulers—was the worst form of this evil practice. In 1075 Pope Gregory embraced these arguments and condemned under penalty of excommunication lay investiture of clergy at any level. He had primarily in mind the emperor's well-established cus-

tom of installing bishops by presenting them with the ring and staff that symbolized episcopal office.

After Gregory's ruling, emperors were no more able to install bishops than they were to install popes. As popes were elected by the College of Cardinals and were not raised up by kings or nobles, so bishops would henceforth be installed in their offices by high ecclesiastical authority empowered by the pope. The spiritual origins and allegiance of episcopal office would thereby be made clear.

Gregory's prohibition came as a jolt to royal authority. Since the days of Charlemagne, emperors had routinely passed out bishoprics to favored clergy. Bishops, who received royal estates, were the emperors' appointees and servants of the state. Henry IV's Carolingian and Ottonian predecessors had carefully nurtured the theocratic character of the empire in both concept and administrative bureaucracy. The Church and religion had become integral parts of government.

Now the emperor, Henry IV, suddenly found himself ordered to secularize the empire by drawing a distinct line between the spheres of temporal and spiritual—royal and ecclesiastical—authority and jurisdiction. But if his key administrators were no longer to be his own carefully chosen and sworn servants, then was not his kingdom in jeopardy? Henry considered Gregory's action a direct challenge to his authority. The territorial princes, on the other hand, ever tending away from the center and eager to see the emperor weakened, were quick to see the advantages of Gregory's ruling. If a weak emperor could not gain a bishop's ear, then a strong prince might, thus bringing the offices of the Church into his orbit of power. In the hope of gaining an advantage over both the emperor and the clergy in their territory, the princes fully supported Gregory's edict.

The lines of battle were quickly drawn. Henry assembled his loyal German bishops at Worms in January 1076 and had them proclaim their independence from Gregory. Gregory promptly responded with the Church's heavy artillery: he excommunicated Henry and absolved all Henry's subjects from loyalty to him. This turn of events delighted the German princes, and Henry found himself facing a general revolt led

Pope Gregory VII Asserts the Power of the Pope

The following "Sayings of the Pope" express the new self-image of the papacy that empowered Gregory's challenge of secular authority.

✦ *Are all of these statements proper for a pope? Would certain statements understandably frighten contemporary rulers and make the pope appear to claim worldly as well as spiritual domination? Where might rulers have thought the pope was going too far?*

That the Roman Church was founded by God alone.

That the Roman Pontiff alone is rightly to be called universal.

That for him alone it is lawful to enact new laws according to the needs of the time, to assemble together new congregations . . . and . . . to divide a rich bishopric and unite the poor ones.

That he alone may use the imperial insignia.

That the Pope is the only one whose feet are to be kissed by all princes.

That his name alone is to be recited in churches.

That his title is unique in the world.

That he may depose emperors.

That he may transfer bishops, if necessary, from one See to another.

That no synod may be called a general one without his order.

That no chapter or book may be regarded as canonical without his authority.

That no sentence of his may be retracted by any one; and that he, alone of all, can retract it.

That he himself may be judged by no one.

That the Roman Church has never erred, nor ever, by the witness of Scripture, shall err to all eternity.

That the Pope may absolve subjects of unjust men from their fealty.

Church and State Through the Centuries: A Collection of Historic Documents, *trans. and ed. by S. Z. Ehler and John B. Morrall (New York: Biblo and Tannen, 1967), pp. 43–44.*

by the duchy of Saxony. He had no recourse but to come to terms with Gregory. In a famous scene Henry prostrated himself outside Gregory's castle retreat at Canossa on January 25, 1077. There he reportedly stood barefoot in the snow off and on for three days before the pope agreed to absolve him.

Papal power had at this moment reached a pinnacle (it would attain even greater heights during the papacy of Innocent III [1198–1216], who also had rulers at his mercy). But heights are also for descending. Gregory's power, as he must have known when he restored Henry to power, was soon to be challenged.

Henry regrouped his forces, regained much of his power within the empire, and soon acted as if the humiliation at Canossa had never occurred. In March 1080 Gregory excommunicated Henry once again, but this time the action was ineffectual. (Historically, repeated excommunications of the same individual have proved to have diminishing returns.) In 1084 Henry, absolutely dominant, installed his own antipope, Clement III, and forced Gregory into exile, where he died the following year. It appeared as if the old practice of kings controlling popes had been restored, and with a vengeance. Clement, however, was never recognized within the Church, and Gregory's followers, who retained wide popular support,

regained power during the pontificates of Victor III (1086–1087) and Urban II (1088–1099).

The settlement of the investiture controversy came in 1122 with the Concordat of Worms. Emperor Henry V (r. 1106–1125), having early abandoned his predecessors' practice of nominating popes and raising up antipopes, formally renounced his power to invest bishops with ring

A twelfth-century German manuscript portrays the struggle between Emperor Henry IV and Pope Gregory VII. In the top panel, Henry installs the puppet pope Clement III and drives Gregory from Rome. Below, Gregory dies in exile. The artist was a monk; his sympathies were with Gregory, not Henry. [Thuringer Universitäts- und Landesbibliothek, Jena]

and staff. In exchange, Pope Calixtus II (1119–1124) recognized the emperor's right to be present and to invest bishops with fiefs before and after their investment with ring and staff by the Church. The old Church–state "back scratching" in this way continued, but now on very different terms. The clergy received their offices and attendant religious powers solely from ecclesiastical authority and no longer from kings and emperors. Rulers continued to bestow lands and worldly goods on high clergy in the hope of influencing them. The Concordat of Worms thus made the clergy more independent but not necessarily less worldly.

The Gregorian party may have won the independence of the clergy, but the price it paid was to encourage division among the feudal forces within the empire. The pope made himself strong by making imperial authority weak. In the end those who profited most from the investiture controversy were the German princes.

The new Gregorian fence between temporal and spiritual power did not prevent kings and popes from being good neighbors if each was willing. Succeeding centuries, however, proved that the aspirations of kings were too often in conflict with those of popes for peaceful coexistence to endure. The most bitter clash between Church and state was still to come. It would occur during the late thirteenth century and early fourteenth century in the confrontation between Pope Boniface VIII and King Philip IV of France (see Chapter 9).

The First Crusades

If an index of popular piety and support for the pope in the High Middle Ages is needed, the Crusades amply provide it. What the Cluny reform was to the clergy, the first Crusades to the Holy Land were to the laity: an outlet for the heightened religious zeal of the late eleventh and the twelfth centuries, Europe's most religious period before the Protestant Reformation.

Late in the eleventh century, the Byzantine Empire was under severe pressure from the Seljuk Turks, and the eastern emperor, Alexius I Comnenus, appealed for western aid. At the Council of Clermont in 1095, Pope Urban II responded positively to this appeal, setting the First Crusade in motion. This event has puzzled

some historians, because the First Crusade was a risky venture. But the pope, the nobility, and western society at large had much to gain by removing large numbers of nobility temporarily from Europe. Too many idle, restless noble youths were spending a great part of their lives feuding with each other and raiding other people's land. The pope recognized that peace and tranquility might be gained at home by sending factious aristocrats abroad with their accouterments of war (100,000 went with the First Crusade). And the nobility recognized there were fortunes to be made in foreign wars. This was especially true of the younger sons of noblemen, who, in an age of growing population and shrinking landed wealth, saw the Crusades as an opportunity to become landowners. Pope Urban may also have envisioned the Crusade leading to a reconciliation and possible reunion with the Eastern church.

Religion was not the only motive inspiring the Crusaders; hot blood and greed were equally influential. But unlike the later Crusades, undertaken for patently mercenary reasons, the early Crusades were to a very high degree inspired by genuine religious piety and were carefully orchestrated by the revived papacy. Popes promised participants in the First Crusade a plenary indulgence should they die in battle, that is, a complete remission of any outstanding temporal punishment for their unrepented mortal sins and hence release from suffering for them in purgatory. In addition to this direct spiritual reward, the Crusaders were also impelled by their enthusiasm for a Holy War against the hated infidel and the romance of a holy pilgrimage to the Holy Land. All these elements combined to make the First Crusade a rousing success (at least from the Christian point of view). Crusading zeal also sparked anti-Jewish riots and massacres in Europe, an expression of intolerance to Jews that would prove to be an enduring feature of militant Christianity.

THE FIRST VICTORY The eastern emperor welcomed any aid against advancing Islamic armies. The western Crusaders did not, however, assemble to defend Europe's borders against aggression. They freely took the offensive to rescue the holy city of Jerusalem, which had been in non-Christian hands since the seventh century, from the Seljuk Turks. To this end three

Pope Urban II (1088–1099)
Preaches the First Crusade

When Pope Urban II summoned the First Crusade in a sermon at the Council of Clermont on November 26, 1095, he painted a most savage picture of the Muslims who controlled Jerusalem. Urban also promised the Crusaders, who responded by the tens of thousands, remission of their unrepented sins and assurance of heaven. Robert the Monk is one of four witnesses who has left us a summary of the sermon.

✦ *Is the pope engaging in a propaganda and smear campaign? What are the images he creates of the enemy and how accurate and fair are they? Did the Christian church have a greater claim to Jerusalem than the people then living there? Does a religious connection with the past entitle one group to confiscate the land of another?*

From the confines of Jerusalem and the city of Constantinople a horrible tale has gone forth and very frequently has been brought to our ears, namely, that a race from the kingdom of the Persians [that is, the Seljuk Turks], an accursed race, a race utterly alienated from God, a generation forsooth which has not directed its heart and has not entrusted its spirit to God, has invaded the lands of those Christians and has depopulated them by the sword, pillage and fire; it has led away a part of the captives into its own country, and a part it has destroyed by cruel tortures; it has either entirely destroyed the churches of God or appropriated them for the rites of its own religion. They destroy the altars, after having defiled them with their uncleanness. They circumcise the Christians, and the blood of the circumcision they either spread upon the altars or pour into the vases of the baptismal font. When they wish to torture people by a base death, they perforate their navels, and dragging forth the extremity of the intestines, bind it to a stake; then with flogging they lead the victim around until the viscera having gushed forth the victim falls prostrate upon the ground. Others they bind to a post and pierce with arrows. Others they compel to extend their necks and then, attacking them with naked swords, attempt to cut through the neck with a single blow. What shall I say of the abominable rape of the women? The kingdom of the Greeks is now dismembered by them and deprived of territory so vast in extent that it can not be traversed in a march of two months. On whom therefore is the labor of avenging these wrongs and of recovering this territory incumbent, if not upon you? . . .

Jerusalem is the navel of the world; the land is fruitful above others, like another paradise of delights. This the Redeemer of the human race has made illustrious by His advent, has beautified by residence, has consecrated by suffering, has redeemed by death, has glorified by burial. This royal city, therefore, situated at the centre of the world, is now held captive by His enemies, and is in subjection to those who do not know God, to the worship of the heathens. She seeks therefore and desires to be liberated, and does not cease to implore you to come to her aid. From you especially she asks succor, because, as we have already said, God has conferred upon you above all nations great glory in arms. Accordingly undertake this journey for the remission of your sins, with the assurance of the imperishable glory of the kingdom of heaven.

Translations and Reprints from the Original Sources of European History, Vol. 1 *(Philadelphia: Department of History, University of Pennsylvania, 1910), pp. 5–7.*

A depiction of pilgrims journeying to the Holy Land in a mid-fifteenth century Book of Hours. [Scala/Art Resource, N.Y.]

military discipline and weaponry. It also helped that they had descended upon a politically divided and factious Islamic world that initially lacked the unity to organize an effective resistance.

The victorious Crusaders divided the conquered territory into the feudal states of Jerusalem, Edessa, and Antioch, which they held as alleged fiefs from the pope. Godfrey of Bouillon, leader of the French–German army (and after him his brother Baldwin), ruled over the kingdom of Jerusalem. The Crusaders, however, remained only small islands within a great sea of Muslims, who looked on the western invaders as hardly more than savages. And once settled in the Holy Land, the Crusaders found themselves increasingly on the defensive. Now an occupying rather than a conquering army, they became obsessed with fortifying their position. They built castles throughout the Holy Land, the ruins of many of which are still visible today.

Once secure within their castle enclaves, the Crusaders ceased to live off the land, as they had done since leaving Europe, and relied more and more on imports from home. The once fierce warriors became international businessmen as they developed the economic resources of their new possessions. The Knights Templars, originally a military–religious order, became castle stewards and escorts of western pilgrims to and from the Holy Land, in the process accumulating great wealth and becoming important bankers and moneylenders.

great armies—tens of thousands of Crusaders—gathered in France, Germany, and Italy. Following different routes, they reassembled in Constantinople in 1097 (see Map 7-1).

The convergence of these spirited soldiers on the eastern capital was a cultural shock that only deepened antipathy toward the West. The eastern emperor suspected their true motives, and the common people, whom they pillaged and suppressed, hardly considered them Christian brothers in a common cause. Nonetheless these fanatical Crusaders accomplished what no Eastern army had been able to do. They soundly defeated one Seljuk army after another in a steady advance toward Jerusalem, which fell to them on July 15, 1099. The Crusaders' success resulted from their superior

THE SECOND CRUSADE Native resistence finally broke the Crusaders around mid-century, and the forty-odd-year Latin presence in the East began to crumble. Edessa fell to Islamic armies in 1144. A Second Crusade, preached by the eminent Bernard of Clairvaux (1091–1153), Christendom's most powerful monastic leader, attempted a rescue, but it met with dismal failure. In October 1187, Saladin (r. 1138–1193), king of Egypt and Syria, reconquered Jerusalem itself. Save for a brief interlude in the thirteenth century, it remained thereafter in Islamic hands until modern times.

THE THIRD CRUSADE A Third Crusade in the twelfth century (1189–1192) attempted yet another rescue, enlisting as its leaders the most

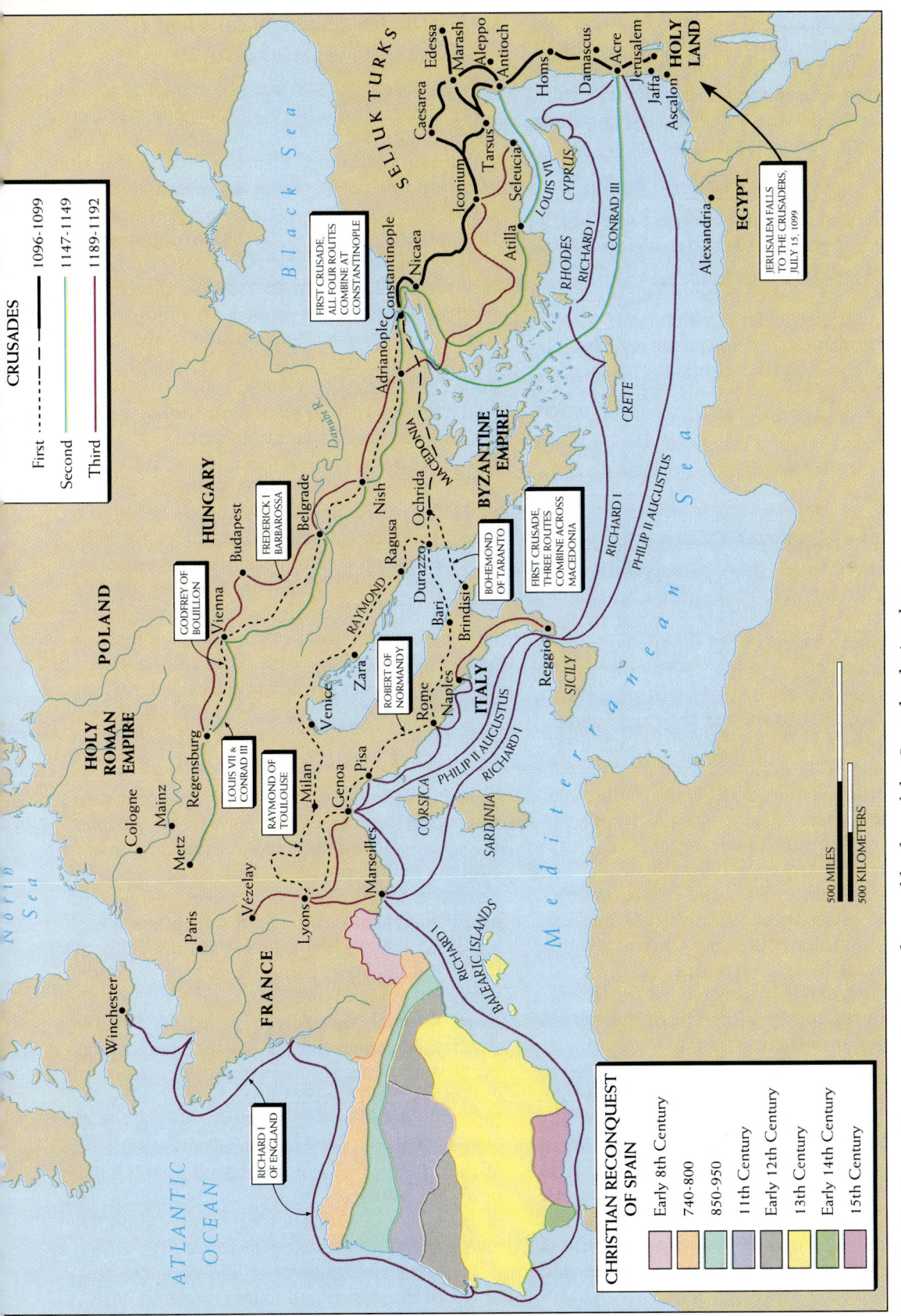

CRUSADES

First	1096-1099
Second	1147-1149
Third	1189-1192

North Sea

Black Sea

SELJUK TURKS

Edessa
Marash
Aleppo
Antioch
Caesarea
Damascus
Homs
Acre
HOLY LAND
Jerusalem
Jaffa
Ascalon

FIRST CRUSADE, ALL FOUR ROUTES COMBINE AT CONSTANTINOPLE

Nicaea
Constantinople
Adrianople
Attila
Iconium
Tarsus
Seleucia
LOUIS VII
CYPRUS
RHODES
RICHARD I
CONRAD III

JERUSALEM FALLS TO THE CRUSADERS, JULY 15, 1099

EGYPT

Alexandria

Danube R.

POLAND

HUNGARY

FREDERICK I BARBAROSSA

Budapest
Belgrade
Nish
Ochrida
MACEDONIA

Vienna

GODFREY OF BOUILLON

BYZANTINE EMPIRE

FIRST CRUSADE, THREE ROUTES COMBINE ACROSS MACEDONIA

Durazzo
Ragusa
RAYMOND
Zara
Venice
Bari
Brindisi
BOHEMOND OF TARANTO

CRETE

RICHARD I
PHILIP II AUGUSTUS

HOLY ROMAN EMPIRE

Cologne
Mainz
Metz
Regensburg

LOUIS VII & CONRAD III

RAYMOND OF TOULOUSE

ROBERT OF NORMANDY

Milan
Genoa
Pisa
Rome
Naples
ITALY
Reggio
SICILY

PHILIP II AUGUSTUS
RICHARD I

CORSICA
SARDINIA

Mediterranean Sea

FRANCE

Paris
Vézelay
Lyons
Marseilles

Winchester

RICHARD I

RICHARD I OF ENGLAND

BALEARIC ISLANDS

ATLANTIC OCEAN

CHRISTIAN RECONQUEST OF SPAIN

	Early 8th Century
	740-800
	850-950
	11th Century
	Early 12th Century
	13th Century
	Early 14th Century
	15th Century

500 MILES
500 KILOMETERS

MAP 7-1 THE EARLY CRUSADES Routes and several leaders of the Crusades during the first century of the movement are shown. The names on this map do not exhaust the list of great nobles who went on the First Crusade. The even showier array of monarchs of the Second and Third Crusades still left the Crusades, on balance, ineffective in achieving their goals.

powerful western rulers: Emperor Frederick Barbarossa; Richard the Lion-Hearted, king of England; and Philip Augustus, king of France. But the Third Crusade proved a tragicomic commentary on the passing of the original crusading spirit. Frederick Barbarossa accidentally drowned while fording the Saleph River, a small stream, near the end of his journey across Asia Minor. Richard the Lion-Hearted and Philip Augustus reached the outskirts of Jerusalem, but their intense personal rivalry shattered the Crusaders' unity and chances of victory. Philip Augustus returned to France and made war on Richard's continental territories. Richard fell captive to the Emperor Henry VI as he was returning to England. (Henry VI suspected Richard of plotting against him with Henry's mortal enemy, Henry the Lion, the duke of Saxony, who happened also to be Richard's brother-in-law.)

The English paid a handsome ransom for their adventurous king's release. Popular resentment of taxes levied for this ransom became part of the background of the revolt against the English monarchy that led to the royal recognition of Magna Carta in 1215 (discussed later in the chapter).

The long-term results of the first three Crusades had little to do with their original purpose. Politically and religiously they were a failure, and the Holy Land reverted as firmly as ever to Muslim hands. The Crusades did, however, act for centuries as a safety valve for violence-prone Europe. More importantly, they stimulated western trade with the East. The merchants of Venice, Pisa, and Genoa followed the Crusaders across to lucrative new markets. The need to resupply the new Christian settlements in the Near East reopened old trade routes that had long been closed by Islamic domination of the Mediterranean and established important new ones as well.

It is a commentary on both the degeneration of the original crusading ideal and the Crusaders' true historical importance that the Fourth Crusade turned into a large commercial venture manipulated by the Venetians. And wherever new trading centers sprang up along the Crusader routes, cultural as well as economic commerce occurred. Western Christians learned firsthand about Islamic culture and Muslims about the Christian West.

The Pontificate of Innocent III (1198–1216)

Pope Innocent III was a papal monarch in the Gregorian tradition of papal independence from secular domination. He proclaimed and practiced as none before him the doctrine of the plenitude of papal power. In a famous statement, he likened the relationship of the pope to the emperor—or the Church to the state—to that of the sun to the moon. As the moon received its light from the sun, so the emperor received his brilliance (that is, his crown) from the hand of the pope—an allusion to the famous precedent set on Christmas Day, 800, when Pope Leo III crowned Charlemagne.

Although this pretentious theory greatly exceeded Innocent's ability to practice it, he and his successors did not hesitate to act on the ambitions it reflected. When Philip II, the king of France, tried unlawfully to annul his marriage, Innocent placed France under interdict, suspending all Church services save baptism and the last rites. The same punishment befell England with even greater force when King John refused to accept Innocent's nominee for archbishop of Canterbury. And as we will see later in the chapter, Innocent intervened frequently and forcefully in the affairs of the Holy Roman Empire.

THE NEW PAPAL MONARCHY Innocent made the papacy a great secular power, with financial resources and a bureaucracy equal to those of contemporary monarchs. During his reign the papacy transformed itself, in effect, into an efficient ecclesio-commercial complex, which would be attacked by reformers throughout the later Middle Ages. Innocent consolidated and expanded ecclesiastical taxes on the laity, the chief of which was Peter's pence. In England, that tax, long a levy on all but the poorest houses, became a lump-sum payment by the English crown during Innocent's reign. Innocent also imposed an income tax of 2.5 percent on the clergy. Annates (the payment of a portion or all of the first year's income received by the holder of a new benefice) and fees for the pallium (an archbishop's symbol of office) became especially favored revenue-gathering devices.

Innocent also reserved to the pope the absolution of many sins and religious crimes, forcing those desirous of pardons or exemptions to bargain directly with Rome. It was a measure of the degree to which the papacy had embraced the new money economy that it employed Lombard merchants and bankers to collect the growing papal revenues.

CRUSADES IN FRANCE AND THE EAST
Innocent's predilection for power politics also expressed itself in his use of the Crusade, the traditional weapon of the Church against Islam, to suppress internal dissent and heresy. Heresy had grown under the influence of native religious reform movements that tried, often naïvely, to disassociate the Church from the growing materialism of the age and to keep it pure of political scheming. A good deal of heresy also stemmed from anticlericalism fed by real abuses of the clergy witnessed directly by the laity, such as immorality, greed, and poor pastoral service.

The idealism of these movements was too extreme for the papacy. In 1209 Innocent launched a Crusade against the Albigensians, or Cathars ("pure ones"). These advocates of an ascetic, dualist religion were concentrated in the area of Albi in Languedoc in southern France, but Catharism also had adherents among the laity in Italy and Spain. The Albigensians generally sought a pure and simple religious life, following the model of the apostles of Jesus in the New Testament. They opposed Christian teaching on several points. They denied the Old Testament and its God of wrath, as well as the Christian belief in God's incarnation in Jesus Christ. They conceived of the Church as an invisible, spiritual force, and resisted it as a legal, financial, and dogmatic institution.

The more radical Cathars opposed human procreation—because to reproduce corporeal bodies was to prolong the imprisonment of immortal souls in dying matter—and avoided it either through extreme sexual asceticism or the use of contraceptives (sponges and acidic ointments) and even abortion. On the other hand, the Cathars' strong dualism justified latitude in sexual behavior on the part of ordinary believers—this in the belief that the flesh and the spirit were so fundamentally different that it mattered little what the former did. It was in opposition to such beliefs that the Church developed its social teachings condemning contraception and abortion.

Pope Innocent III (1198–1215) made the papacy a great wordly power, with financial resources and a bureaucracy equal to those of secular monarchies. [Adros Studio]

The Crusades against the Albigensians were carried out by powerful noblemen from northern France. These great magnates, led by Simon de Montfort, were as much attracted by the great wealth of the area of Languedoc as they were moved by Christian conscience to stamp out heresy. The Crusades also allowed the northerners to extend their political power into the south. They resulted in a succession of massacres and ended with a special Crusade led by King Louis VIII of France from 1225 to 1226 that destroyed the Albigensians as a political entity. Pope Gregory IX (1227–1241) introduced the Inquisition into the region to complete the work of the Crusaders. This institution, a formal tribunal for the detection and punishment of heresy, had been in use by the Church since the mid-twelfth century as a way for bishops to maintain diocesan discipline. During Innocent's pontificate it became centralized in the papacy. Papal legates were dispatched to chosen regions to conduct interrogations and the subsequent trials and executions.

THE FOURTH CRUSADE It was also during Innocent's pontificate that the Fourth Crusade to the Holy Land was launched. In 1202, some 30,000 Crusaders arrived in Venice to set sail for Egypt. When they were unable to pay the price of transport, the Venetians negotiated an alternative to payment: conquest of Zara, a rival Christian port city on the Adriatic. To the shock of Pope Innocent III, the Crusaders obliged. This digression of the Crusaders from their orig-

---

The Crusaders Sack Constantinople

The sack of Constantinople in 1204 by western Crusaders ostensibly en route to the Holy Land deeply divided Christendom down to modern times. It also signaled Italy's dominance of Mediterranean trade and western Europe's expansion as a true world power. This Byzantine description also makes clear the materialism and greed of the Crusaders, who desecrated holy places and confiscated treasures.

◆ *Should Christian Crusaders have been expected to act differently? What was the standard practice of besieging armies then and how did this behavior compare with it? Was there anything in the history of the relationship between Rome and Constantinople, Roman Christianity and Byzantine Christianity, that might have given the Crusaders pause, or urged them on?*

How shall I begin to tell of the deeds wrought by these nefarious men! Alas, the images, which ought to have been adored, were trodden under foot! Alas, the relics of the holy martyrs were thrown into unclean places! . . . They snatched the precious reliquaries, thrust into their bosoms the ornaments which these contained, and used the broken remnants for pans and drinking cups—precursors of Anti-christ, authors and heralds of his nefarious deeds which we momentarily expect. Manifestly, indeed, by that race then, just as formerly, Christ was robbed and insulted and His garments were divided by lot; only one thing was lacking, that His side, pierced by a spear, should pour rivers of divine blood on the ground.

Nor can the violation of the Great Church [of St. Sophia] be listened to with equanimity. For the sacred altar, formed of all kinds of precious materials and admired by the whole world, was broken into bits and distributed among the soldiers, as was all the other sacred wealth of so great and infinite splendor.

When the sacred vases and utensils of unsurpassable art and grace and rare materi-al, and the fine silver, wrought with gold, which encircled the screen of the tribunal and the ambo, of admirable workmanship, and the door and many other ornaments, were to be borne away as booty, mules and saddled horses were led to the very sanctuary of the temple. Some of these which were unable to keep their footing on the splendid and slippery pavement, were stabbed when they fell, so that the sacred pavement was polluted with blood and filth. . . .

No one was without a share in the grief. In the alleys, in the streets, in the temples, complaints, weeping, lamentations, grief, the groaning of men, the shrieks of women, wounds, rape, captivity, the separation of those most closely united. Nobles wandered about ignominiously, those of venerable age in tears, the rich in poverty. Thus it was in the streets, on the corners, in the temple, in the dens, for no place remained unassailed or defended the suppliants. All places everywhere were filled full of all kinds of crime. Oh, immortal God, how great the afflictions of the men, how great the distress!

Translations and Reprints from the Original Sources of European History, Vol. 3 *(Philadelphia: Department of History, University of Pennsylvania, 1909), pp. 15–16.*

inal goal proved to be only their first. They soon besieged Constantinople itself, which was completely in western hands by 1204.

This stunning event brought Venice new lands and maritime rights that assured its domination of the eastern Mediterranean. Constantinople now became the center for western trade throughout the Near East. Although its capture had been an embarrassment to the pope, the papacy soon adjusted to this unforeseen turn of events and shared in the spoils. The Western church had a unique opportunity to extend its presence into the East. A confidant of Innocent's became patriarch of Constantinople and launched a mission to win the Greeks and the Slavs to the Roman church. Western control of Constantinople continued until 1261, when the eastern emperor Michael Paleologus, helped by the Genoese, who envied Venetian prosperity in the East, finally recaptured the city. The more than fifty-year occupation of Constantinople did nothing to heal the political and religious divisions between East and West. When Constantinople returned to eastern hands, East-West relations were at a new low.

THE FOURTH LATERAN COUNCIL Under Innocent's direction, the Fourth Lateran Council met in 1215 to formalize Church discipline throughout the hierarchy, from pope to parish priest. Many important landmarks in ecclesiastical legislation issued from this council. It gave full dogmatic sanction to the controversial doctrine of transubstantiation, according to which the bread and wine of the Lord's Supper become the true body and blood of Christ when consecrated by a priest in the sacrament of the Eucharist. This doctrine has been part of Catholic teaching ever since. It reflects the influence of the Cluniac monks and those of a new order, the Cistercians. During the twelfth century, these orders made the adoration of the Virgin Mary (the patron saint of the Cistercians) and the worship of Christ in the Eucharist the centerpieces of a reformed, Christocentric piety. The doctrine of transubstantiation is an expression of the popularity of this piety. It also enhanced the power and authority of the clergy, because it specified that only they could perform the miracle of the Eucharist.

The council also made annual confession and Easter communion mandatory for every adult Christian. This legislation formalized the sacrament of Penance as the Church's key instrument of religious education and discipline in the later Middle Ages.

FRANCISCANS AND DOMINICANS During his reign, Pope Innocent gave official sanction to two new monastic orders: the Franciscans and the Dominicans. No other action of the pope had more of an effect on spiritual life. Unlike other regular clergy, the members of these mendicant orders, known as friars, did not confine themselves to the cloister. They went out into the world to preach the Church's mission and to combat heresy, begging or working to support themselves (hence the term mendicant).

Lay interest in spiritual devotion, especially among urban women, was particularly intense at the turn of the twelfth century. In addition to the heretical Albigensians, there were movements of Waldensians, Beguines, and Beghards, each of which stressed biblical simplicity in religion and a life of poverty in imitation of Christ. Such movements were especially active in Italy and France. Their heterodox teachings—teachings that, although not necessarily heretical, nonetheless challenged Church orthodoxy—and the critical frame of mind they promoted caused the pope deep concern. Innocent feared they would inspire lay piety to turn militantly against the Church. The Franciscan and Dominican orders, however, emerged from the same background of intense religiosity. By sanctioning them and thus keeping their followers within the confines of Church organization, the pope provided a response to heterodox piety as well as an answer to lay criticism of the worldliness of the papal monarchy.

The Franciscan Order was founded by Saint Francis of Assisi (1182–1226), the son of a rich Italian cloth merchant, who became disaffected with wealth and urged his followers to live a life of extreme poverty. Pope Innocent recognized the order in 1210, and its official rule was approved in 1223. The Dominican Order, the Order of Preachers, was founded by Saint Dominic (1170–1221), a well-educated Spanish cleric, and was sanctioned in 1216. Both orders received special privileges from the pope and were solely under his jurisdiction. This special relationship with Rome gave the friars an inde-

Dominicans (left), and Franciscans (right). Unlike the other religious orders, the Dominicans and Franciscans did not live in cloisters, but wandered about preaching and combating heresy. They depended for support on their own labor and the kindness of the laity. [Bibliothèque Nationale, Paris]

pendence from local clerical authority that bred resentment among some secular clergy.

Pope Gregory IX (1227–1241) canonized Saint Francis only two years after Francis's death—a fitting honor for Francis and a stroke of genius on the part of the pope. By bringing the age's most popular religious figure, one who had even miraculously received the stigmata (bleeding wounds like those of the crucified Jesus), so emphatically within the confines of the Church, he enhanced papal authority over lay piety.

Two years after the canonization, however, Gregory canceled Saint Francis's own *Testament* as an authoritative rule for the Franciscan order. He did so because he found it to be an impractical guide for the order and because the unconventional nomadic life of strict poverty it advocated conflicted with papal plans to enlist the order as an arm of Church policy. Most Franciscans themselves, under the leadership of moderates like Saint Bonaventure, general of the order between 1257 and 1274, also came to doubt the wisdom of extreme asceticism. During the thirteenth century the main branch of the order progressively complied with papal wishes. In the fourteenth century the pope condemned a radical branch, the Spiritual Franciscans,

extreme followers of Saint Francis who considered him almost a new Messiah. In his condemnation, the pope declared absolute poverty a fictitious ideal that not even Christ endorsed.

The Dominicans, a less factious order, combated doctrinal error through visitations and preaching. They conformed convents of Beguines to the Church's teaching, led the Church's campaign against heretics in southern France, and staffed the offices of the Inquisition after its centralization by Pope Gregory IX in 1223. The great Dominican theologian, Thomas Aquinas (d. 1274), was canonized in 1322. His efforts to synthesize faith and reason resulted in a definitive and enduring statement of Catholic belief (see Chapter 8).

The Dominicans and the Franciscans strengthened the Church among the laity. Through the institution of so-called Third Orders, they provided ordinary men and women the opportunity to affiliate with the monastic life and pursue the high religious ideals of poverty, obedience, and chastity, while remaining laymen and laywomen. Laity who joined such orders were known as *tertiaries*. Such organizations helped keep lay piety orthodox and within the Church during a period of heightened religiosity.

England and France: Hastings (1066) to Bouvines (1214)

In 1066 the death of the childless Anglo-Saxon ruler Edward the Confessor (so-named because of his reputation for piety) occasioned the most important change in English political life. Edward's mother was a Norman, giving the duke of Normandy a hereditary claim to the English throne. Before his death, Edward, who was not a strong ruler, acknowledged the duke's claim and even directed that his throne be given to William, the reigning duke of Normandy (d. 1087). But the Anglo-Saxon assembly, which customarily bestowed the royal power, had a mind of its own and vetoed Edward's last wishes, choosing instead Harold Godwinsson. This

Saint Francis of Assisi Sets Out His Religious Ideals

Saint Francis of Assisi (1182–1226) was the founder of the Franciscan Order of friars. The religious principles by which he required his followers to live were stated in the Rule of the Order, *which Pope Honorius III approved in 1223. The chief principle was to lead a life of poverty. The ideal of poverty caused conflict between the order and the pope, who feared some Franciscans carried it too far.*

✦ *Can ideals be so high that they threaten the well-being of an institution? What would have happened to the Church if all clergy, including the pope, had lived a life of poverty, begging, and working with their hands, as the* Rule *of St. Francis instructs? What provisions are there in the* Rule *to assure the pope of the Order's loyalty?*

This is the rule and way of living of the Minorite brothers, namely, to observe the holy Gospel of our Lord Jesus Christ, living in obedience, without personal possessions, and in chastity. Brother Francis promises obedience and reverence to our lord Pope Honorius, and to his successors who canonically enter upon their office, and to the Roman Church. And the other brothers shall be bound to obey Brother Francis and his successors.

I firmly command all the brothers by no means to receive coin or money, of themselves or through an intervening person. But for the needs of the sick and for clothing the other brothers, the ministers alone and the guardians shall provide through spiritual friends, as it may seem to them that necessity demands, according to time, place, and the coldness of the temperature. This one thing being always borne in mind, that, as has been said, they receive neither coin nor money.

Those brothers to whom God has given the ability to labor shall do so faithfully and devoutly, but in such manner that idleness, the enemy of the soul, being averted, they may not extinguish the spirit of holy prayer and devotion, to which other temporal things should be subservient. As a reward, moreover, for their labor, they may receive for themselves and their brothers the necessities of life, but not coin or money; and this humbly, as becomes the servants of God and the followers of most holy poverty.

The brothers shall appropriate nothing to themselves, neither a house, nor a place, nor anything; but as pilgrims and strangers in this world, in poverty and humility serving God, they shall confidently go seeking for alms. Nor need they be ashamed, for the Lord made Himself poor for us in this world.

Frederic Austin Ogg, ed., A Source Book of Mediaeval History: Documents Illustrative of European Life and Institutions from the German Invasions to the Renaissance *(New York: Telegraph Books, 1908), pp. 375–376.*

defiant action triggered the swift conquest of England by the powerful Normans. William's forces defeated Harold's army at Hastings on October 14, 1066. Within weeks of the invasion William was crowned king of England in Westminster Abbey, both by right of heredity and by right of conquest.

William the Conqueror

Thereafter, William embarked on a twenty-year conquest that eventually made all of England his domain. Every landholder, whether large or small, was henceforth his vassal, holding land legally as a fief from the king. William organized his new English nation shrewdly. He established a strong monarchy whose power was not fragmented by independent territorial princes. He kept the Anglo-Saxon tax system and the practice of court writs (legal warnings) as a flexible form of central control over localities. And he took care not to destroy the Anglo-Saxon quasi-democratic tradition of frequent "parleying"—that is, the holding of conferences between the king and lesser powers who had vested interests in royal decisions.

The practice of parleying had been initially nurtured by Alfred the Great (r. 871–899). A strong and willful king who had forcibly unified England, Alfred cherished the advice of his councilors in the making of laws. His example was respected and emulated by Canute (r. 1016–1035), the Dane who restored order and brought unity to England after the civil wars that engulfed the land during the reign of the incompetent Ethelred II (r. 978–1016). The new Norman king, William, although he thoroughly subjugated his noble vassals to the crown, maintained the tradition of parleying by consulting with them regularly about decisions of state. The result was a unique blending of the "one" and the "many," a balance between monarchical and parliamentary elements that has ever since been a feature of English government—although the English Parliament as we know it today did not formally develop as an institution until the late thirteenth century.

For administration and taxation purposes William commissioned a county-by-county survey of his new realm, a detailed accounting known as the *Domesday Book* (1080–1086). The title of the book may reflect the thoroughness and finality of the survey. As none would escape the doomsday judgment of God, so none was overlooked by William's assessors.

The Growing Power and Influence of the Church	
910	Cluny founded by William the Pious
1059	Pope Nicholas II establishes College of Cardinals
1075	Pope Gregory VII condemns lay investiture of clergy under penalty of excommunication
1076	Emperor Henry IV excommunicated by Pope Gregory VII for defying ban on lay investiture
1077	Henry IV begs and receives papal absolution in Canossa
1084	Henry IV installs an antipope and forces Gregory VII into exile
1095	Pope Urban II preaches the First Crusade at the Council of Clermont
1099	Jerusalem falls to the Crusaders; forty-five years of western rule in the Holy Land begins
1122	Concordat of Worms between Emperor Henry V and Pope Calixtus II ends Investiture Controversy
1144	Islamic armies reconquer Edessa
1187	Jerusalem reconquered by Saladin, King of Egypt and Syria
1189–1192	Third Crusade fails to recover the Holy Land from Islamic armies
1202	Fourth Crusade launched; captures Constantinople instead of going to Holy Land
1209	Pope Innocent III launches Albigensian Crusade in southern France; excommunicates King John of England
1210	Pope Innocent III recognizes the Franciscan Order
1215	Fourth Lateran Council sanctions doctrine of transubstantiation and mandates annual confession by all adult Christians
1216	Pope Innocent III recognizes the Dominican Order

William the Conqueror on horseback urging his troops into combat with the English at the Battle of Hastings (October 14, 1066). From the Bayeux Tapestry, about 1073–1083. [Giraudon/Art Resource, N.Y.]

Henry II

William's son, Henry I (r. 1100–1135), died without a male heir, throwing England into virtual anarchy until the accession of Henry II (r. 1154–1189). Son of the duke of Anjou and Matilda, daughter of Henry I, Henry mounted the throne as head of the new Plantagenet dynasty, the family name of the Angevin (or Anjouan) line of kings who ruled England until the death of Richard III in 1485. Henry tried to recapture the efficiency and stability of his grandfather's regime, but in the process he steered the English monarchy rapidly toward an oppressive rule. Partly by inheritance from his father (Anjou) and partly by his marriage to Eleanor of Aquitaine (ca. 1122–1204), Henry brought to the throne greatly expanded French holdings, virtually the entire west coast of France.

The union with Eleanor created the so-called Angevin, or English–French Empire. Eleanor married Henry while he was still the count of Anjou and not yet king of England. The marriage occurred only eight weeks after the annulment of Eleanor's fifteen-year marriage to the ascetic French king Louis VII in March 1152. Although the annulment was granted on grounds of consanguinity (blood relationship), the true reason for the dissolution of the marriage was Louis's suspicion of infidelity (according to rumor, Eleanor had been intimate with a cousin). The annulment was very costly to Louis, who lost Aquitaine together with his wife. Eleanor bore Henry eight children, five of them sons, among them the future kings Richard the Lion-Hearted and John.

In addition to gaining control of most of the coast of France, Henry also conquered a part of Ireland and made the king of Scotland his vassal. Louis VII saw a mortal threat to France in this English expansion. He responded by adopting what came to be a permanent French policy of containment and expulsion of the English from their continental holdings in France. This policy was not finally successful until the mid-fifteenth century, when English power on the continent collapsed after the Hundred Years' War.

Eleanor of Aquitaine and Court Culture

Eleanor of Aquitaine was a powerful influence on both politics and culture in twelfth-century France and England. She had accompanied her first husband, King Louis VII, on the Second Crusade, becoming an example for women of lesser stature, who were also then venturing in increasing numbers into war and business and other areas previously considered the province of men. After marrying Henry, she settled in

Angers, the chief town of Anjou, where she sponsored troubadours and poets at her lively court. There the troubadour Bernart de Ventadorn composed in Eleanor's honor many of the most popular love songs of high medieval aristocratic society. Eleanor spent the years 1154 to 1170 as Henry's queen in England. She separated from Henry in 1170, partly because of his public philandering and cruel treatment, and took revenge on him by joining Louis VII in provoking Henry's three surviving sons, who were unhappy with the terms of their inheritance, into unsuccessful rebellion against their father in 1173. From 1179 until his death in 1189, Henry kept Eleanor under mild house arrest to prevent similar mischief on her part.

After her separation from Henry in 1170 and until Henry confined her in England, Eleanor lived in Poitiers with her daughter Marie, the countess of Champagne; the two made the court of Poitiers a famous center for the literature of courtly love. This genre, with its thinly veiled eroticism, has been viewed as an attack on medieval ascetic values. Be that as it may, it was certainly a commentary on contemporary domestic life within the aristocracy. The troubadours hardly promoted promiscuity at court— the code of chivalry that guided relations between lords and their vassals condemned the seduction of the wife of one's lord as the most heinous of offenses, punishable, in some places, by castration and/or execution. Rather the troubadours presented in a frank and entertaining way stories that satirized carnal love or depicted it with tragic irony while glorifying the ennobling power of friendly or "courteous" love.

The most famous courtly literature was that of Chrétien de Troyes, whose stories of King Arthur and the Knights of the Round Table contained the tragic story of Sir Lancelot's secret and illicit love for Arthur's wife, Guinevere.

Popular Rebellion and Magna Carta

As Henry II acquired new lands abroad, he became more autocratic at home. He forced his will on the clergy in the Constitutions of Clarendon (1164). These measures placed limitations on judicial appeals to Rome, subjected the clergy to the civil courts, and gave the king control over the election of bishops. The result was strong political resistance from both the nobility and the clergy. The archbishop of Canterbury, Thomas à Becket (1118?–1170), once Henry's compliant chancellor, broke openly with the king and fled to Louis VII. Becket's subsequent assassination in 1170 and his canonization by Pope Alexander III in 1172 helped focus popular resentment against the king's heavyhanded tactics. (Two hundred years later, Geoffrey Chaucer, writing in an age made cynical by the Black Death and the Hundred Years' War, had the pilgrims of his *Canterbury Tales* journey to the shrine of Thomas à Becket.)

Under Henry's successors, the brothers Richard the Lion-Hearted (r. 1189–1199) and John (r. 1199–1216), burdensome taxation in support of unnecessary foreign Crusades and a failing war with France turned resistance into outright rebellion. Richard had to be ransomed at a high price from the Holy Roman Emperor

An effigy of Eleanor of Aquitaine, queen by marriage of both France and England. [Giraudon/Art Resource, N.Y.]

Henry VI, who had taken him prisoner during his return from the ill-fated Third Crusade. In 1209 Pope Innocent III, in a dispute with King John over the pope's choice for archbishop of Canterbury, excommunicated the king and placed England under interdict. To extricate himself and keep his throne, John had to make humiliating concessions, even declaring his country a fief of the pope. The last straw for the English, however, was the defeat of the king's forces by the French at Bouvines in 1214. With the full support of the clergy and the townspeople, English barons revolted against John. The popular rebellion ended with the king's grudging recognition of Magna Carta ("Great Charter") in 1215.

This famous document put limits on autocratic behavior of the kind exhibited by Norman kings and their successors, the Angevin or Plantagenet kings. It also secured the rights of the many, at least the privileged many, against the monarchy. In Magna Carta the privileged preserved their right to be represented at the highest levels of government in important matters like taxation. But the monarchy was also preserved and left strong. Some argue that just such a balancing of the one and the many, the stronger and the comparatively weaker—preserving both sides and giving real power to each—was exactly the goal of feudal government.

Political accident clearly had more to do with Magna Carta than political genius. Nevertheless, the English did manage to avoid both a dissolution of the monarchy by the nobility and the abridgment of the rights of the nobility by the monarchy. Although King John continued to resist the Great Charter in every way, and succeeding kings ignored it, Magna Carta nonetheless became a cornerstone of modern English law.

Philip II Augustus

The English struggle in the High Middle Ages was to secure the rights of the many, not the authority of the king. The French, on the other hand, faced the reverse problem. In 987, noblemen chose Hugh Capet to succeed the last Carolingian ruler, replacing the Carolingian dynasty with the Capetian dynasty. For two centuries thereafter, until the reign of Philip II

A depiction of the murder of St. Thomas à Becket in Canterbury cathedral. From the Playfair Book of Hours. *[Victoria and Albert Museum/Art Resource, N.Y., Ms. L 475-1918.]*

Augustus (r. 1180–1223), powerful feudal princes dominated France.

During this period, after a rash initial attempt to challenge the more powerful French nobility before they had enough strength to do so, the Capetian kings concentrated their limited resources on securing the royal domain, their uncontested territory around Paris and the Île-de-France to the northeast. Aggressively exercising their feudal rights, French kings, especially after 1100, gained near absolute obedience from the noblemen in this area, and in the process established a solid base of power. By the reign of Philip II, Paris had become the center of French government and culture and the Capetian dynasty a secure hereditary monarchy. Thereafter, the kings of France could impose their will on the French nobles, who were

The English Nobility Imposes Restraints on King John

The gradual building of a sound English constitutional monarchy in the Middle Ages required the king's willingness to share power. He had to be very strong but could not act as a despot or rule by fiat. The danger of despotism became acute in England under the rule of King John. In 1215 the English nobility forced him to recognize Magna Carta, which reaffirmed traditional rights and personal liberties that are still enshrined in English law.

✦ *Are the rights protected by Magna Carta basic ones or special privileges? Do they suggest there was a sense of "fairness" in the past? Does the granting of such rights in any way weaken the king?*

A free man shall not be fined for a small offense, except in proportion to the gravity of the offense; and for a great offense he shall be fined in proportion to the magnitude of the offense, saving his freehold [property]; and a merchant in the same way, saving his merchandise; and the villein [a free serf, bound only to his lord] shall be fined in the same way, saving his wainage [wagon], if he shall be at [the king's] mercy. And none of the above fines shall be imposed except by the oaths of honest men of the neighborhood. . . .

No constable or other bailiff of [the king] shall take anyone's grain or other chattels without immediately paying for them in money, unless he is able to obtain a postponement at the good will of the seller.

No constable shall require any knight to give money in place of his ward of a castle [i.e., standing guard], if he is willing to furnish that ward in his own person, or through another honest man, if he himself is not able to do it for a reasonable cause; and if we shall lead or send him into the army, he shall be free from ward in proportion to the amount of time which he has been in the army through us.

No sheriff or bailiff of [the king], or any one else, shall take horses or wagons of any free man, for carrying purposes, except on the permission of that free man.

Neither we nor our bailiffs will take the wood of another man for castles, or for anything else which we are doing, except by the permission of him to whom the wood belongs. . . .

No free man shall be taken, or imprisoned, or dispossessed, or outlawed, or banished, or in any way injured, nor will we go upon him, nor send upon him, except by the legal judgment of his peers, or by the law of the land.

To no one will we sell, to no one will we deny or delay, right or justice.

James Harvey Robinson, ed., Readings in European History, Vol. 1 *(Boston: Athenaeum, 1904), pp. 236–237.*

always in law, if not in political fact, the king's sworn vassals.

In an indirect way the Norman conquest of England helped stir France to unity and made it possible for the Capetian kings to establish a truly national monarchy. The duke of Normandy, who after 1066 was master of the whole of England, was also among the vassals of the French king in Paris. Capetian kings understandably watched with alarm as the power of their Norman vassal grew. Other powerful vassals of the king also watched with alarm. King Louis VI, the Fat (r. 1108–1137), entered an alliance with Flanders, traditionally a Norman enemy. King Louis VII (r. 1137–1180), assisted by a brilliant minister, Suger, the abbot of St. Denis and famous for his patronage of Gothic architecture, found allies in the great northern French cities and used their wealth to build a royal army.

When he succeeded Louis VII as king, Philip II Augustus inherited financial resources and a skilled bureaucracy that put him in a strong position. He was able to resist the competition of the French nobility and the clergy and to focus on the contest with the English king. Confronted at the same time with an internal and an international struggle, he proved successful in both. His armies occupied all the English king's territories on the French coast except for Aquitaine. As a showdown with the English neared on the continent, however, Holy Roman Emperor Otto IV (1198–1215) entered the fray on the side of the English, and the French found themselves assailed from both east and west. But when the international armies finally clashed at Bouvines in Flanders on July 27, 1214, in what history records as the first great European battle, the French won handily over the opposing Anglo–Flemish–German army. This victory unified France politically around the monarchy and thereby laid the foundation for French ascendancy in the later Middle Ages. The defeat so weakened Otto IV that he fell from power in Germany. (It also, as we have seen, sparked the rebellion in England that forced King John to accept Magna Carta.)

France in the Thirteenth Century: The Reign of Louis IX

If Innocent III realized the fondest ambitions of medieval popes, Louis IX (r. 1226–1270), the grandson of Philip Augustus, embodied the medieval view of the perfect ruler. Coming to power in the wake of the French victory at Bouvines (1214), Louis inherited a unified and secure kingdom. Although he was endowed with a moral character that far exceeded that of his royal and papal contemporaries, he was also at times prey to naïveté. Not beset by the problems of sheer survival, and a reformer at heart, Louis found himself free to concentrate on what medieval people believed to be the business of civilization.

Generosity Abroad

Magnanimity in politics is not always a sign of strength, and Louis could be very magnanimous. Although in a strong position during negotiations for the Treaty of Paris (1259), which momentarily settled the dispute between France and England, he refused to take advantage of it to drive the English from their French possessions. Had he done so and ruthlessly confiscated English territories on the French coast, he might have lessened, if not averted altogether, the conflict of the Hundred Years' War that began in the fourteenth century. Instead he surrendered disputed territory on the borders of Gascony to the English king, Henry III, and

Philip II Augustus in a romanticized nineteenth century portrait. [Roger-Viollet]

Louis IX embarking on the Seventh Crusade. He later led the Eighth (and last) Crusade, during which he died of dysentery. This illustration was made in the fourteenth century. [Bibliothèque Nationale, Paris]

confirmed Henry's possession of the duchy of Aquitaine.

Although he occasionally chastised popes for their crude political ambitions, Louis remained neutral during the long struggle between the German Hohenstaufen emperor Frederick II and the papacy (discussed later in the chapter); and his neutrality redounded very much to the pope's advantage. Louis also remained neutral when his brother, Charles of Anjou, intervened in Italy and Sicily against the Hohenstaufens, again to the pope's advantage. Urged on by the pope and his noble supporters, Charles was crowned king of Sicily in Rome, and his subsequent defeat of the son and grandson of Frederick II ended the Hohenstaufen dynasty. For such service to the Church, both by action and by inaction, the Capetian kings of the thirteenth century became the objects of many papal favors.

Order and Excellence at Home

Louis's greatest achievements lay at home. The efficient French bureaucracy, which his predecessors had used to exploit their subjects, became under Louis an instrument of order and fair play in local government. He sent forth royal commissioners *(enquêteurs)*, reminiscent of Charlemagne's far less successful *missi dominici*. Their mission was to monitor the royal officials responsible for local governmental administration (especially the *baillis* and *prévôts*, whose offices had been created by his predecessor, Philip Augustus) and to ensure that justice would truly be meted out to all. These royal ambassadors were received as genuine tribunes of the people. Louis further abolished private wars and serfdom within his royal domain. He gave his subjects the judicial right of appeal from local to higher courts, and made the tax system, by medieval standards, more equitable. The French people came to associate their king with justice; consequently, national feeling, the glue of nationhood, grew very strong during his reign.

Respected by the kings of Europe and possessed of far greater moral authority than the pope, Louis became an arbiter among the world's powers. During his reign French society and culture became an example to all of Europe, a pattern that would continue into the modern period. Northern France became the showcase of monastic reform, chivalry, and Gothic art and architecture. Louis's reign also coincided with the golden age of Scholasticism, which saw the convergence of Europe's greatest thinkers on Paris, among them Saint Thomas Aquinas and Saint Bonaventure (see Chapter 8).

Louis's perfection remained, however, that of a medieval king. Like his father, Louis VIII (r. 1223–1226), who had taken part in the Albigensian Crusade, Louis was something of a religious fanatic. He sponsored the French Inquisition. He led two French Crusades against the Muslims, which, although inspired by the purest religious motives, proved to be personal disasters. During the first (1248–1254), Louis was captured and had to be ransomed out of Egypt. He died of a fever during the second in 1270. It was especially for this selfless, but also useless, service on behalf of the Church that Louis later received the rare honor of sainthood. Probably not coincidentally, the Church bestowed this honor when it was under pressure from a more powerful and less than "most Christian" French king, the ruthless Philip IV the Fair (r. 1285–1314). [See Chapter 9.]

The Hohenstaufen Empire (1152–1272)

During the twelfth and thirteenth centuries, stable governments developed in both England and France. In England, Magna Carta balanced the rights of the nobility against the authority of the kings, and in France the reign of Philip II Augustus secured the authority of the king over the competitive claims of the nobility. During the reign of Louis IX, the French exercised international influence over politics and culture. The story within the Holy Roman Empire, which embraced Germany, Burgundy, and northern Italy by the mid-thirteenth century, was very different (see Map 7-2). There, primarily because of the efforts of the Hohenstaufen dynasty to extend imperial power into southern Italy, disunity and blood feuding remained the order of the day for two centuries. It left as a legacy the fragmentation of Germany until modern times.

Frederick I Barbarossa

The investiture struggle had earlier weakened imperial authority. After the Concordat of Worms, the German princes held the dominant lay influence over episcopal appointments and within the rich ecclesiastical territories.

Imperial power seemed to recuperate, however, with the accession to the throne of Frederick I Barbarossa (r. 1152–1190) of the new Hohenstaufen dynasty, the most powerful line of emperors yet to succeed the Ottonians. The Hohenstaufens not only reestablished imperial authority but also started a new phase in the contest between popes and emperors, one that was to prove even deadlier than the investiture struggle had been. Never have kings and popes despised and persecuted one another more than during the Hohenstaufen dynasty.

As Frederick I surveyed his empire, he saw powerful feudal princes in Germany and Lombardy and a pope in Rome who believed that the emperor was his creature. Disaffection was widespread, however, with the incessant feudal strife of the princes and the turmoil caused by the theocratic pretensions of the papacy. Thus popular opinion was on the emperor's side, giving Frederick a foundation on which to rebuild imperial authority, and he was shrewd enough to take advantage of it. In Bologna at the time, Roman law (the law of the Roman Empire, particularly the Justinian *Code*) was undergoing a revival under the scholar Irnerius (d. 1125), and Frederick championed its application within his empire. Roman law served Frederick on both of his fronts. On one hand, it enhanced centralized authority against the nobility; on the other, it stressed the *secular* foundation of imperial power against the tradition of Roman election of the emperor, and especially against the tradition of papal coronation of the emperor, thereby keeping papal influence at a minimum.

Switzerland became Frederick's base of operation. From there he tried to hold the empire together by invoking feudal bonds. He was relatively successful in Germany, thanks largely to the fall from power in 1180 and the exile to Normandy of his strongest German rival, Henry the Lion (d. 1195), the duke of Saxony. Although realistically acknowledging the power

MAP 7-2 GERMANY AND
ITALY IN THE MIDDLE AGES
*Medieval Germany and
Italy were divided lands.
The Holy Roman Empire
(Germany) embraced hun-
dreds of independent territories that the emperor ruled
only in name. The papacy
controlled the Rome area
and tried to enforce its will
on Romagna. Under the
Hohenstaufens (mid-twelfth
to mid-thirteenth century),
internal German divisions
and papal conflict reached
new heights; German rulers
sought to extend their
power to southern Italy and
Sicily.*

of the German duchies, Frederick never missed an opportunity to apprise each of its prescribed duties as a fief of the king. If Frederick was not everywhere ruler in fact, he was clearly so in law, and he permitted no one to forget it. The same tactic had been successfully employed by the Capetian kings of France when they faced superior noble forces.

Italy proved to be the great obstacle to imperial plans. In 1155 Frederick restored Pope Adrian IV (1154–1159) to power in Rome after a religious revolutionary, Arnold of Brescia (d. 1155), had gained control of the city. For his efforts Frederick won a coveted papal coronation—and strictly on his terms, not on those of the pope. The door to Italy thereby opened and an imperial Diet gave official sanction to his Italian claims. But there was fierce resistance to him in Italy, led by Milan.

As this challenge to royal authority was occurring, one of Europe's most skilled lawyers, Cardinal Roland, was elected Pope Alexander III (1159–1181). While a cardinal, he had negotiated an alliance between the papacy and the Norman kingdom of Sicily in a clever effort to strengthen the papacy against imperial influence. Perceiving him to be a very capable foe, Frederick had opposed his election as pope and had even backed a schismatic pope against him in a futile effort to undo Alexander's election. Frederick now found himself at war with the pope, Milan, and Sicily. In 1167 the combined forces of the North Italian communes drove him back into Germany. The final blow to imperial plans in Italy came a decade later, in 1176, when Italian forces soundly defeated

Frederick at Legnano. In the final Peace of Constance in 1183, Frederick recognized the claims of the Lombard cities to full rights of self-rule.

Henry VI and the Sicilian Connection

Frederick's reign ended with stalemate in Germany and defeat in Italy. At his death in 1190 he was not, as a ruler, equal in stature to the kings of England and France. After the Peace of Constance in 1183 he seems himself to have conceded as much, accepting the reality of the empire's indefinite division among the feudal princes of Germany. In the last years of his reign, however, an opportunity both to solve his problem with Sicily, still a papal ally, and to form a new territorial base of power for future emperors presented itself. The Norman ruler of the kingdom of Sicily, William II (r. 1166–1189), sought an alliance with Frederick that would free him to pursue a scheme to conquer Constantinople. In 1186 a most fateful marriage between Frederick's son, the future Henry VI (r. 1190–1197), and Constance, heiress to the kingdom of Sicily, sealed the alliance.

This alliance proved, however, to be only another well-laid political plan that went astray. The Sicilian connection became a fatal distraction for the succeeding Hohenstaufen kings. It led them in the end to sacrifice their traditional territorial base in northern Europe to the temptations of imperialism. Equally ominous, this union of the empire with Sicily left Rome encircled, thereby ensuring the undying hostility of a papacy already thoroughly distrustful of the

Frederick I Barbarossa, wearing the imperial crown, leads the Third Crusade to Jerusalem. He drowned in the Saleph River while en route. [Bürgerbibliothek, Bern]

emperor. The marriage alliance with Sicily proved to be the first step in what soon became a fight to the death between pope and emperor.

When Henry VI came to rule in 1190, he faced a multitude of enemies: a hostile papacy, still smarting from the refusal of his father to recognize territorial claims within the Papal States; supremely independent German princes, led by the archbishop of Cologne; and an England whose adventurous king, Richard the Lion-Hearted, was encouraged to plot against Henry by the exiled duke of Saxony, Henry the Lion.

Into this divided kingdom a son, the future Frederick II, was born in 1194. Heretofore the German princes had not recognized birth alone as entitling the offspring of emperors to the imperial throne, although it did give them an inside track. To stabilize his monarchy, Henry campaigned vigorously for the recognition of the principle of hereditary succession. He won many German princes to this point of view by granting them full hereditary rights to their own fiefs—an appropriate exchange. But the encircled papacy was not disposed to secure Hohenstaufen power by supporting a hereditary right to the imperial throne. The pope wanted, rather, to return to the period before 1152, when imperial power had been diffused among many princes and future emperors could be more easily created from among the pope's allies. He accordingly joined dissident German princes against Henry.

Otto IV and the Welf Interregnum

When Henry died in September 1197, leaving his son Frederick a ward of the pope, chaos was his immediate heir. Henry's brother, Philip of Swabia, succeeded him as German king, but the Welf family, rivals of the Hohenstaufens, put forth a rival claimant, Otto of Brunswick. The English supported Otto; the French, beginning a series of interventions in German affairs, supported the Hohenstaufens; and the papacy supported first one side and then the other as each in turn threatened to encircle Rome. Germany was thrown into anarchy and civil war.

Otto, crowned Otto IV by his supporters in Aachen in 1198, outlasted his rival, and later won general recognition in Germany. Hohenstaufen support remained alive, however,

and Otto reigned over a very divided kingdom. Then, in October 1209, Pope Innocent III (1198–1216) crowned him emperor, enhancing his authority. Innocent, however, was a shrewd pope who was determined to curb imperial power in Italy and restore papal power there, and he was willing to play one German dynasty against the other to do so. When, after his coronation, Otto proceeded to attack Sicily, pursuing an imperial policy that once again threatened to encircle Rome, the pope quickly moved from benefactor to mortal enemy; four months after crowning Otto emperor, the pope excommunicated him.

Frederick II

Pope Innocent, casting about for a counterweight to the treacherous Otto, joined the French, who had remained loyal to the Hohenstaufens against the English-Welf alliance. His new ally, the French king, Philip Augustus, impressed on Innocent that a solution to their problems with Otto IV lay near at hand in the person of Innocent's ward, Frederick of Sicily, the son of the late Hohenstaufen Emperor Henry VI, who was now of age. Unlike Otto, Frederick had an immediate hereditary claim to the imperial throne. In December 1212, the young Frederick, with papal, French, and German support, was crowned king of the Romans in Mainz. Within a year and a half, Philip Augustus ended the reign of Otto IV on the battlefield of Bouvines. In 1215 Frederick, now Frederick II, was crowned emperor again, this time in the imperial city of Aachen.

During his reign, Frederick effectively turned dreams of a unified Germany into a nightmare of disunity, and he may be credited with assuring German fragmentation until modern times. Frederick was Sicilian and dreaded travel beyond the Alps. He spent only nine of his thirty-eight years as emperor in Germany, and six of those were before 1218. Although he pursued his royal interests in Germany, he did so mostly through representatives. He seemed to desire only the imperial title for himself and his sons, and, to secure it, he was willing to give the German princes what they wanted. His eager compliance with their demands laid the foundation for six centuries of German division. In 1220 he recognized the jurisdictional claims of the ecclesiastical princes of Germany. In 1232 he extended the same recognition to the secular princes. Their power greatly enhanced, the German princes were thereafter undisputed lords over their territories.

Frederick's concessions were tantamount to an abdication of imperial responsibility in Germany. They have been characterized as a German equivalent to Magna Carta in the sense that they secured the rights of the German nobility. But unlike the king of England who signed Magna Carta, Frederick did little to secure the rights of monarchy in Germany. Whereas Magna Carta may be said to have had the long-term consequence of promoting a bal-ance of authority between king and parliament, Frederick simply made the German princes little emperors within their realms. Centuries of petty absolutism, not parliamentary government, was the result.

Frederick's relations with the pope were equally disastrous. He was excommunicated no fewer than four times, the first in 1227 for refusing to carry through a Crusade he had begun at the pope's request. The papacy came to view Frederick as the Antichrist, the biblical beast of the Apocalypse whose persecution of the faithful signaled the end of the world. The basis of the conflict lay once again in imperial policies that threatened to encircle Rome.

Frederick II Denounces the Pope

When Frederick II learned that he had again been excommunicated by the pope, this time at the Council of Lyons in 1245, he raged at the presumption of popes to depose kings. His words were recorded in the Greater Chronicle of Matthew of Paris. This condemnation of the temporal power of popes would be heard again and again in the later Middle Ages.

✦ *Is Frederick's rage justified? What was at stake for him? Why is it necessary to separate church and state? Why would life not be more secure under the rule of a religious leader than under a secular one?*

When the Emperor Frederick was made fully aware of all these proceedings [his excommunication by the pope at Lyons] he could not contain himself, but burst into a violent rage, and, darting a scowling look on those who sat around him, he thundered forth: "The Pope in his synod has disgraced me by depriving me of my crown. Whence arises such great audacity? Whence proceeds such rash presumption? Where are my chests which contain my treasures?" And on their being brought and unlocked before him, by his order, he said, "See if my crowns are lost now"; then finding one, he placed it on his head and, being thus crowned, he stood up, and, with threatening eyes and a dreadful voice, unrestrainable from passion, he said aloud, "I have not yet lost my crown, nor will I be deprived of it by any attacks of the Pope or the council without a bloody struggle. Does his vulgar pride raise him to such heights as to enable him to hurl from the imperial dignity me, the chief prince of the world, than whom none is greater—yea, I who am without an equal . . . ? In some things I was bound to obey, at least to respect, him [the pope]; but now I am released from all ties of affection and veneration, and also from the obligation of any kind of peace with him." From that time forth, therefore, Frederick, in order to injure the Pope more effectually . . . did all kinds of harm to his Holiness, to his money, as well as to his friends and relatives.

Frederic Austin Ogg, ed., A Source Book of Mediaeval History: Documents Illustrative of European Life and Institutions from the German Invasions to the Renaissance *(New York: Telegraph Books, 1908), pp. 408–409.*

Major Political Events of High Middle Ages	
955	Otto I defeats Hungarians at Lechfeld, securing Europe's eastern border
1066	Normans win the Battle of Hastings and assume English rule
1152	Frederick I Barbarossa becomes first Hohenstaufen emperor; reestablishes imperial authority
1154	Henry II assumes the English throne as the first Plantagenet or Angevin king
1164	Henry II forces the *Constitutions of Clarendon* on the English clergy
1170	Henry II's defiant archbishop, Thomas à Becket, assassinated
1176	Papal and other Italian armies defeat Frederick I at Legnano
1194	Birth of future Hohenstaufen ruler Frederick II, who becomes a ward of the pope
1198	Welf interregnum in the empire begins under Otto IV
1212	Frederick II crowned emperor in Mainz with papal, French, and German support
1214	French armies under Philip II Augustus defeat combined English and German forces at Bouvines in the first major European battle
1215	English barons revolt against King John and force the king's recognition of *Magna Carta*
1227	Frederick II excommunicated for the first of four times by the pope; conflict between Hohenstaufen dynasty and papacy begins
1250	Frederick II dies, having been defeated by the German princes with papal support
1257	German princes establish their own electoral college to elect future emperors
1270	French king Louis IX, having unified and reformed France, dies a Crusader in the Holy Land

Although Frederick abandoned Germany, he was determined to control Lombardy. His efforts to establish a dominant Lombardy-Sicily axis in Italy brought his excommunication in 1238.

The papacy finally won the long struggle that ensued, although its victory proved in time to be a Pyrrhic one. During this contest, Pope Innocent IV (1243–1254) launched the Church into European politics on a massive scale. This wholesale secularization made the Church highly vulnerable to criticism from religious reformers and royal apologists. Innocent organized and led the German princes against Frederick, who—thanks to Frederick's grand concessions to them—had become a superior force and were in full control of Germany by the 1240s. German and Italian resistance kept Frederick completely on the defensive throughout his last years.

When Frederick died in 1250, the German monarchy died with him. The princes established their own informal electoral college in 1257, which thereafter controlled the succession. Through this institution, which the emperor formally recognized in 1356, the "king of the Romans" became a puppet, but now with firmly attached strings. The princes elected him directly; his offspring had no hereditary right to succeed him.

Between 1250 and 1272 the Hohenstaufen dynasty slowly faded into oblivion. Its legacy was to make permanent the divisions within the empire. Independent princes now controlled Germany. Italy fell to local magnates. The connection between Germany and Sicily, established by Frederick I, was permanently broken. And the papal monarchy emerged as one of Europe's most formidable powers, soon to enter its most costly conflict with the French and the English.

Medieval Russia

In the late tenth century, Prince Vladimir of Kiev (972–1015), at that time Russia's dominant city, received delegations of Muslims, Roman Catholics, Jews, and Greek Orthodox Christians, each of which hoped to see Russians embrace their religion. Vladimir chose Greek Orthodoxy, which became the religion of Russia, adding strong cultural bonds to the close commercial ties that had long linked Russia to the Byzantine Empire.

Politics and Society

Vladimir's successor, Yaroslav the Wise (1016–1054), developed Kiev into a magnificent political and cultural center, with architecture rivaling that of Constantinople. He also sought contacts with the West in an unsuccessful effort to counter the political influence of the Byzantine emperors. After his death, rivalry among their princes slowly divided Russians into three cultural groups: the Great Russians, the White Russians, and the Little Russians (Ukrainians). Autonomous principalities also challenged Kiev's dominance, and it became just one of several national centers.

Government in the principalities combined monarchy (the prince), aristocracy (the prince's council of noblemen), and democracy (a popular assembly of all adult males). The broadest social division was between freemen and slaves. Freemen included the clergy, army officers, boyars (wealthy landowners), townsmen, and peasants. Slaves were mostly prisoners of war. Debtors working off their debts made up a large, semi-free, intermediate group.

Mongol Rule (1243–1480)

In the thirteenth century, Mongol (or Tatar) armies swept over China, much of the Islamic world, and Russia. Ghengis Khan (1155–1227) invaded Russia in 1223, and Kiev fell to Batu Khan in 1240. Russian cities became dependent, tribute-paying principalities of the segment of the Mongol Empire called the *Golden Horde* (a phrase derived from the Tatar words for the color of Batu Khan's tent), which included the steppe region of what is now southern Russia and had its capital at Sarai, on the Lower Volga. The Golden Horde stationed officials in all the principal Russian towns to oversee taxation and the conscription of soldiers into Tatar armies.

Mongol rule created further cultural divisions between Russia and the West. The Mongols intermarried with the Russians and also created harems filled with Russian women. Russians who resisted were sold into slavery in foreign lands. Russian women—under the influence of Islam, which had become the religion of the Golden Horde—began to wear veils and to lead more secluded lives. The Mongols, however, left Russian political and religious institutions largely intact and, thanks to their far-flung trade, brought most Russians greater peace and prosperity than they had enjoyed before.

Russian Liberation

The princes of Moscow cooperated with their overlords in the collection of tribute and grew

The Cathedral of St. Basil in Moscow. Built between 1544 and 1560 during the reign of Ivan the Terrible, it reflects the enduring Byzantine influence on Russian architecture. [Sovfoto]

wealthy under the Mongols. As Mongol rule weakened, the princes took control of the territory surrounding the city. In a process that has come to be known as "the gathering of the Russian Land," they then gradually expanded the principality of Moscow through land purchases, colonization, and conquest.

In 1380, Grand Duke Dimitri of Moscow (1350–1389) defeated Tatar forces at Kulikov Meadow in a victory that marks the beginning of the decline of Mongol hegemony. Another century would pass before Ivan III, called Ivan the Great (d. 1505), would bring all of northern Russia under Moscow's control and end Mongol rule (1480). By the last quarter of the fourteenth century, however, Moscow had become the political and religious center of Russia, replacing Kiev. In Russian eyes it was destined to become the "third Rome" after the fall of Constantinople to the Turks in 1453.

With its borders finally secured, western Europe was free to develop its political institutions and cultural forms during the High Middle Ages. The map of Europe as we know it today began to take shape. England and France can be seen forming into modern nation states, but within Germany and the Holy Roman Empire the story was different. There, imperial rule first revived (under the Ottonians) and then collapsed totally (under the Hohenstaufen dynasty). The consequences for Germany were ominous; thereafter, it became Europe's most fractured land. On a local level, however, an effective organization of society from noble to serf emerged throughout western Europe.

The major disruption of the period was an unprecedented conflict between Church and state, former allies. During the Investiture Struggle and the period of the Crusades, the Church became a powerful monarchy in its own right. For the first time it competed with secular states on the latter's own terms, dethroning emperors, kings, and princes by excommunication and interdict. In doing so, it inadvertently laid the foundation for the Western doctrine of the separation of Church and state.

Having succeeded so brilliantly in defending its spiritual authority against rulers, popes ventured boldly into the realm of secular politics as well, especially during the pontificates of Popes Innocent III and Innocent IV. As the sad story of the Hohenstaufen dynasty attests, they had remarkable, if short-lived, success there also. But the Church was to pay dearly for its successes, both spiritually and politically. Secularization of the papacy during the High Middle Ages left it vulnerable to the attacks of a new breed of unforgiving religious reformers, and the powerful monarchs of the later Middle Ages were to subject it to bold and vengeful bullying.

Review Questions

1. Discuss the rise of the German empire and the accomplishments of the Saxon king, Otto I. How was he able to consolidate political rule over the various German duchies and use the church to his advantage? Does he deserve the title "The Great"?

2. What were the main reasons for the Cluny reform movement? How do you account for its success and how important was the impact of this reform movement on the subsequent history of the medieval Church?

3. Discuss the conflict between Pope Gregory VII and King Henry IV over the issue of lay investiture. What were the causes of the controversy, the actions of the contending parties, and the outcome of the struggle? What was at stake for each of the disputants and what were the ramifications of the struggle?

4. The eighteenth-century French intellectual Voltaire said the Holy Roman Empire was neither holy, nor Roman. What did he mean? Do you agree with him?

5. What major development in western and eastern Europe encouraged the emergence of the crusading movement? Why were the Crusaders unsuccessful in establishing lasting political and religious control over the Holy Land? What were the political, religious, and economic results of the Crusades? Which do you consider most important and why?

6. Hohenstaufen rule proved disastrous for Germany's development as a nation. What were some of the factors preventing German consolidation during that era? Why did Germany remain in feudal chaos while France and England eventually coalesced into reasonably strong states?

Suggested Readings

J. W. BALDWIN, *The Government of Philip Augustus* (1986). An important scholarly work.

M. W. BALDWIN (Ed.), *History of the Crusades, I: The First Hundred Years* (1955). Basic historical narrative.

G. BARRACLOUGH, *The Origins of Modern Germany* (1946). Dated but penetrating political narrative setting modern Germany in the perspective of the Middle Ages.

G. BARRACLOUGH, *The Medieval Papacy* (1968). Brief survey with pictures.

A. CAPELLANUS, *The Art of Courtly Love*, trans. by J. J. Parry (1941). Documents from the court of Marie de Champagne.

M. CLAGETT, G. POST, and R. REYNOLDS (Eds.), *Twelfth-Century Europe and the Foundations of Modern Society* (1966). A demanding but stimulating collection of essays.

H. E. J. Cowdrey, *Popes, Monks, and Crusaders* (1984). Recreation of the atmosphere that gave birth to the Crusades.

R. H. C. Davis, *A History of Medieval Europe: From Constantine to St. Louis* (1972), Part 2. Succinct, lucid survey.

E. M. Hallam, *Capetian France 987–1328* (1980). Very good on politics and heretics.

J. C. Holt, *Magna Carta*, 2nd ed. (1992). The famous document and its interpretation by succeeding generations.

E. H. Kantorowicz, *The King's Two Bodies* (1957). Controversial analysis of political concepts in the High Middle Ages.

H. Leyser, *Hermits and the New Monasticism: A Study of Religious Communities in Western Europe, 1000–1150* (1984). The new power and influence of reformed monasticism.

K. Leyser, *Rule and Conflict in Early Medieval Society: Ottonian Saxony* (1979). Basic and authoritative.

K. Leyser, *Medieval Germany and Its Neighbors, 900–1250* (1982). Basic and authoritative.

P. Mandonnet, *St. Dominic and His Work* (1944). On the origins of the Dominican Order.

H. E. Mayer, *The Crusades*, trans. by John Gilligham (1972). Extremely detailed; the best one-volume account.

J. Moorman, *A History of the Franciscan Order* (1968). The best survey.

J. B. Morrall, *Political Thought in Medieval Times* (1962). Readable and illuminating account.

C. Petit-Dutaillis, *The Feudal Monarchy in France and England from the Tenth to the Thirteenth Century*, trans. by E. D. Hunt (1964). Political narrative in great detail.

S. Reynolds, *Kingdoms and Communities in Western Europe 900–1300* (1984). For the medieval origins of Western political and cultural traditions.

T. Reuter (Ed.), *The Medieval Nobility* (1979). Collection of scholarly essays.

J. Riley-Smith, *The Crusades: A Short History* (1987). Up-to-date, lucid, and readable.

I. Spector, *Russia: A New History* (1935). Admirable simplicity.

B. Tierney, *The Crisis of Church and State* (1964). Extremely useful collection of key documents.

G. Vernadsky, *A History of Russia, I–IV* (1946–1963). A graspable magisterial survey.

W. L. Wakefield and A. P. Evans (Eds.), *Heresies of the High Middle Ages* (1969). A major document collection.

S. Williams (Ed.), *The Gregorian Epoch: Reformation, Revolution, Reaction* (1964). Scholarly debate over Gregory's reign.

R. L. Wolff and H. W. Hazard (Eds.), *History of the Crusades, II: The Later Crusades 1189–1311* (1962).

A lady and her knight going hunting. [Bildarchiv Preussischer Kulturbesitz]

8

The High Middle Ages (1000–1300): People, Towns, and Universities

Key Topics in This Chapter
- The major groups composing medieval society
- The rise of towns and a new merchant class
- The founding of universities and educational curriculum
- How women and children fared in the Middle Ages

Between the tenth and twelfth centuries, European agricultural production steadily improved, due to a warming climate and improved technology. With increased food supplies came something of a population explosion by the eleventh century. The recovery of the countryside in turn stimulated new migration into and trade with the long-dormant towns. A revival of old towns and the creation of new ones resulted. A rich and complex fabric of life developed, closely integrating town and country-side and allowing civilization to flourish in the twelfth and thirteenth centuries as it had not done in the West since the Roman Empire. Beginning with the Crusades, trade also revived with distant towns and foreign lands. With the rise of towns a new merchant class, the ancestors of modern capitalists, came into being. Enormous numbers of skilled artisans and day workers, especially in the cloth-making industries, were the foundation of the new urban wealth.

Urban culture and education also flourished. The revival of eastern trade and contacts with Muslim intellectuals, particularly in Spain, made possible the recovery of ancient scholarship and science. Unlike the comparative dabbling in antiquity during Carolingian times, the twelfth century enjoyed a true renaissance of classical learning. Schools and curricula also broadened beyond the clergy during the twelfth century to educate laity, thereby greatly increasing lay literacy and the role of the laity in government and culture.

In the mid-twelfth century in France, Gothic architecture began to replace the plain and ponderous Romanesque preferred by fortress Europe during the early Middle Ages. Its new grace and beauty—soaring arches, bold flying buttresses, dazzling light, and stained glass—were a testament to the vitality of humankind as well as to the glory of God in this unique period of human achievement.

The Traditional Order of Life

In the art and literature of the Middle Ages, three basic social groups were represented: those who fought as mounted knights (the landed nobility), those who prayed (the clergy), and those who labored in fields and shops (the peasantry and village artisans). After the revival of towns in the eleventh century, there emerged a fourth social group: the long-distance traders and merchants. Like the peasantry, they also labored, but in ways strange to the traditional groups. They were freemen who often possessed great wealth, yet unlike the nobility and the clergy, they owned no land, and unlike the peasantry, they did not toil in fields and shops. Their rise to power caused an important crack in the old social order, for they drew behind them the leadership of the urban artisan groups created by the new urban industries that grew up in the wake of the revival of trade. During the late Middle Ages these new "middling classes" firmly established themselves and their numbers have been enlarging ever since.

Nobles

As a distinctive social group, not all nobles were originally great men with large hereditary lands. Many rose from the ranks of feudal vassals or warrior knights. The successful vassal attained a special social and legal status based on his landed wealth (accumulated fiefs), his exercise of authority over others, and his distinctive social customs—all of which set him apart from others in medieval society. By the late Middle Ages there had evolved a distinguishable higher and lower nobility living in both town and country. The higher were the great landowners and territorial magnates, long the dominant powers in their regions; the lower were petty landlords, the descendants of minor knights, newly rich merchants who could buy country estates, or wealthy farmers patiently risen from ancestral serfdom.

It was a special mark of the nobility that they lived off the labor of others. Basically lords of manors, the nobility of the early and High Middle Ages neither tilled the soil like the peasantry nor engaged in the commerce of merchants—activities considered beneath their dignity. The nobleman resided in a country mansion or, if he were particularly wealthy, a castle. Personal preference drew him to the countryside as much as that his fiefs were usually rural manors.

WARRIORS Arms were the nobleman's profession; his sole occupation and reason for living was waging war. In the eighth century the adoption of stirrups made mounted warriors, or cavalry, the key ingredient of a successful army. (Stirrups had the advantage of permitting the rider to strike a blow without falling to the ground.) Good horses (and a warrior needed several) and the accompanying armor and weaponry of horse warfare were expensive. Only those with means could pursue the life of a cavalryman. The nobleman's fief provided the means to acquire the expensive military equipment that his rank required. He maintained his enviable position as he had gained it, by fighting for his chief.

The nobility accordingly celebrated the physical strength, courage, and constant activity of warfare. Warring gave them both new riches and an opportunity to gain honor and glory. Knights were paid a share in the plunder of victory, and in time of war everything became fair game. Special war wagons, designed for the collection and transport of booty, followed them into battle. Sadness greeted periods of peace, as they meant economic stagnation and boredom. Whereas the peasants and the townspeople counted peace the condition of their occupational success, the nobility despised it as unnatural to their profession.

They looked down on the peasantry as cowards who ran and hid in time of war. Urban merchants, who amassed wealth by business methods strange to feudal society, were held in equal contempt, which increased as the affluence and political power of the townspeople grew. The nobility possessed as strong a sense of superiority over these "unwarlike" people as the clergy did over the general run of laity.

KNIGHTHOOD The nobleman nurtured his sense of distinctiveness within medieval society by the chivalric ritual of dubbing to knighthood. This ceremonial entrance into the noble class became almost a religious sacrament. The ceremony was preceded by a bath of purification, confession, communion, and a prayer vigil. Thereafter, the priest blessed the knight's standard, lance, and sword. As prayers were chanted, the priest girded the knight with his sword and presented him his shield, enlisting him as much in the defense of the Church as in the service of his lord. Dubbing raised the nobleman to a state as sacred in his sphere as clerical ordination made the priest in his. The comparison is legitimate. The clergy and the nobility were medieval society's privileged estates. The appointment of noblemen to high ecclesiastical office and their eager participation in the Church's Crusades had strong ideological and social underpinnings as well as economic and political motives.

In the twelfth century, knighthood was legally restricted to men of high birth. This circumscription of noble ranks came in reaction to the growing wealth, political power, and successful social climbing of newly rich townsmen (mostly merchants), who formed a new urban patriciate that was increasingly competitive with the lower nobility. Kings remained free, however, to raise up knights at will and did not shrink from increasing royal revenues by selling noble titles to wealthy merchants. But the law was building fences—fortunately not without gates—between town and countryside in the High Middle Ages.

SPORTSMEN In peacetime the nobility had two favorite amusements: hunting and tourna-

ments. Where they could, noblemen progressively monopolized the rights to game, forbidding the commoners from hunting in "lords'" forests. This practice built resentment among common people to the level of revolt. Free game, fishing, and access to wood were basic demands in the petitions of grievance and the revolts of the peasantry throughout the High and later Middle Ages.

The pastime of tournaments also sowed seeds of social disruption, but more within the ranks of the nobility itself. Tournaments were designed not only to keep men fit for war, but also to provide the excitement of war without the useless maiming and killing of prized vassals. But as regions competed fiercely with one another for victory and glory, even mock battles with blunted weapons proved to be deadly. Often, tournaments got out of hand, ending with bloodshed and animosity among the com-

Noblewomen watch a tournament. These mock battles were designed to provide the excitement of war without its mayhem. However, they tended to get out of hand, resulting in bloodshed and even death. [University of Heidelberg]

batants. (The intense emotions and occasional violence that accompany interregional soccer in Europe today may be seen as a survival of this kind of rivalry.) The Church came to oppose tournaments as occasions of pagan revelry and senseless violence. Kings and princes also turned against them as sources of division within their realms. Henry II of England proscribed them in the twelfth century. They did not end in France until the mid-sixteenth century, after Henry II of France was mortally wounded by a shaft through his visor during a tournament celebrating his daughter's marriage.

COURTLY LOVE From the repeated assemblies in the courts of barons and kings, set codes of social conduct, or "courtesy," developed in noble circles. With the French leading the way, mannered behavior and court etiquette became almost as important as battlefield expertise. Knights became literate gentlemen, and lyric poets sang and moralized at court. The cultivation of a code of behavior and a special literature to eulogize it was not unrelated to problems within the social life of the nobility. Noblemen were notorious philanderers; their illegitimate children mingled openly with their legitimate offspring in their houses. The advent of courtesy was in part an effort to reform this situation.

Although the poetry of courtly love was sprinkled with frank eroticism and the beloved in these epics were married women pursued by those to whom they were not married, the love recommended by the poet was usually love at a distance, unconsummated by sexual intercourse. It was love without touching, a kind of sex without physical sex, and only as such was it considered ennobling. Court poets depicted those who succumbed to illicit carnal love as reaping at least as much suffering as joy from it.

SOCIAL DIVISIONS No medieval social group was absolutely uniform—not the nobility, the clergy, the townspeople, not even the peasantry. Not only was the nobility a class apart, it also had strong social divisions within its own ranks. Noblemen formed a broad spectrum—from minor vassals without subordinate vassals to mighty barons, the principal vassals of a king or prince, who had many vassals of their own. Dignity and status within the nobility were directly related to the exercise of authority over others; a chief with many vassals obviously far excelled the small country nobleman who served another and was lord over none but himself.

Even among the domestic servants of the nobility, a social hierarchy developed according to assigned manorial duties. Although they were peasants in the eyes of the law, the chief stewards—charged to oversee the operation of the lord's manor and entrusted with the care and education of the noble children—became powerful "lords" within their "domains." Some freemen found the status of the steward enviable enough to surrender their own freedom and become domestic servants in the hope of attaining it. In time the social superiority of the higher ranks of domestic servants won legal recognition as medieval law adjusted to acknowledge the privileges of wealth and power at whatever level they appeared.

By the late Middle Ages, several factors forced the landed nobility into a steep economic and political decline from which it never recovered. Climatic changes and agricultural failures created large famines, while the great plague (see Chapter 9) brought about unprecedented population losses. Changing military tactics occasioned by the use of infantry and heavy artillery during the Hundred Years' War made the noble cavalry nearly obsolete. And the alliance of wealthy towns with the king weakened the nobility within their very own domains. One can speak of a waning of the landed nobility after the fourteenth century. Thereafter, the effective possession of land and wealth counted far more than parentage and lineage as qualification for entrance into the highest social class.

Clergy

Unlike the nobility and the peasantry, the clergy was an open estate. Although the clerical hierarchy reflected the social classes from which the clergy came, one was still a cleric by religious training and ordination, not by the circumstances of birth or military prowess.

REGULAR AND SECULAR CLERICS There were two basic types of clerical vocation: the regular and the secular clergy. The regular clergy were the orders of monks who lived according to a special ascetic rule (*regula*) in cloisters separated from the world. They were the spiritual elite among the clergy, and theirs was not a way of life lightly entered. Canon law required that one be at least twenty-one years of age before making a final profession of the monastic vows of poverty, chastity, and obedience. The monks' personal sacrifices and high religious ideals made them much respected in high medieval society. This popularity was a major factor in the success of the Cluny reform movement and of the Crusades of the eleventh and twelfth centuries. The Crusades provided laypeople a way to participate in the admired life of asceticism and prayer; in these holy pilgrimages they had the opportunity to imitate the suffering and perhaps even the death of Jesus, as the monks imitated his suffering and death by retreat from the world and severe self-denial.

Many monks (and also nuns, who increasingly embraced the vows of poverty, obedience, and chastity without a clerical rank) secluded themselves altogether. The regular clergy, however, were never completely cut off from the secular world. They maintained frequent contact with the laity through such charitable activities as feeding the destitute and tending the sick, through liberal arts instruction in monastic schools, through special pastoral commissions from the pope, and as supplemental preachers and confessors in parish churches during Lent and other peak religious seasons. It became the mark of the Dominican and Franciscan friars to live a common life according to a special rule, and still to be active in a worldly ministry. Some monks, because of their learning and rhetorical skills, even rose to prominence as secretaries and private confessors to kings and queens.

The secular clergy, those who lived and worked directly among the laity in the world (*saeculum*), formed a vast hierarchy. At the top were the high prelates—the wealthy cardinals, archbishops, and bishops, who were drawn almost exclusively from the nobility—and below them the urban priests, the cathedral canons, and the court clerks. Finally, there was the great mass of poor parish priests, who were neither financially nor intellectually very far above the common people they served (the basic educational requirement was an ability to say the Mass). Until the Gregorian reform in the eleventh century, parish priests lived with women in a relationship akin to marriage, and their concubines and children were accepted

Monks singing from a choir book (fifteenth century). [Pierpont Morgan Library, 1994, M.685.f.1r.]

within the communities they served. Because of their relative poverty, it was not unusual for priests to "moonlight" as teachers, artisans, or farmers. Their parishioners also accepted and even admired this practice.

NEW ORDERS One of the results of the Gregorian reform was the creation of new religious orders aspiring to a life of poverty and self-sacrifice in imitation of Christ and the first apostles. The more important were the Canons Regular (founded 1050–1100), the Carthusians (founded 1084), the Cistercians (founded 1098), and the Praemonstratensians (founded 1121). Carthusians, Cistercians, and Praemonstratensians practiced extreme austerity in their quest to recapture the pure religious life of the early Church.

Strictest of them all were the Carthusians. Members lived in isolation and fasted three days a week. They also devoted themselves to long periods of silence and even self-flagellation in their quest for perfect self-denial and conformity to Christ.

The Cistercians (from Cîteaux in Burgundy) were a reform wing of the Benedictine order and were known as the "white monks," a reference to their all-white attire, symbolic of apostolic purity. (The Praemonstratensians also wore white.) They hoped to avoid the materialistic influences of urban society and maintain uncorrupted the original *Rule* of Saint Benedict, which their leaders believed Cluny was compromising. The Cistercians accordingly stressed anew the inner life and spiritual goals of monasticism. They located their houses in remote areas and denied themselves worldly comforts and distractions. Remarkably successful, the order could count 300 chapter houses within a century of its founding, and many others imitated its more austere spirituality.

The Canons Regular were independent groups of secular clergy (and also earnest laity) who, in addition to serving laity in the world, also adopted the *Rule* of Saint Augustine (a monastic guide dating from around the year 500) and practiced the ascetic virtues of regular clerics. There were monks who renounced exclusive withdrawal from the world. There were also priests who renounced exclusive involvement in it. By merging the life of the cloister with traditional clerical duties, the Canons Regular foreshadowed the mendicant friars of the thirteenth century—the Dominicans and the Franciscans, who combined the ascetic ideals of the cloister with a very active ministry in the world.

The monasteries and nunneries of the established orders recruited candidates from among the wealthiest social groups. Crowding in the convents and the absence of patronage gave rise in the thirteenth century to lay satellite convents known as beguine houses. These housed religiously earnest unmarried women from the upper and middle social strata. Cologne established 100 such houses between 1250 and 1350, each containing eight to twelve women. Several of these convents, in Cologne and elsewhere, became heterodox in religious doctrine and practice, falling prey to heresy. Among the responsibilities of the new religious orders of Dominicans and Franciscans was the "regularization" of such convents.

PROMINENCE OF THE CLERGY The clergy constituted a far greater proportion of medieval society than modern society. Estimates suggest that 1.5 percent of fourteenth-century Europe was in clerical garb. The clergy were concentrated in urban areas, especially in towns with universities and cathedrals, where in addition to their studies they found work in a wide variety of religious services. In late-fourteenth-century England there was one cleric for every seventy laypeople, and in counties with a cathedral or a university the proportion rose to one cleric for every fifty laypeople.[1] In large university towns the clergy could exceed 10 percent of the population.

Despite the moonlighting of poorer parish priests, the clergy as a whole, like the nobility, lived on the labor of others. Their income came from the regular collection of tithes and Church taxes according to an elaborate system that evolved in the High and later Middle Ages. The Church was, of course, a major landowner and regularly collected rents and fees. Monastic communities and high prelates amassed great fortunes; there was a popular saying that the granaries were always full in the monasteries. The immense secular power attached to high clerical posts can be seen in the intensity of the investiture struggle. The loss of the right to present chosen clergy with the ring and staff of episcopal office was a direct threat to the emperor's control of his realm. The bishops had become royal agents and were endowed to that purpose with royal lands that the emperor could ill afford to have slip from his control.

During the greater part of the Middle Ages, the clergy were the "first estate," and theology was the queen of the sciences. How did the clergy come into such prominence? A lot of it was self-proclaimed. However, there was also popular respect and reverence for the clergy's role as mediator between God and humanity. The priest brought the very Son of God down to earth when he celebrated the sacrament of the Eucharist; his absolution released penitents from punishment for mortal sin. It was declared improper for mere laypeople to sit in judgment on such a priest.

[1]*Denys Hay,* Europe in the Fourteenth and Fifteenth Centuries, *2nd ed. (New York: Holt, Rinehart, 1966), pp. 58–59.*

Theologians elaborated the distinction between the clergy and the laity very much to the clergy's benefit. The belief in the superior status of the clergy underlay the evolution of clerical privileges and immunities in both person and property. As holy persons, the clergy were not supposed to be taxed by secular rulers without special permission from the proper ecclesiastical authorities. Clerical crimes were under the jurisdiction of special ecclesiastical courts, not the secular courts. Because churches and monasteries were deemed holy places, they, too, were free from secular taxation and legal jurisdiction. Hunted criminals, lay and clerical, regularly sought asylum within them, disrupting the normal processes of law and order. When city officials violated this privilege of asylum, ecclesiastical authorities threatened excommunication and interdict. People feared this suspension of the Church's sacraments, including Christian burial, almost as much as they feared the criminals to whom the Church gave asylum.

By the late Middle Ages, townspeople came increasingly to resent the special immunities of the clergy. They complained that it was not proper for the clergy to have greater privileges yet far fewer responsibilities than all others who lived within the town walls. An early-sixteenth-century lampoon reflected what had by then become a widespread sentiment:

Priests, monks, and nuns
Are but a burden to the earth.
They have decided
That they will not become citizens.
That's why they're so greedy—
They stand firm against our city
And will swear no allegiance to it.
And we hear their fine excuses:
"It would cause us much toil and trouble
Should we pledge our troth as burghers."[2]

The separation of Church and state and the distinction between the clergy and the laity have persisted into modern times. After the fifteenth century, however, the clergy ceased to be the superior class they had been for so much of the Middle Ages. In both Protestant and Catholic lands governments progressively subjected them to the basic responsibilities of citizenship.

[2]Cited by S. Ozment, The Reformation in the Cities (New Haven, Conn.: Yale University Press, 1975), p. 36.

Peasants

The largest and lowest social group in medieval society was the one on whose labor the welfare of all the others depended: the agrarian peasantry. Many peasants lived on and worked the manors of the nobility, the primitive cells of rural social life. All were to one degree or another dependent on their lords and considered their property. The manor in Frankish times was a plot of land within a village, ranging from twelve to seventy-five acres in size, assigned to a certain member by a settled tribe or clan. This member and his family became lords of the land, and those who came to dwell there formed a smaller, self-sufficient community within a larger village community. In the early Middle Ages such manors consisted of the dwellings of the lord and his family, the cottages of the peasant workers, agricultural sheds, and fields.

THE DUTIES OF TENANCY The landowner or lord of the manor required a certain amount of produce (grain, eggs, and the like) and a certain number of services from the peasant families that came to dwell on and farm his land. The tenants were free to divide the labor as they wished; and what goods remained after the lord's levies were met were their own. A powerful lord might own many such manors. Kings later based their military and tax assessments on the number of manors owned by a vassal landlord. No set rules governed the size of manors. There were manors of a hundred acres or less and some of several thousand or more.

There were both servile and free manors. The tenants of the latter had originally been freemen known as *coloni*. Original inhabitants and petty landowners, they swapped their small possessions for a guarantee of security from a more powerful lord, who came in this way to possess their land. Unlike the pure serfdom of the servile manors, whose tenants had no original claim to a part of the land, the tenancy obligations on free manors tended to be limited and the tenants' rights more carefully defined. It was a milder serfdom. Tenants of servile manors were by comparison far more vulnerable to the whims of their landlords. These two types of manor tended, however, to merge. The most common situation was the manor on which tenants of greater and lesser degrees of servitude dwelt together, their services to the lord defined by their personal status and local custom. In many regions free, self-governing peasant communities existed without any overlords and tenancy obligations.

The lord held both judicial and police powers. He owned and operated the machines that processed crops into food and drink. Marc Bloch, the modern authority on manorial society, has vividly depicted the duties of tenancy:

On certain days the tenant brings the lord's steward perhaps a few small silver coins or, more often, sheaves of grain harvested on his fields, chickens from his farmyard, cakes of wax from his beehives or from the swarms of the neighboring forest. At other times he works on the arable or the meadows of the demesne [the lord's plot of land in the manorial fields, between one-third and one-half of that available]. Or else we find him carting casks of wine or sacks of grain on behalf of the master to distant residences. His is the labour which repairs the walls or moats of the castle. If the master has guests the peasant strips his own bed to provide the necessary extra bedclothes. When the hunting season comes round he feeds the pack. If war breaks out he does duty as a footsoldier or orderly, under the leadership of the reeve of the village.[3]

The lord also had the right to subject his tenants to exactions known as *banalities*. He could, for example, force them to breed their cows with his bull, and to pay for the privilege; to grind their bread grains in his mill; to bake their bread in his oven; to make their wine in his wine press; to buy their beer from his brewery; and even to surrender to him the tongues or other choice parts of all animals slaughtered on his lands. The lord also collected as an inheritance tax a serf's best animal. Without the lord's permission, a serf could neither travel nor marry outside the manor in which he served.

THE LIFE OF A SERF Exploited as the serfs may appear to have been from a modern point of view, their status was far from chattel slavery. It was to the lord's advantage to keep his serfs healthy and happy; his welfare, like theirs, depended on a successful harvest. Serfs had their own dwellings and modest strips of land and lived by the produce of their own labor and organization. They were permitted to market for their own profit what surpluses might remain after the harvest. They were free to choose their spouses within the local village, although the lord's permission was required if a wife or husband was sought from another village. And serfs could pass their property (their dwellings and field strips) and worldly goods on to their children.

Peasants lived in timber-framed huts. Except for the higher domestic servants, they seldom ventured far beyond their own villages. The local priest often was their window on the world, and Church festivals were their major communal entertainment. Their religiosity was based in large part on the Church being the only show in town, although their religious beliefs were by no means unambiguously Christian.

Despite the social distinctions between free and servile serfs—and, within these groups, between those who owned ploughs and oxen and those who possessed only hoes—the common dependence on the soil forced close cooperation. The ratio of seed to grain yield was consistently poor; about two bushels of seed were required to produce six to ten bushels of grain in

Men and women harvesting pears. From a Book of Hours (fifteenth century). [Lauros-Giraudon/Art Resource, N.Y.]

[3]*Marc Bloch,* Feudal Society, *trans. by L. A. Manyon (Chicago: University of Chicago Press, 1968), p. 250.*

good times. There was rarely an abundance of bread and ale, the staple peasant foods. Two important American crops, potatoes and corn (maize), were unknown in Europe until the sixteenth century. Pork was the major source of protein, and every peasant household had its pigs. At slaughter time a family might also receive a little tough beef. But basically everyone depended on the grain crops. When they failed or fell short, the peasantry simply went hungry unless the lord had surplus stores that he was willing to share.

CHANGES IN THE MANOR Two basic changes occurred in the evolution of the manor from the early to the later Middle Ages. The first was the fragmentation of the manor and the rise to dominance of the single-family holding. This development was aided by such technological advances as the collar harness (ca. 800), the horseshoe (ca. 900), and the three-field system of crop rotation, which made it easier for smaller familial units to support themselves. As the lords parceled out their land to new tenants, their own plots became progressively smaller.

The Services of a Serf

By the fourteenth century, serfs were paid for their labor. This contract, from a manor in Sussex, England, describes the services required of one serf, John of Cayworth, stipulating the number of days he must devote to each and the pay he is to receive in return. Deductions for meals, which varied in price with the particular service performed, are factored into the serf's take-home pay.

✦ *Do the chores and the number of days the serf must work appear excessive? Was it worthwhile for the serf, given what he received in exchange? Would modern renters of land and lodging consider these payments reasonable today?*

John of Cayworth holds a house and 30 acres of land, and owes yearly 2 s[chillings] at Easter and Michaelmas [in rent to his lord]; and he owes a cock and two hens at Christmas [also in rent] of the value of 4 d[enarii].

And he ought to harrow for 2 days at the Lenten sowing with one man and his own horse and his own harrow, the value of the work being 4d.; and he is to receive from the lord on each day 3 meals, of the value of 5d., and then the lord will be at a loss of 1d. . . .

And he ought to carry the manure of the lord for 2 days with one cart, with his own 2 oxen, the value of the work being 8d.; and he is to receive from the lord each day 3 meals at the value as above. . . .

And he shall find one man for 2 days, for mowing the meadow of the lord, who can mow, by estimation, 1 acre and a half, the value of the mowing of an acre being 6d.; the

sum is there 9d. And he is to receive each day 3 meals of the value given above. . . .

And he ought to carry the hay of the lord for 1 day with a cart and 3 animals of his own, the price of the work being 6d. And he shall have from the lord 3 meals of the value of 2 1/2d. . . . .

And he ought to carry in autumn beans or oats for 2 days with a cart and 3 animals of his own, the value of the work being 12d. And he shall receive from the lord each day 3 meals of the value given above. . . .

And he ought to carry wood from the woods of the lord as far as the manor, for two days in summer, with a cart and 3 animals of his own, the value of the work being 9d. And he shall receive from the lord each day 3 meals of the price given above. . . .

The totals of the rents, with the value of the hens, is 2s. 4d.

James Harvey Robinson, ed., Readings in European History, Vol. 2 (Boston: Athenaeum, 1906), pp. 400–402.

The increase in tenants and the decrease in the lord's fields brought about a corresponding reduction in the labor services exacted from the tenants. Also, the bringing of new fields into production increased individual holdings and modified labor services. In France, by the reign of Louis IX (1226–1270), only a few days a year were required, whereas in the time of Charlemagne peasants had worked the lords' fields several days a week.

As the single-family unit replaced the clan as the basic nuclear group, assessments of goods and services fell on individual fields and households, no longer on manors as a whole. Family farms replaced manorial units. The peasants' carefully nurtured communal life made possible a family's retention of its land and dwelling after the death of the head of the household. In this way, land and property remained in the possession of a single family from generation to generation.

The second change in the evolution of the manor was the conversion of the serf's dues into money payments, a change made possible by the revival of trade and the rise of the towns. This development, completed by the thirteenth century, permitted serfs to hold their land as rent-paying tenants and to overcome their servile status. Although tenants thereby gained greater freedom, they were not necessarily better off materially. Whereas servile workers could have counted on the benevolent assistance of their landlords in hard times, rent-paying workers were left, by and large, to their own devices. Their independence caused some landlords to treat them with indifference and even resentment.

Lands and properties that had been occupied by generations of peasants and were recognized as their own were always under the threat of the lord's claim to a prior right of inheritance and even outright usurpation. As their demesnes declined, the lords were increasingly tempted to encroach on such traditionally common lands. The peasantry fiercely resisted such efforts, instinctively clinging to the little they had. In many regions they successfully organized to gain a voice in the choice of petty rural officials.

By the mid-fourteenth century a declining nobility in England and France, faced with the ravages of the great plague and the Hundred Years' War, tried to turn back the historical clock by increasing taxes on the peasantry and passing laws to restrict their migration into the cities. The peasantry responded with armed revolts in the countryside. These revolts became the rural equivalents of the organization of medieval cities in sworn communes to protect their self-interests against powerful territorial rulers. The revolts of the agrarian peasantry, like those of the urban proletariat, were brutally crushed. They stand out at the end of the Middle Ages as violent testimony to the breakup of medieval society. As growing national sentiment would break its political unity and heretical movements end its nominal religious unity, the peasantry's revolts revealed the absence of medieval social unity.

Towns and Townspeople

In the eleventh and twelfth centuries, towns held only about 5 percent of western Europe's population. By modern comparison they were not very large. Of Germany's 3,000 towns, for example, 2,800 had populations under 1,000. Only 15 German towns exceeded 10,000. The largest, Cologne, had 30,000. In England only London had more than 10,000. Paris was larger than London, but not by much. The largest European towns were in Italy; Florence approached 100,000 and Milan was not far behind. Despite their comparatively small size, towns then, as now, were where the action was. One could find there the whole of medieval society and its most creative segments.

The Chartering of Towns

Towns were originally dominated by feudal lords, both lay and clerical. The lords created the towns by granting charters to those who would agree to live and work within them. The charters guaranteed their safety and gave inhabitants a degree of independence unknown on the land. The purpose was originally to concentrate skilled laborers who could manufacture the finished goods desired by lords and bishops. In this way, manorial society may be seen actually cre-

Many medieval towns, especially in northern Europe, were entirely enclosed by walls for protection. Here is the mid-fifteenth century walled city of Lüneburg in northern Germany. [Foto Makovec]

The Rue du Matelas, a French street in Rouen, Normandy, was preserved intact from the Middle Ages to World War II. Note the narrowness of the street and the open sewer running down its center. The houses were built of rough cast stone, mud, and timber. [Roger-Viollet]

ating its urban challenger and weakening itself. Because they longed for finished goods and for the luxuries that came from faraway places, noblemen had urged their serfs to become skilled at making such things. The new skills required to do this in turn gave serfs a new importance and power. By the eleventh century skilled serfs began to pay their manorial dues in manufactured goods, no longer in field labor, eggs, chickens, and beans. In return for a fixed rent and proper subservience, serfs were also encouraged to settle and work in towns. There they gained special rights and privileges by way of the charters.

As towns grew and beckoned, many serfs fled the countryside with their skills and went directly to the new urban centers. There they found the freedom and profits that could lift an industrious craftsman into higher social ranks. As this migration of serfs to the towns accelerated, the lords in the countryside offered them more favorable terms of tenure to keep them on the land. In this way the growth of towns improved the lot of serfs generally. But serfs could not easily be kept down on the farms after they had discovered the opportunities of town life.

The Rise of Merchants

Rural society not only gave the towns their craftsmen and day laborers, but the first merchants themselves may also have been enterprising serfs. Certainly, some of the long-distance traders were men who had nothing to lose and everything to gain by the enormous risks of

MAP 8-1 SOME MEDIEVAL TRADE ROUTES AND REGIONAL PRODUCTS *Trade in the West varied in intensity and geographical extent in different periods during the Middle Ages. The map shows some of the channels that came to be used in interregional commerce. Labels tell part of what was carried in that commerce.*

foreign trade. They traveled together in armed caravans and convoys, buying goods and products as cheaply as possible at the source, and selling them for all they could get in western ports (see Map 8-1). More than anything else, it was the greed and daring of these rough-hewn men that created Western urban life as we know it today.

At first the merchants were not liked by the traditional social groups of nobility, clergy, and peasantry, who considered them an oddity. As late as the fifteenth century, we find the landed nobility still snubbing the urban patriciate. Such snobbery probably never died out among the older landed nobility, who looked down on the traders as men with poor breeding, little character, and money they did not properly earn or deserve. Over time, however, the powerful grew to respect the merchants, and the weak always tried to imitate them, because wherever the

This is a fanciful illustration of Venice, a major Italian trading center, showing Marco Polo's father and uncle departing the city for the Far East. Their first journey, in 1266, took them to Kaifeng, China, opening trade between Venice and the Far East. Their second and more famous journey, in 1271, included Marco; his detailed diaries of what he saw and experienced provided western Europeans with much of their knowledge about China before the famous sea voyages of the sixteenth century. [The Bodleian Museum]

merchants went, they left a trail of wealth behind.

Challenging the Old Lords

As the traders established themselves in towns, they grew in wealth and numbers, formed their own protective associations, and soon found themselves able to challenge traditional seigneurial authority. Merchants especially wanted to end the arbitrary tolls and tariffs imposed by regional magnates over the surrounding countryside. Such regulations hampered the flow of commerce on which both merchant and craftsman in the growing urban export industries depended. Wherever merchants settled in large numbers they opposed the tolls, tariffs, and other petty restrictions that discouraged the flow of trade. Merchant guilds or protective associations sprang up in the eleventh century, followed in the twelfth by guilds of craftsmen (drapers, haberdashers, furriers, hosiers, goldsmiths, and so on), who worked to advance the business interests of both merchants and craftsmen as well as to enhance the personal well-being of their members. This quickly brought them into conflict with the norms of comparatively static agricultural society.

Townspeople needed simple and uniform laws and a government sympathetic to their new forms of business activity, not the fortress mentality of the lords of the countryside. Such a need could not but create a struggle with the old nobility within and outside the towns. This conflict led towns in the High and later Middle Ages to form their own independent communes and to ally themselves with kings against the nobility in the countryside. This development would eventually rearrange the centers of power in medieval Europe and dissolve classic feudal government.

Because the merchants were so clearly the engine of the urban economy, small shopkeepers and artisans identified far more with them than with the aloof lords and bishops who were a town's original masters. Most townspeople found their own interests best served by the development of urban life in the direction the merchants wanted it to go. Namely, they wanted greater commercial freedom, fewer barriers to trade and business, and a freer secular life; in

The Laws and Customs of Chester

The following laws and customs appear in the Domesday Book *(1080–1086). They were included there because the English town of Chester was among the forty or so towns in which the king had a financial interest. The town paid a portion of the fines it collected for criminal behavior to the king's representative.*

◆ In terms of fine and financial loss, what were the most serious crimes? Was simple negligence punished? Did religion play a role in the setting of any of these fines? Do the fines suggest vigilance or pettiness?

If any free man of the king broke the peace which had been granted and killed a man in his house, all his land and money came to the king, and he himself became an outlaw.

He who shed blood between Monday morning and the ninth hour of Saturday compounded for it with [i.e., paid a fine of] ten shillings. From the ninth hour of Saturday to Monday morning bloodshed was compounded for with twenty shillings. Similarly any one paid twenty shillings who shed blood in the twelve days after Christmas, on the day of the Purification of the Blessed Mary, on the first day after Easter, the first day of Pentecost, Ascension day, on the Assumption or Nativity of the Blessed Mary, and on the day of All Saints. . . .

He who committed theft or robbery, or exercised violence upon a woman in a house, compounded for each of these with forty shillings. . . .

If fire burned the city, he from whose house it started compounded for it with three oras [about two shillings worth] of pennies, and gave to his next neighbor two shillings. Of all these forfeitures, two parts belonged to the king and the third to the earl.

A man or a woman making false measure in the city, and being arrested, compounded for it with four shillings. Similarly a person making bad ale was either placed in the ducking stool or gave four shillings to the reeve [the bailiff]. This forfeiture the officer of the king and of the earl received in the city, in whosesoever land it has been done, either of the bishop or of another man. Similarly also, if any one held the toll back beyond three nights, he compounded for it with forty shillings.

James Harvey Robinson, ed., Readings in European History, Vol. 1 *(Boston: Athenaeum, 1904), pp. 406–407.*

---

sum, a less closed urban life. The lesser nobility (the small knights) outside the towns also recognized the new mercantile economy to be the wave of the future. During the eleventh and twelfth centuries the burgher upper class increased its economic strength and successfully challenged the old urban lords for control of the towns.

New Models of Government

With urban autonomy came new models of self-government. Around 1100 the old urban nobility and the new burgher upper class merged. It was a marriage between those wealthy by birth (inherited property) and those who made their fortunes in long-distance trade. From this new ruling class was born the aristocratic town council, which henceforth came to govern towns.

Enriching and complicating the situation even more, small artisans and craftspeople also slowly developed their own protective associations or guilds and began to gain a voice in government. The towns' ability to provide opportunities for the "little person" had created the slogan, "Town air brings freedom." In the countryside the air one breathed still belonged to the lord of the land; but in the towns residents were treated as freemen. Within town walls people thought of themselves as citizens with basic rights, not subjects liable to their masters' whim. Economic hardship certainly continued to exist among the lower urban groups despite their basic legal and political freedoms. But social mobility was at least a possibility in the towns.

KEEPING PEOPLE IN THEIR PLACES Traditional measures of success had great appeal within the towns. Despite their economic independence, the wealthiest urban groups admired and imitated the lifestyle of the old landed nobility. Although the latter treated the urban patriciate with disdain, successful merchants longed to live the noble, knightly life. They wanted coats of arms, castles, country estates, and the life of a gentleman or a lady on a great manor. This became particularly true in the later Middle Ages, when reliable bills of exchange and international regulation of trade, together with the maturation of merchant firms, allowed merchants to conduct their business by mail. Then only the young apprentices did a lot of traveling, to learn the business from the ground up. When merchants became rich enough to do so, they took their fortunes to the countryside.

Such social-climbing disturbed city councils, and when merchants departed for the country-side, towns often lost out economically. A need to be socially distinguished and distinct pervaded urban society. The merchants were just the tip of the iceberg. Towns tried to control this need by defining grades of luxury in dress and residence for the various social groups and vocations. Overly conspicuous consumption was a kind of indecent exposure punishable by law. Such sumptuary laws restricted the types and amount of clothing one might wear (the length and width of fur pieces, for example) and how one might decorate one's dwelling architecturally. In this way, people were forced to dress and live according to their station in life. The intention of such laws was positive: to maintain social order and dampen social conflict by keeping everyone clearly and peacefully in their place.

SOCIAL CONFLICT AND PROTECTIVE ASSOCIATIONS (GUILDS) Despite unified resistance to external domination, medieval towns were not internally harmonious social units. They were a collection of many selfish and competitive communities, each seeking to advance its own business and family interests.

Skilled workers were an integral component of the commerce of medieval towns. This scene shows the manufacture of cannons in a foundry in Florence. [Scala/Art Resource, N.Y.]

Conflict between haves and have-nots was inevitable, especially because medieval towns had little concept of social and economic equality. Theoretically, poor artisans could work their way up from lower social and vocational levels, and some lucky ones did. But so long as they had not done so, they were excluded from the city council. Only families of long standing in the town who owned property had full rights of citizenship and a direct say in the town's government at the highest levels. Government, in other words, was inbred and aristocratic.

Conflict also existed between the poorest workers in the export trades (usually the weavers and woolcombers) and the economically better off and socially ascending independent workers and small shopkeepers. The better-off workers also had their differences with the merchants, whose export trade often brought competitive foreign goods into the city. So independent workers and small shopkeepers organized to restrict foreign trade to a minimum and corner the local market in certain items.

Over time, the formation of artisan guilds gave workers in the trades a direct voice in government. Ironically, a long-term effect of this gain was to limit the social mobility of the poorest artisans. The guilds gained representation on city councils, where, to discourage imports, they used their power to enforce quality standards and fair prices on local businesses. These actions created tight restrictions on guild membership, squeezing out poorer artisans and trades. As a result, lesser merchants and artisans found their opportunities progressively limited. So rigid and exclusive did the dominant guilds become that they often stifled their own creativity and inflamed the journeymen whom they excluded from their ranks. Unrepresented artisans and craftsmen constituted a true urban proletariat prevented by law from forming their own guilds or entering existing ones. The efforts by guild-dominated governments to protect local craftsmen and industries tended to narrow trade and depress the economy for all.

Towns and Kings

By providing kings with the resources they needed to curb factious noblemen, towns became a major force in the transition from feudal societies to national governments. In many places kings and towns formally allied against the traditional lords of the land. A notable exception to this general development is England, where the towns joined with the barons against the oppressive monarchy of King John (1199–1216), becoming part of the parliamentary opposition to the crown. But by the fifteenth century, kings and towns had also joined forces in England, so much so that by century's end Henry Tudor (1485–1509) was known as the "burgher king."

Towns attracted kings and emperors for obvious reasons. Towns were a ready source of educated bureaucrats and lawyers who knew Roman law, the tool for running kingdoms and empires. Money was also to be found in the towns in great quantity, enabling kings to hire their own armies and free themselves from dependence on the nobility. Towns had the human, financial, and technological resources to empower kings. By such alliances, towns won royal political recognition and had their constitutions guaranteed. This proved somewhat easier to do in the stronger coastal areas than in interior areas, where urban life remained less vigorous and territorial government was on the rise. In France, towns became integrated early into royal government. In Germany, they fell under ever tighter control by the princes. In Italy, uniquely, towns expanded to dominate the surrounding countryside, becoming genuine city-states during the Renaissance.

It was also in the towns' interest to have a strong monarch as their protector against despotic local lords and princes, who were always eager to integrate, or engulf, the towns within their expanding territories. Unlike a local magnate, kings tended to remain at a distance, allowing towns to exercise their precious autonomy. A king was thus the more desirable overlord. It was also an advantage to a town to have its long-distance trade conducted in the name of a known powerful monarch. This gave predators pause and improved official cooperation along the way. Both sides, kings and towns, gained from such alliances.

Between the eleventh and fourteenth centuries, towns had considerable freedom and autonomy. As in Roman times, they again became the flourishing centers of Western civilization. But after the fourteenth century, and even earlier in France and England, the towns, like the Church before them, were steadily bent to the political will of kings and princes in most places. By the seventeenth century few would be truly autonomous, the vast majority integrated thoroughly into the larger purposes of the "state."

Jews in Christian Society

Towns also attracted large numbers of Jews. It was within the major urban centers, particularly in France and Germany, that Jews gathered between the late twelfth and thirteenth centuries. They did so both by choice and for safety in the increasingly hostile Christian world. In cities, Jews plied trades in small businesses, and many became wealthy as moneylenders to kings and popes as well as having urban business-people as clients. After the creation of universities, Jews rented Christian students everything from books to clothes. Jewish intellectual and religious culture had always been very elaborate and sophisticated, both dazzling and threatening to Christians who viewed it from outside. These various factors—the separateness of Jews, their economic power, and their cultural strength—encouraged suspicion and distrust among Christians, whose religious teaching held Jews responsible for the death of Christ.

Between the late twelfth and early fourteenth centuries, Jews were exiled from France and persecuted elsewhere as well. Two factors were behind this unprecedented surge in anti-Jewish sentiment. The first was a desire on the part of kings to confiscate Jewish wealth and property and eliminate the Jews as economic competitors with the monarchy. (French kings acted similarly in the fourteenth century against a wealthy Christian military order known as the Knights Templars; see Chapters 7 and 9.) The other factor behind the exile of Jews was the Church's increasing political vulnerability to the new dynastic monarchies. Faced with the loss of its political power, the Church became more determined than ever to maintain its spiritual hegemony. With the beginning of the Crusades and the creation of new mendicant orders, the Church powerfully reasserted claims to spiritual sovereignty over Europe and beyond, instigating major campaigns against dissenters, heretics, witches, and Jews at home as well as against the infidel abroad.

Schools and Universities

In the twelfth century, Byzantine and Spanish Islamic scholars made it possible for the logical works of Aristotle, the writings of Euclid and Ptolemy, the basic works of Greek physicians and Arab mathematicians, and the larger texts of Roman law to circulate among Western scholars. Islamic scholars especially preserved these works. They also wrote extensive, thought-provoking commentaries on Greek texts that were translated into Latin and made available to Western scholars and students. The result of this renaissance of ancient knowledge was an intellectual ferment that gave rise to Western universities.

University of Bologna

The first important Western university was in Bologna, established by Emperor Frederick Barbarossa in 1158. There we find the first formal organizations of students and masters and the first degree programs—the institutional foundations of the modern university. Originally the term *university* meant simply a corporation of individuals (students and masters) who joined for their mutual protection from overarching episcopal authority (the local bishop oversaw the university) and from the local townspeople. Because townspeople then looked on students as foreigners without civil rights, such protective unions were necessary. They followed the model of an urban trade guild.

Bolognese students also "unionized" to guarantee fair rents and prices from their often reluctant hosts. And students demanded regular, high-quality teaching from their masters. In Italy, students actually hired their own teachers, set pay scales, and drew up desired lecture topics. Masters who did not keep their promises or live up to student expectations were boycotted. Price gouging by townspeople was met with the threat to move the university to another town. This could rather easily be done because the university was not yet tied to a fixed physical

Philip II Augustus Orders Jews Out of France

Long the objects of Christian polemic, hated as moneylenders by ordinary people, and feared by the clergy as successful competitors with Christianity, Jews became easy scapegoats for rulers who wished to exploit fear and prejudice. In 1182, Philip II Augustus, eyeing the wealthy Jews of Paris, ordered all nonconverting Jews out of France and confiscated their property and possessions.

◆ *What is the king's argument for exiling Jews? Did Jewish moneylenders threaten the well-being of Christians? Are economic and political motives apparent in the king's actions? Why was religious pluralism and toleration so difficult for people then?*

[When Philip became king] a great multitude of Jews had been dwelling in France for a long time. . . . [In Paris] they grew so rich that they claimed as their own almost half of the whole city, and they had Christians in their houses as menservants and maidservants, who were backsliders from the faith of Jesus Christ and judaized with the Jews. . . .

And whereas the Lord had said . . . in Deuteronomy (23:19–20): "Thou shall not lend upon usury to thy brother, but to the stranger," the Jews . . . understood by "stranger" every Christian, and they took from the Christians their money at usury. And so heavily burdened in this wise were citizens and soldiers and peasants . . . that many of them were constrained to part with their possessions. Others were bound under oath in houses of the Jews in Paris, held as if captives in prison.

The most Christian King Philip hearing of these things . . . released all Christians of his kingdom from their debts to the Jews, and kept a fifth part of the whole amount for himself. . . . [Then in] 1182, in the month of April . . . an edict went forth from . . . the king . . . that all the Jews of his kingdom should be prepared to go forth by the coming feast of St. John the Baptist. And the king gave them leave to sell each his movable goods before the time fixed.

When faithless Jews heard this edict some of them . . . converted to the Lord [Jesus Christ, and] to them the king, out of regard for the Christian religion, restored all their possessions . . . and gave them perpetual liberty. Others were blinded by their ancient error and persisted in their perfidy. . . . The infidel Jews . . . astonished and stupefied by the strength of mind of Philip the king and his constancy in the Lord . . . prepared to sell all their household goods. The time was now at hand when the king ordered them to leave France. . . . Then did the Jews sell all their movable possessions in great haste, while their landed property reverted to the crown. Thus the Jews, having sold their goods and taken the price for the expenses of their journey, departed with their wives and children and all their households in the . . . year of the Lord 1182.

James Harvey Robinson, ed., Readings in European History, Vol. 2 (Boston: Atheneaum, 1906), pp. 426–428.

---

plant. Students and masters moved freely from town to town as they chose. Such mobility gave them a unique independence from their surroundings.

Masters also formed their own protective associations and established procedures and standards for certification to teach within their ranks. The first academic degree was a certifi-

The University of Bologna in central Italy was distinguished as the center for the revival of Roman law. This carving on the tomb of a Bologna professor of law shows students attending one of his lectures. [Scala/Art Resource, N.Y.]

cate that licensed one to teach, a *licentia docendi*. It granted graduates in the liberal arts program, the program basic to all higher learning, as well as those in the higher professional sciences of medicine, theology, and law, "the right to teach anywhere" (*ius ibique docendi*).

Bologna was famous for the revival of Roman law. During the Frankish era and later, from the seventh to the eleventh centuries, only the most rudimentary manuals of Roman law had survived. With the growth of trade and towns in the late eleventh century, Western scholars had come into contact with the larger and more important parts of the *Corpus Juris Civilis* of Justinian, which had been lost during the intervening centuries. The study and dissemination of this recovered material was now undertaken in Bologna under the direction of a learned man named Irnerius, who flourished in the early twelfth century. He and his students made authoritative commentaries or glosses on existing laws based on their newly broadened knowledge of the *Corpus Juris*. They thereby expanded legal knowledge. Around 1140, a monk named Gratian, also resident in Bologna, created the standard legal text in Church, or canon, law, the

Concordance of Discordant Canons, known simply as Gratian's *Decretum*.

As Bologna was the model for southern European universities (that is, those of Spain, Italy, and southern France) and the study of law, so Paris became the model for northern European universities and the study of theology. Oxford, Cambridge, and (much later) Heidelberg were among its imitators. All these universities required a foundation in the liberal arts for advanced study in the higher sciences of medicine, theology, and law. The arts program consisted of the *trivium* (grammar, rhetoric, and logic) and the *quadrivium* (arithmetic, geometry, astronomy, and music) or, more simply, the language arts and the mathematical arts.

Cathedral Schools

Before the emergence of universities, the liberal arts had been taught in cathedral and monastery schools. The purpose of these schools was to train the clergy, and their curricula tended understandably to be narrowly restricted to this goal. But by the late eleventh and twelfth centuries, cathedral schools also began to provide

The architecture of the early Middle Ages is known as Romanesque because it is closely related to the style of the late Roman Empire. It is characterized by thick stone walls and rounded arches that support the roof. The few windows are often very small, mere slits, giving Romanesque buildings a fortresslike appearance. Shown here is the Abbey of Germigny-des-Prés in northern France. [Giraudon/Art Resource, N.Y.]

Beginning in the mid-twelfth century, the Gothic style evolved from Romanesque architecture. The word Gothic at first meant "barbaric," and was applied to the new style by its critics. Its most distinctive visible features are its ribbed, criss-crossing vaulting, its pointed rather than rounded arches, and its prominent exterior "flying" buttresses. The vaulting, the exterior flying buttresses, and the increased height they made possible give prominence to the strong vertical aspect of Gothic buildings. The buttresses, by shifting much of the structural weight of the buildings off the walls, also made possible wide expanses of windows—hence the extensive use of stained glass and the characteristic colored light that often floods Gothic cathedrals. Use of the windows to show stories from the Bible, saints' lives, and local events was similar to earlier use of mosaics. Shown here is an example of French Gothic, Reims Cathedral, where the kings of France were crowned. [Scala/Art Resource, N.Y.]

lectures for nonclerical students and they broadened their curricula to include some training for purely secular vocations. In 1179, a papal decree obliged cathedrals to provide teachers gratis for laity who wanted to learn.

After 1200, increasing numbers of future notaries and merchants who had no particular interest in becoming priests, but who needed Latin and related intellectual disciplines to fill their secular positions, studied side by side with aspiring priests in cathedral and monastery schools. By the thirteenth century, the demand for secretaries and notaries in the growing urban and territorial governments and for literate personnel in the expanding merchant firms gave rise to special schools for strictly secular vocational preparation. With the appearance of these schools, the Church began for the first time to lose some of its monopoly on higher education.

The most famous of the cathedral schools were those of Rheims and Chartres. Chartres won fame under the direction of such distinguished teachers as Fulbert, Saint Ivo, and Saint Bernard of Chartres (not to be confused with the more famous Saint Bernard of Clairvaux). Gerbert, who later became Pope Sylvester II (r. 999–1003), guided Rheims to greatness in the last quarter of the tenth century. Gerbert was filled with enthusiasm for knowledge and promoted both logical and rhetorical studies. He did much to raise the study of logic to preeminence within the liberal arts, despite his personal belief in the greater relevance of rhetoric to the promotion of Christianity.

University of Paris

The University of Paris grew institutionally out of the cathedral school of Notre Dame, among others. King Philip Augustus and Pope Innocent III gave the new university its charter in 1200. At Paris the college, or house system, originated. At first, a college was just a hospice providing room and board for poor students who could not afford to rent rooms in town. But the educational life of the university quickly expanded into

Ca' d' Oro, Venice, 1422–1440. This late Gothic home (palazzo) of a wealthy person reflects strong Eastern influence in its arches and latticework. [Scala/Art Resource, N.Y.]

fixed structures and began to thrive on their sure endowments. University-run colleges made the overseeing and protection of students easier and gave the university a new prominence as a permanent urban institution.

In Paris, the most famous college was the Sorbonne, founded around 1257 by Robert de Sorbon, chaplain to the king, for the housing of theology students. In Oxford and Cambridge, the colleges became the basic unit of student life and were indistinguishable from the university proper. By the end of the Middle Ages such colleges had tied universities to physical plants and fixed foundations. Their mobility was forevermore restricted and hence also, compared with earlier times, their autonomy and freedom.

As a group, students at Paris had power and prestige. They enjoyed royal protections and privileges denied ordinary citizens. Many Parisian students were well-to-do, and not a few were spoiled and petulant. They did not endear themselves to the townspeople, whom they considered to be inferior. That townspeople sometimes let their resentments of such students lead to violence against them is made clear from the city's ordinances. City law forbade the beating of students. Only those students who had clearly committed serious crimes could be imprisoned. Only in self-defense might a citizen strike a student. All citizens were obligated to testify against anyone seen abusing a student. University laws also required all teachers to be carefully examined before being licensed to teach Parisian students. The law thus recognized students as both a valuable and a vulnerable resource.

The Curriculum

Before the so-called renaissance of the twelfth century, when many Greek and Arabic texts became available to Western scholars and students in Latin translations, the education available within the cathedral and monastery schools had been quite limited. Students learned grammar, rhetoric, and some elementary geometry and astronomy. They had the classical Latin grammars of Donatus and Priscian, Saint Augustine's treatise *On Christian Doctrine,* and Cassiodorus's treatise *On Divine and Secular Learning.* The writings of Boethius provided instruction in arithmetic and music and pre-

served the small body of Aristotle's logical works then known in the West. After the textual finds of the early twelfth century, Western scholars recovered the whole of Aristotle's logic, the astronomy of Ptolemy, the writings of Euclid, and many Latin classics. By the mid-thirteenth century, almost all of Aristotle's works circulated in the West.

In the High Middle Ages the learning process remained very basic. The assumption was that truth already existed; it was not something that one had to go out and find. It was there, requiring only to be properly organized, elucidated, and defended. Such conviction made logic and dialectic the focus of education. Students wrote commentaries on authoritative texts, especially those of Aristotle and the Church fathers. Teachers did not encourage students to strive independently for undiscovered truth. Students rather learned to organize and harmonize the accepted truths of tradition, which were drilled into them.

This method of study, based on logic and dialectic, was known as Scholasticism. It reigned supreme in all the faculties, in law and medicine as well as in philosophy and theology. Students read the traditional authorities in their field, formed short summaries of their teaching, disputed them with their peers by elaborating traditional arguments pro and con, and then drew conclusions. Logic and dialectic dominated arts training because they were the tools that could discipline knowledge and thought. Dialectic is a negative logical inquiry, the art of discovering a truth by finding the contradictions in arguments against it. Astonishingly, medical students did no practical work; they studied and debated the authoritative texts just as the law and theology students did.

Few books existed for students and, because printing with movable type did not yet exist, those available were expensive hand-copied works. So students could not leisurely master a subject in the quiet of their studies. They had rather to learn it in discussion, lecture, and debate. There was a lot of memorizing and the ability to think on one's feet was stressed. Rhetoric, or persuasive argument, was the ultimate goal, that is, the ability to make an eloquent defense of the knowledge one had clarified by logic and dialectic. Successful students became virtual walking encyclopedias; their education

Student Life at the University of Paris

As the following account by Jacques de Vitry makes clear, not all students at the University of Paris in the thirteenth century were there to gain knowledge. Students fought constantly and subjected each other to ethnic insults and slurs.

◆ *Why were students from different lands so prejudiced against one another? Does the rivalry of faculty members appear to have been as intense as that among students? What are the student criticisms of the faculty? Do they sound credible?*

Almost all the students at Paris, foreigners and natives, did absolutely nothing except learn or hear something new. Some studied merely to acquire knowledge, which is curiosity; others to acquire fame, which is vanity; others still for the sake of gain, which is cupidity and the vice of simony. Very few studied for their own edification, or that of others. They wrangled and disputed not merely about the various sects or about some discussions; but the differences between the countries also caused dissensions, hatreds and virulent animosities among them, and they impudently uttered all kinds of affronts and insults against one another.

They affirmed that the English were drunkards and had tails; the sons of France proud, effeminate and carefully adorned like women. They said that the Germans were furious and obscene at their feasts; the Normans, vain and boastful; the Poitevins, traitors and always adventurers. The Burgundians they considered vulgar and stupid. The Bretons were reputed to be fickle and changeable, and were often reproached for the death of Arthur. The Lombards were called avaricious, vicious and cowardly; the Romans, seditious, turbulent and slanderous; the Sicilians, tyrannical and cruel; the inhabitants of Brabant, men of blood, incendiaries, brigands and ravishers; the Flemish, fickle, prodigal, gluttonous, yielding as butter, and slothful. After such insults from words they often came to blows.

I will not speak of those logicians [professors of logic and dialectic] before whose eyes flitted constantly "the lice of Egypt," that is to say, all the sophistical subtleties, so that no one could comprehend their eloquent discourses in which, as says Isaiah, "there is no wisdom." As to the doctors of theology, "seated in Moses' seat," they were swollen with learning, but their charity was not edifying. Teaching and not practicing, they have "become as sounding brass or a tinkling cymbal," or like a canal of stone, always dry, which ought to carry water to "the bed of spices." They not only hated one another, but by their flatteries they enticed away the students of others; each one seeking his own glory, but caring not a whit about the welfare of souls.

Translations and Reprints from the Original Sources of European History, Vol. 2 (Philadelphia: Department of History, University of Pennsylvania, 1902), pp. 19–20.

both filled their heads with knowledge and gave them the ability to recite it impressively.

THE SUMMA The twelfth century saw the rise of the *summa*, an authoritative summary of allegedly all that was known about a particular subject. The summa's main purpose was to conciliate traditional authorities and heap up clari-fied truth. In canon law there was Gratian's *Concordance of Discordant Canons* (around 1142), whose very title embodies the scholastic method. In theology, there was Peter Lombard's *Four Books of Sentences* (1155–1157). Embracing traditional teaching on God, the Creation, Christ, and the sacraments, it was destined to become the standard theological textbook until the Protestant reformers declared it unbiblical. It had evolved from Peter Abelard's *Sic et Non* (around 1122), a much smaller work that juxtaposed seemingly contradictory statements on the same subject by revered authorities. Out of this same tradition came Saint Thomas Aquinas's magnificent *Summa Theologiae* (begun in 1265), to many the last word on theology, which the medieval summa was always intended to be.

University study normally began between the ages of twelve and fifteen. Students coming to

Thomas Aquinas Proves the Existence of God

People in the Middle Ages saw continuity between earth and heaven, the world of the living and the world of the dead. For intellectuals, reason and revelation, while different, were also believed to be connected, so that reasoned argument could prove some of what the Bible revealed to faith. Thomas Aquinas, perhaps the greatest medieval theologian, here states his famous five arguments for the existence of God, which he believed any rational person would agree with.

◆ *Are these arguments persuasive? Which is the most persuasive, which the least? Are they basically the same argument?*

Is there a God?

REPLY: There are five ways in which one can prove that there is a God.

The FIRST . . . is based on change. Some things . . . are certainly in process of change: this we plainly see. Now anything in the process of change is being changed by something else. . . . Hence one is bound to arrive at some first cause of change not itself being changed by anything, and this is what everybody understands by God.

The SECOND way is based on the nature of causation. In the observable world causes are found to be ordered in series. . . . Such a series must however stop somewhere. . . . One is therefore forced to suppose some first cause, to which everyone gives the name "God."

The THIRD way is based on what need not be and on what must be. . . . Some . . . things . . . can be, but need not be for we find them springing up and dying away. . . . Now everything cannot be like this [for then we must conclude that] once upon a time there was nothing. But if that were true there would be nothing even now, because some thing that does not exist can only be brought into being by something already existing. . . . One is forced therefore to suppose something which must be . . . [and] is itself the cause that other things must be.

The FOURTH way is based on the gradation observed in things. Some things are found to be more good, more true, more noble . . . and other things less [so]. But such comparative terms describe varying degrees of approximation to a superlative . . . [something that is] the truest and best and most noble of things. . . . There is something, therefore, which causes in all other things their being, their goodness, and whatever other perfection they have. And this we call "God."

The FIFTH way is based on the guidedness of nature. An orderedness of actions to an end is observed in all bodies obeying natural laws . . . ; they truly tend to a goal and do not merely hit it by accident. . . . Everything in nature, therefore, is directed to its goal by someone with intelligence, and this we call "God."

Thomas Aquinas, Summa Theologiae, I, *ed. by Thomas Gilby (Image Books, New York: 1969), pp. 67–70.*

university were expected to bring with them a good knowledge of Latin gained in local schools or from a private tutor. Once there, students spent four years perfecting their Latin (particularly in the study of the *trivium*) before attaining the bachelor of arts degree. A master's degree thereafter might take three or four years, during which time students studied mathematics, natural science, and philosophy by way of classical texts. A degree in theology at Paris might take more than twenty years of study from beginning to end.

CRITICS OF SCHOLASTICISM Even in the heyday of Scholasticism, this kind of education had its strong critics. Prominent among them were John of Salisbury (ca. 1120–1180) and Saint Bernard of Clairvaux (1090–1153), who thought the scholastic method to be a heartless and presumptuous way to train minds and a threat to the Church.

There were critics also within the ordinary faculty ranks, the so-called *dictatores*. These professional grammarians and rhetoricians, the forerunners of later humanists, gave students practical instruction in the composition of letters and documents. They taught good writing and speaking and, in contrast to the highly abstract logic and dialectic of scholastic education, they stressed practice over theory. (The difference might be compared with that between a modern expository writing program, where execution is the focus, and a modern English department, where theory is the focus.) Later humanists, establishing an approach still favored in modern liberal arts education, would urge scholars to go directly to sources in their original languages and draw their own conclusions.

Philosophy and Theology

Scholastics quarreled over the proper relationship between philosophy (which, for them, meant almost exclusively the writings of Aristotle) and theology (which they believed to be a special "science" based on divine revelation). The problem between philosophy and theology arose because, in Christian eyes, there was a lot of heresy in Aristotle's writings, especially as his teaching was interpreted by certain Islamic commentators. These commentators did not treat his work as a handmaiden to Christianity. For example, Aristotle believed in the eternality of the world (that the world had always been). This plainly called into question the Judeo-Christian teaching that the world had been created in time, as stressed in the book of Genesis. Aristotle also taught that intellect, or mind, was ultimately one, a seeming denial of individuality and hence of Christian teaching about individual responsibility and personal immortality.

When theologians took the logic and metaphysics of Aristotle over into their theologies, some critics believed it posed a threat to biblical teaching and traditional Church authority. Berengar of Tours (d. 1088), for example, was a scholastic who applied logic to the sacrament of the Eucharist; and before long he found himself questioning the Church's teaching on transubstantiation (which was not yet official dogma). Peter Abelard (1079–1142) tried to subject the Trinity to logical examination. He found that, by Aristotle's logic, three could not be one nor one three, in contrast to the Church's teachings about the unity of God the Father, Son, and Holy Ghost.

The boldness of these new logicians shocked conservatives. Monastic leaders especially wondered whether the liberal arts course of study, dominated by Aristotle's writings, was more foe than ally of theological study. The love of learning had clearly gotten in the way of the love of God as far as the critics of Scholasticism were concerned.

A century of such suspicion and criticism of Aristotle's alleged undermining of Christian theology culminated in 1277 when the bishop of Paris condemned 219 philosophical propositions. The condemnation was directed against scholars who seemed to the authorities to be more interested in secular philosophy than in Christian truth. It chilled the relationship between learning and religion. Reason and revelation thereafter became two very different spheres of knowledge, much as Church and state were then also being forced apart in the world of secular politics. William of Ockham (d. 1349) represented conservative opinion on the issue and signaled its future direction when he denied that essential matters of theology could be addressed as if they were empirical. To know God's mind, Christians must content themselves with biblical revelation; reason could not know God directly.

Roles in Medieval Society

Women

The image and the reality of medieval women are two very different things. The image, both for contemporaries and for us today, was strongly influenced by the views of male Christian clergy, whose ideal was the celibate life of chastity, poverty, and obedience. Drawing on classical medical, philosophical, and legal traditions that predated Christianity, as well as on ancient biblical theology, Christian theologians depicted women as physically, mentally, and morally weaker than men.

On the basis of such assumptions, medieval Church and society sanctioned the coercive treatment of women, including corrective wife beating in extreme cases. Christian clergy generally considered marriage a debased state by comparison with the religious life, and in their writings they praised virgins and celibate widows over wives. Women, as the Bible clearly taught, were the "weaker vessel." In marriage their role was to be subject and obedient to their husbands, who, as the stronger, had a duty to protect and discipline them.

This image of the medieval woman suggests that she had two basic options in life: to become either a subjugated housewife or a confined nun. In reality, the vast majority of medieval women were neither.

IMAGE AND STATUS Both within and outside Christianity this image of women—not yet to speak of the reality of their lives—was contradicted. In chivalric romances and courtly love literature of the twelfth and thirteenth centuries, as in the contemporaneous cult of the Virgin Mary, women were presented as objects of service and devotion to be praised and admired, even put on pedestals and treated as superior to men. If the Church shared traditional misogynist sentiments, it also condemned them, as in the case of the *Romance of the Rose*

(late thirteenth century) and other popular "bawdy" literature.

The learned churchman Peter Lombard (1100–1169) sanctioned an image of women that didactic Christian literature often invoked. Why, he asked, was Eve created from Adam's rib and not instead taken from his head or his feet? The answer was clear. God took Eve from Adam's side because he wanted woman neither to rule over nor to be enslaved by man, but to stand squarely at his side, as his companion and partner in mutual aid and trust. By so insisting on the spiritual equality of men and women and their shared responsibility to one another within marriage, the Church also helped to raise the dignity of women.

Germanic law treated women better than Roman law had done. Women had basic rights under law that prevented their being treated as chattel. And there was far greater equality between the sexes. Unlike Roman women, who as teens married men much older than themselves, German women married as adults and their husbands were of similar age. Another practice unknown to the Romans was the groom's conveyance of a marriage portion, or dowry, to his bride to have and to hold as her own in the event of widowhood. All the major Germanic law codes recognized the economic freedom of women, that is, their right to inherit, administer, dispose of, and confer on their children family property and wealth. They could also press charges in court against men for bodily injury and rape. Depending on the country in question, punishments for rape ranged from fines, flogging, and banishment to blinding, castration, and death.

LIFE CHOICES The nunnery was an option for only a very few unmarried women from the higher social classes. Entrance required a dowry (*dos*) and could be almost as expensive as a wedding, although usually it was less. Within the nunnery, a woman could rise to a position of leadership as abbess or mother superior and could exercise an organizational and administrative authority denied her in much of secular life. The nunneries of the established religious orders were also under male supervision, however, so that even abbesses had finally to answer to higher male authority.

Nunneries also provided women an escape from the debilitating effects of multiple pregnancies. In the ninth century, under the influence of Christianity, the Carolingians made monogamous marriage their official policy. Heretofore they had practiced polygyny and concubinage and had permitted divorce. The result was both a boon and a burden to women. On one hand, the selection of a wife now became a very special event, and wives gained greater dignity and legal security. On the other hand, a woman's labor as household manager and bearer of children greatly increased.

The aristocratic wife not only ran a large household but was also the agent of her husband during his absence. In addition to these responsibilities, one wife now had sole responsibility for the propagation of heirs. The Carolingian wife also became the sole object of her husband's wrath and displeasure. Such demands clearly took their toll. The mortality rates of Frankish women increased and their longevity decreased after the ninth century.

Under such conditions the cloister could serve as a welcome refuge to women. The number of women in cloisters was never very great, however. In late medieval England, for example, there are estimated to have been no more than 3,500.

The vast majority of medieval women were neither aristocratic housewives nor nuns, but working women. Much evidence suggests that they were respected and loved by their husbands, perhaps because they worked shoulder by shoulder and hour by hour with them. Between the ages of ten and fifteen, girls were apprenticed in a trade much as were boys, and they learned to be skilled workers. If they married, they might continue their particular trade, operating their bakeshops or dress shops next to their husbands' business, or become assistants and partners in the shops of their husbands. Women appeared in virtually every "blue-collar" trade, from butcher to goldsmith, although they were especially prominent in the food and clothing industries. Women belonged to guilds, just like men, and they became craftmasters. In the later Middle Ages, townswomen increasingly had the opportunity to go to school and to gain vernacular literacy.

It is also true that women did not have as

For unmarried noblewomen and well-to-do burgher women, the cloistered life became an alternative to spinsterhood; however, the number of women entering cloisters was never very great. [Alinari/Art Resource, N.Y.]

wide a range of vocations as men, although the vocational destinies of the vast majority of men were as fixed as those of women. Women were excluded from the learned professions of scholarship, medicine, and law. They often found their freedom of movement within a profession more carefully regulated than a man's. Usually, women performed the same work as men for a wage 25 percent lower. And, as is still true today, women filled the ranks of domestic servants in urban households in disproportionate numbers. Still, women remained as prominent

A fifteenth-century rendering of an eleventh- or twelfth-century marketplace. Medieval women were active in all trades, but especially in the food and clothing industries. [Scala/Art Resource, N.Y.]

and as creative a part of workaday medieval society as men.

Children

The image of medieval children and the reality of their lives seem also to have been two very different things. Until recently historians were inclined to believe that parents were emotionally distant from their children during the Middle Ages. Evidence of low esteem for children comes from a variety of sources.

CHILDREN AS "LITTLE ADULTS" Some historians maintain that children are rarely portrayed as different from adults in medieval art and sculpture. If pictorially children and adults look alike, were people in the Middle Ages aware of childhood as a separate period of life requiring special care and treatment? There was also high infant and child mortality, which, it seems, could only have discouraged parents from making a high emotional investment in their children. How could a parent dare to become attached emotionally to a child who had a 30–50 percent chance of dying before age five?

During the Middle Ages, children assumed adult responsibilities early in life. The children of peasants labored in the fields alongside their parents as soon as they could physically manage the work. Urban artisans and burghers sent their children out of their homes into apprenticeships in various crafts and trades between the ages of eight and twelve. Can such early removal of children from their homes be taken for anything but low affection for children? That children were expected to grow up fast is attested by the canonical ages for marriage, twelve for girls and fourteen for boys (although few married at these ages).

The practice of infanticide is an even more striking suggestion of low esteem for children in ancient and early medieval times. According to Tacitus, the Romans exposed unwanted children, especially girls, at birth. In this way they regulated family size. The surviving children appear to have been given plenty of attention and affection. The Germanic tribes of medieval Europe, by contrast, had large families, but tended to neglect their children in comparison with the Romans. Infanticide, particularly of girls, continued to be practiced in the early Middle Ages, as shown by its condemnation in penance books and by Church synods. Parents were forbidden to sleep with infants and small children to prevent them from being suffocated, either by accident or by design.

Among the German tribes, one paid a much lower *wergild*, or compensatory fine, for injury to a child than for injury to an adult. The *wergild* for injuring a child was only one-fifth that for injuring an adult. That paid for injury to a female child under fifteen was one-half that for injury to a male child—a strong indication that female children were the least esteemed members of German tribal society. Mothers appear also to have nursed boys longer than they did girls, which favored boys' health and survival. A woman's *wergild*, however, increased a full eightfold between infancy and her childbearing years, at which time she had obviously become highly prized.[4]

CHILDHOOD AS A SPECIAL STAGE Despite such varied evidence of parental distance and neglect, there is another side to the story. Since the early Middle Ages, physicians and theologians, at least, have clearly understood childhood to be a distinct and special stage of life. Isidore (560–636), the metropolitan of Seville and a leading intellectual authority throughout the Middle Ages, carefully distinguished six ages

of life, the first four of which were infancy (between one and seven years of age), childhood (seven to fourteen), adolescence, and youth.

According to the medical authorities, infancy proper extended from birth to anywhere between six months and two years (depending on the authority) and covered the period of speechlessness and suckling. The period thereafter, until age seven, was considered a higher level of infancy, marked by the beginning of a child's ability to speak and his or her weaning. At age seven, when a child could think and act decisively and speak clearly, childhood proper began. After this point, a child could be reasoned with, could profit from regular discipline, and could begin to train for a lifelong vocation. At seven a child was ready for schooling, private tutoring, or apprenticeship in a chosen craft or trade. Until physical growth was completed, however—and that could extend to twenty-one years of age—a child or youth was legally under the guardianship of parents or a surrogate authority.

There is evidence that high infant and child mortality, rather than distancing parents from children, actually made parents look on children as all the more precious. The medical authorities respected during the Middle Ages—Hippocrates, Galen, and Soranus of Ephesus—dealt at length with postnatal care and childhood diseases. Both in learned and popular medicine, sensible as well as fanciful cures can be found for the leading killers of children (diarrhea, worms, pneumonia, and fever). When

[4]*David Herlihy, "Medieval Children," in* Essays on Medieval Civilization, *ed. by B. K. Lackner and K. R. Phelp (University of Texas Press, 1978), pp. 109–131.*

Peasant women spinning and carding wool, from a fourteenth-century English manuscript showing women at their daily tasks. [Courtesy of the Trustees of the British Library]

infants and children died, medieval parents grieved as pitiably as modern parents do. In the art and literature of the Middle Ages, we find mothers baptizing dead infants and children or carrying them to pilgrim shrines in the hope of reviving them. There are also examples of mental illness and suicide brought on by the death of a child.[5]

Clear evidence of special attention being paid to children is also found in the great variety of children's toys, and even devices like walkers and potty chairs, that existed in the Middle Ages. The medieval authorities on child rearing widely condemned child abuse and urged moderation in the disciplining of children. In Church art and drama, parents were urged to love their children as Mary loved Jesus. And early apprenticeships may also be interpreted as an expression of parental love and concern rather than indifference and low esteem. For in the Middle Ages, no parental responsibility was thought greater than that of equipping a child for useful and gainful work. Certainly by the High Middle Ages, if not earlier, children were widely viewed as special creatures with their own needs and rights.

———————————◆———————————

During the High Middle Ages, the growth of Mediterranean trade revived old cities and caused the creation of new ones. The Crusades aided and abetted this development. Italian cities especially flourished during the late eleventh and twelfth centuries. Venice dominated Mediterranean trade and extended its political and economic influence throughout the Near East. It had its own safe ports as far away as Syria. As cities grew in population and became rich with successful trade, a new social group, the long-distance traders, rose to prominence. By marriage and political organization, these merchant families organized themselves into an unstoppable force. They successfully challenged the old nobility in and around the cities. A new elite of merchants gained control of city governments almost everywhere. They brought with them a policy of open trade and the blessings

and problems of nascent capitalism. Artisans and small shopkeepers at the lower end of the economic spectrum aspired to follow their example, as new opportunities opened for all. The seeds of social conflict and of urban class struggle had been sown.

One very positive result of the new wealth of towns was the patronage of education and culture. These matters were given an emphasis not experienced since Roman times. Western Europe's first universities appeared in the eleventh century and universities steadily expanded over the next four centuries. There were twenty by 1300. Not only did Scholasticism flourish, but a new literature, art, and architecture developed as well, reflecting both a new human vitality and the reshaping of society and politics. For all of this, western Europeans had no one to thank so much as the new class of merchants, whose greed, daring, and ambition made it all possible.

Review Questions

1. How did the responsibilities of the nobility differ from those of the clergy and the peasantry during the High Middle Ages? In what ways did each social class contribute to the stability of society?

2. What led to the revival of trade and the growth of towns in the twelfth century? What political and social conditions were essential for a revival of trade? How did towns change medieval society?

3. From your understanding of the functions of the medieval university, assess the strengths and weaknesses of higher education in that period. Comment especially on the curriculum.

4. How would you define Scholasticism? What was the Scholastic program and method of study? Who were the main critics of Scholasticism and what were their complaints?

5. How would you assess the position of women in Germanic law and Roman law? What were the options and responsibilities for women in each social class? What are the differing theories regarding the image of children in the Middle Ages?

[5]*Klaus Arnold,* Kind und Gesellschaft im Mittelalter und Renaissance *(Paderborn: 1980), pp. 31, 37.*

Suggested Readings

E. AMT (Ed.), *Women's Lives in Medieval Europe: A Sourcebook* (1993). Outstanding collection of sources.

P. ARIÈS, *Centuries of Childhood: A Social History of Family Life* (1962). Pioneer effort on the subject.

J. W. BALDWIN, *The Scholastic Culture of the Middle Ages: 1000–1300* (1971). Best brief synthesis available.

R. L. BENSON AND G. CONSTABLE, eds., *Renaissance and Renewal in the Twelfth Century* (1982). The world of twelfth-century education documented in great detail.

M. BLOCH, *French Rural History*, trans. by J. Sondheimer (1966). A classic by a great modern historian.

G. DUBY, *The Three Orders: Feudal Society Imagined*, trans. by A. Goldhammer (1981). Large, comprehensive, authoritative.

E. GILSON, *Heloise and Abelard* (1968). Analysis and defense of medieval scholarly and gender values.

B. A. HANAWALT, *The Ties That Bound: Peasant Families in Medieval England* (1986). Illuminating demographic and economic study of rural life.

C. H. HASKINS, *The Renaissance of the Twelfth Century* (1927). Still the standard account.

C. H. HASKINS, *The Rise of Universities* (1972). A short, minor classic.

D. HERLIHY, *Medieval Households* (1985). Bread-and-butter account of household structure in antiquity and the Middle Ages.

G. KÜNSTLER, *Romanesque Art in Europe* (1973). Standard survey.

G. LEFF, *Paris and Oxford Universities in the Thirteenth and Fourteenth Centuries: An Institutional and Intellectual History* (1968). Very good on Scholastic debates.

R. S. LOOMIS (Ed.), *The Development of Arthurian Romance* (1963). Essays debating its meaning and significance.

R. LOPEZ, *The Commercial Revolution of the Middle Ages 900–1350* (1971). A master's brief survey.

E. MÂLE, *The Gothic Image: Religious Art in France in the Thirteenth Century* (1913). An enduring classic.

L. DE MAUSE (Ed.), *The History of Childhood* (1974). Very substantive and provocative essays with an interest in the inner as well as the material lives of children.

K. MERTES, *The English Noble Household 1250–1600* (1988). Good background for the debate over the structure and quality of English family life.

R. I. MOORE, *The Formation of a Persecuting Society: Power and Deviance in Western Europe, 950–1250* (1987). A sympathetic look at heresy and dissent.

A. MURRAY, *Reason and Society in the Middle Ages* (1978). A view of the Middle Ages as an age of reason as well as of faith.

J. T. NOONAN, *Contraception: A History of Its Treatment by the Catholic Theologians and Canonists* (1967). Fascinating account of medieval theological attitudes toward sexuality and sex-related problems.

E. PANOFSKY, *Gothic Architecture and Scholasticism* (1951). A controversial classic.

H. PIRENNE, *Medieval Cities: Their Origins and the Revival of Trade*, trans. by F. D. Halsey (1970). A minor classic.

H. RASHDALL, *The Universities of Europe in the Middle Ages*, Vols. 1–3 (1936). Dated but still extremely useful for documents of the period.

S. REYNOLDS, *Kingdoms and Communities in Western Europe, 900–1300* (1984). A study of the shaping of Europe.

I. S. ROBINSON, *The Papacy 1073–1198: Continuity and Innovation* (1990). A fresh look at the papacy in this period of its reform and independence.

F. RÖRIG, *The Medieval Town*, trans. by D. J. A. Matthew (1972). Excellent study of the towns of northern Europe.

S. SHAHAR, *The Fourth Estate: A History of Women in the Middle Ages* (1983). A comprehensive survey, making clear the great variety of women's work.

R. W. SOUTHERN, *Medieval Humanism and Other Studies* (1970). Provocative and far-ranging essays on topics in intellectual history.

B. STOCK, *The Implications of Literacy* (1983). How the ability to read changed medieval society.

L. THORNDIKE, *University Records and Life in the Middle Ages* (1975). Rich primary sources for both curricular and extracurricular life.

Europe in Transition, 1300–1750

BETWEEN the early fourteenth and the mid-eighteenth centuries, Europe underwent many far-reaching changes. These were years of massive physical suffering brought on by disease and war and of new political and cultural construction made possible by better government and growing wealth.

The era began with one of the greatest disasters in European history: a bubonic plague, known as the *Black Death,* that had killed an estimated two-fifths of the population by the mid-fourteenth century. A hundred years of sharp conflicts between popes and secular rulers preceded this demographic crisis and a hundred years of warfare between England and France followed it. The emergence of strong, ruthless monarchs accompanied the decline in papal power during the later Middle Ages. Commanding greater economic and military resources, these new rulers gained control over the Church in their lands. By the fourteenth century, the nation-states of Europe were warring with one another, no longer with the armies of the pope.

The fourteenth century also saw the beginning of the great cultural resurgence in Europe known as the *Renaissance.* This rebirth of education and culture was closely associated with the rediscovery of forgotten classical Greek and Latin writings and the rapid growth of colleges and universities throughout western Europe.

The past was not the only previously uncharted region Europeans set out to explore. In the late fifteenth century, they began voyages to America, around Africa, and across the Indian Ocean to Asia that introduced them to unfamiliar cultures and non-Western values. Beginning with Copernicus and culminating

with Sir Isaac Newton, scientists charted a new view of the universe. Between them the voyages of discovery and the Scientific Revolution gave Europeans both new confidence in the power of the human mind and a new perspective on their society.

In the sixteenth century, a religious revolt divided Europe spiritually and led to a major restructuring of western Christendom. The Protestant Reformation began in 1517 when an obscure German professor named Martin Luther challenged the religious teaching and authority of the papacy. Within a quarter century, Europe was permanently divided among a growing variety of Protestant churches and the Roman Catholic church. For a century and a half, these new religious differences also fueled political conflict. Religious warfare devastated France in the second half of the sixteenth century and wreaked havoc on Germany in the first half of the seventeenth century.

By the middle of the seventeenth century, most religious warfare had ended. The religious turmoil had strengthened the hand of the secular state. For many rulers and their subjects, political stability became a higher value than religious allegiance. By the early eighteenth century, Europe's rulers (with the notable exception of the English monarchs, who had the will but not the ability) imitated the French king Louis XIV. Through efficient taxation, a loyal administration, and a powerful standing army, Louis bent France to his will, making it the model of the new absolute state to which rulers everywhere aspired. By the second half of the seventeenth century, the balance of power shifted away from Spain, which had dominated Europe during the sixteenth century. France, Austria, and Prussia joined the new parliamentary monarchy of Great Britain as Europe's new masters. And, for the first time, Russia emerged as a major European power.

With the end of religious conflict, energies turned toward economic expansion. New and more efficient farming methods appeared, and nations took the first steps toward industrialization. In the New World, the colonies grew and were consolidated. By the eighteenth century, competition over trade had replaced religion as the cause of war. The demand for political independence, most notably by the English colonies in America, replaced the earlier demands for religious independence. A new age had dawned, one still believing in the power of God, but increasingly fascinated by human political power. ◆

1300–1400	*1309–1377* Pope resides in Avignon *1337–1453* Hundred Years' War *1356 Golden Bull* formalizes German electoral college
1400–1500	*1415–1433* Hussite revolt in Bohemia *1428–1519* Aztecs expand in central Mexico *1429* Joan of Arc leads French to victory *1434* Medici rule begins in Florence *1453–1471* Wars of the Roses in England *1469* Marriage of Ferdinand and Isabella *1487* Henry Tudor creates Court of Star Chamber
1500–1600	*1519* Charles V crowned Holy Roman emperor *1530 Augsburg Confession* defines Lutheranism *1547* Ivan the Terrible becomes tsar of Russia *1555 Peace of Augsburg* recognizes the legal principle, *cuius regio, eius religio* *1558–1603* Reign of Elizabeth I of England *1572* St. Bartholomew's Day Massacre *1588* English defeat of Spanish Armada *1598* Edict of Nantes gives Huguenots religious and civil rights
1600–1700	*1624–1642* Era of Richelieu in France *1629–1640* Charles I's years of personal rule *1640* Long Parliament convenes *1642* Outbreak of the Civil War in England *1643–1661* Cardinal Mazarin regent for Louis XIV *1648* Peace of Westphalia *1649–1652* The Fronde in France *1649* Charles I executed *1660* Charles II restored to the English throne *1661–1715* Louis XIV's years of personal rule *1682–1725* Reign of Peter the Great *1685* Louis XIV revokes Edict of Nantes *1688* Glorious Revolution in Britain
1700–1789	*1700–1721* Great Northern War *1702–1714* War of Spanish Succession *1713* Peace of Utrecht *1720–1740* Walpole in England, Fleury in France *1740* Maria Theresa succeeds to Habsburg throne *1740–1748* War of the Austrian Succession *1756–1763* Seven Years' War *1767* Legislative Commission in Russia *1772* First Partition of Poland *1776* American Declaration of Independence *1778* France aids the American colonies

Society and Economy	Religion and Culture
	1300–1325 Dante Alighieri writes *Divine Comedy*
1315–1317 Greatest famine of the Middle Ages	1302 Boniface VIII issues bull *Unam Sanctam*
1347–1350 Black Death peaks	1350 Boccaccio, *Decameron*
1358 Jacquerie shakes France	1375–1527 The Renaissance in Italy
1378 Ciompi revolt in Florence	1378–1417 The Great Schism
1381 English peasants' revolt	1380–1395 Chaucer writes *Canterbury Tales*
	1390–1430 Christine de Pisan defends women
	1414–1417 The Council of Constance
1450 Johann Gutenberg invents printing with movable type	1425–1450 Lorenzo Valla exposes the *Donation of Constantine*
	1450 Thomas à Kempis, *Imitation of Christ*
1492 Christopher Columbus encounters the Americas	1492 Expulsion of Jews from Spain
1498 Vasco da Gama reaches India	
	1513 Niccolo Machiavelli, *The Prince*
1519 Hernan Cortes lands in Mexico	1516 Erasmus compiles a Greek New Testament
1519–1522 Magellan circumnavigates the earth	1516 Thomas More, *Utopia*
1525 German Peasants' Revolt	1517 Martin Luther's Ninety-five Theses
1531–1533 Francisco Pizarro conquers the Incas	1534 Henry VIII declared head of English Church
	1540 Jesuit Order founded
1540 Spanish open silver mines in Peru, Bolivia, and Mexico	1541 John Calvin becomes Geneva's reformer
	1543 Copernicus, *On the Revolutions*
	1545–1563 Council of Trent
1550–1600 The great witch panics	1549 English *Book of Common Prayer*
1600–1700 Dutch economic prosperity	1605 Bacon, *The Advancement of Learning*; Shakespeare, *King Lear*; Cervantes, *Don Quixote*
1600–early 1700s Spain maintains commercial monopoly in Latin America	1609 Kepler, *On the Motion of Mars*
1607 English settle Jamestown, Virginia	1611 King James Version of the English Bible
1608 French settle Quebec	1632 Galileo, *Dialogues on the Two Chief Systems of the World*
1618–1648 Thirty Years' War devastates Germany	
1619 First African slaves in Virginia	1637 Descartes, *Discourse on Method*
1650s–1670s Anglo-Dutch commercial rivalry	1651 Hobbes, *Leviathan*
1661–1683 Colbert guides French economy	
	1687 Newton, *Principia Mathematica*
	1689 English Toleration Act
1690 Paris Foundling Hospital established	1690 Locke, *Essay Concerning Human Understanding*
1715–1763 Colonial rivalry in the Caribbean	1739 Wesley begins field preaching
1719 Mississippi Bubble in France	1748 Montesquieu, *Spirit of the Laws*
1733 James Kay's flying shuttle	1750 Rousseau, *Discourse on the Moral Effects of the Arts and Sciences*
1750s Agricultural Revolution in Britain	
1750–1840 Growth of new cities	1751 First volume Diderot's *Encyclopedia*
1763 Britain becomes dominant in India	1762 Rousseau, *Social Contract* and *Émile*
1763–1789 Enlightened absolutist rulers seek to spur economic growth	1763 Voltaire, *Treatise on Toleration*
	1774 Goethe, *Sorrows of Young Werther*
1765 James Hargreaves's spinning jenny	1776 Smith, *Wealth of Nations*
1769 Richard Arkwright's waterframe	1781 Kant, *Critique of Pure Reason*
1771–1775 Pugachev's Rebellion	Joseph II adopts toleration in Austria

In the fourteenth and fifteenth centuries, warfare and plague engulfed Europe as never before, and Europeans discovered the power of death and destruction in new and terrible ways. Here Death leads a physician to his own death, as the physician examines his uroscope in vain (examination of urine was the medieval physician's key diagnostic test). Late fifteenth century.[D.Y./Art Resource]

9

The Late Middle Ages (1300–1527): Centuries of Crisis

Political and Social Breakdown
The Hundred Years' War and the Rise of
National Sentiment
Progress of the War
The Black Death
Preconditions and Causes
Popular Remedies
Social and Economic Consequences

New Conflicts and Opportunities
Ecclesiastical Breakdown and Revival: The
Late Medieval Church
The Thirteenth-Century Papacy
Boniface VIII and Philip the Fair
The Avignon Papacy (1309–1377)
The Great Schism (1378–1417) and the
Conciliar Movement to 1449

Key Topics in This Chapter
◆ The Hundred Years' War between England and France
◆ The effects of the bubonic plague on population and society
◆ The growing power of secular rulers over the papacy
◆ Schism, heresy, and reform of the Church

The late Middle Ages saw almost unprecedented political, social, and ecclesiastical calamity. France and England grappled with each other in a bitter conflict known as the Hundred Years' War (1337–1453), an exercise in seemingly willful self-destruction that was made even more terrible in its later stages by the introduction of gunpowder and the invention of heavy artillery. Bubonic plague, known to contemporaries as the Black Death, swept over almost all of Europe, killing as much as one-third of the population in many regions between 1348 and 1350 and transforming many pious Christians into

believers in the omnipotence of death. A schism emerged within the Church that lasted thirty-nine years (1378–1417) and led, by 1409, to the election of no fewer than three competing popes and colleges of cardinals. In 1453 the Turks marched seemingly invincibly through Constantinople and toward the West. As their political and religious institutions buckled, as disease, bandits, and wolves attacked their cities in the wake of war, and as Islamic armies gathered at their borders, Europeans beheld what seemed to be the imminent total collapse of Western civilization.

It was in this period that such scholars as Marsilius of Padua, William of Ockham, and Lorenzo Valla produced lasting criticisms of medieval assumptions about the nature of God, humankind, and society. Kings worked through parliaments and clergy through councils to place lasting limits on the pope's temporal power. The tradition, derived from Roman law, that a secular ruler is accountable to the body of which he or she is head had already found expression in documents like Magna Carta. It came increasingly to carry the force of accepted principle and conciliarists (advocates of the judicial superiority of a church council over a pope) sought to extend it to establish papal accountability to the Church.

But viewed for their three great calamities—war, plague, and schism—the fourteenth and fifteenth centuries were years in which politics resisted wisdom, nature strained mercy, and the Church was less than faithful to its mandate.

Political and Social Breakdown

The Hundred Years' War and the Rise of National Sentiment

Medieval governments were by no means all-powerful and secure. The rivalry of petty lords kept localities in turmoil and dynastic rivalries could plunge entire lands into war, especially when power was being transferred to a new ruler, and woe to the ruling dynasty that failed to produce a male heir.

To field the armies and collect the revenues that made their existence possible, late medieval rulers depended on carefully negotiated alliances among a wide range of lesser powers. Like kings and queens in earlier centuries, they too practiced the art of feudal government, but on a grander scale and with greater sophistication. To maintain the order they required, the Norman kings of England and the Capetian kings of France fine-tuned traditional feudal relationships, stressing the duties of lesser to higher power and the unquestioning loyalty noble vassals owed the king. The result was a degree of centralized royal power unseen before in these lands and a nascent "national" consciousness that equipped both France and England for international warfare.

THE CAUSES OF THE WAR The conflict that came to be known as the Hundred Years' War began in May 1337 and lasted until October 1453. The English king Edward III (r. 1327–1377), the grandson of Philip the Fair of France (r. 1285–1314), may be said to have started the war by asserting a claim to the French throne when the French king Charles IV (r. 1322–1328), the last of Philip the Fair's surviving sons, died without a male heir. The French barons had no intention of placing the then fifteen-year-old Edward on the French throne, choosing instead the first cousin of

Edward III pays homage to his feudal lord Philip VI of France. Legally, Edward was a vassal of the king of France. [Archives Snark International/ Art Resource, N.Y.]

Charles IV, Philip VI of Valois (r. 1328–1350), the first of a new French dynasty that ruled into the sixteenth century.

But there was more to the war than just an English king's assertion of a claim to the French throne. England and France were then emergent territorial powers in too close proximity to one another. Edward was actually a vassal of Philip's, holding several sizable French territories as fiefs from the king of France, a relationship that went back to the days of the Norman conquest. English possession of any French land was repugnant to the French because it threatened the royal policy of centralization. England and France also quarreled over control of Flanders, which, although a French fief, was subject to political influence from England because its principal industry, the manufacture of cloth, depended on supplies of imported English wool. Compounding these frictions was a long history of prejudice and animosity between the French and English people, who constantly confronted one another on the high seas and in port towns. Taken together, these various factors made the Hundred Years' War a struggle for national identity as well as for control of territory.

FRENCH WEAKNESS France had three times the population of England, was far the wealthier of the two countries, and fought on its own soil. Yet, for the greater part of the conflict, until after 1415, the major battles ended in often stunning English victories (see Map 9-1). The primary reason for these French failures was internal disunity caused by endemic social conflicts. Unlike England, France was still struggling in the fourteenth century to make the transition from a fragmented feudal society to a centralized "modern" state.

Desperate to raise money for the war, French kings resorted to financial policies, such as depreciating the currency and borrowing heavily from Italian bankers, that aggravated internal conflicts. In 1355, in a bid to secure funds, the king convened a representative council of townsmen and noblemen that came to be known as the *Estates General*. Although it levied taxes at the king's request, its members also used the king's plight to enhance their own regional rights and privileges, thereby deepening territorial divisions.

France's defeats also reflected English military superiority. English infantry was more disciplined than the French, and English archers carried a formidable weapon, the longbow, capable of firing six arrows a minute with enough force to pierce an inch of wood or the armor of a knight at two hundred yards.

Finally, French weakness during the Hundred Years' War was due in no small degree to the comparative mediocrity of its royal leadership. English kings were far the shrewder.

Progress of the War

The war had three major stages of development, each ending with a seemingly decisive victory by one or the other side.

THE CONFLICT DURING THE REIGN OF EDWARD III In the first stage of the war, Edward embargoed English wool to Flanders, sparking urban rebellions by merchants and the trade guilds. Inspired by a rich merchant, Jacob van Artevelde, the Flemish cities, led by Ghent, revolted against the French and in 1340 these same cities signed an alliance with England acknowledging Edward as king of France. On June 23 of that same year, in the first great battle of the war, Edward defeated the French fleet in the Bay of Sluys, but his subsequent effort to invade France by way of Flanders failed.

In 1346 Edward attacked Normandy and, after a series of easy victories that culminated at the Battle of Crécy, seized Calais. Exhaustion of both sides and the onset of the Black Death forced a truce in late 1347, and the war entered a brief lull. In 1356, near Poitiers, the English won their greatest victory, routing France's noble cavalry and taking the French king, John II the Good (r. 1350–1364), captive back to England. The defeat brought a complete breakdown of political order to France.

Power in France now lay with the Estates General. Led by the powerful merchants of Paris under Étienne Marcel, it took advantage of royal weakness, demanding and receiving rights similar to those granted the English privileged classes in Magna Carta. But unlike the English Parliament, which represented the interests of a comparatively unified English nobility, the French Estates General was too divided to be an instrument for effective government.

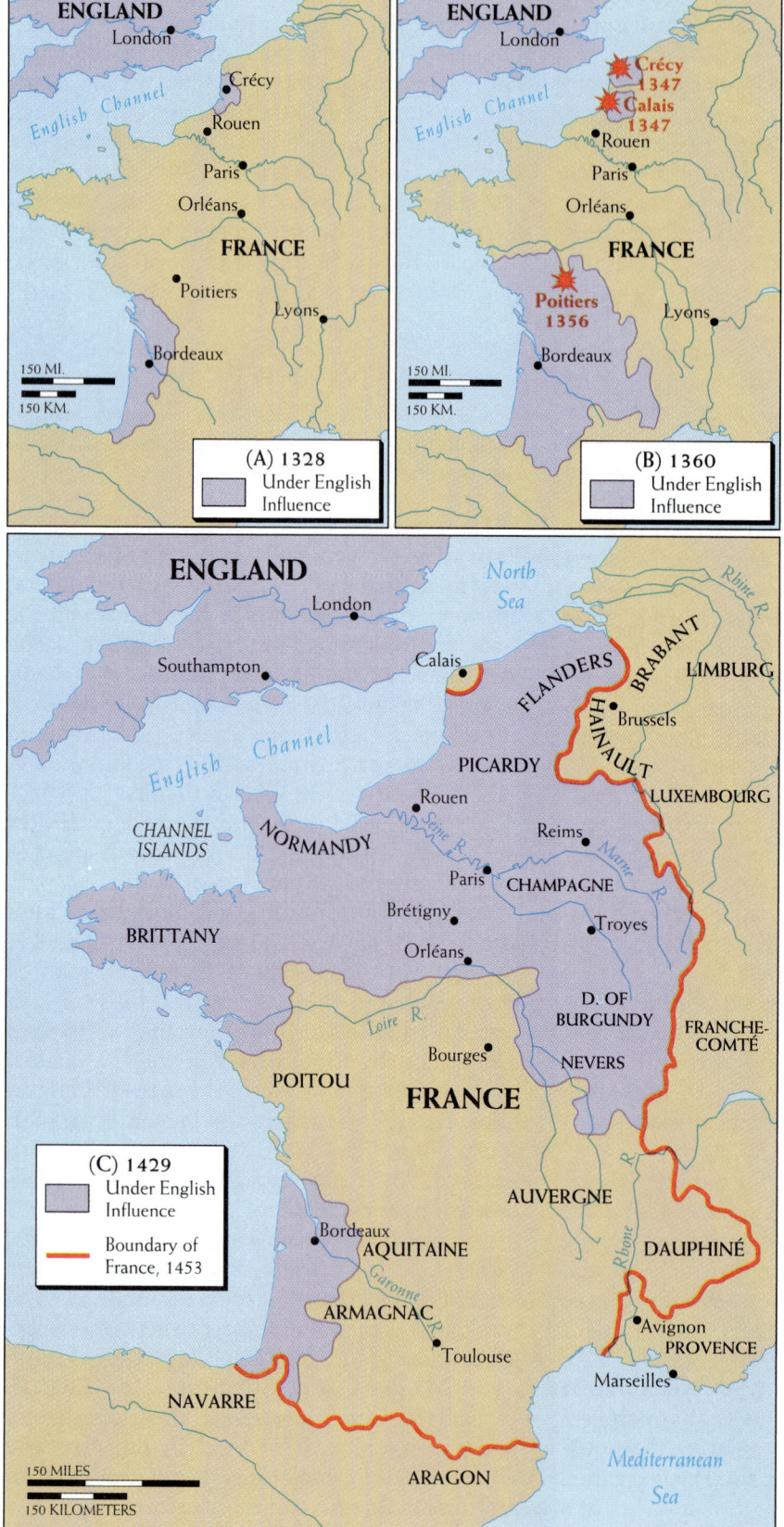

MAP 9-1 THE HUNDRED
YEARS' WAR *The Hundred
Years' War went on inter-
mittently from the late
1330s until 1453. These
maps show the remarkable
English territorial gains up
to the sudden and decisive
turning of the tide of battle
in favor of Joan of Arc in
1429.*

To secure their rights, the French privileged classes forced the peasantry to pay ever-increasing taxes and to repair without compensation the war-damaged properties of the nobility. This bullying became more than the peasants could bear, and they rose up in several regions in a series of bloody rebellions known as the *Jacquerie* in 1358 (after the peasant revolutionary popularly known as "Jacques Bonhomme" or simple Jack). The nobility quickly put down the revolt, matching the rebels atrocity for atrocity.

On May 9, 1360, another milestone of the war was reached when England forced the Peace of Brétigny on the French. This agreement declared an end to Edward's vassalage to the king of France and affirmed his sovereignty over English territories in France (including Gascony, Guyenne, Poitou, and Calais). France also agreed to pay a ransom of three million gold crowns to win King John the Good's release. In return, Edward simply renounced his claim to the French throne.

Such a partition of French territorial control was completely unrealistic, and sober observers on both sides knew it could not last long. France struck back in the late 1360s and by the time of Edward's death in 1377 had beaten the English back to coastal enclaves and the territory of Bordeaux.

FRENCH DEFEAT AND THE TREATY OF TROYES After Edward's death the English war effort lessened, partly because of domestic problems within England. During the reign of Richard II (r. 1377–1399), England had its own version of the *Jacquerie*. In June 1381 long oppressed peasants and artisans joined in a great revolt of the unprivileged classes under the leadership of John Ball, a secular priest, and Wat Tyler, a journeyman. As in France, the revolt was brutally crushed within the year. But it left the country divided for decades.

The war intensified under Henry V (r. 1413–1422), who took advantage of internal French turmoil created by the rise to power of the duchy of Burgundy. With France deeply divided, Henry V struck hard in Normandy. Happy to see the rest of France besieged, the Burgundians foolishly watched from the sidelines while Henry's army routed the opposition led by the count of Armagnac, who had picked up the royal banner, at Agincourt on October 25, 1415. In the years thereafter, belatedly recognizing that the defeat of France would leave them easy prey for the English, the Burgundians closed ranks with French royal forces. This renewed French unity, loose as it was, promised to bring eventual victory over the English, but it was shattered in September 1419 when the

This miniature illustrates two scenes from the English peasant revolt of 1381. On the left, Wat Tyler, one of the leaders of the revolt, is executed in the presence of King Richard II. On the right, King Richard urges armed peasants to end their rebellion. [The Bridgeman Art Library/Art Resource, N.Y.]

duke of Burgundy was assassinated. In the aftermath of this shocking event the duke's son and heir, determined to avenge his father's death, joined forces with the English.

France now became Henry V's for the taking—at least in the short run. The Treaty of Troyes in 1420 disinherited the legitimate heir to the French throne and proclaimed Henry V the successor to the French king, Charles VI. When Henry and Charles died within months of one another in 1422, the infant Henry VI of England was proclaimed in Paris to be king of both France and England. The dream of Edward III that had set the war in motion—to make the ruler of England the ruler also of France—had been realized, at least for the moment.

The son of Charles VI went into retreat in Bourges, where, on the death of his father, he became Charles VII to most of the French people, who ignored the Treaty of Troyes. Displaying unprecedented national feeling inspired by the remarkable Joan of Arc, they soon rallied to his cause and came together in an ultimately victorious coalition.

JOAN OF ARC AND THE WAR'S CONCLUSION
Joan of Arc (1412–1431), a peasant from Domrémy, presented herself to Charles VII in March 1429, declaring that the King of Heaven had called her to deliver besieged Orléans from the English. The king was understandably skeptical, but being in retreat from what seemed to be a hopeless war, he was willing to try anything to reverse French fortunes. And the deliverance of Orléans, a city strategic to the control of the territory south of the Loire, would be a godsend. Charles's desperation overcame his skepticism, and he gave Joan his leave.

Circumstances worked perfectly to her advantage. The English force was already exhausted by a six-month siege of Orléans and at the point of withdrawal when Joan arrived with fresh French troops. After repulsing the English from Orléans, the French enjoyed a succession of victories they popularly attributed to Joan. She deserved much of this credit, but not because she was a military genius. She provided the French with something military experts could not: inspiration and a sense of national identity and self-confidence. Within a few months of the liberation of Orléans, Charles VII received his

A contemporary portrait of Joan of Arc (1412–1431) in the National Archives in Paris. [Giraudon/Art Resource, N.Y.]

The Hundred Years' War (1337–1443)

1340	English victory at Bay of Sluys
1346	English victory at Crécy and seizure of Calais
1347	Black Death strikes
1356	English victory at Poitiers
1358	*Jacquerie* disrupts France
1360	Peace of Brétigny recognizes English holdings in France
1381	English peasants revolt
1415	English victory at Agincourt
1422	Treaty of Troyes proclaims Henry VI ruler of both England and France
1429	Joan of Arc leads French to victory at Orléans
1431	Joan of Arc executed as a heretic
1453	War ends; English retain only coastal town of Calais

crown in Rheims and ended the nine-year "disinheritance" prescribed by the Treaty of Troyes.

Charles forgot his liberator as quickly as he had embraced her. When the Burgundians captured Joan in May 1430, he was in a position to secure her release but did little for her. The Burgundians and the English wanted her publicly discredited, believing this would also discredit Charles VII and demoralize French resistance. She was turned over to the Inquisition in English-held Rouen. The inquisitors broke the courageous "Maid of Orléans" after ten weeks of interrogation, and she was executed as a relapsed heretic on May 30, 1431. Twenty-five years later (1456) Charles reopened her trial, and she was declared innocent of all the charges. In 1920 the Church declared her a saint.

In 1435 the duke of Burgundy made peace with Charles. France, now unified and at peace with Burgundy, continued progressively to force the English back. By 1453, the date of the war's end, the English held only their coastal enclave of Calais.

The Hundred Years' War, with sixty-eight years of at least nominal peace and forty-four of hot war, had lasting political and social consequences. It devastated France, but it also awak-

Joan of Arc Refuses to Recant Her Beliefs

Joan of Arc, threatened with torture, refused to recant her beliefs and instead defended the instructions she had received from the voices that spoke to her.

♦ *In the following excerpt from her self-defense, do you get the impression that the judges have made up their minds about Joan in advance? How does this judicial process, which was based on intensive interrogation of the accused, differ from a trial today? Why was Joan deemed heretical and not insane when she acknowledged hearing voices?*

On Wednesday, May 9th of the same year [1431], Joan was brought into the great tower of the castle of Rouen before us the said judges. And [she] was required and admonished to speak the truth on many different points contained in her trial which she had denied or to which she had given false replies, whereas we possessed certain information, proofs, and vehement presumptions upon them. Many of the points were read and explained to her, and she was told that if she did not confess them truthfully she would be put to the torture, the instruments of which were shown to her all ready in the tower. There were also present by our instruction men ready to put her to the torture in order to restore her to the way and knowledge of truth, and by this means to procure the salvation of her body and soul which by her lying inventions she exposed to such grave perils.

To which the said Joan answered in this manner: "Truly if you were to tear me limb from limb and separate my soul from my body, I would not tell you anything more: and if I did say anything, I should afterwards declare that you had compelled me to say it by force." Then she said that on Holy Cross Day last she received comfort from St. Gabriel; she firmly believes it was St. Gabriel. She knew by her voices whether she should submit to the Church, since the clergy were pressing her hard to submit. Her voices told her that if she desired Our Lord to aid her she must wait upon Him in all her doings. She said that Our Lord has always been the master of her doings, and the Enemy never had power over them. She asked her voices if she would be burned and they answered that she must wait upon God, and He would aid her.

The Trial of Jeanne D'Arc, trans. by W. P. Barrett (New York: Gotham House, 1932), pp. 303–304.

ened French nationalism and hastened the transition there from a feudal monarchy to a centralized state. It saw Burgundy become a major European political power. And it encouraged the English, in response to the seesawing allegiance of the Netherlands throughout the conflict, to develop their own clothing industry and foreign markets. In both France and England the burden of the on-again, off-again war fell most heavily on the peasantry, who were forced to support it with taxes and services.

The Black Death

Preconditions and Causes

In the late Middle Ages, nine-tenths of the population worked the land. The three-field system, in use in most areas since well before the fourteenth century, had increased the amount of arable land and thereby the food supply. The growth of cities and trade had also stimulated agricultural science and productivity. But as the food supply grew, so also did the population. It is estimated that Europe's population doubled between the years 1000 and 1300 and by 1300 had begun to outstrip food production. There were now more people than food to feed them or jobs to employ them, and the average European faced the probability of extreme hunger at least once during his or her expected thirty-five-year life span.

Between 1315 and 1317 crop failures produced the greatest famine of the Middle Ages. Densely populated urban areas like the industrial towns of the Netherlands experienced great suffering. Decades of overpopulation, economic depression, famine, and bad health progressively weakened Europe's population and made it highly vulnerable to a virulent bubonic plague that struck with full force in 1348.

This Black Death, so called by contemporaries because of the way it discolored the body, followed the trade routes from Asia into Europe. Appearing in Sicily in late 1347, it entered Europe through the port cities of Venice, Genoa, and Pisa in 1348, and from there it swept rapidly through Spain and southern France and into northern Europe. Areas that lay outside the major trade routes, like Bohemia, appear to have remained virtually unaffected.

Bubonic plague made numerous reappearances in succeeding decades. By the early fifteenth century, it is estimated that western Europe as a whole had lost as much as two-fifths of its population. There was not a full recovery until the sixteenth century (see Map 9-2).

Popular Remedies

The plague, transmitted by rat- or human-borne fleas, often reached a victim's lungs during the

More than one out of three Europeans died of the Black Death. In many localities so many people died that the traditional rites of death were abandoned in favor of hurried mass burials in communal pits. [Giraudon/Art Resource, N.Y.]

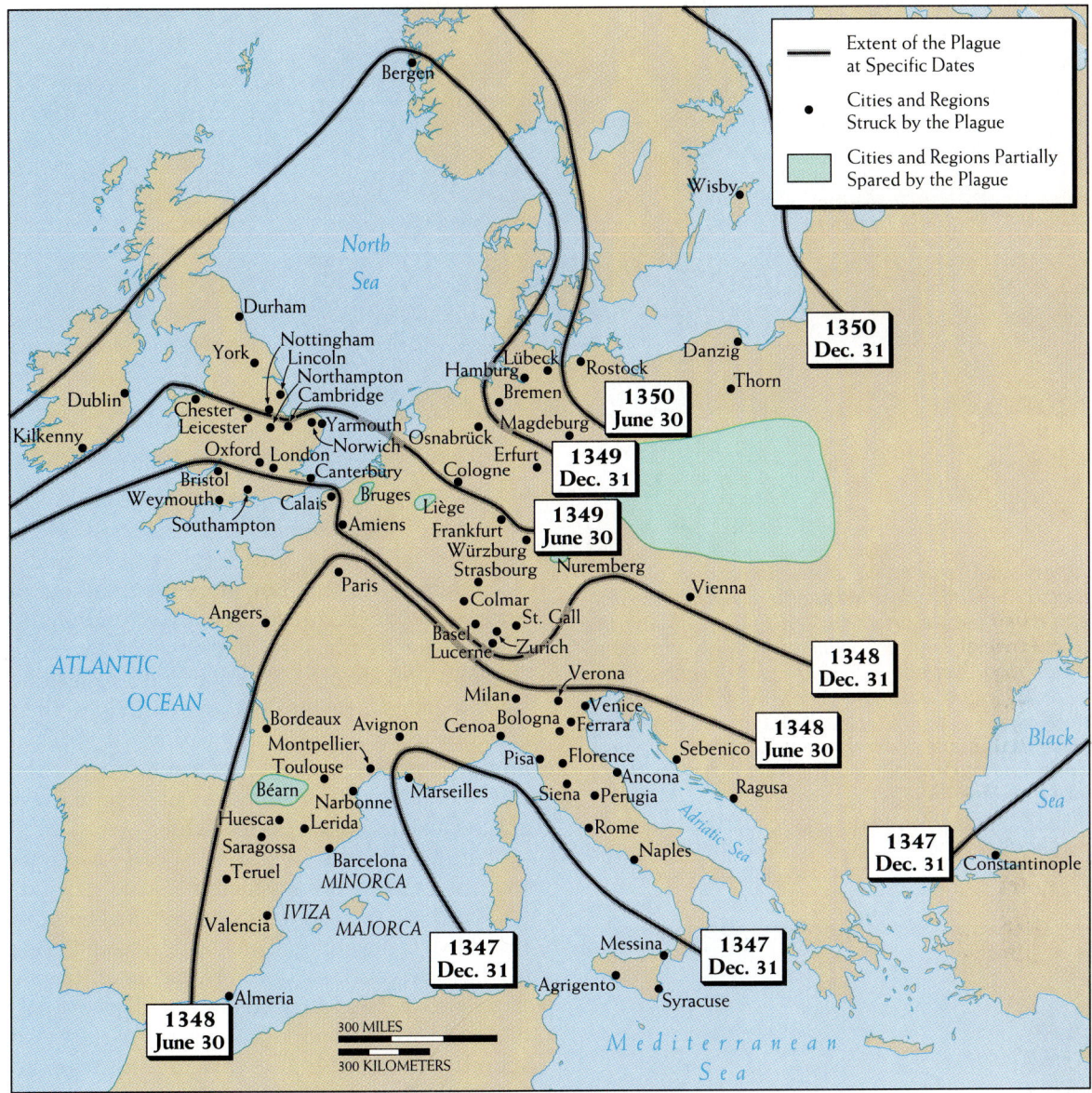

MAP 9-2 SPREAD OF THE BLACK DEATH *Apparently introduced by sea-borne rats from Black Sea areas where plague-infested rodents have long been known, the Black Death brought huge human, social, and economic consequences. One of the lower estimates of Europeans dying is 25,000,000. The map charts the plague's spread in the mid-fourteenth century. Generally following trade routes, the plague reached Scandinavia by 1350, and some believe it then went on to Iceland and even Greenland. Areas off the main trade routes were largely spared.*

course of the disease. From the lungs it could be spread from person to person by the victim's sneezing and wheezing. Contemporary physicians had no understanding of these processes, and so even the most rudimentary prophylaxis against the disease was lacking. To the people of the time the Black Death was a catastrophe with no apparent explanation and against which there was no known defense. Throughout much of western Europe it inspired an obsession with death and dying and a deep pessimism that endured for decades after the plague years.

Popular wisdom held that a corruption in the atmosphere caused the disease. Some blamed

The plague inspired an obsession with death. In this scene from fourteenth-century Lucca in north Italy, the plague cuts people down indiscriminately— bishops, kings, and others alike. [Scala/Art Resource, N.Y.]

In this scene from an illustrated manuscript of Boccaccio's Decameron, *physicians apply leeches to an emperor. The text says he suffered from a disease that caused a terrible stench, which is why the physicians are holding their noses. Bleeding was the agreed-upon best way to prevent and cure illness and was practiced as late as the nineteenth century. Its popularity was rooted in the belief that a build-up of foul matter in the body caused illness by disrupting the body's four humors (blood, phlegm, yellow bile, and black bile). Bleeding released the foul matter and restored equilibrium among the humors, thus preserving good health by strengthening resistance to disease. [Jean-Loup Charmet/Science Photo Library]*

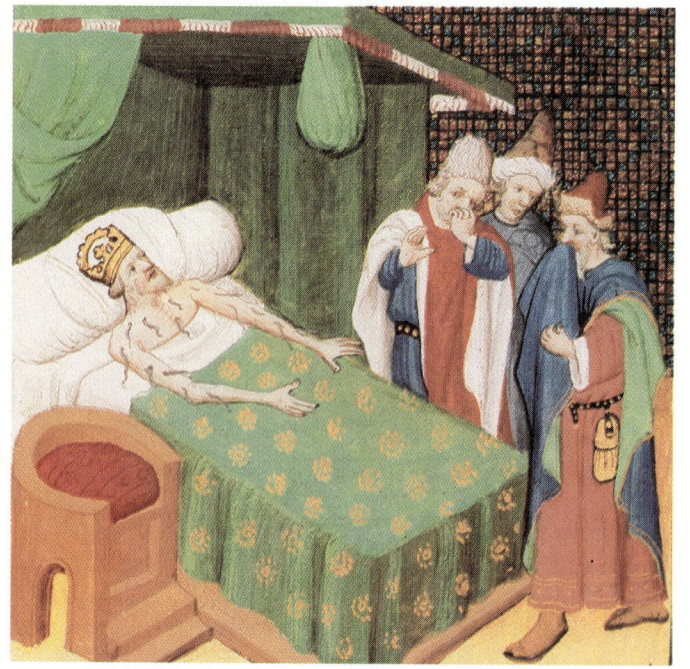

poisonous fumes released by earthquakes. Many adopted aromatic amulets as a remedy. According to the contemporary observations of Boccaccio, who recorded the varied reactions to the plague in the *Decameron* (1353), some sought a remedy in moderation and a temperate life; others gave themselves over entirely to their passions (sexual promiscuity within the stricken areas apparently ran high); and still others, "the most sound, perhaps, in judgment," chose flight and seclusion as the best medicine.

Among the most extreme social reactions were processions of flagellants. These religious fanatics beat themselves in ritual penance until they bled, believing that such action would bring divine intervention. The terror created by the flagellants (whose dirty bodies may have actually served to transport the disease) became so socially disruptive and threatening even to established authority that the Church finally outlawed such processions.

Jews were cast as scapegoats for the plague. Centuries of Christian propaganda had bred hatred toward them, but so too had their willing role as society's moneylenders. Pogroms occurred in several cities, sometimes incited by the arrival of flagellants.

Social and Economic Consequences

Whole villages vanished in the wake of the plague. Among the social and economic consequences of this depopulation were a shrunken

Boccaccio Describes the Ravages of the Black Death in Florence

The Black Death provided an excuse to the poet, humanist, and storyteller Giovanni Boccaccio (1313–1375) to assemble his great collection of tales, the Decameron. *Ten congenial men and women flee Florence to escape the plague and while away the time telling stories. In one of the stories, Boccaccio embedded a fine clinical description of plague symptoms as seen in Florence in 1348 and of the powerlessness of physicians and the lack of remedies.*

✦ *What did people do to escape plague? Was any of it sound medical practice? What does the study of calamities like the Black Death tell us about the people of the past?*

In Florence, despite all that human wisdom and forethought could devise to avert it, even as the cleansing of the city from many impurities by officials appointed for the purpose, the refusal of entrance to all sick folk, and the adoption of many precautions for the preservation of health; despite also humble supplications addressed to God, and often repeated both in public procession and otherwise, by the devout; towards the beginning of the spring of the said year [1348] the doleful effects of the pestilence began to be horribly apparent by symptoms that [appeared] as if miraculous.

Not such were these symptoms as in the East, where an issue of blood from the nose was a manifest sign of inevitable death; but in men and women alike it first betrayed itself by the emergence of certain tumours in the groin or the armpits, some of which grew as large as a common apple, others as an egg, some more, some less, which the common folk called *gavoccioli*. From the two said parts of the body this deadly *gavoccioli* soon began to propagate and spread itself in all directions indifferently; after which the form of the malady began to change, spots black or livid making their appearance in many cases on the arm or the thigh or elsewhere, now few and large, now minute and numerous. And as the *gavoccioli* had been and still were an infallible token of approaching death, such also were these spots on whomsoever they shewed themselves. Which maladies seemed to set entirely at naught both the art of the physician and the virtues of physic; indeed, whether it was that the disorder was of a nature to defy such treatment, or that the physicians were at fault . . . and, being in ignorance of its source, failed to apply the proper remedies; in either case, not merely were those that recovered few, but almost all died within three days of the appearance of the said symptoms . . . and in most cases without any fever or other attendant malady.

The Decameron of Giovanni Boccaccio, *trans. by J. M. Rigg (London: J. M. Dent & Sons, 1930), p. 5.*

labor supply and a decline in the value of the estates of the nobility.

FARMS DECLINE As the number of farm laborers decreased, their wages increased and those of skilled artisans soared. Many serfs now chose to commute their labor services by money payments or to abandon the farm altogether and pursue more interesting and rewarding jobs in skilled craft industries in the cities. Agricultural prices fell because of lowered demand, and the price of luxury and manufactured goods—the work of skilled artisans—rose. The noble landholders suffered the greatest decline in power from this new state of affairs. They were forced to pay more for finished products and for farm labor but received a smaller return on their agricultural produce. Everywhere their rents were in steady decline after the plague.

PEASANTS REVOLT To recoup their losses, some landowners converted arable land to sheep pasture, substituting more profitable wool production for labor-intensive grain crops. Others abandoned the effort to farm their land and simply leased it to the highest bidder. Landowners also sought simply to reverse their misfortune—to close off the new economic opportunities opened for the peasantry by the demographic crisis—through repressive legislation that forced peasants to stay on their farms and froze their wages at low levels. In France the direct tax on

A caricature of physicians (early sixteenth century). In the Middle Ages and later, people recognized the shortcomings of physicians and surgeons and visited them only as a last resort. Here a physician carries a uroscope (for collecting and examining urine); cloudy or discolored urine signaled an immediate need for bleeding. The physician/surgeon wears surgical shoes and his assistant carries a flail—a comment on the risks of medical services. [Hacker Art Books]

the peasantry, the *taille*, was increased, and opposition to it was prominent among the grievances behind the *Jacquerie*. In 1351, the English Parliament passed a Statute of Laborers, which limited wages to preplague levels and restricted the ability of peasants to leave the land of their traditional masters. Opposition to such legislation was also a prominent factor in the English Peasants' Revolt. (See page 333.)

CITIES REBOUND Although the plague hit urban populations especially hard, the cities and their skilled industries came, in time, to prosper from its effects. Cities had always been careful to protect their interests; as they grew, they passed legislation to regulate competition from rural areas and to control immigration. After the plague the reach of such laws was progressively extended beyond the cities to include surrounding lands belonging to impoverished nobles and feudal landlords, many of whom were peacefully integrated into urban life.

The omnipresence of death whetted the appetite for goods that only skilled urban industries could produce. Expensive cloths and jewelry, furs from the north, and silks from the south were in great demand in the second half of the fourteenth century. Faced with life at its worst, people insisted on having the very best. Initially this new demand could not be met. The basic unit of urban industry was the master and his apprentices (usually one or two), whose numbers were purposely kept low and whose privileges were jealously guarded. The craft of the skilled artisan was passed from master to apprentice only very slowly. The first wave of plague transformed this already restricted supply of skilled artisans into a shortage almost overnight. As a result, the prices of manufactured and luxury items rose to new heights and this, in turn, encouraged workers to migrate from the countryside to the city and learn the skills of artisans. Townspeople in effect profited coming and going from the forces that impoverished the landed nobility. As wealth poured into the cities and per capita income rose, the cost to urban dwellers of agricultural products from the countryside, now less in demand, declined.

There was also gain as well as loss for the Church. Although it suffered losses as a great landholder and was politically weakened, it had received new revenues from the vastly increased demand for religious services for the dead and the dying and from the multiplication of gifts and bequests.

New Conflicts and Opportunities

By increasing the importance of skilled artisans, the plague contributed to new conflicts within the cities. The economic and political power of local artisans and trade guilds grew steadily in the late Middle Ages along with the demand for their goods and services. The merchant and patrician classes found it increasingly difficult to maintain their traditional dominance and grudgingly gave guild masters a voice in city government. As the guilds won political power, they encouraged restrictive legislation to protect local industries. These restrictions, in turn, brought confrontations between master artisans, who wanted to keep their numbers low and expand their industries at a snail's pace, and the many journeymen, who were eager to rise to the rank of master. To the long-existing conflict between the guilds and the urban patriciate was now added a conflict within the guilds themselves.

After 1350 the two traditional "containers" of monarchy—the landed nobility and the Church—were politically on the defensive, and to no small degree as a consequence of the plague. Kings took full advantage of the new situation, drawing on growing national sentiment to centralize their governments and economies. As already noted, the plague reduced the economic power of the landed nobility. In the same period the battles of the Hundred Years' War demonstrated the military superiority of paid professional armies over the traditional noble cavalry, thus bringing into question the traditional role of the nobility. The plague also killed many members of the clergy—perhaps one-third of the German clergy fell victim to it as they dutifully ministered to the sick and dying. The reduction in clerical ranks occurred in the same century in which the residence of the pope in Avignon (1309–1377) and the Schism (1378–1415) were undermining much of the Church's popular support.

Ecclesiastical Breakdown and Revival: The Late Medieval Church

At first glance the popes may appear to have been in a very favorable position in the latter half of the thirteenth century. Frederick II had been vanquished and imperial pressure on Rome had been removed. The French king, Louis IX, was an enthusiastic supporter of the Church, as evidenced by his two disastrous Crusades, which won him sainthood. Although it lasted only seven years, a reunion of the Eastern church with Rome was proclaimed by the Council of Lyons in 1274, when the Western church took advantage of Emperor Michael Palaeologus's request for aid against the Turks. But despite these positive events, the Church was not really in as favorable a position as it appeared.

The Thirteenth-Century Papacy

As early as the reign of Pope Innocent III (1198–1216), when papal power reached its height, there were ominous developments. Innocent had elaborated the doctrine of papal plenitude of power and on that authority had declared saints, disposed of benefices, and created a centralized papal monarchy with a clearly political mission. Innocent's transformation of the papacy into a great secular power weakened the Church spiritually even as it strengthened it politically. Thereafter the Church as a papal monarchy and the Church as the "body of the faithful" came increasingly to be differentiated. It was against the "papal church" and in the name of the "true Christian church" that both reformers and heretics raised their voices in protest until the Protestant Reformation.

What Innocent began, his successors perfected. Under Urban IV (r. 1261–1264) the papacy established its own law court, the Rota Romana, which tightened and centralized the Church's legal proceedings. The latter half of the thirteenth century saw an elaboration of the system of clerical taxation; what had begun in the twelfth century as an emergency measure to raise funds for the Crusades became a fixed institution. In the same period, papal power to determine appointments to many major and minor Church offices—the so-called reservation of benefices—was greatly broadened. The thirteenth-century papacy became a powerful political institution governed by its own law and courts, serviced by an efficient international bureaucracy, and preoccupied with secular goals.

Papal centralization of the Church undermined both diocesan authority and popular support. Rome's interests, not local needs, came to control Church appointments, policies, and discipline. Discontented lower clergy appealed to the higher authority of Rome against the disciplinary measures of local bishops. In the second half of the thirteenth century, bishops and abbots protested such undercutting of their power. To its critics, the Church in Rome was hardly more than a legalized, fiscalized, bureaucratic institution. As early as the late twelfth century, heretical movements of Cathars and Waldensians had appealed to the biblical ideal of simplicity and separation from the world. Other reformers unquestionably loyal to the Church, such as Saint Francis of Assisi, would also protest a perceived materialism in official religion.

POLITICAL FRAGMENTATION The Church of the thirteenth century was being undermined by more than internal religious disunity. The demise of imperial power meant that the papacy in Rome was no longer the leader of antiimperial (Guelf, or propapal) sentiment in Italy. Instead of being the center of Italian resistance to the emperor, popes now found themselves on the defensive against their old allies. That was the ironic price paid by the papacy to vanquish the Hohenstaufens.

Rulers with a stake in Italian politics now directed the intrigue formerly aimed at the emperor toward the College of Cardinals. For example, Charles of Anjou, king of Sicily, managed to create a French–Sicilian faction within the college. Such efforts to control the decisions of the college led Pope Gregory X (r. 1271–1276) to establish the practice of sequestering the cardinals immediately on the death of the pope. The purpose of this so-called conclave of cardinals was to minimize extraneous political influence on the election of new popes, but the college had become so politicized that it proved to be of little avail.

In 1294 such a conclave, in frustration after a deadlock of more than two years, chose a saintly but inept Calabrian hermit as Pope Celestine V. Celestine abdicated under suspicious circumstances after only a few weeks in office. He also died under suspicious circumstances; his successor's critics later argued that he had been murdered for political reasons by the powers behind the papal throne to ensure the survival of the papal office. His tragicomic reign shocked a majority of the college into unified action. He was quickly replaced by his very opposite, Pope Boniface VIII (r. 1294–1303), a nobleman and a skilled politician. His pontificate, however, would inaugurate the beginning of the end of papal pretensions to great power status.

Boniface VIII and Philip the Fair

Boniface came to rule when England and France were maturing as nation-states. In England a long tradition of consultation between the king and powerful members of English society evolved into formal "parliaments" during the reigns of Henry III (1216–1272) and Edward I (1272–1307), and these meetings helped to create a unified kingdom. The reign of the French king Philip IV the Fair (1285–1314) saw France become an efficient, centralized monarchy. Philip was no Saint Louis, but a ruthless politician. He was determined to end England's continental holdings, control wealthy Flanders, and establish French hegemony within the Holy Roman Empire.

Boniface had the further misfortune of bringing to the papal throne memories of the way earlier popes had brought kings and emperors to their knees. Very painfully he was to discover that the papal monarchy of the early thirteenth century was no match for the new political powers of the late thirteenth century.

THE ROYAL CHALLENGE TO PAPAL AUTHORITY France and England were on the brink of all-out war when Boniface became pope in 1294. Only Edward I's preoccupation with rebellion in Scotland, which the French encouraged, prevented him from invading France and starting the Hundred Years' War a half century earlier than it did start. As both countries mobi-

Pope Boniface VIII (1294–1303), depicted here, opposed the taxation of the clergy by the kings of France and England and issued one of the strongest declarations of papal authority over rulers, the bull Unam Sanctam. *This statue is in the Museo Civico, Bologna, Italy. [Scala/Art Resource, N.Y.]*

lized for war, they used the pretext of preparing for a Crusade to tax the clergy heavily. In 1215 Pope Innocent III had decreed that the clergy were to pay no taxes to rulers without prior papal consent. Viewing English and French taxation of the clergy as an assault on traditional clerical rights, Boniface took a strong stand against it. On February 5, 1296, he issued a bull, *Clericis Laicos*, which forbade lay taxation of the clergy without prior papal approval and took back all previous papal dispensations in this regard.

In England Edward I retaliated by denying the clergy the right to be heard in royal court, in effect removing from them the protection of the king. But it was Philip the Fair who struck back with a vengeance. In August 1296 he forbade the exportation of money from France to Rome, thereby denying the papacy revenues it needed to operate. Boniface had no choice but to come quickly to terms with Philip. He conceded Philip the right to tax the French clergy "during an emergency," and, not coincidentally, he canonized Louis IX in the same year.

Boniface was then also under siege by powerful Italian enemies, whom Philip did not fail to patronize. A noble family (the Colonnas), rivals of Boniface's family (the Gaetani) and radical followers of Saint Francis of Assisi (the Spiritual Franciscans), were at this time seeking to invalidate Boniface's election as pope on the grounds that Celestine V had resigned the office under coercion. Charges of heresy, simony, and even the murder of Celestine were hurled against Boniface.

In the year 1300, a Jubilee year, Boniface's fortunes appeared to revive. In a Jubilee celebration, all Catholics who visited Rome and fulfilled certain conditions while there received a special indulgence, or remission of their sins. Tens of thousands of pilgrims flocked to Rome in that year, and heady with this display of popular religiosity, Boniface reinserted himself into international politics. He championed Scottish resistance to England, for which he received a firm rebuke from an outraged Edward I and from Parliament.

But once again a confrontation with the king of France proved the more costly. Philip seemed to be spoiling for another fight with the pope. He arrested Boniface's Parisian legate, Bernard Saisset, the bishop of Pamiers and also a powerful secular lord, whose independence Philip had opposed. Accused of heresy and treason, Saisset was tried and convicted in the king's court. Thereafter, Philip demanded that Boniface recognize the process against Saisset, something

Boniface VIII Reasserts the Church's Claim to Temporal Power

Defied by the French and the English, Pope Boniface VIII (r. 1294–1303) boldly reasserted the temporal power of the Church in the bull Unam Sanctam *(November 1302). This document claimed that both spiritual and temporal power on earth were under the pope's jurisdiction, because in the hierarchy of the universe spiritual power both preceded and sat in judgment on temporal power.*

◆ *On what does the pope base his claims to supremacy? Is his argument logical, or does he beg the question? Why did secular rulers find his arguments unpersuasive?*

We are taught by the words of the Gospel that in this church and in her power there are two swords, a spiritual one and a temporal one. . . . Certainly anyone who denies that the temporal sword is in the power of Peter has not paid heed to the words of the Lord when he said, "Put up thy sword into its sheath" (Matthew 26:52). Both then are in the power of the church, the material sword and the spiritual. But the one is exercised for the church, the other by the church, the one by the hand of the priest, the other by the hand of kings and soldiers, though at the will and suffrance of the authority subject to the spiritual power. . . . For, according to the blessed Dionysius, it is the law of divinity for the lowest to be led to the highest through intermediaries. In the order of the universe all things are not kept in order in the same fashion and immediately but the lowest are ordered by the intermediate and inferiors by superiors. But that the spiritual power excels any earthly one in dignity and nobility we ought the more openly to confess in proportion as spiritual things excel temporal ones. Moreover we clearly perceive this from the giving of tithes, from benediction and sanctification, from the acceptance of this power and from the very government of things. For, the truth bearing witness, the spiritual power has to institute the earthly power and to judge it if it has not been good. So it is verified the prophecy of Jeremiah (1:10) concerning the church and the power of the church, "Lo, I have set thee this day over the nations and over kingdoms."

As quoted in Brian Tierney, The Crisis of Church and State 1050–1300 *(Englewood Cliffs, N.J.: Prentice-Hall, 1964), pp. 188–189. Used by permission of the publisher.*

that Boniface could do only if he was prepared to surrender his jurisdiction over the French episcopate. This challenge could not be side-stepped, and Boniface acted swiftly to champion Saisset as a defender of clerical political independence within France. He demanded Saisset's unconditional release, revoked all previous agreements with Philip in the matter of clerical taxation, and ordered the French bishops to convene in Rome within a year. A bull, *Ausculta Fili* ("Listen, My Son"), was sent to Philip in December 1301, pointedly informing him that "God has set popes over kings and kingdoms."

UNAM SANCTAM (1302) Philip unleashed a ruthless antipapal campaign. Two royal apologists, Pierre Dubois and John of Paris, refuted papal claims to the right to intervene in temporal matters. Increasingly placed on the defensive, Boniface made a last-ditch stand against state control of national churches. On November 18, 1302, he issued the bull *Unam Sanctam*. This famous statement of papal power declared that temporal authority was "subject" to the spiritual power of the Church. On its face a bold assertion, *Unam Sanctam* was in truth the desperate act of a besieged papacy.

After *Unam Sanctam* the French and the Colonnas moved against Boniface with force. Guillaume de Nogaret, Philip's chief minister, denounced Boniface to the French clergy as a common heretic and criminal. An army, led by Nogaret and Sciarra Colonna, surprised the pope in mid-August 1303 at his retreat in Anagni. Boniface was badly beaten and almost executed before an aroused populace liberated and returned him safely to Rome. But the ordeal proved too much for him and he died a few months later, in October 1303.

Boniface's immediate successor, Benedict XI (r. 1303–1304), excommunicated Nogaret for his deed, but there was to be no lasting papal retaliation. Benedict's successor, Clement V (r. 1305–1314), was forced into French subservience. A former archbishop of Bordeaux, Clement declared that *Unam Sanctam* should not be understood as in any way diminishing French royal authority. He released Nogaret from excommunication and pliantly condemned the Knights Templars, whose treasure Philip thereafter forcibly expropriated.

In 1309 Clement moved the papal court to Avignon, an imperial city on the southeastern border of France. Situated on land that belonged to the pope, the city maintained its independence from the king. In 1311 Clement made it his permanent residence, both to escape a Rome ridden with strife after the confrontation between Boniface and Philip and to escape pressure from Philip. There the papacy was to remain until 1377.

After Boniface's humiliation, popes never again seriously threatened kings and emperors, despite continuing papal excommunications and political intrigue. In the future the relation between Church and state would tilt in favor of the state and the control of religion within particular monarchies. Ecclesiastical authority would become subordinate to larger secular political purposes.

The Avignon Papacy (1309–1377)

The Avignon papacy was in appearance, although not always in fact, under strong French

The Palace of the Popes in Avignon, France. In 1311, Pope Clement V made the city his permanent residence, and the popes remained there until 1377. [Fritz Henle/Photo Researchers, Inc.]

influence. During Clement V's pontificate the French came to dominate the College of Cardinals, testing the papacy's agility both politically and economically. Finding itself cut off from its Roman estates, the papacy had to innovate to get needed funds. Clement expanded papal taxes, especially the practice of collecting annates, the first year's revenue of a church office or benefice bestowed by the pope. Clement VI (r. 1342–1352) began the practice of selling indulgences, or pardons for unrepented sins. To make the purchase of indulgences more compelling, Church doctrine on purgatory—a place of punishment where souls would atone for venial sins—also developed during this period. By the fifteenth century the church had extended indulgences to cover the souls of people already dead, allowing the living to buy a reduced sentence in purgatory for their deceased loved ones. Such practices contributed to the Avignon papacy's reputation for materialism and political scheming and gave reformers new ammunition.

POPE JOHN XXII Pope John XXII (r. 1316–1334), the most powerful Avignon pope, tried to restore papal independence and to return to Italy. This goal led him into war with the Visconti, the most powerful ruling family of Milan, and a costly contest with Emperor Louis IV. John had challenged Louis's election as emperor in 1314 in favor of the rival Habsburg candidate. The result was a minor replay of the confrontation between Philip the Fair and Boniface VIII. When John obstinately and without legal justification refused to recognize Louis's election, the emperor retaliated by declaring John deposed and setting in his place an antipope. As Philip the Fair had also done, Louis enlisted the support of the Spiritual Franciscans, whose views on absolute poverty John had condemned as heretical. Two outstanding pamphleteers wrote lasting tracts for the royal cause: William of Ockham, whom John excommunicated in 1328, and Marsilius of Padua (ca. 1290–1342), whose teaching John declared heretical in 1327.

In his *Defender of Peace* (1324), Marsilius of Padua stressed the independent origins and autonomy of secular government. Clergy were subjected to the strictest apostolic ideals and confined to purely spiritual functions, and all power of coercive judgment was denied the pope. Marsilius argued that spiritual crimes must await an eternal punishment. Transgressions of divine law, over which the pope had jurisdiction, were to be punished in the next life, not in the present one, unless the secular ruler declared a divine law also a secular law. This assertion was a direct challenge of the power of the pope to excommunicate rulers and place countries under interdict. The *Defender of Peace* depicted the pope as a subordinate member of a society over which the emperor ruled supreme and in which temporal peace was the highest good.

John XXII made the papacy a sophisticated international agency and adroitly adjusted it to the growing European money economy. The more the Curia (or papal court) mastered the latter, however, the more vulnerable it became to criticism. Under John's successor, Benedict XII (r. 1334–1342), the papacy became entrenched in Avignon. Seemingly forgetting Rome altogether, Benedict began construction of the great Palace of the Popes and attempted to reform both papal government and the religious life. His high-living French successor, Clement VI, placed papal policy in lockstep with the French. In this period the cardinals became barely more than lobbyists for policies favorable to their secular patrons.

NATIONAL OPPOSITION TO THE AVIGNON PAPACY As Avignon's fiscal tentacles probed new areas, monarchies took strong action to protect their interests. The latter half of the fourteenth century saw legislation restricting papal jurisdiction and taxation in France, England, and Germany. In England, where the Avignon papacy was identified with the French enemy after the outbreak of the Hundred Years' War, statutes that restricted payments and appeals to Rome and the pope's power to make high ecclesiastical appointments were several times passed by Parliament between 1351 and 1393.

In France ecclesiastical appointments and taxation were regulated by the so-called Gallican liberties. These national rights over religion had long been exercised in fact and were legally acknowledged by the Church in the Pragmatic Sanction of Bourges published by Charles VII (r. 1422–1461) in 1438. This agreement recog-

Marsilius of Padua Denies Coercive Power to the Clergy

According to Marsilius, the Bible gave the pope no right to pronounce and execute sentences on any person. The clergy held a strictly moral and spiritual rule, their judgments to be executed only in the afterlife, not in the present one. Here, on earth, they should be obedient to secular authority. Marsilius argued this point by appealing to the example of Jesus.

◆ *How do Marsilius's arguments compare with those of Pope Boniface in the preceding document? Does Marsilius's argument, if accepted, destroy the worldly authority of the Church? Why was his teaching condemned as heretical?*

We now wish . . . to adduce the truths of the holy Scripture . . . which explicitly command or counsel that neither the Roman bishop called pope, nor any other bishop or priest, or deacon, has or ought to have any rulership or coercive judgment or jurisdiction over any priest or nonpriest, ruler, community, group, or individual of whatever condition. . . . Christ himself came into the world not to dominate men, nor to judge them [coercively] . . . not to wield temporal rule, but rather to be subject as regards the . . . present life; and moreover, he wanted to and did exclude himself, his apostles and disciples, and their successors, the bishops or priests, from all coercive authority or worldly rule, both by his example and by his word of counsel or command. . . . When he was brought before Pontius Pilate . . . and accused of having called himself king of the Jews, and [Pilate] asked him whether he had said this . . . [his] reply included these words . . . "My kingdom is not of this world," that is, I have not come to reign by temporal rule or dominion, in the way . . . worldly kings reign. . . . This, then, is the kingdom concerning which he came to teach and order, a kingdom which consists in the acts whereby the eternal kingdom is attained, that is, the acts of faith and the other theological virtues; not however, by coercing anyone thereto.

Marsilius of Padua: The Defender of Peace: The Defensor Pacis, *trans. by Alan Gewirth (New York: Harper, 1967), pp. 113–116.*

nized the right of the French church to elect its own clergy without papal interference, prohibited the payment of annates to Rome, and limited the right of appeals from French courts to the Curia in Rome. In German and Swiss cities in the fourteenth and fifteenth centuries, local governments also took the initiative to limit and even to overturn traditional clerical privileges and immunities.

JOHN WYCLIFFE AND JOHN HUSS The popular lay religious movements that most successfully assailed the late medieval Church were the Lollards in England and the Hussites in Bohemia. The Lollards looked to the writings of John Wycliffe (d. 1384) to justify their demands, and both moderate and extreme Hussites to the writings of John Huss (d. 1415), although both Wycliffe and Huss would have disclaimed the extremists who revolted in their name.

Wycliffe was an Oxford theologian and a philosopher of high standing. His work initially served the anticlerical policies of the English government. He became within England what William of Ockham and Marsilius of Padua had been at the Bavarian court of Emperor Louis IV: a major intellectual spokesman for the rights of royalty against the secular pretensions of popes.

After 1350 English kings greatly reduced the power of the Avignon papacy to make ecclesiastical appointments and collect taxes within England, a position that Wycliffe strongly supported. His views on clerical poverty followed original Franciscan ideals and, more by accident than by design, gave justification to government restriction and even confiscation of Church properties within England. Wycliffe argued that the clergy "ought to be content with food and clothing."

Wycliffe also maintained that personal merit, not rank and office, was the only basis of religious authority. This was a dangerous teaching because it raised allegedly pious laypeople above allegedly corrupt ecclesiastics, regardless of the latter's official stature. There was a threat in such teaching to secular as well as to ecclesiastical dominion and jurisdiction. At his posthumous condemnation by the pope, Wycliffe was accused of the ancient heresy of Donatism—the teaching that the efficacy of the Church's sacra-

ments did not lie in their sheer performance but also depended on the moral character of the clergy who administered them. Wycliffe also anticipated certain Protestant criticisms of the medieval Church by challenging papal infallibility, the sale of indulgences, the authority of scripture, and the dogma of transubstantiation.

The Lollards, English advocates of Wycliffe's teaching, like the Waldensians, preached in the vernacular, disseminated translations of Holy Scripture, and championed clerical poverty. At first, they came from every social class. Lollards were especially prominent among the groups that had something tangible to gain from the confiscation of clerical properties (the nobility and the gentry) or that had suffered most under the current Church system (the lower clergy and the poor people). After the English Peasants' Revolt of 1381, an uprising filled with egalitarian notions that could find support in Wycliffe's teaching, Lollardy was officially viewed as subversive. Opposed by an alliance of Church and crown, it became a capital offense in England by 1401.

Heresy was not so easily brought to heel in Bohemia, where it coalesced with a strong national movement. The University of Prague, founded in 1348, became the center for both Czech nationalism and a native religious reform movement. The latter began within the bounds of orthodoxy. It was led by local intellectuals and preachers, the most famous of whom was John Huss, the rector of the university after 1403.

The Czech reformers supported vernacular translations of the Bible and were critical of traditional ceremonies and allegedly superstitious practices, particularly those relating to the sacrament of the Eucharist. They advocated lay communion with cup as well as bread. Traditionally, only the priest received communion with both cup and bread, the laity with bread only—a sign of the clergy's spiritual superiority over the laity. Hussites taught that bread and wine remained bread and wine after priestly consecration, and questioned the validity of sacraments performed by priests in mortal sin.

Wycliffe's teaching appears to have influenced the movement very early. Regular traffic between England and Bohemia had existed for decades, ever since the marriage in 1381 of Anne of Bohemia to King Richard II. Czech stu-

A portrayal of Jan Hus as he was led to the stake at Constance. After his execution, his bones and ashes were scattered in the Rhine River to prevent his followers from claiming them as relics. This pen-and-ink drawing is from Ulrich von Richenthal's Chronicle of the Council of Constance *(ca. 1450). [The Bettmann Archive]*

dents studied at Oxford, and many returned with copies of Wycliffe's writings.

Huss became the leader of the pro-Wycliffe faction at the University of Prague. In 1410 his activities brought about his excommunication and the placement of Prague under papal interdict. In 1414 Huss won an audience with the newly assembled Council of Constance. He journeyed to the council eagerly, armed with a safe-conduct pass from Emperor Sigismund, naïvely believing that he would convince his strongest critics of the truth of his teaching. Within weeks of his arrival in early November 1414, he was formally accused of heresy and imprisoned. He died at the stake on July 6, 1415, and was followed there less than a year later by his colleague Jerome of Prague.

The reaction in Bohemia to the execution of these national heroes was fierce revolt. Militant Hussites, the Taborites, set out to transform Bohemia by force into a religious and social paradise under the military leadership of John Ziska. After a decade of belligerent protest, the Hussites won significant religious reforms and control over the Bohemian church from the Council of Basel.

The Great Schism (1378–1417) and the Conciliar Movement to 1449

Pope Gregory XI (r. 1370–1378) reestablished the papacy in Rome in January 1377, ending what had come to be known as the "Babylonian Captivity" of the church in Avignon, a reference to the biblical bondage of the Israelites. The return to Rome proved to be short-lived, however.

URBAN VI AND CLEMENT VII On Gregory's death the cardinals, in Rome, elected an Italian archbishop as Pope Urban VI (r. 1378–1389), who immediately announced his intention to reform the Curia. This was an unexpected challenge to the cardinals, most of whom were French, and they responded by calling for the return of the papacy to Avignon. The French king, Charles V, wanting to keep the papacy within the sphere of French influence, lent his support to a schism.

On September 20, 1378, five months after Urban's election, thirteen cardinals, all but one of whom was French, formed their own conclave

and elected Pope Clement VII (r. 1378–1397), a cousin of the French king. They insisted that they had voted for Urban in fear of their lives, surrounded by a Roman mob demanding the election of an Italian pope. Be that as it may, the papacy now became a "two-headed thing" and a scandal to Christendom. Allegiance to the two papal courts divided along political lines. England and its allies (the Holy Roman Empire, Hungary, Bohemia, and Poland) acknowledged Urban VI, whereas France and those in its orbit (Naples, Scotland, Castile, and Aragon) supported Clement VII. The Roman line of popes has, however, been recognized de facto in subsequent Church history.

Two approaches were initially taken to end the schism. One tried to win the mutual cession of both popes, thereby clearing the way for the election of a new pope. The other sought to secure the resignation of the one in favor of the other. Both approaches proved completely fruitless. Each pope considered himself fully legitimate, and too much was at stake for a magnanimous concession on the part of either. There was one way left: the forced deposition of both popes by a special council of the Church.

CONCILIAR THEORY OF CHURCH GOVERNMENT Legally a church council could be convened only by a pope, but the competing popes were not inclined to summon a council they knew would depose them. Also, the deposition of a legitimate pope against his will by a council of the Church was as serious a matter then as the forced deposition of a monarch by a representative assembly.

The correctness of a conciliar deposition of a pope was thus debated a full thirty years before any direct action was taken. Advocates sought to fashion a church in which a representative council could effectively regulate the actions of the pope. The conciliarists defined the Church as the whole body of the faithful, of which the elected head, the pope, was only one part. And the pope's sole purpose was to maintain the unity and well-being of the church—something that the schismatic popes were far from doing. The conciliarists further argued that a council of the Church acted with greater authority than the pope alone. In the eyes of the pope(s) such a concept of the Church threatened both its political and its religious unity.

THE COUNCIL OF PISA (1409–1410) On the basis of the arguments of the conciliarists, cardinals representing both popes convened a council on their own authority in Pisa in 1409, deposed both the Roman and the Avignon popes, and elected a new pope, Alexander V. To the council's consternation, neither pope accepted its action, and Christendom suddenly faced the spectacle of three contending popes. Although the vast majority of Latin Christendom accepted Alexander and his Pisan successor John XXIII (r. 1410–1415), the popes of Rome and Avignon refused to step down.

THE COUNCIL OF CONSTANCE (1414–1417) This intolerable situation ended when Emperor Sigismund prevailed on John XXIII to summon a new council in Constance in 1414, which the Roman pope Gregory XII also recognized. In a famous declaration entitled *Sacrosancta*, the council asserted their supremacy and proceeded to elect a new pope, Martin V (r. 1417–1431), after the three contending popes had either resigned or been deposed. The council then made provisions for regular meetings of Church councils, within five, then seven, and thereafter every ten years.

Despite its role in ending the schism, in the official eyes of the Church Constance was not a legitimate council. Nor have the schismatic popes of Avignon and Pisa been recognized as legitimate (for this reason, another pope could take the name John XXIII in 1958).

THE COUNCIL OF BASEL (1431–1449) Conciliar government of the Church peaked at the Council of Basel, when the council negotiated church doctrine with heretics. In 1432 the Hussites of Bohemia presented the *Four Articles of Prague* to the council as a basis for the negotiations. This document contained requests for (1) giving the laity the Eucharist with cup as well as bread; (2) free, itinerant preaching; (3) the exclusion of the clergy from holding secular offices and owning property; and (4) just punishment of clergy who commit mortal sins.

In November 1433 an agreement was reached between the emperor, the council, and the Hussites, giving the Bohemians jurisdiction over their church similar to that held by the French and the English. Three of the four Prague articles were conceded: communion with cup, free preaching by ordained clergy, and like punishment of clergy and laity for mortal sins.

The end of the Hussite wars and the reform legislation curtailing the papal power of appointment and taxation were the high points of the Council of Basel. The exercise of such power by a council did not please the pope, and in 1438 he gained the opportunity to upstage the Council of Basel by negotiating reunion with the Eastern church. The agreement, signed in Florence in 1439, was short-lived, but it restored papal prestige and signaled the demise of the conciliar movement. The Council of Basel collapsed in 1449. A decade later Pope Pius II (r. 1458–1464) issued the papal bull *Execrabilis* (1460) condemning appeals to councils as "erroneous and abominable" and "completely null and void."

Although many who had worked for reform now despaired of ever attaining it, the conciliar movement was not a total failure. It planted deep within the conscience of all Western peoples the conviction that the role of the leader of an institution is to provide for the well-being of its members, not just the leader.

A second consequence of the conciliar movement was the devolving of religious responsibility onto the laity and secular government. Without papal leadership, secular control of national or territorial churches increased. Kings asserted power over the Church in England and France. In German, Swiss, and Italian cities magistrates and city councils reformed and regulated religious life. This development could not be reversed by the powerful popes of the High Renaissance. On the contrary, as the papacy became a limited territorial regime, national control of the Church ran apace. Perceived as just one among several Italian states, the Papal States could now be opposed as much on the grounds of "national" policy as for religious reasons.

War, plague, and schism convulsed much of late medieval Europe throughout the fourteenth and into the fifteenth century. Two-fifths of the population, particularly along the major trade routes, died from plague in the fourteenth century. War and famine continued to take untold

The Chronicler Calls the Roll at the Council of Constance

The Council of Constance, in session for three years (1414–1417), not only drew many clergy and political representatives into its proceedings but also required a great variety of supporting personnel. Here is an inventory from the contemporary chronicle by Ulrich Richental.

✦ *What or who do you find surprising on this list? Do the numbers of participants suggest participation in the deliberations by clergy of every rank? Why were there embassies from Asia and Africa?*

Pope John XXIII came with 600 men.
Pope Martin, who was elected pope at Constance, came with 30 men.
5 patriarchs, with 118 men.
33 cardinals, with 3,056 men.
47 archbishops, with 4,700 men.
145 bishops, with 6,000 men.
93 suffragan bishops, with 360 men.
Some 500 spiritual lords, with 4,000 men. 24 auditors and secretaries, with 300 men. 37 scholars from the universities of all nations, with 2,000 men.
217 doctors of theology from the five nations, who walked in the processions, with 2,600 men.
361 doctors of both laws, with 1,260 men.
171 doctors of medicine, with 1,600 men.
1,400 masters of arts and licentiates, with 3,000 men.
5,300 simple priests and scholars, some by threes, some by twos, some alone.
The apothecaries who lived in huts, with 300 men. (16 of them were masters.)
72 goldsmiths, who lived in huts.
Over 1,400 merchants, shopkeepers, furriers, smiths, shoemakers, innkeepers, and handworkers, who lived in huts and rented houses and huts, with their servants.
24 rightful heralds of the King, with their squires.

1,700 trumpeters, fifers, fiddlers, and players of all kinds.
Over 700 harlots in brothels came, who hired their own houses, and some who lay in stables and wherever they could, beside the private ones whom I could not count.
In the train of the Pope were 24 secretaries with 200 men, 16 doorkeepers, 12 beadles who carried silver rods, 60 other beadles for the cardinals, auditors and auditors of the camera, and many old women who washed and mended the clothes of the Roman lords in private and public.
132 abbots, all named, with 2,000 men.
155 priors, all recorded with their names, with 1,600 men.
Our lord King, two queens, and 5 princely ladies.
39 dukes, 32 princely lords and counts, 141 counts, 71 barons, more than 1,500 knights, more than 20,000 noble squires.
Embassies from 83 kings of Asia, Africa, and Europe, with full powers; envoys from other lords without number, for they rode in and out every day. There were easily 5,000.
472 envoys from imperial cities.
352 envoys from baronial cities.
72,460 persons.

Richental's Chronicle of the Council, Constance, *in* The Council of Constance, *ed. by J. H. Mundy and K. M. Woodey, trans. by Louise R. Roomis (New York: Columbia University Press, 1961), pp. 189–190. Used by permission.*

numbers after the plague had passed. The introduction of gunpowder and heavy artillery during
the long years of warfare between England and
France resulted in new forms of human destruction. Periodic revolts erupted in town and countryside as ordinary people attempted to defend
their traditional communal rights and privileges
against the new autocratic territorial regimes.

Even God's house seemed to be a shambles
in 1409, when no fewer than three popes came
to rule simultaneously. The leading intellectual
movement of the period was Ockhamism (after
the philosopher William of Ockham). It stressed
the primacy of the individual and was skeptical
of the ability of reason to know much about
God. It has been viewed as an appropriate philosophy for this afflicted and pessimistic age.

There is, however, another side to the late
Middle Ages. By the end of the fifteenth century
the population losses were rapidly being made
up. Between 1300 and 1500, education became
greatly more accessible, especially for laypeople.
The number of universities increased 250 percent, from twenty to seventy, and the rise in the
number of residential colleges was even more
impressive, especially in France, where sixty-
three were built. The fourteenth century saw
the birth of humanism and the fifteenth century
gave us the printing press. Most impressive were
the artistic and cultural achievements of the
Italian Renaissance during the fifteenth century.
The later Middle Ages were thus a period of
growth and creativity as well as one of waning
and decline.

Review Questions

1. What were the underlying and precipitating
   causes of the Hundred Years' War? What
   advantages did each side have? Why were the
   French finally able to drive the English
   almost entirely out of France?
2. What were the causes of the Black Death and
   why did it spread so quickly throughout
   western Europe? Where was it most virulent?
   What were its effects on European society?
   How important do you think disease is in
   changing the course of history?
3. Discuss the struggle between Pope Boniface
   VIII and King Philip the Fair. Why was

Boniface so impotent in the conflict? How
had political conditions changed since the
reign of Pope Innocent III in the late twelfth
century, and what did that mean for the
papacy?
4. Briefly trace the history of the Church from
   1200 to 1450. How did it respond to political
   threats from the growing power of monarchs?
   How great an influence did the Church have
   on secular events?
5. What was the "Avignon Papacy", and why did
   it occur? What effect did it have on the state
   of the papacy? What relation does it have to
   the Great Schism? How did the Church
   become divided and how was it reunited?
   Why was the Conciliar Movement a setback
   for the papacy?
6. Why were kings in the late thirteenth and
   early fourteenth centuries able to control the
   Church more than it could control them?
   How did kings attack the Church during this
   period? Contrast these events with earlier
   ones in which the pope dominated rulers.

Suggested Readings

C. ALLMAND, *The Hundred Years' War: England and
France at War, c. 1300–c. 1450* (1988). Good
overview of war's development and consequences.

P. ARIES, *The Hour of Our Death* (1983). People's
familiarity with and philosophy of death in the
Middle Ages.

R. BARBER (Ed.), *The Pastons: Letters of a Family in
the War of the Roses* (1984). Revelations of English
family life in an age of crisis.

D. HAY, *Europe in the Fourteenth and Fifteenth
Centuries* (1966). Many-sided treatment of political
history.

J. HUIZINGA, *The Waning of the Middle Ages: A Study
of the Forms of Life, Thought, and Art in France
and the Netherlands in the Dawn of the
Renaissance* (1924). A classic study of "mentality"
at the end of the Middle Ages; exaggerated, but
engrossing.

G. LEFF, *Heresy in the Later Middle Ages, I–II* (1967).
Magisterial survey of all the major heretical movements.

J. LE GOFF, *The Birth of Purgatory,* trans. by A.
Goldhammer (1984). Cultural impact of the idea.

W. H. MCNEILL, *Plagues and Peoples* (1976). The
Black Death in a broader context.

F. OAKLEY, *The Western Church in the Later Middle Ages* (1979). Eloquent, sympathetic survey.

S. OZMENT, *The Age of Reform, 1250–1550* (1980). Highlights of late medieval intellectual and religious history.

E. PERROY, *The Hundred Years' War*, trans. by W. B. Wells (1965). Still the most comprehensive one-volume account.

C. PLATT, *The Castle in Medieval England and Wales* (1982). Has an illustrated chapter on English coastal castles built during the Hundred Years' War.

Y. RENOVARD, *The Avignon Papacy 1305–1403*, trans. by D. Bethell (1970). The standard narrative account.

M. SPINKA, *John Huss's Concept of the Church* (1966). Lucid and authoritative account of Hussite theology.

B. TIERNEY, *Foundations of the Conciliar Theory* (1955). Important study showing the origins of conciliar theory in canon law.

B. TIERNEY, *The Crisis of Church and State 1050–1300* (1964). Part IV provides the major documents in the clash between Boniface VIII and Philip the Fair.

W. ULLMANN, *Origins of the Great Schism* (1948). A basic study by a controversial interpreter of medieval political thought.

C. T. WOOD, *Philip the Fair and Boniface VIII* (1967). Excerpts from the scholarly debate over the significance of this confrontation.

H. B. WORKMAN, *John Wyclif*, Vols. 1 and 2 (1926). Dated but still standard.

P. ZIEGLER, *The Black Death* (1969). Highly readable account.

The famous Pietà (made between 1498 and 1500), by Michelangelo, St. Peter's, Rome. This work of the artist's youth, sculpted between his twenty-third and twenty-fifth years, portrays a Mary who is younger than her son. Unsurpassed in delicacy, realism, and emotional impact, it exemplifies the creative energy of the Italian Renaissance. [Scala/Art Resource, N.Y.]

10

Renaissance and Discovery

Key Topics in This Chapter
◆ The politics, culture, and art of the Italian Renaissance
◆ Political struggle and foreign intervention in Italy
◆ The powerful new monarchies of northern Europe
◆ The thought and culture of the northern Renaissance

If the late Middle Ages saw unprecedented chaos, it also witnessed a rebirth that would continue into the seventeenth century. Two modern Dutch scholars have employed the same word (Herfsttij, "harvesttide") with different connotations to describe the period. One has interpreted the word as a "waning" or "decline" (Johan Huizinga), the other as a true "harvest" (Heiko Oberman). If something was dying away, some ripe fruit and seed grain were also being gathered in. The late Middle Ages were a creative breaking up.

By the late fifteenth century, Europe was recovering well from two of the three crises of the late Middle Ages: the demographic and the political. The great losses in population were being made up, and increasingly able monarchs and rulers were imposing a new political order. A solution to the religious crisis, however, would have to await the Reformation and Counter-Reformation of the sixteenth century.

Although the situation would reverse itself in the sixteenth and seventeenth centuries, the city-states of Italy survived the century and a half between 1300 and 1450 better than the territorial states of northern Europe. This was due to Italy's strategic location between East and West and its lucrative Eurasian trade. Great wealth gave rulers and merchants the ability to work their will on both society and culture. They became patrons of government, education, and the arts, always as much for self-aggrandizement as out of benevolence. For whether a family, a firm, a government, or the Church their endowments enhanced their reputation and power. The result of such patronage was a cultural Renaissance in Italian cities unmatched elsewhere.

With the fall of Constantinople to the Turks in 1453, the shrinkage of Italy's once unlimited trading empire began. City-state soon turned against city-state, and by the 1490s the armies of France invaded Italy. Within a quarter century, Italy's great Renaissance had peaked.

The fifteenth century also saw an unprecedented scholarly renaissance. Italian and northern Humanists made a full recovery of classical knowledge and languages and set in motion educational reforms and cultural changes that would spread throughout Europe in the fifteenth and sixteenth centuries. In the process the Italian Humanists invented, for all practical purposes, critical historical scholarship and exploited a new fifteenth-century invention, the "divine art" of printing with movable type.

In this period the vernacular, the local language, began to take its place alongside Latin, the international language, as a widely used literary and political language. And European lands progressively superseded the universal Church as the community of highest allegiance, as patriotism and incipient nationalism seized hearts and minds as strongly as religion. Nations henceforth "transcended" themselves not by journeys to Rome but by competitive voyages to the Far East and the Americas, as the age of global exploration opened.

For Europe the late fifteenth and sixteenth centuries were a period of unprecedented territorial expansion and ideological experimentation. Permanent colonies were established within the Americas, and the exploitation of the New World's human and mineral resources was begun. Imported American gold and silver spurred scientific invention and a new weapons industry and touched off an inflationary spiral that produced an escalation in prices by the century's end. The new bullion also helped create an international traffic in African slaves as rival African tribes sold their captives to the Portuguese. These slaves were brought in ever-increasing numbers to work the mines and the plantations of the New World as replacements for faltering American natives. These centuries also saw social engineering and political planning on a large scale. Newly centralized governments began to put long-range economic policies into practice, a development that came to be known as mercantilism.

The Renaissance in Italy (1375–1527)

In a famous study, *Civilization of the Renaissance in Italy* (1860), Jacob Burckhardt described the Renaissance as the prototype of the modern world. He believed that in fourteenth- and fifteenth-century Italy, through the revival of ancient learning, new secular and scientific values began to supplant traditional religious beliefs. This was the period in which people began to adopt a rational, objective, and statistical approach to reality and to rediscover the importance of the individual and his or her artistic creativity. The result, in Burckhardt's words, was a release of the "full, whole nature of man."

Other scholars have found Burckhardt's description far too modernizing an interpretation of the Renaissance and have accused him of overlooking the continuity between the Middle Ages and the Renaissance. His critics especially stress the still strongly Christian character of Renaissance Humanism. They point out that earlier "renaissances," especially that of the twelfth century, also saw the revival of the ancient classics, interest in Latin language and Greek science, and appreciation of the worth and creativity of individuals.

Despite the exaggeration and bias of Burckhardt's portrayal of the Renaissance, most scholars agree that the Renaissance was a time of transition from the medieval to the modern world. Medieval Europe, especially before the twelfth century, had been a fragmented feudal society with an agricultural economy, and its thought and culture were largely dominated by the Church. Renaissance Europe, especially after the fourteenth century, was characterized by growing national consciousness and political centralization, an urban economy based on organized commerce and capitalism, and ever greater lay and secular control of thought and culture, including religion.

The distinctive features and achievements of the Renaissance are most strikingly revealed in Italy from roughly 1375 to 1527, the year of the infamous sack of Rome by imperial soldiers. What was achieved in Italy during the late fourteenth and the early sixteenth centuries also deeply influenced northern Europe.

The Italian City-State

Renaissance society was no simple cultural transformation. It first took distinctive shape within the cities of late medieval Italy. Italy had always had a cultural advantage over the rest of Europe because its geography made it the natural gateway between East and West. Venice, Genoa, and Pisa traded uninterruptedly with the Near East throughout the Middle Ages and maintained vibrant urban societies. When commerce revived on a large scale in the eleventh century, Italian merchants quickly mastered the business skills of organization, bookkeeping, scouting new markets, and securing monopolies. During the thirteenth and fourteenth centuries, trade-rich cities expanded to become powerful city-states, dominating the political and economic life of the surrounding countryside. By the fifteenth century, the great Italian cities had become the bankers of much of Europe.

GROWTH OF CITY-STATES The growth of Italian cities and urban culture was assisted by the endemic warfare between the emperor and the pope and the Guelf (propapal) and Ghibelline (proimperial) factions that this warfare had created. Either of these might have successfully challenged the cities had they permitted each other to concentrate on it. They chose instead to weaken one another and thus strengthened the merchant oligarchies of the

Isabella d'Este (1474–1539) was one of the most celebrated princesses of the Renaissance. Isabella was the Duchess of Mantua, a small state in northern Italy, and one of the great patrons of the Renaissance. Her court became a major center for artists, musicians, and humanists This portrait is by Titian (1477–1576), the most popular portrait painter of the age, patronized by the richest and most influential people in Europe. [Kunsthistorisches Museum, Vienna]

cities. Unlike those of northern Europe, which tended to be dominated by kings and territorial princes, the great Italian cities were left free to expand into states. They became independent states, absorbing the surrounding countryside and assimilating the area's nobility in a unique urban meld of old and new rich. There were five

MAP 10-1 RENAISSANCE ITALY *The city-states of Renaissance Italy were self-contained principalities whose internal strife was monitored by their despots and whose external aggression was long successfully controlled by treaty.*

such major, competitive states in Italy: the duchy of Milan; the republics of Florence and Venice; the Papal States; and the kingdom of Naples (see Map 10-1).

Social strife and competition for political power were so intense within the cities that, for sheer survival's sake, most evolved into despotisms by the fifteenth century. Venice was a notable exception. It was ruled by a successful merchant oligarchy with power located in a patrician senate of 300 members and a ruthless judicial body, the Council of Ten, that anticipated and suppressed rival groups. Elsewhere, the new social classes and divisions within society,

produced by rapid urban growth, fueled chronic, near-anarchic conflict.

SOCIAL CLASS AND CONFLICT Florence was the most striking example. There were four distinguishable social groups within the city. The first was the old rich, or *grandi*, the nobles and merchants who traditionally ruled the city. The second group was the emergent new-rich merchant class, capitalists and bankers known as the *popolo grosso*, or "fat people." They began to challenge the old rich for political power in the late thirteenth and early fourteenth centuries. Then there were the middle-burgher ranks of guildmasters, shopowners, and professionals, those smaller businesspeople who, in Florence as elsewhere, tended to take the side of the new rich against the conservative policies of the old rich. Finally, there was the *popolo minuto*, or "the little people," the lower economic classes. In 1457 one-third of the population of Florence, about 30,000 people, were officially listed as paupers, that is, having no wealth at all.

These social divisions produced conflict at every level of society, to which was added the ever-present fear of foreign intrigue. In 1378 there was a great revolt of the poor known as the Ciompi Revolt. It resulted from a combination of three factors that made life unbearable for those at the bottom of society: the feuding between the old and the new rich; the social anarchy that had resulted from the Black Death, which cut the city's population almost in half; and the collapse of the banking houses of Bardi and Peruzzi, which left the poor more economically vulnerable than ever. The successful revolt established a chaotic four-year reign of power by the lower Florentine classes. True stability did not return to Florence until the ascent to power in 1434 of Cosimo dé Medici (1389–1464).

DESPOTISM AND DIPLOMACY The wealthiest Florentine, Cosimo dé Medici, was an astute statesman. He controlled the city internally from behind the scenes, skillfully manipulating the constitution and influencing elections. Florence was governed by a council of six (later eight) members known as the *Signoria*. These men were chosen from the most powerful guilds—those representing the major clothing industries (cloth, wool, fur, and silk) and such other groups as bankers, judges, and doctors.

Florentine women doing needlework, spinning, and weaving. These activities took up much of a woman's time and contributed to the elegance of dress for which Florentine men and women were famed. [Alinari/Art Resource]

Through his informal, cordial relations with the electoral committee, Cosimo was able to keep councillors loyal to him in the *Signoria*. As head of the Office of Public Debt, he was able to favor congenial factions. His grandson Lorenzo the Magnificent (1449–1492, r. 1478–1492) ruled Florence in almost totalitarian fashion during the last quarter of the fifteenth century. The assassination of his brother in 1478 by a rival family, the Pazzi, who plotted with the pope against Medici rule, made Lorenzo a cautious and determined ruler.

Despotism was less subtle elsewhere. To prevent internal social conflict and foreign intrigue from paralyzing their cities, the dominant groups cooperated to install a hired strongman. Known as a *podestà*, his purpose was to maintain law and order. He was given executive, military, and judicial authority. His mandate was direct and simple: to permit, by whatever means required, the normal flow of business activity without which not the old rich, the new rich, nor the poor of a city could long survive. Because these despots could not depend on the divided populace, they operated through merce-

nary armies, which they obtained through military brokers known as *condottieri*.

It was a hazardous job. Despots were not only subject to dismissal by the oligarchies that hired them, but they were also popular objects of assassination attempts. The spoils of success, however, were very great. In Milan, it was as despots that the Visconti family came to power in 1278 and the Sforza family in 1450. Both ruled without constitutional restraints or serious political competition. The latter produced one of Machiavelli's heroes, Ludovico il Moro.

Political turbulence and warfare gave birth to diplomacy. Consequently, the various city-states could stay abreast of foreign military developments and, if shrewd enough, gain power and advantage short of actually going to war. Most city-states established resident embassies in the fifteenth century. Their ambassadors not only represented them in ceremonies and as negotiators but also became their watchful eyes and ears at rival courts.

Whether within the comparatively tranquil republic of Venice, the strong-arm democracy of Florence, or the undisguised despotism of

Cosimo de'Medici (1389–1464), Florentine banker and statesman, in his lifetime the city's wealthiest man and most successful politician. This portrait is by Pontormo. [Erich Lessing, Art Resource, N.Y.]

Milan, the disciplined Italian city proved a most congenial climate for an unprecedented flowering of thought and culture. Italian Renaissance culture was promoted as vigorously by despots as by republicans and by secularized popes as enthusiastically as by the more spiritually minded. Such widespread support occurred because the main requirement for patronage of the arts and letters was the one thing that Italian cities of the High Renaissance had in abundance: great wealth.

Humanism

There are several schools of thought on the essence of Humanism. Those who follow the nineteenth-century historian Jacob Burckhardt, who saw the Italian Renaissance as the birth of modernity, view it as an un-Christian philosophy that stressed the dignity of humankind and championed individualism and secular values. Others argue that Humanists were the very champions of authentic Catholic Christianity, who opposed the pagan teaching of Aristotle and the ineloquent Scholasticism that his writings nurtured. Still others see Humanism as a form of scholarship consciously designed to promote a sense of civic responsibility and political liberty.

An authoritative modern commentator on Humanism is Paul O. Kristeller. He has accused all these views of dealing more with the secondary effects than with the essence of Humanism. Humanism, he believes, was no particular philosophy or value system but simply an educational program that concentrated on rhetoric and sound scholarship for their own sake.

There is truth in each of these definitions. Humanism was the scholarly study of the Latin and Greek classics and the ancient Church fathers both for their own sake and in the hope of a rebirth of ancient norms and values. Humanists advocated the *studia humanitatis*, a liberal arts program of study that embraced grammar, rhetoric, poetry, history, politics, and moral philosophy. Not only were these subjects considered a joy in themselves, they were also seen as celebrating the dignity of humankind and preparing people for a life of virtuous action. The Florentine Leonardo Bruni (ca. 1370–1444) first gave the name *humanitas* ("humanity") to the learning that resulted from such scholarly pursuits. Bruni was a student of Manuel Chrysoloras, a Byzantine scholar who opened the world of Greek scholarship to a generation of young Italian Humanists when he taught at Florence between 1397 and 1403.

The first Humanists were orators and poets. They wrote original literature, in both the classical and the vernacular languages, inspired by and modeled on the newly discovered works of the ancients. They also taught rhetoric within the universities. When Humanists were not employed as teachers of rhetoric, their talents were sought as secretaries, speech writers, and diplomats in princely and papal courts.

The study of classical and Christian antiquity

existed before the Italian Renaissance. There were recoveries of ancient civilization during the Carolingian renaissance of the ninth century, within the cathedral school of Chartres in the twelfth century, during the great Aristotelian revival in Paris in the thirteenth century, and among the Augustinians in the early fourteenth century. These precedents, however, only partially compare with the grand achievements of the Italian Renaissance of the late Middle Ages. The latter was far more secular and lay-dominated, had much broader interests, was blessed with far more recovered manuscripts, and possessed far superior technical skills than had been the case in the earlier "rebirths" of antiquity.

Unlike their Scholastic rivals, Humanists were less bound to recent tradition; they did not focus all their attention on summarizing and comparing the views of recognized authorities on a text or question, but went directly to the original sources themselves. And their most respected sources were classical and biblical, not the medieval philosophers and theologians. Avidly searching out manuscript collections, Italian Humanists made the full sources of Greek and Latin antiquity available to scholars during the fourteenth and fifteenth centuries. Mastery of Latin and Greek was the surgeon's tool of the Humanist. There is a kernel of truth—but only a kernel—in the arrogant boast of the Humanists that the period between themselves and classical civilization was a "dark middle age."

PETRARCH, DANTE, AND BOCCACCIO
Francesco Petrarch (1304–1374) was the father of Humanism. He left the legal profession to pursue his love of letters and poetry. Most of his life was spent in and around Avignon. However, he became caught up in Cola di Rienzo's popular revolt and two-year reign (1347–1349) in Rome as "tribune" of the Roman people. He also served the Visconti family in Milan in his later years.

Petrarch celebrated ancient Rome in his *Letters to the Ancient Dead*, fancied personal letters to Cicero, Livy, Vergil, and Horace. He also wrote a Latin epic poem (*Africa*, a poetic historical tribute to the Roman general Scipio Africanus) and a set of biographies of famous Romans (*Lives of Illustrious Men*). Petrarch's most famous contemporary work was a collec-

tion of highly introspective love sonnets to a certain Laura, a married woman whom he romantically admired from a safe distance.

His critical textual studies, elitism, and contempt for the allegedly useless learning of the Scholastics were features that many later Humanists also shared. Classical and Christian values coexist, not always harmoniously, in his work, and this uneasy coexistence is true, too, of many later Humanists. Medieval Christian values can be seen in Petrarch's imagined dialogues with Saint Augustine and in tracts written to defend the personal immortality of the soul against the Aristotelians.

Petrarch was, however, far more secular in orientation than his famous near-contemporary Dante Alighieri (1265–1321), whose *Vita Nuova* and *Divine Comedy* form with Petrarch's sonnets the cornerstones of Italian vernacular liter-

Petrarch (Francesco Petrarca, 1304–1374) is considered the father of Humanism. [Roger-Viollet]

*Dante Alighieri (1265–1321) portrayed with scenes of hell, purgatory, and paradise from
the* Divine Comedy, *his classic epic poem. [Scala/Art Resource, N.Y.]*

ature. Petrarch's student and friend Giovanni
Boccaccio (1313–1375) was also a pioneer of
Humanist studies. His *Decameron*, 100 often
bawdy tales told by three men and seven women
in a country retreat from the plague that ravaged
Florence in 1348, is both a stinging social commentary (especially in its exposé of sexual and
economic misconduct) and a sympathetic look
at human behavior. An avid collector of manuscripts, Boccaccio also assembled an encyclopedia of Greek and Roman mythology.

EDUCATIONAL REFORMS AND GOALS
Humanists were not bashful scholars. They
delighted in going directly to primary sources

and refused to be slaves to tradition. Such an
attitude not only made them innovative educators, it also kept them constantly in search of
new sources of information. Magnificent manuscript collections were assembled with great
care, as if they were potent medicines for the ills
of contemporary society.

The goal of Humanist studies was to be wise
and to speak eloquently, to know what is good
and to practice virtue. Learning was not to
remain abstract and unpracticed. "It is better to
will the good than to know the truth," Petrarch
had taught, and this became a motto of many
later Humanists, who like Petrarch believed that
learning ennobled people. Pietro Paolo Vergerio

(1349–1420), the author of the most influential Renaissance tract on education, *On the Morals that Befit a Free Man*, left a classic summary of the Humanist concept of a liberal education:

We call those studies liberal which are worthy of a free man; those studies by which we attain and practice virtue and wisdom; that education which calls forth, trains, and develops those highest gifts of body and mind which ennoble men and which are rightly judged to rank next in dignity to virtue only, for to a vulgar temper, gain and pleasure are the one aim of existence, to a lofty nature, moral worth and fame.[1]

The ideal of a useful education and well-rounded people inspired far-reaching reforms in traditional education. Quintilian's *Education of the Orator*, the complete text of which was discovered in 1416, became the basic classical guide for the Humanist revision of the traditional curriculum. Vittorino da Feltre (d. 1446) exemplified the ideals of Humanist teaching. He not only had his students read the difficult works of Pliny, Ptolemy, Terence, Plautus, Livy, and Plutarch, he subjected them as well to vigorous physical exercise and games. Another famous educator, Guarino da Verona (d. 1460), rector of the new University of Ferrara and a student of the age's most renowned Greek scholar, Manuel Chrysoloras, streamlined the study of classical languages there and gave it systematic form.

Humanist learning was not confined to the classroom, as Baldassare Castiglione's (1478–1529) famous *Book of the Courtier* illustrates. Written as a practical guide for the nobility at the court of Urbino, it embodied the highest ideals of Italian Humanism. It depicts the successful courtier as one who knew how to integrate knowledge of ancient languages and history with athletic, military, and musical skills, while practicing good manners and exhibiting moral character.

Noblewomen too played a role at court in education and culture, and among them none more so than Christine de Pisan (1363?–1434). The Italian-born daughter of the physician and astrologer of the French king Charles V, she received at the French court as fine an education

as any man. She became expert in classical, French, and Italian languages and literature. Married at fifteen and the widowed mother of three at twenty-seven, she turned to writing lyric poetry to support herself. She soon became a well-known woman of letters much read throughout the courts of Europe. Her most famous work, *The City of Ladies*, is a chronicle of the accomplishments of the great women of history.

THE FLORENTINE "ACADEMY" AND THE REVIVAL OF PLATONISM Of all the important recoveries of the past made during the Italian Renaissance, none stands out more than the revival of Greek studies, especially the works of Plato, in fifteenth-century Florence. Many factors combined to bring this revival about. An important foundation was laid in 1397 when the city invited Manuel Chrysoloras to come from Constantinople and promote Greek learning. A half century later (1439), the ecumenical Council of Ferrara–Florence, having convened to negotiate the reunion of the Eastern and Western churches, opened the door for many Greek scholars and manuscripts to enter the West. After the fall of Constantinople to the Turks in 1453, Greek scholars fled to Florence for refuge. This was the background against which the Florentine Platonic Academy evolved under the patronage of Cosimo dé Medici and the supervision of Marsilio Ficino (1433–1499) and Pico della Mirandola (1463–1494).

The thinkers of the Renaissance were interested in every variety of ancient wisdom. They were especially attracted, however, to the Platonic tradition and to those Church fathers who tried to synthesize Platonic philosophy and Christian teaching. The Florentine "Academy" was actually not a formal school, but an informal gathering of influential Florentine Humanists devoted to the revival of the works of Plato and the Neoplatonists: Plotinus, Proclus, Porphyry, and Dionysius the Areopagite. To this end, Ficino edited and published the complete works of Plato.

The appeal of Platonism lay in its flattering view of human nature. It distinguished between an eternal sphere of being and the perishable world in which humans actually lived. Human

[1]*Cited by De Lamar Jensen,* Renaissance Europe: Age of Recovery and Reconciliation *(Lexington, Mass.: D. C. Health, 1981), p. 111.*

Christine de Pisan Instructs Women on How to Handle Their Husbands

Renown Renaissance noblewoman Christine de Pisan has the modern reputation of being perhaps the first feminist, and her book, The Treasure of the City of Ladies *(also known as* The Book of Three Virtues*) has been described as the Renaissance woman's survival manual. Here she gives advice to the wives of artisans.*

◆ *How does Christine de Pisan's image of husband and wife compare with other medieval views? Would the Church take issue with her advice in any way? As a noblewoman commenting on the married life of artisans, does her high social standing influence her advice? Would she give similar advice to women of her own social class?*

All wives of artisans should be very painstaking and diligent if they wish to have the necessities of life. They should encourage their husbands or their workmen to get to work early in the morning and work until late. . . . [And] the wife herself should [also] be involved in the work to the extent that she knows all about it, so that she may know how to oversee his workers if her husband is absent, and to reprove them if they do not do well. . . . And when customers come to her husband and try to drive a hard bargain, she ought to warn him solicitously to take care that he does not make a bad deal. She should advise him to be chary of giving too much credit if he does not know precisely where and to whom it is going, for in this way many come to poverty. . . .

In addition, she ought to keep her husband's love as much as she can, to this end: that he will stay at home more willingly and that he may not have any reason to join the foolish crowds of other young men in taverns and indulge in unnecessary and extravagant expense, as many tradesmen do, especially in Paris. By treating him kindly she should protect him as well as she can from this. It is said that three things drive a man from his home: a quarrelsome wife, a smoking fireplace, and a leaking roof. She too ought to stay at home gladly and not go off every day traipsing hither and yon gossiping with the neighbours and visiting her chums to find out what everyone is doing. That is done by slovenly housewives roaming about the town in groups. Nor should she go off on these pilgrimages got up for no good reason and involving a lot of needless expense.

Christine de Pisan, The Treasure of the City of Ladies or The Book of the Three Virtues, *trans. by Sarah Lawson (Penguin Books: New York, 1985), pp. 167–168.*

reason was believed to belong to the former, indeed, to have preexisted in this pristine world and to continue to commune with it, as the present knowledge of mathematical and moral truth bore witness.

Strong Platonic influence can be seen in Pico's *Oration on the Dignity of Man*, perhaps the most famous Renaissance statement on the nature of humankind. Pico wrote the *Oration* as an introduction to a pretentious collection of 900 theses. Published in Rome in December 1486, they were intended to serve as the basis for a public debate on all of life's important topics. The *Oration* drew on Platonic teaching to depict humans as the only creatures in the world who possessed the freedom to be whatever they chose, able at will to rise to the height of angels or to descend to the level of pigs.

CRITICAL WORK OF THE HUMANISTS: LORENZO VALLA Because they were guided by a scholarly ideal of philological accuracy and historical truthfulness, the Humanists could become critics of tradition even when that was not their intention. Dispassionate critical scholarship shook long-standing foundations, not the least of which were those of the medieval Church.

The work of Lorenzo Valla (1406–1457), author of the standard Renaissance text on Latin philology, the *Elegances of the Latin Language* (1444), reveals the explosive character of the new learning. Although a good Catholic, Valla became a hero to later Protestants. His popularity among Protestants stemmed from his defense of predestination against the advocates of free will, and especially from his exposé of the *Donation of Constantine* (see Chapter 6).

This fraudulent document, written in the eighth century, was allegedly a grant of vast territories made by the fourth-century Roman emperor Constantine to the pope. Valla did not intend the exposé of the *Donation* to have the

---

Pico della Mirandola States the Renaissance Image of Man

One of the most eloquent descriptions of the Renaissance image of human beings comes from the Italian Humanist Pico della Mirandola (1463–1494). In his famed Oration on the Dignity of Man *(ca. 1486), Pico describes humans as free to become whatever they choose.*

◆ *How great, really, is the choice outlined here? Are the basic options limited? Do they differ from what the Church thought life's possibilities were? Is the concept of freedom in this passage a modern one?*

The best of artisans [God] ordained that that creature (man) to whom He had been able to give nothing proper to himself should have joint possession of whatever had been peculiar to each of the different kinds of being. He therefore took man as a creature of indeterminate nature and, assigning him a place in the middle of the world, addressed him thus: "Neither a fixed abode nor a form that is thine alone nor any function peculiar to thyself have we given thee, Adam, to the end that according to thy longing and according to thy judgment thou mayest have and possess what abode, what form, and what functions thou thyself shalt desire. The nature of all other beings is limited and constrained within the bounds of laws prescribed by Us. Thou, constrained by no limits, in accordance with thine own free will, in whose hand We have placed thee, shall ordain for thyself the limits of thy nature. We have set thee at the world's center that thou mayest from thence more easily observe whatever is in the world. We have made thee neither of heaven nor of earth, neither mortal nor immortal, so that with freedom of choice and with honor, as though the maker and molder of thyself, thou mayest fashion thyself in whatever shape thou shalt prefer. Thou shalt have the power to degenerate into the lower forms of life, which are brutish. Thou shalt have the power, out of thy soul's judgment, to be reborn into the higher forms, which are divine." O supreme generosity of God the Father, O highest and most marvelous felicity of man! To him it is granted to have whatever he chooses, to be whatever he wills.

Giovanni Pico della Mirandola, Oration on the Dignity of Man, *in* The Renaissance Philosophy of Man, *ed. by E. Cassirer et al. (Chicago: Phoenix Books, 1961), pp. 224–225.*

devastating force that Protestants later attributed to it. He only proved in a careful, scholarly way what others had long suspected. Using the most rudimentary textual analysis and historical logic, Valla proved that the document was filled with such anachronistic terms as *fief* and made references that were meaningless in the fourth century. In the same dispassionate way Valla also pointed out errors in the Latin Vulgate, still the authorized version of the Bible for the Western church.

Such discoveries did not make Valla any less loyal to the Church, nor did they prevent his faithful fulfillment of the office of Apostolic Secretary in Rome under Pope Nicholas V. Nonetheless, historical criticism of this type

served those less loyal to the medieval Church. It was no accident that young Humanists formed the first identifiable group of Martin Luther's supporters.

Civic Humanism Italian Humanists were exponents of applied knowledge; their basic criticism of traditional education was that much of it was useless. Education, they believed, should promote individual virtue and public service. This ideal inspired what has been called *civic Humanism,* by which is meant examples of Humanist leadership of the political and cultural life. The most striking instance is to be found in Florence. There three Humanists served as chancellors: Colluccio Salutati (1331–1406),

Giotto's portrayal of the funeral of St. Francis of Assisi. The saint is surrounded by his admiring brothers and a knight of Assisi (first on the right). Giotto's (1266–1336) work signals the evolution toward Renaissance art. The damaged areas on this fresco resulted from removing nineteenth century restorations. [Scala/Art Resource, N.Y.]

A Contemporary Description of Leonardo

In this passage, Giorgio Vasari (1512–1574), friend and biographer of the great Renaissance painters, sculptors, and architects, claims Leonardo da Vinci's versatility was actually a handicap.

◆ According to Vasari, how does Leonardo's genius work against him? Why do you suppose so many scholars have pointed to Leonardo as the prototypical "Renaissance man"?

The richest gifts are occasionally seen to be showered, as by celestial influence, upon certain human beings; nay, they sometimes supernaturally and marvelously gather in a single person—beauty, grace, and talent united in such a manner that to whatever the man thus favored may turn himself, his every action is so divine as to leave all other men far behind. . . . This was . . . the case of Leonardo da Vinci . . . who had . . . so rare a gift of talent and ability that to whatever subject he turned his attention . . . he presently made himself absolute master of it. . . .

He would without doubt have made great progress in the learning and knowledge of the sciences had he not been so versatile and changeful. The instability of his character led him to undertake many things, which, having commenced, he afterwards abandoned. In arithmetic, for example, he made such rapid progress in the short time he gave his attention to it, that he often confounded the master who was teaching him. . . . He also commenced the study of music and resolved to acquire the art of playing the lute . . . singing to the instrument most divinely. . . .

Being also an excellent geometrician, Leonardo not only worked in sculpture but also in architecture; likewise he prepared . . . designs for . . . entire buildings. . . . While only a youth, he first suggested the formation of a canal from Pisa to Florence by means of certain changes . . . in the river Arno. He made designs for mills, fulling machines, and other engines run by water. But as he had resolved to make painting his profession, he gave the greater part of his time to drawing from nature.

James Harvey Robinson, ed., Readings in European History, Vol. 1 *(Boston: Athenaeum, 1904), pp. 535–536.*

Leonardo Bruni (ca. 1370–1444), and Poggio Bracciolini (1380–1459). Each used his rhetorical skills to rally the Florentines against the aggression of Naples and Milan. Bruni and Poggio also wrote adulatory histories of the city. Another accomplished Humanist scholar, Leon Battista Alberti (1402–1472), was a noted architect and builder in the city. Whether it was Humanism that accounted for such civic activity or just a desire to exercise great power remains a debated issue.

On the other hand, many Humanists became cliquish and snobbish, an intellectual elite concerned only with pursuing narrow, antiquarian interests and writing pure, classical Latin in the quiet of their studies. It was in reaction against this elitist trend that the Humanist historians Niccolò Machiavelli (1469–1527) and Francesco Guicciardini (1483–1540) adopted the vernacular and made contemporary history their primary source and subject matter.

Renaissance Art

In Renaissance Italy, as in Reformation Europe, the values and interests of the laity were no longer subordinated to those of the clergy. In

These two works by Donatello, sculpted fifteen years apart, reveal the psychological complexity of Renaissance artists and their work. On the left is a youthful, sexy David, standing awkwardly and seemingly puzzled on the head of the slain Goliath. Created in 1440, it is the earliest free-standing nude made in the West since Roman times. On the right, sculpted in 1454–55 from poplar wood, is Mary Magdalen returned from her desert retreat; she is a toothless hag, shorn of all dignity. [right, Scala/Art Resource, N.Y.] [left, Art Resource, N.Y.]

education, culture, and religion the laity assumed a leading role and established models for the clergy to imitate. This was a development due in part to the Church's loss of international power during the great crises of the late Middle Ages. It was also encouraged by the rise of national sentiment, the creation of competent national bureaucracies staffed by the laity rather than clerics, and the rapid growth of lay education during the fourteenth and fifteenth centuries. Medieval Christian values were adjusting to a more this-worldly spirit. Men and women began again to appreciate and even glorify the secular world, secular learning, and purely human pursuits as ends in themselves.

This new perspective on life is prominent in the painting and sculpture of the High Renaissance—the late fifteenth and early sixteenth centuries, when Renaissance art reached its full maturity. Whereas medieval art tended to be abstract and formulaic, Renaissance art was emphatically concerned with the observation of the natural world and the communication of human emotions. Renaissance artists also tried to give their works a greater rational (chiefly mathematical) order, a symmetry and proportionality that reflected pictorially their deeply held belief in the harmony of the universe. The interest of Renaissance artists in ancient Roman art was closely allied to an independent interest in humanity and nature.

Renaissance artists had the advantage of new technical skills developed during the fifteenth century. In addition to the availability of oil paints, two special techniques were perfected: that of using shading to enhance naturalness (chiaroscuro) and that of adjusting the size of figures to give the viewer a feeling of continuity with the painting (linear perspective). These techniques permitted the artist to "rationalize" space and paint a more natural world. The result was that, when compared with their flat Byzantine and Gothic counterparts, Renaissance paintings were filled with energy and life and stood out from the canvas in three dimensions.

The new direction was signaled by Giotto (1266–1336), the father of Renaissance painting. An admirer of Saint Francis of Assisi, whose love of nature he shared, Giotto painted a more natural world than his Byzantine and Gothic predecessors. Though still filled with religious seriousness, his work was no longer so

Raphael's portrait (c. 1515) of Baldassare Castiglione (1478–1529), now in the Louvre. Castiglione, author of the Book of the Courtier, *was Raphael's close friend. The self-restraint and inner calm which he considered the chief qualities of the gentleman are also qualities of Raphael's art, reflected in the portrait's perfect balance and harmony. This painting greatly influenced Rembrandt, who later tried unsuccessfully to buy it. [Service Photographique des Musées Nationaux, Paris]*

abstract and unnatural a depiction of the world. The painter Masaccio (1401–1428) and the sculptor Donatello (1386–1466) continued to portray the world around them more literally and naturally. The heights were reached by the great masters of the High Renaissance: Leonardo da Vinci (1452–1519), Raphael (1483–1520), and Michelangelo Buonarroti (1475–1564).

LEONARDO DA VINCI More than any other person in the period, Leonardo exhibited the Renaissance ideal of the universal person. He was a true master of many skills. One of the greatest painters of all time, he was also a military engineer for Ludovico il Moro in Milan, Cesare Borgia in Romagna, and the French king Francis I. Leonardo advocated scientific experimentation, dissected corpses to learn anatomy, and was an accomplished, self-taught botanist. His inventive mind foresaw such modern machines as airplanes and submarines. Indeed, the variety of his interests was so great that it could shorten his attention span, so that he was constantly moving from one activity to another. His great skill in conveying inner moods through complex facial features can be seen in the most famous of his paintings, the *Mona Lisa*, as well as in his self-portrait.

RAPHAEL Raphael, a man of great sensitivity and kindness, was apparently loved by contemporaries as much for his person as for his work. His premature death at thirty-seven cut short his artistic career. He is famous for his tender madonnas, the best known of which graced the monastery of San Sisto in Piacenza and is now in Dresden. Art historians praise his fresco *The School of Athens*, a grandly conceived portrayal of the great masters of Western philosophy, as a virtually perfect example of Renaissance technique. It depicts Plato and Aristotle surrounded by the great philosophers and scientists of antiquity, who are portrayed with features of Raphael's famous contemporaries, including Leonardo and Michelangelo.

MICHELANGELO The melancholy genius Michelangelo also excelled in a variety of arts and crafts. His eighteen-foot godlike sculpture *David*, which long stood majestically in the great square of Florence, is a perfect example of the Renaissance artist's devotion to harmony, symmetry, and proportion, as well as the extreme glorification of the human form. Four different popes commissioned works by Michelangelo. The most famous are the frescoes

Vasari Describes the Magic of Raphael's Personality

In this passage, Vasari describes the painter Raphael as a person with an extraordinary ability to create an atmosphere of harmony among those who worked with him.

◆ *Do you find the personal traits of Raphael, as described by Vasari, also reflected in his paintings? Is the author romanticizing the artist? Compare this with his description of Leonardo in the preceding document.*

There was among his many extraordinary gifts one of such value and importance that I can never sufficiently admire it and always think thereof with astonishment. This was the power accorded him by heaven of bringing all who approached his presence into harmony, an effect . . . contrary to the nature of our artists. Yet all . . . became as of one mind once they began to labor in the society of Raphael, and they continued in such unity and concord that all harsh feelings and evil dispositions became subdued and disappeared at the sight of him. . . . This happened because all were surpassed by him in friendly courtesy as well as in art. All confessed the influence of his sweet and gracious nature. . . . Not only was he honored by men, but even by the very animals who would constantly follow his steps and always loved him.

James Harvey Robinson, ed., Readings in European History, Vol. 1 *(Boston: Athenaeum, 1904), pp. 536–537.*

for the Sistine Chapel, painted during the pontificate of Pope Julius II (1503–1513), who also set Michelangelo to work on the pope's own magnificent tomb. The Sistine frescoes originally covered 10,000 square feet and involved 343 figures, over half of which exceeded 10 feet in height. But it is their originality and perfection as works of art that impress most. This labor of love and piety took four years to complete. A person of incredible energy and endurance who lived to be almost ninety, Michelangelo insisted on doing almost everything himself and permitted his assistants only a few of the many chores involved in his work.

His later works are more complex and suggest deep personal changes. They mark, artistically and philosophically, the passing of High Renaissance painting and the advent of a new style known as *Mannerism,* which reached its peak in the late sixteenth and early seventeenth centuries. A reaction against the simplicity and symmetry of High Renaissance art (which also found expression in music and literature), Mannerism made room for the strange and even the abnormal and gave freer reign to the subjectivity of the artist. Mannerism acquired its name because the artist was permitted to express his or her own individual perceptions and feelings, to paint, compose, or write in a "mannered" or "affected" way. Tintoretto (d. 1594) and especially El Greco (d. 1614) became Mannerism's supreme representatives.

Slavery in the Renaissance

Throughout Renaissance Italy, slavery flourished as extravagantly as art and culture. A thriving western slave market existed as early as the twelfth century, when the Spanish sold Muslim slaves captured in raids and war to wealthy Italians and other interested buyers. Contemporaries looked on such slavery as a merciful act, since these captives would otherwise have been killed. In addition to widespread household or domestic slavery, collective plantation slavery, following East Asian models, also developed during the High Middle Ages in the eastern Mediterranean. In the savannas of Sudan and on Venetian estates on the islands of Cyprus and Crete, gangs of slaves worked sugar

This portrait of Katharina, by Albrecht Dürer, provides evidence of African slavery in Europe during the sixteenth century. Katharina was in the service of one João Bradao, a Portuguese economic minister living in Antwerp, then the financial center of Europe. Dürer became friends with Bradao during his stay in the Low Countries in the winter of 1520–1521. [Bildarchiv Foto Marburg/Art Resource, N.Y.]

cane plantations, the model for later western Mediterranean and New World slavery.

After the Black Death (1348–1350) had reduced the supply of laborers everywhere in western Europe, the demand for slaves soared. Slaves now began to be imported from Africa, the Balkans, Constantinople, Cyprus, Crete, and the lands surrounding the Black Sea. Because slaves were taken randomly from con-

Michelangelo and
Pope Julius II

Vasari here describes how Pope Julius, the most fearsome and worldly of the Renaissance popes, forced Michelangelo to complete the Sistine Chapel before Michelangelo was ready to do so.

◆ *Did Michelangelo hold his own with the pope? What does this interchange suggest about the relationship of patrons and artists in the Renaissance? Were great artists like Michelangelo so revered that they could do virtually as they pleased?*

[The pope was very anxious to see the decoration of the Sistine Chapel completed, and constantly inquired when it would be finished.] On one occasion, therefore, Michelangelo replied, "It will be finished when I shall have done all that I believe is required to satisfy Art." "And we command," rejoined the pontiff, "that you satisfy our wish to have it done quickly," adding that if it were not at once completed, he would have Michelangelo thrown headlong from the scaffolding. Hearing this, our artist, who feared the fury of the pope, and with good cause, without taking time to add what was wanting, took down the remainder of the scaffolding to the great satisfaction of the whole city on All Saints' day, when Pope Julius went into that chapel to sing mass. But Michelangelo had much desired to retouch some portions of the work *a secco* [that is, after the damp plaster upon which the paint had been originally laid *al fresco* had dried], as had been done by the older masters who had painted the stories on the walls. He would also have gladly added a little ultramarine to the draperies and gilded other parts, to the end that the whole might have a richer and more striking effect.

The pope, too, hearing that these things were still wanting, and finding that all who beheld the chapel praised it highly, would now fain have had the additions made. But as Michelangelo thought reconstructing the scaffold too long an affair, the pictures remained as they were, although the pope, who often saw Michelangelo, would sometimes say, "Let the chapel be enriched with bright colors and gold; it looks poor." When Michelangelo would reply familiarly, "Holy Father, the men of those days did not adorn themselves with gold; those who are painted here less than any, for they were none too rich; besides which they were holy men, and must have despised riches and ornaments."

James Harvey Robinson, ed., Readings in European History, Vol. 1 *(Boston: Athenaeum, 1904), pp. 538–539.*

quered people, they consisted of many races: Tatars, Circassians, Greeks, Russians, Georgians, and Iranians as well as Asians and Africans. According to one source, "By the end of the fourteenth century, there was hardly a well-to-do household in Tuscany without at least one slave: brides brought them [to their marriages] as part of their dowry, doctors accepted them from their patients in lieu of fees—and it was not unusual to find them even in the service of a priest."[2]

Owners had complete dominion over their slaves; in Italian law, this meant the "[power] to have, hold, sell, alienate, exchange, enjoy, rent or unrent, dispose of in [their] will[s], judge soul

[2]*Iris Origo,* The Merchant of Prato: Francesco di Marco Datini 1335–1410 *(New York: David Godine, 1986), pp. 90–91.*

and body, and do with in perpetuity whatsoever may please [them] and [their] heirs and no man may gainsay [them]."[3] A strong, young, healthy slave cost the equivalent of the wages paid a free servant over several years. Considering the lifetime of free service thereafter, slaves could be well worth the cost.

The Tatars and Africans appear to have been the worst treated. But as in ancient Greece and Rome, slaves at this time were generally accepted as family members and were integrated into households. Not a few women slaves became mothers of their masters' children. Quite a few children of such unions were adopted and raised as legitimate heirs of their fathers. It was clearly in the interest of their owners to keep slaves healthy and happy; otherwise they were of little use and could even become a threat. Still, slaves remained a foreign and suspected presence in Italian society; they were, as all knew, uprooted and resentful people.

Italy's Political Decline: The French Invasions (1494–1527)

The Treaty of Lodi

As a land of autonomous city-states, Italy's peace and safety from foreign invasion, especially from invasion by the Turks, had always depended on internal cooperation. Such cooperation had been maintained during the last half of the fifteenth century, thanks to a carefully constructed political alliance known as the Treaty of Lodi (1454–1455). The terms of the treaty brought Milan and Naples, long traditional enemies, into alliance with Florence. These three stood together for decades against Venice, which was frequently joined by the Papal States, to create an internal balance of power. When a foreign enemy threatened Italy, however, the five formed a united front.

Around 1490, following the rise to power of the Milanese despot Ludovico il Moro, hostilities between Milan and Naples resumed. The peace made possible by the Treaty of Lodi ended in 1494 when Naples, supported by Florence

[3]Ibid., p. 209.

and the Borgia Pope Alexander VI (r. 1492–1503), prepared to attack Milan. Ludovico made what proved to be a fatal response in these new political alignments; he appealed for aid to the French. French kings had ruled Naples from 1266 to 1435, before they were driven out by Duke Alfonso of Sicily. Breaking a wise Italian rule, Ludovico invited the French to reenter Italy and revive their dynastic claim to Naples. In his haste to check his rival Naples, Ludovico did not recognize sufficiently that France also had dynastic claims to Milan. Nor did he foresee how insatiable the French appetite for Italian territory would become once French armies had crossed the Alps.

Charles VIII's March Through Italy

The French king Louis XI had resisted the temptation to invade Italy, while nonetheless keeping French dynastic claims in Italy alive. His successor, Charles VIII (r. 1483–1498), an eager youth in his twenties, responded to Ludovico's call with lightning speed. Within five months he had crossed the Alps (August 1495) and raced as conqueror through Florence and the Papal States into Naples. As Charles approached Florence, the Florentine ruler, Piero dé Medici, who had allied with Naples against Milan, tried to placate the French king by handing over Pisa and other Florentine possessions. Such appeasement only brought about Piero's forced exile by a population that was revolutionized then by the radical Dominican preacher Girolamo Savonarola (1452–1498). Savonarola convinced most of the fearful Florentines that the French king's arrival was a long-delayed and fully justified divine vengeance on their immorality.

Charles entered Florence without resistance. Thanks to Savonarola's flattery and the payment of a large ransom, the city was spared a threatened destruction. Savonarola continued to exercise virtual rule over Florence for four years after Charles's departure. The Florentines proved, however, not to be the stuff theocracies are made of. Savonarola's moral rigor and antipapal policies made it impossible for him to survive indefinitely. This became especially true after the Italian cities reunited and the ouster of the French invader, whom Savonarola had praised as a godsend, became national policy. Savonarola was imprisoned and executed in May 1498.

Charles's lightning march through Italy also struck terror in non-Italian hearts. Ferdinand of Aragon, who hoped to expand his own possessions in Italy from his kingdom of Sicily, now found himself vulnerable to a French–Italian axis. He took the initiative to create a counteralliance—the League of Venice, formed in March 1495—in which he joined with Venice, the Papal States, and Emperor Maximilian I against the French. The alliance set the stage for a conflict between France and Spain that would not end until 1559.

Ludovico il Moro meanwhile recognized that he had sown the wind; having desired a French invasion only so long as it weakened his enemies, he now saw Milan threatened by the whirlwind of events that he had himself created. In reaction he joined the League of Venice, and this alliance was able to send Charles into retreat by May. Charles remained thereafter on the defensive until his death in April 1498.

Pope Alexander VI and the Borgia Family

The French returned to Italy under Charles's successor, Louis XII (r. 1498–1515). This time they were assisted by a new Italian ally, the Borgia pope, Alexander VI. Alexander was probably the most corrupt pope who ever sat on the papal throne. He openly promoted the political careers of Cesare and Lucrezia Borgia, the children he had had before he became pope, and he placed papal policy in tandem with the efforts of his powerful family to secure a political base in Romagna.

In Romagna several principalities had fallen away from the Church during the Avignon papacy. And Venice, the pope's ally within the League of Venice, continued to contest the Papal States for their loyalty. Seeing that a French alliance could give him the opportunity to reestablish control over the region, Alexander took steps to secure French favor. He annulled Louis XII's marriage to Charles VIII's sister so Louis could marry Charles's widow, Anne of Brittany—a popular political move designed to keep Brittany French. The pope also bestowed a

cardinal's hat on the archbishop of Rouen, Louis's favorite cleric. Most important, Alexander agreed to abandon the League of Venice; this withdrawal of support made the league too weak to resist a French reconquest of Milan. In exchange, Cesare Borgia received the sister of the king of Navarre, Charlotte d'Albret, in marriage, a union that greatly enhanced Borgia military strength. Cesare also received land grants from Louis XII and the promise of French military aid in Romagna.

All in all it was a scandalous trade-off, but one that made it possible for both the French king and the pope to realize their ambitions within Italy. Louis successfully invaded Milan in August 1499. Ludovico il Moro, who had originally opened the Pandora's box of French invasion, spent his last years languishing in a French prison. In 1500 Louis and Ferdinand of Aragon divided Naples between them, while the pope and Cesare Borgia conquered the cities of Romagna without opposition. Alexander awarded his victorious son the title "duke of Romagna."

Pope Julius II

Cardinal Giuliano della Rovere, a strong opponent of the Borgia family, succeeded Alexander VI as Pope Julius II (r. 1503–1513). He suppressed the Borgias and placed their newly conquered lands in Romagna under papal jurisdiction. Julius came to be known as the "warrior pope" because he brought the Renaissance papacy to a peak of military prowess and diplomatic intrigue. Shocked, as were other contemporaries, by this thoroughly secular papacy, the Humanist Erasmus (1466?–1536), who had witnessed in disbelief a bullfight in the papal palace during a visit to Rome, wrote a popular anonymous satire entitled *Julius Excluded from Heaven*. This humorous account purported to describe the pope's unsuccessful efforts to convince Saint Peter that he was worthy of admission to heaven.

Assisted by his powerful allies, Pope Julius succeeded in driving the Venetians out of Romagna in 1509. Thus he ended Venetian claims in the region and fully secured the Papal States. Having realized this long-sought papal goal, Julius turned to the second major undertaking of his pontificate: ridding Italy of his former ally, the French invader. Julius, Ferdinand of Aragon, and Venice formed a second Holy League in October 1511, and within a short period Emperor Maximilian I and the Swiss joined them. By 1512 the league had the French in full retreat, and they were soundly defeated by the Swiss in 1513 at Novara.

The French were nothing if not persistent. They invaded Italy a third time under Louis's successor, Francis I (r. 1515–1547). French armies massacred Swiss soldiers of the Holy League at Marignano in September 1515, revenging the earlier defeat at Novara. The victory won from the pope the Concordat of Bologna in August 1516. This agreement gave the French king control over the French clergy in exchange for French recognition of the pope's superiority over Church councils and his right to collect annates in France. This was an important compromise that helped keep France Catholic after the outbreak of the Protestant Reformation. But the new French entry into Italy also led to the first of four major wars with Spain in the first half of the sixteenth century: the Habsburg–Valois wars, none of which France won.

Niccolò Machiavelli

The period of foreign invasions made a shambles of Italy. The same period that saw Italy's cultural peak in the work of Leonardo, Raphael, and Michelangelo also witnessed Italy's political tragedy. One who watched as French, Spanish, and German armies wreaked havoc on this country was Niccolò Machiavelli (1469–1527). The more he saw, the more convinced he became that Italian political unity and independence were ends that justified any means.

A Humanist and a careful student of ancient Rome, Machiavelli was impressed by the way Roman rulers and citizens had then defended their fatherland. They possessed *Virtù*, the ability to act decisively and heroically for the good of their country. Stories of ancient Roman patriotism and self-sacrifice were Machiavelli's favorites, and he lamented the absence of such traits among his compatriots. Such romanticizing of the Roman past caused some exaggeration of both ancient virtue and contemporary fail-

Santi di Tito's portrait of Machiavelli, perhaps the most famous Italian political theorist, who advised Renaissance princes to practice artful deception and inspire fear in their subjects if they wished to be successful. [Scala/Art Resource, N.Y.]

ings. His Florentine contemporary, Francesco Guicciardini, a more sober historian less given to idealizing antiquity, wrote truer chronicles of Florentine and Italian history.

Machiavelli also held deep republican ideals, which he did not want to see vanish from Italy. He believed that a strong and determined people could struggle successfully with fortune. He scolded the Italian people for the self-destruction their own internal feuding was causing. He wanted an end to that behavior above all, so that a reunited Italy could drive all foreign armies out.

But were his fellow citizens up to such a challenge? The juxtaposition of what Machiavelli believed the ancient Romans had been with the failure of his contemporaries to attain such high

Machiavelli on Why the Princes of Italy Have Lost Their States

Despite his seeming pessimism about the ability of contemporary Romans to act as forcefully as ancient ones, Machiavelli still believed in the ability of free will to control perhaps half of life. Here he presents his views on why rulers fail.

♦ *Is Machiavelli unrealistic to blame failure on an individual's own inertness and resignation to misfortune? Does he consider political and social circumstances to be beyond the individual's control? How much of failure is within, how much outside, the individual?*

If we contemplate those lords who in our own times have lost their dominions in Italy, such as the King of Naples, the Duke of Milan, and others, in the first place we shall see that in respect of arms they have . . . all alike been defective; and next, that some of them have either had the people against them, or if they have had the people with them, they have not known how to secure themselves against their nobles. For without such defects . . . states . . . are never overthrown. . . .

Let those princes of ours, therefore, who . . . have lost their dominions, blame not Fortune but their own inertness. For never having reflected in tranquil times that there might come a change (and it is human nature when the sea is calm not to think of storms), when adversity overtook them, they thought not of defence but only of escape . . . hoping that their people . . . would some day recall them. [But this is an ignoble course of action because] it does not depend on you for its success, and those modes of defence alone are good, certain and lasting, which depend upon yourself and your own worth. . . .

Many have been and are of the opinion that human affairs are so governed by Fortune and by God that men cannot alter them by any prudence of theirs, and indeed have no remedy against them. . . . I am in part inclined to agree with this opinion. . . . Nevertheless, that our free will be not wholly set aside, I think it may be the case that Fortune is the mistress of one half of our actions, and yet leaves the control of the other half, or a little less, to ourselves.

Niccolò Machiavelli, The Prince, *ed. by Charles W. Eliot (New York: P. F. Collier & Son, 1910), pp. 82–84.*

ideals made him the famous cynic whose name—in the epithet *Machiavellian*—has become synonymous with ruthless political expediency. Only a strongman, he concluded in the end, could impose order on so divided and selfish a people; the salvation of Italy required, for the present, a cunning dictator.

It has been argued that Machiavelli wrote *The Prince* in 1513 as a cynical satire on the way rulers actually did behave and not as a serious recommendation of unprincipled despotic rule. To take his advocacy of tyranny literally, it is argued, contradicts both his earlier works and his own strong family tradition of republican service. But Machiavelli seems to have been in earnest when he advised rulers to discover the advantages of fraud and brutality, at least as a temporary means to the higher end of a unified Italy. He apparently hoped to see a strong ruler emerge from the Medici family, which had captured the papacy in 1513 with the pontificate of Leo X (r. 1513–1521). At the same time, the Medici family retained control over the powerful territorial state of Florence. The situation was similar to that of Machiavelli's hero Cesare Borgia and his father Pope Alexander VI, who

Major Political Events of the Italian Renaissance (1375–1527)	
1378–1382	The Ciompi Revolt in Florence
1434	Medici rule in Florence established by Cosimo dé Medici
1454–1455	Treaty of Lodi allies Milan, Naples, and Florence (in effect until 1494)
1494	Charles VIII of France invades Italy
1494–1498	Savonarola controls Florence
1495	League of Venice unites Venice, Milan, the Papal States, the Holy Roman Empire, and Spain against France
1499	Louis XII invades Milan (the second French invasion of Italy)
1500	The Borgias conquer Romagna
1512–1513	The Holy League (Pope Julius II, Ferdinand of Aragon, Emperor Maximilian, and Venice) defeat the French
1513	Machiavelli writes *The Prince*
1515	Francis I leads the third French invasion of Italy
1516	Concordat of Bologna between France and the papacy
1527	Sack of Rome by imperial soldiers

had earlier brought factious Romagna to heel by placing secular family goals and religious policy in tandem. *The Prince* was pointedly dedicated to Lorenzo dè Medici, duke of Urbino and grandson of Lorenzo the Magnificent.

Whatever Machiavelli's hopes may have been, the Medicis were not destined to be Italy's deliverers. The second Medici pope, Clement VII (r. 1523–1534), watched helplessly as Rome was sacked by the army of Emperor Charles V in 1527, also the year of Machiavelli's death.

Revival of Monarchy in Northern Europe

After 1450 there was a progressive shift from divided feudal to unified national monarchies as "sovereign" rulers emerged. This is not to say that the dynastic and chivalric ideals of feudal monarchy vanished. Territorial princes did not pass from the scene; representative bodies persisted and in some areas even grew in influence. But in the late fifteenth and early sixteenth centuries, the old problem of the one and the many was decided in favor of the interests of monarchy.

The feudal monarchy of the High Middle Ages was characterized by the division of the basic powers of government between the king and his semiautonomous vassals. The nobility and the towns had acted with varying degrees of unity and success through evolving representative assemblies such as the English Parliament, the French Estates General, and the Spanish Cortes to thwart the centralization of royal power. Because of the Hundred Years' War and the schism in the Church, the nobility and the clergy were in decline by the late Middle Ages and less able to contain expanding monarchies.

The increasingly important towns began to ally with the king. Loyal, business-wise townspeople, not the nobility and the clergy, increasingly staffed the royal offices and became the king's lawyers, bookkeepers, military tacticians, and foreign diplomats. This new alliance between king and town broke the bonds of feudal society and made possible the rise of sovereign states.

In a sovereign state, the powers of taxation, war making, and law enforcement no longer belong to semiautonomous vassals but are concentrated in the monarch and are exercised by his or her chosen agents. Taxes, wars, and laws become national rather than merely regional matters. Only as monarchs became able to act independently of the nobility and representative assemblies could they overcome the decentralization that had been the basic obstacle to nation building. Ferdinand and Isabella of Spain rarely called the Cortes into session. The French Estates General did not meet at all from 1484 to 1560. Henry VII (r. 1485–1509) of England managed to raise revenues without going begging to Parliament after Parliament voted him customs revenues for life in 1485. Monarchs were also assisted by brilliant theorists, from Marsilius of Padua in the fourteenth century to Machiavelli to Jean Bodin in the sixteenth, who eloquently argued the sovereign rights of monarchy.

The many were, of course, never totally subjugated to the one. But in the last half of the fifteenth century, rulers demonstrated that the law was their creature. They appointed civil servants whose vision was no longer merely local or regional. In Castile, they were the *corregidores*, in England, the justices of the peace, and in France, bailiffs operating through well-drilled lieutenants. These royal ministers and agents could become closely attached to the localities they administered in the ruler's name. And regions were able to secure congenial royal appointments. Throughout England, for example, local magnates served as representatives of the Tudors. Nonetheless these new executives remained *royal* executives, bureaucrats whose outlook was "national" and whose loyalty was to the "state."

Monarchies also began to create standing national armies in the fifteenth century. The noble cavalry receded as the infantry and the artillery became the backbone of royal armies. Mercenary soldiers were recruited from Switzerland and Germany to form the major part of the "king's army." Professional soldiers who fought for pay and booty proved far more efficient than feudal vassals who fought simply for honor's sake. Monarchs who failed to meet their payrolls, however, faced a new danger of mutiny and banditry on the part of foreign troops.

The growing cost of warfare in the fifteenth and sixteenth centuries increased the need of monarchs for new national sources of income, but their efforts to expand royal revenues were hampered by the stubborn belief among the highest classes that they were immune from government taxation. The nobility guarded their properties and traditional rights and despised taxation as an insult and a humiliation. Royal revenues accordingly grew at the expense of those least able to resist, and least able to pay.

The monarchs had several options when it came to raising money. As feudal lords they could collect rents from their royal domain. They could also levy national taxes on basic food and clothing, such as the *gabelle*, or salt tax, in France and the *alcabala*, or 10 percent sales tax on commercial transactions, in Spain. The rulers could also levy direct taxes on the peasantry. This they did through agreeable representative assemblies of the privileged classes in which the peasantry did not sit. The *taille*, which the French kings independently determined from year to year after the Estates General was suspended in 1484, was such a tax. Innovative fund-raising devices in the fifteenth century included the sale of public offices and the issuance of high-interest government bonds. But rulers did not levy taxes on the powerful nobility. They rather borrowed from rich nobles and the great bankers of Italy and Germany. In money matters, the privileged classes remained as much the kings' creditors and competitors as their subjects.

France

Charles VII (r. 1422–1461) was a king made great by those who served him. His ministers created a permanent professional army, which—thanks initially to the inspiration of Joan of Arc—drove the English out of France. And largely because of the enterprise of an independent merchant banker named Jacques Coeur, the French also developed a strong economy, diplomatic corps, and national administration during Charles's reign. These were the sturdy tools with which Charles's son and successor, the ruthless Louis XI (r. 1461–1483), made France a great power.

There were two cornerstones of French nation-building in the fifteenth century. The first was the collapse of the English empire in France following the Hundred Years' War. The second was the defeat of Charles the Bold and his duchy of Burgundy. Perhaps Europe's strongest political power in the mid-fifteenth century, Burgundy aspired to dwarf both France and the Holy Roman Empire as the leader of a dominant middle kingdom. It might have done so had not the continental powers joined in opposition.

When Charles the Bold died in defeat in a battle at Nancy in 1477, the dream of Burgundian empire died with him. Louis XI and Habsburg Emperor Maximilian I divided the conquered Burgundian lands between them, with the treaty-wise Habsburgs getting the better part. The dissolution of Burgundy ended its constant intrigue against the French king and left Louis XI free to secure the monarchy. The newly acquired Burgundian lands and his own Angevin inheritance permitted the king to end his reign with a kingdom almost twice the size of that with which he had started. Louis successfully harnessed the nobility, expanded the trade and industry so carefully nurtured by Jacques Coeur, created a national postal system, and even established a lucrative silk industry at Lyons (later transferred to Tours).

A strong nation is a two-edged sword. Because Louis's successors inherited a secure and efficient government, they felt free to pursue what proved ultimately to be a debilitating foreign policy. Conquests in Italy in the 1490s and a long series of losing wars with the Habsburgs in the first half of the sixteenth century left France by the mid-sixteenth century again a defeated nation almost as divided internally as during the Hundred Years' War.

Spain

Spain, too, became a strong country in the late fifteenth century. Both Castile and Aragon had been poorly ruled and divided kingdoms in the mid-fifteenth century. The union of Isabella of Castile (r. 1474–1504) and Ferdinand of Aragon (r. 1479–1516) changed that situation. The two future sovereigns married in 1469, despite strong protests from neighboring Portugal and France, both of whom foresaw the formidable European power the marriage would create. Castile was by far the richer and more populous of the two, having an estimated five million inhabitants to Aragon's population of under one million. Castile was also distinguished by its lucrative sheep-farming industry, run by a government-backed organization called the *Mesta*, another example of developing centralized economic planning. Although the marriage of Ferdinand and Isabella dynastically united the two kingdoms, they remained constitutionally separated. Each retained its respective government agencies—separate laws, armies, coinage, and taxation—and cultural traditions.

Ferdinand and Isabella could do together what neither was able to accomplish alone: subdue their realms, secure their borders, venture abroad militarily, and Christianize the whole of Spain. Between 1482 and 1492 they conquered the Moors in Granada. Naples became a Spanish possession in 1504. By 1512 Ferdinand had secured his northern borders by conquering the kingdom of Navarre. Internally, Ferdinand and Isabella won the allegiance of the Hermandad, a powerful league of cities and towns, which served them against stubborn landowners. Townspeople allied themselves with the crown and progressively replaced the nobility within the royal administration. The crown also extended its authority over the wealthy chivalric orders, a further circumscription of the power of the nobility.

Spain had long been remarkable among European lands as a place where three religions—Islam, Judaism, and Christianity—coexisted with a certain degree of toleration. This toleration was to end dramatically under Ferdinand and Isabella, who made Spain the prime exemplar of state-controlled religion.

Ferdinand and Isabella exercised almost total control over the Spanish church as they placed religion in the service of national unity. They appointed the higher clergy and the officers of the Inquisition. The Inquisition, run by Tomás de Torquemada (d. 1498), Isabella's confessor, was a key national agency established in 1479 to monitor the activity of converted Jews (*conversos*) and Muslims (*Moriscos*) in Spain. In 1492 the Jews were exiled and their properties were confiscated. In 1502 nonconverting Moors in Granada were driven into exile by Cardinal Francisco Jiménez de Cisneros (1437–1517), the great spiritual reformer and educator. Spanish spiritual life remained largely uniform and successfully controlled. This was a major reason Spain remained a loyal Catholic country throughout the sixteenth century and provided a base of operation for the European Counter-Reformation.

Despite a certain internal narrowness, Ferdinand and Isabella were rulers with wide horizons. They contracted anti-French marriage alliances that came to determine a large part of European history in the sixteenth century. In 1496 their eldest daughter, Joanna, later known as "the Mad," married Archduke Philip, the son of Emperor Maximilian I. The fruit of this union, Charles I of Spain, was the first ruler over a united Spain; by his inheritance and election as emperor in 1519, he came to rule over a European kingdom almost equal in size to that of Charlemagne. A second daughter, Catherine of Aragon, wed Arthur, the son of the English king Henry VII. After Arthur's premature death, she was betrothed to his brother, the future King Henry VIII (r. 1509–1547), whom she married eight years later in 1509. The failure of this marriage became the key factor in the emergence of the Anglican church and the English Reformation.

The new power of Spain was also revealed in Ferdinand and Isabella's promotion of overseas exploration. They sponsored the Genoese adventurer Christopher Columbus (1451–1506), who discovered the islands of the Caribbean while sailing west in search of a shorter route to the spice markets of the Far East. This patronage led to the creation of the Spanish Empire in

These sculptures of Ferdinand (r. 1479–1516) and Isabella (r. 1474–1504) are from the royal chapel in the Cathedral of Granada. Their marriage in 1469 joined the kingdoms of Aragon and Castile and created the Spain we know today. [© Robert Frerck/Odyssey Productions]

Mexico and Peru, whose gold and silver mines helped to make Spain Europe's dominant power in the sixteenth century.

England

The last half of the fifteenth century was a period of especially difficult political trial for the English. Following the Hundred Years' War, a defeated England was subjected to internal warfare between two rival branches of the royal family, the House of York and the House of Lancaster. This conflict, known to us today as the Wars of the Roses (because York's symbol, according to legend, was a white rose, and Lancaster's a red rose), kept England in turmoil from 1455 to 1485.

The Lancastrian monarchy of Henry VI (r. 1422–1461) was consistently challenged by the duke of York and his supporters in the prosperous southern towns. In 1461 Edward IV (r. 1461–1483), son of the duke of York, successfully seized power and instituted a strong-arm rule that lasted more than twenty years; it was only briefly interrupted in 1470–1471 by Henry VI's short-lived restoration. Assisted by loyal and able ministers, Edward effectively increased the power and finances of the monarchy.

His brother, Richard III (r. 1483–1485), usurped the throne from Edward's son, and after Richard's death, the new Tudor dynasty portrayed him as an unprincipled villain who had also murdered Edward's sons in the Tower of London to secure his hold on the throne. The best-known version of this characterization—unjust according to some—is found in Shakespeare's *Richard III*. Be that as it may, Richard's reign saw the growth of support for the exiled Lancastrian Henry Tudor, who returned to England to defeat Richard on Bosworth Field in August 1485.

Henry Tudor ruled as Henry VII (r. 1485–1509), the first of the new Tudor dynasty that would dominate England throughout the sixteenth century. To bring the rival royal families together and to make the hereditary claim of his offspring to the throne uncontestable, Henry married Edward IV's daughter, Elizabeth of York. He succeeded in disciplining the English nobility through a special instrument of the royal will known as the *Court of Star Chamber.*

Created with the sanction of Parliament in 1487, the court was intended to end the perversion of English justice by "over-mighty subjects," that is, powerful noblemen who used intimidation and bribery to win favorable verdicts in court cases. In the Court of Star Chamber, the king's councillors sat as judges and were not swayed by such tactics. The result was a more equitable court system.

It was also a court more amenable to the royal will. Henry shrewdly construed legal precedents to the advantage of the crown, using English law to further the ends of monarchy. He managed to confiscate noble lands and fortunes with such success that he was able to govern without dependence on Parliament for royal funds, always a cornerstone of strong monarchy. In these ways, Henry began to shape a monarchy that would develop into one of early modern Europe's most exemplary governments during the reign of his granddaughter, Elizabeth I.

The Holy Roman Empire

Germany and Italy were the striking exceptions to the steady development of politically centralized lands in the last half of the fifteenth century. Unlike England, France, and Spain, the empire saw the many thoroughly repulse the one. In Germany territorial rulers and cities resisted every effort at national consolidation and unity. As in Carolingian times, rulers continued to partition their kingdoms, however small, among their sons. By the late fifteenth century, Germany was hopelessly divided into some 300 autonomous political entities.

The princes and the cities did work together to create the machinery of law and order, if not of union, within the divided empire. The emperor and the major German territorial rulers reached an agreement in 1356, the *Golden Bull.* It established a seven-member electoral college consisting of the archbishops of Mainz, Trier, and Cologne; the duke of Saxony; the margrave of Brandenburg; the count Palatine; and the king of Bohemia. This group also functioned as an administrative body. They elected the emperor and, in cooperation with him, provided what transregional unity and administration existed.

Emperor Maximilian (r. 1493–1519) and his family, as painted in 1515 by Bernard Strigel. [Kunsthistorisches Museum, Vienna]

The figure of the emperor gave the empire a single ruler in law, if not in fact. The conditions of his rule and the extent of his powers over his subjects, especially the seven electors, were renegotiated with every imperial election. Therefore, the rights of the many (the princes) were always balanced against the power of the one (the emperor).

In the fifteenth century an effort was made to control incessant feuding by the creation of an imperial diet (*Reichstag*). This was a national assembly of the seven electors, the nonelectoral princes, and the sixty-five imperial free cities. The cities were the weakest of the three bodies represented in the diet. During such an assembly in Worms in 1495, the members won from Emperor Maximilian I (r. 1493–1519) an imperial ban on private warfare and the creation of a Supreme Court of Justice to enforce internal peace, and an imperial Council of Regency to coordinate imperial and internal German policy. The latter was very grudgingly conceded by the emperor because it gave the princes a share in executive power.

Although important, these reforms were still a poor substitute for true national unity. In the sixteenth and seventeenth centuries, the territorial princes became virtually sovereign rulers in their various domains. Such disunity aided religious dissent and conflict. It was in the cities and territories of still-feudal, fractionalized, backward Germany that the Protestant Reformation broke out in the sixteenth century.

The Northern Renaissance

The scholarly works of northern Humanists created a climate favorable to religious and educational reforms on the eve of the Reformation.

Northern Humanism was initially stimulated by the importation of Italian learning through such varied intermediaries as students who had studied in Italy, merchants who traded there, and the Brothers of the Common Life. This last was an influential lay religious movement that began in the Netherlands and permitted men and women to live a shared religious life without making formal vows of poverty, chastity, and obedience.

The northern Humanists, however, developed their own distinctive culture. They tended to come from more diverse social backgrounds and to be more devoted to religious reforms than their Italian counterparts. They were also more willing to write for lay audiences as well as for a narrow intelligentsia. Thanks to the invention of printing with movable type, it became possible for Humanists to convey their educational ideals to laymen and clerics alike. Printing gave new power and influence to elites in both Church and state, who now could popularize their viewpoints freely and widely.

The Printing Press

A variety of forces converged in the fourteenth and fifteenth centuries to give rise to the invention of the printing press. Since the days of Charlemagne, kings and princes had encouraged schools and literacy to help provide educated bureaucrats to staff the offices of their kingdoms. Without people who could read, think critically, and write reliable reports, no kingdom, large or small, could be properly governed. By the fifteenth century, a new literate lay public had been created, thanks to the enormous expansion of schools and universities during the late Middle Ages (universities more than tripled between 1300 and 1500, from twenty to seventy).

The invention of a process of cheap paper manufacture also helped to make books economical and to broaden their content. Manuscript books had been inscribed on vellum, a cumbersome and expensive medium. (It required 170 calfskins or 300 sheepskins to make a single vellum Bible.) Single-sheet woodcuts had long been printed. This involved carving a block of wood and inking it, then stamp-

An early printing press. Between 1435 and 1455, Johannes Gutenberg worked out the complete technology of casting individual letters into rectangular metal type, composing the type into pages held together by pressure, and printing those pages on an adaptation of the wooden standing press using ink made of lampblack mixed with oil varnish. This new technology made it possible for the first time in the West to manufacture numerous identical copies of written works. [Huntington Library]

ing out as many copies as one could make before the wood deteriorated. The end product was much like a modern poster.

In response to the demand for books created by the expansion of lay literacy, Johann Gutenberg (d. 1468) invented printing with movable type in the mid-fifteenth century in the German city of Mainz, the center of printing for the whole of western Europe. Thereafter, books were rapidly and handsomely produced on top-

The printing press made possible the diffusion of Renaissance learning. But no book stimulated thought more at this time than did the Bible. With Gutenberg's publication of a printed Bible in 1454, scholars gained access to a dependable, standardized text, so that Scripture could be discussed and debated as never before. [Huntington Library]

ics both profound and practical, and intended for ordinary lay readers, scholars, and clerics alike. Especially popular in the early decades of print were books of piety and religion, calendars and almanacs, and how-to books (on child rearing, making brandies and liquors, curing animals, and farming successfully).

The new technology proved enormously profitable to printers, whose numbers exploded. By 1500, within a scant fifty years of Gutenberg's press, printing presses operated in at least 60 German cities and in more than 200 cities throughout Europe. The printing press was a boon to the careers of Humanists, who now gained international audiences.

Literacy deeply affected people everywhere, nurturing self-esteem and a critical frame of mind. By standardizing texts, the print revolution made anyone who could read an instant authority. Rulers in Church and state now had to deal with a less credulous and docile laity. Print was also a powerful tool for political and religious propaganda as well. Kings could now indoctrinate people as never before, and the clergy found themselves able to mass produce both indulgences and pamphlets.

Erasmus

The far-reaching influence of Desiderius Erasmus (1466?–1536), the most famous of the northern Humanists and the reputed "prince of the Humanists," illustrates the impact of the printing press. Erasmus gained fame as both an educational and a religious reformer. His life and work make clear that many loyal Catholics wanted major reforms long before the Reformation made them a reality.

Erasmus earned his living by tutoring when patrons were scarce. He prepared short Latin dialogues for his students that were intended to teach them how to speak and live well, inculcating good manners and language by encouraging them to imitate what they read.

These dialogues were published under the title *Colloquies;* they grew in number and length in consecutive editions, coming also to embrace anticlerical dialogues and satires on popular religious superstition. Erasmus collected ancient and contemporary proverbs as well, which he published under the title *Adages.* Beginning with about 800 examples, he increased his collection to more than 5,000 in the final edition of the work. Among the sayings that the *Adages* popularized are such common modern expressions as "to leave no stone unturned" and "where there is smoke, there is fire."

Erasmus aspired to unite the classical ideals of humanity and civic virtue with the Christian ideals of love and piety. He believed that disciplined study of the classics and the Bible, if begun early enough, was the best way to reform both individuals and society. He summarized his own beliefs with the phrase *philosophia Christi,* a simple, ethical piety in imitation of Christ. He set this ideal in starkest contrast to what he believed to be the dogmatic, ceremonial, and factious religious practice of the later Middle Ages. What most offended him about the Scholastics, both those of the late Middle Ages and, increasingly, the new Lutheran ones, was their letting doctrine and disputation overshadow humble piety and Christian practice.

To promote his own religious beliefs, Erasmus labored to make the ancient Christian sources available in their original versions. He believed that only as people drank from the pure, unadulterated sources could moral and

Albrecht Dürer's portrait of Erasmus (1466?–1536), the Dutch Humanist who influenced all of the reform movements of the sixteenth century. Erasmus was popularly said to have "laid the egg that Luther hatched." [Louvre, Paris, Cabinet des Dessins]

religious health result. He edited the works of the Church fathers and produced a Greek edition of the New Testament (1516), which became the basis for his new, more accurate Latin translation (1519).

These various enterprises did not please Church authorities. They were unhappy with both Erasmus's "improvements" on the Vulgate, Christendom's Bible for over a thousand years, and his popular anticlerical satires. At one point in the mid-sixteenth century, all of Erasmus's works were placed on the *Index of Forbidden Books.* Erasmus also received Luther's unqualified condemnation for his views on the freedom of human will. Still, Erasmus's works became basic tools of reform in the hands of both Protestant and Catholic reformers.

Humanism and Reform

In France, Spain, England, and Germany, Humanism stirred both educational and religious reform.

GERMANY Rudolf Agricola (1443–1485), the father of German Humanism, spent ten years in Italy and he introduced Italian learning to Germany when he returned. Conrad Celtis (d. 1508), the first German poet laureate, and Ulrich von Hutten (1488–1523), a fiery knight, gave German Humanism a nationalist coloring hostile to non-German cultures, especially Roman. von Hutten especially illustrates the union of Humanism, German nationalism, and Luther's religious reform. A poet who admired Erasmus, he attacked indulgences and published an edition of Valla's exposé of the *Donation of Constantine* (see the earlier section on Valla). He died in 1523 the victim of a hopeless knights' revolt against the princes.

The *cause célèbre* that brought von Hutten onto the historical stage and unified reform-minded German Humanists was the Reuchlin affair. Johann Reuchlin (1455–1522) was Europe's foremost Christian authority on Hebrew and Jewish learning. He wrote the first reliable Hebrew grammar by a Christian scholar and was personally attracted to Jewish mysticism. Around 1506 a converted Jew named Pfefferkorn, supported by the Dominican Order in Cologne, began a movement to suppress Jewish writings. When Pfefferkorn attacked Reuchlin, many German Humanists, in the name of academic freedom and good scholarship and not for any pro-Jewish sentiment, rushed to Reuchlin's defense. The controversy lasted several years and produced one of the great satires of the period, the *Letters of Obscure Men* (1515), a merciless satire of monks and Scholastics to which von Hutten contributed. When Martin Luther came under attack in 1517 for his famous ninety-five theses against indulgences, many German Humanists saw a repetition of the Scholastic attack on Reuchlin and rushed to his side.

Thomas More (1478–1535), painted by Hans Holbein the Younger in 1527. The English statesman and author was beheaded by Henry VIII for his refusal to recognize the king's sovereignty over the English church. [The Frick Collection]

ENGLAND Italian learning came to England by way of English scholars and merchants and visiting Italian prelates. Lectures by William Grocyn (d. 1519) and Thomas Linacre (d. 1524) at Oxford and those of Erasmus at Cambridge marked the scholarly maturation of English Humanism. John Colet (1467–1519), dean of Saint Paul's Cathedral, patronized Humanist studies for the young and promoted religious reform as well.

Thomas More (1478–1535), a close friend of Erasmus, is the best known English Humanist. His *Utopia* (1516), a conservative criticism of contemporary society, rivals the plays of Shakespeare as the most-read sixteenth-century

English work. *Utopia* depicted an imaginary society based on reason and tolerance that overcame social and political injustice by holding all property and goods in common and requiring everyone to earn their bread by their own work.

More became one of Henry VIII's most trusted diplomats. But his repudiation of the Act of Supremacy (1534), which made the king of England head of the English church in place of the pope (see Chapter 11), and his refusal to recognize the king's marriage to Anne Boleyn led to his execution in July 1535. Although More remained Catholic, Humanism in England, as also in Germany, played an important role in preparing the way for the English Reformation.

FRANCE The French invasions of Italy made it possible for Italian learning to penetrate France, stirring both educational and religious reform. Guillaume Budé (1468–1540), an accomplished Greek scholar, and Jacques Lefèvre d'Étaples (1454–1536), a biblical authority, were the leaders of French Humanism. Lefèvre's scholarly works exemplified the new critical scholarship and influenced Martin Luther. Guillaume Briçonnet (1470–1533), the bishop of Meaux, and Marguerite d'Angoulême (1492–1549), sister of King Francis I, the future queen of Navarre, and a successful spiritual writer in her own right, cultivated a generation of young reform-minded Humanists. The future Protestant reformer John Calvin was a product of this native reform circle.

SPAIN Whereas in England, France, and Germany, Humanism prepared the way for Protestant reforms, in Spain it entered the service of the Catholic church. Here the key figure was Francisco Jiménez de Cisneros (1437–1517), a confessor to Queen Isabella, and after 1508 the Grand Inquisitor—a position that allowed him to enforce the strictest religious orthodoxy. Jiménez founded the University of Alcalá near Madrid in 1509, printed a Greek edition of the New Testament, and translated many religious tracts designed to reform clerical life and better direct lay piety. His great achievement, taking fifteen years to complete, was the *Complutensian Polyglot Bible*, a six-volume work that placed the Hebrew, Greek, and Latin versions of the Bible in parallel columns. Such

scholarly projects and internal Church reforms joined with the repressive measures of Ferdinand and Isabella to keep Spain strictly Catholic throughout the Age of Reformation.

Voyages of Discovery and the New Empire in the West

On the eve of the Reformation, the geographical as well as the intellectual horizons of Western people were changing. The fifteenth century saw the beginning of western Europe's global expansion and the transference of commercial supremacy from the Mediterranean and the Baltic to the Atlantic seaboard (see Map 10-2).

Gold and Spices

Mercenary motives, reinforced by traditional missionary ideals, inspired Prince Henry the Navigator (r. 1394–1460) to sponsor the Portuguese exploration of the African coast. His main object was the gold trade, which for centuries Muslims had monopolized. By the last decades of the fifteenth century, gold from Guinea was entering Europe by way of Portuguese ships calling at the port cities of Lisbon and Antwerp, rather than by the traditional Arab land routes. Antwerp became the financial center of Europe, a commercial crossroads where the enterprise and derring-do of the Portuguese, the Spanish, and especially the Flemish met the capital funds of the German banking houses of Fugger and Welser.

The rush for gold quickly expanded into a rush for the spice markets of India. In the fifteenth century the diet of most Europeans was a dull combination of bread and gruel, cabbage, turnips, peas, lentils, and onions, together with what meat became available during seasonal periods of slaughter. Spices, especially pepper and cloves, were in great demand both to preserve and to enhance the taste of food.

Bartholomew Dias (d. 1500) opened the Portuguese empire in the East when he rounded the Cape of Good Hope at the tip of Africa in 1487. A decade later, in 1498, Vasco da Gama (d. 1524) reached the coast of India. When he returned to Portugal, he brought with him a

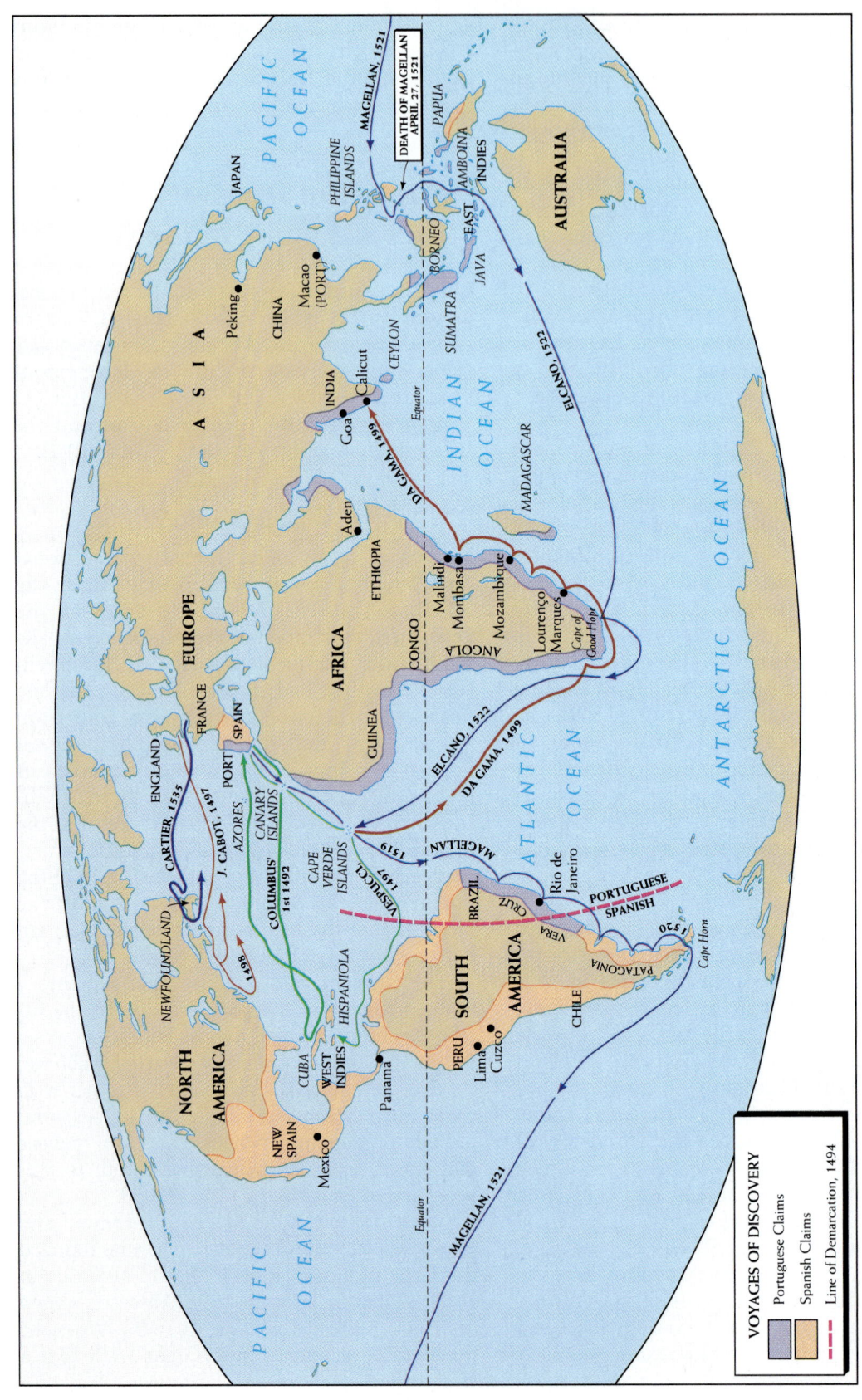

MAP 10-2 EUROPEAN VOYAGES OF DISCOVERY AND THE COLONIAL CLAIMS OF SPAIN AND
PORTUGAL IN THE FIFTEENTH AND SIXTEENTH CENTURIES *The map dramatizes the expansion of the area of European interest in the fifteenth and sixteenth centuries. Not until
today's "space age" has a comparable widening of horizons been possible.*

cargo worth sixty times the cost of the voyage. Later, the Portuguese established themselves firmly on the Malabar Coast with colonies in Goa and Calcutta and successfully challenged the Arabs and the Venetians for control of the European spice trade.

While the Portuguese concentrated on the Indian Ocean, the Spanish set sail across the Atlantic. They did so in the hope of establishing a shorter route to the rich spice markets of the East Indies. But rather than beating the Portuguese at their own game, Christopher Columbus (1451–1506) discovered the Americas instead.

Amerigo Vespucci (1451–1512) and Ferdinand Magellan (1480–1521) showed that these new lands were not the outermost territory of the Far East, as Columbus died believing. Their travels proved the lands to be an entirely new continent that opened on the still greater Pacific Ocean. Magellan, in search of a westward route to the East Indies, died in the Philippines.

The Spanish Empire in the New World

Columbus's voyage of 1492 marked, unknowingly to those who undertook and financed it, the beginning of more than three centuries of Spanish conquest, exploitation, and administration of a vast American empire. That imperial venture produced important results for the cultures of both the European and the American continents. The gold and silver extracted from its American possessions financed Spain's major role in the religious and political conflicts of the age and contributed to European inflation of the sixteenth century.

In large expanses of both South and North America, Spanish government set an imprint of Roman Catholicism, economic dependence, and hierarchical social structure that has endured to the present day. Such influence was already clear with Columbus. On October 12, 1492, after a thirty-three day voyage from the Canary Islands, he landed in San Salvador (Watlings Island) in the eastern Bahamas. He thought that he was on an outer island of Japan (or what he called Cipangu); he had undertaken his journey in the mistaken notion that the island of Japan would be the first land mass he would reach as he sailed west. This belief was based on Marco

Polo's accounts of his years in China in the thirteenth century and the first globe map of the world, by Martin Behaim. That map, published in 1492, showed only ocean between the west coast of Europe and the east coast of Asia. Not until his third voyage to the Caribbean did Columbus realize that the island of Cuba was not Japan and that the South American continent beyond it was not China.

When Columbus landed in San Salvador, his three ships were met on the beach by naked and extremely friendly natives. Like all the natives Columbus met on his first voyage, they were Taino Indians, who spoke a variant of a language known as Arawak. From the start, the natives' generosity amazed Columbus. They freely gave his men all the corn and yams they desired and many sexual favors as well. "They never say no," Columbus marveled. At the same time Columbus observed how very easily they could be enslaved.

A Conquered World

Mistaking the islands where he landed for the East Indies, Columbus called the native peoples whom he encountered *Indians*. That name persisted even after it had become clear that a new continent had been discovered. These native peoples had migrated across the Bering Straits from Asia onto the American landmass many thousands of years before the European voyages of discovery, creating communities all the way from Alaska to South America

Native Americans had established advanced civilizations that date to as early as the first millennium B.C. in two parts of what is today known as Latin America: Mesoamerica, which stretches from central Mexico into the Yucatan and Guatemala, and the Andean region of South America, primarily modern-day Peru and Bolivia. The earliest civilization in Mesoamerica, that of the Olmec, dates to about 1200 B.C. By the early centuries of the first millennium A.D. much of the region was dominated by the powerful city of Teotihuacán, which at the time was one of the largest urban centers in the world. The first millennium A.D. saw the flowering of the remarkable civilization of the Mayas in the Yucatan region. The Mayans built large cities with immense pyramids and achieved considerable skills in mathematics and astronomy.

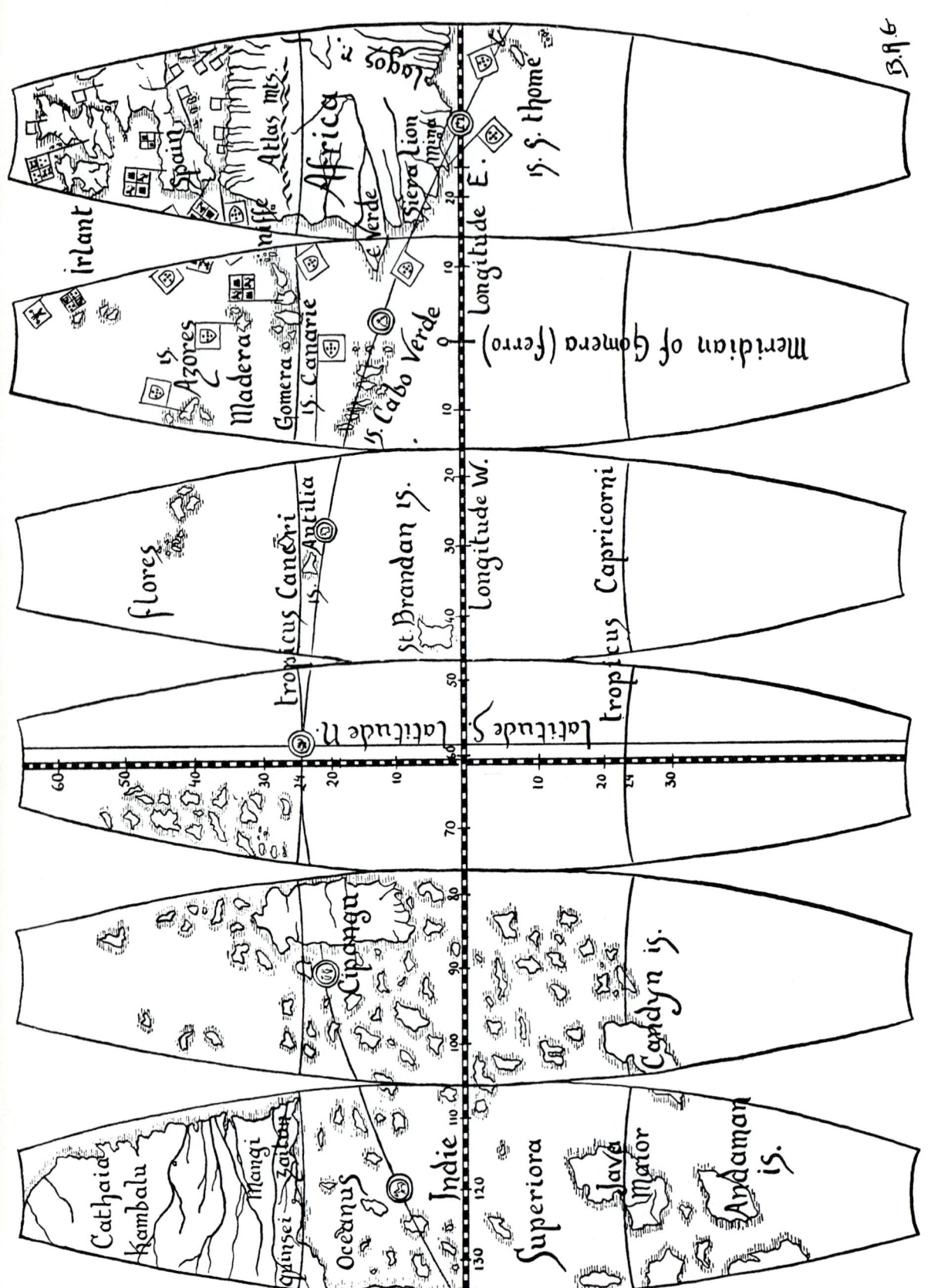

What Columbus knew of the world in 1492 was contained in this map by the Nuremberg geographer Martin Behaim, creator of the first spherical globe of the earth. The ocean section of Behaim's globe is reproduced here. Departing the Canary Islands (in the second section from the right), Columbus expected his first major landfall to be Japan (Cipangu, in the second section from the left). When he landed at San Salvador, he thought he was on the outer island of Japan. And when he arrived in Cuba, he thought he was in Japan.

The first great interregional civilization in Andean South America, that of Chavín, emerged during the first millennium B.C. Regional cultures of the succeeding Early Intermediate Period (A.D. 100–600) included the Nazca on the south coast of Peru and the Moche on the north coast. The Huari-Tiahuanco culture again imposed interregional conformity during the Middle Horizon (600–1000). In the Late Intermediate Period, the Chimu Empire (800–1400) dominated the valleys of the Peruvian north coast. These early Andean societies built major ceremonial centers throughout the Andes, constructed elaborate irrigation systems, canals, and highways, and created exquisite pottery, textiles, and metalwork.

At the time of the arrival of the first Spanish explorers, the Aztec Empire dominated Mesoamerica and the Inca Empire dominated Andean South America (see Map 10-3). Both were very rich, and their conquest promised the Spanish the possibility of acquiring large quantities of gold.

THE AZTECS IN MEXICO The forebears of the Aztecs had arrived in the Valley of Mexico early in the twelfth century, where they lived as a subservient people. In 1428, under the leadership of Chief Itzcoatl, they rebelled against their rulers. That rebellion opened a period of Aztec conquest that reached its climax just after 1500. Their capital, Tenochtitlán (modern-day Mexico City) was located on an island in the center of a lake. By the time the Spanish conquerors arrived, the Aztecs governed many smaller tribes harshly, forcing labor and tribute from them. Believing that the gods must literally be fed with human bodies to guarantee continuing sunshine and soil fertility, the Aztecs also demanded and received thousands of captives each year to be sacrificed to their gods. Such policies left the Aztecs surrounded by terrorized tribes that felt no loyalty to them and longed for a liberator.

In 1519, Hernán Cortés landed on the coast of Mexico with a force of about 600 men. He opened communication with tribes nearby and then with Montezuma, the Aztec ruler. Mont-

A sixteenth-century Aztec drawing depicts the Spanish conquest of Mexico. [The Bettmann Archive]

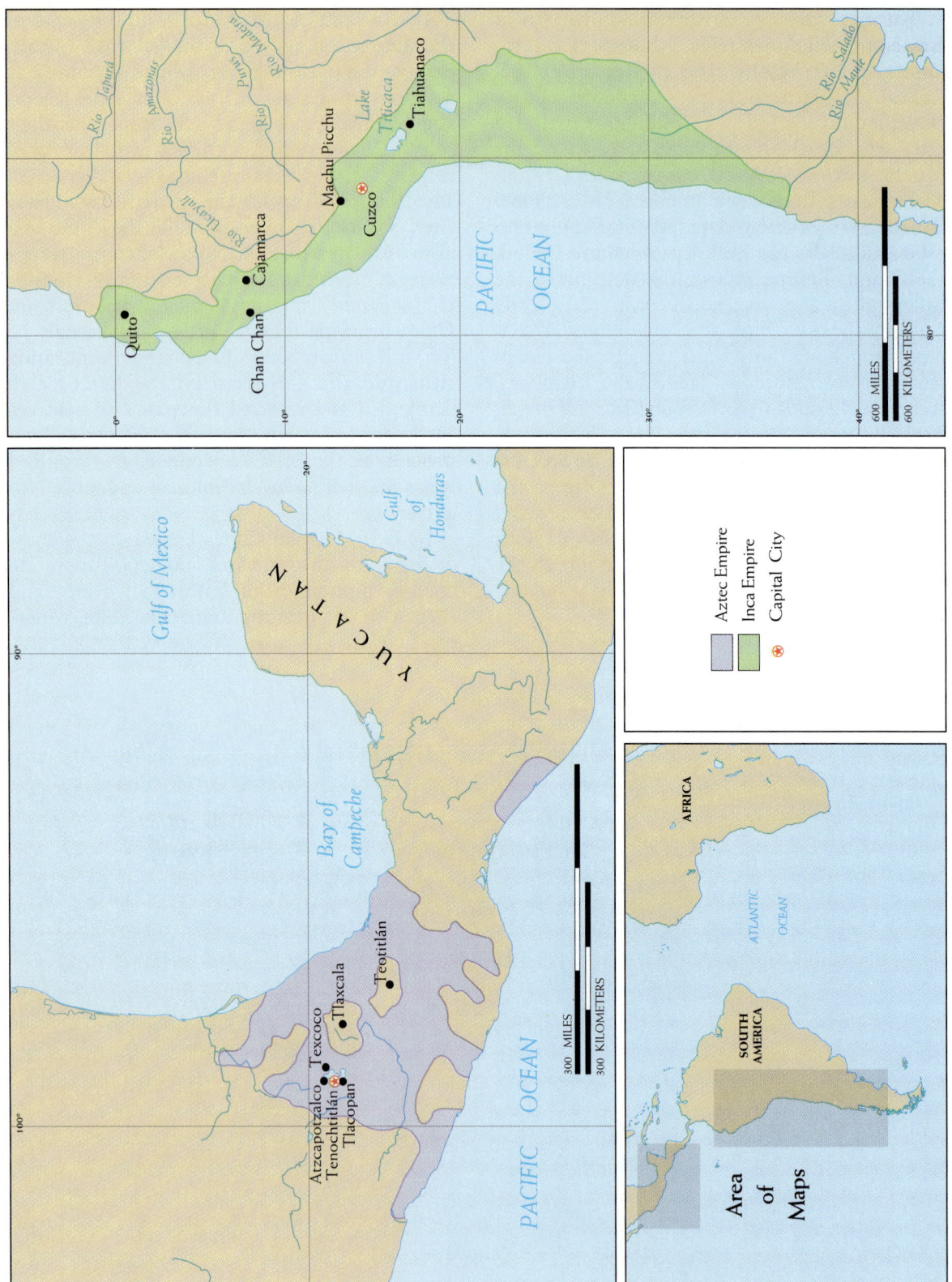

The map contains the following labels:

Top map (South America / Inca Empire):
- Rio Japurá
- Rio Amazonas
- Rio Purús
- Rio Madeira
- Rio Salado
- Rio Maule
- Rio Ucayali
- Lake Titicaca
- Tiahuanaco
- Machu Picchu
- Cuzco
- Cajamarca
- Chan Chan
- Quito
- PACIFIC OCEAN
- 0°, 10°, 20°, 30°, 40°, 80°
- 600 MILES
- 600 KILOMETERS

Bottom-left map (Mesoamerica / Aztec Empire):
- Gulf of Mexico
- Gulf of Honduras
- YUCATAN
- Bay of Campeche
- Teotitlán
- Tlaxcala
- Texcoco
- Atzcapotzalco
- Tenochtitlán
- Tlacopan
- PACIFIC OCEAN
- 90°, 100°, 20°
- 300 MILES
- 300 KILOMETERS

Legend:
- Aztec Empire
- Inca Empire
- Capital City

Inset map:
- AFRICA
- SOUTH AMERICA
- ATLANTIC OCEAN
- Area of Maps

MAP 10-3 THE AZTEC AND INCA EMPIRES ON THE EVE OF THE SPANISH CONQUEST

ezuma initially believed Cortés to be a god. Aztec religion contained the legend of a priest named Quetzalcoatl who had been driven away four centuries earlier and had promised to return in the very year in which Cortés arrived. Montezuma initially attempted to appease Cortés with gifts of gold. The Indians had recently been ravaged by epidemic diseases of European origin, principally smallpox, and were in no position to oppose him. After several weeks of negotiations and the forging of alliances with subject tribes, Cortés's forces marched on Tenochtitlán, conquered it, and imprisoned Montezuma, who later died under unexplained circumstances. The Aztecs tried to drive the Spanish out, but by late 1521 they were defeated after great loss of life. Cortés proclaimed the former Aztec Empire to be New Spain.

THE INCAS IN PERU The second great Indian civilization conquered by the Spanish was that of the Incas, located in the highlands of Peru. Like the Aztecs, they had conquered many neighboring states and tribes and by the early sixteenth century ruled harshly over several million subject people, whom they compelled to build their roads and cities, farm their lands, and fight their wars.

In 1531, largely inspired by Cortés's example in Mexico, Francisco Pizarro sailed from Panama and landed on the western coast of South America to undertake a campaign against the Inca Empire. His force included perhaps 200 men armed with guns and swords and equipped with horses, the military power of which the Incas did not fathom.

In late 1531, Pizarro lured the Inca chief Atahualpa into a conference, where he captured him and killed many of his followers. Atahualpa attempted to ransom himself by having a vast horde of gold transported from all over Peru to Pizarro. Discovering that he could not turn Atahualpa into a puppet ruler, Pizarro executed him in 1533. Division within the ranks of the Spanish conquerors prevented effective royal control of the sprawling Inca civilization until the late 1560s.

The conquests of Mexico and Peru stand among the most brutal episodes in modern Western history. One civilization armed with advanced weaponry subdued, in a remarkably brief time, two powerful peoples. Beyond the drama and bloodshed, these conquests made it very difficult for Indian civilizations to have a major impact on Western civilization. Some scholars believe, however, that the Iroquois tribes of North America set examples of freedom of speech, assembly, and religion that may have influenced the framers of the American Constitution.

The Spanish and the Indians made some accommodations to each other, but in the end European values, religion, economic goals, and language dominated. No group that retained indigenous religion, language, or values could become part of the new dominant culture or of the political power elite. In that sense, the Spanish conquests of the early sixteenth century marked the beginning of the process whereby South America was transformed into Latin America.

The Economy of Exploitation

From the beginning, the native peoples of America and their lands were drawn into the Atlantic economy and the world of competitive European commercialism. For the Indians of Latin America and somewhat later the blacks of Africa, that drive for gain meant various arrangements of forced labor.

There were three major components in the colonial economy of Latin America: mining, agriculture, and shipping. Each of them involved either labor or servitude or a relationship of dependence of the New World economy on that of Spain.

MINING The early conquistadores ("conquerors") were primarily interested in gold, but by the middle of the sixteenth century, silver mining provided the chief source of metallic wealth. The great mining centers were Potosí in Peru and somewhat smaller sites in northern Mexico. The Spanish crown was particularly interested in mining because it received one-fifth (the quinto) of all mining revenues. For this reason, the crown maintained a monopoly over the production and sale of mercury, required in the silver-mining process. Exploring for silver never lost predominance

Montaigne on "Cannibals" in Foreign Lands

The French philosopher Michel de Montaigne (1533–1592) had seen a Brazilian native in Rouen in 1562, an alleged cannibal brought to France by the explorer Villegagnon. The experience gave rise to an essay on the subject of what constitutes a savage. Montaigne concluded that no people on earth were more barbarous than Europeans who take natives of other lands captive.

◆ *Is Montaigne romanticizing New World natives? Is he being too hard on Europeans? Had the Aztecs or Incas had the ability to discover and occupy Europe, would they have enslaved and exploited Europeans?*

Now, to return to my subject, I think there is nothing barbarous and savage in that nation [Brazil], from what I have been told. . . . Each man calls barbarism whatever is not his own practice; for indeed it seems we have no other test of truth and reason than the example and pattern of the opinions and customs of the country we live in. *There* [we] always [find] the perfect religion, the perfect government, the perfect and accomplished manners in all things. Those [foreign] people are wild, just as we call wild the fruits that Nature has produced by herself and in her normal course; where really it is those that we have changed artificially and led astray from the common order that we should rather call wild. The former retain alive and vigorous their genuine virtues and properties, which we have debased in the latter by adapting them to gratify our corrupted taste. And yet for all that, the savor and delicacy of some uncultivated fruits of those countries is quite as excellent, even to our taste, as that of our own. It is not reasonable that [our human] art should win the place of honor over our great and powerful mother Nature. We have so overloaded the beauty and richness of her works by our inventions that we have quite smothered her. Yet wherever her purity shines forth, she wonderfully puts to shame our vain and frivolous attempts: "Ivy comes readier without our care;/In lonely caves the arbutus grows more fair;/No art with artless bird song can compare."[1] All our efforts cannot even succeed in reproducing the nest of the tiniest little bird, its contexture, its beauty and convenience; or even the web of the puny spider. All things, says Plato,[2] are produced by nature, by fortune, or by art; the greatest and most beautiful by one or the other of the first two, the least and most imperfect by the last.

These nations, then, seem to me "barbarous" in this sense, that they have been fashioned very little by the human mind, and are still very close to their original naturalness. The laws of nature still rule them, very little corrupted by ours; and they are in such a state of purity that I am sometimes vexed that they were unknown earlier, in the days when there were men able to judge them better than we.

[1]*Propertius, 1.11.10*
[2]*Laws, 10*

The Complete Essays of Montaigne, *trans. by Donald M. Frame (Stanford: Stanford University Press, 1958), pp. 153–154.*

---

during the colonial era. Its production by forced labor for the benefit of Spaniards and the Spanish crown epitomized the wholly extractive economy that stood at the foundation of colonial life.

AGRICULTURE The major rural and agricultural institution of the Spanish colonies was the *hacienda*. This was a large landed estate owned by persons originally born in Spain (*peninsulares*) or persons of Spanish descent born in

America (creoles). Laborers on the hacienda usually stood in some relation of formal servitude to the owner and were rarely free to move from the services of one landowner to another.

The hacienda economy produced two major products: foodstuffs for mining areas and urban centers and leather goods used in mining machinery. Both farming and ranching were subordinate to the mine economy.

In the West Indies, the basic agricultural unit was the plantation. On Cuba, Hispaniola, Puerto Rico, and other islands, the labor of black slaves from Africa produced sugar to supply an almost insatiable demand for the product in Europe.

A final major area of economic activity in the Spanish colonies was urban service occupations. These included government offices, the legal profession, and shipping. Their practitioners were either *peninsulares* or *creoles,* with the former dominating more often than not.

LABOR SERVITUDE All of this extractive and exploitive economic activity required labor, and the Spanish in the New World decided very early that the native population would supply that labor. A series of social devices was used to draw them into the new economic life imposed by the Spanish.

The first of these was the *encomienda.* This was a formal grant of the right to the labor of a specific number of Indians, usually a few hundred, but sometimes thousands, for a particular period of time. The institution stood in decline by the middle of the sixteenth century because the Spanish monarchs feared that the holders of *encomienda* might become a powerful independent nobility in the New World. They were also persuaded on humanitarian grounds against this particular kind of exploitation of the Indians.

The passing of the *encomienda* led to a new arrangement of labor servitude, the *repartimiento.* This device required adult male Indians to devote a certain number of days of labor annually to Spanish economic enterprises. In the mines of Peru, the *repartimiento* was known as the *mita,* the Inca term for their labor tax. *Repartimiento* service was often extremely harsh, and in some cases Indians did not survive their stint. The limitation of labor time led some Spanish managers to abuse their workers

on the assumption that fresh workers would soon be appearing on the scene.

The eventual shortage of workers and the crown's pressure against extreme versions of forced labor led to the use of free labor. The freedom, however, was more in appearance than reality. Free Indian laborers were required to purchase goods from the land or mine owner, to whom they became forever indebted. This form of exploitation, known as *debt peonage,* continued in Latin America long after the nineteenth-century wars of liberation.

Black slavery was the final mode of forced or subservient labor in the New World. Both the Spanish and the Portuguese had earlier used African slaves in Europe. The sugar plantations of the West Indies now became the major center of black slavery.

The conquest, the forced labor of the economy of exploitation, and the introduction of European diseases had devastating demographic consequences for the Indian population. For centuries Europeans had lived in a far more complex human and animal environment than Native Americans. They had frequent contact with different ethnic and racial groups and with a variety of domestic animals. Such interaction helped them develop strong immune systems that enabled them to survive the ravages of measles, smallpox, and typhoid. Native Americans by contrast grew up in a simpler and more sterile environment and were completely defenseless against these diseases. Within a generation the native population of New Spain (Mexico) was reduced to an estimated 8 percent of its numbers, from 25,000,000 to 2,000,000.

The Impact on Europe

The influx of spices and precious metals into Europe from the new Spanish Empire was a mixed blessing. It contributed to a steady rise in prices during the sixteenth century that created an inflation rate estimated at 2 percent a year. The new supply of bullion from the Americas joined with enlarged European production to increase greatly the amount of coinage in circulation, and this increase in turn fed inflation. Fortunately, the increase in prices was by and large spread over a long period and was not sudden. Prices doubled in Spain by mid-century, quadrupled by 1600. In Luther's Wittenberg, the

A Contemporary Describes Forced Indian Labor at Potosí

The Potosí range, in modern Bolivia, was the site of a great silver-mining industry in the Spanish Empire. The vast amount of wealth contained in the region became legendary almost as soon as mining began there in the 1540s. Indians, most of whom were forced laborers working under the mita system of conscription, did virtually all the work underground. This description, written by a Spanish friar in the early seventeenth century, portrays both the large size of the enterprise and the harsh conditions that the Indians endured. At any one time, only one-third of the 13,300 conscripted Indians were employed. The labor force was changed every four months.

◆ *How efficient does the description suggest the mines were? What would have been the likely effects of working so long underground surrounded by burning candles?*

According to His Majesty's warrant, the mine owners on this massive range have a right to the mita [conscripted labor] of 13,300 Indians in the working and exploitation of the mines, both those which have been discovered, those now discovered, and those which shall be discovered. It is the duty of the Corregidor [municipal governor] of Potosí to have them rounded up and to see that they come in from all the provinces. . . .

The mita Indians go up every Monday morning to the locality of Guayna Potosí which is at the foot of the range; the Corregidor arrives with all the provincial captains or chiefs who have charge of the Indians assigned them, and he there checks off and reports to each mine and smelter owner the number of Indians assigned him for his miner or smelter; that keeps him busy till 1 P.M., by which time the Indians are already turned over to these mine and smelter owners.

After each has eaten his ration, they climb up the hill, each to his mine, and go in, staying there from that hour until Saturday evening without coming out of the mine; their wives bring them food, but they stay constantly underground, excavating and carrying out the ore from which they get the silver. They all have tallow candles, lighted day and night; that is the light they work with, for as they are underground, they have need of it all the time. . . .

These Indians have different functions in the handling of the silver ore; some break it up with bar or pick, and dig down in, following the vein in the mine; others bring it up; others up above keep separating the good and the poor in piles; others are occupied in taking it down from the range to the mills on herds of llamas; every day they bring up more than 8,000 of these native beasts of burden for this task. These teamsters who carry the metal do not belong to the mita, but are mingados—hired.

Antonio Vázquez de Espinosa, Compendium and Description of the Indies *(ca. 1620), trans. by Charles Upson Clark (Washington, D.C.: Smithsonian Institution Press, 1968), p. 62.*

cost of basic food and clothing increased almost 100 percent between 1519 and 1540. Generally wages and rents remained well behind the rise in prices.

The new wealth enabled governments and private entrepreneurs to sponsor basic research and expansion in the printing, shipping, mining, textile, and weapons industries. There is also evidence of large-scale government planning in such ventures as the French silk industry and the Habsburg–Fugger development of mines in Austria and Hungary.

In the thirteenth and fourteenth centuries capitalist institutions and practices had already begun to develop in the rich Italian cities (one may point to the activities of the Florentine banking houses of Bardi and Peruzzi). Those who owned the means of production, either privately or corporately, were clearly distinguished from the workers who operated them. Wherever possible, entrepreneurs created monopolies in basic goods. High interest was charged on loans—actual, if not legal, usury. And the "capitalist" virtues of thrift, industry, and orderly planning were everywhere in evidence—all intended to permit the free and efficient accumulation of wealth.

The late fifteenth and the sixteenth centuries saw the maturation of this type of capitalism together with its attendant social problems. The Medicis of Florence grew very rich as bankers of the pope, as did the Fuggers of Augsburg, who bankrolled Habsburg rulers. The Fuggers lent Charles I of Spain more than 500,000 florins to buy his election as Holy Roman Emperor in 1519, boasting that they had created the emperor. The new wealth and industrial expansion also raised the expectations of the poor and the ambitious and heightened the reactionary tendencies of the wealthy. This effect, in turn, aggravated the traditional social divisions between the clergy and the laity, the urban patriciate and the guilds, and the landed nobility and the agrarian peasantry.

These divisions may indirectly have prepared the way for the Reformation as well by making many people critical of traditional institutions and open to new ideas—especially those that seemed to promise greater freedom and a chance at a better life.

———————————— ◆ ————————————

As it recovered from national wars during the late Middle Ages, Europe saw the establishment of permanent centralized states and regional governments. The foundations of modern France, Spain, England, Germany, and Italy were laid at this time. As rulers imposed their will on regions outside their immediate domains, the "one" progressively took control of the "many," and previously divided lands came together as nations.

Thanks to the work of Byzantine and Islamic scholars, ancient Greek science and scholarship found their way into the West in these centuries. Europeans had been separated from their classical cultural heritage for almost eight centuries. No other world civilization had experienced such a disjunction from its cultural past. The discovery of classical civilization occasioned a rebirth of intellectual and artistic activity in both southern and northern Europe. One result was the splendor of the Italian Renaissance, whose scholarship, painting, and sculpture remain among western Europe's most impressive achievements.

Ancient learning was not the only discovery of the era. New political unity spurred both royal greed and national ambition. By the late fifteenth century, Europeans were in a position to venture far away to the shores of Africa, the southern and eastern coasts of Asia, and to the New World of the Americas. Discovery was not the only outcome of these voyages; the exploitation of the peoples and lands of the New World revealed a dark side of Western civilization. Some penalties were paid even then. The influx of New World gold and silver created new human and economic problems on the European mainland. In some circles Europeans even began to question their civilization's traditional values.

Review Questions

1. Discuss Jacob Burkhardt's interpretation of the Renaissance. What criticisms have been leveled against it? How would you define the term *Renaissance* in the context of fifteenth- and sixteenth-century Italy?

2. How would you define *Renaissance Humanism?* In what ways was the Renaissance a break with the Middle Ages, and in what ways did it owe its existence to medieval civilization?

3. Who were some of the famous literary and artistic figures of the Italian Renaissance? What did they have in common that might be described as "the spirit of the Renaissance"?

4. Why did the French invade Italy in 1494? How did this event trigger Italy's political decline? How do the actions of Pope Julius II

and the ideas of Niccolò Machiavelli signify a new era in Italian civilization?

5. A common assumption is that creative work proceeds best in periods of calm and peace. Given the combination of political instability and cultural productivity in Renaissance Italy, do you think this assumption is valid?

6. How did the Northern Renaissance differ from the Italian Renaissance? In what ways was Erasmus the embodiment of the Northern Renaissance?

7. What factors lead to the voyages of discovery? How did the Spanish establish their empire in the Americas? Why was the conquest so violent? What was the experience of native peoples during and after the conquest?

Suggested Readings

L. B. ALBERTI, *The Family in Renaissance Florence,* trans. by R. N. Watkins (1962). A contemporary Humanist, who never married, explains how a family should behave.

M. ASTON, *The Fifteenth Century: The Prospect of Europe* (1968). Crisp social history, with pictures.

R. H. BAINTON, *Erasmus of Christendom* (1960). Charming presentation.

H. BARON, *The Crisis of the Early Italian Renaissance,* Vols. 1 and 2 (1966). A major work, setting forth the civic dimension of Italian Humanism.

B. BERENSON, *Italian Painters of the Renaissance* (1957). Eloquent and authoritative.

C. BOXER, *Four Centuries of Portuguese Expansion, 1415–1825* (1961). Comprehensive survey by the leading authority.

G. A. BRUCKER, *Renaissance Florence* (1969). Comprehensive survey of all facets of Florentine life.

G. A. BRUCKER, *Giovanni and Lusanna: Love and Marriage in Renaissance Florence* (1986). Love in the Renaissance shown to be more Bergman than Fellini.

J. BURCKHARDT, *The Civilization of the Renaissance in Italy* (1867). The old classic that still has as many defenders as detractors.

R. E. CONRAD, *Children of God's Fire: A Documentary History of Black Slavery in Brazil* (1983). Not for the squeamish.

A. W. CROSBY, *The Columbian Exchange: Biological and Cultural Consequences of 1492* (1973). A study of the epidemiological disaster that Columbus visited upon Native Americans.

E. L. EISENSTEIN, *The Printing Press As an Agent of Change: Communications and Cultural Transformations in Early Modern Europe,* 2 vols. (1979). Bold, stimulating account of the centrality of printing to all progress in the period.

W. K. FERGUSON, *Europe in Transition, 1300–1520* (1962). A major survey that deals with the transition from medieval society to Renaissance society.

C. GIBSON, *Spain in America* (1956). A splendidly clear and balanced narrative.

C. GIBSON, *The Aztecs Under Spanish Rule: A History of the Indians of the Valley of Mexico* (1964). Exceedingly interesting book.

F. GILBERT, *Machiavelli and Guicciardini* (1984). The two great Renaissance historians lucidly compared.

M. GILMORE, *The World of Humanism, 1453–1517* (1952). A comprehensive survey, especially strong in intellectual and cultural history.

W. L. GUNDERSHEIMER (Ed.), *French Humanism, 1470–1600* (1969). Essays summarizing research and provoking further study.

J. R. HALE, *Renaissance Europe: The Individual and Society, 1480–1520* (1971). A galloping social history.

L. HANKE, *Bartholome de Las Casas: An Interpretation of His Life and Writings* (1951). Biography of the great Dominican critic of Spanish exploitation of Native Americans.

J. HANKINS, *Plato in the Renaissance* (1992). A magisterial study of how Plato was read and interpreted by Renaissance scholars.

D. HERLIHY, *The Family in Renaissance Italy* (1974). Excellent on family structure and general features.

D. HERLIHY and C. KLAPISCH-ZUBER, *Tuscans and Their Families* (1985). Important work based on unique demographic data that gives the reader a new appreciation of quantitative history.

D. L. JENSEN, *Renaissance Europe: Age of Recovery and Reconciliation* (1981). Up-to-date and comprehensive survey.

F. KATZ, *The Ancient American Civilizations* (1972). An excellent introduction.

B. KEEN and M. WASSERMAN, *A Short History of Latin America* (1984). A good survey with very helpful bibliographical guides.

R. KELSO, *Doctrine of the Lady of the Renaissance* (1978). Noblewomen in the Renaissance.

C. KLAPISCH-ZUBER, *Women, Family, and Ritual in Renaissance Italy* (1985). Provocative, wide-ranging essays documenting the Renaissance as very much a man's world.

P. O. KRISTELLER, *Renaissance Thought: The Classic, Scholastic, and Humanist Strains* (1961). A master shows the many sides of Renaissance thought.

I. MACLEAN, *The Renaissance Notion of Women* (1980). An account of the views of Renaissance intellectuals and their sources in antiquity.

R. MARIUS, *Thomas More: A Biography* (1984). Eloquent analysis of the man as well as of the saint.

L. MARTINES, *Power and Imagination: City States in Renaissance Italy* (1980). Stimulating account of cultural and political history.

H. A. MISKIMIN, *The Economy of Early Renaissance Europe, 1300–1460* (1975). Shows interaction of social, political, economic, and cultural change.

S. E. MORRISON, *Admiral of the Ocean Sea: A Life of Christopher Columbus* (1946). Still the authoritative biography.

E. PANOFSKY, *Meaning in the Visual Arts* (1955). Eloquent treatment of Renaissance art.

J. H. PARRY, *The Age of Reconnaissance* (1964). A comprehensive account of exploration in the years 1450–1650.

P. PARTNER, *Renaissance Rome, 1500–1559: A Portrait of a Society* (1976). A description of the city from an insider's perspective.

M. M. PHILLIPS, *Erasmus and the Northern Renaissance* (1956). A learned, rewarding account of the man and the movement.

J. B. A. POCOCK, *The Machiavellian Moment in Florentine Political Thought and the Atlantic Republican Tradition* (1975). Traces the influence of Florentine political thought in early modern Europe.

I. A. RICHTER (Ed.), *The Notebooks of Leonardo da Vinci* (1985). The master in his own words.

Q. SKINNER, *The Foundations of Modern Political Thought I: The Renaissance* (1978). Broad survey, including absolutely every known political theorist, major and minor.

Lutherans made Jesus' blessing of infants and small children (Mark 10:13) a new theme in art and a forceful polemic against both Catholics, who believed good works to be a condition of salvation, and Anabaptists, who rejected infant baptism. Lucas Cranach the Elder painted over twenty versions of this scene. Here he portrays Jesus directly accessible to those with simple childlike faith, who do no special good works and have nothing to recommend them except God's grace. The painting also expresses the Protestant affirmation of marriage and family and rejection of celibacy and of clerical polemics against women and sex. [Elke Walford, Hamburger Kunsthalle]

11

The Age of Reformation

> **Key Topics in This Chapter**
> ◆ The social and religious background to the Reformation
> ◆ Martin Luther's challenge to the Church and the course of the Reformation in Germany
> ◆ The Reformation in Switzerland, France, and England
> ◆ Transitions in family life between medieval and modern times

In the second decade of the sixteenth century, a powerful religious movement began in Saxony in Germany and rapidly spread throughout northern Europe, deeply affecting society and politics as well as the spiritual lives of men and women. Attacking what they believed to be burdensome superstitions that robbed people of both their money and their peace of mind,

Protestant reformers led a broad revolt against the medieval Church. In a short span of time, hundreds of thousands of people from all social classes set aside the beliefs of centuries and adopted a more simplified religious practice.

The Protestant Reformation challenged aspects of the Renaissance, especially its tendency to follow classical sources in glorifying human nature and its loyalty to traditional religion. Protestants were more impressed by the human potential for evil than by the inclination to do good; they encouraged parents, teachers, and magistrates to be firm disciplinarians. On the other hand, Protestants also embraced many Renaissance values, especially in the sphere of educational reform and particularly with regard to training in ancient languages. Like the Italian Humanists, the Protestant reformers prized the tools that allowed them to go directly to the original sources. For them this meant the study of the Hebrew and Greek Scriptures, enabling them to root their consequent challenges to traditional institutions in biblical authority.

Society and Religion

The Protestant Reformation occurred at a time of sharp conflict between the emerging nation-states of Europe, bent on conformity and centralization within their realms, and the self-governing small towns and regions, long accustomed to running their own affairs. Since the fourteenth century, the king's law and custom had progressively overridden local law and custom almost everywhere. Many towns and territories were keenly sensitive to the loss of traditional rights and freedoms. Many townspeople and village folk perceived in the religious revolt an ally in their struggle to remain politically free and independent. The Reformation came to be closely identified in the minds of its supporters with what we today might call states' rights or local control.

Social and Political Conflict

The Reformation broke out first in the free imperial cities of Germany and Switzerland. There were about sixty-five such cities, and each was in a certain sense a little kingdom unto itself. The great majority had Protestant movements, but with mixed success and duration. Some quickly turned Protestant and remained so. Some were Protestant only for a short time. Others developed mixed confessions, frowning on sectarianism and aggressive proselytizing, and letting Catholics and Protestants live side by side with appropriate barriers.

What seemed a life-and-death struggle with higher princely or royal authority was not the only conflict cities were experiencing. They also suffered deep internal social and political divisions. Certain groups favored the Reformation more than others. In many places, guilds whose members were economically prospering and socially rising were in the forefront of the Reformation. The printers' guild is a prominent example. Its members were literate, sophisticated about the world, in a rapidly growing industry, and economically very ambitious. They also had an economic stake in fanning religious conflict with Protestant propaganda, which many of course also sincerely believed. Guilds with a history of opposition to reigning governmental authority also stand out among early Protestant supporters, regardless of whether their members were literate.

There is, in brief, evidence to suggest that people who felt pushed around and bullied by either local or distant authority—a guild by an autocratic local government, an entire city or region by a powerful prince or king—often perceived in the Protestant movement an ally, at least initially.

Social and political experience thus coalesced with the larger religious issues in both town and countryside. A Protestant sermon or pamphlet seemed directly relevant, for example, to the townspeople of German and Swiss cities who faced incorporation into the territory of a powerful local prince, who looked on them as obedient subjects rather than as free citizens. When Martin Luther and his comrades wrote, preached, and sang about a priesthood of all believers, scorned the authority of ecclesiastical landlords, and ridiculed papal laws as arbitrary human inventions, they touched political as well as religious nerves. And this was as true in the villages as in the towns. Like city dwellers, the peasants on the land also heard in the Protestant sermon and pamphlet a promise of political liberation and even a degree of social betterment. More

The Reformation broke out against a background of deep social and political divisions that bred resentment against authority. This early sixteenth-century woodcut by Georg Pencz presents a warning against tyranny. It shows a world turned upside down, with the hunted becoming the hunters. The rabbits capture the hunters and their dogs and subject them to the same brutal treatment—skinning, butchering, and cooking—that the hunters and dogs routinely inflict on rabbits. The message: tyranny eventually begets rebellion. [Hacker Art Books]

than the townspeople, the peasants found their traditional liberties—from fishing and hunting rights to representation at local diets—progressively being chipped away by the great secular and ecclesiastical landlords who ruled over them.

Popular Religious Movements and Criticism of the Church

The Protestant Reformation could also not have occurred without the monumental crises of the medieval Church during the "exile" in Avignon, the Great Schism, the conciliar period, and the Renaissance papacy. For increasing numbers of people, the medieval Church had ceased to provide a viable foundation for religious piety. Many intellectuals and laypeople felt a sense of

crisis about the traditional teaching and spiritual practice of the Church. Between the secular pretensions of the papacy and the dry teaching of Scholastic theologians, laity and clerics alike began to seek a more heartfelt, idealistic, and—often, in the eyes of the pope—increasingly heretical religious piety. The late Middle Ages were marked by independent lay and clerical efforts to reform local religious practice and by widespread experimentation with new religious forms.

A variety of factors contributed to the growth of lay criticism of the Church. The laity in the cities were becoming increasingly knowledgeable about the world and those who controlled their lives. They traveled widely—as soldiers, pilgrims, explorers, and traders. New postal sys-

Injustice. This woodcut by an unknown artist compares the law, represented by the court scene in the center, to a spider's web, shown in the window on the right. Just as the web traps small, weak insects, the law ensnares the poor, seen hanging on the gallows and the wheel through the window on the left. And just as the large bee flies easily through the web, the rich and powerful escape punishment for their crimes. [Hacker Art Books]

This sculpture illustrates the new piety of feeling that emerged in the fifteenth century in reaction to the cold, ritualized religious practice that had become predominant. Here the Virgin Mary is caught as she swoons over the crucifixion of her Son. During the sixteenth century, both Protestants and Catholics tried to accommodate the desire for personal involvement in religion. [Bebenhausen, Württembergisches Landesmuseum]

tems and the printing press increased the information at their disposal. The new age of books and libraries raised literacy and heightened curiosity. Laypeople were increasingly able to take the initiative in shaping the cultural life of their communities.

From the Albigensians, Waldensians, Beguines, and Beghards in the thirteenth century to the Lollards and Hussites in the fifteenth, lay religious movements shared a common goal of religious simplicity in imitation of Jesus. Almost without exception they were inspired by an ideal of apostolic poverty in religion; that is, all wanted a religion of true self-sacrifice like that of Jesus and the first disciples. The laity sought a more egalitarian Church, one that gave the members as well as the head of the Church a voice, and a more spiritual Church, one that

lived manifestly according to its New Testament model.

THE MODERN DEVOTION   One of the most constructive lay religious movements in northern Europe on the eve of the Reformation was that of the Brothers of the Common Life, or what came to be known as the *Modern Devotion.* The brothers fostered religious life outside formal ecclesiastical offices and apart from formal religious vows. Established by Gerard Groote (1340–1384), the Modern Devotion was centered at Zwolle and Deventer in the Netherlands. The brother and (less numerous) sister houses of the Modern Devotion, however, spread rapidly throughout northern Europe and influenced parts of southern Europe as well. In these houses clerics and laity came together to share a common life, stressing individual piety and practical religion. Lay members were not expected to take special religious vows or to wear special religious dress, nor did they abandon their ordinary secular vocations.

The brothers were also active in education. They worked as copyists, sponsored many religious and a few classical publications, ran hospices for poor students, and conducted schools for the young, especially for boys preparing for the priesthood or a monastic vocation. As youths, Nicholas of Cusa, Johann Reuchlin, and Desiderius Erasmus were looked after by the brothers. Thomas à Kempis (d. 1471) summarized the philosophy of the brothers in what became the most popular religious book of the period, the *Imitation of Christ.* This semimystical guide to the inner life was intended primarily for monks and nuns, but was widely appropriated by laity who also wanted to pursue the ascetic life.

The Modern Devotion has been seen as the source of Humanist, Protestant, and Catholic reform movements in the sixteenth century. Some scholars, however, believe that it represented an individualistic approach to religion, indifferent and even harmful to the sacramental piety of the Church. It was actually a very conservative movement. The brothers retained the old clerical doctrines and values, while placing them within the new framework of an active common life. Their practices clearly met a need for a more personal piety and a better-informed religious life. Their movement appeared at a time when the laity were demanding good preaching in the vernacular and were even taking the initiative to endow special preacherships to ensure it. The Modern Devotion permitted laypeople to practice a full religious life without surrendering their life in the world.

LAY CONTROL OVER RELIGIOUS LIFE On the eve of the Reformation, Rome's international network of Church offices, which had unified Europe religiously during the Middle Ages, began to fall apart in many areas. This collapse was hurried along by a growing sense of regional identity—incipient nationalism—and local secular administrative competence. The long-entrenched benefice system of the medieval Church had permitted important ecclesiastical posts to be sold to the highest bidders and had left residency requirements in parishes unenforced. Such a system did not result in a vibrant local religious life. The substitutes hired by nonresident holders of benefices lived elsewhere, mostly in Rome. They milked the revenues of their offices, often performed their chores mechanically, and had neither firsthand knowledge of nor much sympathy with local needs and problems. Rare was the late medieval German town that did not have complaints about the maladministration, concubinage, or fiscalism of their clergy, especially the higher clergy (bishops, abbots, and prelates).

Communities had protested loudly the financial abuses of the medieval Church long before Luther published his famous summary of economic grievances in 1520 in the *Address to the Christian Nobility of the German Nation*. The sale of indulgences in particular had been repeatedly attacked before Luther came on the scene. On the eve of the Reformation, this practice had expanded to permit people to buy release from time in purgatory for both themselves and their deceased loved ones. Rulers and magistrates had little objection to their sale, and might even encourage it so long as a generous portion of the income they generated remained in the local coffers. But when an indulgence was offered primarily for the benefit of distant interests, as with the Saint Peter's indulgence protested by Luther, resistance arose for strictly financial reasons, because their sale drained away local revenues.

The sale of indulgences would not end until rulers found new ways to profit from religion, and the laity found a more effective popular remedy for religious anxiety. The Reformation provided the former by sanctioning the secular dissolution of monasteries and the confiscation of ecclesiastical properties. It held out the latter in its new theology of justification by faith.

City governments also undertook to improve local religious life on the eve of the Reformation by endowing preacherships. These positions, supported by benefices, provided for well-trained and dedicated pastors who could provide regular preaching and pastoral care that went beyond the routine performance of the Mass and traditional religious functions. In many instances these preacherships became platforms for Protestant preachers.

Magistrates also carefully restricted the growth of ecclesiastical properties and clerical privileges. During the Middle Ages, canon and civil law had come to recognize special clerical rights in both property and person. Because they were holy places, churches and monasteries had been exempted from the taxes and laws that affected others. They were treated as special places of "sacral peace" and asylum. It was considered inappropriate for holy persons (clergy) to be burdened with such "dirty jobs" as military service, compulsory labor, standing watch at city gates, and other obligations of citizenship. Nor was it thought right that the laity, of whatever rank, should sit in judgment on those who were their shepherds and intermediaries with God. The clergy, accordingly, came to enjoy an immunity of place (which exempted ecclesiastical properties from taxes and recognized their right of asylum) and an immunity of person (which exempted the clergy from the jurisdiction of civil courts).

On the eve of the Reformation measures were passed to restrict these privileges and to end their abuses. Among them we find efforts to regulate ecclesiastical acquisition of new property, to circumvent the right of asylum in churches and monasteries (a practice that posed a threat to the normal administration of justice), and to bring the clergy under the local tax code. Governments had understandably tired of ecclesiastical interference in what to them were strictly political spheres of competence and authority.

Martin Luther and German Reformation to 1525

Unlike France and England, late medieval Germany lacked the political unity to enforce "national" religious reforms during the late Middle Ages. There were no lasting Statutes of Provisors and *Praemunire,* as in England, nor a Pragmatic Sanction of Bourges, as in France, limiting papal jurisdiction and taxation on a national scale. What happened on a unified national level in England and France occurred only locally and piecemeal within German territories and towns. As popular resentment of clerical immunities and ecclesiastical abuses, especially over the selling of indulgences, spread among German cities and towns, an unorganized "national" opposition to Rome formed. German Humanists had long given voice to such criticism, and by 1517 it was pervasive enough to provide a solid foundation for Martin Luther's reform.

Luther (1483–1546) was the son of a successful Thüringian miner. He was educated in Mansfeld, Magdeburg (where the Brothers of the Common Life were his teachers), and Eisenach. Between 1501 and 1505 he attended the University of Erfurt, where the nominalist teachings of William of Ockham and Gabriel Biel (d. 1495) prevailed. After receiving his master of arts degree in 1505, Luther registered with the Law Faculty following his parents' wishes. But he never began the study of law. To the disappointment of his family, he instead entered the Order of the Hermits of Saint Augustine in Erfurt on July 17, 1505. This decision had apparently been building for some time and was resolved during a lightning storm in which a terrified Luther, crying out to Saint Anne for assistance (Saint Anne was the patron saint of travelers in distress), promised to enter a monastery if he escaped death.

Ordained in 1507, Luther pursued a traditional course of study. In 1510 he journeyed to Rome on the business of his order, finding there justification for the many criticisms of the Church he had heard in Germany. In 1511 he moved to the Augustinian monastery in Wittenberg, where he earned his doctorate in theology in 1512. Thereafter, he became a leader within the monastery, the new university, and the spiritual life of the city.

Justification by Faith Alone

Reformation theology grew out of a problem then common to many of the clergy and the laity: the failure of traditional medieval religion to provide either full personal or intellectual satisfaction. Luther was especially plagued by the disproportion between his own sense of sinfulness and the perfect righteousness that medieval theology taught that God required for salvation. Traditional Church teaching and the sacrament of penance proved to be of no consolation. Luther wrote that he came to despise the phrase "righteousness of God," for it seemed to demand of him a perfection he knew neither he nor any other human being could ever achieve. His insight into the meaning of "justification by faith alone" was a gradual process that extended between 1513 and 1518. The righteousness that God demands, he concluded, did not result from many religious works and ceremonies but was given in full measure to those who believe and trust in Jesus Christ, who alone is the perfect righteousness satisfying to God. To believe in Christ meant to stand before God clothed in Christ's sure righteousness.

The Attack on Indulgences

An indulgence was a remission of the temporal penalty imposed by priests on penitents as a "work of satisfaction" for their mortal sins. According to medieval theology, after the priest absolved a penitent of guilt for his sins, the penitent remained under an eternal penalty, a punishment God justly imposed for sin. After absolution, however, this eternal penalty was said to be transformed into a temporal penalty, a manageable "work of satisfaction" that the penitent could perform here and now (for example, prayers, fasting, almsgiving, retreats, and pilgrimages). Penitents who defaulted on such prescribed works of satisfaction could expect to suffer for them in purgatory.

At this point, indulgences, which had earlier been given to Crusaders who did not complete their penances because they had fallen in battle, became an aid to laity, made genuinely anxious

Martin Luther Discovers Justification by Faith Alone

Many years after the fact, Martin Luther described his famous discovery that God's righteousness was not active and punishing but passive and transforming. It made those who believed in Christ as holy in God's eyes as Christ was holy.

✦ *Why did Luther find the monastic life so unsatisfying? Did he misunderstand the Church's teaching about God's love and mercy? How does his discovery of God's "passive righteousness" give him peace of mind?*

Though I lived as a monk without reproach, I felt that I was a sinner before God with an extremely disturbed conscience. I could not believe that he was placated by my satisfaction. I did not love, yes, I hated the righteous God who punishes sinners, and secretly, if not blasphemously, certainly murmuring greatly, I was angry with God, and said, "As if, indeed, it is not enough, that miserable sinners, eternally lost through original sin, are crushed by every kind of calamity by the law of the decalogue, without having God add pain to pain by the gospel and also by the gospel threatening us with his righteousness and wrath!" Thus I raged with a fierce and troubled conscience. Nevertheless, I beat importunately upon Paul at that place, most ardently desiring to know what St. Paul wanted.

At last, by the mercy of God, meditating day and night, I gave heed to the context of the words, namely, 'In it the righteousness of God is revealed, as it is written, 'He who through faith is righteous shall live'" [Romans 1:17]. There I began to understand that the righteousness of God is that by which the righteous [man] lives by a gift of God, namely by faith. And this is the meaning: the righteousness of God is revealed by the gospel, namely, the passive righteousness with which merciful God justifies us by faith, as it is written, "He who through faith is righteous shall live." Here I felt that I was altogether born again and had entered paradise itself through open gates. There a totally other face of the entire Scripture showed itself to me. Thereupon I ran through the Scriptures from memory. I also found in other terms an analogy, as, the work of God, that is, what God does in us, the power of God, with which he makes us strong, the wisdom of God, with which he makes us wise, the strength of God, the salvation of God, the glory of God.

And I extolled my sweetest word with a love as great as the hatred with which I had before heated the word "righteousness of God." Thus that place in Paul was for me truly the gate to paradise.

Preface to the Complete Edition of Luther's Latin Writings (1545), in Luther's Works, Vol. 34, ed. by Lewis W. Spitz (Philadelphia: Muhlenberg Press, 1960) pp. 336–337.

by their belief in a future suffering in Purgatory for neglected penances or unrepented sins. In 1343 Pope Clement VI (r. 1342–1352) had proclaimed the existence of a "treasury of merit," an infinite reservoir of good works in the Church's possession that could be dispensed at the pope's discretion. On the basis of this declared treasury the Church sold "letters of indulgence," which covered the works of satisfaction owed by penitents. In 1476 Pope Sixtus IV (r. 1471–1484) extended indulgences also to Purgatory.

Originally, indulgences had been given only for the true self-sacrifice of going on a Crusade to the Holy Land. By Luther's time, they were regularly dispensed for small cash payments (very modest sums that were regarded as a good work of almsgiving). They were presented to the laity as remitting not only their own future punishments, but also those of their dead relatives presumed to be suffering in purgatory.

In 1517 a Jubilee indulgence was proclaimed during the pontificate of Pope Julius II (r. 1503–1513) to raise funds for the rebuilding of Saint Peter's in Rome. It was preached on the borders of Saxony in the territories of Archbishop Albrecht of Mainz. Albrecht was much in need of revenues because of the large debts he had incurred in order to hold, contrary to Church law, three ecclesiastical appointments. The selling of the indulgence was a joint venture by Albrecht, the Augsburg banking-house of Fugger, and Pope Leo X, half the proceeds going to the pope and half to Albrecht and his creditors. The famous indulgence preacher John Tetzel (d. 1519) was enlisted to preach the indulgence in Albrecht's territories because he was a seasoned professional who knew how to stir ordinary people to action. As he exhorted on one occasion:

A contemporary caricature depicts John Tetzel, the famous indulgence preacher. The last lines of the jingle read: "As soon as gold in the basin rings, right then the soul to Heaven springs." It was Tetzel's preaching that spurred Luther to publish his ninety-five theses. [Staatliche Lutherhalle, Wittenberg]

Don't you hear the voices of your dead parents and other relatives crying out, "Have mercy on us, for we suffer great punishment and pain. From this you could release us with a few alms. . . . We have created you, fed you, cared for you, and left you our temporal goods. Why do you treat us so cruelly and leave us to suffer in the flames, when it takes only a little to save us?"[1]

When on October 31, 1517, Luther, according to tradition, posted his ninety-five theses against indulgences on the door of Castle Church in Wittenberg, he protested especially against the impression created by Tetzel that indulgences actually remitted sins and released the dead from punishment in purgatory. Luther believed these claims went far beyond the traditional practice and seemed to make salvation something that could be bought and sold.

Election of Charles V

The ninety-five theses were embraced by Humanists and other proponents of reform. They made Luther famous overnight and prompted official proceedings against him. In October he was called before the general of the Dominican Order in Augsburg. But as sanctions were being prepared against Luther, Emperor Maximilian I died (January 12, 1519), and this event, fortunate for the Reformation, turned attention away from heresy in Saxony to the contest for a new emperor.

The pope backed the French king, Francis I. However, Charles I of Spain, a youth of nineteen, succeeded his grandfather and became Emperor Charles V (see Map 11-1). Charles was assisted by both a long tradition of Habsburg imperial rule and a massive Fugger campaign chest, which secured the votes of the seven electors. The electors, who traditionally enhanced their power at every opportunity, wrung new concessions from Charles for their votes. The emperor agreed to a revival of the Imperial Supreme Court and the Council of Regency and promised to consult with a diet of the empire on all major domestic and foreign affairs that affected the empire. These measures also helped the development of the Reformation by preventing unilateral imperial action against the Germans, something Luther could be thankful for in the early years of the Reformation.

[1]*Die Reformation in Augenzeugen berichten, ed. by Helmar Junghaus (Düsseldorf: Karl Rauch Verlag, 1967), p. 44.*

MAP 11-1 THE EMPIRE OF CHARLES V *Dynastic marriages and simple chance concentrated into Charles's hands rule over the lands shown here, plus Spain's overseas possessions. Crowns and titles rained down on him; election in 1519 as emperor gave him new burdens and responsibilities.*

Luther's Excommunication and the Diet of Worms

In the same month in which Charles was elected emperor, Luther entered a debate in Leipzig (June 27, 1519) with the Ingolstadt professor John Eck. During this contest, Luther challenged the infallibility of the pope and the inerrancy of Church councils, appealing, for the first time, to the sovereign authority of Scripture alone. He burned all his bridges to the old Church when he further defended certain teachings of John Huss condemned by the Council of Constance.

In 1520 Luther signaled his new direction with three famous pamphlets. The *Address to the Christian Nobility of the German Nation* urged the German princes to force reforms on the Roman church, especially to curtail its political and economic power in Germany. The *Babylonian Captivity of the Church* attacked the traditional seven sacraments, arguing that only two, Baptism and the Eucharist, were proper, and exalted the authority of Scripture, Church councils, and secular princes over that of the pope. The eloquent *Freedom of a Christian* summarized the new teaching of salvation by faith alone.

On June 15, 1520, Leo's papal bull *Exsurge Domine* condemned Luther for heresy and gave him sixty days to retract. The final bull of excommunication, *Decet Pontificem Romanum,* was issued on January 3, 1521.

In April 1521 Luther presented his views before a diet of the empire in Worms, over which the newly elected Emperor Charles V presided. Ordered to recant, Luther declared that

German Peasants Protest Rising Feudal Exactions

In the late fifteenth and early sixteenth centuries, German feudal lords, both secular and ecclesiastical, tried to increase the earnings from their lands by raising demands on their peasant tenants. As the personal freedoms of peasants were restricted, their properties confiscated, and their traditional laws and customs overridden, massive revolts occurred in southern Germany in 1525. Some historians see this uprising and the social and economic conditions that gave rise to it as the major historical force in early modern history. The following, from Memmingen, in modern Germany, is the most representative and well-known statement of peasant grievances.

◆ *Are the peasants' demands reasonable given the circumstances of the sixteenth century? Are peasants more interested in material than in spiritual freedom? Which of the demands are the most revolutionary?*

1. It is our humble petition and desire . . . that in the future . . . each community should choose and appoint a pastor, and that we should have the right to depose him should he conduct himself improperly. . . .

2. We are ready and willing to pay the fair tithe of grain. . . . The small tithes [of cattle], whether [to] ecclesiastical or lay lords, we will not pay at all, for the Lord God created cattle for the free use of man. . . .

3. We . . . take it for granted that you will release us from serfdom as true Christians, unless it should be shown us from the Gospel that we are serfs.

4. It has been the custom heretofore that no poor man should be allowed to catch venison or wildfowl or fish in flowing water, which seems to us quite unseemly

---

to do so would be to act against Scripture, reason, and his own conscience. On May 26, 1521, he was placed under the imperial ban and thereafter became an "outlaw" to secular as well as to religious authority. For his own protection, friends hid him in a secluded castle, where he spent almost a year, from April 1521 to March 1522. During his stay, he translated the New Testament into German, using Erasmus's new Greek text, and he attempted by correspondence to oversee the first stages of the Reformation in Wittenberg.

Imperial Distractions: France and the Turks

The Reformation was greatly helped in these early years by the emperor's war with France and the advance of the Ottoman Turks into eastern Europe. Against both adversaries Charles V, who also remained a Spanish king with dynastic responsibilities outside the empire, needed German troops, and to that end he promoted friendly relations with the German princes. Between 1521 and 1559 Spain (the Habsburg dynasty) and France (the Valois dynasty) fought four major wars over disputed territories in Italy and along their borders. In 1526 the Turks overran Hungary at the Battle of Mohacs, while in western Europe the French-led League of Cognac formed against Charles for the second Habsburg–Valois war.

Thus preoccupied, the emperor agreed through his representatives at the German Diet of Speyer in 1526 that each German territory was free to enforce the Edict of Worms (1521) against Luther "so as to be able to answer in good conscience to God and the emperor." That concession, in effect, gave the German princes

and unbrotherly as well as selfish and not agreeable to the Word of God. . . .

5. We are aggrieved in the matter of wood-cutting, for the noblemen have appropriated all the woods to themselves. . . .

6. In regard to the excessive services demanded of us which are increased from day to day, we ask that this matter be properly looked into so that we shall not continue to be oppressed in this way. . . .

7. We will not hereafter allow ourselves to be further oppressed by our lords, but will let them demand only what is just and proper according to the word of the agreement between the lord and the peasant. The lord should no longer try to force more services or other dues from the peasant without payment. . . .

8. We are greatly burdened because our holdings cannot support the rent exacted from them. . . . We ask that the lords may appoint persons of honor to inspect these holdings and fix a rent in accordance with justice. . . .

9. We are burdened with a great evil in the constant making of new laws. . . . In our opinion we should be judged according to the old written law. . . .

10. We are aggrieved by the appropriation . . . of meadows and fields which at one time belonged to a community as a whole. These we will take again into our own hands. . . .

11. We will entirely abolish the due called *Todfall* [that is, heriot or death tax, by which the lord received the best horse, cow, or garment of a family upon the death of a serf] and will no longer endure it, nor allow widows and orphans to be thus shamefully robbed against God's will, and in violation of justice and right. . . .

12. It is our conclusion and final resolution, that if any one or more of the articles here set forth should not be in agreement with the Word of God, as we think they are, such article we will willingly retract.

Translations and Reprints from the Original Sources of European History, Vol. 2 (Philadelphia: Department of History, University of Pennsylvania, 1897).

territorial sovereignty in religious matters and the Reformation time to put down deep roots. Later (in 1555) the Peace of Augsburg would enshrine such local princely control over religion in imperial law.

How the Reformation Spread

In the late 1520s and 1530s, the Reformation passed from the hands of the theologians and pamphleteers into those of the magistrates and princes. In many cities, the magistrates quickly followed the lead of the Protestant preachers and their sizable congregations in mandating the religious reforms they preached. In numerous instances, magistrates had themselves worked for decades to bring about basic church reforms and thus welcomed the preachers as new allies. Reform now ceased to be merely slogans and became laws which all townspeople had to obey.

The religious reform became a territorial political movement as well, led by the Elector of Saxony and the prince of Hesse, the two most powerful German Protestant rulers. Like the urban magistrates, the German princes quickly recognized the political and economic opportunities offered them by the demise of the Roman Catholic church in their regions. Soon they too were pushing Protestant faith and politics onto their neighbors. By the 1530s, Protestant cities and lands formed powerful defensive alliances and prepared for war with the Catholic emperor.

The Peasants' Revolt

In its first decade the Protestant movement suffered more from internal division than from imperial interference. By 1525 Luther had become as much an object of protest within Germany as was the pope. Original allies, sympathizers, and fellow travelers declared their independence from him.

Like the German Humanists, the German peasantry also had at first believed Luther to be an ally. The peasantry had been organized since the late fifteenth century against efforts by territorial princes to override their traditional laws and customs and to subject them to new regulations and taxes. Peasant leaders, several of whom were convinced Lutherans, saw in Luther's teaching about Christian freedom and his criticism of monastic landowners a point of view close to their own. They openly solicited Luther's support of their political and economic rights, including their revolutionary request for release from serfdom.

The peasant revolt of 1524–1525 frightened both Protestant and Catholic rulers, who united to suppress it. Many peasants died in the revolt, but in its early stages the peasant armies inflicted substantial casualties and committed atrocities of their own. Here Albrecht Dürer (1471–1528) portrays three armed peasants conversing. [Sachsische Landesbibliothek, Abteilung Deutsche Fotothek]

Luther and his followers sympathized with the peasants. Indeed, for several years Lutheran pamphleteers made *Karsthans*, the burly, honest peasant who earned his bread by the sweat of his brow and sacrificed his own comfort and well-being for others, a symbol of the simple life that God desired all people to live. The Lutherans, however, were not social revolutionaries. When the peasants revolted against their masters in 1524–1525, Luther, not surprisingly, condemned them in the strongest possible terms as "un-Christian" and urged the princes to crush their revolt without mercy. Tens of thousands of peasants (estimates run between 70,000 and 100,000) died by the time the revolt was put down.

For Luther, the freedom of the Christian was to be found in an inner release from guilt and anxiety, not in a right to restructure society by violent revolution. Had Luther supported the Peasants' Revolt, he would not only have contradicted his own teaching, but would probably also have ended any chance of the survival of his reform beyond the 1520s. Still, many believe that his decision ended the promise of the Reformation as a social revolution.

The Reformation Elsewhere

Although Luther's was the first, Switzerland and France had their own independent reform movements almost simultaneously with Germany's. From them developed new churches as prominent and lasting as the Lutheran.

Zwingli and the Swiss Reformation

Switzerland was a loose confederacy of thirteen autonomous cantons, or states, and allied areas (see Map 11-2). Some cantons became Protestant, some remained Catholic, and a few other cantons and regions managed to effect a compromise. There were two main preconditions of the Swiss Reformation. First was the growth of national sentiment occasioned by popular opposition to foreign mercenary service (providing mercenaries for Europe's warring nations was a major source of Switzerland's livelihood). Second was a desire for Church reform that had persisted in Switzerland since the councils of Constance (1414–1417) and Basel (1431–1449).

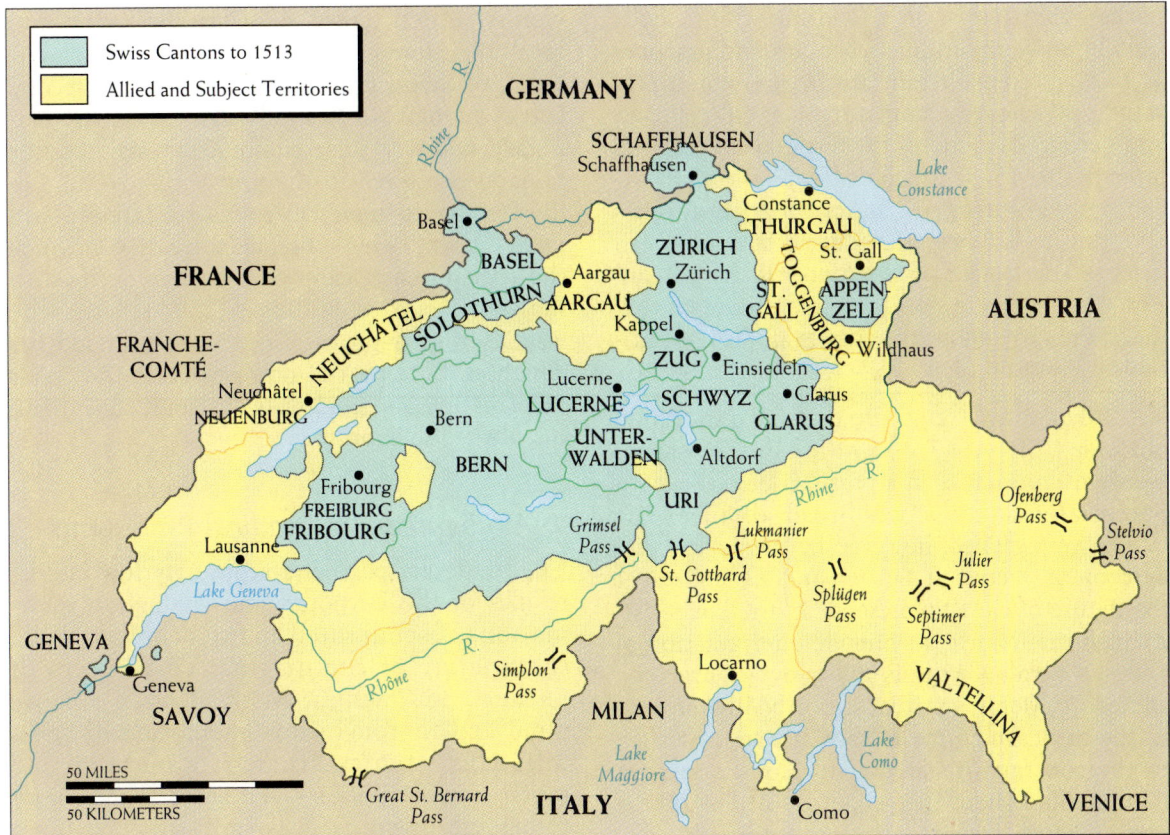

MAP 11-2 THE SWISS CONFEDERATION *While nominally still a part of the Holy Roman Empire, Switzerland grew from a loose defensive union of the central "forest cantons" in the thirteenth century to a fiercely independent association of regions with different languages, histories, and, finally, religions.*

THE REFORMATION IN ZURICH Ulrich Zwingli (1484–1531), the leader of the Swiss Reformation, had been humanistically educated in Bern, Vienna, and Basel. He was strongly influenced by Erasmus, whom he credited with having set him on the path to reform. He served as a chaplain with Swiss mercenaries during the disastrous Battle of Marignano in Italy in 1515 and thereafter became an eloquent critic of mercenary service. Zwingli believed that this service threatened both the political sovereignty and the moral well-being of the Swiss confederacy. By 1518 Zwingli was also widely known for opposition to the sale of indulgences and to religious superstition.

In 1519 he entered the competition for the post of people's priest in the main church of Zurich. His candidacy was contested because of his acknowledged fornication with a barber's daughter, an affair he successfully minimized in a forcefully written self-defense. Actually, his conduct was less scandalous to his contemporaries, who sympathized with the plight of the celibate clergy, than it may be to the modern reader. One of Zwingli's first acts as a reformer was to petition for an end to clerical celibacy and for the right of all clergy to marry, a practice that quickly became accepted in all Protestant lands.

From his new position as people's priest in Zurich, Zwingli engineered the Swiss Reformation. In March 1522 he was party to the breaking of the Lenten fast—an act of protest analogous to burning one's national flag today. Zwingli's reform guideline was very simple and very effective. Whatever lacked literal support in Scripture was to be neither believed nor practiced. As had also happened with

Luther, that test soon raised questions about such honored traditional teachings and practices as fasting, transubstantiation, the worship of saints, pilgrimages, purgatory, clerical celibacy, and certain sacraments. A disputation held on January 29, 1523, concluded with the city government granting its sanction to Zwingli's Scripture test. Thereafter Zurich became to all intents the center of the Swiss Reformation. The new regime imposed a harsh discipline that made the city one of the first examples of puritanical Protestantism.

THE MARBURG COLLOQUY Landgrave Philip of Hesse (1504–1567) sought to unite Swiss and German Protestants in a mutual defense pact, a potentially significant political alliance. His efforts were spoiled, however, by theological disagreements between Luther and Zwingli over the nature of Christ's presence in the Eucharist. Zwingli maintained a symbolic interpretation of Christ's words, "This is my body"; Christ, he argued, was only spiritually, not bodily, present in the bread and wine of the Eucharist. Luther, to the contrary, insisted that Christ's human nature could share the properties of His divine nature; hence, where Christ was spiritually present, He could also be bodily present, for His was a special nature. Luther wanted no part of an abstract, spiritualized Christ. Zwingli, on the other hand, feared that Luther had not broken sufficiently with medieval sacramental theology.

Philip of Hesse brought the two Protestant leaders together in his castle in Marburg in early October 1529, but they were unable to work out their differences on this issue. Luther left thinking Zwingli a dangerous fanatic. Although cooperation between the two sides did not cease, the disagreement splintered the Protestant movement theologically and politically. Separate defense leagues formed, and semi-Zwinglian theological views came to be embodied in the *Tetrapolitan Confession*. This confession of faith was prepared by the Strasbourg reformers Martin Bucer and Caspar Hedio for presentation to the Diet of Augsburg (1530) as an alternative to the Lutheran *Augsburg Confession*.

SWISS CIVIL WARS As the Swiss cantons divided between Protestantism and Catholicism, civil wars began. There were two major battles, both at Kappel, one in June 1529 and a second in October 1531. The first ended in a Protestant victory, which forced the Catholic cantons to break their foreign alliances and to recognize the rights of Swiss Protestants. During the second battle Zwingli was found wounded on the battlefield and was unceremoniously executed, his remains scattered to the four winds so his followers would have no relics to console and inspire them. The subsequent treaty confirmed the right of each canton to determine its own religion. Heinrich Bullinger (1504–1575), who was Zwingli's protégé and later married his daughter, became the new leader of the Swiss Reformation and guided its development into an established religion.

Anabaptists and Radical Protestants

The moderate pace and seemingly low ethical results of the Lutheran and Zwinglian reformations discontented many people, among them some of the original co-workers of Luther and Zwingli. Many desired a more rapid and thorough implementation of apostolic Christianity—that is, a more visible moral transformation—and accused the major reformers of going only halfway. The most important of these radical groups were the Anabaptists, the sixteenth-century ancestors of the modern Mennonites and Amish. The Anabaptists were especially distinguished by their rejection of infant baptism and their insistence on only adult baptism (*Anabaptism* derives from the Greek word meaning "to rebaptize"). They believed that baptism performed on a consenting adult conformed to Scripture and was more respectful of human freedom.

CONRAD GREBEL AND THE SWISS BRETHREN Conrad Grebel (1498–1526), with whom Anabaptism originated, performed the first adult rebaptism in Zurich in January 1525. Initially a co-worker with Zwingli and an even greater biblical literalist, Grebel broke openly with Zwingli. In a religious disputation in October 1523, Zwingli supported the city government's plea for a gradual removal of traditional religious practices.

The alternative of the Swiss Brethren, as Grebel's group came to be called, was embodied in the *Schleitheim Confession* of 1527. This document distinguished Anabaptists not only by

Zwingli Lists the Errors of the Roman Church

Religious argument can become confusing. A clear summary of issues is often helpful—both to the disputants and to interested bystanders. Before the first Zurich Disputation (1523), which effectively introduced the Protestant Reformation in Zurich, the reformer Zwingli prepared such a summary of the new Evangelical truths and the errors of the Roman church, known as the Sixty-Seven Articles. Here are some of them.

◆ *Are these the same errors that Luther condemned? How would the Church have been affected if it had conceded these errors to Zwingli?*

All who consider other teachings equal to or higher than the Gospel err, and they do not know what the Gospel is.

In the faith rests our salvation, and in unbelief our damnation; for all truth is clear in Christ.

In the Gospel one learns that human doctrines and decrees do not aid in salvation.

That Christ, having sacrificed himself once, is to eternity a certain and valid sacrifice for the sins of all faithful, wherefrom it follows that the Mass is not a sacrifice, but is a remembrance of the sacrifice and assurance of the salvation which Christ has given us.

That God desires to give us all things in his name, whence it follows that outside of this life we need no [intercession of the saints or any] mediator except himself.

That no Christian is bound to do those things which God has not decreed, therefore one may eat at all times all food, wherefrom one learns that the decree about cheese and butter [i.e., fasting from such foods at certain times of the year] is a Roman swindle.

That no special person can impose the ban upon [i.e., excommunicate] anyone, but the Church, that is, the congregation of those among whom the one to be banned dwells, together with their watchman, i.e., the pastor.

All that the so-called spiritual [i.e., the papal church] claims to have of power and protection belongs to the lay [i.e., the secular magistracy], if they wish to be Christians.

Greater offense I know not than that one does not allow priests to have wives, but permits them to hire prostitutes.

Christ has borne all our pains and labor. Hence whoever assigns to works of penance what belongs to Christ errs and slanders God.

The true divine Scriptures know naught about purgatory after this life.

The Scriptures know no priests except those who proclaim the word of God.

Ulrich Zwingli: Collected Works, *Samuel M. Jackson, ed. (Philadelphia: University of Pennsylvania Press, 1972), pp. 111–117.*

their practice of adult baptism but also by their refusal to go to war, to swear oaths, and to participate in the offices of secular government. Anabaptists physically separated from society to form a more perfect community in imitation of what they believed to be the example of the first Christians. Because of the close connection between religious and civic life in this period, the political authorities viewed such separatism as a threat to basic social bonds.

THE ANABAPTIST REIGN IN MÜNSTER At first, Anabaptism drew its adherents from all social classes. But as Lutherans and Zwinglians joined with Catholics in opposition to the Anabaptists and persecuted them within the cities, a more rural, agrarian class came to make up the great majority. In 1529, rebaptism became a capital offense throughout the Holy Roman Empire. Estimates are that between 1525 and 1618 at least 1,000 and perhaps as many as 5,000 men and women were executed for rebaptizing themselves as adults. Brutal measures were universally applied against non-conformists after Anabaptist extremists came to power in the German city of Münster in 1534–1535.

Led by two Dutch emigrants, a baker, Jan Matthys of Haarlem, and a tailor, Jan Beukelsz of Leiden, the Anabaptist majority in this city forced Lutherans and Catholics either to convert or to emigrate. The Lutherans and Catholics left and the city was blockaded by besieging armies. Münster transformed itself into an Old Testament theocracy, replete with charismatic leaders and the practice of polygamy. The latter was undertaken as a measure of social control because there were so many more women, recently widowed or deserted, than men in the city. Many women revolted against the practice and were allowed to leave the resented polyga-mous marriages.

The outside world was deeply shocked by such developments in Münster. Protestant and Catholic armies united to crush the radicals. The skeletons of their leaders long hung in pub-lic view as a warning to all who would so offend traditional Christian sensitivities. After this episode, moderate, pacifistic Anabaptism became the norm among most nonconformists. The moderate Anabaptist leader Menno Simons (1496–1561), the founder of the Mennonites, set the example for the future.

SPIRITUALISTS Another radical movement, that of the *Spiritualists*, was made up mostly of isolated individuals distinguished by their dis-dain of all traditions and institutions. They believed that the only religious authority was God's spirit, which spoke here and now to every individual. Among them were several former Lutherans. Thomas Müntzer (d. 1525), who had close contacts with Anabaptist leaders in Germany and Switzerland, died as a leader of a peasants' revolt. Sebastian Franck (d. 1541), a free-lance critic of all dogmatic religion, pro-claimed the religious autonomy of every individ-ual soul. Caspar Schwenckfeld (d. 1561) was a prolific writer and wanderer after whom the Schwenckfeldian church is named.

ANTITRINITARIANS A final group of radical Protestants was the Antitrinitarians, exponents of a commonsense, rational, and ethical reli-gion. Chief among this group were the Spaniard Michael Servetus (1511–1553), executed in 1553 in Geneva for "blasphemies against the Holy Trinity," and the Italians Lelio (d. 1562) and Faustus Sozzini (d. 1604), the founders of Socinianism. These thinkers were the strongest opponents of Calvinism, especially its belief in original sin and predestination, and have a deserved reputation as defenders of religious tol-eration.

John Calvin and the Genevan Reformation

In the second half of the sixteenth century, Calvinism replaced Lutheranism as the domi-nant Protestant force in Europe. Calvinism was the religious ideology that inspired or accompa-nied massive political resistance in France, the Netherlands, and Scotland. It established itself within the Palatinate during the reign of Elector Frederick III (r. 1559–1576). Calvinists believed strongly in both divine predestination and the individual's responsibility to reorder society according to God's plan. They became zealous reformers determined to transform and order society so that men and women would act exter-nally as they believed, or should believe, inter-nally and were presumably destined to live eter-nally.

In a famous study, *The Protestant Ethic and the Spirit of Capitalism* (1904), the German sociologist Max Weber argued that this peculiar combination of religious confidence and self-dis-ciplined activism produced an ethic that stimu-lated and reinforced the spirit of emergent capi-talism. According to this argument, there was thus a close association between Calvinism and other later forms of Puritanism and the develop-ment of modern capitalist societies.

The founder of Calvinism, John Calvin (1509–1564), was born into a well-to-do family, the son of the secretary to the bishop of Noyon in Picardy. He received church benefices at age twelve, which financed the best possible educa-tion at Parisian colleges and a law degree at Orléans. In the 1520s, he associated with the indigenous French reform party. (See page 387.) Although he would finally reject this group as ineffectual, its members contributed to his preparation as a religious reformer.

It was probably in the spring of 1534 that Calvin experienced that conversion to Protestantism by which he said his "long stubborn heart" was "made teachable" by God. His own experience became a personal model of reform that he would later apply to the recalcitrant citizenry of Geneva. His mature theology stressed the sovereignty of God over all creation and the necessity of man's conformity to His will. In May 1534 he dramatically surrendered the benefices he had held for so long and at such profit and joined the Reformation.

POLITICAL REVOLT AND RELIGIOUS REFORM IN GENEVA Whereas in Saxony religious reform paved the way for a political revolution against the emperor, in Geneva a political revolution against the local prince-bishop laid the foundation for the religious change. Genevans successfully revolted against their resident prince-bishop in the late 1520s, and the city council assumed his legal and political powers in 1527.

In late 1533 the Protestant city of Bern dispatched two reformers to Geneva: Guillaume Farel (1489–1565) and Antoine Froment (1508–1581). In the summer of 1535, after much internal turmoil, the Protestants triumphed, and the traditional Mass and other religious practices were removed. On May 21, 1536, the city voted officially to adopt the Reformation: "to live according to the Gospel and the Word of God . . . without . . . any more masses, statues, idols, or other papal abuses."

Calvin arrived in Geneva after these events, in July 1536. He was actually en route to a scholarly refuge in Strasbourg, in flight from the persecution of Protestants in France, when warring between France and Spain forced him to turn sharply south to Geneva. Farel successfully pleaded with him to stay in the city and assist the Reformation, threatening Calvin with divine vengeance if he turned away from this task.

Before a year had passed, Calvin had drawn up articles for the governance of the new church as well as a catechism to guide and discipline the people. Both were presented for approval to the city councils in early 1537. Because of the strong measures they proposed to govern Geneva's moral life, many suspected the reformers were intent upon creating a "new papacy." Opponents attacked Calvin and Farel, fearing

A portrait of the young John Calvin. [Bibliothèque Publique et Universitaire, Geneva]

that they were going too far too fast. Geneva's powerful Protestant ally, Bern, which had adopted a more moderate Protestant reform, pressured Geneva's magistrates to restore traditional religious ceremonies and holidays that Calvin and Farel had abolished. When the reformers opposed these actions, they were exiled from the city.

Calvin went to Strasbourg, a model Protestant city, where he became pastor to the French exiles there and he wrote biblical commentaries and a second edition of his masterful *Institutes of the Christian Religion*, which many consider the definitive theological statement of the Protestant faith. Most important, he learned from the Strasbourg reformer Martin Bucer how to implement his goals successfully.

CALVIN'S GENEVA In 1540 Geneva elected syndics who were both favorable to Calvin and determined to establish full Genevan political and religious independence from Bern. They knew Calvin would be a valuable ally in this project and invited him to return. This he did in September 1540, never to leave the city again. Within months of his return, the city imple-

A caricature of drunkenness by Hans Weidt, The Winebag and His Wheelbarrow *addressed the very serious problem of alcoholism that plagued the sixteenth century. Both Catholic and Protestant clergy railed against it.* [Hacker Art Books]

of the elders and the pastors and was presided over by one of the four syndics. It enforced the strictest moral discipline.

Among the many personal conflicts in Geneva that gave Calvin his reputation as a stern moralist, none proved more damaging than his active role in the capture and execution of the Spanish physician and amateur theologian Michael Servetus in 1553. Servetus had earlier been condemned by the Inquisition. He died at the stake in Protestant Geneva for denying the doctrine of the Trinity, a subject on which he had written a scandalous book.

After 1555, the city's syndics were all devout Calvinists, greatly strengthening Calvin's position and Geneva became home to thousands of exiled Protestants who had been driven out of France, England, and Scotland. Refugees (more than 5,000), most of them utterly loyal to Calvin, eventually made up more than one-third of the population of Geneva.

To the thousands of persecuted Protestants who flocked to Geneva in mid-century, the city was a beacon and a refuge, Europe's only free city. During Calvin's lifetime Geneva also gained the reputation of being a "woman's paradise" because the laws there severely punished men who beat their wives.

mented new ecclesiastical ordinances that provided for cooperation between the magistrates and the clergy in matters of internal discipline.

Following the Strasbourg model, the Genevan church was organized into four offices: (1) pastors, of whom there were five; (2) teachers, or doctors, to instruct the populace in and to defend true doctrine; (3) elders, a group of twelve laymen chosen by and from the Genevan councils and empowered to "oversee the life of everybody"; and (4) deacons to dispense church goods and services to the poor and the sick.

Calvin and his followers were motivated above all by a desire to transform society morally. Faith, Calvin taught, did not sit idly in the mind but conformed one's every action to God's law. The "elect" should live in a manifestly God-pleasing way, if they were truly God's elect. In the attempted realization of this goal, Calvin spared no effort. The consistory became his instrument of power. This body was composed

Political Consolidation of the Lutheran Reformation

By 1530, the Reformation was in Europe to stay. It would, however, take several decades and major attempts to eradicate it, before all would recognize this fact. With the political triumph of Lutheranism in the empire by the 1550s, Protestant movements elsewhere gained a new lease on life.

The Diet of Augsburg

Emperor Charles V, who spent most of his time on politics and military maneuvers outside the empire, especially in Spain and Italy, returned to the empire in 1530 to direct the Diet of Augsburg. This meeting of Protestant and Catholic representatives assembled to impose a settlement of the religious divisions. With its

Rules Governing Genevan Moral Behavior

During Calvin's lifetime, Geneva gained the reputation of being a model evangelical city. Persecuted Protestants in the outside world considered it Europe's freest and most godly city. Strict moral enforcement conformed faith and practice. It also gave the city and the new church the order they needed to survive against their enemies. The following selections are from ordinances governing the village churches around Geneva.

✦ *Are Calvin's rules designed primarily to protect the Reformation? What do these rules suggest that he fears most? Are the penalties heavy or slaps on the wrist? Is it a sign of the failure of his reform that the Genevan people never stopped doing these things?*

Concerning the Time of Assembling at Church

That the temples be closed for the rest of the time [when religious services are not being held] in order that no one shall enter therein out of hours, impelled thereto by superstition; and if any one be found engaged in any special act of devotion therein or near by he shall be admonished for it: if it be found to be of a superstitious nature for which simple correction is inadequate, then he shall be chastised.

Blasphemy

Whoever shall have blasphemed, swearing by the body or by the blood of our Lord, or in similar manner, he shall be made to kiss the earth for the first offence; for the second to pay 5 sous, and for the third 6 sous, and for the last offence be put in the pillory for one hour.

Drunkenness

1. That no one shall invite another to drink under penalty of 3 sous.
2. That taverns shall be closed during the sermon, under penalty that the tavern-keeper shall pay 3 sous, and whoever may be found therein shall pay the same amount.
3. If any one be found intoxicated he shall pay for the first offence 3 sous and shall be remanded to the consistory; for the second offence he shall be held to pay the sum of 6 sous, and for the third 10 sous and be put in prison.
4. That no one shall make *roiaumes* [great feasts] under penalty of 10 sous.

Songs and Dances

If any one sing immoral, dissolute or outrageous songs, or dance the *virollet* or other dance, he shall be put in prison for three days and then sent to the Consistory.

Usury

That no one shall take upon interest or profit more than five per cent upon penalty of confiscation of the principal and of being condemned to make restitution as the case may demand.

Games

That no one shall play at any dissolute game or at any game whatsoever it may be, neither for gold nor silver nor for any excessive stake, upon penalty of 5 sous and forfeiture of stake played for.

Translations and Reprints from the Original Sources of European History, Vol. 3 *(Philadelphia Department of History, University of Pennsylvania, 1909), pp. 10–11.*

terms dictated by the Catholic emperor, the diet adjourned with a blunt order to all Lutherans to revert to Catholicism.

The Reformation was by this time too firmly established for that to occur. In February 1531 the Lutherans responded with the formation of their own defensive alliance, the Schmalkaldic League. The league took as its banner the *Augsburg Confession,* a moderate statement of Protestant beliefs that had been spurned by the emperor at the Diet of Augsburg. In 1538 Luther drew up a more strongly worded Protestant confession known as the *Schmalkaldic Articles.* Under the leadership of Landgrave Philip of Hesse and Elector John Frederick of Saxony, the league achieved a stalemate with the emperor, who was again distracted by renewed war with France and the ever-resilient Turks.

The Expansion of the Reformation

In the 1530s German Lutherans formed regional consistories, judicial bodies composed of theologians and lawyers, which oversaw and administered the new Protestant churches. These consistories replaced the old Catholic episcopates. Philip Melanchthon, the "praeceptor of Germany," oversaw the enactment of educational reforms that provided for compulsory primary education, schools for girls, a Humanist revision of the traditional curriculum, and catechetical instruction of the laity in the new religion.

The Reformation also entrenched itself elsewhere. Introduced into Denmark by Christian II (r. 1513–1523), Lutheranism thrived there under Frederick I (r. 1523–1533), who joined the Schmalkaldic League. Under Christian III (r. 1536–1559), Lutheranism became the official state religion.

In Sweden, Gustavus Vasa (r. 1523–1560), supported by a Swedish nobility greedy for Church lands, embraced Lutheranism, confiscated Church property, and subjected the clergy to royal authority at the Diet of Vesteras (1527).

In politically splintered Poland, Lutherans, Anabaptists, Calvinists, and even Antitrinitarians found room to practice their beliefs. Poland, primarily because of the absence of a central political authority, became a model of religious pluralism and toleration in the second half of the sixteenth century.

Reaction Against Protestants: The Interim

Charles V made abortive efforts in 1540–1541 to enforce a compromise agreement between Protestants and Catholics. As these and other conciliar efforts failed, he turned to a military solution. In 1547 imperial armies crushed the Protestant Schmalkaldic League, defeating John Frederick of Saxony in April and taking Philip of Hesse captive shortly thereafter.

The emperor established puppet rulers in Saxony and Hesse and issued as imperial law the *Augsburg Interim,* a new order that Protestants everywhere must readopt old Catholic beliefs and practices. Protestants were granted a few cosmetic concessions, for example, clerical marriage (with papal approval of individual cases) and communion in both kinds (that is, bread *and* wine). Although the *Interim* met only surface acceptance within Germany, it forced many Protestant leaders into exile. The Strasbourg reformer Martin Bucer, for example, departed to England, where he would play an important role in drafting the religious documents of the English Reformation during the reign of Edward VI. In Germany, the city of Magdeburg became a refuge for persecuted Protestants and the center of Lutheran resistance.

The Peace of Augsburg

The Reformation was too entrenched by 1547 to be ended even by brute force. Maurice of Saxony, hand-picked by Charles V to rule Saxony, recognized the inevitable and shifted his allegiance to the Protestants. Confronted by fierce resistance and weary from three decades of war, the emperor was forced to relent. After suffering a defeat by Protestant armies in 1552, Charles reinstated the Protestant leaders and guaranteed Lutheran religious freedoms in the Peace of Passau (August 1552). With this declaration he effectively surrendered his lifelong quest for European religious unity.

The Peace of Augsburg in September 1555 made the division of Christendom permanent. This agreement recognized in law what had already been well established in practice: *cuius regio, eius religio,* meaning that the ruler of a land would determine the religion of the land. Lutherans were permitted to retain all Church lands forcibly seized before 1552. An "ecclesiastical reservation" was added, however, that was intended to prevent high Catholic prelates who converted to Protestantism from taking their lands, titles, and privileges with them. Those discontented with the religion of their region were permitted to migrate to another.

The Peace of Augsburg did not extend official recognition to Calvinism and Anabaptism as legal forms of Christian belief and practice. Anabaptists had long adjusted to such exclusion by forming their own separatist communities. Calvinists, however, were not separatists and could not choose that route. They remained determined not only to secure the right to worship publicly as they pleased but also to shape society according to their own religious convictions. While Anabaptists retreated and Lutherans enjoyed the security of an established religion, Calvinists organized to lead national revolutions throughout northern Europe in the second half of the sixteenth century.

The English Reformation to 1533

Late medieval England had a well-earned reputation for maintaining the rights of the crown against the pope. Edward I (r. 1272–1307) had rejected efforts by Pope Boniface VIII to prevent secular taxation of the clergy. Parliament passed the first Statutes of Provisors and *Praemunire* in the mid-fourteenth century curtailing payments and judicial appeals to Rome as well as papal appointments in England. Lollardy, Humanism, and widespread anticlerical sentiment prepared the way religiously and intellectually for Protestant ideas, which entered England in the early sixteenth century.

The Preconditions of Reform

In the early 1520s future English reformers met at the White Horse Inn in Cambridge to discuss Lutheran writings smuggled into England by merchants and scholars. One of these future reformers was William Tyndale (ca. 1492–1536), who translated the New Testament into English in 1524–1525, while in Germany. Printed in Cologne and Worms, Tyndale's New Testament began to circulate in England in 1526.

Progress of Protestant Reformation on the Continent	
1513–1517	Fifth Lateran Council fails to bring about reform in the Church
1517	Luther posts ninety-five theses against indulgences
1519	Charles I of Spain elected Holy Roman Emperor (as Charles V)
1519	Luther challenges authority of pope and inerrancy of Church councils at Leipzig Debate
1521	Papal bull excommunicates Luther for heresy
1521	Diet of Worms condemns Luther
1521–1522	Luther translates the New Testament into German
1524–1525	Peasants' Revolt in Germany
1527	The *Schleitheim Confession* of the Anabaptists
1529	Marburg Colloquy between Luther and Zwingli
1530	Diet of Augsburg fails to settle religious differences
1531	Formation of Protestant Schmalkaldic League
1534–1535	Anabaptists assume political power in city of Münster
1536	Calvin arrives in Geneva
1540	Jesuits, founded by Ignatius of Loyola, recognized as order by pope
1546	Luther dies
1547	Armies of Charles V crush Schmalkaldic League
1548	Augsburg *Interim* outlaws Protestant practices
1555	Peace of Augsburg recognizes rights of Lutherans to worship as they please
1545–1563	Council of Trent institutes reforms and responds to the Reformation

Cardinal Thomas Wolsey (ca. 1475–1530), the chief minister of King Henry VIII (r. 1509–1547), and Sir Thomas More (1478–1535), Wolsey's successor, guided royal opposition to incipient English Protestantism. The king himself defended the seven sacraments against Luther, receiving as a reward the title "Defender of the Faith" from Pope Leo X. Following Luther's intemperate reply to Henry's amateur theological attack, More wrote a lengthy *Response to Luther* in 1523.

The King's Affair

While Lollardy and Humanism may be said to have provided the native seeds for religious reform, it was Henry's unhappy marriage that broke the soil and allowed the seeds to take root. Henry had married Catherine of Aragon (d. 1536), daughter of Ferdinand and Isabella of Spain, and the aunt of Emperor Charles V. By 1527 the union had produced no male heir to the throne and only one surviving child, a daughter, Mary. Henry was justifiably concerned about the political consequences of leaving only a female heir. In this period, people believed it unnatural for women to rule over men. At best, a woman ruler meant a contested reign; at worst, turmoil and revolution.

Henry even came to believe that his union with Catherine, who had many miscarriages and stillbirths, had been cursed by God, because Catherine had first been the wife of his brother, Arthur. Henry's father, King Henry VII, had betrothed Catherine to Henry after Arthur's untimely death to keep the English alliance with Spain intact. They were officially married in 1509, a few days before Henry VIII received his crown. Because marriage to the wife of one's brother was prohibited by both canon and biblical law (see Leviticus 18:16, 20:21), the marriage had required a special dispensation from Pope Julius II.

By 1527 Henry was thoroughly enamored of Anne Boleyn, one of Catherine's ladies in waiting. He determined to put Catherine aside and take Anne as his wife. This he could not do in Catholic England, however, without papal annulment of the marriage to Catherine. And therein lay a special problem. The year 1527 was also the year when soldiers of the Holy Roman Empire mutinied and sacked Rome. The reigning pope, Clement VII, was at the time a prisoner of Charles V, who happened also to be Catherine's nephew. Even if this had not been the case, it would have been virtually impossible for the pope to grant an annulment of a marriage that not only had survived for eighteen years but had been made possible in the first place by a special papal dispensation.

Cardinal Wolsey, who aspired to become pope, was placed in charge of securing the royal annulment. Lord Chancellor since 1515 and papal legate-at-large since 1518, Wolsey had long been Henry's "heavy" and the object of much popular resentment. When he failed to secure the annulment, through no fault of his own, he was dismissed in disgrace in 1529. Thomas Cranmer (1489–1556) and Thomas Cromwell (1485–1540), both of whom harbored Lutheran sympathies, thereafter became the king's closest advisers. Finding the way to a papal annulment closed, Henry's new advisers struck a different course. Why not simply declare the king supreme in English spiritual affairs as he was in English temporal affairs? Then the king could settle the king's affair himself .

The Reformation Parliament

In 1529 Parliament convened for what would be a seven-year session that earned it the title the "Reformation Parliament." During this period, it passed a flood of legislation that harassed and finally placed royal reins on the clergy. In doing so, it established a precedent that would remain a feature of English government: whenever fundamental changes are made in religion, the monarch must consult with and work through Parliament. In January 1531 the clergy in Convocation (a legislative assembly representing the English clergy) publicly recognized Henry as head of the Church in England "as far as the law of Christ allows." In 1532 Parliament published official grievances against the Church ranging from alleged indifference to the needs of the laity to an excessive number of religious holidays. In the same year Parliament passed the Submission of the Clergy, effectively placing canon law under royal control and thereby the clergy under royal jurisdiction.

In January 1533 Henry wed the pregnant Anne Boleyn, with Thomas Cranmer officiating. In February 1533 Parliament made the king the highest court of appeal for all English subjects. In March 1533 Cranmer became archbishop of Canterbury and led the Convocation in invalidating the king's marriage to Catherine. In 1534 Parliament ended all payments by the English clergy and laity to Rome and gave Henry sole jurisdiction over high ecclesiastical appointments. The Act of Succession in the same year made Anne Boleyn's children legitimate heirs to the throne, and the Act of Supremacy declared Henry "the only supreme head in earth of the Church of England."

When Thomas More and John Fisher, bishop of Rochester, refused to recognize the Act of Succession and the Act of Supremacy, Henry had them executed, making clear his determina-

tion to have his way regardless of the cost. In 1536 and 1538 Parliament dissolved England's monasteries and nunneries.

Wives of Henry VIII

Henry's domestic life proved to lack the consistency of his political life. In 1536 Anne Boleyn was executed for alleged treason and adultery, and her daughter, Elizabeth, was declared illegit-

---

The Execution of Fisher and More

In 1535 Bishop John Fisher, a long-time pamphleteer for Queen Catherine's cause, and Sir Thomas More, famed humanist and former lord chancellor, were beheaded for refusing to recognize the king's supremacy. They were the most distinguished of Henry VIII's adversaries and victims. As reported by Hall's Chronicle, More managed to find humor in the proceedings.

◆ *How could More die so boldly? What does the author mean by asking whether he was a foolish wise man or a wise foolish man? Is the description propaganda? What impact did More's execution have on Henry's reign?*

The twenty-second day of the same month John Fisher, bishop of Rochester, was beheaded, and his head set upon London Bridge. This bishop was of very many men lamented; for he was reported to be a man of great learning, and a man of very good life, but therein wonderfully deceived, for he maintained the pope to be supreme head of the Church, and very maliciously refused the king's title of supreme head. . . .

Also the sixth day of July was Sir Thomas More beheaded for the like treason before rehearsed, which, as you have heard, was for the denying of the king's Majesty's supremacy. This man was also counted learned, and, as you have heard before, he was lord chancellor of England, and in that time a great persecutor of such as detested the supremacy of the bishop of Rome, which he himself so highly favored that he stood to it until he was brought to the scaffold on the Tower Hill, where on a block his head was stricken from his shoulders and had no more harm.

I cannot tell whether I should call him a

foolish wise man or a wise foolish man, for undoubtedly he, beside his learning, had a great wit, but it was so mingled with taunting and mocking, that it seemed to them that best knew him that he thought nothing to be well spoken except he had ministered some mock in the communication, insomuch as at his coming to the Tower one of the officers demanded his upper garment for his fee, meaning his gown, and he answered he should have it and took him his cap, saying that it was the uppermost garment that he had. . . .

Also the hangman kneeled down to him asking him forgiveness of his death (as the manner is), to whom he said, "I forgive thee, but I promise thee that thou shalt never have honesty of the striking of my head, my neck is so short." Also even when he should lay down his head on the block he, having a great gray beard, struck out his beard, and said to the hangman, "I pray you let me lay my beard over the block lest ye should cut it." Thus with a mock he ended his life.

James Harvey Robinson, ed., Readings in European History, Vol. 2 (Boston, Athenaeum: 1906), pp. 142–143.

---

imate. Henry had four further marriages. His third wife, Jane Seymour, died in 1537 shortly after giving birth to the future Edward VI. Henry wed Anne of Cleves sight unseen on the advice of Cromwell, the purpose being to create by the marriage an alliance with the Protestant princes. Neither the alliance nor Anne—whom Henry thought to have a remarkable resemblance to a horse—proved worth the trouble; the marriage was annulled by Parliament, and Cromwell was dismissed and eventually executed. Catherine Howard, Henry's fifth wife, was beheaded for adultery in 1542. His last wife, Catherine Parr, a patron of Humanists and reformers, for whom Henry was the third husband, survived him to marry still a fourth time—obviously she was a match for the English king.

The King's Religious Conservatism

Henry's boldness in politics and his domestic affairs did not extend to religion. True, because of his actions the pope had ceased to be head of the English Church and English Bibles were placed in English churches, but despite the break with Rome, Henry remained decidedly conservative in his religious beliefs. With the Ten Articles of 1536, he made only mild concessions to Protestant tenets, otherwise maintaining Catholic doctrine in a country filled with Protestant sentiment. Despite his many wives and amorous adventures, Henry absolutely forbade the English clergy to marry and threatened any clergy who were twice caught in concubinage with execution.

An allegorical depiction of the Tudor succession by the painter Lucas de Heere (1534–1584). On Henry VIII's right stands his Catholic daughter Mary (1533–1558) and her husband Philip II of Spain. They are accompanied by Mars, the god of war. Henry's son, Edward VI (1547–1553), kneels at the king's left. Elizabeth I (1558–1603) is shown standing in the foreground attended by Peace and Plenty, allegorical figures of what her reign brought to England. [Sudeley Castle]

Angered by the growing popularity of Protestant views, even among his chief advisers, Henry struck directly at them in the Six Articles of 1539. These reaffirmed transubstantiation, denied the Eucharistic cup to the laity, declared celibate vows inviolable, provided for private masses, and ordered the continuation of auricular confession. (Protestants referred to the articles as the "whip with six stings.") Although William Tyndale's English New Testament grew into the Coverdale Bible (1535) and the Great Bible (1539), and the latter was mandated for every English parish, England had to await Henry's death before it could become a genuinely Protestant country.

The Protestant Reformation Under Edward VI

When Henry died, his son and successor, Edward VI (r. 1547–1553), was only ten years old. Edward reigned under the successive regencies of Edward Seymour, who became the duke of Somerset (1547–1550), and the earl of Warwick, who became known as the duke of Northumberland (1550–1553). During this time England fully enacted the Protestant Reformation. The new king and Somerset corresponded directly with John Calvin. During Somerset's regency, Henry's Six Articles and laws against heresy were repealed, and clerical marriage and communion with cup were sanctioned.

In 1547 the chantries, places where endowed masses had traditionally been said for the dead, were dissolved. In 1549 the Act of Uniformity imposed Thomas Cranmer's *Book of Common Prayer* on all English churches. Images and altars were removed from the churches in 1550. After Charles V's victory over the German princes in 1547, German Protestant leaders had fled to England for refuge. Several of these refugees now directly assisted the completion of the English Reformation, Martin Bucer prominent among them.

The Second Act of Uniformity, passed in 1552, imposed a revised edition of the *Book of Common Prayer* on all English churches. A forty-two-article confession of faith, also written by Thomas Cranmer, was adopted, setting forth a moderate Protestant doctrine. It taught justifi-

cation by faith and the supremacy of Holy Scripture, denied transubstantiation (although not real presence), and recognized only two sacraments.

All these changes were short-lived, however. In 1553 Catherine of Aragon's daughter succeeded Edward (who had died in his teens) to the English throne as Mary I (r. 1553–1558) and proceeded to restore Catholic doctrine and practice with a singlemindedness that rivaled that of her father. It was not until the reign of Anne Boleyn's daughter, Elizabeth I (r. 1558–1603), that a lasting religious settlement was worked out in England.

Catholic Reform and Counter-Reformation

The Protestant Reformation did not take the medieval Church completely by surprise. There were many internal criticisms and efforts at reform before there was a Counter-Reformation in reaction to Protestant successes.

Sources of Catholic Reform

Before the Reformation began, ambitious proposals had been made for Church reform. But sixteenth-century popes, ever mindful of how the councils of Constance and Basel had stripped the pope of his traditional powers, quickly squelched such efforts to bring about basic changes in the laws and institutions of the Church. They preferred the charge given to the Fifth Lateran Council (1513–1517) in the keynote address by the superior general of the Hermits of Saint Augustine: "Men are to be changed by, not to change, religion."

Despite such papal foot-dragging, the Church was not without its reformers. Many new religious orders also sprang up in the sixteenth century to lead a broad revival of piety within the Church. The first of these was the Theatines, founded in 1524 to groom devout and reform-minded leaders at the higher levels of the Church hierarchy. One of the co-founders was Bishop Gian Pietro Carafa, the future Pope Paul IV. Another new order, whose mission pointed in the opposite direction, was the Capuchins.

ments the Spanish mystics Saint Teresa of Avila (1515–1582) and Saint John of the Cross (1542–1591) revived and popularized the mystical piety of medieval monasticism.

Ignatius of Loyola and the Jesuits

Of the various reform groups, none was more instrumental in the success of the Counter-Reformation than the Society of Jesus, the new order of Jesuits. Organized by Ignatius of Loyola in the 1530s, it was officially recognized by the Church in 1540. The society grew within the space of a century from its original 10 members to more than 15,000 members scattered throughout the world, with thriving missions in India, Japan, and the Americas.

The Ecstasy of St. Teresa of Avila, by Gianlorenzo Bernini (1598–1680). Mystics like Saint Teresa and Saint John of the Cross helped revive the traditional piety of medieval monasticism. [Scala/Art Resource, N.Y.]

Recognized by the pope in 1528, they sought to return to the original ascetic and charitable ideals of Saint Francis and became very popular among the ordinary people to whom they directed their ministry. The Somaschi, who became active in the mid-1520s, and the Barnabites, founded in 1530, directed their efforts at repairing the moral, spiritual, and physical damage done to people in war-torn areas of Italy.

For women, there was the new order of Ursulines, founded in 1535. It established convents in Italy and France for the religious education of girls from all social classes and became very influential. Another new religious order, the Oratorians, officially recognized in 1575, was an elite group of secular clerics who devoted themselves to the promotion of religious literature and Church music. Among their members was the great Catholic hymnist and musician Giovanni Palestrina (1526–1594).

In addition to these lay and clerical move-

The founder of the Jesuits, Ignatius of Loyola (1491–1556), was a heroic figure. A dashing courtier and caballero in his youth, he began his spiritual pilgrimage in 1521 after he had been seriously wounded in the legs during a battle with the French. During a lengthy and painful convalescence, he passed the time by reading Christian classics. So impressed was he with the heroic self-sacrifice of the Church's saints and their methods of overcoming mental anguish and pain that he underwent a profound religious conversion. Henceforth, he, too, would serve the Church as a soldier of Christ.

After recuperating, Ignatius applied the lessons he had learned during his convalescence to a program of religious and moral self-discipline that came to be embodied in the *Spiritual Exercises*. This psychologically perceptive devotional guide contained mental and emotional exercises designed to teach one absolute spiritual self-mastery over one's feelings. It taught that a person could shape his or her own behavior, even create a new religious self, through disciplined study and regular practice.

Whereas in Jesuit eyes Protestants had distinguished themselves by disobedience to Church authority and religious innovation, the exercises of Ignatius were intended to teach good Catholics to deny themselves and submit without question to higher Church authority and spiritual direction. Perfect discipline and self-control were the essential conditions of such obedience. To these were added the enthusiasm of traditional spirituality and mysticism and uncompromising loyalty to the Church's cause above all else. This was a potent combination that helped counter the Reformation and win many Protestants back to the Catholic fold, especially in Austria and Bavaria and along the Rhine.

The Council of Trent (1545–1563)

The broad success of the Reformation and the insistence of the Emperor Charles V forced Pope Paul to call a general council of the Church to reassert Church doctrine. In anticipation, the pope appointed a reform commission, chaired by Caspar Contarini (1483–1542), a leading liberal theologian. His report, presented to the pope in February 1537, bluntly criticized the fiscality and simony of the papal Curia as the pri-

mary source of the Church's loss of esteem. The report was so critical that Pope Paul attempted unsuccessfully to suppress its publication and Protestants reprinted and circulated it as justification of their criticism.

The long-delayed council of the Church met in 1545 in the imperial city of Trent in northern Italy. There were three sessions, spread over eighteen years, with long interruptions due to war, plague, and imperial and papal politics. The council met from 1545 to 1547, from 1551 to 1552, and from 1562 to 1563, a period that spanned the careers of four different popes.

Unlike the general councils of the fifteenth century, Trent was strictly under the pope's control, with high Italian prelates very prominent in the proceedings. Initially four of the five attending archbishops and twenty-one of the twenty-three attending bishops were Italians. Even at its final session in 1562, more than three-quarters of the council fathers were Italians. Voting was limited to high churchmen; university theologians, the lower clergy, and the laity were not permitted to share in the council's decisions.

The council's most important reforms concerned internal Church discipline. Steps were taken to curtail the selling of Church offices and other religious goods. Many bishops who resided in Rome rather than within their dioceses were forced to move to their appointed seats of authority. Trent strengthened the authority of local bishops so they could effectively discipline popular religious practice. The bishops were also subjected to new rules that required them not only to reside in their dioceses, but also to be highly visible by preaching regularly and conducting annual visitations. Trent also sought to give the parish priest a brighter image by requiring him to be neatly dressed, better educated, strictly celibate, and active among his parishioners. To this end, Trent also called for the construction of a seminary in every diocese.

Not a single doctrinal concession was made to the Protestants, however. In the face of Protestant criticism the Council of Trent gave a ringing reaffirmation to the traditional Scholastic education of the clergy; the role of good works in salvation; the authority of tradition; the seven sacraments; transubstantiation; the withholding of the Eucharistic cup from the laity; clerical celibacy; the reality of purgatory;

MAP 11-3 THE RELIGIOUS SITUATION ABOUT 1560 *By 1560 Luther, Zwingli, and Loyola were dead, Calvin near the end of his life, the English break from Rome fully accomplished, and the last session of the Council of Trent about to assemble. Here is the religious geography of western Europe then.*

the veneration of saints, relics, and sacred images; and the granting of letters of indulgence. The council resolved medieval Scholastic quarrels in favor of the theology of Saint Thomas Aquinas, further enhancing his authority within the Church. Thereafter, the Church offered its strongest resistance to groups like the Jansenists, who strongly endorsed the medieval Augustinian tradition, a source of alternative Catholic as well as many Protestant doctrines.

Rulers initially resisted Trent's reform decrees, fearing a revival of papal political power within their lands. But with the passage of time and the pope's assurances that religious reforms were his sole intent, the new legislation took hold and parish life revived under the guidance of a devout and better-trained clergy.

The Church in Spanish America

Roman Catholic priests had accompanied the earliest explorers and the conquerors of the Indians. Because of internal reforms within the Spanish church at the turn of the sixteenth century, these first clergy tended to be imbued with many of the social and religious ideals of Christian Humanism. They believed that they could foster Erasmus's concept of the "philosophy of Christ" in the New World. Consequently these missionary priests were filled with zeal not only to convert the inhabitants to Christianity but also to bring to them learning and civilization of a European kind.

A very real tension existed between the early Spanish conquerors and the mendicant friars who sought to minister to the Indians. Without conquest, the Church could not convert the Indians, but the priests often deplored the harsh labor conditions imposed on them. During the first three-quarters of a century of Spanish domination, priests were among the most eloquent and persuasive defenders of the rights of native peoples in the New World.

Bartolomé de Las Casas, a Dominican, contended that conquest was not necessary for conversion. One result of his campaign was new royal regulation of conquest after 1550. Another result was the "Black Legend," which portrayed all Spanish treatment of Indians as unprincipled and inhumane. Those who held this point of view drew heavily on Las Casas's writings. Although largely true, the "Black Legend" nonetheless exaggerated the case against Spain and has been exploited by Spanish critics. Many of the Indian rulers had also been exceedingly cruel, as witnessed by the Aztec demands for

The Council of Trent Orders Reform of Bishops

Recognizing that effective reform requires strong local leadership, the Council of Trent gave bishops new power and responsibility. In return, it expected a higher level of discipline from them.

✦ *Why had the Church not given bishops such power and responsibility sooner? Might the Reformation have been avoided if it had?*

It is to be desired that those who undertake the office of bishop shall understand what their portion is, and comprehend that they are called, not to their own convenience, not to riches or luxury, but to labors and cares, for the glory of God. For it is not to be doubted that the rest of the faithful also will be more easily excited to religion and innocence if they shall see those who are set over them not fixing their thoughts on the things of this world, but on the salvation of souls and on their heavenly country. Wherefore this holy Council, being minded that these things are of the greatest importance towards restoring ecclesiastical discipline, admonishes all bishops that, often meditating thereon, they show themselves conformable to their office by their actual deeds and the actions of their lives, which is a kind of perpetual sermon; but, above all, that they so order their whole conversation that others may be able to derive examples of frugality, modesty, continency, and that holy humility which so much commends us to God.

Wherefore . . . this Council not only orders that bishops be content with modest furniture and a frugal table and diet, but that they also give heed that in the rest of their manner of living and in their whole house, there be nothing seen which is alien to this holy institution, and which does not manifest simplicity, zeal toward God, and a contempt of vanities.

James Harvey Robinson, ed., Readings in European History, Vol. 2 *(Boston: Athenaeum, 1906).*

Bartolomé de Las Casas (1474–1566) was the most outspoken and effective defender of the Indians of the New World against Spanish exploitation. [Bildarchiv Preussischer Kulturbesitz]

human sacrifice, and both the Aztecs and the Incas enslaved other peoples. Had the Aztecs discovered Spain and held the upper hand there, the persecution of native Europeans would likely have been as great as that of native Americans at the hands of the Spanish.

By the end of the sixteenth century, the Church in Spanish America had become largely an institution upholding the colonial status quo. On many occasions, individual priests did defend the communal rights of Indian tribes, but the colonial Church also prospered as the Spanish elite prospered. The Church became a great landowner through crown grants and through bequests from Catholics who died in the New World. The monasteries took on an economic as well as a spiritual life of their own. Whatever its concern for the spiritual welfare of the Indians, the Church remained one of the indications that Spanish America was a conquered world. And those who spoke for the Church did not challenge Spanish domination or any but the most extreme modes of Spanish economic exploitation. By the end of the colonial era in the late eighteenth century, the Roman Catholic church had become one of the most conservative forces in Latin America.

The Social Significance of the Reformation in Western Europe

It was a common trait of the Lutheran, Zwinglian, and Calvinist reformers to work within the framework of reigning political power. Luther, Zwingli, and Calvin saw themselves and their followers as subject to definite civic responsibilities and obligations. Their conservatism in this regard has led scholars to characterize them as "magisterial reformers," meaning not only that they were the leaders of the major Protestant movements but also that they succeeded by the force of the magistrate's sword. Some have argued that this willingness to resort to coercion led the reformers to compromise their principles. They themselves, however, never contemplated reform outside or against the societies of which they were members. They wanted it to take shape within the laws and institutions of the sixteenth century. To that end, they remained highly sensitive to what was politically and socially possible in their age. Some scholars believe that the reformers were too conscious of the historically possible, that their reforms went forward with such caution that they changed late medieval society very little and actually encouraged acceptance of the sociopolitical status quo.

The Revolution in Religious Practices and Institutions

The Reformation may have been politically conservative, but by the end of the sixteenth century it had brought about radical changes in traditional religious practices and institutions in those lands where it succeeded.

RELIGION IN FIFTEENTH-CENTURY LIFE In the fifteenth century, on the streets of the great cities of central Europe that later turned Protestant (for example, Zurich, Strasbourg, Nuremberg, or Geneva), the clergy and the religious were everywhere. They made up 6 to 8 percent of the total urban population, and they exercised considerable political as well as spiritual power. They legislated and taxed; they tried cases in special Church courts; and they enforced their laws with threats of excommunication.

A Defense of American Natives

Bartolomé de Las Casas (1474–1566), a Dominican missionary to the New World, describes the native people of the islands of the Caribbean and their systematic slaughter by the Spanish.

◆ *Is Las Casas romanticizing the American natives? Does he truly respect their native culture and beliefs?*

This infinite multitude of people was so created by God that they were without fraud . . . subtilty or malice. . . . Toward the Spaniards whom they serve, patient, meek, and peaceful, [they] lay aside all contentious and tumultuous thoughts, and live without any hatred or desire of revenge. The people are most delicate and tender, enjoying such a feeble constitution of body as does not permit them to endure labour. . . . The[ir] nation [the West Indies] is very poor and indigent, possessing little, and by reason that they gape not after temporal goods, [being] neither proud nor ambitious. Their diet is such that the most holy hermit cannot feed more sparingly in the wildernesse. They go naked . . . and a poor shag mantle . . . is their greatest and their warmest covering. They lie upon mats; only those who have larger fortunes lie upon a kind of net which is tied at the four corners and so fasten'd to the roof, which the Indians in their natural language call Hamecks [hammocks]. They are of a very apprehensive and docile wit, and capable of all good learning, and very apt to receive our Religion, which when they have but once tasted [it], they are carried [off] with a very ardent and zealous desire to make further progress in it; so that I have heard divers Spaniards confess that they had nothing else to hinder them from enjoying heaven, but the ignorance of the true God.

To these quiet Lambs, endued with such blessed qualities, came the Spaniards like most cruel Tygres, Wolves, and Lions . . . for these forty years, minding nothing else but the slaughter of these unfortunate wretches . . . [whom] they have so cruelly and inhumanely butchered, [so] that of three millions of people which Hispaniola [modern Haiti and Dominican Republic] itself did contain, there are left remaining alive scarce three hundred persons. And the island of Cuba . . . lies wholly desert, untilled and ruined. The islands of St. John and Jamaica lie waste and desolate. The Lycayan islands neighboring to the north upon Cuba and Hispaniola . . . are now totally unpeople and destroyed; the inhabitants thereof amounting to above 500,000 souls, partly killed, and partly forced away to work in other places. . . . Other islands there were near the island of St. John more than thirty in number, which were totally made desert. All which islands . . . lie now altogether solitary without any people or inhabitant.

Bartolomé de Las Casas, The Tears of the Indians, *trans. by John Phillips (1656), from reprint of original edition (Academic Reprints, Stanford, Calif., n.d.), pp. 2–4.*

The Church calendar regulated daily life. About one-third of the year was given over to some kind of religious observance or celebration. There were frequent periods of fasting. On almost a hundred days out of the year a pious Christian could not, without special dispensation, eat eggs, butter, fat, or meat.

Monasteries and especially nunneries were prominent and influential institutions. The children of society's most powerful citizens resided there. Local aristocrats were closely identified with particular churches and chapels, whose walls recorded their lineage and proclaimed their generosity. On the streets, friars from near and far begged alms from passersby. In the churches the Mass and liturgy were read entirely in Latin. Images of saints were regularly displayed, and on certain holidays their relics were paraded about and venerated.

There was a booming business at local religious shrines. Pilgrims gathered there by the hundreds, even thousands, many sick and dying, all in search of a cure or a miracle, but also for diversion and entertainment. Several times during the year special preachers arrived in the city to sell letters of indulgence.

Many clergy walked the streets with concubines and children, although they were sworn to celibacy and forbidden marriage. The Church tolerated such relationships upon payment of penitential fines.

People everywhere could be heard complaining about the clergy's exemption from taxation and, in many instances, also from the civil criminal code. People also grumbled about having to support Church offices whose occupants actually lived and worked elsewhere. Townspeople also expressed concern that the Church had too much influence over education and culture.

RELIGION IN SIXTEENTH-CENTURY LIFE In these same cities after the Reformation had firmly established itself, few changes in politics and society were evident. The same aristocratic families governed as before, and the rich generally got richer and the poor poorer. But overall numbers of clergy fell by two-thirds and religious holidays shrunk by one-third. Monasteries and nunneries were nearly absent. Many were transformed into hospices for the sick and poor or into educational institutions, their endowments also turned over to these new purposes. A few cloisters remained for very devout old monks and nuns, who could not be pensioned off or who lacked families and friends to care for them. But these remaining cloisters died out with their inhabitants.

In the churches, which had also been reduced in number by at least one-third, worship was conducted almost completely in the vernacular. In some, particularly those in Zwinglian cities, the walls were stripped bare and whitewashed to make sure the congregation meditated only on God's word. The laity observed no obligatory fasts. Indulgence preachers no longer appeared. Local shrines were closed down, and anyone found openly venerating saints, relics, and images was subject to fine and punishment.

Copies of Luther's translation of the New Testament or, more often excerpts from it, could be found in private homes, and meditation on them was encouraged by the new clergy. The clergy could marry, and most did. They paid taxes and were punished for their crimes in civil courts. Domestic moral life was regulated by committees composed of roughly equal numbers of laity and clergy, over whose decisions secular magistrates had the last word.

Not all Protestant clergy remained enthusiastic about this new lay authority in religion. And the laity themselves were also ambivalent about certain aspects of the Reformation. Over half of the original converts returned to the Catholic fold before the end of the sixteenth century. Whereas one-half of Europe could be counted in the Protestant camp in the mid-sixteenth century, only one-fifth would be there by the mid-seventeenth century.[2]

The Reformation and Education

Another important cultural achievement of the Reformation was its implementation of many of the educational reforms of Humanism in the new Protestant schools and universities. Many Protestant reformers in Germany, France, and England were Humanists. Even when their views on Church doctrine and humankind separated them from the Humanist movement, the Protestant reformers continued to share with the Humanists a common opposition to Scholasticism and a belief in the unity of wisdom, eloquence, and action. The Humanist program of studies, which provided the language skills to deal authoritatively with original sources, proved to be a more appropriate tool for the elaboration of Protestant doctrine than did Scholastic dialectic, which remained ascendant in the Counter-Reformation.

The Catholic counterreformers recognized the close connections between Humanism and the Reformation. Ignatius of Loyola observed the way in which the new learning had been embraced by and served the Protestant cause. In

[2]*Geoffrey Parker,* Europe in Crisis, 1598–1648 *(Ithaca, N.Y.: Cornell University Press, 1979), p. 50.*

his *Spiritual Exercises,* he insisted that when the Bible and the Church fathers were read directly, they be read under the guidance of the authoritative Scholastic theologians: Peter Lombard, Bonaventura, and Thomas Aquinas. The latter, Ignatius argued, being "of more recent date," had the clearer understanding of what Scripture and the Fathers meant and therefore should guide the study of the past.

When in August 1518 Philip Melanchthon (1497–1560), a young Humanist and professor of Greek, arrived at the University of Wittenberg, his first act was to implement curricular reforms on the Humanist model. In his inaugural address, entitled *On Improving the Studies of the Young,* Melanchthon presented himself as a defender of good letters and classical studies against "barbarians who practice barbarous arts." By the latter he meant the Scholastic theologians of the later Middle Ages, whose methods of juxtaposing the views of conflicting authorities and seeking to reconcile them by disputation had, he believed, undermined both good letters and sound biblical doctrine. Scholastic dominance in the universities was seen by Melanchthon as having bred contempt for the Greek language and learning and as having encouraged neglect of the study of mathematics, sacred studies, and the art of oratory. Melanchthon urged the careful study of history, poetry, and other Humanist disciplines.

Together Luther and Melanchthon restructured the University of Wittenberg's curriculum. Commentaries on Lombard's *Sentences* were dropped, as was canon law. Straightforward historical study replaced old Scholastic lectures on Aristotle. Students read primary sources directly, not by way of accepted Scholastic commentators. Candidates for theological degrees defended the new doctrine on the basis of their own exegesis of the Bible. New chairs of Greek and Hebrew were created. Luther and Melanchthon also pressed for universal compulsory education so both boys and girls could reach vernacular literacy in the Bible.

In Geneva, John Calvin and his successor, Theodore Beza, founded the Genevan Academy, which later evolved into the University of Geneva. That institution, created primarily for training Calvinist ministers, pursued ideals similar to those set forth by Luther and Melanchthon. Calvinist refugees trained in the academy carried Protestant educational reforms to France, Scotland, England, and the New World. Through such efforts a working knowledge of Greek and Hebrew became commonplace in educated circles in the sixteenth and seventeenth centuries.

Some contemporaries decried what they saw as a narrowing of the original Humanist program as Protestants took it over. Erasmus, for example, came to fear the Reformation as a threat to the liberal arts and good learning. Sebastian Franck pointed to parallels between Luther's and Zwingli's debates over Christ's presence in the Eucharist and such old Scholastic disputations as that over the Immaculate Conception of the Virgin.

Humanist culture and learning nonetheless remained indebted to the Reformation. The Protestant endorsement of the Humanist program of studies remained as significant for the Humanist movement as the latter had been for the Reformation. Protestant schools and universities consolidated and preserved for the modern world many of the basic pedagogical achievements of Humanism. There the *studia humanitatis,* although often as little more than a handmaiden to theological doctrine, found a permanent home, one that remained hospitable even in the heyday of Protestant Scholasticism.

The Reformation and the Changing Role of Women

The Protestant reformers took a positive stand on clerical marriage and strongly opposed monasticism and the celibate life. From this position they challenged the medieval tendency alternately to degrade women as temptresses (following the model of Eve) and to exalt them as virgins (following the model of Mary). Protestants opposed the popular antiwoman and antimarriage literature of the Middle Ages. They praised woman in her own right, but especially in her biblical vocation as mother and housewife. Although from a modern perspective, women remained subject to men, new marriage laws gave them greater security and protection.

Relief of sexual frustration and a remedy of fornication were prominent in Protestant arguments for marriage. But the reformers also viewed their wives as indispensable companions in their work, and this not solely because they took domestic cares off their husbands' minds. Luther, who married in 1525 at the age of forty-two, wrote of women:

Imagine what it would be like without women. The home, cities, economic life, and government would virtually disappear. Men cannot do without women. Even if it were possible for men to beget and bear children, they still could not do without women.[3]

John Calvin wrote at the death of his wife:

I have been bereaved of the best companion of my life, of one who, had it been so ordered, would not only have been the willing sharer of my indigence, but even of my death. During her life she was the faithful helper of my ministry.[4]

Such tributes were intended in part to overcome Catholic criticism that marriage distracted the cleric from his ministry. They were primarily the expression of a new value placed on the estate of marriage and family life. In opposition to the celibate ideal of the Middle Ages, Protestants stressed as no religious movement before them the sacredness of home and family. This attitude contributed to a more respectful and sharing relationship between husbands and wives and between parents and children.

The ideal of the companionate marriage— that is, of husband and wife as coworkers in a special God-ordained community of the family, sharing authority equally within the household—led to an important expansion of the grounds for divorce in Protestant cities as early as the 1520s. Women now had an equal right with men to divorce and remarry in good conscience—unlike in Catholicism, where only a separation from bed and table, not divorce and remarriage, was permitted a couple in a failed marriage. The reformers were actually more willing to permit divorce and remarriage on grounds of adultery and abandonment than were secular magistrates, who feared liberal divorce laws would lead to social upheaval.

Protestant doctrines were as attractive to women as they were to men. Renegade nuns wrote exposés of the nunnery in the name of Christian freedom and justification by faith, declaring that the nunnery was no special

Albrecht Dürer's portrait of a young girl (1515). The Protestant movement encouraged girls to be literate in their native languages. [Kupferstichkabinett Staatliche Museen, Preussischer Kulturbesitz, Berlin]

woman's place at all and that supervisory male clergy (who alone could hear the nuns' confessions and administer sacraments to them) made their lives as unpleasant and burdensome as any abusive husband. Women in the higher classes, who enjoyed new social and political freedoms during the Renaissance, found in Protestant theology a religious complement to their greater independence in other walks of life. Some cloistered noblewomen, however, protested the closing of nunneries. They believed the cloister provided them a more interesting and independent way of life than they would have known in the secular world.

Because they wanted women to become pious housewives, Protestants also encouraged the education of girls to literacy in the vernacular, expecting them thereafter to model their lives on the Bible. During their studies, however,

[3]Luther's Works, Vol. 54: Table Talk, ed. and trans. by Theodore G. Tappert (Philadelphia: Fortress Press, 1967), p. 161.
[4]Letters of John Calvin, Vol. 2, trans. by J. Bonnet (Edinburgh: T. Constable, 1858), p. 216.

women found biblical passages that suggested they were equal to men in the presence of God. Education also gave some women a role as independent authors in the Reformation. From a modern perspective, these may seem like small advances, but they were significant, if indirect, steps in the direction of the emancipation of women.

Family Life in Early Modern Europe

Changes in the timing and duration of marriage, in family size, and in infant and child care suggest that family life was under a variety of social and economic pressures in the sixteenth and seventeenth centuries. The Reformation was a factor in these changes, but not the only or even the major one.

Marriage

Men and women married for the first time at later ages than they had in previous centuries. Men tended to be in their middle to late twenties rather than in their late teens and early twenties, and women in their early to mid-twenties rather than in their teens. The church-sanctioned minimum age for marriage remained fourteen for men and twelve for women, and betrothal could still occur at these young ages if the parents agreed. As it had done throughout the High and later Middle Ages, the Church also recognized as valid the free, private exchange of vows between a man and a woman of canonical age. After the Reformation condemned such "clandestine" unions, however, the Church increasingly required both parental consent and public vows for a fully licit marriage, a procedure it had actually always preferred, but had found very difficult to enforce.

A village wedding as portrayed by Pieter Bruegel the Younger (1564–1638). [Scala/Art Resource, N.Y.]

A young couple in love (ca. 1480) by an anonymous artist. [Bildarchiv Preussischer Kulturbesitz]

Late marriage reflected the difficulty couples had supporting themselves independently. Family size had grown with population in the fifteenth and early sixteenth centuries and larger families meant more heirs, a greater division of resources, and a longer time for the average couple to prepare materially for marriage. Later marriages also meant that couples would not have as much time together as they would if they had married younger. This shorter duration of marriage also contributed to more frequent remarriage. Because older women were less able to endure the rigors of successive pregnancies, later marriage also increased maternal mortality. And as the rapid growth of orphanages and foundling homes between 1600 and 1800 attests, delayed marriage increased out-of-wedlock pregnancies.

Marriages were often "arranged" in the sense that the male heads of two families met and discussed the terms of a marriage before they informed the prospective bride and bridegroom.

It was rare, however, for the two people involved not to know each other in advance or to have no prior relationship. Parents did not force total strangers to live together, and children had a legal right to protest and resist an unwanted marriage. A forced marriage was, by definition, invalid, and no one believed an unwanted marriage would last. The best marriage was one desired by both parties and supported by their families.

Family Size

The early modern family was conjugal or nuclear; it consisted of a father and a mother and the two to four of their children who managed to live into adulthood. The average husband and wife had six to eight children, a birth about every two years. Of these, an estimated one-third died by age five, and one-half were gone by age twenty. Rare was the family at any social level that did not learn firsthand about infant mortality and child death. The Protestant reformer Martin Luther fathered six children, two of whom he lost, an infant daughter at eight months and another at thirteen years.

Birth control had been practiced since antiquity in the form of acidic ointments, sponges, and *coitus interruptus* (male withdrawal before ejaculation). The Church's frequent condemnation of this last practice in the thirteenth and fourteenth centuries suggests that conscious and regular efforts at birth control were growing more common in the late Middle Ages. Birth control was not, however, very effective. For both historical and moral reasons the Church firmly opposed it. According to Saint Thomas Aquinas, a moral act must always aid and abet, never frustrate, the natural end of a creaturely process. In the eyes of the Church, the natural end of sex was the production of children and their subsequent rearing to the glory of God within the bounds of matrimony and the community of the Church.

Despite the Church's official opposition to contraception, Christian moral teaching may inadvertently have reinforced a contraceptive mentality within the early modern family by making husbands more sensitive to the suffering and unhappiness that multiple pregnancies forced upon their wives.

Infant and Child Care

But the Church allied with the physicians of early modern Europe on another intimate family matter. It condemned upper-class women who put their newborn children out to wet nurses (for as long as eighteen months), virtually abandoning the primary care of their infants. Wet nurses were women who had recently had a baby or were suckling a child of their own and who, for a fee, agreed to suckle another child. The practice increased the risk of infant mortality because it exposed the infant to a strange and often shared milk supply from a woman who often was not as healthy as its own mother and who usually lived under less sanitary conditions.

Nursing a child was a chore some upper-class women found distasteful. Among women, vanity and convenience appear to have been primary motives for turning to wet nurses. For husbands, even more seemed to be at stake in the practice. The Church forbade sexual intercourse while a woman was lactating and sexual intercourse was believed to spoil a lactating woman's milk (pregnancy ended the supply). Thus, a nursing wife often became a reluctant lover. Nursing also has a contraceptive effect, and there is evidence that some women prolonged nursing precisely to delay a new pregnancy. For wealthy burghers and noblemen who wanted an abundance of male heirs, nursing seemed to rob them of both sex and offspring and to jeopardize their patrimony, hence their support of wet nursing.

Loving Families?

The early modern family had features that seem cold, unloving, even cruel, in retrospect. Not only did well-to-do parents give infants to wet nurses, but later, when the children were between the ages of eight and thirteen, parents generally placed them in apprenticeships or in employment in the homes and businesses of relatives, friends, or acquaintances. The affective ties between spouses seem to have been equally tenuous. Widowers and widows sometimes remarried within a few months of their spouses' death, occasionally within weeks. Marriages with extreme disparity in age, especially between old men and young women, have also been cited as evidence that marriage at the time was based purely on material considerations.

Love and affection, however, are as relative to time and culture as other values. A kindness in one historical period can seem a cruelty in another. Like the medieval parent, an early modern parent would surely have asked a modern critic, "What greater love can parents have for their children than to prepare them for useful and gainful work?"

Because of primitive living conditions, contemporaries could also appreciate the utilitarian and humane side of marriage and thus wink at quick remarriages. On the other hand, marriages with extreme disparity in age were actually no more the norm in early modern Europe than was the practice of wet nursing. Yet both practices received much criticism. The weight of the evidence suggests that premodern parents were as capable of loving one another and their children as modern parents are.

The family of Hans Holbein the Younger (1497–1534), as painted by the artist himself. [Via Foto Hans Hinz, Basel]

The Instructions of a Father to His Youngest Son

At age fourteen, in the year 1539, Christoph Ravensburg departed Augsburg, Germany, for an apprenticeship in Lyons, France, bearing with him these words of advice from his father.

◆ *What are the father's overriding concerns as his son leaves home for the first time? What does his father consider to be the traits of a "true man"? On what is Christoph to rely in time of temptation and danger?*

Dear son Christoph, . . . If you heed the instructions that follow, you will become a true man.

Love God and be mindful of Him, and see to the keeping of His commandments. Attend the traditional religious service in the land where you will be, as other devout and honorable people there do. And argue neither little nor much over any matter of faith, for that will put you at a disadvantage and even threaten your life.

Sebastian Weyer and his brother [the father's business associates in Lyons] will try to place you with a proper master. . . . They will also look after your basic needs, be it clothing or something else. Therefore, try your best to do what they tell you. And when you are with your master, do what he and his wife tell you, and do it with the utmost diligence, always willingly and obediently.

Above all else, take care that you do not lie and steal. Should you have the merchants' money in your hand or see their many wares lying before you, take none of it for yourself. For it often happens that money or something else is purposefully placed before one such as you as a test. So as dear to you as

your life and my favor are, for the sake of life and limb, be false to no one about anything.

Avoid bad company, and when you sometimes hear it said, or actually see other Germans acting improperly and wanting to be Junkers [wealthy noblemen indulging themselves], let it be an example and a warning to you that you not do so.

Do not let your master's other servants or maids with whom you will be living teach you to steal anything in the house, be it food, drink, or anything else that it is wrong to take, for this may bring you great misfortune. They will tempt one such as you to see if he lets himself be led astray.

When bathing or swimming, avoid the great threatening waters of the Saone and the Rhone [which meet in Lyons]. Do not enter them; if you are tempted to do so, resist, as I have told you many times before. Use other waters for your needs, so that you do not drown. . . .

Avoid strong drink by mixing a lot of water in with the wine. Resolve not to get drunk either during your journey or upon your arrival. When you are thirsty, drink only water or well-watered wine, because your nat-

---

◆

During the early Middle Ages, Christendom had been divided into Western and Eastern churches with irreconcilable theological differences. When, in 1517, Martin Luther posted ninety-five theses questioning the selling of indulgences and the traditional sacrament of penance that lay behind them, he created a division within Western Christendom itself—an internal division between Protestants and Catholics.

The Lutheran protest came at a time of political and social discontent with the Church. Not only princes and magistrates, but many ordinary people as well resented traditional clerical rights and privileges. In many instances the clergy were exempted from secular laws and taxes, while remaining powerful landowners whose personal lifestyles were not all that different from those of the laity. Spiritual and secular protest combined to make the Protestant Reformation a successful assault on the old

ural disposition is to eat and drink a lot. Take care of yourself in this way so that you become all the less susceptible to illness.

Avoid gambling, whoring, partying, cursing, and other bad associations and vices. Place yourself in the company of honest people, whom you know to be good and accomplished, and from whom you can learn something good yourself. And when you can find the time, be sure to practice your writing and arithmetic so that you do not forget them, . . .

Keep yourself and your clothes clean, and take good care of your clothes. Be always ready and willing, not argumentative. And do not give up too soon when someone reproaches you for something, for they do it for your own good.

Concentrate on your needs and be frugal and sparing. Don't spend money needlessly, because when you are larger and older, you will want and need it. Do not take comfort in [any expected] wealth [from me]; resolve to learn how to earn [your own] money and to spend it wisely.

As you well know, great expenditures are now being made on your behalf and they will also be made on behalf of your brothers and sisters, so that after my death, you will discover all the less [money for yourself]. Therefore, look to your own needs; plan well now to support yourself and also to be in a position to help the children of your brothers and sisters as well.

Take care that in your innocence you not let yourself be talked into entering a marriage on your own or become entangled [with some woman]. Stay away from dishonest women so that you do not get the pox [syphilis] and other maladies that flow from them.

Keep your feet warm and dry, for the world is an unholy bath; this will make you less vulnerable to foot ailments.

Do not go about the streets at night unless your master sends you out. He will instruct you and arrange things so that you may go safely. Many corrupt youth hang out on the bridge over the Saone and villainy often occurs there.

. . .

Write often to me and your mother, and let me know what kind of master you have there, what his name is and what he does, also how many servants he has and how he treats you.

Finally, as I said at the beginning and as has long been your custom, above all else be godfearing with your reading, prayer, etc. and act as other devout people there do. Buy yourself a Latin prayerbook like the others there have so that almighty God may help you and you suffer no want. May the Lord God care for you.

Written by your father in Augsburg,
26 March, 1539.
Leo Ravenspurg

Friedrich Beyschlag, ed., "Ein Vater an seinen Sohn (1539)," Archiv für Kulturgeschichte 4 (1906): 296–302, trans. by S. Ozment.

Church. In town after town and region after region within Protestant lands, the major institutions and practices of traditional piety were significantly transformed.

It soon became clear, however, that the division would not stop with the Lutherans. Making Scripture the only arbiter in religion had opened a Pandora's box. People proved to have very different ideas about what Scripture taught. Indeed, there seemed to be as many points of view as there were readers. Rapidly the

Reformation created Lutheran, Zwinglian, Anabaptist, Spiritualist, Calvinist, and Anglican versions of biblical religion—a splintering of Protestantism that still endures.

Catholics had been pursuing reform before the Reformation broke out in Germany, although without papal enthusiasm, and certainly not along clear Protestant lines. When major reforms finally came in the Catholic church around the mid-sixteenth century, they were doctrinally reactionary but administratively and spiritually flexible. The Church enforced strict obedience and conformity to its teaching, but it also provided the laity with a better educated and disciplined clergy. For laity who wanted a deeper and more individual piety, experimentation with proven spiritual practices was now permitted. By century's end, such measures had successfully countered and in some areas even spectacularly reversed Protestant gains.

After the Reformation, pluralism steadily became a fact of Western religious life. It did so at first only by sheer force, since no one religious body was then prepared to concede the validity of alternative Christian beliefs and practices. During the sixteenth and seventeenth centuries, only those groups that fought doggedly for their faith gained the right to practice it freely. Despite these struggles, religious pluralism endured. Never again would there be only a Catholic Christian church in Europe.

Review Questions

1. What were the main problems of the Church that contributed to the Protestant Reformation? Why was the Church unable to suppress dissent as it had earlier?
2. What were the basic similarities and differences between the ideas of Luther and Zwingli? Between Luther and Calvin? Did the differences tend to split the Protestant ranks and thereby lessen the effectiveness of the movement?
3. Why did the Reformation begin in Germany? What political factors contributed to the success of the Reformation there as opposed to France or Italy?
4. What was the Catholic reformation and what principal decisions and changes were instituted by the Council of Trent? Was the Protestant Reformation a healthy movement for the Catholic church?
5. Why did Henry VIII finally break with the Catholic church? Was the "new" religion he established really Protestant? What problems did his successors face as a result of Henry's move?
6. What impact did the Reformation have on women in the sixteenth and seventeenth cen-

turies? What new factors and pressures affected relations between men and women, family size, and child care during this period?

Suggested Readings

W. BOUWSMA, *John Calvin. A Sixteenth Century Portrait* (1988). Interpretation of Calvin against background of Renaissance intellectual history.

J. DELUMEAU, *Catholicism Between Luther and Voltaire: A New View of the Counter Reformation* (1977). Programmatic essay for a social history of the Counter-Reformation.

A. G. DICKENS, *The Counter Reformation* (1969). Brief narrative with pictures.

A. G. DICKENS, *The English Reformation* (1974). The best one-volume account.

A. G. DICKENS and JOHN M. TONKIN, *The Reformation in Historical Thought* (1985). The standard critical guide to the main developments in Reformation studies.

G. DONALDSON, *The Scottish Reformation* (1960). Dependable, comprehensive narrative.

G. ELTON, *Reform and Reformation: England, 1509–1558* (1977). Standard political narrative.

H. O. EVENNETT, *The Spirit of the Counter Reformation* (1968). Essay on the continuity of Catholic reform and its independence from the Protestant Reformation.

J. FLANDRIN, *Families in Former Times* (1979). Family life in France.

B. GOTTLIEB, *The Family in the Western World* (1992). Accessible overview with up-to-date annotated bibliographies.

R. HOULBROOKE, *English Family Life, 1450–1716. An Anthology from Diaries* (1988). A rich collection of documents illustrating family relationships.

R. P. HSIA (Ed.), *The German People and the Reformation* (1988). Substantial excerpts from the latest research.

J. L. IRWIN (Ed.), *Womanhood in Radical Protestantism, 1525–1675* (1979). Sources illustrating images of women in sectarian Protestant thought.

H. JEDIN, *A History of the Council of Trent*, Vols. 1 and 2 (1957–1961). Comprehensive, detailed, authoritative.

D. L. JENSEN, *Reformation Europe, Age of Reform and Revolution* (1981). Excellent, up-to-date survey.

W. K. JORDAN, *Edward VI: The Young King* (1968). The basic biography.

R. M. KINGDON (Ed.), *Transition and Revolution: Problems and Issues of European Renaissance and Reformation History* (1974). Covers politics, printing, theology, and witchcraft.

A. MacFarlane, *The Family Life of Ralph Josselin: A Seventeenth Century Clergyman* (1970). A model study of Puritan family life!

J. F. McNeill, *The History and Character of Calvinism* (1954). The most comprehensive account and very readable.

E. W. Monter, *Calvin's Geneva* (1967). Dependable sketch derived from authoritative studies.

H. A. Oberman, *Luther: Man Between God and the Devil* (1989). Perhaps the best account of Luther's life, by a Dutch master.

J. O'Malley, *The First Jesuits* (1993). Extremely detailed account of the creation of the Society of Jesus and its original purposes.

S. Ozment, *The Age of Reform 1250–1550: An Intellectual and Religious History of Late Medieval and Reformation Europe* (1980). A broad survey of major religious ideas and beliefs.

S. Ozment, *When Fathers Ruled: Family Life in Reformation Europe* (1983). A survey of sixteenth-century attitudes toward marriage and parenthood.

S. Ozment, *Three Behaim Boys: Growing Up in Early Modern Germany* (1990). The lives of three boys in their late teens and early adulthood told in their own words.

S. Ozment, *Protestants: The Birth of a Revolution* (1992). The Reformation in Germany as a religious and cultural movement.

R. R. Post, *The Modern Devotion* (1968). Currently the authoritative interpretation.

E. F. Rice, Jr., *The Foundations of Early Modern Europe 1460–1559* (1970). Broad, succinct narrative.

J. G. Ridley, *Thomas Cranmer* (1962). The basic biography.

J. J. Scarisbrick, *The Reformation and the English People* (1990). Eloquent argument that the Reformation changed little religiously, that it was a political, not a spiritual, triumph.

Q. Skinner, *The Foundations of Modern Political Thought II: The Age of Reformation* (1978). A comprehensive survey that treats *every* political thinker and tract.

L. W. Spitz, *The Protestant Reformation 1517–1559* (1985). Sweeping survey with rich bibliographies.

D. Starkey, *The Reign of Henry VIII* (1985). Portrayal of the king as in control of neither his life nor his court.

J. Stayer, *Anabaptists and the Sword* (1972). The political philosophies of sectarians.

L. Stone, *The Family, Sex and Marriage in England 1500–1800* (1977). Controversial but in many respects still reigning view of English family history.

G. Strauss (Ed. and Trans.), *Manifestations of Discontent in Germany on the Eve of the Reformation* (1971). Rich collection of sources for both rural and urban scenes.

G. Strauss, *Luther's House of Learning: The Indoctrination of the Young in the German Reformation* (1978). Account of Protestant efforts to rear children in the new faith, stressing the negative side.

R. H. Tawney, *Religion and the Rise of Capitalism* (1947). Advances beyond Max Weber's arguments relating Protestantism and capitalist economic behavior.

E. Troeltsch, *The Social Teaching of the Christian Churches*, Vols. 1 and 2, trans. by O. Wyon (1960). Old, liberal account of the Reformation and its critics with fondness for the latter.

M. Weber, *The Protestant Ethic and the Spirit of Capitalism*, trans. by T. Parsons (1958). First appeared in 1904–1905 and has continued to stimulate debate over the relationship between religion and society.

F. Wendel, *Calvin: The Origins and Development of His Religious Thought*, trans. by P. Mairet (1963). The best treatment of Calvin's theology.

G. H. Williams, *The Radical Reformation* (1962). Broad survey of the varieties of dissent within Protestantism.

The St. Bartholemew's Day Massacre, as depicted by the contemporary Protestant painter François Dubois. In this notorious event, 3,000 Protestants were slaughtered in Paris and an estimated 20,000 others died throughout France. The massacre transformed the religious struggle in France from a contest for political power into a war for survival between Protestants and Catholics. [Musée Cantonal des Beaux Arts, Palais de Rumine, Lausanne]

12

The Age of Religious Wars

> **Key Topics in This Chapter**
> ◆ The war between Calvinists and Catholics in France
> ◆ The Spanish occupation of the Netherlands
> ◆ The struggle for supremacy between England and Spain
> ◆ The devastation of central Europe during the Thirty Years' War

The late sixteenth century and the first half of the seventeenth centuries are described as an "age of religious wars" because of the bloody opposition of Protestants and Catholics across Europe. Both genuine religious conflict and bitter dynastic rivalries fueled the wars. In France, the Netherlands, England, and Scotland in the second half of the sixteenth century, Calvinists fought Catholic rulers for the right to govern their own territories and to practice their chosen religion openly. In the first half of the seventeenth century, Lutherans, Calvinists, and Catholics marched against one another in central and northern Europe during the Thirty Years' War. By the middle of the seventeenth century, English Puritans had successfully revolted against the Stuart monarchy and the Anglican church.

Renewed Religious Struggle

During the first half of the sixteenth century, religious conflict had been confined to central Europe and was primarily a struggle by Lutherans to secure rights and freedoms for themselves. In the second half of the sixteenth century, the focus shifted to western Europe—to France, the Netherlands, England, and Scotland—and became a struggle by Calvinists for recognition. After the Peace of Augsburg (1555), and with it acceptance of the principle that a region's ruler would determine its religion (*cuius regio, eius religio*), Lutheranism became a legal religion in the Holy Roman Empire. The Peace of Augsburg did not, however, extend recognition to non-Lutheran Protestants. Both Catholics and Lutherans scorned Anabaptists and other sectarians as anarchists, and Calvinists were not yet strong enough to demand legal standing.

Outside the empire the struggle for Protestant religious rights had intensified in most countries by the mid-sixteenth century. After the Council of Trent adjourned in 1563, Catholics began a Jesuit-led international counteroffensive against Protestants. At the time of John Calvin's death in 1564, Geneva had become both a refuge for Europe's persecuted Protestants and an international school for Protestant resistance, producing leaders fully equal to the new Catholic challenge.

Genevan Calvinism and Catholicism as revived by the Council of Trent were two equally

The religious conflicts of the sixteenth and seventeenth centuries are reflected in the art and architecture of the period. This eighteenth-century cloister-church in Ottobeuren in Bavaria, designed by Johann Michael Fischer, is in the baroque style congenial to the Catholic Counter-Reformation. The interior explodes with energy and is filled with sculptures and paintings and magnificent woodwork that catch the eye. The intent was to inspire and move the worshipper to self-transcendence. [Bildarchiv Preussischer Kulturbesitz]

In stark contrast to the baroque style, this seventeenth-century Calvinist church in the Palatinate has no interior decoration to distract the worshipper from the Word of God. The intent was to create an atmosphere of quiet introspection and reflection on one's spiritual life and God's Word. [German National Museum, Nuremberg]

dogmatic, aggressive, and irreconcilable church systems. Calvinists may have looked like "new papists" to critics when they dominated cities like Geneva. Yet when, as minorities, they found their civil and religious rights denied, they became true firebrands and revolutionaries. Calvinism adopted a presbyterian organization that magnified regional and local religious authority. Boards of presbyters, or elders, representing the many individual congregations of Calvinists, directly shaped the policy of the church at large.

By contrast, the Counter-Reformation sponsored a centralized episcopal church system, hierarchically arranged from pope to parish priest, that stressed absolute obedience to the person at the top. The high clergy—the pope and his bishops—not the synods of local churches, ruled supreme. Calvinism proved attractive to proponents of political decentralization who opposed totalitarian rulers, whereas Catholicism remained congenial to proponents of absolute monarchy determined to maintain "one king, one church, one law."

The opposition between the two religions can be seen even in the art and architecture that each came to embrace. The Catholic Counter-Reformation found the Baroque style congenial. A successor to Mannerism, Baroque art is a grandiose, three-dimensional display of life and energy. Great Baroque artists like Peter Paul Rubens (1571–1640) and Gianlorenzo Bernini (1598–1680) were Catholics. Protestants by contrast opted for a simpler and more restrained art and architecture, as can be seen in the English churches of Christopher Wren

(1632–1723) and the gentle, searching portraits of the Dutch Mennonite Rembrandt van Rijn (1606–1669).

As religious wars engulfed Europe, the intellectuals perceived the wisdom of religious pluralism and toleration more quickly than did the politicians. A new skepticism, relativism, and individualism in religion became respectable in the sixteenth and seventeenth centuries (see Chapter 14). Sebastian Castellio's (1515–1563) pithy censure of John Calvin for his role in the execution of the Antitrinitarian Michael Servetus summarized a growing sentiment: "To kill a man is not to defend a doctrine, but to kill a man."[1] The French essayist Michel de Montaigne (1533–1592) asked in scorn of the dogmatic mind: "What do I know?" And the Lutheran Valentin Weigel (1533–1588), surveying a half century of religious strife in Germany, advised people to look within themselves for religious truth and no longer to churches and creeds.

Such skeptical views gained currency in larger political circles only at the cost of painful experience. Religious strife and civil war were best held in check where rulers tended to subordinate theological doctrine to political unity, urging tolerance, moderation, and compromise—even indifference—in religious matters. Rulers of this kind came to be known as *politiques*, and the most successful among them was Elizabeth I of England. By contrast, rulers like Mary I of England, Philip II of Spain, and Oliver Cromwell, who took their religion with the utmost seriousness and refused every compromise, did not in the long run achieve their political goals.

As we shall see, the wars of religion were both internal national conflicts and truly international wars. Catholic and Protestant subjects struggled against one another for control of the crown of France, the Netherlands, and England. The Catholic governments of France and Spain conspired and finally sent armies against Protestant regimes in England and the Netherlands. The outbreak of the Thirty Years' War in 1618 made the international dimension of the religious conflict especially clear; before it ended in 1648, the war drew every major European nation directly or indirectly into its deadly net.

[1]*Contra libellum Calvini (N.P., 1562), p. E 2 a.*

The French Wars of Religion (1562–1598)

Anti-Protestant Measures and the Struggle for Political Power

French Protestants are known as *Huguenots*, a term derived from Besançon Hugues, the leader of Geneva's political revolt against the House of Savoy in the 1520s, a prelude to that city's Calvinist Reformation. They were under surveillance in France already in the early 1520s, when Lutheran writings and doctrines began to circulate in Paris. The capture of the French king Francis I by the forces of Emperor Charles V at the Battle of Pavia in 1525 provided a motive for the first wave of Protestant persecution in France. The French government hoped thereby to pacify their Habsburg conqueror, a fierce opponent of German Protestants, and to win their king's swift release.

A second major crackdown came a decade later. When Protestants plastered Paris and other cities with anti-Catholic placards on October 18, 1534, mass arrests of suspected Protestants followed. The government retaliation drove John Calvin and other members of the French reform party into exile. In 1540 the Edict of Fontainebleau subjected French Protestants to the Inquisition. Henry II (r. 1547–1559) established new measures against Protestants in the Edict of Chateaubriand in 1551. Save for a few brief interludes, the French monarchy remained a staunch foe of the Protestants until the ascension to the throne of Henry of Navarre in 1589.

The Habsburg–Valois wars (see Chapter 11) had ended with the Treaty of Cateau-Cambrésis in 1559, after which Europe experienced a moment of peace. But the same year marked the beginning of internal French conflict and the shift of the European balance of power away from France to Spain. The shift began with an accident. During a tournament held to celebrate the marriage of his thirteen-year-old daughter to Philip II, the son of Charles V and heir to the Spanish Habsburg lands, the French king, Henry II, was mortally wounded when a lance pierced his visor. This unforeseen event brought to the throne his sickly fifteen-year-old son, Francis II, under the regency of the queen mother, Catherine de Médicis. With the monarchy so weakened by Henry's death, three powerful families saw their chance to control France and began to compete for the young king's ear. They were the Bourbons, whose power lay in the south and west; the Montmorency-Chatillons, who controlled the center of France; and the Guises, who were dominant in eastern France.

The Guises were by far the strongest and had little trouble establishing firm control over the young king. Francis, duke of Guise, had been Henry II's general, and his brothers, Charles and Louis, were cardinals of the Church. Mary Stuart, Queen of Scots and wife of Francis II, was their niece. Throughout the latter half of the sixteenth century, the name of Guise remained interchangeable with militant, reactionary Catholicism.

The Bourbon and Montmorency-Chatillon families, in contrast, developed strong Huguenot sympathies, largely for political reasons. The Bourbon Louis I, prince of Condé (d. 1569), and the Montmorency-Chatillon Admiral Gaspard de Coligny (1519–1572) became the political leaders of the French Protestant resistance. They collaborated early in an abortive plot to kidnap Francis II from his Guise advisers in the Conspiracy of Amboise in 1560. This conspiracy was strongly condemned by John Calvin, who considered such tactics a disgrace to the Reformation.

Appeal of Calvinism

Often for quite different reasons ambitious aristocrats and discontented townspeople joined Calvinist churches in opposition to the Guise-dominated French monarchy. In 1561 more than 2,000 Huguenot congregations existed throughout France. Yet Huguenots were a majority of the population in only two regions: Dauphiné and Languedoc. Although they made up only about one fifteenth of the population, Huguenots were in important geographic areas and were heavily represented among the more powerful segments of French society. More than two-fifths of the French aristocracy became Huguenots. Many apparently hoped to establish within France a principle of territorial sovereignty akin to that secured within the Holy Roman Empire by the Peace of Augsburg. In this way,

Calvinism indirectly served the forces of political decentralization.

John Calvin and Theodore Beza consciously sought to advance their cause by currying favor with powerful aristocrats. Beza converted Jeanne d'Albert, the mother of the future Henry IV. The prince of Condé was apparently converted in 1558 under the influence of his Calvinist wife. For many aristocrats—Condé probably among them—Calvinist religious convictions were attractive primarily as aids to long-sought political goals.

The military organization of Condé and Coligny progressively merged with the religious organization of the French Huguenot churches, creating a potent combination that benefitted both political and religious dissidents. Calvinism gave political resistance justification and inspiration, and the forces of political resistance made Calvinism a viable religious alternative in Catholic France. Each side had much to gain from the other. The confluence of secular and religious motives, although beneficial to aristocratic resistance and Calvinist religion alike, tended to cast suspicion on the religious appeal of Calvinism. Clearly religious conviction was neither the only nor always the main reason for becoming a Calvinist in France in the second half of the sixteenth century.

Catherine de Médicis and the Guises

Following Francis II's death in 1560, Catherine de Médicis continued as regent for her minor son, Charles IX (r. 1560–1574). At a colloquy in Poissy, she tried unsuccessfully to reconcile the Protestant and Catholic factions. Fearing the power and guile of the Guises, Catherine, whose first concern was always to preserve the monarchy, sought allies among the Protestants. In 1562, after conversations with Beza and Coligny, she issued the January Edict, a measure that granted Protestants freedom to worship publicly outside towns—although only privately within them—and to hold synods. In March this royal toleration came to an abrupt end when the duke of Guise surprised a Protestant congregation at Vassy in Champagne and proceeded to massacre several score. That event marked the beginning of the French wars of religion (March 1562).

Catherine de Médicis (1519–1589) exercised power in France during the reigns of her three sons Francis II (r. 1559–1560), Charles IX (r. 1560–1574), and Henry III (r. 1574–1589). [Roger-Viollet]

Had Condé and the Huguenot armies rushed immediately to the queen's side after this attack, Protestants might well have secured an alliance with the crown. The queen mother's fear of Guise power was great at this time. But the hesitation of the Protestant leaders, due primarily to indecision on the part of Condé, placed the young king and the queen mother, against their deepest wishes, in firm Guise control. Cooperation with the Guises became the only alternative to capitulation to the Protestants.

THE PEACE OF SAINT-GERMAIN-EN-LAYE
During the first French war of religion, fought between April 1562 and March 1563, the duke of Guise was assassinated. It is a measure of the international character of the struggle in France

that troops from Hesse and the Palatinate fought alongside the Huguenots. A brief resumption of hostilities in 1567–1568 was followed by the bloodiest of all the conflicts, between September 1568 and August 1570. In this period, Condé was killed and Huguenot leadership passed to Coligny. This was actually a blessing in disguise for the Protestants because Coligny was far the better military strategist. In the Peace of Saint-Germain-en-Laye (1570), which ended the third war, the crown, acknowledging the power of the Protestant nobility, granted the Huguenots religious freedoms within their territories and the right to fortify their cities.

Perpetually caught between fanatical Huguenot and Guise extremes, Queen Catherine had always sought to balance one side against the other. Like the Guises, she wanted a Catholic France; she did not, however, desire a Guise-dominated monarchy. After the Peace of Saint-Germain-en-Laye the crown tilted manifestly toward the Bourbon faction and the Huguenots, and Coligny became Charles IX's most trusted adviser. Unknown to the king, Catherine began to plot with the Guises against the ascendant Protestants. As she had earlier sought Protestant support when Guise power threatened to subdue the monarchy, she now sought Guise support as Protestant influence grew.

There was reason for Catherine to fear Coligny's hold on the king. Louis of Nassau, the leader of Protestant resistance to Philip II in the Netherlands, had gained Coligny's ear. Coligny used his position of influence to win the king of France over to a planned French invasion of the Netherlands in support of the Dutch Protestants. Such a course of action would have placed France squarely on a collision course with mighty Spain. Catherine recognized far better than her son that France stood little chance in such a contest. She and her advisers had been much sobered in this regard by news of the stunning Spanish victory over the Turks at Lepanto in October 1571 (to be discussed later).

THE SAINT BARTHOLOMEW'S DAY MASSACRE
When Catherine lent her support to the infamous Saint Bartholomew's Day Massacre of Protestants, she did so out of a far less reasoned judgment. Her decision appears to have been

made in a state of near panic. On August 22, 1572, four days after the Huguenot Henry of Navarre had married the king's sister, Marguerite of Valois—still another sign of growing Protestant power—Coligny was struck down, although not killed, by an assassin's bullet. Catherine had apparently been party to this Guise plot to eliminate Coligny. After its failure, she feared both the king's reaction to her complicity with the Guises and the Huguenot response under a recovered Coligny. Catherine convinced Charles that a Huguenot coup was afoot, inspired by Coligny, and that only the swift execution of Protestant leaders could save the crown from a Protestant attack on Paris.

On Saint Bartholomew's Day, August 24, 1572, Coligny and 3,000 fellow Huguenots were butchered in Paris. Within three days an estimated 20,000 Huguenots were executed in coordinated attacks throughout France. It is a date that has ever since lived in infamy for Protestants.

Pope Gregory XIII and Philip II of Spain reportedly greeted the news of the Protestant massacre with special religious celebrations. Philip especially had good reason to rejoice. By throwing France into civil war, the massacre ended for the moment any planned French opposition to his efforts to subdue his rebellious subjects in the Netherlands. But the massacre of thousands of Protestants also gave the discerning Catholic world cause for new alarm. The event changed the nature of the struggle between Protestants and Catholics both within and beyond the borders of France. It was thereafter no longer an internal contest between Guise and Bourbon factions for French political influence, nor was it simply a Huguenot campaign to win basic religious freedoms. Henceforth, in Protestant eyes, it became an international struggle to the death for sheer survival against an adversary whose cruelty now justified any means of resistance.

PROTESTANT RESISTANCE THEORY Only as Protestants faced suppression and sure defeat did they begin to sanction active political resistance. At first, they tried to practice the biblical precept of obedient subjection to worldly authority (Romans 13:1). Luther had only grudgingly approved resistance to the emperor after the

Diet of Augsburg in 1530. In 1550 Lutherans in Magdeburg had published a highly influential defense of the right of lower authorities to oppose the emperor's order that all Lutherans return to the Catholic fold.

Calvin, who never faced the specter of total political defeat after his return to Geneva in September 1540, had always condemned willful disobedience and rebellion against lawfully constituted governments as un-Christian. But he also taught that lower magistrates, as part of the lawfully constituted government, had the right and duty to oppose tyrannical higher authority.

The exiled Scottish reformer John Knox, who had seen his cause crushed by Mary of Guise, the Regent of Scotland, and Mary I of England, laid the groundwork for later Calvinist resistance. In his famous *First Blast of the Trumpet Against the Terrible Regiment of Women* (1558), he declared that the removal of a heathen tyrant was not only permissible, but a Christian duty. He had the Catholic queen of England in mind.

After the great massacre of French Protestants on Saint Bartholomew's Day, 1572, Calvinists everywhere came to appreciate the need for an active defense of their religious rights. Classical Huguenot theories of resistance appeared in three major works of the 1570s. The first was the *Franco-Gallia* of François Hotman (1573), a Humanist argument that the representative Estates General of France historically held higher authority than the French king. The second was Theodore Beza's *On the Right of Magistrates over Their Subjects* (1574), which, going beyond Calvin's views, justified the correction and even the overthrow of tyrannical rulers by lower authorities. Finally, Philippe du Plessis Mornay's *Defense of Liberty Against Tyrants* (1579) admonished princes, nobles, and magistrates beneath the king, as guardians of the rights of the body politic, to take up arms against tyranny in other lands.

The Rise to Power of Henry of Navarre

Henry III (r. 1574–1589) was the last of Henry II's sons to wear the French crown. He found the monarchy wedged between a radical Catholic League, formed in 1576 by Henry of Guise, and vengeful Huguenots. Neither group would have been reluctant to assassinate a ruler

Theodore Beza Defends the Right to Resist Tyranny

One of the oldest problems in political and social theory has been that of knowing when resistance to repression in matters of conscience is justified. Since Luther's day, Protestant reformers had urged their followers to obey established political authority. After the 1572 Massacre of Saint Bartholomew's Day, how-ever, Protestant pamphleteers urged Protestants to resist tyrants and persecutors with armed force. In 1574 Theodore Beza pointed out the obligation of rulers to act in the best interests of their subjects and the latter's right to resist them when they did not.

◆ *When does a ruler go too far according to Beza? To whom may subjects appeal against a tyrant? Does Beza believe that individuals may take the law into their own hands?*

It is apparent that there is a mutual obligation between the king and the officers of a kingdom; that the government of the kingdom is not in the hands of the king in its entirety, but only the sovereign degree; that each of the officers has a share in accord with his degree; and that there are definite conditions on either side. If these conditions are not observed by the inferior officers, it is the part of the sovereign to dismiss and punish them. . . . If the king, hereditary or elective, clearly goes back on the conditions without which he would not have been recognized and acknowledged, can there be any doubt that the lesser magistrates of the kingdom, of the cities, and of the provinces, the administration of which they have received from the sovereignty itself, are free of their oath, at least to the extent that they are entitled to resist flagrant oppression of the realm which they swore to defend and protect according to their office and their particular jurisdiction? . . .

We must now speak of the third class of subjects, which though admittedly subject to the sovereign in a certain respect, is, in another respect, and in cases of necessity the protector of the rights of the sovereignty itself, and is established to hold the sovereign to his duty, and even, if need be, constrain and punish him. . . . The people is prior to all the magistrates, and does not exist for them, but they for it. . . . Whenever law and equity prevailed, nations neither created nor accepted kings except upon definite conditions. From this it follows that when kings flagrantly violate these terms, those who have the power to give them their authority have no less power to deprive them of it.

Constitutionalism and Resistance in the Sixteenth Century: Three Treatises by Hotman, Beza, and Mornay, trans. and ed. by Julian H. Franklin (New York: Pegasus, 1969), pp. 111–114.

whom they considered heretical and a tyrant. Like the queen mother, Henry sought to steer a middle course. In this effort he received support from a growing body of neutral Catholics and Huguenots, who put the political survival of France above its religious unity. Such *politiques* were prepared to compromise religious creeds as might be required to save the nation.

The Peace of Beaulieu in May 1576 granted the Huguenots almost complete religious and civil freedom. France, however, was not ready then for such sweeping toleration. Within seven months of the Peace of Beaulieu, the Catholic League forced Henry to return to the illusory quest for absolute religious unity in France. In October 1577 the king truncated the Peace of

Beaulieu and once again circumscribed areas of permitted Huguenot worship. Thereafter Huguenot and Catholic factions quickly returned to their accustomed anarchical military solutions. The Protestants were led by Henry of Navarre, now heir to the French throne by virtue of his marriage to Margaret of Valois, Henry III's sister.

In the mid-1580s the Catholic League, supported by the Spanish, became completely dominant in Paris. In what came to be known as the Day of the Barricades, Henry III attempted to rout the league with a surprise attack in 1588. The effort failed badly, and the king had to flee Paris. Forced by his weakened position into unkingly guerilla tactics, and also emboldened by news of the English victory over the Spanish Armada in 1588, Henry successfully plotted the assassination of both the duke and the cardinal of Guise. These assassinations sent France reeling once again. Led by still another Guise brother, the Catholic League reacted with a fury that matched the earlier Huguenot response to the Massacre of Saint Bartholomew's Day. The king now had only one course of action. He struck an alliance with the Protestant Henry of Navarre in April 1589.

As the two Henrys prepared to attack the Guise stronghold of Paris, however, a fanatical Jacobin friar stabbed and killed Henry III. Thereupon the Bourbon Huguenot Henry of Navarre succeeded the childless Valois king to the French throne as Henry IV (r. 1589–1610). Pope Sixtus V and Philip II stood aghast at the sudden prospect of a Protestant France. They had always wanted France to be religiously Catholic and politically weak, and they now acted to achieve that end. Spain rushed troops to support the besieged Catholic League. Philip II apparently even harbored hopes of placing his eldest daughter, Isabella, the granddaughter of Henry II and Catherine de Médicis, on the French throne.

Direct Spanish intervention in the affairs of France seemed only to strengthen Henry IV's grasp on the crown. The French people viewed his right to hereditary succession more seriously than his espoused Protestant confession. Henry was also widely liked. Notoriously informal in dress and manner—a factor that made him especially popular with the soldiers—Henry also had the wit and charm to neutralize the strongest enemy in a face-to-face confrontation. He came to the throne as a *politique*, long weary

Henry IV of France (r. 1589–1610) on horseback, painted in 1594. [Giraudon/Art Resource, N.Y.]

with religious strife and fully prepared to place political peace above absolute religious unity. He believed that a royal policy of tolerant Catholicism would be the best way to achieve such peace. On July 25, 1593, he publicly abjured the Protestant faith and embraced the traditional and majority religion of his country. "Paris is worth a mass," he is reported to have said.

It was, in fact, a decision he had made only after a long period of personal agonizing. The Huguenots were understandably horrified by this turnabout, and Pope Clement VIII remained skeptical of Henry's sincerity. But most of the French church and people, having known internal strife too long, rallied to the king's side. By 1596 the Catholic League was dispersed, its ties with Spain were broken, and the wars of religion in France, to all intents, had ground to a close.

The Edict of Nantes

On April 13, 1598, Henry IV's famous Edict of Nantes proclaimed a formal religious settlement. The following month, on May 2, 1598, the Treaty of Vervins ended hostilities between France and Spain.

In 1591 Henry IV had already assured the Huguenots of at least qualified religious freedoms. The Edict of Nantes made good that promise. It recognized and sanctioned minority religious rights within what was to remain an officially Catholic country. This religious truce—and it was never more than that—granted the Huguenots, who by this time numbered well over one million, freedom of public worship, the right of assembly, admission to public offices and universities, and permission to maintain fortified towns. Most of the new freedoms, however, were to be exercised within their own towns and territories. Concession of the right to fortify their towns reveals the continuing distrust between French Protestants and Catholics. As significant as it was, the edict only transformed a long hot war between irreconcilable enemies into a long cold war. To its critics it had only created a state within a state.

A Catholic fanatic assassinated Henry IV in May 1610. Although he is best remembered for the Edict of Nantes, the political and economic policies he put in place were equally important.

They laid the foundations for the transformation of France into the absolute state it would become under Cardinal Richelieu and Louis XIV. Ironically, in pursuit of the political and religious unity that had escaped Henry IV, Louis XIV, calling for "one king, one church, one law," would revoke the Edict of Nantes in 1685 (see Chapter 13). This action would force France and Europe to learn again by bitter experience the hard lessons of the wars of religion. Rare is the politician who learns from the lessons of history rather than repeating its mistakes.

Imperial Spain and the Reign of Philip II (1556–1598)

Pillars of Spanish Power

Until the English defeated the mighty Spanish Armada in 1588, no one person stood larger in the second half of the sixteenth century than Philip II of Spain. Philip was heir to the intensely Catholic and militarily supreme western Habsburg kingdom. The eastern Habsburg lands of Austria, Bohemia, and Hungary had been given over by his father, Charles V, to Philip's uncle, the Emperor Ferdinand I. These lands,

Main Events of French Wars of Religion	
1559	Treaty of Cateau-Cambrésis ends Habsburg–Valois wars
1559	Francis II succeeds to French throne under regency of his mother, Catherine de Médicis
1560	Conspiracy of Amboise fails
1562	Protestant worshipers massacred at Vassy in Champagne by the duke of Guise
1572	The Saint Bartholomew's Day Massacre leaves thousands of Protestants dead
1589	Assassination of Henry III brings the Huguenot Henry of Navarre to throne as Henry IV
1593	Henry IV embraces Catholicism
1598	Henry IV grants Huguenots religious and civil freedoms in the Edict of Nantes
1610	Henry IV assassinated

Henry IV Recognizes Huguenot Religious Freedom

By the Edict of Nantes (April 13, 1598) Henry IV recognized Huguenot religious freedoms and the rights of Protestants to participate in French public institutions. Here are some of its provisions.

✦ *Are Huguenots given equal religious standing with Catholics? Are there limitations on their freedoms?*

We have by this perpetual and irrevocable Edict pronounced, declared, and ordained and we pronounce, declare and ordain:

Art. I. Firstly, that the memory of everything done on both sides from the beginning of the month of March, 1585, until our accession to the Crown and during the other previous troubles, and at the outbreak of them, shall remain extinct and suppressed, as if it were something which had never occurred. . . .

Art. II. We forbid all our subjects, of whatever rank and quality they may be, to renew the memory of these matters, to attack, be hostile to, injure or provoke each other in revenge for the past, whatever may be the reason and pretext . . . but let them restrain themselves and live peaceably together as brothers, friends, and fellow-citizens. . . .

Art. III. We ordain that the Catholic, Apostolic, and Roman religion shall be restored and re-established in all places and districts of this our kingdom and the countries under our rule, where its practice has been interrupted. . . .

. . . .

Art. VI. And we permit those of the so-called Reformed religion to live and dwell in all the towns and districts of this our kingdom and the countries under our rule, without being annoyed, disturbed, molested or constrained to do anything against their conscience, or for this cause to be sought out in their houses and districts where they wish to live, provided that they conduct themselves in other respects to the provisions of our present Edict. . . .

. . . .

Art. XXI. Books dealing with the matters of the aforesaid so-called Reformed religion shall not be printed and sold publicly, except in the towns and districts where the public exercise of the said religion is allowed. . . .

Art. XXII. We ordain that there shall be no difference or distinction, because of the aforesaid religion, in the reception of students to be instructed in Universities, Colleges, and schools, or of the sick and poor into hospitals, infirmaries, and public charitable institutions. . . .

. . . .

Art. XXVII. In order to reunite more effectively the wills of our subjects, as is our intention, and to remove all future complaints, we declare that all those who profess or shall profess the aforesaid so-called Reformed religion are capable of holding and exercising all public positions, honours, offices, and duties whatsoever . . . in the towns of our kingdom . . . notwithstanding all contrary oaths.

Church and State Through the Centuries: A Collection of Historic Documents, *trans. and ed. by S. Z. Ehler and John B. Morrall (New York: Biblo and Tannen, 1967), pp. 185–187.*

together with the imperial title, remained in the possession of the Austrian branch of the family.

NEW WORLD RICHES Populous and wealthy Castile gave Philip a solid home base. The regular arrival in Seville of bullion from the Spanish colonies in the New World provided additional wealth. In the 1540s great silver mines had been opened in Potosí in present-day Bolivia and in Zacatecas in Mexico. These gave Philip the

Titian's portrait of Philip II of Spain (r. 1556–1598), the most powerful ruler of his time. [Alinari/Art Resource]

The new American wealth brought dramatic social change to the peoples of Europe during the second half of the sixteenth century. As Europe became richer, it was also becoming more populous. In the economically and politically active towns of France, England, and the Netherlands, populations had tripled and quadrupled by the early seventeenth century. Europe's population exceeded 70 million by 1600.

The combination of increased wealth and population triggered inflation. A steady 2 percent a year rise in prices in much of Europe had serious cumulative effects by mid-century. There were more people than before and greater coinage in circulation, but less food and fewer jobs; wages stagnated while prices doubled and tripled in much of Europe.

This was especially the case in Spain. Because the new wealth was concentrated in the hands of a few, the traditional gap between the "haves"—the propertied, privileged, and educated classes—and the "have-nots" greatly widened. Nowhere did the unprivileged suffer more than in Spain, where the Castilian peasantry, the backbone of Philip II's great empire, became the most heavily taxed people of Europe. Those whose labor contributed most to making possible Spanish hegemony in Europe in the second half of the sixteenth century prospered least from it.

EFFICIENT BUREAUCRACY AND MILITARY A subjugated peasantry and wealth from the New World were not the only pillars of Spanish strength. Philip II shrewdly organized the lesser nobility into a loyal and efficient national bureaucracy. A reclusive man, he managed his kingdom by pen and paper rather than by personal presence. He was also a learned and pious Catholic, although some popes suspected that he used religion as much for political as for devotional purposes. That he was a generous patron of the arts and culture can be seen in his unique retreat outside Madrid, the Escorial, a combination palace, church, tomb, and monastery. Philip also knew personal sorrows. His mad and treacherous son, Don Carlos, died under suspicious circumstances in 1568—some contemporaries suspected that Philip had him quietly executed—only three months before the death of the queen.

great sums needed to pay his bankers and mercenaries. He nonetheless never managed to erase the debts left by his father nor to finance his own foreign adventures fully. He later contributed to the bankruptcy of the Fuggers when, at the end of his life, he defaulted on his enormous debts.

A view of the Escorial, Philip II's massive palace-monastery-mausoleum northwest of Madrid. Built between 1563 and 1584, it was a monument to the piety and power of the king. Philip vowed to build the complex after the Spanish defeated the French at Saint-Quentin on St. Lawrence's day in 1577. The floor plan of the Escorial resembles a grill, the symbol of St. Lawrence (who, according to legend, was martyred by being roasted alive on a grill). [Odyssey Productions]

SUPREMACY IN THE MEDITERRANEAN During the first half of Philip's reign, attention focused almost exclusively on the Mediterranean and the Turkish threat. By history, geography, and choice, Spain had traditionally been Catholic Europe's champion against Islam. During the 1560s the Turks advanced deep into Austria, while their fleets dominated the Mediterranean. Between 1568 and 1570 armies under Philip's half-brother, Don John of Austria, the illegitimate son of Charles V, suppressed and dispersed the Moors in Granada.

In May 1571 a Holy League of Spain, Venice, and the pope, again under Don John's command, formed to check Turkish belligerence in the Mediterranean. In what was the largest naval battle of the sixteenth century, Don John's fleet engaged the Ottoman navy under Ali Pasha off Lepanto in the Gulf of Corinth on October 7, 1571. Before the engagement ended, over one-third of the Turkish fleet had been sunk or captured and 30,000 Turks had died. The Mediterranean for the moment belonged to Spain, and the Europeans were left to fight each other. Philip's armies also succeeded in putting down

resistance in neighboring Portugal, which Spain annexed in 1580. The conquest of Portugal not only added to Spanish seapower but also brought the magnificent Portuguese overseas empire in Africa, India, and the Americas into the Spanish orbit.

The Revolt in the Netherlands

The spectacular Spanish military success in southern Europe was not repeated in northern Europe. When Philip attempted to impose his will within the Netherlands and on England and France, he learned the lessons of defeat. The resistance of the Netherlands especially proved the undoing of Spanish dreams of world empire (see Map 12-1).

CARDINAL GRANVELLE The Netherlands was not only the richest area of Philip's Habsburg kingdom, but of Europe as well. In 1559 Philip had departed the Netherlands for Spain, never again to return. His half-sister, Margaret of Parma, assisted by a special council of state, became regent in his absence. The

The battle of Lepanto occurred off the coast of Greece on October 7, 1571. In the largest naval engagement of the sixteenth century, the Spanish and their Italian allies under Don John of Austria smashed the Turkish fleet and ended the Ottoman threat in the western Mediterranean. [National Maritime Museum, London]

council was headed by Philip's hand-picked lieutenant, the extremely able Antoine Perrenot (1517–1586), after 1561 Cardinal Granvelle. Granvelle hoped to check Protestant gains by internal Church reforms. He planned to break down the traditional local autonomy of the seventeen Netherlands provinces by stages and establish in its place a centralized royal government directed from Madrid. A politically docile and religiously uniform country was the goal.

The merchant towns of the Netherlands were, however, Europe's most independent; many, like magnificent Antwerp, were also Calvinist strongholds. By tradition and habit the people of the Netherlands inclined far more toward variety and toleration than toward obeisant conformity and hierarchical order. Two members of the council of state formed a stubborn opposition to the Spanish overlords, who now sought to reimpose their traditional rule with a vengeance. They were the Count of Egmont (1522–1568) and William of Nassau, the Prince of Orange (1533–1584), known as

"the Silent" because of his extremely small circle of confidants.

Like other successful rulers in this period, William of Orange placed the Netherlands' political autonomy and well-being above religious creeds. He personally passed through successive Catholic, Lutheran, and Calvinist stages. In 1561 he married Anne of Saxony, the daughter of the Lutheran Elector Maurice and the granddaughter of the late Landgrave Philip of Hesse. He maintained his Catholic practices until 1567, when he turned Lutheran. After the Saint Bartholomew's Day Massacre (1572), Orange (as he was called) became an avowed Calvinist.

In 1561 Cardinal Granvelle proceeded with a planned ecclesiastical reorganization of the Netherlands. It was intended to tighten the control of the Catholic hierarchy over the country and to accelerate its consolidation as a Spanish ward. Orange and Egmont, organizing the Dutch nobility in opposition, succeeded in gaining Granvelle's removal from office in 1564. Aristocratic control of the country after Granvelle's departure, however, proved woefully inefficient. Popular unrest continued to grow, especially among urban artisans, who joined the congregations of radical Calvinist preachers in increasing numbers.

THE COMPROMISE The year 1564 also saw the first fusion of political and religious opposition to Margaret's government. This opposition resulted from Philip II's unwise insistence that the decrees of the Council of Trent be enforced throughout the Netherlands. William of Orange's younger brother, Louis of Nassau, who had been raised a Lutheran, led the opposition, and it received support from the Calvinist-inclined lesser nobility and townspeople. A

MAP 12-1 THE NETHERLANDS DURING THE REFORMATION *The northern and southern provinces of the Netherlands. The former, the United Provinces, were mostly Protestant in the second half of the sixteenth century, while the southern Spanish Netherlands made peace with Spain and remained largely Catholic.*

national covenant was drawn up called the *Compromise*, a solemn pledge to resist the decrees of Trent and the Inquisition. Grievances were loudly and persistently voiced. When Regent Margaret's government spurned the protesters as "beggars" in 1566, Calvinists rioted through the country. Louis called on French Huguenots and German Lutherans to send aid to the Netherlands, and a full-scale rebellion against the Spanish regency appeared imminent.

THE DUKE OF ALBA The rebellion failed to materialize, however, because the Netherlands' higher nobility would not support it. Their shock at Calvinist iconoclasm and anarchy was as great as their resentment of Granvelle's more subtle repression. Philip, determined to make an example of the Protestant rebels, dispatched the duke of Alba to suppress the revolt. His army of 10,000 journeyed northward from Milan in 1567 in a show of combined Spanish and papal might. A special tribunal, known to the Spanish as the Council of Troubles and among the Netherlanders as the Council of Blood, reigned over the land. The counts of Egmont and Horn and several thousand suspected heretics were publicly executed before Alba's reign of terror ended.

The Spanish levied new taxes, forcing the Netherlands to pay for the suppression of its own revolt. One of these taxes, the "tenth penny," a 10 percent sales tax, met such resistance from merchants and artisans that it remained uncollectible in some areas even after a reduction to 3 percent. Combined persecution and taxation sent tens of thousands fleeing from the Netherlands during Alba's cruel six-year rule. Alba came to be more hated than Granvelle or the radical Calvinists had ever been.

RESISTANCE AND UNIFICATION William of Orange was an exile in Germany during these turbulent years. He now emerged as the leader of a broad movement for the Netherlands' independence from Spain. The northern, Calvinist-inclined provinces of Holland, Zeeland, and Utrecht, of which Orange was the *stadholder*, or governor, became his base. As in France, political resistance in the Netherlands gained both organization and inspiration by merging with Calvinism.

The early victories of the resistance attest to the popular character of the revolt. A case in point is the capture of the port city of Brill by the "Sea Beggars." These men were an international group of anti-Spanish exiles and crimi-

The Milch Cow, *a sixteenth-century satirical painting depicting the Netherlands as a cow in whom all the great powers of Europe have an interest. Elizabeth of England is feeding her (England had long-standing commercial ties with Flanders); Philip II of Spain is attempting to ride her (Spain was trying to reassert its control over the entire area); William of Orange is trying to milk her (he was the leader of the anti-Spanish rebellion); and the king of France holds her tail (France hoped to profit from the rebellion at Spain's expense). [Rijksmuseum, Amsterdam]*

nals, among them many Englishmen. William of Orange did not hesitate to enlist their services. Their brazen piracy, however, had forced Queen Elizabeth to disassociate herself from them and to bar their ships from English ports. In 1572 the Beggars captured Brill and other seaports in Zeeland and Holland. Mixing with the native population, they quickly sparked rebellions against Alba in town after town and spread the resistance southward. In 1574 the people of Leiden heroically resisted a long Spanish siege. The Dutch opened the dikes and flooded their country to repulse the hated Spanish. The faltering Alba had by that time ceded power to Don Luis de Requesens, who replaced him as commander of Spanish forces in the Netherlands in November 1573.

THE PACIFICATION OF GHENT The greatest atrocity of the war came after Requesens's death in 1576. Spanish mercenaries, leaderless and unpaid, ran amok in Antwerp on November 4, 1576, leaving 7,000 people dead in the streets. The event came to be known as the Spanish Fury.

These atrocities accomplished in four short days what neither religion nor patriotism had previously been able to do. The ten largely Catholic southern provinces (what is roughly modern Belgium) now came together with the seven largely Protestant northern provinces (what is roughly the modern Netherlands) in unified opposition to Spain. This union, known as the Pacification of Ghent, was accomplished on November 8, 1576. It declared internal regional sovereignty in matters of religion, a key clause that permitted political cooperation among the signatories, who were not agreed over religion. It was a Netherlands version of the territorial settlement of religious differences brought about in the Holy Roman Empire in 1555 by the Peace of Augsburg. Four provinces initially held out, but they soon made the resistance unanimous by joining the all-embracing Union of Brussels in January 1577. For the next two years the Spanish faced a unified and determined Netherlands.

Don John, the victor over the Turks at Lepanto in 1571, had taken command of Spanish land forces in November 1576. He now experienced his first defeat. Confronted by unified Netherlands resistance, he signed the humiliat-

ing Perpetual Edict in February 1577. The treaty provided for the removal of all Spanish troops from the Netherlands within twenty days. This withdrawal of troops gave the country to William of Orange and effectively ended for the time being whatever plans Philip may have had for using the Netherlands as a staging area for an invasion of England.

THE UNION OF ARRAS AND THE UNION OF UTRECHT The Spanish, however, were nothing if not persistent. Don John and Alessandro Farnese of Parma, the regent Margaret's son, revived Spanish power in the southern provinces, where constant fear of Calvinist extremism had moved the leaders to break the Union of Brussels. In January 1579 the southern provinces formed the Union of Arras, and within five months they made peace with Spain. These provinces later served the cause of the Counter-Reformation. The northern provinces responded with the formation of the Union of Utrecht.

NETHERLANDS INDEPENDENCE Seizing what now appeared to be a last opportunity to break the back of Netherlands resistance, Philip II declared William of Orange an outlaw and placed a bounty of 25,000 crowns on his head. The act predictably stiffened the resistance of the northern provinces. In a famous defiant speech to the Estates General of Holland in December 1580, known as the *Apology,* Orange publicly denounced Philip as a heathen tyrant whom the Netherlands need no longer obey.

On July 22, 1581, the member provinces of the Union of Utrecht met in The Hague and formally declared Philip no longer their ruler. They turned instead to the French duke of Alençon, Catherine de Médicis's youngest son. The southern provinces had also earlier looked to him as a possible middle way between Spanish and Calvinist overlordship. All the northern provinces save Holland and Zeeland accepted Alençon as their "sovereign" (Holland and Zeeland distrusted him almost as much as they did Philip II), but with the understanding that he would be only a titular ruler. But Alençon, an ambitious failure, saw this as his one chance at greatness. When he rashly attempted to take actual control of the provinces in 1583, he was deposed and returned to France.

William of Orange Defies Spain

After having been declared an outlaw and facing possible assassination, William of Orange addressed the Netherlands' Assembly in 1581.

◆ *Is this a personal or a political statement? Is his offer to die if the Assembly wishes real or rhetorical?*

What could be more gratifying in this world . . . to one engaged in the great . . . task of securing liberty for a good people oppressed by evil men, than to be mortally hated by one's enemies . . . ? Such is the pleasure that the Spaniards and their adherents have prepared for me . . . by that infamous proscription by which they sought to ruin me. . . .

I am falsely accused of being an ingrate, infidel, heretic, and hypocrite, a new Judas and Cain, a disturber of the peace, a rebel, foreigner, enemy of the human race, a public pest of the Christian comonwealth, a traitor and a scoundrel; that I am [now] to be killed like a beast, with a reward for any assassin or poisoner who will undertake the job. . . .

My enemies object that I have "established liberty of conscience." I confess that the glow of fires in which so many poor Christians have been tormented [because of their religious beliefs] is not an agreeable sight to me, although it may rejoice the eyes of the duke of Alba and the Spaniards. . . . They denounce me as a hypocrite, which is absurd enough. . . . As their friend, I told them quite frankly that they were twisting a rope to hang themselves when they began the barbarous policy of persecution. . . . When later I became their opponent . . . in the interest of your freedom, I do not see what hypocrisy they could discover [in it] . . . unless they call it hypocrisy to . . . chase them out of the country and inflict upon them, without disguise, all the harm that the law of war permits. . . .

They say that the war can never come to an end so long as I am among you. Might it please God that my . . . exile, or even my death, should bring you a true deliverance from all the evils . . . which the Spaniards are preparing . . . ! how agreeable to me would be such a banishment? how sweet [such a] death! If, then, gentlemen, you believe that my exile, or even my death, may serve you, I am ready to obey your behests. Here is my head, over which no prince or monarch has authority save you. Dispose of it as you will for the safety and preservation of our commonwealth.

James Harvey Robinson, ed., Readings in European History, Vol. 2 *(Boston: Athenaeum, 1906), pp. 177–179.*

Spanish efforts to reconquer the Netherlands continued into the 1580s. William of Orange, assassinated in July 1584, was succeeded by his seventeen-year-old son, Maurice (1567–1625), who, with the assistance of England and France, continued Dutch resistance. Fortunately for the Netherlands, Philip II began now to meddle directly in French and English affairs. He signed a secret treaty with the Guises (the Treaty of Joinville in December 1584) and sent armies under Farnese into France in 1590. Hostilities with the English, who had openly aided the Dutch rebels, also increased. Gradually they built toward a climax in 1588, when Philip's great Armada was defeated in the English Channel.

These new fronts overextended Spain's resources, strengthening the Netherlands. Spanish preoccupation with France and England permitted the northern provinces to drive out all Spanish soldiers by 1593. In 1596 France and England formally recognized the independence of these provinces. Peace was not, however, concluded with Spain until 1609, when the Twelve

Years' Truce gave the northern provinces virtual independence. Full recognition came finally in the Peace of Westphalia in 1648.

England and Spain (1553–1603)

Mary I

Before Edward VI died in 1553, he agreed to a device to make Lady Jane Grey, the teenage daughter of a powerful Protestant nobleman and, more important, the granddaughter on her mother's side of Henry VIII's younger sister Mary, his successor in place of the Catholic Mary Tudor (r. 1553–1558). But popular support for the principle of hereditary monarchy was too strong to deprive Mary of her rightful rule. Popular uprisings in London and elsewhere led to Jane Grey's removal from the throne within days of her crowning, and she was eventually beheaded.

Once enthroned, Mary proceeded to act even beyond the worst fears of the Protestants. In 1554 she entered a highly unpopular political marriage with Prince Philip (later Philip II) of Spain, a symbol of militant Catholicism to English Protestants. At his direction she pursued a foreign policy that in 1558 cost England its last enclave on the Continent, Calais.

Mary's domestic measures were equally shocking to the English people and even more divisive. During her reign, Parliament repealed the Protestant statutes of Edward and reverted to the Catholic religious practice of her father, Henry VIII. The great Protestant leaders of the Edwardian Age—John Hooper, Hugh Latimer, and Thomas Cranmer—were executed for heresy. Hundreds of Protestants either joined them in martyrdom (282 were burned at the stake during Mary's reign) or took flight to the Continent. These "Marian exiles" settled in Germany and Switzerland, forming especially large communities in Frankfurt, Strasbourg, and Geneva. (John Knox, the future leader of the Reformation in Scotland, was prominent among them.) There they worshiped in their own congregations, wrote tracts justifying armed resistance, and waited for the time when a Protestant counteroffensive could be launched in their homelands. They were also exposed to religious beliefs more radical than any set forth during Edward VI's reign. Many of these exiles later held positions in the Church of England during Elizabeth I's reign.

Elizabeth I

Mary's successor was her half-sister, Elizabeth I (r. 1558–1603), the daughter of Henry VIII and Anne Boleyn. Elizabeth had remarkable and enduring successes in both domestic and foreign policy. Assisted by a shrewd adviser, Sir William Cecil (1520–1598), she built a true kingdom on the ruins of Mary's reign. Between 1559 and 1563, she and Cecil guided a religious settlement through Parlia-ment that prevented England from being torn asunder by religious differences in the sixteenth century, as the Continent was. Another ruler who subordinated

Elizabeth I (1558–1603) standing on a map of England in 1592. An astute politician in both foreign and domestic policy, Elizabeth was perhaps the most successful ruler of the sixteenth century. [National Portrait Gallery, London]

A Description of Mary Tudor

In 1557 the Venetian Ambassador reported to his government on the state of England, including a description of Mary I. At the time he wrote, she was receiving widespread criticism of her rule, particularly of her foreign policy, which the critics felt tied England too closely to the interests of Spain.

◆ *Does the gender of its subject color this description? Would a king be similarly described? What does the ambassador see as Mary's weaknesses and strengths?*

Queen Mary, the daughter of Henry VIII and of his queen Catherine, daughter of Ferdinand the Catholic, king of Aragon, is a princess of great worth. In her youth she was rendered unhappy by the event of her mother's divorce; by the ignominy and threats to which she was exposed after the change of religion in England, she being unwilling to unbend to the new one; and by the dangers to which she was exposed by the duke of Northumberland, and the riots among the people when she ascended the throne.

She is of short stature, well made, thin and delicate, and moderately pretty; her eyes are so lively that she inspires reverence and respect, and even fear, wherever she turns them; nevertheless she is very shortsighted. Her voice is deep, almost like that of a man. She understands five languages—English, Latin, French, Spanish, and Italian, in which last, however, she does not venture to converse. She is also much skilled in ladies' work, such as producing all sorts of embroidery with the needle. She has a knowledge of music, chiefly on the lute, on which she plays exceedingly well. As to the qualities of her mind, it may be said of her that she is rash, disdainful, and parsimonious rather than liberal. She is endowed with great humility and patience, but withal high-spirited, courageous, and resolute, having during the whole course of her adversity not been guilty of the least approach to meanness of deportment; she is, moreover, devout and staunch in the defense of her religion.

Some personal infirmities under which she labors are the causes to her of both public and private affliction; to remedy these recourse is had to frequent bloodletting, and this is the real cause of her paleness and the general weakness of her frame. These have also given rise to the unfounded rumor that the queen is in a state of pregnancy. The cabal she has been exposed to, the evil disposition of the people toward her, the present poverty and the debt of the crown, and her passion for King Philip, from whom she is doomed to live separate, are so many other causes of the grief with which she is overwhelmed. She is, moreover, a prey to the hatred she bears my Lady Elizabeth, and which has its source in the recollection of the wrongs she experienced on account of her mother, and in the fact that all eyes and hearts are turned towards my Lady Elizabeth as successor to the throne. . . .

James Harvey Robinson, ed., Readings in European History, Vol. 2 *(Boston: Athenaeum, 1906), pp. 149–150.*

religious to political unity, Elizabeth merged a centralized episcopal system, which she firmly controlled, with broadly defined Protestant doctrine and traditional Catholic ritual. In the resulting Anglican church inflexible religious extremes were not permitted.

In 1559 an Act of Supremacy passed Parliament repealing all the anti-Protestant legislation of Mary Tudor and asserting Elizabeth's right as "supreme governor" over both spiritual and temporal affairs. An Act of Uniformity in the same year mandated a revised version of the second *Book of Common Prayer* (1552) for every English parish. The issuance of the Thirty-Nine

Articles on Religion in 1563—which were a revision of Thomas Cranmer's original forty-two—made a moderate Protestantism the official religion within the Church of England.

CATHOLIC AND PROTESTANT EXTREMISTS

Elizabeth hoped to avoid both Catholic and Protestant extremism at the official level by pursuing a middle way. Her first archbishop of Canterbury, Matthew Parker (d. 1575), represented this ideal. But Elizabeth could not prevent the emergence of subversive Catholic and Protestant zealots. When she ascended the throne, Catholics were in the majority in England. The extremists among them, encouraged by the Jesuits, plotted against her. Catholic radicals were also encouraged and later directly assisted by the Spanish, who were piqued both by Elizabeth's Protestant sympathies and by her refusal to follow the example of her half-sister

An Unknown Contemporary Describes Queen Elizabeth

No sixteenth-century ruler governed more effectively than Elizabeth I of England (r. 1558–1603), who was both loved and feared by her subjects. An unknown contemporary has left the following description, revealing not only her intelligence and political cunning but also something of her immense vanity.

◆ *How does this description compare with that of Mary I? How do their personal qualities and political skills differ?*

I will proceed with the description of the queen's disposition and natural gifts of mind and body, wherein she either matched or exceeded all the princes of her time, as being of a great spirit yet tempered with moderation, in adversity never dejected, in prosperity rather joyful than proud; affable to her subjects, but always with due regard to the greatness of her estate, by reason whereof she was both loved and feared.

In her later time, when she showed herself in public, she was always magnificent in apparel; supposing haply thereby that the eyes of her people (being dazzled by the glittering aspect of her outward ornaments) would not so easily discern the marks of age and decay of natural beauty; and she came abroad the more seldom, to make her presence the more grateful and applauded by the multitude, to whom things rarely seen are in manner as new.

She suffered not, at any time, any suitor to depart discontented from her, and though ofttimes he obtained not that he desired, yet he held himself satisfied with her manner of speech, which gave hope of success in the second attempt. . . .

Latin, French, and Italian she could speak very elegantly, and she was able in all those languages to answer ambassadors on the sudden. . . . Of the Greek tongue she was also not altogether ignorant. She took pleasure in reading of the best and wisest histories, and some part of Tacitus's *Annals* she herself turned into English for her private exercise. She also translated Boethius's *On the Consolation of Philosophy* and a treatise of Plutarch, *On Curiosity*, with divers others. . . .

It is credibly reported that not long before her death, she had a great apprehension of her own age and declination by seeing her face (then lean and full of wrinkles) truly represented to her in a glass, which she a good while very earnestly beheld; perceiving thereby how often she had been abused by flatterers (whom she held in too great estimation) that had informed her the contrary.

James Harvey Robinson, ed., Readings in European History, Vol. 2 *(Boston: Athenaeum, 1906), pp. 191–193.*

Mary and take Philip II's hand in marriage. Elizabeth remained unmarried throughout her reign, using the possibility of a marriage alliance very much to her diplomatic advantage.

Catholic extremists hoped eventually to replace Elizabeth with Mary Stuart, Queen of Scots. Unlike Elizabeth, who had been declared illegitimate during the reign of her father, Mary Stuart had an unblemished claim to the throne by way of her grandmother Margaret, the sister of Henry VIII. Elizabeth acted swiftly against Catholic assassination plots and rarely let emotion override her political instincts. Despite proven cases of Catholic treason and even

Elizabeth I before Parliament. The artist shows the Queen small and in the background, and places Parliament prominently in the foreground, suggesting that England, despite the enormous power of the Queen, is a land where parliamentary government reigns supreme. [Folger Shakespeare Library]

attempted regicide, she executed fewer Catholics during her forty-five years on the throne than Mary Tudor had executed Protestants during her brief five-year reign. She showed little mercy, however, to separatists and others who threatened the unity of her rule.

Elizabeth dealt cautiously with the Puritans, who were Protestants working within the national church to "purify" it of every vestige of "popery" and to make its Protestant doctrine more precise. The Puritans had two special grievances: (1) the retention of Catholic ceremony and vestments within the Church of England, which made it appear to the casual observer that no Reformation had occurred, and (2) the continuation of the episcopal system of Church governance, which conceived of the English church theologically as the true successor to Rome, while placing it politically under the firm hand of the queen and her compliant archbishop.

Sixteenth-century Puritans were not separatists. They enjoyed wide popular support and were led by widely respected men like Thomas Cartwright (d. 1603). They worked through Parliament to create an alternative national church of semiautonomous congregations governed by representative presbyteries (hence, Presbyterians), following the model of Calvin and Geneva. Elizabeth dealt firmly but subtly with this group, conceding absolutely nothing that lessened the hierarchical unity of the Church of England and her control over it.

The more extreme Puritans wanted every congregation to be autonomous, a law unto itself, with neither higher episcopal nor presbyterian control. They came to be known as *Congregationalists*. Elizabeth and her second archbishop of Canterbury, John Whitgift (d. 1604), refused to tolerate this group, whose views on independence they found patently subversive. The Conventicle Act of 1593 gave such separatists the option of either conforming to the practices of the Church of England or facing exile or death.

DETERIORATION OF RELATIONS WITH SPAIN A series of events led inexorably to war between England and Spain, despite the sincerest desires on the part of both Philip II and Elizabeth to avoid a confrontation. In 1567 the Spanish duke of Alba marched his mighty army into the Netherlands, which was, from the English point of view, simply a convenient staging area for a Spanish invasion of England. Pope Pius V (r. 1566–1572), who favored a military conquest of Protestant England, "excommunicated" Elizabeth for heresy in 1570. This mischievous act only encouraged both internal resistance and international intrigue against the queen. Two years later, as already noted, the piratical Sea Beggars, many of whom were Englishmen, occupied the port city of Brill in the Netherlands and aroused the surrounding countryside against the Spanish.

Following Don John's demonstration of Spain's awesome seapower at the famous naval battle of Lepanto in 1571, England signed a mutual defense pact with France. Also in the 1570s, Elizabeth's famous seamen, John Hawkins (1532–1595) and Sir Francis Drake (1545?–1596), began to prey regularly on Spanish shipping in the Americas. Drake's circumnavigation of the globe between 1577 and 1580 was one in a series of dramatic demonstrations of English ascendancy on the high seas.

After the Saint Bartholomew's Day Massacre, Elizabeth was the only protector of Protestants in France and the Netherlands. In 1585 she signed the Treaty of Nonsuch, which provided English soldiers and cavalry to the Netherlands. Funds that had previously been funneled covertly to support Henry of Navarre's army in France now flowed openly.

MARY, QUEEN OF SCOTS These events made a tinderbox of English–Spanish relations. The spark that finally touched it off was Elizabeth's execution of Mary, Queen of Scots (1542–1587).

Mary Stuart was the daughter of King James V of Scotland and Mary of Guise and had resided in France from the time she was six years old. This thoroughly French and Catholic queen had returned to Scotland after the death of her husband, the French king Francis II, in 1561. There she found a successful, fervent Protestant Reformation that had won legal sanction the year before in the Treaty of Edinburgh (1560). As hereditary heir to the throne of Scotland, Mary remained queen by divine and human right. She was not intimidated by the Protestants who controlled her realm. She established an international French court culture, the gaiety and sophistication of which impressed many Protestant nobles, whose religion often made their lives exceedingly dour.

Mary was closely watched by the ever-vigilant Scottish reformer John Knox. He fumed publicly and always with effect against the queen's private Mass and Catholic practices, which Scottish law made a capital offense for everyone else. Knox won support in his role of watchdog from Elizabeth and Cecil. Elizabeth personally despised Knox and never forgave him for writing the *First Blast of the Trumpet Against the Terrible Regiment of Women,* a work aimed at provoking a revolt against Mary Tudor but published in the year of Elizabeth's ascent to the throne. Elizabeth and Cecil tolerated Knox because he served their foreign policy, never permitting Scotland to succumb to the young Mary and her French and Catholic ways.

In 1568 a public scandal forced Mary's abdication and flight to her cousin Elizabeth in England. Mary's reputed lover, the earl of Bothwell, was, with cause, suspected of having killed her legal husband, Lord Darnley. When a packed court acquitted Bothwell, he subsequently married Mary. The outraged reaction from Protestant nobles forced Mary to surrender the throne to her one-year-old son, who became James VI of Scotland (and, later, Elizabeth's successor as King James I of England). Because of Mary's clear claim to the English throne, she remained an international symbol of a possible Catholic England, and she was consumed by the desire to be queen of England. Her presence in England, where she resided under house arrest for nineteen years, was a constant discomfort to Elizabeth.

In 1583 Elizabeth's vigilant secretary, Sir Francis Walsingham, uncovered a plot against Elizabeth involving the Spanish ambassador Bernardino de Mendoza. After Mendoza's deportation in January 1584, popular antipathy toward Spain and support for Protestant resistance in France and the Netherlands became massive throughout England.

In 1586 Walsingham uncovered still another plot against Elizabeth, the so-called Babington plot (after Anthony Babington, who was caught seeking Spanish support for an attempt on the queen's life). This time he had uncontestable proof of Mary's complicity. Elizabeth believed that the execution of a sovereign, even a dethroned sovereign, weakened royalty everywhere. She was also aware of the outcry that Mary's execution would create throughout the Catholic world, and Elizabeth sincerely wanted peace with English Catholics. But she really had no choice in the matter and consented to Mary's execution on February 18, 1587. This event dashed all Catholic hopes for a bloodless reconversion of Protestant England. After the execution of the Catholic queen of Scotland, Pope Sixtus V (r. 1585–1590), who feared Spanish domination almost as much as he abhorred English Protestantism, could no longer withhold public support for a Spanish invasion of England. Philip II ordered his Armada to make ready.

THE ARMADA Spain's war preparations were interrupted in the spring of 1587 by Sir Francis Drake's successful shelling of the port city of Cadiz, an attack that inflicted heavy damage on Spanish ships and stores. After "singeing the beard of Spain's king," Drake raided the coast of Portugal, further incapacitating the Spanish. The success of these strikes forced the Spanish to postpone their planned invasion of England until the spring of 1588.

On May 30 of that year, a mighty fleet of 130 ships bearing 25,000 sailors and soldiers under the command of the duke of Medina-Sidonia set sail for England. In the end, however, the English won a stunning victory. The invasion barges that were to transport Spanish soldiers from the galleons onto English shores were prevented from leaving Calais and Dunkirk. The swifter English and Netherlands ships, helped by what came to be known as an "English wind," dispersed the waiting Spanish fleet, over one-third of which never returned to Spain.

The news of the Armada's defeat gave heart to Protestant resistance everywhere. Although Spain continued to win impressive victories in the 1590s, it never fully recovered from this defeat. Spanish soldiers faced unified and inspired French, English, and Dutch armies. By the time of Philip's death on September 13, 1598, his forces had been successfully rebuffed on all fronts. His seventeenth-century successors were all inferior leaders who never knew responsibilities equal to Philip's. Nor did Spain ever again know such imperial grandeur. The French soon dominated the Continent, while in the New World the Dutch and the English progressively whittled away Spain's once glorious overseas empire.

Elizabeth died on March 23, 1603, leaving behind her a strong nation poised to expand into a global empire.

The Thirty Years' War (1618–1648)

The Thirty Years' War in the Holy Roman Empire was the last and most destructive of the wars of religion. Religious and political differences had long set Catholics against Protestants

In 1588 Philip II sent a massive naval armada to invade England. The English, however, with the help of the weather and the Dutch, dispersed and destroyed the Spanish fleet. Spain never fully recovered from this defeat. [Art Resource, N.Y.]

The horror of the Thirty Year's War is captured in this painting by Jan Brueghel (1568–1625) and Sebastien Vranx (1573–1647). During the breaks in fighting, marauding armies ravaged the countryside, destroying villages and massacring the rural population. [Kunsthistorisches Museum, Vienna]

and Calvinists against Lutherans. What made the Thirty Years' War so devastating was the now-entrenched hatred of the various sides and their seeming determination to sacrifice all for their religious beliefs. As the conflicts multiplied, virtually every major European land, especially Lutheran Denmark and Sweden, became involved either directly or indirectly. When the hostilities ended in 1648, the peace terms shaped much of the map of northern Europe as we know it today.

Preconditions for War

FRAGMENTED GERMANY In the second half of the sixteenth century, Germany was an almost ungovernable land of about 360 autonomous political entities. There were independent secular principalities (duchies, landgraviates, and marches); ecclesiastical principalities (archbishoprics, bishoprics, and abbeys); numerous free cities; and castle regions dominated by knights. The Peace of Augsburg (1555) had given each a significant degree of sovereignty within its own borders. Each levied its own tolls and tariffs and coined its own money, practices that made land travel and trade between the various regions difficult, where not impossible. In addition, many of these little lands were filled with great power pretensions. Political decentralization and fragmentation characterized Germany as the seventeenth century opened; it

was not a unified nation like Spain, England, or even strife-filled France.

Because of its central location, Germany had always been Europe's highway for merchants and traders going north and south and east and west. During the Thirty Years' War it became its stomping ground. Europe's rulers pressed in on Germany both for reasons of trade and because some of them held lands or legal privileges within certain German principalities. German princes, in their turn, looked to import and export markets beyond German borders. They opposed any efforts to consolidate the Holy Roman Empire, lest their territorial rights, confirmed by the Peace of Augsburg, be overturned. German princes were not loath to turn to Catholic France or to the kings of Denmark and Sweden for allies against the Habsburg emperor. The princes perceived the emperor's dynastic connections with Spain, and the policies he generated as a result, to be against their territorial interests. Even the pope found political reasons for supporting Bourbon France against the menacing international kingdom of the Habsburgs.

After the Council of Trent, Protestants in the empire suspected the existence of an imperial and papal conspiracy to recreate the Catholic Europe of pre-Reformation times. The imperial diet, which was controlled by the German princes, demanded strict observance of the constitutional rights of Germans, as set forth in agreements with the emperor since the mid-fourteenth century. Consequently, it effectively countered every move by the emperor to impose his will in the empire. In the late sixteenth century, the emperor ruled only to the degree to which he was prepared to use force of arms against his subjects.

RELIGIOUS DIVISION Religious conflict accentuated the international and internal political divisions (see Map 12-2). During this period the population within the Holy Roman Empire was about equally divided between Catholics and Protestants, the latter having perhaps a slight numerical edge by 1600. The terms of the Peace of Augsburg had attempted to freeze the territorial holdings of the Lutherans and the Catholics. In the intervening years, however, the Lutherans had gained political control in some Catholic areas, as had the Catholics in a few previously Lutheran areas. Such territorial reversals, or the threat of them, only increased the suspicion and antipathy between the two sides.

The Lutherans had been far more successful in securing their rights to worship in Catholic lands than the Catholics had been in securing such rights in Lutheran lands. The Catholic rulers, who were in a weakened position after the Reformation, had no choice but to make concessions to Protestant communities within their territories. These communities remained a sore point. Also, the Catholics wanted strict enforcement of the "Ecclesiastical Reservation" of the Peace of Augsburg, which Protestants had made little effort to recognize. The Catholics demanded that all ecclesiastical princes, electors, archbishops, bishops, and abbots who had deserted the Catholic for the Protestant side be immediately deprived of their religious offices and positions and that their ecclesiastical principalities be promptly returned to Catholic control. The Lutherans, and especially the Calvinists in the Palatinate, ignored this stipulation at every opportunity.

There was religious strife in the empire not only between Protestants and Catholics but also between liberal and conservative Lutherans and between Lutherans and the growing numbers of Calvinists. The last half of the sixteenth century was a time of warring Protestant factions within German universities. In addition to the heightened religious strife, the challenge of the new scientific and material culture that was becoming ascendant in intellectual and political circles increased the anxiety of religious people of all persuasions.

CALVINISM AND THE PALATINATE As elsewhere in Europe, Calvinism was the political and religious leaven within the Holy Roman Empire on the eve of the Thirty Years' War. Calvinism was unrecognized as a legal religion by the Peace of Augsburg. It gained a strong foothold within the empire, however, when Frederick III (r. 1559–1576), a devout convert to Calvinism, became Elector Palatine (ruler within the Palatinate) and made it the official religion of his domain. Heidelberg became a German Geneva in the 1560s: both a great intellectual center of Calvinism and a staging area for Calvinist penetration into the empire. By 1609 Palatine Calvinists headed a Protestant defensive alliance that received outside support from Spain's sixteenth-century enemies: England, France, and the Netherlands.

The Lutherans came to fear the Calvinists almost as much as they did the Catholics. Palatine Calvinists seemed to the Lutherans directly to threaten the Peace of Augsburg—and hence the legal foundation of the Lutheran states—by their bold missionary forays into the empire. Also, outspoken Calvinist criticism of the doctrine of Christ's real presence in the Eucharist shocked the more religiously conservative Lutherans. The Elector Palatine once expressed his disbelief in transubstantiation by publicly shredding the host and mocking it as a "fine God." To Lutherans, such religious disrespect and aggressiveness disgraced the Reformation.

MAXIMILIAN OF BAVARIA AND THE CATHOLIC LEAGUE If the Calvinists were active within the Holy Roman Empire, so also were their Catholic counterparts, the Jesuits. Staunchly Catholic Bavaria, supported by Spain, became militarily and ideologically for the Counter-Reformation what the Palatinate was for Protestantism. From there, the Jesuits launched successful missions throughout the empire, winning such major cities as Strasbourg and Osnabrück back to the Catholic fold by 1600. In 1609 Maximilian, duke of Bavaria, organized a Catholic League to counter a new Protestant alliance that had been formed in the same year under the leadership of the Calvinist Elector

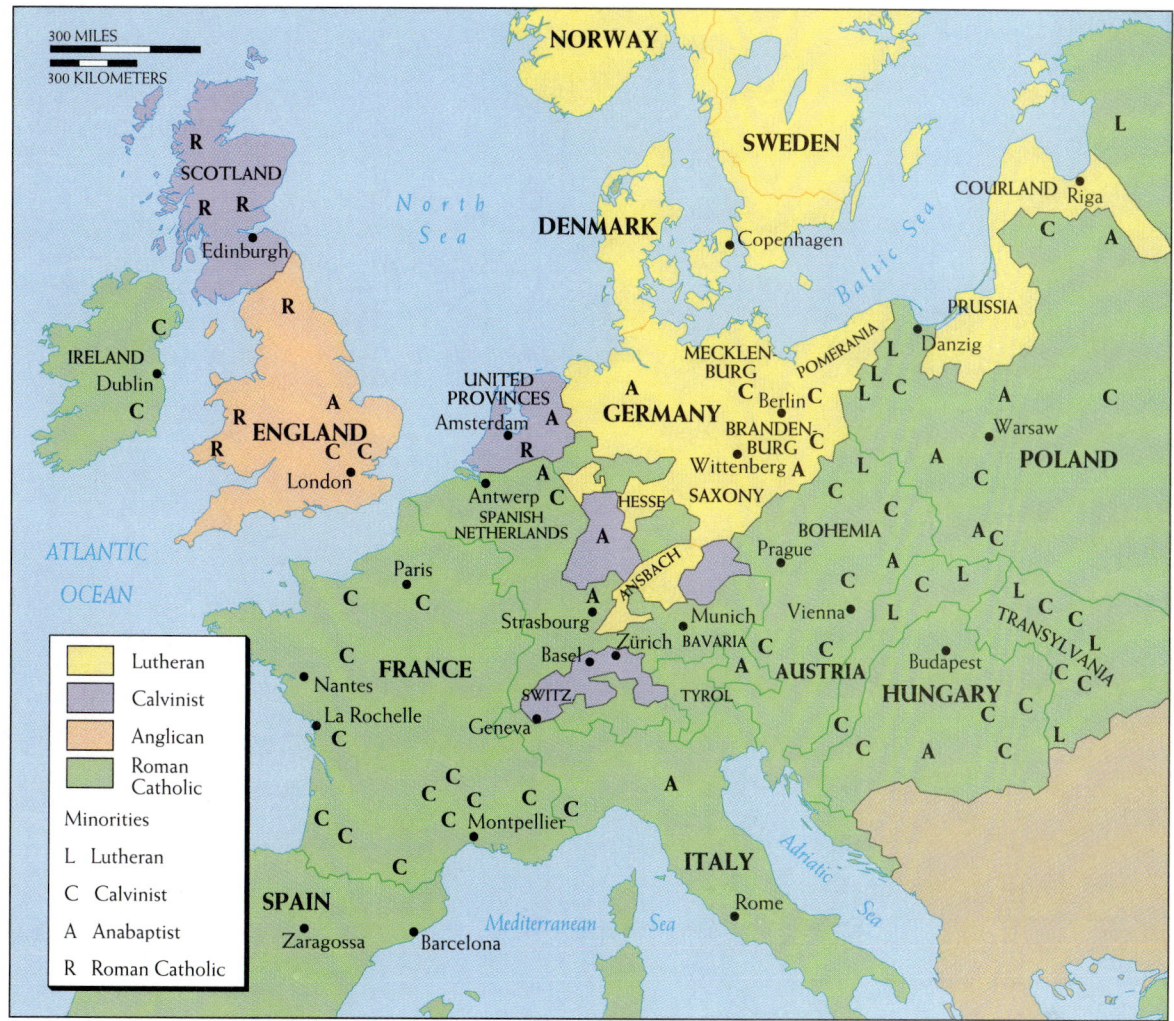

Palatine, Frederick IV (r. 1583–1610). When the league fielded a great army under the command of Count Johann von Tilly, the stage was set, both internally and internationally, for the worst of the religious wars, the Thirty Years' War (see Map 12-3).

Four Periods of War

The war went through four distinguishable periods. During its course it drew in every major western European nation—at least diplomatically and financially if not by direct military involvement. The four periods were the Bohemian (1618–1625); the Danish (1625–1629); the Swedish (1630–1635); and the Swedish–French (1635–1648).

THE BOHEMIAN PERIOD The war broke out in Bohemia after the ascent to the Bohemian throne in 1618 of the Habsburg Ferdinand, the archduke of Styria, who was also in the line of succession to the imperial throne. Educated by the Jesuits and a fervent Catholic, Ferdinand was determined to restore the traditional faith throughout Austria, Bohemia, and Poland—the eastern Habsburg lands.

MAP 12-3   THE HOLY ROMAN EMPIRE ABOUT 1618   *On the eve of the Thirty Years' War,*
the Holy Roman Empire was politically and religiously fragmented, as this somewhat sim-
plified map reveals. Lutherans dominated the north and Catholics the south, while
Calvinists controlled the United Provinces and the Palatinate and were important in
Switzerland and Brandenburg.

No sooner had Ferdinand become king of Bohemia than he revoked the religious freedoms of Bohemian Protestants. In force since 1575, these freedoms had even been recently broadened by Emperor Rudolf II (r. 1576–1612) in his Letter of Majesty in 1609. The Protestant nobil-

ity in Prague responded to Ferdinand's act in May 1618 by literally throwing his regents out the window. The event has ever since been known as the "defenestration of Prague." The three officials fell fifty feet into a dry moat that, fortunately, was padded with manure, which cushioned their fall and spared their lives. In the following year Ferdinand became Holy Roman Emperor as Ferdinand II, by the unanimous vote of the seven electors. The Bohemians, however, defiantly deposed him in Prague and declared the Calvinist Elector Palatine, Frederick V (r. 1616–1623), their overlord.

What had begun as a revolt of the Protestant nobility against an unpopular king of Bohemia thereafter escalated into an international war. Spain sent troops to Ferdinand, who found more immediate allies in Maximilian of Bavaria and the opportunistic Lutheran Elector John George I of Saxony (r. 1611–1656). John George saw a sure route to territorial gain by joining in an easy victory over the weaker Elector Palatine. This was not the only time politics and greed would overshadow religion during this long conflict, although Lutheran–Calvinist religious animosity also overrode a common Protestantism.

Ferdinand's army under Tilly routed Frederick V's troops at the Battle of White Mountain in 1620. By 1622 Ferdinand had managed not only to subdue and re-Catholicize Bohemia but to conquer the Palatinate as well. While he and his allies enjoyed the spoils of these victories, the fighting extended into northwestern Germany as the duke of Bavaria pressed the conflict. Laying claim to land as he went, he continued to pursue Ernst von Mansfeld, one of Frederick's surviving mercenary generals, into the north.

THE DANISH PERIOD The emperor's subjugation of Bohemia and the Palatinate and Maximilian's forays into northwestern Germany raised new fears that a reconquest and re-Catholicization of the whole empire now loomed. This was in fact precisely Ferdinand II's design. The Lutheran King Christian IV (r. 1588–1648) of Denmark, who already held territory within the empire as the duke of Holstein, was eager to extend Danish influence over the coastal towns of the North Sea. Encouraged by the English, the French, and the Dutch, he picked up the Protestant banner of resistance, opening the Danish period of the conflict (1625–1629). Christian's forces were not, however, up to the challenge. Entering Germany with his army in 1626, he was quickly humiliated by Maximilian and forced to retreat into Denmark.

As military success made Maximilian stronger and more difficult to control, Ferdinand II sought a more pliant tool for his policies by hiring a powerful, complex mercenary, Albrecht of Wallenstein (1583–1634). Wallenstein was another opportunistic Protestant who had gained a great deal of territory by joining Ferdinand during the conquest of Bohemia. A brilliant and ruthless military strategist, Wallenstein not only completed Maximilian's work by bringing the career of the elusive Ernst von Mansfeld to an end but also penetrated Denmark with an occupying army. By 1628 Wallenstein commanded a crack army of more than 100,000 and became a law unto himself within the empire, completely outside the emperor's control. Pandora's box had now been fully opened.

Wallenstein broke Protestant resistance so successfully that Ferdinand issued the Edict of Restitution in 1629. This proclamation dramatically reasserted the Catholic safeguards of the Peace of Augsburg (1555). It reaffirmed the illegality of Calvinism—a completely unrealistic move in 1629. It also ordered the return of all Church lands acquired by the Lutherans since 1552, an equally unrealistic mandate. Compliance would have involved the return of no less than sixteen bishoprics and twenty-eight cities and towns to Catholic allegiance. Although based on legal precedent and certainly within Ferdinand's power to command, the expectations of the edict were not adjusted to the political realities of 1629. It struck panic in the hearts of Protestants and Habsburg opponents everywhere, who now saw clearly the emperor's plan to recreate a Catholic Europe. Resistance quickly reignited.

THE SWEDISH PERIOD Gustavus Adolphus of Sweden (r. 1611–1632), a deeply pious king of a unified Lutheran nation, became the new leader of Protestant forces within the empire, opening the Swedish period of the war (1630–1635). He was handsomely bankrolled by two very interested bystanders: the French minister Cardinal Richelieu, whose foreign policy was to protect French interests by keeping Habsburg armies tied down in Germany, and the Dutch, who had not forgotten Spanish Habsburg domination in the sixteenth century. The Swedish king found ready allies in the electors of Brandenburg and Saxony and soon won a smashing victory at Breitenfeld in 1630. The Protestant victory at Breitenfeld so dramatically reversed the course of the war that it has been regarded as the most decisive, although far from the final, engagement of the long conflict.

One of the reasons for the overwhelming Swedish victory at Breitenfeld was the military genius of Gustavus Adolphus. The Swedish king brought a new mobility to warfare by having both his infantry and his cavalry employ fire and charge tactics. At six deep, his infantry squares were smaller than the traditional ones, and he filled them with equal numbers of musketeers and pikemen. His cavalry also alternated pistol shot with sword charges. His artillery was lighter and more mobile in battle. Each unit of his army—infantry, cavalry, and artillery—had *both* defensive and offensive capability and could quickly change from one to the other.

Gustavus Adolphus died at the hands of Wallenstein's forces during the Battle of Lützen (November 1632)—a very costly engagement for both sides that created a brief standstill. Ferdinand had long been resentful of Wallenstein's independence, although he was the major factor in imperial success. In 1634 Ferdinand had Wallenstein assassinated. By that time, Wallenstein had not only served his purpose for the emperor, but, ever opportunistic, he was even trying openly to strike bargains with the

Protestants for his services. The Wallenstein episode is a telling commentary on this war without honor. Despite the deep religious motivations, greed and political gain were the real forces at work in the Thirty Years' War. Even allies that owed one another their success were not above treating each other as mortal enemies.

In the Peace of Prague in 1635 the German Protestant states, led by Saxony, reached a compromise agreement with Ferdinand. The Swedes, however, received continued support from France and the Netherlands. Desiring to maximize their investment in the war, they refused to join the agreement. Their resistance to settlement plunged the war into its fourth and most devastating phase, the Swedish–French period (1635–1648).

THE SWEDISH–FRENCH PERIOD The French openly entered the war in 1635, sending men and munitions as well as financial subsidies. After their entrance the war dragged on for thirteen years, with French, Swedish, and Spanish soldiers looting the length and breadth of Germany—warring, it seemed, simply for the sake of warfare itself. The Germans, long weary of the devastation, were too disunited to repulse the foreign armies; they simply watched and suffered. By the time peace talks began in the Westphalian cities of Münster and Osnabrück in 1644, an estimated one-third of the German population had died as a direct result of the war.

A contemporary engraving portraying the assassination of the opportunistic mercenary Albrecht of Wallenstein. [Bildarchiv Preussischer Kulturbesitz]

It was the worst European catastrophe since the Black Death of the fourteenth century.

The Treaty of Westphalia

The Treaty of Westphalia in 1648 brought all hostilities within the Holy Roman Empire to an end (see Map 12-4). It rescinded Ferdinand's Edict of Restitution and firmly reasserted the major feature of the religious settlement of the Peace of Augsburg, as the ruler of each land was again permitted to determine the religion of his land. The treaty also gave the Calvinists their long-sought legal recognition. The independence of the Swiss Confederacy and the United Provinces of Holland, long recognized in fact, was now proclaimed in law. And the treaty elevated Bavaria to the rank of an elector state. The provisions of the treaty made the German princes supreme over their principalities. Yet, as guarantors of the treaty, Sweden and France found many occasions to meddle in German affairs until the century's end, France to considerable territorial gain. Brandenburg–Prussia emerged as the most powerful northern German state. Because the treaty broadened the legal status of Protestantism, the pope opposed it altogether, but he had no power to prevent it.

France and Spain remained at war outside the empire until 1659, when French victories forced on the Spanish the humiliating Treaty of the Pyrenees. Thereafter France became Europe's dominant power, and the once vast Habsburg kingdom waned.

By confirming the territorial sovereignty of Germany's many political entities, the Treaty of Westphalia perpetuated German division and political weakness into the modern period. Only two German states attained any international significance during the seventeenth century: Austria and Brandenburg–Prussia. The petty regionalism within the empire also reflected on a small scale the drift of larger European politics. In the seventeenth century, distinctive nation-states, each with its own political, cultural, and religious identity, reached maturity and firmly established the competitive nationalism of the modern world.

———————————— ◆ ————————————

Both religion and politics played major roles in each of the great conflicts of the Age of Religious Wars—the internal struggle in France, Spain's unsuccessful effort to subdue the Netherlands, England's successful resistance of Spain, and the steady march of virtually every major European power through the hapless empire during the first half of the seventeenth century. Parties and armies of different religious persuasions are visible in each conflict, and in each we also find a life-or-death political struggle.

The wars ended with the recognition of minority religious rights and a guarantee of the traditional boundaries of political sovereignty. In France, the Edict of Nantes (1598) brought peace by granting Huguenots basic religious and civil freedoms and by recognizing their towns and territories. Peace and sovereignty came to the Netherlands with the departure of the Spanish, guaranteed initially by the Twelve Years' Truce (1609) and secured fully by the Peace of Westphalia (1648). The conflict between England and Spain ended with the removal of the Spanish threat to English sovereignty in politics and religion, which resulted from the execution of Mary, Queen of Scots (1587), and the English victory over the Armada (1588). In the Holy Roman Empire, peace came with the reaffirmation of the political principle of the Peace of Augsburg (1555), as the Peace of Westphalia brought the Thirty Years' War to an end by again recognizing the sovereignty of rulers within their lands and their right to determine the religious beliefs of their subjects. Europe at mid-century had real, if brief, peace.

Review Questions

1. What part did politics play in the religious positions of the French leaders? How did the king (or his regent) decide which side to favor? What led to the infamous St. Bartholomew's Day Massacre, and what did it achieve?

2. How did Spain achieve a position of dominance in the sixteenth century? What were its strengths and weaknesses as a nation? What were Philip II's goals? Which was he unable to achieve and why?

3. Henry of Navarre (Henry IV of France), Elizabeth I, and William of Orange were all *politiques*. Define the term and explain why it applies to these three rulers.

MAP 12-4 EUROPE IN 1648 At the end of the Thirty Years' War, Spain still had extensive possessions. Austria and Brandenburg-Prussia were prominent, the independence of the

4. Discuss the background to the establishment of the Anglican church in England. What were the politics of Mary I? What was Elizabeth I's settlement, and how difficult was it to impose on all of England? Who were her detractors and what were their criticisms?

5. Why was the Thirty Years' War fought? To what extent did politics determine the outcome of the war? Discuss the Treaty of Westphalia in 1648. Could matters have been resolved without war?

6. "The Thirty Years' War is the outstanding example in European history of meaningless conflict." Evaluate this statement and provide specific reasons.

Suggested Readings

F. BRAUDEL, *The Mediterranean and the Mediterranean World in the Age of Philip the Second*, Vols. 1 and 2 (1976). Widely acclaimed work of a French master historian.

N. Z. DAVIS, *Society and Culture in Early Modern France* (1975). Essays on popular culture.

R. DUNN, *The Age of Religious Wars 1559–1689* (1979). Excellent brief survey of every major conflict.

J. H. ELLIOTT, *Europe Divided 1559–1598* (1968). Direct, lucid narrative account.

G. R. ELTON, *England Under the Tudors* (1955). Masterly account.

J. H. FRANKLIN (Ed. and Trans.), *Constitutionalism and Resistance in the Sixteenth Century: Three Treatises by Hotman, Beza, and Mornay* (1969). Three defenders of the right of people to resist tyranny.

P. GEYL, *The Revolt of the Netherlands, 1555–1609* (1958). The authoritative survey.

J. GUY, *Tudor England* (1990). The standard history and good synthesis of recent scholarship.

C. HAIGH, *Elizabeth I* (1988). Elizabeth portrayed as a magnificent politician and propagandist.

D. LOADES, *Mary Tudor* (1989). Authoritative and good story-telling.

J. LYNCH, *Spain Under the Habsburg I: 1516–1598* (1964). Political narrative.

W. MacCAFFREY, *Queen Elizabeth and the Making of Policy 1572-1588* (1985). Very good on the intricacy of Elizabethan religious policy.

G. MATTINGLY, *The Armada* (1959). A masterpiece and novel-like in style.

J. E. NEALE, *The Age of Catherine de Medici* (1962). Short, concise summary.

J. E. NEALE, *Queen Elizabeth I* (1934). Superb biography.

G. PARKER, *Philip II* (1978). Readable, admiring account.

G. PARKER, *Europe in Crisis, 1598–1648* (1979). The big picture at a gallop.

T. K. RABB (Ed.), *The Thirty Years' War* (1972). Excerpts from the scholarly debate over the war's significance.

J. G. RIDLEY, *John Knox* (1968). Large, detailed biography.

J. H. M. SALMON (Ed.), *The French Wars of Religion: How Important Were the Religious Factors?* (1967). Scholarly debate over the relation between politics and religion.

J. H. M. SALMON, *Society in Crisis: France in the Sixteenth Century* (1976). Standard narrative account.

A. SOMAN (Ed.), *The Massacre of St. Bartholomew's Day: Reappraisals and Documents* (1974). Results of an international symposium on the anniversary of the massacre.

K. THOMAS, *Religion and the Decline of Magic* (1971). Provocative, much acclaimed work focused on popular culture.

C. V. WEDGWOOD, *The Thirty Years' War* (1939). Extremely detailed account that downplays the war's achievements.

C. V. WEDGWOOD, *William the Silent* (1944). Excellent political biography of William of Orange.

J. WORMALD, *Mary, Queen of Scots: A Study in Failure* (1991). Mary portrayed as a queen who did not understand her country and was out of touch with the times.

Louis XIV of France (r. 1643–1715) was the dominant European monarch in the second half of the seventeenth century. The powerful centralized monarchy he created established the prototype for the mode of government later termed absolutism. *[Giraudon/Art Resource, N.Y.]*

13

Paths to Constitutionalism and Absolutism: England and France in the Seventeenth Century

---

Key Topics in This Chapter

◆ The factors behind the divergent political paths of England and France in the seventeenth century

◆ The conflict between Parliament and the king over taxation and religion in early Stuart England, the English Civil War, and the abolition of the monarchy

◆ The Restoration and the development of Parliament's supremacy over the monarchy after the "Glorious Revolution"

◆ The establishment of an absolutist monarchy in France under Louis XIV

◆ The wars of Louis XIV

During the seventeenth century England and France moved in two very different political directions. By the close of the century, after decades of fierce civil and religious conflict that *pitted Parliament and monarch against each other, England had developed into a parliamentary monarchy with a policy of religious toleration. Parliament, composed of the House of*

Lords and the House of Commons, shared responsibility for government with the monarch. It met regularly and the Commons, composed primarily of wealthy landed gentry, had to stand for election every three years. By contrast, France developed an absolutist, centralized form of government dominated by a monarchy that shared little power with any other national institutions. Its authority resided rather in a complex set of relationships with local nobility, guilds, and towns and in its ability to support the largest standing army in Europe. In the seventeenth century France also abandoned Henry IV's policy of religious toleration and proscribed all but the Roman Catholic church.

These English and French forms of government became models for other nations. The French model, termed absolutism *in the nineteenth century, would be imitated by other monarchies across the continent during the eighteenth century. The English model would later inspire the political creed known in the nineteenth century as* liberalism. *Like all such political terms, these labels, although useful, can conceal considerable complexity. English monarchs did not share all power with Parliament; they controlled the army, foreign policy, and much patronage. Likewise the absolute monarchs of France and their later imitators elsewhere in Europe were not truly absolute; laws, traditions, and many local institutions and customs limited their power.*

Two Models of European Political Development

In the second half of the sixteenth century, changes in military organization, weapons, and tactics sharply increased the cost of warfare. Because traditional sources of revenue were inadequate to finance these growing costs—as well as the costs of government—monarchs sought new ones. Only monarchies that succeeded in building a secure financial base that was not deeply dependent on the support of noble estates, diets, or assemblies achieved absolute rule. The French monarchy succeeded in this effort after mid-century, whereas the English monarchy failed. The paths to that success and failure led to the two models of government—absolutism in France and parliamentary

monarchy in England—that shaped subsequent political development in Europe.

In their pursuit of adequate income, English monarchs of the seventeenth century threatened the local political interests and economic well-being of the country's nobility and others of great landed and commercial wealth. These politically active groups, invoking traditional English liberties in their defense, effectively resisted the monarchs' attempted intrusions throughout the century.

The experience of Louis XIV, the French king, was different. During the second half of the seventeenth century, he would make the French nobility dependent upon his goodwill and patronage. In turn, he would support their local influence and their place in a firm social hierarchy. But even the French king's dominance of the nobility was not wholly complete. Louis accepted the authority of the noble-dominated *Parlement* of Paris to register royal decrees before they officially became law, and he permitted regional *parlements* to exercise considerable authority over local administration and taxation. Funds from taxes levied by the central monarchy found their way into many local pockets.

Religious factors also affected the political destinies of England and France. A strong Protestant religious movement known as Puritanism arose in England and actively opposed the Stuart monarchy. Puritanism represented a nonpolitical force that sought at first to limit and eventually to overturn the English monarchy. Louis XIV, in contrast, crushed the Protestant communities of France. He was generally supported in these efforts by Roman Catholics who saw religious uniformity enforced by the monarchy working to their advantage.

There were also major institutional differences between the two countries. In Parliament, England possessed a political institution that had long bargained with the monarch over political issues. In the early seventeenth century, to be sure, Parliament did not meet regularly and was not the strong institution it would become by the close of the century. Nor was there anything certain or inevitable about the transformation it underwent over the course of the century. The institutional basis for it, however, was in place. Parliament was there and expected to be consulted from time to time. Its members—

nobility and gentry—had experience organizing and speaking, writing legislation, and criticizing royal policies. Furthermore, the English had a legal and political tradition based on concepts of liberty to which members of Parliament and their supporters throughout the country could and did appeal in their conflict with the monarchy.

For all intents, France lacked a similarly strong tradition of broad liberties, representation, and bargaining between the monarchy and other national institutions. The Estates General had met from time to time to grant certain revenues to the monarch, but it played no role after the early seventeenth century. It met in 1614, but thereafter the monarchy was able to find other sources of income, and the Estates General was not called again until the eve of the French Revolution in 1789. Consequently, whatever political forces might have wished to oppose or limit the monarchy lacked both an institutional base from which to operate and a tradition of meetings during which the necessary political skills might have been developed.

Finally, personalities played an important role. During the first half of the century, France profited from the guidance of two of its most able statesmen, Cardinals Richelieu and Mazarin. Mazarin trained Louis XIV to be a hard-working, if not always wise, monarch. Louis drew strong and capable ministers about himself. The four Stuart monarchs of England, on the other hand, had trouble simply making people trust them. They did not always keep their word. They acted on whim. They often displayed faulty judgment. In a political situation that demanded compromise, they rarely offered any. They offended significant groups of their subjects unnecessarily. In a nation that saw itself as strongly Protestant, they were suspected, sometimes accurately, of Catholic sympathies. Many of Charles's opponents in Parliament, of course, had flaws of their own, but the nature of the situation focused attention and criticism on the king.

In both England and France, the nobility and large landowners stood at the top of the social hierarchy and sought to protect their privileges and local interests. Important segments of the British nobility and landed classes came to distrust the Stuart monarchs, whom they believed sought to undermine their local political control and social standing. Parliamentary government was the result of the efforts of these English landed classes to protect their concerns and limit the power of the monarchy to interfere with life on the local level. The French nobility under Louis XIV, in contrast, eventually concluded that the best way to secure their own interests was to support his monarchy. He provided them with many forms of patronage, and he protected their tax exemptions, their wealth, and their local social standing.

The divergent developments of England and France in the seventeenth century would have surprised most people in 1600. It was not inevitable that the English monarchy would have to govern through Parliament or that the French monarchy would avoid dealing with national political institutions that could significantly limit its authority. The Stuart kings of England certainly aspired to the autocracy Louis XIV achieved, and some English political philosophers eloquently defended the divine right of kings and absolute rule. At the beginning of the seventeenth century, the English monarchy was strong. Queen Elizabeth, after a reign of almost forty-five years, was much revered. Parliament met only when called to provide financial support to the monarch. France, on the other hand, was emerging from the turmoil of its religious wars. The strife of that conflict had torn the society asunder. The monarchy was relatively weak. Henry IV, who had become king in 1589, pursued a policy of religious toleration. The French nobles had significant military forces at their disposal and in the middle of the seventeenth century confronted the king with rebellion. These conditions would change dramatically in both nations by the late seventeenth century.

Constitutional Crisis and Settlement in Stuart England

James I

In 1603 James VI of Scotland (r. 1603–1625), the son of Mary Stuart, Queen of Scots, without opposition or incident succeeded the childless Elizabeth as James I of England. His was a difficult situation. The elderly queen had been very popular and was totally identified with the nation. James was not well known, would never be popular, and, as a Scot, was an outsider. He inherited not only the crown but also a large royal debt and a fiercely divided church—problems that his politically active subjects expected him to address. The new king strongly advocated the divine right of kings, a subject on which he had written a book—*A Trew Law of Free Monarchies*—in 1598. He expected to rule with a minimum of consultation beyond his own royal court.

James quickly managed to anger many of his new subjects, but he did not wholly alienate them. In this period Parliament met only when the monarch summoned it, which James hoped to do rarely. Its chief business was to grant certain sources of income. The real value of these revenues, however, had been falling during the past half century, limiting their importance and thus the importance of Parliament to the king. To meet his needs, James developed other sources of income, largely by levying—solely on the authority of ill-defined privileges claimed to be attached to the office of king—new custom duties known as *impositions*. These were a version of the older customs duties known as *tonnage and poundage*. Members of Parliament resented these independent efforts to raise revenues as an affront to their authority over the royal purse, but they did not seek a serious confrontation. Rather, throughout James's reign they wrangled and negotiated behind the scenes.

The religious problem also festered under James. Puritans within the Church of England had hoped that James's experience with the Scottish Presbyterian church and his own Protestant upbringing would incline him to favor their efforts to further the reformation of the English church. Since the days of Elizabeth, they had sought to eliminate elaborate religious ceremonies and replace the hierarchical episcopal system of Church governance with a more representative Presbyterian form like that of the Calvinist churches on the Continent.

In January 1604, the Puritans had their first direct dealing with the new king. James responded in that month to a statement of Puritan grievances, the so-called Millenary Petition, at a special religious conference at Hampton Court. The political implications of the demands in this petition concerned him, and their tone offended him. To the dismay of

This elegant painting portrays a very quiet London of the mid-1630s. During the next sixty years it would suffer wrenching political turmoil and the devastation of a great fire (depicted on page 490.) [Yale Center for British Art]

King James I Defends Popular Recreation Against the Puritans

The English Puritans believed in strict observance of the Sabbath, disapproving any sports, games, or general social conviviality on Sunday. James I thought these strictures prevented many Roman Catholics from joining the Church of England. In 1618 James ordered the clergy of the Church of England to read the Book of Sports from their pulpits. In this declaration, he permitted people to engage in certain sports and games after church services. His hope was to allow innocent recreations on Sunday while encouraging people to attend the Church of England. Despite the king's good intentions, the order offended the Puritans. The clergy resisted his order and he had to withdraw it.

✦ *What motives of state might have led James I to issue this declaration? How does he attempt to make it favorable to the Church of England? Why might so many clergy have refused to read this statement to their congregations?*

With our own ears we heard the general complaint of our people, that they were barred from all lawful recreation and exercise upon the Sunday's afternoon, after the ending of all divine service, which cannot but produce two evils: the one the hindering of the conversion of many [Roman Catholic subjects], whom their priests will take occasion hereby to vex, persuading them that no honest mirth or recreation is lawful or tolerable in our religion, which cannot but breed a great discontentment in our people's hearts, especially as such as are peradventure upon the point of turning [to the Church of England]: the other inconvenience is, that this prohibition barreth the common and meaner sort of people from using such exercises as may make their bodies more able for war, when we or our successors shall have occasion to use them; and in place thereof sets up filthy tipplings and drunkenness, and breeds a number of idle and discontented speeches in their ale-houses. For when shall the common people have leave to exercise, if not upon the Sundays and holy days, seeing they must apply their labor and win their living in all working days? . . .

[A]s for our good people's lawful recreation, our pleasure likewise is, that after the end of divine service our good people be not disturbed, . . . or discouraged from any lawful recreation, such as dancing, either men or women; archery for men, leaping, vaulting, or any other such harmless recreation, or from having of Hay-games, Whitsun-ales, and Morris-dances; and the setting up of May-poles and other sports therewith used; . . . but withal we do here account still as prohibited all unlawful games to be used upon Sundays only, as bear and bull-baitings . . . and at all times in the meaner sort of people by law prohibited, bowling.

And likewise we bar from this benefit and liberty all such known as recusants [Roman Catholics], either men or women, as will abstain from coming to church or divine service, being therefore unworthy of any lawful recreation after the said service, that will not first come to the church and serve God; prohibiting in like sort the said recreations to any that, though [they] conform in religion [i.e., members of the Church of England], are not present in the church at the service of God, before their going to the said recreations.

Henry Bettenson, ed., Documents of the Christian Church, 2nd ed. *(London: Oxford University Press, 1963), pp. 400–403.*

the Puritans, he firmly declared his intention to maintain and even enhance the Anglican episcopacy. "A Scottish presbytery," he snorted, "agreeth as well with monarchy as God and the devil. No bishops, no king." James was not simply being arbitrary. Elizabeth also had not accommodated the Puritan demands. To have done so would have created strife within the Church of England.

Both sides left the conference with their suspicions of one another largely confirmed. The Hampton Court conference did, however, sow one fruitful seed. A commission was appointed to render a new translation of the Bible. That mission was fulfilled in 1611 with the publication of the eloquent Authorized, or King James, Version.

James also offended the Puritans with his opposition to their narrow view of human life and social activities. The Puritans believed that Sunday should be a day taken up largely with religious observances and little leisure or recreation. James believed recreation and sports were innocent activities and good for his people. He also believed Puritan narrowness discouraged Roman Catholics from converting to the Church of England. Consequently, in 1618 he issued the *Book of Sports*, which permitted games on Sunday for people who attended Church of England services. The clergy refused to read his order from the pulpit, and he had to rescind it.

It was during James's reign that some religious dissenters began to leave England. In 1620 Puritan separatists founded Plymouth Colony in Cape Cod Bay in North America, preferring flight from England to Anglican conformity. Later in the 1620s, a larger, better financed group of Puritans left England to found the Massachusetts Bay Colony. In each case, the colonists believed that reformation had not gone far enough in England and that only in America could they worship freely and organize a truly reformed Church.

Although James inherited a difficult situation, he also created special problems for himself. His court became a center of scandal and corruption. He governed by favorites, the most influential of whom was the duke of Buckingham, whom rumor made the king's homosexual lover. Buckingham controlled royal patronage and openly sold peerages and titles to the highest bidders—a practice that angered the nobility because it cheapened their rank. There had always been court favorites, but never before had a single person so controlled access to the monarch.

James's foreign policy also roused opposition. He regarded himself as a peacemaker. Peace reduced pressures on royal revenues and the need for larger debts. The less his demands for money, the less the king had to depend on the goodwill of Parliament. In 1604 he concluded a much-needed peace with Spain, England's chief adversary during the second half of the sixteenth century. His subjects viewed this peace as a sign of pro-Catholic sentiment. James further increased suspicions when he tried unsuccessfully to relax the penal laws against Catholics. The English had not forgotten the brutal reign of Mary Tudor and the acts of treason by Catholics during Elizabeth's reign. In 1618 James hesitated, not unwisely, to rush English troops to the aid of Protestants in Germany at the outbreak of the Thirty Years' War. This hesitation caused some to question his loyalty to the Anglican church. These suspicions increased when he tried to arrange a marriage between his son Charles and the Spanish Infanta (the daughter of the king of Spain). In the king's last years, as his health failed and the reins of government passed increasingly to his son Charles and to Buckingham, parliamentary opposition and Protestant sentiment combined to undo his pro-Spanish foreign policy. In 1624, shortly before James's death, England entered a continental war against Spain largely in response to the pressures of members of Parliament.

Charles I

Parliament had favored the war with Spain but would not adequately finance it because its members distrusted Buckingham. Unable to gain adequate funds from Parliament, Charles I (r. 1625–1649), like his father, resorted to extraparliamentary measures. He levied new tariffs and duties and attempted to collect discontinued taxes. He even subjected the English people to a so-called *forced loan* (a tax theoretically to be repaid), imprisoning those who refused to pay. The government quartered troops in transit to war zones in private homes. All these actions

English Puritans Explain Their Emigration to America

Conditions in England during the reign of Charles I deteriorated so much that some English people chose to emigrate to Holland and New England. Writing in 1629, John Winthrop, a Suffolk gentleman who would become the governor of the Massachusetts Bay Colony, cited his reasons for going to America. He makes clear the religious and moral zeal that inspired the first settlers in New England.

◆ *How does Winthrop put the emigration of the Puritans into the pattern of biblical history? What are the signs of religious conviction that he sees in Europe and England? What steps, if any, might the English monarchy have taken to persuade such people to remain in England?*

1. It will be a service to the Church of great consequence to carry the gospel into those parts of the world, . . . and to raise a bulwark against the kingdom of Antichrist which the Jesuits labor to rear up in those parts.

2. All other churches of Europe are brought to desolation, and our sins, for which the Lord begins already to frown upon us and to cut us short, do threaten evil times to be coming upon us; and who knows but that God hath provided this place to be a refuge for many whom he means to save out of the general calamity, and seeing the Church hath no place left to fly into but the wilderness, what better work can there be than to go and provide tabernacles and food for her. . . .

3. This land [England] grows weary of her inhabitants, so as man, who is the most precious of all creatures, is here more vile and base than the earth we tread upon, and of less price among us than an horse or a sheep . . . and thus it is come to pass that children, servants, and neighbors, especially if they be poor, are counted the greatest burdens, which, if things were right, would be the chiefest earthly blessings.

4. The whole earth is the Lord's garden, and he hath given it to the sons of men with a general commission (Gen. i. 28) to increase and multiply, and replenish the earth and subdue it, which was again renewed to Noah; the end is double and natural, that man might enjoy the fruits of the earth and God might have his due glory from the creature. Why then should we stand here striving for places of habitation, etc. (many men spending as much labor and cost to recover or keep sometimes an acre or two of land as would procure them many, and as good or better, in another country), and in the meantime suffer a whole continent as fruitful and convenient for the use of man to lie waste without any improvement? . . .

. . . .

7. What can be a better work and more honorable and worthy a Christian than to help raise and support a particular church while it is in its infancy, and join his forces with such a company of faithful people as by a timely assistance may grow strong and prosper, and for want of it may be put to great hazard, if not wholly ruined?

James Harvey Robinson, ed., Readings in European History, Vol. 2 *(Boston: Athenaeum, 1906), pp. 225–226.*

Charles I ruled for several years without calling Parliament, but once he began a war with Scotland, he needed revenues that only Parliament could supply. [Photographique de la Réunion des Musées Nationaux]

intruded on life at the local level and challenged the power of the local nobles and landowners to control their districts.

When Parliament met in 1628, its members were furious. Taxes were being illegally collected for a war that was going badly for England and that now, through royal blundering, involved France as well as Spain. Parliament expressed its displeasure by making the king's request for new funds conditional on his recognition of the Petition of Right. This important declaration of constitutional freedom required that henceforth there should be no forced loans or taxation without the consent of Parliament, that no freeman should be imprisoned without due cause, and that troops should not be billeted in private homes. It was thus an expression of resentment

and resistance to the intrusion of the monarchy on the local level. Though Charles agreed to the petition, there was little confidence that he would keep his word.

YEARS OF PERSONAL RULE   In August 1628, Charles's chief minister, Buckingham, with whom Parliament had been in open dispute since 1626, was assassinated. His death, while sweet to many, did not resolve the hostility between the king and Parliament. In January 1629, Parliament further underscored its resolve to limit royal prerogative. It declared that religious innovations leading to "popery"—by this it meant Charles's high-church policies—and the levying of taxes without parliamentary consent were acts of treason. Perceiving that things were getting out of hand, Charles promptly dissolved Parliament and did not recall it again until 1640, when war with Scotland forced him to do so.

To conserve his limited resources, Charles made peace with France in 1629 and Spain in 1630. This policy again roused fears among some of his subjects that he was too friendly to Roman Catholic powers. The French and Roman Catholic background of Charles's wife furthered these suspicions. Part of her marriage contract permitted her to hear Mass daily at the English court. Charles's attitude toward the Church of England also raised suspicions. He supported a group within the Church, known as Arminians, who rejected many Puritan doctrines and favored elaborate, high-church practices. The Puritans were convinced these practices would bring a return to Roman Catholicism.

To allow Charles to rule without renegotiating financial arrangements with Parliament, his chief minister, Thomas Wentworth (after 1640, earl of Stafford), instituted a policy known as *thorough*. This policy imposed strict efficiency and administrative centralization in government. Its goal was absolute royal control of England. Its success depended on the king's ability to operate independently of Parliament, which no law required him to summon.

Charles's ministers exploited every legal fundraising device. They enforced previously neglected laws and extended existing taxes into new areas. For example, starting in 1634, they gradually extended inland to the whole of

England a tax called *ship money*, normally levied only on coastal areas to pay for naval protection. A great landowner named John Hampden mounted a legal challenge to the extension of this tax. Although the king prevailed in what was a close legal contest, his victory was costly. It deepened the animosity toward him among the powerful landowners, who would elect and sit in Parliament should he need to summon it.

During these years of personal rule, Charles surrounded himself with an elaborate court and patronized some of the greatest artists of the day. Like his father, he sold noble titles and knighthoods, lessening their value and the social exclusiveness conferred on those who already possessed them. Nobles and great landowners feared that the growth of the court, the king's relentless pursuit of revenue, and the inflation of titles and honors would reduce their local influence and social standing. They also feared that the monarch might actually succeed in governing without ever again calling Parliament into session.

Charles might very well have ruled indefinitely without Parliament had not his religious policies provoked war with Scotland. James I had allowed a wide variety of religious observances in England, Scotland, and Ireland. Charles by contrast hoped to impose religious conformity at least within England and Scotland. William Laud (1573–1645), who was first Charles's religious advisor and, after 1633, archbishop of Canterbury, held a high-church view of Anglicanism. He favored powerful bishops, elaborate liturgy, and personal religious observance and devotion rather than the preaching and listening favored by the Puritans. As a member of the Court of High Commission, Laud had already radicalized the English Puritans by denying them the right to publish and preach. In 1637 Charles and Laud, against the opposition of the English Puritans as well as the Scots, tried to impose on Scotland the English episcopal system and a prayerbook almost identical to the Anglican Book of Common Prayer.

The Scots rebelled, and Charles, with insufficient resources for a war, was forced to call Parliament. The members of Parliament opposed his policies almost as much as they

The religious policies of Archbishop Laud provoked strong Puritan opposition. He was executed in 1645. [Robert Harding Picture Library, London]

wanted to crush the rebellion. Led by John Pym (1584–1643), they refused even to consider funds for war until the king agreed to redress a long list of political and religious grievances. The king, in response, immediately dissolved Parliament—hence its name, the Short Parliament (April–May 1640). When the Presbyterian Scots invaded England and defeated an English army at the Battle of Newburn in the summer of 1640, Charles reconvened Parliament, this time on its terms, for a long and most fateful duration.

THE LONG PARLIAMENT The landowners and the merchant classes represented by Parliament had resented the king's financial measures and paternalistic rule for some time. The Puritans in Parliament resented his religious policies and deeply distrusted the influence of the Roman

Catholic queen. The Long Parliament (1640–1660) thus acted with widespread support and general unanimity when it convened in November 1640.

The House of Commons impeached both the earl of Stafford and Archbishop Laud. Disgraced and convicted by a parliamentary bill of attainder (a judgment of treason entailing loss of civil rights), Stafford was executed in 1641. Laud was imprisoned and also later executed (1645). Parliament abolished the Court of Star Chamber and the Court of High Commission, royal instruments of political and religious *thorough,* respectively. The levying of new taxes without consent of Parliament and the inland extension of ship money now became illegal. Finally, Parliament resolved that no more than three years should elapse between its meetings and that it could not be dissolved without its own consent. Parliament was determined that neither Charles nor any future English king could again govern without consulting it.

Despite its cohesion on these initial actions, Parliament was divided over the precise direction to take on religious reform. Both moderate Puritans (the Presbyterians) and more extreme Puritans (the Independents) wanted the complete abolition of the episcopal system and the Book of Common Prayer. The majority Presbyterians sought to reshape England religiously along Calvinist lines, with local congregations subject to higher representative governing bodies (presbyteries). Independents wanted a much more fully decentralized Church with every congregation as its own final authority. Finally, many conservatives in both houses of Parliament were determined to preserve the English church in its current form. Their numbers fell dramatically after 1642, however, when many of them left the House of Commons with the outbreak of civil war.

These divisions further intensified in October 1641, when a rebellion erupted in Ireland and Parliament was asked to raise funds for an army to suppress it. Pym and his followers, loudly reminding the House of Commons of the king's past behavior, argued that Charles could not be trusted with an army and that Parliament should become the commander-in-chief of English armed forces. Parliamentary conservatives, on the other hand, were appalled by such a bold departure from tradition.

ERUPTION OF CIVIL WAR Charles saw the division within Parliament as a chance to reassert his power. On December 1, 1641, Parliament presented him with the "Grand Remonstrance," a more-than-200-article summary of popular and parliamentary grievances against the crown. In January 1642, he invaded Parliament with his soldiers. He intended to arrest Pym and the other leaders, but they had been forewarned and managed to escape. The king then withdrew from London and began to raise an army. Shocked by his action, a majority of the House of Commons passed the Militia Ordinance, which gave Parliament authority to raise an army of its own. The die was now cast. For the next four years (1642–1646), civil war engulfed England.

Charles assembled his forces at Nottingham, and the war began in August. It was fought over two main issues:

- Would an absolute monarchy or a parliamentary government rule England?
- Would English religion be controlled by the king's bishops and conform to high Anglican practice or adopt a decentralized, Presbyterian system of church governance?

Charles's supporters, known as Cavaliers, were located in the northwestern half of England. The parliamentary opposition, known as Roundheads because of their close-cropped hair, had its stronghold in the southeastern half of the country. Supporters of both sides included nobility, gentry, and townspeople. The chief factor distinguishing them was religion; the Puritans tended to favor Parliament.

Oliver Cromwell and the Puritan Republic

Two factors led finally to Parliament's victory. The first was an alliance with Scotland consummated in 1643 when John Pym persuaded Parliament to accept the terms of the Solemn League and Covenant. This agreement committed Parliament, with the Scots, to a Presbyterian system of Church government. This policy meant for the Scots that they would never again be confronted with an attempt to impose the English prayerbook on their religious services. The second factor was the reorganization of the parliamentary army under Oliver Cromwell (1599–1658), a middle-aged country squire of iron discipline and strong Independent religious sentiment. Cromwell and his "godly men" favored neither the episcopal system of the king nor the pure Presbyterian system of the Solemn League and Covenant. They were willing to tolerate an established majority Church, but only if it also permitted Protestant dissenters to worship outside it.

The allies won the Battle of Marston Moor in 1644, the largest engagement of the war. In June

Oliver Cromwell's New Model Army defeated the royalists in the English Civil War. After the execution of Charles I in 1649, Cromwell dominated the short-lived English republic, conquered Ireland and Scotland, and ruled as Lord Protector from 1653 until his death in 1658. [Historical Pictures/Stock Montage, Inc.]

The English Civil War 1642-1646

- Controlled by the Parliamentarians, Beginning of 1645.
- Controlled by the Royalists, Beginning of 1645.
- Conquered by the Parliamentarians, in 1645.
- ✸ Battle Site

MAP 13-1 THE ENGLISH CIVIL WAR *This map shows the rapid deterioration of the Royalist position in 1645.*

1645, Cromwell's newly reorganized forces, known as the New Model Army, fighting with disciplined fanaticism, won a decisive victory over the king at Naseby (see Map 13-1).

Defeated militarily, Charles tried again to take advantage of divisions within Parliament, this time seeking to win the Presbyterians and the Scots over to the royalist side. But Cromwell and his army firmly foiled him. In December 1648, Colonel Thomas Pride physically barred the Presbyterians, who made up a majority of Parliament, from taking their seats. After "Pride's Purge," only a "rump" of fewer than fifty members remained. Though small in numbers, this Independent Rump Parliament did not

The Rump Parliament Abolishes Kingship

On January 30, 1649, Charles I was executed. Approximately six weeks later, on March 17, the Rump Parliament passed an act, quoted here, that abolished the monarchy in England, paving the war for England to become a republic. Both the execution of the king and the establishment of a republic amazed most European observers. Compare this document to Bishop Bossuet's defense of the divine right of kings that appears later in this chapter.

◆ *What are the offenses of Charles I to which this document points? By what authority does Parliament claim the power to abolish the monarchy? What objections might a supporter of the monarchy have raised in to these claims? What provisions does Parliament make for its own succession?*

And whereas it is and hath been found by experience, that the office of a King in this nation and Ireland, and to have the power thereof in any single person, is unnecessary, burdensome, and dangerous to the liberty, safety, and public interest of the people, and that for the most part, use hath been made of the regal power and prerogative to oppress and impoverish and enslave the subject; and that usually and naturally any one person in such power makes it his interest to incroach upon the just freedom and liberty of the people, and to promote the setting up of their own will and power above the laws, that so they might enslave these kingdoms to their own lust; be it therefore enacted and ordained by this present Parliament, and by authority of the same, that the office of a King in this nation shall not henceforth reside in or be exercised by any one single person; and that no one person whatsoever shall or may have, or hold the office, style, dignity, power, or authority of King of the said kingdoms and dominions, or any of them, or of the Prince of Wales, any law, statute, usuage, or custom to the contrary thereof in any wise notwithstanding. . . .

And whereas by the abolition of the kingly office provided for in this Act, a most happy way is made for this nation (if God see it good) to return to its just and ancient right, of being governed by its own representatives or national meetings in council, from time to time chosen and entrusted for that purpose by the people, it is therefore resolved and declared by the Commons assembled in Parliament that they will put a period to the sitting of this present Parliament, and dissolve the same so soon as may possibly stand with the safety of the people that hath betrusted them, and with what is absolutely necessary for the preserving and upholding the Government now settled in the way of a Commonwealth: and that they will carefully provide for the certain choosing, meeting, and sitting of the next and future representatives, with such other circumstances of freedom in choice and equality in distribution of members to be elected thereunto, as shall most conduce to the lasting freedom and good of this Commonwealth.

S. R. Gardiner, Constitutional Documents of the Puritan Revolution *(Oxford: The Clarendon Press, 1906), pp. 384–386.*

hesitate to use its power. On January 30, 1649, after a trial by a special court, the Rump Parliament executed Charles as a public criminal and thereafter abolished the monarchy, the House of Lords, and the Anglican church. What had begun as a civil war had at this point become a revolution.

From 1649 to 1660, England became officially a Puritan republic, although for much of that time it was dominated by Cromwell. During this period, Cromwell's army conquered Ireland and Scotland, creating the single political entity of Great Britain. Cromwell, however, was a military man and no politician. He was increasingly frustrated by what seemed to him to be pettiness and dawdling on the part of Parliament. When in 1653 the House of Commons entertained a motion to disband his expensive army of 50,000, Cromwell responded by marching in and disbanding Parliament. He ruled thereafter as Lord Protector.

This military dictatorship, however, proved no more effective than Charles's rule had been and became just as harsh and hated. Cromwell's great army and foreign adventures inflated his budget to three times that of Charles. Near chaos reigned in many places, and commerce suffered throughout England. Cromwell was as intolerant of Anglicans as Charles had been of Puritans. People deeply resented his Puritan prohibitions of drunkenness, theatergoing, and dancing. Political liberty vanished in the name of religious liberty.

Cromwell's challenge had been to devise a political structure to replace that of monarch and Parliament. He tried various arrangements, none of which worked. He quarreled with the various Parliaments elected while he was Lord Protector. By the time of his death in 1658, most of the English were ready to end the Puritan religious experiment and the republican political experiment and return to their traditional institutions of government. Negotiations between leaders of the army and the exiled Charles II (r. 1660–1685), son of Charles I, led to the restoration of the Stuart monarchy in 1660.

Charles II and the Restoration of the Monarchy

Charles II returned to England amid great rejoicing. A man of considerable charm and political skill, Charles set a refreshing new tone after eleven years of somber Puritanism. His restoration returned England to the status quo of 1642, with a hereditary monarch once again on the throne, no legal requirement that he summon Parliament regularly, and the Anglican church, with its bishops and prayerbook, supreme in religion.

Charles II (r. 1660–1685) was a person of considerable charm and political skill. Here he is portrayed as the founder of the Royal Society. [Robert Harding Picture Library, London]

The king, however, had secret Catholic sympathies and favored a policy of religious toleration. He wanted to allow all those outside the Church of England, Catholics as well as Puritans, to worship freely so long as they remained loyal to the throne. But in Parliament, even the ultraroyalist Anglicans did not believe patriotism and religion could be separated. Between 1661 and 1665, through a series of laws known as the Clarendon Code, Parliament excluded Roman Catholics, Presbyterians, and Independents from the religious and political life of the nation. These laws imposed penalties for attending non-Anglican worship services, required strict adherence to the Book of Common Prayer and the Thirty-Nine Articles, and demanded oaths of allegiance to the Church of England from all persons serving in local government.

The Great Fire of London of 1666 destroyed much of the city. It was rebuilt under the architectural guidance of Sir Christopher Wren. [Yale Center for British Art, Paul Mellon Collection]

At the time of the Restoration, England adopted Navigation Acts that required all imports to be carried either in English ships or in ships registered to the country from which the cargo originated. Dutch ships carried cargo from many nations, and such laws struck directly at Dutch dominance in the shipping industry. A series of naval wars between England and Holland ensued. Charles also attempted to tighten his grasp on the rich English colonies in North America and the Caribbean, many of which had been settled and developed by separatists who desired independence from English rule.

Although Parliament strongly supported the monarchy, Charles, following the pattern of his predecessors, required greater revenues than Parliament appropriated. These he obtained in

part by increased customs duties. Because England and France were both at war with Holland, he also received aid from France. In 1670 England and France formally allied against the Dutch in the Treaty of Dover. In a secret portion of this treaty, Charles pledged to announce his conversion to Catholicism as soon as conditions in England permitted. In return for this announcement (which was never made), Louis XIV of France promised to pay a substantial subsidy to England.

In an attempt to unite the English people behind the war with Holland, and as a sign of good faith to Louis XIV, Charles issued a Declaration of Indulgence in 1672. This document suspended all laws against Roman Catholics and Protestant nonconformists. But again, the conservative Parliament proved less generous than the king and refused to grant money for the war until Charles rescinded the measure. After he did, Parliament passed the Test Act, which required all officials of the crown, civil and military, to swear an oath against the doctrine of transubstantiation—a requirement that no loyal Roman Catholic could honestly meet.

Parliament had aimed the Test Act largely at the king's brother, James, duke of York, heir to the throne and a recent, devout convert to Catholicism. In 1678 a notorious liar named Titus Oates swore before a magistrate that Charles's Catholic wife, through her physician, was plotting with Jesuits and Irishmen to kill the king so James could assume the throne. The matter was taken before Parliament, where Oates was believed. In the ensuing hysteria, known as the Popish Plot, several people were tried and executed. Riding the crest of anti-Catholic sentiment and led by the earl of Shaftesbury (1621–1683), opposition members of Parliament, called Whigs, made an impressive but unsuccessful effort to enact a bill excluding James from succession to the throne.

More suspicious than ever of Parliament, Charles II turned again to increased customs duties and the assistance of Louis XIV for extra income. By these means he was able to rule from 1681 to 1685 without recalling Parliament. In these years, Charles suppressed much of his opposition. He drove the earl of Shaftesbury into exile, executed several Whig leaders for treason, and bullied local corporations into electing members of Parliament submissive to the royal will. When Charles died in 1685 (after a deathbed conversion to Catholicism), he left James the prospect of a Parliament filled with royal friends.

James II and Renewed Fears of a Catholic England

James II (r. 1685–1688) did not know how to make the most of a good thing. He alienated Parliament by insisting on the repeal of the Test Act. When Parliament balked, he dissolved it and proceeded openly to appoint known Catholics to high positions in both his court and the army. In 1687 he issued a Declaration of Indulgence, which suspended all religious tests and permitted free worship. Local candidates for Parliament who opposed the declaration were removed from their offices by the king's soldiers and were replaced by Catholics. In June 1688, James went so far as to imprison seven Anglican bishops who had refused to publicize his suspension of laws against Catholics.

Parliament Passes the Test Act

In 1672 Parliament enacted the Test Act, designed to prevent Roman Catholics from holding any significant political position in England. The act was directed against the effort of Charles II to pursue a more tolerant policy and to give notice to his brother, James, duke of York, who had recently converted to Catholicism, that he could not bring Roman Catholics into the government. This law remained in effect until 1828.

✦ *What would prevent devout Roman Catholics from taking this oath? Why did Parliament wish to keep Roman Catholics from office? What were the pressures on Charles II to admit them to office? What does this Act tell you about the general political and religious climate in England during the years of the Restoration?*

For preventing dangers which may happen from popish recusants, and quieting the minds of his majesty's good subjects, be it enacted . . . that all and every person or persons, as well peers as commoners, that shall bear any office or offices, civil or military, or shall receive any pay, salary, fee, or wages by reason of any patent or grant from his majesty, or shall have command or place of trust from or under his majesty, or from any of his majesty's predecessors, or by his or their authority, or by authority derived from him or them . . . or shall be of the household or in the service or employment of his majesty, or of his royal highness the Duke of York . . . take the several oaths of supremacy and allegiance . . . by law established; . . . and the said respective officers aforesaid shall also receive the sacrament of the Lord's Supper, according to the usage of the Church of England. . . .

And be it further enacted by the authority aforesaid, that at the same time when the person concerned in this Act shall take the aforesaid oaths of supremacy and allegiance, they shall likewise make and subscribe this declaration following, under the same penalties and forfeitures as by this Act is appointed:

"I, A. B., do declare that I do believe that there is not any transubstantiation in the Sacrament of the Lord's Supper, or in the elements of bread and wine, at or after the consecration thereof by any person whatsoever."

Of which subscription there shall be the like register kept, as of the taking oaths aforesaid.

Henry Bettenson, ed., Documents of the Christian Church (London: Oxford University Press, 1963), pp. 418–420.

Each of these actions represented a direct royal attack on the local power and authority of nobles, landowners, the Church, and other corporate bodies whose members believed they possessed particular legal privileges. James was attacking English liberty and challenging all manner of social privileges and influence.

Under the guise of a policy of enlightened toleration, James was actually seeking to subject all English institutions to the power of the monarchy. His goal was absolutism, and even conservative, loyalist Tories, as the royal supporters were called, could not abide this policy. The English feared, with reason, that James planned to imitate the religious intolerance of Louis XIV. In 1685 Louis had revoked the Edict of Nantes (which had protected French Protestants for almost a century) and imposed Catholicism on the entire nation, using his dragoons against those who protested or resisted.

James soon faced united opposition. When his Catholic second wife gave birth to a son and Catholic male heir to the throne on June 20, 1688, opposition turned to action. The English had hoped that James would die without a male heir so the throne would pass to Mary, his Protestant eldest daughter. Mary was the wife of William III of Orange, stadtholder of the Netherlands, great-grandson of William the Silent, and the leader of European opposition to Louis XIV's imperial designs. Within days of the birth of James's son, Whig and Tory members of Parliament formed a coalition and invited Orange to invade England to preserve "traditional liberties," that is, the Anglican church and parliamentary government.

The "Glorious Revolution"

William of Orange arrived with his army in November 1688 and was received without opposition by the English people. In the face of sure defeat, James fled to France and the protection of Louis XIV. With James gone, Parliament declared the throne vacant and on its own authority in 1689 proclaimed William and Mary the new monarchs, completing the successful bloodless "Glorious Revolution." William and Mary, in turn, recognized a Bill of Rights that limited the powers of the monarchy and guaranteed the civil liberties of the English privileged classes. Henceforth, England's monarchs would be subject to law and would rule by the consent

William and Mary became the monarchs of England in 1689. Their accession brought England's economic and military resources into the balance against the France of Louis XIV. [Robert Harding Picture Library, London]

of Parliament, which was to be called into session every three years. The Bill of Rights also pointedly prohibited Roman Catholics from occupying the English throne. The Toleration Act of 1689 permitted worship by all Protestants and outlawed Roman Catholics and anti-Trinitarians (those who denied the Christian doctrine of the Trinity).

The measure closing this century of strife was the Act of Settlement in 1701. This bill provided for the English crown to go to the Protestant House of Hanover in Germany if none of the children of Queen Anne (r. 1702–1714), the second daughter of James II and the last of the Stuart monarchs, was alive at her death. She outlived all of her children, and so in 1714, the Elector of Hanover became King George I of England, the third foreign monarch to occupy the English throne in just over a century.

The "Glorious Revolution" of 1688 established a framework of government by and for the governed that seemed to bear out the arguments of John Locke's *Second Treatise of Government* (1690). In this work, Locke described the relationship of a king and his people as a bilateral contract. If the king broke that contract, the people, by whom Locke meant the privileged and powerful, had the right to depose him. Locke had written the essay before the revolution, but it came to be read as a justification for it. Although neither in fact nor in theory a "popular" revolution such as would occur in America and France a hundred years later, the Glorious Revolution did establish in England a permanent check on monarchical power by the classes represented in Parliament. At the same time, as will be seen in Chapter 15, in its wake

England in the Seventeenth Century	
1603	James VI of Scotland becomes James I of England
1604	Hampton Court Conference
1611	Publication of the Authorized, or King James, Version of the English Bible
1625	Charles I becomes English monarch
1628	Petition of Right
1629	Charles I dissolves Parliament and embarks on eleven years of personal rule
1640	April–May, Short Parliament November, Long Parliament convenes
1641	Great Remonstrance
1642	Outbreak of the Civil War
1645	Charles I defeated at Naseby
1648	Pride's Purge
1649	Charles I executed
1649–1660	Various attempts at a Puritan Commonwealth
1660	Charles II restored to the English throne
1670	Secret Treaty of Dover between France and England
1672	Parliament passes the Test Act
1678	Popish Plot
1685	James II becomes king of England
1688	Glorious Revolution
1689	William and Mary come to the throne of England
1701	Act of Settlement provides for Hanoverian succession
1702–1715	Reign of Queen Anne, the last of the Stuarts

the English government had achieved a secure financial base that would allow it to pursue a century of warfare.

Rise of Absolute Monarchy in France

Seventeenth-century France, in contrast to England, saw both discontent among the nobility and religious pluralism smothered by the absolute monarchy and the closed Catholic state of Louis XIV (r. 1643–1715). An aggressive ruler who sought glory (*la gloire*) in foreign wars, Louis XIV subjected his subjects at home to "one king, one law, one faith."

Historians once portrayed Louis XIV's reign as a time when the rising central monarchy exerted far-reaching, direct control of the nation at all levels. A somewhat different picture is now emerging. Louis's predecessors and their chief ministers in the half century before his reign had already tried to impose direct rule, arousing discontent and, at mid-century, a rebellion among the nobility. Louis's genius was to make the monarchy the most important and powerful political institution in France while also assuring the nobles and other wealthy groups of their social standing and political and social influence on the local level. Rather than destroying existing local social and political institutions, Louis largely worked through them. Once nobles understood the king would support their local authority, they supported his central royal authority. In other words, the king and the nobles came to recognize that they needed each other. Nevertheless, Louis made it clear to all concerned that he was the senior partner in the relationship.

Louis's royal predecessors laid the institutional foundations for absolute monarchy and also taught him certain practices to avoid. Just as the emergence of a strong Parliament was not inevitable in England, neither was the emergence of an absolute monarchy in France.

Henry IV and Sully

Coming to the throne after the French wars of religion, Henry IV (r. 1589–1610; see Chapter 12) sought to curtail the privileges of the French nobility. His targets were the provincial governors and the regional *parlements*, especially the powerful *Parlement* of Paris, where a divisive spirit lived on. Here were to be found the old privileged groups, tax-exempt magnates who were largely preoccupied with protecting their self-interests. During the reign of Louis XIII (r. 1610–1643), royal civil servants known as *intendants* subjected these privileged groups to stricter supervision, implementing the king's will with some success in the provinces. An important function of the *intendants* was to prevent abuses from the sale of royal offices that conferred the right to collect revenues, sell licenses, or carry out other remunerative forms of administration. It was usually nobles who acquired these lucrative offices, which was one reason for their ongoing influence.

After decades of religious and civil war, an economy more amenable to governmental regulation emerged during Henry IV's reign. Henry and his finance minister, the duke of Sully (1560–1641), established government monopolies on gunpowder, mines, and salt, preparing the way for the mercantilist policies of Louis XIV and his minister Colbert. They began a canal system to link the Atlantic and the Mediterranean by joining the Saône, the Loire, the Seine, and the Meuse rivers. They introduced the royal *corvée*, a labor tax that created a national force of drafted workers used to improve roads and the conditions of internal travel. Sully even dreamed of organizing the whole of Europe politically and commercially into a kind of common market.

Louis XIII and Richelieu

Henry IV was assassinated in 1610, and the following year Sully retired. Because Henry's son and successor, Louis XIII, was only nine years old at his father's death, the task of governing fell to the queen mother, Marie de Médicis (d. 1642). Finding herself in a vulnerable position, she sought security abroad by signing a ten-year mutual defense pact with France's arch rival Spain in the Treaty of Fontainebleau (1611). This alliance also arranged for the later marriage of Louis XIII to the Spanish Infanta as well as for the marriage of the queen's daughter Elizabeth to the heir to the Spanish throne. The queen sought internal security against pressures from the French nobility by promoting the career of Cardinal Richelieu (1585–1642) as the king's chief adviser. Richelieu, loyal and shrewd, aspired to make France a supreme European power. He, more than any other person, was the secret of French success in the first half of the seventeenth century.

An apparently devout Catholic who also believed that the Church best served both his own ambition and the welfare of France, Richelieu pursued a strongly anti-Habsburg policy. Although he supported the Spanish alliance of the queen and Catholic religious unity within France, he was determined to contain Spanish power and influence, even when that meant aiding and abetting Protestant Europe. It is an indication both of Richelieu's awkward political situation and of his diplomatic agility that he could, in 1631, pledge funds to the Protestant army of Gustavus Adolphus, the king of Sweden, while also insisting that Catholic Bavaria be spared from attack and that

Cardinal Richelieu laid the foundations for the political ascendancy of the French monarchy. [The National Gallery, London]

Catholics in conquered countries be permitted to practice their religion. One measure of the success of Richelieu's foreign policies can be seen in France's substantial gains in land and political influence when the Treaty of Westphalia (1648) ended hostilities in the Holy Roman Empire (see Chapter 12) and the Treaty of the Pyrenees (1659) sealed peace with Spain.

At home, Richelieu pursued centralizing policies utterly without qualm. Supported by the king, who let his chief minister make most decisions of state, Richelieu stepped up the campaign against separatist provincial governors and *parlements*. He made it clear that there was only one law, that of the king, and none could stand above it. When disobedient nobles defied his edicts, they were imprisoned and even executed. Such treatment of the nobility won Richelieu much enmity, even from the queen mother, who, unlike Richelieu, was not always willing to place the larger interests of the state above the pleasure of favorite nobles.

Richelieu started the campaign against the Huguenots that would end in 1685 with Louis XIV's revocation of the Edict of Nantes. Royal armies conquered major Huguenot cities in 1629. The subsequent Peace of Alais (1629) truncated the Edict of Nantes by denying Protestants the right to maintain garrisoned cities, separate political organizations, and independent law courts. Only Richelieu's foreign policy, which involved France in ties with Protestant powers, prevented the earlier implementation of the policy of extreme intolerance that marked the reign of Louis XIV. In the same year that Richelieu rescinded the independent political status of the Huguenots in the Peace of Alais, he also entered negotiations to make Gustavus Adolphus his counterweight to the expansion of Habsburg power within the Holy Roman Empire. By 1635 the Catholic soldiers of France were fighting openly with Swedish Lutherans against the emperor's army in the final phase of the Thirty Years' War (see Chapter 12).

Richelieu employed the arts and the printing press to defend his actions and to indoctrinate the French people in the meaning of *raison d'état* ("reason of state"). This also set a precedent for Louis XIV, who made elaborate use of royal propaganda and spectacle to assert and enhance his power.

This medallion shows Anne of Austria, the wife of Louis XIII, with her son, Louis XIV. She wisely placed political authority in the hands of Cardinal Mazarin, who prepared Louis to govern France. [Giraudon/Art Resource, N.Y.]

Young Louis XIV and Mazarin

Although Richelieu helped lay the foundations for a much expanded royal authority, his immediate legacy was strong resentment of the monarchy among the French nobility and wealthy commercial groups. The crown's steady multiplication of royal offices, its replacement of local authorities by "state" agents, and its reduction of local sources of patronage undermined the traditional position of the privileged groups in French society. Among those affected were officers of the crown in the law courts and other royal institutions.

Louis XIV was only five years old when Louis XIII died in 1643. During his minority, the queen mother, Anne of Austria (d. 1666), placed the reins of government in the hands of Cardinal Mazarin (1602–1661), who continued Richelieu's determined policy of centralization. During his regency, long-building resentment produced a backlash. Between 1649 and 1652, in a series of widespread rebellions known as the Fronde (after the slingshot used by street boys), segments of the nobility and townspeople sought to reverse the drift toward absolute monarchy and to preserve local autonomy.

The *Parlement* of Paris initiated the revolt in 1649, and the nobility at large soon followed. Urging them on were the influential wives of princes whom Mazarin had imprisoned for treason. The many (the nobility) briefly triumphed over the one (the monarchy) when Mazarin released the imprisoned princes in February 1651. He and Louis XIV thereafter entered a short exile (Mazarin leaving France, Louis fleeing Paris). They returned in October 1652 after an interlude of inefficient and nearly anarchic rule by the nobility. The period of the Fronde convinced most French people that the rule of a strong king was preferable to the rule of many regional powers with competing and irreconcilable claims. At the same time, Louis XIV and his later advisors learned that heavy-handed policies like those of Richelieu and Mazarin could endanger the monarchy. Louis would ultimately concentrate unprecedented authority in the monarchy, but his means would be more clever than those of his predecessors.

The Years of Louis's Personal Rule

On the death of Mazarin, Louis XIV assumed personal control of the government. Unlike his royal predecessors, he appointed no single chief minister. One result was to make revolt more difficult. Rebellious nobles would now be challenging the king directly; they could not claim to be resisting only a bad minister.

Mazarin prepared Louis XIV well to rule France. The turbulent events of his youth also made an indelible impression on the king. Louis wrote in his memoirs that the Fronde caused him to loathe "kings of straw," and he followed two strategies to assure he would never become one.

First, Louis and his advisors became masters of propaganda and political image creation. Indoctrinated with a strong sense of the grandeur of his crown, Louis never missed an opportunity to impress it on the French people. When the dauphin (the heir to the French throne) was born in 1662, for example, Louis

appeared for the celebration dressed as a Roman emperor.

Second, Louis made sure the French nobles and other major social groups would benefit from the growth of his own authority. Although he maintained control over foreign affairs and limited the influence of noble institutions on the monarchy, he never tried to abolish those institutions or limit their authority at the local level. The crown, for example, usually conferred informally with regional *parlements* before making rulings that would affect them. Likewise, the crown would rarely enact economic regulations without consulting local opinion. Local *parlements* enjoyed considerable latitude in all regional matters. In an exception to this pattern, Louis did clash with the *Parlement* of Paris, with which he had to register laws, and eventually in 1673 he curtailed much of its power. Many regional *parlements* and other regional authorities, however, had resented the power of that body.

Employing these strategies of propaganda and cooperation, Louis set out to anchor his rule in the principle of the divine right of kings, to domesticate the French nobility by binding them to the court rituals of Versailles, and to crush religious dissent.

King by Divine Right

Reverence for the king and the personification of government in his person had been nurtured in France since Capetian times. It was a maxim of French law and popular opinion that "the king of France is emperor in his realm" and the king's wish the law of the land. Building on this reverence, Louis XIV defended absolute royal authority on the grounds of divine right.

An important source for Louis's concept of royal authority was his devout tutor, the political theorist Bishop Jacques-Bénigne Bossuet (1627–1704). An ardent champion of the Gallican liberties—the traditional rights of the French king and Church in matters of ecclesiastical appointments and taxation—Bossuet defended what he called the "divine right of kings." In support of his claims he cited examples of Old Testament rulers divinely appointed by and answerable only to God. As medieval popes had insisted that only God could judge a pope, so Bossuet argued that none save God could judge the king. Kings may have remained duty-bound to reflect God's will in their rule—in this sense, Bossuet considered them always subject to a higher authority. Yet as God's regents on earth they could not be bound to the dictates of mere princes and parliaments. Such assumptions lay behind Louis XIV's alleged declaration: *"L'état, c'est moi"* ("I am the state").

Versailles

More than any other monarch of the day, Louis XIV used the physical setting of his royal court to exert political control. The palace court at Versailles on the outskirts of Paris became Louis's permanent residence after 1682. It was a true temple to royalty, architecturally designed and artistically decorated to proclaim the glory

---

Bishop Bossuet Defends the Divine Right of Kings

The revolutions of the seventeenth century caused many to fear anarchy far more than tyranny, among them the influential French bishop Jacques-Bénigne Bossuet (1627–1704), the leader of French Catholicism in the second half of the seventeenth century. Louis XIV made him court preacher and tutor to his son, for whom Bossuet wrote a celebrated Universal History. In the following excerpt, Bossuet defends the divine right and absolute power of kings. He depicts kings as embracing in their person the whole body of the state and the will of the people they govern and, as such, as being immune from judgment by any mere mortal.

◆ *Why might Bossuet have wished to make such extravagant claims for absolute royal power? How might these claims be transferred to any form of government? What are the religious bases for Bossuet's argument? How does this argument for absolute royal authority lead also to the need for a single uniform religion in France?*

The royal power is absolute. . . . The prince need render account of his acts to no one. "I counsel thee to keep the king's commandment, and that in regard of the oath of God. Be not hasty to go out of his sight; stand not on an evil thing for he doeth whatsoever pleaseth him. Where the word of a king is, there is power; and who may say unto him, What doest thou? Whoso keepeth the commandment shall feel no evil thing" [Eccles. 8:2–5]. Without this absolute authority the king could neither do good nor repress evil. It is necessary that his power be such that no one can hope to escape him, and finally, the only protection of individuals against the public authority should be their innocence. This confirms the teaching of St. Paul: "Wilt thou then not be afraid of the power? Do that which is good" [Rom. 13:3].

God is infinite, God is all. The prince, as prince, is not regarded as a private person: he is a public personage, all the state is in him; the will of all the people is included in his. As all perfection and all strength are united in God, so all the power of individuals is united in the person of the prince. What grandeur that a single man should embody so much! . . .

Behold an immense people united in a single person; behold this holy power, paternal and absolute; behold the secret cause which governs the whole body of the state, contained in a single head: you see the image of God in the king, and you have the idea of royal majesty. God is holiness itself, goodness itself, and power itself. In these things lies the majesty of God. In the image of these things lies the majesty of the prince.

From Politics Drawn from the Very Words of Holy Scripture, *as quoted in James Harvey Robinson, ed.,* Readings in European History, Vol. 2 *(Boston: Athenaeum, 1906), pp. 275–276.*

of the Sun King, as Louis was known. A spectacular estate with magnificent fountains and acres of orange groves, it became home to thousands of the more important nobles, royal officials, and servants. Although its physical maintenance and new additions, which continued throughout Louis's lifetime, consumed over half his annual revenues, Versailles paid significant political dividends.

Because Louis ruled personally, he was the chief source of favors and patronage in France. To emphasize his prominence, he organized life at court around every aspect of his own daily routine. He encouraged nobles to approach him directly, but required them to do so through elaborate court etiquette. Polite and fawning nobles sought his attention, entering their names on waiting lists to be in attendance at especially favored moments. The king's rising and dressing in particular were times of rare intimacy, when nobles could whisper their special requests in his ear. Fortunate nobles held his night candle as they accompanied him to his bed.

Although only five feet four inches in height, the king had presence and was always engaging in conversation. He turned his own sexuality to political ends and encouraged the belief at court that it was an honor to lie with him. Married to the Spanish Infanta Marie Thérèse for political reasons in 1660, he kept many mistresses. After Marie's death in 1683, he settled down in a secret marriage to Madame de Maintenon and apparently became much less the philanderer.

Court life was a carefully planned and successfully executed effort to domesticate and trivialize the nobility. Barred by law from high government positions, the ritual and play kept them busy and dependent so they had little time to plot revolt. Dress codes and high-stakes gambling contributed to their indebtedness and dependency on the king. Members of the court spent the afternoons hunting, riding, or strolling about the lush gardens of Versailles. Evenings

Versailles, as painted in 1668 by Pierre Patel the Elder (1605–1676). The central building is the hunting lodge built for Louis XIII earlier in the century. The wings that appear here were some of Louis XIV's first expansions. [Giraudon/Art Resource, N.Y.]

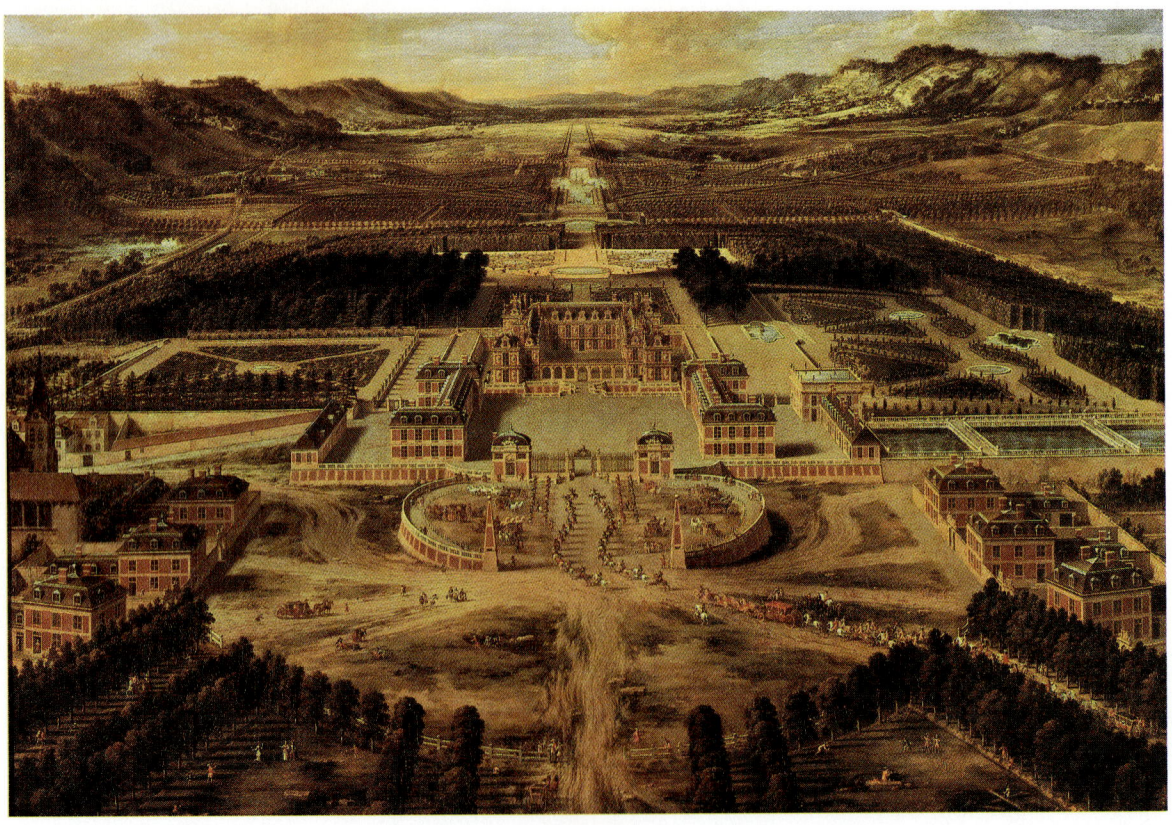

were given over to planned entertainment in the large salons (plays, concerts, gambling, and the like), followed by supper at 10:00 P.M. Even the king's retirement was part of the day's spectacle.

Moments near the king were important to most court nobles because they were effectively excluded from the real business of government. Louis ruled through powerful councils that controlled foreign affairs, domestic relations, and economic regulations. Each day after morning Mass, which Louis always observed, he spent hours with the chief ministers of these councils, whom he chose from families long in royal service or from among people just beginning to rise in the social structure. Unlike the nobles at court, they had no real or potential power bases in the provinces and depended solely on the king for their standing in both government and society.

Some nobles, of course, did not attend Versailles. Some tended to their local estates and cultivated their local influence. Many others were simply too poor to cut a figure at court. All the nobility understood, however, that Louis, unlike Richelieu and Mazarin, would not threaten their local social standing. Louis supported France's traditional social structure and the social privileges of the nobility.

Suppression of the Jansenists

Like Richelieu before him, Louis believed that political unity and stability required religious conformity. His first move in this direction, which came early in his personal reign, was against the Roman Catholic Jansenists.

The French crown and the French Church had by long tradition—originating with the so-called Gallican liberties in the fourteenth century—jealously guarded their independence from Rome. A great influx of Catholic religious orders, the Jesuits prominent among them, followed Henry IV's conversion to Catholicism. Because of their leadership at the Council of Trent and their close connections to Spain, the Jesuits had been banned from France by Catherine de Médicis. Henry IV, however, lifted the ban in 1603, with certain conditions: He required members of the order to swear an oath of allegiance to the king, he limited the number of new colleges they could open, and he required

them to have special licenses for public activities.

The Jesuits were not, however, easily harnessed. They rapidly monopolized the education of the upper classes, and their devout students promoted the religious reforms and doctrine of the Council of Trent throughout France. In a measure of their success, Jesuits served as confessors to Henry IV, Louis XIII, and Louis XIV.

Jansenism arose in the 1630s as part of an intra-Catholic opposition to the theology and the political influence of the Jesuits. Jansenists adhered to the Augustinian tradition that had also spawned many Protestant teachings. Serious and uncompromising, they particularly opposed Jesuit teachings about free will. They believed with Saint Augustine that original sin so corrupted humankind that individuals could do nothing good nor secure their own salvation without divine grace. The namesake of the movement, Cornelius Jansen (d. 1638), was a Flemish theologian and the bishop of Ypres. His posthumously published *Augustinus* (1640) assailed Jesuit teaching on grace and salvation.

Through one of Jansen's close friends, a prominent Parisian family, the Arnaulds, became Jansenist allies, adding a political element to the Jansenists' theological objections to the Jesuits. Like many other French people, the Arnaulds believed the Jesuits had been behind the assassination of Henry IV in 1610.

The Arnaulds dominated Jansenist communities at Port-Royal and Paris during the 1640s. In 1643 Antoine Arnauld published a work entitled *On Frequent Communion*, in which he criticized the Jesuits for confessional practices that permitted the easy redress of almost any sin. The Jesuits, in turn, condemned the Jansenists as "crypto-Calvinists."

On May 31, 1653, Pope Innocent X declared heretical five Jansenist theological propositions on grace and salvation. In 1656 the pope banned Jansen's *Augustinus* and the Sorbonne censured Antoine Arnauld. In this same year, Antoine's friend, Blaise Pascal (1623–1662), the most famous of Jansen's followers, published the first of his *Provincial Letters* in defense of Jansenism. A deeply religious man, Pascal tried to reconcile the "reasons of the heart" with growing seventeenth-century reverence for the clear and distinct ideas of the mind (see Chapter 14). He objected to Jesuit moral theology not

Cornelis Jansen, Bishop of Ypres (1585–1638), wrote that individuals could do nothing to contribute to their salvation unless they were assisted by divine grace. This teaching, which came to be called Jansenism, was condemned as heretical by the Church because it seemed to deny the doctrine of human free will. [Giraudon/Art Resource, N.Y.]

Louis's Early Wars

Louis's France was in many ways like much of the rest of contemporary Europe. It had a largely subsistence economy and its cities enjoyed only limited commercial prosperity. It did not, in other words, achieve the economic strength of a modern industrial economy. By the 1660s, however, France was superior to any other European nation in administrative bureaucracy, armed forces, and national unity. Louis had sufficient resources at his disposal to raise and maintain a large and powerful army, and by every external measure he was in a position to dominate Europe. He spent most of the rest of his reign attempting to do so.

GOVERNING FOR WARFARE Three remarkable French ministers established and supported Louis XIV's great war machine: Colbert, Louvois, and Vauban.

The policies of Jean-Baptiste Colbert (1619–1683) transformed France into a major commercial power. [Erich Lessing/Art Resource, N.Y.]

only as being lax and shallow, but also because he felt its rationalism failed to do full justice to the religious experience.

In 1660 Louis permitted the papal bull *Ad Sacram Sedem* (1656) to be enforced in France, thus banning Jansenism. He also closed down the Port-Royal community. Thereafter, Jansenists either retracted their views or went underground. Much later, in 1710, Louis lent his support to a still more thorough purge of Jansenist sentiment.

Jansenism had offered the prospect of a Catholicism broad enough to appeal to France's Protestant Huguenots. By suppressing it, Louis also eliminated the best hope for bringing peaceful religious unity to his country.

Colbert Revives French Manufacture and Trade

Political power goes hand in hand with economic power. In this letter to the officials of Marseilles (1664), Louis XIV summarized the new policies proposed by Colbert to improve French business. Every effort was made to improve the means of manufacture and trade by freeing merchants from restrictive regulations and by subsidizing new ventures from the royal treasury.

◆ *What does this document suggest were the major obstacles to economic growth Colbert wished to overcome? What specific steps does Colbert propose to aid the economy? What kind of occupations or commerce might most benefit from these steps? To what extent does the French government appear to be entering the economic process and to what extent does it seem to be trusting the market?*

Considering how advantageous it would be to this realm to reestablish its foreign and domestic commerce, . . . we have resolved to establish a council particularly devoted to commerce, to be held every fortnight in our presence, in which all the interests of merchants and the means conducive to the revival of commerce shall be considered and determined upon, as well as all that which concerns manufactures.

We also inform you that we are setting apart, in the expenses of our state, a million livres each year for the encouragement of manufactures and the increase of navigation, to say nothing of the considerable sums which we cause to be raised to supply the companies of the East and West Indies;

That we are working constantly to abolish all the tolls which are collected on the navigable rivers;

That there has already been expended more than a million livres for the repair of the public highways, to which we shall also devote our constant attention;

That we will assist by money from our royal treasury all those who wish to reestablish old manufactures or to undertake new ones;

That we are giving orders to all our ambassadors or residents at the courts of the princes, our allies, to make, in our name, all proper efforts to cause justice to be rendered in all cases involving our merchants, and to assure for them entire commercial freedom;

That we will comfortably lodge at our court each and every merchant who has business there during all the time that he shall be obliged to remain there, having given orders to the grand marshal of our palace to indicate a proper place for that purpose, which shall be called the House of Commerce; . . .

That all the merchants and traders by sea who purchase vessels, or who build new ones, for traffic or commerce shall receive from us subsidies for each ton of merchandise which they export or import on the said voyages.

James Harvey Robinson, ed., Readings in European History, Vol. 2 *(Boston: Athenaeum, 1906), pp. 280–281.*

Jean-Baptiste Colbert (1619–1683), controller general of finances and Louis's most brilliant minister, created the economic base Louis needed to finance his wars. Colbert worked to centralize the French economy with the same rigor that Louis had worked to centralize the French government. Colbert tried, with modest success, to organize much economic activity under state supervision and, through tariffs, carefully regulated the flow of imports and exports. He sought to create new national industries and organized factories around a tight regimen of work and ideology. He simplified the administrative bureaucracy, abolished unnecessary positions, and reduced the number of tax-exempt nobles. He also increased the *taille*, a direct tax on the peasantry and a major source of royal income.

This kind of close government control of the economy came to be known as *mercantilism* (a term invented by later critics of the policy). Its aim was to maximize foreign exports and internal reserves of bullion, the gold and silver necessary for making war. Modern scholars argue that Colbert overcontrolled the French economy and cite his "paternalism" as a major reason for the failure of French colonies in the New World. Be that as it may, his policies unquestionably transformed France into a major commercial power, with foreign bases in Africa, in India, and in the Americas, from Canada to the Caribbean.

Louis's army, about a quarter of a million strong, was the creation of Michelle Tellier and his more famous son, the marquis of Louvois (1641–1691). Louis's war minister from 1677 to 1691, Louvois was a superior military tactician.

Before Louvois, the French army had been an amalgam of local recruits and mercenaries, uncoordinated groups whose loyalty could not always be counted on. Without regular pay or a way to supply their everyday needs, troops often lived by pillage. Louvois instituted good salaries and improved discipline, making soldiering a respectable profession. He limited military commissions and introduced a system of promotion by merit, bringing dedicated fighters into the ranks. Enlistment was for four years and was restricted to single men. *Intendants*, the king's ubiquitous civil servants, monitored conduct at all levels.

Because it was well disciplined, this new, large, and powerful standing army had considerable public support. Unlike its undisciplined predecessor, the new army no longer threatened the lives, homes, or well-being of the people it was supposed to protect. It thus provides an excellent example of the kinds of benefits many saw in the growing authority of the central monarchy.

What Louvois was to military organization, Sebastien Vauban (1633–1707) was to military engineering. He perfected the arts of fortifying and besieging towns. He also devised the system of trench warfare and developed the concept of defensive frontiers that remained basic to military tactics through World War I.

THE WAR OF DEVOLUTION Louis's first great foreign adventure was the War of Devolution (1667–1668). It was fought, as would be the later and more devastating War of the Spanish Succession, over Louis's claim to the Spanish Belgian provinces through his wife, Marie Thérèse (1638–1683). According to the terms of the Treaty of the Pyrenees (1659), Marie had renounced her claim to the Spanish succession on condition that a 500,000-crown dowry be

Throughout the age of the splendor at the court of Louis XIV millions of French peasants lived lives of poverty and harship. [Erich Lessing/Art Resource, N.Y.]

paid to Louis within eighteen months of the marriage, a condition that was not met. When Philip IV of Spain died in September 1665, he left all his lands to his sickly four-year-old son by a second marriage, Charles II (r. 1665–1700), and explicitly denied any lands to his daughter. Louis had always harbored the hope of turning the marriage to territorial gain and even before Philip's death had argued that Marie was entitled to a portion of the inheritance.

Louis had a legal argument on his side, which gave the war its name. He maintained that in certain regions of Brabant and Flanders, which were part of the Spanish inheritance, property "devolved" to the children of a first marriage rather than to those of a second. Therefore, Marie had a higher claim than Charles II to these regions. The argument was not accepted, for such regional laws could hardly bind the king of Spain. Louis, however, was not deterred from sending his armies, under the viscount of Turenne, into Flanders and the Franche-Comté in 1667. In response to this aggression, England, Sweden, and the United Provinces of Holland formed the Triple Alliance, a force sufficient to compel Louis to agree to peace under the terms in the Treaty of Aix-la-Chapelle (1668). According to the treaty, he gained control of certain towns bordering the Spanish Netherlands (see Map 13-2).

INVASION OF THE NETHERLANDS In 1670, with the signing of the Treaty of Dover, England and France became allies against the Dutch. Without the English, the Triple Alliance crumbled. This left Louis in a stronger position to invade the Netherlands for a second time, which he did in 1672. This time he aimed di-rectly at Holland, which had organized the Triple Alliance in 1667, foiling French designs in Flanders. Dutch boasting after the Treaty of Aix-la-Chapelle had mightily offended Louis. Cartoons like one depicting the sun (Louis was called the "Sun King") eclipsed by a great moon of Dutch cheese distressed him. Without neutralizing Holland, he knew he could never hope to acquire land in the Spanish Netherlands, much less fulfill his dreams of European hegemony.

Louis's successful invasion of the United Provinces in 1672 brought the downfall of Dutch statesmen Jan and Cornelius De Witt. Replacing them was the twenty-seven-year-old Prince of Orange, destined after 1689 to become King William III of England. Orange was the great-grandson of William the Silent, who had repulsed Philip II and dashed Spanish hopes of dominating the Netherlands in the sixteenth century.

Orange, an unpretentious Calvinist, who was in almost every way Louis's opposite, galvanized the seven provinces into a fierce fighting unit. In 1673 he united the Holy Roman Emperor, Spain, Lorraine, and Brandenburg in an alliance against Louis. His enemies now saw the French king as a "Christian Turk," a menace to the whole of western Europe, Catholic and Protestant alike. In the ensuing warfare, both sides experienced gains and losses. Louis lost his ablest generals, Turenne and Condé, in 1675, but a victory by Admiral Duquesne over the Dutch fleet in 1676 gave France control of the Mediterranean. The Peace of Nijmwegen, signed with different parties in successive years (1678, 1679), ended the hostilities of this second war. There were various minor territorial adjustments but no clear victor except the United Netherlands, which retained all of its territory.

Revocation of the Edict of Nantes

In the decade after his invasion of the Netherlands, Louis made his second major move to assure religious conformity. Following the proclamation of the Edict of Nantes in 1598, relations between the great Catholic majority (nine-tenths of the French population) and the Protestant minority remained hostile. There were about 1.75 million Huguenots in France in the 1660s, but their numbers were declining in the second half of the seventeenth century. The French Catholic church had long denounced Calvinists as heretical and treasonous and had supported their persecution as both pious and patriotic.

Following the Peace of Nijmwegen in 1678–1679, which halted for the moment his aggression in Europe, Louis launched a methodical government campaign against the French Huguenots in a determined effort to unify France religiously. He hounded the Huguenots out of public life, banning them from government office and excluding them from such professions as printing and medicine. He used sub-

MAP 13-2 THE WARS OF LOUIS XIV *This map shows the territorial changes resulting from Louis XIV's first three major wars. The War of the Spanish Succession was yet to come.*

sidies and selective taxation to encourage Huguenots to convert to Catholicism. And in 1681 he bullied them by quartering his troops in their towns. In the final stage of the persecution, Louis revoked the Edict of Nantes in October 1685. As a result, Protestant churches and schools were closed, Protestant ministers exiled, nonconverting laity forced to be galley slaves, and Protestant children ceremonially baptized by Catholic priests.

In 1685 Louis XIV revoked the Edict of Nantes, thus ending religious toleration in France. [Robert Harding Picture Library, London]

The revocation of the Edict of Nantes was a major blunder. Louis was afterwards viewed in Protestant countries as a new Philip II, intent on a Catholic reconquest of the whole of Europe, who must be resisted at all costs. The revocation prompted the voluntary emigration of more than a quarter million French people, who formed new communities and joined the resistance to France in England, Germany, Holland, and the New World. Thousands of French Huguenots served in the army of Louis's arch foe, William of Orange, later King William III of England. Many of those who remained in France became part of an uncompromising guerilla resistance to the king. Despite the many domestic and foreign liabilities it brought him, Louis, to his death, considered the revocation to be his most pious act, one that placed God in his debt.

Louis's Later Wars

THE LEAGUE OF AUGSBURG AND THE NINE YEARS' WAR After the Treaty of Nijmwegen, Louis maintained his army at full strength and restlessly probed beyond his perimeters. In 1681 his forces conquered the free city of Strasbourg,

prompting new defensive coalitions to form against him. One of these, the League of Augsburg, created in 1686 to resist French expansion into Germany, had grown by 1689 to include England, Spain, Sweden, the United Provinces, and the electorates of Bavaria, Saxony, and the Palatinate. It also had the support of the Austrian emperor Leopold. Between 1689 and 1697, the League and France battled each other in the Nine Years' War. During the same period, England and France struggled for control of North America in what came to be known as King William's War.

The Nine Years' War ended when stalemate and exhaustion forced both sides to accept an interim settlement. The Peace of Ryswick, signed in September 1697, was a triumph for William of Orange, now William III of England, and Emperor Leopold. It secured Holland's borders and thwarted Louis's expansion into Germany.

WAR OF THE SPANISH SUCCESSION: TREATIES OF UTRECHT AND RASTADT After Ryswick, Louis, who seemed to thrive on partial success, made still a fourth attempt to realize his grand design to dominate Europe. This time an unforeseen turn of events helped

Louis XIV Revokes the Edict of Nantes

Believing that a country could not be under one king and one law unless it was also under one religious system, Louis XIV stunned much of Europe in October 1685 by revoking the Edict of Nantes, which had protected the religious freedoms and civil rights of French Protestants since 1598. Compare this document to the one in Chapter 15 in which the Elector of Brandenburg welcomes displaced French Protestants into his domains.

✦ *What specific actions does this declaration order against Protestants? Does it offer any incentives for Protestants to convert to Catholicism? How does this declaration compare with the English Test Act?*

Art. 1. Know that we . . . with our certain knowledge, full power and royal authority, have by this present, perpetual and irrevocable edict, suppressed and revoked the edict of the aforesaid king our grandfather, given at Nantes in the month of April, 1598, in all its extent . . . together with all the concessions made by [this] and other edicts, declarations, and decrees, to the people of the so-called Reformed religion, of whatever nature they be . . . and in consequence we desire . . . that all the temples of the people of the aforesaid so-called Reformed religion situated in our kingdom . . . should be demolished forthwith.

Art. 2. We forbid our subjects of the so-called Reformed religion to assemble any more for public worship of the above-mentioned religion. . . .

Art. 3. We likewise forbid all lords, of whatever rank they may be, to carry out heretical services in houses and fiefs . . . the penalty for . . . the said worship being confiscation of their body and possessions.

Art. 4. We order all ministers of the aforesaid so-called Reformed religion who do not wish to be converted and to embrace the Catholic, Apostolic, and Roman religion, to depart from our kingdom and the lands subject to us within fifteen days from the publication of our present edict . . . on pain of the galleys.

Art. 5. We desire that those among the said [Reformed] ministers who shall be converted [to the Catholic religion] shall continue to enjoy during their life, and their wives shall enjoy after their death as long as they remain widows, the same exemptions from taxation and billeting of soldiers, which they enjoyed while they fulfilled the function of ministers. . . .

Art. 8. With regard to children who shall be born to those of the aforesaid so-called Reformed religion, we desire that they be baptized by their parish priests. We command the fathers and mothers to send them to the churches for that purpose, on penalty of a fine of 500 livres or more if they fail to do so; and afterwards, the children shall be brought up in the Catholic, Apostolic, and Roman religion. . . .

Art. 10. All our subjects of the so-called Reformed religion, with their wives and children, are to be strongly and repeatedly prohibited from leaving our aforesaid kingdom . . . or of taking out . . . their possessions and effects. . . .

The members of the so-called Reformed religion, while awaiting God's pleasure to enlighten them like the others, can live in the towns and districts of our kingdom . . . and continue their occupation there, and enjoy their possessions . . . on condition . . . that they do not make public profession of [their religion].

S. Z. Ehler and John B. Morrall, ed. and trans., Church and State Through the Centuries: A Collection of Historic Documents *(New York: Biblo and Tannen, 1967), pp. 209–213.*

him. On November 1, 1700, Charles II of Spain, known as "the Sufferer" because of his genetic deformities and lingering illnesses, died.

Both Louis and the Austrian emperor Leopold had claims to the Spanish inheritance through their grandsons: Louis through his marriage to Marie Thérèse and Leopold through his marriage to her younger sister, Margaret Thérèse. Although Louis's grandson, Philip of Anjou, had the better claim (because Marie Thérèse was Margaret Thérèse's older sister), Marie Thérèse had renounced her right to the Spanish inheritance in the Treaty of the Pyrenees (1659), and the inheritance was expected to go to Leopold's grandson.

Louis nurtured fears that the Habsburgs would dominate Europe should they gain control of Spain as well as the Holy Roman Empire. Most of the nations of Europe, however, feared France more than the Habsburgs and determined to prevent a union of the French and Spanish crowns. As a result, before Charles II's death, negotiations began among the nations involved to partition his inheritance in a way that would preserve the existing balance of power.

Charles II upset these negotiations by leaving his entire inheritance to Philip of Anjou, Louis's grandson. At a stroke, Spain and its possessions had fallen to France. Although Louis had been party to the partition agreements that preceded Charles's death, he now saw God's hand in Charles's will; he chose to enforce its terms over those of the partition agreement. Philip of Anjou moved to Madrid and became Philip V of Spain. Louis, in what was interpreted as naked French aggression, sent his troops again into Flanders, this time to remove Dutch soldiers from Spanish territory in the name of the new French king of Spain. Louis also declared Spanish America open to French ships.

In September 1701, England, Holland, and the Holy Roman Empire formed the Grand Alliance to counter Louis. They sought to preserve the balance of power by once and for all securing Flanders as a neutral barrier between Holland and France and by gaining for the emperor his fair share of the Spanish inheritance. After the formation of the Grand Alliance, Louis increased the stakes of battle by recognizing the claim of James Edward, the son of James II of England, to the English throne.

The Reign of Louis XIV (1643–1715)	
1643	Louis ascends the French throne at the age of 5
1643–1661	Cardinal Mazarin directs the French government
1648	Peace of Westphalia
1649–1652	The Fronde revolt
1653	The Pope declares Jansenism a heresy
1659	Treaty of Pyrenées between France and Spain
1660	Papal ban on Jansenists enforced in France
1661	Louis commences personal rule
1667–1668	War of Devolution
1670	Secret Treaty of Dover between France and Great Britain
1672–1679	French war against the Netherlands
1685	Louis revokes the Edict of Nantes
1689–1697	War of the League of Augsburg
1701	Outbreak of the War of the Spanish Succession
1713	Treaty of Utrecht between France and Great Britain
1714	Treaty of Rastatt between France and Spain
1715	Death of Louis XIV

In 1701 the thirteen-year War of the Spanish Succession (1701–1714) began, and once again total war enveloped western Europe. France, for the first time, went to war with inadequate finances, a poorly equipped army, and mediocre military leadership. The English, in contrast, had advanced weaponry (flintlock rifles, paper cartridges, and ring bayonets) and superior tactics (thin, maneuverable troop columns rather than the traditional deep ones). John Churchill, the duke of Marlborough, who succeeded William of Orange as military leader of the alliance, bested Louis's soldiers in every major engagement. He routed French armies at Blenheim in August 1704 and on the plain of Ramillies in 1706—two decisive battles of the war. In 1708–1709 famine, revolts, and uncollectible taxes tore France apart internally. Despair pervaded the French court. Louis wondered aloud how God could forsake one who had done so much for Him.

MAP 13-3 EUROPE IN 1714 *The War of the Spanish Succession ended in the year before the death of the aged Louis XIV. By then France and Spain, although not united, were both ruled by members of the Bourbon family, and Spain had lost its non-Iberian possessions.*

Though ready to make peace in 1709, Louis could not bring himself to accept the stiff terms of the alliance. These included a demand that he transfer all Spanish possessions to the emperor's grandson Charles and remove Philip V from Madrid. Hostilities continued, and a clash of forces at Malplaquet (September 1709) left carnage on the battlefield unsurpassed until modern times.

France finally signed an armistice with England at Utrecht in July 1713 and concluded

hostilities with Holland and the emperor in the Treaty of Rastadt in March 1714. This agreement confirmed Philip V as king of Spain but gave Gibraltar to England, making it a Mediterranean power (see Map 13-3). It also won Louis's recognition of the right of the House of Hanover to accede to the English throne.

Politically, the eighteenth century would belong to England as the sixteenth had belonged to Spain and the seventeenth to France.

Although France remained intact and strong, the realization of Louis XIV's territorial ambitions had to await the rise of Napoleon Bonaparte. On his deathbed on September 1, 1715, Louis fittingly warned his heir, the dauphin, not to imitate his love of buildings and his liking for war.

Louis XIV's Legacy

Louis XIV left France a mixed legacy. His wars had brought widespread death and destruction, and his armies had shelled civilian populations. Although the monarchy was still strong at his death, it was more feared than admired. Its finances were insecure and dependent on debt. Continued warfare in the eighteenth century would weaken its finances further, leading eventually to the crises that sparked the French Revolution. Louis's policies of centralization would later make it difficult for France to develop effective institutions of representation and self-government. The aristocracy, after its years of domestication at Versailles, would have difficulty providing the nation with effective leaders and ministers.

Yet Louis's reign also had a positive side. He may have loved war too much, but he also built the magnificent palace of Versailles and brought a new majesty to France. He skillfully manipulated the fractious French aristocracy and bourgeoisie, he elevated skilled and trustworthy ministers, councillors, and *intendants*, and he created a new French empire by expanding trade into Asia and colonizing North America.

Louis's rule was not so absolute as to exert oppressive control over the daily lives of his subjects as in the police states of the nineteenth and twentieth centuries. His absolutism functioned primarily in the classic areas of European

The foreign policy of Louis XIV brought warfare to all of Europe. This eighteenth-century painting by Benjamin West memorializes the British victory over France in the battle of La Hogue in 1692. [National Gallery of Art]

state action—the making of war and peace, the regulation of religion, and the oversight of economic activity. Even at the height of his power, local institutions, some controlled by townspeople and others by nobles, continued to exert administrative authority at the local level. The king and his ministers supported the high status and tax exemptions of these local elites. But in contrast to the Stuart kings of England, Louis firmly prevented them from capturing or significantly limiting his authority on the national level. Not until the French monarchy was so weakened by financial crisis at the end of the eighteenth century would it succumb to demands for a more representative form of government.

◆

In the seventeenth century, England and France developed divergent forms of government. England became the model for parliamentary monarchy, France for absolute monarchy.

The politically active English elite—the nobility along with the wealthy landowning and commercial classes—struggled throughout the century to limit the authority of rulers—including Oliver Cromwell as well as the Stuart monarchs—over local interests. In the process, they articulated a political philosophy that stressed the need to prevent the central concentration of political power. The Bill of Rights (1689) and the Toleration Act that followed the "Glorious Revolution" of William and Mary seemed to achieve the goals of this philosophy. These acts brought neither democracy nor full religious freedom in a modern sense; the Bill of Rights protected only the privileged, not all the English people, and the Toleration Act outlawed Catholics and Unitarians. Still, they firmly established representative government in England and extended legal recognition, at least in principle, to a variety of religious beliefs. The Bill of Rights required the monarch to call Parliament regularly.

In France, by contrast, the monarchy remained supreme. Although the king had to mollify privileged local elites, by considering the interests of the nobility and the traditional rights of towns and regions, France had no national institution like Parliament through which he had to govern. Louis XIV was able, on his own authority, to fund the largest army in Europe.

He could and did crush religious dissent. His own propaganda and the fear of his adversaries may have led to an exaggerated view of Louis's power, but his reign nonetheless provided a model of effective centralized power that later continental rulers tried to follow.

Review Questions

1. By the end of the seventeenth century, England and France had different systems of government with different religious policies. What were the main differences? Similarities? Why did each nation develop as it did?

2. Why did the English king and Parliament come into conflict in the 1640s? What were the most important issues behind the war between them and who bears more responsibility for it? What role did religion play in the conflict?

3. What was the Glorious Revolution and why did it take place? What were James II's mistakes and what were the issues involved in the events of 1688? What kind of settlement emerged from the revolution? How did England in 1700 differ from England in 1600?

4. Discuss the development of absolutism in France. What policies of Henry IV and Louis XIII were essential in creating the absolute monarchy?

5. What were the chief ways Louis XIV consolidated his monarchy? What limits were there on his authority? What was Louis's religious policy?

6. Assess the success of Louis XIV's foreign policy. What were his aims? Were they realistic? To what extent did he attain them?

Suggested Readings

M. Ashley, *England in the Seventeenth Century* (1980). Readable survey.

W. Beik, *Absolutism and Society in Seventeenth-Century France* (1985). An important study that questions the extent of royal power.

R. Bonney, *Political Change in France Under Richelieu and Mazarin, 1624–1661* (1978). A careful examination of how these two cardinals lay the foundation for Louis XIV's absolutism.

R. Briggs, *Early Modern France, 1560–1715* (1977). A useful brief survey.

P. Burke, *The Fabrication of Louis XIV* (1992). Examines the manner in which the public image of Louis XIV was forged in art.

P. Collinson, *The Religion of Protestants: The Church in English Society 1559–1625* (1982). The best recent introduction to Puritanism.

B. Coward, *Cromwell* (1991). A brief biography.

R. S. Dunn, *The Age of Religious Wars, 1559–1715* (1979). Lucid survey setting the conflicting political systems of France and England in larger perspective.

D. Hirst, *Authority and Conflict: England 1603–1658* (1986). Scholarly survey integrating history and historiography.

R. Hutton, *Charles the Second, King of England, Scotland, and Ireland* (1989). Replaces all previous biographies.

P. Lake, *Anglicans and Puritans: Presbyterianism and English Conformist Thought from Whitgift to Hooker* (1988). An important study of religious thought.

W. H. Lewis, *The Splendid Century* (1953). Focuses on society, especially in the age of Louis XIV.

R. Lockyer, *Buckingham* (1984). Biography of the English court favorite.

R. Mettam, *Power and Faction in Louis XIV's France* (1988). Examines the political intricacies of the reign and suggests the limits to absolutism.

G. Parker, *Europe in Crisis 1598–1648* (1979). Examines the entire scope of early seventeenth-century Europe.

D. L. Rubin (Ed.), *The Sun King: The Ascendancy of French Culture During the Reign of Louis XIV* (1992). A collection of useful essays.

C. Russell, *The Causes of the English Civil War* (1990). A major revisionist account, which should be read with Stone's book.

K. Sharpe, *The Personal Rule of Charles I* (1992). A major narrative work.

J. Spur, *The Restoration Church of England, 1646–1689* (1992). Now the standard work on this subject.

L. Stone, *The Causes of the English Revolution 1529–1642* (1972). Brief survey stressing social history and ruminating over historians and historical method.

V. Tapié, *France in the Age of Louis XIII and Richelieu* (1984). A narrative account.

G. R. R. Treasure, *Seventeenth Century France* (1966). Broad, detailed survey of entire century.

N. Tyacke, *Anti-Calvinists: The Rise of English Arminianism c. 1590–1640* (1987). The most important recent study of Archbishop Laud's policies and his predecessors.

D. Underdown, *Revel, Riot, and Rebellion* (1985). On popular culture and the English Civil War.

M. Walzer, *The Revolution of the Saints: A Study in the Origins of Radical Politics* (1965). Effort to relate ideas and politics that depicts Puritans as true revolutionaries.

C. V. Wedgwood, *Richelieu and the French Monarchy* (1950). Fine biography.

J. B. Wolf, *Louis XIV* (1968). Very detailed political biography.

Hans Holbein's painting of "The Ambassadors" (1533) features the French ambassador (left) and a scholarly friend (right) standing at the ends of a two-tiered table on which lie musical and scientific instruments together with books. Each of these represents one of the four major areas of the university curriculum: arithmetic, astronomy, geometry, and music. The bottom shelf contains a globe of the earth, which is showing the New World. [Courtesy of the Trustees, National Gallery, London]

512

14

New Directions in Thought and Culture in the Sixteenth and Seventeenth Centuries

Key Topics in This Chapter
◆ The astronomical theories of Copernicus, Brahe, Kepler, Galileo, and Newton and the emergence of the scientific worldview
◆ Witchcraft and witch hunts
◆ The literary imagination in a changing world
◆ The philosophical foundations of modern thought

The sixteenth and seventeenth centuries witnessed a sweeping change in the scientific view of the universe. An earth-centered picture gave way to one in which the earth was only another planet orbiting about the sun. The sun itself became one of millions of stars. This transformation of humankind's perception of its place in the larger scheme of things led to a profound rethinking of moral and religious matters as well as of scientific theory. Faith and reason needed new modes of reconciliation, as did faith and science. The new ideas and methods of science challenged modes of thought associated with medieval times and Scholasticism. The new outlook on physical nature touched the literary imagination, and religious thinkers had to reconsider many traditional ideas. Philosophers applied rational, scientific thought to the realm of politics. Some supported absolutism; others, parliamentary systems.

The new scientific concepts and the methods of their construction were so impressive that they set the standard for assessing the validity of knowledge in the Western world thereafter.

A late-seventeenth-century armillary sphere, an astronomical device composed of rings representing the orbits of important celestial bodies. This one portrays Copernicus's construction of the heavens. [The Bettmann Archive]

Perhaps no single intellectual development proved to be more significant for the future of European and Western civilization.

Side by side with enlightenment and science, however, came a new wave of superstition and persecution. The changing world of religion and politics also created profound fear and anxiety among both the simple and the learned, resulting in Europe's worst witch hunts.

The Scientific Revolution

The process by which the new view of the universe and of scientific knowledge came to be established is normally termed the *Scientific Revolution*. This metaphor must be used carefully, however. The word *revolution* normally denotes rapid political change involving large numbers of people. The Scientific Revolution was not rapid, nor did it involve more than a few hundred human beings. It was a complex movement with many false starts and many brilliant people with wrong as well as useful ideas. It took place in the studies and the crude laboratories of thinkers in Poland, Italy, Bohemia, France, and Great Britain.

The Scientific Revolution stemmed from two major tendencies. The first, illustrated by Nicolaus Copernicus, was the imposition of important small changes on existing models of thought. The second, embodied by Francis Bacon, was the desire to pose new kinds of questions and to use new methods of investigation. In both cases, scientific thought changed current and traditional opinions in other fields.

Nicolaus Copernicus: Rejection of an Earth-Centered Universe

Nicolaus Copernicus (1473–1543) was a Polish astronomer who enjoyed a high reputation throughout his life. He had been educated in Italy and corresponded with other astronomers throughout Europe. He had not been known, however, for strikingly original or unorthodox thought. In 1543, the year of his death, Copernicus published *On the Revolutions of the Heavenly Spheres*. Because he died near the time of publication, the fortunes of his work are not the story of one person's crusade for progressive science. Copernicus's book was "a revolution-making rather than a revolutionary text."[1] What Copernicus did was to provide an intellectual springboard for a complete criticism of the then-dominant view of the position of the earth in the universe.

THE PTOLEMAIC SYSTEM At the time of Copernicus, the standard explanation of the place of the earth in the heavens was that associated with Ptolemy and his work entitled the *Almagest* (A.D. 150). Commentators on the original work had developed several alternative Ptolemaic systems over the centuries. Most of these assumed that the earth was the center of the universe. Above the earth lay a series of crystalline spheres, one of which contained the moon, another the sun, and still others the planets and the stars. This was the astronomy found in such works as Dante's *Divine Comedy*. At the outer regions of these spheres lay the realm of God and the angels. Aristotelian physics provided the intellectual underpinnings of the Ptolemaic systems. The earth had to be the center because of its heaviness. The stars and the other heavenly bodies had to be enclosed in the crystalline spheres so that they could move. Nothing could move unless something was actually moving it. The state of rest was natural; motion was the condition that required explanation.

Numerous problems were associated with this system, and these had long been recognized. The most important was the observed motions of the planets, which included noncircular patterns around the earth. At certain times the planets actually appeared to be going backward. The Ptolemaic systems explained these strange motions primarily through *epicycles*. An epicycle is an orbit upon an orbit, like a spinning jewel on a ring. The planets were said to make a second revolution in an orbit tangent to their primary orbit around the earth. Other intellectual but nonobservational difficulties related to the immense speed at which the spheres had to move around the earth. To say the least, the Ptolemaic systems were cluttered.

[1]*Thomas S. Kuhn*, The Copernican Revolution: Planetary Astronomy in the Development of Western Thought *(New York: Vintage, 1959), p. 135.*

They were effective, however, as long as one assumed Aristotelian physics and the Christian belief that the earth rested at the center of the created universe.

COPERNICUS'S UNIVERSE Copernicus's *On the Revolutions of the Heavenly Spheres* challenged this picture in the most conservative manner possible. It suggested that if the earth were assumed to move about the sun in a circle, many of the difficulties with the Ptolemaic systems would disappear or become simpler. Although not wholly eliminated, the number of epicycles would be somewhat fewer. The motive behind this shift away from the earth-centered universe was to find a solution to the problems of planetary motion. By allowing the earth to move around the sun, Copernicus was able to construct a more mathematically elegant basis for astronomy. He had been discontented with the traditional system because it was mathematically clumsy and inconsistent. The primary appeal of his new system was its mathematical aesthetics. With the sun at the center of the universe, mathematical astronomy would make more sense. A change in the conception of the position of the earth meant that the planets were actually moving in circular orbits and only seemed to be doing otherwise because of the position of the observers on earth.

Except for this modification in the position of the earth, Copernicus retained Ptolemaic ideas in most of the other parts of his book. The path of the planets remained circular. Genuine epicycles still existed in the heavens. His system was no more accurate than the existing ones for predicting the location of the planets. He had used no new evidence. The major impact of his work was to provide another way of confronting some of the difficulties inherent in Ptolemaic astronomy. It did not immediately replace the old astronomy, but it allowed other people who were also discontented with the Ptolemaic systems to think in new directions.

Copernicus's concern about the relationship between mathematics and the observed behavior of planets is an example of the single most important factor in the developing new science: the fusion of mathematics with empirical data and observation. Mathematics provided the model to which the new scientific thought

Copernicus Ascribes Movement to the Earth

Copernicus published De Revolutionibus Orbium Caelestium (On the Revolutions of the Heavenly Spheres) *in 1543. In his preface, addressed to Pope Paul III, he explained what had led him to think that the earth moved around the sun and what he thought were some of the scientific consequences of the new theory.*

◆ *How does Copernicus justify his argument to the pope? How important was historical precedent and tradition to the pope? Might Copernicus have thought that the pope would be especially susceptible to such argument, even though what Copernicus proposed (the movement of the earth) contradicted the Bible?*

I may well presume, most Holy Father, that certain people, as soon as they hear that in this book about the Revolutions of the Spheres of the Universe I ascribe movement to the earthly globe, will cry out that, holding such views, I should at once be hissed off the stage. . . .

So I should like your Holiness to know that I was induced to think of a method of computing the motions of the spheres by nothing else than the knowledge that the Mathematicians [who had previously considered the problem] are inconsistent in these investigations.

For, first, the mathematicians are so unsure of the movements of the Sun and Moon that they cannot even explain or observe the constant length of the seasonal year. Secondly, in determining the motions of these and of the other five planets, they use neither the same principles and hypotheses nor the same demonstrations of the apparent motions and revolutions. . . . Nor have they been able thereby to discern or deduce the principal thing—namely the shape of the Universe and the unchangeable symmetry of its parts. . . .

I pondered long upon this uncertainty of mathematical tradition in establishing the motions of the system of the spheres. At last I began to chafe that philosophers could by no means agree on any one certain theory of the mechanism of the Universe, wrought for us by a supremely good and orderly Creator. . . . I therefore took pains to read again the works of all the philosophers on whom I could lay hand to seek out whether any of them had ever supposed that the motions of the spheres were other than those demanded by the [Ptolemaic] mathematical schools. I found first in Cicero that Hicetas [of Syracuse, fifth century B.C.] had realized that the Earth moved. Afterwards I found in Plutarch that certain others had held the like opinion. . . .

Thus assuming motions, which in my work I ascribe to the Earth, by long and frequent observations I have at last discovered that, if the motions of the rest of the planets be brought into relation with the circulation of the Earth and be reckoned in proportion to the circles of each planet, not only do their phenomena presently ensue, but the orders and magnitudes of all stars and spheres, nay the heavens themselves, become so bound together that nothing in any part thereof could be moved from its place without producing confusion of all the other parts of the Universe as a whole.

As quoted in Thomas S. Kuhn, The Copernican Revolution: Planetary Astronomy in the Development of Western Thought *(New York: Vintage Books, 1959), pp. 137–139, 141–142.*

would conform; new empirical evidence helped persuade the learned ublic of its validity.

Tycho Brahe and Johannes Kepler: New Scientific Observations

The next major step toward the conception of a sun-centered system was taken by Tycho Brahe (1546–1601). He actually spent most of his life opposing Copernicus and advocating a different kind of earth-centered system. He suggested that the moon and the sun revolved around the earth and that the other planets revolved around the sun. In attacking Copernicus, however, he gave the latter's ideas more publicity. More important, this Danish astronomer's major weapon against Copernican astronomy was a series of new naked-eye astronomical observations. Brahe constructed the most accurate tables of observations that had been drawn up for centuries.

When Brahe died, these tables came into the possession of Johannes Kepler (1571–1630), a German astronomer. Kepler was a convinced Copernican, but his reasons for taking that position were not scientific. Kepler was deeply influenced by Renaissance Neoplatonism, which held the sun in special honor. He was determined to find mathematical harmonies in Brahe's numbers that would support a sun-centered universe. After much work Kepler discovered that to keep the sun at the center of things, he must abandon the Copernican concept of circular orbits. The mathematical relationships that emerged from a consideration of Brahe's observations suggested that the orbits of the planets were elliptical. Kepler published his findings in 1609 in a book, *On the Motion of Mars*. He had solved the problem of planetary orbits by using Copernicus's sun-centered universe and Brahe's empirical data.

Kepler had also defined a new problem. None of the available theories could explain why the planetary orbits were elliptical. That solution awaited the work of Sir Isaac Newton.

Galileo Galilei: A Universe of Mathematical Laws

From Copernicus to Brahe to Kepler, there had been little new information about the heavens that might not have been known to Ptolemy. In

Tycho Brahe in the Uranienburg observatory on the Danish island of Hven (1587). Brahe made the most important observations of the stars since antiquity. Kepler used his data to solve the problem of planetary motion in a way that supported Copernicus's sun-centered view of the universe. Ironically, Brahe himself had opposed Copernicus's view. [Bildarchiv Preussischer Kulturbesitz]

the same year that Kepler published his volume on Mars, however, an Italian scientist named Galileo Galilei (1564–1642) first turned a telescope on the heavens. Through that recently invented instrument he saw stars where none had been known to exist, mountains on the moon, spots moving across the sun, and moons orbiting Jupiter. The heavens were far more complex than anyone had formerly suspected. None of these discoveries proved that the earth orbited the sun, but they did suggest the complete inadequacy of the Ptolemaic system. It simply could not accommodate itself to all these

book brought down on him the condemnation of the Roman Catholic church. He was compelled to recant his opinions. He is reputed, however, to have muttered after the recantation, *"E pur si muove"* ("It [the earth] still moves").

Galileo's discoveries and his popularization of the Copernican system were of secondary importance in his life work. His most important achievement was to articulate the concept of a universe totally subject to mathematical laws. More than any other writer of the century, he argued that nature in its most minute details displayed mathematical regularity. He once wrote:

Philosophy is written in that great book which ever lies before our eyes—I mean the universe—but we cannot understand it if we do not first learn the language and grasp the symbols in which it is written. This book is written in the mathematical language, and the symbols are triangles, circles, and other geometrical figures, without whose help it is impossible to comprehend a single word of it; without which one wanders through a dark labyrinth.[2]

The universe was rational; however, its rationality was not that of Scholastic logic but of mathematics. Copernicus had thought that the heavens conformed to mathematical regularity; Galileo saw this regularity throughout all physical nature. He believed that the smallest atom behaved with the same mathematical precision as the largest heavenly sphere.

A world of quantity was replacing one of qualities. All aspects of the world—including color, beauty, and taste—would increasingly be described in terms of the mathematical relationships among quantities. Mathematical models would eventually be applied even to social relations. Nature was cold, rational, mathematical, and mechanistic. What was real and lasting was what was mathematically measurable. Few intellectual shifts have wrought such momentous changes for Western civilization.

Isaac Newton: The Laws of Gravitation

Englishman Isaac Newton (1642–1727) drew on the work of his predecessors and his own brilliance to solve the major remaining problem of

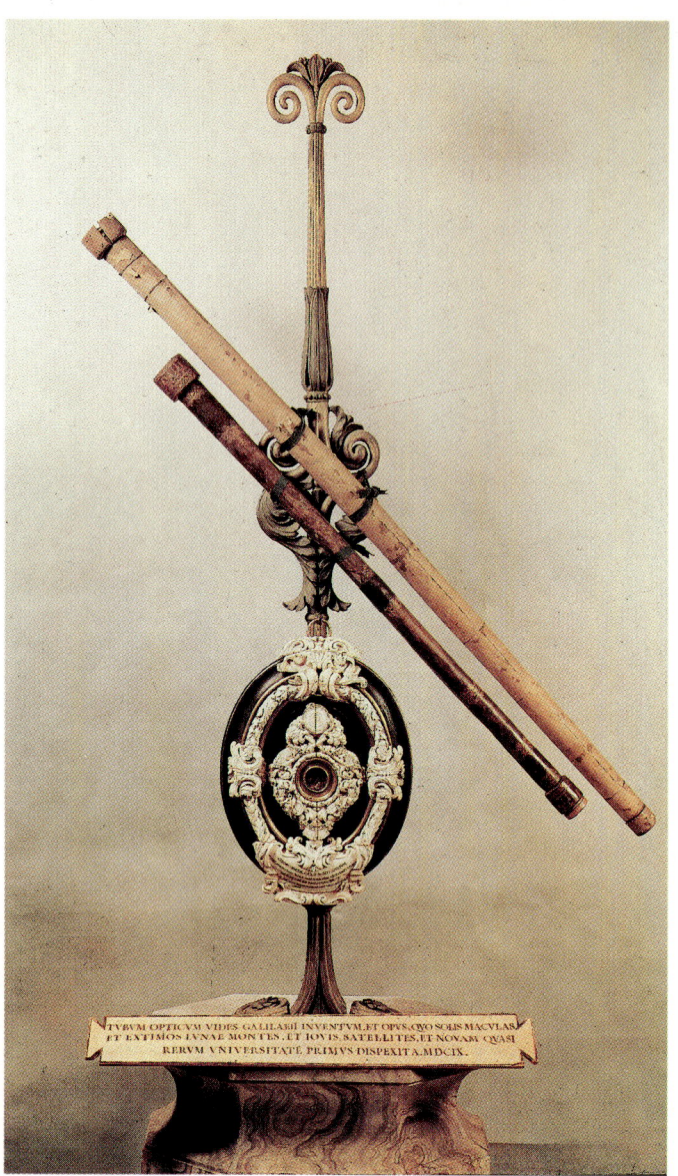

The telescope with which Galileo worked after 1609. He observed earth's moon and the cyclical phases of the planet Venus and discovered the most prominent moons of Jupiter. These observations had revolutionary intellectual and theological implications in the seventeenth century. [Istituto e Museo de Storia della Scienza, Scala/Art Resource, N.Y.]

new phenomena. Some of Galileo's colleagues at the University of Padua were so unnerved that they refused to look through the telescope.

Galileo publicized his findings and arguments for the Copernican system in numerous works, the most famous of which was his *Dialogues on the Two Chief Systems of the World* (1632). This

[2]*Quoted in E. A. Burtt,* The Metaphysical Foundations of Modern Physical Science *(Garden City, N.Y.: Anchor-Doubleday, 1954), p. 75.*

Galileo Discusses the Relationship of Science and the Bible

The religious authorities were often critical of the discoveries and theories of sixteenth- and seventeenth-century science. For years before his condemnation by the Roman Catholic church in 1633, Galileo had contended that scientific theory and religious piety were compatible. In his Letter to the Grand Duchess Christiana *(of Tuscany) written in 1615, he argued that God had revealed truth in both the Bible and physical nature and that the truth of physical nature did not contradict the Bible if the latter were properly understood.*

✦ *Is Galileo's argument based on science or theology? Did the Church believe that nature was as much a revelation of God as the Bible? As Galileo describes them, which is the surer revelation of God, nature or the Bible? Why might the pope reject Galileo's argument?*

The reason produced for condemning the opinion that the earth moves and the sun stands still is that in many places in the Bible one may read that the sun moves and the earth stands still. . . .

With regard to this argument, I think in the first place that it is very pious to say and prudent to affirm that the holy Bible can never speak untruth—whenever its true meaning is understood. But I believe nobody will deny that it is often very abstruse, and may say things which are quite different from what its bare words signify. . . .

This being granted, I think that in discussions of physical problems we ought to begin not from the authority of scriptural passages, but from sense-experiences and necessary demonstrations; for the holy Bible and the phenomena of nature proceed alike from the divine Word, the former as the dictate of the Holy Ghost and the latter as the observant executrix of God's commands. It is necessary for the Bible, in order to be accommodated to the understanding of every man, to speak many things which appear to differ from the absolute truth so far as the bare meaning of the words is concerned. But Nature, on the other hand, is inexorable and immutable; she never transgresses the laws imposed upon her, or cares a whit whether her abstruse reasons and methods of operation are understandable to men. For that reason it appears that nothing physical which sense-experience sets before our eyes, or which necessary demonstrations prove to us, ought to be called in question (much less condemned) upon the testimony of biblical passages which may have some different meaning beneath their words. For the Bible is not chained in every expression to conditions as strict as those which govern all physical effects; nor is God any less excellently revealed in Nature's actions than in the sacred statements of the Bible. . . .

From this I do not mean to infer that we need not have an extraordinary esteem for the passages of holy Scripture. On the contrary, having arrived at any certainties in physics, we ought to utilize these as the most appropriate aids in the true exposition of the Bible and in the investigation of those meanings which are necessarily contained therein for these must be concordant with demonstrated truths. I should judge the authority of the Bible was designed to persuade men of those articles and propositions which, surpassing all human reasoning, could not be made credible by science, or by any other means than through the very mouth of the Holy Spirit. . . .

But I do not feel obliged to believe that the same God who has endowed us with senses, reason, and intellect has intended to forgo their use and by some other means to give us knowledge which we can attain by them.

Discoveries and Opinions of Galileo, *trans. and ed. by Stillman Drake (Garden City, N.Y.: Doubleday Anchor Books, 1957), pp. 181–183.*

planetary motion and to establish a basis for physics that endured more than two centuries. The question that continued to perplex seventeenth-century scientists who accepted the theories of Copernicus, Kepler, and Galileo was how the planets and other heavenly bodies moved in an orderly fashion. The Ptolemaic and Aristotelian answer had been the crystalline spheres and a universe arranged in the order of the heaviness of its parts. Many unsatisfactory theories had been set forth to deal with the question.

In 1687 Newton published *The Mathematical Principles of Natural Philosophy*, better known by its Latin title of *Principia Mathematica*. Much of the research and thinking for this great work had taken place more than fifteen years earlier. Newton was heavily indebted to the work of Galileo and particularly to the latter's view that inertia applied to bodies both at rest and in motion. Galileo's mathematical bias permeated Newton's thought. Newton reasoned that the planets and all other physical objects in the universe moved through mutual attraction, or gravity. Every object in the universe affected every other object through gravity. The attraction of gravity explained why the planets moved in an orderly rather than a chaotic manner. He had found that "the force of gravity towards the whole planet did arise from and was compounded of the forces of gravity towards all its parts, and towards every one part was in the inverse proportion of the squares of the distances from the part."[3] Newton proved this relationship mathematically. He made no attempt to explain the nature of gravity itself.

Newton was a great mathematical genius, but he also upheld the importance of empirical data and observation. Like Francis Bacon (see pages 532–535), he believed that one must observe phenomena before attempting to explain them. The final test of any theory or hypothesis for him was whether it described what could actually be observed. He was a great opponent of the rationalism of the French philosopher Descartes (see pages 535–536), which he believed included insufficient guards against error. As Newton's own theory of universal gravitation became increasingly accepted, so too was Baconian empiricism.

[3]*Quoted in A. Rupert Hall*, From Galileo to Newton, 1630–1720 *(London: Fontana, 1970), p. 300.*

Sir Isaac Newton discovered the mathematical and physical laws governing the force of gravity. Newton believed that religion and science were compatible and mutually supportive, and that the study of nature gave one a beter understanding of the Creator. This portrait of Newton is by Sir Godfrey Kneller. [Bildarchiv Preussischer Kulturbesitz]

Newton's Reconciliation of Science and Faith

With the work of Newton, the natural universe became a realm of law and regularity. Beliefs in spirits and divinities were no longer necessary to explain its operation. Thus, the Scientific Revolution liberated human beings from the fear of a chaotic or haphazard universe. Most of the scientists were very devout people. They saw in the new picture of physical nature a new picture also of God. The Creator of this rational, lawful nature must also be rational. To study nature was to come to a better understanding of that Creator. Science and religious faith were not only compatible but mutually supporting. As

Newton Contemplates the Nature of God

Isaac Newton believed there was a close relationship between his scientific theory and the truths of religion. He and many other scientists of his generation were convinced that the investigation of physical nature would lead to proofs of the existence of God. In this passage, taken from comments he added to later editions of the Principia Mathematica, *Newton explains how the character of planetary motion leads one to conclude that God exists.*

◆ *How do Newton's arguments for God's existence compare with those of Thomas Aquinas (see Chapter 8, page 316)? If the pope could accept Aquinas's arguments, why not also those of Galileo and Newton? Why is Newton, like Copernicus and Galileo before him, so convinced that science and religion are in harmony? Are they still "medieval" men, or did the times in which they lived force them to argue this way to justify their work?*

The six primary planets are revolved about the sun in circles concentric with the sun. . . . Ten moons are revolved about the earth, Jupiter, and Saturn in circles concentric with them . . . ; but it is not to be conceived that mere mechanical causes could give birth to so many regular motions. . . . This most beautiful system of sun, planets, and comets could only proceed from the counsel and dominion of an intelligent and powerful Being. And if the fixed stars are the centers of other like systems, these, being formed by the like wise counsel, must be all subject to the dominion of One, especially since the light of the fixed stars is of the same nature with the light of the sun and from every system light passes into all the other systems; and lest the systems of the fixed stars should, by their gravity, fall on each other, he hath placed those systems at immense distances from one another.

This Being governs all things, not as the soul of the world, but as Lord over all; and on account of his dominion he is wont to be called "Lord God." . . . The word "God" usually signifies "Lord," but every lord is not a God. It is the dominion of a spiritual being which constitutes a God: a true, supreme, or imaginary dominion makes a true, supreme, or imaginary god. And from his true dominion it follows that the true God is a living, intelligent, and powerful Being; and, from his other perfections, that he is supreme or most perfect. He is eternal and infinite, omnipotent, and omniscient; that is, his duration reaches from eternity to eternity; his presence from infinity to infinity; he governs all things and knows all things that are or can be done. He is not eternity and infinity, but eternal and infinite; he is not duration or space, but he endures and is present. He endures forever and is everywhere present; and, by existing always and everywhere, he constitutes duration and space. . . . We have ideas of his attributes, but what the real substance of anything is we know not. . . . We know him only by his most wise and excellent contrivances of things and final causes; we admire him for his perfections, but we reverence and adore him on account of his dominion, for we adore him as his servants; and a god without dominion, providence, and final causes is nothing else but Fate and Nature.

H. S. Thayer, ed., Newton's Philosophy of Nature: Selections from His Writings *(New York: Hafner Press, 1974), pp. 42–44.*

Major Works of the Scientific Revolution	
1543	*On the Revolutions of the Heavenly Spheres* (Copernicus)
1605	*The Advancement of Learning* (Bacon)
1609	*On the Motion of Mars* (Kepler)
1620	*Novum Organum* (Bacon)
1632	*Dialogues on the Two Chief Systems of the World* (Galileo)
1637	*Discourse on Method* (Descartes)
1687	*Principia Mathematica* (Newton)

Newton wrote, "The main Business of Natural Philosophy is to argue from Phaenomena without feigning Hypothesis, and to deduce Causes from Effects, till we come to the very first Cause, which certainly is not mechanical."[4]

This reconciliation of faith and science allowed the new physics and astronomy to spread rapidly. At the very time when Europeans were finally tiring of the wars of religion, the new science provided the basis for a view of God that might lead away from irrational disputes and wars over religious doctrine. Faith in a rational God encouraged faith in the rationality of human beings and in their capacity to improve their lot once liberated from the traditions of the past. The Scientific Revolution provided the great model for the desirability of change and of criticism of inherited views. The new science, however, caused some people to feel that the mystery had been driven from the universe and that the rational Creator was less loving and less near to humankind than the God of earlier ages.

Continuing Superstition: Witch Hunts and Panic

The new science by no means swept away all other thought. Traditional beliefs and fears long retained their hold on the culture. During the

[4]*Quoted in Franklin Baumer,* Main Currents of Western Thought, *4th ed. (New Haven: Yale, 1978) p. 323.*

sixteenth and seventeenth centuries many Europeans remained preoccupied with sin, death, and the Devil. Religious people, including many among the learned and many who were sympathetic to the emerging scientific ideas, continued to believe in the power of magic and the occult. Until the end of the seventeenth century almost all Europeans in one way or another believed in the power of demons.

Nowhere is the dark side of early modern thought and culture better seen than in the witch hunts and panics that erupted in almost every Western land. Between 1400 and 1700, courts sentenced an estimated 70,000–100,000 people to death for harmful magic (*maleficium*) and diabolical witchcraft. In addition to inflicting harm on their neighbors, these witches were said to attend mass meetings known as *sabbats*, to which they were believed to fly. They were also accused of indulging in sexual orgies with the Devil, who appeared at such gatherings in animal form, most often as a he-goat. Still other charges against them were cannibalism (they were alleged to be especially fond of small Christian children) and a variety of ritual acts and practices designed to insult every Christian belief and value.

Where did such beliefs come from, and how could seemingly enlightened people believe them? Their roots were in both popular and elite cultures, especially in clerical culture.

Village Origins

In village societies, so-called cunning folk played a positive role in helping people cope with calamity. People turned to them for help when such natural disasters as plague and famine struck or when such physical disabilities as lameness or inability to conceive offspring befell either humans or animals. The cunning folk provided consolation and gave people hope that such natural calamities might be averted or reversed by magical means. In this way they provided an important service and kept village life moving forward.

Possession of magical powers, for good or ill, made one an important person within village society. Not surprisingly, claims to such powers most often were made by the people most in need of security and influence, namely, the old and the impoverished, especially single or widowed women. Witch beliefs in village society may also have been a way of defying urban Christian society's attempts to impose its laws and institutions on the countryside. From this perspective, village Satanism became a fanciful substitute for an impossible social revolt, a way of spurning the values of one's new masters. It is also possible, although unlikely, that witch beliefs in rural society had a foundation in local fertility cults, whose semipagan practices, designed to ensure good harvests, may have acquired the features of diabolical witchcraft under Church persecution.

Influence of the Clergy

Popular belief in magic was the essential foundation of the great witch hunts of the sixteenth and seventeenth centuries. Had ordinary people not believed that certain gifted individuals could aid or harm others by magical means, and had they not been willing to make accusations, the hunts could never have occurred. Yet the contribution of learned society was equally great. The Christian clergy also practiced magic, that of the holy sacraments, and the exorcism of demons had been one of their traditional functions within society. Fear of demons and the Devil, which the clergy actively encouraged, allowed the clergy to assert their moral authority over people and to enforce religious discipline and conformity.

In the late thirteenth century the Church declared that only its priests possessed legitimate magical power. Since such power was not human, theologians reasoned, it had to come either from God or from the Devil. If it came from God, then it was properly confined to and exercised only on behalf of the Church. Those who practiced magic outside the Church evidently derived their power from the Devil. From such reasoning grew accusations of "pacts" between non-Christian magicians and Satan. This made the witch hunts a life-and-death struggle against Christian society's worst heretics and foes, those who had directly sworn allegiance to the Devil himself.

The Church based its intolerance of magic outside its walls on sincere belief in and fear of the Devil. But attacking witches was also a way for established Christian society to extend its power and influence into new areas. To accuse, try, and execute witches was also a declaration of moral and political authority over a village or territory. As the cunning folk were local spiritual authorities, revered and feared by people, their removal became a major step in establishing a Christian beachhead in village society.

Role of Women

A good 80 percent of the victims of witch hunts were women, the vast majority between forty-five and sixty years of age and single. This fact has suggested to some that misogyny fueled the witch hunts. Based in male hatred and sexual fear of women, and occurring at a time when women threatened to break out from under male control, witch hunts, it is argued, were simply woman hunts. Older single women may, however, have been vulnerable for more basic social reasons. They were a largely dependent social group in need of public assistance and natural targets for the peculiar "social engineering" of the witch hunts. Some accused witches were women who sought to protect and empower themselves within their communities by claiming supernatural powers.

It may be, however, that gender played a largely circumstantial role. Because of their economic straits, more women than men laid claim to the supernatural powers that made them influential in village society. For this reason, they found themselves on the front lines in disproportionate numbers when the Church declared war against all who practiced magic without its blessing. Also, the involvement of many of these women in midwifery associated them with the deaths of beloved wives and infants and thus made them targets of local resentment and accusations. Both the Church and their neighbors were prepared to think and say the worst about these women. It was a deadly combination.

Witch Panics

Why did the great witch panics occur in the second half of the sixteenth and early seventeenth centuries? The misfortune created by religious

Three witches suspected of practicing harmful magic are burned alive on a pyre in Baden. On the left, two of them are shown feasting and cavorting with demons at a Sabbat. [Bildarchiv Preussischer Kulturbesitz]

division and warfare were major factors. The new levels of violence exacerbated fears and hatreds and encouraged scapegoating. But political self-aggrandizement also played a role. As governments expanded and attempted to control their realms, they, like the Church, wanted to eliminate all competition for the loyalty of their subjects. Secular rulers as well as the pope could pronounce their competitors "devilish."

Some argue that the Reformation was responsible for the witch panics. Having weakened the traditional religious protections against demons and the Devil, while at the same time portray-ing them as still powerful, the Reformation is said to have forced people to protect themselves by executing perceived witches.

End of the Witch Hunts

Why did the witch hunts come to an end in the seventeenth century? Many factors played a role. The emergence of a new, more scientific worldview made it difficult to believe in the powers of witches. When in the seventeenth century mind and matter came to be viewed as two independent realities, words and thoughts

Why More Women Than Men Are Witches

A classic of misogyny, The Hammer of Witches *(1486), written by two Dominican monks, Heinrich Krämer and Jacob Sprenger, was sanctioned by Pope Innocent VIII as an official guide to the Church's detection and punishment of witches. Here Krämer and Sprenger explain why they believe that the great majority of witches are women rather than men.*

✦ *Why would two Dominican monks say such things about women? What are the biblical passages that they believe justify them? Do their descriptions have any basis in the actual behavior of women then? What is the rivalry between married and unmarried people that they refer to?*

Why are there more superstitious women than men? The first [reason] is that they are more credulous; and since the chief aim of the devil is to corrupt faith, therefore he rather attacks them. . . . The second reason is that women are naturally more impressionable and ready to receive the influence of a disembodied spirit. . . . The third reason is that they have slippery tongues and are unable to conceal from their fellow-women those things which by evil arts they know; and since they are weak, they find an easy and secret manner of vindicating themselves by witchcraft. . . . [Therefore] since women are feebler both in mind and body, it is not surprising that they should come more under the spell of witchcraft. For as regards intellect, or the understanding of spiritual things, they seem to be of a different nature from men, a fact which is vouched for by the logic of the authorities, backed by various examples from the Scriptures. . . .

But the natural reason [for woman's proclivity to witchcraft] is that she is more carnal than a man, as is clear from her many carnal abominations. And it should be noted that there was a defect in the formation of the first woman, since she was formed from a bent rib, that is, a rib of the breast, which is bent as it were in a contrary direction to a man. And since through this defect she is an imperfect animal, she always deceives. . . .

As to her other mental quality, her natural will, when she hates someone whom she formerly loved, then she seethes with anger and impatience in her whole soul, just as the tides of the sea are always heaving and boiling. . . .

Truly the most powerful cause which contributes to the increase of witches is the woeful rivalry between married folk and unmarried women and men. This [jealousy or rivalry exists] even among holy women, so what must it be among the others . . . ?

Just as through the first defect in their intelligence women are more prone [than men] to abjure the faith, so through their second defect of inordinate affections and passions they search for, brood over, and inflict various vengeances, either by witchcraft or by some other means. Wherefore it is no wonder that so great a number of witches exist in this sex. . . . [Indeed, witchcraft] is better called the heresy of witches than of wizards, since the name is taken from the more powerful party [that is, the greater number, who are women]. Blessed be the Highest who has so far preserved the male sex from so great a crime.

Malleus Maleficarum, *trans. by Montague Summers (Bungay, Suffolk: John Rodker, 1928), pp. 41–47.*

lost the ability to affect things. A witch's curse was merely words. With advances in medicine and the beginning of insurance companies, people learned to rely on themselves when faced with natural calamity and physical affliction and no longer searched for supernatural causes and solutions. Witch hunts also tended to get out of hand. Accused witches sometimes alleged that important townspeople had also attended sabbats; even the judges could be so accused. At this point the trials ceased to serve the purposes of those who were conducting them. They not only became dysfunctional but threatened anarchy as well.

Although Protestants, like Catholics, hunted witches, the Reformation may also have contributed to an attitude of mind that put the Devil in a more manageable perspective. Protestants ridiculed the sacramental magic of the old Church as superstition and directed their faith to a sovereign God absolutely supreme over time and eternity. Even the Devil was believed to serve God's purposes and acted only with His permission. Ultimately God was the only significant spiritual force in the universe. This belief made the Devil a less fearsome creature. "One little word can slay him," Luther wrote of the Devil in the great hymn of the Reformation.

Finally, the imaginative and philosophical literature of the sixteenth and seventeenth centuries (see below), while continuing to display concern for religion and belief in the supernatural, also suggested that human beings have a significant degree of control over their own lives and need not be constantly fearing demons and resorting to supernatural aid.

Literary Imagination in Transition

The world of the new science developed in the midst of a society where medieval outlooks and religious values remained very much alive. Literary figures of the same period often reflected both the new and the old. In Cervantes one sees a brilliant writer raising questions about the adequacy of medieval values of chivalry and honor and probing the nature of human perceptions of reality. Shakespeare's dramas provide an insight into virtually the entire range of late sixteenth- and early seventeenth-century English worldviews. John Milton could attempt to justify the ways of the Christian God to doubting human beings and in the same work have characters debate the adequacy of the Ptolemaic and Copernican systems. During the same years that Newton reached his deepest insights about nature, John Bunyan could write one of the classic works of simple Christian piety. It is the combination of past and future worldviews that makes the thought of the seventeenth century so remarkable and rich.

Miguel de Cervantes Saavedra: Rejection of Idealism

Spanish literature of the sixteenth and seventeenth centuries reflects the peculiar religious and political history of Spain in this period. Spain was a deeply Catholic country, and this was a major influence on its literature. Since the joint reign of Ferdinand and Isabella (1479–1504), the Church had received the unqualified support of reigning political power. Although there was religious reform in Spain, a Protestant Reformation never occurred, thanks largely to the entrenched power of the Church and the Inquisition.

A second influence on Spanish literature was the aggressive piety of Spanish rulers, and this intertwining of Catholic piety and political power underlay a third influence: preoccupation with medieval chivalric virtues—in particular, questions of honor and loyalty. The novels and plays of the period almost invariably focus on a special decision involving a character's reputation as his honor or loyalty is tested. In this regard Spanish literature may be said to have remained more Catholic and medieval than that of England and France, where major Protestant movements had occurred. Two of the most important Spanish writers in this period became priests (Lope de Vega and Pedro Calderón de la Barca). The one generally acknowledged to be the greatest Spanish writer of all time, Cervantes, was preoccupied in his work with the strengths and weaknesses of religious idealism.

Cervantes (1547–1616) had only a smattering of formal education. He educated himself by wide reading in popular literature and immersion in the "school of life." As a young man he worked in Rome for a Spanish cardinal. As a soldier he was decorated for gallantry in the Battle of Lepanto (1571). He also spent five years as a slave in Algiers after his ship was pirated in 1575. Later, while working as a tax collector, he was several times imprisoned for padding his accounts, and it was in prison that he began, in 1603, to write his most famous work, *Don Quixote*.

The first part of *Don Quixote* appeared in 1605. The intent of this work seems to have been to satirize the chivalric romances then popular in Spain. But Cervantes could not conceal his deep affection for the character he created as an object of ridicule, Don Quixote. The work is satire only on the surface and has remained as much an object of study by philosophers and theologians as by students of Spanish literature. Cervantes presented Don Quixote as a none-too-stable middle-aged man. Driven mad by reading too many chivalric romances, he had come to believe he was an aspiring knight who had to prove his worthiness by brave deeds. To this end, he donned a rusty suit of armor and chose for his inspiration a quite unworthy peasant girl (Dulcinea), whom he fancied to be a noble lady to whom he could, with honor, dedicate his life.

Don Quixote's foil—Sancho Panza, a clever, worldly-wise peasant who serves as his squire—watched with bemused skepticism as his lord did battle with a windmill (which he mistook for a dragon) and repeatedly made a fool of himself as he galloped across the countryside. The story ends tragically with Don Quixote's humiliating defeat by a well-meaning friend, who, disguised as a knight, bests Don Quixote in combat and forces him to renounce his quest for knighthood. The humiliated Don Quixote does not, however, come to his senses as a result. He returns sadly to his village to die a shamed and broken-hearted old man.

Throughout *Don Quixote*, Cervantes juxtaposes the down-to-earth realism of Sancho Panza with the old-fashioned religious idealism of Don Quixote. The reader perceives that Cervantes admired the one as much as the

Miguel de Cervantes Saavedra (1547–1616), the author of Don Quixote, *considered by many to be Spain's greatest writer. [Art Resource, N.Y.]*

other and meant to portray both as representing attitudes necessary for a happy life.

William Shakespeare: Dramatist of the Age

There is much less factual knowledge about Shakespeare (1564–1616) than one would expect of the greatest playwright in the English language. He married at the early age of eighteen, in 1582, and he and his wife, Anne Hathaway, were the parents of three children (including twins) by 1585. He apparently worked as a schoolteacher for a time and in this capacity gained his broad knowledge of Renaissance learning and literature. His own reading and enthusiasm for the learning of his day are manifest in the many literary allusions that appear in his plays.

Shakespeare lived the life of a country gentleman. There is none of the Puritan distress over worldliness in his work. He took the new commercialism and the bawdy pleasures of the Elizabethan Age in stride and with amusement. He was a radical neither in politics nor religion. The few allusions in his works to the Puritans seem more critical than complimentary.

That Shakespeare was interested in politics is apparent from his history plays and the references to contemporary political events that fill all his plays. He viewed government through the character of the individual ruler, whether Richard III or Elizabeth Tudor, not in terms of ideal systems or social goals. By modern standards he was a political conservative, accepting the social rankings and the power structure of his day and demonstrating unquestioned patriotism.

Shakespeare knew the theater as one who participated in every phase of its life—as a playwright, an actor, and part owner of a theater. He was a member and principal writer of a famous company of actors known as the King's Men. Between 1590 and 1610, many of his plays were performed at court, where he moved with comfort and received both Queen Elizabeth's and King James's enthusiastic patronage.

Elizabethan drama was already a distinctive form when Shakespeare began writing. Unlike French drama of the seventeenth century, which was dominated by classical models, English drama developed in the sixteenth and seventeenth centuries as a blending of many forms: classical comedies and tragedies, medieval morality plays, and contemporary Italian short stories.

A view of London indicating the Swan Theatre, where many of Shakespeare's plays were performed. [Folger Shakespeare Library]

Two contemporaries, Thomas Kyd and Christopher Marlowe, influenced Shakespeare's tragedies. Kyd (1558–1594) wrote the first dramatic version of *Hamlet*. The tragedies of Marlowe (1564–1593) set a model for character, poetry, and style that only Shakespeare among the English playwrights of the period surpassed. Shakespeare synthesized the best past and current achievements. A keen student of human motivation and passion, he had a unique talent for getting into people's minds.

Shakespeare wrote histories, comedies, and tragedies. *Richard III* (1593), a very early play, stands out among the histories, although some scholars have criticized as Tudor propaganda the picture it presents of Richard as an unprincipled villain. Shakespeare's comedies, although not attaining the heights of his tragedies, surpass his history plays in originality.

The tragedies are considered his unique achievement. Four of these were written within a three-year period: *Hamlet* (1603), *Othello* (1604), *King Lear* (1605), and *Macbeth* (1606). The most original of the tragedies, *Romeo and Juliet* (1597), transformed an old popular story into a moving drama of "star-cross'd lovers." Both Romeo and Juliet, denied a marriage by their warring families, die tragic deaths. Romeo, finding Juliet and thinking her dead after she has taken a sleeping potion, poisons himself. Juliet, awakening to find Romeo dead, kills herself with his dagger.

Throughout his lifetime and ever since, Shakespeare was immensely popular with both the playgoer and the play reader. The works of no other dramatist from his age are performed in theaters, and even on the screen, more regularly today.

John Milton: Puritan Poet

John Milton (1608–1674) was the son of a devout Puritan father. As a student, he avidly read the Christian and pagan classics. In 1638 he traveled to Italy, where he found in the lingering Renaissance a very congenial intellectual atmosphere. The Phlegraean Fields near Naples, a volcanic region, later became the model for hell in *Paradise Lost,* and it is suspected by some scholars that the Villa d'Este provided the model for paradise in *Paradise Regained*. Milton remained throughout his life a man more at home in the Italian Renaissance, with its high ideals and universal vision, than in the war-torn England of the seventeenth century.

A man of deep inner conviction and principle, Milton believed that standing a test of character was the most important thing in a person's life. This belief informed his own personal life and is the subject of much of his literary work.

In 1639 Milton joined the Puritan struggle against Charles I and Archbishop Laud. Employing his writing talent, he defended the Presbyterian form of Church government against the episcopacy and supported other Puritan reforms. After a month-long unsuccessful marriage in 1642 (a marriage later reconciled), he wrote several tracts in defense of the right to divorce. These writings became targets of a Parliamentary censorship law in 1643, against which Milton wrote an eloquent defense of freedom of the press entitled *Areopagitica* (1644).

Until the upheavals of the civil war moderated his views, Milton believed that government should have the least possible control over the

John Milton (1608–1674). [Courtesy of the Prints Division, Library of Congress.]

private lives of individuals. When Parliament divided into Presbyterians and Independents, he took the side of the latter, who wanted to dissolve the national church altogether in favor of the local autonomy of individual congregations. He also defended the execution of Charles I in a tract entitled *On the Tenure of Kings and Magistrates*. After his intense labor on this tract, his eyesight failed. Milton was totally blind when he wrote his masterpieces.

Paradise Lost, completed in 1665 and published in 1667, is a study of the destructive qualities of pride and the redeeming possibilities of humility. It elaborates in traditional Christian language and concept the revolt of Satan in heaven and the fall of Adam on earth. The motives of Satan and all who rebel against God intrigued Milton. His proud but tragic Satan, who preferred to reign in hell than to serve in heaven, is one of the great figures in world literature and represented for Milton the absolute corruption of potential greatness.

Milton wanted *Paradise Lost* to be for England what Homer's *Iliad* was for Greece and Vergil's *Aeneid* for Rome. In choosing biblical subject matter, he revealed the great influence of contemporary theology on his mind. Milton tended to agree with the Arminians, followers of the Dutch Protestant theologian Arminius (1560–1609), who, unlike the extreme Calvin-

John Milton Defends Freedom to Print Books

During the English Civil War, the Parliament passed a very strict censorship measure. In Areopagitica (1644), John Milton attacked this law and contributed one of the major defenses for the freedom of the press in the history of Western culture. In the following passage, he compares the life of a book with the life of a human being.

◆ *Why does Milton think that it may be more dangerous and harmful to attack a book than to attack a person? Was life cheaper and intelligence rarer in his time? Does he have particular kinds of books in mind? What can a book do for society that people cannot?*

I deny not but that it is of greatest concern in the Church and Commonwealth to have a vigilant eye how books demean themselves as well as men; and thereafter to confine, imprison, and do sharpest justice on them as [if they were criminals]; for books are not absolutely dead things, but do contain a progeny of life in them to be as active as that soul was whose progeny they are; nay, they do preserve as in a vial the purest efficacy and extraction of that living intellect that bred them. . . . He who kills a man kills a reasonable creature, God's Image; but he who destroys a good book, kills reason itself, kills the Image of God, as it were. . . . Many a man lives [as] a burden to the Earth; but a good book is the precious life-blood of a master spirit, embalmed and treasured up on purpose to a life beyond life. It is true, no age can restore a life, whereof, perhaps there is no great loss; and revolutions of ages do not oft recover the loss of a rejected truth, for the want of which whole nations fare the worse. We should be wary, therefore, what persecution we raise against the living labours of public men, how we spill that seasoned life of man preserved and stored up in books; since we see a kind of homicide may be thus committed, sometimes a martyrdom, and if it extends to the whole impression, a kind of massacre, whereof the execution ends not in the slaying of an elemental life, but strikes at that ethereal . . . essence, the breath of reason itself; slays an immortality rather than a life.

J. A. St. John, ed., The Prose Works of John Milton *(London: H. G. Bohn, 1843–1853), 2:8–9.*

ists, did not believe that all worldly events, including the Fall of Man, were immutably fixed in the eternal decree of God. Milton shared the Arminian belief that human beings must take responsibility for their fate and that human efforts to improve character could, with God's grace, bring salvation.

Perhaps his own blindness, joined with the hope of making the best of the failed Puritan revolution, inclined Milton to sympathize with those who urged people to make the most of what they had, even in the face of defeat. That is a manifest concern of his last works, *Samson Agonistes*, which recounts the biblical story of Samson, and *Paradise Regained*, the story of Christ's temptation in the wilderness, both published in 1671.

John Bunyan: Visions of Christian Piety

Bunyan (1628–1688) was the English author of two classics of sectarian Puritan spirituality: *Grace Abounding* (1666) and *The Pilgrim's Progress* (1678). A Bedford tinker, his works speak especially for the seventeenth-century working people and popular religious culture. He received only the most basic education before taking up his father's craft, and he served in Oliver Cromwell's revolutionary army for two years. The visionary fervor of the New Model Army influenced his work, which is filled with the language of battle.

After the restoration of the monarchy in 1660, Bunyan went to prison for his fiery preaching and remained there for twelve years. During these years, he wrote his famous autobiography, *Grace Abounding*, both a very personal statement and a model for the faithful. Like *The Pilgrim's Progress*, Bunyan's later masterpiece, *Grace Abounding* is Puritan piety at its most fervent. Puritans believed that individuals could do absolutely nothing to save themselves, and this made them extremely restless and introspective. People could only trust that God had placed them among the elect and try each day to live a life that reflected such favored status. So long as men and women struggled successfully against the flesh and the world, they had presumptive evidence that they were among God's elect. To falter or to become complacent in the face of temptation was to cast doubt on one's

faith and salvation and even to raise the specter of eternal damnation.

This anxious questing for salvation is the subject of *The Pilgrim's Progress*, a work unique in its contribution to Western religious symbolism and imagery. It is the story of the journey of Christian and his friends Hopeful and Faithful to the Celestial City. It teaches that one must deny spouse, children, and all earthly security and go in search of "Life, life, eternal life." During the long journey, the travelers must resist the temptations of Worldly-Wiseman and Vanity Fair, pass through the Slough of Despond, and endure a long dark night in Doubting Castle, their faith being tested at every turn. Bunyan later wrote a work tracing the progress of Christian's opposite, *The Life and Death of Mr. Badman* (1680), which told the story of a man so addicted to the bad habits of Restoration society, of which Bunyan strongly disapproved, that he journeyed steadfastly not to heaven but to hell.

Philosophy in the Wake of Changing Science

By the end of the sixteenth century, many people, weary of religious strife, no longer embraced either the old Catholic or the new Protestant absolutes. The century that followed was a period of intellectual as well as political transition. The thinkers of the Renaissance, reacting against the dogmatic thinking of medieval Scholasticism, had laid the groundwork for this change.

Major Works of Seventeenth-Century Literature and Philosophy	
1605	*King Lear* (Shakespeare)
1605	*Don Quixote*, Part I (Cervantes)
1651	*Leviathan* (Hobbes)
1656–1657	*Provincial Letters* (Pascal)
1667	*Paradise Lost* (Milton)
1677	*Ethics* (Spinoza)
1678	*The Pilgrim's Progress* (Bunyan)
1690	*Treatises of Government* (Locke)
1690	*An Essay Concerning Human Understanding* (Locke)

The revolution in scientific thought contributed directly to a major reconsideration of Western philosophy. Several of the most important figures in the Scientific Revolution, such as Descartes and Bacon, were also philosophers

The microscope of Robert Hooke (1535–1703). The microscope became the telescope's companion as a major optical instrument in the seventeenth century. Several scientists, including Galileo, had a hand in its development, but the Englishman Hooke and the Dutchman Anton von Leeuwenhoek (1632–1723) did the most to perfect it. [Historical Collections, National Museum of Health and Medicine, Armed Forces Institute of Pathology]

discontented with the Scholastic heritage. Bacon stressed the importance of empirical research. Descartes attempted to find certainty through the exploration of his thinking processes. Newton's interests likewise extended to philosophy; he wrote broadly on many topics, including scientific method and theology.

The new methods of science had a broad impact on philosophers. The emphasis that Galileo placed on mathematics spread to other areas of thought. Pascal, a gifted mathematician, became concerned about the issue of certain knowledge and religious faith. Spinoza would write his ethical discourses in the form of geometrical theorems. Hobbes produced a great political treatise through a mode of rational reasoning resembling mathematics. Locke would attempt to explore the human mind in a fashion that he believed resembled Newton's approach to the physical universe. Virtually all of these writers found a tension that they hoped to resolve between the new science and religious belief.

Francis Bacon: Empirical Method

Bacon (1561–1626) was an Englishman of almost universal accomplishment. He was a lawyer, a high royal official, and the author of histories, moral essays, and philosophical discourses. Traditionally, he has been regarded as the father of empiricism and of experimentation in science. Much of this reputation is unearned. Bacon was not a scientist except in the most amateur fashion. His accomplishment was setting a tone and helping to create a climate conducive to scientific work.

In books such as *The Advancement of Learning* (1605), the *Novum Organum* (1620), and the *New Atlantis* (1627), Bacon attacked the Scholastic belief that most truth had already been discovered and only required explanation, as well as the Scholastic reverence for intellectual authority in general. He believed that Scholastic thinkers paid too much attention to tradition and to the knowledge of the ancients. He urged contemporaries to strike out on their own in search of a new understanding of nature. He wanted seventeenth-century Europeans to have confidence in themselves and their own abilities rather than in the people and methods of the past. Bacon was one of the first major European writers to champion the desirability of innovation and change.

Bacon believed that human knowledge should produce useful results. In particular, knowledge of nature should be brought to the aid of the human condition. These goals required the modification or abandonment of Scholastic modes of learning and thinking. Bacon contended, "The [Scholastic] logic now in use serves more to fix and give stability to the errors which have their foundation in commonly received notions than to help the search after truth."[5] Scholastic philosophers could not escape from their syllogisms to examine the foundations of their thought and intellectual presuppositions. Bacon urged that philosophers and investigators of nature examine the evidence of their senses before constructing logical speculations. In a famous passage, he divided all philosophers into "men of experiment and men of dogmas." He observed:

The men of experiment are like the ant, they only collect and use; the reasoners resemble spiders, who make cobwebs out of their own substance. But the bee takes a middle course: it gathers its material from the flowers of the garden and of the field, but transforms and digests it by a power of its own. Not unlike this is the true business of philosophy.[6]

By directing scientists toward an examination of empirical evidence, Bacon hoped that they would achieve new knowledge and thus new capabilities for humankind.

Bacon compared himself with Columbus plotting a new route to intellectual discovery. The comparison is significant, because it displays the consciousness of a changing world that appears so often in writers of the late sixteenth and early seventeenth centuries. They were rejecting the past not from simple hatred but rather from a firm understanding that the world was much more complicated than their medieval forebears had thought.

Neither Europe nor European thought could

Sir Francis Bacon (1561–1626), champion of the inductive method of gaining knowledge. [By courtesy of the National Portrait Gallery, London]

remain self-contained. Like the new worlds on the globe, new worlds of the mind were also emerging. Most of the people in Bacon's day, including the intellectuals, thought that the best era of human history lay in antiquity. Bacon dissented vigorously from that view. He looked to a future of material improvement achieved through the empirical examination of nature. His own theory of induction from empirical evidence was quite unsystematic, but his insistence on appeal to experience influenced others whose methods were more productive.

Bacon believed that science had a practical purpose and its goal was human improvement.

[5]*Quoted in Baumer, p. 281.*
[6]*Quoted in Baumer, p. 288.*

Bacon Attacks the Idols That Harm Human Understanding

Francis Bacon wanted the men and women of his era to have the courage to change the way they thought about physical nature. In this famous passage from the Novum Organum *(1620), he attempted to explain why it is so difficult to ask new questions and seek new answers.*

✦ *Is Bacon's view of human nature pessimistic? Are people hopelessly trapped in overlapping worlds of self-interest and fantasy imposed by their nature and cultural traditions? How did Bacon expect people to overcome such formidable barriers?*

The idols and false notions which are now in possession of the human understanding and have taken deep root therein . . . . so beset men's minds that truth can hardly find entrance. . . . There are four classes of Idols which beset men's minds. To these for distinction's sake I have assigned names,—calling the first class *Idols of the Tribe*; the second, *Idols of the Cave*; the third, *Idols of the Marketplace*; the fourth, *Idols of the Theatre*.

The Idols of the Tribe have their foundation in human nature itself; and in the tribe or race of men. For it is a false assertion that the sense of man is the measure of things. On the contrary, all perceptions as well as the sense as of the mind are according to the measure of the universe. And the human understanding is like a false mirror, which, receiving rays irregularly, distorts and discolours the nature of things by mingling its own nature with it.

The Idols of the Cave are the idols of the individual man. For every one (besides the errors common to human nature in general) has a cave or den of his own, which refracts and discolours the light of nature; owing either to his own proper and peculiar nature; or to his education and conversation with others; or to the reading of books, and the authority of those whom he esteems and admires. . . .

There are also Idols formed by the intercourse and association of men with each other, which I call Idols of the Marketplace, on account of the commerce and consort of men there. For it is by discourse that men associate; and words are imposed according to the apprehension of the vulgar. And therefore the ill and unfit choice of words wonderfully obstructs the understanding. . . .

Lastly, there are Idols which have immigrated into men's minds from the various dogmas of philosophies, and also from wrong laws of demonstration. These I call Idols of the Theatre; because in my judgment all the received systems are but so many stage plays, representing worlds of their own creation after an unreal and scenic fashion.

Francis Bacon, Essays, Advancement of Learning, New Atlantis, and Other Pieces, *ed. by Richard Foster Jones (New York: Odyssey, 1937), pp. 278–280.*

Some scientific investigation does have this character. Much pure research does not. Bacon, however, linked science and material progress in the public mind. This was a powerful idea and has continued to influence Western civilization to the present day. It has made science and those who can appeal to the authority of science major forces for change and innovation. Thus, though not making any major scientific contribution himself, Bacon directed investigators of nature to a new method and a new purpose.

René Descartes: The Method of Rational Deduction

Descartes (1596–1650) was a gifted mathematician who invented analytic geometry. His most important contribution, however, was to develop a scientific method that relied more on deduction than empirical observation and induction.

In 1637 he published his *Discourse on Method,* in which he attempted to provide a basis for all thinking founded on a mathematical model. The work appeared in French rather than in Latin because he wanted it to have wide circulation and application. He began by saying that he would doubt everything except those propositions about which he could have clear and distinct ideas. This approach rejected all forms of intellectual authority except the conviction of his own reason. He concluded that he could not doubt his own act of thinking and his own existence. From this base he proceeded to deduce the existence of God. The presence of God was important to Descartes because God guaranteed the correctness of clear and distinct ideas. Because God was not a deceiver, the ideas of God-given reason could not be false.

On the basis of such assumptions, Descartes concluded that human reason could fully comprehend the world. He divided existing things into two basic categories: things thought and things occupying space, mind and body. Thinking was characteristic of the mind and extension (things occupying space) of the body. Within the material world, the world of extension, mathematical laws reigned supreme and could be grasped by reason. Because they were mathematical, they could be deduced from each other and constituted a complete system. The world of extension was the world of the scientist. It had no place for spirits, divinity, or anything nonmaterial. Descartes separated mind from body to banish such things from the realm of scientific speculation. Reason was to be applied only to the mechanical and mathematical realm of matter.

Descartes's emphasis on deduction and rational speculation exercised broad influence. His deductive methodology, however, eventually lost favor to scientific induction, in which the scientist draws generalizations from data derived from empirical observations.

Blaise Pascal: Reason and Faith

Pascal (1623–1662) was a French mathematician and a physical scientist who surrendered all his wealth to pursue an austere, self-disciplined life. Torn between dogmatism (which he saw epitomized by the Jesuits) and skepticism, he aspired to write a work that would refute both. He considered the Jesuits' casuistry (i.e., arguments designed to minimize and excuse sinful acts) a distortion of Christian teaching. He rejected the skeptics of his age because they either denied religion altogether (atheists) or accepted it only as it conformed to reason

René Descartes (1596–1650) believed that because the material world operated according to mathematical laws, it could be accurately understood by the exercise of human reason. [Erich Lessing/Art Resource, N.Y.]

(deists). He never produced a definitive refutation of the two sides. Rather he formulated his views on these matters in piecemeal fashion in a provocative collection of reflections on humankind and religion published posthumously under the title *Pensées*.

Pascal allied himself with the Jansenists, seventeenth-century Catholic opponents of the Jesuits. His sister was a member of the Jansenist community of Port-Royal, near Paris. The Jansenists shared with the Calvinists Saint Augustine's belief in human beings' total sinfulness, their eternal predestination by God, and their complete dependence on faith and grace for knowledge of God and salvation.

Pascal believed that reason and science were of no avail in matters of religion. Here only the reasons of the heart and a "leap of faith" could prevail. He saw two essential truths in the Christian religion: that a loving God, worthy of human attainment, exists, and that human beings, because they are corrupt by nature, are

---

Pascal Meditates on Human Beings As Thinking Creatures

Pascal was both a religious and a scientific writer. Unlike other scientific thinkers of the seventeenth century, he was not overly optimistic about the ability of science to improve the human condition. But science and philosophy might help human beings to understand their situation better. In these passages from his Pensées (Thoughts), *he ponders the uniqueness of human beings as thinking creatures.*

✦ *Is this an intellectual's view of human nature? Where does the idea that man is a rational creature come from, that human reason is more noble than the universe? Does Pascal ignore human will and emotion, selfishness, and destructive-*

339

I can well conceive a man without hands, feet, head (for it is only experience which teaches us that the head is more necessary than feet). But I cannot conceive man without thought; he would be a stone or a brute.

344

Reason commands us far more imperiously than a master; for in disobeying the one we are unfortunate, and in disobeying the other we are fools.

346

Thought constitutes the greatness of man.

347

Man is but a reed, the most feeble thing in nature; but he is a thinking reed. The entire universe need not arm itself to crush him. A vapour, a drop of water suffices to kill him. But, if the universe were to crush him, man would still be more noble than that which killed him, because he knows that he dies and the advantage which the universe has over him; the universe knows nothing of this.

All our dignity consists, then, in thought. By it we must elevate ourselves, and not by space and time which we cannot fill. Let us endeavour, then, to think well; this is the principle of morality.

348

A thinking reed—It is not from space that I must seek my dignity, but from the government of my thought. I shall have no more if I possess worlds. By space the universe encompasses and swallows me up like an atom; by thought I comprehend the world.

Blaise Pascal, Pensées and The Provincial Letters *(New York: Modern Library, 1941), pp. 115–116.*

utterly unworthy of God. He believed that the atheists and the deists of his age had spurned the clear lesson of reason. For him rational analysis of the human condition revealed utter mortality and corruption and exposed the weakness of reason itself in resolving the problems of human nature and destiny. Reason properly drove those who truly heed it to faith in God and reliance on divine grace.

Pascal made a famous wager with the skeptics. It is a better bet, he argued, to believe that God exists and to stake everything on His promised mercy than not to do so. This is because if God does exist, everything will be gained by the believer, whereas, should He prove not to exist, the loss incurred by having believed in Him is by comparison very slight.

Convinced that belief in God improved life psychologically and disciplined it morally (regardless of whether God proved in the end to exist), Pascal worked to strengthen traditional religious belief. He urged his contemporaries to seek self-understanding by "learned ignorance" and to discover humankind's greatness by recognizing its misery. He hoped thereby to counter what he believed to be the false optimism of the new rationalism and science.

Baruch Spinoza: The World As Divine Substance

The most controversial thinker of the seventeenth century may have been Baruch Spinoza (1632–1677), the son of a Jewish merchant of

Pascal invented this adding machine, the ancestor of mechanical calculators, around 1644. It has eight wheels with ten cogs each, corresponding to the numbers 0–9. The wheels move forward for addition, backward for subtraction. [Bildarchiv Preussischer Kulturbesitz]

Amsterdam. His philosophy caused his excommunication by his own synagogue in 1656. During his lifetime, both Jews and Protestants attacked him as an atheist.

Spinoza's most influential writing, the *Ethics*, appeared after his death in 1677. Religious leaders universally condemned it for its apparent espousal of pantheism (a doctrine equating God and nature). Spinoza so closely identified God and nature that little room seemed left either for divine revelation in Scripture or for the personal immortality of the soul—a position equally repugnant to Jews and to Christians. The *Ethics* was written, in the spirit of the new science, as a geometrical system of definitions, axioms, and propositions. Spinoza divided the work into five parts, which dealt with God, the mind, emotions, human bondage, and human freedom.

The most controversial part of the *Ethics* deals with the nature of substance and of God. According to Spinoza, there is only one substance, which is self-caused, free, and infinite, and that substance is God. From this definition it follows that everything that exists is in God and cannot even be conceived of apart from Him. Such a doctrine was not literally pantheistic because God was still seen to be more than the created world that He, as primal substance, embraced. But in Spinoza's view, statements about the natural world were also statements about divine nature. Mind and matter are thus seen to be extensions of the infinite substance of God; what transpires in the world of people and nature is also an expression of the divine.

Such teaching seemed to portray the world as eternal and human actions as unfree and inevitable. Jews and Christians had traditionally condemned such teachings because they deny the creation of the world by God in time and destroy any voluntary basis for personal reward and punishment.

Although his contemporaries condemned him, Spinoza found enthusiastic supporters among many nineteenth-century thinkers who, unable to accept traditional religious language and doctrines, found in his teaching a congenial rational religion.

Thomas Hobbes: Apologist for Absolutism

Thomas Hobbes (1588–1679) was the most original political philosopher of the seventeenth century. Although he never broke with the Church of England, he embraced basic Calvinist beliefs, particularly their low view of human nature and the ideal of a commonwealth based on a divine–human covenant.

An urbane and much-traveled man, Hobbes enthusiastically supported the new scientific movement. During the 1630s, he visited Paris, where he came to know Descartes, and he spent time with Galileo in Italy as well. He took special interest in the works of William Harvey (1578–1657), famous for his discovery of the circulation of blood through the body. And Hobbes was also a superb classicist. His first published work was a translation of Thucydides' *History of the Peloponnesian War*, the first English translation of this work, still reprinted today.

The English Civil War made Hobbes a political philosopher and inspired his *Leviathan* (1651). Written as the concluding part of a broad philosophical system that analyzed physical bodies and human nature, the work established Hobbes as a major European thinker.

Hobbes viewed people and society in a thoroughly materialistic and mechanical way. All psychological processes begin with and are derived from bare sensation, and all motivations are egoistical, intended to increase pleasure and minimize pain. The human power of reasoning, which Hobbes defined as the process of adding and subtracting the consequences of agreed-upon general names of things, develops only after years of concentrated industry. Human will he defined as simply "the last appetite before choice."

Despite this mechanistic view of human nature, Hobbes believed people could accomplish much by the reasoned use of science. Such progress, however, was contingent on their prior correct use of that greatest of human creations, the commonwealth, in which people were freely united by mutual agreement in one all-powerful sovereign government.

The key to Hobbes' political philosophy can be found in a brilliant myth he created about the original state of humankind. According to this account, people in their natural state are inclined to "perpetual and restless desire" for power. Because all people want and, in their natural state, possess a natural right to everything, their equality breeds enmity, competition, diffidence, and perpetual quarreling—"a way of every man against every man." As Hobbes put it in a famous summary:

In such condition there is no place for industry, because the fruit thereof is uncertain; and consequently no culture of the earth; no navigation nor use of the commodities that may be imported by sea; no commodious building; no instruments of moving and removing such things as require much force; no knowledge of the face of the earth; no account of time; no arts; no letters; no society; and, which is worst of all, continual fear and danger of violent death; and the life of man solitary, poor, nasty, brutish, and short.[7]

Whereas earlier and later philosophers saw the original human state as a paradise from which humankind had fallen, Hobbes saw it as a corruption from which only society could deliver people. Contrary to Aristotle and Christian thinkers like Thomas Aquinas, Hobbes did not believe human beings were naturally sociable; they were self-centered beasts and utterly without a master until one was imposed by force.

People escape this terrible state of nature, according to Hobbes, only by entering a social contract, that is, by agreeing to live in a commonwealth tightly ruled by a recognized sovereign. They are driven to this solution by their desire for "commodious living" and fear of death. The social contract obliges every person, for the sake of peace and self-defense, to agree to set aside personal rights to all things and to be content with as much liberty against others as he or she would allow others against himself or herself. All agree to live according to a secularized version of the golden rule: "Do not that to another which you would not have done to yourself."[8]

Because words and promises are insufficient to guarantee this state, the social contract also establishes the coercive use of force to compel compliance. Believing the dangers of anarchy to be always greater than those of tyranny, Hobbes thought that rulers should be absolute and unlimited in their power, once established in office. There is no room in Hobbes's political philosophy for protest in the name of individual

A portrait of Thomas Hobbes (1588–1679), whose political treatise, Leviathan, portrayed rulers as absolute lords over their lands, incorporating in their persons the individual wills of all their people. [Bildarchiv Preussischer Kulturbesitz]

conscience, nor for resistance to legitimate authority by private individuals. Contemporary Catholics and Puritans alike criticized these features of the Leviathan. To his critics, Hobbes pointed out the alternative:

The greatest that in any form of government can possibly happen to the people in general is scarce sensible in respect of the miseries and horrible calamities that accompany a civil war or that dissolute condition of masterless men, without subjection to laws and a coercive power to tie their hands from rapine and revenge.[9]

[7]Thomas Hobbes, Leviathan Parts I and II, ed. by H. W. Schneider (Indianapolis: Bobbs-Merrill, 1958), pp. 86, 106–107.

[8]Hobbes, p. 130.

[9]Hobbes, p. 152.

It is puzzling why Hobbes believed that absolute rulers would be more benevolent and less egoistic than all other people. He simply placed the highest possible value on a strong, efficient ruler who could save human beings from the chaos attendant on the state of nature. In the end, it mattered little to Hobbes whether that ruler was Charles I, Oliver Cromwell, or Charles II, each of whom received Hobbes's enthusiastic support—once he was established in power.

John Locke: Defender of Moderate Liberty

Locke (1632–1704) has proved to be the most influential political thinker of the seventeenth century. Although he was not as original as Hobbes, his political writings became a major source of the later Enlightenment criticism of absolutism. They gave inspiration to both the American and the French revolutions.

Locke's sympathies lay with the Puritans and the parliamentary forces that challenged the Stuart monarchy. His father fought with the parliamentary army during the English Civil War. Locke read deeply in the works of Francis Bacon, René Descartes, and Isaac Newton and was a close friend of the English physicist and chemist Robert Boyle (1627–1691). Some view Locke as synthesizing the rationalism of Descartes and the experimental science of Bacon, Newton, and Boyle.

Locke came for a brief period also under the influence of Hobbes. This ended, however, after his association with Anthony Ashley Cooper, the earl of Shaftesbury. Shaftesbury was considered by his contemporaries to be a radical in both religion and politics. He organized an unsuccessful rebellion against Charles II in 1682, after which both he and Locke, who lived with him, were forced to flee to Holland.

In his *Essay Concerning Human Understanding* (1690), Locke explored the function of the human mind. He portrayed it at birth as a blank tablet. There are no innate ideas, he argued; all knowledge is derived from direct sensual experience. What people know is not the external world in itself but the results of the interaction of the mind with the outside world.

Locke also denied the existence of innate moral norms. Moral ideas are the product of people's subordination of self-love to reason—a free act of self-discipline so that conflict in conscience may be avoided and happiness attained. Locke also believed the teachings of Christianity to be identical to what uncorrupted reason taught. A rational person would therefore always live according to Christian moral precepts. Although Locke firmly denied toleration to Catholics and atheists—both of whom were considered subversive in England—he otherwise sanctioned a variety of Protestant religious practice.

During the reign of Charles II, Locke wrote *Two Treatises of Government*. Here he opposed the argument, set forth by Sir Robert Filmer and Thomas Hobbes, that rulers are absolute in

John Locke (1632–1704), defender of the rights of the people against rulers who think their power absolute. [By courtesy of the National Portrait Gallery, London]

their power. Filmer was the author of *Patriarcha, or the Natural Power of Kings* (1680), which compared the rights of kings over their subjects to those of fathers over their children. Locke devoted his entire first treatise to a refutation of this argument, maintaining that both fathers and rulers were bound to the law of nature. The voice of reason teaches that "all mankind [are] equal and independent, [and] no one ought to harm another in his life, health, liberty, or possessions,"[10] inasmuch as all humans are made in the image of God. According to Locke, people enter into social contracts, empowering legislatures and monarchs to "umpire" their disputes, precisely to preserve their natural rights, not to give rulers an absolute power over them. Rulers are "entrusted" with the preservation of the law of nature and transgress it at their peril:

Whenever that end [the preservation of life, liberty, and property] is manifestly neglected or opposed, the trust must necessarily be forfeited and the power devolve into the hands of those that gave it, who may place it anew where they think best for their safety and security.[11]

From Locke's point of view, absolute monarchy was "inconsistent" with civil society and can be "no form of civil government at all."

Locke's main differences with Hobbes stemmed from the latter's negative views of human nature. Locke believed that the natural human state was one of perfect freedom and equality in which everyone enjoyed, in unregulated fashion, the natural rights of life, liberty, and property. Contrary to Hobbes, human beings in their natural state were creatures not of monomaniacal passion but of extreme goodwill and rationality. And they did not surrender their natural rights unconditionally when they entered the social contract. Rather they established a means whereby these rights could be better preserved. The warfare that Hobbes believed characterized the state of nature emerged for Locke only when rulers failed to preserve people's natural freedom and attempted to enslave them by absolute rule. The preservation and protection of human freedom, not its suppression, was government's mandate.

───────────── ◆ ─────────────

The Scientific Revolution and the thought of writers whose work was contemporaneous with it mark a major turning point in the history of Western thought and eventually had a worldwide impact. The scientific and political ideas of the late sixteenth and seventeenth centuries gradually overturned many of the most fundamental premises of the medieval worldview. The sun replaced the earth as the center of the solar system. The solar system itself came to be viewed as one of many possible systems in the universe. The new knowledge of the physical universe provided occasions for challenges to the authority of the Church and of Scripture. Mathematics began to replace theology and metaphysics as the tool for understanding nature.

Parallel to these developments and sometimes related to them, political thought became much less concerned with religious issues. Hobbes generated a major theory of political obligation with virtually no reference to God. Locke theorized about politics with a recognition of God but with little attention to Scripture. Both Locke and Spinoza championed greater freedom of religious and political expression. Locke produced a psychology that emphasized the influence of environment on human character and action. All of these new ideas gradually displaced or reshaped theological and religious modes of thought and placed humankind and life on earth at the center of Western thinking. Intellectuals in the West consequently developed greater self-confidence in their own capacity to shape the world and their own lives.

None of this came easily, however. The new science and enlightenment were accompanied by new anxieties that were reflected in a growing preoccupation with sin, death, and the Devil. The worst expression of this preoccupation was a succession of witch hunts and trials that took the lives of as many as 100,000 people between 1400 and 1700.

---

[10]John Locke, The Second Treatise of Government, *ed. by T. P. Peardon (Indianapolis: Bobbs-Merrill, 1952), Ch. 2, sects. 4–6, pp. 4–6.*
[11]*Locke, Ch. 13, sect. 149, p. 84.*

Review Questions

1. Discuss the contributions of Copernicus, Brahe, Kepler, Galileo, and Newton to the Scientific Revolution. Which do you think made the most important contributions and why? What did Francis Bacon contribute to the foundation of scientific thought?

2. How would you define the term *Scientific Revolution*? In what ways was it truly revolutionary? Which is more enduring, a political revolution or an intellectual one?

3. How did Isaac Newton reconcile his scientific discoveries with his faith in God? Compare his experience with that of Galileo or Pascal. Are reason and faith compatible?

4. Compare and contrast the political philosophies of Thomas Hobbes and John Locke. How did each view human nature? Would you rather live under a government designed by Hobbes or by Locke? Why?

5. How do you explain the phenomenon of witchcraft and witch hunts in an age of scientific enlightenment? Why did the witch panics occur in the late sixteenth and early seventeenth centuries? How might the Reformation have contributed to them?

6. How do the literary works of Cervantes, Shakespeare, and Milton reflect concern about the adequacy of past values and how did they shape the world view of their own seventeenth century society?

Suggested Readings

R. ASHCRAFT, *Revolutionary Politics and Locke's Two Treatises of Government* (1986). The most important study of Locke to appear in recent years.

V. M. BRITTAIN, *Valiant Pilgrim: The Story of John Bunyan and Puritan England* (1950). Illustrated historical biography.

K. C. BROWN, *Hobbes Studies* (1965). A collection of important essays.

H. BUTTERFIELD, *The Origins of Modern Science 1300–1800* (1949). An authoritative survey.

J. CAIRD, *Spinoza* (1971). Intellectual biography by a philosopher.

I. B. COHEN, *Revolution in Science* (1985). A general consideration of the concept and of historical examples of change in scientific thought.

H. CRAIG, *Shakespeare: A Historical and Critical Study with Annotated Texts of Twenty-one Plays* (1958). Everything the Shakespeare scholar needs.

M. CRANSTON, *Locke* (1961). Brief biographical sketch.

J. DUNN, *The Political Thought of John Locke; An Historical Account of the "Two Treatises of Government"* (1969). An excellent introduction.

M. DURAN, *Cervantes* (1974). Detailed biography.

M. A. FINOCCHIARO, *The Galileo Affair: A Documentary History* (1989). A collection of all the relevant documents and introductory commentary.

GALILEO GALILEI, *Discoveries and Opinions of Galileo*, ed. and trans. by S. Drake (1957). Useful selections.

A. R. HALL, *The Scientific Revolution 1500–1800: The Formation of the Modern Scientific Attitude* (1966). Traces undermining of traditional science and rise of new sciences.

C. HILL, *Milton and the English Revolution* (1977). A major biography.

M. HUNTER, *Science and Society in Restoration England* (1981). Examines the social relations of scientists and scientific societies.

M. JACOB, *The Newtonians and the English Revolution* (1976). A controversial book that attempts to relate science and politics.

D. JOHNSTON, *The Rhetoric of Leviathan: Thomas Hobbes and the Politics of Cultural Transformation* (1986). An important study that links Hobbes's thought to the rhetoric of the Renaissance.

R. KIECKHEFER, *European Witch Trials: Their Foundations in Popular and Learned Culture 1300–1500* (1976). Excellent background for understanding the great witch panic.

A. KORS and E. PETERS, eds., *European Witchcraft, 1100–1700* (1972). Collection of major documents.

A. KOYRÉ, *From the Closed World to the Infinite Universe* (1957). Treated from perspective of the historian of ideas.

T. S. KUHN, *The Copernican Revolution* (1957). A scholarly treatment.

C. LARNER, *Enemies of God: The Witchhunt in Scotland* (1981). Perhaps the most exemplary local study of the subject.

P. LASLETT, *Locke's Two Treatises of Government*, 2nd ed. (1970). Definitive texts with very important introductions.

B. LEVACK, *The Witch Hunt in Early Modern Europe* (1986). Lucid, up-to-date survey of research.

D. LINDBERG and R. L. NUMBERS (Eds.), *God and Nature: Historical Essays on the Encounter Between Christianity and Science* (1986). The best collection of essays on the subject.

O. MAYER, *Authority, Liberty, and Automatic Machinery in Early Modern Europe* (1986). A lively study that seeks to relate thought about machinery to thought about politics.

R. POPKIN, *The History of Scepticism from Erasmus to Spinoza* (1979). A classic study of the fear of loss of intellectual certainty.

P. REDONDI, *Galileo: Heretic* (1987). A controversial work that examines the relationship of Galileo's thought to the Church's teaching on the Eucharist rather than to planetary motion.

S. SHAPIN and S. SCHAFFER, *Leviathan and the Air-Pump: Hobbes, Boyle, and the Experimental Life* (1985). A study of the debate over the validity of scientific experiment during the age of the Scientific Revolution.

B. SHAPIRO, *Probability and Certainty in Seventeenth-Century England: A Study of the Relationships Between Natural Science, Religion, History, Law, and Literature* (1983). As the title indicates, a very broad study and an important one.

K. THOMAS, *Religion and the Decline of Magic* (1971). Provocative, much acclaimed work focused on popular culture.

R. S. WESTFALL, *Never at Rest: A Biography of Isaac Newton* (1981). A new important major study.

John III Sobieski (1624–1696) was elected king of Poland in 1674. Sobieski led the Polish Army in repulsing the Turkish siege of Vienna in 1683, an event discussed in one of the documents in this chapter. Despite this victory Sobieski failed to establish a strong central monarchy in Poland. [Erich Lessing/Art Resource, N.Y.]

15

Successful and Unsuccessful Paths to Power (1686–1740)

Key Topics in This Chapter
◆ The decline of Spain and the Netherlands relative to France and England among the maritime powers
◆ French aristocratic resistance to the monarchy
◆ Early eighteenth-century British political stability
◆ The efforts of the Habsburgs to secure their holdings
◆ The emergence of Prussia as a major power under the Hohenzollerns
◆ The efforts of Peter the Great to transform Russia into a powerful centralized nation along Western lines

---

The late seventeenth and early eighteenth centuries witnessed significant shifts of power and influence among the states of Europe. Nations that had been strong lost their status as significant military and economic units. Other countries that in some cases had figured only marginally in international relations came to the fore. Great Britain, France, Austria, Russia, and Prussia emerged during this period as the powers that would dominate Europe until at least

World War I. Their political and economic dominance occurred at the expense of Spain, the United Netherlands, Poland, Sweden, and the Ottoman Empire. Equally essential to their rise was the weakness of the Holy Roman Empire after the Treaty of Westphalia (1648), which ended the Thirty Years' War.

The successful competitors for international power were those states that created strong central political authorities. Farsighted observers in the late seventeenth century already understood that in the future those domains that would become or remain great powers must imitate the political and military organization of Louis XIV's France. Strong monarchy alone could impose unity of purpose on the state. The turmoil of seventeenth-century civil wars and aristocratic revolts had impressed people with the value of a strong monarch as the guarantor of minimum domestic tranquility.

Imitation of French absolutism involved more than belief in a strong monarchy. It usually required building a standing army, organizing an efficient tax structure to support the army, and establishing a bureaucracy to collect the taxes. Moreover, the political classes of the country, especially the nobles, had to be converted to a sense of duty and loyalty to the central government that was more intense than their loyalty to other competing political and social institutions.

The waning powers were those that failed to achieve such effective organization. They were unable to employ their political, economic, and human resources to resist external aggression or to overcome the forces of domestic dissolution. Internal and external failures were closely related. If a state did not maintain or establish a central political authority with sufficient power over the nobility, the cities, the guilds, and the Church, it could not raise a strong army to defend its borders or its economic interests. More often than not, the key element leading to success or failure was the character, personality, and energy of the monarch.

The Maritime Powers

In western Europe, Britain and France emerged as the dominant powers. This development represented a shift of influence away from Spain and the United Netherlands. Both the latter countries had been strong and important during the sixteenth and seventeenth centuries, but they became politically and militarily marginal during the eighteenth century. Neither, however, disappeared from the map, and both retained considerable economic vitality and influence. The difference was that France and Britain

attained so much more power and economic strength.

Spain

Spanish power had depended on the influx of wealth from the Americas and on the capacity of the Spanish monarchs to rule the still largely autonomous provinces of the Iberian Peninsula. The economic life of Spain was never healthy. Except for wool, it had virtually no exports to pay for its imports. Instead of promoting domestic industries, the Spanish government financed imports by using the gold and silver mined in its New World empire. This external source of wealth was uncertain because the treasure fleets from the New World (discussed more fully in Chapter 17) could be and sometimes were captured by pirates or hostile navies.

The political life of Spain was also weak. Within its divisions of Castile, Aragon, Navarre, the Basque provinces, and other districts, the royal government could not operate without the cooperation of strong local nobles and the Church. From the defeat of the Armada in 1588 to the Treaty of the Pyrenees in 1659 after Spain's defeat by France, Spain suffered a series of foreign policy reverses that harmed the domestic prestige of the monarchy. Furthermore, between 1665 and 1700, the physically malformed, dull-witted, and sexually impotent Charles II was monarch. Throughout his reign, the provincial estates and the nobility increased their power. After his death, the other powers of Europe fought over who would succeed him in the War of the Spanish Succession (1701–1714).

The Treaty of Utrecht (1713), which ended the war, gave the Spanish crown to Philip V (r. 1700–1746), a grandson of Louis XIV. The new king should have tried to consolidate his internal power and protect Spanish overseas trade. However, his second wife, Elizabeth Farnese, used Spanish power to secure thrones for her two sons in Italy. Such diversions of government resources allowed the nobility and the provinces to continue to assert their privileges against the monarchy. Not until the reign of Charles III (r. 1759–1788) did Spain have a monarch concerned with efficient domestic and imperial administration and internal improvement. By the third quarter of the century, Spain was bet-

In the mid-eighteenth century, when this picture of the Amsterdam Exchange was painted, Amsterdam had replaced the cities of Italy and south Germany as the leading banking center of Europe. Amsterdam retained this position until the late eighteenth century. [Museum Boymans-van Beuningen, Rotterdam]

ter governed, but it could no longer compete effectively in great power politics.

The Netherlands

The decline of the United Provinces of the Netherlands occurred wholly within the eighteenth century. After the death of William III of Britain in 1702, the various local provinces successfully prevented the emergence of another strong stadtholder. Unified political leadership

therefore vanished. During the earlier long wars of the Netherlands with Louis XIV and Britain, naval supremacy had slowly but steadily passed to the British. The fishing industry declined, and the Dutch lost their technological superiority in shipbuilding. Countries between which Dutch ships had once carried goods now traded directly with each other. For example, the British began to use their own vessels in the Baltic traffic with Russia.

Similar stagnation overtook the Dutch domestic industries, such as textile finishing, paper making, and glass blowing. The disunity of the provinces and the absence of vigorous leadership hastened this economic decline and prevented action that might have slowed or halted it.

What saved the United Provinces from becoming completely insignificant in European matters was their continued financial dominance. Well past the middle of the century, their banks continued to provide loans and financing for European trade.

France After Louis XIV

Despite its military reverses in the War of the Spanish Succession, France remained a great power. It was less strong in 1715 than in 1680, but it still possessed the largest European population, an advanced if troubled economy, and the administrative structure bequeathed it by Louis XIV. Moreover, even if France and its resources had been drained by the last of Louis's wars, the other major states of Europe were similarly debilitated. What France required was economic recovery and consolidation, wiser political leadership, and a less ambitious foreign policy. It did enjoy a period of recovery, but its leadership was at best indifferent. Louis XIV was succeeded by his five-year-old great-grandson Louis XV (r. 1715–1774). The young boy's uncle, the duke of Orléans, became regent and remained so until his death in 1720. The regency, marked by financial and moral scandals, further undermined the faltering prestige of the monarchy.

JOHN LAW AND THE MISSISSIPPI BUBBLE The duke of Orléans was a gambler, and for a time he turned over the financial management of the kingdom to John Law (1621–1729), a Scottish mathematician and fellow gambler. Law believed that an increase in the paper-money supply would stimulate France's economic recovery. With the permission of the regent, he established a bank in Paris that issued paper money. Law then organized a monopoly, called the Mississippi Company, on trading privileges with the French colony of Louisiana in North America.

The Mississippi Company also took over the management of the French national debt. The company issued shares of its own stock in exchange for government bonds, which had fallen sharply in value. To redeem large quantities of bonds, Law encouraged speculation in Mississippi Company stock. In 1719 the price of the stock rose handsomely. Smart investors, however, took their profits by selling their stock in exchange for paper money from Law's bank, which they then sought to exchange for gold. The bank, however, lacked enough gold to redeem all the paper money brought to it.

In February 1720, all gold payments were halted in France. Soon thereafter Law himself fled the country. The Mississippi Bubble, as the affair was called, had burst. The fiasco brought disgrace on the government that had sponsored Law. The Mississippi Company was later reorganized and functioned profitably, but fear of paper money and speculation marked French economic life for decades.

RENEWED AUTHORITY OF THE PARLEMENTS The duke of Orléans made a second decision that also lessened the power of the monarchy. He attempted to draw the French nobility once again into the decision-making processes of the government. Louis XIV had filled his ministries and bureaucracies with persons from nonnoble families. The regent, under pressure from the nobility, tried to restore a balance. He set up a system of councils on which nobles were to serve along with bureaucrats. The years of idle noble domestication at Versailles, however, had worked too well, and the nobility seemed to lack both the talent and the desire to govern. The experiment failed.

Despite this failure, the great French nobles did not surrender their ancient ambition to assert their rights, privileges, and local influence over those of the monarchy. The chief feature of eighteenth-century French political life was the attempt of the nobility to use its authority to limit the power of the monarchy. The most effective instrument in this process was the parlements, or courts dominated by the nobility.

The French parlements were different from the English Parliament. These French courts, the most important of which was the Parlement of Paris, could not legislate. Rather, they had the power to recognize or not to recognize the legality of an act or law promulgated by the monarch.

The impending collapse of John Law's bank triggered a financial panic throughout France. Desperate investors, such as those shown here in the city of Rennes, sought to exchange their paper currency for gold and silver before the bank's supply of precious metals was exhausted. [Musse de Bretagne, Rennes]

By long tradition their formal approval had been required to make a royal law valid. Louis XIV had often restricted stubborn, uncooperative *parlements*. In another major political blunder, however, the duke of Orléans had formally approved the full reinstitution of the *parlements'* power to allow or disallow laws. Thereafter the growing financial and moral weakness of the monarchy allowed these aristocratic judicial institutions to reassert their authority. This situation meant that until the

revolution in 1789 the *parlements* became natural centers for aristocratic resistance to royal authority.

ADMINISTRATION OF CARDINAL FLEURY
In 1726 Cardinal Fleury (1653–1743) became the chief minister of the French court. He was the last of the great churchmen who loyally and effectively served the French monarchy. Like his seventeenth-century predecessors, the cardinals Richelieu and Mazarin, Fleury was a realist. He

Cardinal Fleury (1653–1743) was the tutor and chief minister of Louis XV from 1726 to 1743. Fleury gave France a period of peace and prosperity, but was unable to solve the state's long-term financial problems. This portrait is by Hyacinthe Rigaud (1659–1743). [Photographie Bulloz]

understood the political ambition and incapacity of the nobility and worked quietly to block their undue influence. He was also aware of the precarious financial situation of the royal treasury.

The cardinal, who was seventy-three years old when he came to office, was determined to give the country a period of peace. He surrounded himself with able assistants who tried to solve France's financial problems. Part of the national debt was repudiated. New industries enjoying special privileges were established, and roads and bridges built. On the whole the nation prospered,

but Fleury could never draw from the nobles or the Church sufficient tax revenues to put the state on a stable financial footing.

Fleury died in 1743, having unsuccessfully attempted to prevent France from intervening in the war then raging between Austria and Prussia. The cost of this intervention was to undo all his financial pruning and planning.

Another failure must also be credited to this elderly churchman. Despite his best efforts, he had not trained Louis XV to become an effective monarch. Louis XV possessed most of the vices and almost none of the virtues of his great-grandfather Louis XIV. He wanted to hold on to absolute power but was unwilling to work the long hours required. He did not choose many wise advisers after Fleury. He was tossed about by the gossip and intrigues of the court. His personal life was scandalous. Louis XV was not an evil person but a mediocre one. And in a monarch, mediocrity was unfortunately often a greater fault than vice.

Despite this political drift, France remained a great power. France's army at mid-century was still the largest and strongest military force on the Continent. Its commerce and production expanded. Its colonies produced wealth and spurred domestic industries. Its cities grew and prospered. The wealth of the nation waxed as the absolutism of the monarchy waned. France did not lack sources of power and strength, but the political leadership could not organize, direct, or inspire its people.

Great Britain: The Age of Walpole

In 1713 Britain had emerged as a victor over Louis XIV, but the nation required a period of recovery. As an institution, the British monarchy was not in the degraded state of the French monarchy, yet its stability was not certain.

THE HANOVERIAN DYNASTY In 1714 the Hanoverian dynasty, as designated by the Act of Settlement (1701), came to the throne. Almost immediately, George I (r. 1714–1727) faced a challenge to his new title. The Stuart pretender James Edward (1688–1766), the son of James II, landed in Scotland in December 1715. His forces marched southward but met defeat less than two months later. Although militarily successful against the pretender, the new dynasty and its supporters saw the need for consolidation.

WHIGS AND TORIES   During the seventeenth century, England had been one of the most politically restive countries in Europe. The closing years of Queen Anne's reign (1702–1714) had seen sharp clashes between the political factions of Whigs and Tories over whether to end the war with France. The Tories had urged a rapid peace settlement and after 1710 had opened negotiations with France. During the same period, the Whigs were seeking favor from

Madame de Pompadour (1721–1764) was the mistress of Louis XV. She exercised considerable political influence at the court and was a notable patron of artists, craftsmen, and writers. This 1763 portrait is by Hubert Drouais (1727–1775) [Roger-Viollet]

the Elector of Hanover, the future George I, who would soon be their monarch. His concern for his domains in Hanover made him unsympathetic to the Tory peace policy. In the final months of Anne's reign, some Tories, fearing that they would lose power under the waiting Hanoverian dynasty, opened channels of communication with the Stuart pretender; and a few even rallied to his cause.

Under these circumstances, George I, on his arrival in Britain, clearly favored the Whigs. Previously the differences between the Whigs and the Tories had been vaguely related to principle. The Tories emphasized a strong monarchy, low taxes for landowners, and firm support of the Anglican church. The Whigs supported monarchy but wanted Parliament to retain final sovereignty. They favored urban commercial interests as well as the prosperity of the landowners. They encouraged a policy of religious toleration toward the Protestant nonconformists in England. Socially both groups supported the status quo.

Neither group was organized like a modern political party. Outside Parliament, each party consisted of political networks based on local connections and economic influence. Each group acknowledged a few national spokesmen, who articulated positions and principles. After the Hanoverian accession and the eventual Whig success in achieving the firm confidence of George I, the chief difference for almost forty years between the Whigs and the Tories was that one group had access to public office and patronage and the other did not. This early Hanoverian proscription of Tories from public life was one of the most prominent features of the age.

THE LEADERSHIP OF ROBERT WALPOLE The political situation after 1715 remained in flux, until Robert Walpole (1676–1745) took over the helm of government. Walpole had been active in the House of Commons since the reign of Queen Anne and had been a cabinet minister. What gave him special prominence under the new dynasty was a British financial scandal similar to the French Mississippi Bubble.

Management of the British national debt had been assigned to the South Sea Company, which exchanged government bonds for company

stock. As in the French case, the price of the stock soared, only to crash in 1720 when prudent investors sold their holdings and took their speculative profits. Parliament intervened and, under Walpole's leadership, adopted measures to honor the national debt. To most contemporaries, Walpole had saved the financial integrity of the country and had thus proved himself a person of immense administrative capacity and political ability.

George I gave Walpole his full confidence. For this reason Walpole has often been regarded as the first *prime minister* of Great Britain and the originator of the cabinet system of government. Walpole generally demanded that all the ministers in the cabinet agree on policy, but he could not prevent frequent public differences among them. Unlike a modern English prime minister, he was not chosen by the majority of the House of Commons. The real sources of his power were the personal support of the king, George I and later George II (r. 1727–1760), his ability to handle the House of Commons, and his iron-fisted control of government patronage. To oppose Walpole meant the almost certain loss of government patronage for oneself, one's family, or one's friends. Through the skillful use of patronage, Walpole bought support for himself and his policies from people who wanted to receive jobs, appointments, favors, and government contracts. Such corruption supplied the glue of political loyalty.

Walpole's favorite slogan was "Quieta non movere" (roughly, "Let sleeping dogs lie"). To that end, he pursued peace abroad and supported the status quo at home. In this regard he much resembled Cardinal Fleury.

THE STRUCTURE OF PARLIAMENT The structure of the eighteenth-century British House of Commons aided Walpole in his pacific policies. It was neither a democratic nor a representative body. Each of the counties into which Britain was divided elected two members. But if the more powerful landed families in a county agreed on the candidates, there was no contest. Most members, however, were elected from a variety of units called boroughs. A few boroughs were large enough for elections to be relatively democratic, but most had few electors. For example, a local municipal corporation or council of only a dozen members might have the right to elect a member of Parliament. In Old Sarum, one of the most famous corrupt, or "rotten," boroughs, the Pitt family simply bought up those pieces of property to which a vote was attached and thus in effect owned a seat in the House of Commons. Through proper electoral management, which involved favors to the electors, the House of Commons could be controlled.

The structure of Parliament and the manner in which the House of Commons was elected meant that the owners of property, especially wealthy nobles, dominated the government of England. They did not pretend to represent people and districts or to be responsive to what would later be called public opinion. They regarded themselves as representing various economic and social interests, such as the West Indian interest, the merchant interest, or the landed interest. These owners of property were suspicious of an administrative bureaucracy controlled by the crown or its ministers. To diminish royal influence, they or their agents served as local government administrators, judges, militia commanders, and tax collectors. In this sense, the British nobility and large landowners actually did govern the nation. And because they regarded the Parliament as the political sovereign, there was no absence of central political authority and direction. Consequently, the supremacy of Parliament gave

Britain the unity that absolute monarchy provided elsewhere in Europe.

These parliamentary structures also helped to strengthen the financial position of the British government. The British monarch could not raise taxes the way his continental counterparts could, but the British government consisting of the monarch and Parliament could and did raise vast sums of tax revenue and loans to wage war throughout the eighteenth century. All Britons paid taxes. There were virtually no exemptions. The British credit market was secure through the regulation of the Bank of England, founded in 1693. This strong system of finance and tax collection was one of the cornerstones of eighteenth-century British power.

FREEDOM OF POLITICAL LIFE British political life was genuinely more free than that on the Continent. There were real limits on the power of Robert Walpole. Parliament could not wholly ignore popular political pressure. Even with the extensive use of patronage, many members of Parliament maintained independent views. Newspapers and public debate flourished. There was freedom of speech and association. There was no

France and Great Britain in the Early Eighteenth Century	
1713	Treaty of Utrecht ends the War of the Spanish Succession
1714	George I becomes king of Great Britain and establishes the Hanoverian dynasty
1715	Louis XV becomes King of France
1715–1720	Regency of the duke of Orléans in France
1720	Mississippi Bubble bursts in France and South Sea Bubble bursts in Great Britain
1720–1742	Robert Walpole dominates British politics
1726–1743	Cardinal Fleury serves as Louis XV's chief minister
1727	George II becomes king of Great Britain
1733	Excise bill crisis in Britain
1739	War of Jenkins's Ear begins between England and Spain

This series of four Hoga[r]
etchings satirizes the no[t]
ously corrupt English ele[c]
toral system. Hogarth sh[ows]
the voters going to the p[olls]
after having been bribed [and]
intoxicated with free gin.
(Voting was then in pub[lic.]
The secret ballot was no[t]
introduced in England u[ntil]
1872.) The fourth etchi[ng]
"Chairing the Member,"
shows the triumphal pro[ces-]
sion of the victorious ca[n-]
didate, which is clearly
turning into a brawl. [Me[tro-]
politan Museum of Art,
Harris Brisbane Dick Fu[nd,]
1932. Acc. #32.35.(124[.)]

Lady Mary Wortley Montagu (1689–1762) was a famous writer of letters and an extremely well-traveled woman of the eighteenth century. As the document on page 557 suggests, she was also a shrewd and toughminded political advisor to her husband. [National Portrait Gallery, London]

large standing army. Those Tories barred from political office and the Whig enemies of Walpole could and did openly oppose his policies—which would have been impossible on the Continent.

For example, in 1733 Walpole presented to the House of Commons a scheme to expand the scope of the excise tax, a tax that resembled a modern sales tax. The outcry in the press, on the public platform, and in the streets was so great that he eventually withdrew the measure. What the British regarded as their traditional political rights raised a real and potent barrier to the power of the government. Again in 1739 the public outcry over the alleged Spanish treatment of British merchants in the Caribbean pushed Britain into a war that Walpole opposed and deplored.

Walpole's ascendancy, which lasted until 1742, did little to raise the level of British political morality, but it brought a kind of stability that Britain had not enjoyed for a century. Its foreign trade grew steadily and spread from New England to India. Agriculture became more productive. All forms of economic enterprise seemed to prosper. The navy became stronger. As a result of this political stability and economic growth, Great Britain became a European power of the first order and stood at the beginning of its era as a world power. Its government and economy during the next generation became a model for all progressive Europeans.

Central and Eastern Europe

The major factors in the shift of political influence among the maritime nations were naval strength, economic progress, foreign trade, and sound domestic administration. The conflicts among them occurred less in Europe than on

---

Lady Mary Wortley Montagu Advises Her Husband on Election to Parliament

In this letter of 1714, Lady Mary Wortley Montagu discussed with her husband the various paths that he might follow to gain election to the British House of Commons. Note her emphasis on knowing the right people and on having large amounts of money to spend on voters. Eventually, her husband was elected to Parliament in a borough that was controlled through government patronage.

✦ *What are the various ways in which candidates and their supporters used money to campaign? What role did friendships play in the campaigning? How important do the political ideas or positions of the candidates seem to be? Women could not vote in eighteenth-century parliamentary elections, but what kind of influence do they seem to exert?*

You seem not to have received my letters, or not to have understood them: you had been chose undoubtedly at York, if you had declared in time; but there is not any gentleman or tradesman disengaged at this time; they are treating every night. Lord Carlisle and the Thompsons have given their interest to Mr. Jenkins. I agree with you of the necessity of your standing this Parliament, which, perhaps, may be more considerable than any that are to follow it; but, as you proceed, 'tis my opinion, you will spend your money and not be chose. I believe there is hardly a borough unengaged. I expect every letter should tell me you are sure of some place; and, as far as I can perceive you are sure of none. As it has been managed, perhaps it will be the best way to deposit a certain sum in some friend's hands, and buy some little Cornish borough: it would, undoubtedly, look better to be chose for a considerable town; but I take it to be now too late. If you have any thoughts of

Newark, it will be absolutely necessary for you to enquire after Lord Lexington's interest; and your best way to apply yourself to Lord Holdernesse, who is both a Whig and an honest man. He is now in town, and you may enquire of him if Brigadier Sutton stands there; and if not, try to engage him for you. Lord Lexington is so ill at the Bath, that it is a doubt if he will live 'till the elections; and if he dies, one of his heiresses, and the whole interest of his estate, will probably fall on Lord Holdernesse.

'Tis a surprize to me, that you cannot make sure of some borough, when a number of your friends bring in so many Parliament-men without trouble or expense. 'Tis too late to mention it now, but you might have applied to Lady Winchester, as Sir Joseph Jekyl did last year, and by her interest the Duke of Bolton brought him in for nothing; I am sure she would be more zealous to serve me, than Lady Jekyl.

Lord Wharncliffe, ed., Letters and Works of Lady Mary Wortley Montagu, 3rd ed., Vol. 1 (London, 1861), p. 211.

---

the high seas and in their overseas empires. These nations existed in well-defined geographical areas with established borders. Their populations generally accepted the authority of the central government.

Central and eastern Europe were different. Except for the Baltic ports, the economy was agrarian. There were fewer cities and many more large estates populated by serfs. The states in this region did not possess overseas empires. Changes in the power structure normally involved changes in borders or, at least, in which prince ruled a particular area. Military conflicts took place at home rather than overseas.

The political structure of this region, which lay largely east of the Elbe River, was very "soft." The almost constant warfare of the seventeenth century had led to a habit of temporary and shifting political loyalties. The princes and aristocracies of small states and principalities were unwilling to subordinate themselves to a central monarchical authority. Consequently, the political life of the region and the kind of state that emerged there were different from those of western Europe.

Beginning in the last half of the seventeenth century, eastern and central Europe began to assume the political and social contours that would characterize it for the next two centuries. After the Peace of Westphalia, the Austrian Habsburgs recognized the basic weakness of the position of Holy Roman Emperor and began to consolidate their power outside Germany. At the same time, Prussia emerged as a factor in North German politics and as a major challenger to Habsburg domination of Germany. Most important, Russia at the opening of the eighteenth century became a military power of the first order. These three states (Austria, Prussia, and Russia) achieved their new status largely as a result of the political decay or military defeat of Sweden, Poland, and the Ottoman Empire.

Sweden: The Ambitions of Charles XII

Under Gustavus Adolphus II (r. 1611–1632), Sweden had played an important role as a Protestant combatant in the Thirty Years' War. During the rest of the seventeenth century, Sweden had consolidated its control of the Baltic, thus preventing Russian possession of a Baltic port and permitting Polish and German access to the sea only on Swedish terms. The Swedes also possessed one of the better armies in Europe. Sweden's economy, however, based primarily on the export of iron, was not strong enough to ensure continued political success.

In 1697 Charles XII (r. 1697–1718) came to the throne. He was headstrong, to say the least, and perhaps insane. In 1700 Russia began a drive to the west against Swedish territory. The Russian goal was a foothold on the Baltic. In the resulting Great Northern War (1700–1721), Charles XII led a vigorous and often brilliant campaign, but one that eventually resulted in the defeat of Sweden. In 1700 he defeated the Russians at the Battle of Narva, but then he turned south to invade Poland. The conflict dragged on, and the Russians were able to strengthen their forces.

In 1708 the Swedish monarch began a major invasion of Russia but became bogged down in the harsh Russian winter. The next year his army was decisively defeated at the Battle of Poltava. Thereafter the Swedes could maintain only a holding action against their enemies. Charles himself sought refuge in Turkey and did not return to Sweden until 1714. He was killed four years later while fighting the Norwegians.

The Great Northern War came to a close in 1721. Sweden had exhausted its military and economic resources and had lost its monopoly on the Baltic coast. Russia had conquered a large section of the eastern Baltic, and Prussia had gained a part of Pomerania. Internally, after the death of Charles XII, the Swedish nobles were determined to reassert their power over the monarchy. They did so but then quarreled among themselves. Sweden played a very minor role in European affairs thereafter.

The Ottoman Empire

At the southeastern extreme of Europe, the Ottoman Empire was a barrier to the territorial ambitions of the Austrian Habsburgs, Poland, and Russia. The empire in the late seventeenth century still controlled most of the Balkan Peninsula and the entire coastline of the Black Sea. In theory the empire existed to enhance the spread of Islam. Its population, however, was exceedingly diverse both ethnically and religiously. The empire ruled these people not on a territorial but on a religious basis. That is, it created units, called *millets*, that included all persons of a particular religious faith. Various laws and regulations applied to the persons who belonged to a particular millet rather than to a particular administrative territory. Non-Islamic persons in the empire were known as *zimmis*. They could practice their religion, but they were second class citizens who could not rise in the service of the empire or profit much from its successes. This mode of government maintained the self-identity of these various peoples and allowed for little religious integration or interaction.

From the fifteenth century onward, the Ottoman Empire had tried to push further westward in Europe. The empire made its greatest military invasion into Europe in 1683, when it unsuccessfully besieged Vienna. In addition, many Christians in the Balkans and on the Aegean islands had converted to Islam. Many of these people had earlier been forced to convert to Roman Catholicism by the Venetians and welcomed the Turks and their faith as vehicles for political liberation. Much of the Islamic presence in the Balkans today dates to these conversions.

By the last third of the seventeenth century, however, the Ottomans had overextended themselves politically, economically, and militarily. From the mid-sixteenth century, the Ottoman rulers spent so much time at war that they could not attend to meetings of governmental bodies in Constantinople. As time passed, political groups in the capital resisted any substantial strengthening of the central government or of the role of the sultan. Rivalries for power among army leaders and nobles, as well as their flagrant efforts to enrich themselves, weakened the effectiveness of the government. In the outer provinces, such as Transylvania, Wallachia, and Moldavia (all parts of modern Romania), the empire depended on the goodwill of local rulers, who paid tribute but never submitted themselves fully to the imperial power. The empire's economy was weak, and its exports were primarily raw materials. Moreover, the actual conduct of most of its trade had been turned over to representatives of other nations.

Charles XII of Sweden (r. 1697–1718) led his nation into a number of disastrous wars. These confllicts exhausted the country's resources, preventing Sweden from playing a major role in later eighteenth-century power politics. [Roger-Viollet]

By the early eighteenth century, the weakness of the Ottoman Empire meant that a political vacuum that would grow during the next two centuries had come into existence on the southeastern perimeter of Europe. The various European powers who had created strong armies and bureaucracies would begin to probe and eventually dismember the Ottoman Empire. In 1699 the Turks concluded a treaty with their longtime Habsburg enemy and surrendered all pretensions of control over and consequent receipt of revenues from Hungary, Transylvania, Croatia, and Slavonia. From this time onward, Russia also attempted to extend its territory and influence at the expense of the empire. By the early nineteenth century, many of the peoples who lived in the Balkans and around the Black Sea would seek to create their own national states. The retreat and decay of the Ottoman Empire and the scramble of other states and regional peoples to assume control of southeastern Europe would cause political and ethnic turmoil there from the eighteenth century to our own day.

Poland: Absence of Strong Central Authority

In no other part of Europe was the failure to maintain a competitive political position so complete as in Poland. In 1683 King John III Sobieski (r. 1674–1696) had led a Polish army to rescue Vienna from the Turkish siege. Following that spectacular effort, however, Poland became a byword for the dangers of aristocratic independence. In Poland as nowhere else on the Continent, the nobility became the single most powerful political factor in the country. Unlike the British nobility and landowners, the Polish nobility would not even submit to a central authority of their own making. There was no effective central authority in the form of either a king or a parliament.

The Polish monarchy was elective, but the deep distrust and divisions among the nobility prevented their electing a king from among themselves. Sobieski was a notable exception. Most of the Polish monarchs were foreigners and were the tools of foreign powers. The Polish nobles did have a central legislative body called the *Sejm*, or Diet. It included only the nobles and specifically excluded representatives from corporate bodies, such as the towns. In the Diet, however, there existed a practice known as the *liberum veto*, whereby the staunch opposition of any single member could require the body to disband. Such opposition was termed "exploding the Diet." This practice was most often the work of a group of dissatisfied nobles rather than of one person. Nonetheless, the requirement of unanimity was a major stumbling block to effective government.

Government as it was developing elsewhere in Europe simply was not tolerated in Poland. Localism reminiscent of the Middle Ages continued to hold sway as the nobles used all their energy to maintain their traditional "Polish liberties." There was no way to collect enough taxes to build up an army. The price of this noble liberty would eventually be the disappear-

ance of Poland from the map of Europe during the last half of the eighteenth century.

The Habsburg Empire and the Pragmatic Sanction

The close of the Thirty Years' War marked a fundamental turning point in the history of the Austrian Habsburgs. Previously, in alliance with the Spanish branch of the family, they had hoped to dominate all of Germany and to return it to the Catholic fold. They did not achieve either goal, and the decline of Spanish power meant that in future diplomatic relations the Austrian Habsburgs were on their own. The Treaty of Westphalia in 1648 permitted Protestantism within the Holy Roman Empire and also recognized the political autonomy of more than 300 corporate German political entities within the empire. These included large units (such as Saxony, Hanover, Bavaria, and Brandenburg) and scores of small cities, bishoprics, principalities, and petty territories of independent knights.

After 1648 the Habsburgs retained a firm hold on the title of Holy Roman Emperor, but the effectiveness of the title depended less on force of arms than on the cooperation that the emperor could elicit from the various political bodies in the empire. The Diet of the empire sat at Regensburg from 1663 until the empire was dissolved in 1806. The Diet and the emperor generally regulated the daily economic and political life of Germany. The post-Westphalian Holy Roman Empire resembled Poland in its lack of central authority. Unlike its Polish neighbor, however, the Holy Roman Empire was reorganized from within as the Habsburgs attempted to regain their authority. As will be seen shortly, Prussia set out on its course toward European power at the same time.

CONSOLIDATION OF AUSTRIAN POWER While concentrating on their hereditary Austrian holdings among the German states, the Habsburgs also began to consolidate their power and influence within their other hereditary possessions (see Map 15-1). These included, first, the Crown of Saint Wenceslas, encompassing the kingdom of Bohemia (in the modern Czech Republic and Slovakia) and the duchies of Moravia and Silesia and, second, the Crown of

The King of Poland Frees Vienna from the Turks

In 1683 the Ottoman Empire had laid siege to Vienna. The Habsburg monarchy found itself under enormous military pressure. The military forces of John III Sobieski, the king of Poland, rescued the city and repulsed the last great Turkish advance upon central Europe.

✦ *What role did religious sentiments and prejudice play in this description? In that regard, how was the battle portrayed as a conflict between two different religions and two different cultures? How is the ruler of Austria portrayed so as to make the king of Poland the hero of the account? What factors appear to have led the leader of the Ottoman forces to retreat? What were the physical fruits of battle for the victors?*

The Victory which the King of Poland hath obtained over the Infidels, is so great and so compleat that past Ages can scarce parallel the fame; and perhaps future Ages will never see any thing like it. . . . On the one hand we see Vienna besieged by three hundred thousand Turks; reduced to the last extremity; its Outworks taken; the Enemy fixed to the Body of the Place; . . . : We see an Emperor [the Habsburg ruler] chased from his Capital; retired to a Corner of his Dominions; all his Country at the mercy of the Tartars, who have filled the Camp with an infinite Number of unfortunate Slaves that had been forcibly carried away out of Austria. On the other hand, we see the King of Poland, who goes out of his Kingdom, with part of his Army, and hastens to succour his . . . Allies, . . . to march against the Enemies of the Christian Religon willing to act in Person on this Occasion, as a true Buckler of Religion. . . .

The Battle was fought on the 12th, it lasted 14 or 15 Hours; the slaughter was horrible, and the loss of the Turks inestimable, for they left the Field of Battle, besides the Dead and Prisoners, all their Canon, Equipage, Tents and infinite Riches that they had been six Years gathering together throughout the whole Ottoman Empire. . . .

The Night was spent in slaughter, and the unhappy Remnant of this Army saved their Lives by flight, having abandoned all to the Victors; even an infinite Number of Waggons, loaden with Ammunition, and some Field pieces, that designed to have carried with them; and which were found the next Day upon the Road they had taken; which makes us suspect that they'll not be able to rally again, . . .

The King [of Poland] understood afterwards by Deserters, who come every hour in Troops to surrender themselves to him, as well as the Renegadoes, that the Visier [the Turkish leader], seeing the defeat of the Army, called his Sons to him, embraced them, bitterly bewailed their Misfortune, and turned towards the Han of the Tartars [an ally of the Turks], and said, 'And thou, wilt not thou succour me?' To whom the Tartar Prince replied, That he knew the King of Poland by more than one Proof, and that the Visier would be very happy if he could save himself by flight, as having no other way for his Security, and that he was going to show him Example.

The Grand Visier being thus abandoned, took the same way, and retired in Disorder with only one Horse. . . . The Booty that was taken in this Action is infinite and inestimable; The Field of Battle was sowed with Gold Sabres, . . . and such a prodigious Quantity of other things that the Pillage which has already lasted three Days, will scarce be over in a whole Week. . . .

From Polish Manuscripts: or the Secret History of the Reign of John Sobieski, the III of That Name, King of Poland, *trans. by M. Delerac (London: D. Rhodes, 1700), pp. 355–364, as quoted in Alfred J. Bannan and Achilles Edelenyi, eds.,* Documentary History of Eastern Europe *(New York: Twayne Publishers, Inc., 1970), pp. 112–116.*

MAP 15-1 THE AUSTRIAN HABSBURG EMPIRE, 1521–1772 *The Empire had three main units—Austria, Bohemia, and Hungary. Expansion was mainly eastward: East Hungary from the Ottomans (seventeenth century) and Galicia from Poland (1772). Meantime, Silesia was lost, but the Habsburgs retained German influence as Holy Roman Emperors.*

Saint Stephen, which included Hungary, Croatia, and Transylvania. In the middle of the seventeenth century, much of Hungary remained occupied by the Turks and was liberated only at the end of the century.

In the early eighteenth century, the family further extended its domains, receiving the former Spanish (thereafter Austrian) Netherlands, Lombardy in northern Italy, and briefly, the kingdom of Naples in southern Italy through the Treaty of Utrecht in 1713. During the eighteenth and nineteenth centuries, the Habsburgs' power and influence in Europe were based primarily on their territories outside Germany.

In the second half of the seventeenth century and later, the Habsburgs faced immense problems in these hereditary territories. In each they ruled by virtue of a different title and had to gain the cooperation of the local nobility. The most difficult province was Hungary, where the Magyar nobility seemed ever ready to rebel. There was almost no common basis for political unity among peoples of such diverse languages,

customs, and geography. Even the Habsburg zeal for Roman Catholicism no longer proved a bond for unity as they confronted the equally zealous Calvinism of many of the Magyar nobles. The Habsburgs established various central councils to chart common policies for their far-flung domains. Virtually all of these bodies dealt with only part of the Habsburgs' holdings. Repeatedly, the Habsburgs had to bargain with nobles in one part of Europe to maintain their position in another.

Despite all these internal difficulties, Leopold I (r. 1657–1705) rallied his domains to resist the advances of the Turks and the aggression of Louis XIV. He achieved Ottoman recognition of his sovereignty over Hungary in 1699 and began the suppression of a long rebellion by his new Magyar subjects that lasted from 1703 to 1711. He also conquered much of the Balkan Peninsula and western Romania. These southeastward extensions allowed the Habsburgs to hope to develop Mediterranean trade through the port of Trieste. The expansion at the cost of the Ottoman Empire also helped them to compensate for their loss of domination over the Holy Roman Empire. Strength in the East gave them greater political leverage in Germany. Leopold I was succeeded by Joseph I (r. 1705–1711), who continued his policies.

THE HABSBURG DYNASTIC PROBLEM When Charles VI (r. 1711–1740) succeeded Joseph, he had no male heir, and there was only the weakest of precedents for a female ruler of the Habsburg domains. Charles feared that on his death the Austrian Habsburg lands might fall

Maria Theresa Discusses One Weakness of Her Throne

Scattered subjects of the multilingual Austrian Empire (Germans, Hungarians, Czechs, Slovaks, Slovenes, Croatians, Italians, and Romanians, for example) made impossible the unifying of the empire into a strong centralized monarchy. Maria Theresa, writing in 1745, explained how previous Habsburg rulers had impoverished themselves by attempting, with little success, to purchase the political and military support of the nobles in different provinces. The more privileges they gave the nobles, the more they were expected to give.

♦ *How had the pursuit of war led to financial weakness on the part of the Habsburgs? How had each new Habsburg ruler been persuaded to make large grants to the nobles? How had the behavior of earlier rulers increased the power of ministers and decreased the power of the monarch?*

To return once again to my ancestors, these individuals not only gave away most of the crown estates, but absorbed also the debts of those properties confiscated in time of rebellion, and these debts are still in arrears. Emperor Leopold [1658–1705] found little left to give away, but the terrible wars he fought no doubt forced him to mortgage or pawn additional crown estates. His successors did not relieve these burdens, and when I became sovereign, the crown revenues barely reached eighty thousand gulden. Also in the time of my forebears, the ministers received enormous payments from the crown and from the local Estates because they knew not only how to exploit selfishly the good will, grace, and munificence of the Austrian house by convincing each ruler that [his] predecessor had won fame by giving freely but also how to win the ears of the provincial lords and clergy so that these ministers

acquired all that they wished. In fact they spread their influence so wide that in the provinces they were more feared and respected than the ruler himself. And when they had finally taken everything from the sovereign, these same ministers turned for additional compensation to their provinces, where their great authority continuously increased. Even though complaints reached the monarch, out of grace and forebearance toward the ministers, he simply allowed the exploitations to continue. . . .

This system gave the ministers such authority that the sovereign himself found it convenient for his own interests to support them because he learned by experience that the more prestige enjoyed by the heads of the provinces, the more of the sovereign's demands these heads could extract from their Estates.

Maria Theresa, Political Testament, *cited in Karl A. Roider, ed. and trans.,* Maria Theresa *(Englewood Cliffs, N.J.: Prentice-Hall, 1973), pp. 32–33.*

prey to the surrounding powers, as had those of the Spanish Habsburgs in 1700. He was determined to prevent that disaster and to provide his domains with the semblance of legal unity. To those ends, he devoted most of his reign to seeking the approval of his family, the estates of his realms, and the major foreign powers for a document called the Pragmatic Sanction.

This instrument provided the legal basis for a single line of inheritance within the Habsburg dynasty through Charles VI's daughter Maria Theresa (r. 1740–1780). Other members of the Habsburg family recognized her as the rightful heir. The nobles of the various Habsburg domains did likewise after extracting various concessions from Charles. So, when Charles VI died in October 1740, he believed that he had secured legal unity for the Habsburg Empire and a safe succession for his daughter.

Charles VI had indeed established a permanent line of succession and the basis for future legal bonds within the Habsburg holdings. He had failed, however, to protect his daughter from foreign aggression, either through the Pragmatic Sanction or, more important, by leaving her a strong army and a full treasury. Less than two months after his death, the fragility of the foreign agreements became apparent. In December 1740, Frederick II of Prussia invaded the Habsburg province of Silesia. Maria Theresa had to fight to defend her inheritance.

Prussia and the Hohenzollerns

The Habsburg achievement had been to draw together into an uncertain legal unity a collection of domains possessed through separate feudal titles. The achievement of the Hohenzollerns of Brandenburg-Prussia was to acquire a similar collection of titular holdings and then to forge them into a centrally administered unit. Despite the geographical separation of their territories and the paucity of their natural economic resources, they transformed feudal ties and structures into bureaucratic ones. They subordinated every social class and most economic pursuits to the strengthening of the institution that united their far-flung realms: the army. They thus made the term "Prussian" synonymous with administrative rigor and military discipline.

A STATE OF DISCONNECTED TERRITORIES
The rise of Prussia occurred within the German power vacuum created after 1648 by the Peace of Westphalia. It is the story of the extraordinary Hohenzollern family, which had ruled the German territory of Brandenburg since 1417 (see Map 15-2). Through inheritance the family had acquired the duchy of Cleves and the counties of Mark and Ravensburg in 1609, the duchy of East Prussia in 1618, and the duchy of Pomerania in 1637. Except for Pomerania, none of these lands was contiguous with Brandenburg. East Prussia lay inside Poland and outside the authority of the Holy Roman Emperor. All of the territories lacked good natural resources, and many of them were devastated during the Thirty Years' War. At Westphalia the Hohenzollerns lost part of Pomerania to Sweden but were compensated by receiving three more bishoprics and the promise of the archbishopric of Magdeburg when it became vacant, as it did in 1680. By the late seventeenth century, the scattered Hohenzollern holdings represented a block of territory within the Holy Roman Empire second in size only to that of the Habsburgs.

Despite its size, the Hohenzollern conglomerate was weak. The areas were geographically separate, with no mutual sympathy or common concern among them. In each, local noble estates limited the power of the Hohenzollern prince. The various areas were also exposed to foreign aggression.

FREDERICK WILLIAM, THE GREAT ELECTOR
The person who began to forge these areas and nobles into a modern state was Frederick William (r. 1640–1688), who became known as the Great Elector (the ruler of Brandenburg was called an *Elector* because he was one of the princes who elected the Holy Roman Emperor). He established himself and his successors as the central uniting power by breaking the local noble estates, organizing a royal bureaucracy, and establishing a strong army.

Between 1655 and 1660, Sweden and Poland engaged in a war that endangered the Great Elector's holdings in Pomerania and East Prussia. Frederick William had neither the military nor the financial resources to confront this threat. In 1655 the Brandenburg estates refused to grant his new taxes; however, he proceeded to

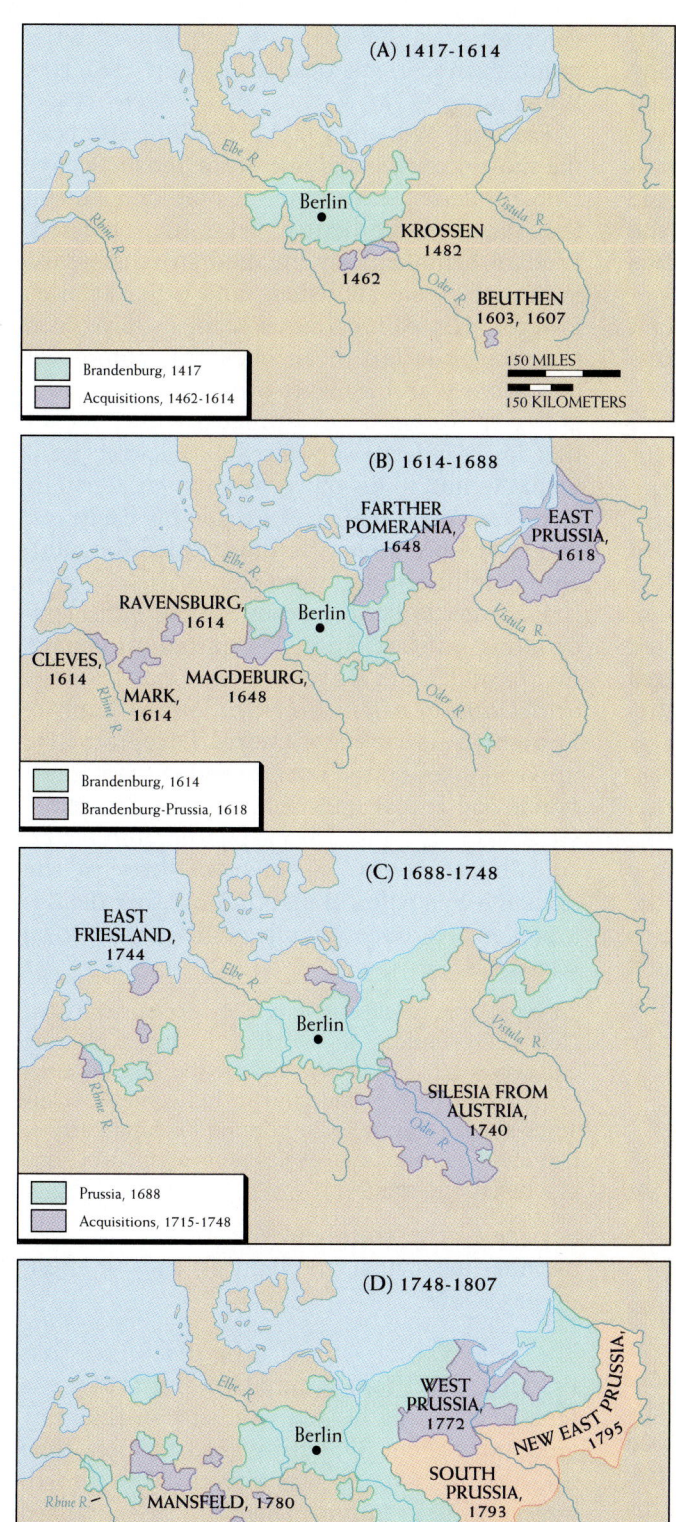

MAP 15-2 EXPANSION OF BRANDENBURG-PRUSSIA
In the seventeenth-century, Brandenburg-Prussia expanded mainly by acquiring dynastic titles in geographically separated lands. In the eighteenth-century, it expanded through aggression to the east, seizing Silesia in 1740 and various parts of Poland in 1772, 1793, and 1795.

(A) 1417-1614

Berlin

KROSSEN
1482

1462

BEUTHEN
1603, 1607

Elbe R.

Vistula R.

Rhine R.

Oder R.

150 MILES

150 KILOMETERS

☐ Brandenburg, 1417
☐ Acquisitions, 1462-1614

(B) 1614-1688

FARTHER
POMERANIA,
1648

EAST
PRUSSIA,
1618

RAVENSBURG,
1614

Berlin

CLEVES,
1614

MARK,
1614

MAGDEBURG,
1648

Elbe R.

Vistula R.

Rhine R.

Oder R.

☐ Brandenburg, 1614
☐ Brandenburg-Prussia, 1618

(C) 1688-1748

EAST
FRIESLAND,
1744

Berlin

SILESIA FROM
AUSTRIA,
1740

Elbe R.

Vistula R.

Rhine R.

Oder R.

☐ Prussia, 1688
☐ Acquisitions, 1715-1748

(D) 1748-1807

WEST
PRUSSIA,
1772

NEW EAST PRUSSIA,
1795

Berlin

SOUTH
PRUSSIA,
1793

MANSFELD, 1780

Elbe R.

Rhine R.

Oder R.

Vistula R.

☐ Prussia, 1748
☐ Acquisitions, 1748-1772
☐ Temporary Acquisitions,
1793-1795 to 1807.

collect the required taxes by military force. In 1659 a different grant of taxes, originally made in 1653, elapsed; Frederick William continued to collect them as well as those he had imposed by his own authority. He used the money to build up an army that allowed him to continue to enforce his will without the approval of the nobility. Similar threats and coercion took place against the nobles in his other territories.

There was, however, a political and social trade-off between the Elector and his various nobles. These Junkers, or German noble landlords, were allowed almost complete control over the serfs on their estates. In exchange for their obedience to the Hohenzollerns, the Junkers received the right to demand obedience from their serfs. Frederick William also tended to choose as the local administrators of the tax structure men who would normally have been members of the noble estates. He thus co-opted potential opponents into his service. The taxes fell most heavily on the backs of the peasants and the urban classes.

As the years passed, sons of Junkers increasingly dominated the army officer corps, and this practice became even more pronounced during the eighteenth century. All officials and army officers took an oath of loyalty directly to the Elector. The army and the Elector thus came to embody the otherwise absent unity of the state. The existence of the army made Prussia a valuable potential ally and a state with which other powers needed to curry favor.

FREDERICK WILLIAM I, KING OF PRUSSIA Yet, even with the considerable accomplishments of the Great Elector, the house of Hohenzollern did not possess a crown. The achievement of a royal title was one of the few state-building accomplishments of Frederick I (r. 1688–1713). This son of the Great Elector was the least "Prussian" of his family during these crucial years. He built palaces, founded Halle University (1694), patronized the arts, and lived luxuriously. In 1701, however, at the outbreak of the War of the Spanish Succession, he put his army at the disposal of the Habsburg Holy Roman Emperor. In exchange for this loyal service, the emperor permitted Frederick to assume the title of "King in Prussia." Thereafter

Frederick became Frederick I, and he passed the much-desired royal title to his son Frederick William I in 1713.

Frederick William I (r. 1713–1740) was both the most eccentric and one of the most effective Hohenzollerns. After giving his father a funeral that matched the luxury of his life, Frederick William I immediately imposed strict austerity. Some jobs were abolished, and other salaries lowered. His political aims seem to have been the consolidation of an obedient, compliant bureaucracy and a bigger army. He initiated a policy of *Kabinett* government, which meant that lower officials submitted all relevant documents to him in his office, or *Kabinett*. Then he alone examined the papers, made his decisions, and issued his orders. He thus skirted the influence of ministers and ruled alone.

Frederick William I organized the bureaucracy along military lines. He united all departments under the *General-Ober Finanz-Kriegs-und-Domänen-Direktorium*, more happily known to us as the General Directory. He imposed taxes on the nobility and changed most remaining feudal dues into money payments. He sought to transform feudal and administrative loyalties into a sense of duty to the monarch as a political institution rather than as a person. He once described the perfect royal servant as

an intelligent, assiduous, and alert person who after God values nothing higher than his king's pleasure and serves him out of love and for the sake of honor rather than money and who in his conduct solely seeks and constantly bears in mind his king's service and interests, who, moreover, abhors all intrigues and emotional deterrents.[1]

Service to the state and the monarch was to become impersonal, mechanical, and, in effect, unquestioning.

THE PRUSSIAN ARMY The discipline that Frederick William applied to the army was fanatical. During his reign the size of the army grew from about 39,000 in 1713 to more than 80,000 in 1740. It was the third or fourth largest army in Europe, whereas Prussia ranked thirteenth in population. Rather than using re-

---

[1]*Quoted in Hans Rosenberg,* Bureaucracy, Aristocracy, and Autocracy *(Boston: Beacon Press, 1958), p. 93.*

The Great Elector Welcomes Protestant Refugees from France

The Hohenzollern dynasty of Brandenburg-Prussia pursued a policy of religious toleration. The family itself was Calvinist, whereas most of its subjects were Lutherans. When Louis XIV of France revoked the Edict of Nantes in 1685 (see the document in Chapter 13), Frederick William, the Great Elector, seized the opportunity to invite into his realms French Protestants. As his proclamation indicates, he wanted to attract persons with productive skills who could aid the economic development of his domains.

✦ *In reading this document, do you believe religious or economic concerns more nearly led the Elector of Brandenburg to welcome the French Protestants? What specific privileges did the Elector extend to them? To what extent were these privileges a welcoming measure and to what extent were they inducements to emigrate to Brandenburg? In what kind of economic activity does the Elector expect the French refugees to engage?*

We, Friedrich Wilhelm, by Grace of God Margrave of Brandenburg. . . .

Do hereby proclaim and make known to all and sundry that since the cruel persecutions and rigorous ill-treatment in which Our co-religionists of the Evangelical-Reformed faith have for some time past been subjected in the Kingdom of France, have caused many families to remove themselves and to betake themselves out of the said Kingdom into other lands, We now . . . have been moved graciously to offer them through this Edict . . . a secure and free refuge in all Our Lands and Provinces. . . .

Since Our Lands are not only well and amply endowed with all things necessary to support life, but also very well-suited to the reestablishment of all kinds of manufactures and trade and traffic by land and water, We permit, indeed, to those settling therein free choice to establish themselves where it is most convenient for their profession and way of living. . . .

The personal property which they bring with them, including merchandise and other wares, is to be totally exempt from any taxes, customs dues, licenses, or other imposts of any description, and not detained in any way. . . .

As soon as these Our French co-religionists of the Evangelical-Reformed faith have settled in any town or village, they shall be admitted to the domiciliary rights and craft freedoms customary there, gratis and without payments of any fee; and shall be entitled to the benefits, rights, and privileges enjoyed by Our other, native, subjects, residing there. . . .

Not only are those who wish to establish manufacture of cloth, stuffs, hats, or other objects in which they are skilled to enjoy all necessary freedoms, privileges and facilities, but also provision is to be made for them to be assisted and helped as far as possible with money and anything else which they need to realize their intention. . . .

Those who settle in the country and wish to maintain themselves by agriculture are to be given a certain plot of land to bring under cultivation and provided with whatever they need to establish themselves initially. . . .

C. A. Macartney, ed., The Habsburg and Hohenzollern Dynasties in the Seventeenth and Eighteenth Centuries *(New York: Walker, 1970), pp. 270–273.*

Though economically weak and with a small population, Prussia became an important state because it developed a large, well-trained army. Prussian troops were known for their discipline, the result of constant drill and harsh punishment. In this mid-eighteenth-century engraving one soldier is being whipped while another is about to run a gauntlet of other soldiers. [Bildarchiv Preussischer Kulturbesitz]

cruiters, the king made each canton or local district responsible for supplying a quota of soldiers.

After 1725 Frederick William always wore an officer's uniform. He formed one regiment from the tallest soldiers he could find in Europe. Separate laws applied to the army and to civilians. Laws, customs, and royal attention made the officer corps the highest social class of the state. Military service attracted the sons of Junkers. Thus, the army, the Junker nobility, and the monarchy were forged into a single political entity. Military priorities and values

dominated Prussian government, society, and daily life as in no other state of Europe. It has often been said that whereas other nations possessed armies, the Prussian army possessed its nation.

Although Frederick William I built the best army in Europe, he avoided conflict. He wanted to drill his soldiers but not to order them into battle. Although he terrorized his family and associates and on occasion knocked out teeth with his walking stick, he was not militarily aggressive. The army was for him a symbol of

Prussian power and unity, not an instrument to be used for foreign adventures or aggression.

At his death in 1740, he passed to his son Frederick II "the Great" (r. 1740–1786) this superb military machine, but he could not also pass on the wisdom to refrain from using it. Almost immediately on coming to the throne, Frederick II upset the Pragmatic Sanction and invaded Silesia. He thus crystallized the Austrian–Prussian rivalry for control of Germany that would dominate central European affairs for over a century.

The Entry of Russia into the European Political Arena

Though ripe with consequences for the future, the rise of Prussia and the new consolidation of the Austrian Habsburg domains seemed to many at the time only another shift in the long-troubled German scene. The emergence of Russia, however, as an active European power was a wholly new factor in European politics. Previously Russia had been considered part of Europe only by courtesy. Geographically and politically it lay on the periphery. Hemmed in by Sweden on the Baltic and by the Ottoman Empire on the Black Sea, the country had no warm-water ports. Its chief outlet to the west was Archangel on the White Sea, which was ice free for only part of the year. There was little trade. What Russia did possess was a vast reserve of largely undeveloped natural and human resources.

Birth of the Romanov Dynasty

The reign of Ivan the Terrible, which had begun so well and closed so frighteningly, was followed by anarchy and civil war known as the "Time of Troubles." In 1613, hoping to restore stability, an assembly of nobles elected as tsar a seventeen-year-old boy named Michael Romanov (r. 1613–1654). Thus began the dynasty that despite palace revolutions, military conspiracies, assassinations, and family strife ruled Russia until 1917.

Michael Romanov and his two successors, Alexis I (r. 1654–1676) and Theodore III (r.

Austria and Prussia in the Late Seventeenth and Early Eighteenth Centuries	
1640–1688	Reign of Frederick William, the Great Elector
1657–1705	Leopold I rules Austria and resists the Turkish invasions
1683	Turkish siege of Vienna
1688–1713	Reign of Frederick I of Prussia
1699	Peace treaty between Turks and Habsburgs
1711–1740	Charles VI rules Austria and secures agreement to the Pragmatic Sanction
1713–1740	Frederick William I builds up the military power of Prussia
1740	Maria Theresa succeeds to the Habsburg throne
1740	Frederick II violates the Pragmatic Sanction by invading Silesia

1676–1682), brought stability and some bureaucratic centralization to Russia. The country remained, however, weak and impoverished. The bureaucracy after years of turmoil was still largely controlled by the *boyars*, the old nobility. This administrative apparatus could barely supress a revolt of peasants and Cossacks (horsemen who lived on the steppe frontier) under Stepan Razin in 1670–1671. Furthermore, the government and the tsars faced the danger of mutiny from the *streltsy*, or guards of the Moscow garrison.

Peter the Great

In 1682 another boy—ten years old at the time—ascended the fragile Russian throne as coruler with his half brother. His name was Peter (r. 1682–1725), and Russia would never be the same after him. He and the ill Ivan V had come to power on the shoulders of the streltsy, who expected to be rewarded for their support. Much violence and bloodshed had surrounded the disputed succession. Matters became even more confused when the boys' sister, Sophia, was named regent. Peter's followers overthrew her in 1689. From that date onward, Peter ruled

Peter the Great (r. 1682–1725) seeking to make Russia a major military power, reorganized the country's political and economic structures. His reign saw Russia enter fully into European power politics. [The Bettmann Archive]

the first order. The products and workers from the West who had filtered into Russia impressed and intrigued him. In 1697 he made a famous visit in transparent disguise to western Europe. There he dined and talked with the great and the powerful, who considered this almost seven-foot-tall ruler both crude and rude. His happiest moments on the trip were spent inspecting shipyards, docks, and the manufacture of military hardware.

Peter returned to Moscow determined to copy what he had seen abroad, for he knew that warfare would be necessary to make Russia a great power. The tsar's drive toward westernization, though unsystematic, had four general goals: taming the boyars and the streltsy, achieving secular control of the Church, reorganizing the internal administration, and developing the economy. Peter pursued each of these goals ruthlessly. His effort was unprecedented in Russian history in both its intensity and scope.

TAMING THE BOYARS AND STRELTSY Peter made a sustained attack on the boyars. In 1698, immediately on his return from abroad, he personally shaved the long beards of the court boyars and sheared off the customary long, hand-covering sleeves of their shirts and coats, which had made them the butt of jokes throughout Europe. More important, he demanded that the nobles serve his state.

In 1722 he published a Table of Ranks that equated a person's social position and privileges with his rank in the bureaucracy or the army rather than with his position in the nobility. Peter thus intended to make the social standing of individual boyars a function of their willingness to serve the central state. Unlike Prussian Junkers, however, the Russian nobility never became perfectly loyal to the state. They repeatedly sought to reassert their independence and their control of the Russian imperial court and to bargain with later tsars over local authority and the nobles' dominance of the serfs.

The streltsy fared less well than the boyars. In 1698 they had rebelled while Peter was on his European tour. On his return, he brutally suppressed the revolt. There were private tortures and public executions, in which Peter's own ministers took part. Almost 1,200 of the rebels

personally, although in theory he shared the crown until Ivan died in 1696. The dangers and turmoil of his youth convinced Peter of two things. First, the power of the tsar must be made secure from the jealousy of the boyars and the greed of the streltsy. Second, the military power of Russia must be increased. In that respect he resembled Louis XIV of France, who had experienced the turmoil of the Fronde during his youth and resolved to establish a strong monarchy.

Western Europe, particularly its military resources, fascinated Peter I, who became known as Peter the Great. He was an imitator of

Rise of Russian Power	
1533–1584	Reign of Ivan the Terrible
1584–1613	Time of Troubles
1613	Michael Romanov becomes tsar
1682	Peter the Great becomes tsar as a boy
1689	Peter assumes personal rule
1696	Russia captures Azov on the Black Sea from the Turks
1697	European tour of Peter the Great
1698	Peter returns to Russia to put down the revolt of the streltsy
1700	The Great Northern War opens between Russia and Sweden; Russia defeated at Narva by Swedish Army of Charles XII
1703	Saint Petersburg founded
1709	Russia defeats Sweden at the Battle of Poltava
1718	Charles XII of Sweden dies
1718	Son of Peter the Great dies under mysterious circumstances in prison
1721	Peace of Nystad ends the Great Northern War
1721	Peter establishes a synod for the Russian church
1722	Peter issues the Table of Ranks
1725	Peter dies leaving an uncertain succession

were put to death, and their corpses remained on public display to discourage future disloyalty.

ACHIEVING SECULAR CONTROL OF THE CHURCH Peter dealt with the potential independence of the Russian Orthodox church with similar ruthlessness. Here again, he had to confront a problem that had arisen in the turbulent decades that had preceded his reign. The Russian church had long opposed the scientific as well as the theological thought of the West. In the mid-seventeenth century, a reformist movement led by Patriarch Nikon introduced certain changes into Church texts and ritual. These reforms caused great unrest among the Old Believers, a group of Russian Christians who strongly opposed these changes. Although condemned by the hierarchy, the Old Believers persisted in their opposition. Thousands of them committed suicide rather than submit to the new rituals. The Old Believers represented a rejection of change and innovation; their opposition discouraged the Church hierarchy from making any further substantial accommodations with modern thought.

In the future Peter wanted to avoid two kinds of difficulties with the Church. First, the clergy must not be able to oppose change and westernization. Second, the hierarchy of the Church must not be permitted to cause again the kind of controversy that had inspired the Old Believers. Consequently, in 1721, Peter simply abolished the position of patriarch. In its place he established a synod headed by a layman, called the Procurator General, to rule the Church in accordance with secular requirements. So far as transforming a traditional institution was concerned, this action toward the Church was the most radical policy of Peter's reign. It produced still further futile opposition from the Old Believers, who saw the tsar as leading the Church into new heresy.

REORGANIZING DOMESTIC ADMINISTRATION In his reorganization of domestic administration, Peter looked to institutions then used in Sweden. These were "colleges," or bureaus, of several persons rather than departments headed by a single minister. These colleges, which he imposed on Russia, were to look after matters such as the collection of taxes, foreign relations, war, and economic affairs. This new organization was an attempt to breathe life into Russia's stagnant and inefficient administration.

In 1711 he created a central senate of nine members who were to direct the Moscow government when the tsar was away with the army. The purpose of these and other local administrative reforms was to establish a bureaucracy that could support an efficient army.

DEVELOPING THE ECONOMY AND WAGING WAR The economic development advocated by Peter the Great was closely related to his military needs. He encouraged the establishment of an iron industry in the Ural Mountains, and by mid-century Russia had become the largest iron producer in Europe. He sent promising young Russians abroad to acquire technical and organizational skills. He tried to attract West European craftsmen to live and work in Russia.

Peter the Great built St. Petersburg on the Gulf of Finland to provide Russia with better contact with Western Europe. He moved Russia's capital there from Moscow in 1703. This is an eighteenth-century view of the city. [John R. Freeman]

Except for the striking growth of the iron industry, which nevertheless later languished, these efforts had only marginal success.

The goal of these internal reforms and political departures was to support a policy of warfare. Peter was determined to secure warm-water ports that would allow Russia to trade with the West and to have a greater impact on European affairs. This policy led him into wars with the Ottoman Empire and Sweden. His armies began fighting the Turks in 1695 and captured Azov on the Black Sea in 1696. It was a temporary victory, for in 1711 he was compelled to return the port.

Peter had more success against Sweden, where the inconsistency and irrationality of Charles XII were no small aid. In 1700 Russia invaded the Swedish Baltic possessions. The Swedish king's failure to follow up his victory at Narva in 1700 allowed Peter to regroup his forces and reserve his resources. In 1709, when Charles XII returned to fight Russia again, Peter was ready, and the Battle of Poltava sealed the fate of Sweden. In 1721 the Peace of Nystad, which ended the Great Northern War, confirmed the Russian conquest of Estonia, Livonia, and part of Finland. Henceforth Russia possessed warm-water ports and a permanent influence on European affairs.

At one point the domestic and foreign policies of Peter the Great literally intersected. This was at the spot on the Gulf of Finland where he founded his new capital city of Saint Petersburg. There he built government structures and compelled the boyars to construct town houses. He thus imitated those European monarchs who had copied Louis XIV by constructing smaller versions of Versailles. The founding of Saint Petersburg went beyond establishing a central imperial court, however. It symbolized a new western orientation of Russia and Peter's determination to hold his position on the Baltic coast. He had begun the construction of the city and had moved the capital there in 1703, even before his victory over Sweden was assured.

Despite his notable success on the Baltic,

Peter's reign ended with a great question mark. He had long quarreled with his only son, Alexis. Peter was jealous of the young man and feared he might undertake sedition. In 1718 Peter had his son imprisoned, and during this imprison-ment, Alexis died mysteriously. Thereafter Peter claimed for himself the right to name a succes-sor, but he could never bring himself to desig-nate one either orally or in writing. Conse-quently, when he died in 1725, there was no

Peter the Great Establishes Building Requirements in Saint Petersburg

By constructing Saint Petersburg on the Gulf of Finland, Peter the Great tried to consolidate his military efforts in the Great Northern War. The city was to pro-vide Russia with a permanent outlet to the West and to be the site of its new capital. The construction of this city consequently served symbolic political ends as well as military and economic ones. In this document, Peter explains how he expected the city to be constructed.

◆ *Why might Peter have been so concerned that the work on the city progress rapidly? What are the difficulties in construction in Russia that this document reveals? What do those difficulties tell you about Russia's society and its econ-omic resources? Why might Peter have been concerned that only houses face on the streets of the new city?*

1. On the City Island and the Admiralty Island in Saint Petersburg, as likewise on the banks of the greater Neva and its more important arms, wood buildings are forbid-den, only adobe houses being allowed. The two above-mentioned islands and the embankments excepted, wood may be used for buildings, the plans to be obtained from the architect. . . . The roofs are to be cov-ered either with two thicknesses of turf laid on rafters with cross-ribs (not on laths or boards), or with tiles. No other roof covering is allowed under penalty of severe fines. The streets should be bordered directly by the houses, not with fences or stables.

2. The most illustrious and mighty Peter the Great, Emperor and Autocrat of all Russia, has commanded his imperial decree to be proclaimed to people of all ranks. Whereas stone construction here is advancing very slowly, it being difficult to obtain stone-masons and other artisans of this craft even for good pay; for this reason all stone buildings of any description are forbidden in the whole state for a few years, until construction has sufficiently progressed here, under penalty of confiscation of the offend-er's property and exile. This decree is to be announced in all the cities and districts of the Saint Petersburg province, except this city, so that none may plead ignorance as an excuse.

3. The following is ordered: no building shall be undertaken in Petersburg on the grounds of houses, between neighboring back yards, until all the main and side streets are entirely built up. However, if after this any person needs more buildings, he may build on his grounds, along the neighbor's lot. No stables or barns may be built facing the street, but only inside the grounds. Along the streets and side streets all the space must be filled by residences, as ordered. In the loca-tions where, as ordered by previous decrees, wooden houses may be built, they must be made of squared logs. If the logs are used as they are, the walls must be faced with boards and coated with red, or painted to look like brick.

From Marthe Blinoff, ed., Life and Thought in Old Russia, (University Park: The Pennsylvania State University Press, 1961), pp. 16–17.

firm policy on the succession to the throne. For more than thirty years, soldiers and nobles again determined who ruled Russia. Peter had laid the foundations of a modern Russia, but he had failed to lay the foundations of a stable state.

◆

By the second quarter of the eighteenth century, the major European powers were not yet nation-states in which the citizens felt themselves united by a shared sense of community, culture, language, and history. They were still monarchies in which the personality of the ruler and the personal relationships of the great noble families exercised considerable influence over public affairs. The monarchs, except in Great Britain, had generally succeeded in making their power greater than the nobility's. The power of the aristocracy and its capacity to resist or obstruct the policies of the monarch were not destroyed, however. In Britain, of course, the nobility had tamed the monarchy, but even there tension between nobles and monarchs would continue throughout the rest of the century.

In foreign affairs the new arrangement of military and diplomatic power established early in the century prepared the way for two long conflicts. The first was a commercial rivalry for trade and overseas empire between France and Great Britain. During the reign of Louis XIV, these two nations had collided over the French bid for dominance in Europe. During the eighteenth century, they dueled for control of commerce on other continents. The second arena of warfare was in central Europe, where Austria and Prussia fought for the leadership of the German states.

Behind these international conflicts and the domestic rivalry of monarchs and nobles, however, the society of eighteenth-century Europe began to change. The character and the structures of the societies over which the monarchs ruled were beginning to take on some features associated with the modern age. These economic and social developments would eventually transform the life of Europe to a degree beside which the state building of the early eighteenth-century monarchs paled.

Review Questions

1. Explain why Britain and France remained leading powers in western Europe while Spain and the United Netherlands declined.
2. How did the stricture of British government change under the political leadership of Robert Walpole? What were the chief sources of Walpole's political strength?
3. How was the Hohenzollern family able to forge a conglomerate of diverse land holdings into the state of Prussia? Who were the major personalities involved in this process and what were their individual contributions? Why was the military so important in Prussia?
4. Compare and contrast the varying success with which the Hohenzollerns and Habsburgs each handled their problems. Which family was more successful and why? Why were Sweden, the Ottoman Empire, and Poland each less successful?
5. How and why did Russia emerge as a great power? Discuss the character of Peter the Great. How were his reforms related to his military ambitions? What were his methods of reform? To what extent did he succeed? What were Russia's domestic problems before Peter came to power?
6. "Peter the Great was a rational ruler, interested in the welfare of his people." Do you agree with this statement? Why? Can you make a case for Peter as a bloody tyrant, concerned only with promoting his own glory?

Suggested Readings

T. M. BARKER, *Army, Aristocracy, Monarchy: Essays in War, Society and Government in Austria, 1618–1780* (1982). Examines the intricate power relationships among these major institutions.

J. BLACK, *Eighteenth-Century Europe 1700–1789* (1990). An excellent survey.

J. BREWER, *The Sinews of Power: War, Money and the English State, 1688–1783* (1989). An extremely important study of the financial basis of English power.

R. BROWNING, *Political and Constitutional Ideas of the Court Whigs* (1982). An excellent overview of the ideology of Walpole's supporters.

F. L. Carsten, *The Origins of Prussia* (1954). Discusses the groundwork laid by the Great Elector in the seventeenth century.

J. C. D. Clark, *English Society: 1688–1832: Social Structure and Political Practice During the Ancien Regime* (1985). An important, controversial work that emphasizes the role of religion in English political life.

A. Cobban, *A History of Modern France*, 2nd ed., Vol. 1 (1961). A lively and opinionated volume.

L. Colley, *In Defiance of Oligarchy: The Tory Party, 1714–60* (1982). An important study that challenges much conventional opinion about eighteenth-century British politics.

N. Davis, *God's Playground*, Vol. 1 (1991). Excellent on prepartition Poland.

P. M. G. Dickson, *Finance and Government Under Maria Theresa* (1987). A definitive work.

W. Doyle, *The Old European Order, 1660–1800* (1992). The most thoughtful treatment of the subject.

P. Dukes, *The Making of Russian Absolutism: 1613–1801* (1982). An overview based on recent scholarship.

R. R. Ergang, *The Potsdam Führer* (1941). The biography of Frederick William I.

R. J. W. Evans, *The Making of the Habsburg Monarchy, 1550–1700: An Interpretation* (1979). Places much emphasis on intellectual factors and the role of religion.

F. Ford, *Robe and Sword: The Regrouping of the French Aristocracy After Louis XIV* (1953). An important book for political, social, and intellectual history.

G. P. Gooch, *Maria Theresa and Other Studies* (1951). A sound introduction to the problems of the Habsburgs.

G. P. Gooch, *Louis XV, The Monarchy in Decline* (1956). A discussion of the problems of France after the death of Louis XIV.

J. M. Hittle, *The Service City: State and Townsmen in Russia, 1600–1800* (1979). Examines the relationship of cities in Russia to the growing power of the central government.

H. Holborn, *A History of Modern Germany, 1648–1840* (1966). The most comprehensive survey in English.

R. A. Kann and Z. V. David, *The Peoples of the Eastern Habsburg Lands, 1526–1918* (1984). A helpful overview of the subject.

D. McKay and H. M. Scott, *The Rise of the Great Powers 1648–1815* (1983). Now the standard survey.

W. H. McNeil, *Europe's Steppe Frontier, 1500–1800* (1964). An interpretive essay on the history of southeastern Europe.

R. K. Massie, *Peter the Great: His Life and His World* (1980). A good popular biography.

L. B. Namier and J. Brooke, *The History of Parliament: The House of Commons, 1754–1790*, 3 vols. (1964). A detailed examination of the unreformed British House of Commons and electoral system.

J. B. Owen, *The Eighteenth Century* (1974). An excellent introduction to England in this period.

G. Parker, *The Military Revolution: Military Innovation and the Rise of the West (1500–1800)* (1988). A major work in every respect.

J. H. Plumb, *Sir Robert Walpole*, 2 vols. (1956, 1961). A masterful biography ranging across the sweep of European politics.

J. H. Plumb, *The Growth of Political Stability in England, 1675–1725* (1969). An important interpretive work.

N. V. Riasanovsky, *The Image of Peter the Great in Russian History and Thought* (1985). Examines the legacy of Peter in Russian history.

N. V. Riasanovsky, *A History of Russia*, 5th ed. (1992). The best one-volume introduction.

H. Rosenberg, *Bureaucracy, Aristocracy, and Autocracy: The Prussian Experience, 1660–1815* (1960). Emphasizes the organization of Prussian administration.

P. F. Sugar, *Southeastern Europe Under Ottoman Rule, 1354–1804* (1977). An extremely clear presentation.

B. H. Sumner, *Peter the Great and the Emergence of Russia* (1951). This remains a classic study.

E. N. Williams, *The Ancien Régime in Europe* (1972). A state-by-state survey of very high quality.

During the eighteenth century, most goods were produced in small workshops, such as this English blacksmith shop painted by Joseph Wright of Derby (1734–1797), or in the homes of artisans. Not until very late in the century, with the early stages of industrialization, did a few factories appear. [Yale Center for British Art, Paul Mellon Collection]

16

Society and Economy Under the Old Regime in the Eighteenth Century

> **Key Topics in This Chapter**
> ◆ The varied privileges and powers of Europe's aristocracies in the Old Regime and their efforts to increase their wealth
> ◆ The plight of rural peasants
> ◆ Family structure and family economy
> ◆ The transformation of Europe's economy by the agricultural and industrial revolutions
> ◆ Urban growth and the social tensions that accompanied it
> ◆ The strains on the institutions of the Old Regime brought about by social change

During the French Revolution and the turmoil spawned by that upheaval, it became customary to refer to the patterns of social, political, and economic relationships that had existed in France before 1789 as the ancien régime, or the "Old Regime." The term has come to be applied generally to the life and institutions of prerevolutionary Europe. Politically, it meant the rule of theoretically absolute monarchies with growing bureaucracies and aristocratically led armies. Economically, scarcity of food, predominance of agriculture, slow transport, a low level of iron production, comparatively unsophisticated financial institutions, and, in some cases, competitive commercial overseas empires characterized the Old Regime. Socially, men and women living during the period saw themselves less as individuals than as members of distinct corporate bodies that possessed certain privileges or rights as a group.

Tradition, hierarchy, corporateness, and privilege were the chief social characteristics of the Old Regime. Yet it was by no means a static society. Change and innovation were fermenting in its midst. Farming became more commercialized, and both food production and the size of the population increased. The early stages of the Industrial Revolution made more consumer goods available, and domestic consumption expanded throughout the century. The colonies in the Americas provided strong demand for European goods and manufactures. Merchants in seaports and other cities were expanding their businesses. By preparing their states for war, European governments put new demands on the resources and the economic organizations of their nations. The spirit of rationality that had been so important to the Scientific Revolution of the seventeenth century continued to manifest itself in the economic life of the eighteenth century. The Old Regime itself fostered the changes that eventually transformed it into a different kind of society.

Major Features of Life in the Old Regime

Socially, prerevolutionary Europe was based on (1) aristocratic elites possessing a wide variety of inherited legal privileges; (2) established churches intimately related to the state and the aristocracy; (3) an urban labor force usually organized into guilds; and (4) a rural peasantry subject to high taxes and feudal dues. Of course, the men and women living during this period did not know it was the Old Regime. Most of them earned their livelihoods and passed their lives as their forebears had done for generations before them and as they expected their children to do after them.

Maintenance of Tradition

During the eighteenth century, the past weighed more heavily on people's minds than did the future. Few persons outside the government bureaucracies, the expanding merchant groups, and the movement for reform called the *Enlightenment* (see Chapter 18) considered change or innovation desirable. This was especially true of social relationships. Both nobles and peasants, for different reasons, repeatedly called for the restoration of traditional or customary rights. The nobles asserted what they considered their ancient rights against the intrusion of the expanding monarchical bureaucracies. The peasants, through petitions and revolts, called for the revival or the maintenance of the customary manorial rights that allowed them access to particular lands, courts, or grievance procedures.

Except for the early industrial development in Britain and the accompanying expansion of personal consumption, the eighteenth-century economy was also predominantly traditional. The quality and quantity of the grain harvest remained the most important fact of life for most of the population and the gravest concern for governments.

Hierarchy and Privilege

Closely related to this traditional social and economic outlook was the hierarchical structure of the society. The medieval sense of rank and degree not only persisted but became more rigid during the century. In several continental cities, *sumptuary laws* regulating the dress of the different classes remained on the books. These laws forbade persons in one class or occupation to wear clothes like those worn by their social superiors. These laws, which sought to make the social hierarchy easily visible, were largely ineffective by this time. What really enforced the hierarchy was the corporate nature of social relationships.

Each state or society was considered a community composed of numerous smaller communities. Eighteenth-century Europeans did not enjoy what Americans regard as individual rights. Instead a person enjoyed such rights and privileges as were guaranteed to the particular communities or groups of which she or he was a part. The "community" might include the village, the municipality, the nobility, the Church, the guild, a university, or the parish. In turn, each of these bodies enjoyed certain privileges, some great, some small. The privileges might involve exemption from taxation or from some especially humiliating punishment, the right to practice a trade or craft, the right of one's children to pursue a particular occupation, or, for the Church, the right to collect the tithe.

The Aristocracy

The eighteenth century was the great age of the aristocracy. The nobility constituted approximately 1 to 5 percent of the population of any given country. In every country, it was the single wealthiest sector of the population, had the widest degree of social, political, and economic power, and set the tone of polite society. In most countries, the nobility had their own separate house in the parliament, estates, or diet. Only nobles had any kind of representation in Hungary and Poland. Land continued to provide the aristocracy with its largest source of income, but aristocrats did not merely own estates. Their influence was felt throughout social and economic life. In much of Europe, however, it was felt that manual labor was regarded as beneath a noble. In Spain, it was assumed that even the poorer nobles would lead lives of idleness. In other nations, however, the nobility often fostered economic innovation and embraced the commercial spirit. Such willingness to change helped protect their wealth.

Varieties of Aristocratic Privilege

To be an aristocrat was a matter of birth and legal privilege. This much the aristocracy had in common across the Continent. In almost every other respect, they differed markedly from country to country.

BRITISH NOBILITY   The smallest, wealthiest, best-defined, and most socially responsible aristocracy resided in Great Britain. It consisted of about 400 families, whose eldest male member sat in the House of Lords. Through the corruptions of the electoral system, these families also controlled many seats in the House of Commons. The estates of the British nobility ranged from a few thousand to fifty thousand acres, from which they received rents. The nobles owned about one-fourth of all the arable land in the country. Increasingly the British aris-

The foundation of aristocratic life was the possession of land. English aristocrats and large landowners controlled local government as well as the English Parliament. This painting of Robert Andrews and his wife by Thomas Gainsborough (1728–1788) shows an aristocratic couple on their estate. The gun and the hunting dog in this portrait suggest the importance landowners assigned to the virtually exclusive hunting privileges they enjoyed on their land. [The National Gallery, London]

tocracy invested its wealth in commerce, canals, urban real estate, mines, and even industrial ventures. Because only the eldest son inherited the title and the land, younger sons moved into commerce, the army, the professions, and the Church. British landowners in both houses of Parliament levied taxes and also paid them. They had few significant legal privileges, but their direct or indirect control of local government gave them immense political power and social influence. The aristocracy dominated the society and politics of the English counties. Their country houses, many of which were built in the eighteenth century, were centers for local society.

FRENCH NOBILITY The situation of the continental nobilities was less clear-cut. In France, the approximately 400,000 nobles were divided between nobles of the sword and those of the robe. The former families' nobility was derived from military service; the latter had either gained their titles by serving in the bureaucracy or had purchased them. The two groups had quarreled in the past but often cooperated during the eighteenth century to defend their common privileges.

The French nobility were also divided between those who held office or favor with the royal court at Versailles and those who did not. The court nobility reaped the immense wealth that could be gained from holding high office. The noble hold on such offices intensified during the century. By the late 1780s, appointments to the Church, the army, and the bureaucracy, as well as other profitable positions, tended to go to the nobles already established in court circles. Whereas these well-connected aristocrats were rich, the provincial nobility, called *hobereaux*, were often little better off than wealthy peasants.

Despite differences in rank, origin, and wealth, certain hereditary privileges set all French aristocrats apart from the rest of society. They were exempt from many taxes. For example, most French nobles did not pay the *taille*, or land tax, the basic tax of the Old Regime. The nobles were technically liable for payment of the *vingtième*, or the "twentieth," which resembled an income tax, but they rarely had to pay it in full. The nobles were not liable for the royal *corvées*, or forced labor on public works, which fell on the peasants. In addition to these exemp-

tions, French nobles could collect feudal dues from their tenants and enjoyed exclusive hunting and fishing privileges.

EASTERN EUROPEAN NOBILITIES East of the Elbe River, the character of the nobility became even more complicated and repressive. Throughout the area, the military traditions of the aristocracy remained important. In Poland, there were thousands of nobles, or *szlachta,* who after 1741 were entirely exempt from taxes. Until 1768 these Polish aristocrats possessed the right of life and death over their serfs. Most of the Polish nobility were relatively poor. A few rich nobles who had immense estates exercised political power in the fragile Polish state.

In Austria and Hungary, the nobility continued to possess broad judicial powers over the peasantry through their manorial courts. They also enjoyed various degrees of exemption from taxation. The wealthiest of them, Prince Esterhazy of Hungary, owned ten million acres of land.

In Prussia, after the accession of Frederick the Great in 1740, the position of the Junker nobles became much stronger. Frederick's various wars required their full support. He drew his officers almost wholly from the Junker class. Nobles also increasingly made up the bureaucracy. As in other parts of eastern Europe, the Prussian nobles had extensive judicial authority over the serfs.

In Russia, the eighteenth century saw what amounted to the creation of the nobility. Peter the Great's (r. 1682–1725) linking of state service and noble social status through the Table of Ranks (1722) established among Russian nobles a self-conscious class identity that had not previously existed. Thereafter they were determined to resist compulsory state service. In 1736 Empress Anna (r. 1730–1740) reduced such service to twenty-five years. In 1762 Peter III (r. 1762) exempted the greatest nobles entirely from compulsory service. In 1785, in the Charter of the Nobility, Catherine the Great (r. 1762–1796) legally defined noble rights and privileges in exchange for the assurance that the nobility would serve the state voluntarily. Noble privileges included the right of transmitting noble status to one's wife and children, the judicial protection of noble rights and property, considerable power over the serfs, and exemption from personal taxes.

Aristocratic Resurgence

The Russian Charter of the Nobility constituted one aspect of the broader European-wide development termed the *aristocratic resurgence*. The aristocratic resurgence was the nobility's reaction to the threat to their social position and privileges that they felt from the expanding power of the monarchies. This resurgence took several forms in the eighteenth century. First, all nobilities tried to preserve their exclusiveness by making it more difficult to become a noble. Second, they pushed to reserve appointments to the officer corps of the armies, the bureaucracies, the government ministries, and the Church exclusively for nobles. They thus hoped to control the power of the monarchies.

Third, the nobles attempted to use the authority of existing aristocratically controlled institutions against the power of the monarchies. These institutions included the British Parliament, the French courts, or *parlements*, and the local aristocratic estates and provincial diets in Germany and the Habsburg empire. Fourth, the nobility sought to improve its financial position by gaining further exemptions from taxation or by collecting higher rents or long-forgotten feudal dues from the peasantry. The nobility tried to shore up its position by various appeals to traditional and often ancient privileges that had lapsed over time. This aristocratic challenge to the monarchies was a fundamental political fact of the day.

The Land and Its Tillers

Land was the economic basis of eighteenth-century life and the foundation of the status and power of the nobility. Well over three-fourths of all Europeans lived in the country, and few of them ever traveled more than a few miles from their birthplace. Except for the nobility and the wealthier nonaristocratic landowners, most people who dwelled on the land were poor. They lived in various states of economic and social dependency, exploitation, and vulnerability.

Peasants and Serfs

Rural social dependency related directly to the land. The nature of the dependency differed sharply for free peasants, such as English tenants and most French cultivators, and for the serfs of Germany, Austria, and Russia, who were legally bound to a particular plot of land and a particular lord. But everywhere, the class that owned most of the land also controlled the local government and the courts. For example, in

Grain production lay at the heart of eighteenth-century farming. In this engraving farm workers can be seen threshing wheat, winnowing the grain, and finally putting the grain in bags so it can be carried to a mill and ground into flour. In many cases the mill would be owned by the local landlord, who would charge peasants for its use. [Bildarchiv Preussischer Kulturbesitz]

Great Britain, all farmers and smaller tenants had the legal rights of English citizens. The justices of the peace, however, who presided over the county courts and who could call out the local militia, were always substantial landowners, as were the members of Parliament, who made the laws. In eastern Europe, the landowners presided over the manorial courts. On the Continent, the burden of taxation fell on the tillers of the soil.

OBLIGATIONS OF PEASANTS Landlord power increased as one moved across Europe from west to east. Most French peasants owned some land, but there were a few serfs in eastern France. Nearly all French peasants were subject to certain feudal dues, called *banalités*. These included the required use-for-payment of the lord or seigneur's mill to grind grain and his oven to bake bread. The seigneur could also require a certain number of days each year of the peasant's labor. This practice of forced labor was termed the *corvée*. Because even landowning French peasants rarely possessed enough

land to support their families, they had to rent more land from the seigneur and were also subject to feudal dues attached to those plots. In Prussia and Austria, despite attempts by the monarchies late in the century to improve the lot of the serfs, the landlords continued to exercise almost complete control over them. In many of the Habsburg lands, law and custom required the serfs to provide service, or *robot*, to the lords.

Serfs were worst off in Russia. There nobles reckoned their wealth by the number of "souls" (that is, male serfs) owned rather than by the acreage the landlord possessed. Russian landlords, in effect, regarded serfs merely as economic commodities. They could demand as many as six days a week of labor, known as *barshchina*, from the serfs. Like Prussian and Austrian landlords, they enjoyed the right to punish their serfs. On their own authority, Russian landlords could even exile a serf to Siberia. Serfs had no legal recourse against the orders and whims of their lords. There was little difference between Russian serfdom and slavery.

Eighteenth-century France had some of the best roads in the world, but they were often built with forced labor. French peasants were required to work part of each year on such projects. This system, called the corvée, *was not abolished until the French Revolution in 1789. [Giraudon/Art Resource, N.Y.]*

A Commission of Inquiry Describes the Burden of Bohemian Serfs

During her reign, the Habsburg Empress Maria Theresa (r. 1740–1780) became increasingly concerned about the plight of serfs in her domains. By the 1760s she would have abolished serfdom except for the strong resistance of the landlords. She did, however, order an official Commission of Enquiry into the situation of serfs in Bohemia. The Commission reported in June 1769 and included the following comments in its report. Robot is the Slavonic term for payments of compulsory labor by serfs to landlords.

◆ *How did the status of serfs make them especially vulnerable to exploitation and subject to harsh living conditions? What actions could serfs take to protect themselves or their families from harsh masters? How does the relationship of these Bohemian serfs to their lords compare with the French peasants under the* métayer *system described by Turgot in another document in this chapter?*

The *robot* gives rise to continual vexations. Even those nobles who have the best intentions are unable to protect their peasants, because their agents are rough, evil, violent and grasping. These burdens are terrifyingly heavy, and it is not surprising that the peasants try to evade them by every means. In consequence of the arbitrary allocation of the *robot*, the peasants live in a condition of real slavery; they become savage and brutalized, and cultivate the lands in their charge badly. . . . In their ruinous huts, the parents sleep on straw, the children naked on the wide shelves of earthenware stoves; they never wash, which promotes the spread of epidemics; there are no doctors to look after them. . . . Even their personal effects are not safe from the greed of the great lords. If they own a good horse, the lord forces them to sell it to him. . . . In many places the serfs are forced to buy sick sheep from their lord at an arbitrarily fixed price. Implements of torture are set up in every village market square, or in front of the castle; recalcitrant peasants are thrown into irons, they are forced to sit astride a sharp wooden horse, which cuts deeply into their flesh; stones are hung on their legs; for the most trifling offence they are given fifty strokes of the rod; the serf who arrives late for his *robot*, be it only half an hour, is beaten half-dead. Many flee into Prussia to escape this reign of terror; there are hundreds of huts which their occupants have abandoned because they threatened to collapse and they had not the means to repair them. In other places the thatches have been taken off to feed the horses for lack of fodder, because these wretched creatures are forbidden to gather leaves in the forest for fear of their disturbing the game. Even when the harvest has been good they are obliged to ask for seed from their lord, and he sells it to them at an extortionate price. The big landlords drive away the Jews, who make loans on better terms. . . . The Kingdom of Bohemia is like a statue which is collapsing because its pedestal has been taken away, because all the charges of the Kingdom are born by the peasants, who are the sole taxpayers.

C. A. Macartney, *The Habsburg and Hohenzollern Dynasties in the Seventeenth and Eighteenth Centuries (New York: Walker and Company, 1970), pp. 173–174.*

In southeastern Europe, where the Ottoman Empire held sway, peasants were free though landlords tried to exert authority in every way. The domain of the landlords was termed a *çift*. The landlord was often an absentee who managed the estate through an overseer. During the seventeenth and eighteenth centuries, these landlords, like those elsewhere in Europe, often became more commercially oriented and turned to the production of commercial crops, such as cotton, vegetables, potatoes, and maize.

Scarcity of labor rather than recognition of legal rights supported the independence of the southeastern European peasants. A peasant might migrate from one landlord to another. Because the second landlord needed the peasant's labor, he had no reason to return him to the original landlord. During the seventeenth and eighteenth centuries, however, disorder originating in the capital of Constantinople (now Istanbul) spilled over into the Balkan Peninsula. In this climate, landlords increased their authority by offering their peasants protection from bandits or rebels who might destroy peasant villages. As in medieval times, the manor house or armed enclosure of a local landlord became the peasants' refuge. These landlords also owned all the housing and tools required by the peasants and furnished their seed grain. Consequently, despite legal independence, Balkan peasants under the Ottoman Empire became largely dependent upon the landlords, though never to the extent of serfs in Eastern Europe or Russia.

PEASANT REBELLIONS The Russian monarchy itself contributed to the further degradation of the serfs. Peter the Great gave whole villages to favored nobles. Later in the century, Catherine the Great confirmed the authority of the nobles over their serfs in exchange for the landowners' political cooperation. Russia experienced vast peasant unrest with well over fifty peasant revolts occurring between 1762 and 1769. These culminated between 1773 and 1775 in Pugachev's Rebellion, when Emelyan Pugachev (1726–1775) promised the serfs land of their own and freedom from their lords. All of southern Russian was in turmoil until the government brutally suppressed the rebellion. Thereafter, any thought of liberalizing or improving the condition of the serfs was set aside for a generation.

Pugachev's was the largest peasant uprising of the eighteenth century, but smaller peasant revolts or disturbances took place in Bohemia in 1775, in Transylvania in 1784, in Moravia in 1786, and in Austria in 1789. There were almost no revolts in western Europe, but England experienced many rural riots. Rural rebellions were violent, but the peasants and serfs normally directed their wrath against property rather than persons. The rebels usually sought to reassert traditional or customary rights against practices that they perceived as innovations. Their targets were carefully chosen and included unfair pricing, onerous new or increased feudal dues, changes in methods of payment or land use, unjust officials, or extraordinarily brutal overseers and landlords. Peasant revolts were thus conservative in nature.

Aristocratic Domination of the Countryside: The English Game Laws

One of the clearest examples of aristocratic domination of the countryside and of aristocratic manipulation of the law to its own advantage was English legislation on hunting.

Between 1671 and 1831, English landowners had the exclusive legal right to hunt game animals. These specifically included hares, partridges, pheasants, and moorfowl. Similar legislation covered other animals such as deer, the killing of which by an unauthorized person became a capital offense in the eighteenth century. By law, only persons owning a particular amount of landed property could hunt these animals. Excluded from the right to hunt were all persons renting land, wealthy city merchants who did not own land, and poor people in cities, villages, and the countryside. The poor were excluded because the elite believed that allowing the poor to enjoy the sport of hunting would undermine their work habits. The city merchants were excluded because the landed gentry in Parliament wanted to demonstrate visibly and legally the superiority of landed wealth over commercial wealth. Thus, the various game laws upheld the superior status of the aristocracy and the landed gentry.

The game laws represent a prime example of class legislation. The gentry who benefitted from the laws and whose parliamentary representatives had passed them also served as the local justices of the peace who administered the laws and punished their violation. The justices of the peace could levy fines and even have poachers impressed into the army. Gentry could also take civil legal action against wealthier poachers, such as rich farmers who rented land, and thus saddle them with immense legal fees. The gentry also employed gamekeepers to protect game from poachers. The gamekeepers were known to kill the dogs belonging to people suspected of poaching. By the middle of the century, gamekeepers had devised trapguns to shoot poachers who tripped their hidden levers.

A small industry arose to circumvent the game laws, however. Many poor people living either on an estate or in a nearby village would kill game for food. They believed that the game actually belonged to the community, and this poaching increased during hard times. Poaching was thus one way for the poor to find food.

Even more important was the black market in game animals sustained by the demand of urban people for this kind of luxury meat. Here arose the possibility of poaching for profit, and indeed, poaching technically meant the stealing or killing of game for sale. Local people from both the countryside and the villages would steal the game and then sell it to middlemen called higglers. Later, coachmen took over this function. The higglers and the coachmen would smuggle the game into the cities, where poulterers would sell it at a premium price. Everyone involved made a bit of money along the way. During the second half of the century, English aristocrats began to construct large game preserves. The rural poor, who had lost their rights to communal land as a result of its enclosure by the large landowners, deeply resented these preserves, which soon became hunting grounds to organized gangs of poachers.

Penalties against poaching increased in the 1790s after the outbreak of the French Revolution, but so did the amount of poaching as the economic hardships caused by Britain's participation in the wars of the era put a greater burden on poor people and as the demand for food in English cities grew along with their pop-

Emelyan Pugachev (1726–1775) led the largest peasant revolt in Russian history. In this contemporary propaganda picture he is shown in chains. An inscription in Russian and German was printed below the picture decrying the evils of revolution and insurrection. [Bildarchiv Preussischer Kulturbesitz]

ulation. By the 1820s, both landowners and reformers called for a change in the law. In 1831 Parliament rewrote the game laws, retaining the landowners' possession of the game but permitting them to allow other people to hunt it. Poaching continued, but the exclusive right of the landed classes to hunt game had ended.

Family Structures and the Family Economy

In preindustrial Europe, the *household* was the basic unit of production and consumption. Few productive establishments employed more than a handful of people not belonging to the family of the owner, and those rare exceptions were in cities. The overwhelming majority of Europeans, however, lived in rural areas. There, as well as in small towns and cities, the household mode of organization predominated on farms, in artisans' workshops, and in small merchants' shops. With that mode of economic organization, there developed what is known as the *family economy*. Its structure as described here had prevailed over most of Europe for centuries.

Households

What was a household in the preindustrial Europe of the Old Regime? There were two basic models, one characterizing northwestern Europe and the other eastern Europe.

NORTHWESTERN EUROPE In northwestern Europe, the household almost invariably consisted of a married couple, their children through their early teenage years, and their servants. Except for the few wealthy people, households were small, usually consisting of not more than five or six members. Furthermore, in these households, more than two generations of a family rarely lived under the same roof. High mortality and late marriage prevented families of three generations. In other words, grandparents rarely lived in the same household as their grandchildren and families consisted of parents and children. The family structure of northwestern Europe was thus nuclear rather than extended.

This particular characteristic of the northwestern European household is one of the major discoveries of recent research into family history. Previously historians had assumed that before industrialization Europeans lived in extended familial settings with several generations living together in a household. Recent demographic investigation has sharply reversed this picture. Children lived with their parents only until their early teens. Then they normally left home, usually to enter the work force of young servants who lived and worked in another household. A child of a skilled artisan might remain with his or her parents to learn a valuable skill; but only rarely would more than one child do so because children's labor was more remunerative outside the home.

These young men and women who had left home would eventually marry and form an independent household of their own. This practice of moving away from home is known as *neolocalism*. These young people married relatively late. Men were usually over twenty-six, and women over twenty-three. The new couple usually had children as soon after marriage as possible. Frequently, the woman was already pregnant at marriage. Family and community pressure often compelled the man to marry her. In any case, premarital sexual relations were common, though illegitimate births were rare. The new couple would soon employ a servant, who together with their growing children would undertake whatever form of livelihood the household used to support itself.

The word *servant* in this context may be confusing. It does not refer to someone looking after the needs of wealthy people. Rather, in preindustrial Europe, a servant was a person—either male or female—who was hired, often under a clear contract, to work for the head of the household in exchange for room, board, and wages. The servant was usually young and by no means always socially inferior to his or her employer. Normally, the servant was an integral part of the household and ate with the family.

Young men and women became servants when their labor was no longer needed in their parents' household or when they could earn more money for their family outside the parental household. Being a servant for several years—often as many as eight or ten—allowed young people to acquire the productive skills and the monetary savings necessary to begin their own household. These years spent as servants largely account for the late age of marriage in northwestern Europe.

EASTERN EUROPE As one moved eastward across the continent, the structure of the household and the pattern of marriage changed. There both men and women usually married before the age of twenty. Consequently, children were born to much younger parents. Often, especially among Russian serfs, wives were older than their husbands. Eastern European households were generally larger than those in the West. Often a rural Russian household consisted of more than nine and possibly more than twenty members, with three or perhaps even four generations of the same family living together. Early marriage made this situation more likely. In Russia, marrying involved not starting a new household but remaining in and expanding one already established.

The landholding structure in eastern Europe accounts, at least in part, for these patterns of marriage and the family. The lords of the manor who owned land wanted to ensure that it would be cultivated so they could receive their rents. Thus, for example, in Poland, landlords might forbid marriage between their own serfs and those from another estate. They might also require widows and widowers to remarry to assure adequate labor for a particular plot of land. Polish landlords also frowned on the hiring of free laborers—the equivalent of servants in the West—to help cultivate land. The landlords preferred to use other serfs. This practice inhibited the formation of independent households. In Russia, landlords ordered the families of young people in their villages to arrange marriages within a short, set time. These lords discouraged single-generation family households because the death or serious illness of one person in such a household might mean that the land assigned to it would go out of cultivation.

The Family Economy

Throughout Europe, most people worked within the family economy. That is to say, the household was the basic unit of production and consumption. Almost everyone lived within a household of some kind because it was virtually impossible for ordinary people to support themselves independently. Indeed, except for members of religious orders, people living outside a household were viewed with great suspicion. They were considered potentially criminal or disruptive or, at least, potentially dependent on the charity of others. Everywhere beggars met deep hostility.

Depending on their ages and skills, everyone in the household worked. The need to survive poor harvests or economic slumps meant that no one could be idle. Within this family economy, all goods and income produced went to the benefit of the household rather than to the individual family member. On a farm much of the effort went directly into raising food or producing other agricultural goods that could be exchanged for food. Few western Europeans, however, had enough land to support their household from farming alone. Thus one or more family members might work elsewhere and send wages home. For example, the father or older children might work as a harvest picker or might fish or might engage in other labor, either in the neighborhood or farther from home. If the father was such a migrant worker, the burden of farm work would fall on his wife and their younger children. This was not an uncommon pattern.

The family economy also dominated the life of skilled urban artisans. The father was usually the chief artisan. He normally employed one or more servants, but would expect his children to work in the enterprise also. His eldest child was usually trained in the trade. His wife often sold his wares or opened a small shop of her own. Wives of merchants also often ran their husbands' businesses, especially when the husband traveled to purchase new goods. In any case, everyone in the family was involved. If business was poor, family members would look for employment elsewhere, not to support themselves as individuals but to ensure the survival of the family unit.

In western Europe, the death of a father often brought disaster to the economy of the household. The continuing economic life of the family usually depended on his land or skills. The widow might take on the farm or the business, or his children might do so. The widow usually sought to remarry quickly to restore the labor and skills of a male to the household and to prevent herself from falling into a state of dependence.

The high mortality rate of the time meant that many households were reconstituted second family groups that included stepchildren. Because of the advanced age of the widow or economic hard times, however, some households might simply dissolve. The widow became dependent on charity or relatives. The children became similarly dependent or entered the workforce of servants earlier than they would otherwise. In other cases, the situation could be so desperate that they would resort to crime or to begging. The personal, emotional, and economic vulnerability of the family economy cannot be overemphasized.

In eastern Europe, the family economy functioned in the context of serfdom and landlord domination. Peasants clearly thought in terms of their families and expanding the land avail-

Rules Are Established for the Berlin Poor House

Poverty was an enormous problem in eighteenth-century Europe, often forcing family members to work away from home and creating thousands of migrant workers and beggars. Governments were hostile to beggars and sometimes migrant workers, whom they regarded as a potential source of crime and disorder. Many of these concerns are evident in the regulations for the Berlin Poor House.

♦ *What were the distinctions made between the poor who deserved sympathy and those who did not? How would such a distinction affect social policy? Why might beggars have been regarded as dangers to public order? What attitudes toward work are displayed in these regulations?*

Whereas His Majesty . . . has renewed the prohibition of begging in the streets and in houses and has made all giving of alms punishable; it is decided to inform the public of the present measures for the relief of the poor, and to acquaint it with the main outlines of the above order:

1. In the new workhouse, . . . the genuinely needy and the poor deserving sympathy shall be cared for better than hitherto, but the deliberate beggars shall more resolutely be made to work.

2. The past organization of this house has therefore been totally altered, so that all persons to be received in it shall be divided into two entirely separate main classes, differentiated both in the status of their work and its location, in their dormitory and in their board.

3. The first class is meant for the old and for other persons deserving help and sympathy, who cannot entirely live by their work and do not wish to beg. Those report to the Poor's Chest in the Town Hall of Berlin, with

able for cultivation. The village structure may have mitigated the pressures of the family economy, as did the multigenerational family. Dependence on the available land was the chief fact of life. There were many fewer artisan and merchant households, and there was far less geographical mobility than in western Europe.

Women and the Family Economy

The family economy established many of the chief constraints on the lives and personal experiences of women in preindustrial society. Most of the historical research that has been undertaken on this subject relates to western Europe. There, a woman's life experience was largely the function of her capacity to establish and maintain a household. For women, marriage was an economic necessity as well as an institution that fulfilled sexual and psychological needs.

Outside a household a woman's life was vulnerable and precarious. Some women succeeded in becoming economically independent. They were the exception. Normally, unless she were an aristocrat or a member of a religious order, a woman probably could not support herself solely by her own efforts. Consequently, a woman devoted much of her life first to maintaining her parents' household and then to devising some means of getting her own household to live in as an adult. Bearing and rearing children were usually subordinate to these goals.

By the age of seven, a girl would have begun to help with the household work. On a farm, this might mean looking after chickens, watering animals, or carrying food to adults working the land. In an urban artisan's household, she would do light work, perhaps cleaning or carrying and later sewing or weaving. The girl would remain in her parents' home as long as she

a certificate from the Minister of their Church, showing their hitherto unblemished character, and after their references have been checked, they shall be accepted. They spin in the house as much wool as their age and health permits, and if they spin more than the cost of their keep, the surplus shall be paid out to them. . . .

. . . .

5. The second main class is destined for those who do not wish to make use of this benefaction, but would rather live by begging. These deliberate beggars will be arrested by the Poor Law Constables, if necessary with the assistance of the Police, irrespective of age or status, whether they be vagabonds, journeymen, citizens, discharged soldiers, their wives or children, and will be sent to the workhouse.

6. Those who are caught begging for the first time shall be put into this class for three months at least, for the second time, for a year, and for the third and later times for several years, according to circumstances, for life.

7. Similarly, this class is destined for those who after due process of law have been sent for punishment as runaway servants and apprentices, for a period of time determined by the Court.

8. All the persons under numbers 5, 6, and 7 shall be forced to spin and prepare wool, and shall be kept on a minimum standard, clearly differentiated from the first class, both in the status and quantity of their work in their board and their lodging.

9. The children shall be cared for separately, . . . and shall receive education for several hours a day. . . .

10. Before a beggar is discharged, he must, in order that he shall not again become a public nuisance, prove an occupation in prospect or the existence of relations or of other persons, who will look after him and will put him up at once. . . .

Kruegeger, Geschichte der Manufacturen . . . , *as quoted and translated in S. Pollard and C. Holmes, eds.,* Documents of European Economic History, Vol. I *(London: Edward Arnold, 1968), pp. 166–167.*

made a real contribution to the family enterprise or as long as her labor elsewhere was not more remunerative to the family.

An artisan's daughter might not leave home until marriage because at home she could learn increasingly valuable skills associated with the trade. The situation was different for the much larger number of girls growing up on farms. Their parents and brothers could often do all the necessary farm work, and a girl's labor at home quickly became of little value to her family. She would then leave home, usually between the ages of twelve and fourteen. She might take up residence on another farm, but more likely she would migrate to a nearby town or city. She would rarely travel more than thirty miles from her parents' household. She would then normally become a servant, once again living in a household, but this time in the household of an employer.

Having migrated from home, the young woman's chief goal was to accumulate enough capital for a dowry. Her savings would make her eligible for marriage because they would allow her to make the necessary contribution to form a household with her husband. Marriage within the family economy was a joint economic undertaking, and the wife was expected to make an immediate contribution of capital for establishing the household. A young woman might well work for ten years or more to accumulate a dowry. This practice meant that marriage was usually postponed until her mid- to late twenties.

Within marriage, earning enough money or producing enough farm goods to ensure an adequate food supply dominated women's concerns. Domestic duties, childbearing, and child rearing were subordinate to economic pressures. Consequently, couples tried to limit the number of children, usually through the practice of

(a)

(b)

These four scenes were painted by the English ar[tist] Francis Wheatley (1747–1801) near the close of th[e] eighteenth century. They illustrate in a very idealiz[ed] manner the life of a farm family in the morning (a,[)] noon (b), in the evening [(c),] and at night (d). Note the artist's assumptions abou[t] the division of labor by ge[n]der. Men work in the field[s,] women work in the home [to] look after the needs of m[en] and children. As other illu[s]trations in this chapter sh[ow,] many eighteenth-century women in fact worked ou[t]side the home, but consid[er]able social pressure was developing at this time to restrict them to domestic roles. These paintings are thus more prescriptive th[an] descriptive, intended in p[art] to persuade their viewers that women belonged in their separate family sph[ere.] Many, perhaps most, fam[i]lies living in the countrys[ide] could not maintain the clo[se]ness that these paintings extol. To survive, many h[ad] to send members to work on other farms or even in other regions of the count[ry] following the harvest. [Ya[le] Center for British Art, Pau[l] Mellon Collection]

(c)

(d)

Priscilla Wakefield Demands More Occupations Be Opened to Women

At the end of the eighteenth century, several English women writers began to demand a wider life for women. Priscilla Wakefield was among such authors. She was concerned that women found themselves only able to pursue occupations that paid poorly. Often they were excluded from work on the grounds of their alleged physical weakness. She also believed that women should receive equal wages for equal work. Many of the issues she raised have yet to be adequately addressed on behalf of women.

◆ *From reading this passage, what do you understand to have been the arguments at the end of the eighteenth century to limit the kinds of employment that women might enter? Why did women receive lower wages for work similar to or the same as that done by men? What occupations traditionally filled by men does Wakefield believe women might also pursue?*

Another heavy discouragement to the industry of women, is the inequality of the reward of their labor, compared with that of men; an injustice which pervades every species of employment performed by both sexes.

In employments which depend on bodily strength, the distinction is just; for it cannot be pretended that the generality of women can earn as much as men, when the produce of their labor is the result of corporeal exertion; but it is a subject of great regret, that this inequality should prevail even where an equal share of skill and application is exerted. Male stay-makers, mantua-makers, and hairdressers, are better paid than female artists of the same professions; but surely it will never be urged as an apology for this disproportion, that women are not as capable of making stays, gowns, dressing hair, and similar arts, as men; if they are not superior to them, it

---

coitus interruptus, the withdrawal of the male before ejaculation. Parents often placed young children with wet nurses so the mother could continue to make her economic contribution to the household. The wet nurse, in turn, contributed to the economic welfare of her own household. The child would be fully reintegrated into its own family when it was weaned and would then be expected to aid the family at an early age.

The work of married women differed markedly between city and country and was in many ways a function of their husbands' occupations. If the peasant household had enough land to support itself, the wife spent much of her time quite literally carrying things for her husband—water, food, seed, harvested grain, and the like. There were few such adequate landholdings, however. If the husband had to do work besides farming, such as fishing or migrant labor, the wife might

actually be in charge of the farm and do the ploughing, planting, and harvesting. In the city, an artisan or merchant's wife might well be in charge of the household finances and actively participate in managing the trade or manufacturing enterprise. When her husband died, she might take over the business and perhaps hire an artisan. Finally, if economic disaster struck the family, it was usually the wife who organized what Olwen Hufton has called the "economy of expedients,"[1] within which family members might be sent off to find work elsewhere or even to beg in the streets.

Through all this economic activity women found many occupations and professions closed

[1]*Olwen Hufton, "Women and the Family Economy in Eighteenth-Century France," French Historical Studies, 9 (1976): 19.*

can only be accounted for upon this principle, that the prices they receive for their labor are not sufficient to repay them for the expense of qualifying themselves for their business; and that they sink under the mortification of being regarded as artisans of inferior estimation. . . .

Besides these employments which are commonly performed by women, and those already shown to be suitable for such persons as are above the condition of hard labor, there are some professions and trades customarily in the hands of men, which might be conveniently exercised by either sex.—Watchmaking requiring more ingenuity than strength, seems peculiarly adapted to women; as do many parts of the business of stationer, particularly, ruling account books or making pens. The compounding of medicines in an apothecary's shop, requires no other talents than care and exactness; and if opening a vein occasionally be a indispensable requisite,

a woman may acquire the capacity of doing it, for those of her own sex at least, without any reasonable objection. . . . Pastry and confectionery appear particularly consonant to the habits of women, though generally performed by men; perhaps the heat of the ovens, and the strength requisite to fill and empty them, may render male assistants necessary; but certain women are most eligible to mix up the ingredients, and prepare the various kinds of cakes for baking.—Light turnery and toy-making depend more upon dexterity and invention than force, and are therefore suitable work for women and children. . . .

Farming, as far as respects the theory, is commensurate with the powers of the female mind: nor is the practice of inspecting agricultural processes incompatible with the delicacy of their frames if their constitution be good.

Priscilla Wakefield, Reflections on the Present Condition of the Female Sex (1798), *(London, 1817), pp. 125–127, as quoted in Bridget Hill, ed.*, Eighteenth-Century Women: An Anthology *(London: George Allen & Unwin, 1984), pp. 227–228.*

to them because they were women. They labored with less education than men, because in this society women in all levels of life consistently found fewer opportunities for education than men. They often received lower wages than men for the same work.

Children and the World of the Family Economy

For women of all social ranks, childbirth was a time of fear and personal vulnerability. Contagious diseases endangered both mother and child. Puerperal fever was frequent, as were other infections from unsterilized medical instruments. Not all midwives were skillful practitioners. Furthermore, most mothers and children immediately encountered immense poverty and wretched housing. Assuming that both mother and child survived, the mother

might nurse the infant, but often the child would be sent to a wet nurse. Convenience may have led to this practice among the wealthy, but economic necessity dictated it for the poor. The structures and customs of the family economy did not permit a woman to devote herself entirely to rearing a child. The wet-nursing industry was well organized, with urban children being frequently transported to wet nurses in the country, where they would remain for months or even years.

Throughout Europe, however, the birth of a child was not always welcome. The child might represent another economic burden on an already hard-pressed household. Or it might be illegitimate. The number of illegitimate births seems to have increased during the eighteenth century, possibly because increased population migration led to fleeting romances.

An Edinburgh Physician Describes the Dangers of Childbirth

Death in childbirth was a common occurrence throughout Europe until the twentieth century. This brief letter from an Edinburgh physician illustrates how devastating infectious diseases could be to women at the time of childbirth.

◆ *How does this passage illustrate a health danger that only women confronted? How might the likelihood of the death of oneself or a spouse in childbirth have affected one's attitudes toward children? How does this passage illustrate limitations on knowledge about disease in the eighteenth century?*

We had puerperal fever in the infirmary last winter. It began about the end of February, when almost every woman, as soon as she was delivered, or perhaps about twenty-four hours after, was seized with it; and all of them died, though every method was tried to cure the disorder. What was singular, the women were in good health before they were brought to bed, though some of them had been long in the hospital before delivery. One woman had been dismissed from the ward before she was brought to bed; came into it some days after with her labor upon her; was easily delivered, and remained perfectly well for twenty-four hours, when she was seized with a shivering and the other symptoms of the fever. I caused her to be removed to another ward; yet notwithstanding all the care that was taken of her she died in the same manner as the others.

From a letter to Mr. White from a Dr. Young of Edinburgh, 21 November, 1774, cited in C. White, Treatise on the Management of Pregnant and Lying-In Women (London, 1777), pp. 45–46, as quoted in Bridget Hill, ed., Eighteenth-Century Women: An Anthology (London: George Allen & Unwin, 1984), p. 102.

Through at least the end of the seventeenth century, unwanted or illegitimate births could lead to infanticide, especially among the poor. The parents might smother the infant or expose it to the elements. These practices were one result of both the ignorance and the prejudice surrounding contraception.

The late seventeenth and the early eighteenth centuries saw a new interest in preserving the lives of abandoned children. Although foundling hospitals established to care for abandoned children had existed before, their size and number expanded during these years. Two of the most famous were the Paris Foundling Hospital (1670) and the London Foundling Hospital (1739). Such hospitals cared for thousands of European children, and the demands for their services increased during the eighteenth century. For example, early in the century, an average of 1,700 children a year were admitted to the Paris Foundling Hospital. In the peak year of 1772, however, that number rose to 7,676 children. Not all of those children came from Paris. Many had been brought to the city from the provinces, where local foundling homes and hospitals were overburdened. The London Foundling Hospital lacked the income to deal with all the children brought to it. In the middle of the eighteenth century, the hospital found itself compelled to choose children for admission by a lottery system.

Sadness and tragedy surrounded abandoned children. Most of them were illegitimate infants from across the social spectrum. Many, however, were left with the foundling hospitals because their parents could not support them. There was a close relationship between rising food prices and increasing numbers of abandoned children in Paris. Parents would sometimes leave personal tokens or saints' medals on the abandoned baby in the vain hope that they might one day be able to reclaim the child. Few children were reclaimed. Leaving a child at a foundling hospital did not guarantee its survival. Again, to cite the situation in Paris, only about 10 percent of all abandoned children lived to the age of ten.

Despite all of these perils of early childhood, children did grow up and come of age across Europe. The world of the child may not have received the kind of attention that it does today, but during the eighteenth century, the seeds of that modern sensibility were sown. Particularly among the upper classes, new interest arose in the education of children. In most areas education remained firmly in the hands of the churches. As economic skills became more demanding, literacy became more valuable, and literacy rates rose during the century. Yet most Europeans remained illiterate. Not until the late nineteenth century was the world of childhood inextricably linked to the process of education. Then children would be reared to become members of a national citizenry. In the Old Regime, they were reared to make their contribution to the economy of their parents' family and then to set up their own households.

The Revolution in Agriculture

Thus far this chapter has examined those groups who sought stability and who, except for certain members of the nobility, resisted change. Other groups, however, wished to pursue significant new directions in social and economic life. The remainder of this chapter will consider those forces and developments that would during the next century transform European life. These developments first appeared in agriculture.

The main goal of traditional peasant society was a stability that would ensure the local food supply. Despite differences in rural customs throughout Europe, the tillers resisted changes that might endanger the sure supply of food, which they generally believed that traditional cultivation would provide. The food supply was never certain, and the farther east one traveled, the more uncertain it became. Failure of the harvest meant not only hardship but death from either outright starvation or protracted debility. Often, people living in the countryside had more difficulty finding food than did city dwellers, whose local government usually stored reserve supplies of grain.

Poor harvests also played havoc with prices.

Few children in the eighteenth century were as privileged as these in this landed English family. Most began working to help support their families as soon as they were physically able. It was during the eighteenth century, however, that Europeans apparently began to view childhood as a distinct period in human development. Even though Arthur Devis has painted these children to look something like little adults, he has included various toys associated with childhood. [Yale Center for British Art, Paul Mellon Collection]

Smaller supplies or larger demand raised grain prices. Even small increases in the cost of food could exert heavy pressure on peasant or artisan families. If prices increased sharply, many of those families fell back on poor relief from their local municipality or county or the Church.

During the eighteenth century, historians now believe, bread prices slowly but steadily rose, spurred largely by population growth. Since bread was their main food, this inflation put pressure on all of the poor. Prices rose faster than urban wages and brought no appreciable advantage to the small peasant producer. On the other hand, the rise in grain prices benefitted landowners and those wealthier peasants who had surplus grain to sell.

The rising grain prices gave landlords an opportunity to improve their incomes and lifestyle. To achieve those ends, landlords in western Europe began a series of innovations in farm production that became known as the *Agricultural Revolution.* Landlords commercialized agriculture and thereby challenged the traditional peasant ways of production. Peasant revolts and disturbances often resulted. The governments of Europe, hungry for new taxes and dependent on the goodwill of the nobility, used their armies and militias to smash peasants who defended the past.

NEW CROPS AND NEW METHODS The drive to improve agricultural production began during the sixteenth and seventeenth centuries in the Low Countries, where the pressures of the growing population and the shortage of land required changes in cultivation. Dutch landlords and farmers devised better ways to build dikes and to drain land, so that they could farm more extensive areas. They also experimented with new crops, such as clover and turnips, that would increase the supply of animal fodder and restore the soil. These improvements became so famous that early in the seventeenth century English landlords hired Cornelius Vermuyden, a Dutch drainage engineer, to drain thousands of acres of land around Cambridge.

English landlords provided the most striking examples of eighteenth-century agricultural improvement. They originated almost no genuinely new farming methods, but they popularized ideas developed in the previous century either in the Low Countries or in England.

Some of these landlords and agricultural innovators became famous. For example, Jethro Tull (1674–1741) was willing to experiment himself and to finance the experiments of others. Many of his ideas, such as the refusal to use manure as fertilizer, were wrong. Others, however, such as using iron plows to turn earth more deeply and planting wheat by a drill rather than by casting, were excellent. His methods permitted land to be cultivated for longer periods without having to be left fallow.

Charles "Turnip" Townsend (1674–1738) encouraged other important innovations. He learned from the Dutch how to cultivate sandy soil with fertilizers. He also instituted crop rotation, using wheat, turnips, barley, and clover. This new system of rotation replaced the fallow field with one sown with a crop that both restored nutrients to the soil and supplied animal fodder. The additional fodder meant that more livestock could be raised. These fodders allowed animals to be fed during the winter and assured a year-round supply of meat. The larger number of animals increased the quantity of manure available as fertilizer for the grain crops. Consequently, in the long run, there was more food for both animals and human beings.

A third British agricultural improver was Robert Bakewell (1725–1795), who pioneered new methods of animal breeding that produced more and better animals and more milk and meat.

These and other innovations received widespread discussion in the works of Arthur Young (1741–1820), who edited the *Annals of Agriculture.* In 1793 he became secretary of the British Board of Agriculture. Young traveled widely across Europe, and his books are among the most important documents of life during the second half of the eighteenth century.

ENCLOSURE REPLACES OPEN-FIELD METHOD Many of the agriculture innovations, which were adopted only slowly, were incompatible with the existing organization of land in England. Small cultivators who lived in village communities still farmed most of the soil. Each farmer tilled an assortment of unconnected strips. The two- or three-field systems of rotation left large portions of land fallow and unproductive each year. Animals grazed on the common land in the summer and on the stubble of the harvest in the winter. Until at least the middle of the eighteenth century, the decisions about what crops would be planted were made communally. The entire system discouraged improvement and favored the poorer farmers, who needed the common land and stubble fields for their animals. The village method precluded expanding the pasture land to raise more animals that would, in turn, produce more manure, which could be used for fertilizer. Thus, the methods of traditional production aimed at a steady, but not a growing, supply of food.

In 1700 approximately half the arable land in England was farmed by this open-field method. By the second half of the century, the rising price of wheat encouraged landlords to consolidate or enclose their lands to increase production. The enclosures were intended to use land more rationally and to achieve greater commercial profits. The process involved the fencing of common lands, the reclamation of previously untilled waste, and the transformation of strips into block fields. These procedures brought turmoil to the economic and social life of the countryside. Riots often ensued.

Because many English farmers either owned their strips or rented them in a manner that amounted to ownership, the larger landlords had usually to resort to parliamentary acts to legalize the enclosure of the land, which they owned but rented to the farmers. Because the large landowners controlled Parliament, such measures passed easily. Between 1761 and 1792, almost 500,000 acres were enclosed through parliamentary act, compared with 75,000 acres between 1727 and 1760. In 1801 a general enclosure act streamlined the process.

The enclosures were controversial at the time and have remained so among historians. They permitted the extension of both farming and innovation and thus increased food production on larger agricultural units. They also disrupted small traditional communities; they forced off the land independent farmers, who had needed the common pasturage, and poor cottagers, who had lived on the reclaimed waste land. The enclosures, however, did not depopulate the countryside. In some counties where the enclosures took place, the population increased. New soil had come into production, and services subsidiary to farming also expanded.

The enclosures did not create the labor force for the British Industrial Revolution. What the enclosures most conspicuously displayed was the introduction of the entrepreneurial or capitalistic attitude of the urban merchant into the countryside. This commercialization of agriculture, which spread from Britain slowly across the Continent during the next century, strained the paternal relationship between the governing and governed classes. Previously, landlords often had looked after the welfare of the lower orders through price controls or waiving rents during depressed periods. As the landlords became increasingly concerned about profits, they began to leave the peasants to the mercy of the marketplace.

LIMITED IMPROVEMENTS IN EASTERN EUROPE Improving agriculture tended to characterize farm production west of the Elbe. Dutch farming was quite efficient. In France, despite the efforts of the government to improve agriculture, enclosures were restricted. Yet there was much discussion in France about improving agricultural methods. These new procedures benefitted the ruling classes because better agriculture increased their incomes and assured a larger food supply, which discouraged social unrest.

In Prussia, Austria, Poland, and Russia, agricultural improvement was limited. Nothing in the relationship of the serfs to their lords encouraged innovation. In eastern Europe, the chief method of increasing production was to bring previously untilled lands under the plow. The landlords or their agents rather than the villages normally directed farm management. By extending tillage, the great landlords sought to squeeze more labor from their serfs rather than greater productivity from the soil. East European landlords, like their western counterparts, sought to increase their profits, but they were much less ambitious and successful. The only significant nutritional gain achieved through their efforts was the introduction of maize and the potato. Livestock production did not increase significantly.

Population Expansion

The population explosion with which the entire world must contend today had its origins in the

Turgot Describes French Landholding

The economy of Europe until the nineteenth century was overwhelmingly rural. That meant that economic growth and political stability depended largely on agricultural production. During the eighteenth century, many observers became keenly aware that different kinds of landholding led to different attitudes toward work and to different levels of production. Robert Jacques Turgot (1727–1781), who later became finance minister of France, analyzed these differences in an effort to reform French agriculture. He was especially concerned with arrangements that encouraged long-term investment. The métayer *system, discussed by Turgot, was an arrangement whereby landowners arranged to have land farmed by peasants who received part of the harvest as payment for their working the land. The peasant had no long-term interest in improving the land. Virtually all observers regarded the system as inefficient.*

◆ *Why does Turgot clearly favor those farmers who can make investments in the land they rent from a proprietor? What are the structures of the* métayer *system? Why did it necessarily lead to poor investments and lesser harvests? What is Turgot's attitude toward work and entrepreneurship?*

1. What really distinguishes the area of large-scale farming from the areas of small-scale production is that in the former areas the proprietors find farmers who provide them with a permanent revenue from the land and who buy from them the right to cultivate it for a certain number of years. These farmers undertake all the expenses of cultivation, the ploughing, the sowing and the stocking of the farm with cattle, animals and tools. They are really agricultural entrepreneurs, who possess, like the entrepreneurs in all other branches of commerce, considerable funds, which they employ in the cultivation of land. . . .

They have not only the brawn but also the wealth to devote to agriculture. They have to work, but unlike workers they do not have to earn their living by the sweat of their brow, but by the lucrative employment of their cap-

---

eighteenth century. Before this time, Europe's population had experienced dramatic increases, but plagues, wars, or famine had redressed the balance. Beginning in the second quarter of the eighteenth century, the population began to increase steadily. The need to feed this population caused food prices to rise, which spurred agricultural innovation. The need to provide everyday consumer goods for the expanding numbers of people fueled the demand side of the Industrial Revolution.

Our best estimates suggest that in 1700 Europe's population, excluding the European provinces of the Ottoman Empire, was between 100 million and 120 million people. By 1800 the figures had risen to almost 190 million, and by 1850 to 260 million. The population of England and Wales rose from 6 million in 1750 to more than 10 million in 1800. France grew from 18 million in 1715 to about 26 million in 1789. Russia's population increased from 19 million in 1722 to 29 million in 1766. Such extraordinary, sustained growth put new demands on all resources and considerable pressure on existing social organization.

The population expansion occurred across the Continent in both the country and the cities. Only a limited consensus exists among scholars about the causes of this growth. There was a clear decline in the death rate. There were fewer wars and somewhat fewer epidemics in the eighteenth century. Hygiene and sanitation

ital, just as the shipowners of Nantes and Bordeaux employ theirs in maritime commerce.

2. *Métayer System* The areas of small-scale farming, that is to say at least 4/7ths of the kingdom, are those where there are no agricultural entrepreneurs, where a proprietor who wishes to develop his land cannot find anyone to cultivate it except wretched peasants who have no resources other than their labor, where he is obliged to make, at his own expense, all the advances necessary for tillage, beasts, tools, sowing, even to the extent of advancing to his *métayer* the wherewithal to feed himself until the first harvest, where consequently a proprietor who did not have any property other than his estate would be obliged to allow it to lie fallow.

After having deducted the costs of sowing and feudal dues with which the property is burdened, the proprietor shares with the *métayer* what remains of the profits, in accordance with the agreement they have concluded. The proprietor runs all the risks of harvest failure and any loss of cattle: he is the real entrepreneur. The *métayer* is nothing more than a mere workman, a farm hand to whom the proprietor surrenders a share of his profits instead of paying wages. But in his work the proprietor enjoys none of the advantages of the farmer who, working on his own behalf, works carefully and diligently; the proprietor is obliged to entrust all his advances to a man who may be negligent or a scoundrel and is answerable for nothing.

This *métayer*, accustomed to the most miserable existence and without the hope and even the desire to obtain a better living for himself, cultivates badly and neglects to employ the land for valuable and profitable production; by preference he occupies himself in cultivating those things whose growth is less troublesome and which provide him with more foodstuffs, such as buck wheat and chestnuts which do not require any attention. He does not worry very much about his livelihood; he knows that if the harvest fails, his master will be obliged to feed him in order not to see his land neglected.

A. M. R. Turgot, Oeuvres, et documents le concernant, *ed. by F. Schelle, 5 vols. (Paris, 1914), Vol. II, pp. 448–450, as quoted and translated in S. Pollard and C. Holmes, eds.,* Documents of European Economic History, Vol. I *(London: Edward Arnold, 1968), pp. 38–39.*

also improved. Better medical knowledge and techniques were once thought to have contributed to the decline in deaths. This factor is now discounted because the more important medical advances came after the initial population explosion or would not have contributed directly to it.

Rather, changes in the food supply itself may have allowed population growth to be sustained. Improved and expanding grain production made one contribution. Another and even more important change was the cultivation of the potato. This tuber was a product of the New World and came into widespread European production during the eighteenth century. On a single acre enough potatoes could be raised to feed one peasant's family for an entire year. This more certain food supply enabled more children to survive to adulthood and rear children of their own.

The impact of the population explosion can hardly be overestimated. It created new demands for food, goods, jobs, and services. It provided a new pool of labor. Traditional modes of production and living had to be revised. More people lived in the countryside than could find employment there. Migration increased. There were also more people who might become socially and politically discontented. And because the population growth fed on itself, these pressures and demands continued to increase. The society and the social practices of the Old Regime literally outgrew their traditional bounds.

The Industrial Revolution of the Eighteenth Century

The second half of the eighteenth century witnessed the beginning of the industrialization of the European economy. The Industrial Revolution constituted the achievement of sustained economic growth. Previously, production had been limited. The economy of a province or a country might grow, but growth soon reached a plateau. Since the late eighteenth century, however, the economy of Europe has managed to expand almost uninterrupted. Depressions and recessions have been temporary, and even during such economic downturns, the Western economy has continued to grow.

At considerable social cost, industrialization made possible the production of more goods and more services than ever before in human history. Industrialization in Europe eventually overcame the economy of scarcity. The new means of production demanded new kinds of skills, new discipline in work, and a large labor force. The goods produced met immediate consumer demand and also created new demands. In the long run, industrialization clearly raised the standard of living and overcame the poverty that most Europeans who lived during the eighteenth century and earlier had taken for granted. It gave human beings greater control over the forces of nature than they had ever known before; yet industrialism would also by the middle of the nineteenth century cause new and unanticipated problems with the environment.

During the eighteenth century, people did not call these economic developments a *revolution*. That term came to be applied to the British economic phenomena only after the French Revolution. Then continental writers observed that what had taken place in Britain was the economic equivalent of the political events in France, hence an *Industrial Revolution*. It was revolutionary less in its speed, which was on the whole rather slow, than in its implications for the future of European society.

A Revolution in Consumption

The most familiar side of the Industrial Revolution was the invention of new machinery, the establishment of factories, and the creation of a new kind of workforce. Recent studies, however, have emphasized the demand side of the Industrial Revolution and the vast increase in both the desire and the possibility of consuming goods and services that arose in the early eighteenth century.

The inventions of the Industrial Revolution increased the supply of consumer goods as never before in history. The supply of goods was only one side of the economic equation, however. The supply had been called forth by an unprecedented demand for humble goods of everyday life. Those goods included everyday consumer items such as clothing of all kinds, buttons, toys, china, furniture, rugs, kitchen utensils, candlesticks, brassware, silverware, pewterware, glassware, watches, jewelry, soap, beer, wines, and foodstuffs. It was the ever-increasing demand for these goods that sparked the ingenuity of designers and inventors. Furthermore, there seemed to be no limits to consumer demand.

Many social factors came into play to establish the markets for these consumer goods. During the seventeenth century, the Dutch had enjoyed enormous prosperity and had led the way in new forms of both everyday consumption and that of luxury goods. For reasons that are still not clear, during the eighteenth century, increasing numbers first of the English and then of people living on the Continent came to have more disposable income. This wealth may have resulted from the improvements in agriculture. Those incomes allowed people to buy consumer goods that previous generations either did not possess or waited until they had inherited. What is key to this change in consumption is that it depended primarily upon expanding the various domestic markets in Europe.

This revolution, if that is not too strong a term, in consumption was not automatic. People became persuaded that they needed or wanted new consumer goods. Often, entrepreneurs caused it to happen by developing new methods of marketing. An enterprising manufacturer such as the porcelain manufacturer

Consumption of all forms of consumer goods increased greatly in the eighteenth century. This engraving illustrates a shop, probably in Paris. Here women, working apparently for a woman manager, are making dresses and hats to meet the demands of the fashion trade. As the document on pages 592–593 demonstrates, some women writers urged more such employment opportunities for women. [Bildarchiv Preussischer Kulturbesitz]

Josiah Wedgwood (1730–1795) first attempted to find customers among the royal family and the aristocracy. Once he had gained their business with luxury goods, he would then produce a somewhat less expensive version of the chinaware for middle-class customers. He also used advertising. He opened showrooms in London and had salesmen traveling all over England with samples and catalogues of his wares. On the Continent, he equipped salesmen with bilingual catalogues. There seemed to be no limit to the markets for different kinds of consumer goods that could be stimulated by social emulation on the one hand and advertising on the other.

Furthermore, the process of change in style itself became institutionalized. New fashions and inventions were always better than old ones. If new kinds of goods could be produced, there usually was a market for them. If one product did not find a market, its failure provided a lesson for the development of a different new product.

This expansion of consumption quietly but steadily challenged the social assumptions of the day. Fashion publications made all levels of society aware of new styles. Clothing fashions could be copied. Servants could begin to dress well if not luxuriously. There were changes in the consumption of food and drink that also called forth demand for new kinds of dishware for the home. Tea and coffee became staples. The brewing industry became fully commercialized. Those developments entailed the need for new kinds of cups and mugs and many more of them.

There would always be critics of this consumer economy. The vision of luxury and comfort it offered contrasted with the asceticism of ancient Sparta and contemporary Christian ethics. Yet ever-increasing consumption and production of the goods of everyday life became a hallmark of modern Western society from the eighteenth century to our own day. It would be difficult to overestimate the importance of the desire for consumer goods and the increasing material standard of living that they made possible in Western history after the eighteenth century. The presence and accessibility of such goods became the hallmark of a nation's prosperity. It is perhaps relevant to note that it was the absence of such consumer goods as well as of civil liberties that during the 1980s led to such deep discontent with the Communist regimes in eastern Europe and the former Soviet Union.

Industrial Leadership of Great Britain

Great Britain was the home of the Industrial Revolution and, until the middle of the nineteenth century, maintained the industrial leadership of Europe. Several factors contributed to the early start in Britain.

Great Britain took the lead in the consumer revolution that expanded the demand for goods that could be efficiently supplied. London was by far the largest city in Europe. It was the center of a world of fashion and taste to which hundreds of thousands if not millions of British citizens were exposed each year. In London, these people learned to want the consumer goods they saw on visits for business and pleasure. Newspapers thrived in Britain during the eighteenth century, allowing for advertising that increased consumer wants. The social structure of Britain allowed and even encouraged people to imitate the lifestyles of their social superiors. It seems to have been in Britain that a world of fashion first developed that led people to want to accumulate goods. In addition to the domestic consumer demand, the British economy benefited from demand from the colonies in North America.

Britain was also the single largest free-trade area in Europe. The British had good roads and waterways without internal tolls or other trade barriers. The country was endowed with rich deposits of coal and iron ore. Its political structure was stable, and property was absolutely secure. The sound systems of banking and public credit established a stable climate for investment. Taxation in Britain was heavy, but it was efficiently and fairly collected, largely from indirect taxes. Furthermore, British taxes received legal approval through Parliament with all social classes and all regions of the nation paying the same taxes. In contrast to the Continent, there was no pattern of privileged tax exemptions.

Finally, British society was mobile by the standards of the time. Persons who had money or could earn money could rise socially. The British aristocracy would receive into its midst people who had amassed large fortunes. Even persons of wealth not admitted to the aristocracy could enjoy their riches, receive social prominence, and exert political influence. No one of these factors preordained the British advance toward industrialism. Together, however, when added to the progressive state of British agriculture, they provided the nation with the marginal advantage to create a new mode of economic production.

New Methods of Textile Production

The industry that pioneered the Industrial Revolution and met growing consumer demand was the production of textiles for clothing. It provides the key example of industrialism emerging to supply the demands of an ever-growing market for everyday goods. Furthermore, it illustrates the surprising fact that much of the earliest industrial change took place not in cities but in the countryside.

Although eighteenth-century society was primarily agricultural, manufacturing also permeated rural areas. The peasant family living in a one- or two-room cottage was the basic unit of production rather than the factory. The same peasants who tilled the land in spring and summer often spun thread or wove textiles in the winter.

Under what is termed the *domestic* or *putting-out system*, agents of urban textile merchants took wool or other unfinished fibers to the homes of peasants, who spun it into thread. The agent then transported the thread to other peasants, who wove it into the finished product. The merchant sold the wares. In thousands of peasant cottages from Ireland to Austria, there stood a spinning wheel or a handloom. Sometimes the spinners or weavers owned their own equipment, but more often than not by the middle of the century, the merchant capitalist owned the machinery as well as the raw material.

The domestic system of textile production was a basic feature of this family economy and would continue to be so in Britain and on the Continent well into the nineteenth century. By mid-century, however, a series of production bottlenecks had developed within the domestic system. The demand for cotton textiles was growing more rapidly than production, especially in Great Britain, which had a large domestic and North American market for cotton textiles. Inventors devised some of the most famous machines of the early Industrial Revolution in response to this consumer demand for cotton textiles.

THE SPINNING JENNY Cotton textile weavers had the technical capacity to produce the quantity of fabric demanded. The spinners, however, did not have the equipment to produce as much thread as the weavers needed. James Kay's invention of the flying shuttle, which increased the productivity of the weavers, had created this imbalance during the 1730s. Thereafter, various groups of manufacturers and merchants offered prizes for the invention of a machine to eliminate this bottleneck.

About 1765 James Hargreaves (d. 1778) invented the spinning jenny. Initially, this machine allowed 16 spindles of thread to be spun, but by the close of the century its capacity had been increased to as many as 120 spindles.

THE WATER FRAME The spinning jenny broke the bottleneck between the productive capacity of the spinners and the weavers, but it was still a piece of machinery used in the cottage. The invention that took cotton textile manufacture out of the home and put it into the factory was Richard Arkwright's (1732–1792)

water frame, patented in 1769. This was a water-powered device designed to permit the production of a purely cotton fabric rather than a cotton fabric containing linen fiber for durability. Eventually Arkwright lost his patent rights, and other manufacturers could use his invention freely. As a result, many factories sprang up in the countryside near streams that provided the necessary waterpower. From the 1780s onward, the cotton industry could meet an ever-expanding demand. Cotton output increased by 800 percent between 1780 and 1800. By 1815 cotton composed 40 percent of the value of British domestic exports, and by 1830 just over 50 percent.

The Industrial Revolution had commenced in earnest by the 1780s, but the full economic and social ramifications of this unleashing of human productive capacity were not really felt until the early nineteenth century. The expansion of industry and the incorporation of new inventions often occurred rather slowly. For example, Edmund Cartwright (1743–1822) invented the power loom for machine weaving in the late 1780s. Yet not until the 1830s were there more power-loom weavers than handloom weavers in Britain. Nor did all the social ramifications of industrialism appear immediately. The first cotton mills used waterpower, were located in the country, and rarely employed more than two dozen workers. Not until the late-century application of the steam engine, perfected by James Watt (1736–1819) in 1769, to the running of textile machinery could factories easily be located in or near existing urban centers. The steam engine not only vastly increased and regularized the available energy but also made possible the combination of urbanization and industrialization.

The Steam Engine

More than any other invention, the steam engine permitted industrialization to grow on itself and to expand into one area of production after another. This machine provided for the first time in human history a steady and essentially unlimited source of inanimate power. Unlike engines powered by water or the wind, the steam engine, driven by the burning of coal, provided a portable source of industrial power that did not fail or falter as the seasons of the year changed. Unlike human or animal power, the steam engine depended on mineral energy that did not tire during a day. Finally, the steam engine could be applied to many industrial and, eventually, transportation uses.

The first practical engine using steam power had been the invention of Thomas Newcomen (1663–1729) in the early eighteenth century. The piston of this device was moved when the steam that had been induced into the cylinder condensed, causing the piston to fall. The Newcomen machine was large, inefficient in its use of energy because both the condenser and the cylinder were heated, and practically untransportable. Despite these problems, English mine operators used the Newcomen machines to pump water out of coal and tin mines. By the third quarter of the eighteenth century, almost 100 Newcomen machines were operating in the mining districts of England.

During the 1760s, James Watt, a Scottish engineer and machine maker, began to experiment with a model of a Newcomen machine at the University of Glasgow. He gradually understood that separating the condenser from the piston and the cylinder would achieve much greater efficiency. In 1769 he patented his new invention, but transforming his idea into application presented difficulties. His design required precise metalwork. Watt soon found a partner in Matthew Boulton (1728–1809), a successful toy and button manufacturer in Birmingham, the city with the most skilled metalworkers in Britain. Watt and Boulton, in turn, consulted with John Wilkinson (1728–1808), a cannon manufacturer, to find ways to drill the precise metal cylinders required by Watt's design. In 1776 the Watt steam engine found its first commercial application pumping water from mines in Cornwall.

The use of the steam engine spread slowly because until 1800 Watt retained the exclusive patent rights. He was also reluctant to make further changes in his invention that would permit the engine to operate more rapidly. Boulton

This painting shows the pithead of an eighteenth-century coal mine in England. The machinery on the left includes a steam engine that powered equipment to bring mined coal to the surface or to pump water from the mine. Britain's rich veins of coal were one of the factors contributing to its early industrialization. [Board of Trustees of the National Museums and Galleries on Merseyside, Walker Art Gallery, Liverpool]

Major Inventions in the Textile-Manufacturing Revolution	
1733	James Kay's flying shuttle
1765	James Hargreaves's spinning jenny (patented 1770)
1769	James Watt's steam engine patent
1769	Richard Arkwright's water frame patent
1787	Edmund Cartwright's power loom

eventually persuaded him to make modifications and improvements. These allowed the engines to be used not only for pumping but also for running cotton mills. By the early nineteenth century, the steam engine had become the prime mover for all industry. With its application to ships and then to wagons on iron rails, the steam engine also revolutionized transportation.

Iron Production

The manufacture of high-quality iron has been basic to modern industrial development. It is the chief element of all heavy industry and land or sea transport. Iron has also been the material out of which most productive machinery itself has been manufactured. During the early eighteenth century, British ironmakers produced somewhat less than 25,000 tons annually. Three factors held back the production of the metal. First, charcoal rather than coke was used to smelt the ore. Charcoal, derived from wood, was becoming scarce and does not burn at as high a temperature as coke, derived from coal. Second, until the perfection of the steam engine, insufficient blasts could be achieved in the furnaces. Finally, the demand for iron was limited. The elimination of the first two problems also eliminated the third.

Eventually, British ironmakers began to use coke, and the steam engine provided new power for the blast furnaces. Coke was an abundant fuel because of Britain's large coal deposits. The existence of the steam engine both improved iron production and increased the demand for iron.

In 1784 Henry Cort (1740–1800) introduced a new puddling process, that is, a new method for melting and stirring the molten ore. Cort's process allowed more slag (the impurities that bubbled to the top of the molten metal) to be removed and a purer iron to be produced. Cort also developed a rolling mill that continuously shaped the still-molten metal into bars, rails, or other forms. Previously the metal had been pounded into these forms.

All these innovations achieved a better, more versatile product at a lower cost. The demand for iron grew as its price became lower. By the early nineteenth century, the British produced over a million tons annually. The lower cost of iron, in turn, lowered the cost of steam engines and allowed them to be used more widely.

Cities

Remarkable changes occurred in the pattern of city growth between 1500 and 1800. In 1500 within Europe (excluding Hungary and Russia) there were 156 cities with a population greater than 10,000. Only 4 of those cities—Paris, Milan, Venice, and Naples—had populations larger than 100,000. By 1800, 363 cities had 10,000 or more inhabitants, and 17 of them had populations larger than 100,000. The percentage of the European population living in urban areas had risen from just over 5 percent to just over 9 percent. There had also occurred a major shift in urban concentration from southern, Mediterranean Europe to the north.

Patterns of Preindustrial Urbanization

The eighteenth century witnessed a considerable growth of towns, closely related to the tumult of the day and the revolutions with which the century closed. London grew from about 700,000 inhabitants in 1700 to almost 1 million in 1800. By the time of the French Revolution, Paris had more than 500,000 inhabitants. Berlin's population tripled during the century, reaching 170,000 in 1800. Warsaw had 30,000 inhabitants in 1730, but almost 120,000 in 1794. Saint Petersburg, founded in 1703, numbered more than 250,000 inhabitants a century later. In addition to the growth of these capitals, the number of smaller cities of 20,000–50,000 people increased considerably. This urban growth must, however, be kept in

Frederick the Great Grants Special Privileges to an Ironworks

To encourage investment in plant and equipment, some continental monarchies, like governments today, would give certain producers special privileges that relieved them from taxes and make working for them particularly attractive. Frederick the Great (r. 1740–1786), who was always concerned about armaments that required metal, granted such privileges to an ironworks.

✦ *What kinds of taxes did Frederick use to raise revenues in his kingdom? What other practices did he follow to keep from spending money? What are the labor arrangements that might have made this ironworks a place where workers might have preferred to work? By looking at the special privileges given to the workers at this ironworks, what can you conclude about the situation of workers employed in factories, mines, or foundries that did not enjoy special privileges?*

. . . in order that the newly discovered iron stone in Pomerania . . . shall not be without benefit but be used for the good of his lands and loyal subjects in Pomerania . . . H. M. [His Majesty King Frederick] is graciously pleased . . . to grant the following liberties to their servants and workmen, or to those to be employed by them in the future.

(1) It is H. M. highest wish and command that each and every man and servant accept-ed by the said works or volunteering for them, shall be exempt together with all his family from all quartering of troops, . . . from all taxes and services, such as Contributions, Cavalry Tax, Land and Roof Tax, War contribution, Income Taxes, and all other burden, of whatever title, which have been enacted or may be enacted in the future, for now and for evermore as long as they remain employees of the furnaces. . . .

perspective. Even in France and Great Britain, probably somewhat less than 20 percent of the population lived in cities. And the town of 10,000 inhabitants was much more common than the giant urban center.

These raw figures conceal significant changes that took place in how cities grew and how the population distributed itself. The major urban development of the sixteenth century had been followed by a leveling off and even a decline in the seventeenth. New growth began in the early eighteenth century and accelerated during the late eighteenth and the early nineteenth centuries. Between 1500 and 1750 the major urban expansion took place within already established and generally already large cities. After 1750 the pattern changed with the birth of new cities and the rapid growth of older smaller cities.

GROWTH OF CAPITALS AND PORTS In particular, between 1600 and 1750, the cities that grew most vigorously were capitals and ports. This situation reflects the success of monarchical state building during those years and the consequent burgeoning of bureaucracies, armies, courts, and other groups who lived in the capitals. The growth of port cities, in turn, reflects the expansion of European overseas trade and most especially that of the Atlantic routes. Except for Manchester in England and Lyons in France, the new urban conglomerates were non-industrial cities.

Furthermore, between 1600 and 1750, cities with populations of fewer than 40,000 inhabitants declined. These included older landlocked trading centers, medieval industrial cities, and ecclesiastical centers. They contributed less to the new political regimes, and the expansion of the putting-out system transferred to the countryside much production that had once occurred in medieval cities. Rural labor was cheaper than urban labor, and cities with concentrations of

Further, the said servants and workmen employed about the furnaces shall remain subject to the laws of the land regarding prohibited goods and in other respects, and shall refrain from smuggling, on pain of incurring the usual penalties, provided that the searches which may become necessary in this regard about the furnaces shall be in the presence of the appropriate factor, so that disorders may be avoided and the factor be made responsible for the prevention of smuggling.

(2) The furnace servants and workmen are hereby given the right and the liberty to purchase all that they need for themselves and their families in the way of necessities, food, drink and otherwise, from anywhere in the King's dominions, either in the country or in the towns, wherever they can best be got.

(3) All the servants and workmen employed in the said iron furnaces and rolling mills, . . . as well as their families, shall be wholly exempt from impressment and recruitment.

(4) They shall be paid their wages promptly and in cash, and they shall in no manner be forced to accept against their will food or other truck in place of ready cash, as happens quite often at other furnaces, and whereby the poor workmen may be cheated of their hard-earned wage.

(5) All furnace servants and workmen receive free lodging and firing, but the latter is to consist of windfall twigs and branches only, gathered by members of their families.

(6) If one or other of the furnace servants or workmen should wish, after the expire of the term of his binding [i.e., expiration of his work contract], to remove to his home or elsewhere with his property, brought with him, acquired later or earned in the Royal dominions at work at the furnace, he shall be allowed to do so freely and without hindrance, and no deduction shall be demanded from his goods or money.

From Privilegium für die Hütten-Bediente und Arbeiter bey den Königlichen Chur-Mäkschen, Pommerschen und Neumärckschen Eisen Hütten und Blech Werken (Berlin, 1 November 1768), *as quoted and translated in* S. Pollard *and* C. Holmes, *eds.*, Documents of European Economic History, Vol. I *(London: Edward Arnold, 1968), pp. 71–72.

labor declined as production was moved from the urban workshop into the country.

EMERGENCE OF NEW CITIES AND GROWTH OF SMALL TOWNS In the middle of the eighteenth century, a new pattern emerged. The rate of growth of existing large cities declined, while new cities began to emerge and existing smaller cities began to grow. Several factors were at work in the process, which Jan De Vries has termed "an urban growth from below."[2] First, there was the general overall population increase. Second, the early stages of the Industrial Revolution, particularly in Britain, occurred in the countryside and fostered the growth of smaller towns and cities located nearby the factories. Factory organization itself led to new concentrations of population.

[2]Jan De Vries, *"Patterns of Urbanization in Pre-Industrial Europe, 1500–1800,"* in H. Schmal, ed., Patterns of Urbanization Since 1500 *(London: Croom Helm, 1981), p. 103.*

Cities also grew, however, where there was little industrialization because of the new prosperity of European agriculture. Improved agricultural production promoted the growth of nearby market towns and other urban centers that served agriculture or allowed more prosperous farmers to have access to the consumer goods and recreation they wanted. This new pattern of urban growth—new cities and the expansion of smaller existing ones—would continue into the nineteenth century.

Urban Classes

Social divisions were as marked in the cities of the eighteenth century as they were in the industrial centers of the nineteenth. Visible segregation often existed between the urban rich and the urban poor. The nobles and the upper middle class lived in fashionable town houses,

Until it was destroyed by Allied bombing in World War II, Dresden was regarded as one of the most beautiful cities in Europe. Life in this city, as in many others in Germany, centered on the royal court and the economic activity it generated. Cities like this were usually centers for the arts as well as for politics. [Bildarchiv Preussischer Kulturbesitz]

often constructed around newly laid-out green squares. The poorest town dwellers usually congregated along the rivers. Small merchants and artisans lived above their shops. Whole families might live in a single room. Modern sanitary facilities were still unknown. There was little pure water. Cattle, pigs, goats, and other animals walked the streets with the people. All reports on the cities of Europe during this period emphasize both the striking grace and beauty of the dwellings of the wealthy and the dirt, filth, and stench that filled the streets.

Poverty was not just an urban problem; it was usually worse in the countryside. In the city, however, poverty was more visible in the form of crime, prostitution, vagrancy, begging, and alcoholism. Many a young man or woman from the countryside migrated to the nearest city to seek a better life, only to discover poor housing, little food, disease, degradation, and finally death. It did not require the Industrial Revolution and the urban factories to make the cities into hellholes for the poor and the dispossessed. The full darkness of London life during the mid-century

"gin age," when consumption of that liquor blinded and killed many poor people, is evident in the engravings of William Hogarth (1697–1764). See Chapter 15.

Also contrasting with the serenity of the aristocratic and upper-commercial-class lifestyle were the public executions that took place all over Europe, the breaking of men and women on the wheel in Paris, and the public floggings in Russia. Brutality condoned and carried out by the ruling classes was simply a fact of everyday life.

THE UPPER CLASSES At the top of the urban social structure stood a generally small group of nobles, large merchants, bankers, financiers, clergy, and government officials. These men (and they were always men) controlled the political and economic affairs of the town. Normally, they constituted a self-appointed and self-electing oligarchy who governed the city through its corporation or city council. These rights of self-government had normally been granted by some form of royal charter that gave the city corporation its authority and the power to select its own members. In a few cities on the Continent, artisan guilds controlled the corporations, but more generally the councils were under the influence of the local nobility and the wealthiest commercial people.

THE MIDDLE CLASS Another group in the city was the prosperous but not always immensely wealthy merchants, tradesmen, bankers, and professional people. They were the most dynamic element of the urban population and constituted the persons traditionally regarded as the middle class, or *bourgeoisie*. The concept of the middle class was much less clear-cut than that of the nobility. The middle class itself was and would remain diverse and divided with persons employed in the professions often resentful of those who drew their incomes from commerce. Less wealthy members of the middle

Manchester's Calico Printers Protest the Use of New Machinery

The introduction of the new machines associated with the Industrial Revolution stirred much protest. With machines able to duplicate the skills of laborers, workers feared the loss of jobs and the resulting loss of status when their chief means of livelihood lay in their possession of those displaced and now mechanized skills. The following letter was sent anonymously to a Manchester manufacturer by English workers. It shows the outrage of those workers, the intimidation they were willing to use as threats, and their own economic fears.

♦ *How might new machines adversely affect the livelihood of workers? Did the workers have other complaints against Mr. Taylor in addition to the introduction of new machinery? How have these workers reached an agreement to protect the interests of James Hobson? How do the workers combine the threat of violent actions with claims that other actions they have taken are legal?*

Mr. Taylor, If you dont discharge James Hobson from the House of Correction we will burn your House about your Ears for we have sworn to stand by one another and you must immediately give over any more Mashen Work for we are determined there shall be no more of them made use of in the Trade and it will be madness for you to contend with the Trade as we are combined by Oath to fix Prices we can afford to pay him a Guinea Week and not hurt the fund if you was to keep him there till Dumsday therefore mind you comply with the above or by God we will keep our Words with you we will make some rare Bunfires in this Countey and at your Peril to call any more Meetings mind that we will make the Mosney Pepel shake in their Shoes we are determined to destroy all Sorts of Masheens for Printing in the Kingdom for there is more hands then is work for so no more from the ingerd Gurnemen Rember we are a great number sworn nor you must not advertise the Men that you say run away from you when your il Usage was the Cause of their going we will punish you for that our Meetings are legal for we want nothing but what is honest and to work for selvs and familers and you want to starve us but it is better for you and a few more which we have marked to die then such a Number of Pore Men and their famerles to be starved.

London Gazette, 1786, p. 36, as reprinted in Douglas Hay, ed., Albion's Fatal Tree *(New York: Pantheon Books, 1975), p. 318.*

class of whatever occupation resented wealthier members who might be connected to the nobility through social or business relationships.

The middle class had less wealth than most nobles but more than urban artisans. Middle-class people lived in the cities and towns, and their sources of income had little or nothing to do with the land. In one way or another, they all benefitted from expanding trade and commerce whether as merchants, as lawyers, or as small factory owners. Theirs was a world in which the earning and saving of money allowed for rapid social mobility and change in lifestyle. They saw themselves as people willing to use their capital and energy to work, while they portrayed the nobility as idle. The members of the middle class tended to be economically aggressive and socially ambitious. People often made fun of them for these characteristics and were jealous of their success. The middle class normally supported reform, change, and economic growth. The bourgeoisie also wanted more rational regulations for trade and commerce, as did some of the more progressive aristocrats.

The middle class were the people whose lives fostered the revolution in consumption. On one hand, as owners of factories and of wholesale and retail businesses, they produced and sold goods for the expanding consumer market; on the other hand, members of the middle class were also among the chief consumers. It was to their homes that the vast array of new consumer goods made their way. They were also the people whose social values clearly embraced most fully the commercial spirit. They might not enjoy the titles or privileges of the nobility, but they could enjoy considerable material comfort and prosperity. It was this style of life that less well-off people could still emulate as they sought to acquire consumer goods for themselves.

During the eighteenth century, the relationship between the middle class and the aristocracy was complicated. On one hand, the nobles, especially in England and France, increasingly embraced the commercial spirit associated with the middle class by improving their estates and investing in cities. On the other hand, wealthy members of the middle class

This engraving illustrates a metalworking shop such as might have been found in almost any town of significance in Europe. Most of the people employed in the shop probably belonged to the same family. Note that two women are also working. The wife may very well have been the person in charge of keeping the accounts of the business. The two younger boys might be children of the owner or apprentices in the trade, or both. [Bildarchiv Preussischer Kulturbesitz]

often tried to imitate the lifestyle of the nobility by purchasing landed estates. The aspirations of the middle class for social mobility, however, conflicted with the determination of the nobles to maintain and reassert their own privileges and to protect their own wealth. The middle-class commercial figures—traders, bankers, manufacturers, and lawyers—often found their pursuit of both profit and prestige blocked by the privileges of the nobility and its social exclusiveness, by the inefficiency of monarchical bureaucracies dominated by the nobility, or by aristocrats who controlled patronage and government contracts.

The bourgeoisie were not rising to challenge the nobility; rather, both were seeking to add new dimensions to their existing political power and social prestige. The tensions that arose between the nobles and the middle class during the eighteenth century normally involved issues of power sharing or access to political influence rather than clashes over values or goals associated with class.

The middle class in the cities also feared the lower urban classes as much as they envied the nobility. The lower orders were a potentially violent element in society, a potential threat to property, and, in their poverty, a drain on national resources. The lower classes, however, were much more varied than either the city aristocracy or the middle class cared to admit.

ARTISANS Shopkeepers, artisans, and wage earners were the single largest group in any city. They were grocers, butchers, fishmongers, carpenters, cabinetmakers, smiths, printers, handloom weavers, and tailors, to give a few examples. They had their own culture, values, and institutions. Like the peasants of the countryside, they were in many respects conservative. Their economic position was highly vulnerable. If a poor harvest raised the price of food, their own businesses suffered. These urban classes also contributed to the revolution in consumption, however. They could buy more goods than ever before, and many of them sought to the extent their incomes permitted to copy the domestic consumption of the middle class.

The lives of these artisans and shopkeepers centered on their work and their neighborhoods. They usually lived near or at their place of employment. Most of them worked in shops with fewer than a half dozen other artisans. Their primary institution had historically been the guild, but by the eighteenth century, the guilds rarely had the influence of their predecessors in medieval or early modern Europe.

Nevertheless, the guilds were not to be ignored. They played a conservative role. Rather than seeking economic growth or innovation, they tried to preserve the jobs and skills of their members. The guilds were still able in many countries to determine who could pursue a particular craft. To lessen competition, they attempted to prevent too many people from learning a particular skill.

The guilds also provided a framework for social and economic advancement. At an early age, a boy might become an apprentice to learn a craft or trade. After several years he would be made a journeyman. Still later, if successful and sufficiently competent, he might become a master. The artisan could also receive certain social benefits from the guilds. These might include aid for his family during sickness or the promise of admission for his son. The guilds were the chief protection for artisans against the operation of the commercial market. They were particularly strong in central Europe.

The Urban Riot

The artisan class, with its generally conservative outlook, maintained a rather fine sense of social and economic justice. These ideals were based largely on traditional practices. If the collective sense of what was economically "just" was offended, artisans frequently manifested their displeasure by rioting. The most sensitive area was the price of bread, the staple food of the poor. If a baker or a grain merchant announced a price that was considered unjustly high, a bread riot might well ensue. Artisan leaders would confiscate the bread or grain and sell it for what the urban crowd considered a "just price." They would then give the money paid for the grain or bread to the baker or merchant.

The potential for bread riots restrained the greed of merchants. Such disturbances represented a collective method of imposing the "just price" in place of the price set by the commercial marketplace. Thus, bread and food riots, which occurred throughout Europe, were not irrational acts of screaming hungry people but

The Gordon Riots of 1780, in London, triggered by anti-Catholic bigotry, were among the most destructive civil disturbances in the history of Europe. [The Bettmann Archive]

highly ritualized social phenomena of the Old Regime and its economy of scarcity.

Other kinds of riots also characterized eighteenth-century society and politics. The riot was a way in which people who were excluded in every other way from the political processes could make their will known. Sometimes urban rioters were incited by religious bigotry. For example, in 1753 London Protestant mobs compelled the government ministry to withdraw an act to legalize Jewish naturalization. In 1780 the same rabidly Protestant spirit manifested itself in the Gordon riots. Lord George Gordon (1751–1793) had raised the specter of an imaginary Catholic plot after the government relieved military recruits from having to take specifically anti-Catholic oaths.

In these riots and in food riots, violence was normally directed against property rather than against people. The rioters themselves were not "riff-raff" but usually small shopkeepers, freeholders, artisans, and wage earners. They usually wanted only to restore a traditional right or practice that seemed endangered. Nevertheless, considerable turmoil and destruction could result from their actions.

During the last half of the century, urban riots increasingly involved political ends. Though often simultaneous with economic disturbances, the political riot always had nonartisan leadership or instigators. In fact, the "crowd" of the eighteenth century was often the tool of the upper classes. In Paris, the aristocratic *Parlement* often urged crowd action in their disputes with the monarchy. In Geneva, middle-class citizens supported artisan riots against the local urban oligarchy. In Great Britain in 1792, the government incited mobs to attack English sympathizers of the French Revolution. Such outbursts of popular unrest suggest that the crowd or mob first entered the European political and social arena well before the revolution in France.

The Jewish Population: The Age of the Ghetto

Although the small Jewish communities of Amsterdam and other West European cities became famous for their intellectual life and financial institutions, the vast majority of European Jews lived in eastern Europe. In the eighteenth century and thereafter, the Jewish population of Europe was concentrated in Poland, Lithuania, and the Ukraine, where no fewer than three million Jews dwelled. There were perhaps as many as 150,000 in the Habsburg lands, primarily Bohemia, around 1760. Fewer than 100,000 lived in Germany. There were approximately 40,000 in France. Much smaller Jewish populations resided in England and Holland, each of which had a Jewish population of less than 10,000. There were even smaller groups of Jews elsewhere.

In 1762 Catherine the Great of Russia specifically excluded Jews from a manifesto that welcomed foreigners to settle in Russia. She somewhat relaxed the exclusion a few years later. After the first partition of Poland of 1772, to be discussed in Chapter 18, Russia included a large Jewish population. There were also larger Jewish communities in Prussia and under Austrian rule.

Jews dwelled in most nations without enjoying the rights and privileges of other subjects of the monarchs unless such rights were specifically granted to them. They were regarded as a kind of resident alien whose residence might well be temporary or changed at the whim of local rulers or the monarchical government.

No matter where they dwelled, the Jews of Europe under the Old Regime lived apart in separate communities from non-Jewish Europeans. These communities might be distinct districts of cities known as *ghettos* or in primarily Jewish villages in the countryside. Jews were also treated as a distinct people religiously and legally. In Poland for much of the century, they were virtually self-governing. In other areas, they lived under the burden of discriminatory legislation. Except in England, Jews could not and did not mix in the mainstream of the societies in which they dwelled. This period, which really may be said to have begun with the expulsion of the Jews from Spain at the end of the fifteenth century, is known as the age of the ghetto or separate community.

During the seventeenth century, a few Jews had helped finance the wars of major rulers. These financiers often became close to the rulers and were known as "court Jews." Perhaps the most famous was Samuel Oppenheimer (1630–1703), who helped the Habsburgs finance their struggle against the Turks and the defense of Vienna. Even these privileged Jews, including Oppenheimer, however, often failed to have their loans repaid. The court Jews and their financial abilities became famous. They tended to marry among themselves.

The overwhelming majority of the Jewish population of Europe, however, lived in poverty. They occupied the most undesirable sections of cities or poor rural villages. They pursued moneylending in some cases, but often worked at the lowest occupations. Their religious beliefs, rituals, and community set them apart. Virtually all laws and social institutions kept them apart from their Christian neighbors in situations of social inferiority.

Under the Old Regime, it is important to emphasize, all of this discrimination was based on religious separateness. Jews who converted to Christianity were welcomed, even if not always warmly, into the major political and social institutions of gentile European society. Until the last two decades of the eighteenth century, in every part of Europe, however, those Jews who remained loyal to their faith were subject to various religious, civil, and social disabilities. They could not pursue the professions freely; often they could not change residence freely; and they stood outside the political structures of the nations in which they lived. Jews could be expelled from the cities where they lived, and their property could be confiscated. They were regarded as socially and religiously inferior. They could be required to listen to sermons that insulted them and their religion. Jews might find their children taken away from them and given Christian instruction. They knew that their non-Jewish neighbors might suddenly turn against them and kill them or their fellow religious believers.

As will be seen in subsequent chapters, the end of the Old Regime brought major changes in the lives of these Jews and in their relationship to the larger culture.

Near the close of the eighteenth century, European society was on the brink of a new era. That society had remained traditional and corporate largely because of the economy of scarcity. Beginning in the eighteenth century, the commercial spirit and the values of the marketplace, although not new, were permitted fuller play than ever before in European history. The newly unleashed commercial spirit led increasingly to a conception of human beings as individuals rather than as members of communities. In particular that spirit manifested itself in agricultural and industrial revolutions, as well as in the drive toward greater consumption. Together those two vast changes in production overcame most of the scarcity that had haunted Europe and the West generally. The accompanying changes in landholding and production would bring major changes to the European social structure.

The expansion of population provided a further stimulus for change. More people meant more labor, more energy, and more minds contributing to the creation and solution of social difficulties. Cities had to accommodate themselves to expanding populations. Corporate groups, such as the guilds, had to confront the existence of a larger labor force. New wealth meant that birth would eventually become less and less a determining factor in social relationships, except in regard to the social roles assigned to the two sexes. Class structure and social hierarchy remained, but the boundaries became somewhat blurred.

Finally, the conflicting ambitions of monarchs, the nobility, and middle class generated innovation. In the pursuit of new revenues, the monarchs interfered with the privileges of the nobles. In the name of ancient rights, the nobles attempted to secure and expand their existing social privileges. The middle class, in all of its diversity, was growing wealthier from trade, commerce, and the practice of the professions. Its members wanted social prestige and influence equal to their wealth. They resented privileges, frowned on hierarchy, and rejected tradition.

All these factors meant that the society of the eighteenth century stood at the close of one era in European history and at the opening of another.

Review Questions

1. Describe the life of an English aristocrat at the beginning of the eighteenth century and toward its close. How did the English aristocrat differ from the French aristocrat in this regard? What kind of privileges separated European aristocrats from other social groups?

2. How would you define the term *family economy*? What were some of the particular characteristics of the northwestern European household as opposed to that in eastern Europe? In what ways were the lives of women constrained by the family economy in preindustrial Europe?

3. What caused the Agricultural Revolution? How did technological innovations help change European agriculture? To what extent did the English aristocracy contribute to the Agricultural Revolution? What were some of the reasons for peasant revolts in Europe in the eighteenth century?

4. What factors explain the increase in Europe's population in the eighteenth century? What were the effects of the population explosion? How did population growth contribute to changes in consumption?

5. What caused the Industrial Revolution of the eighteenth century? What were some of the technological innovations and why were they important? Why did Great Britain take the lead in the Industrial Revolution? How did the consumer contribute to the Industrial Revolution?

6. Describe city life during the eighteenth century. Were all European cities of the same character? What changes had taken place in the distribution of population in cities and towns? Compare the lifestyle of the upper class with that of the middle and lower classes. What were some of the causes of urban riots?

Suggested Readings

I. T. BEREND and G. RANKI, *The European Periphery and Industrialization, 1780–1914* (1982). Examines the experience of eastern and Mediterranean Europe.

J. BLUM, *Lord and Peasant in Russia from the Ninth to the Nineteenth Century* (1961). A thorough and wide-ranging discussion.

J. BLUM, *The End of the Old Order in Rural Europe* (1978). The most comprehensive treatment of life in rural Europe, especially central and eastern, from the early eighteenth through the mid-nineteenth centuries.

F. BRAUDEL, *Capitalism and Material Life, 1400–1800* (1974). An investigation of the physical resources and human organization of preindustrial Europe.

F. BRAUDEL, *The Structures of Everyday Life: The Limits of the Possible*, trans. by M. Kochan (1982). A magisterial survey by the most important social historian of our time.

J. BREWER and R. PORTER, *Consumption and the World of Goods* (1993). A large, wide-ranging collection of essays.

J. CANNON, *Aristocratic Century: The Peerage of Eighteenth-Century England* (1985). A useful treatment based on the most recent research.

P. DEANE, *The First Industrial Revolution*, 2nd ed. (1979). A well-balanced and systematic treatment.

J. DE VRIES, *The Economy of Europe in an Age of Crisis, 1600–1750* (1976). An excellent overview that sets forth the main issues.

J. De Vries, *European Urbanization 1500–1800* (1984). The most important and far-ranging recent treatment of the subject.

W. Doyle, *The Old European Order: 1660–1800* (1992). The best one-volume treatment.

P. Earle, *The Making of the English Middle Class: Business, Community, and Family Life in London, 1660–1730* (1989). The most careful study of the subject.

M. W. Flinn, *The European Demographic System, 1500–1820* (1981). A major summary.

R. Forster, *The Nobility of Toulouse in the Eighteenth Century* (1960). A local study that displays the variety of noble economic activity.

R. Forster and O. Ranum, *Deviants and Abandoned in French Society* (1978). This and the following volume contain important essays from the French journal *Annales*.

R. Forster and O. Ranum, *Medicine and Society in France* (1980).

D. V. Glass and D. E. C. Eversley (Eds.), *Population in History: Essays in Historical Demography* (1965). Fundamental for understanding the eighteenth-century increase in population.

A. Goodwin (Ed.), *The European Nobility in the Eighteenth Century* (1953). Essays on the nobility in each state.

P. Goubert, *The Ancien Régime: French Society, 1600–1750*, trans. by S. Cox (1974). A superb account of the peasant social order.

D. Hay (Ed.), *Albion's Fatal Tree: Crime and Society in Eighteenth-Century England* (1975). Separate essays on a previously little explored subject.

O. H. Hufton, *The Poor of Eighteenth-Century France, 1750–1789* (1975). A brilliant study of poverty and the family economy.

R. M. Isherwood, *Farce and Fantasy: Popular Entertainment in Eighteenth-Century Paris* (1986). A study that concentrates primarily on the theater and related spectacles.

C. Jones, *Charity and Bienfaisance: The Treatment of the Poor in the Montpellier Region, 1740–1815* (1982). An important local French study.

E. L. Jones, *Agriculture and Economic Growth in England, 1650–1815* (1968). A good introduction to an important subject.

A. Kahan, *The Plow, the Hammer, and the Knout: An Economic History of Eighteenth-Century Russia* (1985). An extensive and detailed treatment.

H. Kamen, *European Society, 1500–1700* (1985). The best one-volume treatment.

R. K. McClure, *Coram's Children: The London Foundling Hospital in the Eighteenth Century* (1981). A moving work that deals with the plight of all concerned with the problem.

N. McKenderick (Ed.), *The Birth of a Consumer Society: The Commercialization of Eighteenth-Century England* (1982). Deals with several aspects of the impact of commercialization.

F. E. Manuel, *The Broken Staff: Judaism Through Christian Eyes* (1992). An important discussion of Christian interpretations of Judaism.

M. A. Meyer, *The Origins of the Modern Jew: Jewish Identity and European Culture in Germany, 1749–1824* (1967). A general introduction organized around individual case studies.

P. B. Munsche, *Gentlemen and Poachers: The English Game Laws, 1671–1831* (1981). An excellent analysis of these laws.

S. Pollard, *The Genesis of Modern Management: A Study of the Industrial Revolution in Great Britain* (1965). Treats the issue of industrialization from the standpoint of factory owners.

S. Pollard, *Peaceful Conquest: The Industrialization of Europe, 1760–1970* (1981). A useful survey.

A. Ribeiro, *Dress in Eighteenth Century Europe, 1715–1789* (1985). An interesting examination of the social implication of style in clothing.

G. Rudé, *The Crowd in History 1730–1848* (1964). A pioneering study.

S. Schama, *The Embarrassment of Riches: An Interpretation of Dutch Culture in the Golden Age* (1987). A broad examination of the impact of wealth on the Dutch.

H. Schmal (Ed.), *Patterns of European Urbanization Since 1500* (1981). Major revisionist essays.

L. Stone, *The Family, Sex and Marriage in England 1500–1800* (1977). A pioneering study of a subject receiving increasing interest from historians.

L. Stone, *An Open Elite?* (1985). Raises important questions about the traditional view of open access to social mobility in England.

T. Tackett, *Priest and Parish in Eighteenth-Century France: A Social and Political Study of the Curés in a Diocese of Dauphiné, 1750–1791* (1977). An important local study that displays the role of the Church in the fabric of social life in the Old Regime.

R. Wall (Ed.), *Family Forms in Historic Europe* (1983). Essays that cover the entire continent.

E. A. Wrigley, *Continuity, Chance and Change: The Character of the Industrial Revolution in England* (1988). A major conceptual reassessment.

E. A. Wrigley and R. S. Schofield, *The Population History of England, 1541–1871: A Reconstruction* (1982). One of the most ambitious demographic studies ever undertaken.

During the seventeenth and eighteenth centuries European maritime nations established overseas empires, and set up trading monopolies within them, in an effort to magnify their economic strength. As this painting of the Old Custom House Quay in London suggests, trade from these empires and the tariffs imposed on it were expected to generate revenue for the home country. But trade rivalries between imperial powers also generated wars. And behind many of the goods carried in the great sailing ships in the harbor and landed on these docks lay the labor of African slaves working on the plantations of North and South America. [Michael Holford]

616

17

Empire, War, and Colonial Rebellion

Key Topics in This Chapter
◆ Europe's mercantilist empires
◆ Spain's vast colonial empire in the Americas
◆ The wars of the mid-eighteenth century in Europe and the colonies
◆ The struggle for independence in Britain's North American colonies

The middle of the eighteenth century witnessed a renewal of European warfare on a worldwide scale. The conflict involved two separate but interrelated rivalries. Austria and Prussia fought for dominance in central Europe, while Great Britain and France dueled for commercial and colonial supremacy. The wars were long, extensive, and costly in both effort and money. They resulted in a new balance of power on the Continent and on the high seas. Prussia emerged as a great power, and Great Britain gained a world empire.

Moreover, the expense of these wars led every major European government after the Peace of Paris of 1763 to reconstruct its policies of taxation and finance. These revised fiscal programs produced internal conditions for the monarchies of Europe that had most significant results for the rest of the century. These included the American Revolution, enlightened absolutism on the Continent, a continuing financial crisis for the French monarchy, and reform of the Spanish Empire in South America.

Periods of European Overseas Empires

Since the Renaissance, European contacts with the rest of the world have gone through four distinct stages. The first was that of the European discovery, exploration, initial conquest, and settlement of the New World. This period had closed by the end of the seventeenth century.

The second era, which is largely the concern of this chapter, was one of colonial trade rivalry among Spain, France, and Great Britain. The Anglo-French side of the contest has often been compared to a second Hundred Years' War. During this second period, both the British colonies of the North American seaboard and the Spanish colonies of Mexico and Central and South America emancipated themselves from European control. This era may be said to have closed during the 1820s.

The third stage of European contact with the non-European world occurred in the nineteenth century. During that period, European governments carved new formal empires involving the European administration of indigenous peoples in Africa and Asia. Those nineteenth-century empires also included new areas of European settlement, such as Australia, New Zealand, and South Africa. The bases of these empires were trade, national honor, and military strategy.

The last period of European empire occurred during the mid-twentieth century, with the decolonization of peoples who had previously been under European colonial rule.

During the four and a half centuries before decolonization, Europeans exerted political dominance over much of the rest of the world that was far disproportional to the geographical size or population of Europe. Europeans frequently treated other peoples as social, intellectual, and economic inferiors. They ravaged existing cultures because of greed, religious zeal, or political ambition. These actions are major facts of European history and significant factors in the contemporary relationship of Europe and its former colonies. What allowed the Europeans to exert such influence and domination for so long over so much of the world was not any innate cultural superiority but a technological supremacy related to naval power and gunpowder. Ships and guns allowed the Europeans to exercise their will almost wherever they chose.

Eighteenth-Century Empires

Eighteenth-century European empires existed primarily to enrich trade. They were empires based on commerce, and the trade of these empires helped to establish the consumer revolution discussed in the previous chapter. Extensive trade rivalries sprang up around the world. Consequently, the protection of these empires required extensive naval power. Spain dominated the largest of these empires and constructed elaborate naval, commercial, and political structures to exploit and govern it. Finally, these empires depended largely upon slave labor. Indeed, the Atlantic slave trade itself represented one of the major ways in which European merchants enriched themselves. That trade in turn forcibly brought the peoples of Africa into the life and culture of the New World.

Mercantile Empires

Navies and merchant shipping were the keystones of the mercantile empires that were meant to bring profit to a nation rather than to provide areas for settlement. The Treaty of Utrecht (1713) established the boundaries of empire during the first half of the century.

Except for Brazil, which was governed by Portugal, Spain controlled all of mainland South America. In North America, it ruled Florida, Mexico, California, and the Southwest. The Spanish also governed the islands of Cuba, Puerto Rico, and half of Hispaniola.

The British Empire consisted of the colonies along the North Atlantic seaboard, Nova Scotia, Newfoundland, Jamaica, and Barbados. Britain also possessed a few trading stations on the Indian subcontinent.

The French domains covered the Saint Lawrence River valley and the Ohio and Mississippi river valleys. They included the West Indian islands of Saint Domingue, Guadeloupe, and Martinique and also stations in India. To the French and British merchant communities, India appeared as a vast potential market for European goods as well as the source of calicos and spices that were much in demand in Europe.

The Dutch controlled Surinam, or Dutch Guiana, in South America, and various trading stations in Ceylon and Bengal. Most important,

The Dutch established a major trading base at Batavia in the East Indies. The city they called Batavia is now Djakarta, Indonesia. [Bildarchiv Preussischer Kulturbesitz]

they controlled the trade with Java in what is now Indonesia. The Dutch had opened these markets largely in the seventeenth century and had created a vast trading empire far larger in extent, wealth, and importance than the geographical size of the United Netherlands would have led one to expect. The Dutch had been daring sailors and had made important technological innovations in sailing.

All of these powers also possessed numerous smaller islands in the Caribbean. So far as eighteenth-century developments were concerned, the major rivalries existed among the Spanish, the French, and the British.

MERCANTILIST GOALS Where any formal economic theory lay behind the conduct of these empires, it was *mercantilism*, that practical creed of hard-headed business persons. The terms *mercantilism* and *mercantile system* were invented by opponents of the system whereby governments heavily regulated trade and commerce in hope of increasing national wealth. Economic writers believed it necessary for a nation to gain a favorable trade balance of gold and silver bullion. They regarded bullion as the measure of a country's wealth, and a nation was truly wealthy only if it amassed more bullion than its rivals.

From beginning to end, the economic well-being of the home country was the primary concern of mercantilist writers. Colonies were to provide markets and natural resources for the industries of the home country. In turn, the home country was to furnish military security and political administration for the colonies. For decades both sides assumed that the colonies were the inferior partner in the relationship. The mercantilist statesmen and traders regarded the world as an arena of scarce resources and economic limitation. They assumed that one national economy could grow only at the expense of others. The home country and its colonies were to trade exclusively with each other. To that end, they tried to forge trade-tight systems of national commerce through navigation laws, tariffs, bounties to encourage production, and prohibitions against trading with the subjects of other monarchs. National monopoly was the ruling principle.

Mercantilist ideas had always been neater on paper than in practice. By the early eighteenth century, mercantilist assumptions were far removed from the economic realities of the colonies. The colonial and home markets simply did not mesh. Spain could not produce enough goods for South America. Economic production in the British North American colonies challenged English manufacturing and led to British attempts to limit certain colonial industries, such as iron and hat making.

The Mercantilist Position Stated

One of the earliest discussions of the economic theory of mercantilism appeared in England's Treasure by Forraign Trade *(1664) by Thomas Mun (1571–1641). In this passage from that work, Mun explained why it was necessary to the prosperity of the nation for more goods to be exported than imported. Although mercantilist theory later became more sophisticated, all writers in the eighteenth century emphasized the necessity of a favorable balance of trade.*

✦ *Why does Mun emphasize foreign trade rather than the development of a domestic market? Why might persons of Mun's day have put so much stress on the possession of gold and silver bullion? How does the outlook of this passage assume a world of scarce goods rather than one in which economies might grow through the production of new kinds of products?*

The ordinary means therefore to increase our wealth and treasure is by Forraign Trade wherein wee must ever observe this rule; to sell more to strangers yearly than wee consume of theirs in value. For suppose that when this Kingdom is plentifully served with the Cloth, Lead, Tinn, Iron, Fish and other native commodities, we doe yearly export the overplus to forraign countries to the value of twenty two hundred thousand pounds; by which means we are enabled beyond the Seas to buy and bring in forraign wares for our use and Consumptions, to the value of twenty hundred thousand pounds; By this order duly kept in our trading, we may rest assured that the Kingdom shall be enriched yearly two hundred thousand pounds, which must be brought to us in so much Treasure; because that part of our stock which is not returned to us in wares must necessarily be brought home in treasure [i.e., gold or silver bullion].

Thomas Mun, England's Treasure by Forraign Trade, *as quoted in Charles Wilson,* England's Apprenticeship, 1603–1763 *(London: Longman, 1965), p. 60.*

Colonists of different countries wished to trade with each other. English colonists could buy sugar more cheaply from the French West Indies than from English suppliers. The traders and merchants of one nation always hoped to break the monopoly of another. For all these reasons the eighteenth century became the "golden age of smugglers."[1] The governments could not control the activities of all their subjects. Clashes among colonists could and did bring about conflict between governments.

FRENCH–BRITISH RIVALRY Major flash points existed between France and Britain in North America. Their colonists quarreled endlessly with each other. Both groups of settlers coveted the lower Saint Lawrence River valley, upper New England, and later the Ohio River valley. There were other rivalries over fishing rights, fur trade, and alliances with Native American tribes.

India was another area of Anglo-French rivalry. On the Indian subcontinent, both France and Britain traded through privileged, chartered companies that enjoyed a legal monopoly. The East India Company was the English institution; the French equivalent was the *Compagnie des Indes.* The trade of India and Asia figured only marginally in the economics of empire. Nevertheless, enterprising Europeans always hoped to develop profitable commerce with India. Others regarded India as a springboard into the even larger potential market of China. The original European footholds in India were trading posts called *factories.* They existed

[1]*Walter Dorn,* Competition for Empire, 1740–1763 *(New York: Harper, 1940), p. 266.*

through privileges granted by various Indian governments.

Two circumstances in the middle of the eighteenth century changed this situation in India. First, the indigenous administration and government of several Indian states had decayed. Second, Joseph Dupleix (1697–1763) for the French and Robert Clive (1725–1774) for the British saw this developing power vacuum as opportunities for expanding the control of their respective companies. To maintain their own security and to expand their privileges, each of the two companies began in effect to take over the government of some regions. Each group of Europeans hoped to checkmate the other.

The Spanish Colonial System

Spanish control of its American empire involved both a system of government and one of monopolistic trade regulation. Both were more rigid in appearance than in practice. Actual government was often informal, and the trade monopoly was frequently breached.

COLONIAL GOVERNMENT Because Queen Isabella of Castile (r. 1474–1504) had commissioned Columbus, the technical legal link between the New World and Spain was the crown of Castile. Its powers both at home and in America were subject to few limitations. The Castilian monarch assigned the government of America to the Council of the Indies, which, with the monarch, nominated the viceroys of New Spain (Mexico) and Peru. These viceroys served as the chief executives in the New World and carried out the laws promulgated by the Council of the Indies.

Each of the viceroyalties was divided into several subordinate judicial councils, known as *audiencias*. There was also a variety of local officers, the most important of which were the *corregidores*, who presided over municipal councils. All of these offices provided the monarchy with a vast array of patronage, usually bestowed on persons born in Spain. Virtually all power flowed from the top of this political structure downward; in effect, local initiative or self-government scarcely existed.

TRADE REGULATION The colonial political structures functioned largely to support Spanish commercial self-interest. The *Casa de Contrat-ación* (House of Trade) in Seville regulated all trade with the New World. Cadiz was the only port authorized for use in the American trade. The Casa de Contratación was the most influential institution of the Spanish Empire. Its members worked closely with the *Consulado* (Merchant Guild) of Seville and other groups involved with the American commerce in Cadiz.

A complicated system of trade and bullion fleets administered from Seville was the key for maintaining the trade monopoly. Each year, a fleet of commercial vessels (the *flota*) controlled by Seville merchants, escorted by warships, carried merchandise from Spain to a few specified ports in America. These included Portobello, Veracruz, and Cartagena. There were no authorized ports on the Pacific Coast. Areas far to the south, such as Buenos Aires on the Rio de la Plata, received goods only after the shipments had been unloaded at one of the authorized ports. After selling their wares, the ships were loaded with silver and gold bullion, usually wintered in heavily fortified Caribbean ports, and

The fortress of El Morro in the harbor of San Juan, Puerto Rico. This massive citadel protected the Spanish treasure fleets that carried gold and silver each year to Spain from the mines of Mexico and Peru. [Comstock]

Visitors Describe the Portobello Fair

The Spanish tried to restrict all trade within their Latin American empire to a few designated ports. Each year a fair was held in certain of these ports. The most famous of these was Portobello on the Isthmus of Panama. In the 1730s, two visitors saw the event and described it. This fair was the chief means of facilitating trade between the western coast of South America and Spain.

◆ *What products were sold at this fair? How might the actual sale of gold bullion at this fair have led to attitudes such as were seen in the earlier document by Thomas Mun? How does this passage illustrate the inefficiency of monopoly trade in the Spanish empire and the many chances for smuggling?*

The town of Portobello, so thinly inhabited, by reason of its noxious air, the scarcity of provisions, and the soil, becomes, at the time of the [Spanish] galleons one of the most populous places in all South America. . . .

The ships are no sooner moored in the harbour, than the first work is, to erect, in the square, a tent made of the ship's sails, for receiving its cargo; at which the proprietors of the goods are present, in order to find their bales, by the marks which distinguish them. These bales are drawn on sledges, to their respective places by the crew of every ship, and the money given them is proportionally divided.

Whilst the seamen and European traders are thus employed, the land is covered with droves of mules from Panama, each drove consisting of above an hundred, loaded with chests of gold and silver, on account of the merchants of Peru. Some unload them at the exchange, others in the middle of the square; yet, amidst the hurry and confusion of such crowds, no theft, loss, or disturbance, is ever known. He who has seen this place during the tiempo muerto, or dead time, solitary, poor, and a perpetual silence reigning everywhere; the harbour quite empty, and every place wearing a melancholy aspect; must be filled with astonishment at the sudden change, to see the bustling multitudes, every

house crowded, the square and streets encumbered with bales and chests of gold and silver of all kinds; the harbour full of ships and vessels, some bringing by the way of Rio de Chape the goods of Peru, such as cacao, quinquina, or Jesuit's bark, Vicuña wool, and bezoar stones; others coming from Carthagena, loaded with provisions; and thus a spot, at all times detested for its deleterious qualities, becomes the staple of the riches of the old and new world, and the scene of one of the most considerable branches of commerce in the whole earth.

The ships being unloaded, and the merchants of Peru, together with the president of Panama, arrived, the fair comes under deliberation. And for this purpose the deputies of the several parties repair on board the commodore of the galleons, where, in the presence of the commodore, and the president of Panama, . . . the prices of the several kinds of merchandizes are settled. . . . The purchases and sales, as likewise the exchanges of money, are transacted by brokers, both from Spain and Peru. After this, every one begins to dispose of his goods; the Spanish brokers embarking their chests of money, and those of Peru sending away the goods they have purchased, in vessels called chatas and bongos, up the river Chagres. And thus the fair of Portobello ends.

George Juan and Antonio de Ulloa, A Voyage to South America, Vol. 1 *(London, 1772), pp. 103–110, as quoted in Benjamin Keen, ed.,* Readings in Latin-American Civilization 1492 to the Present *(New York: Houghton Mifflin, 1955), pp. 107–108.*

then sailed back to Spain. The flota system always worked imperfectly, but trade outside it was illegal. Regulations prohibited the Spanish colonists within the American empire from establishing direct trade with each other and from building their own shipping and commercial industry. Foreign merchants were also forbidden to breach the Spanish monopoly.

COLONIAL REFORM UNDER THE SPANISH BOURBON MONARCHS A crucial change occurred in the Spanish colonial system in the early eighteenth century. The War of the Spanish Succession (1701–1714) and the Treaty of Utrecht (1713) replaced the Spanish Habsburgs with the Bourbons of France on the Spanish throne. Philip V (r. 1700–1746) and his successors tried to use French administrative skills to reassert the imperial trade monopoly, which had decayed under the last Spanish Habsburgs, and thus to improve the domestic economy and revive Spanish power in European affairs.

Under Philip V, Spanish coastal patrol vessels tried to suppress smuggling in American waters. An incident arising from this policy (to be discussed later in this chapter) led to war with England in 1739. In 1739 Philip established the viceroyalty of New Granada in the area that today includes Venezuela, Colombia, and Ecuador. The goal was to increase direct royal government in the area.

During the reign of Ferdinand VI (r. 1746–1759), the great mid-century wars exposed the vulnerability of the empire to naval attack and economic penetration. As an ally of France, Spain emerged as one of the defeated powers in 1763. Government circles became convinced that further changes in the colonial system had to be undertaken.

Charles III (r. 1759–1788), the most important of the royal imperial reformers, attempted to reassert Spain's control of the empire. Like his two Bourbon predecessors, Charles III emphasized royal ministers rather than councils. Thus, the role of both the Council of the Indies and the Casa de Contratación diminished. After 1765 Charles abolished the monopolies of Seville and Cadiz and permitted other Spanish cities to trade with America. He also opened more South American and Caribbean ports to trade and authorized some commerce between Spanish ports in America. In 1776 he organized a fourth viceroyalty in the region of Rio de la Plata, which included much of present-day Argentina, Uruguay, Paraguay, and Bolivia (see Map 17-1).

While relaxing Spanish trade with and in America, Charles III attempted to increase the efficiency of tax collection and to end bureaucratic corruption. To achieve those ends, he introduced the institution of the *intendent* into the Spanish Empire. These loyal, royal bureaucrats were patterned on the French *intendants* made so famous and effective as agents of the absolutism of Louis XIV.

These late-eighteenth-century Bourbon reforms did stimulate the imperial economy. Trade expanded and became more varied. These reforms, however, also brought the empire more fully under direct Spanish control. Many *peninsulares* (persons born in Spain) entered the New World to fill new posts. Expanding trade brought more Spanish merchants to Latin America. The economy remained export oriented, and economic life was still organized to benefit Spain. As a result of these policies, the *creoles* (persons of European descent born in the Spanish colonies) came to feel that they were second-class subjects. In time their resentment would provide a major source of the discontent leading to the wars of independence in the early nineteenth century. The imperial policies of Charles III were the Spanish equivalent of the new colonial measures undertaken by the British government in 1763, which led to the American Revolution.

Black African Slavery, the Plantation System, and the Atlantic Economy

The heart of the eighteenth-century colonial rivalry lay in the West Indies. These islands, close to the American continents, were the jewels of empire. The West Indies raised tobacco, cotton, indigo, coffee, and, above all, sugar, for which there existed strong markets in Europe. These commodities were becoming part of daily life especially in western Europe; they represented one aspect of those major changes in consumption that marked eighteenth-century European culture. Sugar in particular had become a staple rather than a luxury. It was

MAP 17-1 VICEROYALTIES IN LATIN AMERICA IN 1780 *The late-eighteenth century viceroy-alties in Latin America display the effort of the Spanish Bourbon monarchy to establish more direct control of the continent. They sought this control through the introduction of more royal officials and by establishing more governmental districts.*

used in coffee, tea, and cocoa, for making candy and preserving fruits, and in the brewing industry. There seemed no limit to its uses, and no limit to consumer demand for it.

Slavery was basic to the economies of the West Indies, the Spanish and Portuguese settlements in South America, and the British colonies on the South Atlantic seaboard of North America. The major source of slaves was black West Africans.

Slavery had existed in various parts of Europe since ancient times. Before the eighteenth century, little or no moral or religious stigma attached to slave owning or slave trading. It had had a continuous existence in the Mediterranean world, where only the sources of slaves changed over the centuries. After the conquest of Constantinople in the mid-fifteenth century, the Ottoman Empire forbade the exportation of white slaves from regions under its control. The Portuguese had then begun to import African slaves into the Iberian Peninsula from the Canary Islands and West Africa. Black slaves from Africa were also not uncommon in other parts of the Mediterranean, and a few found their way into northern Europe. There they might be used as personal servants or displayed because of the novelty of their color in the courts of royalty or homes of the wealthy.

THE PLANTATION SYSTEM Once the New World was discovered and settled, the conquering Spanish and Portuguese faced a severe shortage of labor. They and most of the French and English settlers who came later had no intention of undertaking manual work themselves. At first, they used Native Americans as laborers, but during the sixteenth and seventeenth centuries, disease killed hundreds of thousands of Native Americans. As a result labor soon became scarce. The Spanish and Portuguese then turned to the labor of imported African slaves. By the late sixteenth century, in the islands of the West Indies and the major cities of South America, black slaves equaled or surpassed the numbers of white European settlers.

On much of the South American continent dominated by Spain, the numbers of slaves declined during the late seventeenth century, and the institution became less fundamental there than elsewhere. Slavery continued to pros-

per, however, in Brazil and in the Caribbean. Later, slavery spread into the British North American colonies. The first slaves were brought to Jamestown in 1619. They soon became a fundamental institution in North American colonial life, where at one time or another slaves were held in all the colonies.

One of the forces that led to the spread of slavery in Brazil and the West Indies was the cultivation of sugar. Small landowners could not cultivate sugar because it required a large investment in land and equipment. Only slave labor could provide enough workers for the extremely large and profitable sugar plantations. By the close of the seventeenth century, the Caribbean islands were the world center for the production of sugar and the chief supplier for the ever growing consumer demand for the product. As the production of sugar expanded, so also did the demand for slaves and their consequent importation. By 1725, it has been estimated, almost 90 percent of the population of Jamaica was black slaves. The situation was similar throughout the West Indies. There and elsewhere, in Brazil and the southern British colonies, prosperity and slavery went hand in hand. The wealthiest and most prized of the colonies were those that raised staples such as sugar, rice, tobacco, or cotton by slave labor. In Brazil, slave labor sustained first sugar production and then late in the eighteenth century gold mining and coffee cultivation.

The plantation to which the slaves eventually arrived was always in a more or less isolated rural setting, but its products rapidly entered a larger integrated transatlantic economy. The plantation might raise food for its owners and their slaves, but the main production, whether sugar, tobacco, or later cotton and coffee, was intended for export. The production of the plantations was thus drawn into the world of transatlantic trade, manufacture, and consumption. In turn, the plantation owners imported virtually all the finished or manufactured goods used or consumed on the plantation from Europe.

Colonial trade followed roughly a geographic triangle. European goods were carried to Africa to be exchanged for slaves, who were then taken to the West Indies, where they were traded for sugar and other tropical products, which were then shipped to Europe. Not all ships covered all three legs of the triangle. Another major trade pattern existed between New England and the West Indies with New England fish or ship stores being traded for sugar.

Slavery and the slave trade touched most of the economy of the transatlantic world. The prosperity of cities such as Newport, Rhode Island; Liverpool, England; and Nantes, France, rested almost entirely on the slave trade. Cities in the British North American colonies profited from slavery sometimes by trading in slaves but more often by supplying other goods to the West Indian market. It was not the New World planters and slave traders alone, however, who were involved in the trade. Slavery touched most of the economy of the transatlantic world. All the shippers who handled cotton, tobacco, and sugar depended on slavery, though they might not have had direct contact with the institution, as did all the manufacturers and merchants who produced the finished products for the consumer market.

SLAVE EXPERIENCE   The Spanish, Portuguese, Dutch, French, and English traders who participated in the slave trade forcibly transported several million (perhaps more than nine million) Africans to the New World. During the first four centuries of settlement, far more black slaves came involuntarily to the New World than did free European settlers. The conditions of their passage across the Atlantic were wretched. Quarters were unspeakably cramped; food was bad; disease was rampant. Many Africans died on the crossing. Yet the trade persisted because of the demand for labor in America, where it was cheaper to import new slaves than it was to rear slave children to adulthood. The mortality rate of slaves in the West Indies and elsewhere was very high. More and more new Africans had to be bought into slavery simply to keep a steady supply.

The life conditions of plantation slaves differed from colony to colony. Black slaves living in Portuguese areas had the fewest legal protections. In the Spanish colonies, the Church

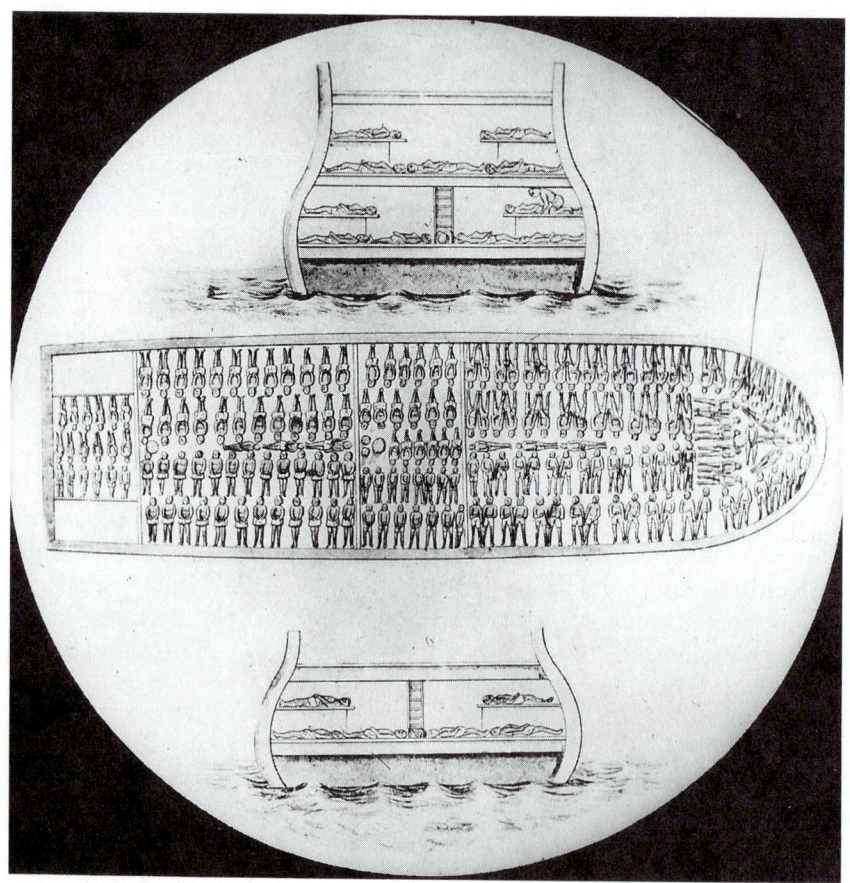

African captives imported into the Americas were carried across the Atlantic in unspeakable conditions on ships designed to maximize the number of human beings carried as cargo. This cross-section illustrates how the human cargo was arranged. The document on page 627 describes the Atlantic passage. [Bildarchiv Preussischer Kulturbesitz]

A Slave Trader Describes the Atlantic Passage

During 1693 and 1694, Captain Thomas Phillips carried slaves from Africa to Barbados on the ship Hannibal. The financial backer of the voyage was the Royal African Company of London, which held an English crown monopoly on slave trading. Phillips sailed to the west coast of Africa, where he purchased the Africans who were sold into slavery by an African king. Then he set sail westward.

♦ *Who are the various people described in this document who in one way or another were involved in or profited from the slave trade? What dangers did the Africans face on the voyage? What contemporary attitudes could have led this ship captain to treat and think of his human cargo simply as goods to be transported? What are the grounds of his self-pity for the difficulties he met?*

Having bought my complement of 700 slaves, 480 men and 220 women, and finish'd all my business at Whidaw [on the Gold Coast of Africa], I took my leave of the old king and his cappasheirs [attendants], and parted, with many affectionate expressions on both sides, being forced to promise him that I would return again the next year, with several things he desired me to bring from England. . . . I set sail the 27th of July in the morning, accompany'd with the East-India Merchant, who had bought 650 slaves, for the Island of St. Thomas . . . from which we took our departure on August 25th and set sail for Barbadoes.

We spent in our passage from St. Thomas to Barbadoes two months eleven days, from the 25th of August to the 4th of November following: in which time there happened such sickness and mortality among my poor men and Negroes. Of the first we buried 14, and of the last 320, which was a great detriment to our voyage, the Royal African Company losing ten pounds by every slave that died, and the owners of the ship ten pounds ten shillings, being the freight agreed on to be paid by the charter-party for every Negro delivered alive ashore to the African Company's agents at Barbadoes. . . . The loss in all amounted to near 6500 pounds sterling.

The distemper which my men as well as the blacks mostly died of was the white flux, which was so violent and inveterate that no medicine would in the least check it, so that when any of our men were seized with it, we esteemed him a dead man, as he generally proved. . . .

The Negroes are so incident to the small-pox that few ships that carry them escape without it, and sometimes it makes vast havock and destruction among them. But tho' we had 100 at a time sick of it, and that it went thro' the ship, yet we lost not above a dozen by it. All the assistance we gave the diseased was only as much water as they desir'd to drink, and some palm-oil to annoint their sores, and they would generally recover without any other helps but what kind nature gave them. . . .

But what the small pox spar'd, the flux swept off, to our great regret, after all our pains and care to give them their messes in due order and season, keeping their lodgings as clean and sweet as possible, and enduring so much misery and stench so long among a parcel of creatures nastier than swine, and after all our expectations to be defeated by their mortality. . . .

No gold-finders can endure so much noisome slavery as they do who carry Negroes; for those have some respite and satisfaction, but we endure twice the misery; and yet by their mortality our voyages are ruin'd, and we pine and fret ourselves to death, and take so much pains to so little purpose.

Thomas Phillips, "Journal," A Collection of Voyages and Travels, Vol. VI, *ed. by Awnsham and John Churchill (London, 1746), as quoted in Thomas Howard, ed.,* Black Voyage: Eyewitness Accounts of the Atlantic Slave Trade *(Boston: Little, Brown and Company, 1971), pp. 85–87.*

TO BE SOLD on board the Ship *Bance-Ifland*, on tuefday the 6th of *May* next, at *Afhley-Ferry*; a choice cargo of about 250 fine healthy NEGROES, juft arrived from the Windward & Rice Coaft. —The utmoft care has already been taken, and fhall be continued, to keep them free from the leaft danger of being infected with the SMALL-POX, no boat having been on board, and all other communication with people from *Charles-Town* prevented.

Auftin, Laurens, & Appleby.

N. B. Full one Half of the above Negroes have had the SMALL-POX in their own Country.

Those Africans who survived the voyage across the Atlantic were immediately sold into slavery in the Americas. This slave-auction notice relates to a group of slaves whose ship had stopped at Charleston, South Carolina, and then landed elsewhere in the region to auction its human cargo. Notice the concern to assure potential buyers that the slaves were healthy. [The Bettmann Archive]

The daily life of most slaves during these centuries was one of hard agricultural labor, poor diet, and inadequate housing. Slave families could be separated by the owner during his life or sold separately after his death. Their welfare and their lives were sacrificed to the continuing expansion of the sugar, rice, and tobacco plantations that made their owners wealthy and that produced goods for European consumers. Scholars have sometimes concluded that slaves in one area lived better than in another. Today, it is generally accepted that all the slaves in plantation societies led exposed and difficult lives with little variation among them.

The African slaves who were transported to the Americas, were, like the Native Americans, converted to Christianity. In the Spanish, French, and Portuguese domains, they became Roman Catholics, and in the English colonies they became Protestants of one denomination or another. In either case, although some African practices survived in muted forms, these practices were gradually separated from African religious belief. Although slaves did manage to mix Christianity with their previous African religions, their conversion to Christianity was nonetheless another example, like that of the Native Americans, of the crushing of a set of non-European cultural values in the context of the New World economies and social structures.

The European settlers in the Americas and the slave traders also carried with them prejudices against black Africans. Many Europeans considered Africans to be savages or less than civilized. Still others looked down upon them simply because they were slaves. Both Christians and Muslims had shared these attitudes in the Mediterranean world, where European slavery had for so long existed. Furthermore, many European languages and cultures attached negative connotations to the idea and image of blackness. In virtually all these plantation societies, race was an important element in keeping black slaves in a position of marked subservience. Although racial thinking in regard to slavery became important primarily in the nineteenth century, the fact of slaves being differentiated from the rest of the population by race as well as by their being chattel property was fundamental to the system. All of these factors formed the racial prejudice that

attempted to provide some protection for black slaves but devoted more effort toward protecting the Native Americans. Slave codes were developed in the British and the French colonies during the seventeenth century, but they provided only the most limited protection. Virtually all slaveowners feared a slave revolt, and legislation and other regulations were intended to prevent one. All slave laws favored the master rather than the slave. Slave masters were permitted to whip slaves and inflict other exceedingly harsh corporal punishment. Furthermore, slaves were often forbidden to gather in large groups lest they plan a revolt. In most of these slave societies, the marriages of slaves were not recognized by law. The children of slaves continued to be slaves and were owned by the owner of their parents.

continues to plague society in the former slave-owning regions.

The plantations that stretched from the middle Atlantic colonies of North America through the West Indies and into Brazil constituted a vast corridor of slave societies in which social and economic subordination was based on both involuntary servitude and race. It had not existed before the European discovery and exploitation of the resources of the Americas. This kind of society in its extent and totality of dependence on slave labor and racial differences was novel in both European and world history. As already noted, its social and economic influence touched not only the plantation societies themselves but West Africa, western Europe, and New England. It existed from the sixteenth century through the second half of the nineteenth century, when slave emancipation had been completed through the British effort to outlaw the slave trade during the first half of the nineteenth century, the Latin American Wars of Independence, the Emancipation Proclamation of 1863 in the United States, and the Brazilian emancipation of 1888. To the present day, every society where this form of plantation slavery once existed still contends with the long-term effects of that institution.

Slaves in Brazil washing diamond ore to isolate gems. Notice the ratio of white overseers with whips to black slaves. [Bildarchiv Preussischer Kulturbesitz]

Mid-Eighteenth-Century Wars

The War of Jenkins's Ear

In the middle of the eighteenth century, the West Indies had become a hotbed of trade rivalry. Spain attempted to tighten its monopoly, and English smugglers, shippers, and pirates attempted to pierce it. Matters came to a climax in the late 1730s.

The Treaty of Utrecht (1713) gave two special privileges to Great Britain in the Spanish Empire. The British received a thirty-year *asiento*, or contract, to furnish slaves to the Spanish. Britain also gained the right to send one ship each year to the trading fair at Portobello, a major Caribbean seaport on the Panamanian coast. These two privileges allowed British traders and smugglers potential inroads into the Spanish market. Little but friction arose from these rights. During the night offshore, British

ships often resupplied the annual legal Portobello ship with additional goods as it lay in port. Much to the chagrin of the British, the Spanish government took its own alleged trading monopoly seriously and maintained coastal patrols, which boarded and searched English vessels to look for contraband.

In 1731, during one such boarding operation, there was a fight, and the Spaniards cut off the ear of an English captain named Robert Jenkins. Thereafter he carried about his severed ear preserved in a jar of brandy. This incident was of little importance until 1738, when Jenkins appeared before the British Parliament, reportedly brandishing his ear as an example of Spanish atrocities to British merchants in the West Indies. The British merchant and West Indies interests put great pressure on Parliament to relieve Spanish intervention in their trade. Sir Robert Walpole (1676–1745), the British prime minister, could not resist these pressures. In late 1739, Great Britain went to war with Spain. This war might have been a relatively minor incident, but because of developments in continental European politics, it became the opening encounter to a series of European wars fought across the world until 1815.

The War of the Austrian Succession (1740–1748)

In December 1740, after being king of Prussia for less than seven months, Frederick II seized the Austrian province of Silesia in eastern Germany. The invasion shattered the provisions

Maria Theresa of Austria provided the leadership that saved the Habsburg Empire from possible disintegration after the Prussian invasion of Silesia in 1740. [Kunsthistorisches Museum, Vienna]

of the Pragmatic Sanction (see Chapter 15) and upset the continental balance of power as established by the Treaty of Utrecht. The young king of Prussia had treated the House of Habsburg simply as another German state rather than as the leading power in the region. Silesia itself rounded out Prussia's possessions, and Frederick was determined to keep his ill-gotten prize.

MARIA THERESA PRESERVES THE HABSBURG EMPIRE The Prussian seizure of Silesia could have marked the opening of a general hunting season on Habsburg holdings and the beginning of revolts by Habsburg subjects. Instead it led to new political allegiances. Maria Theresa's great achievement was not the reconquest of Silesia, which eluded her, but the preservation of the Habsburg Empire as a major political power.

Maria Theresa was then only twenty-three and had succeeded to the Habsburg realms only two months before the invasion. She won loyalty and support from her various subjects not merely through her heroism but more specifically by granting new privileges to the nobility. Most significant, the empress recognized Hungary as the most important of her crowns and promised the Magyars considerable local autonomy. She thus preserved the Habsburg state, but at considerable cost to the power of the central monarchy.

Hungary would continue to be, as it had been in the past, a particularly troublesome area in the Habsburg Empire. When the monarchy enjoyed periods of strength and security, guarantees made to Hungary could be ignored. At times of weakness, or when the Magyars could stir enough opposition, the monarchy promised new concessions.

FRANCE DRAWS GREAT BRITAIN INTO THE WAR The war over the Austrian succession and the British–Spanish commercial conflict could have remained separate disputes. What quickly united them was the role of France. Just as British merchant interests had pushed Sir Robert Walpole into war, a group of aggressive court aristocrats compelled the elderly Cardinal Fleury (1653–1743), first minister of Louis XV, to abandon his planned naval attack on British trade and instead to support the Prussian aggression against Austria, the traditional enemy of France. This was among the more fateful decisions in French history.

In the first place, aid to Prussia consolidated a new and powerful state in Germany. That new power could, and indeed later did, endanger France. Second, the French move against Austria brought Great Britain into the Continental war, as Britain sought to assure that the Low Countries remained in the friendly hands of Austria, not France. In 1744 the British–French conflict expanded beyond the Continent, as France decided to support Spain against Britain

---

Maria Theresa Agrees to Appoint Hungarian Councillors

Maintaining the loyalty of Hungary was always one of the chief difficulties of the Habsburgs. Maria Theresa's coronation as Queen of Hungary occurred in 1741 shortly after Frederick the Great's invasion of Silesia; therefore, she especially needed Hungarian support. Toward the end of the ceremonies, there occurred a famous scene in which the Hungarian nobles pledged their loyalty to the young queen as she stood before them holding her infant son. Maria Theresa, however, had paid a high price for this loyalty and the continuation of stable Habsburg rule in Hungary. She had agreed to a series of laws that convinced the Hungarians that they would be secure under her rule and be able largely to direct their own affairs. These agreements were typical of the kind of bargaining that Habsburg monarchs had to engage in with their various realms.

◆ *What are the specific goals of these regulations in regard to Hungarian participation in the government of Maria Theresa? To what extent do these regulations both assure Hungarian influence and promise royal patronage to Hungarians? There is an adage that all politics is local politics. How might the concerns of the Hungarians be said to reflect that outlook?*

Law XI of the agreement of 1741 included the following provisions.

On Hungarian affairs and business: that these are to be conducted through Hungarians.

1. Her Majesty has further graciously resolved that She will conduct, and have conducted, the affairs and business of the country, both inside and outside the country, through Hungarians.

2. Consequently, also in Her august Court, in matters dependent on the supreme power enjoyed by Her, She will, in accordance with Her august judgment and royal prerogative, make use of the assistance and counsel of Her loyal Hungarian Councillors.

4. And She will deign to take men of Hungarian nationality into the Ministry of State itself.

5. And inside the Kingdom [of Hungary] She will in the future also duly conduct all administration and matters concerning the public affairs of the same Kingdom in the manner determined by the laws of the land, through the channel of the Vice-Regal Council. . . .

6. And in cases of future vacancies in the said Vice-Regal Council She will appoint suitable landed Hungarians from all parts of the Kingdom, men acquainted with the business and constitution of the Kingdom.

C. A. Macartney, ed., The Habsburg and Hohenzollern Dynasties in the Seventeenth and Eighteenth Centuries *(New York: Walker and Company, 1970), pp. 135–136.*

The Battle of Fontenoy was fought in 1745 during the War of the Austrian Succession. There the French under Maréchal de Saxe defeated an English army that was defending the territory of Maria Theresa in the Austrian Netherlands. This painting of the battle is by Pierre Lenfant (1704–1787). [Giraudon/Art Resource, N.Y.]

in the New World. As a result, French military and economic resources were badly divided. France could not bring sufficient strength to the colonial struggle. Having chosen to continue the old struggle with Austria, France lost the struggle for the future against Great Britain. The war ended in stalemate in 1748 with the Treaty of Aix-la-Chapelle. Prussia retained Silesia, and Spain renewed the *asiento* agreement with Great Britain. Most observers thought the treaty was a truce rather than a permanent peace.

The "Diplomatic Revolution" of 1756

Before the rivalries again erupted into war, a dramatic shift of alliances took place. In 1756 Prussia and Great Britain signed the Convention of Westminster, a defensive alliance aimed at preventing the entry of foreign troops into the Germanies. Frederick II feared invasions by both Russia and France. The convention meant that Great Britain, the ally of Austria since the wars of Louis XIV, had now

joined forces with Austria's major eighteenth-century enemy.

Maria Theresa was despondent over this development. It delighted her foreign minister, Prince Wenzel Anton Kaunitz (1711–1794), however. He had long hoped for an alliance with France to help dismember Prussia. The Convention of Westminster made this alliance, unthinkable a few years earlier, possible. France was agreeable because Frederick had not consulted it before coming to his understanding with Britain. So, later in 1756, France and Austria signed a defensive alliance. Kaunitz had succeeded in completely reversing the direction that French foreign policy had followed since the sixteenth century. France would now fight to restore Austrian supremacy in central Europe.

The Seven Years' War (1756–1763)

Although the Treaty of Aix-la-Chapelle had brought peace in Europe, France and Great Britain continued to struggle unofficially on the colonial front. There were continual clashes between their settlers in the Ohio River valley and in upper New England. These were the prelude to what is known in American history as the French and Indian War. Once again, however, Frederick II precipitated a European war that extended into a colonial theater.

FREDERICK THE GREAT OPENS HOSTILITIES In August 1756, Frederick II opened what would become the Seven Years' War by invading Saxony. Frederick considered this to be a pre-emptive strike against a conspiracy by Saxony, Austria, and France to destroy Prussian power. He regarded this invasion as a continuation of the defensive strategy of the Convention of Westminster. The invasion itself, however, created the very destructive alliance that Frederick feared. In the spring of 1757, France and Austria made a new alliance dedicated to the destruction of Prussia. They were eventually joined by Sweden, Russia, and many of the smaller German states.

Frederick the Great Rallies His Officers for Battle

In December 1757, Frederick the Great of Prussia addressed his officers before the Battle of Leuthen with the Austrians. Although he had recently defeated the French at Rossbach, he remained in a difficult position with Berlin in the hands of enemy forces.

✦ *How does Frederick appeal to patriotism and also to fear of humiliation on the part of his officers? How does he anticipate overcoming his numerical disadvantage? What evidence does this document provide about the kind of obedience and discipline Frederick expected?*

You are aware, gentlemen, that Prince Karl of Lorraine has succeeded in taking Schweidnitz, defeating the duke of Bevern and making himself master of Breslau, while I was engaged in checking the advance of the French and imperial forces. A part of Schleswig, my capital, and all the military stores it contained, are lost, and I should feel myself in dire straits indeed if it were not for my unbounded confidence in your courage, your constancy, and your love for the fatherland, which you have proved to me on so many occasions in the past.

. . . I should feel that I had accomplished nothing if Austria were left in possession of Schleswig. Let me tell you that I propose, in defiance of all the rule of the art of war, to attack the army of Prince Karl, three times as large as ours, wherever I find it. It is here no question of the numbers of the enemy nor of the importance of the positions they have occupied; all this I hope to overcome by the devotion of my troops and the careful carry-ing out of my plans. I must take this step or all will be lost; we must defeat the enemy, else we shall all lie buried under his batteries. So I believe—so I shall act.

Communicate my decision to all the officers of the army; prepare the common soldier for the exertions that are to come, and tell him that I feel justified in expecting unquestioning obedience from him. Remember that you are Prussians and you cannot show yourselves unworthy of that distinction.

. . . The regiment of cavalry that does not immediately on the receipt of orders throw itself upon the enemy I will have unmounted immediately after the battle and make it a garrison regiment. The battalion of infantry that even begins to hesitate, no matter what the danger may be, shall lose its flags and its swords and have the gold lace stripped from its uniforms.

And now, gentlemen, farewell; erelong we shall either have defeated the enemy or we shall see each other no more.

James Harvey Robinson, ed., Readings in European History, Vol. 2 *(New York: Ginn & Company, 1906), pp. 323–324.*

William Pitt the Elder guided Great Britain to a stunning victory in the Seven Years' War. [National Portrait Gallery, London]

Two factors in addition to Frederick's stubborn leadership (it was after this war that he came to be called Frederick the Great) saved Prussia. First, Britain furnished considerable financial aid. Second, in 1762 Empress Elizabeth of Russia died. Her successor was Tsar Peter III (he was murdered the same year), whose admiration for Frederick was boundless. He immediately made peace with Prussia, thus relieving Frederick of one enemy and allowing him to hold off Austria and France. The Treaty of Hubertusburg of 1763 ended the continental conflict with no significant changes in prewar borders. Silesia remained Prussian, and Prussia clearly stood among the ranks of the great powers.

WILLIAM PITT'S STRATEGY FOR WINNING NORTH AMERICA The survival of Prussia was less impressive to the rest of Europe than the victories of Great Britain in every theater of conflict. The architect of these victories was William Pitt the Elder (1708–1778). Pitt was a person of colossal ego and administrative genius who had grown up in a commercial family. Although he had previously criticized British involvement with the continent, once he became secretary of state in charge of the war in 1757, he reversed himself and pumped huge financial subsidies to Frederick the Great. He regarded the German conflict as a way to divert French resources and attention from the colonial struggle. He later boasted of having won America on the plains of Germany.

North America was the center of Pitt's real concern. Put quite simply, he wanted all of North America east of the Mississippi for Great Britain, and that was exactly what he won. He sent more than 40,000 regular English and colonial troops against the French in Canada. Never had so many soldiers been devoted to a field of colonial warfare. He achieved unprecedented cooperation with the American colonies, whose leaders realized that they might finally defeat their French neighbors.

The French government was unwilling and unable to direct similar resources against the English in America. Their military administration was corrupt; the military and political command in Canada were divided; and France could not adequately provision its North American forces. In September 1759, on the Plains of Abraham overlooking the valley of the Saint Lawrence River at Quebec City, the British army under General James Wolfe defeated the French under Lieutenant General Louis Joseph de Montcalm. The French empire in Canada was ending.

Pitt's colonial vision, however, extended beyond the Saint Lawrence Valley and the Great Lakes Basin. The major islands of the French West Indies fell to British fleets. Income from the sale of captured sugar helped finance the British war effort. British slave interests captured the bulk of the French slave trade. Between 1755 and 1760 the value of the French colonial trade fell by more than 80 percent. In India, the British forces under the command of Robert Clive defeated the French in 1757 at the Battle of Plassey. This victory opened the way for the eventual conquest of Bengal in northeast

India and later of all India by the British East India Company. Never had Great Britain or any other European power experienced such a complete worldwide military victory.

THE TREATY OF PARIS OF 1763 The Treaty of Paris of 1763 reflected somewhat less of a victory than Britain had won on the battlefield. Pitt was no longer in office. George III (r. 1760–1820) and Pitt had quarreled over policy, and the minister had departed. His replacement was the earl of Bute (1713–1792), a favorite of the new monarch. Bute was responsible for the peace settlement. Britain received all of Canada, the Ohio River valley, and the eastern half of the Mississippi River valley. Britain returned Pondicherry and Chandernagore in India and the West Indian sugar islands of Guadeloupe and Martinique to the French.

The Seven Years' War had been a vast conflict. Tens of thousands of soldiers and sailors had been killed or wounded. Major battles had been fought around the globe. At great internal sacrifice, Prussia had permanently wrested Silesia from Austria and had turned the Holy Roman Empire into an empty shell. Habsburg power now depended largely on the Hungarian domains. France, though still having sources of colonial income, was no longer a great colonial power. The Spanish Empire remained largely intact, but the British were still determined to penetrate its markets.

On the Indian subcontinent, the British East India Company was able to continue to impose its own authority on the decaying indigenous governments. The results of that situation would be felt until the middle of the twentieth century. In North America, the British government faced the task of organizing its new territories. From this time until World War II, Great Britain was a world power, not just a European one.

The quarter century of warfare also caused a long series of domestic crises among the European powers. The French defeat convinced many people in that nation of the necessity for political and administrative reform. The financial burdens of the wars had astounded all contemporaries. Every power had to begin to find ways to increase revenues to pay its war debt and to finance its preparation for the next com-

Conflicts of the Mid-Eighteenth Century	
1713	Treaty of Utrecht
1739	Outbreak of War of Jenkins's Ear between England and Spain
1740	War of the Austrian Succession commences
1748	Treaty of Aix-la-Chapelle
1756	Convention of Westminster between England and Prussia
1756	Seven Years' War opens
1757	Battle of Plassey
1759	British forces capture Quebec
1763	Treaty of Hubertusburg
1763	Treaty of Paris

bat. Nowhere did this search for revenue lead to more far-ranging consequences than in the British colonies in North America.

The American Revolution and Europe

The revolt of the British colonies in North America was an event in both transatlantic and European history. It erupted from problems of revenue collection common to all the major powers after the Seven Years' War. The War of the American Revolution was a continuation of the conflict between France and Great Britain. The French support of the Americans deepened the existing financial and administrative difficulties of the French monarchy.

Resistance to the Imperial Search for Revenue

After the Treaty of Paris of 1763, the British government faced two imperial problems. The first was the sheer cost of empire, which the British felt they could no longer carry alone. The national debt had risen considerably, as had domestic taxation. Since the American colonies had been the chief beneficiaries of the conflict, the British felt that it was rational for the colonies henceforth to bear part of the cost of their protection and administration. The second

ministry of George Grenville (1712–1770). The measure attempted to produce more revenue from imports into the colonies by the rigorous collection of what was actually a lower tax. Smugglers who violated the law were to be tried in admiralty courts without juries. The next year, Parliament passed the Stamp Act, which put a tax on legal documents and certain other items such as newspapers. The British considered these taxes legal because the decision to collect them had been approved by Parliament and regarded them as just because the money was to be spent in the colonies.

The Americans responded that they alone through their assemblies had the right to tax themselves and that they were not represented in Parliament. Furthermore, the expenditure in

George III (r. 1760–1820) succeeded to the English throne near the end of the Seven Years' War and presided over policies that led to the revolt and loss of the American colonies. Although he tried to reassert some of the monarchical influence on Britain's politics that had eroded under George I and George II, the first two Hanoverian kings, George III never sought to make himself a tyrant as his critics charged. This portrait is by Benjamin West (1728–1820). [Royal Collection Enterprises]

MAP 17-2 NORTH AMERICA IN 1763 *In the year of the victory over France, the English colonies lay along the Atlantic seaboard. The difficulties of organizing authority over the previous French territory in Canada and west of the Appalachian Mountains would contribute to the coming of the American Revolution.*

problem was the vast expanse of new territory in North America that the British had to organize. This included all the land from the mouth of the Saint Lawrence River to the Mississippi River, with its French settlers and, more importantly, its Native American possessors (see Map 17-2).

The British drive for revenue began in 1764 with the passage of the Sugar Act under the

the colonies of the revenue levied by Parliament did not reassure the colonists. They feared that if colonial government were financed from outside, they would lose control over it. In October 1765, the Stamp Act Congress met in America and drew up a protest to the crown. There was much disorder in the colonies, particularly in Massachusetts, roused by groups known as the

The Stamp Act Congress Addresses George III

In 1765 the Stamp Act Congress met to protest the British imposition of taxes on the colonies. The resolutions of the Congress made it very clear that American leaders believed that Great Britain had no right to impose such taxation.

✦ *What are the rights of English citizens that the Americans claim? How has the Stamp Act violated them? Why do they believe the British Parliament has no right to tax them? Do the colonists believe it possible for themselves to be represented in Parliament?*

The Members of this Congress, sincerely devoted, with the warmest sentiments of affection and duty to His Majesty's person and government . . . and with minds deeply impressed by a sense of the present and impending misfortunes of the British colonies on this continent; having considered as maturely as time will permit, the circumstances of the said colonies, esteem it our indispensable duty to make the following declarations of our humble opinion, respecting the most essential rights and liberties of the colonists, and of the grievances under which they labor, by reason of several late acts of Parliament.

I. That His Majesty's subjects in these colonies, own the same allegiance to the crown of Great Britain, that is owing from his subjects born within the realm, and all due subordination to that august body the Parliament of Great Britain.

II. That His Majesty's liege subjects in these colonies are entitled to all the inherent rights and liberties of his natural born subjects, within the kingdom of Great Britain.

III. That it is inseparably essential to the freedom of a people, and the undoubted right of Englishmen, that no taxes be imposed on them but with their own consent, given personally, or by their representatives.

IV. That the people of these colonies are not, and cannot, be represented in the House of Commons in Great Britain.

V. That the only representatives of the people of these colonies are persons chosen therein by themselves, and that no taxes ever have been, or can be constitutionally imposed on them, but by their respective legislatures.

VI. That all supplies to the crown being free gifts of the people, it is unreasonable and inconsistent with the principles and spirit of the British constitution, for the people of Great Britain to grant to His Majesty the property of the colonists.

VII. That trial by jury, is the inherent and invaluable right of every British subject in these colonies.

VIII. That the late act of Parliament entitled, *An act for granting and supplying certain stamp duties, and other duties, in the British colonies and plantations, in America, etc.* by imposing taxes on the inhabitants of these colonies, and the said act, and several other acts, by extending the jurisdiction of the courts of admiralty beyond its ancient limits, have a manifest tendency to subvert the rights and liberties of the colonists.

Journal of the First Congress of the American Colonies . . . 1765 *(New York, 1845), pp. 27–29, as quoted in Oscar Handlin, ed.,* Readings in American History *(New York: Alfred A. Knopf, 1957), pp. 116–117.*

Sons of Liberty. The colonists agreed to refuse to import British goods. In 1766 Parliament repealed the Stamp Act, but through the Declaratory Act said that it had the power to legislate for the colonies.

The Stamp Act crisis set the pattern for the next ten years. Parliament, under the leadership of a royal minister, would approve revenue or administrative legislation. The Americans would then resist by reasoned argument, economic pressure, and violence. Then the British would repeal the legislation, and the process would begin again. Each time, tempers on both sides became more frayed and positions more irreconcilable. With each clash the Americans more fully developed their own thinking about political liberty.

The Crisis and Independence

In 1767 Charles Townshend (1725–1767), as Chancellor of the Exchequer, the British finance

This view of the "Boston Massacre" of March 5, 1770 by Paul Revere owes more to propaganda than fact. There was no order to fire and the innocent citizens portrayed here were really an angry, violent mob. [New-York Historical Society]

minister, led Parliament to pass a series of revenue acts relating to colonial imports. The colonists again resisted. The ministry sent over its own customs agents to administer the laws. To protect these new officers, the British sent troops to Boston in 1768. The obvious tensions resulted. In March 1770, the Boston Massacre, in which British troops killed five citizens, took place. That same year, Parliament repealed all of the Townshend duties except the one on tea.

In May 1773, Parliament passed a new law relating to the sale of tea by the East India Company. The measure permitted the direct importation of tea into the American colonies. It actually lowered the price of tea while retaining the tax imposed without the colonists' consent. In some cities, the colonists refused to permit the unloading of the tea; in Boston, a shipload of tea was thrown into the harbor.

The British ministry of Lord North (1732–1792) was determined to assert the authority of Parliament over the resistant colonies. During 1774 Parliament passed a series of laws known in American history as the Intolerable Acts. These measures closed the port of Boston, reorganized the government of Massachusetts, allowed troops to be quartered in private homes, and removed the trials of royal customs officials to England. The same year, Parliament approved the Quebec Act for the future administration of Canada. It extended the boundaries of Quebec to include the Ohio River valley. The Americans regarded the Quebec Act as an attempt to prevent the extension of their mode of self-government westward beyond the Appalachian Mountains.

During these years, citizens critical of British policy had established committees of correspondence throughout the colonies. They made the various sections of the eastern seaboard aware of common problems and aided united action. In September 1774, these committees organized the gathering of the First Continental Congress in Philadelphia. This body hoped to persuade Parliament to restore self-government in the colonies and to abandon its attempt at direct supervision of colonial affairs. Conciliation, however, was not forthcoming. By April 1775, the Battles of Lexington and Concord had been fought. In June, the colonists suffered defeat at the Battle of Bunker Hill. Despite that defeat, the colonial assemblies soon began to meet under their own authority rather than under that of the king.

The Second Continental Congress gathered in May 1775. It still sought conciliation with Britain, but the pressure of events led it to begin to conduct the government of the colonies. By August 1775, George III had declared the colonies in rebellion. During the winter, Thomas Paine's (1737–1809) pamphlet *Common Sense* galvanized public opinion in favor of separation from Great Britain. A colonial army and navy were organized. In April 1776, the Continental Congress opened American ports to the trade of all nations. And on July 4, 1776, the Continental Congress adopted the Declaration of Independence. Thereafter, the War of the American Revolution continued until 1781, when the forces of George Washington defeated those of Lord Cornwallis at Yorktown. Early in 1778, however, the war had widened into a European conflict when Benjamin Franklin (1706–1790) persuaded the French government to support the rebellion. In 1779 the Spanish also came to the aid of the colonies. The 1783 Treaty of Paris concluded the conflict, and the thirteen American colonies had established their independence.

American Political Ideas

The political ideas of the American colonists had largely arisen out of the struggle of seventeenth-century English aristocrats and gentry against the absolutism of the Stuart monarchs. The American colonists looked to the English Revolution of 1688 as having established many of their own fundamental political liberties as well as those of the English. The colonists claimed that, through the measures imposed from 1763 to 1776, George III and the British Parliament were attacking those liberties and dissolving the bonds of moral and political allegiance that had formerly united the two peoples. Consequently, the colonists employed a theory that had developed to justify an aristocratic rebellion to support their own popular revolution.

These Whig political ideas, largely derived from the writings of John Locke, were, however, only a part of the English ideological heritage that affected the Americans. Throughout the eighteenth century, they had become familiar with a series of British political writers called the *Commonwealthmen*. These writers held republican political ideas that had their intellectual roots in the most radical thought of the Puritan revolution. During the early eighteenth century, these writers, the most influential of whom were John Trenchard (1662–1723) and Thomas Gordon (d. 1750) in *Cato's Letters* (1720–1723), had relentlessly criticized the government patronage and parliamentary management of Sir Robert Walpole and his successors. They argued that such government was corrupt and that it undermined liberty. They regarded much parliamentary taxation as simply a means of financing political corruption. They also considered standing armies instruments of tyranny. In Great Britain, this republican political tradition had only a marginal impact. The writers

Thomas Paine was the author of Common Sense, *a political pamphlet published early in 1776 that helped galvanize American opinion in favor of independence from Great Britain. [Bildarchiv Preussischer Kulturbesitz]*

were largely ignored because most British subjects regarded themselves as the freest people in the world. Three thousand miles away, however, colonists read these radical books and pamphlets and often accepted them at face value. The policy of Great Britain toward America following the Treaty of Paris of 1763 and certain political events in Britain had made many colonists believe that the worst fears of the Commonwealthmen were coming true. All of these events coincided with the accession of George III to the throne.

Events in Great Britain

George III (r. 1760–1820) believed that a few powerful Whig families and the ministries that they controlled had bullied and dominated his two immediate royal predecessors. George III also believed that he should have ministers of his own choice and that Parliament should function under royal rather than aristocratic management. When William Pitt resigned after a disagreement with George over war policy, the king appointed the earl of Bute as his first minister. In doing so, he ignored the great Whig families that had run the country since 1715. The king sought the aid of politicians whom the Whigs hated. Moreover, he tried to use the same kind of patronage techniques developed by Walpole to achieve royal control of the House of Commons.

Between 1761 and 1770, George tried one minister after another, but each in turn failed to gain enough support from the various factions in the House of Commons. Finally, in 1770 he turned to Lord North, who remained the king's first minister until 1782. The Whig families and other political spokespersons claimed that George III was attempting to impose a tyranny. What they meant was that the king was attempting to curb the power of a particular group of the aristocracy. George III certainly was seeking to restore more royal influence to the government of Great Britain, but he was not attempting to make himself a tyrant.

THE CHALLENGE OF JOHN WILKES Then, in 1763, began the affair of John Wilkes (1725–1797). This London political radical and member of Parliament published a newspaper called *The North Briton.* In issue Number 45 of this paper, Wilkes strongly criticized Lord Bute's handling of the peace negotiations with France. Wilkes was arrested under the authority of a general warrant issued by the secretary of state. He pleaded the privileges of a member of Parliament and was released. The courts also later ruled that the vague kind of general warrant by which he had been arrested was illegal. The House of Commons, however, ruled that issue Number 45 of *The North Briton* constituted libel and expelled Wilkes. He soon fled the country and was outlawed. Throughout these procedures there was widespread support for Wilkes, and many popular demonstrations were held in his cause.

In 1768 Wilkes returned to England and again stood for election to Parliament. He won the election, but the House of Commons, under the influence of George III's friends, refused to seat him. He was elected three more times. After the fourth election, the House of Commons simply ignored the results and seated the government-supported candidate. As had happened earlier in the decade, large, popular, unruly demonstrations of shopkeepers, artisans, and small property owners supported Wilkes. He also received aid from some aristocratic politicians who wished to humiliate George III. Wilkes himself contended during all his troubles that his was the cause of English liberty. "Wilkes and Liberty" became the slogan of all political radicals and many noble opponents of the monarch. Wilkes was finally seated in 1774, after having become the lord mayor of London.

The American colonists closely followed these developments. Events in Britain confirmed their fears about a monarchical and parliamentary conspiracy against liberty. The king, as their Whig friends told them, was behaving like a tyrant. The Wilkes affair displayed the arbitrary power of the monarch, the corruption of the House of Commons, and the contempt of both for popular electors. That same monarch and Parliament were attempting to overturn the traditional relationship of Great Britain to its colonies by imposing parliamentary taxes. The same government had then landed troops in Boston, changed the government of Massachusetts, and undermined the traditional right of jury trial. All of these events fulfilled too exactly the portrait of political tyranny that had developed over the years in the minds of articulate colonists.

MOVEMENT FOR PARLIAMENTARY REFORM

The political influences between America and Britain operated both ways. The colonial demand for no taxation without representation and the criticism of the adequacy of the British system of representation struck at the core of the eighteenth-century British political structure. British subjects at home who were no more directly represented in the House of Commons than were the Americans could adopt the colonial arguments. The colonial questioning of the taxing authority of the House of Commons was related to the protest of John Wilkes. Both the Americans and Wilkes were challenging the power of the monarch and the authority of Parliament. Moreover, both the colonial leaders and Wilkes appealed over the head of legally constituted political authorities to popular opinion and popular demonstrations. Both were protesting the power of a largely self-selected aristocratic political body. The British ministry was fully aware of these broader political implications of the American troubles.

The American colonists also demonstrated to Europe how a politically restive people in the Old Regime could fight tyranny and protect political liberty. They established revolutionary but orderly political bodies that could function outside the existing political framework: the congress and the convention. These began with the Stamp Act Congress of 1765 and culminated in the Constitutional Convention of 1787. The legitimacy of those congresses and conventions lay not in existing law but in the alleged consent of the governed. This approach represented a new way to found a government.

Toward the end of the War of the American Revolution, calls for parliamentary reform arose in Britain itself. The method proposed for changing the system was the extralegal Association Movement.

THE YORKSHIRE ASSOCIATION MOVEMENT

By the close of the 1770s, many in Britain resented the mismanagement of the American war, the high taxes, and Lord North's ministry. In northern England in 1778, Christopher Wyvil (1740–1822), a landowner and retired clergyman, organized the Yorkshire Association Movement. Property owners, or freeholders, of Yorkshire met in a mass meeting to demand rather moderate changes in the corrupt system of parliamentary elections. They organized corresponding societies elsewhere. They intended that the association examine—and suggest reforms for—the entire government. The Association Movement was thus a popular attempt to establish an extralegal institution to reform the government.

The movement collapsed during the early 1780s because its supporters, unlike Wilkes and the American rebels, were not willing to appeal for broad popular support. Nonetheless, the agi-

This satirical portrait of John Wilkes is by William Hogarth. It depicts Wilkes with unattractive personal characteristics and questions the sincerity of his calls for liberty. [Charles Farrell Collection]

Major Cartwright Calls for the Reform of Parliament

During the years of the American Revolution, there were many demands in England itself for a major reform of Parliament. In this pamphlet of 1777, Major John Cartwright (1740–1824) demanded that many more English citizens be allowed to vote for members of the House of Commons.

♦ *What does Cartwright mean by "deep parliamentary corruption"? Does it extend beyond Parliament itself? Why are annual parliaments and equal representation a solution? Why are the claims of the few who now send representatives to Parliament rejected by Cartwright?*

Suffering as we do, from a deep parliamentary corruption, it is no time to tamper with silly correctives, and trifle away the life of public freedom: but we must go to the bottom of the stinking sore and cleanse it thoroughly: we must once more infuse into the constitution the vivifying spirit of liberty and expel the very last dregs of this poison. *Annual parliaments* with an *equal representation of the commons* are the only specifics in this case: and they would effect a radical cure. That a house of commons, formed as ours is, should maintain septennial elections, and laugh at every other idea is no wonder. The wonder is, that the British nation which, but the other day, was the greatest nation on earth, should be so easily laughed out of its liberties. . . .

Those who now claim the *exclusive* right of sending to parliament the 513 representatives for about six million souls (amongst whom are one million five hundred thousand males, *competent as electors*) consist of about two hundred and fourteen thousand persons; and 254 of these representatives are elected by 5,723. . . . Their pretended rights are many of them, derived from *royal favour*; some from ancient usage and prescription; and some indeed from act of parliament; but neither the most authentic acts of royalty, nor precedent, nor prescription, nor even parliament can establish any flagrant injustice; much less can they strip one million two hundred and eighty six thousand of an inalienable right, to vest it in a number amounting to only one seventh of that multitude. . . .

John Cartwright, Legislative Rights of the Commonality Vindicated *(1777), cited in S. Maccoby,* The English Radical Tradition, 1763–1914 *(London: Adam and Charles Black, 1966), pp. 32–33.*

---

tation of the Association Movement provided many people with experience in political protest. Several of its younger figures lived to raise the issue of parliamentary reform after 1815.

Parliament was not insensitive to the demands of the Association Movement. In April 1780, the Commons passed a resolution that called for lessening the power of the crown. In 1782 Parliament adopted a measure for "economical" reform, which abolished some patronage at the disposal of the monarch. These actions, however, did not prevent George III from appointing a minister of his own choice. In

1783 shifts in Parliament obliged Lord North to form a ministry with Charles James Fox (1749–1806), a long-time critic of George III. The monarch was most unhappy with the arrangement.

In 1783 the king approached William Pitt the Younger (1759–1806), son of the victorious war minister, to manage the House of Commons. During the election of 1784, Pitt received immense patronage support from the crown and constructed a House of Commons favorable to the monarch. Thereafter, Pitt sought to formulate trade policies that would give his ministry broad popularity. He attempted in 1785 one measure of modest parliamentary reform. When it failed, the young prime minister, who had been only twenty-four at the time of his appointment, abandoned the cause of reform.

By the mid-1780s, George III had achieved a part of what he had sought since 1761. He had reasserted the influence of the monarchy in political affairs. It proved a temporary victory because his own mental illness, which would finally require a regency, weakened the royal power. The cost of his years of dominance had been high, however. On both sides of the Atlantic, the issue of popular sovereignty had been raised and widely discussed. The American colonies had been lost. Economically, this loss did not prove disastrous. British trade with America after independence actually increased.

The Americans—through the state constitutions, the Articles of Confederation, and the federal Constitution adopted in 1788—had demonstrated to Europe the possibility of government without kings and hereditary nobilities. They had established the example of a nation in which written documents based on popular consent and popular sovereignty—rather than on divine law, natural law, tradition, or the will of kings—were the highest political and legal authority. The political novelty of these assertions should not be ignored.

As the crisis with Britain unfolded during the 1760s and 1770s, the American colonists had come to see themselves as first preserving traditional English liberties against the tyrannical crown and corrupt Parliament and then as developing a whole new sense of liberty. By the mid-1770s, the colonists had rejected monarchical government and embraced republican political ideals. They would govern themselves through elected assemblies without any presence of a monarchical authority. Once a constitution was adopted, they would insist on a bill of rights specifically protecting a whole series of civil liberties. The Americans would reject the aristocratic social hierarchy that had existed in the colonies. They would embrace democratic ideals even if the franchise remained limited. They would assert the equality of white male citizens not only before the law but in ordinary social relations. They would reject social status based on birth and inheritance and assert the necessity of the liberty for all citizens to

improve their social standing and economic lot by engaging in free commercial activity. They did not free their slaves nor did they address issues of the rights of women or of Native Americans, but the American colonists of the eighteenth century in making their revolution produced a society more free than any the world had seen and one that would eventually expand the circle of political and social liberty. In all these respects, the American Revolution was a genuinely radical movement, the influence of which would expand as Americans moved across the continent and as other peoples began to question traditional modes of European government.

———————————◆———————————

Throughout the eighteenth century, the great European powers fought in two major arenas—their overseas commercial empires and central Europe.

In the New World, Britain, France, and Spain battled for commercial dominance. France and Britain also clashed over their spheres of influence in India. By the third quarter of the century, Britain had succeeded in ousting France from most of its major holdings in North America and from any significant presence in India. Spain, though no longer a military power of the first order, had managed to maintain its vast colonial empire in Latin America and a large measure of its monopoly over the region's trade.

On the Continent, France, Austria, and Prussia collided over conflicting territorial and dynastic ambitions. Britain became involved to protect its continental interests and to use the continental wars to divert France from the colonial arena. Prussia with British aid had emerged in 1763 as a major continental power. Austria had lost considerable territory to Prussia. France had accumulated a vast debt.

The mid-century conflicts in turn led to major changes in all the European states. Each of the monarchies needed more money and tried to govern itself more efficiently. This problem led Britain to attempt to tax the North American colonies, which led to a revolution and the colonies' independence. Already deeply in debt, the French monarchy aided the Americans, fell into a deeper financial crisis, and soon sharply clashed with the nobility as royal ministers tried to find new revenues. That clash eventually unleashed the French Revolution. Spain moved to administer its Latin American empire more efficiently, which increased revolutionary discontent in the early nineteenth century. In preparation for future wars, the rulers of Prussia, Austria, and Russia pursued a mode of activist government known as Enlightened Absolutism. This will be examined in the next chapter. In that regard, the mid-eighteenth-century wars set in motion most of the major political developments of the next half century.

Review Questions

1. What were the fundamental ideas associated with mercantile theory? Did they work? Which European country was most successful in establishing a mercantile empire? Least successful? Why?

2. What were the main points of conflict between Britain and France in North America, the West Indies, and India? How did the triangles of trade function between the Americas, Europe, and Africa?

3. How was the Spanish colonial empire in the Americas organized and managed? What changes did the Bourbon monarchs institute in the Spanish empire?

4. What was the nature of slavery in the Americas? How was it linked to the economies of the Americas, Europe, and Africa? What was the plantation system and how did it contribute to the inhumane treatment of slaves?

5. The Seven Years' War was a major conflict with battles fought around the globe. What were the results of this war? Which countries emerged in a stronger position and why?

6. Discuss the American Revolution in the context of European history. To what extent were the colonists influenced by European ideas and political developments? To what extent did their actions influence Europe in turn?

Suggested Readings

B. BAILYN, *The Ideological Origins of the American Revolution* (1967). An important work illustrating the role of English radical thought in the perceptions of the American colonists.

B. BAILYN, *The Peopling of British North America: An Introduction* (1988). A study of the immigrants to the British colonies on the eve of the Revolution.

C. A. BAYLY, *Imperial Meridian: The British Empire and the World, 1780–1830* (1989). A major study of the empire after the loss of America.

C. BECKER, *The Declaration of Independence: A Study in the History of Political Ideas* (1922). Remains an important examination of the political and imperial theory of the Declaration.

L. BETHELL (Ed.), *The Cambridge History of Latin America*, Vols. 1 and 2 (1984). Excellent essays on the colonial era.

J. BLACK, *Pitt the Elder* (1992). The most recent biography.

C. BONWICK, *English Radicals and the American Revolution* (1977). Explores the relationship between English radical politics and events in America.

D. BRADING, *The First America* (1991). A major study of colonial Latin America.

J. Brewer, *Party Ideology and Popular Politics at the Accession of George III* (1976). An important series of essays on popular radicalism.

J. Brewer, *The Sinews of Power: War, Money, and the English State, 1688–1783* (1989). A study that emphasizes the financial power behind British military success.

J. Brooke, *King George III* (1972). The best biography.

K. N. Chaudhuri, *The Trading World of Asia and the English East India Company* (1978). Examines the impact of trade on both Asians and Europeans.

L. Colley, *Britons: Forging the Nation, 1707–1837* (1992). A major work with important discussions of the recovery from the loss of America.

P. Curtin, *The Atlantic Slave Trade* (1969). The best work on the subject.

D. B. Davis, *The Problem of Slavery in Western Culture* (1966). A brilliant and far-ranging discussion.

D. B. Davis, *The Problem of Slavery in the Age of Revolution, 1770–1823* (1975). A major work for both European and American history.

R. Davis, *The Rise of the Atlantic Economies* (1973). A major synthesis.

W. Dorn, *Competition for Empire, 1740–1763* (1940). Still one of the best accounts of the mid-century struggle.

C. Gibson, *Spain in America* (1966). A splendidly clear and balanced discussion.

L. H. Gipson, *The British Empire Before the American Revolution*, 13 vols. (1936–1967). A magisterial account of the mid-century wars from an imperial viewpoint.

P. Langford, *A Polite and Commercial People: England 1717–1783* (1989). An excellent survey of mid-century Britain based on the most recent scholarship covering social history as well as politics, the overseas wars, and the American Revolution.

J. Lockhardt and S. B. Schwartz, *Early Latin America: A History of Colonial Spanish America and Brazil* (1983). The new standard work.

J. R. McNeil, *Atlantic Empires of France and Spain: Louisbourg and Havana, 1700–1763* (1985). An examination of imperial policies for two key overseas outposts.

R. Middleton, *The Bells of Victory: The Pitt–Newcastle Ministry and the Conduct of the Seven Years' War, 1757–1762* (1985). A careful study of the intricacies of eighteenth-century cabinet government that questions the centrality of Pitt's role in the British victory.

S. W. Mintz, *Sweetness and Power: The Place of Sugar in Modern History* (1985). Traces the role of sugar in the world economy and how sugar has had an impact on world culture.

J. H. Parry, *Trade and Dominion: The European Overseas Empires in the Eighteenth Century* (1971). A comprehensive account with attention to the European impact on the rest of the world.

J. G. A. Pocock, *The Machiavellian Moment: Florentine Political Thought and the Atlantic Republican Tradition* (1975). An important book that traces the origins of Anglo-American radicalism to Renaissance Florence.

J. G. A. Pocock, *Virtue, Commerce, and History: Essays on Political Thought and History, Chiefly in the Eighteenth Century* (1985). Important articles.

C. D. Rice, *The Rise and Fall of Black Slavery* (1975). An excellent survey of the subject with careful attention to the numerous historiographical controversies.

J. C. Riley, *The Seven Years' War and the Old Regime in France: The Economic and Financial Toll* (1986). A useful analysis of pressures that would undermine the French monarchy.

G. Rudé, *Wilkes and Political Liberty* (1962). A close analysis of popular political behavior.

K. W. Schweizer, *Frederick the Great, William Pitt, and Lord Bute: The Anglo-Prussian Alliance, 1756–1763* (1991). The most recent study of this complex diplomacy.

I. K. Steele, *The English Atlantic, 1675–1740: An Exploration of Communication and Community* (1986). An exploration of culture and commerce in the transatlantic world.

R. L. Stein, *The French Sugar Business in the Eighteenth Century* (1988). A study that covers all aspects of the French sugar trade.

J. Thornton, *Africa and Africans in the Making of the Atlantic World, 1400–1680* (1992). A discussion of the role of Africans in the emergence of the transatlantic economy.

J. West, *Gunpower, Government, and War in the Mid-Eighteenth Century* (1991). A study of how warfare touched much of government.

G. Wills, *Inventing America: Jefferson's Declaration of Independence* (1978). An important study that challenges much of the analysis in the Becker volume.

G. S. Wood, *The Creation of the American Republic, 1776–1787* (1969). A far-ranging work dealing with Anglo-American political thought.

G. S. Wood, *The Radicalism of the American Revolution* (1991). A major interpretation.

Enlightenment and Revolution

BETWEEN approximately 1750 and 1850, certain extraordinary changes occurred in Western civilization. Although of immediate significance primarily for the nations of Europe and the Americas, these developments in the long run had an immense worldwide impact. Eventually, all civilizations were to feel the influence of the European intellectual ferment and political turmoil of these years. Most of the intellectual, political, economic, and social characteristics associated with the modern world came into being during this era. Europe became the great exporter of ideas and technologies that in time transformed one area after another of human experience.

An intellectual movement known as the *Enlightenment*, characterized by ideals of reform and challenge to traditional cultural authority, captured the imagination of numerous writers. The Enlightenment drew confidence from the scientific worldview that had emerged during the seventeenth century. Its exponents urged the application of the spirit of critical rationalism in one area of social and political life after another. They posed serious historical and moral questions to the Christian faith. They contended that laws of society and economics could be discovered and could then be used to improve the human condition. They embraced the idea of economic growth and development. They called for political reform and more efficient modes of government. They upheld the standard of rationality in order to cast doubt on traditional modes of thought and behavior that seemed to them less than rational. As a result of their labors, initially in Europe and ultimately throughout the world, the idea of change as a positive value, which

has played so important a role in modern life, emerged for the first time.

For many people, however, change seemed to come too rapidly and violently when revolution erupted in France in 1789. Beginning as an aristocratic revolt against the monarchy, the revolution rapidly spread to every corner of French political and social life. The rights of man and citizen displaced those of the monarchy, the aristocracy, and the Church. By 1792 the revolution had become a genuinely popular movement and had established a French republic whose armies challenged the other major European monarchies. The reign of terror that saw the execution of the French king unleashed civil violence unlike anything witnessed in Europe since the age of the religious wars. By the end of the 1790s, to restore order, French political leaders turned themselves over to the leadership of Napoleon. Thereafter, for more than a decade, his armies uprooted institutions of the Old Regime across the Continent. Only in 1815, after the Battle of Waterloo, was the power of France and Napoleon finally contained.

The French Revolution in one way or another served as a model for virtually all later popular revolutions. It unleashed new forces and political creeds in one area of the world after another. The French Revolution, with its broad popular base, brought the *people* to the forefront of world political history. In defining the early goals of the revolution—to establish a legal framework of limited monarchical power, secure citizen rights, and make possible relatively free economic activity—its supporters developed the political creed of *liberalism*.

The wars of the French Revolution and of Napoleon, stretching from 1792 to 1815, awakened the political force of nationalism, which has proved to be the single most powerful ideology of the modern world. Loyalty to the nation defined in ethnic terms of a common language, history, and culture replaced loyalty to dynasties. As a political ideology, nationalism could be used both to liberate a people from the domination of another nation and to justify wars of aggression. Nationalism was put to both uses in Europe and throughout the rest of the world in the two centuries following the revolution in France. Nationalism became a kind of secular religion that aroused a degree of loyalty and personal self-sacrifice previously prompted only by the great religious traditions.

Finally, between 1750 and 1850, Europe became not only an exporter of reform and revolution but also of manufactured commodities. The technology and the society associated with industrialism took root throughout the western portion of the continent. Europeans achieved a productive capacity that, in cooperation with their naval power, permitted them to dominate the markets of the world. Thereafter, to be strong, independent, and modern seemed to require industrialization and imitation of the manufacturing techniques of Europe and, later, of the United States.

Industrialism and its society, however, fostered immense social problems, dislocations, and injustices. The major intellectual and political response to these was socialism, several varieties of which emerged from the European social and economic turmoil of the 1830s and 1840s. History eventually proved the most significant of these to be that espoused by Karl Marx, whose *Communist Manifesto* appeared in 1848.

Remarkable ironies are attached to the European achievements of the late eighteenth and the early nineteenth centuries. Enlightenment, revolution, and industrialism contributed to an awakening of European power that permitted the continent to dominate the world for a time at the end of the nineteenth century. Yet those same movements produced various intellectual critiques, political ideas, and economic skills that twentieth-century non-European peoples would turn against their temporary European masters. It is for that reason that the age of enlightenment and revolution in the West proved so important, not only for Europe, but for the history of the entire modern world. ◆

1700–1789	*1713* Peace of Utrecht *1713–1740* Frederick William I builds Prussian military *1720–1740* Walpole in England, Fleury in France *1739* War of Jenkins's Ear *1740* Maria Theresa succeeds to Habsburg throne *1740–1748* War of the Austrian Succession *1756–1763* Seven Years' War *1767* Legislative Commission in Russia *1772* First Partition of Poland *1775–1783* American Revolution *1785* Catherine the Great of Russia issues Charter of Nobility
1789–1815	*1789* Gathering of the Estates General at Versailles; fall of the Bastille; Declaration of the Rights of Man and Citizen *1791* French monarchy abolished *1793* Louis XVI executed *1793–1794* Reign of Terror *1795* The Directory established in France *1799* Napoleon named First Consul in France *1803* War resumes between Britain and France *1804* Napoleonic Code; Napoleon crowned emperor *1805* Third Coalition formed against France; battles of Trafalgar and Austerlitz *1806* Napoleon establishes the Continental System *1807* Treaty of Tilsit between France and Russia *1808* Spanish resistance to Napoleon stiffens *1812* Napoleon invades Russia; meets defeat *1814* Napoleon abdicates; Congress of Vienna opens; Louis XVIII restored in France *1815* Napoleon defeated at Waterloo
1815–1850	*1819* Carlsbad Decrees in Germanies; Peterloo Massacre and the Six Acts, Britain *1820* Spanish Revolution begins *1821* Greek Revolution begins *1823* France intervenes in Spanish Revolution *1825* Decembrist Revolt in Russia *1829* Catholic Emancipation Act in Great Britain *1830* Revolution in France, Belgium, and Poland; Serbia gains independence *1832* Great Reform Bill in Britain *1848* Revolutions sweep across Europe

Society and Economy	Religion and Culture
1715–1763 Colonial rivalry in the Caribbean	1721 Montesquieu, *Persian Letters*
1733 James Kay's flying shuttle	1733 Voltaire, *Letters on the English*
1750s Agricultural Revolution in Britain	1738 Voltaire, *Elements of the Philosophy of Newton*
1750–1840 Growth of new cities	1739 Wesley begins field preaching
1763 British establish dominance in India	1748 Hume, *Inquiry into Human Nature*
1763–1789 Enlightened absolutist rulers seek to spur economic growth	1748 Montesquieu, *Spirit of the Laws*
1765 James Hargreaves's spinning jenny	1750 Rousseau, *Discourse on the Moral Effects of the Arts and Sciences*
1769 Richard Arkwright's waterframe	1751 First volume of Diderot's *Encyclopedia*
1771–1775 Pugachev's Rebellion	1762 Rousseau, *Social Contract* and *Émile*
1780 Gordon riots in London	1763 Voltaire, *Treatise on Toleration*
1787 Edmund Cartwright's power loom	1774 Goethe, *Sorrows of Young Werther*
	1776 Smith, *Wealth of Nations*
	1779 Lessing, *Nathan the Wise*
	1781 Joseph II adopts toleration in Austria
	1781 Kant, *Critique of Pure Reason*
1789–1802 Revolutionary legislation restructures French economic life	1789 Blake, *Songs of Innocence*
	1790 Civil Constitution of the Clergy; Burke, *Reflections on the Revolution in France*
	1792 Wollstonecraft, *Vindication of the Rights of Woman*
	1793 France proclaims Cult of Reason
1794–1824 Wars of Independence in Latin America break the colonial system	1794 France proclaims Cult of the Supreme Being
	1798 Wordsworth and Coleridge, *Lyrical Ballads*; Malthus, *Essay on the Principle of Population*
	1799 Schleiermacher, *Speeches on Religion to Its Cultured Despisers*
	1802 Chateaubriand, *Genius of Christianity*
	1802 Napoleon, Concordat with the Papacy
	1806 Hegel, *Phenomenology of Mind*
	1807 Fichte, *Addresses to the German Nation*
	1808 Goethe, *Faust*, Part I
1810 Abolition of serfdom in Prussia	1812 Byron, *Childe Harold's Pilgrimage*
1800–1850 British industrial dominance	1817 Ricardo, *Principles of Political Economy*
1825 Stockton and Darlington Railway opens	1819 Byron, *Don Juan*
1828–1850 First European police departments	1829 Catholic Emancipation Act in Great Britain
1830–1850 Railway building in western Europe	1830–1842 Comte, *The Positive Philosophy*
1833 English Factory Act to protect children	1830 Lyell, *Principles of Geology*
1834 German *Zollverein* established	1833 Russia begins "Official Nationality" policy
1842 Chadwick, *Report on the Sanitary Condition of the Labouring Population*	1835 Strauss, *Life of Jesus*
1846 Corn Laws repealed in Britain	1840 Villermé, *Catalogue of the Physical and Moral State of Workers*
1847 Ten Hour Act passed in Britain	1843 Kierkegaard, *Fear and Trembling*
1848 Serfdom abolished in Austria and Hungary	1848 Marx and Engels, *Communist Manifesto*

Philosopher, dramatist, poet, historian, and popularizer of scientific ideas, Voltaire (1694–1778) was the most famous and influential of the eighteenth-century philosophes. His sharp satire and criticism of religious institutions opened the way for a more general critique of the European political and social status quo. [Bildarchiv Preussischer Kulturbesitz]

18

The Age of Enlightenment: Eighteenth-Century Thought

Key Topics in This Chapter
◆ The intellectual and social background of the Enlightenment
◆ The *philosophes* of the Enlightenment and their agenda of intellectual and political reform
◆ Efforts of "Enlightened" monarchs in central and eastern Europe to increase the economic and military strength of their domains
◆ The partition of Poland by Prussia, Russia, and Austria

During the eighteenth century, the conviction began to spread throughout the literate sectors of European society that change and reform were both possible and desirable. This attitude is now commonplace, but it came into its own only after 1700. It represents one of the primary intellectual inheritances from that age. The movement of people and ideas that fostered such thinking is called the Enlightenment.

Its leading voices combined confidence in the human mind inspired by the Scientific Revolution and faith in the power of rational criticism to challenge the intellectual authority of tradition and the Christian past. These writers *stood convinced that human beings could comprehend the operation of physical nature and mold it to the ends of material and moral improvement, economic growth, and political reform. The rationality of the physical universe became a standard against which the customs and traditions of society could be measured and criticized. Such criticism penetrated every corner of contemporary society, politics, and religious opinion. As a result, the spirit of innovation and improvement came to characterize modern Europe and Western society.*

Some of the ideas and outlooks of the Enlightenment had a direct impact on several rulers in central and eastern Europe. These rulers, whose policies became known by the term enlightened absolutism, sought to centralize their authority so as to reform their countries. They often attempted to restructure religious authority and to sponsor economic growth. Although they were often associated with the writers of the Enlightenment, many of their policies were in direct opposition to enlightened ideals. Nonetheless, both the Enlightenment writers and these monarchs were forces for modernization in European life.

Formative Influences

The Newtonian worldview, the stability and prosperity of Great Britain after 1688, the need for reform in France after the wars of Louis XIV, and the consolidation of what is known as a *print culture* were the chief factors that fostered the ideas of the Enlightenment and the call for reform throughout Europe.

Ideas of Newton and Locke

Isaac Newton (1642–1727) and John Locke (1632–1704) were the major intellectual forerunners of the Enlightenment. Newton's formulation of the law of universal gravitation exemplified the power of the human mind. By example and in his writing, he encouraged Europeans to approach the study of nature directly and to avoid metaphysics and supernaturalism. Newton had always insisted on empirical support for his general laws and constantly used empirical experience to check his rational speculations. This emphasis on concrete experience became a key feature of Enlightenment thought.

Newton also seemed to have revealed a pattern of rationality in the physical world. During the eighteenth century, thinkers began to apply this insight to society. If nature was rational, they reasoned, society too should be organized rationally.

As noted in Chapter 14, Newton's success in physics inspired his countryman John Locke to explain human psychology in terms of experience. In *An Essay Concerning Human Understanding* (1690), Locke argued that all humans enter the world a *tabula rasa*, or blank page. Personality is the product of the sensations that impinge on an individual from the external world throughout his or her life. Thus, experience, and only experience, shapes character. The implication of this psychology was that human nature is changeable and can be molded by modifying the surrounding physical and social environment. Locke's was a reformer's psychology. It suggested the possibility of improving the human condition. Locke's psychology also, in effect, rejected the Christian doctrine that human beings are permanently flawed by sin. Human beings need not wait for the grace of God or other divine aid to better their lives. They could take charge of their own destiny.

The Example of British Toleration and Stability

Newton's physics and Locke's psychology provided the theoretical basis for a reformist approach to society. The domestic stability of Great Britain after the Revolution of 1688 furnished a living example of a society in which enlightened reforms appeared to function for the benefit of all. England permitted religious toleration to all except Unitarians and Roman Catholics, and even they were not actually persecuted. Relative freedom of the press and free speech prevailed. The authority of the monarchy was limited, and political sovereignty resided in Parliament. The courts protected citizens from arbitrary government action. The army was small. In the view of reformist observers on the Continent, these liberal policies had produced not disorder and instability

The Newtonian world view inspired much of the confidence of the Enlightenment. In this painting from the studio of Joseph Wright of Derby, an anonymous philosopher presents a lecture on the orrery, an eighteenth-century model of the heavens. [Yale Center for British Art, Paul Mellon Collection]

but prosperity, stability, and a loyal citizenry. This view may have been idealized, but England was nonetheless significantly freer than any other European nation at the time.

Need for Reform in France

If the example of Great Britain suggested that change and freedom need not be disastrous, France seemed to illustrate those aspects of European politics and society that most demanded reform. Its legacy from Louis XIV was absolute monarchy, a large standing army, heavy taxation, and religious persecution. Louis's policies had ultimately brought defeat in war and left his people so miserable that many celebrated when he died. His successors continued to curb liberties. The regime restricted freedom of worship and censored the press and literary expression. Authors often had their works printed in Switzerland to avoid these restraints. Critics of the regime were subject to arbitrary arrest, although some of them reached accommodations with the authorities. State regulations hampered economic growth. Many aristocrats, regarding themselves as part of a military class, upheld traditional militaristic values.

Yet France, because it confronted its political thinkers so sharply with the need for reform, became a major center for the Enlightenment.

The Emergence of a Print Culture

The Enlightenment was the first major intellectual movement of European history to flourish in a print culture, a culture in which books, journals, newspapers, and pamphlets had achieved a status of their own. Although printed books and pamphlets played a significant role during the Reformation and Counter-Reformation, the powerful messages of those movements were spread mostly by preaching. During the eighteenth century, the volume of printed material—books, journals, magazines, and daily newspapers—increased sharply throughout Europe, most notably in Britain. Prose came to be valued as highly as poetry and the novel emerged as a distinct genre. The printed word had become the chief vehicle for the communication of ideas and would remain so until the electronic revolution of our own day.

A growing concern with everyday life and material concerns—with secular as opposed to religious issues—accompanied this expansion of printed forms. Toward the end of the seventeenth century, half the books published in Paris were religious; by the 1780s, only about 10 percent were.

Books were not inexpensive in this era, but they, and the ideas they conveyed, circulated in a variety of ways to reach a broad public. Private and public libraries grew in number, allowing single copies to reach many readers. Authors might also publish the same material in different formats. The English essayist, critic, and dictionary author Samuel Johnson (1709–1784), for example, published as books collections of essays that had first appeared in newspapers or journals.

Familiarity with books and secular ideas came increasingly to be expected within aristocratic and middle-class society. Popular publications such as Joseph Addison (1672–1719) and Richard Steele's (1672–1729) *The Spectator*

(begun in 1711) fostered the value of polite conversation and the reading of books. Coffee houses became centers for the discussion of writing and ideas. The lodges of Freemasons, the meeting places for members of a movement that began in Britain and spread to the Continent, provided another site for the consideration of secular ideas in secular books.

The expanding market for printed matter allowed writers to earn a living from their work for the first time, making authorship an occupation. Parisian ladies sought out popular writers for their fashionable salons. Some writers, notably Alexander Pope (1688–1744) and Voltaire, grew wealthy, providing an example for their aspiring young colleagues. In a challenge to older aristocratic values, status for authors in this new print culture was based on merit and commercial competition, not heredity and patronage.

A division, however, soon emerged between high and low literary culture. Successful authors of the Enlightenment addressed themselves to monarchs, nobles, the upper middle classes, and professional groups and were read and accepted in these upper levels of society. Other authors found social and economic disappointment. They lived marginally, writing professionally for whatever newspaper or journal would pay for their pages. Many of these lesser writers grew resentful, blaming a corrupt society for their lack of success. From their anger, they often espoused radical ideas or carried Enlightenment ideas to radical extremes, transmitting them in this embittered form to their often lower-class audience. The new print culture thus circulated the ideas of the Enlightenment to virtually all literate groups in society.

An expanding literate public and the growing influence of secular printed materials created a new and increasingly influential social force called *public opinion*. This force—the collective effect on political and social life of views circulated in print and discussed in the home, the workplace, and centers of leisure—seems not to have existed as a vital force before the middle of the eighteenth century. Books and newspapers could have thousands of readers, who in effect supported the writers whose works they bought, discussing their ideas and circulating them widely. The writers, in turn, had to answer only

The world of the Enlightenment has often been portrayed as entirely optimistic. Such was hardly the case. Some people feared that the expansion of knowledge might bring danger as well as liberation. In this famous painting of the bird in an air pump, Joseph Wright of Derby captures some of that uncertainty. The scene is suffused in light, a metaphor for scientific enlightenment, but the bird will probably die as a result of the experiment. The group gathered around it are clearly having varied reactions to what they are witnessing. [The National Gallery, London]

to their readers. The result changed the cultural and political climate in Europe. In 1775 a new member of the French Academy declared:

A tribunal has arisen independent of all powers and that all powers respect, that appreciates all talents, that pronounces on all people of merit. And in an enlightened century, in a century in which each citizen can speak to the entire nation by way of print, those who have a talent for instructing men and a gift for moving them—in a word, men of letters— are, amid the public dispersed, what the orators of Rome and Athens were in the middle of the public assembled.[1]

Governments could no longer operate wholly in secret or with disregard to the larger public sphere. They, as well as their critics, had to

[1] *Chrétien-Guillaume Malesherbes, as quoted in Roger Chartier,* The Cultural Origins of the French Revolution, *trans. by Lydia G. Cochran (Durham, N.C.: Duke University Press, 1991), pp. 30–31.*

explain and discuss their views and policies openly.

Continental European governments sensed the political power of the new print culture. They regulated the book trade, censored books and newspapers, confiscated offending titles, and imprisoned offending authors. The eventual expansion of freedom of the press represented also an expansion of the print culture—with its independent readers, authors, and publishers—and the challenge it represented to traditional intellectual, social, and political authorities.

The *Philosophes*

The writers and critics who forged the new attitudes favorable to change, who championed reform, and who flourished in the emerging print culture were the *philosophes*. Not usually philosophers in a formal sense, they sought rather to apply the rules of reason and common sense to nearly all the major institutions and social practices of the day. The most famous of their number included Voltaire, Montesquieu, Diderot, Rousseau, Hume, Gibbon, Smith, Lessing, and Kant.

A few of these *philosophes* occupied professorships in universities. Most, however, were free agents who might be found in London coffee houses, Edinburgh drinking spots, the salons of fashionable Parisian ladies, the country houses of reform-minded nobles, or the courts of the most powerful monarchs on the Continent. In eastern Europe, they were often to be found in the royal bureaucracies. They were not an organized group; they disagreed on many issues. Their relationship with each other and with lesser figures of the same turn of mind has quite appropriately been compared with that of a family, in which despite quarrels and tensions a basic unity still remains.[2]

The chief bond among the *philosophes* was their common desire to reform thought, society, and government for the sake of human liberty. As Peter Gay has suggested, this goal included "freedom from arbitrary power, freedom of

speech, freedom of trade, freedom to realize one's talents, freedom of aesthetic response, freedom, in a word, of moral man to make his way in the world."[3] No other single set of ideas has done so much to shape the modern world. The literary vehicles through which the *philosophes* delivered their message included books, pamphlets, plays, novels, philosophical treatises, encyclopedias, newspapers, and magazines. During the Reformation and the religious wars, writers had used the printed word to debate the proper mode of faith in God. The *philosophes* of the Enlightenment employed the printed word to proclaim a new faith in the capacity of humankind to improve itself without the aid of God.

Many of the *philosophes* were of middle-class origins. The bulk of their readership was also drawn from the prosperous commercial and professional people of the eighteenth-century towns and cities. These people discussed the reformers' writings and ideas in local philosophical societies, Freemason lodges, and clubs. They had enough income and leisure time to buy and read the *philosophes'* works. Although the writers of the Enlightenment did not consciously champion the goals or causes of the middle class, they did provide an intellectual ferment and a major source of ideas that could be used to undermine existing social practices and political structures. They taught their contemporaries how to pose pointed, critical questions. Moreover, the *philosophes* generally supported the economic growth, the expansion of trade, and the improvement of transport that were transforming the society and the economy of the eighteenth century and enlarging the middle class.

The Enlightenment evolved over the course of the century and involved writers living at different times in various countries. Its early exponents popularized the rationalism and scientific ideas of the seventeenth century (see Chapter 14). They worked to expose contemporary social and political abuses and argued that reform was necessary and possible. Their progress in this cause was anything but steady. Among the obstacles they met were vested interests, political oppression, and religious condemnation.

[2]*Peter Gay*, The Enlightenment: An Interpretation, Vol. 1 *(New York: Knopf, 1967), p. 4.*

[3]*Gay, p. 3.*

Immanuel Kant Defines Enlightenment

Immanuel Kant was one of the most important German philosophers associated with the Enlightenment. His work is more fully discussed in Chapter 20. The passage here is from one of his more accessible articles, written in 1784 for a broad audience. He equates Enlightenment with the courage of the individual to use his or her reason. He indicates that this is difficult because so many people have come by habit to depend upon others for guidance. He discusses the freedom the use of reason requires.

◆ *What were some of the authorities Kant saw the liberated intellect having the courage to question? Why does Kant believe intellectual liberation requires effort and the rejection of laziness and cowardice? Why does Kant link enlightenment with freedom?*

Enlightenment is man's emergence from his self-imposed nonage. Nonage is the inability to use one's own understanding without another's guidance. This nonage is self-imposed if its causes lie not in lack of understanding but in indecision and lack of courage to use one's own mind without another's guidance. *Dare to know! (Sapere aude)* "Have the courage to use your own understanding," is therefore the motto of the enlightenment.

Laziness and cowardice are the reasons why such a large part of mankind gladly remain minors all their lives, long after nature has freed them from external guidance. They are the reasons why it is so easy for others to set themselves up as guardians. It is so comfortable to be a minor. If I have a book that thinks for me, a pastor who acts as my conscience, a physician who prescribes my diet, and so on—then I have no need to exert myself. I have no need to think, if only I can pay; others will take care of that disagreeable business for me. . . .

Thus it is very difficult for the individual to work himself out of the nonage which has become almost second nature to him. He has even grown to like it and is at first really incapable of using his own understanding, because he has never been permitted to try it. Dogmas and formulas, these mechanical tools designed for reasonable use—or rather abuse—of his natural gifts, are the fetters of an everlasting nonage. The man who casts them off would make an uncertain leap over the narrowest ditch, because he is not used to such movement. That is why there are only a few men who walk firmly, and who have emerged from nonage by cultivating their own minds.

It is more nearly possible, however, for the public to enlighten itself; indeed, if it is only given freedom, enlightenment is almost inevitable. There will always be a few independent thinkers, even among the self-appointed guardians of the multitude. Once such men have thrown off the yoke of nonage, they will spread about them the spirit of a reasonable appreciation of man's value and of his duty to think for himself. . . .

This enlightenment requires nothing but *freedom*—and the most innocent of all that may be called "freedom": freedom to make public use of one's reason in all matters.

Immanuel Kant, "What is Enlightenment?" trans. by Peter Gay, in Introduction to Contemporary Civilization in the West, *2nd ed., Vol. 2 (New York: Columbia University Press, 1954), pp. 1071–1072.*

Yet, by mid-century, they had brought enlightened ideas to the European public in a variety of formats. The *philosophes'* "family" had come into being. They corresponded with each other, wrote for each other as well as for the public, and defended each other against the political and religious authorities.

By the second half of the century, they were sufficiently safe to quarrel among themselves on occasion. They had stopped talking in generalities, and their major advocates were addressing specific abuses. Their books and articles had become more specialized and more practical. They had become more concerned with politics than with religion. Having convinced Europeans that change was a good idea, they began to suggest exactly what changes were most desirable. They had become honored figures.

Voltaire's Agenda of Intellectual Reform

One of the earliest and by far the most influential of the *philosophes* was François Marie Arouet, known to posterity as Voltaire (1694–1778). During the 1720s, Voltaire had offended the French authorities by certain of his writings. He was arrested and put in prison for a brief time.

Later Voltaire went to England, visiting its best literary circles, observing its tolerant intellectual and religious climate, relishing the freedom he felt in its moderate political atmosphere, and admiring its science and economic prosperity. In 1733 he published *Letters on the English*, which appeared in French the next year. The book praised the virtues of the English and indirectly criticized the abuses of French society. In 1738 he published *Elements of the Philosophy of Newton*, which popularized the thought of the great scientist. Both works were well received and gave Voltaire a reputation as an important writer.

Thereafter Voltaire lived part of the time in France and part near Geneva, just across the French border, where the royal authorities could not bother him. He wrote essays, history, plays, stories, and letters that made him the literary dictator of Europe. He used the bitter venom of his satire and sarcasm against one evil after another in French and European life. In his most famous satire, *Candide* (1759), he attacked war, religious persecution, and what he regarded as unwarranted optimism about the human condition.

Like most *philosophes*, Voltaire believed that improvement of human society was necessary and possible. But he was never certain that reform, if achieved, would be permanent. The optimism of the Enlightenment was a tempered hopefulness rather than a glib certainty. An undercurrent of pessimism characterized most of the works of the period.

The Encyclopedia

The mid-century witnessed the publication of the *Encyclopedia*, one the greatest monuments of the Enlightenment. Under the heroic leadership of Denis Diderot (1713–1784), and Jean le Rond d'Alembert (1717–1783), the first volume appeared in 1751. Numbering seventeen volumes of text and eleven of plates (illustrations), the project reached completion in 1772.

The *Encyclopedia*, in part a collective plea for freedom of expression, reached fruition only after many attempts to censor it and to halt its publication. It was the product of the collective effort of more than 100 authors, and its editors had at one time or another solicited articles from all the major French *philosophes*. It included the most advanced critical ideas of the time on religion, government, and philosophy. To avoid official censure, these ideas often had to be hidden in obscure articles or under the cover of irony. The *Encyclopedia* also included important articles and illustrations on manufacturing, canal building, ship construction, and improved agriculture, making it an important source of knowledge about eighteenth-century social and economic life.

Between 14,000 and 16,000 copies of various editions of the *Encyclopedia* were sold before 1789. The project had been designed to secularize learning and to undermine intellectual assumptions that lingered from the Middle Ages and the Reformation. The articles on politics, ethics, and society ignored divine law and concentrated on humanity and its immediate well-being. The encyclopedists looked to antiquity rather than to the Christian centuries for their intellectual and ethical models. For them, the future welfare of humankind lay not in pleasing

God or following divine commandments but rather in harnessing the power and resources of the earth and in living at peace with one's fellow human beings. The good life lay here and now and was to be achieved through the application of reason to human relationships. With the publication of the *Encyclopedia,* Enlightenment thought became more fully diffused over the Continent, penetrating German and Russian intellectual and political circles.

The Enlightenment and Religion

For many but not all *philosophes* of the eighteenth century, ecclesiastical institutions were the chief impediment to human improvement and happiness. Voltaire's cry, "Crush the Infamous Thing" summed up the attitude of a number of *philosophes* toward the Church and Christianity. Almost all varieties of Christianity, but especially Roman Catholicism, felt their criticism.

The critical *philosophes* complained that the churches hindered the pursuit of a rational life and the scientific study of humanity and nature. The clergy taught that humans were basically depraved, becoming worthy only through divine grace. According to the doctrine of original sin, Protestant or Catholic, meaningful improvement in human nature on earth was impossible. Religion thus turned attention away from this world to the world to come. For example, the *philosophes* argued that the Calvinist doctrine of predestination denied a relationship between virtuous actions in this life and the fate of the soul after death. Mired in conflicts over obscure doctrinal differences, the churches promoted intolerance and bigotry, inciting torture, war, and other forms of human suffering.

With this attack, the *philosophes* were challenging not only a set of ideas but also some of Europe's most powerful institutions. The churches were deeply enmeshed in the power structure of the old regime. They owned large amounts of land and collected tithes from peasants before any secular authority collected its taxes. Most clergy were legally exempt from taxes and made only annual voluntary grants to the government. The upper clergy in most countries were relatives of aristocrats. Churchmen were actively involved in politics, serving in the British House of Lords and advising princes on the Continent. In Protestant countries, the leading local landowner usually appointed the clergyman of a particular parish. Across the Continent, membership in the predominant denomination of the kingdom gave certain subjects political advantages. Nonmembership often excluded other subjects from political participation. Clergymen of all faiths preached the sinfulness of political disobedience. They provided intellectual justification for the social and political status quo, and they were active agents of religious and literary censorship.

Deism

The *philosophes,* although critical of many religious institutions and frequently anticlerical, were not opposed to all religion. In Scotland, for example, the enlightened historian William Robertson (1721–1793) was the head of the Scottish Kirk. In England, clergy of the established Church did much to popularize the thought of Newton. What the *philosophes* sought, however, was religion without fanaticism and intolerance, a religious life that would not substitute Church authority for the authority of human reason. The Newtonian worldview had convinced many writers that nature was rational. Therefore, the God who had created nature must also be rational, and the religion through which that God was worshiped should be rational. Most of them believed that the life of religion and of reason could be combined, giving rise to a movement known as *deism.*

The title of one of the earliest deist works, *Christianity Not Mysterious* (1696) by John Toland (1670–1722), indicates the general tenor of this religious outlook. Toland and later deist writers promoted religion as a natural and rational, rather than a supernatural and mystical, phenomenon. In this respect they differed from Newton and Locke, both of whom regarded themselves as distinctly Christian. Newton believed God could interfere with the natural order, whereas the deists regarded God as a kind of divine watchmaker who had created the mechanism of nature, set it in motion, and then departed. Most of the deist writers were also strongly anticlerical and for that reason regarded as radical.

There were two major points in the deists' creed. The first was a belief in the existence of God, which they thought could be empirically justified by the contemplation of nature. Joseph Addison's poem on the spacious firmament (1712) illustrates this idea:

The spacious firmament on high,
With all the blue ethereal sky,
And spangled heav'n, a shining frame,
Their great Original proclaim:
Th' unwearied Sun, from day to day,
Does his Creator's power display,
And publishes to every land
The work of an Almighty hand.

Because nature provided evidence of a rational God, that deity must also favor rational morality. So the second point in the deists' creed was a belief in life after death, when rewards and punishments would be meted out according to the virtue of the lives people led on this earth.

Deism was empirical, tolerant, reasonable, and capable of encouraging virtuous living. Voltaire declared:

The great name of Deist, which is not sufficiently revered, is the only name one ought to take. The only gospel one ought to read is the great book of Nature, written by the hand of God and sealed with his seal. The only religion that ought to be professed is the religion of worshiping God and being a good man.[4]

Deists hoped that wide acceptance of their faith would end rivalry among the various Christian sects and with it religious fanaticism, conflict, and persecution. They also felt deism would remove the need for priests and ministers, who, in their view, were often responsible for fomenting religious differences and denominational hatred.

Toleration

According to the *philosophes*, religious toleration was a primary social condition for the virtuous life. Again Voltaire took the lead in championing this cause. In 1762 the Roman Catholic political authorities in Toulouse ordered the exe-

cution of a Huguenot named Jean Calas. He stood accused of having murdered his son to prevent him from converting to Roman Catholicism. Calas was viciously tortured and publicly strangled without ever confessing his guilt. The confession would not have saved his life, but it would have given the Catholics good propaganda to use against Protestants.

Voltaire learned of the case only after Calas's death. He made the dead man's cause his own. In 1763 he published his *Treatise on Tolerance* and hounded the authorities for a new investigation. Finally, in 1765 the judicial decision against the unfortunate man was reversed. For Voltaire, the case illustrated the fruits of religious fanaticism and the need for rational reform of judicial processes. Somewhat later in the century, the German playwright and critic Gotthold Lessing (1729–1781) wrote *Nathan the Wise* (1779), a plea for toleration not only of different Christian sects but also of religious faiths other than Christianity.

The premise behind all of these calls for toleration was, in effect, that life on earth and human relationships should not be subordinated to religion. Secular values and considerations were more important than religious ones.

Radical Enlightenment Criticism of Religion

Some *philosophes* went beyond the formulation of a rational religious alternative to Christianity and the advocacy of toleration to attack the churches and the clergy with great vehemence. Voltaire repeatedly questioned the truthfulness of priests and the morality of the Bible. In his *Philosophical Dictionary* (1764) he humorously pointed out inconsistencies in biblical narratives and immoral acts of the biblical heroes. The Scottish philosopher David Hume (1711–1776), in "Of Miracles," a chapter in his *Inquiry into Human Nature* (1748), argued that no empirical evidence supported the belief in divine miracles central to much of Christianity. For Hume, the greatest miracle was that people believed in miracles. In *The Decline and Fall of the Roman Empire* (1776), Edward Gibbon (1737–1794), the English historian, explained the rise of Christianity in terms of natural causes rather than the influence of miracles and piety.

[4]*Quoted in J. H. Randall, The Making of the Modern Mind,* rev. ed. *(New York: Houghton Mifflin, 1940), p. 292.*

Voltaire Attacks Religious Fanaticism

The chief complaint of the philosophes *against Christianity was that it bred a fanaticism that led people to commit crimes in the name of religion. In this passage from his* Philosophical Dictionary *(1764), Voltaire directly reminded his readers of the intolerance of the Reformation era and indirectly referred to examples of contemporary religious excesses. He argued that the philosophical spirit can overcome fanaticism and foster toleration and more humane religious behavior. Shocking many of his contemporaries, he praised the virtues of Confucianism over those of Christianity.*

✦ *What concrete examples of religious fanaticism might Voltaire have had in mind? Why does Voltaire contend that neither religion nor laws can contain religious fanaticism? Why does Voltaire admire the Chinese?*

Fanaticism is to superstition what delirium is to fever and rage to anger. The man visited by ecstasies and visions, who takes dreams for realities and his fancies for prophecies, is an enthusiast; the man who supports his madness with murder is a fanatic. . . .

The most detestable example of fanaticism was that of the burghers of Paris who on St. Bartholomew's Night [1572] went about assassinating and butchering all their fellow citizens who did not go to mass, throwing them out of windows, cutting them in pieces.

Once fanaticism has corrupted a mind, the malady is almost incurable. . . .

The only remedy for this epidemic malady is the philosophical spirit which, spread gradually, at last tames men's habits and prevents the disease from starting; for once the disease has made any progress, one must flee and wait for the air to clear itself. Laws and religion are not strong enough against the spiritual pest; religion, far from being healthy food for infected brains, turns to poison in them. . . .

Even the law is impotent against these attacks of rage; it is like reading a court decree to a raving maniac. These fellows are certain that the holy spirit with which they are filled is above the law, that their enthusiasm is the only law they must obey.

What can we say to a man who tells you that he would rather obey God than men, and that therefore he is sure to go to heaven for butchering you?

Ordinarily fanatics are guided by rascals, who put the dagger into their hands; these latter resemble that Old Man of the Mountain who is supposed to have made imbeciles taste the joys of paradise and who promised them an eternity of the pleasures of which he had given them a foretaste, on condition that they assassinated all those he would name to them. There is only one religion in the world that has never been sullied by fanaticism, that of the Chinese men of letters. The schools of philosophy were not only free from this pest, they were its remedy; for the effect of philosophy is to make the soul tranquil, and fanaticism is incompatible with tranquility. If our holy religion has so often been corrupted by this infernal delirium, it is the madness of men which is at fault.

Voltaire, Philosophical Dictionary, *trans. by P. Gay (New York: Basic Books, 1962), pp. 267–269.*

A few *philosophes* went further. Baron d'Holbach (1723–1789) and Julien Offray de La Mettrie (1709–1751) embraced positions very near to atheism and materialism. Theirs was distinctly a minority position, however. Most of the *philosophes* sought not the abolition of religion but its transformation into a humane force that would encourage virtuous living.

The *philosophes'* criticisms of traditional religion nonetheless often reflected an implicit con-

David Hume (1711–1776), the Scottish philosopher, argued against belief in miracles and, by implication, against belief in Christianity itself. [The Bettmann Archive]

tempt not only for Christianity but also, and sometimes more vehemently, for Judaism. Their attack on the veracity of biblical miracles and biblical history undermined the authority of the Hebrew scriptures as well as the Christian, and their satirical barbs were aimed most often at personalities from the Hebrew scriptures. Some *philosophes* characterized Judaism as a more primitive faith than Christianity. The Enlightenment view of religion thus served in some ways to further stigmatize Jews and Judaism in the eyes of non-Jewish Europeans.

The Enlightenment and Society

Although the *philosophes* wrote much on religion, humanity was the center of their interest. As one writer in the *Encyclopedia* observed, "Man is the unique point to which we must refer everything, if we wish to interest and please amongst considerations the most arid and details the most dry."[5] The *philosophes* believed that the application of human reason to society would reveal laws in human relationships similar to those found in physical nature. At the same time, the use of the word *man* in this passage was not simply an accident of language. Most *philosophes* were thinking primarily of men, not women, when they framed their reformist ideas. With a few exceptions, as will be seen later in this chapter, they had little interest in expanding women's intellectual and social opportunities.

Although the term did not appear until later, the idea of social science originated with the Enlightenment. *Philosophes* hoped to end human cruelty by discovering social laws and making people aware of them. These concerns are most evident in the *philosophes'* work on law and prisons.

Beccaria and Reform of Criminal Law

In 1764 Cesare Beccaria (1738–1794), an Italian *philosophe*, published *On Crimes and Punishments*, in which he applied critical analysis to the problem of making punishments both effective and just. He wanted the laws of monarchs and legislatures—that is, positive law—to conform with the rational laws of nature. He rigorously and eloquently attacked both torture and capital punishment. He thought that the criminal justice system should ensure speedy trial and certain punishment, and that the intent of punishment should be to deter further crime. The purpose of laws was not to impose the will of God or some other ideal of perfection; its purpose was to secure the greatest good or happiness for the greatest number of human beings. This utilitarian philosophy based on happiness in this life permeated most of Enlightenment writing on practical reforms.

The Physiocrats and Economic Freedom

Economic policy was another area where the *philosophes* saw existing legislation and administration preventing the operation of natural

[5]*Quoted in F. L. Baumer, Main Currents of Western Thought, 4th ed. (New Haven, Conn.: Yale University Press, 1978), p. 374.*

Cesare Beccaria (1738–1794) sought to apply Enlightenment ideas to the issue of crime and punishment and to bring a rational approach to criminal law. [Bildarchive Preussischer Kulturbesitz]

Adam Smith and The Wealth of Nations

The most important economic work of the Enlightenment was Adam Smith's (1723–1790) *Inquiry into the Nature and Causes of the Wealth of Nations* (1776). Smith, who was for a time a professor at Glasgow, believed that economic liberty was the foundation of a natural economic system. As a result, he urged that the mercantile system of England—including the navigation acts, the bounties, most tariffs, special trading monopolies, and the domestic regulation of labor and manufacture—be abolished. These regulations were intended to preserve the wealth of the nation, to capture wealth from other nations, and to maximize the work available for the nation's laborers. Smith argued,

Adam Smith was the author of The Wealth of Nations, *published in 1776. In this work he set forth forceful arguments for the benefits of a free market economy that continue to influence economic thinking.* [Bildarchiv Preussischer Kulturbesitz]

social laws. They believed that mercantilist legislation (designed to protect a country's trade from external competition) and the regulation of labor by governments and guilds actually hampered the expansion of trade, manufacture, and agriculture. In France, these economic reformers were called the *physiocrats*. Their leading spokesmen were François Quesnay (1694–1774) and Pierre Dupont de Nemours (1739–1817).

The physiocrats believed that the primary role of government was to protect property and to permit its owners to use it freely. They particularly felt that all economic production depended on sound agriculture. They favored the consolidation of small peasant holdings into larger, more efficient farms. Here as elsewhere there was a close relationship between the rationalism of the Enlightenment and the spirit of improvement at work in eighteenth-century European economic life.

however, that they hindered the expansion of wealth and production. The best way to encourage economic growth, he maintained, was to unleash individuals to pursue their own selfish economic interest. As self-interested individuals sought to enrich themselves by meeting the needs of others in the marketplace, the economy would expand. Consumers would find their wants met as manufacturers and merchants competed for their business.

It was a basic assumption of mercantilism that the earth's resources are limited and scarce, so that one nation can only acquire wealth at the expense of others. Smith's book challenged this assumption. He saw the resources of nature—water, air, soil, and minerals—as boundless. To him, they demanded exploitation for the enrichment and comfort of humankind. In effect, Smith was saying that the nations and peoples of Europe need not be poor.

The idea that humans should exploit nature's infinite bounty for their benefit, which dominated Western economic activity until recently, thus stemmed directly from the Enlightenment. When Smith wrote, the population of the world was smaller, its people poorer, and the quantity of undeveloped resources per capita much greater than now. For people of the eighteenth century, true improvement of the human condition seemed to lie in the uninhibited exploitation of natural resources.

Smith is usually regarded as the founder of laissez-faire economic thought and policy, which favors a limited role for the government in economic life. *The Wealth of Nations* was, however, a complex book. Smith was no simple dogmatist. For example, he did not oppose all government activity touching the economy. The state, he argued, should provide schools, armies, navies, and roads. It should also undertake certain commercial ventures, such as the opening of dangerous new trade routes that were economically desirable but too expensive or risky for private enterprise.

Political Thought of the *Philosophes*

Nowhere was their appreciation of the complexity of the problems of contemporary society clearer than in the *philosophes'* political thought. Nor did any other area of their reformist enterprise so clearly illustrate the tension and conflict within the "family" of the Enlightenment. Most *philosophes* were discontented with certain political features of their countries, but they were especially discontented in France. There the corruptness of the royal court, the blundering of the bureaucracy, the less than glorious mid-century wars, and the power of the Church compounded all problems. Consequently, the most important political thought of the Enlightenment occurred in France. The French *philosophes*, however, stood quite divided as to the proper solution to their country's problems. Their attitudes spanned a wide political spectrum from aristocratic reform to democracy to absolute monarchy.

Montesquieu and The Spirit of the Laws

Charles Louis de Secondat, Baron de Montesquieu (1689–1755), was a lawyer, noble of the robe, and a member of a provincial *parlement.* He also belonged to the Bordeaux Academy of Science, before which he presented papers on scientific topics.

Although living comfortably within the bosom of French society, he saw the need for reform. In 1721 he published *The Persian Letters* to satirize contemporary institutions. The book consisted of letters purportedly written by two Persians visiting Europe. They explained to friends at home how European behavior contrasted with Persian life and customs. Behind the humor lay the cutting edge of criticism and an exposition of the cruelty and irrationality of much contemporary European life.

In his most enduring work, *The Spirit of the Laws* (1748), Montesquieu held up the example of the British constitution as the wisest model for regulating the power of government. With his interest in science, his hope for reform, and his admiration for Britain, he embodied all the major elements of the Enlightenment mind.

Montesquieu's *Spirit of the Laws*, perhaps the single most influential book of the century, exhibits the internal tensions of the Enlightenment. In it, Montesquieu pursued an empirical method, taking illustrative examples from the political experience of both ancient and modern nations. From these he concluded there could be no single set of political laws that applied to all

Charles de Secondat, Baron de Montesquieu (1689–1755) was the author of The Spirit of the Laws, *possibly the most influential work of political thought of the eighteenth century. [Bettmann/Hulton]*

other corporate bodies that enjoyed liberties the monarch had to respect. These corporate bodies might be said to represent various segments of the general population and thus of public opinion. In France, he regarded the aristocratic courts, or *parlements*, as the major example of an intermediary association. Their role was to limit the power of the monarchy and thus to preserve the liberty of its subjects.

In championing these aristocratic bodies and the general role of the aristocracy, Montesquieu was a political conservative. He adopted this conservatism in the hope of achieving reform, however, for he believed the oppressive and inefficient absolutism of the monarchy accounted for the degradation of French life.

One of Montesquieu's most influential ideas was that of the division of power in government. For his model of a government with authority wisely separated among different branches, he took contemporary Great Britain. There, he believed, executive power resided in the king, legislative power in the Parliament, and judicial power in the courts. He thought any two branches could check and balance the power of the other. His perception of the eighteenth-century British constitution was incorrect because he failed to see how patronage and electoral corruption allowed a handful of powerful aristocrats to dominate the government. Moreover, he was also unaware of the emerging cabinet system, which was slowly making the executive power a creature of the Parliament.

Nevertheless, Montesquieu's analysis illustrated his strong sense that monarchs should be subject to constitutional limits on their power and that a separate legislature, not the monarch, should formulate laws. For this reason, although he set out to defend the political privileges of the French aristocracy, Montesquieu's ideas had a profound and still-lasting effect on the constitutional form of liberal democracies of the next two centuries.

Rousseau: A Radical Critique of Modern Society

Jean-Jacques Rousseau (1712–1778) held a view of the exercise and reform of political power quite different from Montesquieu's. Rousseau was a strange, isolated genius who never felt particularly comfortable with the other

peoples at all times and in all places. The good political life depended rather on the relationship among many political variables. Whether the best form of government for a country was a monarchy or a republic, for example, depended on its size, population, social and religious customs, economic structure, traditions, and climate. Only a careful examination and evaluation of these elements could reveal what mode of government would prove most beneficial to a particular people.

So far as France was concerned, Montesquieu had some definite ideas. He believed in a monarchical government tempered and limited by various sets of intermediary institutions. These included the aristocracy, the towns, and the

The writings of Jean Jacques Rousseau (1712–1778) raised some of the most profound social and ethical questions of the Enlightenment. This portrait by Maurice Quentin was made around 1740. [Bildarchiv Preussischer Kulturbesitz]

philosophes. His own life was troubled. He could form few close friendships. He sired numerous children whom he abandoned to foundling hospitals. Yet perhaps more than any other writer of the mid-eighteenth century, he transcended the political thought and values of his own time. Rousseau had a deep antipathy toward the world and the society in which he lived. It seemed to him impossible for human beings living according to contemporary commercial values to achieve moral, virtuous, or sincere lives. In 1750, in his *Discourse on the Moral Effects of the Arts and Sciences,* he contended that the process of civilization and enlightenment had corrupted human nature. In

1755, in his *Discourse on the Origin of Inequality,* Rousseau blamed much of the evil in the world on the uneven distribution of property.

In both works Rousseau brilliantly and directly challenged the social fabric of the day. He drew into question the concepts of material and intellectual progress and the morality of a society in which commerce and industry were regarded as the most important human activities. He felt that the real purpose of society was to nurture better people. In this respect Rousseau's vision of reform was much more radical than that of other contemporary writers. The other *philosophes* believed that life would improve if people could enjoy more of the fruits of the earth or could produce more goods. Rousseau raised the more fundamental question of what constitutes the good life. This question has haunted European social thought ever since the eighteenth century.

Rousseau carried these same concerns into his political thought. His most extensive discussion of politics appeared in *The Social Contract* (1762). Although the book attracted rather little immediate attention, by the end of the century it was widely read in France. *The Social Contract,* compared with Montesquieu's *Spirit of the Laws,* is a very abstract book. It does not propose specific reforms but outlines the kind of political structure that Rousseau believed would overcome the evils of contemporary politics and society.

In the tradition of John Locke, most eighteenth-century political thinkers regarded human beings as individuals and society as a collection of individuals pursuing personal, selfish goals. These writers wished to liberate individuals from the undue bonds of government. Rousseau picked up the stick from the other end. His book opens with the declaration, "All men are born free, but everywhere they are in chains."[6] The rest of the volume is a defense of the chains of a properly organized society over its members.

Rousseau suggested that society is more important than its individual members, because they are what they are only because of their relationship to the larger community. Independent

[6]*Jean-Jacques Rousseau,* The Social Contract and Discourses, *trans. by G. D. H. Cole (New York: Dutton, 1950), p. 3.*

human beings living alone can achieve very little. Through their relationship to the larger community, they become moral creatures capable of significant action. The question then becomes what kind of community allows people to behave morally. In his two previous discourses, Rousseau had explained that contemporary European society was not such a community. It was merely an aggregate of competing individuals whose chief social goal was to preserve selfish independence in spite of all potential social bonds and obligations.

Rousseau envisioned a society in which each person could maintain personal freedom while behaving as a loyal member of the larger community. Drawing on the traditions of Plato and Calvin, he defined freedom as obedience to law. In his case, the law to be obeyed was that created by the general will. In a society with virtuous customs and morals in which citizens have adequate information on important issues, the concept of the general will is normally equivalent to the will of a majority of voting citizens. Democratic participation in decision making would bind the individual citizen to the community. Rousseau believed that the general will, thus understood, must always be right and that to obey the general will is to be free. This argument led him to the notorious conclusion that under certain circumstances some people must be forced to be free. Rousseau's politics thus constituted a justification for radical direct democracy and for collective action against individual citizens.

Rousseau had in effect launched an assault on the eighteenth-century cult of the individual and the fruits of selfishness. He stood at odds with the commercial spirit that was transforming the society in which he lived. Rousseau would have disapproved of the main thrust of Adam Smith's *Wealth of Nations*, which he may or may not have read, and would no doubt have preferred a study on the virtue of nations. Smith wanted people to be prosperous; Rousseau wanted them to be good even if being good meant that they might remain poor. He saw human beings not as independent individuals but as creatures enmeshed in necessary social relationships. He believed that loyalty to the community should be encouraged. As one device to that end, he suggested a civic religion based on the creed of deism. Such a shared tolerant religious faith would help unify a society.

Rousseau's chief source of intellectual inspiration was Plato and the ancient Greek *polis*. Especially in Sparta, he thought he had discovered human beings dwelling in a moral society inspired by a common purpose. He hoped that modern human beings might also create such a moral commonwealth in which virtuous living would be valued over commercial profit.

Rousseau had only a marginal impact on his own time. The other *philosophes* questioned his critique of material improvement. Aristocrats and royal ministers could hardly be expected to welcome his proposal for radical democracy. Too many people were either making or hoping to make money to appreciate his criticism of commercial values. He proved, however, to be a figure to whom later generations returned. Many leaders in the French Revolution were familiar with his writing, and he influenced most writers in the nineteenth and twentieth centuries who were critical of the general tenor and direction of Western culture. Rousseau hated much about the emerging modern society in Europe, but he contributed much to modernity by exemplifying for later generations the critic who dared to call into question the very foundations of social thought and action.

Women in the Thought and Practice of the Enlightenment

Women, especially in France, helped significantly to promote the careers of the *philosophes*. In Paris, the salons of women such as Marie-Thérèse Geoffrin (1699–1777), Julie de Lespinasse (1733–1776), and Claudine de Tencin (1689–1749) gave the *philosophes* access to useful social and political contacts and a receptive environment in which to circulate their ideas. Association with a fashionable salon brought *philosophes* increased social status and added luster and respectability to their ideas. They clearly enjoyed the opportunity to be the center of attention that a salon provided, and their presence at them could boost the sales of their works. The women who organized the salons were well-connected to major political figures who could help protect the *philosophes* and secure them pensions. The marquise de

The salon of Mme. Marie-Thérèse Geoffrin (1699–1777) was one of the most important gathering spots for Enlightenment writers during the middle of the eighteenth century. Well-connected women such as Mme. Geoffrin were instrumental in helping the philosophes *they patronized to bring their ideas to the attention of influential people in French society and politics. [Giraudon/Art Resource, N.Y.]*

Pompadour, the mistress of Louis XV (1721–1764), played a key role in overcoming efforts to censor the *Encyclopedia*. She also helped block the circulation of works attacking the *philosophes*. Other salon hostesses purchased the writings of the *philosophes* and distributed them among their friends. Madame de Tencin was responsible for promoting Montesquieu's *Spirit of the Laws* in this way.

Despite this help and support from the learned women of Paris, the *philosophes* were on the whole not strong feminists. Many urged better and broader education for women. They criticized the education women did receive as overly religious, and they tended to reject ascetic views of sexual relations. But in general they displayed rather traditional views toward

women and advocated no radical changes in the social condition of women.

Montesquieu, for example, illustrates some of these tensions in the views of Enlightenment writers toward women. He maintained in general that the status of women in a society was the result of climate, the political regime, culture, and women's physiological nature. He believed women were not naturally inferior to men and should have a wider role in society. He showed himself well aware of the kinds of personal, emotional, and sexual repression European women endured in his day. He sympathetically observed the value placed on women's appearance and the prejudice women met as they aged. In *The Persian Letters*, he included a long exchange about the repression of women in a

Rousseau Argues for Separate Spheres for Men and Women

Rousseau published Émile, *a novel about education, in 1762. In it he made one of the strongest and most influential arguments of the eighteenth century for distinct social roles for men and women. Furthermore, he portrayed women as fundamentally subordinate to men. See pages 670, 671 for a contempory rebuttal.*

✦ *How does Rousseau move from the physical differences between men and women to an argument for distinct social roles and social spheres? What would be the proper kinds of social activities for women in Rousseau's vision? What kind of education would he think appropriate for women?*

There is no parity between the two sexes in regard to the consequences of sex. The male is male only at certain moments. The female is female her whole life or at least during her whole youth. Everything constantly recalls her sex to her; and, to fulfill its functions well, she needs a constitution which corresponds to it. She needs care during her pregnancy; she needs rest at the time of childbirth; she needs a soft and sedentary life to suckle her children; she needs patience and gentleness, a zeal and an affection that nothing can rebuff in order to raise her children. She serves as the link between them and their father; she alone makes him love them and gives him the confidence to call them his own. How much tenderness and care is required to maintain the union of the whole family! And, finally, all this must come not from virtues but from tastes, or else the human species would soon be extinguished.

The strictness of the relative duties of the two sexes is not and cannot be the same. When woman complains on this score about unjust man-made inequality, she is wrong. This inequality is not a human institution—or, at least, it is the work not of prejudice but of reason. It is up to the sex that nature has charged with the bearing of children to be responsible for them to the other sex. Doubtless it is not permitted to any one to violate his faith, and every unfaithful husband who deprives his wife of the only reward of the austere duties of her sex is an unjust and barbarous man. But the unfaithful woman does more; she dissolves the family and breaks all the bonds of nature. . . .

Once it is demonstrated that man and woman are not and ought not be constituted in the same way in either character or temperament, it follows that they ought not to have the same education. In following nature's directions, man and woman ought to act in concert, but they ought not to do the same things. The goal of their labors is common, but their labors themselves are different, and consequently so are the tastes directing them. . . .

The good constitution of children initially depends on that of their mothers. The first education of men depends on the care of women. Men's morals, their passions, their tastes, their pleasures, their very happiness also depend on women. Thus the whole education of women ought to relate to men. To please men, to be useful to them, to make herself loved and honored by them, to raise them when young, to care for them when grown, to counsel them, to console them, to make their lives agreeable and sweet—these are the duties of women at all times, and they ought to be taught from childhood. So long as one does not return to this principle, one will deviate from the goal, and all the precepts taught to women will be of no use for their happiness or for ours.

Jean-Jacques Rousseau, Émile; or, On Education, *trans. by Allan Bloom (New York: Basic Books, Inc., 1979), pp. 361, 363, 365.*

Mary Wollstonecraft Criticizes Rousseau's View of Women

Mary Wollstonecraft published A Vindication of the Rights of Woman *in 1792, thirty years after Rousseau's* Émile *had appeared. In this pioneering feminist work, she criticized and rejected Rousseau's argument for distinct and separate spheres for men and women. She portrayed that argument as defending the continued bondage of women to men and as hindering the wider education of the entire human race.*

✦ *What specific criticisms does Wollstonecraft direct against Rousseau's views? Why does Wollstonecraft put so much emphasis on a new kind of education for women? How might Wollstonecraft's arguments be seen as embodying the high ideals of enlightenment that Immanuel Kant set forth in an earlier selection in this chapter?*

The most perfect education . . . is such an exercise of the understanding as is best calculated to strengthen the body and form the heart. Or, in other words, to enable the individual to attain such habits of virtue as will render it independent. In fact, it is a farce to call any being virtuous whose virtues do not result from the exercise of its own reason. This was Rousseau's opinion respecting men: I extend it to women. . . .

I may be accused of arrogance; still I must declare what I firmly believe, that all the writers who have written on the subject of female education and manners from Rousseau to Dr. Gregory [a Scottish physician], have contributed to render women more artificial, weak characters, than they would other wise have been; and, consequently, more useless members of society. . . .

. . . Strengthen the female mind by enlarging it, and there will be an end to blind obedience; but, as blind obedience is ever sought for by power, tyrants and sensualists are in the right when they endeavour to keep women in the dark, because the former only wants slaves, and the latter a play-thing. The sensualist, indeed, has been the most dangerous of tyrants, and women have been duped by their lovers, as princes by their ministers, whilst dreaming that they reigned over them.

. . . Rousseau declares that a woman

Persian harem, condemning by implication the restrictions on women in European society. Yet there were limits to Montesquieu's willingness to consider social change in regard to the role of women in European life. Although in *The Spirit of the Laws* he indicated a belief in the equality of the sexes, he still retained a traditional view of marriage and family and expected men to dominate those institutions. Furthermore, although he supported the right of women to divorce and opposed laws directly oppressive of women, he upheld the ideal of female chastity.

The views about women expressed in the *Encyclopedia* were less generous than those of Montesquieu. It suggested some ways to improve women's lives, but in general it did not include the condition of women as a focus of reform. The editors, Diderot and d'Alembert, recruited men almost exclusively as contributors, and there is no indication they saw a need to include many articles by women. Most of the articles that dealt with women specifically or that discussed women in connection with other subjects often emphasized their physical weakness and inferiority, usually attributed to menstruation or childbearing. Contributors disagreed on the social equality of women. Some favored it, others opposed it, and still others were indifferent. The articles conveyed a general sense that women were reared to be frivolous

should never, for a moment, feel herself independent, that she should be governed by fear to exercise her natural cunning, and made a coquetish slave in order to render her a more alluring object of desire, a *sweeter* companion to man, whenever he chooses to relax himself. He carries the arguments, which he pretends to draw from the indications of nature, still further, and insinuates that truth and fortitude, the corner stones of all human virtue, should be cultivated with certain restrictions, because, with respect to the female character, obedience is the grand lesson which ought to be impressed with unrelenting rigour.

What nonsense! when will a great man arise with sufficient strength of mind to put away the fumes which pride and sensuality have thus spread over the subject! If women are by nature inferior to men, their virtues must be the same in quality, if not in degree, or virtue is a relative idea; consequently, their conduct should be founded on the same principles, and have the same aim.

Connected with man as daughters, wives, and mothers, their moral character may be estimated by their manner of fulfilling those simple duties; but the end, the grand end of their exertions should be to unfold their own faculties and acquire the dignity of conscious virtue. . . .

But avoiding . . . any direct comparison of the two sexes collectively, or frankly acknowledging the inferiority of women, according to the present appearance of things, I shall only insist that men have increased that inferiority till women are almost sunk below the standard of rational creatures. Let their faculties have room to unfold, and their virtues to gain strength, and then determine where the whole sex must stand in the intellectual scale. . . .

. . . I . . . will venture to assert, that till women are more rationally educated, the progress of human virtue and improvement in knowledge must receive continual checks. . . .

The mother, who wishes to give true dignity of character to her daughter, must, regardless of the sneers of ignorance, proceed on a plan diametrically opposite to that which Rousseau has recommended with all the deluding charms of eloquence and philosophical sophistry: for his eloquence renders absurdities plausible, and his dogmatic conclusions puzzle, without convincing, those who have not ability to refute them.

Mary Wollstonecraft, A Vindication of the Rights of Woman, *ed. by Carol H. Poston (New York: W. W. Norton & Co., Inc., 1975), pp. 21, 22, 24–26, 35, 40, 41.*

and unconcerned with important issues. The encyclopedists discussed women primarily in a family context—as daughters, wives, and mothers—and present motherhood as their most important occupation. And on sexual behavior, the encyclopedists upheld an unquestioned double standard.

In contrast to the articles, however, illustrations in the *Encyclopedia* showed women deeply involved in the economic activities of the day. The illustrations also showed the activities of lower- and working-class women, about whom the articles have little to say.

One of the most surprising and influential analyses of the position of women came from Jean-Jacques Rousseau. This most radical of all Enlightenment political theorists urged a very traditional and conservative role for women. In his novel *Émile* (1762, discussed again in Chapter 20), he set forth a radical version of the view that men and women occupy separate spheres. He declared that women should be educated for a position subordinate to men, emphasizing especially women's function in bearing and rearing children. In his vision there was little else for women to do but make themselves pleasing to men. He portrayed them as weaker and inferior to men in virtually all respects except perhaps for their capacity for feeling and giving love. He excluded them from political life. The world of citizenship, political action, and civic virtue was to be populated by men. Women were assigned the domestic sphere alone. Many of these attitudes were not new—some have roots as ancient as Roman law—but Rousseau's powerful presentation and the influence of his other writings gave them new life in the late eighteenth century. Rousseau deeply influenced many leaders of the French Revolution, who, as will be seen in the next chapter, often incorporated his view on gender roles in the policies they implemented.

Paradoxically, in spite of these views and in spite of his own ill treatment of the many women who bore his many children, Rousseau achieved a vast following among women in the eighteenth century. He is credited with persuading thousands of upper-class women to breast feed their own children rather than putting them out to wet nurses. One explanation for this influence is that his writings, although they did not advocate liberating women or expanding their social or economic roles, did stress the importance of their emotions and subjective feelings. He portrayed the domestic life and the role of wife and mother as a noble and fulfilling vocation, giving middle- and upper-class women a sense that their daily occupations had purpose. He assigned them a degree of influence in the domestic sphere that they could not have competing with men outside it.

In 1792, in *A Vindication of the Rights of Woman*, Mary Wollstonecraft (1759—1797) brought Rousseau before the judgment of the rational Enlightenment ideal of progressive knowledge. The immediate incentive for this essay was her opposition to certain policies of the French Revolution, unfavorable to women, which were inspired by Rousseau. Wollstonecraft (who, like so many women of her day, died shortly after childbirth of puerperal fever) accused Rousseau and others after him who upheld traditional roles for women of attempting to narrow women's vision and limit their experience. She argued that to confine women to the separate domestic sphere because of supposed limitations of their physiological nature was to make them the sensual slaves of men. Confined in this separate sphere, they were the victims of male tyranny, their obedience was

blind, and they could never achieve their own moral or intellectual identity. Denying good education to women would impede the progress of all humanity. With these arguments, Wollstonecraft was demanding for women the kind of liberty that male writers of the Enlightenment had been championing for men for more than a century. In doing so, she placed herself among the *philosophes* and broadened the agenda of the Enlightenment to include the rights of women as well as those of men.

Enlightened Absolutism

Most of the *philosophes* favored neither Montesquieu's reformed and revived aristocracy nor Rousseau's democracy as a solution to contem-

---

Major Publication Dates of the Enlightenment

1687	Newton's *Principia Mathematica*
1690	Locke's *Essay Concerning Human Understanding*
1696	Toland's *Christianity Not Mysterious*
1721	Montesquieu's *Persian Letters*
1733	Voltaire's *Letters on the English*
1738	Voltaire's *Elements of the Philosophy of Newton*
1748	Montesquieu's *Spirit of the Laws*
1748	Hume's *Inquiry into Human Nature*, with the chapter "Of Miracles"
1750	Rousseau's *Discourse on the Moral Effects of the Arts and Sciences*
1751	First volume of the *Encyclopedia*, edited by Diderot
1755	Rousseau's *Discourse on the Origin of Inequality*
1759	Voltaire's *Candide*
1762	Rousseau's *Social Contract* and *Émile*
1763	Voltaire's *Treatise on Toleration*
1764	Voltaire's *Philosophical Dictionary*
1764	Beccaria's *On Crimes and Punishments*
1776	Gibbon's *Decline and Fall of the Roman Empire*
1776	Smith's *Wealth of Nations*
1779	Lessing's *Nathan the Wise*
1792	Wollstonecraft's *Vindication of the Rights of Woman*

---

porary political problems. Like other thoughtful people of the day in other stations and occupations, they looked to the existing monarchies. Voltaire was a very strong monarchist. He and others—such as Diderot, who visited Catherine II of Russia, and the physiocrats, some of whom were ministers to the French kings—did not wish to limit the power of monarchs. Rather, they sought to redirect that power toward the rationalization of economic and political structures and the liberation of intellectual life. Most *philosophes* were not opposed to power if they could find a way of using it for their own purposes.

During the last third of the century, it seemed to some observers that several European rulers had actually embraced many of the reforms set forth by the *philosophes. Enlightened absolutism* is the term used to describe this phenomenon. The phrase indicates monarchical government dedicated to the rational strengthening of the central absolutist administration at the cost of other lesser centers of political power. The monarchs most closely associated with it are Frederick II of Prussia, Joseph II of Austria, and Catherine II of Russia.

Frederick II corresponded with the *philosophes,* for a time provided Voltaire with a place at his court, and even wrote history and political tracts. Catherine II, adept at what would later be called public relations, consciously sought to create the image of being enlightened. She read the works of the *philosophes,* became a friend of Diderot and Voltaire, and made frequent references to their ideas, all in the hope that her nation might seem more modern and Western. Joseph II continued numerous initiatives begun by his mother, Maria Theresa. He imposed a series of religious, legal, and social reforms that contemporaries believed he had derived from suggestions of the *philosophes.*

The relationship between these rulers and the writers of the Enlightenment was, however, more complicated than these appearances suggest. The humanitarian and liberating zeal of the Enlightenment writers was only part of what motivated the policies of the rulers. Frederick II, Joseph II, and Catherine II were also determined that their nations would play major diplomatic and military roles in Europe. In no small mea-

sure, they adopted Enlightenment policies favoring the rational economic and social integration of their realms because these policies also increased their military strength. All the states of Europe had emerged from the Seven Years' War knowing they would need stronger armies for future wars and increased revenue to finance those armies. The search for new revenues and internal political support was one of the incentives prompting the "enlightened" reforms of the monarchs of Russia, Prussia, and Austria. Consequently, they and their advisers used rationality to pursue many goals admired by the *philosophes* but also to further what the *philosophes* considered irrational militarism.

Frederick the Great of Prussia

Frederick II (the Great, r. 1740–1786) sought the recovery and consolidation of Prussia in the wake of its suffering and near defeat in the mid-century wars. He succeeded, at great military and financial cost, in retaining Silesia, which he had seized from Austria in 1740, and worked to promote it as a manufacturing district. Like his Hohenzollern forebears, he continued to import workers from outside Prussia. He directed new attention to Prussian agriculture. Under state supervision, swamps were drained, new crops introduced, and peasants encouraged and sometimes compelled to migrate where they were needed. For the first time in Prussia, potatoes and turnips came into general production. Frederick also established a Land-Mortgage Credit Association to help landowners raise money for agricultural improvements.

The impetus for these economic policies came from the state. The monarchy and its bureaucracy were the engine for change. Most Prussians, however, did not prosper under Frederick's reign. The burden of taxation continued to fall disproportionally on peasants and townspeople.

Frederick's noneconomic policies met with somewhat more success. Continuing the Hohenzollern policy of toleration, he allowed Catholics and Jews to settle in his predominantly Lutheran country, and he protected the Catholics living in Silesia. This policy permitted

Frederick II, the Great (r. 1740–1786), sought to create prosperity for all parts of the Prussian economy and would make personal visits to factories and shops to inspect the goods being made and sold in his kingdom. Here he visits a fashionable shop. [Bildarchiv Preussischer Kulturbesitz]

the state to benefit from the economic contribution of foreign workers. Frederick, however, virtually always appointed Protestants to major positions in the government and army.

Frederick also ordered a new codification of Prussian law, completed after his death. His object was to rationalize the existing legal system, making it more efficient, eliminating regional peculiarities, and reducing aristocratic influence. Frederick shared this concern for legal reform with the other enlightened monarchs, who saw it as a means of extending and strengthening royal power.

Reflecting an important change in the European view of the ruler, Frederick liked to describe himself as "the first servant of the State." The impersonal state was beginning to replace the personal monarchy. Kings might come and go, but the apparatus of government—the bureaucracy, the armies, the laws, the courts, and the combination of power, service, and protection that compelled citizen loyalty—remained. The state as an entity separate from the personality of the ruler came into its own after the French Revolution, but it was born in the monarchies of the old regime.

Joseph II of Austria

No eighteenth-century ruler so embodied rational, impersonal force as the emperor Joseph II of Austria. He was the son of Maria Theresa and coruler with her from 1765 to 1780. During the next ten years he ruled alone. He was an austere and humorless person. During much of his life, he slept on straw and ate little but beef. He prided himself on a narrow, passionless rationality, which he sought to impose by his own will on the various Habsburg domains. Despite his eccentricities and the coldness of his personality, Joseph II sincerely wished to improve the lot of his people. He was much less a political opportunist and cynic than either Frederick the Great of Prussia or Catherine the Great of Russia. The ultimate result of his well-intentioned efforts was a series of aristocratic and peasant rebellions extending from Hungary to the Austrian Netherlands.

CENTRALIZATION OF AUTHORITY As explained in Chapter 15, of all the rising states of the eighteenth century, Austria was the most diverse in its people and problems. Robert Palmer likened it to "a vast holding company."[7] The Habsburgs never succeeded in creating either a unified administrative structure or a strong aristocratic loyalty. To preserve the monarchy during the War of the Austrian Succession (1740–1748), Maria Theresa had guaranteed the aristocracy considerable independence, especially in Hungary.

During and after the conflict, however, Maria Theresa took steps to strengthen the power of the crown outside of Hungary, building more of a bureaucracy than had previous Habsburg rulers. In Austria and Bohemia, through major administrative reorganization, she imposed a much more efficient system of tax collection that extracted funds even from the clergy and the nobles. She also established several central councils to deal with governmental problems. To assure her government a sufficient supply of educated officials, she sought to bring all educational institutions into the service of the crown. She also expanded primary education on the local level.

Maria Theresa was concerned about the welfare of the peasants and serfs. She brought them some assistance by extending the authority of the royal bureaucracy over local nobles and decreeing limits on the amount of labor, or *robot,* landowners could demand from peasants. Her concern was not particularly humanitarian; rather, it arose from her desire to assure a good pool from which to draw military recruits. In all these policies and in her general desire to stimulate prosperity and military strength by royal initiative, Maria Theresa anticipated the policies of her son.

Joseph II was more determined than his mother and his projected reforms were more

Joseph II of Austria (r. 1765–1790), shown here in the center, with his brother Leopold (later Leopold II) on his right, attempted to impose exceedingly rational policies on the Habsburg empire. Joseph urged religious toleration and confiscated church lands. His attempts to tax the nobility stirred up a revolt that Leopold settled after Joseph's death by rescinding his policies. [Kunsthistorisches Museum, Vienna]

[7]Robert R. Palmer, The Age of Democratic Revolution, Vol. 1 (Princeton, N.J.: Princeton University Press, 1959), p. 103.

Maria Theresa and Joseph II of Austria Debate the Question of Toleration

In 1765 Joseph, the eldest son of the Empress Maria Theresa, had become coregent with his mother. He began to believe that some measure of religious toleration should be introduced into the Habsburg realms. Maria Theresa, whose opinions on many political issues were quite advanced, adamantly refused to consider adopting a policy of toleration. This exchange of letters sets forth their sharply differing positions. The toleration of Protestants in dispute related only to Lutherans and Calvinists. Maria Theresa died in 1780; the next year Joseph issued an edict of toleration.

✦ *How does Joseph define toleration, and why does Maria Theresa believe it is the same as religious indifference? Why does Maria Theresa fear that toleration will bring about political as well as religious turmoil? Why does Maria Theresa think the belief in toleration has come from Joseph's acquaintance with wicked books?*

Joseph to Maria Theresa, July 20, 1777

It is only the word "toleration" which has caused the misunderstanding. You have taken it in quite a different meaning [from mine expressed in an earlier letter]. God preserve me from thinking it a matter of indifference whether the citizens turn Protestant or remain Catholic, still less, whether they cleave to, or at least observe, the cult which they have inherited from their fathers! I would give all I possess if all the Protestants of your states would go over to Catholicism.

The word "toleration," as I understand it, means only that I would employ any persons, without distinction of religion, in purely temporal matters, allow them to own property, practice trades, be citizens, if they were qualified and if this would be of advantage to the State and its industry. Those who, unfortunately, adhere to a false faith, are far further

---

wide-ranging. He aimed to extend the borders of his territories in the direction of Poland, Bavaria, and the Ottoman Empire. His greatest ambition, however, was to increase the authority of the Habsburg emperor over his various realms. He sought to overcome the pluralism of the Habsburg holdings by imposing central authority in areas of political and social life where Maria Theresa had wisely chosen not to exert authority.

In particular, Joseph sought to reduce Hungarian autonomy. To avoid having to guarantee Hungary's existing privileges or extend new ones at the time of his coronation, he refused to have himself crowned king of Hungary and even had the Crown of Saint Stephen sent to the Imperial Treasury in Vienna. He reorganized local government in Hungary to increase the authority of his own officials. He also required the use of German in all governmental matters. The Magyar nobility resisted these measures, and in 1790 Joseph had to rescind most of them.

ECCLESIASTICAL POLICIES Another target of Joseph's assertion of royal absolutism was the Church. From the reign of Charles V in the sixteenth century to that of Maria Theresa, the Habsburgs had been the most important dynastic champion of Roman Catholicism. Maria Theresa was devout, but she had not allowed the Church to limit her authority. Although she had attempted to discourage certain of the more extreme modes of Roman Catholic popular religious piety, such as public flagellation, she adamantly opposed toleration.

from being converted if they remain in their own country than if they migrate into another, in which they can hear and see the convincing truths of the Catholic faith. Similarly, the undisturbed practice of their religion makes them far better subjects and causes them to avoid irreligion, which is a far greater danger to our Catholics than if one lets them see others practice their religion unimpeded.

Maria Theresa to Joseph, Late July, 1777

Without a dominant religion? Toleration, indifference are precisely the true means of undermining everything, taking away every foundation; we others will then be the greatest losers. . . . He is no friend of humanity, as the popular phrase is, who allows everyone his own thoughts. I am speaking only in the political sense, not as a Christian; nothing is so necessary and salutary as religion. Will you allow everyone to fashion his own religion as he pleases? No fixed cult, no subordination to the Church—what will then become of us? The result will not be quiet and contentment; its outcome will be the rule of the stronger and more unhappy times like those which we have already seen. A manifesto by you to this effect can produce the utmost distress and make you responsible for many thousands of souls. And what are my own sufferings, when I see you entangled in opinions so erroneous? What is at stake is not only the welfare of the State but your own salvation. . . . Turning your eyes and ears everywhere, mingling your spirit of contradiction with the simultaneous desire to create something, you are ruining yourself and dragging the Monarchy down with you into the abyss. . . . I only wish to live so long as I can hope to descend to my ancestors with the consolation that my son will be as great, as religious as his forebears, that he will return from his erroneous views, from those wicked books whose authors parade their cleverness at the expense of all that is most holy and most worthy of respect in the world, who want to introduce an imaginary freedom which can never exist and which degenerates into license and into complete revolution.

As quoted in C. A. Macartney, ed., The Habsburg and Hohenzollern Dynasties in the Seventeenth and Eighteenth Centuries *(New York: Walker,* 1970), pp. 151–153.

Joseph II was also a practicing Catholic, but from the standpoint of both enlightenment and pragmatic politics, he favored a policy of toleration. In October 1781, Joseph issued a Toleration Patent (decree) that extended freedom of worship to Lutherans, Calvinists, and the Greek Orthodox. They were permitted to have their own places of worship, to sponsor schools, to enter skilled trades, and to hold academic appointments and positions in the public service. From 1781 through 1789, Joseph issued a series of patents and other enactments that relieved the Jews in his realms of certain taxes and signs of personal degradation. He also extended to them the right of private worship. Although these actions benefitted the Jews, they did not grant them full equality with other Habsburg subjects.

Joseph also sought to bring the various institutions of the Roman Catholic church directly under royal control. He forbade direct communication between the bishops of his realms and the pope. Viewing religious orders as unproductive, he dissolved more than 600 monasteries and confiscated their lands. He excepted, however, certain orders that ran schools or hospitals. He dissolved the traditional Roman Catholic seminaries, which instilled in priests too great a loyalty to the papacy and too little concern for their future parishioners. In their place he sponsored eight general seminaries where the training emphasized parish duties. He also issued decrees creating new parishes in areas with a shortage of priests, funding them with money from the confiscated monasteries. In effect, Joseph's policies made Roman Catholic priests the employees of the state, ending the influence of the Roman Catholic church as an independent institution in Habsburg lands. In many respects the ecclesiastical policies of Joseph II, known as *Josephinism*, prefigured those of the French Revolution.

ECONOMIC AND AGRARIAN REFORM Like Frederick of Prussia, Joseph sought to improve the economic life of his domains. He abolished many internal tariffs and encouraged road building and the improvement of river transport. He went on personal inspection tours of farms and manufacturing districts. Joseph also reconstructed the judicial system to make laws more uniform and rational and to lessen the influence of local landlords. National courts with power over the landlord courts were established. All of these improvements were expected to bring new unity to the state and more taxes into the imperial coffers in Vienna.

Joseph's policies toward serfdom and the land were a far-reaching extension of those Maria Theresa had initiated. Over the course of his reign he introduced a series of reforms that touched the very heart of the rural social structure. He did not seek to abolish the authority of landlords over their peasants, but he did seek to make that authority more moderate and subject to the oversight of royal officials. He abolished serfdom as a legally sanctioned state of servitude. He granted peasants a wide array of personal freedoms, including the right to marry, to engage in skilled work, and to have their children trained in skilled work without the landlord's permission.

Joseph reformed the procedures of the manorial courts and opened avenues of appeal to royal officials. He also encouraged landlords to change land leases so it would be easier for peasants to inherit them or to transfer them to other peasants. His goal in all of these efforts to reduce traditional burdens on peasants was to make them more productive and industrious farmers.

Near the end of his reign, Joseph proposed a new and daring system of land taxation. He decreed in 1789 that all proprietors of the land were to be taxed regardless of social status. No longer were the peasants alone to bear the burden of taxation. He abolished *robot* (the services due a landlord from peasants) and commuted it into a monetary tax, only part of which was to go to the landlord, the rest reverting to the state. Resistant nobles blocked the implementation of this decree, and after Joseph died in 1790 it was never put into effect. This and other of Joseph's earlier measures, however, brought turmoil throughout the Habsburg realms. Peasants revolted over disagreements about the interpretation of their newly granted rights. The nobles of the various realms protested the taxation scheme. The Hungarian Magyars resisted Joseph's centralization measures and forced him to rescind them.

On Joseph's death, the crown went to his brother Leopold II (r. 1790–1792). Although sympathetic to Joseph's goals, Leopold found himself forced to repeal many of the most controversial decrees, such as that on taxation. In other areas, Leopold thought his brother's policies simply wrong. For example, he returned much political and administrative power to local nobles because he thought it expedient for them to have a voice in government. Still, he did not repudiate his brother's policies wholesale. He retained, in particular, Joseph's religious policies and maintained political centralization to the extent he thought possible.

Catherine the Great of Russia

Joseph II never grasped the practical necessity of forging political constituencies to support his policies. Catherine II (r. 1762–1796), who had been born a German princess but who became empress of Russia, understood only too well the fragility of the Romanov dynasty's base of power.

After the death of Peter the Great in 1725, the court nobles and the army repeatedly determined the Russian succession. As a result, the crown fell primarily into the hands of people with little talent. Peter's wife, Catherine I, ruled for two years (1725–1727) and was succeeded for three years by Peter's grandson, Peter II. In 1730 the crown devolved on Ann, a niece of Peter the Great. During 1740 and 1741, a child named Ivan VI, who was less than a year old, was the nominal ruler. Finally, in 1741 Peter the Great's daughter Elizabeth came to the throne. She held the title of empress until 1762, but her reign was not notable for new political departures or sound administration. Her court was a shambles of political and romantic intrigue. Much of the power possessed by the tsar at the opening of the century had vanished.

At her death in 1762, Elizabeth was succeeded by Peter III, one of her nephews. He was a weak ruler whom many contemporaries considered mad. He immediately exempted the nobles from compulsory military service and then rapidly made peace with Frederick the Great, for whom he held unbounded admiration. That decision probably saved Prussia from military defeat in the Seven Years' War. The one positive feature of this unbalanced creature's life was his marriage in 1745 to a young German princess born in Anhalt Zerbst. This was the future Catherine the Great.

For almost twenty years she lived in misery and frequent danger at the court of Elizabeth. During that time she befriended important nobles and read widely in the books of the *philosophes*. She was a shrewd person whose experience in a court crawling with rumors, intrigue, and conspiracy had taught her how to survive. She exhibited neither love nor fidelity toward her demented husband. A few months after his accession as tsar, Peter was deposed and murdered with Catherine's approval, if not her aid, and she was immediately proclaimed empress.

Catherine's familiarity with the Enlightenment and the general culture of western Europe convinced her that Russia was very backward and that it must make major reforms if it was to remain a great power. She understood that any major reform must have a wide base of political and social support, especially since she had assumed the throne through a palace coup. In 1767 she summoned a Legislative Commission to advise her on revisions in the law and government of Russia. There were more than 500 delegates, drawn from all sectors of Russian life. Before the commission convened, Catherine issued a set of *Instructions*, partly written by herself. They contained many ideas drawn from the political writings of the *philosophes*. The commission considered the *Instructions* as well as other ideas and complaints raised by its members.

The revision of Russian law, however, did not occur for more than half a century. In 1768

Catherine dismissed the commission before several of its key committees had reported. Yet the meeting had not been useless, for a vast amount of information had been gathered about the conditions of local administration and economic life throughout the realm. The inconclusive debates and the absence of programs from the delegates themselves suggested that most Russians saw no alternative to an autocratic monarchy. For her part, Catherine had no intention of departing from absolutism.

LIMITED ADMINISTRATIVE REFORM Catherine proceeded to carry out limited reforms on her own authority. She gave strong support to the rights and local power of the nobility. In 1777 she reorganized local government to solve problems brought to light by the Legislative Commission. She put most local offices in the hands of nobles rather than creating a royal bureaucracy. In 1785 Catherine issued the Charter of the Nobility, which guaranteed many noble rights and privileges. In part, the empress had no choice but to favor the nobles. They had the capacity to topple her from the throne. There were too few educated subjects in her realm to establish an independent bureaucracy, and the treasury could not afford an army strictly loyal to the crown. So Catherine wisely made a virtue of necessity. She strengthened the stability of her crown by making convenient friends with her nobles.

ECONOMIC GROWTH Part of Catherine's program was to continue the economic development begun under Peter the Great. She attempted to suppress internal barriers to trade. Exports of grain, flax, furs, and naval stores grew dramatically. She also favored the expansion of the small Russian urban middle class so vital to trade. And through all of these departures Catherine tried to maintain ties of friendship and correspondence with the *philosophes*. She knew that if she treated them kindly, they would be sufficiently flattered to give her a progressive reputation throughout Europe.

TERRITORIAL EXPANSION Catherine's limited administrative reforms and her policy of economic growth had a counterpart in the diplomatic sphere. The Russian drive for warm-water ports continued (see Map 18-1). This goal

Catherine the Great, here portrayed as a young princess, ascended to the Russian throne after the murder of her husband. She tried initially to enact major reforms but she never intended to abandon absolutism. She assured the nobility of their rights and by the end of her reign had imposed press censorship. [The Bettmann Archive]

province of the Crimea became an independent state, which Catherine painlessly annexed in 1783.

The Partition of Poland

These military successes obviously brought the empress much domestic political support, but they made the other states of eastern Europe uneasy. These anxieties were overcome by an extraordinary division of Polish territory known as the First Partition of Poland.

The Russian victories along the Danube River were most unwelcome to Austria, which also harbored ambitions of territorial expansion in that direction. At the same time, the Ottoman Empire was pressing Prussia for aid against Russia. Frederick the Great made a proposal to Russia and Austria that would give each something it wanted, prevent conflict among the powers, and save appearances. After long, complicated, secret negotiations the three powers

required warfare with the Turks. In 1769, as a result of a minor Russian incursion, the Ottoman Empire declared war on Russia. The Russians responded in a series of strikingly successful military moves.

During 1769 and 1770, the Russian fleet sailed all the way from the Baltic Sea into the eastern Mediterranean. The Russian army won several major victories that by 1771 gave Russia control of Ottoman provinces on the Danube River and the Crimean coast of the Black Sea. The conflict dragged on until 1774, when it was closed by the Treaty of Kuchuk-Kainardji. The treaty gave Russia a direct outlet on the Black Sea, free navigation rights in its waters, and free access through the Bosporus. Moreover, the

Russia from Peter the Great Through Catherine the Great	
1725	Death of Peter the Great
1725–1727	Catherine I
1727–1730	Peter II
1730–1741	Anne
1740–1741	Ivan VI
1741–1762	Elizabeth
1762	Peter III
1762	Catherine II (the Great) becomes empress
1767	Legislative Commission summoned
1769	War with Turkey begins
1771–1775	Pugachev's Rebellion
1772	First Partition of Poland
1774	Treaty of Kuchuk-Kainardji ends war with Turkey
1775	Reorganization of local government
1783	Russia annexes the Crimea
1785	Catherine issues the Charter of the Nobility
1793	Second Partition of Poland
1795	Third Partition of Poland
1796	Death of Catherine the Great

MAP 18-1 EXPANSION OF RUSSIA 1689–1796 *The overriding territorial aim of Peter the Great in the first quarter and of Catherine the Great in the last half of the eighteenth century was to secure year-round navigable outlets to the sea for the vast Russian Empire, hence Peter's push to the Baltic Sea and Catherine's to the Black Sea. Catherine also managed to acquire large areas of Poland through the partitions of that country.*

In September 1772, the helpless Polish aristocracy, paying the price for maintaining their internal liberties at the expense of developing a strong central government, ratified this seizure of nearly one-third of their territory. The loss was not necessarily fatal to Poland's continued existence, and it inspired a revival of national feeling. Real attempts were made to adjust the Polish political structures to the realities of the time. These proved, however, to be too little and too late. The political and military strength of Poland could not match that of its stronger, more ambitious neighbors. The partition of Poland clearly demonstrated that any nation

MAP 18-2 PARTITIONS OF POLAND, 1772–1793–1795 *The callous eradication of Poland from the map displayed eighteenth-century power politics at its most extreme. Poland, without strong central governmental institutions, fell victim to those states in central and eastern Europe that had developed such institutions.*

agreed that Russia would abandon the conquered Danubian provinces. In compensation Russia received a large portion of Polish territory with almost two million inhabitants. As a reward for remaining neutral, Prussia annexed most of the territory between East Prussia and Prussia proper. This land allowed Frederick to unite two previously separate sections of his realm. Finally, Austria took Galicia, with its important salt mines, and other Polish territory with more than two and one-half million inhabitants (see Map 18-2).

Frederick the Great Examines the Political Weakness of Poland

During the last quarter of the eighteenth century, Prussia, Russia, and Austria partitioned Poland, removing it from the map of Europe for over a century. These partitions were regarded as among the most astonishing diplomatic moves of the day. Yet several years before the first partition occurred, Frederick the Great outlined the vulnerability of Poland and the reasons it commanded so little respect among the great powers of Europe.

◆ *What are the specific weaknesses of Polish political structures? Why is Frederick so critical of the Polish nobility? In what ways had late-eighteenth-century Poland failed to achieve a strong central government?*

Poland can scarcely be counted among the European Powers. The lack of population in that kingdom, arising from the fact that the landowners treat their subjects as slaves, is one of the defects of that republic. There are many others which contribute to its low rating, such as poor financial administration, and a force of only 13,000 men instead of an army. All the faults of the old feudal forms of government have been preserved there to our own day: elections of their kings, followed by civil wars; turbulent Diets, of which not one runs its course; no legislation, no justice. It is the reign of anarchy. Poland would long ago have been subjugated, had not her jealous neighbors restrained by armed deterrence the ambitious rulers who sought to subdue her.

Torn by factions, Poland is always weak: as long as her present form of government lasts, she will be little to be feared by her enemies and a burden on her allies. The nobility is proud and arrogant in prosperity, cowardly in misfortune, corrupt and incapable of taking vigorous measures or following them through. In a word, in my opinion, Poland is the least important nation in Europe.

From "*Testament politique*" (1768), Die Politischen Testamente Friedrichs des Grossen, *G. B. Volz, ed. (Berlin, 1920), p. 99, as quoted in A. Lentin,* Enlightened Absolutism (1760–1790): A Documentary Sourcebook *(London: Avero, 1985), p. 219.*

that had not established a strong monarchy, bureaucracy, and army could no longer compete within the European state system.

Russia and Prussia partitioned Poland again in 1793, and Russia, Prussia, and Austria partitioned it a third time in 1795, removing it from the map of Europe for more than a century. Each time, the great powers contended that they were saving themselves, and by implication the rest of Europe, from Polish anarchy. The fact of the matter was that the Poland's political weakness left it vulnerable to plunderous aggression. The partitions of 1793 and 1795 took place in the shadow of the French Revolution, which left the absolute monarchies of eastern Europe concerned for their own stability. As a result, they reacted harshly even to minor attempts at reform by the Polish nobles, fearing they might infect their own domains.

The End of the Eighteenth Century in Central and Eastern Europe

During the last two decades of the eighteenth century, all three regimes based on enlightened absolutism became more conservative and politically repressive. In Prussia and Austria, the innovations of the rulers stirred resistance among the nobility. In Russia, fear of peasant unrest was the chief factor.

Frederick the Great of Prussia grew remote during his old age, leaving the aristocracy to fill important military and administrative posts. A reaction to Enlightenment ideas also set in among Prussian Lutheran writers.

In Austria, Joseph II's plans to restructure society and administration in his realms provoked growing frustration and political unrest, with the nobility calling for an end to innovation. In response, Joseph turned increasingly to censorship and his secret police.

Russia faced a peasant uprising, the Pugachev Rebellion, between 1771 and 1775, and Catherine the Great never fully recovered from the fears of social and political upheaval it raised. Once the French Revolution broke out in 1789, the Russian empress censored books based on Enlightenment thought and sent offensive authors into Siberian exile.

By the close of the century, fear of and hostility to change permeated the ruling classes of central and eastern Europe. This reaction began before 1789, but the events in France bolstered and sustained it for almost half a century. Paradoxically, nowhere did the humanity and liberalism of the Enlightenment encounter greater rejection than in those states that had been governed by "enlightened" rulers.

Although the enlightened absolute monarchs lacked the humanity of the *philosophes*, they had embraced the Enlightenment spirit of innovation. They wanted to change the political, social, and economic structures of their realms. From the close of the Seven Years' War (1763) until the opening of the French Revolution in 1789, the monarchies of both western and eastern Europe had been the major agents of institutional change. In every case they provoked aristocratic, and sometimes popular, resistance and resentment. George III of Britain fought for years with Parliament and lost the colonies of North America in the process. Frederick II of Prussia succeeded with his program of reform only because he accepted new aristocratic influence over the bureaucracy and the army. Catherine II of Russia had to come to terms with Russia's nobility. Joseph II, who did not consult with the nobility of his domains, left those domains in turmoil.

This French engraving is a satirical comment on the first partition of Poland (1772) by Russia, Austria, and Prussia. The distressed monarch attempting to retain his crown is Stanislaus of Poland. Catherine of Russia, Joseph of Austria, and Frederick of Prussia point out their respective shares of the loot. [Bildarchiv Preussischer Kulturbesitz]

These monarchs pushed for innovations from a desire for increased revenue. In France also, the royal drive for adequate fiscal resources led to aristocratic resistance. In France, however, neither the monarchy nor the aristocracy could control the social and political forces their quarrel unleashed.

◆

The writers of the Enlightenment, known as philosophes, *charted a major new path in modern European and Western thought. They oper-*

Alexander Radishchev Attacks Russian Censorship

Alexander Radishchev (1749–1802) was an enlightened Russian landowner who published A Journey from Saint Petersburg to Moscow *in 1790. The book criticized many aspects of Russian political and social life, including the treatment of serfs. Shortly after its publication, Catherine the Great, fearing the kind of unrest associated with the French Revolution might spread to Russia, had Radishchev arrested. He was tried and sentenced to death, but Catherine commuted the sentence to a period of Siberian exile. All but eighteen copies of his book were destroyed. It was not published in Russia again until 1905. These passages criticizing censorship illustrate how a writer filled with the ideas of the Enlightenment could question some of the fundamental ways in which an enlightened absolutist ruler, such as Catherine, governed.*

◆ *How does Radishchev satirize censorship and the censors? Why does he contend that public opinion rather than the government will act as an adequate censor? Would work censored by public opinion be truly free from censorship? Why might Catherine the Great or other enlightened absolutist rulers have feared opinions like these?*

Having recognized the usefulness of printing, the government has made it open to all; having further recognized that control of thought might invalidate its good intention in granting freedom to set up presses, it turned over the censorship or inspection of printed works to the Department of Public Morals. Its duty in this matter can only be the prohibition of the sale of objectionable works. But even this censorship is superfluous. A single stupid official in the Department of Public Morals may do the greatest harm to enlightenment and may for years hold back the progress of reason: he may prohibit a useful discovery, a new idea, and may rob everyone of something great. Here is an example on a small scale. A

---

ated within a print culture that made public opinion into a distinct cultural force. Admiring Newton and the achievements of physical science, they tried to apply reason and the principles of science to the cause of social reform. They believed also that passions and feelings were essential parts of human nature. Throughout their writings they championed reasonable moderation in social life. More than any other previous group of Western thinkers, they strongly opposed the authority of the established churches and especially of Roman Catholicism. Most of them championed some form of religious toleration. They also sought to achieve a science of society that could discover how to maximize human productivity and material happiness. The great dissenter among them was Rousseau, who also wished to reform society but in the name of virtue rather than material happiness.

The political influence of these writers went in several directions. The founding fathers of the American republic looked to them for political guidance, as did moderate liberal reformers throughout Europe, especially within royal bureaucracies. The autocratic rulers of eastern Europe consulted the *philosophes* in the hope that Enlightenment ideas might allow them to rule more efficiently. The revolutionaries in France would honor them. This diverse assortment of followers illustrates the diverse character of the *philosophes* themselves. It also shows that Enlightenment thought cannot be reduced to a single formula. Rather it should be seen as an outlook that championed change and reform, giving central place to humans

translation of a novel is brought to the Department of Public Morals for its imprimatur. The translator, following the author in speaking of love calls it "the tricky god." The censor in uniform and in the fullness of piety strikes out the expression saying, "It is improper to call a divinity tricky." He who does not understand should not interfere. . . .

Let anyone print anything that enters his head. If anyone finds himself insulted in print, let him get his redress at law. I am not speaking in jest. Words are not always deeds, thoughts are not crimes. These are the rules in the *Instruction for a New Code of Laws*. But an offense in words or in print is always an offense. Under the law no one is allowed to libel another, and everyone has the right to bring suit. But if one tells the truth about another, that cannot, according to the law, be considered a libel. What harm can there be if books are printed without a police stamp? Not only will there be no harm; there will be an advantage, an advantage from the first to the last, from the least to the greatest, from the Tsar to the last citizen. . . .

I will close with this: the censorship of what is printed belongs properly to society, which gives the author a laurel wreath or uses his sheets for wrapping paper. Just so, it is the public that gives its approval to a theatrical production, and not the director of the theater. Similarly the Censor can give neither glory nor dishonor to the publication of a work. The curtain rises, and every one eagerly watches the performance. If they like it, they applaud; if not, they stamp and hiss. Leave what is stupid to the judgment of public opinion, stupidity will find a thousand censors. The most vigilant policy cannot check worthless ideas as well as a disgusted public. They will be heard just once; they will die, never to rise again. But once we have recognized the uselessness of the censorship, or, rather, its harmfulness in the realm of knowledge, we must also recognize the vast and boundless usefulness of freedom of the press.

Alexander Radishchev, A Journey from Saint Petersburg to Moscow (Cambridge, Mass.: Harvard University Press, 1958), pp. 9–19, as quoted in Thomas Riha, ed., Readings in Russian Civilization, 2nd ed., rev., Vol. II (Chicago: The University of Chicago Press, 1969), pp. 269–271.

and their welfare on earth rather than to God and the hereafter.

Review Questions

1. How did the Enlightenment change basic Western attitudes toward reform, faith, and reason? What were the major formative influences on the *philosophes*? How important were Voltaire and the *Encyclopedia* in the success of the Enlightenment?

2. Why did the *philosophes* consider organized religion to be their greatest enemy? Discuss the basic tenets of Deism. What criticism might a Deist direct at traditional Christianity and how might he or she improve it?

3. What were the attitudes of the *philosophes* toward women? What was Rousseau's view of women? What were the separate spheres he imagined men and women occupying? What were Mary Wollstonecraft's criticisms of Rousseau's view?

4. Compare the arguments of the mercantilists with those of Adam Smith in his book, *The Wealth of Nations*. How did both sides view the earth's resources? Why might Smith be regarded as an advocate of the consumer?

5. Discuss the political views of Montesquieu and Rousseau. Was Montesquieu's view of England accurate? Was Rousseau a child of the Enlightenment or its enemy? Which did Rousseau value more, the individual or society?

6. Were the enlightened monarchs true believers in the ideal of the *philosophes* or was

their enlightenment a mere veneer? Were they really absolute in power? What motivated their reforms? What does the partition of Poland indicate about the spirit of *enlightened absolutism*?

Suggested Readings

R. P. Bartlett, *Human Capital: The Settlement of Foreigners in Russia, 1762–1804* (1979). Examines Catherine's policy of attracting farmers and skilled workers to Russia.

D. Beales, *Joseph II: In the Shadow of Maria Theresa, 1741–1780* (1987). The best treatment in English of the early political life of Joseph II.

C. Becker, *The Heavenly City of the Eighteenth Century Philosophers* (1932). An influential but very controversial discussion.

C. B. A. Behrens, *Society, Government, and the Enlightenment: The Experiences of Eighteenth-Century France and Prussia* (1985). A wide-ranging comparative study.

T. Bestermann, *Voltaire* (1969). A biography by the editor of Voltaire's letters.

D. D. Bien, *The Calas Affair: Persecution, Toleration, and Heresy in Eighteenth-Century Toulouse* (1960). The standard treatment of the famous case.

E. Cassirer, *The Philosophy of the Enlightenment* (1951). A brilliant but difficult work by one of the great philosophers of the twentieth century.

R. Chartier, *The Cultural Origins of the French Revolution* (1991). A wide-ranging discussion of the emergence of the public sphere and the role of books and the book trade during the Enlightenment.

H. Chisick, *The Limits of Reform in the Enlightenment: Attitudes Toward the Education of the Lower Classes in Eighteenth-Century France* (1981). An attempt to examine the impact of the Enlightenment on nonelite classes.

G. R. Cragg, *The Church and the Age of Reason* (1961). A general survey of eighteenth-century religious life.

R. Darnton, *The Business of Enlightenment: A Publishing History of the* Encyclopedia, *1775–1800* (1979). A wide-ranging examination of the printing and dispersion of the *Encyclopedia*.

R. Darnton, *The Literary Underground of the Old Regime* (1982). Essays on the world of printers, publishers, and booksellers.

T. S. Dock, *Women in the* Encyclopédie: *A Compendium* (1983). An analysis of the articles from the *Encyclopedia* that deal with women.

P. Fussell, *The Rhetorical World of Augustan Humanism* (1969). Examines writers during the Enlightenment.

J. Gagliardo, *Enlightened Despotism* (1967). A discussion of the subject in its European context.

P. Gay, *The Enlightenment: An Interpretation,* 2 vols. (1966, 1969). The most important and far-reaching treatment.

C. C. Gillispie, *Science and Polity in France at the End of the Old Regime* (1980). A major survey of the subject.

N. Hampson, *A Cultural History of the Enlightenment* (1969). A useful introduction.

M. C. Jacob, *The Radical Enlightenment: Pantheists, Freemasons, and Republicans* (1981). A treatment of frequently ignored figures in the age of the Enlightenment.

M. C. Jacob, *Living the Enlightenment: Freemasonry and Politics in Eighteenth-Century Europe* (1991). The best treatment in English of Freemasonry.

A. Kernan, *Printing Technology, Letters, and Samuel Johnson* (1987). A discussion of print culture and its impact on English letters.

R. Kreiser, *Miracles, Convulsions, and Ecclesiastical Politics in Early Eighteenth-Century Paris* (1978). An important study of the kind of religious life that the *philosophes* opposed.

J. B. Landes, *Women and the Public Sphere in the Age of the French Revolution* (1988). An extended essay on the role of women in public life during the eighteenth century.

C. A. Macartney, *The Habsburg Empire, 1790–1918* (1971). Provides useful coverage of major mid-eighteenth century developments.

J. W. McClellan III, *Science Reorganized: Scientific Societies in the Eighteenth Century* (1985). An examination of the organization of science and its relationship to popular culture.

I. de Madariaga, *Russia in the Age of Catherine the Great* (1981). The best discussion in English.

F. Manuel, *The Eighteenth Century Confronts the Gods* (1959). A broad examination of the *philosophes'* treatment of Christian and pagan religion.

R. R. Palmer, *Catholics and Unbelievers in Eighteenth Century France* (1939). A discussion of the opponents of the *philosophes*.

G. Ritter, *Frederick the Great* (trans. 1968). A useful biography.

R. O. Rockwood (Ed.), *Carl Becker's Heavenly City Revisited* (1958). Important essays qualifying Becker's thesis.

J. Schwartz, *The Sexual Politics of Jean-Jacques Rousseau* (1984). A controversial reading of Rousseau's political thought organized around gender issues.

R. B. Sher, *Church and University in the Scottish Enlightenment: The Moderate Literati of Edinburgh* (1985). A major study that examines the role of religious moderates in aiding the goals of the Enlightenment.

J. N. Shklar, *Men and Citizens, a Study of Rousseau's Social Theory* (1969). A thoughtful and provocative overview of Rousseau's political thought.

D. Spadafora, *The Idea of Progress in Eighteenth Century Britain* (1990). A recent major study that covers many aspects of the Enlightenment in Britain.

S. I. Spencer, *French Women and the Age of Enlightenment* (1984). An outstanding collection of essays that cover the political, economic, and cultural roles of women.

R. E. Sullivan, *John Toland and the Deist Controversy: A Study in Adaptation* (1982). An important and informative discussion.

A. M. Wilson, *Diderot* (1972). A splendid biography of the person behind the *Encyclopedia* and other major Enlightenment publications.

To symbolize the beginning of a new era in human history French revolutionary legislators established a new calendar. The year 1793 became Year One in this new calendar, and all the months of the year were given new names. This calendar for Year Two proclaims the indivisible unity of the revolution and the goals of Liberty, Equality, and Fraternity. [Bildarchiv Preussischer Kulturbesitz]

19

The French Revolution

Key Topics in This Chapter

◆ The financial crisis that impelled the French monarchy to call the Estates General

◆ The transformation of the Estates General into the National Assembly, the Declaration of the Rights of Man and Citizen, and the reconstruction of the political and ecclesiastical institutions of France

◆ The second revolution, the end of the monarchy, and the turn to more radical reforms

◆ The war between France and the rest of Europe

◆ The Reign of Terror, the Thermidorian Reaction, and the establishment of the Directory

In the spring of 1789, the long-festering conflict between the French monarchy and the aristocracy erupted into a new political crisis. This dispute, unlike earlier ones, quickly outgrew the issues of its origins and produced the wider disruption known as the French Revolution. Before the turmoil settled, small-town provincial lawyers and Parisian street orators exercised more influence over the fate of the Continent than did aristocrats, royal ministers, or monarchs. Armies commanded by people of low birth and filled by conscripted village youths emerged victorious over forces composed of professional soldiers led by officers of noble birth. The very existence of the Roman Catholic faith in France was challenged. Politically and socially neither France nor Europe would ever be the same after these events.

The Crisis of the French Monarchy

Although the French Revolution was a turning point in *modern* European history, it grew out of the tensions and problems that characterized practically all late-eighteenth-century states. The French monarchy emerged from the Seven Years' War (1756–1763) both defeated and in debt and was unable afterward to put its finances on a sound basis. French support of the American revolt against Great Britain further deepened the financial difficulties of the government. On the eve of the revolution, the interest and payments on the royal debt amounted to just over one-half of the entire budget. Given the economic vitality of the nation, the debt was neither overly large nor disproportionate to the debts of other European powers. The problem lay with the inability of the royal government to tap the wealth of the French nation through taxes to service and repay the debt. Paradoxically France was a rich nation with an impoverished government.

The Monarchy Seeks New Taxes

The debt was symptomatic of the failure of the late eighteenth-century French monarchy to come to terms with the resurgent social and political power of aristocratic institutions and in particular the *parlements*. For twenty-five years after the Seven Years' War there was a stand-off between them as one royal minister after another attempted to devise new tax schemes that would tap the wealth of the nobility, only to be confronted by the opposition of both the *Parlement* of Paris and provincial *parlements*. Both Louis XV (r. 1715–1774) and Louis XVI (r. 1774–1792) lacked the character and the resolution to carry the dispute to a successful conclusion. The moral and political corruption of both their courts and the indecision of Louis XVI meant that the monarchy could not rally the French public to its side. In place of a consistent policy to deal with the growing debt and aristocratic resistance to change, the monarchy gave way to hesitancy, retreat, and even duplicity.

In 1770 Louis XV appointed René Maupeou (1714–1792) as chancellor. The new minister was determined to break the *parlements* and increase taxes on the nobility. He abolished the *parlements* and exiled their members to different parts of the country. He then began an ambitious program of reform and efficiency. What ultimately doomed Maupeou's policy was less the resistance of the nobility than the death of Louis XV in 1774. His successor, Louis XVI, in an attempt to regain what he conceived to be popular support, restored all the *parlements* and confirmed their old powers.

France's successful intervention on behalf of the American colonists against the British did nothing to relieve the government's financial difficulties. By 1781, as a result of the aid to America, its debt was larger and its sources of revenues were unchanged. The new director-general of finances, Jacques Necker (1732–1804), a Swiss banker, then produced a public report that suggested that the situation was not so bad as had been feared. He argued that if the expenditures for the American war were removed, the budget was in surplus. Necker's report also revealed that a large portion of royal expenditures went to pensions for aristocrats and other royal court favorites. This revelation angered court aristocratic circles, and Necker soon left office. His financial sleight of hand, nonetheless, made it more difficult for later government officials to claim a real need to raise new taxes.

The monarchy hobbled along until 1786. By this time, Charles Alexandre de Calonne

This late-eighteenth-century cartoon satirizes the French social structure. It shows a poor man in chains, who represents the vast majority of the population, supporting an aristocrat, a bishop, and a noble of the robe. The aristocrat is claiming feudal rights, the bishop holds papers associating the church with religious persecution and clerical privileges, and the noble of the robe holds a document listing the rights of the noble-dominated parlements. [The Bettmann Archive]

(1734–1802) was the minister of finance. Calonne proposed to encourage internal trade, to lower some taxes, such as the *gabelle* on salt, and to transform peasants' services to money payments. More important, Calonne urged the introduction of a new land tax that would require payments from all landowners regardless of their social status. If this tax had been imposed, the monarchy could have abandoned other indirect taxes. The government would also have had less need to seek additional taxes that required approval from the aristocratically dominated *parlements*. Calonne also intended to establish new local assemblies to approve land taxes; in these assemblies the voting power would have depended on the amount of land owned rather than on the social status of the owner. All these proposals would have undermined both the political and the social power of the French aristocracy.

The Aristocracy and the Clergy Resist Taxation

Calonne's policies and the country's fiscal crisis made a new clash with the nobility unavoidable, and the monarchy had very little room to maneuver. The creditors were at the door; the treasury was nearly empty. In 1787 Calonne met with an Assembly of Notables drawn from the upper ranks of the aristocracy and the Church to seek support and approval for his plan. The assembly adamantly refused any such action; rather, it demanded that the aristocracy be allowed a greater share in the direct government of the kingdom. The notables called for the reappointment of Necker, who they believed had left the country in sound fiscal condition. Finally, they claimed that they had no right to consent to new taxes and that such a right was vested only in the medieval institution of the

Well-meaning but weak and vacillating, Louis XVI (r. 1774–1792) stumbled from concession to concession until he finally lost all power to save his throne. [Giraudon/Art Resource, N.Y.]

General could do so. Shortly thereafter Brienne appealed to the Assembly of the Clergy to approve a large subsidy to allow funding of that part of the debt then coming due for payment. The clergy, like the *Parlement* dominated by aristocrats, not only refused the subsidy but also reduced their existing contribution, or *don gratuit*, to the government.

As these unfruitful negotiations were taking place at the center of political life, local aristocratic *parlements* and estates in the provinces were making their own demands. They wanted a restoration of the privileges they had enjoyed during the early seventeenth century, before Richelieu and Louis XIV had crushed their independence. Consequently, in July 1788, the king, through Brienne, agreed to convoke the Estates General the next year. Brienne resigned and Necker replaced him. The institutions of the aristocracy—and to a lesser degree, of the Church—had brought the French monarchy to its knees. In the country of its origin, royal absolutism had been defeated.

The Revolutions of 1789

The year 1789 proved to be one of the most remarkable in the history of both France and Europe. The French aristocracy had forced Louis XVI to call the Estates General into session. Yet the aristocrats' triumph proved to be quite brief. From the moment the monarch summoned the Estates General, the political situation in France drastically changed. Social and political forces that neither the nobles nor the king could control were immediately unleashed.

From that calling of the Estates General to the present, historians have heatedly debated the meaning of the event and the turmoil that followed over the next decade. Many historians long believed that the calling and gathering of the Estates General unleashed a clash between the bourgeoisie and the aristocracy that had been building in the decades before 1789. More recently other historians have countered that the two groups actually had much in common by 1789 and that many Frenchmen from both the bourgeoisie and the aristocracy resented and opposed the clumsy absolutism of the late-eighteenth-century monarchy. This second

Estates General of France, which had not met since 1614. The notables believed that calling the Estates General, which had been traditionally organized to allow aristocratic and Church dominance, would produce a victory for the nobility over the monarchy.

Again Louis XVI backed off. He dismissed Calonne and replaced him with Étienne Charles Loménie de Brienne (1727–1794), archbishop of Toulouse and the chief opponent of Calonne at the Assembly of Notables. Once in office Brienne found, to his astonishment, that the situation was as bad as his predecessor had asserted. Brienne himself now sought to impose the land tax. The *Parlement* of Paris, however, took the new position that it lacked authority to authorize the tax and said that only the Estates

group of historians contends that the funda-mental issue of 1789 was the determination of various social groups to reorganize the French government to assure the future political influ-ence of all forms of wealth.

As this complicated process was being worked out, the argument goes, distrust arose between the aristocracy and the leadership of the bourgeoisie. Those leaders then turned to the tradespeople of Paris, building alliances with them to achieve their goals. That alliance radi-calized the revolution. When revolutionary poli-cies and actions became too radical, aristocratic and middle-class leaders once again cooperated in the mid-1790s to reassert the security of all forms of private wealth and property. According to this view, there did exist conflict among dif-ferent social groups during the years of the revo-lution, but its causes were immediate, not hid-den in the depths of French economic and social development.

Other historians also look to the influence of immediate rather than long-term causes. They believe that the faltering of the monarchy and the confusion following the calling, election, and organization of the Estates General created a political vacuum. Various leaders and social groups, often using the political vocabulary of the Enlightenment, stepped into that vacuum, chal-lenging each other for dominance. This debate and conflict over the language, and hence values, of political life and activity had been made possi-ble by the emergence of the new print culture with its reading public and numerous channels for the circulation of books, pamphlets, and newspapers. Emerging from this culture were a large number of often-unemployed authors who were resentful of their situation and ready to use their skills to radicalize the discussion. The result was a political debate wider than any before in European history. The events of the era represented a continuing effort to dominate pub-lic opinion about the future course of the nation. The French Revolution, according to this view, thus illustrates the character of a new political culture created by changes in the technology and distribution of print communication.

Yet another group of historians maintains that the events of 1789 through 1795 are only one chapter in a longer-term political reorganization of France following the paralysis of monarchical government, a process that was not concluded until the establishment of the Third Republic in the 1870s. According to this interpretation, the core accomplishment of the revolution of the 1790s was to lay the foundations for a republic that could assure both individual liberty and the safety of property. It was not until the last quar-ter of the nineteenth century, however, that such a republic actually came into existence.

To some extent, how convincing one finds each of these interpretations depends on which years or even months of the revolution one examines. The various interpretations are not, in any case, always mutually exclusive. Certainly, the weakness and ultimate collapse of the monarchy influenced events more than was once acknowledged. All sides did indeed make use of the new formats and institutions of the print culture. Individual leaders shifted their positions and alliances quite frequently, some-times out of principle, more often for policital expediency. Furthermore, the actual political sit-uation differed from city to city and from region to region. The controversial and divisive reli-gious policies of the revolutionary government were often determining factors in the attitudes that French citizens assumed toward the revolu-tion. What does seem clear is that much of the earlier consensus—that the revolution arose almost entirely from conflict between the aris-tocracy and bourgeoisie—no longer stands except with many qualifications. The interpre-tive situation is now much more complicated, and a new consensus has yet to emerge.

The Estates General Becomes the National Assembly

Almost immediately after the Estates General was called, the three groups, or Estates, repre-sented within it clashed with each other. The First Estate was the clergy, the Second Estate the nobility, and the Third Estate theoretically everyone else in the kingdom, although its rep-resentatives were drawn primarily from wealthy members of the commercial and professional middle classes. All the representatives in the Estates General were men. During the wide-spread public discussions preceding the meeting of the Estates General, representatives of the Third Estate made it clear that they would not permit the monarchy and the aristocracy to decide the future of the nation.

Abbé Siéyès Presents the Cause of the Third Estate

Among the many pamphlets that appeared after the calling of the Estates General, one of the most famous was What Is the Third Estate? *by Abbé Emmanuel Siéyès. In this pamphlet Siéyès contrasted the vital contributions of the Third Estate to the nation with its exclusion from political and social privilege. He presents an image of the Third Estate in direct conflict with the aristocracy rather than with the monarchy. On the basis of this pamphlet many later observers and historians argued that the revolution was a conflict between the middle class and the aristocracy. The social structure of France, however, and the interactions of those two groups was much more complicated than Siéyès suggests. Both groups were discontented with monarchical government.*

✦ How does Siéyès define the Third Estate? What injustices does he claim it suffers? What are the complaints that he makes on behalf of the Third Estate against the aristocracy? Why does Siéyès make a distinction between the court and the monarchy?

Who, then would dare to say that the third estate has not within itself all that is necessary to constitute a complete nation? It is the strong and robust man whose one arm remains enchained. If the privileged order were abolished, the nation would be not something less but something more. Thus, what is the third estate? Everything; but an everything shackled and oppressed. . . .

The third estate must be understood to mean the mass of the citizens belonging to the common order. Legalized privilege in any form deviates from the common order, constitutes an exception to the common law, and, consequently, does not appertain to the third estate at all. We repeat, a common law and a common representation are what constitute ONE nation. It is only too true that one is NOTHING in France when one has only the protection of the common law; if one does not possess some privilege, one must resign oneself to enduring contempt, injury, and vexations of every sort. . . .

But here we have to consider the order of the third estate less in its civil status than in its relation with the constitution. Let us examine its position in the Estates General.

Who have been its so-called representatives? The ennobled or those privileged for a period of years. These false deputies have not even been always freely elected by the people. . . .

Add to this appalling truth that, in one manner or another, all branches of the executive power also have fallen to the case which furnishes the Church, the Robe, and the Sword. A sort of spirit of brotherhood causes the nobles to prefer themselves . . . to the rest of the nation. Usurpation is complete; in truth they reign.

. . . it is a great error to believe that France is subject to a monarchical regime.

. . . it is the court, and not the monarch, that has reigned. It is the court that makes and unmakes, appoints and discharges ministers, creates and dispenses positions, etc. And what is the court if not the head of this immense aristocracy which overruns all parts of France; which through its members attains all and everywhere does whatever is essential in all parts of the commonwealth?

John Hall Stewart, A Documentary Survey of the French Revolution *(New York: The Macmillan Company, 1951), pp. 44–45.*

A comment by the Abbé Siéyès (1748–1836) in a pamphlet published in 1789 captures the spirit of the Third Estate's representatives: "What is the Third Estate? Everything. What has it been in the political order up to the present? Nothing. What does it ask? To become something."[1]

DEBATE OVER ORGANIZATION AND VOTING

The initial split between the aristocracy and the Third Estate occurred before the Estates General gathered. The public debate over the proper organization of the body drew the lines of basic disagreement. The aristocracy made two moves to limit the influence of the Third Estate. First, they demanded an equal number of representatives for each estate. Second, in September 1788, the *Parlement* of Paris ruled that voting in the Estates General should be conducted by order rather than by head—that is, each estate, or order, should have one vote, rather than each

member. This procedure would ensure that the aristocratic First and Second Estates could always outvote the Third. Both moves exposed the hollowness of the aristocracy's alleged concern for French liberty and revealed it as a group determined to maintain its privileges. Spokesmen for the Third Estate denounced the arrogant claims of the aristocracy. This debate should not, however, obscure the fact that the aristocracy and the Third Estate shared many economic interests and goals; throughout the country, nobles and the elite of the Third Estate mixed socially and their families intermarried.

The royal council eventually decided that the cause of the monarchy and fiscal reform would best be served by a strengthening of the Third Estate. In December 1788, the council announced that the Third Estate would elect twice as many representatives as either the nobles or the clergy. This so-called doubling of the Third Estate meant that it could easily dominate the Estates General if voting were allowed by head rather than by order. It was correctly assumed that liberal nobles and clergy would

[1]*Quoted in Leo Gershoy,* The French Revolution and Napoleon *(New York: Appleton-Century-Crofts, 1964), p. 102.*

The Estates-General opened at Versailles in 1789 with much pomp and splendor. This print shows the representatives of the three Estates seated in the hall and Louis XVI on a throne at its far end. [Giraudon/Art Resource, N.Y.]

support the Third Estate, confirming that these groups shared some important interests. The method of voting was settled by the king only after the Estates General had gathered at Versailles in May 1789.

THE *CAHIERS DE DOLÉANCES* When the representatives came to the royal palace, they brought with them *cahiers de doléances,* or lists of grievances, registered by the local electors, to be presented to the king. Many of these have survived and provide considerable information about the state of the country on the eve of the revolution. These documents recorded criticisms of government waste, indirect taxes, Church taxes and corruption, and the hunting rights of the aristocracy. They included calls for periodic meetings of the Estates General, more equitable taxes, more local control of administration, unified weights and measures to facilitate trade and commerce, and a free press. The overwhelming demand of the cahiers was for equality of rights among the king's subjects.

These complaints and demands could not, however, be discussed until the questions of organization and voting had been decided. From the beginning, the Third Estate, whose members consisted largely of local officials, professional men, lawyers, and other persons of property, refused to sit as a separate order as the king desired. For several weeks there was a stand-off. Then, on June 1, the Third Estate invited the clergy and the nobles to join them in organizing a new legislative body. A few members of the lower clergy did so. On June 17, that body declared itself the National Assembly.

THE TENNIS COURT OATH Three days later, finding themselves accidentally locked out of their usual meeting place, the National Assembly moved to a nearby tennis court. There its members took an oath to continue to sit until they had given France a constitution. This was the famous *Tennis Court Oath.* Louis XVI ordered the National Assembly to desist from their actions, but shortly afterward a majority of the clergy and a large group of nobles joined the assembly.

On June 27, the king capitulated and formally requested the First and Second Estates to meet with the National Assembly, where voting would occur by head rather than by order. Had nothing further occurred, the government of France would have been transformed. Government by privileged orders had ended. The National Assembly, which renamed itself the National Constituent Assembly, was composed of people from all three orders, who shared liberal goals for the administrative, constitutional, and economic reform of the country. The revolution in France against government by privileged hereditary orders had begun.

Fall of the Bastille

Two new forces soon intruded on the scene. The first was Louis XVI himself, who attempted to regain the political initiative by mustering royal troops near Versailles and Paris. It appeared that he might, following the advice of Queen Marie Antoinette (1755–1793), his brothers, and the most conservative nobles, be contemplating disruption of the National Constituent Assembly. On July 11, without consulting assembly leaders, Louis abruptly dismissed his minister of finance, Necker. These actions marked the beginning of a steady, but consistently poorly executed, royal attempt to undermine the assembly and halt the revolution. Most of the National Constituent Assembly wished to establish some form of constitutional monarchy, but from the start Louis's refusal to cooperate thwarted that effort. The king fatally decided to throw his lot in with the conservative aristocracy against the wide spectrum of emerging political and social interests.

The second new factor to impose itself on the events at Versailles was the populace of Paris. The mustering of royal troops created anxiety in the city, where throughout the winter and spring of 1789 there had been several bread riots. The Parisians who had elected their representatives to the Third Estate had continued to meet after the elections. By June they were organizing a citizen militia and collecting arms. They regarded the dismissal of Necker as the opening of a royal offensive against the National Constituent Assembly and the city.

On July 14, somewhat more than 800 people, most of them small shopkeepers, tradespeople, artisans, and wage earners, marched to the Bastille in search of weapons for the militia. This great fortress, with ten-foot-thick walls, had once held political prisoners. Through miscalculations and ineptitude on the part of the

This painting of the Tennis Court Oath, June 20, 1789, is by Jacques-Louis David (1748–1825). In the center foreground are members of different Estates joining hands in cooperation as equals. The presiding officer is Jean-Sylvain Bailly, soon to become mayor of Paris. [Giraudon/Art Resource, N.Y.]

governor of the fortress, the troops in the Bastille fired into the crowd, killing ninety-eight people and wounding many others. Thereafter the crowd stormed the fortress and eventually gained entrance. They released the seven prisoners, none of whom was there for political reasons, and killed several troops and the governor. They found no weapons.

On July 15, the militia of Paris, by then called the National Guard, offered its command to the marquis de Lafayette (1757–1834). This hero of the American Revolution gave the guard a new insignia: the red and blue stripes of Paris separated by the white stripe of the king. This emblem became the revolutionary cockade (badge) and eventually the flag of revolutionary France.

The attack on the Bastille marked the first of many crucial *journées,* days on which the populace of Paris redirected the course of the revolution. The fall of the fortress signaled that the

National Constituent Assembly alone would not decide the political future of the nation. As the news of the taking of the Bastille spread, similar disturbances took place in provincial cities. A few days later, Louis XVI again bowed to the force of events and personally visited Paris, where he wore the revolutionary cockade and recognized the organized electors as the legitimate government of the city. The king also recognized the National Guard. The citizens of Paris were, for the time being, satisfied. They also had established themselves as an independent political force with which other political groups might ally for their own purposes.

The Great Fear and the Surrender of Feudal Privileges

Simultaneous with the popular urban disturbances, a movement known as the Great Fear

On July 14, 1789, crowds stormed the Bastille, a prison in Paris. This event, whose only practical effect was to free a few prisoners, marked the first time the populace of Paris redirected the course of the revolution. [Giraudon/Art Resource, N.Y.]

swept across much of the French countryside. Rumors had spread that royal troops would be sent into the rural districts. The result was an intensification of the peasant disturbances that had begun during the spring. The Great Fear saw the burning of chateaux, the destruction of records and documents, and the refusal to pay feudal dues. The peasants were determined to take possession of food supplies and land that they considered rightfully theirs. They were reclaiming rights and property that they had lost through the aristocratic resurgence of the last quarter century, as well as venting their general anger against the injustices of rural life.

On the night of August 4, 1789, aristocrats in the National Constituent Assembly attempted to halt the spreading disorder in the countryside. By prearrangement, several liberal nobles and churchmen rose in the assembly and renounced their feudal rights, dues, and tithes. In a scene of great emotion, hunting and fishing rights, judicial authority, and special exemptions were surrendered. These nobles gave up what they had already lost and what they could not have regained without civil war in the rural areas. Later they would also, in many cases, receive compensation for their losses. Nonetheless, after the night of August 4, all French citizens were subject to the same and equal laws. That dramatic session of the assembly paved the way for the legal and social reconstruction of the nation. Without those renunciations, the

The National Assembly Decrees Civic Equality in France

These famous decrees of August 4, 1789, in effect created civic equality in France. The special privileges previously possessed or controlled by the nobility were removed.

✦ *What institutions and privileges are included in "the feudal regime"? How do these decrees recognize that the abolition of some privileges and former tax arrangements will require new kinds of taxes and government financing to support religious, educational, and other institutions? To what extent, if any, does the abolition of these privileges answer the complaints of Abbé Siéyès in the earlier document in this chapter? Or do these abolished privileges touch only life in the French countryside?*

1. The National Assembly completely abolishes the feudal regime. It decrees that, among the rights and dues . . . all those originating in real or personal serfdom, personal servitude, and those which represent them, are abolished without indemnification; all others are declared redeemable, and that the price and mode of redemption shall be fixed by the National Assembly. . . .

2. The exclusive right to maintain pigeon-houses and dove-cotes is abolished. . . .

3. The exclusive right to hunt and to maintain unenclosed warrens is likewise abolished. . . .

4. All manorial courts are suppressed without indemnification.

5. Tithes of every description and the dues which have been substituted for them . . . are abolished, on condition, however, that some other method be devised to provide for the expenses of divine worship, the support of the officiating clergy, the relief of the poor, repairs and rebuilding of churches and parsonages, and for all establishments, seminaries, schools, academies, asylums, communities, and other institutions, for the maintenance of which they are actually devoted. . . .

. . . .

7. The sale of judicial and municipal offices shall be suppressed forthwith. . . .

8. Pecuniary privileges, personal or real, in the payment of taxes are abolished forever. . . .

. . . .

11. All citizens, without distinction of birth, are eligible to any office or dignity, whether ecclesiastical, civil or military. . . .

Frank Maloy Anderson, ed. and trans., The Constitutions and Other Select Documents Illustrative of the History of France, 1789–1907, 2nd. ed., rev. and enl. (Minneapolis: H. W. Wilson, 1908), pp. 11–13.

constructive work of the National Constituent Assembly would have been much more difficult.

Both the attack on the Bastille and the Great Fear displayed characteristics of the rural and urban riots that had occurred often in eighteenth-century France. Louis XVI first thought that the turmoil over the Bastille was simply another bread riot. Indeed, the popular disturbances were only partly related to the events at Versailles. A deep economic downturn had struck France in 1787 and continued into 1788. The harvests for both years had been poor, and food prices in 1789 were higher than at any time since 1703. Wages had not kept up with the rise in prices. Throughout the winter of 1788–1789, an unusually cold one, many people suffered from hunger. Several cities had experienced wage and food riots. These economic problems helped the revolution reach the vast proportions it did.

The political, social, and economic grievances of many sections of the country became combined. The National Constituent Assembly could look to the popular forces as a source of strength against the king and the conservative aristocrats. When the various elements of the assembly later fell into quarrels among themselves, the resulting factions appealed for support to the politically sophisticated and well-organized shopkeeping and artisan classes. They, in turn, would demand a price for their cooperation.

The Declaration of the Rights of Man and Citizen

In late August 1789, the National Constituent Assembly decided that before writing a new constitution, it should set forth a statement of broad political principles. On August 27, the assembly issued the Declaration of the Rights of Man and Citizen. This declaration drew upon much of the political language of the Enlightenment and was also influenced by the Declaration of Rights adopted by Virginia in America in June 1776.

The French declaration proclaimed that all men were "born and remain free and equal in rights." The natural rights so proclaimed were "liberty, property, security, and resistance to oppression." Governments existed to protect those rights. All political sovereignty resided in the nation and its representatives. All citizens were to be equal before the law and were to be "equally admissible to all public dignities, offices, and employments, according to their capacity, and with no other distinction than that of their virtues and talents." There were to be due process of law and presumption of innocence until proof of guilt. Freedom of religion was affirmed. Taxation was to be apportioned equally according to capacity to pay. Property constituted "an inviolable and sacred right."[2]

Although these statements were rather abstract, almost all of them were directed against specific abuses of the old aristocratic and absolutist regime. If any two principles of the future governed the declaration, they were civic equality and protection of property. The

Declaration of the Rights of Man and Citizen has often been considered the death certificate of the Old Regime.

It was not accidental that the Declaration of the Rights of Man and Citizen specifically applied to men and not to women. As discussed in the previous chapter, much of the political language of the Enlightenment, and most especially that associated with Rousseau, separated men and women into distinct gender spheres. According to this view, which influenced the legislation of the revolutionary era, men were suited for citizenship, women for motherhood and the domestic life. Nonetheless, in the charged atmosphere of the summer of 1789, many politically active and informed French women hoped the guarantees of the declaration

Civic equality was one of the hallmarks of the revolutionary era. This figure of Equality holds in her hand a copy of the Declaration of the Rights of Man and Citizen. [The Bettmann Archive]

[2]*Quoted in Georges Lefebvre,* The Coming of the French Revolution, *trans. by R. R. Palmer (Princeton, N.J.: Princeton University Press, 1967), pp. 221–223.*

would be extended to them. Their issues of particular concern related to property, inheritance, family, and divorce. Some people saw in the declaration a framework within which women might eventually enjoy the rights and protection of citizenship.

The Royal Family Forced to Return to Paris

Louis XVI stalled before ratifying both the declaration and the aristocratic renunciation of feudalism. The longer he hesitated, the stronger grew suspicions that he might again try to resort to the use of troops. Moreover, bread continued to be scarce. On October 5, a crowd of as many as 7,000 Parisian women armed with pikes, guns, swords, and knives marched to Versailles demanding more bread. They milled about the palace, and many stayed the night. Intimidated by these Parisian women, the king agreed to sanction the decrees of the assembly. The next day he and his family appeared on a balcony

before the crowd. The Parisians, however, were deeply suspicious of the monarch and believed that he must be kept under the watchful eye of the people. They demanded that Louis and his family return to Paris. The monarch had no real choice in the matter. On October 6, 1789, his carriage followed the crowd into the city, where he and his family settled in the palace of the Tuileries.

The march of the women of Paris was the first example of a popular insurrection employing the language of popular sovereignty directed against the monarch. The National Constituent Assembly also soon moved into Paris. Thereafter, both Paris and France remained relatively stable and peaceful until the summer of 1792.

The Reconstruction of France

Once established in Paris, the National Constituent Assembly set about reorganizing France. In government, it pursued a policy of

The women of Paris marched to Versailles on October 5, 1789. The following day the royal family was forced to return to Paris with them. Henceforth, the French government would function under the constant threat of mob violence. [Giraudon/Art Resource]

à Versaille à Versaille. du 5 Octobre 1789.

constitutional monarchy; in administration, rationalism; in economics, unregulated freedom; and in religion, anticlericalism. Throughout its proceedings the assembly was determined to protect property in all its forms. In those policies the aristocracy and the middle-class elite stood united. The assembly also sought to limit the impact on national life of the unpropertied elements of the nation and even of possessors of small amounts of property. Although championing civic equality before the law, the assembly spurned social equality and extensive democracy. In all these ways the assembly charted a general course that, to a greater or lesser degree, nineteenth-century liberals across Europe would follow.

Political Reorganization

The Constitution of 1791, the product of the National Constituent Assembly's deliberations, established a constitutional monarchy. The major political authority of the nation would be a unicameral Legislative Assembly, in which all laws would originate. The monarch was allowed a suspensive veto that could delay but not halt legislation. Powers of war and peace were vested in the assembly.

ACTIVE AND PASSIVE CITIZENS The constitution provided for an elaborate system of indirect elections intended to thwart direct popular pressure on the government. The citizens of France were divided into active and passive categories. Only active citizens—that is, men paying annual taxes equal to three days of local labor wages—could vote. They chose electors, who then in turn voted for the members of the legislature. At the level of electors or members, still further property qualifications were imposed. Only about fifty thousand citizens of a population of about twenty-five million could qualify as electors or members of the Legislative Assembly. Women could neither vote nor hold office.

These constitutional arrangements effectively transferred political power from aristocratic wealth to all forms of propertied wealth in the nation. Political authority would no longer be achieved through hereditary privilege or through purchase of titles, but through the accumulation of land and commercial property. These new political arrangements based on property rather than birth recognized the new complexities of French society that had developed over the past century and allowed more social and economic interests to have a voice in the governing of the nation.

The laws that excluded women from both voting and holding office did not pass unnoticed. In 1791 Olympe de Gouges (d. 1793), a butcher's daughter from Montauban who became a major revolutionary radical in Paris, composed a *Declaration of the Rights of Woman*, which she ironically addressed to Queen Marie Antoinette. Much of the document reprinted the Declaration of the Rights of Man and Citizen adding the word *woman* to the various original clauses. That strategy demanded that women be regarded as citizens and not merely as daughters, sisters, wives, and mothers of citizens. Olympe de Gouges further outlined rights that would permit women to own property and require men to recognize the paternity of their children. She called for equality of the sexes in marriage and improved education for women. She declared, "Women, wake up; the tocsin of reason is being heard throughout the whole universe; discover your rights."[3] Her declaration illustrated how the simple listing of rights in the Declaration of the Rights of Man and Citizen created a structure of universal civic expectations even for those it did not cover. The National Assembly had established a set of values against which it was itself to be measured. It provided criteria for liberty, and those to whom it had not extended full liberties could demand to know why and could claim that the revolution was incomplete until they enjoyed those freedoms.

DEPARTMENTS REPLACE PROVINCES In reconstructing the local and judicial administration, the National Constituent Assembly applied the rational spirit of the Enlightenment. It abolished the ancient French provinces, such as Burgundy and Brittany, and established in their place eighty-three departments (*départements*) of generally equal size named after rivers, mountains, and other geographical features (see Map 19-1). The departments in turn

[3]*Quoted in Sara E. Melzer and Leslie W. Rabine, eds.,* Rebel Daughters: Women and the French Revolution *(New York: Oxford University Press, 1992), p. 88.*

(A) FRENCH PROVINCES BEFORE 1789

FLANDERS AND HAINAUT
ARTOIS
PICARDY
NORMANDIE
ILE DE FRANCE
METZ AND VERDUN
CHAMPAGNE AND BRIE
ALSACE
LORRAINE
BRETAGNE
MAINE
ORLÉANAIS
ANJOU
TOURAINE
BERRY
NIVERNAIS
BURGUNDY
FRANCHE COMTÉ
SAUMUROIS
POITOU
BOURBONNAIS
AUNIS
MARCHE
SAINTONGE AND ANGOUMOIS
LIMOUSIN
LYONNAIS
AUVERGNE
DAUPHINÉ
GUIENNE AND GASCONY
BÉARN
LANGUEDOC
PROVENCE
FOIX
ROUSSILLON
Paris

ATLANTIC OCEAN

SPAIN

Mediterranean Sea

CORSICA

200 MILES
200 KILOMETERS

(B) FRENCH REVOLUTIONARY DEPARTMENTS AFTER 1789

200 MILES
200 KILOMETERS

PAS-DE-CALAIS
NORD
SOMME
SEINE-INFÉRIEURE
AISNE
ARDENNES
MANCHE
OISE
CALVADOS
EURE
Paris
MARNE
MEUSE
MOSELLE
BAS-RHIN
ORNE
SEINE-ET-MARNE
MEURTHE
CÔTES-DU-NORD
FINISTÈRE
ILLE-ET-VILAINE
MAYENNE
SARTHE
EURE-ET-LOIR
SEINE-ET-OISE
AUBE
HAUTE-MARNE
VOSGES
HAUT-RHIN
MORBIHAN
LOIRET
YONNE
HAUTE-SAÔNE
LOIRE-INFÉRIEURE
MAINE-ET-LOIRE
INDRE-ET-LOIRE
LOIR-ET-CHER
CHER
NIÈVRE
CÔTE-D'OR
DOUBS
VENDÉE
DEUX-SÈVRES
VIENNE
INDRE
SAÔNE-ET-LOIRE
JURA
ALLIER
AIN
CHARENTE-INFÉRIEURE
CHARENTE
CREUSE
HAUTE-VIENNE
PUY-DE-DÔME
RHÔNE
LOIRE
ISÈRE
CORRÈZE
GIRONDE
DORDOGNE
CANTAL
HAUTE-LOIRE
ARDÈCHE
DRÔME
HAUTES-ALPES
LOT-ET-GARONNE
LOT
AVEYRON
LOZÈRE
LANDES
TARN-ET-GARONNE
GERS
TARN
GARD
VAUCLUSE
BASSES-ALPES
HAUTE-GARONNE
HÉRAULT
BOUCHES-DU-RHÔNE
VAR
BASSES-PYRÉNÉES
HAUTES-PYRÉNÉES
ARIÈGE
AUDE
PYRÉNÉES-ORIENTALES

ATLANTIC OCEAN

SPAIN

Mediterranean Sea

GOLO
LIAMONE

(C) FIRST FRENCH REPUBLIC 1792-1799

200 MILES
200 KILOMETERS

ENGLAND
BATAVIAN REPUBLIC
PRUSSIA
Amiens
Antwerp
Cologne
Paris
Lunéville
Strasbourg
FRANCE
HELVETIAN REP.
AUSTRIA
Lyons
CISALPINE REP.
TUSCANY
Marengo
ITALY
Avignon
LIGURIAN REP.
ROMAN EMPIRE
Toulon
SPAIN
PARTHENOPEAN REP.
Mediterranean Sea

■ French Republic, 1792
■ Annexations in 1795
■ Independent Republics, 1799

MAP 19-1 FRENCH PROVINCES AND THE REPUBLIC *In 1789 the National Constituent Assembly redrew the map of France. The ancient provinces (A) were replaced with a larger number of new, smaller departments (B). This redrawing of the map was part of the assembly's effort to impose greater administrative rationality in France. The borders of the republic (C) changed as the French army conquered new territory.*

were subdivided into districts, cantons, and communes. Most local elections were also indirect. The departmental reconstruction proved to be a permanent achievement of the assembly. The departments exist to the present day.

All the ancient judicial courts, including the seigneurial courts and the *parlements*, were also abolished. Uniform courts with elected judges and prosecutors were organized in their place. Procedures were simplified, and the most degrading punishments were removed from the books.

Economic Policy

In economic matters the National Constituent Assembly continued the policies formerly advocated by Louis XVI's reformist ministers. It suppressed the guilds and liberated the grain trade. The assembly established the metric system to provide the nation with uniform weights and measures.

WORKERS' ORGANIZATIONS FORBIDDEN These policies of economic freedom and uniformity disappointed both peasants and urban workers caught in the cycle of inflation. By decrees in 1789, the assembly placed the burden of proof on the peasants to rid themselves of the residual feudal dues for which compensation was to be paid. On June 14, 1791, the assembly crushed the attempts of urban workers to protect their wages by enacting the Chapelier Law, which forbade workers' associations. Peasants and workers were henceforth to be left to the freedom and mercy of the marketplace.

CONFISCATION OF CHURCH LANDS While these various reforms were being put into effect, the original financial crisis that had occasioned the calling of the Estates General persisted. The assembly did not repudiate the royal debt, because it was owed to the bankers, the merchants, and the commercial traders of the Third Estate. The National Constituent Assembly had suppressed many of the old, hated indirect taxes and had substituted new land taxes, but these proved insufficient. Moreover, there were not enough officials to collect them. The continuing financial problem led the assembly to take what may well have been, for the future of French life and society, its most decisive action. The assembly decided to finance the debt by confiscating and then selling the land and property of the Roman Catholic church in France. The results were further inflation, religious schism, and civil war. In effect, the National Constituent Assembly had opened a new chapter in the relations of Church and state in Europe.

THE *ASSIGNATS* Having chosen to plunder the land of the Church, in December 1789 the

The assignats *were government bonds that were backed by confiscated church lands. They circulated as money. When the government printed too many of them, inflation resulted and their value fell. [Bildarchiv Preussischer Kulturbesitz]*

The Revolutionary Government Forbids Worker Organizations

The Chapelier Law of June 14, 1791, was one of the most important pieces of revolutionary legislation. It abolished the kinds of labor organizations that had protected skilled workers under the Old Regime. The principles of this legislation prevented effective labor organization in France for well over half a century.

◆ *Why are workers' organizations declared to be contrary to the principles of liberty? Why were guilds seen as one of the undesirable elements of the Old Regime? What are the coercive powers that are to be brought to bear against workers' organizations? In light of this legislation, what courses of actions were left open to workers as they confronted the operation of the market economy?*

1. Since the abolition of all kinds of corporations of citizens of the same occupation and profession is one of the fundamental bases of the French Constitution, reestablishment thereof under any pretext or form whatsoever is forbidden.

2. Citizens of the same occupation or profession, entrepreneurs, those who maintain open shop, workers, and journeymen of any craft whatsoever may not, when they are together, name either president, secretaries, or trustees, keep accounts, pass decrees or resolutions, or draft regulations concerning their alleged common interests.

. . . .

4. If, contrary to the principles of liberty and the Constitution, some citizens associated in the same professions, arts, and crafts hold deliberations or make agreements among themselves tending to refuse by mutual consent or to grant only at a determined price the assistance of their industry or their labor, such deliberations and agreements, whether accompanied by oath or not, are declared unconstitutional, in contempt of liberty and the Declaration of the Rights of Man, and noneffective; administrative and municipal bodies shall be required so to declare them. . . .

. . . .

8. All assemblies composed of artisans, workers, journeymen, day laborers, or those incited by them against the free exercise of industry and labor appertaining to every kind of person and under all circumstances arranged by private contract, or against the action of police and the execution of judgments rendered in such connection, as well as against public bids and auctions of divers enterprises, shall be considered as seditious assemblies, and as such shall be dispersed by the depositories of the public force, upon legal requisitions made thereupon, and shall be punished according to all the rigor of the laws concerning authors, instigators, and leaders of the said assemblies, and all those who have committed assaults and acts of violence.

John Hall Stewart, A Documentary Survey of the French Revolution *(New York: Macmillan, 1951),* pp. 165–166.

---

assembly authorized the issuance of *assignats,* or government bonds. Their value was guaranteed by the revenue to be generated from the sale of Church property. Initially a limit was set on the quantity of *assignats* to be issued. The bonds, however, proved so acceptable to the public that they began to circulate as currency. The assembly decided to issue an ever larger number of them to liquidate the national debt and to create a large body of new property owners with a direct stake in the revolution. Within a few months, however, the value of the *assignats* began to fall and inflation increased, putting new stress on the lives of the urban poor.

The Civil Constitution of the Clergy

The confiscation of Church lands required an ecclesiastical reconstruction. In July 1790, the National Constituent Assembly issued the Civil Constitution of the Clergy, which transformed the Roman Catholic church in France into a branch of the secular state. This legislation reduced the number of bishoprics from 135 to 83 and brought the borders of the dioceses into conformity with those of the new departments. It also provided for the election of priests and bishops, who henceforth became salaried employees of the state. The assembly consulted neither the pope nor the French clergy about these broad changes. The king approved the measure only with the greatest reluctance.

The Civil Constitution of the Clergy was the major blunder of the National Constituent Assembly. It created embittered relations between the French church and state that have persisted to the present day. The measure immediately created immense opposition within the French church even from bishops who had long championed Gallican liberties over papal domination. In the face of this resistance, the assembly unwisely ruled that all clergy must take an oath to support the Civil Constitution. Only seven bishops and about half the clergy did so. In reprisal, the assembly designated the clergy who had not taken the oath as "refractory" and removed them from their clerical functions.

Further reaction was swift. Refractory priests attempted to celebrate Mass. In February 1791, the pope condemned not only the Civil Constitution of the Clergy but also the Declaration of the Rights of Man and Citizen. That condemnation marked the opening of a Roman Catholic offensive against liberalism and the revolution that continued throughout the nineteenth century. Within France itself, the pope's action created a crisis of conscience and political loyalty for all sincere Catholics. Religious devotion and revolutionary loyalty became incompatible for many people. French citizens were divided between those who supported the constitutional priests and those who resorted to the refractory clergy. Louis XVI and his family favored the refractory clergy.

Counterrevolutionary Activity

The revolution had other enemies besides the pope and the devout Catholics. As it became clear that the old political and social order was undergoing fundamental and probably permanent change, many aristocrats left France. Known as the *émigrés*, they settled in countries near the French border, where they sought to foment counterrevolution. Among the most important of their number was the king's younger brother, the count of Artois (1757–1836). In the summer of 1791, his agents and the queen persuaded Louis XVI to attempt to flee the country.

FLIGHT TO VARENNES On the night of June 20, 1791, Louis and his immediate family, disguised as servants, left Paris. They traveled as far as Varennes on their way to Metz. At Varennes the king was recognized, and his flight was halted. On June 24, a company of soldiers escorted the royal family back to Paris. The leaders of the National Constituent Assembly, determined to save the constitutional monarchy, announced that the king had been abducted from the capital. Such a convenient public fiction could not cloak the realities that the chief counterrevolutionary in France now sat on the throne and that the constitutional monarchy might not last long.

DECLARATION OF PILLNITZ Two months later, on August 27, 1791, under pressure from a group of *émigrés*, Emperor Leopold II of Austria, who was the brother of Marie Antoinette, and Frederick William II (r. 1786–1797), the king of Prussia, issued the Declaration of Pillnitz. The two monarchs promised to intervene in France to protect the royal family and to preserve the monarchy *if* the other major European powers agreed. This provision rendered the statement meaningless because at the time Great Britain would not have given its consent. The declaration was not, however, so read in France, where the revolutionaries saw the nation surrounded by aristocratic and monarchical foes.

The National Constituent Assembly drew to a close in September 1791. Its task of reconstructing the government and the administration of France had been completed. One of its last acts was the passage of a measure that forbade any of its own members to sit in the

In June 1791, Louis XVI and his family attempted to flee France. They were recognized in the town of Varennes, where their flight was halted and they were returned to Paris. This ended any realistic hope for a constitutional monarchy. [The Bettmann Archive]

Legislative Assembly then being elected. The new body met on October 1 and had to confront the immense problems that had emerged during the earlier part of the year. Within the Legislative Assembly major political divisions also soon developed over the future course of the nation and the revolution. Those groups whose members had been assigned to passive citizenship began to demand full political participation in the nation.

A Second Revolution

By the autumn of 1791, the government of France had been transformed into a constitutional monarchy. Virtually all the other administrative and religious structures of the nation had also been reformed. The situation both inside and outside France, however, remained unstable. Louis XVI had reluctantly accepted the constitution on July 14, 1790. French aristocrats resented their loss of position and plotted to overthrow the new order. In the west of France, peasants resisted the revolutionary changes especially as they affected the Church. In Paris, many groups of workers believed the revolution had not gone far enough. Furthermore, during these same months women's groups in Paris began to organize both to support the revolution and to demand a wider civil role and civic protection for women. Radical members of the new Legislative Assembly also believed the revolution should go further. The major foreign powers saw the French Revolution as dangerous to their own domestic political order. By the spring of 1792, all these unstable elements had begun to overturn the first revolutionary settlement and led to a second series of revolutionary changes far more radical and democratically extensive than the first.

End of the Monarchy

The issues raised by the Civil Constitution of the Clergy and Louis XVI's uncertain trustworthiness undermined the unity of the newly organized nation. Factionalism plagued the Legislative Assembly throughout its short life (1791–1792). Ever since the original gathering of the Estates General, deputies from the Third Estate had organized themselves into clubs composed of politically like-minded persons. The most famous and best organized of these were the Jacobins, whose name derived from the fact that Dominican friars were called Jacobins, and the group met in a Dominican monastery in Paris. The Jacobins had also established a network of local clubs throughout the provinces. They had been the most advanced political group in the National Constituent Assembly and had pressed for a republic rather than a constitutional monarchy. Their political language and rhetoric were drawn from the most radical thought of the Enlightenment. That thought and language became all the more effective because the events of 1789–1791 had destroyed the old political framework and the old monarchical political vocabulary was less and less relevant. The political language and rhetoric of a republic filled that vacuum and for a time supplied the political values of the day. The events of the summer of 1791 led to the reassertion of demands for establishing a republic.

In the Legislative Assembly, a group of Jacobins known as the Girondists (because many of them came from the department of the Gironde) assumed leadership.[4] They were determined to oppose the forces of counterrevolution. They passed one measure ordering the *émigrés* to return or suffer loss of property and another requiring the refractory clergy to support the Civil Constitution or lose their state pensions. The king vetoed both acts.

Furthermore, on April 20, 1792, the Girondists led the Legislative Assembly to declare war

[4]*The Girondists are also frequently called the Brissotins after Jacques-Pierre Brissot (1754–1793), their chief spokesman in early 1792.*

on Austria, by this time governed by Francis II (r. 1792–1835) and allied to Prussia. The Girondists believed that the pursuit of the war would preserve the revolution from domestic enemies and bring the most advanced revolutionaries to power. Paradoxically, Louis XVI and other monarchists also favored the war. They thought that the conflict would strengthen the executive power (the monarchy). The king also entertained the hope that foreign armies might defeat French forces and restore the Old Regime. Both sides were playing dangerously foolish politics.

The war radicalized the revolution and led to what is usually called the *second revolution*, which overthrew the constitutional monarchy and established a republic. Both the country and the revolution seemed in danger. As early as March 1792, a group of women led by Pauline Léon had petitioned the Legislative Assembly for the right to bear arms and to fight for the protection of the revolution. Earlier she had led an effort to allow women to serve in the National Guard. These demands to serve, voiced in the universal language of citizenship, illustrated how the words and rhetoric of the revolution could be used to challenge traditional social roles and the concept of separate social spheres for men and women. Furthermore, the pressure of war raised the possibility that the military needs of the nation could not be met if the ideal of separate spheres were honored. Once the war began, some French women did enlist in the army and served with distinction.

Initially the war effort went quite poorly. In July 1792, the duke of Brunswick, commander of the Prussian forces, issued a manifesto promising the destruction of Paris if harm came to the French royal family. This statement stiffened support for the war and increased the already significant distrust of the king.

Late in July, under radical working-class pressure, the government of Paris passed from the elected council to a committee, or commune, of representatives from the sections (municipal wards) of the city. On August 10, 1792, a very large Parisian crowd invaded the Tuileries palace and forced Louis XVI and Marie Antoinette to take refuge in the Legislative Assembly itself. The crowd fought with the royal Swiss guards. When Louis was finally able to call off the troops, several hundred of them and many

On August 10, 1793, the Swiss Guards of Louis XVI fought Parisians who attacked the Tuileries Palace. Several hundred troops and citizens were killed, and Louis XVI and his family were forced to take refuge with the Legislative Assembly. After this event, the monarch virtually ceased to influence events in France. [Giraudon/Art Resource, N.Y.]

Parisian citizens lay dead. The monarchy itself was also a casualty of that melee. Thereafter the royal family was imprisoned in comfortable quarters, but the king was allowed to perform none of his political functions. The recently established constitutional monarchy no longer had a monarch.

The Convention and the Role of the Sans-culottes

Early in September the Parisian crowd again made its will felt. During the first week of the month, in what are known as the September Massacres, the Paris Commune summarily executed or murdered about 1,200 people who were in the city jails. Many of these people were aristocrats or priests, but the majority were simply common criminals. The crowd had assumed that the prisoners were all counterrevolutionaries.

The Paris Commune then compelled the Legislative Assembly to call for the election by universal manhood suffrage of a new assembly to write a democratic constitution. That body, called the *Convention* after its American counterpart of 1787, met on September 21, 1792. The previous day the French army had halted the Prussian advance at the Battle of Valmy in eastern France. The victory of democratic forces at home had been confirmed by victory on the battlefield. As its first act, the Convention declared France a republic, that is, a nation governed by an elected assembly without a king.

GOALS OF THE SANS-CULOTTES The second revolution had been the work of Jacobins more radical than the Girondists and of the peo-

French Women Petition to Bear Arms

The issue of women serving in the revolutionary French military appeared early in the revolution. In March 1791, Pauline Léon presented a petition to the National Assembly on behalf of more than 300 Parisian women asking the right to bear arms and train for military service for the revolution. Similar requests were made during the next two years. Some women did serve in the military, but in 1793 legislation specifically forbade women in military service. The grounds for that refusal was the argument that women belonged in the domestic sphere and military service would lead them to abandon family duties.

◆ Citoyenne *is the feminine form of the French word for citizen. How does this petition seek to challenge the concept of citizenship in the French Declaration of the Rights of Man and Citizen? How do these petitioners relate their demand to bear arms to their role as women in French society? How do the petitioners relate their demands to the use of all national resources against the enemies of the revolution?*

Patriotic women come before you to claim the right which any individual has to defend his life and liberty.

. . . We are *citoyennes* [female citizens], and we cannot be indifferent to the fate of the fatherland.

. . . Yes, Gentlemen, we need arms, and we come to ask your permission to procure them. May our weakness be no obstacle; courage and intrepidity will supplant it, and the love of the fatherland and hatred of tyrants will allow us to brave all dangers with ease. . . .

No, Gentlemen, We will [use arms] only to defend ourselves the same as you; you cannot refuse us, and society cannot deny the right nature gives us, unless you pretend the Declaration of Rights does not apply to women and that they should let their throats be cut like lambs, without the right to defend themselves. For can you believe the tyrants would spare us? . . . Why then not terrorize

---

ple of Paris known as the *sans-culottes*. The name of this group means "without breeches" and derived from the long trousers that, as working people, they wore instead of aristocratic knee breeches. The sans-culottes were shopkeepers, artisans, wage earners, and, in a few cases, factory workers. The persistent food shortages and the revolutionary inflation had made their difficult lives even more burdensome. The politics of the Old Regime had ignored them, and the policies of the National Constituent Assembly had left them victims of unregulated economic liberty. The government, however, required their labor and their lives if the war was to succeed. From the summer of 1792 until the summer of 1794, their attitudes, desires, and ideals were the primary factors in the internal development of the revolution.

The sans-culottes generally knew what they wanted. The Parisian tradespeople and artisans sought immediate relief from food shortages and rising prices through price controls. They believed that all people had a right to subsistence and profoundly resented most forms of social inequality. This attitude made them intensely hostile to the aristocracy and the original leaders of the revolution of 1789, who they believed simply wanted to share political power, social prestige, and economic security with the aristocracy. The sans-culottes' hatred of inequality did not take them so far as to demand the abolition of property. Rather, they advocated a community of small property owners who would also participate in the political nation.

In politics they were antimonarchical, strongly republican, and suspicious even of rep-

aristocracy and tyranny with all the resources of civic effort and the pure zeal, zeal which cold men can well call fanaticism and exaggeration, but which is only the natural result of a heart burning with love for the public weal? . . .

. . . If, for reasons we cannot guess, you refuse our just demands, these women you have raised to the ranks of *citoyennes* by granting that title to their husbands, these women who have sampled the promises of liberty, who have conceived the hope of placing free men in the world, and who have sworn to live free or die—such women, I say, will never consent to concede the day to slaves; they will die first. They will uphold their oath, and a dagger aimed at their breasts will deliver them from the misfortunes of slavery! They will die, regretting not life, but the uselessness of their death; regretting moreover, not having been able to drench their hands in the impure blood of the enemies of the fatherland and to avenge some of their own!

But, Gentlemen, let us cast our eyes away from these cruel extremes. Whatever the rages and plots of aristocrats, they will not succeed in vanquishing a whole people of united brothers armed to defend their rights. We also demand only the honor of sharing their exhaustion and glorious labors and of making tyrants see that women also have blood to shed for the service of the fatherland in danger.

Gentlemen, here is what we hope to obtain from your justice and equity:

1. Permission to procure pikes, pistols, and sabres (even muskets for those who are strong enough to use them), within police regulations.

2. Permission to assemble on festival days and Sundays on the *Champ de la Fédération*, or in other suitable places, to practice maneuvers with these arms.

3. Permission to name the former French Guards to command us, always in conformity with the rules which the mayor's wisdom prescribes for good order and public calm.

From Pauline Léon, Addresse individuelle à l'Assemblée nationale, par des citoyennes de la Capitale, le 6 mars 1791 *(Paris, n.d.), as quoted and translated in Darline Gay Levy, Harriet Branson Applewhite, and Mary Durham Johnson, eds.,* Women in Revolutionary Paris, 1789–1795 *(Urbana: University of Illinois Press, 1979), pp. 72–73.*

resentative government. They believed that the people should make the decisions of government to as great an extent as possible. In Paris, where their influence was most important, the sans-culottes had gained their political experience in meetings of the Paris sections. Those gatherings exemplified direct community democracy and were not unlike a New England town meeting. The economic hardship of their lives made them impatient to see their demands met.

THE POLICIES OF THE JACOBINS The goals of the sans-culottes were not wholly compatible with those of the Jacobins. The latter were republicans who sought representative government. Jacobin hatred of the aristocracy and hereditary privilege did not extend to a general suspicion of wealth. Basically, the Jacobins favored an unregulated economy. From the time of Louis XVI's flight to Varennes onward, however, the more extreme Jacobins began to cooperate with leaders of the Parisian sans-culottes and the Paris Commune for the overthrow of the monarchy. Once the Convention began its deliberations, these Jacobins, known as the *Mountain* because of their seats high in the assembly hall, worked with the sans-culottes to carry the revolution forward and to win the war. This willingness to cooperate with the forces of the popular revolution separated the Mountain from the Girondists, who were also members of the Jacobin Club.

EXECUTION OF LOUIS XVI By the spring of 1793, several issues had brought the Mountain

A Pamphleteer Describes a Sans-culotte

This pamphlet is a 1793 description of a sans-culotte written either by one or by a sympathizer. It describes the sans-culotte as a hard-working, useful, patriotic citizen who bravely sacrifices himself to the war effort. It contrasts those virtues to the lazy and unproductive luxury of the noble and the personally self-interested plottings of the politician.

◆ *What social resentments appear in this description? How could these social resentments be used to create solidarity among the sans-culottes to defend the revolution? How does this document relate civic virtue to work? Do you see any relationship between the social views expressed in this document and the abolition of workers' organizations in a previous document? Where does this document suggest the sans-culotte may need to confront enemies of the republic?*

A *sans-culotte* you rogues? He is someone who always goes on foot, who has no millions as you would all like to have, no chateaux, no valets to serve him, and who lives simply with his wife and children, if he has any, on a fourth or fifth story.

He is useful, because he knows how to work in the field, to forge iron, to use a saw, to use a file, to roof a house, to make shoes, and to shed his last drop of blood for the safety of the Republic.

And because he works, you are sure not to meet his person in the Café de Chartres, or in the gaming houses where others conspire and game; nor at the National theatre . . . nor in the literary clubs. . . .

In the evening he goes to his section, not powdered or perfumed, or smartly booted in the hope of catching the eye of the citizenesses in the galleries, but ready to support good proposals with all his might, and to crush those which come from the abominable faction of politicians.

Finally, a *sans-culotte* always has his sabre sharp, to cut off the ears of all enemies of the Revolution; sometimes he even goes out with his pike; but at the first sound of the drum he is ready to leave for the Vendée, for the army of the Alps or for the army of the North. . . .

"Reply to an Impertinent Question: What is a Sans-culotte?" *April 1793. Reprinted in Walter Markov and Albert Soboul, eds.,* Die Sansculotten von Paris, *and republished trans. by Clive Emsley in Merryn Williams, ed.,* Revolutions: 1775–1830 *(Baltimore: Penguin Books, in association with the Open University, 1971), pp. 100–101.*

and its sans-culottes allies to domination of the Convention and the revolution. In December 1792, Louis XVI was put on trial as mere "Citizen Capet," the family name of extremely distant forebears of the royal family. The Girondists looked for some way to spare his life, but the Mountain defeated the effort. Louis was convicted, by a very narrow majority, of conspiring against the liberty of the people and the security of the state. He was condemned to death and was beheaded on January 21, 1793.

The next month the Convention declared war on Great Britain, Holland, and Spain. Soon thereafter the Prussians renewed their offensive and drove the French out of Belgium. To make matters worse, General Dumouriez (1739–1823), the Girondist victor of Valmy, deserted to the enemy. Finally, in March 1793, a royalist revolt led by aristocratic officers and priests erupted in the Vendée in western France and roused much popular support. Thus, the revolution found itself at war with most of Europe and much of the French nation. The Girondists had led the country into the war but had proved themselves incapable either of winning it or of suppressing the enemies of the revolution at

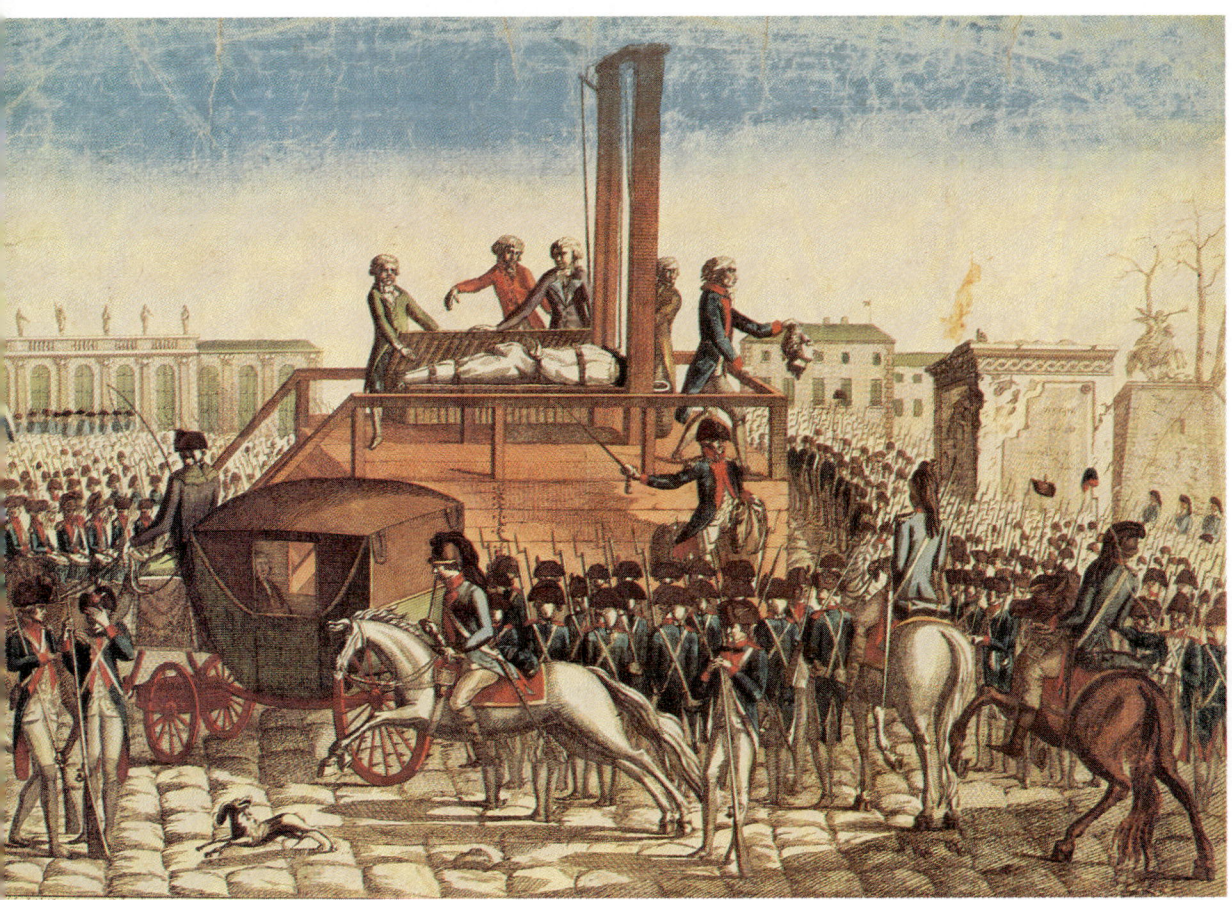

Louis XVI was executed on January 21, 1793. [Giraudon/Art Resource, N.Y.]

home. The Mountain stood ready to take up the task. Every major European power was now hostile to the revolution.

Europe at War with the Revolution

Initially the rest of Europe had been ambivalent toward the revolutionary events in France. Those people who favored political reform regarded the revolution as wisely and rationally reorganizing a corrupt and inefficient government. The major foreign governments thought that the revolution meant that France would cease to be an important factor in European affairs for several years.

Edmund Burke Attacks the Revolution

In 1790, however, the Irish-born writer and British statesman Edmund Burke (1729–1799) argued a different position in *Reflections on the Revolution in France*. Burke regarded the reconstruction of French administration as the application of a blind rationalism that ignored the historical realities of political development and the complexities of social relations. He also forecast further turmoil as people without political experience tried to govern France. As the revolutionaries proceeded to attack the Church, the monarchy, and finally the rest of Europe, Burke's ideas came to have many admirers. His *Reflections* became the handbook of European conservatives for decades.

By the outbreak of the war with Austria in April 1792, the other European monarchies recognized the danger of both the ideas and the

Edmund Burke (1729–1799) published Reflections on the Revolution in France *in 1790. It became the most famous of all conservative denunciations of the revolution. [National Portrait Gallery, London]*

aggression of revolutionary France. The ideals of the Rights of Man and Citizen were highly exportable and applicable to the rest of Europe. In response, one government after another turned to repressive domestic policies.

Suppression of Reform in Britain

In Great Britain, William Pitt the Younger (1759–1806), the prime minister, who had unsuccessfully supported moderate reform of Parliament during the 1780s, turned against both reform and popular movements. The government suppressed the London Corresponding Society, founded in 1792 as a working-class reform group. In Birmingham, the government sponsored mob action to drive Joseph Priestley (1733–1804), a famous chemist and a radical political thinker, out of the country. In early 1793, Pitt secured parliamentary approval for acts suspending habeas corpus and making it possible to commit treason in writing. With less success Pitt attempted to curb freedom of the press. All political groups who dared oppose the

government faced being associated with revolutionary sedition.

The End of Enlightened Absolutism in Eastern Europe

In eastern Europe, the revolution brought an end to enlightened absolutism. The aristocratic resistance to the reforms of Joseph II in the Habsburg lands led his brother, Leopold II, to come to terms with the landowners. Leopold's successor, Francis II (r. 1792–1835), became a major leader of the counterrevolution. In Prussia, Frederick William II (r. 1786–1797), the nephew of Frederick the Great, looked to the leaders of the Lutheran church and the aristocracy to discourage any potential popular uprisings, such as those of the downtrodden Silesian weavers. In Russia, Catherine the Great burned the works of her onetime friend Voltaire. She also exiled Alexander Radishchev (1749–1802) to Siberia for publishing his *Journey from Saint Petersburg to Moscow*, a work critical of Russian social conditions. (See the document in Chapter 18 on pp. 684–685.)

In 1793 and 1795, the eastern powers once again combined against Poland. In that unhappy land, aristocratic reformers had finally achieved the abolition of the *liberum veto* and had organized a new constitutional monarchy in 1791. Russia and Prussia, which already had designs on Polish territory, saw or pretended to see a threat of revolution in the new Polish constitution. In 1793 they annexed large sections of the country; in 1795 Austria joined the two other powers in a final partition that removed Poland from the map of Europe until after World War I. The governments of eastern Europe had used the widely shared fear of further revolutionary disorder to justify old-fashioned eighteenth-century aggression.

War with Europe

In a paradoxical fashion the very success of the revolution in France brought a rapid close to reform movements in the rest of Europe. The French invasion of the Austrian Netherlands and the revolutionary reorganization of that territory roused the rest of Europe to the point of active hostility. In November 1792, the Convention declared that it would aid all peoples who wished to cast off the burdens of aristocratic and monarchical oppression. The Convention had also proclaimed the Scheldt River in the Netherlands open to the commerce of all nations and thus had violated a treaty that Great Britain had made with Austria and Holland. The British were on the point of declaring war on France over this issue when the Convention in February 1793 issued its own declaration of hostilities.

By April 1793, when the Mountain began to direct the French government, the nation was at war with Austria, Prussia, Great Britain, Spain, Sardinia, and Holland. The governments of those nations, allied in what is known as the First

Burke Condemns the Work of the French National Assembly

Edmund Burke was undoubtedly the most important and articulate foreign critic of the French Revolution. He believed that governments could not be quickly created or organized, as seemed to have occurred in France. He was also deeply opposed to democracy, which he thought would lead to unwise, extreme actions on the part of government. Burke left a legacy of brilliantly argued conservative thought that remained a comfort to many followers and a serious challenge to liberals in nineteenth-century Europe. This passage is from his 1790 Reflections on the Revolution in France.

✦ *Why does Burke associate free government with moderation? Why does Burke associate democracy with the failure of leadership? What actions of the National Assembly might Burke have approved and which one would he have condemned?*

To make a government requires no great prudence. Settle the seat of power; teach obedience: and the work is done. To give Freedom is still more easy. It is not necessary to guide; it only requires to let go the rein. But to form a free government; that is, to temper together these opposite elements of liberty and restraint in one consistent work, requires much thought, deep reflection, a sagacious, powerful, and combining mind. This I do not find in those who take the lead in the National Assembly. Perhaps they are not so miserably deficient as they appear. I rather believe it. It would put them below the common level of human understanding. But when the leaders choose to make themselves bidders at an auction of popularity, their talents, in the construction of the state, will be of no service. They will become flatterers instead of legislators; the instruments, not the guides, of the people. If any of them should happen to propose a scheme of liberty, soberly limited, and defined with proper qualifications, he will be immediately outbid by his competitors, who will produce something more splendidly popular. Suspicions will be raised of his fidelity to his cause. Moderation will be stigmatized as the virtue of cowards; and compromise as the prudence of traitors; until, in hopes of preserving the credit which may enable him to temper, and moderate, on some occasions, the popular leader is obliged to become active in propagating doctrines, and establishing powers, that will afterwards defeat any sober purpose at which he ultimately might have aimed.

. . . The improvements of the National Assembly are superficial, their errors fundamental.

Edmund Burke, Reflections on the Revolution in France, *in* The Works of the Right Honourable Edmund Burke, *Vol. 2 (London: Henry G. Bohn, 1864), pp. 515–516.*

Coalition, were attempting to protect their social structures, political systems, and economic interests against the aggression of the revolution.

The Reign of Terror

The outbreak of war in the winter and spring of 1793 brought new, radical political actions within France. The government mobilized both itself and the nation for conflict. Throughout the nation there was the sense that a new kind of war had erupted. In this war the major issue was not protection of national borders as such but rather the defense of the bold new republican political and social order that had emerged during the past four years. The French people understood that the achievements of the revolution were in danger. To protect those achievements the government took extraordinary actions that touched almost every aspect of national life.

The Republic Defended

To mobilize for war, the revolutionary government organized a collective executive in the form of powerful committees. These in turn sought to organize all French national life on a wartime footing. The result was an immense military effort dedicated to both the protection and advance of revolutionary ideals. Ironically, this war effort brought the suppression of many liberties within France itself and led ultimately to a destructive search for internal enemies of the revolution.

THE COMMITTEE OF PUBLIC SAFETY In April 1793, the Convention established a Committee of General Security and a Committee of Public Safety to perform the executive duties of the government. The latter committee became more important and eventually enjoyed almost dictatorial power. The most prominent leaders of the Committee of Public Safety were Jaques Danton (1759–1794), who had provided heroic leadership in September 1792; Maximilien Robespierre (1758–1794), who became for a time the single most powerful member of the committee; and Lazare Carnot (1753–1823), who was in charge of the military. All of these men and the other figures on the committee were strong republicans who had opposed the weak policies of the Girondists. They conceived

of their task as saving the revolution from mortal enemies at home and abroad. They enjoyed a working political relationship with the sans-culottes of Paris, but this was an alliance of expediency on the part of the committee.

THE *LEVÉE EN MASSE* The major problem for the Convention was to wage the war and at the same time to secure domestic support for the effort. In early June 1793, the Parisian sans-culottes invaded the Convention and successfully demanded the expulsion of the Girondist members. That action further radicalized the Convention and gave the Mountain complete control. On June 22, the Convention approved a fully democratic constitution but delayed its implementation until the conclusion of the war emergency. In point of fact, it was never implemented. On August 23, Carnot began a mobilization for victory by issuing a *levée en masse,* a military requisition on the entire population, conscripting males into the army and directing economic production to military purposes. On September 17, a ceiling on prices was established in accord with sans-culotte demands. During these same months the armies of the revolution also successfully crushed many of the counterrevolutionary disturbances in the provinces.

Never before had Europe seen a nation organized in this way nor one defended by a citizen army. Other events within France astounded Europeans even more. The Reign of Terror had begun. Those months of quasi-judicial executions and murders stretching from the autumn of 1793 to the mid-summer of 1794 are probably the most famous or infamous period of the revolution. They can be understood only in the context of the war on one hand and the revolutionary expectations of the Convention and the sans-culottes on the other.

The Republic of Virtue

The presence of armies closing in on the nation made it easy to dispense with legal due process. The people who sat in the Convention and composed the Committee of Public Safety, however, did not see their actions simply in terms of expediency made necessary by war. They also believed they had created something new in world history, a republic of virtue. In this republic, civic virtue would flourish in place of aristo-

The French Convention Calls Up the Entire Nation

This proclamation of the levée en masse, *August 23, 1793, marked the first time in European history that all citizens of a nation were called to contribute to a war effort. The decree set the entire nation on a wartime footing under the centralized direction of the Committee of Public Safety.*

✦ *How did this declaration put the entire nation on a wartime footing? How does this remarkable call to patriotism and opposition to the enemies of the revolution turn extraordinary power over to the revolutionary government? How could the government believe it would receive the wartime support of the workers whose organizations it had forbidden (see the document entitled "The Revolutionary Government Forbids Worker Organizations," earlier in this chapter)?*

1. From this moment until that in which the enemy shall have been driven from the soil of the Republic, all Frenchmen are in permanent requisition for the service of the armies.

The young men shall go to battle; the married men shall forge arms and transport provisions; the women shall make tents and clothing and shall serve in the hospitals; the children shall turn old linen into lint; the aged shall betake themselves to the public places in order to arouse the courage of the warriors and preach the hatred of kings and the unity of the Republic.

2. The national buildings shall be converted into barracks, the public places into workshops for arms, the soil of the cellars shall be washed in order to extract therefrom the saltpetre.

3. The arms of the regulation calibre shall be reserved exclusively for those who shall march against the enemy; the service of the interior shall be performed with hunting pieces and side arms.

4. The saddle horses are put in requisition to complete the cavalry corps; the draughthorses, other than those employed in agriculture, shall convey the artillery and the provisions.

5. The Committee of Public Safety is charged to take all the necessary measures to set up without delay an extraordinary manufacture of arms of every sort which corresponds with the ardor and energy of the French people. . . .

. . . .

8. The levy shall be general. . . .

Frank Maloy Anderson, ed. and trans., The Constitutions and Other Select Documents Illustrative of the History of France, 1789–1907, *2nd ed., rev. and enl. (Minneapolis: H. W. Wilson, 1908), pp. 184–185.*

---

cratic and monarchical corruption. The republic of virtue manifested itself in many ways: in the renaming of streets from the egalitarian vocabulary of the revolution; in republican dress copied from that of the sans-culottes or the Roman Republic; in the absence of powdered wigs; in the suppression of plays that were insufficiently republican; and in a general attack against crimes, such as prostitution, that were supposedly characteristic of aristocratic society.

THE SOCIETY OF REVOLUTIONARY REPUBLICAN WOMEN Revolutionary women established their own distinct institutions during these months. In May 1793, Pauline Léon and Claire Lacombe founded the Society of Revolutionary Republican Women. Their purpose was to fight the internal enemies of the revolution. They saw themselves as militant citizens. Initially the Jacobin leaders welcomed the organization. Its members and other women filled

Maximilien Robespierre (1758–1794) emerged as the most powerful revolutionary figure in 1793 and 1794, dominating the Committee of Public Safety. He considered the Terror essential for the success of the revolution. [Giraudon/Art Resource, N.Y.]

the galleries of the Convention to hear the debates and cheer their favorite speakers. The Society became increasingly radical, however. Its members sought stricter controls on the price of food and other commodities, worked to ferret out food hoarders, and brawled with working market women thought to be insufficiently revolutionary. The women of the Society also demanded the right to wear the revolutionary cockade usually worn only by male citizens. By October 1793, the Jacobins in the Convention had begun to fear the turmoil the Society was causing and banned all women's clubs and societies. The debates over these decrees show that the Jacobins believed the Society opposed many of their economic policies, but the deputies used the Rousseauian language of separate spheres

for men and women to justify their exclusion of women from active political life.

There were other examples of repression of women in 1793. Olympe de Gouges, author of the *Declaration of the Rights of Woman*, opposed the Terror and accused certain Jacobins of corruption. She was tried and guillotined in November 1793. The same year, women were formally excluded from serving in the French army. They were also excluded from the galleries of the Convention. In a very real sense the exclusion of women from public political life was a part of the establishment of the Jacobin republic of virtue, because in such a republic men would be active citizens in the military and political sphere and women would be active in the domestic sphere.

DECHRISTIANIZATION The most dramatic departure of the republic of virtue, and one that illustrates the imposition of political values that would justify the Terror, was an attempt by the Convention to dechristianize France. In November 1793, the Convention proclaimed a new calendar dating from the first day of the French Republic. There were twelve months of thirty days with names associated with the seasons and climate. Every tenth day, rather than every seventh, was a holiday. Many of the most important events of the next few years became known by their dates on the revolutionary calendar.[5] In November 1793, the convention decreed the Cathedral of Notre Dame to be a Temple of Reason. The legislature then sent trusted members, known as deputies on mission, into the provinces to enforce dechristianization by closing churches, persecuting clergy and believers, and occasionally forcing priests to marry. This religious policy roused much opposition and deeply separated the French provinces from the revolutionary government in Paris.

ROBESPIERRE During the crucial months of late 1793 and early 1794, the person who emerged as the chief figure on the Committee of Public Safety was Robespierre. This complex figure has remained controversial to the present day. He was utterly selfless and from the earliest

---

[5]*From summer to spring the months on the revolutionary calendar were Messidor, Thermidor, Fructidor, Vendémiaire, Brumaire, Frimaire, Nivose, Pluviose, Ventose, Germinal, Floreal, and Prairial.*

days of the revolution had favored a republic. The Jacobin Club provided his primary forum and base of power. A shrewd and sensitive politician, Robespierre had opposed the war in 1792 because he feared it might aid the monarchy. He largely depended on the support of the sans-culottes of Paris, but he continued to dress as he had before the revolution and opposed dechristianization as a political blunder. For him, the republic of virtue meant wholehearted support of republican government and the renunciation of selfish gains from political life. He once told the Convention:

If the mainspring of popular government in peace-time is virtue, amid revolution it is at the same time virtue and terror: virtue, without which terror is fatal; terror, without which virtue is impotent. Terror is nothing but prompt, severe, inflexible justice; it is therefore an emanation of virtue.[6]

Robespierre and those who supported his policies were among the first of a succession of secular ideologues of the left and the right who, in the name of humanity, would bring so much suffering to Europe in the next two centuries.

Progress of the Terror

The Reign of Terror manifested itself through a series of revolutionary tribunals established by the Convention during the summer of 1793. The mandate of these tribunals was to try the enemies of the republic, but the definition of enemy was uncertain and shifted as the months passed. It included those who might aid other European powers, those who endangered republican virtue, and finally good republicans who opposed the policies of the dominant faction of the government. In a very real sense the Terror of the revolutionary tribunals systematized and channeled the popular resentment that had manifested itself in the September Massacres of 1792.

The first victims of the Terror were Marie Antoinette, other members of the royal family, and some aristocrats, who were executed in October 1793. They were followed by certain Girondist politicians who had been prominent in the Legislative Assembly. These executions took place in the same weeks that the

On the way to her execution in 1793, Marie Antoinette was sketched from life by David as she passed his window. [Giraudon/Art Resource, N.Y.]

Convention had moved against the Society of Revolutionary Republican Women, whom it had also seen as endangering Jacobin control.

By the early months of 1794, the Terror had moved to the provinces, where the deputies on mission presided over the summary execution of thousands of people who had allegedly supported internal opposition to the revolution. One of the most infamous incidents occurred in Nantes, where several hundred people were simply tied to rafts and drowned in the river. The victims of the Terror were now coming from every social class, including the sans-culottes.

REVOLUTIONARIES TURN AGAINST THEMSELVES In Paris during the late winter of 1794, Robespierre began to orchestrate the Terror against republican political figures of the left and right. On March 24, he secured the execu-

[6]Quoted in Richard T. Bienvenu, The Ninth of Thermidor: The Fall of Robespierre (New York: Oxford University Press, 1968), p. 38.

The Convention Establishes the Worship of the Supreme Being

On May 7, 1794, the Convention passed an extraordinary piece of revolutionary legislation. It established the worship of the Supreme Being as a state cult. Although the law drew on the religious ideas of deism, the point of the legislation was to provide a religious basis for the new secular French state. The reader should pay particular attention to Article 7, which outlines the political and civic values that the Cult of the Supreme Being was supposed to nurture.

✦ *How does this declaration reflect the ideas of the Enlightenment? Why has it been seen as establishing a civil religion? What personal and social values was this religion supposed to nurture?*

1. The French people recognize the existence of the Supreme Being and the immortality of the soul.

2. They recognize that the worship worthy of the Supreme Being is the observance of the duties of man.

3. They place in the forefront of such duties detestation of bad faith and tyranny, punishment of tyrants and traitors, succoring of unfortunates, respect of weak persons, defence of the oppressed, doing to others all the good that one can, and being just towards everyone.

4. Festivals shall be instituted to remind man of the concept of the Divinity and of the dignity of his being.

5. They shall take their names from the glorious events of our Revolution, or from the virtues most dear and most useful to man, or from the greatest benefits of nature.

7. On the days of *décade* [the name given to a particular day in each month of the revolutionary calendar] it shall celebrate the following festivals:

To the Supreme Being and to nature; to the human race; to the French people; to the benefactors of humanity; to the martyrs of liberty; to liberty and equality; to the Republic; to the liberty of the world; to the love of the Patrie [Fatherland]; to the hatred of tyrants and traitors; to truth; to justice; to modesty; to glory and immortality; to friendship; to frugality; to courage; to good faith; to heroism; to disinterestedness; to stoicism; to love; to conjugal love; to paternal love; to maternal tenderness; to filial piety; to infancy; to youth; to manhood; to old age; to misfortune; to agriculture; to industry; to our forefathers; to posterity; to happiness.

John Hall Stewart, A Documentary Survey of the French Revolution *(New York: Macmillan, 1951), pp. 526–527.*

tion of certain extreme sans-culottes leaders known as the *enragés*. They had wanted further measures regulating prices, securing social equality, and pressing dechristianization. Robespierre then turned against more conservative republicans, including Danton. They were accused of being insufficiently militant on the war, profiting monetarily from the revolution, and rejecting any link between politics and moral virtue. Danton was executed during the first week in April. In this fashion, Robespierre exterminated the leadership from both groups that might have threatened his position. Finally, on June 10, he secured passage of the Law of 22 Prairial, which permitted the revolutionary tribunal to convict suspects without hearing substantial evidence. The number of executions was growing steadily.

FALL OF ROBESPIERRE In May 1794, at the height of his power, Robespierre, considering the worship of Reason too abstract for most citizens, abolished it and established the Cult of the Supreme Being. This deistic cult reflected Rousseau's vision of a civic religion that would induce morality among citizens. Robespierre, however, did not long preside over his new religion.

On July 26, he made an ill-tempered speech in the Convention declaring that other leaders of the government were conspiring against himself and the revolution. Such accusations against unnamed persons had usually preceded his earlier attacks. On July 27—the Ninth of Thermidor—members of the Convention, by prearrangement, shouted him down when he rose to make another speech. That night Robespierre was arrested, and the next day he was executed. The revolutionary sans-culottes of Paris would not save him because he had deprived them of their chief leaders. The other Jacobins turned against him because after Danton's death they feared becoming the next victims. Robespierre had destroyed rivals for leadership without creating supporters for himself. In that regard, he was the selfless creator of his own destruction.

The fall of Robespierre might simply have been one more shift in the turbulent politics of the revolution. Instincts of self-preservation rather than major policy differences motivated those who brought about his demise. They had generally supported the Terror and the executions. Yet within a short time the Reign of Terror, which ultimately claimed more than 25,000 victims, came to a close. The largest number of executions had involved peasants and sans-culottes who had joined rebellions against the revolutionary government. By the late summer of 1794, those provincial uprisings had been crushed, and the war against foreign enemies was also going well. Those factors, combined with the feeling in Paris that the revolution had consumed enough of its own children, brought the Terror to an end.

The Thermidorian Reaction

This tempering of the revolution, called the Thermidorian Reaction, began in July 1794. It consisted of the destruction of the machinery of

The Festival of the Supreme Being, which took place in June 1794, inaugurated Robespierre's new civic religion. Its climax occurred when a statue of Atheism was burned and another statue of Wisdom rose from the ashes. [Giraudon/Art Resource, N.Y.]

The closing of the Jacobin Club in November 1794 was a major event in the Thermidorean Reaction that began with the fall of Robespierre. [Roger-Viollet, © Collection Viollet]

terror and the institution of a new constitutional regime. It was the result of a widespread feeling that the revolution had become too radical. In particular, it displayed a weariness of the Terror and a fear that the sans-culottes were exerting far too much political influence.

The End of the Terror

The influence of generally wealthy middle-class and professional people soon replaced that of the sans-culottes. Within days and weeks of Robespierre's execution, the Convention allowed the Girondists who had been in prison or hiding to return to their seats. There was a general amnesty for political prisoners. The Convention restructured the Committee of Public Safety and gave it much less power. The Convention also repealed the notorious Law of 22 Prairial. Some, though by no means all, of the people responsible for the Terror were removed from public life. Leaders of the Paris Commune and certain deputies on mission

were executed. The Paris Commune itself was outlawed. The Paris Jacobin Club was closed, and Jacobin clubs in the provinces were forbidden to correspond with each other.

The executions of former terrorists marked the beginning of "the white terror." Throughout the country, people who had been involved in the Reign of Terror were attacked and often murdered. Jacobins were executed with little more due process than they had extended to their victims a few months earlier. The Convention itself approved some of these trials. In other cases, gangs of youths who had aristocratic connections or who had avoided serving in the army roamed the streets beating known Jacobins. In Lyons, Toulon, and Marseilles, these "bands of Jesus" dragged suspected terrorists from prisons and murdered them much as alleged royalists had been murdered during the September Massacres of 1792.

The republic of virtue gave way, if not to one of vice, at least to one of frivolous pleasures.

The dress of the sans-culottes and the Roman Republic disappeared among the middle class and the aristocracy. New plays appeared in the theaters, and prostitutes again roamed the streets of Paris. Families of victims of the Reign of Terror gave parties in which they appeared with shaved necks like the victims of the guillotine and red ribbons tied about them. Although the Convention continued to favor the Cult of the Supreme Being, it allowed Catholic services to be held. Many refractory priests returned to the country. One of the unanticipated results of the Thermidorian Reaction was a genuine revival of Catholic worship.

The Thermidorian Reaction also saw the repeal of legislation that had been passed in 1792 making divorce more equitable for women. As this suggests, the reaction did not result in any extension of women's rights or an improvement in women's education. The Thermidorians and their successors had seen enough attempts at political and social change. They sought to return family life to its status before the outbreak of the revolution. Political authorities and the Church articulated a firm determination to reestablish separate spheres for men and women and to reinforce traditional gender roles. As a result, French women may have had somewhat less freedom after 1795 than before 1789.

Establishment of the Directory

The Thermidorian Reaction involved further political reconstruction. The fully democratic constitution of 1793, which had never gone into effect, was abandoned. The Convention issued in its place the Constitution of the Year III, which reflected the Thermidorian determination to reject both constitutional monarchy and democracy. The new document provided for a legislature of two houses. Members of the upper body, or Council of Elders, were to be men over forty years of age who were either husbands or widowers. The lower Council of Five Hundred was to consist of married or single men at least thirty years old. The executive body was to be a five-person Directory chosen by the Elders from a list submitted by the Council of Five Hundred. Property qualifications limited the franchise, except for soldiers, who even without property were permitted to vote.

The term *Thermidor* has come to be associated with political reaction. If the French Revolution had originated in political conflicts characteristic of the eighteenth century, however, it had by 1795 become something very different. A society and a political structure based on rank and birth had given way to one based on civic equality and social status based on property ownership. People who had never been allowed direct, formal access to political power had, to different degrees, been granted it. Their entrance in political life had given rise to questions of property distribution and economic regulations that could not again be ignored. Representation had been established as a principle of politics. Henceforth the question before France and eventually before all of Europe would be which new groups would be permitted representation. In the *levée en masse* the French had demonstrated to Europe the power of the secular ideal of nationhood.

The post-Thermidorian course of the French Revolution did not void these stunning changes in the political and social contours of Europe. What triumphed in the Constitution of the Year III was the revolution of the holders of property. For this reason the French Revolution has often been considered a victory of the bourgeoisie, or middle class. The property that won the day, however, was not industrial wealth but the wealth stemming from commerce, the professions, and from land. The largest new propertied class to emerge from the revolutionary turmoil was the peasantry, who, as a result of the destruction of aristocratic privileges, now owned their land. And unlike peasants liberated from traditional landholding in other parts of Europe during the next century, French peasants had to pay no monetary compensation.

Removal of the Sans-culottes from Political Life

The most decisively reactionary element in the Thermidorian Reaction and the new constitution was the removal of the sans-culottes from political life. With the war effort succeeding, the Convention severed its ties with the sans-culottes. True to their belief in an unregulated economy, the Thermidorians repealed the ceiling on prices. As a result, the winter of 1794–1795 brought the worst food shortages of the

The French Revolution

1789	
May 5	The Estates General opens at Versailles
June 17	The Third Estate declares itself the National Assembly
June 20	The National Assembly takes the Tennis Court Oath
July 14	Fall of the Bastille in the city of Paris
Late July	The Great Fear spreads in the countryside
August 4	The nobles surrender their feudal rights in a meeting of the National Constituent Assembly
August 27	Declaration of the Rights of Man and Citizen
October 5–6	Parisian women march to Versailles and force Louis XVI and his family to return to Paris
1790	
July 12	Civil Constitution of the Clergy adopted
July 14	A new political constitution is accepted by the king
1791	
June 14	Chapelier Law
June 20–24	Louis XVI and his family attempt to flee France and are stopped at Varennes
August 27	The Declaration of Pillnitz
October 1	The Legislative Assembly meets
1792	
April 20	France declares war on Austria
August 10	The Tuileries palace is stormed, and Louis XVI takes refuge with the Legislative Assembly
September 2–7	The September Massacres
September 20	France wins the Battle of Valmy
September 21	The Convention meets, and the monarchy is abolished
1793	
January 21	Louis XVI is executed
February 1	France declares war on Great Britain
March	Counterrevolution breaks out in the Vendée
April	The Committee of Public Safety is formed
June 22	The Constitution of 1793 is adopted but not implemented
July	Robespierre enters the Committee of Public Safety
August 23	*Levée en masse* proclaimed
September 17	Maximum prices set on food and other commodities
October 16	Queen Marie Antoinette is executed
October 30	Women's societies and clubs banned
November 10	The Cult of Reason is proclaimed; the revolutionary calendar, beginning on September 22, 1792, is adopted
1794	
March 24	Execution of the leaders of the *sans-culottes*, known as the *enragés*
April 6	Execution of Danton
May 7	Cult of the Supreme Being proclaimed
June 8	Robespierre leads the celebration of the Festival of the Supreme Being
June 10	The Law of 22 Prairial is adopted
July 27	The Ninth of Thermidor and the fall of Robespierre
July 28	Robespierre is executed
1795	
August 22	The Constitution of the Year III is adopted, establishing the Directory

period. There were many food riots, which the Convention put down with force to prove that the era of the *sans-culottes journées* had come to a close. Royalist agents, who aimed to restore the monarchy, tried to take advantage of their discontent. On October 5, 1795—13 Vendémiaire—the sections of Paris led by the royalists rose up against the Convention. The government turned the artillery against the royalist rebels. A general named Napoleon Bonaparte (1769–1821) commanded the cannon, and with a "whiff of grapeshot" he dispersed the crowd.

By the Treaty of Basel in March 1795, the Convention concluded peace with Prussia and Spain. The legislators, however, feared a resurgence of both radical democrats and royalists in the upcoming elections for the Council of Five Hundred. Consequently, the Convention ruled that at least two-thirds of the new legislature must have been members of the older body. The Thermidorians did not even trust the property owners as voters.

The next year, the newly established Directory again faced social unrest. In Paris, Gracchus Babeuf (1760–1797) led the Conspiracy of Equals. He and his followers called for more radical democracy and for more equality of property. They declared at one point, "The aim of the French Revolution is to destroy inequality and to re-establish the general welfare. . . . The Revolution is not complete, because the rich monopolize all the property and govern exclusively, while the poor toil like slaves, languish in misery, and count for nothing in the state."[7] They were in a sense correct. The Directory fully intended to resist any further social changes in France that might endanger property. Babeuf was arrested, tried, and executed. This minor plot became famous many decades later when European socialists attempted to find their historical roots in the French Revolution.

The suppression of the sans-culottes, the narrow franchise of the constitution, the rule of the two-thirds, and the Catholic royalist revival presented the Directory with problems that it never succeeded in overcoming. It lacked any broad base of meaningful political support. It particularly required active loyalty because France remained at war with Austria and Great Britain. Consequently, the Directory came to depend on the power of the army rather than on constitutional processes for governing the country. All the soldiers could vote. Moreover, within the army, created and sustained by the revolution, were officers who were eager for power and ambitious for political conquest. The results of the instability of the Directory and the growing role of the army held profound consequences not only for France but for the entire Western world.

[7]Quoted in John Hall Stewart, A Documentary Survey of the French Revolution (New York: The Macmillan Company, 1966), pp. 656–657.

◆

The French Revolution is the central political event of modern European history. It unleashed political and social forces that shaped events in Europe and much of the rest of the world for the next two centuries. The revolution began with a clash between the monarchy and the nobility. Once the Estates General gathered, however, discontent could not be contained within the traditional boundaries of eighteenth-century political life. The Third Estate, in all of its diversity, demanded real influence in government. Initially, that meant the participation of middle-class members of the Estates General, but quite soon the people of Paris and the peasants of the countryside made their demands known. Thereafter, popular nationalism exerted itself on French political life and the destiny of Europe.

Revolutionary legislation and popular uprisings in Paris, the countryside, and other cities transformed the social as well as the political life of the nation. Nobles surrendered traditional social privileges. The Church saw its property confiscated and its operations brought under state control. For a time there was an attempt to dechristianize the nation. Vast amounts of landed property changed hands, and France became a nation of peasant landowners. Urban workers lost much of the protection they had enjoyed under the guilds and became much more subject to the forces of the marketplace.

Great violence accompanied many of the revolutionary changes. The Reign of Terror took the lives of thousands. France also found itself at war with virtually all of the rest of Europe. Resentment, fear, and a new desire for stability brought the Terror to an end. That desire for stability, combined with a determination to defeat the foreign enemies of the revolution and to carry it abroad, would in turn work to the advantage of the army. Eventually Napoleon Bonaparte would claim leadership in the name of stability and national glory.

Review Questions

1. "Paradoxically, France was a rich nation with an impoverished government." Explain this statement. How did the financial weaknesses

of the French monarchy lay the foundations of the revolution of 1789?

2. Discuss the role of Louis XVI in the French Revolution. What were some of Louis XVI's most serious mistakes? Had Louis been a more able ruler, could the French Revolution have been avoided, or might a constitutional monarchy have succeeded? Or did the revolution ultimately have little to do with the competence of the monarch?

3. How was the Estates General transformed into the National Assembly? How does the Declaration of the Rights of Man and Citizen reflect the social and political values of the eighteenth-century Enlightenment? What were the chief ways in which France and its government were reorganized in the early years of the revolution? Why has the Civil Constitution of the Clergy been called the greatest blunder of the National Assembly?

4. Why were some political factions dissatisfied with the constitutional settlement of 1791? What was the revolution of 1792 and why did it occur? Who were the *sans-culottes* and how did they become a factor in the politics of the period? How influential were they during the Terror in particular? Why did the *sans-culottes* and the Jacobins cooperate at first? Why did that cooperation end?

5. Why did France go to war with Austria in 1792? What were the benefits and drawbacks for France of fighting an external war while in the midst of a domestic political revolution? What were the causes of the Terror? How did the rest of Europe react to the French Revolution and the Terror?

6. A motto of the French Revolution was "equality, liberty and fraternity." How did the revolution both support and violate this motto? Did French women benefit from the revolution? Did French peasants benefit from it?

Suggested Readings

K. M. BAKER, *Inventing the French Revolution: Essays on French Political Culture in the Eighteenth Century* (1990). Important essays on political thought before and during the revolution.

K. M. BAKER and C. LUCAS (Eds.), *The French Revolution and the Creation of Modern Political Culture,*

3 vols. (1987). A splendid collection of important original articles on all aspects of politics during the revolution.

C. BLUM, *Rousseau and the Republic of Virtue: The Language of Politics in the French Revolution* (1986). An exploration of the role of Rousseau's political ideals in the debates of the French Revolution.

R. COBB, *The Police and the People: French Popular Protest, 1789–1820* (1970). An interesting and imaginative treatment of the question of social control during the revolution.

R. COBB, *The People's Armies* (1987). The best treatment in English of the revolutionary army.

A. COBBAN, *Aspects of the French Revolution* (1970). One of the earliest criticisms of a class interpretation of the revolution.

W. DOYLE, *Origins of the French Revolution* (1980). An outstanding summary of historiographical interpretations.

J. EGRET, *The French Pre-Revolution, 1787–88* (1978). A useful survey of the coming crisis for the monarchy.

K. EPSTEIN, *The Genesis of German Conservatism* (1966). A major study of antiliberal forces in Germany before and during the revolution.

F. FEHÉR, *The French Revolution and the Birth of Modernity* (1990). A wide-ranging collection of essays on political and cultural facets of the revolution.

A. FORREST, *The French Revolution and the Poor* (1981). A study that expands consideration of the revolution beyond the standard social boundaries.

M. FREEMAN, *Edmund Burke and the Critique of Political Radicalism* (1980). A study of Burke's thought in the general context of modern political theory.

F. FURET, *Interpreting the French Revolution* (1981). A collection of controversial revisionist essays that cast doubt on the role of class conflict in the revolution.

F. FURET, *Revolutionary France, 1770–1880* (1988). An important survey by an historian who argues the revolution must be seen in the perspective of an entire century.

J. GODECHOT, *The Taking of the Bastille, July 14, 1789* (1970). The best modern discussion of the subject and one that places the fall of the Bastille in the context of crowd behavior in the eighteenth century.

J. GODECHOT, *The Counter-Revolution: Doctrine and Action, 1789–1803* (1971). An examination of opposition to the revolution.

A. GOODWIN, *The Friends of Liberty: The English Democratic Movement in the Age of the French Revolution* (1979). A major new work that explores the impact of the French Revolution on English radicalism.

C. Hesse, *Publishing and Cultural Politics in Revolutionary Paris* (1991). Probes the world of print culture during the French Revolution.

L. Hunt, *Politics, Culture, and Class in the French Revolution* (1986). A series of essays that focus on the modes of symbolic expression for revolutionary values and political ideals.

D. Johnson (Ed.), *French Society and the Revolution* (1976). A useful collection of important essays on the social history of the revolution.

E. Kennedy, *A Cultural History of the French Revolution* (1989). An important examination of the role of the arts, schools, clubs, and intellectual institutions.

M. Kennedy, *The Jacobin Clubs in the French Revolution: The First Years* (1982). A careful scrutiny of the organizations chiefly responsible for the radicalizing of the revolution.

M. Kennedy, *The Jacobin Clubs in the French Revolution: The Middle Years* (1988). A continuation of the previously listed study.

G. Lefebvre, *The French Revolution*, 2 vols. (1962–1964). The leading study of the scholar noted for his subtle class interpretation of the revolution.

D. G. Levy, H. B. Applewhite, and M. D. Johnson (Eds. and Trans.), *Women in Revolutionary Paris, 1789–1795* (1979). A remarkable collection of documents on the subject.

G. Lewis and C. Lucas (Eds.), *Beyond the Terror: Essays in French Regional and Social History, 1794–1815* (1983). Explorations of the counter-terror that followed in the wake of the Thermidorian Reaction.

M. Lyons, *France Under the Directory* (1975). A brief survey of the post-Thermidorian governmental experiment.

T. W. Margadant, *Urban Rivalries in the French Revolution* (1992). Examines the political tensions between the central government in Paris and the cities and towns of the provinces.

S. E. Melzer and L. W. Rabine (Eds.), *Rebel Daughters: Women and the French Revolution* (1992). A collection of essays exploring various aspects of the role and image of women in the French Revolution.

C. C. O'Brien, *The Great Melody: A Thematic Biography of Edmund Burke* (1992). The best recent biography.

M. Ozouf, *Festivals and the French Revolution* (1988). A pioneering study of the role of the public festivals in the revolution.

R. R. Palmer, *Twelve Who Ruled: The Committee of Public Safety During the Terror* (1941). A clear narrative and analysis of the policies and problems of the committee.

R. R. Palmer, *The Age of Democratic Revolution: A Political History of Europe and America, 1760–1800*, 2 vols. (1959, 1964). An impressive survey of the political turmoil in the trans-Atlantic world.

C. Proctor, *Women, Equality, and the French Revolution* (1990). An examination of how the ideas of the Enlightenment and the attitudes of revolutionaries affected the legal status of women.

A. Soboul, *The Parisian Sans-Culottes and the French Revolution, 1793–94* (1964). The best work on the subject.

A. Soboul, *The French Revolution* (trans., 1975). An important work by a Marxist scholar.

B. S. Stone, *The French Parlements and the Crisis of the Old Regime* (1988). A study that considers the role of the aristocratic courts in bringing on the collapse of monarchical government.

D. G. Sutherland, *France, 1789–1815: Revolution and Counterrevolution* (1986). A major synthesis based on recent scholarship in social history.

T. Tackett, *Religion, Revolution, and Regional Culture in Eighteenth-Century France: The Ecclesiastical Oath of 1791* (1986). The most important study of this topic.

J. M. Thompson, *Robespierre*, 2 vols. (1935). The best biography.

C. Tilly, *The Vendée* (1964). A significant sociological investigation.

M. Walzer (Ed.), *Regicide and Revolution: Speeches at the Trial of Louis XVI* (1974). An important and exceedingly interesting collection of documents with a useful introduction.

Napoleon Bonaparte used his military successes to consolidate his political leadership as First Consul and later as Emperor of France. In this heroic portrait Jacques-Louis David portrays Napoleon as a force of nature conquering not only the armies of the enemies of France but also the Alps. On the rocks in the foreground his name follows those of Hannibal and Charlemagne, other great generals who had led armies over the Alps. [Bildarchiv Preussischer Kulturbesitz]

20

The Age of Napoleon and the Triumph of Romanticism

The Rise of Napoleon Bonaparte
Early Military Victories
The Constitution of the Year VIII
The Consulate in France (1799–1804)
Suppressing Foreign Enemies and Domestic Opposition
Concordat with the Roman Catholic Church
The Napoleonic Code
Establishing a Dynasty
Napoleon's Empire (1804–1814)
Conquering an Empire
The Continental System
European Response to the Empire
German Nationalism and Prussian Reform
The Wars of Liberation
The Invasion of Russia
European Coalition

The Congress of Vienna and the European Settlement
Territorial Adjustments
The Hundred Days and the Quadruple Alliance
The Romantic Movement
Romantic Questioning of the Supremacy of Reason
Rousseau and Education
Kant and Reason
Romantic Literature
The English Romantic Writers
The German Romantic Writers
Religion in the Romantic Period
Methodism
New Directions in Continental Religion
Romantic Views of Nationalism and History
Herder and Culture
Hegel and History

Key Topics in This Chapter
◆ Napoleon's rise, his coronation as emperor, and his administrative reforms
◆ Napoleon's conquests, the creation of a French Empire, and Britain's enduring resistance
◆ The invasion of Russia and Napoleon's decline
◆ The reestablishment of a European order at the Congress of Vienna
◆ Romanticism and the reaction to the Enlightenment

By the late 1790s, there existed a general wish for stability in France, especially among property owners, who now included the peasants. The government of the Directory was not providing *this stability. The one force that was able to take charge of the nation as a symbol of both order and popular national will was the army. The most politically astute of the army generals was*

Napoleon Bonaparte. He had been a radical during the early revolution, a victorious general in Italy, and a supporter of the attempt to suppress revolutionary disturbances after Thermidor. Furthermore, as a general, he was a leader in the French army, the institution seen most clearly to embody the popular values of the nation and the revolution.

Once in power, Napoleon consolidated many of the achievements of the revolution. He also repudiated much of it by establishing an empire. Thereafter, his ambitions drew France into wars of conquest and liberation throughout the continent. For over a decade Europe was at war, with only brief periods of armed truce. In leading the French armies across the Continent, Napoleon spread many of the ideas and institutions of the revolution and overturned much of the old political and social order. He also provoked popular nationalism in opposition to his conquest. This new force and the great diplomatic alliances that arose against France eventually defeated Napoleon.

Throughout these Napoleonic years, new ideas and sensibilities, known by the term romanticism, grew across Europe. Many of the ideas had originated in the eighteenth century, but they flourished in the turmoil of the French Revolution and the Napoleonic Wars. The events and values of the revolution spurred the imagination of poets, painters, and philosophers. Some romantic ideas, such as romantic nationalism, supported the revolution; others, such as the emphasis on history and religion, opposed the values of the revolution.

The Rise of Napoleon Bonaparte

The chief danger to the Directory came from the royalists, who hoped to restore the Bourbon monarchy by legal means. Many of the *émigrés* had returned to France. Their plans for a restoration drew support from devout Catholics and from those citizens disgusted by the excesses of the revolution. Monarchy seemed to promise stability. The spring elections of 1797 replaced most incumbents with constitutional monarchists and their sympathizers, thus giving them a majority.

To preserve the republic and prevent a peaceful restoration of the Bourbons, the antimonarchist Directory staged a coup d'état on 18 Fructidor (September 4, 1797). They put their own supporters into the legislative seats won by their opponents. They then imposed censorship and exiled some of their enemies. At the request of the Directors, Napoleon Bonaparte, the general in charge of the Italian campaign, had sent one of his subordinates to Paris to guarantee the success of the coup. In 1797, as in 1795, the army and Bonaparte had saved the day for the government installed in the wake of the Thermidorian Reaction.

Napoleon Bonaparte was born in 1769 to a poor family of lesser nobles at Ajaccio, Corsica. Because France had annexed Corsica in 1768, he went to French schools, pursued a military career, and in 1785 obtained a commission as a French artillery officer. He strongly favored the revolution and was a fiery Jacobin. In 1793 he played a leading role in recovering the port of Toulon from the British. In reward for his service, he was appointed a brigadier general. His previous radical associations threatened his career during the Thermidorian Reaction, but his defense of the new regime on 13 Vendémiaire won him another promotion and a command in Italy.

Early Military Victories

By 1795 French arms and diplomacy had shattered the enemy coalition, but France's annexation of Belgium guaranteed continued fighting with Britain and Austria. The attack on Italy aimed at depriving Austria of the provinces of Lombardy and Venetia. In a series of lightning victories, Bonaparte crushed the Austrian and Sardinian armies. On his own initiative, and in many ways against the wishes of the government in Paris, he concluded the Treaty of Campo Formio in October 1797. The treaty took Austria out of the war and crowned Napoleon's campaign and independent policy with success. Before long, all of Italy and Switzerland had fallen under French domination.

In November 1797, the triumphant Bonaparte returned to Paris to be hailed as a hero and to confront France's only remaining enemy,

Britain. He judged it impossible to cross the channel and invade England at that time. Instead, he chose to attack British interests through the eastern Mediterranean. He set out to capture Egypt from the Ottoman Empire. By this strategy he hoped to drive the British fleet from the Mediterranean, cut off British communications with India, damage British trade, and threaten the British Empire.

Even though Napoleon overran Egypt, the invasion was a failure. Admiral Horatio Nelson (1758–1805) destroyed the French fleet at Abukir on August 1, 1798. Cut off from France, the French army could then neither accomplish anything of importance in the Near East nor get home. To make matters worse, the situation in Europe was deteriorating. The invasion of Egypt had alarmed Russia, which had its own ambitions in the Near East. The Russians, the Austrians, and the Ottomans soon joined Britain to form the Second Coalition. In 1799 the Russian and Austrian armies defeated the French in Italy and Switzerland and threatened to invade France.

The Constitution of the Year VIII

Economic troubles and the dangerous international situation eroded the already fragile support of the Directory. One of the Directors, the Abbé Siéyès, proposed a new constitution. The author of the pamphlet *What Is the Third Estate?* (1789) wanted to establish a vigorous executive body independent of the whims of electoral politics, a government based on the principle of "confidence from below, power from above." The change would require another coup d'état with military support. News of France's diplomatic misfortunes had reached Napoleon in Egypt. Without orders and leaving his doomed army behind, he returned to France in October 1799. Although some people thought that he deserved a court-martial for desertion, he received much popular acclaim. He soon joined Siéyès. On 19 Brumaire (November 10, 1799), his troops drove out the legislators and ensured the success of the coup.

Siéyès appears to have thought that Napoleon could be used and then dismissed, but if so, he badly misjudged his man. The proposed constitution divided executive authority among three

Admiral Viscount Horatio Nelson (1758–1805) was the greatest naval commander of his age. From the battle of Abukir in 1798 to his death at the battle of Trafalgar in 1805, he won a series of brilliant victories that gave Britain mastery of the seas. [Bettmann Newsphotos]

consuls. Bonaparte quickly pushed it aside, as he did Siéyès, and in December 1799, he issued the Constitution of the Year VIII. Behind a screen of universal male suffrage that suggested democratic principles, a complicated system of checks and balances that appealed to republican theory, and a Council of State that evoked memories of Louis XIV, the new constitution in fact established the rule of one man—the First Consul, Bonaparte. To find an appropriate historical analogy, one must go back to Caesar and Augustus and the earlier Greek tyrants. The career of Bonaparte, however, pointed forward to the dictators of the twentieth century. He was the first modern political figure to use the rhetoric of revolution and nationalism, to back it with military force, and to combine those elements into a mighty weapon of imperial expansion in the service of his own power and ambition.

The Consulate in France (1799–1804)

Establishing the Consulate, in effect, closed the revolution in France. The leading elements of the Third Estate—that is, officials, landowners, doctors, lawyers, and financiers—had achieved most of their goals by 1799. They had abolished hereditary privilege, and the careers thus opened to talent allowed them to achieve the wealth, status, and security for their property they sought. The peasants were also satisfied. They had gained the land they had always wanted and had destroyed oppressive feudal privileges as well. The newly established dominant classes were profoundly conservative. They had little or no desire to share their new privileges with the lower social orders. Bonaparte seemed just the person to give them security. When he submitted his constitution to the voters in a plebiscite, they overwhelmingly approved it.

Suppressing Foreign Enemies and Domestic Opposition

Bonaparte quickly justified the public's confidence by making peace with France's enemies. Russia had already quarreled with its allies and left the Second Coalition. A campaign in Italy brought another victory over Austria at Marengo in 1800. The Treaty of Luneville early in 1801 took Austria out of the war and confirmed the earlier settlement of Campo Formio. Britain was now alone and, in 1802, concluded the Treaty of Amiens, which brought peace to Europe.

Bonaparte also restored peace and order at home. He used generosity, flattery, and bribery to win over some of his enemies. He issued a general amnesty and employed in his own service persons from all political factions. He required only that they be loyal to him. Some of the highest offices were occupied by persons who had been extreme radicals during the Reign of Terror, others by persons who had fled the

Terror and favored constitutional monarchy, and still others by former high officials of the old monarchical government.

On the other hand, Bonaparte was ruthless and efficient in suppressing opposition. He established a highly centralized administration in which prefects directly responsible to the central government in Paris managed all departments. He employed secret police. He stamped out once and for all the royalist rebellion in the West and made the rule of Paris effective in Brittany and the Vendée for the first time in many years.

Napoleon also used and invented opportunities to destroy his enemies. When a plot on his life surfaced in 1804, the event provided an excuse to attack the Jacobins, though the bombing was the work of the royalists. In 1804 his forces violated the sovereignty of the German state of Baden to seize the Bourbon duke of Enghien (1772–1804). The duke was accused of participation in a royalist plot and put to death, though Bonaparte knew him to be innocent. The action was a flagrant violation of international law and of due process. Charles Maurice de Talleyrand-Périgord (1754–1838), Bonaparte's foreign minister, later termed the act "worse than a crime—a blunder," because it helped to provoke foreign opposition. On the other hand, it was popular with the former Jacobins, for it seemed to preclude the possibility of a Bourbon restoration. The executioner of a Bourbon was hardly likely to restore the royal family. The execution also seems to have put an end to royalist plots.

Concordat with the Roman Catholic Church

A major obstacle to internal peace was the steady hostility of French Catholics. Refractory clergy continued to advocate counterrevolution. The religious revival that dated from the Thermidorian Reaction increased discontent with the secular state created by the revolution. Bonaparte regarded religion as a political matter. He approved its role in preserving an orderly society but was suspicious of any such power independent of the state.

In 1801, to the shock and dismay of his anti-clerical supporters, Napoleon concluded a concordat with Pope Pius VII (r. 1800–1823). The

Napoleon Makes Peace with the Papacy

In 1801 Napoleon concluded a concordat with Pope Pius VII. This document was the cornerstone of Napoleonic religious policy. The concordat, which was announced on April 8, 1802, allowed the Roman Catholic church to function freely in France only within the limits of Church support for the government as indicated in the oath included in Article 6.

◆ *Why was it to Napoleon's political advantage to make this agreement with the papacy? What privileges or advantages does the Church achieve in this document? Would the highest loyalty of a bishop who took the oath in Article 6 reside with the Church or the French state?*

The Government of the French Republic recognizes that the Roman, catholic and apostolic religion is the religion of the great majority of French citizens.

His Holiness likewise recognizes that this same religion has derived and in this moment again expects the greatest benefit and grandeur from the establishment of the catholic worship in France and from the personal profession of it which the consuls of the Republic make.

In consequence, after this mutual recognition, as well for the benefit of religion as for the maintenance of internal tranquility, they have agreed as follows:

1. The catholic, apostolic and Roman religion shall be freely exercised in France: its worship shall be public, and in conformity with the police regulations which the government shall deem necessary for the public tranquility.

. . . .

4. The First Consul of the Republic shall make appointments, within the three months

which shall follow the publication of the bull of His Holiness, to the archbishoprics and bishoprics of the new circumscription. His Holiness shall confer the canonical institution, following the forms established in relation to France before the change of government.

. . . .

6. Before entering upon their functions, the bishops shall take directly, at the hands of the First Consul, the oath of fidelity which was in use before the change of government, expressed in the following terms:

"I swear and promise to God, upon the holy scriptures, to remain in obedience and fidelity to the government established by the constitution of the French Republic. I also promise not to have any intercourse, nor to assist by any counsel, nor to support any league, either within or without, which is inimical to the public tranquility; and if, within my diocese or elsewhere, I learn that anything to the prejudice of the state is being contrived, I will make it known to the government."

Frank Maloy Anderson, ed. and trans., The Constitutions and Other Select Documents Illustrative of the History of France 1789–1907, *2nd ed., rev. and enl. (Minneapolis: H. W. Wilson, 1908), pp. 296–297.*

---

settlement gave Napoleon what he most wanted. The agreement required both the refractory clergy and those who had accepted the revolution to resign. Their replacements received their spiritual investiture from the pope, but the state named the bishops and paid their salaries and the salary of one priest in each parish. In return, the Church gave up its claims on its confiscated property.

The concordat declared, "Catholicism is the religion of the great majority of French citizens." This was merely a statement of fact and fell far short of what the pope had wanted: religious dominance for the Roman Catholic church. The clergy had to swear an oath of loyalty to the state. The Organic Articles of 1802, which were actually distinct from the concordat, established the supremacy of state over Church. Similar laws were applied to the Protestant and Jewish communities as well, reducing still further the privileged position of the Catholic church.

The Napoleonic Code

In 1802 a plebiscite ratified Napoleon as consul for life, and he soon produced another constitution that granted him what amounted to full power. He thereafter set about reforming and codifying French law. The result was the Civil Code of 1804, usually known as the Napoleonic Code.

The Napoleonic Code safeguarded all forms of property and tried to make French society secure against internal challenges. All the privileges based on birth that had marked the Old Regime and that had been overthrown during the revolution remained abolished. Employment of salaried officials chosen on the basis of merit replaced the purchase of offices.

The conservative attitudes toward labor and women that had emerged during the revolutionary years, however, received full support. Workers' organizations remained forbidden, and workers had fewer rights than their employers. Within families, fathers were granted extensive control over their children and men over their wives. At the same time, laws of primogeniture remained abolished, and property was distributed among all children, including women. Married women could only dispose of their own property with the consent of their husbands. Divorce remained more difficult for women than for men. French law before this code had been a patchwork that differed from region to region. Within that confused set of laws, women had had opportunities to assert and protect their

The coronation of Napoleon, December 2, 1804, as painted by David. Having first crowned himself, the emperor is shown about to place the crown on the head of Josephine. Napoleon instructed David to paint Pope Pius VII with his hand raised in blessing. [Giraudon/Art Resource, N.Y.]

interests. The universality of the Napoleonic Code ended those possibilities.

Establishing a Dynasty

In 1804 Bonaparte seized on the bomb attack on his life to make himself emperor. He argued that establishing a dynasty would make the new regime secure and make further attempts on his life useless. Another new constitution was promulgated in which Napoleon Bonaparte was called Emperor of the French, instead of First Consul of the Republic. This constitution was also overwhelmingly ratified in a plebiscite.

To conclude the drama, Napoleon invited the pope to Notre Dame to take part in the coronation. At the last minute, however, the pope agreed that Napoleon should place the crown on his own head. The emperor had no intention of allowing anyone to think that his power and authority depended on the approval of the Church. Henceforth, he was called Napoleon I.

Napoleon's Empire (1804–1814)

Between his coronation as emperor and his final defeat at Waterloo (1815), Napoleon conquered most of Europe in a series of military campaigns that astonished the world. France's victories changed the map of Europe. The wars put an end to the Old Regime and its feudal trappings throughout western Europe and forced the eastern European states to reorganize themselves to resist Napoleon's armies.

Everywhere Napoleon's advance unleashed the powerful force of nationalism. His weapon was the militarily mobilized French nation, one of the achievements of the revolution. Napoleon could put as many as 700,000 men under arms at one time, risk as many as 100,000 troops in a single battle, endure heavy losses, and return to fight again. He could conscript citizen soldiers in unprecedented numbers, thanks to their loyalty to the nation and to their remarkable leader. No single enemy could match such resources. Even coalitions were unsuccessful until Napoleon finally overreached himself and made mistakes that led to his own defeat.

Conquering an Empire

The Peace of Amiens (1802) between France and Great Britain was merely a truce. Napoleon's unlimited ambitions shattered any hope that it might last. He sent an army to restore the rebellious colony of Haiti to French rule. This move aroused British fears that he was planning the renewal of a French empire in America, because Spain had restored Louisiana to France in 1800. More serious were his interventions in the Dutch Republic, Italy, and Switzerland and his role in the reorganization of Germany. The Treaty of Campo Formio had required a redistribution of territories along the Rhine River, and the petty princes of the region engaged in a shameful scramble to enlarge their holdings. Among the results were the reduction of Austrian influence in Germany and the emergence of a smaller number of larger German states in the west, all dependent on Napoleon.

BRITISH NAVAL SUPREMACY The British found these developments alarming enough to justify an ultimatum. When Napoleon ignored it, Britain declared war in May 1803. William Pitt the Younger returned to office as prime minister in 1804 and began to construct the Third Coalition. By August 1805, he had persuaded Russia and Austria to move once more

In this early-nineteenth-century cartoon England, personified by a caricature of Williams Pitt, and France, personified by a caricature of Napoleon, are carving out their areas of interest around the globe. [Bettmann Archives]

Napoleon's victory at the battle of Austerlitz is considered his most brilliant. A French army of 73,000 crushed an Austro-Russian army of 86,000 under the command of the Tsar and the Emperor of Austria. [Giraudon/Art Resource, N.Y.]

against French aggression. A great naval victory soon raised the fortunes of the allies. On October 21, 1805, the British admiral Horatio, Lord Nelson, destroyed the combined French and Spanish fleets at the Battle of Trafalgar just off the Spanish coast. Nelson died in the battle, but the British lost no ships. The victory of Trafalgar put an end to all French hope of invading Britain and guaranteed British control of the sea for the rest of the war.

NAPOLEONIC VICTORIES IN CENTRAL EUROPE On land the story was different. Even before Trafalgar, Napoleon had marched to the Danube River to attack his continental enemies.

In mid-October he forced a large Austrian army to surrender at Ulm and soon occupied Vienna. On December 2, 1805, in perhaps his greatest victory, Napoleon defeated the combined Austrian and Russian forces at Austerlitz. The Treaty of Pressburg that followed won major concessions from Austria. The Austrians withdrew from Italy and left Napoleon in control of everything north of Rome. He was recognized as king of Italy.

Napoleon also made extensive political changes in Germany. In July 1806, he organized the Confederation of the Rhine, which included most of the western German princes. The withdrawal of these princes from the Holy Roman Empire led Francis II of Austria to dissolve that ancient political body and henceforth to call himself Emperor of Austria.

Prussia, which had carefully remained neutral up to this point, was now provoked into war against France. Napoleon's forces quickly crushed the famous Prussian army at the battles of Jena and Auerstädt on October 14, 1806. Two weeks later, Napoleon was in Berlin. There, on November 21, he issued the Berlin Decrees forbidding his allies to import British goods. On June 13, 1807, Napoleon defeated the Russians at Friedland and went on to occupy Königsberg, the capital of East Prussia. The French emperor was master of all Germany.

TREATY OF TILSIT Unable to fight another battle and unwilling to retreat into Russia, Tsar Alexander I (r. 1801–1825) was ready to make peace. He and Napoleon met on a raft in the middle of the Niemen River while the two armies and the nervous king of Prussia watched from the bank. On July 7, 1807, they signed the Treaty of Tilsit, which confirmed France's gains. Moreover, the treaty reduced the Prussian state to half its previous size, and only the support of Alexander saved it from extinction. Prussia openly and Russia secretly became allies of Napoleon in his war against Britain.

Napoleon organized conquered Europe much like the domain of a Corsican family. The great French Empire was ruled directly by the head of the clan, Napoleon. On its borders lay several satellite states carved out as the portions of the several family members. His stepson ruled Italy for him, and three of his brothers and his brother-in-law were made kings of other conquered states. Napoleon denied a kingdom only to his brother Lucien, of whose wife he disapproved. The French emperor expected his relatives to take orders without question. When they failed to do so, he rebuked and even punished them. This establishment of the Napoleonic family as the collective sovereigns of Europe was unpopular and provoked political opposition that needed only encouragement and assistance to flare up into serious resistance.

The Continental System

After the Treaty of Tilsit, such assistance could come only from Britain, and Napoleon knew

that he must defeat the British before he could feel safe. Unable to compete with the British navy, he continued the economic warfare begun by the Berlin Decrees. He planned to cut off all British trade with the European continent and thus to cripple British commercial and financial power. He hoped to cause domestic unrest and revolution, and thus to drive the British from the war. The Milan Decree of 1807 went further and attempted to stop neutral nations from trading with Britain.

Despite initial drops in exports and domestic unrest, the British economy survived. British control of the seas assured access to the growing markets of North and South America and of the eastern Mediterranean. At the same time, the Continental System did badly hurt the European economies (see Map 20-1). Napoleon rejected advice to turn his empire into a free-trade area. Such a policy would have been both popular and helpful. Instead, his tariff policies favored France, increased the resent-

Napoleon and the Continental System	
1806 (Nov. 21)	Napoleon establishes the Continental System prohibiting all trade with England.
1807 (July 7)	The peace conference at Tilsit results in Russia joining the Continental System and becoming an ally of Napoleon.
1809 and 1810	Napoleon at the peak of his power.
1810 (Dec. 31)	Russia withdraws from the Continental System and resumes relations with Britain. Napoleon plans to crush Russia militarily.
1812 (June–December)	Napoleon invades Russia. The Russians adopt a scorched-earth policy and burn Moscow. The thwarted Napoleon deserts his dwindling army and rushes back to Paris.

Napoleon Advises His Brother to Rule Constitutionally

As Napoleon conquered Europe, he set his relatives on the thrones of various conquered kingdoms and then imposed written constitutions on them. In this letter of November 1807, Napoleon sent his brother Jerome (1784–1860) a constitution for the Kingdom of Westphalia in Germany. The letter provides a good description of how Napoleon spread the political ideas and institutions of the French Revolution across Europe. Napoleon ignored, however, the possibility of nationalistic resentment that French conquest aroused even when that conquest brought more liberal political institutions. Such nationalism would be one of the causes of his downfall.

✦ *What are the benefits that Napoleon believes his conquest and subsequent rule by his brother will bring to their new subjects? How does he believe these rather than military victory will achieve new loyalty? How does Napoleon suggest playing off the resentment of the upper classes to consolidate power? What is the relationship between having a* written *constitution such as Napoleon is sending his brother and the power of public opinion that he mentions toward the close of the letter?*

I enclose the constitution for your Kingdom. You must faithfully observe it. I am concerned for the happiness of your subjects, not only as it affects your reputation, and my own, but also for its influence on the whole European situation.

Don't listen to those who say that your subjects are so accustomed to slavery that they will feel no gratitude for the benefits you give them. There is more intelligence in the Kingdom of Westphalia than they would have you believe; and your throne will never be firmly established except upon the trust and affection of the common people. What German opinion impatiently demands is that men of no rank, but of marked ability, shall have an equal claim upon your favour and your employment, and that every trace of serfdom, or of a feudal hierarchy between the sovereign and the lowest class of his subjects shall be done away with. The benefits of the Code Napoleon, public trial, and the introduction of juries, will be the leading features of your Government. And to tell you the truth, I count more upon their effects, for the extension and consolidation of your rule, than upon the most resounding victories. I want your subjects to enjoy a degree of liberty, equality, and prosperity hitherto unknown to the German people. . . . Such a method of government will be a stronger barrier between you and Prussia than the Elbe, the fortresses, and the protection of France. What people will want to return under the arbitrary Prussian rule, once it has tasted the benefits of a wise and liberal administration? In Germany, as in France, Italy, and Spain, people long for equality and liberalism. I have been managing the affairs of Europe long enough now to know that the burden of the privileged classes was resented everywhere. Rule constitutionally. Even if reason, and the enlightenment of the age, were not sufficient cause, it would be good policy for one in your position; and you will find that the backing of public opinion gives you a great natural advantage over the absolute kings who are your neighbors.

J. M. Thompson, ed., Napoleon's Letters *(London: Dent, 1954), pp. 190–191, as quoted in Maurice Hutt, ed.,* Napoleon *(Englewood Cliffs, N.J.: Prentice-Hall, Inc., 1972), p. 34.*

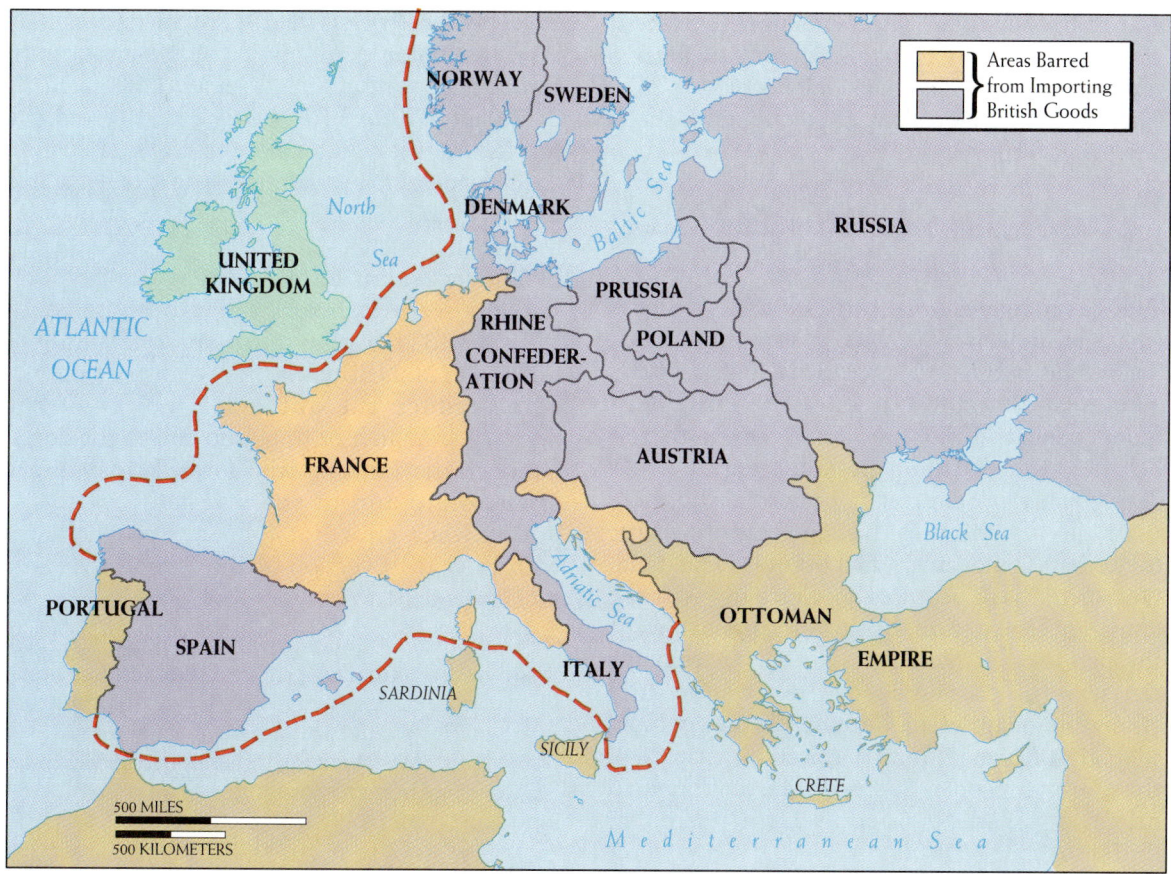

MAP 20-1 THE CONTINENTAL SYSTEM, 1806–1810 *Napoleon hoped to cut off all British trade with the European continent and thereby drive the British from the war.*

ment of foreign merchants, and made them less willing to enforce the system and more ready to engage in smuggling. It was in part to prevent smuggling that Napoleon invaded Spain in 1808. The resulting peninsular campaign in Spain and Portugal helped to bring on his ruin.

European Response to the Empire

Napoleon's conquests stimulated the two most powerful political forces in nineteenth-century Europe: liberalism and nationalism. The export of his version of the French Revolution directly and indirectly spread the ideas and values of the Enlightenment and the principles of 1789.

Wherever Napoleon ruled, the Napoleonic Code was imposed, and hereditary social distinctions were abolished. Feudal privileges disappeared, and the peasants were freed from serfdom and manorial dues. In the towns, the guilds and the local oligarchies that had been dominant for centuries were dissolved or deprived of their power. New freedom thus came to serfs, artisans, workers, and entrepreneurs outside the privileged circles. The established churches lost their traditional independence and were made subordinate to the state. Church monopoly of religion was replaced by general toleration.

These reforms were not undone by the fall of Napoleon. Along with the demand for representative, constitutional government, they remained the basis of later liberal reforms. It also became clear, however, that Napoleon's policies were intended first for his own glory and that of France. The Continental System demonstrated that France, rather than Europe generally, was to be enriched by Napoleon's rule. Consequently, before long the conquered states and peoples grew restive.

German Nationalism and Prussian Reform

The German response to Napoleon's success was particularly interesting and important. There had never been a unified German state. The great German writers of the Enlightenment, such as Immanuel Kant, Friedrich von Schiller, and Gotthold Lessing, were neither deeply politically engaged nor nationalistic.

At the beginning of the nineteenth century, the romantic movement had begun to take hold. One of its basic features in Germany was the emergence of nationalism. Nationalism went through two distinct stages. Initially, nationalistic writers emphasized the unique and admirable qualities of German culture, which, they argued, arose from the peculiar history of the German people. Such cultural nationalism prevailed until Napoleon's humiliation of Prussia at Jena in 1806.

At that point many German intellectuals began to urge resistance to Napoleon on the basis of German nationalism. The French conquest endangered the independence and achievements of all German-speaking people. Many nationalists were also critical of the German princes, who ruled selfishly and inefficiently and who seemed ever ready to lick the boots of Napoleon. Only a people united through its language and culture could resist the French onslaught. No less important in forging a German national sentiment was the example of France itself, which had attained greatness by enlisting the active support of the entire people in the patriotic cause. Henceforth many Germans sought to solve their internal political problems by attempting to establish a unified German state, reformed to harness the energies of the entire people.

After Tilsit, only Prussia could arouse such patriotic feelings. Elsewhere German rulers were either under Napoleon's thumb or actively collaborating with him. Defeated, humiliated, and diminished, Prussia continued to resist, however feebly. To Prussia fled German nationalists from other states, calling for reforms and unification that were, in fact, feared and hated by Frederick William III (r. 1797–1840) and the Junker nobility. Reforms came about despite such opposition because the defeat at Jena had made clear the necessity of new departures for the Prussian state.

The Prussian administrative and social reforms were the work of Baron vom Stein (1757–1831) and Count von Hardenberg (1750–1822). Neither of these reformers intended to reduce the autocratic power of the Prussian monarch or to put an end to the dominance of the Junkers, who formed the bulwark of the state and of the army officer corps. Rather, they aimed at fighting French power with their own version of the French weapons. As Hardenberg declared:

Our objective, our guiding principle, must be a revolution in the better sense, a revolution leading directly to the great goal, the elevation of humanity through the wisdom of those in authority. . . . Democratic rules of conduct in a monarchical administration, such is the formula . . . which will conform most comfortably with the spirit of the age.[1]

Although the reforms came from the top, they wrought important changes in Prussian society.

Stein's reforms broke the Junker monopoly of landholding. Serfdom was abolished. The power of the Prussian Junkers, however, did not permit the total end of the system in Prussia as was occurring in the western principalities of Germany. In Prussia, peasants remaining on the land were forced to continue manorial labor, although they were free to leave the land if they chose. They could obtain the ownership of the land they worked only if they forfeited a third of it to the lord. The result was that Junker holdings grew larger. Some peasants went to the cities to find work, others became agricultural laborers, and some did actually become small freeholding farmers. In Prussia and elsewhere, serfdom had ended, but new social problems had been created as a landless labor force was enlarged by the population explosion.

Military reforms sought to increase the supply of soldiers and to improve their quality. Jena

[1]*Quoted in Geoffrey Brunn,* Europe and the French Imperium *(New York: Harper & Row, 1938), p. 174.*

had shown that an army of free patriots commanded by officers chosen on merit rather than by birth could defeat an army of serfs and mercenaries commanded by incompetent nobles. To remedy the situation, the Prussian reformers abolished inhumane military punishments, sought to inspire patriotic feelings in the soldiers, opened the officer corps to commoners, gave promotions on the basis of merit, and organized war colleges that developed new theories of strategy and tactics.

These reforms soon enabled Prussia to regain its former power. Because Napoleon strictly limited the size of the Prussian army to 42,000 men, however, universal conscription could not be introduced until 1813. Before that date, the Prussians evaded the limit by training one group each year, putting them into the reserves, and then training a new group the same size. Prussia could thus boast an army of 270,000 by 1814.

The Wars of Liberation

SPAIN   In Spain more than elsewhere in Europe, national resistance to France had deep social roots. Spain had achieved political unity as early as the sixteenth century. The Spanish peasants were devoted to the ruling dynasty and especially to the Roman Catholic church. France and Spain had been allies since 1796. In 1807, however, a French army came into the Iberian Peninsula to force Portugal to abandon its traditional alliance with Britain. The army stayed in Spain to protect lines of supply and communication. When a revolt broke out in Madrid in 1808, Napoleon used it as a pretext to depose the Spanish Bourbons and to place his brother Joseph (1768–1844) on the Spanish throne. Attacks on the privileges of the Church increased public outrage. Many members of the upper classes were prepared to collaborate with Napoleon, but the peasants, urged on by the lower clergy and the monks, rose in a general rebellion.

In Spain, Napoleon faced a new kind of warfare. Guerilla bands cut lines of communication, killed stragglers, destroyed isolated units, and then disappeared into the mountains. The British landed an army under Sir Arthur Wellesley (1769–1852), later the duke of Wellington, to support the Spanish insurgents.

Thus began the long peninsular campaign that would drain French strength from elsewhere in Europe and play a critical role in Napoleon's eventual defeat.

AUSTRIA   The French troubles in Spain encouraged the Austrians to renew the war in 1809. Since their defeat at Austerlitz, they had sought a war of revenge. The Austrians counted on Napoleon's distraction in Spain, French war weariness, and aid from other German princes. Napoleon was fully in command in France, however; and the German princes did not move. The French army marched swiftly into Austria and won the Battle of Wagram. The resulting Peace of Schönbrunn deprived Austria of much territory and three and a half million subjects.

Another spoil of victory was the Austrian archduchess Marie Louise (1791–1847), daughter of the emperor. Napoleon's wife, Josephine de Beauharnais (1763–1814), was forty-six and had borne him no children. His dynastic ambitions, as well as the desire for a marriage matching his new position as master of Europe, led him to divorce his wife and to marry the eighteen-year-old Austrian princess. Napoleon had also considered marrying the sister of Tsar Alexander but had received a polite rebuff.

The Invasion of Russia

The failure of Napoleon's marriage negotiations with Russia emphasized the shakiness of the Franco-Russian alliance concluded at Tilsit. The alliance was unpopular with Russian nobles because of the liberal politics of France and because the Continental System prohibited timber sales to Britain. Only French aid in gaining Constantinople could justify the alliance in their eyes, but Napoleon gave them no help against the Ottoman Empire. The organization of the Grand Duchy of Warsaw as a Napoleonic satellite on the Russian doorstep and its enlargement in 1809 after the Battle of Wagram angered Alexander. Napoleon's annexation of Holland in violation of the Treaty of Tilsit, his recognition of the French Marshal Bernadotte (1763–1844) as the future King Charles XIV of Sweden, and his marriage to an Austrian princess further disturbed the tsar. At the end of

The Spanish artist Francisco Goya (1746–1828) was horrified by the atrocities perpetrated by both sides during the guerrilla warfare that followed Napoleon's occupation of Spain. This painting, entitled "The Third of May," depicts French troops executing Spanish insurgents. Events like this roused popular resistance in Spain. The British soon began to assist the insurgency. [Erich Lessing/Art Resource, N.Y.]

1810, Russia withdrew from the Continental System and began to prepare for war (see Map 20-2).

Napoleon was determined to end the Russian military threat. He amassed an army of more than 600,000 men, including a core of Frenchmen and more than 400,000 other soldiers drawn from the rest of his empire. He intended the usual short campaign crowned by a decisive battle, but the Russians disappointed him by retreating before his advance. His vast superiority in numbers—the Russians had only about 160,000 troops—made it foolish for them to risk a battle. Instead they followed a "scorched-earth" policy, destroying all food and supplies as

they retreated. The so-called Grand Army of Napoleon could not live off the country, and the expanse of Russia made supply lines too long to maintain. Terrible rains, fierce heat, shortages of food and water, and the courage of the Russian rear guard eroded the morale of Napoleon's army. Napoleon's advisers urged him to abandon the venture, but he feared that an unsuccessful campaign would undermine his position in the empire and in France. He pinned his faith on the Russians' unwillingness to abandon Moscow without a fight.

In September 1812, Russian public opinion forced the army to give Napoleon the battle he

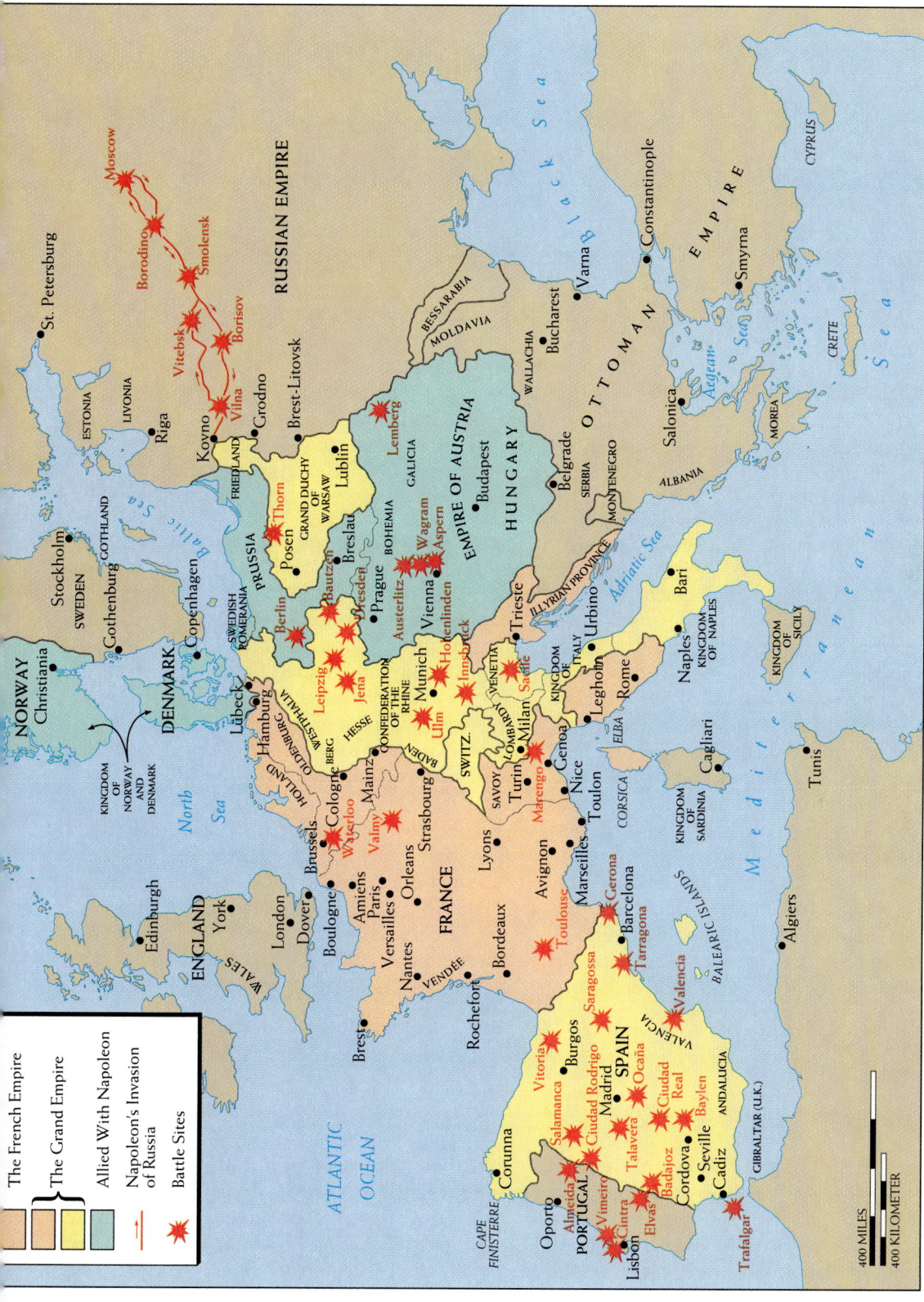

MAP 20-2 NAPOLEONIC EUROPE IN LATE 1812 By mid-1812 the areas shown in peach were incorporated into France, and most of the rest of Europe was directly controlled by or allied with Napoleon. But Russia had withdrawn from the failing Continental System, and the decline of Napoleon was about to begin.

The French Empire
The Grand Empire
Allied With Napoleon
Napoleon's Invasion of Russia
Battle Sites

A German Writer Describes the War of Liberation

The German resistance to Napoleon as his army retreated from Moscow was the first time in modern German history that people from virtually all German-speaking lands cooperated together. The memory of that action became one of the defining moments in the emergence of a sense of German nationhood. Ernest Moritz Arndt (1769–1860) described the excitement and enthusiasm of that moment. This passage was frequently reprinted in German history textbooks for more than a century.

◆ *Why does Arndt claim each of these various groups wanted war? This passage portrays a vast number of German-speaking people resisting Napoleon, but how also does it serve to project the possibility of a united nation that did not yet actually exist? What qualities of action in this passage are similar or dissimilar to the* levée en masse *declared during the French Revolution and reprinted in the previous chapter? Is it possible that Arndt wished to portray the actions of Germans as resembling or equaling the national spirit of the French during the Revolution?*

Fired with enthusiasm, the people rose, "with God for King and Fatherland." Among the Prussians there was only one voice, one feeling, one anger and one love, to save the Fatherland and to free Germany. The Prussians wanted war; war and death they wanted; peace they feared because they could hope for no honorable peace from Napoleon. War, war, sounded the cry from the Carpathians to the Baltic, from the Niemen to the Elbe. War! cried the nobleman and landed proprietor who had become impoverished. War! that peasant who was driving his last horse to death. . . . War! the citizen who was growing exhausted from quartering soldiers and paying taxes. War! the widow who was sending her only son to the front. War! the young girl who, with tears of pride and pain, was leaving her betrothed. Youths who were hardly able to bear arms, men with gray hair, officers who on account of wounds and mutilations had long ago been honorably discharged, rich landed proprietors and officials, fathers of large families and managers of extensive businesses—all were unwilling to remain behind. Even young women, under all sorts of disguises, rushed to arms; all wanted to drill, arm themselves and fight and die for the Fatherland. . . .

The most beautiful thing about all this holy zeal and happy confusion was that all differences of position, class, and age were forgotten . . . that the one great feeling for the Fatherland, its freedom and honor, swallowed all other feelings, caused all other considerations and relationships to be forgotten.

Ernst Moritz Arndt, Das preussische Volk und Heer (1813), *quoted in P. Jennrich, K. Krause, and W. Viernow, eds.,* Geschichte für Mittelschulen *(Halle on Saale, 1941), pp. 111–112, as quoted and translated in Louis L. Snyder, ed.,* Documents of German History *(New Brunswick, N.J.: Rutgers University Press, 1958), pp. 148-149.*

wanted despite the canny Russian General Kutuzov's (1745–1813) wish to avoid the fight and to let the Russian winter defeat the invader. At Borodino, not far west of Moscow, the bloodiest battle of the Napoleonic era cost the French 30,000 casualties and the Russians almost twice as many. Yet the Russian army was not destroyed. Napoleon won nothing substantial, and the battle was regarded as a defeat for him.

Fires, set by the Russians, soon engulfed Moscow and left Napoleon far from home with a badly diminished army lacking adequate supplies as winter came to a vast and unfriendly country. Napoleon, after capturing the burned city, addressed several peace offers to Alexander, but the tsar ignored them. By October, what was left of the Grand Army was forced to retreat. By December, Napoleon realized that the Russian fiasco would encourage plots against him at home. He returned to Paris, leaving the remnants of his army to struggle westward. Perhaps only as many as 100,000 lived to tell the tale of their terrible ordeal.

European Coalition

Even as the news of the disaster reached the West, the final defeat of Napoleon was far from certain. He was able to put down his opponents in Paris and raise another 350,000 men. Neither the Prussians nor the Austrians were eager to risk another bout with Napoleon, and even the Russians hesitated. The Austrian foreign minister, Prince Klemens von Metternich (1773–1859), would have been glad to make a negotiated peace that would leave Napoleon on the throne of a shrunken and chastened France rather than see Europe dominated by Russia. Napoleon might have won a reasonable settlement by negotiation had he been willing to make concessions that would have split his jealous opponents. He would not consider that solution, however. As he explained to Metternich:

Your sovereigns born on the throne can let themselves be beaten twenty times and return to their capitals. I cannot do this because I am an upstart soldier. My domination will not survive the day when I cease to be strong, and therefore feared.[2]

In 1813 patriotic pressure and national ambition brought together the last and most powerful coalition against Napoleon. The Russians drove westward, and Prussia and then Austria joined them. All were assisted by vast amounts of British money. From the west Wellington marched his peninsular army into France. Napoleon's new army was inexperienced and poorly equipped. His generals had lost confidence and were tired. The emperor himself was worn out and sick. Still he waged a skillful campaign in central Europe and defeated the allies at Dresden. In October, however, he was deci-

Arthur Wellesley, the duke of Wellington, first led troops against Napoleon in Spain and later defeated him at the battle of Waterloo, June 18, 1815. Unlike his great naval contemporary, Nelson, he survived to become an elder statesman of Britain. [Bildarchiv Preussischer Kulturbesitz]

sively defeated by the combined armies of the enemy at Leipzig in what the Germans called the Battle of the Nations. At the end of March 1814, the allied army marched into Paris. A few days later, Napoleon abdicated and went into exile on the island of Elba off the coast of northern Italy.

The Congress of Vienna and the European Settlement

Fear of Napoleon and hostility to his ambitions had held the victorious coalition together. As soon as he was removed, the allies pursued their

[2]Quoted in Felix Markham, Napoleon and the Awakening of Europe (New York: Macmillan, 1965), pp. 115–116.

Castlereagh Discusses British Goals on the Continent

Lord Castlereagh was the chief British representative in the negotiations concluding the Napoleonic Wars. He believed that the moment of victory over Napoleon presented Great Britain and the other powers with a unique opportunity to cooperate in establishing a new European diplomatic order. He was particularly concerned to preserve the power and influence of Prussia in northern Europe.

◆ *What are the factors that for the moment could allow the major powers to act in a unified manner? Why was it to Britain's advantage for the other powers to continue to have a sense of the danger posed by revolutionary forces? Why does Castlereagh place so much emphasis on the future role of Prussia?*

The existing state of European relations may possibly not endure beyond the danger which originally gave them birth, and which has recently confirmed them; but it is our duty, as well as our interest, to retard, if we cannot avert, the return of a more contentious order of things: and our insular situation places us sufficiently out of the reach of danger to admit of our pursuing a more generous and confiding policy.

In the present state of Europe, it is the province of Great Britain to turn the confidence she has inspired to the account of peace, by exercising a conciliatory influence between the Powers, rather than put her self at the head of any combinations of Courts to keep others in check. The necessity for such a system of connexion may recur, but this necessity should be no longer problematical when it is acted upon. The immediate object to be kept in view is to inspire the States of Europe, as long as we can, with a sense of the dangers which they have surmounted by their union, of the hazards they will incur by a relaxation of vigilance, [and] to make them feel that the existing concert is their only perfect security against the revolutionary embers more or less existing in every State of Europe; and that their true wisdom is to keep down the petty contentions of ordinary times, and to stand together in support of the established principles of social order. . . .

. . . every consideration of common interest must make me partial to the conservation of its [Prussia's] preponderance as a great Power, inasmuch as Prussia must be the basis of every system in the north of Europe to preserve Holland as an independent State, and to keep France in check; but, with all that partiality and a grateful admiration of the conduct of that nation and its armies in the war, I fairly own that I look with considerable anxiety to the tendency of their politics. There certainly, at this moment, exists a great fermentation in all orders of the State . . . very free notions of Government, if not principles actually revolutionary, are prevalent, and the army is by no means subordinate to the civil authorities. It is impossible to say where these impulses may stop, when they find a representative system in which they may develop themselves.

I call your attention to these circumstances, not as any motive for interference on your part, but in order to impress your mind with the importance (and especially to Prussia herself) of keeping up a good understanding amongst the adjoining States, on which these disorganizing principles have made less impression, till the internal state of both France and of the north of Germany is more assured than it can now be considered to be.

From Memoirs and Correspondence of Viscount Castlereagh, Vol. XI *(London, 1853), pp. 104–107, as quoted in Mack Walker, ed.,* Metternich's Europe *(New York: Walker and Company, 1968), pp. 40–41.*

separate ambitions. The key person in achieving eventual agreement among them was Robert Stewart, Viscount Castlereagh (1769–1822), the British foreign secretary. Even before the victorious armies had entered Paris, he brought about the signing of the Treaty of Chaumont on March 9, 1814. It provided for the restoration of the Bourbons to the French throne and the contraction of France to its frontiers of 1792. Even more important was the agreement by Britain, Austria, Russia, and Prussia to form a Quadruple Alliance for twenty years to guarantee the peace terms and to act together to preserve whatever settlement they later agreed on. Remaining problems—and there were many—and final details were left for a conference to be held at Vienna.

Territorial Adjustments

The Congress of Vienna assembled in September 1814 but did not conclude its work until November 1815. Although a glittering array of heads of state attended the gathering, the four great powers conducted the important work of the conference. The only full session of the congress met to ratify the arrangements made by the big four. The easiest problem facing the great powers was France. All the victors agreed that no single state should be allowed to dominate Europe, and all were determined to see that France should be prevented from doing so again. The restoration of the French Bourbon monarchy, which was temporarily popular, and a nonvindictive boundary settlement were designed to keep France calm and satisfied.

The leading statesmen of the Congress of Vienna are here portrayed in a single group. Metternich, in white breeches, is standing on the left. Lord Castlereagh is sitting in the center with his legs crossed. Talleyrand is seated on the right with his arm on the table. [Royal Library, Windsor Castle]

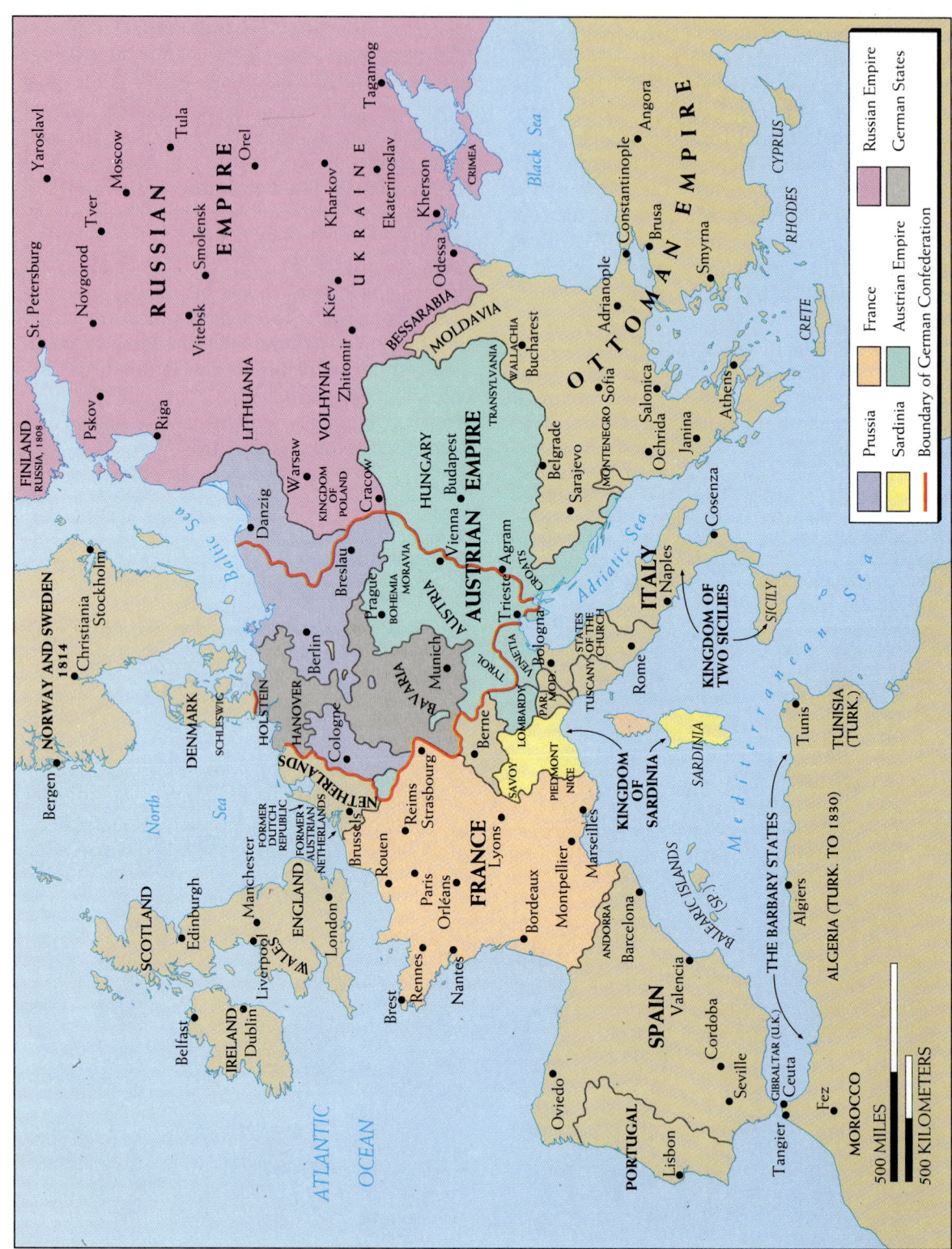

Map 20-3 Europe, After The Congress of Vienna, 1815 *The Congress of Vienna achieved the post-Napoleonic territorial adjustments shown on the map. The most*

Legend:
- Russian Empire
- German States
- France
- Austrian Empire
- Prussia
- Sardinia
- Boundary of German Confederation

The powers also built up a series of states to serve as barriers to any new French expansion (see Map 20-3). They established the kingdom of the Netherlands, including Belgium, in the north and added Genoa to Piedmont in the south. Prussia, whose power was increased by accessions in eastern Europe, was given important new territories along the Rhine River to deter French aggression in the west. Austria was given full control of northern Italy to prevent a repetition of Napoleon's conquests there. As for the rest of Germany, most of Napoleon's arrangements were left untouched. The venerable Holy Roman Empire, which had been dissolved in 1806, was not revived. In all these areas, the congress established the rule of legitimate monarchs and rejected any hint of the republican and democratic politics that had flowed from the French Revolution.

On these matters agreement was not difficult, but the settlement of eastern Europe sharply divided the victors. Alexander I of Russia wanted all Poland under his rule. Prussia was willing to give it to him in return for all of Saxony. Austria, however, was unwilling to surrender its share of Poland or to see Prussian power grow or Russia penetrate deeper into central Europe. The Polish–Saxon question brought the congress to a standstill and almost caused a new war among the victors. But defeated France provided a way out. The wily Talleyrand, now representing France at Vienna, suggested that the weight of France added to that of Britain and Austria might bring Alexander to his senses. When news of a secret treaty among the three leaked out, the tsar agreed to become ruler of a smaller Poland, and Frederick William III of Prussia accepted only part of Saxony (see Map 20-4). Thereafter, France was included as a fifth great power in all deliberations.

The Hundred Days and the Quadruple Alliance

Unity among the victors was further restored by Napoleon's return from Elba on March 1, 1815. The French army was still loyal to the former emperor, and many of the French people thought that their fortunes might be safer under his rule than under that of the restored Bourbons. The coalition seemed to be dissolving

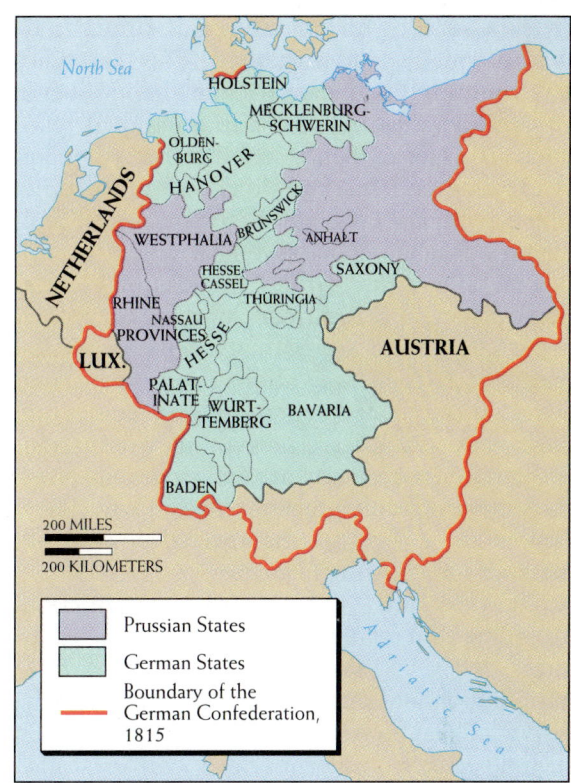

MAP 20-4 THE GERMAN STATES AFTER 1815 *As noted, German states were also reorganized.*

in Vienna. Napoleon seized the opportunity, escaped to France, and was soon restored to power. He promised a liberal constitution and a peaceful foreign policy. The allies were not convinced. They declared Napoleon an outlaw (a new device under international law) and sent their armies to crush him. Wellington, with the crucial help of the Prussians under Field Marshal von Blücher (1742–1819), defeated Napoleon at Waterloo in Belgium on June 18, 1815. Napoleon again abdicated and was sent into exile on Saint Helena, a tiny Atlantic island off the coast of Africa, where he died in 1821.

The Hundred Days, as the period of Napoleon's return is called, frightened the great powers and made the peace settlement harsher for France. In addition to some minor territorial adjustments, the victors imposed a war indemnity and an army of occupation on France. Alexander proposed a Holy Alliance, whereby the monarchs promised to act together in accordance with Christian principles. Austria and

Prussia signed; but Castlereagh thought it absurd and England abstained. The tsar, who was then embracing mysticism, believed his proposal a valuable tool for international relations. The Holy Alliance soon became a symbol of extreme political reaction. The Quadruple Alliance among England, Austria, Prussia, and Russia was renewed on November 20, 1815.

The chief aims of the Congress of Vienna were to prevent a recurrence of the Napoleonic nightmare and to arrange an acceptable settlement for Europe that might produce lasting peace. It succeeded remarkably in achieving these goals. France accepted the new situation without undue resentment. The victorious powers settled difficult problems reasonably. They established a legalistic balance of power and methods for adjusting to change.

The work of the congress has been criticized for failing to recognize and provide for the great forces that would stir the nineteenth century—nationalism and democracy. Such criticism is inappropriate, however. The settlement, like all such agreements, was aimed at solving past ills, and in that it succeeded. The powers would have had to have been more than human to have anticipated future problems or to have yielded to forces of which they disapproved. Perhaps it was unusual enough to produce a settlement that remained essentially intact for almost half a century and that allowed Europe to suffer no general war for a hundred years.

The Romantic Movement

The years of the French Revolution and the conquests of Napoleon saw the emergence of a new and important intellectual movement throughout Europe. *Romanticism* in its various manifestations was a reaction against much of the thought of the Enlightenment. Romantic writers opposed what they considered the excessive scientific narrowness of the eighteenth-century *philosophes*. They accused the latter of subjecting everything to geometrical and mathematical models and thereby demeaning feelings and imagination. Romantic thinkers refused to conceive of human nature as primarily rational. They wanted to interpret both physical nature

Napoleonic Europe	
1797	Napoleon concludes the Treaty of Campo Formio
1798	Nelson defeats the French navy in the habor of Abukir in Egypt
1799	Consulate established in France
1801	Concordat between France and the papacy
1802	Treaty of Amiens
1803	War renewed between France and Britain
1804	Execution of Duke of Enghien
1804	Napoleonic Civil Code issued
1804	Napoleon crowned as emperor
1805	Nelson defeats French fleet at Trafalgar (October 21)
1805	Austerlitz (December 2)
1806	Jena
1806	Continental System established by Berlin Decrees
1807	Friedland
1807	Treaty of Tilsit
1808	Beginning of Spanish resistance to Napoleonic domination
1809	Wagram
1809	Napoleon marries Archduchess Marie Louise of Austria
1812	Invasion of Russia and French defeat at Borodino
1813	Leipzig (Battle of the Nations)
1814	Treaty of Chaumont (March) establishes Quadruple Alliance
1814	Congress of Vienna convenes (September)
1815	Napoleon returns from Elba (March 1)
1815	Waterloo (June 18)
1815	Holy Alliance formed at Congress of Vienna (September 26)
1815	Quadruple Alliance renewed at Congress of Vienna (November 20)
1821	Napoleon dies on Saint Helena

and human society in organic rather than mechanical terms and categories. The Enlightenment *philosophes* had often criticized religion and faith; the romantics in contrast saw religion as basic to human nature and faith as a means to knowledge.

Some historians, most notably Arthur O. Lovejoy, have warned against speaking of a single European-wide romantic movement. They have pointed out that a variety of such movements—occurring almost simultaneously in Germany, England, and France—arose independently and had their own particular courses of development. Such considerations have not, however, prevented the designation of a specific historical period, dated roughly from 1780 to 1830, as the Age of Romanticism or the romantic movement.

Despite national differences, a shared reaction to the Enlightenment marked all of these writers and artists. They saw the imagination or some such intuitive intellectual faculty supplementing reason as a means of perceiving and understanding the world. Many of these writers urged a revival of Christianity, such as had permeated Europe during the Middle Ages. And unlike the *philosophes,* the romantics liked the art, literature, and architecture of medieval times. They were also deeply interested in folklore, folk songs, and fairy tales. The romantics were fascinated by dreams, hallucinations, sleepwalking, and other phenomena that suggested the existence of a world beyond that of empirical observation, sensory data, and discursive reasoning.

Romantic Questioning of the Supremacy of Reason

Several historical streams fed the romantic movement. These included the individualism of the Renaissance and the Reformation, the pietism of the seventeenth century, and the eighteenth-century English Methodist movement. The latter influence encouraged a heartfelt, practical religion in place of dogmatism, rationalism, and deism. The sentimental novels of the eighteenth century, such as Samuel Richardson's (1689–1761) *Clarissa* (1747), also paved the way for thinkers who would emphasize feeling and emotion. The so-called *Sturm und Drang* ("storm and stress") period of German literature and German idealist philosophy were important to the romantics. Two writers who were also closely related to the Enlightenment, however, provided the immediate intellectual foundations for romanticism. They were Jean-Jacques Rousseau and Immanuel Kant, both of whom raised questions

about the sufficiency of the rationalism so dear to the *philosophes.*

Rousseau and Education

It has already been pointed out in Chapter 18 that Jean-Jacques Rousseau, though sharing in the reformist spirit of the Enlightenment, opposed many of its other facets. What romantic writers especially drew from Rousseau was his conviction that society and material prosperity had corrupted human nature. In his works, Rousseau had portrayed humankind as happy and innocent by nature and originally living in a state of equilibrium, able to do what it desired and desiring only what it was able to do. To

In "A Philosopher in a Moonlit Churchyard," the British artist Philip James de Loutherbourg captured many of the themes of the Romantic movement. The painting suggests a sense of history, a love of Gothic architecture, a sense of the importance of religion, and a belief that the world is essentially mysterious. [Yale Center for British Art]

become happy again, humankind must remain true to its natural being while still attempting to realize the new moral possibilities of life in society. In the *Social Contract* (1762), Rousseau had provided his prescription for the reorganization of political life that would achieve that goal.

Rousseau set forth his view on the individual's development toward the good and happy life in his novel *Émile* (1762), also discussed in Chapter 19 in regard to his views on gender. Initially this treatise on education was far more influential than the *Social Contract*. In *Émile*, Rousseau stressed the difference between children and adults. He distinguished the stages of human maturation and urged that children be raised in maximum individual freedom. Each child should be allowed to grow freely, like a plant, and to learn by trial and error what reality is and how best to deal with it. The parent or teacher would help most by providing the basic necessities of life and warding off what was manifestly harmful. Beyond that, the adult should stay completely out of the way, like a gardener who waters and weeds a garden but otherwise lets nature take its course. As noted in Chapter 19, Rousseau thought that men and women because of their physical differences would naturally grow into social roles with different spheres of activity.

Rousseau thought that the child's sentiments as well as its reason should be permitted to flourish. To romantic writers, this concept of human development vindicated the rights of nature over those of artificial society. They thought that such a form of open education would eventually lead to a natural society. In its fully developed form, this view of life led the romantics to value the uniqueness of each individual and to explore childhood in great detail. Like Rousseau, the romantics saw humankind, nature, and society as organically interrelated.

Kant and Reason

Immanuel Kant (1724–1804) wrote the two greatest philosophical works of the late eighteenth century: *The Critique of Pure Reason* (1781) and *The Critique of Practical Reason* (1788). He sought to accept the rationalism of the Enlightenment and still to preserve a belief in human freedom, immortality, and the existence of God. Against Locke and other philosophers who saw knowledge rooted in sensory experience alone, Kant argued for the subjective character of human knowledge. For Kant, the human mind did not simply reflect the world around it like a passive mirror; rather, the mind actively imposed on the world of sensory experience "forms of sensibility" and "categories of understanding." The mind itself generated these categories. In other words, the human mind perceives the world as it does because of its own internal mental categories. This meant that human perceptions were as much the product of the mind's own activity as of sensory experience.

Kant found the sphere of reality that was accessible to pure reason to be quite limited. He believed, however, that beyond the phenomenal world of sensory experience, over which "pure reason" was master, there existed what he called the "noumenal" world. This world was a sphere of moral and aesthetic reality known by "practical reason" and conscience. Kant thought that all human beings possessed an innate sense of moral duty or an awareness of what he called a *categorical imperative.* This term referred to an inner command to act in every situation as one would have all other people always act in the same situation. Kant regarded the existence of this imperative of conscience as incontrovertible proof of humankind's natural freedom. On the basis of humankind's moral sense, Kant postulated the existence of God, eternal life, and future rewards and punishments. He believed that these transcendental truths could not be proved by discursive reasoning. Still, he was convinced that they were realities to which every reasonable person could attest.

To many romantic writers, Kantian philosophy constituted a decisive refutation of the narrow rationality of the Enlightenment. Whether they called it "practical reason," "fancy," "imagination," "intuition," or simply "feeling," the romantics believed in the presence of a special power in the human mind that could penetrate beyond the limits of largely passive human understanding as set forth by Hobbes, Locke, and Hume. Most of them also believed that poets and artists possessed these powers in abundance. Other romantic writers appealed to the limits of human reason to set forth new religious ideas or political thought that was often at odds with Enlightenment writers.

Romantic Literature

The term *romantic* appeared in English and French literature as early as the seventeenth century. Neoclassical writers then used the word to describe literature that they considered unreal, sentimental, or excessively fanciful. In the eighteenth century, the English writer Thomas Warton (1728–1790) associated romantic literature with medieval romances. In Germany, a major center of the romantic literary movement, Johann Gottfried Herder (1744–1803) used the terms *romantic* and *Gothic* interchangeably. In both England and Germany, the term came to be applied to all literature that did not observe classical forms and rules and that gave free play to the imagination.

As an alternative to such dependence on the classical forms, August Wilhelm von Schlegel (1767–1845) praised the "romantic" literature of Dante, Petrarch, Boccaccio, Shakespeare, the Arthurian legends, Cervantes, and Calderón. According to Schlegel, romantic literature was to classical literature what the organic and living were to the merely mechanical. He set forth his views in *Lectures on Dramatic Art and Literature* (1809–1811).

The romantic movement had peaked in Germany and England before it became a major force in France under the leadership of Madame de Staël (1766–1817) and Victor Hugo (1802–1885). So influential was the classical tradition in France that not until 1816 did a French writer openly declare himself a romantic. That was Henri Beyle (1783–1842), who wrote under the pseudonym Stendhal. He praised Shakespeare and Lord Byron and criticized his own countryman, the seventeenth-century classical dramatist Jean Racine (1639–1699).

The English Romantic Writers

The English romantics believed that poetry was enhanced by freely following the creative impulses of the mind. In this belief, they directly opposed Lockean psychology, which regarded the mind as a passive receptor and poetry as a mechanical exercise of "wit" following prescribed rules. For William Blake and Samuel Taylor Coleridge, the artist's imagination was God at work in the mind. As Coleridge expressed his views, the imagination was "a repetition in the finite mind of the eternal act of creation in the infinite I AM." So conceived of, poetry could not be considered idle play. It was the highest of human acts, humankind's self-fulfillment in a transcendental world.

BLAKE   William Blake (1757–1827) considered the poet a seer and poetry to be translated vision. He thought it a great tragedy that so many people understood the world only rationally and could perceive no innocence or beauty in it. In the 1790s, he went through a deep personal depression that seems to have been related to his own inability to perceive the world as he believed it to be. The better one got to know the world, the more the life of the imagination and its spiritual values seemed to recede. Blake saw this problem as evidence of the materialism and injustice of English society. He was deeply impressed by the strong sense of contradiction between a true childlike vision of the world and conceptions of it based on experience.

COLERIDGE   Samuel Taylor Coleridge (1772–1834) was the master of Gothic poems of the supernatural, such as "Christabel," "The Ancient Mariner," and "Kubla Khan." "The Ancient Mariner" relates the story of a sailor cursed for killing an albatross. The poem treats the subject as a crime against nature and God and raises the issues of guilt, punishment, and the redemptive possibilities of humility and penance. At the end of the poem, the mariner discovers the unity and beauty of all things. Having repented, he is delivered from his awful curse, which has been symbolized by the dead albatross hung around his neck:

> O happy living things! no tongue
> Their beauty might declare:
> A spring of love gushed from my heart,
> And I blessed them unaware . . .
> The self-same moment I could pray;
> And from my neck so free
> The Albatross fell off, and sank
> Like lead into the sea.

Coleridge also made major contributions to romantic literary criticism in his lectures on

Shakespeare and in *Biographia Literaria* (1817), which presents his theories of poetry.

WORDSWORTH William Wordsworth (1770–1850) was Coleridge's closest friend. Together they published *Lyrical Ballads* in 1798 as a manifesto of a new poetry that rejected the rules of eighteenth-century criticism. Among Wordsworth's most important later poems is his "Ode on Intimations of Immortality" (1803), written in part to console Coleridge, who was suffering a deep personal crisis. Its subject is the loss of poetic vision, something Wordsworth also keenly felt then in himself. Nature, which he had worshiped, no longer spoke freely to him, and he feared that it might never speak to him again:

> There was a time when meadow, grove, and
>   stream,
> The earth, and every common sight,
> To me did seem
> Appareled in celestial light,
> The glory and the freshness of a dream.
> It is not now as it hath been of yore—
> Turn whereso'er I may,
> By night or day,
> The things which I have seen I now can
>   see no more.

He had lost what he believed that all human beings lose in the necessary process of maturation: their childlike vision and closeness to spiritual reality. For both Wordsworth and Coleridge, childhood was the bright period of creative imagination. Wordsworth held a theory of the soul's preexistence in a celestial state before its creation. The child, being closer in time to its eternal origin and undistracted by worldly experience, recollects the supernatural world much more easily. Aging and urban living corrupt and deaden the imagination, making one's inner feelings and the beauty of nature less important. In his book-length poem *The Prelude* (1850), Wordsworth presented a long autobiographical account of the growth of the poet's mind.

LORD BYRON A true rebel among the romantic poets was Lord Byron (1788–1824). In Britain, even most of the other romantic writers distrusted and disliked him. He had little sympathy for their views of the imagination. Outside England, however, Byron was regarded as the embodiment of the new person of the

Lord Byron may well have been the most famous European poet of the first quarter of the nineteenth century. This portrait by the contemporary artist Géricault captures the poet in a brooding, introspective mood. [Bildarchiv Preussischer Kulturbesitz]

French Revolution. He rejected the old traditions (he was divorced and famous for his amours) and championed the cause of personal liberty. Byron was outrageously skeptical and mocking, even of his own beliefs. In *Childe Harold's Pilgrimage* (1812), he created a brooding, melancholy romantic hero. In *Don Juan* (1819), he wrote with ribald humor, acknowledged nature's cruelty as well as its beauty, and even expressed admiration for urban life.

The German Romantic Writers

Much romantic poetry was also written on the Continent, but almost all major German romantics wrote at least one novel. Romantic novels often were highly sentimental and borrowed material from medieval romances. The characters of romantic novels were treated as symbols of the larger truth of life. Purely realistic description was avoided. The first German romantic novel was Ludwig Tieck's (1773–1853) *William Lovell* (1793–1795). It contrasts the young Lovell, whose life is built on love and imagination, with those who live by cold reason alone and who thus become an easy prey to unbelief, misanthropy, and egoism. As the novel rambles to its conclusion, Lovell is ruined by a mixture of philosophy, materialism, and skepticism, administered to him by two women whom he naïvely loves.

SCHLEGEL   Friedrich Schlegel (1767–1845) wrote a progressive early romantic novel, *Lucinde* (1799), which attacked contemporary prejudices against women as capable of being little more than lovers and domestics. Schlegel's novel reveals the ability of the romantics to become involved in the social issues of their day. He depicted Lucinde as the perfect friend and companion, as well as the unsurpassed lover, of the hero. Like other early romantic novels, the work shocked contemporary morals by frankly discussing sexual activity and by describing Lucinde as equal in all ways to the male hero.

GOETHE   Towering above all of these German writers stood the figure of Johann Wolfgang von Goethe (1749–1832). Perhaps the greatest German writer of modern times, Goethe defies any easy classification. Part of his literary production fits into the romantic mold, and part of it was a condemnation of romantic excesses. The book that made his early reputation was *The Sorrows of Young Werther*, published in 1774. This novel, like many others in the eighteenth century, is composed of a series of letters. The hero falls in love with Lotte, another man's wife. The letters explore this relationship and display the emotional sentimentalism that was characteristic of the age. Eventually Werther and Lotte part, but in his grief over his abandoned love, Werther takes his own life. This novel became popular throughout Europe. Virtually all later romantic authors, and especially those in Germany, admired it because of its emphasis on feeling and on living outside the bounds of polite society.

Much of Goethe's early poetry was also erotic in nature. As he became older, however, Goethe became much more serious and self-consciously moral. He published many other works, including *Iphigenia at Tauris* (1787) and *Wilhelm*

Johann Wolfgang von Goethe (1749–1832), the greatest German writer of modern times, is portrayed here in the garb of a pilgrim against a Romantic background of classical ruins in the fields outside Rome. [Städelisches Kunstinstitut, Frankfurt/Artothek]

Meister's Apprenticeship (1792–1800) that explored how human beings come to live moral lives while still acknowledging the life of the senses.

Goethe's greatest masterpiece was *Faust,* a long dramatic work of poetry in two parts. Part I was published in 1808. It tells the story of Faust, who, weary of life, makes a pact with the Devil—he will exchange his soul for greater knowledge than other human beings possess. As the story progresses, Faust seduces a young woman named Gretchen. She dies but is received into heaven as the grief-stricken Faust realizes that he must continue to live.

In Part II, completed in the year of Goethe's death (1832), Faust is taken through a series of strange adventures involving witches and various mythological characters. This portion of the work has never been admired as much as Part I. At the conclusion, however, Faust dedicates his life, or what remains of it, to the improvement of humankind. In this dedication he feels that he has found a goal that will allow him to overcome the restless striving that first induced him

to make the pact with the Devil. That new knowledge breaks the pact. Faust then dies and is received by angels.

In this great work, Goethe obviously was criticizing much of his earlier thought and that of contemporary romantic writers. He was also attempting to portray the deep spiritual problems that Europeans would encounter as the traditional moral and religious values of Christianity were abandoned. Yet Goethe himself could not reaffirm those values. In that respect, both he and his characters symbolized the spiritual struggle of the nineteenth century.

Religion in the Romantic Period

During the Middle Ages, the foundation of religion had been the Church. The Reformation leaders had appealed to the authority of the Bible. Then, later Enlightenment writers had attempted to derive religion from the rational nature revealed by Newtonian physics. Romantic religious thinkers, on the other hand, appealed to the inner emotions of humankind for the foundation of religion. Their forerunners were the mystics of Western Christianity. One of the first great examples of a religion characterized by romantic impulses—Methodism—arose in England.

Methodism

Methodism originated in the middle of the eighteenth century as a revolt against deism and rationalism in the Church of England. The Methodist revival formed an important part of the background of English romanticism. The leader of the Methodist movement was John Wesley (1703–1791). His education and religious development had been carefully supervised by his remarkable mother, Susannah Wesley, who bore eighteen children in addition to John.

While at Oxford, Wesley organized a religious group known as the "Holy Club." He soon left England for missionary work in Georgia in America, where he arrived in 1735. While crossing the Atlantic, a group of German Moravians on the ship had deeply impressed him. These German pietists exhibited unshakable faith and confidence during a violent storm at sea, while

John Wesley (1703–1791) was the founder of Methodism. He emphasized the role of emotional experience in Christain conversion. [The Bettmann Archive]

Wesley despaired of his life. Wesley concluded that they knew far better than he the meaning of justification by faith. When he returned to England in 1738 after an unhappy missionary career, Wesley began to worship with Moravians in London. There, in 1739, he underwent a conversion experience that he described in the words, "My heart felt strangely warmed." From that point on, he felt assured of his own salvation.

Wesley discovered that he could not preach his version of Christian conversion and practical piety in Anglican church pulpits. Therefore, late in 1739, he began to preach in the open fields near the cities and towns of western England. Thousands of humble people responded to his message of repentance and good works. Soon he and his brother Charles (1707–1788), who became famous for his hymns, began to organize Methodist societies. By the late eighteenth century, the Methodists had become a separate church. They ordained their own clergy and sent missionaries to America, where they eventually achieved their greatest success and most widespread influence.

Methodism stressed inward, heartfelt religion and the possibility of Christian perfection in this life. John Wesley described Christianity as "an inward principle . . . the image of God impressed on a created spirit, a fountain of peace and love springing up into everlasting life." True Christians were those who were "saved in this world from all sin, from all unrighteousness . . . and now in such a sense perfect as not to commit sin and . . . freed from evil thoughts and evil tempers."[3]

Many people, weary of the dry rationalism that derived from deism, found Wesley's ideal relevant to their own lives. The Methodist preachers emphasized the role of enthusiastic emotional experience as part of Christian conversion. After Wesley, religious revivals became highly emotional in style and content.

New Directions in Continental Religion

Similar religious developments based on feeling appeared on the Continent. After the Thermidorian Reaction, a strong Roman Catholic revival took place in France. Its followers disap-

proved of both the religious policy of the revolution and the anticlericalism of the Enlightenment. The most important book to express these sentiments was *The Genius of Christianity* (1802) by Viscount François René de Chateaubriand (1768–1848). In this work, which became known as the "Bible of romanticism," Chateaubriand argued that the essence of religion was "passion." The foundation of faith in the Church was the emotion that its teachings and sacraments inspired in the heart of the Christian.

Against the Newtonian view of the world and of a rational God, the romantics found God immanent in nature. No one stated the romantic religious ideal more eloquently or with greater impact on the modern world than Friedrich Schleiermacher (1768–1834). In 1799 he published *Speeches on Religion to Its Cultured Despisers*. It was a response to Lutheran orthodoxy, on the one hand, and to Enlightenment rationalism, on the other. The advocates of both were the "cultured despisers" of real, or heartfelt, religion. According to Schleiermacher, religion was neither dogma nor a system of ethics. It was an intuition or feelings of absolute dependence on an infinite reali-

Friedrich Schleiermacher (1768–1834) was the most important Protestant theologian of the first half of the nineteenth century. He stressed the importance of feelings in religious experience. [Bildarchiv Preussischer Kulturbesitz]

[3]*Quoted in Albert C. Outler (Ed.),* John Wesley: A Representative Collection of His Writings *(New York: Oxford University Press, 1964), p. 220.*

Chateaubriand Describes the Appeal of a Gothic Church

Throughout most of the eighteenth century, writers had harshly criticized virtually all aspects of the Middle Ages, then considered an unenlightened time. One of the key elements of romanticism was a new appreciation of all things medieval. In this passage from The Genius of Christianity, *Chateaubriand praised the beauty of the Middle Ages and the strong religious feelings produced by stepping into a Gothic church. The description exemplifies the typically romantic emphasis on feelings as the chief foundation of religion.*

♦ *Why does the capacity of a Gothic church to carry Chateaubriand back in time add to its power of inducing a religious feeling? How does Chateaubriand unite the church with nature to emphasize its religious character? Is this vision of religion dependent upon the authority of an organized church or of sacred writings, such as the Bible?*

You could not enter a Gothic church without feeling a kind of awe and a vague sentiment of the Divinity. You were all at once carried back to those times when a fraternity of cenobites [a particular order of monks], after having meditated in the woods of their monasteries, met to prostrate themselves before the altar and to chant the praises of the Lord, amid the tranquility and the silence of the night. . . .

Everything in a Gothic church reminds you of the labyrinths of a wood; everything excites a feeling of religious awe, of mystery, and of the Divinity.

The two lofty towers erected at the entrance of the edifice overtop the elms and yew trees of the church yard, and produce the most picturesque effect on the azure of heaven. Sometimes their twin heads are illumined by the first rays of dawn; at others they appear crowned with a capital of clouds or magnified in a foggy atmosphere. The birds themselves seem to make a mistake in regard to them, and to take them for the trees of the forests; they hover over their summits, and perch upon their pinnacles. But, lo! confused noises suddenly issue from the tops of these towers and scare away the affrighted birds. The Christian architect, not content with building forests, has been desirous to retain their murmurs; and, by means of the organ and of bells, he has attached to the Gothic temple the very winds and thunders that roar in the recesses of the woods. Past ages, conjured up by these religious sounds, raise their venerable voices from the bosom of the stones, and are heard in every corner of the vast cathedral. The sanctuary reechoes like the cavern of the ancient Sibyl; loud-tongued bells swing over your head, while the vaults of death under your feet are profoundly silent.

Viscount François René de Chateaubriand, The Genius of Christianity, *trans. by C. I. White (Baltimore: J. Murphy, 1862), as quoted in Howard E. Hugo, ed.,* The Romantic Reader *(New York: Viking, 1957), pp. 341–342.*

ty. Religious institutions, doctrines, and moral activity expressed that primal religious feeling only in a secondary or indirect way.

Although Schleiermacher considered Christianity the "religion of religions," he also believed that every world religion was unique in its expression of the primal intuition of the infinite in the finite. He thus turned against the universal natural religion of the Enlightenment, which he termed "a name applied to loose, unconnected impulses," and defended the meaningfulness of the numerous world reli-

The philosopher J. G. Fichte (1762–1814), shown here in the uniform of a Berlin home guard. Fichte glorified the role of the great individual in history. [Bildarchiv Preussischer Kulturbesitz]

gions. Every such religion was seen to be a unique version of the emotional experience of dependence on an infinite being. In so arguing, Schleiermacher interpreted the religions of the world in the same way that other romantic writers interpreted the variety of unique peoples and cultures.

Romantic Views of Nationalism and History

A distinctive feature of romanticism, especially in Germany, was its glorification of both the individual person and individual cultures. Behind these views lay the philosophy of German idealism, which understood the world as the creation of subjective egos. J. G. Fichte (1762–1814), an important German philosopher and nationalist, identified the individual ego with the Absolute that underlies all existing things. According to him and similar philosophers, the world is truly the creation of humankind. The world is as it is because especially strong persons conceive of it in a particular way and impose their wills on the world and other people. Napoleon served as the contemporary example of such a great person. This philosophy has ever since served to justify the glorification of great persons and their actions in overriding all opposition to their will and desires.

Herder and Culture

In addition to this philosophy, the influence of new historical studies lay behind the German glorification of individual cultures. German romantic writers went in search of their own past in reaction to the copying of French manners in eighteenth-century Germany, the impact of the French Revolution, and the imperialism of Napoleon. An early leader in this effort was Johann Gottfried Herder (1744–1803). Herder had early resented the French cultural preponderance in Germany. In 1778 he published an influential essay entitled "On the Knowing and Feelings of the Human Soul." In it, he vigorously rejected the mechanical explanation of nature so popular with Enlightenment writers. He saw human beings and societies as developing organically, like plants, over time. Human beings were different at different times and places.

Herder revived German folk culture by urging the collection and preservation of distinctive German songs and sayings. His most important followers in this work were the Grimm brothers, Jakob (1785–1863) and Wilhelm (1786–1859), famous for their collection of fairy tales. Believing that each language and culture were the unique expression of a people, Herder opposed both the concept and the use of a "common" language, such as French, and "universal" institutions, such as those imposed on Europe by Napoleon. These, he believed, were forms of tyranny over the individuality of a people. Herder's writings led to a broad revival of interest in history and philosophy. Although initially directed toward the identification of German origins, such work soon expanded to embrace other world cultures as well. Eventually the ability of the romantic imagination to be at home in any age or culture spurred the study of non-Western religion, comparative literature, and philology.

Hegel and History

The most important person to write about history during the romantic period was the German Georg Wilhelm Friedrich Hegel (1770–1831). He is one of the most difficult and important philosophers in the history of Western civilization.

Hegel believed that ideas develop in an evolutionary fashion that involves conflict. At any given time, a predominant set of ideas, which he termed the thesis, holds sway. The thesis is challenged by other conflicting ideas, which Hegel termed the antithesis. As these patterns of thought clash, a synthesis emerges that eventually becomes the new thesis. Then the process begins all over again. Periods of world history receive their character from the patterns of thought predominating during them.

Several important philosophical conclusions followed from this analysis. One of the most significant was the belief that all periods of history have been of almost equal value because each was, by definition, necessary to the achievements of those that came later. Also, all cultures are valuable because each contributes to the necessary clash of values and ideas that allows humankind to develop. Hegel discussed these concepts in *The Phenomenology of Mind* (1806), *Lectures on the Philosophy of History* (1822–1831), and other works, many of which were published only after his death. During his lifetime, his ideas became widely known through his university lectures at Berlin.

This colored lithograph of G. W. F. Hegel shows him attired in the robes of a university professor. Hegel was the most important philosopher of history in the Romantic period. [Bildarchiv Preussischer Kulturbesitz]

♦

These various romantic ideas made a major contribution to the emergence of nationalism, which proved to be one of the strongest motivating forces of the nineteenth and twentieth centuries. The writers of the Enlightenment had generally championed a cosmopolitan outlook on the world. The romantic thinkers, however, emphasized the individuality and worth of each separate people and culture. A people or a nation was defined by a common language, a

Hegel Explains the Role of Great Men in History

Hegel believed that behind the development of human history from one period to the next lay the mind and purpose of what he termed the "World-Spirit," a concept somewhat resembling the Christian God. Hegel thought particular heroes from the past (such as Caesar) and in the present (such as Napoleon) were the unconscious instruments of that Spirit. In this passage from his lectures on the philosophy of history, Hegel explained how these heroes could change the course of history. All these concepts are characteristic of the romantic belief that human beings and human history are always intimately connected with larger, spiritual forces at work in the world. The passage also reflects the widespread belief of the time that the world of civic or political action pertained to men and that of the domestic sphere belonged to women.

✦ *How might the career of Napoleon have inspired this passage? What are the antidemocratic implications of this passage? In this passage, do great men make history or do historical developments make great men? Why do you think Hegel does not associate this power of shaping history with women as well as men? In that regard, note how he relates history with political developments rather than with those of the private social sphere.*

Such are all great historical men—whose own particular aims involve those large issues which are the will of the World-Spirit. They may be called Heroes, inasmuch as they have derived their purposes and their vocation, not from the calm, regular course of things, sanctioned by the existing order, but from a concealed fount—one which has not attained to phenomenal, present existence—from that inner Spirit, still hidden beneath the surface, which, impinging on the outer world as on a shell, bursts it in pieces, because it is another kernel than that which belonged to the shell in question. They are men, therefore, who appear to draw the impulse of their life from themselves; and whose deeds have produced a condition of things and a complex of historical relations which appear to be only their interest, and their work.

Such individuals had no consciousness of the general Idea they were unfolding, while prosecuting those aims of theirs; on the contrary, they were practical, political men. But at the same time they were thinking men, who had an insight into the requirements of the time—what was ripe for development. This was the very Truth for their age, for their world; the species next in order, so to speak, and which was already formed in the womb of time. It was theirs to know this nascent principle; the necessary, directly sequent step in progress, which their world was to take; to make this their aim, and to expend their energy in promoting it. World-historical men—the Heroes of an epoch—must, therefore, be recognized as its clear-sighted ones; their deeds, their words are the best of that time.

G. W. F. Hegel, The Philosophy of History, *trans. by J. Sibree (New York: Dover, 1956), pp. 30–31.*

---

common history, a homeland that possessed historical associations, and common customs. This cultural nationalism gradually became transformed into a political creed. It came to be widely believed that every people, ethnic group, or

nation should constitute a separate political entity, and that only when it so existed could the nation be secure in its own character.

The example of France under the revolutionary government and then Napoleon had demon-

strated the power of nationhood. Other peoples came to desire similar strength and confidence. Napoleon's toppling of ancient political structures, such as the Holy Roman Empire, proved the need for new political organization in Europe. By 1815 these were the aspirations of only a few Europeans, but as time passed, such yearnings came to be shared by scores of peoples from Ireland to Ukraine. The Congress of Vienna could ignore such feelings, but for the rest of the nineteenth century, as will be seen in subsequent chapters, statesmen had to confront the growing reality of the power these feelings unleashed.

Review Questions

1. How did Napoleon rise to power? What groups supported him? What were the stages by which he eventually made himself emperor? What were his major domestic achievements? Did his rule more nearly fulfill or betray the ideals of the French Revolution?

2. What regions made up Napoleon's realm and what status did each region have within it? How did Napoleon rule his empire? Did his administration show foresight or did the empire ultimately become a burden he could not afford?

3. Why did Napoleon decide to invade Russia? Why did the operation fail? Can Napoleon be considered a "military genius"? Why or why not? To what extent was his brilliance dependent on the ineptitude of his enemies?

4. Who were the principal personalities and what were the most significant problems of the Congress of Vienna? What were the results of the Congress and why were they significant?

5. Compare the role of feelings for romantic writers with the role of reason for Enlightenment writers. What questions did Rousseau and Kant raise about reason?

6. Why did poetry become important to romantic writers? How did the romantic concept of religion differ from Reformation Protestantism and Enlightenment Deism? How did romantic writers use the idea of history?

Suggested Readings

M. H. ABRAMS, *The Mirror and the Lamp: Romantic Theory and the Critical Tradition* (1958). A standard text on romantic literary theory that looks at English romanticism in the context of German romantic idealism.

M. H. ABRAMS, *Natural Supernaturalism: Tradition and Revolution in Romantic Literature* (1971). A brilliant survey of romanticism across West European literature.

J. S. ALLEN, *Popular French Romanticism: Authors, Readers, and Books in the Nineteenth Century* (1981). Relates romanticism to popular culture.

F. C. BEISER, *Enlightenment, Revolution, and Romanticism: The Genesis of Modern German Political Thought, 1790–1800* (1992). The best recent study of the subject.

L. BERGERON, *France Under Napoleon* (1981). An in-depth examination of Napoleonic administration.

J. F. BERNARD, *Talleyrand: A Biography* (1973). A useful account.

E. CASSIRER, *Kant's Life and Thought* (1981). A brilliant work by one of the major philosophers of this century.

D. G. CHANDLER, *The Campaigns of Napoleon* (1966). A good military study.

D. G. CHARLTON, *New Images of the Natural in France* (1984). An examination of the changing attitude toward nature in France during the romantic era.

K. CLARK, *The Romantic Rebellion* (1973). A useful discussion that combines both art and literature.

O. CONNELLY, *Napoleon's Satellite Kingdoms* (1965). The rule of Napoleon and his family in Europe.

A. D. CULLER, *The Victorian Mirror of History* (1985). Studies in the writing of the nineteenth century with emphasis on romantic influences.

J. ENGELL, *The Creative Imagination: Enlightenment to Romanticism* (1981). An important book on the role of the imagination in romantic literary theory.

M. GLOVER, *The Peninsular War, 1807–1814: A Concise Military History* (1974). An interesting account of the military campaign that so drained Napoleon's resources in western Europe.

F. W. J. HEMMINGS, *Culture and Society in France: 1789–1848* (1987). Discusses French romantic literature, theater, and art.

H. HONOUR, *Romanticism* (1979). The best introduction to the subject in terms of the fine arts.

G. N. IZENBERG, *Impossible Individuality: Romanticism, Revolution, and the Origins of Modern Selfhood, 1787–1802* (1992). Explores the concepts of individualism in Germany, England, and France.

H. KISSINGER, *A World Restored: Metternich, Castlereagh and the Problems of Peace, 1812–1822*

(1957). A provocative study by an author who became an American Secretary of State.

S. Körner, *Kant* (1955). A clear introduction to a difficult thinker.

M. LeBris, *Romantics and Romanticism* (1981). A lavishly illustrated work that relates politics and romantic art.

G. Lefebvre, *Napoleon*, 2 vols., trans. by H. Stockhold (1969). The fullest and finest biography.

F. Markham, *Napoleon and the Awakening of Europe* (1954). Emphasizes the growth of nationalism.

H. Nicolson, *The Congress of Vienna* (1946). A good, readable account.

Z. A. Pelczynski, *The State and Civil Society: Studies in Hegel's Political Philosophy* (1984). An important series of essays.

R. Plant, *Hegel: An Introduction* (1983). Emphasis on his political thought.

R. Porter and M. Teich (Eds.), *Romanticism in National Context* (1988). Essays on the phenomenon of romanticism in the major European nations.

B. M. G. Reardon, *Religion in the Age of Romanticism: Studies in Early Nineteenth-Century Thought* (1985). The best recent introduction to this important subject.

S. B. Smith, *Hegel's Critique of Liberalism: Rights in Context* (1989). An excellent introduction to Hegelian political thought.

J. L. Talmon, *Romanticism and Revolt: Europe, 1815–1848* (1967). An effort to sketch the romantic movements and relate them to one another and to the larger political history of the period.

C. Taylor, *Hegel* (1975). The best one-volume introduction.

J. M. Thompson, *Napoleon Bonaparte: His Rise and Fall* (1952). A sound biography.

J. E. Toews, *Hegelianism: The Path Toward Dialectical Humanism, 1805–1841* (1980). A brilliant treatment of German philosophy after Hegel.

A. Walicki, *Philosophy and Romantic Nationalism: The Case of Poland* (1982). Examines how philosophy influenced the character of Polish nationalism.

W. R. Ward, *The Protestant Evangelical Awakening* (1992). Examines the religious revivals of the eighteenth and nineteenth century from a transatlantic perspective.

B. Yack, *The Longing for Total Revolution: Philosophic Sources of Social Discontent from Rousseau to Marx and Nietzsche* (1986). A major exploration of the political philosophy associated with romanticism.

T. Ziolkowski, *German Romanticism and Its Institutions* (1990). An exploration of how institutions of intellectual life influenced creative literature.

The Greeks began a revolution against Ottoman rule in 1821 and had secured national independence by 1830. Greek nationalism inspired liberals across Europe. In "Greece Dying on the Ruins of Missolonghi," the French artist Eugène Delacroix (1798–1863) recalled a particularly difficult moment for the Greeks in their struggle. [Giraudon/Art Resource, N.Y.]

Restoration, Reaction, and Reform (1815–1832)

Key Topics in This Chapter

◆ The challenge of nationalism and liberalism to the conservative order in the early nineteenth century

◆ The domestic and international politics of the conservative order from the Congress of Vienna through the 1820s

◆ The wars of independence in Latin America

◆ The revolutions of 1830 on the Continent and the passage of the Great Reform Bill in Britain

The close of the Congress of Vienna was followed by a decade in which reactionary political forces controlled virtually all of Europe. These forces were determined to restore the authority of monarchies and aristocracies after the turmoil wrought by the French Revolution and Napoleon. Two sets of critics challenged this conservative order. Nationalists wished to see the map of Europe drawn according to the boundaries of nationalities or ethnic groups. Liberals sought moderate political reform and freer economic markets. The goals of nationalists and liberals threatened the dominance of landed aristocracies and the rule of monarchs who governed by virtue of dynastic inheritance rather than nationality. Still another challenge *to the status quo came from the efforts of Europe's Latin American colonies to gain independence.*

For the first fifteen years after the Congress of Vienna, the forces of conservatism were successful except for their failure to retain control of Latin America. Late in the 1820s, however, the conservatives faced stronger challenges. Thereafter, certain major liberal goals were achieved when a revolution occurred in France in 1830 and a sweeping reform bill passed through the British Parliament in 1832. During the same period, however, Russia and other countries in eastern and central Europe continued to resist political and social change.

The Challenges of Nationalism and Liberalism

Observers have frequently regarded the nineteenth century as the great age of *isms.* Throughout the Western world, secular ideologies began to take hold of the learned and popular imaginations in opposition to the political and social status quo. These included nationalism, liberalism, republicanism, socialism, and communism. Earlier in this century, a noted historian called all such words "trouble-breeding and usually thought-obscuring terms."[1] They are just that, if one uses them as an excuse to avoid thinking or if one fails to see the variety of opinions concealed beneath each of them.

The Emergence of Nationalism

Nationalism proved to be the single most powerful European political ideology of the nineteenth and early twentieth centuries. It has reasserted itself in present-day Europe following the collapse of Communist governments in eastern Europe and in the former Soviet Union. As a political outlook, nationalism was and is based on the relatively modern concept that a nation is composed of people who are joined together by the bonds of common language, customs, culture, and history and who, because of those bonds, should be administered by the same government. That is to say, nationalists in the past and the present contend that political and ethnic boundaries should coincide. Political units had not been so defined or governed earlier in European history. The idea came into its own during the late eighteenth and the early nineteenth centuries.

OPPOSITION TO THE VIENNA SETTLEMENT Early-nineteenth-century nationalism directly opposed the principle upheld at the Congress of Vienna that legitimate monarchies or dynasties, rather than ethnicity, provide the basis for political unity. Nationalists naturally protested multinational states such as the Austrian or Russian empires. They also objected to peoples of the same ethnic group, such as Germans and Italians, dwelling in political units smaller than that of the ethnic nation. Consequently, nationalists challenged both the domestic and the international order of the Vienna settlement.

Behind the concept of nationalism usually, though not always, lay the idea of popular sovereignty, since the qualities of peoples rather than rulers determine national character. But this aspect of nationalism frequently led to confusion or conflict because of the presence of minorities. Within many territories where one national group has predominated, there have also existed significant minority ethnic enclaves whom the majority has had every intention of governing with or without their consent. In some cases, a nationalistically conscious group would dominate in one section of a country, but people of the same ethnicity in another region would not have nationalistic aspirations. The former might then attempt to impose their aspirations on the latter.

CREATING NATIONS   In point of fact, it was nationalists who actually created nations in the nineteenth century. During the first half of the century, a particular group of nationalistically minded writers or other intellectual elite, usually small, using the printed word spread a nationalistic concept of the nation. They were frequently historians who chronicled a people's past or writers and literary scholars who established a national literature by collecting and publishing earlier writings in the people's language. In effect, they gave a people a sense of their past and a literature of their own. As time passed, schoolteachers, by imparting a nation's

[1]*Arthur O. Lovejoy,* The Great Chain of Being: A Study in the History of an Idea *(New York: Harper Torchbooks, 1963), p. 6.*

official language and history, played an important role in spreading nationalistic ideas. These small groups of early nationalists established the cultural beliefs and political expectations upon which the later mass-supported nationalism of the second half of the century would grow.

The language to be used in the schools and in government offices was always a point of contention for nationalists. In France and Italy, official versions of the national language were imposed in the schools and replaced local dialects. In parts of Scandinavia and eastern Europe, nationalists attempted to resurrect from earlier times what they regarded as purer versions of the national language. Often these resurrected languages were virtually invented by modern scholars or linguists. This process of establishing national languages led to far more linguistic uniformity in European nations than had existed prior to the nineteenth century. Yet even in 1850 perhaps less than half of the inhabitants of France spoke official French.

Language could become such an effective cornerstone in the foundation of nationalism thanks in large measure to the emergence of the print culture discussed in Chapter 18. The presence of large numbers of printed books, journals, magazines, and newspapers "fixed" language in a more permanent fashion than did the spoken word. This uniform language found in printed works could overcome regional spoken dialects and establish itself as dominant. In most countries, spoken and written proficiency in the official printed language became a path to social and political advancement. The growth of a uniform language helped to persuade people who had not thought of themselves as constituting a nation that they did so.

MEANING OF NATIONHOOD Nationalists used a whole variety of arguments and metaphors to express what they meant by nationhood. Some argued that gathering, for example, Italians into a unified Italy or Germans into a unified Germany, thus eliminating the petty dynastic states that governed those regions, would promote economic and administrative efficiency. Adopting a tenet from political liberalism, certain nationalist writers suggested that nations determining their own destinies resembled individuals exploiting personal talents to determine their own careers. Some nationalists claimed that nations, like biological species in the natural world, were distinct creations of God. Other nationalists claimed a place for their nations in the divine order of things. Throughout the nineteenth century, for example, Polish nationalists portrayed Poland as the suffering Christ among nations, thus implicitly suggesting that Poland, like Christ, would experience resurrection and a new life.

A significant difficulty for nationalism was, and is, determining which ethnic groups could be considered nations, with claims to territory and political autonomy. In theory, any of them could, but in reality nationhood came to be associated with groups that were large enough to support a viable economy, that had a history of significant cultural association, that possessed a cultural elite that could nourish and spread the national language, and that had the capacity to conquer other peoples or to establish and protect their own independence. Throughout the century many smaller ethnic groups claimed to fulfill these criteria but could not effectively achieve either independence or recognition. They could and did, however, create domestic unrest within the political units they inhabited.

REGIONS OF NATIONALISTIC PRESSURE During the nineteenth century, nationalists challenged the political status quo in six major areas of Europe. England had brought Ireland under direct rule in 1800, allowing the Irish to elect members to the British Parliament in Westminster. Irish nationalists, however, wanted independence or at least larger measures of self-government. The "Irish problem," as it was called, would haunt British politics for the next two centuries. German nationalists sought political unity for all German-speaking peoples, challenging the multinational structure of the Austrian Empire and pitting Prussia and Austria against each other. Italian nationalists sought to unify Italian-speaking peoples on the Italian peninsula and to drive out the Austrians. Polish nationalists, targeting primarily their Russian rulers, struggled to restore Poland as an independent nation. In eastern Europe, a whole host of national groups, including Hungarians, Czechs, Slovenes, and others sought either independence or formal recognition within the

Mazzini Defines Nationality

No political force in the nineteenth century was stronger than nationalism. It replaced dynastic political loyalty with loyalty based on ethnic considerations. In 1835 the Italian nationalist and patriot Giuseppe Mazzini (1805–1872) explained his understanding of the concept. Note how he combined a generally democratic view of politics with a religious concept of the divine destiny of nations.

♦ *What are the specific qualities of a people that Mazzini associates with nationalism? How and why does Mazzini relate nationalism to divine purposes? How does this view of nationality relate to the goals of liberal freedom?*

The essential characteristics of a nationality are common ideas, common principles and a common purpose. A nation is an association of those who are brought together by language, by given geographical conditions or by the role assigned them by history, who acknowledge the same principles and who march together to the conquest of a single definite goal under the rule of a uniform body of law.

The life of a nation consists in harmonious activity (that is, the employment of all individual abilities and energies comprised within the association) towards this single goal. . . .

But nationality means even more than this. Nationality also consists in the share of mankind's labors which God assigns to a people. This mission is the task which a people must perform to the end that the Divine Idea shall be realized in this world; it is the work which gives a people its rights as a member of Mankind; it is the baptismal rite which endows a people with its own character and its rank in the brotherhood of nations. . . .

Nationality depends for its very existence upon its sacredness within and beyond its borders.

If nationality is to be inviolable for all, friends and foes alike, it must be regarded inside a country as holy, like a religion, and outside a country as a grave mission. It is necessary too that the ideas arising within a country grow steadily, as part of the general law of Humanity which is the source of all nationality. It is necessary that these ideas be shown to other lands in their beauty and purity, free from any alien mixture, from any slavish fears, from any skeptical hesitancy, strong and active, embracing in their evolution every aspect and manifestation of the life of the nation. These ideas, a necessary component in the order of universal destiny, must retain their originality even as they enter harmoniously into mankind's general progress.

The people must be the basis of nationality; its logically derived and vigorously applied principles its means; the strength of all its strength; the improvement of the life of all and the happiness of the greatest possible number its results; and the accomplishment of the task assigned to it by God its goal. This is what we mean by nationality.

Herbert H. Rown, ed., From Absolutism to Revolution, 1648–1848, 2nd ed. (New York: The Macmillan Company; London: Collier-Macmillan Limited, 1969), pp. 277, 280.

Austrian Empire. Finally, in southeastern Europe on the Balkan Peninsula and eastward, national groups, including Serbs, Greeks, Albanians, Romanians, and Bulgarians, sought independence from Ottoman and Russian control. Although there were never disturbances in all six areas at one time, any one of them could erupt into turmoil. In each area, nationalist activity ebbed and flowed. The dominant governments often thought they needed only to repress the activity or ride it out until stability returned. Over the course of the century, however, nationalists changed the political map and political culture of Europe.

Early-Nineteenth-Century Political Liberalism

The word *liberal* as applied to political activity entered the European and American vocabulary during the nineteenth century. Its meaning has varied over time. Nineteenth-century European conservatives often regarded as "liberal" almost anyone or anything that challenged their own political, social, or religious values. For twentieth-century Americans the word *liberal* carries with it meanings and connotations that have little or nothing to do with its significance to nineteenth-century Europeans. European conservatives of the last century saw liberals as more radical than they actually were; present-day Americans often think of nineteenth-century liberals as more conservative than they were.

POLITICAL GOALS   Nineteenth-century liberals derived their political ideas from the writers of the Enlightenment, the example of English liberties, and the so-called principles of 1789 embodied in the French Declaration of the Rights of Man and Citizen. They sought to establish a political framework of legal equality, religious toleration, and freedom of the press. Their general goal was a political structure that would limit the arbitrary power of government against the persons and property of individual citizens. They generally believed that the legitimacy of government emanated from the freely given consent of the governed. The popular basis of such government was to be expressed through elected representative, or parliamentary, bodies. Most important, free government required that state or crown ministers be responsible to the representatives rather than to the monarch. Liberals sought to achieve these political arrangements through the device of written constitutions. Their desire was to see constitutionalism and constitutional governments installed across the Continent.

These goals may seem very limited, and they were. Responsible constitutional government, however, existed nowhere in Europe in 1815. Even in Great Britain, the cabinet ministers were at least as responsible to the monarch as to the House of Commons. Conservatives were suspicious of written constitutions, associating them with the French Revolution and Napoleonic regimes. They also were certain that all necessary political wisdom could not be reduced to writing.

Those who espoused liberal political structures often were educated, wealthy people who were excluded in one manner or another from the existing political processes. Because of their wealth and education, they felt their exclusion was unjustified. Liberals were often academics, members of the learned professions, and people involved in the rapidly expanding commercial and manufacturing segments of the economy. They believed in and were products of the career open to talent. The monarchical and aristocratic regimes as restored after the Congress of Vienna often failed to recognize sufficiently their new status and to provide for their economic and professional interests.

Although liberals wanted broader political participation, they did not advocate democracy. What they wanted was to extend representation to the propertied classes. Second only to their hostility to the privileged aristocracies was their general contempt for the lower, unpropertied classes. Liberals transformed the eighteenth-century concept of aristocratic liberty into a new concept of privilege based on wealth and property rather than birth. As the French liberal theorist Benjamin Constant (1767–1830) wrote in 1814:

Those whom poverty keeps in eternal dependence are no more enlightened on public affairs than children, nor are they more interested than foreigners in national prosperity, of which they do not understand the basis and of which they enjoy the advantages only indirectly. Property alone, by giving sufficient leisure, renders a man capable of exercising his political rights.[2]

By the middle of the century, this widely shared attitude meant that throughout Europe liberals had separated themselves from both the rural and the urban working class, a division that was to have important consequences.

ECONOMIC GOALS   The economic goals of nineteenth-century liberals also served to divide them from working people. The manufacturers of Great Britain, the landed and manufacturing

[2]*Quoted in Frederick B. Artz,* Reaction and Revolution, 1814–1832 *(New York: Harper, 1934), p. 94.*

Benjamin Constant Discusses the Character of Modern Liberty

In 1819 the French liberal theorist Benjamin Constant (1767–1830) delivered lectures on the character of ancient and modern liberty. In the passage given here, he emphasized the close relationship of modern liberty to economic freedom and a free private life. He then tied the desire for a free private life to the need for representative government.

◆ *According to Constant, what are the specific ways in which a modern citizen is free of government control and interference? What is Constant's defense of representative government? On the basis of this passage, why do you believe that Constant was opposed to democratic government?*

[Modern liberty] is, for each individual, the right not to be subjected to anything but the law, not to be arrested, or detained, or put to death, or mistreated in any manner, as a result of the arbitrary will of one or several individuals. It is each man's right to express his opinions, to choose and exercise his profession, to dispose of his property and even abuse it, to come and go without obtaining permission and without having to give an account of either his motives or his itinerary. It is the right to associate with other individuals, either to confer about mutual interests or profess the cult that he and his associates prefer or simply to fill his days and hours in the manner most conforming to his inclinations and fantasies. Finally, it is each man's right to exert influence on the administration of government, either through the election of some or all of its public functionaries, or through remonstrances, petitions, and demands which authorities are more or less obliged to take into account. . . .

Just as the liberty we now require is distinct from that of the ancients, so this new liberty itself requires an organization different from that suitable for ancient liberty. For the latter, the more time and energy a man consecrated to the exercise of his political rights, the more free he believed himself to be. Given the type of liberty to which we are now susceptible, the more the exercise of our political rights leaves us time for our private interests, the more precious we find liberty to be. From this . . . stems the necessity of the representative system. The representative system is nothing else than an organization through which a nation unloads on several individuals what it cannot and will not do for itself. Poor men handle their own affairs; rich men hire managers. This is the story of ancient and modern nations. The representative system is the power of attorney given to certain men by the mass of the people who want their interests defended but who nevertheless do not always have the time to defend these interests themselves.

Benjamin Constant, Ancient and Modern Liberty, *as translated and quoted in Stephen Holmes,* Benjamin Constant and the Making of Modern Liberalism *(New Haven, Conn.: Yale University Press, 1984), pp. 66, 74.*

middle class of France, and the commercial interests of Germany and Italy, following the Enlightenment ideas of Adam Smith, sought the removal of the economic restraints associated with mercantilism or the regulated economies of enlightened absolutists. They wanted to manufacture and sell goods freely. To that end, they favored the removal of international tariffs and internal barriers to trade. Economic liberals opposed the old paternalistic legislation that established wages and labor practices by government regulation or by guild privileges. They saw labor as simply one more commodity to be bought and sold freely.

Liberals wanted an economic structure in which people were at liberty to use whatever talents and property they possessed to enrich themselves. Such a structure, they contended, would produce more goods and services for everyone at lower prices and provide the basis for material progress.

Because the social and political circumstances of various countries differed, the specific programs of liberals also differed. In Great Britain, the monarchy was already limited and most individual liberties had been secured. With reform, Parliament could provide more nearly representative government. Links between land, commerce, and industry were in place. France likewise had many structures favored by liberals. The Napoleonic Code gave them a modern legal system. They could justify calls for greater rights by appealing to the widely accepted "principles of 1789." As in England, representatives of the different economic interests had worked together. The problem for liberals in both countries was to protect civil liberties, define the respective powers of the monarch and the elected representative body, and to expand the electorate moderately while avoiding democracy.

The complex political situation in German-speaking Europe was different from that in France or Britain, and German liberalism differed accordingly from its French and British counterparts. Monarchs and aristocrats offered stiffer resistance to liberal ideas, leaving German liberals less access to direct political influence. A distinct social divide separated the aristocratic landowning classes, which filled the bureaucracies and officer corps, from the small middle-class commercial and industrial interests. There was little or no precedent for middle-class participation in the government or the military and no strong tradition of civil or individual liberty. From the time of Martin Luther through Kant and Hegel, freedom in Germany had meant conformity to a higher moral law rather than participation in politics.

Most German liberals favored a united Germany and looked either to Austria or Prussia as the instrument of unification. As a result they were more tolerant of strong state and monarchical power than other liberals. They believed a freer social and political order would emerge once unification had been achieved. Unfortunately, the monarchies in Austria and Prussia refused to cooperate with these dreams of unification, leaving German liberals frus-

trated and forcing them to be satisfied with more modest achievements such as the lowering of internal trade barriers.

RELATIONSHIP OF NATIONALISM AND LIBERALISM Nationalism was not necessarily or even logically linked to liberalism. Indeed, many aspects of nationalism were directly opposed to liberal political values. Some nationalists wished their own particular ethnic group to dominate minority national or ethnic groups within a particular region. This was true of the Hungarian Magyars, who sought political control over non-Magyar peoples living within the historical boundaries of Hungary. Nationalists also often defined their own national group in opposition to other national groups whom they might regard as cultural inferiors or as historical enemies. This darker side of nationalism would emerge starkly in the second half of the nineteenth century and would poison European political life early and late in the twentieth century. Furthermore, conservative nationalists might seek political autonomy for their own ethnic group but would have no intention of establishing liberal political institutions thereafter.

Nonetheless, although liberalism and nationalism were not identical, they were often compatible. By espousing the cause of representative government, civil liberties, and economic freedom, nationalist groups in one country could gain the support of liberals elsewhere in Europe who might not otherwise share their nationalist interests. Many nationalists in Germany, Italy, and much of the Austrian Empire adopted this tactic. Some nationalists took other symbolic steps to arouse sympathy. Nationalists in Greece, for example, made Athens their capital because they believed it would associate their struggle for independence with ancient Athenian democracy, which English and French liberals revered.

Conservative Governments on the Domestic Scene

Despite the challenges of liberalism and nationalism, the domestic political order established by the restored conservative institutions of

Europe, particularly in Great Britain and eastern Europe, showed remarkable staying power. Not until World War I did their power and pervasive influence come to an end.

Conservative Outlooks

The major pillars of nineteenth-century conservatism were legitimate monarchies, landed aristocracies, and established churches. The institutions themselves were ancient, but the self-conscious alliance of throne, land, and altar was new. Throughout the eighteenth century, these groups had engaged in frequent conflict. Only the upheavals of the French Revolution and the Napoleonic era transformed them into natural, if sometimes, reluctant, allies. In that regard, conservatism as an articulated outlook and set of cooperating institutions was as new a feature on the political landscape as nationalism and liberalism.

The more theoretical political and religious ideas of the conservative classes were associated with romantic thinkers, such as Edmund Burke (see Chapter 19) and Friedrich Hegel (see Chapter 20). Conservatives shared other, less formal attitudes forged by the revolutionary experience. The fate of Louis XVI convinced most monarchs that they could trust only aristocratic governments or governments of aristocrats in alliance with the wealthiest middle-class and professional people. The European aristocracies believed that their property and influence would rarely be safe under any form of genuinely representative government. All conservatives spurned the idea of a written constitution unless they were permitted to promulgate the document themselves. Even then, some could not be reconciled to the concept.

The churches were equally apprehensive of popular movements except their own revivals. The ecclesiastical leaders throughout the Continent regarded themselves as entrusted with the educational task of supporting the social and political status quo. They also feared and hated most of the ideas associated with the Enlightenment, because those rational concepts and reformist writings enshrined the critical spirit and undermined revealed religion.

Conservatives retained their former arrogance but not their former privileges or their old confidence. They saw themselves surrounded by enemies, standing permanently on the defensive against the forces of liberalism, nationalism, and popular sovereignty. They knew they could be toppled by political groups that hated them. They understood that revolution in one country could spill over into another. These potential sources of unrest had to be confronted both at home and abroad.

Liberalism and Nationalism Resisted in Austria and the Germanies

The early-nineteenth-century statesman who more than any other epitomized conservatism was the Austrian prince Metternich (1773–1859). This devoted servant of the Habsburg emperor had been, along with Britain's Viscount Castlereagh (1769–1822), the chief architect of the Vienna settlement. It was he who seemed to exercise chief control over the forces of the European reaction.

DYNASTIC INTEGRITY OF HABSBURG EMPIRE The Austrian government could make no serious compromises with the new political

Prince Clemens von Metternich (1773–1859) epitomized nineteenth-century conservatism. [Royal Library, Windsor Castle]

forces in Europe. To no other country were the programs of liberalism and nationalism potentially more dangerous. Germans and Hungarians, as well as Poles, Czechs, Slovaks, Slovenes, and other ethnic groups, peopled the Habsburg domains. Through puppet governments Austria also dominated the Italian peninsula.

So far as Metternich and other Austrian officials were concerned, the recognition of the political rights and aspirations of any of the various national groups would mean the probable dissolution of the empire. If Austria permitted representative government, Metternich feared that the national groups would fight their battles internally at the probable cost of Austrian international influence.

Pursuit of dynastic integrity required Austrian domination of the newly formed German Confederation to prevent the formation of a German national state that might absorb the heart of the empire and exclude the other realms governed by the Habsburgs. The Congress of Vienna had created the German Confederation to replace the defunct Holy Roman Empire. It consisted of thirty-nine states under Austrian leadership. Each state remained more or less autonomous, but Austria was determined to prevent any movement toward constitutionalism in as many of them as possible.

DEFEAT OF PRUSSIAN REFORM An important victory for this holding policy came in Prussia in the years immediately after the Congress of Vienna. In 1815 Frederick William III (r. 1797–1840), caught up in the exhilaration that followed the War of Liberation, as Germans called the last part of their conflict with Napoleon, had promised some mode of constitutional government. After stalling on keeping his pledge, he formally reneged on it in 1817. Instead, he created a new Council of State, which, although it improved administrative efficiency, was not constitutionally based.

In 1819 the king moved further from reform. After a major disagreement over the organization of the army, his chief reform-minded ministers resigned, to be replaced with hardened conservatives. On their advice, in 1823 Frederick William III established eight provincial estates, or diets. These bodies were dominated by the Junkers and exercised only an advisory function. The old bonds linking monarchy, army, and landholders in Prussia had been reestablished. The members of this alliance would oppose the threats posed by the aspirations of German nationalists to the conservative social and political order.

STUDENT NATIONALISM AND THE CARLSBAD DECREES Three southern German states—Baden, Bavaria, and Württemberg—had received constitutions after 1815 as their monarchs tried to secure wider political support. None of these constitutions, however, recognized popular sovereignty, and all defined political rights as the gift of the monarch. In the minds and hearts of many young Germans, however, nationalist and liberal expectations raised with the defeat of the French armies remained alive.

The most important of these groups was composed of university students who had grown up during the days of the reforms of Stein and Hardenberg and the initial circulation of the writings of Fichte and other German nationalists. Many of them or their friends had fought Napoleon. When they went to the universities, they continued to dream of a united Germany. They formed *Burschenschaften*, or student associations. Like student groups today, these clubs served numerous social functions, one of which was to sever old provincial loyalties and replace them with loyalty to the concept of a united German state. It should also be noted that these clubs were often anti-Semitic.

In 1817 in Jena, one such student club organized a large celebration for the fourth anniversary of the Battle of Leipzig and the tercentenary of Luther's Ninety-five Theses. There were bonfires, songs, and processions as more than 500 people gathered for the festivities. The event made German rulers uneasy, for it was known that some republicans were involved with the student clubs.

Two years later, in March 1819, a young man named Karl Sand (d. 1820), a *Burschenschaft* member, assassinated the conservative dramatist August von Kotzebue (1761–1819). Sand, who was tried, condemned, and publicly executed, became a martyr in the eyes of some nationalists. Although the assassin had acted alone, Metternich decided to use the incident to suppress the student clubs and other potential institutions of liberalism.

In the fall of 1817, students from across Germany gathered near Wartburg castle to celebrate their sense of national identity. Such events frightened conservative political forces in the German states. [Bildarchiv Preussischer Kulturbesitz]

In May, 1820, Karl Sand, a German student and a member of a Burschenschaft, *was executed for his murder of the conservative playwright August von Kotzebue the previous year. In the eyes of many young German nationalists, Sand was a political martyr. [Bildarchiv Preussischer Kulturbesitz]*

The German Confederation Issues the Carlsbad Decrees

In 1819 the German Confederation, fearful of nationalistic student activism, issued the Carlsbad Decrees under the guidance of Prince Metternich. These decrees limited the activities of German students, faculty, and publishers.

◆ *By what devices did the government attempt to replace the university discipline of students with government discipline? What kind of actions by faculty and students do these decrees forbid or discourage? How was the censorship of newspapers to work?*

Regarding University Life

1. There shall be appointed for each university a special representative of the ruler of each state, the said representatives to have appropriate instructions and extended powers, and they shall have their place of residence where the university is located. . . .

This representative shall enforce strictly the existing laws and disciplinary regulations; he shall observe with care the attitude shown by the university instructors in their public lectures and registered courses; and he shall, without directly interfering in scientific matters or in teaching methods, give a beneficial direction to the teaching, keeping in view the future attitude of the students. Finally, he shall give . . . attention to everything that may promote morality . . . among the students. . . .

2. The confederated governments mutually pledge themselves to eliminate from the universities or any other public educational institutions all instructors who shall have obviously proved their unfitness for the important work entrusted to them by openly deviating from their duties, or by going beyond the boundaries of their functions, or by abusing their legitimate influence over young minds, or by presenting harmful ideas hostile to public order or subverting existing governmental instructions. . . .

Any instructor who has been removed in this manner becomes ineligible for a position in any other public institution of learning in another state of the Confederation.

3. The laws that have for some time been directed against secret and unauthorized societies in the universities shall be strictly enforced. . . . The special representatives of the government are enjoined to exert great care in watching these organizations.

The governments mutually agree that all individuals who shall be shown to have maintained their membership in secret or unauthorized associations, or shall have taken membership in such associations, shall not be eligible for any public office.

4. No student who shall have been expelled from any university by virtue of a decision of the university senate ratified or initiated by the special representative . . . , shall be admitted by any other university. . . .

Regarding the Press

1. As long as this edict remains in force, no publication which appears daily, or as a serial not exceeding twenty sheets of printed matter, shall be printed in any state of the Confederation without the prior knowledge and approval of the state officials. . . .

. . . .

4. Each state of the Confederation is responsible, not only to the state against which the offense is directly committed but to the entire Confederation, for any publication printed within the limits of its jurisdiction, in which the honor or security of other states is impinged upon or their constitution or administration attacked. . . .

. . . .

7. When a newspaper or periodical is suppressed by a decision of the Diet, the editor of such publication may not within five years edit a similar publication in any state of the Confederation.

Quoted from P. A. G. von Meyer, Corpus juris confoederationis Germanicae, *2nd ed., Vol. II (Frankfort on Main, 1833), pp. 138 ff., as quoted and translated in Louis L. Snyder, ed.,* Documents of German History *(New Brunswick, N.J.: Rutgers University Press, 1958), pp. 158–160.*

In July 1819, Metternich persuaded representatives of the major German states to issue the Carlsbad Decrees, which dissolved the *Burschenschaften*. The decrees also provided for university inspectors and press censors. The next year the German Confederation promulgated the Final Act, which limited the subjects that might be discussed in the constitutional chambers of Bavaria, Württemberg, and Baden. The measure also asserted the right of the monarchs to resist demands of constitutionalists. For many years thereafter, the secret police of the various German states harassed potential dissidents. In the opinion of the princes, these included almost anyone who sought even moderate social or political change.

Repression in Great Britain

The years 1819 and 1820 marked a high tide for conservative influence and repression in western as well as eastern Europe. After 1815 Great Britain experienced two years of poor harvests. At the same time, discharged sailors and soldiers and out-of-work industrial workers swelled the ranks of the unemployed.

LORD LIVERPOOL'S MINISTRY AND POPULAR UNREST The Tory ministry of Lord Liverpool (1770–1828) was unprepared for these problems of postwar dislocation. Instead, it sought to protect the interests of the landed and other wealthy classes. In 1815 Parliament passed a Corn Law to maintain high prices for domestically produced grain through import duties on foreign grain. The next year Parliament abolished the income tax paid by the wealthy and replaced it with excise or sales taxes on consumer goods paid by both the wealthy and the poor. These laws continued a legislative trend that marked the abandonment by the British ruling class of its traditional role of paternalistic protector of the poor. In 1799 Parliament had passed the Combination Acts, outlawing workers' organizations or unions. During the war, wage protection had been removed. And many in the taxpaying classes called for the abolition of the poor law that provided public relief for the destitute and unemployed.

In light of these policies and the postwar economic downturn, it is hardly surprising that the lower social orders began to doubt the wisdom of their rulers and to call for a reform of the political system. Mass meetings calling for the reform of Parliament were held. Reform clubs were organized. Radical newspapers, such as William Cobbett's *Political Registrar*, demanded political change. In the hungry, restive agricultural and industrial workers the government could see only images of continental sans-culottes crowds ready to hang aristocrats from the nearest lamppost. Government ministers regarded radical leaders, such as Cobbett (1763–1835), Major John Cartwright (1740–1824), and Henry "Orator" Hunt (1773–1835), as demagogues who were seducing the people away from allegiance to their natural leaders.

The answer of the government to the discontent was repression. In December 1816, an unruly mass meeting took place at Spa Fields near London. This disturbance provided Parliament an excuse to pass the Coercion Act of March 1817. These measures temporarily suspended habeas corpus and extended existing laws against seditious gatherings.

"PETERLOO" AND THE SIX ACTS This initial repression, accompanied by improved harvests, brought calm for a time to the political landscape. By 1819, however, the people were restive again. In the industrial north, many well-organized mass meetings were held to demand the reform of Parliament. The radical reform campaign culminated on August 16, 1819, with a meeting in Manchester at Saint Peter's Fields. Royal troops and the local militia were on hand to ensure order. As the speeches were about to begin, a local magistrate ordered the militia to move into the audience. The result was panic and death. At least eleven people in the crowd were killed; scores were injured. The event became known as the "Peterloo" Massacre, a phrase that drew a contemptuous comparison with the victory at Waterloo.

Peterloo had been the act of the local Manchester officials, whom the Liverpool ministry felt it must support. The cabinet also decided to act once and for all to end these troubles. Most of the radical leaders were arrested and taken out of circulation. In December 1819,

In August, 1819, local troops dispersed a political rally in Manchester, killing a number of the participants. The event became known as the "Peterloo Massacre." [Bildarchiv Preussischer Kulturbesitz]

a few months after the German Carlsbad Decrees, Parliament passed a series of laws called the Six Acts. These (1) forbade large unauthorized, public meetings, (2) raised the fines for seditious libel, (3) speeded up the trials of political agitators, (4) increased newspaper taxes, (5) prohibited the training of armed groups, and (6) allowed local officials to search homes in certain disturbed counties. In effect, the Six Acts attempted to remove the instruments of agitation from the hands of radical leaders and to provide the authorities with new powers.

Two months after the passage of the Six Acts, the Cato Street Conspiracy was unearthed. Under the guidance of a possibly demented figure named Thistlewood, a group of extreme radicals had plotted to blow up the entire British cabinet. The plot was foiled. The leaders were arrested and tried, and four of them were executed. Although little more than a half-baked plot, the conspiracy helped further to discredit the movement for parliamentary reform.

Bourbon Restoration in France

The abdication of Napoleon in 1814 opened the way for a restoration of Bourbon rule in the homeland of the great revolution. The new king was the former count of Provence and a brother of Louis XVI. The son of the executed monarch had died in prison. Royalists had regarded the dead boy as Louis XVII, and so his uncle became Louis XVIII (r. 1814–1824). This fat, awkward man had become a political realist during his more than twenty years of exile. He understood that he could not govern if he attempted to turn back the clock. France had undergone too many irreversible changes. Consequently, Louis XVIII agreed to become a constitutional monarch, but under a constitution of his own making.

THE CHARTER The constitution of the French restoration was the Charter. It provided for a hereditary monarchy and a bicameral legislature. The monarch appointed the upper house; the lower house, the Chamber of Deputies, was elected according to a very narrow franchise with a high property qualification. The Charter guaranteed most of the rights enumerated by the Declaration of the Rights of Man and Citizen. There was to be religious toleration, but Roman Catholicism was designated as the official religion of the nation. Most important for thousands of French people at all social levels who had profited from the revolution, the Charter promised not to challenge the property rights of the current owners of land that had been confiscated from aristocrats and the Church. With this provision, Louis XVIII hoped to reconcile to his regime those who had benefitted from the revolution.

ULTRAROYALISM This moderate spirit did not penetrate deeply into the ranks of royalist supporters whose families had suffered at the hands of the revolution. Rallying around the count of Artois (1757–1836), those people who were more royalist than the monarch now demanded their revenge. In the months after Napoleon's final defeat at Waterloo, royalists in the south and west carried out a White Terror against former revolutionaries and supporters of the deposed emperor. The king could do little or nothing to halt this bloodbath. Similar extreme royalist sentiment could be found in the Chamber of Deputies. The ultraroyalist majority elected in 1816 proved so dangerously reactionary that the king soon dissolved the chamber. The majority returned by the second election was more moderate. Several years of political give-and-take followed with the king making mild accommodations to liberals.

In February 1820, however, the duke of Berri, son of Artois and heir to the throne after his father, was murdered by a lone assassin. The ultraroyalists persuaded Louis XVIII that the murder was the result of his ministers' cooperation with liberal politicians, and the king responded with repressive measures. Electoral laws were revised to give wealthy electors two votes. Press censorship was imposed, and people suspected of dangerous political activity were made subject to easy arrest. By 1821 the government placed secondary education under the control of the Roman Catholic bishops.

All these actions revealed the basic contradiction of the French restoration. By the early 1820s, the veneer of constitutionalism had worn away. Liberals were being driven out of politics and into a near-illegal status.

The Conservative International Order

At the Congress of Vienna, the major powers—Russia, Austria, Prussia, and Great Britain—had agreed to consult with each other from time to time on matters affecting Europe as a whole. The vehicle for this consultation was a series of postwar congresses, or conferences. Later, as differences arose among the powers, the consultations became more informal. This arrangement for resolving mutual foreign policy issues was known as the Concert of Europe. It prevented one nation from taking a major action in international affairs without the assent of the others.

The French Bourbons were restored to the throne in 1815 but would rule only until 1830. This picture shows Louis XVIII, seated, second from left, and his brother, the Count of Artois, who would become Charles X, standing on the left. Notice the bust of Henry IV in the background, placed there to associate the restored rulers with their popular late-sixteenth, early-seventeenth-century forebear. [Bildarchiv Preussischer Kulturbesitz]

The Period of Political Reaction	
1814	French monarchy restored
1815	Russia, Austria, Prussia form Holy Alliance
1815	Russia, Austria, Prussia, and Britain renew Quadruple Alliance
1818	Congress of Aix-la-Chapelle
1819 (July)	Carlsbad Decrees
1819 (August 16)	Peterloo Massacre
1819 (December)	Great Britain passes Six Acts
1820 (January)	Spanish revolution
1820 (October)	Congress of Troppau
1821 (January)	Congress of Laibach
1821 (February)	Greek revolution
1822	Congress of Verona
1823	France helps crush Spanish revolution

The Spanish Revolution of 1820

When the Bourbon Ferdinand VII (r. 1814–1833) was placed on his throne following Napoleon's downfall, he had promised to govern according to a written constitution. Once securely in power, however, he ignored his pledge, dissolved the parliament (the Cortes), and ruled alone. In 1820 a group of army officers about to be sent to suppress revolution in Spain's Latin American colonies rebelled. In March Ferdinand once again announced that he would abide by the provisions of the constitution. For the time being, the revolution had succeeded.

Almost at the same time, in July 1820, revolution erupted in Naples, where the king of the Two Sicilies quickly accepted a constitution. There were other, lesser revolts in Italy, but none of them succeeded.

The major goal of the Concert of Europe was to maintain the balance of power against new French aggression and against the military might of Russia. The Concert of Europe continued to function on large and small issues until the third quarter of the century.

The Congress System

The years that witnessed the domestic conservative consolidation of power also saw a generally successful functioning of the congress system. The first congress took place in 1818 at Aix-la-Chapelle. As a result of this gathering, the four major powers removed their troops from France, which had paid its war reparations, and readmitted that nation to good standing among European nations. Despite unanimity on these decisions, the conference was not without friction. Tsar Alexander I (r. 1801–1825), displaying his full reactionary colors, suggested that the Quadruple Alliance (see Chapter 20) agree to uphold the borders and the existing governments of all European countries. Castlereagh, representing Britain, flatly rejected the proposal. He contended that the Quadruple Alliance was intended only to prevent future French aggression. These disagreements appeared somewhat academic until a series of revolutions began in southern Europe in 1820.

Tsar Alexander I (r. 1801–1825). A mild reformer when he succeeded to the throne, Alexander became increasingly reactionary after 1815. [The Bettmann Archive]

The Congress of Troppau Justifies Intervention Against Revolution

At the Congress of Troppau, which met in 1820, the major continental powers agreed to use their armed forces to block revolution that broke out in other European countries. They were especially concerned with events in Spain and Italy. Metternich proposed an initial policy statement, and then the entire Congress adopted a statement that was circulated to the ambassadors of various of its member nations.

◆ *Why did the powers believe that revolution in one state would necessarily spill over into neighboring states? What are the precedents for cooperation to which they point? Why do they claim they are not interested in conquest?*

Metternich's Preliminary Protocol, November 15, 1820

States which have undergone a change of Government due to revolution, the results of which threaten other states, *ipso facto*, cease to be members of the European Alliance, and remain excluded from it until their situation gives guarantees for legal order and stability. If, owing to such alterations, immediate danger threatens other states, the Powers bind themselves, by peaceful means, or if need be by arms, to bring back the guilty state into the bosom of the Great Alliance.

Circular Despatch from the Courts of Austria, Russia, and Prussia to their Ambassadors in the German Courts, December 8, 1820

The events of March 8 in Spain, and July 2 in Naples, and the catastrophe in Portugal, must cause in all those who have to care for the peace of States a deep feeling of grief and anxiety, and, at the same time, a necessity for meeting, in order to consider how best to meet the evils which threaten to break out all over Europe.

It was natural that these feelings should be

These events frightened the ever-nervous Metternich. Italian disturbances were especially troubling to him. Austria hoped to dominate the peninsula to provide a buffer against the spread of revolution on its own southern flank. The other powers were divided on the best course of action. Britain opposed joint intervention in either Italy or Spain. Metternich turned to Prussia and Russia, the other members of the Holy Alliance formed in 1815, for support. The three eastern powers, along with unofficial delegations from Britain and France, met at the Congress of Troppau in late October 1820. Led by Tsar Alexander, the members of the Holy Alliance issued the Protocol of Troppau. This declaration asserted that stable governments might intervene to restore order in countries experiencing revolution. Yet even Russia hesi-

tated to authorize Austrian intervention in Italian affairs. That decision was finally reached in January 1821 at the Congress of Laibach. Shortly thereafter Austrian troops marched into Naples and restored the king of the Two Sicilies to nonconstitutional government.

The final postwar congress took place in October 1822 at Verona. Its primary purpose was to resolve the situation in Spain. Once again Britain balked at joint action. Shortly before the meeting, Castlereagh had committed suicide. George Canning (1770–1827), the new foreign minister, was much less sympathetic to Metternich's goals. At Verona, Britain, in effect, withdrew from continental affairs. Austria, Prussia, and Russia agreed to support French intervention in Spain. In April 1823, the French army crossed the Pyrenees and within a few

very active in those particular Powers which had lately conquered revolution, and now saw it raising its head again; and also natural that these Powers, in resisting the revolution for the third time, should resort to the same means which they had used so happily in the memorable combat which delivered Europe from a twenty years' yoke.

Everything justified the hope that this union, formed under the most dangerous circumstances, crowned with the most brilliant success, fostered by the negotiations of 1814, 1815, and 1818, as it had released the European continent from the military despotism of the representative of revolution, and brought peace to the world, would be able to curb a new force not less tyrannical and not less to be despised—the power of rebellion and outrage. . . .

The Powers exercise an indisputable right in contemplating common measure of safety against States in which the Government has been overthrown by rebellion, and which, if only as an example, must consequently be treated as hostile to all lawful constitutions and Governments. The exercise of this right

becomes still more urgent when revolutionists spread to neighboring countries the misfortunes which they had brought upon themselves, scattering rebellion and confusion around.

Such a position, such proceedings are an evident violation of contract, which guarantees to all the European Governments, besides the inviolability of their territories, the enjoyment of those peaceful relations which exclude the possibility of encroachment on either side. . . .

No further proof . . . is required that the Powers have not been guided in their resolutions by the thought of conquest or the desire of interfering with the internal affairs of other Governments. They want nothing but to maintain peace, to free Europe from the scourge of revolution, and to avert, or shorten as much as possible, the mischief arising from the violation of all the principles of order and morality. Under such conditions they think themselves justified in claiming the unanimous approbation of the world as a reward for their cares and their efforts.

From Walter A. Phillips, The Confederation of Europe, 2nd ed. *(London: Longmans, Green & Co., 1920), pp. 208–209, as quoted in Mack Walker, ed.,* Metternich's Europe *(New York: Walker and Company, 1968), pp. 127–130.*

months suppressed the Spanish revolution. Liberals and revolutionaries were tortured, executed, and driven from the country. The intervention in Spain in 1823 was one of the bloodiest expressions of reactionary politics during the entire century.

There was a second diplomatic result of the Congress of Verona and the Spanish intervention. George Canning was much more interested in the fate of British commerce and trade than Castlereagh had been. Thus Canning sought to prevent the politics of European reaction from being extended to Spain's colonies in Latin America, which were then in revolt (to be discussed later). He intended to exploit these South American revolutions to break the old Spanish trading monopoly with its colonies and gain access for Britain to Latin American trade.

To that end, the British foreign minister supported the American Monroe Doctrine in 1823, prohibiting further colonization and intervention by European powers in the Americas. Britain soon recognized the Spanish colonies as independent states. Through the rest of the century, British commercial interests dominated Latin America. In this fashion, Canning may be said to have brought to a successful conclusion the War of Jenkins's Ear (1739).

The Greek Revolution of 1821

While the powers were plotting conservative restorations in Italy and Spain, a third Mediterranean revolt erupted in Greece. The Greek revolution became one of the most famous of the century, because it attracted the support and participation of many illustrious literary figures. Liberals throughout Europe, who were seeing their own hopes crushed at home, imagined that the ancient Greek democracy was being reborn. Lord Byron went to fight in Greece and in 1824 died in the cause of Greek liberty. Philhellenic societies were founded in nearly every major country.

The Greeks were rebelling against the Ottoman Empire. The weakness of that empire troubled Europe throughout the nineteenth century, raising what was known as *the eastern question:* What should the European powers do about Ottoman inability to assure political and administrative stability in its holdings in and around the eastern Mediterranean? Most of the major powers had a keen interest in those territories. Russia and Austria coveted land in the Balkans. France and Britain were concerned with the empire's commerce and with control of key naval positions in the eastern Mediterranean. Also at issue was access for Christians to the shrines in the Holy Land. The goals of the great powers often conflicted with the desire for independence of the many national groups in the Ottoman Empire. But because the powers had little desire to strengthen the empire, they were often more sympathetic to nationalistic aspirations there than elsewhere in Europe.

These conflicting interests, as well as mutual distrust, prevented any direct intervention in Greek affairs for several years. Eventually, however, Britain, France, and Russia concluded that an independent Greece would benefit their strategic interests and would not threaten their domestic security. In 1827 they signed the Treaty of London, demanding Turkish recognition of Greek independence, and sent a joint fleet to support the Greek revolt. In 1828 Russia sent troops into the Ottoman holdings in what is today Romania, ultimately gaining control of that territory in 1829 with the Treaty of Adrianople. The treaty also stipulated that the Turks would allow Britain, France, and Russia to decide the future of Greece. In 1830 a second Treaty of London declared Greece an independent kingdom. Two years later, Otto I (r. 1832–1862), the son of the king of Bavaria, was chosen to be the first king of the new Greek royal dynasty.

Serbian Independence

The year 1830 also saw the establishment of a second independent state on the Balkan Peninsula. Since the late eighteenth century, Serbia had sought independence from the Ottoman Empire. During the Napoleonic wars its fate had been linked to Russian policy and Russian relations to the Ottoman Empire. Between 1804 and 1813, a remarkable leader, Karageorge (1762–1817), had led a guerilla war against the Ottoman authorities. This ultimately unsuccessful revolution helped build national self-identity and attracted the interest of the great powers.

In 1815 and 1816, a new leader, Milos (1780–1860), succeeded in negotiating greater administrative autonomy for some Serbian territory, but a majority of Serbs lived outside the borders of this new entity. In 1830 the Ottoman sultan formally granted independence to Serbia, and by the late 1830s the major powers had also extended it their recognition. The political structure of the new nation, however, remained in doubt for many years after 1830.

In 1833 Milos, now a hereditary prince, pressured the Ottoman authorities to extend the borders of Serbia, which they did. These new boundaries pertained until 1878. Serbian leaders continued to seek additional territory, however, creating tensions with Austria. The status of minorities, particularly Muslims, within Serbian territory, also created tensions.

Beginning in the mid-twenties, Russia became Serbia's formal protector, despite the Austrian territory that separated them. In 1856 Serbia came under the collective protection of the great powers, but the special relationship between Russia and Serbia would continue until the First World War and would play a decisive role in the outbreak of that conflict.

The Wars of Independence in Latin America

The wars of the French Revolution and more particularly those of Napoleon sparked movements for independence from European domination throughout Latin America. In less than two decades, between 1804 and 1824, France was driven from Haiti, Portugal lost control of Brazil, and Spain was forced to withdraw from all of its American empire except Cuba and Puerto Rico. Three centuries of Iberian colonial government over the South American continent came to an end (see Map 21-1).

Haiti achieved independence in 1804, following a slave revolt that began in 1794 led by Toussaint L'Ouverture (1746–1803) and Jean-Jacques Dessalines (1758–1806). Haiti's revolution involved the popular uprising of a repressed social group, which proved to be the great exception in the Latin American drive for liberty from European masters. Generally speaking, on the South American continent it was the Creole elite—merchants, landowners, and professional people of Spanish descent—who led the movements against Spain and Portugal. Very few Indians, blacks, mestizos, mulattos, or slaves became involved in or benefitted from the end of Iberian rule. Indeed, the example of the Haitian slave revolt haunted the Creoles, as did the revolt of Indians in the Andes in 1780 and 1781. The Creoles were determined that any drive for political independence from Spain and

Toussaint L'Ouverture (1743–1803) began the revolt that led to Haitian independence in 1804. [Historical Pictures/Stock Montage, Inc.]

Portugal should not cause social disruption or the loss of their existing social and economic privileges. In this respect, the Creole revolutionaries were not unlike American revolutionaries in the southern colonies who wanted to reject British rule but keep their slaves, or French revolutionaries who wanted to depose the king but not to extend liberty to the French working class.

CREOLE DISCONTENT Creole discontent with Spanish colonial government had many sources. (The Brazilian situation will be discussed separately.) Latin American merchants wanted to trade more freely within the region and with North American and European markets. They wanted commercial regulations that would benefit them rather than Spain. They had also experienced increases in taxation by the Spanish crown.

Creoles were also deeply resentful of Spanish policies favoring *peninsulares*—whites born in Spain—for political patronage, including appointments in the colonial government, Church, and army. The Creoles believed the *peninsulares* improperly secured all the best positions. Seen in this light, the royal patronage system represented another device with which Spain extracted wealth and income from America for its own people rather than its colonial subjects.

Creole leaders had read the Enlightenment *philosophes* and regarded their reforms as potentially beneficial to the region. They were also well aware of the events and the political philosophy of the American Revolution. Something more than reform programs and revolutionary example, however, was required to transform Creole discontent into revolt against the Spanish government. That transforming event occurred in Europe when Napoleon toppled the Portuguese monarchy in 1807 and the Spanish government in 1808 and then placed his own brother on the thrones of both countries. The Portuguese royal family fled to Brazil and established its government there. But the Bourbon monarchy of Spain stood, for the time being, wholly vanquished. That situation created an imperial political vacuum throughout Spanish Latin America and provided both the opportunity and the necessity for action by Creole leaders.

MAP 21-1 LATIN AMERICA IN 1830 *By 1830 Latin America had been liberated from European government. This map illustrates the early borders of the states of the region with the dates of their independence.*

The Creole elite feared that a liberal Napoleonic monarchy in Spain would attempt to impose reforms in Latin America that would harm their economic and social interests. They also feared that a Spanish monarchy controlled by France would try to drain the region of the wealth and resources needed for Napoleon's wars. To protect their interests and to seize the opportunity to take over direction of their own political destiny, between 1808 and 1810 various Creole juntas, or political committees, claimed the right to govern different regions of Latin America. Many of them quite insincerely declared that they were ruling in the name of the deposed Spanish monarch Ferdinand VII. After the establishment of these local juntas, the Spanish would not again directly govern the continent; after ten years of politically and economically exhausting warfare, they were required to make Latin American independence permanent. The establishment of the juntas also ended the privileges of the *peninsulares,* whose welfare had always depended on the favors of the Spanish crown, and made positions in the government and army more easily available to Creoles.

SAN MARTÍN IN RIO DE LA PLATA The vast size of Latin America, its geographical barriers, its distinct regional differences, and the absence of an even marginally integrated econ-omy meant there would be several different paths to independence. The first region to assert itself was the Rio de la Plata, or modern Argentina. The center of revolt was Buenos Aires, whose citizens, as early as 1806, had fought off a British invasion against the Spanish commercial monopoly and thus had learned that they could look to themselves rather than Spain for effective political and military action. In 1810 the junta in Buenos Aires not only thrust off Spanish authority but also sent forces into both Paraguay and Uruguay in the cause of liberation from Spain and control by their own region. The armies were defeated, but Spanish control was nonetheless lost in the two areas. Paraguay asserted its own independence. Uruguay was eventually absorbed by Brazil.

The Buenos Aires government was not discouraged by these early defeats and remained determined to liberate Peru, the greatest stronghold of royalist power and loyalty on the conti-

nent. By 1814 José de San Martín (1778–1850) had become the leading general of the Rio de la Plata forces. He organized a disciplined army and led his forces in a daring march over the Andes Mountains. By early 1817, he had occupied Santiago in Chile, where the Chilean independence leader Bernardo O'Higgins (1778–1842) was established as supreme dictator. From Santiago, San Martín oversaw the construction and organization of a naval force that, in 1820, he employed to carry his army by sea to an assault on Peru. The next year, San Martín drove royalist forces from Lima and took for himself the title of Protector of Peru.

SIMÓN BOLÍVAR'S LIBERATION OF VENEZUELA While the army of San Martín had been liberating the southern portion of the continent, Simón Bolívar (1783–1830) had been pursuing a similar task in the north. Bolívar had been involved in the organization of a liberating junta in Caracas, Venezuela, in 1810. He was a firm advocate of both independence and republican modes of government. Between 1811 and 1814, civil war broke out throughout Venezuela as both royalists, on one hand, and slaves and *llaneros* (Venezuelan cowboys), on the other, challenged the authority of the republican government. Bolívar had to go into exile first in

Simón Bolívar was the liberator of much of Latin America. He inclined toward a policy of political liberalism. [Bettmann/Hulton]

Colombia and then in Jamaica. In 1816, with help from Haiti, he launched a new invasion against Venezuela. He first captured Bogota, capital of New Granada (including modern Colombia, Bolivia, and Ecuador), to secure a base for attack on Venezuela. The tactic worked. By the summer of 1821, Bolívar's forces had captured Caracas and he had been named president.

A year later, in July 1822, the armies of Bolívar and San Martín joined as they moved to liberate Quito. At a famous meeting of the two liberators in Guayaquil, a sharp disagreement occurred about the future political structure of Latin America. San Martín believed that monarchies were required; Bolívar maintained his republicanism. Not long after the meeting, San Martín quietly retired from public life and went into exile in Europe. Meanwhile, Bolívar purposefully allowed the political situation in Peru to fall into confusion, and in 1823 he sent in troops to establish his control. On December 9, 1824, at the Battle of Ayacucho, the Spanish royalist forces suffered a major defeat at the hands of the liberating army. The battle marked the conclusion of the Spanish effort to retain their American empire.

INDEPENDENCE IN NEW SPAIN The drive for independence in New Spain, which included present-day Mexico as well as Texas, California, and the rest of the southwest United States, illustrates better than that in any other region the socially conservative outcome of the Latin American colonial revolutions. As elsewhere, a local governing junta was organized. Before it had undertaken any significant measures, however, a Creole priest, Miguel Hidalgo y Costilla (1753–1811), issued a call for rebellion to the Indians in his parish. They and other repressed groups of black and mestizo urban and rural workers responded. Father Hidalgo set forth a program of social change, including hints of changes in landholding. Soon he stood at the head of a loosely organized group of 80,000 followers, who captured several major cities and then marched on Mexico City. Hidalgo's forces and the royalist army that opposed them committed many atrocities. In July 1811, the revolutionary priest was captured and executed. Leadership of his movement then fell to José

Father Miguel Hidalgo y Costilla (d. 1811) led an unsuccessful peasant revolt in 1810–1811 that marked the beginning of Mexico's struggle for independence. [Courtesy of the Organization of American States]

María Morelos y Pavón (1765–1815), a mestizo priest. Far more radical than Hidalgo, he called for an end to forced labor and for substantial land reforms. He was executed in 1815, ending five years of popular uprising.

The uprising and its demand for fundamental social reforms united all conservative political groups in Mexico, both Creole and Spanish. These groups were unwilling to undertake any kind of reform that might cause loss of their privileges. In 1820, however, they found their recently achieved security challenged from an unexpected source. As already explained, the revolution in Spain had forced Ferdinand VII to accept a liberal constitution. Conservative Mexicans feared that the new liberal monarchy would attempt to impose liberal reforms on Mexico. Therefore, for the most conservative of reasons, they rallied to a former royalist general, Augustín de Iturbide (1783–1824), who in 1821 declared Mexico independent of Spain. Shortly thereafter, Iturbide was declared emperor. His own regime did not last long, but an independent Mexico, governed by persons determined to resist any significant social reform, had been created.

BRAZILIAN INDEPENDENCE Brazilian independence, in contrast to that of Spanish Latin America, came relatively simply and peacefully. As already noted, the Portuguese royal family, along with several thousand government officials and members of the court, took refuge in Brazil in 1807. Their arrival immediately transformed Rio de Janeiro into a court city. The prince regent João addressed many of the local complaints, equivalent to those of the Spanish Creoles, by, for example, taking measures that expanded trade. In 1815 he made Brazil a kingdom, which meant that it was no longer to be regarded merely as a colony of Portugal. This change was in many respects long overdue since Brazil was far larger and more prosperous than Portugal itself. Then, in 1820, a revolution occurred in Portugal, and its leaders demanded João's return to Lisbon. They also demanded the return of Brazil to colonial status. João, who had become João VI in 1816 (r. 1816–1826), returned to Portugal, but left his son Dom Pedro as regent in Brazil and encouraged him to be sympathetic to the political aspirations of the Brazilians. In September 1822, Dom Pedro embraced the cause of Brazilian independence against the recolonizing efforts of Portugal. By the end of the year, he had become emperor of an independent Brazil, which maintained an imperial form of government until 1889. Thus, in contrast to virtually all other nations of Latin America, Brazil achieved independence in a way that left no real dispute as to where the center of political authority lay.

Two other factors aided the peaceful transition to independence in Brazil. First, the political leaders of Brazil were frightened by the destruction that had been unloosed in the Spanish American Empire by the wars of independence. They wanted to avoid that experience. Second, the political and social elite in Brazil had every intention of preserving slavery.

The wars of independence elsewhere had generally led to the abolition of slavery or moved the independent states closer to abolition. Any attempt to gain independence from Portugal through warfare might have caused social as well as political turmoil that would open the slavery question.

CONSEQUENCES OF LATIN AMERICAN INDEPENDENCE The era of the wars of independence left Latin America liberated from direct colonial control but economically exhausted and politically unstable. Only Brazil prospered immediately. Independence there had come peacefully and resulted in the establishment of a clearly recognized political authority prepared to pursue policies desired by the economic elite. In contrast to Brazil, the new republics of the former Spanish Empire felt weak and vulnerable. Because the wars of independence had been largely civil wars, disaffected populations threatened all the new governments. Economic life contracted, and in 1830 overall production was lower than it had been in 1800. Mines had fallen into disrepair or had been flooded. Livestock had been confiscated or destroyed. There were few institutions to foster interregional trade or address the difficult terrain that impeded it. The disruption of old trade patterns reduced overseas trade. Funds for investment were scarce. Many wealthy *peninsulares* returned to Spain or went to Cuba. Consequently, Latin American governments and businesses looked to Britain for protection and for markets and capital investment.

The Conservative Order Shaken in Europe

During the first half of the 1820s, the institutions of the restored conservative order had in general successfully resisted the forces of liberalism. The two exceptions to this success, the Greek Revolution and the Latin American wars of independence, both occurred on the periphery of the European world. Beginning in the middle of the 1820s, however, the conservative governments of Russia, France, and Great Britain faced new stirrings of political discontent (see Map

21-2). In Russia, the result was suppression; in France, revolution; and in Britain, accommodation.

Russia: The Decembrist Revolt of 1825

Tsar Alexander I had come to the Russian throne in 1801 after a palace coup against his father, Tsar Paul (r. 1796–1801). After a brief flirtation with Enlightenment ideas, Alexander turned permanently away from reform. Both at home and abroad, he took the lead in suppressing liberalism and nationalism. There would be no significant challenge to tsarist autocracy until his death.

UNREST IN THE ARMY As Russian forces drove Napoleon's army across Europe and then occupied defeated France, many Russian officers were exposed to the ideas of the French Revolution and the Enlightenment. Some of them, realizing how economically backward and politically stifled their own nation remained, developed reformist sympathies. Unable to express themselves openly because of Alexander's repressive policies, they formed secret societies. One of these, the Southern Society, was led by an officer named Pestel. It

MAP 21-2 CENTERS OF REVOLUTION, 1820–1831 *The conservative order imposed by the great powers in post-Napoleonic Europe was challenged by various uprisings and revolutions, beginning in 1820–1821 in Spain, Naples, and Greece, then later in the decade in Russia, Poland, France, and Belgium.*

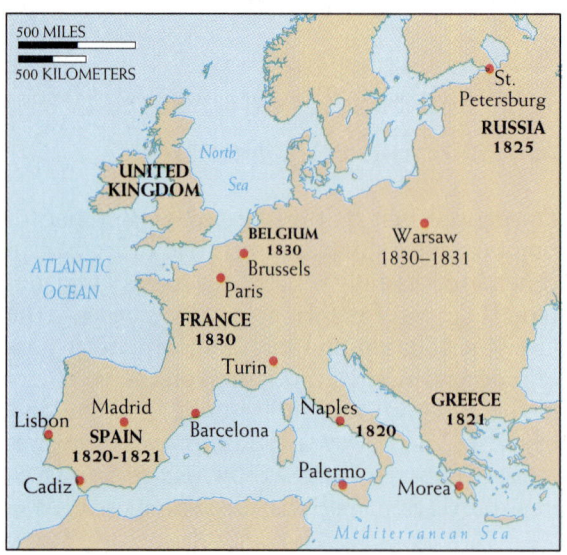

advocated representative government and the abolition of serfdom. Pestel himself even favored limited independence for Poland and democracy. Another secret society, the Northern Society, was more moderate. It favored constitutional monarchy and the abolition of serfdom but wanted protection for the interests of the aristocracy. Both societies were very small and often in conflict with each other. They agreed only that Russia's government must change. Sometime during 1825 they apparently decided to carry out a coup d'état in 1826.

DYNASTIC CRISIS In late November 1825, Tsar Alexander I died unexpectedly. His death created two crises. The first was dynastic. Alexander had no direct heir. His brother Constantine, the next in line to the throne and at the time the commander of Russian forces in occupied Poland, had married a woman who was not of royal blood. He had thus excluded himself from the throne and was more than willing to renounce any claim to it. Through a series of secret instructions made public only after his death, Alexander had named his younger brother, Nicholas (r. 1825–1855), as the new tsar.

Once Alexander was dead, the legality of these instructions became uncertain. Constantine acknowledged Nicholas as tsar, and Nicholas acknowledged Constantine. This family muddle continued for about three weeks, during which to the astonishment of all Europe Russia actually had no ruler. Then, during the early days of December, the army command reported to Nicholas the existence of a conspiracy among certain officers. Able to wait no longer for the working out of legal niceties, Nicholas had himself declared tsar, much to the delight of the by-now-exasperated Constantine.

The second crisis then proceeded to unfold. Several junior officers had indeed plotted to rally the troops under their command to the cause of reform. On December 26, 1825, the army was to take the oath of allegiance to Nicholas, who was less popular than Constantine and who was regarded as more conservative. Nearly all regiments did so. But the Moscow regiment, whose chief officers, surprisingly, were not secret society members, marched into the Senate Square in Saint Petersburg and refused to swear allegiance. Instead, they called for a constitution and the installation of Constantine as tsar. Attempts to settle the situation peacefully failed. Late in the afternoon, Nicholas ordered the cavalry and the artillery to attack the insurgents. More than sixty people were killed. Early in 1826 Nicholas himself presided over the commission that investigated the Decembrist Revolt and the secret army societies. Five of the plotters were executed and more than 100 others were exiled to Siberia.

Although the Decembrist Revolt completely failed, it was the first rebellion in modern Russian history whose instigators had had specific political goals. They wanted constitutional government and the abolition of serfdom. As the century passed, the Decembrists, in their political martyrdom, came to symbolize the yearnings of all the never very numerous Russian liberals.

THE AUTOCRACY OF NICHOLAS I Although Nicholas was neither an ignorant nor a bigoted reactionary, he came to symbolize the most extreme form of nineteenth-century autocracy. Although he knew that economic growth and social improvement in Russia required reform, he was quite simply afraid of change. In 1842 he told his State Council, "There is no doubt that serfdom, in its present form, is a flagrant evil which everyone realizes, yet to attempt to remedy it now would be, of course, an evil more disastrous."[3] To remove serfdom would necessarily, in his view, have undermined the nobles' support of the tsar. So Nicholas turned his back on this and practically all other reforms. Literary and political censorship and a widespread system of secret police flourished throughout his reign. There was little attempt to forge even an efficient and honest administration. The only significant reform of his rule was a codification of Russian law published in 1833.

OFFICIAL NATIONALITY In place of reform, Nicholas and his closest advisers embraced a program called *Official Nationality*. Presiding over this program was Count S. S. Uvarov, minister of education from 1833 to 1849. Its slogan, published repeatedly in government documents, newspapers, journals, and schoolbooks, was "Orthodoxy, Autocracy, and Nationalism." The

Tsar Nicholas I (r. 1825–1855) resisted all attempts to reform Russia and offered the use of Russian troops to other rulers threatened by revolution. [Historical Pictures Collection]

Russian Orthodox faith was to provide the basis for morality, education, and intellectual life. The Church, which since the days of Peter the Great had been an arm of the secular government, controlled the schools and universities. Young Russians were taught to accept their place in life and to spurn social mobility.

The program of autocracy championed the unrestrained power of the tsar as the only authority that could hold the vast expanse of Russia and its peoples together. Political writers stressed that only under the autocracy of Peter the Great, Catherine the Great, and Alexander I had Russia prospered and exerted a major influence on world affairs.

Through the glorification of Russian nationality, Russians were urged to see their religion, language, and customs as a source of perennial wisdom that separated them from the moral corruption and political turmoil of the West. One result of this program was to leave serious Russian intellectuals profoundly alienated from the tsarist government.

REVOLT AND REPRESSION IN POLAND Nicholas I was also extremely conservative in foreign affairs, as became apparent in Poland in the 1830s. Poland, which had been partitioned

[3]Quoted in Michael T. Florinsky, Russia: A History and an Interpretation, Vol. 2 (New York: Macmillan, 1953), p. 755.

in the late eighteenth century and ceased to exist as an independent state, remained under Russian domination after the Congress of Vienna but was granted a constitutional government. Under this arrangement, the tsar was Poland's ruler. Both Alexander and Nicholas delegated their brother, the Grand Duke Constantine (1779–1831), to run Poland's government. Although both tsars frequently infringed on the constitution and quarreled with the Polish Diet, this arrangement held through the 1820s. Nevertheless, Polish nationalists continued to agitate for change.

In late November 1830, after news of the French and Belgian revolutions of that summer had reached Poland, a small insurrection of soldiers and students broke out in Warsaw. Disturbances soon spread throughout the rest of the country. On December 18, the Polish Diet declared the revolution to be a nationalist movement. Early the next month, the Diet voted to depose Nicholas as ruler of Poland. The tsar reacted by sending troops into the country and firmly suppressing the revolt. In February 1832, Nicholas issued the Organic Statute, declaring Poland to be an integral part of the Russian Empire. Although this statute guaranteed certain Polish liberties, these guarantees were systematically ignored. The Polish uprising had confirmed all the tsar's worst fears. Henceforth Russia and Nicholas became the gendarme of Europe, ever ready to provide troops to suppress liberal and nationalist movements.

Revolution in France (1830)

The Polish revolt was the most distant of several disturbances that flowed from the overthrow of the Bourbon dynasty in France during July 1830. When Louis XVIII had died in 1824, his brother, the count of Artois, the leader of the ultraroyalist faction at the time of the restoration, succeeded him as Charles X (r. 1824–1830). The new king was a firm believer in rule by divine right.

THE REACTIONARY POLICIES OF CHARLES X His first action was to have the Chamber of Deputies in 1824 and 1825 indemnify aristocrats who had lost their lands in the revolution. He did this by lowering the interest rates on government bonds to create a fund to pay an

annual sum to the survivors of the *émigrés* who had forfeited land. Middle-class bondholders, who lost income, naturally resented this measure. In another action, Charles restored the rule of primogeniture, whereby only the eldest son of an aristocrat inherited the family domains. And, in support of the Roman Catholic church, he enacted a law that punished sacrilege with imprisonment or death. Liberals disapproved of all of these measures.

In the elections of 1827 the liberals gained enough seats in the Chamber of Deputies to compel conciliatory actions from the king. He appointed a less conservative ministry. Laws against the press and those allowing the government to dominate education were eased. The liberals, however, wanted a genuinely constitutional regime and remained unsatisfied. In 1829 the king decided that his policy of accommodation had failed. He replaced his moderate ministry with an ultraroyalist ministry headed by the Prince de Polignac (1780–1847). The opposition, in desperation, opened negotiations with the liberal Orléanist branch of the royal family.

THE JULY REVOLUTION In 1830 Charles X called for new elections, in which the liberals scored a stunning victory. Instead of accommodating the new Chamber of Deputies, the king and his ministers decided to attempt a royalist seizure of power. In June and July 1830, Polignac had sent a naval expedition against Algeria. Reports of its victory and the founding of a French empire in North Africa reached Paris on July 9. Taking advantage of the euphoria created by this victory, Charles X issued the Four Ordinances on July 25, 1830, staging what amounted to a royal coup d'état. These ordinances restricted freedom of the press, dissolved the recently elected Chamber of Deputies, restricted the franchise to the wealthiest people in the country, and called for new elections under the new royalist franchise.

The Four Ordinances provoked swift and decisive popular political reactions. Liberal newspapers called on the nation to reject the monarch's actions. The laboring populace of Paris, burdened since 1827 by an economic downturn, took to the streets and erected barricades. The king called out troops, and more than 1,800 people died during the ensuing battles in the city.

Russia Reasserts Its Authority in Poland

During 1830 Poland rebelled against Russian administration. The revolt failed after several months. Nicholas I then imposed even more direct and repressive control over Poland.

✦ *In what variety of specific ways does this proclamation attempt to offend and repress Polish nationalism? What rights are given to the Poles? What evidence is there of any institutions being established to protect those rights? Is there anything in this proclamation aimed at gaining the support of some parts of the Polish population?*

Now that an end has been put by force of arms to the rebellion in Poland, and that the nation, led away by agitators, has returned to its duty, and is restored to tranquillity, we deem it right to carry into execution our plan with regard to the introduction of the new order of things, whereby the tranquillity and union of the two nations, which Providence has entrusted to our care, may be forever guarded against new attempts. . . . The kingdom of Poland, again subject to our sceptre, will regain tranquillity, and again flourish in the bosom of peace, restored to it under the auspices of a vigilant government. Hence we consider it one of our most sacred duties to watch with paternal care over the welfare of our faithful subjects, and to use every means in our power to prevent the recurrence of similar catastrophes, by taking from the ill-disposed the power of disturbing public tranquillity. . . .

Art. 1. The kingdom of Poland is forever to be reunited to the Russian empire and form an inseparable part of that empire. . . .

Art. 2. The Crown of the kingdom of Poland is hereditary in our person and in our heirs and successors, agreeably to the order of succession to the throne prescribed by all the Russians.

Art. 3. The Coronation of the Emperors of all the Russians and Kings of Poland shall be one and the same ceremonial which shall take place at Moscow, in the presence of a deputation from the kingdom of Poland, which shall assist at that solemnity with the deputies from the other parts of the empire. . . .

. . . .

Art. 5. The freedom of worship is guaranteed. . . . The Roman Catholic religion, being that of the majority of our Polish subjects, shall be the object of especial protection of the Government. . . .

. . . .

Art. 7. The protection of the laws is assured to all the inhabitants without distinction of rank or class. . . .

. . . .

Art. 13. Publication of sentiments by means of the press, shall be subjected to restrictions which will protect religion, the inviolability of superior authority, the interests of morals, and personal considerations. . . .

Art. 14. The kingdom of Poland shall proportionably contribute to the general expenditure and to the wants of the empire. . . .

. . . .

Art. 20. Our army in the empire and in the kingdom shall compose one in common, without distinction of Russian or Polish troops. . . .

Art. 21. Those of our subjects of the empire of Russia, who are established in the kingdom of Poland, who possess or shall possess, real property in that country, shall enjoy all the rights of natives. It shall be the same with those of our subjects in the kingdom of Poland, who shall establish themselves, and shall possess property, in the other provinces of the empire.

Published in Joseph Hordynaki, *History of the Late Polish Revolution and the Events of the Campaign* (Boston: Printed for Subscribers, 1833), pp. 424–428, as quoted in Alfred J. Bannan and Achilles Edelenyi, *Documentary History of Eastern Europe* (New York: Twayne Publishers, Inc., 1970), pp. 133–137.

On August 2, Charles X abdicated and left France for exile in England. The Chamber of Deputies named a new ministry composed of constitutional monarchists. In an act that finally ended the Bourbon dynasty, it also proclaimed Louis Philippe (r. 1830–1848), the duke of Orléans, the new king of France.

In the Revolution of 1830, the liberals of the Chamber of Deputies had filled a power vacuum created by the popular Paris uprising and the failure of effective royal action. Had Charles X provided himself with sufficient troops in Paris, the outcome could have been quite different. Moreover, had the liberals, who favored constitutional monarchy, not acted quickly, the workers and shopkeepers of Paris might have attempted to form a republic. By seizing the moment, the middle class, the bureaucrats, and the moderate aristocratic liberals overthrew the restoration monarchy and still avoided a republic. These liberals feared a new popular revolution such as had swept France in 1792. They had no desire for another sans-culottes republic. A fundamental political and social tension thus underlay the new monarchy. The revolution had succeeded thanks to a temporary alliance between hard-pressed laborers and the prosperous middle class, but these two groups soon realized that their basic goals had been quite different.

MONARCHY UNDER LOUIS PHILIPPE Politically the July Monarchy, as it was called, was more liberal than the restoration government. Louis Philippe was called the king of the French rather than king of France. The tricolor flag of the revolution replaced the white flag of the Bourbons. The new constitution was regarded as a right of the people rather than a concession of the monarch. Catholicism became the religion of a majority of the people rather than the official religion. The new government was strongly anticlerical. Censorship was abolished. The franchise became somewhat wider but remained on the whole restricted. The king had to cooperate with the Chamber of Deputies; he could not dispense with laws on his own authority.

Socially, however, the Revolution of 1830 proved quite conservative. The hereditary peerage was abolished in 1831, but the everyday economic, political, and social influence of the landed oligarchy continued. Money was the path to power and influence in the government. There was much corruption.

Most important, the liberal monarchy displayed little or no sympathy for the lower and

Liberty Leading the People *by Eugène Delacroix is a famous evocation of the Revolution of 1830. [Giraudon/Art Resource, N.Y.]*

working classes. The Paris workers in 1830 had called for the protection of jobs, better wages, and the preservation of the traditional crafts rather than for the usual goals of political liberalism. The government of Louis Philippe ignored their demands and their plight. The laboring classes of Paris and the provincial cities seemed just one more possible source of disorder. In late 1831, troops suppressed a workers' revolt in Lyons. In July 1832, an uprising occurred in Paris during the funeral of a popular Napoleonic general. Again the government called out troops, and more than 800 people were killed or wounded. In 1834 a very large strike of silkworkers in Lyons was crushed. Such discontent might be smothered for a time, but without attention to the social and economic conditions creating it, new turmoil would eventually erupt.

Belgium Becomes Independent (1830)

The July Days in Paris sent sparks to other political tinder on the Continent. The revolutionary fires first lighted in neighboring Belgium. The former Austrian Netherlands,

Belgium, had been merged with the kingdom of Holland in 1815. The two countries differed in language, religion, and economy, however, and the Belgian upper classes never reconciled themselves to Dutch rule.

On August 25, 1830, disturbances broke out in Brussels following the performance of an opera about a rebellion in Naples against Spanish rule. To end the rioting, the municipal authorities and people from the propertied classes formed a provisional national government. When compromise between the Belgians and the Dutch failed, William of Holland (r. 1815–1840) sent troops and ships against Belgium. By November 10, 1830, the Dutch had been defeated. A national congress then wrote a liberal Belgian constitution, which was promulgated in 1831.

Although the major powers saw the revolution in Belgium as upsetting the boundaries established by the Congress of Vienna, they were not inclined to intervene to reverse it. Russia was preoccupied with the Polish revolt. Prussia and the other German states were suppressing small uprisings in their own domains. The Austrians were busy putting down distur-

Despite laws forbidding disrespect to the government, political cartoonists had a field day with Louis Philippe. Here, an artist emphasizes the king's resemblance to a pear and in the process attacks restraints on freedom of the press. [The Bettmann Archive]

bances in Italy. France under Louis Philippe favored an independent Belgium and hoped to dominate it. Britain felt that it could tolerate a liberal Belgium as long as it was free of foreign domination.

In December 1830, Lord Palmerston (1784–1865), the British foreign minister, gathered representatives of the powers in London. Through skillful negotiations he persuaded them to recognize Belgium as an independent and neutral state. In July 1831, Leopold of Saxe-Coburg (r. 1831–1865) became king of the Belgians. Belgian neutrality was guaranteed by the Convention of 1839 and remained an article of faith in European international relations for almost a century.

Both Belgium and Serbia gained independence in 1830, and ironically, diplomatic circumstances involving both led to World War I. The assassination of an Austrian archduke by a Serbian nationalist in Sarajevo triggered the war, and German violation of Belgian neutrality brought Britain into it.

The Great Reform Bill in Britain (1832)

The revolutionary year of 1830 saw in Great Britain the election of a House of Commons that debated the first major bill to reform Parliament. The death of George IV (r. 1820–1830) and the accession of William IV (r. 1830–1837) required the calling of a Parliamentary election, held in the summer of 1830. Historians once believed that the July revolution in France influenced voting in Britain, but close analysis of the time and character of individual county and borough elections has shown otherwise. The passage of the Great Reform Bill, which became law in 1832, was the result of a series of events very different from those that occurred on the Continent. In Britain, the forces of conservatism and reform made accommodations with each other.

POLITICAL AND ECONOMIC REFORM Several factors contributed to this spirit of accommodation. First, the commercial and industrial class was larger in Britain than in other countries. No matter what group might control the government, British prosperity required attention to their economic interests.

Second, Britain's liberal Whig aristocrats, who regarded themselves as the protectors of constitutional liberty, represented a long tradition in favor of moderate reforms that would make revolutionary changes unnecessary. Early Whig sympathy for the French Revolution reduced their influence. After 1815, however, they reentered the political arena. Finally, British law, tradition, and public opinion all showed a strong respect for civil liberties.

In 1820, the year after the passage of the notorious Six Acts (discussed earlier), Lord Liverpool shrewdly moved to change his cabinet. The new members continued to favor generally conservative policies, but they also believed the government must accommodate itself to the changing social and economic life of the nation. They favored policies of greater economic freedom and repealed earlier Combination Acts that had prohibited labor organizations.

CATHOLIC EMANCIPATION ACT Economic considerations had generally led to these moderate reforms. English determination to maintain the union with Ireland brought about another key reform. England's relationship to Ireland was similar to that of Russia to Poland or Austria to its several national groups. In 1800, fearful that Irish nationalists might again rebel as they had in 1798 and perhaps turn Ireland into a base for a French invasion, William Pitt the Younger had persuaded Parliament to pass the Act of Union between Ireland and England. Ireland now sent 100 members to the House of Commons. Only Protestant Irishmen, however, could be elected to represent their overwhelmingly Roman Catholic nation.

During the 1820s, under the leadership of Daniel O'Connell (1775–1847), Irish nationalists organized the Catholic Association to agitate for Catholic emancipation. In 1828 O'Connell secured his own election to Parliament, where he could not legally take his seat. The British ministry of the duke of Wellington realized that henceforth an entirely Catholic delegation might be elected from Ireland. If they were not seated, civil war might erupt across the Irish Sea. Consequently, in 1829 Wellington and Robert Peel steered the Catholic Emancipation Act through Parliament. Roman Catholics could now become members of Parliament. This measure, together with the repeal in 1828 of restrictions against Protestant nonconformists, ended the Anglican monopoly on British political life.

Catholic emancipation was a liberal measure passed for the conservative purpose of preserving order in Ireland. It included a provision raising the franchise in Ireland so that only the wealthier Irish could vote. Nonetheless, this measure alienated many of Wellington's Anglican Tory supporters in the House of Commons. The election of 1830 returned many supporters of parliamentary reform to Parliament. Even some Tories supported reform because they thought Catholic emancipation could have been passed only by a corrupt House of Commons. The Tories, consequently, were badly divided, and the Wellington ministry soon fell. King William IV then turned to the leader of the Whigs, Earl Grey (1764–1845) to form a government.

LEGISLATING CHANGE The Whig ministry soon presented the House of Commons with a major reform bill that had two broad goals. The first was to abolish "rotten" boroughs, which had very few voters, and to replace them with

Events Associated with Liberal Reform and Revolution	
1824	Charles X becomes king of France
1825	Decembrist Revolt in Russia
1828	Repeal of restrictions against British Protestant Noncomformists
1829	Catholic Emancipation Act passed in Great Britain
1830 (July 9)	News of French colonial conquest in Algeria reaches Paris
1830 (July 25)	Charles X issues the Four Ordinances
1830 (August 2)	Charles X abdicates; Louis Philippe proclaimed king
1830 (August 25)	Belgian revolution
1830 (November 29)	Polish revolution
1832	Organic statute makes Poland an integral part of Russian Empire
1832	Great Reform Bill passed in Great Britain

Daniel O'Connell was the most dynamic and effective Irish nationalist leader in the first half of the nineteenth century. [The Bettmann Archive]

representatives for the previously unrepresented manufacturing districts and cities. Second, the number of voters in England and Wales was to be increased by about 50 percent through a series of new franchises. In 1831 the House of Commons narrowly defeated the bill. Grey called for a new election, in which a majority in favor of the bill was returned. The House of Commons passed the reform bill, but the House of Lords rejected it. Mass meetings were held throughout the country. Riots broke out in several cities.

Finally, William IV agreed to create enough new peers to give a third reform bill a majority in the House of Lords. Under this pressure the House of Lords yielded, and in 1832 the measure became law.

The Great Reform Bill expanded the size of the English electorate, but it was not a democratic measure. It increased the number of voters by more than 200,000, or almost 50 percent,

Thomas Babington Macaulay Defends the Great Reform Bill

Macaulay (1800–1859) was a member of the House of Commons that passed the Great Reform Bill in 1831, only to have it rejected by the House of Lords before another measure was successfully enacted in 1832. His speeches in support of the bill reflect his views on the need for Parliament to give balanced representation to major elements in the population without embracing democracy. His arguments had wide appeal.

✦ *Who does Macaulay think should be represented in Parliament? Why does he oppose universal suffrage? Why does he regard the Reform Bill as "a measure of conservation"?*

[The principle of the ministers] is plain, rational, and consistent. It is this,—to admit the middle class to a large and direct share in the Representation, without any violent shock to the institutions of our country. . . . I hold it to be clearly expedient, that in a country like this, the right of suffrage should depend on a pecuniary qualification. Every argument . . . which would induce me to oppose Universal Suffrage, induces me to support the measure which is now before us. I oppose Universal Suffrage, because I think that it would produce a destructive revolution. I support this measure, because I am sure that it is our best security against a revolution . . . I . . . do entertain great apprehension for the fate of my country. I do in my conscience believe, that unless this measure, or some similar measure, be speedily adopted, great and terrible calamities will befall us. Entertaining this opinion, I think myself bound to state it, not as a threat, but as a reason. I support this measure as a means of Reform: But I support it still more as a measure of conservation. That we may exclude those whom it is necessary to exclude, we must admit those whom it may be safe to admit. . . . All history is full of revolutions, produced by causes similar to those which are now operating in England. A portion of the community which had been of no account, expands and becomes strong. It demands a place in the system, suited, not to its former weakness, but to its present power. If this is granted, all is well. If this is refused, then comes the struggle between the young energy of one class, and the ancient privileges of another. . . . Such . . . is the struggle which the middle classes in England are maintaining against an aristocracy of mere locality.

Hansard's Parliamentary Debates, 3rd ser., Vol. 2, pp. 1191–1197.

but it kept a property qualification for the franchise. (Gender was also a qualification. No thought was given to enfranchising women.) Some members of the working class actually lost the right to vote because of the abolition of certain old franchise rights. New urban boroughs were created to allow the growing cities to have a voice in the House of Commons. Yet the passage of the reform act did not, as was once thought, constitute the triumph of middle-class interests in England. For every new urban electoral district a new rural district was also drawn, and the aristocracy was expected to dominate rural elections. What the bill permitted was a wider variety of property to be represented in the House of Commons.

The success of the reform bill was to reconcile previously unrepresented property owners and economic interests to the political institutions of the country. The act laid the groundwork for further orderly reforms of the Church, municipal government, and commercial policy.

At the first meeting of the House of Commons following the passage of the Great Reform Bill, most seats were still filled by the gentry and the wealthy. But the elimination of rotten boroughs and the election of members from the new urban centers began to transform the House into a representative national body. [National Portrait Gallery, London]

By admitting into the political forum people who sought change and giving them access to the legislative process, it made revolution in Britain unnecessary. In this manner, Great Britain maintained its traditional institutions of government while allowing an increasingly diverse group of people to influence them.

◆

In the fifteen years between the conclusion of the Congress of Vienna and the Revolution of 1830 in France, the Congress system succeeded in holding back revolutionary and nationalistic disturbances in Europe, with the exception only of the Greek revolution of 1821. In Russia, the Decembrist Revolt of 1825 failed almost before it had begun. The only truly successful revolutionary activity during these years occurred in Latin America, where wars of independence ended Spain's centuries-old colonial domination.

Nonetheless, during the 1820s, liberal political ideas and some liberal political figures began to make inroads into the otherwise conservative

order. In 1830 revolution and reform again began to move across Europe. The French rejected the restored Bourbon monarchy and established a more liberal monarchy. Belgium also achieved independence with a liberal government. Perhaps most important, Great Britain moved slowly toward a more liberal position. During the 1820s, Great Britain had become unenthusiastic about a political role that placed it in opposition to all change. For its own commercial reasons, it favored independence for Latin America. Popular pressures at home led the British aristocratic leadership to enact a moderate reform bill in 1832. Thereafter, Britain would be viewed as the leading liberal state in Europe and one that would support nationalistic causes.

Review Questions

1. Define nationalism. What were the goals of nationalists? What were the difficulties they confronted in realizing those goals? Why was nationalism a special threat to the Austrian

Empire? What areas saw significant nationalist movements between 1815 and 1830? Which were successful and which unsuccessful?

2. What were the tenets of liberalism? Who were the liberals and how did liberalism affect the political developments of the early nineteenth century? What relationship does liberalism have to nationalism?

3. What difficulties did the conservatives in Austria, Prussia, and Russia face in the years after the Napoleonic wars? How did they respond on both national and international levels? What were the aims of the concert of Europe? What did it accomplish and why did Britain withdraw?

4. What political changes took place in Latin America in the twenty years between 1804 and 1824? What were the main reasons for Creole discontent with Spanish rule and to what extent were the Creole leaders influenced by Enlightenment political philosophy? Who were some of the primary leaders of Latin American independence and why were they successful?

5. Describe the constitution of the restored monarchy in France. Was the government truly constitutional? What did Charles X hope to accomplish? How much support did he have? What were the causes of the revolution of 1830? What did this revolution achieve, and at what cost?

6. Before 1820, Britain appeared to be moving down the same reactionary road as the other major powers. What factors led to a different outcome in Britain? What was the purpose of the Great Reform Bill? What did it achieve? Would you call it a "revolutionary" document?

Suggested Readings

P. ALTER, *Nationalism* (1985). A useful brief introduction.

B. ANDERSON, *Imagined Communities*, rev. ed. (1991). A discussion of the forces that have fostered national identity.

D. BEALES, *From Castlereagh to Gladstone, 1815–1885* (1969). A survey to be read in conjunction with the Briggs book.

M. BERDAHL, *The Politics of the Prussian Nobility: The Development of a Conservative Ideology, 1770–1848* (1988). A major examination of German conservative outlooks.

G. DE BERTIER DE SAUVIGNY, *The Bourbon Restoration* (trans., 1966), and *Metternich and His Times* (1962). Sympathetic, but not uncritical, studies of the forces of political conservatism.

R. J. BEZUCHA, *The Lyon Uprising of 1834: Social and Political Conflict in the Early July Monarchy* (1974). An excellent discussion of the tensions in France after the Revolution of 1830.

A. BRIGGS, *The Making of Modern England* (1959). Remains the best survey of English history during the first half of the nineteenth century.

M. BROCK, *The Great Reform Act* (1974). The standard work.

G. A. CRAIG, *The Politics of the Prussian Army, 1640–1945* (1955). A splendid study of the conservative political influence of the army on Prussian development.

D. DAKIN, *The Struggle for Greek Independence* (1973). An excellent explanation of the intricacies of the Greek independence question.

J. DROZ, *Europe Between Revolutions, 1815–1848* (1967). An examination of Europe as created by the Vienna settlement.

E. GELLNER, *Nations and Nationalism* (1983). A major theoretical work.

R. GILDEA, *Barricades and Borders: Europe 1800–1914* (1987). A useful survey.

E. HALÉVY, *England in 1815* (1913). One of the most important and influential books written on nineteenth-century Britain.

E. J. HOBSBAWM, *The Age of Revolution, 1789–1848* (1962). A comprehensive survey emphasizing the social ramifications of the liberal democratic and industrial revolutions.

E. J. HOBSBAWM, *Nations and Nationalism since 1780: Programme, Myth, Reality*, rev. ed. (1992). The best recent introduction to the subject.

S. HOLMES, *Benjamin Constant and the Making of Modern Liberalism* (1984). An outstanding study of a major liberal theorist.

A. JARDIN and A. J. TUDESQ, *Restoration and Reaction, 1815–1848* (1984). Surveys this period in France.

B. JELAVICH, *Russia's Balkan Entanglements, 1899–1914* (1991). Now the standard discussion of this topic.

C. JELAVICH and B. JELAVICH, *The Establishment of the Balkan National States, 1804–1920* (1977). A standard, clear introduction.

W. B. KAUFMANN, *British Policy and the Independence of Latin America, 1802–1828* (1951). A standard discussion of an important relationship.

W. B. LINCOLN, *Nicholas I: Emperor and Autocrat of All the Russians* (1978). A serious scholarly treatment.

J. Lynch, *The Spanish American Revolutions, 1808–1826* (1973). An excellent one-volume treatment.

C. A. Macartney, *The Habsburg Empire, 1790–1918* (1971). An outstanding survey.

A. Palmer, *Alexander I: Tsar of War and Peace* (1974). An interesting biography that captures much of the mysterious personality of this ruler.

P. Pilbeam, *The 1830 Revolution in France* (1991). An account that emphasizes the restoration accommodation to various interest groups.

D. H. Pinkney, *The French Revolution of 1830* (1972). The best account in English.

M. Raeff, *The Decembrist Movement* (1966). An examination of the unsuccessful uprising, with documents.

N. V. Riasanovsky, *Nicholas I and Official Nationality in Russia, 1825–1855* (1959). A lucid discussion of the conservative ideology that made Russia the major opponent of liberalism.

C. A. Ruud, *Fighting Words: Imperial Censorship and the Russian Press, 1804–1906* (1982). Examines the government attempt to shape and control public opinion.

J. Sheehan, *German History, 1770–1866* (1989). A very long work that is now the best available survey of the subject.

A. B. Ulam, *Russia's Failed Revolutionaries* (1981). Contains a useful discussion of the Decembrists as a background for other nineteenth-century Russian revolutionary activity.

P. S. Wandycz, *The Lands of Partitioned Poland, 1795–1918* (1974). The best study of Poland during the nineteenth century.

Cities all across the continent grew during the first half of the nineteenth century. Some developed with little planning into bewildering places. Others—as this Berlin street scene suggests—developed in ways more congenial to their residents, with neighborhoods that continued to combine workshops, stores, and residences. [Bildarchiv Preussischer Kulturbesitz]

22

Economic Advance and Social Unrest (1830–1850)

Key Topics in This Chapter
◆ The development of industrialism and its effects on the organization of labor
   and the family
◆ The changing role of women in industrial society
◆ The establishment of police forces and reform of prisons
◆ Early developments in European socialism
◆ The revolutions of 1848

By 1830 Europe was headed toward an industrial society. Only Great Britain had already
attained that status, but the pounding of new
machinery and the grinding of railway engines
soon began to echo across much of the Continent. Yet what characterized the second quarter
of the century was not the triumph of industrialism but the final protests of those economic
groups who opposed it. Intellectually, the period
saw the formulation of the major creeds sup-

porting and criticizing the newly emerging society.

These were years of uncertainty for almost everyone. Even the most confident entrepreneurs knew that the trade cycle might bankrupt them in a matter of weeks. For the industrial workers and the artisans, unemployment became a haunting and recurring problem. For the peasants, the question was sufficiency of food. It was a period of self-conscious transition that culminated in 1848 with a continent-wide outbreak of revolution. People knew that one mode of life was passing, but no one knew what would replace it.

Toward an Industrial Society

During the first half of the nineteenth century, industrial production of both manufacturing and consumer goods that had begun earlier in Great Britain began to spread across much of Europe. This slow but steady conversion of the European economy to industrial manufacturing generally took place in cities. Thus, it brought about new migrations of people from the countryside to urban settings and caused a painful reorganization in the lives of European workers. Many of those who possessed valuable preindustrial skills saw those skills displaced by machines. Industrialism and the accompanying urban growth no less than the political revolutions that derived from the French Revolution overturned the social order of the Old Regime.

Britain's Industrial Leadership

The Industrial Revolution had begun in eighteenth-century Great Britain with the advances in textile production described in Chapter 16. Natural resources, adequate capital, native technological skills, a growing food supply, a social structure that allowed considerable mobility, and strong foreign and domestic demand for goods had given Britain an edge in achieving a vast new capacity for production in manufacturing. British factories and recently invented machines allowed producers to furnish customers with a greater number of products whose quality was higher and whose prices were lower than those of any competitors. The French Revolution and the wars of Napoleon had also finally destroyed the French Atlantic trade and

had for two decades disrupted continental economic life. The Latin American wars of independence opened the markets of South America to British goods. In North America, both the United States and Canada demanded British products. Through its control of India, Britain commanded the markets of southern Asia.

The British textile industry was a vast worldwide economic network. Much of the raw cotton that fed the new British textile mills came from the plantations of the southern United States. The British textile industry was thus dependent on the labor of black American slaves, though Britain itself had since 1807 been trying to end the slave trade. Then in turn the finished textiles were shipped all over the world along sea lanes protected by the British navy. The wealth that Britain gained through textile production and its other industries of ironmaking, shipbuilding, china production, and the manufacture of other finished goods was invested all over the world but especially in the United States and Latin America. This enormous activity provided the economic foundation for British dominance of the world scene in the nineteenth century.

Despite the economic lag, the continental nations were beginning to make material progress. By the 1830s, in Belgium, France, and Germany, the number of steam engines in use was growing steadily. Exploitation of the coalfields of the Ruhr and the Saar basins had begun. Coke was replacing charcoal in iron and steel production.

Industrial areas on the Continent were generally less concentrated than in Britain, and large manufacturing districts, such as the British Midlands, did not yet exist there. Major pockets of production, such as Lyons, Rouen, Liège, and Lille, did exist in western Europe, but most continental manufacturing still took place in the countryside. New machines were integrated into the existing domestic system. The extreme slowness of continental imitation of the British example meant that at mid-century peasants and urban artisans remained more important politically than industrial factory workers.

Population and Migration

While the process of industrialization spread, the population of Europe continued to grow on the base of the eighteenth-century population explosion. The number of people in France rose from 32.5 million in 1831 to 35.8 million in 1851. The population of Germany rose from 26.5 million to 33.5 million during approximately the same period. That of Britain grew from 16.3 million to 20.8 million. More and more of the people of Europe lived in cities. By mid-century, one-half of the population of England and Wales had become town dwellers; the proportion for France and Germany was about one-quarter. Eastern Europe by contrast remained overwhelmingly rural with little industrial manufacturing.

The sheer numbers of human beings put considerable pressure on the physical resources of the cities. Migration from the countryside meant that existing housing, water, sewers, food supplies, and lighting were completely inadequate. Slums with indescribable filth grew, and disease, especially cholera, ravaged the population. Crime increased and became a way of life for those who could make a living in no other manner. Human misery and degradation in many early-nineteenth-century cities seemed to have no bounds.

The situation in the countryside was scarcely better. During the first half of the century, the productive use of the land remained the basic fact of life for most Europeans. The enclosures of the late eighteenth century, the land redistribution of the French Revolution, and the emancipation of serfs in Prussia and later in Austria (1848) and Russia (1861) commercialized landholding. Liberal reformers had hoped that the legal revolution in ownership would transform peasants into progressive, industrious farmers. Instead, most peasants had become conservative landholders without enough land to make agricultural innovations or, often, even to support themselves.

It is important to note the differing dates of rural emancipation across Europe. In England, France, and the Low Countries, persons living in the countryside could move freely between country and town. In Germany, eastern Europe, and Russia, such migration was difficult until after emancipation of the serfs. Even when emancipation did occur, as throughout Germany early in the century, it did not make migration simple. So from Germany eastward, the pace of industrialization was much slower in part because of the absence of a fluid market for free labor moving to the cities.

The specter of poor harvests still haunted Europe. The worst such experience of the century was the Irish famine of 1845–1847. Perhaps as many as half a million Irish peasants with no land or small plots simply starved when disease blighted the potato crop. Hundreds of thousands emigrated. By mid-century, the revolution in landholding had led to greater agricultural production. It also resulted in a vast uprooting of people from the countryside into cities and from Europe into the rest of the world. The countryside thus provided many of the workers for the new factories as well as people with few economic skills who slowly emigrated to cities in hope of finding work.

Railways

Industrial advance itself had also contributed to this migration. The 1830s and 1840s were the great age of railway building. The Stockton and Darlington Line opened in England in 1825. By 1830 another major line had been built between Manchester and Liverpool and had several hundred passengers a day. Belgium had undertaken railway construction by 1835. The first French line opened in 1832, but serious construction came only in the 1840s. Germany entered the railway age in 1835. At mid-century, Britain had 9,797 kilometers of railway; France, 2,915; and Germany, 5,856.

The railroads, plus canals and improved regular roads, meant that people could leave the place of their birth more easily than ever before. The improvement in transportation also allowed cheaper and more rapid passage of raw materials and finished products.

Railways epitomized the character of the industrial economy during the second quarter of the century. They represented investment in capital goods rather than in consumer goods. There was consequently a shortage of consumer goods at cheap prices. This favoring of capital over consumer production was one reason that the working class often found itself able to purchase so little for its wages. The railways in and of themselves also brought about still more industrialization. Embodying the most dramatic application of the steam engine, they created a sharply increased demand for iron and steel and

A view of one of the first French railways, the line between Paris and the suburb of St. Germain. The line was built by Baron James de Rothschild of the famous Jewish banking family. [Roger-Viollet]

then for a more skilled labor force. The new iron and steel capacity soon permitted the construction of ironclad ships and iron machinery rather than wooden ones. These great capital industries led to the formation of vast industrial fortunes that would be invested in still newer enterprises. Industrialism had begun to grow on itself.

The Labor Force

The composition and experience of the early nineteenth-century labor force was varied. No single description could include all the factory workers, urban artisans, domestic system craftsmen, household servants, miners, countryside peddlers, farm workers, or railroad navvies. The workforce was composed of some persons who were reasonably well off, enjoying steady employment and decent wages. It also numbered the "laboring poor," who held jobs but who earned little more than subsistence wages. There were others, such as the women and children who worked naked in the mines of Wales, whose conditions of life shocked all of Europe when a parliamentary report in the early 1840s publicized them. Furthermore, the conditions of workers varied from decade to decade and from industry to industry within any particular decade.

Although historians have traditionally emphasized the role and experience of industrial factory workers, only the textile-manufacturing industry became thoroughly mechanized and moved into the factory setting during the first half of the century. Far more of the nonrural, nonagricultural workforce consisted of skilled artisans living in cities or small towns. They were attempting to maintain the value of their skills and control over their trades in the face of changing features of production. All these working people faced possible unemployment, with little or no provision for their security. They confronted during their lives the dissolution of many of the traditional social ties of custom and community.

Proletarianization of Factory Workers and Urban Artisans

During the century, both artisans and factory workers underwent a process of *proletarianization.* This term is used to indicate the entry of workers into a wage economy and their gradual loss of significant ownership of the means of production, such as tools and equipment, and of control over the conduct of their own trades. The process occurred rapidly wherever the factory system arose. The factory owner provided the financial capital to construct the factory, to purchase the machinery, and to secure the raw materials. The factory workers contributed their labor for a wage. The process could also occur outside the factory setting if a new invention, such as a mechanical printing press, could do

Andrew Ure Praises the Factory System

The factory was itself as much an invention of the industrial revolution as were the new machines that the factory often housed. The factory required a new organization of labor. It also made possible the production of vast new quantities of manufactured goods. Andrew Ure (1778–1857), a generally uncritical observer of the factory system, explains the changes brought about by the new sites of production.

♦ *What does Ure understand to be new about the factory system? Why does he emphasize the willingness of workers to be employed in factories? How does he portray the factory system as creating the possibility of new abundance?*

The term *Factory*, in technology, designates the combined operation of many orders of work-people, adult and young, in tending with assiduous skill a system of productive machines continuously impelled by a central power. This definition includes such organizations as cotton-mills, flax-mills, silk-mills, woolen-mills, and certain engineering works. . . . I conceive that this title, in its strictest sense, involves the idea of a vast automaton, composed of various mechanical and intellectual organs, acting in uninterrupted concert for the production of a common object, all of them being subordinated to a self-regulated moving force. . . .

In its precise acceptation, the Factory system is of recent origin, and may claim England for its birthplace. . . .

When the first water-frames for spinning cotton were erected at Cromford, in the romantic valley of the Derwent, about sixty years ago, mankind were little aware of the mighty revolution which the new system of labor was destined by Providence to achieve, not only in the structure of British society, but in the fortunes of the world at large.

Arkwright alone had the sagacity to discern, and the boldness to predict in glowing language, how vastly productive human industry would become, when no longer proportioned in its results to muscular effort, which is by its nature fitful and capricious, but when made to consist in the task of guiding the work of mechanical fingers and arms, regularly impelled with great velocity by some indefatigable physical power. . . .

In my recent tour, continued during several months, through the manufacturing districts, I have seen tens of thousands of old, young, and middle-aged of both sexes, many of them too feeble to get their daily bread by any of the former modes of industry, earning abundant food, raiment, and domestic accommodation, without perspiring at a single pore, screened meanwhile from the summer's sun and the winter's frost, in apartments more airy and salubrious than those of the metropolis, in which our legislative and fashionable aristocracies assemble. In those spacious halls the benignant power of steam summons around him his myriads of willing menials, and assigns to each the regulated task, substituting for painful muscular effort on their part, the energies of his own gigantic arm, and demanding in return only attention and dexterity to correct such little aberrations as casually occur in his workmanship. . . . Such is the factory system, replete with prodigies in mechanics and political economy, which promises, in its future growth, to become the great minister of civilization to the terraqueous globe, enabling this country, as its heart, to diffuse along with its commerce, the life-blood of science and religion to myriads of people still lying "in the region and shadow of death."

Andrew Ure, The Philosophy of Manufactures; or, An Exposition of the Scientific, Moral, and Commercial Economy of the Factory System (London, 1835), pp. 13 ff., as quoted in Mack Walker, ed., Metternich's Europe (New York: Walker and Company, 1968), pp. 275–276, 278–279.

the work of several artisans within a workshop setting.

Factory workers also submitted to various kinds of factory discipline that was virtually always unpopular and difficult to impose. This discipline meant that the demands for smooth operation of the machinery largely determined work conditions. Closing of factory gates to late workers, fines for such lateness, dismissal for drunkenness, and public scolding of faulty laborers were attempts to create human discipline that would match the regularity of the cables, wheels, and pistons. The factory worker had no direct say about the quality of the product or its price.

For all the difficulties of factory conditions, however, the economic situation was often better than for the textile workers who resisted the factory mode of production. In particular, English handloom weavers, who continued to work in their homes, experienced decades of declining trade and growing poverty in their unsuccessful competition with power looms.

Urban artisans in the nineteenth century experienced proletarianization more slowly than factory workers, and machinery had little to do with the process. The emergence of factories in and of itself did not harm urban artisans. Many even prospered from the development. For

example, the construction and maintenance of the new machines generated major demand for metalworkers, who consequently prospered. The actual erection of factories and the expansion of cities benefitted all craftsmen in the building trades, such as carpenters, roofers, joiners, and masons. The lower prices for machine-made textiles aided artisans involved in the making of clothing, such as tailors and hatters, by reducing the costs of their raw materials. Where the urban artisans encountered difficulty and where they found their skills and livelihood threatened were in the organization of production.

In the eighteenth century, a European town or city workplace had usually consisted of a few artisans laboring for a master. They labored first as apprentices and then as journeymen, according to established guild regulations and practices. The master owned the workshop and the larger equipment, and the apprentices and journeymen owned their tools. The journeyman could expect to become a master. This guild system had allowed considerable worker control over labor recruitment and training, pace of production, quality of product, and price.

In the nineteenth century, it became increasingly difficult for artisans to continue to exercise corporate or guild direction and control over their trades. The legislation of the French

A parliamentary report in the early 1840s revealed the deplorable conditions of women and children working underground in Welsh mines, shocking British public opinion and inspiring labor reforms. [Bildarchiv Preussischer Kulturbesitz]

Revolution had outlawed such organizations in France. Across Europe, political and economic liberals disapproved of labor and guild organizations and attempted to ban them.

Other destructive forces were also at work. The masters often found themselves under increased competitive pressure from larger, more heavily capitalized establishments or from the introduction of machine production into a previously craft-dominated industry. In many workshops masters began to follow a practice, known in France as *confection*, whereby goods, such as shoes, clothing, and furniture, were produced in standard sizes and styles rather than by special orders for individual customers.

This practice increased the division of labor in the workshop. Each artisan produced a smaller part of the more-or-less uniform final product. Thus, less skill was required of each artisan, and the particular skills possessed by a worker became less valuable. Masters also tried to increase production and reduce costs by lowering the wages paid for piecework. Those attempts often led to work stoppages or strikes. Migrants from the countryside or small towns into the cities created, in some cases, a surplus of relatively unskilled workers. They were willing to work for lower wages or under less favorable and protected conditions than traditional artisans. This situation made it much more difficult for urban journeymen ever to hope to become masters with their own workshops in which they would be in charge. Increasingly, these artisans became lifetime wage laborers whose skills were simply bought and sold in the marketplace.

Working-Class Political Action: The Example of British Chartism

By the middle of the century, such artisans, proud of their skills and frustrated in their social expectations, became the most radical political element in the European working class. From at least the 1830s onward, these artisans took the lead in one country after another in attempting to formulate new ways of protecting their social and economic interests.

By the late 1830s, significant numbers of people in the British working class linked the solution of their economic plight to a program of political reform known as *Chartism*. In 1836 William Lovett (1800–1877) and other London radical artisans formed the London Working Men's Association. In 1838 the group issued the Charter, demanding six specific reforms. The Six Points of the Charter included universal manhood suffrage, annual election of the House of Commons, the secret ballot, equal electoral districts, abolition of property qualifications for members of the House of Commons, and payment of salaries to members of the House of Commons.

This engraving depicts the final great Chartist demonstration in London in 1848. Chartism was the first large-scale working-class political movement in Europe. [Bildarchiv Preussischer Kulturbesitz]

For more than ten years, the Chartists, who were never tightly organized, agitated for their reforms. On three occasions the Charter was presented to Parliament, which refused to pass it. Petitions with millions of signatures were presented to the House of Commons. Strikes were called. The Chartists published a newspaper, *The Northern Star*. Feargus O'Connor (1794–1855), the most important Chartist leader, made speeches across Britain. Despite this vast activity, Chartism as a national movement failed. Its ranks were split between those who favored violence and those who wanted to use peaceful tactics. On the local level, however, the Chartists scored several successes and controlled the city councils in Leeds and Sheffield.

As prosperity returned after the depression of the late 1830s and early 1840s, many working people abandoned the movement. Chartists' demonstrations in 1848 fizzled. Nevertheless, Chartism was the first large-scale European working-class political movement. It had specific goals and largely working-class leadership. Eventually, several of the Six Points were enacted into law. Continental working-class observers saw in Chartism the kind of mass movement that workers must eventually adopt if they were to improve their situation.

Family Structures and the Industrial Revolution

It is more difficult to generalize about the European working-class family structure in the age of early industrialism than under the Old Regime. Industrialism developed at such different rates across the Continent, and the impact of industrialism cannot be separated from that of migration and urbanization. Furthermore, industrialism did not touch all families directly. The structures and customs of many peasant families changed little for much of the nineteenth century.

Much more is known about the relationships of the new industry to the family in Great Britain than elsewhere. Many of the British developments foreshadowed those in other countries as the factory system spread.

The Family in the Early Factory System

Contrary to the opinion historians and other observers once held, the adoption of new machinery and factory production did not destroy the working-class family. Before the late-eighteenth-century revolution in textile production in England, the individual family involved in textiles was the chief unit of production. The earliest textile inventions, such as the spinning jenny, did not change that situation. The new machine was simply brought into the home to spin the thread. It was the mechanization of weaving that led to the major change. The father who became a machine weaver was then employed in a factory. His work was thus separated from his home. Although one should not underestimate the changes and pressures in family life that occurred when the father left for the factory, the structure of early English factories allowed the father to preserve certain of his traditional family roles as they had existed before the factory system.

In the domestic system of the family economy, the father and mother had worked with their children in textile production as a family unit. They had trained and disciplined the children within the home setting. Their home life and their economic life were largely the same. Early factory owners and supervisors permitted the father to employ his wife and children as his assistants. Parental training and discipline were thus transferred from the home into the early factory. In some cases, in both Britain and France, whole families would move near a new factory so the family as a unit could work there. Those accommodations to family life nonetheless did not relieve any family members of having to face the new work discipline of the factory setting.

A major shift in this family and factory structure began in the mid-1820s in England and had been more or less completed by the mid-1830s. As spinning and weaving were put under one roof, the size of factories and of the machinery became larger. These newer machines required fewer skilled operators but many relatively unskilled attendants. Machine tending became the work of unmarried women and of children. Factory owners found that these workers would accept lower wages and were less likely than adult men to try to form worker or union organizations.

Factory wages for the more skilled adult males, however, became sufficiently high to allow some fathers to remove their children from the factory and to send them to school. The children who were now working in the factories as assistants were often the children of the economically depressed handloom weavers. The wives of the skilled operatives also usually did not work in the factories any longer. So, the original links of the family in the British textile factory that had existed for well over a quarter century largely disappeared. Men were supervising women and children who did not belong to their families.

CONCERN FOR CHILD LABOR It was at this point in the 1830s that workers became concerned about the plight of child labor, because parents were no longer exercising discipline over their own children in the factories. The English Factory Act of 1833 forbade the employment of children under age nine, limited the workday of children aged nine to thirteen to nine hours, and required that these children be given two hours of education a day paid for by the factory owner. The effect was further to divide work and home life. The workday for adult males and older teenagers remained twelve hours. Younger children often worked in relays of four or six hours. Consequently, the parental link was thoroughly broken. The education requirement began the process of removing nurturing and training from the home and family to a school, where a teacher rather than the parents was in charge of education.

After this act was passed, many of the British working class demanded shorter workdays for adults. They desired to reunite, in some manner, the workday of adults with that of their children, or at least to allow adults to spend more time with their children. In 1847 Parliament mandated a ten-hour day. By present standards, this was long. At that time, however, it allowed parents and children more hours together as a domestic unit since their relationship as a work or production unit had ceased wherever the factory system prevailed. By the middle of the 1840s, in the lives of industrial workers, the roles of men as breadwinners and as fathers and husbands had become distinct in the British textile industry.

CHANGING ECONOMIC ROLE FOR THE FAMILY What occurred in Britain presents a general pattern for what would happen elsewhere with the spread of industrial capitalism and public education. The European family was passing from being the chief unit of both production and consumption to becoming the chief unit of consumption alone. This development did not mean the end of the family as an economic unit. Parents and children, however, now came to depend on sharing wages often derived from several sources rather than on sharing work in the home or factory.

Ultimately, the wage economy meant that families were less closely bound together than in the past. Because wages could be sent over long

As textile production became increasingly automated in the nineteenth century, textile factories required fewer skilled workers and more unskilled attendants. To fill these unskilled positions, factory owners turned increasingly to unmarried women and widows, who worked for lower wages than men and were less likely to form labor organizations. [Bildarchiv Preussischer Kulturbesitz]

distances to parents, children might now move farther away from home. Once they moved far away, the economic link was, in time, often broken. On the other hand, when a family settled in an industrial city, the wage economy might, in that or the next generation, actually discourage children from leaving home as early as they had in the past. Children could find wage employment in the same city and then live at home until they had accumulated enough savings to marry and begin their own household. That situation meant that children often remained with their parents longer than in the past.

Women in the Early Industrial Revolution

The industrial economy ultimately produced an immense impact on the home and family life of women. First, it took virtually all productive work out of the home and allowed many families to live on the wages of the male spouse. That transformation prepared the way for a new concept of gender-determined roles in the home and in domestic life generally. Women came to be associated with domestic duties, such as housekeeping, food preparation, child rearing and nurturing, and household management. The man came to be associated almost exclu-

sively with breadwinning. Children were reared to match these expected gender patterns. Previously, this domestic division of labor into separate spheres had prevailed only among the relatively small middle class and the gentry. During the nineteenth century, that division came to characterize the working class as well.

Opportunities and Exploitation in Employment

Because the early Industrial Revolution had begun in textile production, women and their labor were deeply involved from the start. While both spinning and weaving were still domestic industries, women usually worked in all stages of production. Hand spinning was virtually always a woman's task. At first, when spinning was moved into factories and involved large machines, women often were displaced by men. Furthermore, the higher wages commanded by male cotton-factory workers allowed many married women not to work or to work only to supplement their husbands' wages.

WOMEN IN FACTORIES With the next generation of machines in the 1820s, however, unmarried women rapidly became employed in the factories. But their new jobs there often demanded fewer skills than those they had previously exercised in the home production of tex-

This pen-manufacturing factory in Birmingham, England employed only women. [The Bettmann Archive]

tiles. Women's factory work also required fewer skills than most work done by men. Tending a machine required less skill than actually spinning or weaving or acting as foreman. There was thus a certain paradox in the impact of the factory on women. Many new jobs were opened to them, but the level of skills was lowered.

Moreover, almost always, the women in the factories were young single women or widows. Upon marriage or perhaps after the birth of the first child, young women usually found that their husbands earned enough money for them to leave the factory. Or they found themselves unwanted by the factory owners, who disliked employing married women because of the likelihood of pregnancy, the influence of their husbands, and the duties of child rearing. Widows might return to factory work because they then lacked their husbands' income.

WORK ON THE LAND AND IN THE HOME In Britain and elsewhere by mid-century, industrial factory work still accounted for less than half of all employment for women. The largest group of employed women in France continued to work on the land. In England, they were domestic servants. Through western Europe, domestic industries, such as lacemaking, glove making, garment making, and other kinds of needlework, employed a vast number of women. In almost all such cases, their conditions of labor were harsh, whether they worked in their homes or in sweated workshops. It cannot be overemphasized that all work by women commanded low wages and involved low skills. They had virtually no effective modes of protecting themselves from exploitation. The charwoman was a common sight across the Continent and symbolized the plight of working women.

The low wages of women workers in all areas of employment sometimes led to their becoming prostitutes to supplement their wage income. This situation prevailed across Europe throughout the century. In 1844 Louise Aston (1814–1871), a German political radical, portrayed this situation in a poem looking at the experience of a Silesian woman weaver as she confronts a factory owner upon whom her family depends to purchase the cloth they have woven:

The factory owner has come,
And he says to me: 'My darling child,

I know your people
Are living in misery and sorrow;
So if you want to lie with me
For three or four nights,
See this shiny gold coin!
It's yours immediately.'[1]

Such sexual exploitation of women was hardly new to European society, but the particular pressures of the transformation of the economy from one of skilled artisans to unskilled factory workers made many women especially vulnerable.

Changing Expectations in Working-Class Marriage

Movement to cities and entrance into the wage economy gave women wider opportunities for marriage. Cohabitation before marriage was not uncommon. Parents had less to do with arranging marriages than in the past. Marriage now usually meant that a woman would leave the workforce to live on her husband's earnings. If all went well, that arrangement might improve her situation. If the husband became ill or died, however, or if he deserted his wife, she would have to reenter the market for unskilled labor at an advanced age.

Despite these changes, many of the traditional practices associated with the family economy survived into the industrial era. As a young woman came of age, both family needs and her desire to marry still directed what she would do with her life. The most likely early occupation for a young woman was domestic service. A girl born in the country normally migrated to a nearby town or city for such employment, often living initially with a relative. As in the past, she would try to earn enough in wages to give her a dowry, so that she might marry and set up her own household. If she became a factory worker, she would probably live in a supervised dormitory. Such dormitories were one of the ways that factory owners attracted young women into their employ by convincing parents that their daughters would be safe.

The life of young women in the cities was more precarious than earlier. There were fewer family and community ties. There were also

[1]As quoted in Lia Secci, "German Women Writers and the Revolution of 1848," in John C. Fout, ed., German Women in the Nineteenth Century: A Social History (New York: Holmes & Meier, 1984), p. 162.

Women Industrial Workers Explain
Their Economic Situation

In 1832 there was much discussion in the British press about factory legislation. Most of that discussion was concerned with the employment of children, but the Examiner newspaper made the suggestion that any factory laws should not only address the problem of child labor but also in time eliminate women from employment in factories. That article provoked the following remarkable letter to the editor, composed by or on behalf of women factory workers, which eloquently stated the real necessity of such employment for women and the unattractive alternatives.

♦ *What are the reasons these women enumerate to prove the necessity of their holding manufacturing jobs? What changes in production methods have led women from the home to the factory? How does the situation of these women relate to the possibility of their marrying? Compare the plight of these English working-class women with that of the French middle-class woman in the next document.*

Sir,

Living as we do, in the densely populated manufacturing districts of Lancashire, and most of us belonging to that class of females who earn their bread either directly or indirectly by manufactories, we have looked with no little anxiety for your opinion on the Factory Bill. . . . You are for doing away with our services in manufactories altogether. So much the better, if you had pointed out any other more eligible and practical employment for the surplus female labour, that will want other channels for a subsistence. If our competition were withdrawn, and short hours substituted, we have no doubt but the effects would be as you have stated, "not to lower wages, as the male branch of the family would be enabled to earn as much as the whole had done," but for the thousands of females who are employed in manufactories, who have no legitimate claim on any male relative for employment or support, and who have, through a variety of circumstance, been early thrown on their own resources for a livelihood, what is to become of them?

In this neighbourhood, hand-loom has been almost totally superseded by power-loom weaving, and no inconsiderable number of females, who must depend on their own exertions, or their parishes for support, have been forced, of necessity into the manufactories, from their total inability to earn a livelihood at home.

It is a lamentable fact, that, in these parts of the country, there is scarcely any other mode of employment for female industry, if we except servitude and dressmaking. Of the former of these, there is no chance of employment for one-twentieth of the candidates that would rush into the field, to say nothing of lowering the wages of our sisters of the same craft; and of the latter, galling as some of the hardships of manufactories are (of which the indelicacy of mixing with the men is not the least), yet there are few women who have been so employed, that would change conditions with the ill-used genteel little slaves, who have to lose sleep and health, in catering to the whims and frivolities of the butter-flies of fashion.

We see no way of escape from starvation, but to accept the very tempting offers of the newspapers, held out as baits to us, fairly to ship ourselves off to Van Dieman's Land [Tasmania] on the very delicate errand of husband hunting, and having safely arrived at the "Land of Goshen," jump ashore, with a "Who wants me?" . . .

THE FEMALE OPERATIVES
OF TODMORDEN

The Examiner, February 26, 1832, as quoted in Ivy Pinchbeck, Women Workers and the Industrial Revolution, 1750–1850 *(New York: Augustus M. Kelley, 1969), pp. 199–200.*

A Young Middle-Class French Woman Writes to Her Father About Marriage

Stéphanie Jullien was a young middle-class woman whose father wished her to marry a man who was courting her. She had already rejected one suitor and was thus a great concern to her father. In this letter, she explains to her father the matters that disturb her and make her wish to delay her decision. Ultimately, she did marry the man in question, and the marriage appears to have been happy.

◆ *How does Stéphanie Jullien distinguish between the vocational and social opportunities available to a woman and those to a man? What are her expectations of a relationship with a husband? What does the letter also tell you about her sense of her relationship to her father? Compare this letter with the preceding letter by English working-class women. What problems do the women share? How are their lives different? What does a comparison of the two letters tell you about the difference in class experience in the early nineteenth century?*

You men have a thousand occupations to distract you: society, business, politics, and work absorb you, exhaust you, upset you. . . . As for us women who, as you have said to me from time to time, have only the roses in life, we feel more profoundly in our solitude and in our idleness the sufferings that you can slough off. I don't want to make a comparison here between the destiny of man and the destiny of woman: each sex has its own lot, its own troubles, its own pleasures. I only want to explain to you that excess of moroseness of which you complain and of which I am the first to suffer. . . . I am not able to do anything for myself and for those around me. I am depriving my brothers in order to have a dowry. I am not even able to live alone, being obliged to take from others, not only in order to live but also in order to be protected, since social convention does not allow me to have independence. And yet the world finds me guilty of being the only person that I am at liberty to be; not having useful or productive work to do, not having any calling except marriage, and not being able to look by myself for someone who will suit me, I am full of cares and anxieties. . . .

I am asking for more time [before responding to a marriage proposal]. It is not too much to want to see and know a man for ten months, even a year when it is a matter of passing one's life with him. There is no objection to make, you say. But the most serious and the most important presents itself: *I do not love him.* Don't think I am talking about a romantic and impossible passion or an ideal love, neither of which I ever hope to know. I am talking of a feeling that makes one want to see someone, that makes his absence painful and his return desirable, that makes one interested in what another is doing, that makes one want another's happiness almost in spite of oneself, that makes, finally, the duties of a woman toward her husband pleasures and not efforts. It is a feeling without which marriage would be hell, a feeling that cannot be born out of esteem, and which to me, however, seems to be the very basis of conjugal happiness. I can't feel these emotions immediately. . . . Let me have some time. I want to love, not out of any sense of duty, but for myself and for the happiness of the one to whom I attach my life, who will suffer if he only encounters coldness in me, when he brings me love and devotion.

From the Jullien Family Papers, 39 AP 4, Archives Nationales, Paris, trans. by Barbara Corrado Pope, as quoted in Erna Olafson Hellerstein, Leslie Parker Hume, and Karen M. Offen, eds., Victorian Women: A Documentary Account of Women's Lives in Nineteenth-Century England, France, and the United States *(Stanford, Calif.: Stanford University Press, 1981), pp. 247–248.*

perhaps more available young men. These men, who worked for wages rather than in the older apprenticeship structures, were more mobile, so that relationships between men and women often were more fleeting. In any case, illegitimate births increased; fewer women who became pregnant before marriage found the father willing to marry them.

Marriage in the wage industrial economy was also different in certain respects from earlier marriages. It still involved the starting of a separate household, but the structure of gender relationships within the household was different. Marriage was less an economic partnership. The husband's wages might well be able to support the entire family. The wage economy and the industrialization separating workplace from home made it difficult for women to combine domestic duties with work. When married women worked, it was usually in the nonindustrial sector of the economy. More often than not, children were sent to work rather than the wife. This may help explain the increase of fertility within marriages, as children in the wage economy usually were an economic asset. Married women worked outside the home only when family needs or illness or the death of a spouse forced them to do so.

In the home, working-class women were by no means idle. Their domestic duties were an essential factor in the family wage economy. If work took place elsewhere, someone had to be directly in charge of maintaining the home front. Homemaking came to the fore when a life at home had to be organized separate from the place of work. Wives were primarily concerned with food and cooking, but they often also were in charge of the family's finances. The role of the mother expanded when the children still living at home became wage earners. She was now providing home support for her entire wage-earning family. She created the environment to which the family members returned after work. The longer period of home life of working children may also have increased and strengthened familial bonds of affection between those children and their hardworking, homebound mothers. In all these respects, the culture of the working-class marriage and family tended to imitate the family patterns of the middle and upper classes, whose members had often accept-ed the view of separate gender spheres set forth by Rousseau and popularized in hundreds of novels, journals, and newspapers.

Problems of Crime and Order

Throughout the nineteenth century, the political and economic elite in Europe were profoundly concerned about social order. The revolutions of the late eighteenth and early nineteenth centuries made them fearful of future disorder and threats to life and property. The process of industrialization and urbanization also contributed to this problem of order. Thousands of Europeans migrated from the countryside to the towns and cities. There they often encountered poverty or unemployment and general social frustration and disappointment. Cities became places associated with criminal activity and especially crimes against property, such as theft and arson. Throughout the first sixty years of the nineteenth century, crime appears to have increased slowly but steadily before more or less reaching a plateau.

Historians and social scientists are divided about the reasons for this rise in the crime rate. So little is known about crime in rural settings that comparisons with the cities are difficult. There are also many problems with crime statistics in the nineteenth century. No two nations kept them in the same manner. Different legal codes and systems of judicial administration were in effect in different areas of the Continent, thus giving somewhat different legal definitions of criminal activity. The result has been confusion, difficult research, and tentative conclusions.

New Police Forces

From the propertied elite classes, two major views about containing crime and criminals emerged during the nineteenth century: prison reform and better systems of police. The result of these efforts was the triumph in Europe of the idea of a policed society. This concept means the presence of a paid, professionally trained group of law-enforcement officers charged with keeping order, protecting property and lives, investigating crime, and apprehending offenders. These officers are distinct from the army and are charged specifically with domestic security. It is to them that the civilian population normally turns for law enforcement. One of the key features of the theory of a policed society is that crime may be prevented by the visible presence of law-enforcement officers. These police forces, at least in theory, did not perform a political role, though in many countries that distinction was often ignored. Police forces also became one of the major areas of municipal government employment.

Such professional police forces did not really exist until the early nineteenth century. They differed from one country to another in both authority and organization, but their creation proved to be one of the main keys to the emergence of an orderly European society. The prefect of Paris set forth the chief principles that lay behind the founding of all of these new police units when he announced in 1828:

Safety by day and night, free traffic movement, clean streets, the supervision of and precaution against accidents, the maintenance of order in public places, the seeking out of offences and their perpetrators. . . . The municipal police is a parental police.[2]

---

[2]*Quoted in Clive Emsley,* Policing and Its Context, 1750–1870 *(London: Macmillan, 1983), p. 58.*

Professional police forces appeared in Paris in 1828. The same year the British Parliament passed legislation sponsored by Sir Robert Peel (1788–1850) that placed police on London streets. They were soon known as *bobbies* after the sponsor of the legislation. Similar police departments were deployed in Berlin after the Revolution of 1848. All of these forces were distinguished by an easily recognizable uniform. Police on the Continent were armed; those in Britain were not.

Although citizens sometimes viewed police with a certain suspicion, by the end of the century, most Europeans held friendly views toward police and regarded them as their protectors. Persons from the upper and middle classes felt their property to be more secure. Persons from the working class also frequently turned to the police to protect their lives and property and to aid them in other ways in emergencies. Of course, such was not the attitude toward political or secret police, who were hated and dreaded wherever governments created them.

Prison Reform

Before the nineteenth century, European prisons were local jails or state prisons, such as the Bastille. Governments also sent criminals to

London policemen, 1850. Professional police forces did not exist before the early nineteenth century. The London police force was created by Parliament in 1828. [Mansell Collection]

prison ships called *hulks*. Some Mediterranean nations sentenced prisoners to naval galleys, where, chained to their benches, they rowed until they died or were eventually released. Prisons inmates lived under wretched conditions. Men, women, and children were housed together. Persons guilty of minor offenses were left in the same room with those guilty of the most serious offenses.

Beginning in the late eighteenth century, the British government used the penalty of transportation for persons convicted of the most serious offenses. Transportation to the colony of New South Wales in Australia was regarded as an alternative to capital punishment and was used by the British until the middle of the nineteenth century, when the colonies began to object. Thereafter the British government established public works prisons in Britain to house long-term prisoners.

By the close of the eighteenth century and the early decades of the nineteenth century, reformers, such as John Howard (1726–1790) and Elizabeth Fry (1780–1845) in England and Charles Lucas (1803–1889) in France, exposed the horrendous conditions in prisons and demanded change. Reform came slowly because of the expense of constructing new prisons and a general lack of sympathy for criminals.

In the 1840s, however, both the French and the English undertook several bold efforts at prison reform. These reform efforts would appear to indicate a shift in opinion whereby crime was seen not as an assault on order or on authority but as a mark of a character fault in the criminal. Thereafter part of the goal of imprisonment was to rehabilitate or transform the prisoner during the period of incarceration. The result of this change was the creation of exceedingly repressive prison systems designed according to the most advanced scientific modes of understanding criminals and criminal reform.

Europeans used various prison models originally established in the United States. All these experiments depended on separating prisoners from each other. One was known as the Auburn system after Auburn Prison in New York State. According to it, prisoners were separated during the night but could associate in work time during the day. The other was the Philadelphia system, in which prisoners were kept rigorously separated at all times.

The chief characteristics of all of these systems were an individual cell for each prisoner and long periods of separation and silence between prisoners. The most famous example of this kind of prison in Europe was Pentonville Prison near London. There each prisoner occupied a separate cell and was never allowed to speak to or see another prisoner. Each prisoner wore a mask when in the prison yard; in the chapel, each had a separate stall. The point of

Often treadmills like these were the only exercise available for English prisoners. [Bildarchiv Preussischer Kulturbesitz]

the system was to turn the prisoner's mind in on itself to a mode of contemplation that would reform criminal tendencies. As time passed, the system became more relaxed because the intense isolation often led to mental collapse.

In France, imprisonment became more repressive as the century passed. The French constructed prisons similar to Pentonville in the 1840s. In 1875 the French also adopted a firm general policy of isolation of inmates in prison. Sixty prisons based on this principle were constructed by 1908. Prisoners were supposed to be trained in some kind of trade or skill while in prison so they could reemerge as reformed citizens.

The vast increase in repeat offenses led the French government in 1885 to declare transportation the penalty for repeated serious crimes. It did this long after the British had abandoned the practice. The French sent serious repeat offenders to places, such as the infamous Devil's Island off the coast of South America, literally to purge the nation of its worst criminals and to ensure that they would never return.

All of these attempts to create a police force and to reform prisons illustrate the new post–French Revolution concern about order and stability by European political and social elites. On the whole, by the end of the century, an orderly society had been established, and the new police and prisons had no small role in that development.

Classical Economics

Economists whose thought largely derived from Adam Smith's *Wealth of Nations* (1776) dominated private and public discussions of industrial and commercial policy. Their ideas are often associated with the phrase *laissez-faire*. Although they thought that the government should perform many important functions, the classical economists favored economic growth through competitive free enterprise. They conceived of society as consisting of atomistic individuals whose competitive efforts met the demands of consumers in the marketplace. Most economic decisions should be made through the mechanism of the marketplace. They distrusted government action, believing it

to be mischievous and corrupt. The government should maintain a sound currency, enforce contracts, protect property, impose low tariffs and taxes, and leave the remainder of economic life to private initiative. The economists naturally assumed that the state would maintain enough armed forces and naval power to protect the nation's economic structure and foreign trade. The emphasis on thrift, competition, and personal industriousness voiced by the political economists appealed to the middle classes.

Malthus on Population

The classical economists suggested complicated and pessimistic ideas about the working class. Thomas Malthus (1766–1834) and David Ricardo (1772–1823), probably the most influential of all these writers, suggested, in effect, that the condition of the working class could not be improved. In 1798 Malthus published the first edition of his *Essay on the Principle of*

Thomas Robert Malthus, in his Essay on the Principle of Population, *predicted that overpopulation would bring misery to human society. [The Bettmann Archive]*

Population. His ideas have haunted the world ever since. He contended that population must eventually outstrip the food supply. Although the human population grows geometrically, the food supply can expand only arithmetically. There was little hope of averting the disaster, in Malthus's opinion, except through late marriage, chastity, and contraception, the last of which he considered a vice. It took three-quarters of a century for contraception to become a socially acceptable method of containing the population explosion.

Malthus contended that the immediate plight of the working class could only become worse. If wages were raised, the workers would simply produce more children, who would, in turn, consume both the extra wages and more food. Later in his life, Malthus suggested, in a more optimistic vein, that if the working class could be persuaded to adopt a higher standard of living, their increased wages might be spent on consumer goods rather than on more children.

Ricardo on Wages

In the *Principles of Political Economy* (1817), David Ricardo transformed the concepts of Malthus into the Iron Law of Wages. If wages were raised, more children would be produced. They, in turn, would enter the labor market, thus expanding the number of workers and lowering wages. As wages fell, working people would produce fewer children. Wages would then rise, and the process would start all over again. Consequently, in the long run, wages would always tend toward a minimum level. These arguments simply confirmed employers in their natural reluctance to raise wages and also provided strong theoretical support for opposition to labor unions. The ideas of the economists were spread to the public during the 1830s through journals, newspapers, and even short stories, such as Harriet Martineau's (1802–1876) series of *Illustrations of Political Economy.*

Government Policies Based on Classical Economics

The working class of France and Great Britain, needless to say, resented these attitudes, but the governments embraced them. Louis Philippe (1773–1850) and his minister François Guizot (1787–1874) told the French to go forth and enrich themselves. People who simply displayed sufficient energy need not be poor. A number of the French middle class did just that. The July Monarchy (1830–1848) saw the construction of major capital-intensive projects, such as roads, canals, and railways. Little, however, was done about the poverty in the cities and the countryside.

In Germany, the middle classes made less headway. The Prussian reformers after the Napoleonic wars, however, had seen the desirability of abolishing internal tariffs that impeded economic growth. In 1834 all the major German states, except Austria, formed the *Zollverein,* or free trading union. Classical economics had less

Harriet Martineau (1802–1876) popularized the ideas of the British classical economists, using moral tales to illustrate their principles. [The Bettmann Archive]

influence in Germany because of the tradition dating from enlightened absolutism of state direction of economic development. The German economist Friedrich List (1789–1846) argued for this approach to economic growth during the second quarter of the century.

Britain was the home of the major classical economists, and their policies were widely accepted. The utilitarian thought of Jeremy Bentham (1748–1832) increased their influence. Although utilitarianism did not originate with him, Bentham sought to create codes of scientific law that were founded on the principle of utility, that is, the greatest happiness for the greatest number. In his *Fragment on Government* (1776) and *The Principles of Morals and Legislation* (1789), Bentham explained that the application of the principle of utility would overcome the special interests of privileged groups who prevented rational government. He regarded the existing legal and judicial systems as burdened by traditional practices that harmed the very people whom the law should serve. The application of reason and utility would remove the legal clutter that prevented justice from being realized. He believed the principle of utility could be applied to other areas of government administration.

Bentham gathered round him political disciples who combined his ideas with those of classical economics. In 1834 the reformed House of Commons passed a new Poor Law that had been prepared by followers of Bentham. This measure established a Poor Law Commission that set out to make poverty the most undesirable of all social situations. Government poor relief was to be disbursed only in workhouses. Life in the workhouse was consciously designed to be more unpleasant than life outside. Husbands and wives were separated; the food was bad; and the enforced work was distasteful. The social stigma of the workhouse was even worse. The law and its administration presupposed that people would not work because they were lazy. The laboring class, not unjustly, regarded the workhouses as new "bastilles."

The second British monument to applied classical economics was the repeal of the Corn Laws in 1846. The Anti–Corn Law League, organized by manufacturers, had sought this goal for more than six years. The league wanted to abolish the tariffs protecting the domestic price of grain. That change would lead to lower food prices, which would then allow lower wages at no real cost to the workers. In turn, the prices on British manufactured goods could also be lowered to strengthen their competitive position in the world market.

The actual reason for Sir Robert Peel's repeal of the Corn Laws in 1846 was the Irish famine. Peel had to open British ports to foreign grain to feed the starving Irish. He realized that the Corn Laws could not be reimposed. Peel accompanied the abolition measure with a program for government aid to modernize British agriculture and to make it more efficient. The repeal of the Corn Laws was the culmination of the lowering of British tariffs that had begun during the 1820s. The repeal marked the opening of an era of free trade that continued until late in the century.

Early Socialism

During the twentieth century, the socialist movement, in the form of either communist or social democratic political parties, constituted one of the major political forces in Europe. Less than 150 years ago, the advocates of socialism lacked any meaningful political following, and their doctrines appeared blurred and confused to most of their contemporaries.

The early socialists generally applauded the new productive capacity of industrialism. They denied, however, that the free market could adequately produce and distribute goods the way the classical economists claimed. In the capitalist order, the socialists saw primarily mismanagement, low wages, maldistribution of goods, and suffering arising from the unregulated industrial system. Moreover, the socialists thought that human society should be organized as a community rather than merely as a conglomerate of atomistic, selfish individuals.

Utopian Socialism

Among the earliest people to define the social question were a group of writers called the *utopian socialists* by their later critics. They were considered utopian because their ideas were often visionary and because they frequently advocated the creation of ideal communities. They were called socialists because they questioned the structures and values of the existing capitalistic framework. In some cases, they actually deserved neither description. A significant factor in the experience of almost all these groups was the discussion and sometimes the practice of radical ideas in regard to sexuality and the family. People who might have been sympathetic to their economic concerns were profoundly unsympathetic to their views on free love and open family relationships.

SAINT-SIMONIANISM Count Claude Henri de Saint-Simon (1760–1825) was the earliest of the socialist pioneers. As a young liberal French aristocrat, he had fought in the American Revolution. Later he welcomed the French Revolution, during which he made and lost a fortune. By the time of Napoleon's ascendancy, he had turned to a career of writing and social criticism.

Above all else, Saint-Simon believed that modern society would require rational management. Private wealth, property, and enterprise should be subject to an administration other than that of its owners. His ideal government would have consisted of a large board of directors organizing and coordinating the activity of individuals and groups to achieve social harmony. In a sense he was the ideological father of technocracy. Not the redistribution of wealth but its management by experts would alleviate the poverty and social dislocation of the age.

When Saint-Simon died in 1825, he had persuaded only a handful of people that his ideas were correct. Nonetheless, Saint-Simonian societies were always centers for lively discussion of advanced social ideals. Some of the earliest debates in France over feminism took place within those societies. During the late 1820s and 1830s, the Saint-Simonians became well known for advocating sexuality outside marriage. Interestingly enough, several of Saint-Simon's disciples became leaders in the French railway industry during the 1850s.

OWENISM The major British contributor to the early socialist tradition was Robert Owen (1771–1858), a self-made cotton manufacturer. In his early twenties, Owen became a partner in one of the largest cotton factories in Britain at New Lanark, Scotland. Owen was a firm believer in the environmentalist psychology of the Enlightenment. If human beings were placed in the correct surroundings, they and their character could be improved. Moreover, Owen saw no incompatibility between creating a humane industrial environment and making a good profit.

At New Lanark, he put his ideas into practice. Workers were provided with good quarters. Recreational possibilities abounded, and the children received an education. There were several churches, although Owen himself was a notorious freethinker on matters of religion and sex. In the factory itself, various rewards were given for good work. His plant made a fine profit. Visitors flocked from all over Europe to see what Owen had accomplished through enlightened management.

In numerous articles and pamphlets, as well as in letters to influential people, Owen pleaded for a reorganization of industry based on his own successful model. He envisioned a series of communities shaped like parallelograms in which factory and farm workers might live together and produce their goods in cooperation. During the 1820s, Owen sold his New Lanark factory and then went to the United States, where he established the community of New Harmony, Indiana. When quarrels among the members led to the community's failure, he refused to give up his reformist causes. He returned to Britain, where he became the moving force behind the organization of the Grand National Union. This was an attempt to draw all British trade unions into a single body. It collapsed with other labor organizations during the early 1830s.

FOURIERISM Charles Fourier (1772–1837) was the French intellectual counterpart of Owen. He was a commercial salesman who never succeeded in attracting the same kind of public attention as Owen. He wrote his books and articles and waited at home each day at noon, hoping to meet a patron who would undertake his program. No one ever arrived to meet him. Fourier believed that the industrial order ignored the passionate side of human nature. Social discipline ignored all the pleasures that human beings naturally seek.

Fourier advocated the construction of communities, called phalanxes, in which liberated living would replace the boredom and dullness of industrial existence. Agrarian rather than industrial production would predominate in these communities. Sexual activity would be relatively free, and marriage was to be reserved only for later life. Fourier also urged that no person be required to perform the same kind of work for the entire day. People would be both happier and more productive if they moved from one task to another. Through his emphasis on the problem of boredom, Fourier isolated one of the key difficulties of modern economic life.

Saint-Simon, Owen, and Fourier expected some existing government to carry out their ideas. They failed to confront the political difficulties of their envisioned social transformations. Other figures paid more attention to the politics of the situation. In 1839 Louis Blanc (1811–1882) published *The Organization of Labor*. Like other socialist writers, this Frenchman demanded an end to competition, but he did not seek a wholly new society. He called for political reform that would give the vote to the working class. Once so empowered, workers could use the vote to turn the political processes to their own economic advantage. A state controlled by a working-class electorate would finance workshops to employ the poor. In time, such workshops might replace private enterprise, and industry would be organized to ensure jobs. Blanc recognized the power of the state to improve life and the conditions of labor. The state itself could become the great employer of labor.

Anarchism

Other writers and activists of the 1840s, however, rejected both industry and the dominance of government. These were the anarchists. They are usually included in the socialist tradition, although they do not exactly fit. Some favored programs of violence and terrorism; others were peaceful. Auguste Blanqui (1805–1881) was a major spokesman for terror. He spent most of his adult life in jail. Seeking the abolition of both capitalism and the state, Blanqui urged the development of a professional revolutionary vanguard to attack capitalist society. His ideas for the new society were vague, but in his call for professional revolutionaries he foreshadowed

Lenin.

Pierre Joseph Proudhon (1809–1865) represented the other strain of anarchism. In his most famous work, *What Is Property?* (1840), Proudhon attacked the banking system, which rarely extended credit to small property owners or the poor. He wanted credit expanded to allow such people to engage in economic enterprise. Society should be organized on the basis of *mutualism*, which amounted to a system of small businesses. There would be peaceful cooperation and exchange of goods among these groups. With such a social system, the state as it then existed would be unnecessary. His ideas later influenced the French labor movement, which was generally less directly political in its activities than the movements in Britain or Germany.

Marxism

Too often the history of European socialism is regarded as a linear development leading naturally or necessarily to the late-century triumph of Marxism. Nothing could be further from the truth. Marxist socialist ideas did eventually triumph over much, though not all, of Europe, but only through competition with other socialist formulas. At mid-century, the ideas of Karl Marx were simply one more contribution to a heady mixture of concepts and programs criticizing the emerging industrial capitalist society. Marxism differed from its competitors in its authors' claims to scientific accuracy, their rejection of reform, and their call for revolution, though the character of that revolution was not well defined.

Karl Marx (1818–1883) was born in the Rhineland. His family was Jewish, but his father had converted to Lutheranism. Judaism played no role in his education. Marx's middle-class parents sent him to the University of Berlin, where he became deeply involved in Hegelian philosophy and radical politics. During 1842 and 1843, he edited the radical *Rhineland Gazette (Rheinische Zeitung)*. Soon the German authorities drove him from his native land. He lived as an exile in Paris, then in Brussels, and finally, after 1849, in London.

PARTNERSHIP WITH ENGELS In 1844 Marx met Friedrich Engels (1820–1895), another

Karl Marx's socialist philosophy eventually triumphed over most alternative versions of socialism in Europe, but his monumental work has been subject to varying interpretations, criticisms, and revisions that continue to this day. [Bildarchiv Preussischer Kulturbesitz]

than fifty pages, the *Manifesto* would become the most influential political document of modern European history, but that development lay in the future. At the time it was simply one more political tract. Moreover, neither Marx nor his thought had any effect on the revolutionary events of 1848.

SOURCES OF MARX'S IDEAS The major ideas of the *Manifesto* and of Marx's later work, including *Capital* (Vol. I, 1867), were derived from German Hegelianism, French socialism, and British classical economics. Marx applied to social and economic development Hegel's concept that thought develops from the clash of thesis and antithesis into a new intellectual synthesis. For Marx, the conflict between dominant and subordinate social groups generated conditions that led to the emergence of a new dominant social group. These new social relationships, in turn, generated new discontent, conflict, and development.

The French socialists provided Marx with a portrayal of the problems of capitalist society and had raised the issue of property redistribution. Both Hegel and Saint-Simon led Marx to see society and economic conditions as developing through historical stages. The classical economists had produced the analytical tools for an empirical, scientific examination of industrial capitalist society. Marx later explained to a friend:

What I did that was new was to prove: (1) that the existence of classes is bound up with particular historical phases in the development of production; (2) that the class struggle necessarily leads to the dictatorship of the proletariat; (3) that this dictatorship itself only constitutes the transition to the abolition of all classes and to a classless society.[3]

REVOLUTION THROUGH CLASS CONFLICT In *The Communist Manifesto*, Marx and Engels contended that human history must be understood rationally and as a whole. History is the record of humankind's coming to grips with physical nature to produce the goods necessary for survival. That basic productive process deter-

young middle-class German, whose father owned a textile factory in Manchester, England. The next year Engels published *The Conditions of the Working Class in England*, which presented a devastating picture of industrial life. The two men became fast friends. Late in 1847, they were asked to write a pamphlet for a newly organized and ultimately short-lived secret Communist League. *The Communist Manifesto*, published in German, appeared early in 1848. Marx, Engels, and the league had adopted the name *communist* because the term was much more self-consciously radical than socialist. Communism implied the outright abolition of private property rather than some less extensive rearrangement of society. A work of fewer

[3]*Albert Fried and Ronald Sanders, eds.,* Socialist Thought: A Documentary History *(Garden City, N.Y.: Anchor Doubleday, 1964), p. 295.*

mines the structures, values, and ideas of a society. Historically, the organization of the means of production has always involved conflict between the classes who owned and controlled the means of production and those classes who worked for them. That necessary conflict has provided the engine for historical development; it is not an accidental by-product of mismanagement or bad intentions. Thus, piecemeal reforms cannot eliminate the social and economic evils that are inherent in the very structures of production. A radical social transformation is required. The development of capitalism will make such a revolution inevitable.

In Marx's and Engels's eyes, the class conflict that had characterized previous Western history had become simplified during the early nineteenth century into a struggle between the bourgeoisie and the proletariat, or between the middle class and the workers. The character of capitalism ensured the sharpening of the struggle. Capitalist production and competition would steadily increase the size of the unpropertied proletariat. Large-scale mechanical production crushed both traditional and smaller industrial producers into the ranks of the proletariat. As the business structures grew larger and larger, the competitive pressures would squeeze out smaller middle-class units. Competition among the few remaining giant concerns would lead to more intense suffering for the proletariat.

As the workers suffered increasingly from the competition among the ever-enlarging firms, Marx contended, they would eventually begin to foment revolution. Finally, they would overthrow the few remaining owners of the means of production. For a time the workers would organize the means of production through a dictatorship of the proletariat. This would eventually give way to a propertyless and classless communist society.

This proletarian revolution was inevitable, according to Marx and Engels. The structure of capitalism required competition and consolidation of enterprise. Although the class conflict involved in the contemporary process resembled that of the past, it differed in one major respect. The struggle between the capitalistic bourgeoisie and the industrial proletariat would culminate in a wholly new society that would be free of class conflict. The victorious proletariat, by its

Major Works of Economic and Political Commentary	
1776	Adam Smith, *The Wealth of Nations*
1798	Thomas Malthus, *Essay on the Principle of Population*
1817	David Ricardo, *Principles of Political Economy*
1830s	Harriet Martineau, *Illustrations of Political Economy*
1839	Louis Blanc, *The Organization of Labor*
1845	Friedrich Engels, *The Condition of the Working Class in England*
1848	Karl Marx and Friedrich Engels, *The Communist Manifesto*

very nature, could not be a new oppressor class: "The proletarian movement is the self-conscious, independent movement of the immense majority, in the interest of the immense majority."[4] The result of the proletarian victory would be "an association, in which the free development of each is the condition for the free development of all."[5] The victory of the proletariat over the bourgeoisie would represent the culmination of human history. For the first time in human history, one group of people would not be oppressing another.

The economic environment of the 1840s had conditioned Marx's analysis. The decade had seen much unemployment and deprivation. During the later part of the century, however, capitalism did not collapse as he had predicted, nor did the middle class become proletarianized. Rather, more and more people came to benefit from the industrial system. Nonetheless, within a generation Marxism had captured the imagination of many socialists, especially in Germany, and large segments of the working class. Marxist doctrines appeared to be based on the empirical evidence of hard economic fact. This scientific claim of Marxism helped the ideology as science became more influential during the second half of the century.

[4]*Robert C. Tucker, ed.,* The Marx–Engels Reader *(New York: W. W. Norton, 1972), p. 353.*
[5]*Ibid.*

1848: Year of Revolutions

In 1848 a series of liberal and nationalistic revolutions erupted across the Continent. No single factor caused this general revolutionary groundswell; rather, similar conditions existed in several countries. Severe food shortages had prevailed since 1846. Grain and potato harvests had been poor. The famine in Ireland was simply the worst example of a more widespread situation. The commercial and industrial economy was also depressed. Unemployment was widespread. All systems of poor relief were overburdened. These difficulties, added to the wretched living conditions in the cities, heightened the sense of frustration and discontent of the urban artisan and laboring classes.

The dynamic force for change in 1848 originated, however, not with the working classes but with the political liberals, who were generally drawn from the middle classes. Throughout the Continent, liberals were pushing for their program of more representative government, civil liberty, and unregulated economic life. The repeal of the English Corn Laws and the example of peaceful agitation by the Anti–Corn Law League encouraged them. The liberals on the Continent wanted to pursue similar peaceful tactics. To put additional pressure on their governments, however, they began to appeal for the support of the urban working classes. The goals of the latter were improved working and economic conditions rather than a liberal framework of government. Moreover, the tactics of the working classes were frequently violent rather than peaceful. The temporary alliance of liberals and workers in several states overthrew or severely shook the old order; then the allies began to fight each other.

Finally, outside France, nationalism was an important common factor in the uprisings. Germans, Hungarians, Italians, Czechs, and smaller national groups in eastern Europe sought to create national states that would reorganize or replace existing political entities. The Austrian Empire, as usual, was the state most profoundly endangered by nationalism. At the same time, however, various national groups clashed with each other during these revolutions.

The immediate results of the 1848 revolutions were stunning. Never in a single year had Europe known so many major uprisings. The French monarchy fell, and many other thrones were badly shaken. Yet the revolutions proved a false spring for progressive Europeans. Without exception, the revolutions failed to establish genuinely liberal or national states. The conservative order proved stronger and more resilient than anyone had expected. Moreover, the liberal middle-class political activists in each country discovered that they could no longer push for political reform without also raising the social question. The liberals refused to follow political revolution with social reform and thus isolated themselves from the working classes. Once separated from potential mass support, the liberal revolutions became an easy prey to the armies of the reactionary classes.

France: The Second Republic and Louis Napoleon

As had happened twice before, the revolutionary tinder first blazed in Paris. The liberal political opponents of the corrupt regime of Louis Philippe and his minister Guizot had organized a series of political banquets. These occasions were used to criticize the government and to demand further middle-class admission to the political process. The poor harvests of 1846 and 1847 and the resulting high food prices and unemployment brought working-class support to the liberal campaign. On February 21, 1848, the government forbade further banquets. A large one had been scheduled for the next day. On February 22, disgruntled Parisian workers paraded through the streets demanding reform and Guizot's ouster. The next morning the crowds grew, and by afternoon Guizot had resigned. The crowds had erected barricades, and numerous clashes had occurred between the citizenry and the municipal guard. On February 24, 1848, Louis Philippe abdicated and fled to England.

THE NATIONAL ASSEMBLY AND PARIS WORKERS The liberal opposition, led by the poet Alphonse de Lamartine (1790–1869), organized a provisional government. They intended to call an election for an assembly that would write a republican constitution. The various working-class groups in Paris had other ideas; they wanted a social as well as a political revolu-

During the February days of the French Revolution of 1848 crowds in Paris burned the throne of Louis Philippe. [Bildarchiv Preussischer Kulturbesitz]

tion. Led by Louis Blanc, they demanded representation in the cabinet. Blanc and two other radical leaders were made ministers. Under their pressure, the provisional government organized national workshops to provide work and relief for thousands of unemployed workers.

On Sunday, April 23, an election based on universal manhood suffrage chose the new National Assembly. The result was a legislature dominated by moderates and conservatives. In the French provinces, there had been much resentment against the Paris radicals. The Church and the local notables still exercised considerable influence. Small landowning peasants feared possible confiscation of their holdings by Parisian socialists. The new conservative National Assembly had little sympathy for the expensive national workshops, which they incorrectly perceived to be socialistic.

Throughout May, government troops and the Parisian crowd of unemployed workers and artisans clashed. As a result, the assembly closed the workshops to new entrants and planned the removal of many enrolled workers. By late June, barricades again appeared in Paris. On June 24, under orders from the government, General Cavaignac (1802–1857), with troops drawn largely from the conservative countryside, moved to destroy the barricades and to quell potential disturbances. During the next two days, more than 400 people were killed. Thereafter, troops hunted down another 3,000 persons in street-to-street fighting. The drive for social revolution had ended.

EMERGENCE OF LOUIS NAPOLEON The so-called June Days confirmed the political predominance of conservative property holders in French life. They wanted a state safe for small property. This search for social order received further confirmation late in 1848. The victor in the presidential election was Louis Napoleon Bonaparte (1808–1873), a nephew of the great emperor. For most of his life, he had been an

L'ILLUSTRATION,
JOURNAL UNIVERSEL.

Ab pour Paris, 3 mois, 8 fr. — 6 mois, 16 fr. — Un an, 30 fr.
Prix de chaque N°, 75 c. — La collection mensuelle, br., 2 fr. 75.

N°° 279-280. Vol. XI. — SAMEDIS 1er - 8 JUILLET 1848.
Bureaux : rue Richelieu, 60.

Ab pour les dép. — 3 mois, 9 fr. — 6 mois, 17 fr. — Un an, 32 fr.
Ab. pour l'Étranger, — 10 fr. — 20 fr. — 40 fr.

SOMMAIRE.

Insurrection de juin 1848. — 13 gravures — Barricades du faubourg Saint-Martin, du faubourg Saint-Antoine, de cité Saint-Lazare, Saint-Maur, etc. — La Population pendant et après le combat. — Aspect de Paris. — Portraits de l'archevêque de Paris, du général Négrier, et cinq gardes mobiles. — Exposition du général Bréa et la convocadures au Panthéon. — Casses de prisonniers. — Destruction des ambulances. — Épreuves divers. — Combat dans les carrières Montmartre. — Revue, Faits, etc.

Insurrection de juin 1848.

Nous avons une œuvre spéciale à accomplir, c'est de montrer, autant que peut le faire l'art qui sert de moyen et d'instrument à notre publication, les principaux épisodes de l'horrible attentat qui vient d'épouvanter la France et de mettre en péril la civilisation. Nous ne retracerons pas, après tant d'autres témoins oculaires,

après tant de récits empruntés aux acteurs même du drame, tous les traits déjà recueillis dans la mémoire de nos lecteurs. Notre récit se bornera aux faits principaux, aux traits saillants, aux actes qui serviront plus tard la source où puisera l'historien de ces tristes journées.

Nous aurons d'ailleurs à revenir, à l'occasion de la pompe funèbre qui vient d'émouvoir tout Paris en deuil, sur ceux qui ont succombé; nous citerons les dévouements sublimes et les pertes irréparables : l'héroïsme de Brea, de Dornès, que la mort, on

Le général Lamoricière et le colonel Bapatel, à la tête d'un détachement du 11° léger et de la 3° compagnie du 4° bataillon de la 9° légion commandé par les capitaines Oud t et Ferelle, parlementant avec les insurgés de la barricade de la caserne du faubourg Saint-Martin.

During June 1848, troops moved against the insurrection in Paris. This edition of a French journal is reporting those events and illustrates a moment before a clash between troops and revolutionaries. [Bildarchiv Preussischer Kulturbesitz]

---

adventurer living outside France. Twice he had attempted to lead a coup against the July Monarchy. The disorder of 1848 gave him a new opportunity to enter French political life. After the corruption of Louis Philippe and the turmoil of the early months of the Second Republic, the voters turned to the name of Bonaparte as a source of stability and greatness.

The election of the "Little Napoleon" doomed the Second Republic. Louis Napoleon was dedicated to his own fame rather than to republican institutions. He was the first of the modern dictators who, by playing on unstable politics and social insecurity, greatly changed European life. He constantly quarreled with the National Assembly and claimed that he rather than they represented the will of the nation. In 1851 the assembly refused to amend the constitution to allow the president to run for reelection. Consequently, on December 2, 1851, the anniversary of the great Napoleon's victory at Austerlitz, Louis Napoleon seized personal power. Troops dispersed the assembly, and the president called for new elections. More than 200 people died resisting the coup, and more than 26,000 persons were arrested throughout the country. Almost 10,000 persons who opposed the coup were transported to Algeria.

Yet, in the plebiscite of December 21, 1851, more than 7.5 million voters supported the actions of Louis Napoleon and approved a new constitution that consolidated his power. Only about 600,000 citizens dared to vote against him. A year later, in December 1852, an empire was proclaimed, and Louis Napoleon became Emperor Napoleon III. Again a plebiscite approved the action. For the second time in just over fifty years, France had turned from republicanism to caesarism.

FRENCH WOMEN IN 1848 The years between the February Revolution of 1848 and the Napoleonic coup of 1852 saw major feminist activity on the part of French women. Especially in Paris, women seized the opportunity of the collapse of the July Monarchy to voice demands for reform of their social conditions. They joined the wide variety of political clubs that emerged in the wake of the revolution. Some of these clubs particularly emphasized women's rights. Some women even tried unsuccessfully to vote in the various elections of 1848. Both middle-class and working-class women were involved in these activities. The most radical group of women called themselves the *Vesuvians,* after the volcano in Italy. They claimed it was time for the demands of women to come forth like pent-up lava. They demanded full domestic household equality between men and women, the right of women to serve in the military, and similarity in dress for both sexes. They also conducted street demonstrations. The radical character of their demands and actions lost them the support of more moderate women.

Certain Parisian women quickly attempted to use for their own cause the liberal freedoms that suddenly had become available. They organized the *Voix des femmes (The Women's Voice),* a daily newspaper that addressed issues of concern to women. The newspaper insisted that improving the lot of men would not necessarily improve the condition of women. They soon organized a society with the same name as the newspaper. Many of the women involved in the newspaper and society had earlier been involved in Saint-Simonian or Fourierist groups. The *Voix des femmes* group were relatively conservative feminists. They cooperated with male political groups, and they urged the integrity of the family and fidelity in marriage. They furthermore warmly embraced the maternal role for women, but tried to use that social function to raise the importance of women in society. Because motherhood and child rearing are so important to a society, they argued, women must receive better educations, the right to work, economic security, equal civil rights, property rights, and the right to vote. The provisional government made no move to enact these rights, although some members of the assembly supported the women's groups. The emphasis on family and motherhood represented in part a defensive strategy to prevent conservative women and men from accusing the advocates of women's rights of seeking to destroy the family and traditional marriage.

The fate of French feminists in 1848 was similar to that of the radical workers. They were thoroughly defeated, and their efforts wholly frustrated. Once the elections were held that spring, the new government expressed no sympathy for their causes. The closing of the national workshops adversely affected women workers as well as men and blocked one outlet that women had used to make their needs known. The conservative crackdown on political clubs closed another arena in which women had participated. Women were soon specifically forbidden to participate in political clubs either by themselves or with men. These repressive actions repeated what had happened to politically active French women and their organizations in 1793.

At this point, women associated with the *Voix des femmes* attempted to organize workers' groups to improve the economic situation for working-class women. Two leaders of this effort, Jeanne Deroin (d. 1894) and Pauline Roland (1805–1852), were arrested, tried, and imprisoned for these activities. The former eventually went into exile from France; the latter was sent off to Algeria during the repression after the coup of Louis Napoleon. By 1852 the entire feminist movement that had sprung up in 1848 had been thoroughly eradicated.

Alexis de Tocqueville Laments the Coup of Napoleon III

Alexis de Tocqueville (1805–1859) was one of the shrewdest political observers of the first half of the nineteenth century. He was deeply troubled by what he saw as a tendency in French politics to swing from democratic excesses to dictatorship. When Louis Napoleon carried out his coup in 1851, a new dictatorship was established in France. In this letter, de Tocqueville expresses his disappointment, anger, and concern about the future.

◆ *Why does de Tocqueville blame both Louis Philippe and the revolutionaries for the emergence of Louis Napoleon? How does he portray Louis Napoleon as appealing to conservative groups in France? Why does he think it will require a foreign policy disaster to oust Louis Napoleon from power?*

. . . When I finally want to speak of our affairs, even to my best friends (. . .), a sadness so bitter and so profound seizes me that I have trouble continuing such distressing conversations or correspondence. . . . What has happened can be defined: the most odious conduct of revolutionaries has been employed to serve the grudges and above all to calm the fears of the conservative party. Indeed, one has to go back to the Committee of Public Safety and the Terror to find anything analogous in our history to what we are seeing now. . . . [De Tocqueville discusses arbitrary arrests and the exile without trial of persons to Algeria and Guiana.] But what is heartbreaking is to see the bulk of the nation applaud and feel that it is not suppressed, but supreme. Nothing shows two things more clearly: the first, the softening of souls, which the immoral government of Louis Philippe brought about; the second, the dreadful terror into which this violent, but above all mad, Revolution of February [1848] has thrown these souls, softened and ready to bear anything with joy and even to assist in anything provided that the phantom of socialism that disturbed their enjoyment by threatening their future would disappear.

Although this government has been established by one of the greatest crimes known in history [the coup of Louis Napoleon], nevertheless it will last a long enough time, unless it hastens itself to ruin. Its excesses, its wars, its corruption must make the country forget its fear of the socialist, which necessarily requires time. God be willing, in the meantime it will not find its end in a fashion nearly as prejudicial to us as to itself, in some mad foreign adventure. We know this only too well in France; governments never escape the law of their origins. This one, which arrives by means of the army, which can only endure by means of the army, which minds its popularity and even its reason for existing only in the memories of military glory, this government will be dragged fatally into wanting territorial expansion, spheres of influence, in other words, into war. This is, at least, what I fear, and what all sensible people dread with me. In war, it will surely find death, but perhaps then its death will cost us very dearly.

Alexis de Tocqueville to Henry Reeve, January, 9, 1852, as quoted in Alexis de Tocqueville, Selected Letters on Politics and Society, *ed. by Roger Boesche, trans. by James Toupin and Roger Boesche (Berkeley: University of California Press, 1985), pp. 283–284.*

The Habsburg Empire: Nationalism Resisted

The events of February 1848 in Paris immediately reverberated throughout the Habsburg domains. The empire was susceptible to revolutionary challenge on every score. Its government rejected liberal institutions. Its borders cut across national lines. Its society perpetuated serfdom. During the 1840s, even Metternich had urged reform, but none was forthcoming. In 1848 the regime confronted major rebellions in Vienna, Prague, Hungary, and Italy. It was also intimately concerned about the disturbances that broke out in Germany.

THE VIENNA UPRISING The Habsburg troubles began on March 3, 1848, when Louis Kossuth (1802–1894), a Magyar nationalist and member of the Hungarian Diet, attacked Austrian domination of Hungary, called for the independence of Hungary, and demanded a responsible ministry under the Habsburg dynasty. Ten days later, inspired by Kossuth's speeches, students led a series of major disturbances in Vienna. The army failed to restore order. Metternich resigned and fled the country. The feebleminded Emperor Ferdinand (r. 1835–1848) promised a moderately liberal constitution. Unsatisfied, the radical students then formed democratic clubs to press the revolution further. On May 17, the emperor and the imperial court fled to Innsbruck. The government of Vienna at this point lay in the hands of a committee of more than 200 persons primarily concerned with alleviating the economic plight of Viennese workers.

What the Habsburg government actually most feared was not the urban rebellions but a potential uprising of the serfs in the countryside. Already there had been isolated instances of serfs invading manor houses and burning records. Almost immediately after the Vienna uprising, the imperial government had emancipated the serfs in much of Austria. The Hungarian Diet also abolished serfdom in March 1848. These actions smothered the most serious potential threat to order in the empire. The emancipated serfs now had little reason to support the revolutionary movement in the cities. These emancipations were one of the most important permanent results of the Revolutions of 1848.

THE MAGYAR REVOLT The Vienna revolt had further encouraged the Hungarians. The Magyar leaders of the Hungarian March Revolution were primarily liberals supported by

Louis Kossuth, a Magyar nationalist, seeking to raise troops to fight for Hungarian independence during the revolutionary disturbances of 1848. [Bildarchiv Preussischer Kulturbesitz]

nobles who wanted their aristocratic liberties guaranteed against the central government in Vienna. The Hungarian Diet passed a series of March Laws that ensured equality of religion, jury trials, the election of a lower chamber, a relatively free press, and payment of taxes by the nobility. Emperor Ferdinand approved these measures, because in the spring of 1848 he could do little else.

The Magyars also hoped to establish a separate Hungarian state within the Habsburg domains. They would retain considerable local autonomy while Ferdinand remained their emperor. As part of this scheme for a partially independent state, the Hungarians attempted to annex Transylvania, Croatia, and other eastern territories of the Habsburg Empire. That policy of annexation would have brought Romanians, Croatians, and Serbs under Magyar government. These national groups resisted the drive toward Magyarization, the most important element of which was the imposition upon them of the Hungarian language. The national groups now being repressed by the Hungarians believed that they had a better chance of maintaining their national or ethnic identity, their languages, and their economic self-interest under Habsburg control. In late March the Vienna government sent Count Joseph Jellachich (1801–1859) to aid the national groups who were rebelling against the rebellious Hungarians. By early September 1848, he was leading an invasion force against Hungary with the strong support of the national groups who were resisting Magyarization. These events in Hungary represented a prime example of the clash between liberalism and nationalism. The state that the Hungarian March Laws would have governed was liberal in political structure, but it would not have allowed autonomy to the non-Magyar peoples within its borders.

CZECH NATIONALISM In the middle of March 1848, with Vienna and Budapest in revolt, Czech nationalists had demanded that Bohemia and Moravia be permitted to constitute an autonomous Slavic state within the empire similar to that just constituted in Hungary. Conflict immediately developed, however, between the Czechs and the Germans living in these regions. The Czechs summoned a congress of the Slavs including Poles, Ruthenians, Czechs, Slovaks, Croats, Slovenes, and Serbs, who met in Prague during early June. Under the leadership of Francis Palacky (1798–1876), this first Pan-Slavic Congress issued a manifesto calling for the national equality of Slavs within the Habsburg Empire. The manifesto also protested the repression of all Slavic peoples under Habsburg, Hungarian, German, and Ottoman domination. The docu-

The Pan-Slavic Congress Calls for the Liberation of Slavic Nationalities

The first Pan-Slavic Congress met in Prague in June 1848. In this "Manifesto" it called for the reorganization of the Austrian Empire and the political reorganization of most of the rest of eastern Europe. Its calls for changes in the national standing of the various Slavic peoples would have touched the Russian, Austrian, and Ottoman empires as well as some of the then un-united states of Germany. The national aspirations voiced in this document would affect Europe from that time to the present. It is also important to note that the authors recognize that the principle of nationality as adapted to the political life of Slavic peoples is relatively new in 1848.

◆ *How did the authors of this manifesto apply the individual freedoms associated with the French Revolution to the fate of individual nations? What are the specific areas of Europe that these demands would have changed? What potential national or ethnic differences among the Slavic peoples does this manifesto ignore or gloss over?*

The Slavic Congress in Prague is something unheard-of, in Europe as well as among the Slavs themselves. For the first time since our appearance in history, we, the scattered members of a great race, have gathered in great numbers from distant lands in order to become reacquainted as brothers and to deliberate our affairs peacefully. We have understood one another not only through our beautiful language, spoken by eighty millions, but also through the consonance of our hearts and the similarity of our spiritual qualities. . . .

It is not only in behalf of the individual within the state that we raise our voices and make known our demands. The nation, with all its intellectual merit, is as sacred to us as are the rights of an individual under natural law. . . .

In the belief that the powerful spiritual stream of today demands new political forms and that the state must be re-established upon altered principles, if not within new boundaries, we have suggested to the Austrian Emperor, under whose constitutional government we, the majority [of Slavic peoples] live, that he transform his imperial state into a union of equal nations. . . .

. . . We raise our voices vigorously in behalf of our unfortuante brothers, the Poles, who were robbed of their national identity by insidious force. We call upon the governments to rectify this curse and these old onerous and hereditary sins in their administrative policy, and we trust in the compassion of all Europe. . . . We demand that the Hungarian Ministry abolish without delay the use of inhuman and coercive means toward the Salvic races in Hungary, namely the Serbs, Croats, Slovaks, and Ruthenians, and that they promptly be completely assured of their national rights. Finally, we hope that the inconsiderate policies of the Porte will no longer hinder our Slavic brothers in Turkey from strongly claiming their nationality and developing it in a natural way. If, therefore, we formally express our opposition to such despicable deeds, we do so in the confidence that we are working for the good of freedom. Freedom makes the peoples who hitherto have ruled more just and makes them understand that injustice and arrogance bring disgrace not to those who must endure it but to those who act in such a manner.

From the "Manifesto of the First Pan-Slavic Congress," trans. by Max Riedlsperger from I. I. Udalzow, Aufzeichnungen über die Geschichte des nationalen und politischen Kampfes in Böhme im Jahre 1848 *(Berlin: Rutten & Loening, 1953), pp. 223–226, as quoted in Stephen Fischer-Galati, ed.,* Man, State, and Society in East European History *(New York: Praeger Publishers, 1970), pp. 156–159.*

ment raised the vision of a vast East European Slavic nation or federation of Slavic states that would extend from Poland south and eastward through Ukraine and within which Russian interests would surely dominate. Although such a state never came into being, the prospect of a unified Slavic people freed from Ottoman and Habsburg control was an important political factor in later European history. Panslavism would become a tool that Russia would use in attempts to gain the support of nationalist minorities in eastern Europe and the Balkans and to bring pressure against both the Habsburg Empire and Germany.

On June 12, the day the Pan-Slavic Congress closed, a radical insurrection broke out in Prague. General Prince Alfred Windischgraetz (1787–1862), whose wife had been killed by a stray bullet, moved his troops against the uprising. The local middle class was happy to see the radicals suppressed, as they were by June 17. The Germans in the area approved the smothering of Czech nationalism. The policy of "divide and conquer" had succeeded.

REBELLION IN NORTHERN ITALY While repelling the Hungarian and Czech bids for autonomy, the Habsburg government also faced war in northern Italy. A revolution against Habsburg domination began in Milan on March 18. Five days later the Austrian commander General Count Joseph Wenzel Radetzky (1766–1858) retreated from the city. King Charles Albert of Piedmont (r. 1831–1849), who wanted to expand the influence of his kingdom in Lombardy (the province of which Milan is the capital), aided the rebels. The Austrian forces fared badly until July, when Radetzky, reinforced by new troops, defeated Piedmont and suppressed the revolution. For the time being, Austria had held its position in northern Italy.

Vienna and Hungary remained to be recaptured. In midsummer the emperor returned to the capital. A newly elected assembly was trying to write a constitution, while within the city the radicals continued to press for further concessions. The imperial government decided to reassert its control. When a new insurrection occurred in October, the imperial army bombarded Vienna and crushed the revolt. On December 2, Emperor Ferdinand, now clearly too feeble to govern, abdicated in favor of his young nephew Francis Joseph (r. 1848–1916). Real power now lay with Prince Felix Schwarzenberg (1800–1852), who intended to use the army with full force.

On January 5, 1849, troops occupied Budapest. By March the triumphant Austrian forces had imposed military rule over Hungary, and the new emperor repudiated the recent constitution. The Magyar nobles attempted one last revolt. In August Austrian troops reinforced by 200,000 soldiers happily furnished by Tsar Nicholas I of Russia (r. 1825–1855) finally crushed the Hungarian revolt. Croatians and other nationalities who had resisted Magyarization welcomed the collapse of the Hungarian revolt. The imperial Habsburg government had survived its gravest internal challenge because of the divisions among its enemies and its own willingness to use military force with a vengeance.

Italy: Republicanism Defeated

The brief Piedmont–Austrian war of 1848 marked only the first stage of the Italian revolution. Many Italians hoped that King Charles Albert of Piedmont would drive Austria from the peninsula and thus prepare the way for Italian unification. The defeat of Piedmont was a sharp disappointment to them. Liberal and nationalist hopes then shifted to the pope. Pius IX (r. 1846–1878) had a liberal reputation. He had reformed the administration of the Papal States. Nationalists believed that some form of a united Italian state might emerge under the leadership of this pontiff.

In Rome, however, as in other cities, political radicalism was on the rise. On November 15, 1848, a democratic radical assassinated Count Pelligrino Rossi (r. 1787–1848), the liberal minister of the Papal States. The next day, popular demonstrations forced the pope to appoint a radical ministry. Shortly thereafter, Pius IX fled to Naples for refuge. In February 1849, the radicals proclaimed the Roman Republic. Republican nationalists from all over Italy, including Giuseppe Mazzini (1805–1872) and Giuseppe Garibaldi (1807–1882), two of the most prominent, flocked to Rome. They hoped to use the new republic as a base of operations to unite the rest of Italy under a republican government.

In March 1849, radicals in Piedmont forced Charles Albert to renew the patriotic war against Austria. After the almost immediate defeat of Piedmont at the Battle of Novara, the king abdicated in favor of his son, Victor Emmanuel II (r. 1849–1878). The defeat meant that the Roman Republic must defend itself alone. The troops that attacked Rome and restored the pope came from France. The French wanted to prevent the rise of a strong, unified state on their southern border. Moreover, protection of the pope was good domestic politics for the French Republic and its president, Louis Napoleon. In early June 1849, 10,000 French soldiers laid siege to Rome. By the end of the month, the Roman Republic had dissolved. Garibaldi attempted to lead an army north against Austria but was defeated. On July 3, Rome fell to the French forces, which stayed there to protect the pope until 1870.

Pius IX returned, having renounced his previous liberalism. He became one of the archconservatives of the next quarter century. Leadership toward Italian unification would have to come from another direction.

Germany: Liberalism Frustrated

The revolutionary contagion had also spread rapidly through numerous states of Germany. Württemberg, Saxony, Hanover, and Bavaria all experienced insurrections calling for liberal government and greater German unity. The major revolution, however, occurred in Prussia.

REVOLUTION IN PRUSSIA By March 15, 1848, large popular disturbances had erupted in Berlin. Frederick William IV (r. 1840–1861), believing that the trouble stemmed from foreign conspirators, refused to turn his troops on the Berliners. He even announced certain limited reforms. Nevertheless, on March 18, several citizens were killed when troops cleared a square near the palace.

The monarch was still hesitant to use his troops forcefully, and there was much confusion in the government. The king also called for a Prussian constituent assembly to write a constitution. The next day, as angry Berliners crowded around the palace, Frederick William IV appeared on the balcony to salute the corpses of his slain subjects. He made further concessions and implied that henceforth Prussia would aid the movement toward German unification. For all practical purposes, the Prussian monarchy had capitulated.

Frederick William IV appointed a cabinet headed by David Hansemann (1790–1864), a widely respected moderate liberal. The Prussian constituent assembly, however, proved to be rad-

German revolutionaries behind a street barricade in Berlin prepare for an assault from forces loyal to King Frederick William IV, March 18–19, 1848. [The Bettmann Archive]

ical and democratic. As time passed, the king and his conservative supporters decided that they would ignore the assembly. The liberal ministry resigned and was replaced by a conservative one. In April 1849, the assembly was dissolved, and the monarch proclaimed his own constitution. One of its key elements was a system of three-class voting. All adult males were allowed to vote. They voted, however, according to three classes arranged by ability to pay taxes. Thus, the largest taxpayers, who constituted only about 5 percent of the population, elected one-third of the Prussian Parliament. This system prevailed in Prussia until 1918. In the finally revised Prussian constitution of 1850, the ministry was responsible to the king alone. Moreover, the Prussian army and officer corps swore loyalty directly to the monarch.

THE FRANKFURT PARLIAMENT While Prussia was moving from revolution to reaction, other events were unfolding in Germany as a whole. On May 18, 1848, representatives from all the German states gathered in Saint Paul's Church in Frankfurt to revise the organization of the German Confederation. The Frankfurt Parliament intended to write a moderately liberal constitution for a united Germany. The liberal character of the Frankfurt Parliament alienated both German conservatives and the German working class. The offense to the conservatives was simply the challenge to the existing political order. The Frankfurt Parliament lost the support of the industrial workers and artisans by refusing to restore the protection once afforded by the guilds. The liberals were too attached to the concept of a free labor market to offer meaningful legislation to workers. This failure marked the beginning of a profound split between German liberals and the German working class. For the rest of the century, German conservatives would be able to play on that division.

As if to demonstrate its disaffection from workers, in September 1848, the Frankfurt Parliament called in troops of the German Confederation to suppress a radical insurrection in the city. The liberals in the parliament wanted nothing to do with workers who erected barricades and threatened the safety of property.

The Frankfurt Parliament also floundered on the issue of unification. Members differed over including Austria in the projected united Germany. The large German (*grossdeutsch*) solution favored inclusion, whereas the small German (*kleindeutsch*) solution advocated exclusion. The latter formula prevailed because Austria rejected the whole notion of German unification, which raised too many other nationality problems within the Habsburg domains. Consequently, the Frankfurt Parliament looked to Prussian rather than Austrian leadership.

On March 27, 1849, the parliament produced its constitution. Shortly thereafter, its delegates offered the crown of a united Germany to Frederick William IV of Prussia. He rejected the offer, asserting that kings ruled by the grace of God rather than by the permission of manmade constitutions. On his refusal, the Frankfurt Parliament began to dissolve. Not long afterward troops drove off the remaining members.

German liberals never fully recovered from this defeat. The Frankfurt Parliament had alienated the artisans and the working class without gaining any compensating support from the conservatives. The liberals had proved themselves to be awkward, hesitant, unrealistic, and ultimately dependent on the armies of the monarchies. They had failed to unite Germany or to confront effectively the realities of political power in the German states. The various revolutions did achieve an extension of the franchise in some of the German states and the establishment of conservative constitutions. The gains were not negligible, but they were a far cry from the hopes of March 1848.

———————————◆———————————

The first half of the nineteenth century had witnessed enormous, unprecedented social change in Europe. The foundations of the industrial economy were laid. Virtually no existing institution was untouched by that emerging economy. Railways crossed the Continent. New consumer goods were available. Family patterns changed, as did the social and economic expectations of women. The crowding of cities presented new social and political problems. Issues of social order came to the fore with the new concern about crime and the establishment of new police forces. An urban working class became

The Revolutionary Crisis of 1848–1851

1848

February 22–24 Revolution in Paris forces the abdication of Louis Philippe

February 26 National workshops established in Paris

March 3 Kossuth attacks the Habsburg domination of Hungary

March 13 Revolution in Vienna

March 15 The Habsburg emperor accepts the Hungarian March Revolution Laws in Berlin

March 18 Frederick William IV of Prussia promises a constitution Revolution in Milan

March 19 Frederick William IV is forced to salute the corpses of slain revolutionaries in Berlin

March 22 Piedmont declares war on Austria

April 23 Election of the French National Assembly

May 15 Worker protests in Paris lead the National Assembly to close the national workshops

May 17 Habsburg Emperor Ferdinand flees from Vienna to Innsbruck

May 18 The Frankfurt Assembly gathers to prepare a German constitution

June 2 Pan-Slavic Congress gathers in Prague

June 17 A Czech revolution in Prague is suppressed

June 23–26 A workers' insurrection in Paris is suppressed by the troops of the National Assembly

July 24 Austria defeats Piedmont

September 17 General Jellachich invades Hungary

October 31 Vienna falls to the bombardment of General Windisch-Graetz

November 15 Papal minister Rossi is assassinated in Rome

November 16 Revolution in Rome

November 25 Pope Pius IX flees Rome

December 2 Habsburg Emperor Ferdinand abdicates and Francis Joseph becomes emperor

December 10 Louis Napoleon is elected president of the Second French Republic

1849

January 5 General Windischgraetz occupies BudapestFebruary 2 The Roman Republic is proclaimed

March 12 War is resumed between Piedmont and Austria

March 23 Piedmont is defeated, and Charles Albert abdicates the crown of Piedmont in favor of Victor Emmanuel II

March 27 The Frankfurt Parliament completes a constitution for Germany

March 28 The Frankfurt Parliament elects Frederick William IV of Prussia to be emperor of Germany

April 21 Frederick William IV of Prussia rejects the crown offered by the Frankfurt Parliament

June 18 The remaining members of the Frankfurt Parliament are dispersed by troops

July 3 Collapse of the Roman Republic after invasion by French troops

August 9–13 The Hungarian forces are defeated by Austria aided by Russian troops

1851

December 2 Coup d'état of Louis Napoleon

---

one of the chief facts of both political and social life. The ebb and flow of the business cycle caused increased economic anxiety for workers and property owners alike.

While all these fundamental social changes took place, Europe was also experiencing contin-uing political strife. The turmoil of 1848 through 1850 ended the era of liberal revolution that had begun in 1789. Liberals and nationalists had discovered that rational argument and small insurrections would not achieve their goals. The political initiative passed for a time to the conservative political groups. Nationalists hence-forth were less romantic and more hardheaded. Railways, commerce, guns, soldiers, and devious diplomacy rather than language and cultural heritage became the future weapons of national unification. The working class also adopted new tactics and organization. The era of the riot and urban insurrection was also ending. In the future, workers would turn to trade unions and political parties to achieve their political and social goals.

Perhaps most important after 1848, the European middle class ceased to be revolutionary. It became increasingly concerned about protecting its property against radical political and social movements associated with socialism and, increasingly, as the century passed, with Marxism. The middle class remained politically liberal only so long as liberalism seemed to promise economic stability and social security for its own style of life.

Review Questions

1. What inventions were particularly important in the development of industrialism? What changes did industrialism make in society? Why were the years covered in this chapter so difficult for artisans? What is meant by the expression, "the proletarianization of workers"?

2. In what ways did the industrial economy change the working-class family? What roles and duties did various family members assume? Most specifically, how did the role of women change in the new industrial era?

3. What were the goals of the working class in the new industrial society and how did they differ from middle-class goals? How do you explain the separation of working-class and middle-class goals?

4. How did police change in the nineteenth century and why were new systems of enforcement instituted? In what ways were prisons improved and how do you account for the reform movement that led to the improvements?

5. How would you define socialism? What were the chief ideas of the early socialists? How did the ideas of Karl Marx differ from earlier writers?

6. What factors, old and new, led to the widespread outbreak of revolutions in 1848? Were the causes in the various countries essentially the same or did each have its own particular set of circumstances? Why did these revolutions fail throughout Europe? What roles did liberals and nationalists play in these revolutions? Why did they sometimes clash?

Suggested Readings

B. S. ANDERSON and J. P. ZINSSER, *A History of Their Own: Women in Europe from Prehistory to the Present*, Vol. II (1988). A wide-ranging survey.

S. AVINERI, *The Social and Political Thought of Karl Marx* (1969). An advanced treatment.

I. BERLIN, *Karl Marx: His Life and Environment* (1948). An excellent introduction.

P. BROCK, *The Slovak National Awakening* (1976). A standard work.

R. B. CARLISLE, *The Proffered Crown: Saint-Simonianism and the Doctrine of Hope* (1987). The best treatment of the broad social doctrines of Saint-Simonianism.

W. COLEMAN, *Death Is a Social Disease: Public Health and Political Economy in Early Industrial France* (1982). One of the first works in English to study this problem.

I. DEAK, *The Lawful Revolution: Louis Kossuth and the Hungarians, 1848–1849* (1979). The most significant study of the topic in English.

J. ELSTER, *An Introduction to Karl Marx* (1985). The best volume to provide a discussion of Marx's fundamental concepts.

T. HAMEROW, *Restoration, Revolution, and Reaction: Economics and Politics in Germany, 1815–1871* (1958). Traces the forces that worked toward the failure of revolution in Germany.

R. F. HAMILTON, *The Bourgeois Epoch: Marx and Engels on Britain, France, and Germany* (1991). Examines Marx and Engels's observations against what is known to have been the situation in each nation.

J. F. C. HARRISON, *Quest for the New Moral World: Robert Owen and the Owenites in Britain and America* (1969). Now the standard work.

R. HEILBRONER, *The Worldly Philosophers*, rev. ed. (1972). A useful, elementary introduction to nineteenth-century economic thought.

G. HIMMELFARB, *The Idea of Poverty: England in the Early Industrial Age* (1984). A major work covering the subject from the time of Adam Smith through 1850.

M. Ignatieff, *A Just Measure of Pain: The Penitentiary in the Industrial Revolution, 1750–1850* (1978). An important treatment of early English penal thought and practice.

K. Kolakowski, *Main Currents of Marxism: Its Rise, Growth, and Dissolution*, 3 vols. (1978). An important and comprehensive survey.

D. Landes, *The Unbound Prometheus: Technological Change and Industrial Development in Western Europe from 1750 to the Present* (1969). The best one-volume treatment of technological development in a broad social and economic context.

W. L. Langer, *Political and Social Upheaval, 1832–1852* (1969). A remarkably thorough survey strong in both social and intellectual history as well as political narrative.

F. Manuel, *The Prophets of Paris* (1962). A stimulating treatment of French utopian socialism and social reform.

T. W. Margadant, *French Peasants in Revolt: The Insurrection of 1851* (1979). A study of the rural resistance to Louis Napoleon.

J. M. Merriman, *The Agony of the Republic: The Repression of the Left in Revolutionary France, 1848–1851* (1978). A major study of how the Second French Republic and popular support for it were suppressed.

C. G. Moses, *French Feminism in the Nineteenth Century* (1984). Includes important chapters on French feminism in 1848.

P. O'Brien, *The Promise of Punishment: Prisons in Nineteenth-Century France* (1982). An excellent treatment of the problems of life within the prison.

H. Perkin, *The Origins of Modern English Society, 1780–1880* (1969). A provocative attempt to look at the society as a whole.

I. Pinchbeck, *Women Workers and the Industrial Revolution, 1750–1850* (1930, rep. 1969). A pioneering study that remains of great value.

D. H. Pinkney, *Decisive Years in France, 1840–47* (1986). A detailed and careful examination of the years leading up to the Revolution of 1848.

P. Robertson, *An Experience of Women: Pattern and Change in Nineteenth-Century Europe* (1982). A useful survey.

W. H. Sewell, Jr., *Work and Revolution in France: The Language of Labor from the Old Regime to 1848* (1980). A fine analysis of French artisans.

N. Smelzer, *Social Change in the Industrial Revolution: An Application of Theory to the British Cotton Industry* (1959). Important sections on the working-class family.

D. Sorkin, *The Transformation of German Jewry, 1780–1840* (1987). An examination of the decades of Jewish emancipation in Germany.

P. Stearns, *Eighteen Forty-Eight: The Tide of Revolution in Europe* (1974). A good discussion of the social background.

L. S. Strumingher, *Women and the Making of the Working Class: Lyon, 1830–1870* (1979). A local study from which broader generalizations can be made.

G. D. Sussman, *Selling Mother's Milk: The Wetnursing Business in France, 1715–1914* (1982). An examination of an important subject in the history of the family and of women.

D. Thompson, *The Chartists: Popular Politics in the Industrial Revolution* (1984). An important study.

E. P. Thompson, *The Making of the English Working Class* (1964). An influential and controversial work.

L. A. Tilly and J. W. Scott, *Women, Work, and Family* (1978). A useful and sensitive survey.

A. S. Wohl, *Endangered Lives: Public Health in Victorian Britain* (1983). A wide-ranging examination of the health problems created by urbanization and industrialization.

C. Woodham-Smith, *The Great Hunger: Ireland, 1845–1849* (1962). A moving account of one of the great social tragedies of the nineteenth century.

G. Wright, *Between the Guillotine and Liberty: Two Centuries of the Crime Problem in France* (1983). A useful overview.

H. Zehr, *Crime and the Development of Modern Society: Patterns of Criminality in Nineteenth-Century Germany and France* (1976). An examination of crimes against property in urban society.

Toward the Modern World

THE CENTURY between approximately 1850 and 1945 may quite properly be regarded as the European era of world history. The nations of Europe achieved and exercised an unprecedented measure of political, economic, and military power across the globe. No less impressive than the extent of this influence was its brevity. By 1945 much of Europe, from Britain to the Soviet Union, literally lay in ruins. Within a few years, the United States and the Soviet Union would emerge as superpowers with whom no European state could compete. Furthermore, nations throughout Asia, Africa, and Latin America that had once experienced direct or indirect European rule would soon thrust off their colonial status. Both the rise and the decline of European world dominance fostered violence, warfare, and human exploitation all over the globe.

The half century after 1850 witnessed political consolidation and economic expansion that paved the way for the momentary dominance of Europe. The skillful diplomats and armies of the conservative monarchies of Piedmont and Prussia united Italy and Germany by military force. As a major new political and economic power in central Europe, Germany loomed as a potential rival to Great Britain, France, and Russia. For a time, shrewd diplomacy and a series of complex alliances contained that rivalry. At the same time, while sorting out the new power relationships on the continent, the nations of Europe exported potential conflicts overseas. The result of this externalized rivalry was a period of imperialistic ventures. By the turn of the century, these had resulted in the outright partition of Africa into areas directly governed by Europeans and in the penetration of China by European merchants, administrators, and missionaries.

What permitted this unprecedented situation to arise was the economic and technological base of late-nineteenth-century European civilization. Europeans possessed the productive capacity to dominate world markets. Their banks controlled or influenced vast amounts of capital throughout the world. Their engineers constructed and later often managed railways on all the continents. Their military technology, especially their navies, allowed them to back up economic power with armed force.

With the expansion of industrial power, new political ideologies came to the fore in Europe. Across the continent, socialists challenged the ideology of liberalism and spawned internal disputes that have influenced European political life to the present day. The supporters of nationalism, the other dominant political ideology, challenged the legitimacy of any political arrangement that was not based on ethnicity or failed to recognize it. Nowhere was nationalism a more troubling force than in the multinational Habsburg Empire.

In 1914 Europe's general dominance came to an abrupt end when war, growing out of imperialistic and nationalistic rivalry, erupted among its major states. That conflict may be regarded as the central event of the twentieth century. Its effects continue to influence the world today. The Austro-Hungarian monarchy collapsed. Germany became a republic. The revolutionary socialist government of the Bolsheviks replaced the imperial government of the Russian tsars.

Social turmoil and economic dislocation accompanied the political revolutions. The victorious nations of Britain, France, and Italy had lost millions of young men, and much of their wealth had been exhausted by wartime expenditures. The military and financial participation of the United States blocked the establishment of independent economic policy by the European powers. Continuing nationalistic resentments fostered by the Paris Peace Settlement of 1919, in combination with the political and economic pressures of the 1920s and 1930s, created stressful conditions from which arose the authoritarian movements of Italian Fascism and German Nazism. By 1939 the aggression of Germany and the hesitant response of the other major powers led again to the outbreak of war in Europe. From that conflict, Europe failed to reemerge as the dominant political or economic force in the world.

Two other developments also contributed to the end of the European era of world history. First, the principle of national self-determination, applied to Europeans in the 1919 settlement, was adopted by colonial peoples asserting their own right to national independence. Second, the demand for self-determination soon became linked to a critique of foreign capitalist domination of colonial economic life, a critique flowing directly from the spread of communist ideas throughout the colonial world after the Russian Revolution. Thus, the peoples of Asia, Africa, and Latin America adopted the European ideologies of nationalism and revolutionary socialism as a solution to their own problems, turning them against their source. ◆

1850–1890	*1851* Louis Napoleon seizes power in France *1854–1856* Crimean War *1861* Proclamation of the Kingdom of Italy *1862* Bismarck becomes prime minister of Prussia *1864* First International founded *1867* Austro-Hungarian Dual Monarchy founded *1868* Gladstone becomes British prime minister *1869* Suez Canal completed *1870* Franco-Prussian War; French Republic proclaimed *1871* German Empire proclaimed; Paris Commune *1874* Disraeli becomes British prime minister *1875* Britain gains control of Suez *1880s* Britain establishes Protectorate in Egypt *1881* People's Will assassinates Alexander II; Three Emperor's League is renewed *1882* Italy, Germany, Austria form Triple Alliance *1884–1885* Germany forms African protectorates *1888* William II becomes German emperor

1890–1918	*1894* Dreyfus convicted in France; Nicholas II
	    becomes tsar of Russia
	1898 Germany begins to build a battleship navy
	1902 British Labour Party formed
	1903 Bolshevik–Menshevik split
	1904 Britain and France in Entente Cordiale
	1905 Revolution in St. Petersburg suppressed; first
	    Moroccan crisis
	1906 Dreyfus conviction set aside
	1908–1909 Bosnian crisis
	1911 Second Moroccan crisis
	1912 Third Irish Home Rule Bill passed
	1912–1913 First and Second Balkan Wars
	1914–1918 World War I
	1917 Russian Revolution; Bolsheviks seize power

1918–1939	*1919* Paris Peace Conference; Weimar Constitution
	    proclaimed in Germany
	1922 Mussolini takes power in Italy
	1923 France invades the Ruhr; Hitler's Beer Hall
	    Putsch; first Labour government in Britain
	1924 Death of Lenin
	1925 Locarno Agreements
	1931 National Government formed in Great Britain
	1933 Hitler appointed chancellor of Germany
	1935 Nuremburg Laws; Italy invades Ethiopia
	1936 Popular Front in France; purge trials in the
	    Soviet Union; Spanish Civil War begins
	1938 Munich Conference; *Kristallnacht* in
	    Germany
	1939 Germany invades Poland, starts World War II

Society and Economy	Religion and Culture
1850–1910 Height of European outward migration	*1850–1880* Jewish emancipation in much of Europe
1853–1870 Haussmann redesigns Paris	*1853–1854* Gobineau, *Essay on the Inequality of the Human Races*
1857 Bessemer steel-making process	
1861 Serfdom abolished in Russia	*1857* Flaubert, *Madame Bovary*
	1859 Darwin, *The Origin of Species*
	1864 Pius IX, *Syllabus of Errors*
1870 Education Act and first Irish Land Act, Britain	*1867* Mill, *The Subjection of Women*
	1869 Disestablishment of the Irish church
	1871 Darwin, *The Descent of Man;* Religious tests abolished at Oxford and Cambridge
1875 Public Health and Artisan Dwelling Acts, Britain	*1872* Nietzsche, *The Birth of Tragedy*
	1873–1876 Bismarck's *Kulturkampf*
1881 Second Irish Land Act	*1879* Ibsen, *A Doll's House*
	1880s Growing anti-Semitism in Europe
	1880 Zola, *Nana*
	1883 Mach, *The Science of Mechanics*
1886 Daimler invents internal combustion engine	*1883* Nietzsche, *Thus Spake Zarathustra*
1890s Oil begins its impact on world economy	*1892* Ibsen, *The Master Builder*
1894 Union of German Women's Organizations founded	*1893* Shaw, *Mrs. Warren's Profession*
	1896 Herzl, *The Jewish State*
1895 Diesel engine invented	*1899* Bernstein, *Evolutionary Socialism*
1897 German and Czech language equality in Austrian Empire; Russia mandates eleven-and-a-half hour workday	*1900* Freud, *The Interpretation of Dreams;* Key, *The Century of the Child*
	1902 Lenin, *What Is to Be Done?*
1901 National Council of French Women founded	*1903* Shaw, *Man and Superman*
1903 Third Irish Land Act; British Women's Social and Political Union founded; Wright brothers fly the first airplane	*1905* Weber, *The Protestant Ethic and the Spirit of Capitalism;* Termination of the Napoleonic Concordat in France
1906 Land redemption payments canceled for Russian peasants	*1907* Bergson, *Creative Evolution*
	1908 Sorel, *Reflections of Violence*
1907 Women vote on national issues in Norway	*1910* Pope Pius X requires anti-Modernist oath
1918 Vote granted to some British women	*1914* Joyce, *Portrait of the Artist as a Young Man*
1920s Worldwide commodity crisis	*1919* Barth, *Commentary on the Epistle to the Romans*
1921 Soviet Union begins New Economic Policy	*1920* Keynes, *Economic Consequences of the Peace*
1922 French Senate rejects vote for women	
1923 Rampant inflation in Germany	*1922* Joyce, *Ulysses*
1926 General strike in Great Britain	*1924* Hitler, *Mein Kampf*
1928 Britain extends full franchise to women	*1925* Woolf, *Mrs. Dalloway*
1928–1933 First Five Year Plan and agricultural collectivization in the Soviet Union	*1927* Heidegger, *Being and Time;* Mann, *Buddenbrooks*
1929 Wall Street crash	*1927* Woolf, *To the Lighthouse;* Mann, *Magic Mountain*
1932 Lausanne Conference ends German reparations	*1929* Woolf, *A Room of One's Own*
mid-1930s Nazis stimulate German economy through public works and defense spending	*1936* Keynes, *General Theory of Employment, Interest, and Money*
	1937 Orwell, *Road to Wigan Pier*
	1938 Sartre, *Nausea*

Prince Otto von Bismarck (1815–1898) was the most important statesman of the second half of the nineteenth century. He used warfare and shrewd diplomacy to lead Prussia to unify Germany. Having achieved this goal, he worked for the rest of his career to keep the peace. [Bildarchiv Preussischer Kulturbesitz]

23

The Age of Nation-States

Key Topics in This Chapter
- The unification of Italy and Germany
- The shift from empire to republic in France
- The emergence of dual monarchy in Austria-Hungary
- Reforms in Russia, including the emancipation of the serfs
- The emergence of Great Britain as the exemplary liberal state and its confrontation with Irish nationalists

---

The revolutions of 1848 had collapsed in defeat for both liberalism and nationalism. Throughout the early 1850s, conservative regimes entrenched themselves across the Continent. Yet only a quarter century later, many of the major goals of early-nineteenth-century liberals and nationalists had been accomplished. Italy and Germany were each finally united under constitutional monarchies. The Habsburg emperor had accepted constitutional government and recognized the liberties of the Magyars of

Hungary. In Russia, the tsar had emancipated the serfs. France was again a republic. Liberalism and even democracy flourished in Great Britain.

Paradoxically, most of these developments occurred under conservative leadership. Events within European international affairs compelled some governments to pursue new policies at home as well as abroad. They had to find novel methods of maintaining the loyalty of their subjects. Some conservative leaders preferred to carry out a popular policy on their own terms, so that they, rather than the liberals, would receive credit. Other leaders acted as they did because they had no choice.

The Crimean War (1853–1856)

As has so often been true in modern European history, the impetus for change originated in war. The Crimean War (1853–1856) was rooted in the long rivalry between Russia and the Ottoman Empire. Two disputes led to the conflict. First, the Ottoman Empire had recently granted Catholic France rather than Orthodox Russia the oversight of the Christian shrines in the Holy Land. Second, Russia wanted to extend its control over the Ottoman provinces of Moldavia and Walachia (now in Romania). The tsar's duty to protect Orthodox Christians in the Ottoman Empire furnished the pretext for the Russian aggression. Russia occupied the two provinces in the summer of 1853. The Ottoman Empire declared war on Russia in the autumn of that year.

The other great powers soon became involved, and a war among major European states resulted. Both France and Great Britain opposed Russian expansion in the eastern Mediterranean, where they had extensive naval and commercial interests. Napoleon III also thought that an activist foreign policy would shore up domestic support for his regime. On March 28, 1854, France and Britain declared war on Russia. Much to the disappointment of Tsar Nicholas I, Austria and Prussia remained neutral. The Austrians had their own ambitions in the Balkans, and, for the moment, Prussia followed Austrian leadership.

Both sides conducted the conflict ineptly. The ill-equipped and poorly commanded armies became bogged down along the Crimean coast of the Black Sea. In September 1855, after a long siege, the Russian fortress of Sevastopol finally fell to the French and British. In March 1856, a conference in Paris concluded the Treaty of Paris, which required Russia to surrender territory near the mouth of the Danube River, to recognize the neutrality of the Black Sea, and to renounce claims of protection over Christians in the Ottoman Empire. Even before the conference, Austria had forced Russia to withdraw from Moldavia and Walachia. The image of an invincible Russia that had prevailed across

A fortress near Sevastopol lies in ruins in August, 1855, following a bombardment during the Crimean War. [Bildarchiv Preussischer Kulturbesitz]

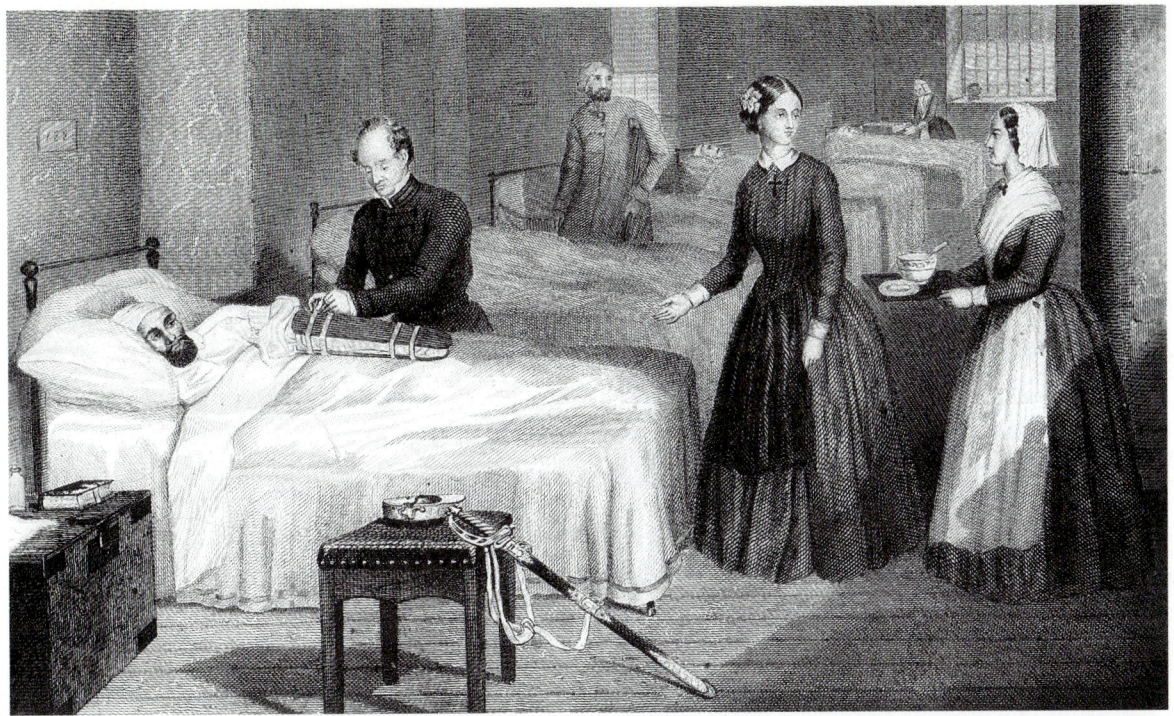

During the Crimean War, Florence Nightingale of Great Britain organized nursing care for the wounded. [The Bettmann Archive]

Europe since the close of the Napoleonic wars was shattered.

Also shattered was the Concert of Europe (see Chapter 21) as a means of dealing with international relations on the Continent. Following the successful repression of the 1848 uprisings, the great powers feared revolution less than they had earlier in the century, and consequently they displayed much less reverence for the Vienna settlement. As historian Gordon Craig once commented, "After 1856 there were more powers willing to fight to overthrow the existing order than there were to take up arms to defend it."[1] Napoleon III had little respect for the Congress of Vienna and favored redrawing the map along lines of nationality. Hoping to compensate for their failure to act during the Crimean War, the Austrians tried to assert more influence within the German Confederation. Prussia became increasingly discontented with a role in Germany subordinate to Austria's. Russia, which had been among the chief defenders of the Vienna settlement, now sought to

overcome the disgrace of the 1856 Treaty of Paris. The mediocre display of British military prowess led that nation to hesitate about future continental involvement.

Consequently, for about twenty-five years after the Crimean War, European affairs were unstable, producing a period of largely unchecked adventurism in foreign policy. Without the restraining influence of the Concert of Europe, each nation believed that only the limits of its military power and its diplomatic influence should constrain its international ambitions. Moreover, foreign policy increasingly became an instrument of domestic policy. The two most significant achievements to result from this new international situation were the unifications of Italy and Germany. Those events, in turn, put further pressures on their neighbors.

Italian Unification

Nationalists had long wanted to unite the small, absolutist principalities of the Italian peninsula

---

[1]The New Cambridge Modern History, Vol. 10 (Cambridge, England: Cambridge University Press, 1967), p. 273.

Giuseppe Mazzini was a fervent republican nationalist. He aroused emotional support for Italian unity, but also frightened moderate Italians. [Bildarchiv Preussischer Kulturbesitz]

thought may be realized in the world."[2] In 1831 he founded the Young Italy Society to drive Austria from the peninsula and establish an Italian republic.

During the 1830s and 1840s, Mazzini and his fellow republican Giuseppe Garibaldi (1807–1882) led insurrections. Both were deeply involved in the ill-fated Roman Republic of 1849. Throughout the 1850s, they continued to conduct what amounted to guerilla warfare. Because both men spent much time in exile, they became well known across the Continent and in the United States.

Republican nationalism frightened moderate Italians, who wanted to rid themselves of Austrian domination but not at the cost of establishing a republic. For a time, these people had looked to the papacy as a possible vehicle for unification. That solution became impossible after the experience of Pius IX with the Roman Republic in 1849. Consequently, at mid-century "Italy" remained a geographical expression rather than a political entity.

Yet between 1852 and 1860, the Italian peninsula was transformed into a nation-state governed by a constitutional monarchy. The process was carried out not by romantic republican nationalists but by Count Camillo Cavour (1810–1861), the moderately liberal prime minister of Piedmont. The method of unification was force of arms tied to secret diplomacy. The spirit of Machiavelli must have smiled over the enterprise.

into a single state. During the first half of the century, however, opinion differed about the manner and goals of Italian unification.

Romantic Republicans

One approach to the issue was romantic republicanism. After the Congress of Vienna, secret republican societies were founded throughout Italy, the most famous of which was the *Carbonari* ("charcoal burners"). They were singularly ineffective.

Following the failure of nationalist uprisings in 1831, the leadership of romantic republican nationalism passed to Giuseppe Mazzini (1805–1872). He became the most important nationalist leader in all Europe and brought new emotional fervor to the cause. He once declared, "Nationality is the role assigned by God to a people in the work of humanity. It is its mission, its task on earth, to the end that God's

Cavour's Policy

Piedmont (officially styled the Kingdom of Sardinia), in northwestern Italy, was the most independent state on the peninsula. The Congress of Vienna had restored the kingdom as a buffer between French and Austrian ambitions. As we have seen, during 1848 and 1849, King Charles Albert of Piedmont, after having promulgated a conservative constitution, twice unsuccessfully fought Austria. Following the second defeat, he abdicated in favor of his son, Victor Emmanuel II (r. 1849–1878). In 1852 the new monarch chose as his prime minister Count Camillo Cavour.

[2]*Quoted in William L. Langer,* Political and Social Upheaval, 1832–1852 *(New York: Harper Torchbooks, 1969), p. 115.*

A cunning statesman, Cavour had begun political life as a strong conservative but had gradually moved toward a moderately liberal position. He had made a fortune by investing in railroads, reforming agriculture on his own estates, and editing a newspaper. He was deeply imbued with the ideas of the Enlightenment, classical economics, and utilitarianism. Cavour was a nationalist of a new breed who had no respect for Mazzini's ideals. A strong monarchist, Cavour rejected republicanism. It was economic and material progress rather than romantic ideals that required a large, unified state on the Italian peninsula.

Cavour believed that if Italians proved themselves to be efficient and economically progressive, the great powers might decide that Italy could govern itself. He joined the Piedmontese Cabinet in 1850 and became premier two years later. He worked for free trade, railway construction, credit expansion, and agricultural improvement. He felt that such material and economic bonds, rather than fuzzy Romantic yearnings, must unite the Italians. Cavour also recognized the need to capture the loyalties of those Italians who believed in other varieties of nationalism. He thus fostered the Nationalist Society, which established chapters in other Italian states to press for unification under the leadership of Piedmont. Finally, the prime minister believed that Italy could be unified only with the aid of France. The recent accession of Napoleon III in France seemed to open the way for such aid.

FRENCH SYMPATHIES Cavour used the Crimean War to bring Italy into European politics. In 1855 Piedmont joined the conflict on the side of France and Britain and sent 10,000 troops to the front. This small but significant participation in the war allowed Cavour to raise the Italian question at the Paris conference. He left Paris with no diplomatic reward, but his intelligence and political capacity had impressed everyone. Cavour also gained the sympathy of Napoleon III. During the rest of the decade, he achieved further international respectability for Piedmont by opposing various plots of Mazzini, who was still attempting to lead nationalist uprisings. By 1858 Cavour represented a moderate liberal alternative to both republicanism and reactionary absolutism in Italy.

Count Camillo Cavour, the moderately liberal prime minister of the Kingdom of Piedmont, was determined to make the idea of a united Italy respectable and acceptable to the rest of Europe. [Bildarchiv Preussischer Kulturbesitz]

Cavour continued to bide his time. Then, in January 1858, an Italian named Orsini attempted to assassinate Napoleon III. The incident made the French emperor, who had once belonged to a nationalist group, newly concerned about the Italian issue. He saw himself continuing his more famous uncle's liberation of the peninsula. He also saw Piedmont as a potential ally against Austria. In July 1858, Cavour and Napoleon III met at Plombières in southern France. Riding alone in a carriage, with the emperor at the reins, the two men plotted to provoke a war in Italy that would permit them to defeat Austria. A formal treaty in December 1858 confirmed the agreement. France was to receive French-speaking Nice and Savoy from Piedmont for its aid.

WAR WITH AUSTRIA In early 1859 tension grew between Austria and Piedmont as Piedmont mobilized its army. On April 22,

Austria demanded that Piedmont demobilize. That demand allowed Piedmont to claim that Austria was provoking a war. France intervened to aid its ally. On June 4, the Austrians were defeated at Magenta, and on June 24 at Solferino. Meanwhile, revolutions had broken out in Tuscany, Modena, Parma, and the Romagna provinces of the Papal States.

With the Austrians in retreat and the new revolutionary regimes calling for union with Piedmont, Napoleon III feared too extensive a Piedmontese victory. On July 11, he indepen-

Cavour Explains Why Piedmont Should Enter the Crimean War

As prime minister of Piedmont, Cavour tried to prove that the Italians were capable of progressive government. In 1855, addressing the Parliament of Piedmont, he urged entry into the Crimean War, so that the other Europeans would consider Piedmont a military power. Earlier, politics in Italy had been characterized by petty absolute princes and romantic nationalist conspiracies, both of which Cavour scorned. He understood that in the nineteenth century a nation must possess good government, economic prosperity, and a strong army.

◆ *Why does Cavour feel it necessary to condemn conspiracies as a political device? What does Cavour believe Italy must do to raise its reputation? Why is war the test of strength and character for Italy?*

The experience of recent years and previous centuries has proved (at least in my opinion) how little Italy has benefited by conspiracies, revolutions and disorderly uprisings. Far from helping her, they have been a tremendous calamity for this beautiful part of Europe. And not only, gentlemen, because individual people so often suffered from them, not only because revolutions became the cause or pretext for repression, but above all because continual conspiracies, repeated revolutions and disorderly uprisings damaged the esteem and, up to a certain point, the sympathy that other European peoples cherished for Italy.

Now, gentlemen, I believe that the principal condition for the improvement of Italy's fate, the condition that stands out above all others, is to lift up her reputation once more, so to act that all the peoples of the world, those governing and those governed, may do justice to her qualities. And for this two things are necessary: first, to prove to Europe that Italy has sufficient civic sense to govern herself freely and according to law, and that she is in a condition to adopt the very best forms of government; second, to prove that her military valor is as great as that of her ancestors.

You have done Italy one service by your conduct over the last seven years. You have shown Europe in the most luminous way that Italians are capable of governing themselves with wisdom, prudence, and trustworthiness. But it still remains for you to do Italy an equal, if not a greater, service; it is our country's task to prove that Italy's sons can fight valiantly on battlefields where glory is to be won. And I am sure, gentlemen, that the laurels that our soldiers will win in Eastern Europe will help the future state of Italy more than all that has been done by those people who hoped to regenerate her by rhetorical speeches and writings.

As quoted in Denis Mack Smith, ed. and trans., The Making of Italy, 1796–1870 *(New York: Walker and Company, 1968), pp. 199–200.*

Giuseppe Garibaldi represented the forces of romantic Italian nationalism. The landing of his Redshirts on Sicily and their subsequent invasion of southern Italy in 1860 forced Cavour to unite the entire peninsula sooner than he had intended. [Bildarchiv Preussischer Kulturbesitz]

dently concluded a peace with Austria at Villafranca. Piedmont received Lombardy, but Venetia remained under Austrian control. Cavour felt betrayed by France, but the war had driven Austria from most of northern Italy. Later that summer, Parma, Modena, Tuscany, and the Romagna voted to unite with Piedmont (see Map 23-1).

GARIBALDI'S CAMPAIGN At this point, the forces of romantic republican nationalism compelled Cavour to pursue the complete unification of northern and southern Italy. In May 1860, Garibaldi landed in Sicily with more than 1,000 troops, who had been outfitted in the north. He captured Palermo and prepared to attack the mainland. By September he controlled the city and kingdom of Naples, probably the most corrupt example of Italian absolutism. Garibaldi had for more than two decades hoped to form a republican Italy, but Cavour forestalled him. He rushed Piedmontese troops south to confront Garibaldi. On the way, they conquered the rest of the Papal States except the area around Rome, which was protected for the pope by French troops. Garibaldi's nationalism won out over his republicanism, and he unhappily accepted the Piedmontese domination. In late 1860 Naples and Sicily voted to join the northern union forged by Piedmont.

The New Italian State

In March 1861, Victor Emmanuel II was proclaimed king of Italy. Three months later Cavour died. The new state more than ever needed his skills because Italy had, in effect, been more nearly conquered than united by Piedmont. The republicans resented the treatment of Garibaldi. The clericals resented the conquest of the Papal States. In the south, armed resistance continued until 1866 against the imposition of Piedmontese-style administration. The economies of north and south Italy were incompatible. The south was rural, poor, and backward. The north was industrializing, and its economy was increasingly linked to the rest of Europe. The social structures of the two regions reflected those differences, with large landholders and peasants dominant in the south and an urban working class emerging in the north.

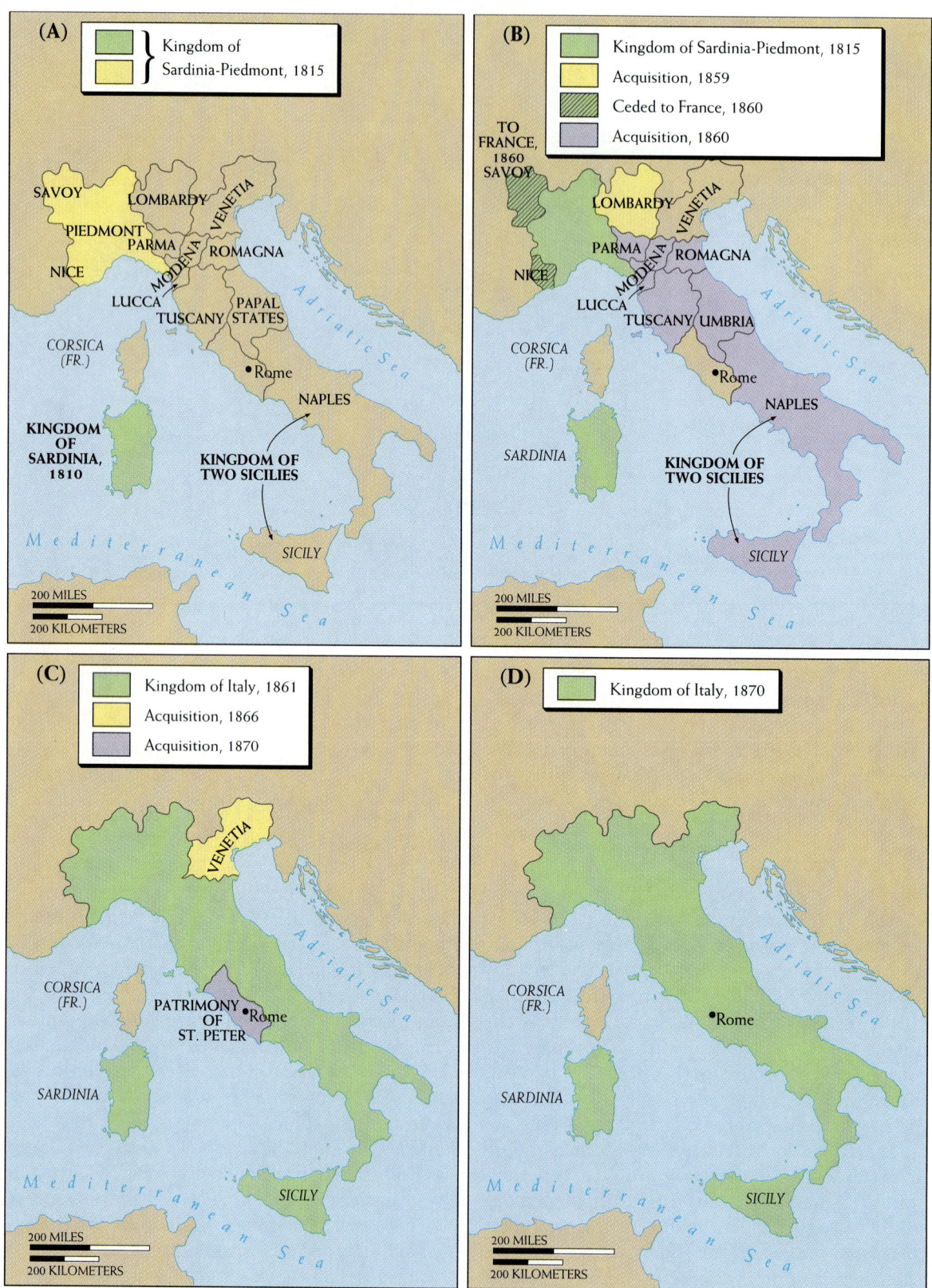

(A)

Kingdom of Sardinia-Piedmont, 1815

SAVOY
LOMBARDY
PIEDMONT
VENETIA
PARMA
NICE
MODENA
ROMAGNA
LUCCA
TUSCANY
PAPAL STATES
CORSICA (FR.)
• Rome
NAPLES
KINGDOM OF SARDINIA, 1810
KINGDOM OF TWO SICILIES
Adriatic Sea
Mediterranean Sea
CORSICA (FR.)
SICILY
200 MILES
200 KILOMETERS

(B)

Kingdom of Sardinia-Piedmont, 1815
Acquisition, 1859
Ceded to France, 1860
Acquisition, 1860

TO FRANCE, 1860 SAVOY
LOMBARDY
VENETIA
NICE
PARMA
MODENA
ROMAGNA
LUCCA
TUSCANY
UMBRIA
CORSICA (FR.)
•Rome
NAPLES
KINGDOM OF TWO SICILIES
SARDINIA
Adriatic Sea
Mediterranean Sea
SICILY
200 MILES
200 KILOMETERS

(C)

Kingdom of Italy, 1861
Acquisition, 1866
Acquisition, 1870

VENETIA
CORSICA (FR.)
PATRIMONY OF ST. PETER
•Rome
SARDINIA
Adriatic Sea
Mediterranean Sea
SICILY
200 MILES
200 KILOMETERS

(D)

Kingdom of Italy, 1870

CORSICA (FR.)
•Rome
SARDINIA
Adriatic Sea
Mediterranean Sea
SICILY
200 MILES
200 KILOMETERS

MAP 23-1   THE UNIFICATION OF ITALY   *Beginning with the association of Sardinia and Piedmont by the Congress of Vienna in 1815, unification was achieved through the expansion of Piedmont between 1859 and 1870. Both Cavour's statesmanship and the campaigns of ardent nationalists played large roles.*

The political framework of the united Italy could not overcome these problems. The constitution, which was that promulgated for Piedmont in 1848, provided for a conservative constitutional monarchy. Parliament consisted of two houses: a Senate appointed by the king, and a Chamber of Deputies elected on a narrow franchise. Ministers were responsible to the monarch, not to Parliament. These arrangements did not foster vigorous parliamentary life. Political leaders often simply avoided major problems. In place of efficient, progressive government, such as Cavour had brought to Piedmont, a system called *transformismo* developed; political opponents were "transformed" into government supporters through bribery, favors, or a seat in the cabinet. Italian politics became a byword for corruption.

Nor was unification complete. Many Italians believed that other territories should be added to their nation. The most important of these were Venetia and Rome. The former was gained in 1866 in return for Italy's alliance with Prussia in the Austro-Prussian War. Rome and the papacy continued to be guarded by French troops, first sent there in 1849, until the Franco-Prussian War of 1870 forced their withdrawal. The Italian state then annexed Rome and made it the capital. The papacy confined itself to the Vatican, and it remained hostile to the Italian state until the two sides concluded a treaty, the Lateran Accord of 1929.

By 1870 only the small province of Trent and the city of Trieste, both ruled by Austria, remained outside Italy. In and of themselves, these areas were not important, but they fueled the continued hostility of Italian nationalists toward Austria. The desire to liberate *Italia Irredenta,* or "Unredeemed Italy," was one reason for the Italian support of the Allies against Austria and Germany during World War I.

In 1860, after the wars that unified Italy, southern Italians formally voted in plebiscites to join the united nation. [Bildarchiv Preussischer Kulturbesitz]

MAP 23-2 THE UNIFICATION OF GERMANY *Under Bismarck's leadership, and with the strong support of its royal house, Prussia used most diplomatic and military means, on both the German and international stages, to forcibly unify the German states into a strong national entity.*

German Unification

The construction of a united Germany was the single most important political development in Europe between 1848 and 1914 (see Map 23-2). It transformed the balance of economic, military, and international power. Moreover, the method of its creation largely determined the character of the new German state. Germany was united by the conservative army, monarchy, and prime minister of Prussia, among whose chief motives was the outflanking of Prussian liberals. A unified Germany, sought for two generations by German liberals, was actually achieved for the most illiberal of reasons.

During the 1850s, German unification still seemed remote. The major states continued to trade with each other through the *Zollverein* (tariff union), and railways linked their economies. Frederick William IV of Prussia had given up thoughts of unification under Prussian leadership. Austria continued to oppose any closer union that might lessen its influence. Liberal nationalists had not recovered from the humiliating experiences of 1848 and 1849. What quickly modified this situation was a series of domestic political changes and problems within Prussia.

In 1858 Frederick William IV was adjudged insane, and his brother William assumed the regency. William I (r. 1861–1888), who became king in his own right in 1861, was less idealistic than his brother and more of a Prussian patriot. In the usual Hohenzollern tradition, his first concern was to strengthen the Prussian army. In 1860 his war minister and chief of staff proposed to enlarge the army, to increase the number of officers, and to extend the period of conscription from two to three years. The Prussian Parliament, created by the Constitution of 1850, refused to approve the necessary taxes. The liberals, who dominated the body, sought to avoid placing additional power in the hands of the monarchy. For two years monarch and Parliament were deadlocked.

Bismarck

In September 1862, William I turned for help to the person who, more than any other single individual, shaped the next thirty years of European history: Otto von Bismarck (1815–1898). Bismarck came from Junker (noble landlord) stock. He attended university, joined a *Burschenschaft* (a student society), and displayed an interest in German unification. Then he retired to his father's estate. During the 1840s he was elected to the provincial diet, where his stand was so reactionary as to disturb even the king. Yet he had made his mark. From 1851 to 1859, Bismarck served as the Prussian minister to the Frankfurt Diet of the German Confederation. Later he became Prussian ambassador to Russia and had just been named ambassador to France when William I appointed him prime minister of Prussia.

Although Bismarck had entered public life as a reactionary, he had mellowed into a conservative. He opposed parliamentary government but not a constitutionalism that provided for a strong monarch. He understood that Prussia— and later, Germany—must have a strong industrial base. His years in Frankfurt arguing with his Austrian counterpart had hardened his Prussian patriotism. In politics, he was a pragmatist who put more trust in power and action than in ideas. As he declared in his first speech as prime minister, "Germany is not looking to Prussia's liberalism but to her power. . . . The great questions of the day will not be decided by speeches and majority decisions—that was the mistake of 1848–1849—but by iron and

blood."[3] Yet this same minister, after having led Prussia into three wars, spent the next nineteen years seeking to preserve peace.

Upon becoming prime minister in 1862, Bismarck immediately moved against the liberal Parliament. He contended that even without new financial levies, the Prussian constitution permitted the government to carry out its functions on the basis of previously granted taxes. Therefore, taxes could be collected and spent despite the parliamentary refusal to vote them. The army and most of the bureaucracy supported this interpretation of the constitution. In 1863, however, new elections sustained the liberal majority in the Parliament. Bismarck had to find some way to attract popular support away from the liberals and toward the monarchy and the army. He therefore set about uniting Germany through the conservative institutions of Prussia.

THE DANISH WAR (1864) Bismarck pursued a *kleindeutsch*, or small German, solution to unification; Austria was to be excluded from a united German state. This goal required complex diplomacy. The Schleswig–Holstein problem gave Bismarck the handle for his policy. These two northern duchies had long been ruled by the kings of Denmark without being part of Denmark itself. Their populations were a mixture of Germans and Danes. Holstein, where Germans predominated, belonged to the German Confederation. In 1863 the Danish parliament moved to incorporate both duchies into Denmark. The smaller states of the German Confederation proposed an all-German war to halt this move. Bismarck wanted Prussia to act alone or only in cooperation with Austria. Together the two large states easily defeated Denmark in 1864.

The Danish defeat increased Bismarck's personal prestige, and over the next two years, he maneuvered Austria into war with Prussia. In August 1865, the two powers negotiated the Convention of Gastein, which put Austria in charge of Holstein and Prussia in charge of Schleswig. Bismarck then moved to mend other

[3]*Quoted in Otto Pflanze,* Bismarck and the Development of Germany: The Period of Unification: 1815–1871 *(Princeton, N.J.: Princeton University Press, 1963), p. 177.*

diplomatic fences. He had gained Russian sympathy by supporting the 1863 suppression of a Polish revolt, and he persuaded Napoleon III to promise neutrality in an Austro-Prussian conflict. In April 1866, Bismarck concluded a treaty with Italy promising that Italy would get Venetia if it attacked Austria in support of Prussia when war broke out. Now Bismarck had to provoke his war.

THE AUSTRO-PRUSSIAN WAR (1866) Constant Austro-Prussian tension had arisen over the administration of Schleswig and Holstein. Bismarck ordered the Prussian forces to be as obnoxious as possible to the Austrians. On June 1, 1866, Austria appealed to the German Confederation to intervene in the dispute. Bismarck claimed that the request violated the terms of the 1864 alliance and the Convention of Gastein. The Seven Weeks' War that resulted in the summer of 1866 led to the decisive defeat of Austria at the Battle of Königgrätz in Bohemia.

The Treaty of Prague, which ended the conflict on August 23, was lenient toward Austria. Austria only lost Venetia, which was ceded to Napoleon III, who in turn ceded it to Italy. Austria refused to give Venetia directly to Italy because the Austrians had crushed the Italians during the war. The treaty and the military defeat permanently excluded the Habsburgs from German affairs. Prussia had thus established itself as the only major power among the German states.

THE NORTH GERMAN CONFEDERATION In 1867 the states of Hanover, Hesse, and Nassau, and the city of Frankfurt, which had all supported Austria during the war, were annexed by Prussia, and their rulers were deposed. All Germany north of the Main River now formed a federation under Prussian leadership, the North German Confederation. Each state retained its own local government, but all military forces were under federal control. The president of the federation was the king of Prussia, represented by his chancellor, Bismarck. There was a legislature consisting of two houses: a federal council, or *Bundesrat*, composed of members appointed by the governments of the states, and a lower house, or *Reichstag*, chosen by universal manhood suffrage.

Bismarck had little fear of this broad franchise, because he sensed that the peasants would vote for conservatives. Moreover, the *Reichstag* had little real power, because the ministers were responsible only to the monarch. The *Reichstag* could not even originate legislation. All laws had to be proposed by the chancellor. The legislature did have the right to approve military budgets, but these were usually submitted to cover several years at a time. The constitution of the confederation, which after 1871 became the constitution of the German Empire, possessed some of the appearances but none of the substance of liberalism. Germany was in effect a military monarchy.

The spectacular success of Bismarck's policy overwhelmed the liberal opposition in the Prussian Parliament. The liberals were split between those who prized liberalism and those who supported unification. In the end, nationalism proved more attractive. In 1866 the Prussian Parliament retroactively approved the earlier disputed military budget. Bismarck had crushed the Prussian liberals by making the monarchy and the army the most popular institutions in the country. The drive toward unification had achieved his domestic political goal.

The Franco-Prussian War and the German Empire (1870–1871)

Bismarck now awaited an opportunity to complete unification by bringing the states of southern Germany into the confederation. Events in Spain gave him the excuse. In 1868 a military coup deposed the corrupt Bourbon queen of Spain, Isabella II (r. 1833–1868). In searching for a new monarch, the Spaniards chose Prince Leopold of Hohenzollern-Sigmaringen, a Catholic cousin of William I of Prussia. On June 19, 1870, Leopold accepted the Spanish crown with Prussian blessings. Bismarck knew that France would react strongly against the idea of a Hohenzollern Spain.

On July 2, the Spanish government announced Leopold's acceptance, and the French reacted as expected. France sent its ambassador Count Vincent Benedetti (1817–1900) to consult with William I, who was vacationing at Bad Ems. They discussed the

government instructed Benedetti to ask William for assurances that he would tolerate no future Spanish candidacy for Leopold. The king refused but said that he might take the question under further consideration. Later that day he sent Bismarck, who was in Berlin, a telegram reporting the substance of the meeting. The chancellor, who desperately wanted a war with France to complete unification, had been disappointed by the peaceful resolution of the controversy. The king's telegram gave him a new opportunity to incite a war. Bismarck released an edited version of the dispatch. The revised Ems telegram made it appear that William had insulted the French ambassador. The idea was to goad France into declaring war.

The French government fell for Bismarck's bait and declared war on July 19. Napoleon III was sick and not eager for war, but his government believed that victory over the North German Confederation would give the empire renewed popular support. Once the conflict erupted, the southern German states, honoring treaties of 1866, enthusiastically joined Prussia against France, whose defeat was not long in coming. On September 1, at the Battle of Sedan, the Germans not only beat the French army but also captured Napoleon III. By late September Paris was besieged; it finally capitulated on January 28, 1871.

Ten days earlier, in the Hall of Mirrors at the Palace of Versailles, the German Empire had been proclaimed. During the war the states of southern Germany had joined the North German Confederation, and their rulers requested William to accept the imperial title of German emperor. The princes remained heads of their respective states within the new federation. From the peace settlement with France, Germany received the additional territory of Alsace and part of Lorraine.

Both the fact and the manner of German unification produced long-range effects in Europe. A powerful new state had been created in north central Europe. It was rich in natural resources and talented citizens. Militarily and economically, the German Empire would be far stronger than Prussia had been alone. The unification of Germany was also a blow to European liberalism, because the new state was a conservative creation. Conservative politics was now backed

matter at several meetings. On July 12, Leopold's father renounced his son's candidacy for the Spanish throne, fearing that the issue would cause war between Prussia and France. William was relieved that conflict had been avoided and that he had not had to order Leopold to renounce the Spanish throne.

There the matter might have rested had it not been for the impetuosity of the French and the guile of Bismarck. On July 13, the French

The proclamation of the German Empire in the Hall of Mirrors at Versailles, January 18, 1871, after the defeat of France in the France–Prussian War. Kaiser Wilhelm I is standing at the top of the steps under the flags. Bismarck is in the center in a white uniform. [Bildarchiv Preussischer Kulturbesitz]

not by a weak Austria or an economically retrograde Russia but by the strongest state on the Continent.

The two nations most immediately affected by German and Italian unification were France and Austria. The emergence of the two new united states revealed the weakness of both France and the Habsburg Empire. Change had to come in each. France returned to republican government, and the Habsburgs came to terms with their Magyar subjects.

France: From Liberal Empire to the Third Republic

Historians have traditionally divided the reign of Emperor Napoleon III (r. 1851–1870) into the years of the authoritarian empire and those of the liberal empire. The point of division is the year 1860. Initially, after the coup in December 1851, Napoleon III had controlled the legislature, strictly censored the press, and harassed political dissidents. His support came from the army, property owners, the French Catholic church, and businessmen. They approved the security he ensured for property, his protection of the pope, and his aid to commerce and rail-

road construction. The French victory in the Crimean War had further confirmed the emperor's popularity.

From the late 1850s onward, Napoleon III began to modify his policy. In 1860 he concluded a free trade treaty with Britain and permitted freer debate in the legislature. By the late 1860s, he had relaxed the press laws and had permitted labor unions. In 1870 he allowed the leaders of the moderates in the legislature to form a ministry, and he also agreed to a liberal constitution that made the ministers responsible to the legislature.

Napoleon III's liberal concessions sought to shore up domestic support to compensate for his failures in foreign policy. By 1860 he had lost control of the diplomacy of Italian unification. Between 1861 and 1867, he had supported a disastrous military expedition against Mexico led by Archduke Maximilian of Austria that ended in defeat and Maximilian's execution. In 1866 France had watched passively while Bismarck and Prussia reorganized German affairs. The war of 1870 against Germany had been the French government's last and most disastrous attempt to shore up its foreign policy and secure domestic popularity.

The Second Empire, but not the war, came to an inglorious end with the Battle of Sedan in September 1870. The emperor was captured, imprisoned, and then allowed to go to England, where he died in 1873. Shortly after news of the Sedan disaster reached Paris, a republic was proclaimed, and a Government of National Defense was established. Paris itself was soon under Prussian siege, and the government was transferred to Bordeaux. Paris finally surrendered in January 1871, but the rest of France had been ready to sue for peace long before.

The Paris Commune

The division between the provinces and Paris became sharper after the fighting with Germany stopped. Monarchists dominated the new National Assembly elected in February. For the time being, the assembly gave executive power to Adolphe Thiers (1797–1877), who had been active in French politics since 1830. He negotiated a settlement with Prussia (the Treaty of Frankfurt) whereby France was charged a large indemnity and remained occupied by Prussian troops until the indemnity had been paid. France also lost Alsace and part of Lorraine. The treaty was officially ratified on May 23.

Many Parisians, having suffered during the siege, resented what they regarded as a betrayal by the monarchist National Assembly sitting at Versailles. The Parisians elected a new municipal government, called the Paris Commune, that was formally proclaimed on March 28, 1871. The Commune intended to administer Paris separately from the rest of France. At one time or another, political radicals and socialists of all stripes participated in the Paris Commune. The National Assembly moved rapidly in early April to surround Paris with an army. On May 8, this army bombarded the city. On May 21, the assembly's forces broke through the city's defenses. During the next seven days, the troops restored order to Paris and killed about 20,000 inhabitants. The communards claimed their own victims as well.

The short-lived Paris Commune quickly became a legend throughout Europe. Marxists regarded it as a genuine proletarian government that the French bourgeoisie had suppressed. This interpretation is mistaken. The Commune, though of shifting composition, was dominated by petty bourgeois members. The socialism of the Commune had its roots in Blanqui and Proudhon's anarchism rather than in Marx's concept of class conflict. The goal of the Commune was not a worker's republic but a nation composed of relatively independent, radically democratic enclaves. Its suppression thus represented not only the protection of property but also the triumph of the centralized nation-state over an alternative political organization. Just as the armies of Piedmont and Prussia had united the small states of Italy and Germany, the army of the French National Assembly destroyed the particularistic political tendencies of Paris and, by implication, those of any other French community.

The Third Republic

The National Assembly backed into a republican form of government indirectly and much against its will. The monarchists, who constituted its majority, were divided in loyalty between the House of Bourbon and the House of Orléans. They could have surmounted this problem because the Bourbon claimant, the count of Chambord, had no children and agreed to accept the Orléanist heir as his successor. Chambord refused to become king, however, if France retained the revolutionary tricolor flag. Even the conservative monarchists would not return to the white flag of the Bourbons, which symbolized extreme political reaction.

While the monarchists quarreled among themselves, time passed, and events marched on. By September 1873, the indemnity had been paid, and the Prussian occupation troops had withdrawn. Thiers was ousted from office because he had displayed clear republican sentiments. The monarchists wanted a more sympathetic executive. They elected as president a conservative army officer, Marshal MacMahon (1808–1893), who was expected to prepare for a monarchist restoration. In 1875 the National Assembly, still monarchist in sentiment but unable to find a king, decided to regularize the political system. It adopted a law that provided for a Chamber of Deputies elected by universal manhood suffrage, a Senate chosen indirectly, and a president elected by the two legislative

The Paris Commune Is Proclaimed

In September 1870, the French Republic was proclaimed, and shortly thereafter a National Assembly was elected. Paris, which had held out against Prussia longer than any other part of France, was hostile to the National Assembly. On March 18, 1871, a revolt against the assembly occurred in Paris. The National Guard of Paris sought to organize the city as a separate part of France. Here is an excerpt of the proclamation of March 28 of Paris as an autonomous commune separate from France. The rebellious Parisians wanted all of France to be organized into a federation of politically autonomous communes. This communal concept was directly opposed to that of the large national state. Two months after this proclamation, the troops of the assembly crushed the commune.

✦ *How does this document interpret the French defeat at the hands of Prussia as a punishment? How does this declaration portray the proclamation of the commune as a continuation of the French Revolution? What are the specific political goals and values of the commune according to this declaration?*

By its revolution of the 18th March, and the spontaneous and courageous efforts of the National Guard, Paris has regained its autonomy. . . . On the eve of the sanguinary and disastrous defeat suffered by France as the punishment it has to undergo for the seventy years of the Empire, and the monarchical, clerical, parliamentary, legal and conciliatory reaction, our country again rises, revives, begins a new life, and retakes the tradition of the Communes of old and of the French Revolution. This tradition, which gave victory to France, and earned the respect and sympathy of past generations, will bring independence, wealth, peaceful glory and brotherly love among nations in the future.

Never was there so solemn an hour. The Revolution which our fathers commenced and we are finishing . . . is going on without bloodshed, by the might of the popular will. . . . To secure the triumph of the Communal idea . . . it is necessary to determine its general principles, and to draw up . . . the programme to be realized. . . .

The Commune is the foundation of all political states, exactly as the family is the embryo of human society. It must have autonomy; that is to say, self-administration and self-government, agreeing with its particular genius, traditions, and wants; preserving, in its political, moral, national, and special groups its entire liberty, its own character, and its complete sovereignty, like a citizen of a free town.

To secure the greatest economic development, the national and territorial independence, and security, association is indispensable; that is to say, a federation of all communes, constituting a united nation.

The autonomy of the Commune guarantees liberty to its citizens; and the federation of all the communes increases, by the reciprocity, power, wealth, markets, and resources of each member, the profit of all. It was the Communal idea . . . which triumphed on the 18th of March, 1871. It implies, as a political form, the Republic, which is alone compatible with liberty and popular sovereignty.

G. A. Kertesz, ed., Documents in the Political History of the European Continent, 1815–1939 (Oxford: Clarendon Press, 1968), pp. 312–313.

Wreaths hang in mourning on the wall of Père Lachaise Cemetery where the last sup-porters of the Paris Commune were shot by the troops of the National Assembly. [Roger-Viollet]

houses. This rather simple republican system had resulted from the bickering and frustration of the monarchists.

After numerous quarrels with the Chamber of Deputies, MacMahon resigned in 1879. His departure meant that dedicated republicans generally controlled the national government despite lingering opposition from the Church, wealthy families, and a part of the army.

The political structure of the Third Republic proved much stronger than many citizens suspected at the time. It survived challenges for leadership from persons such as General George Boulanger (1837–1891), who would have imposed stronger executive authority. It also survived several scandals, such as those involving sales of awards of the Legion of Honor and widespread corruption of politicians by a company that tried to construct a canal in Panama, which made its politics appear increasingly sleazy to conservatives. The institutions of the republic, however, allowed new ministers to replace those whose corruption was exposed.

The Dreyfus Affair

The greatest trauma of the Third Republic occurred over the Dreyfus affair. On December 22, 1894, a French military court found Captain Alfred Dreyfus (1859–1935) guilty of passing secret information to the German army. The evidence for his guilt was flimsy and was later revealed to have been forged. Someone in the officer corps had been passing documents to the Germans, and it suited the army investigators to accuse Dreyfus, who was Jewish. After Dreyfus had been sent to Devil's Island, a notorious prison in French Guiana, however, secrets continued to flow to the German army. In 1896 a new head of French counterintelligence reexamined the Dreyfus file and found evidence of forgery. A different officer was implicated, but a military court acquitted him of all charges.

By then the affair had provoked widespread and sometimes near-hysterical public debate. The army, the French Catholic church, political conservatives, and vehemently anti-Semitic newspapers repeatedly contended that Dreyfus

The prosecution of Captain Alfred Dreyfus, shown here standing on the right at his military trial, provoked the most serious crisis of the Third Republic. [The Bettmann Archive]

was guilty. Such anti-Dreyfus opinion was dominant at the beginning of the affair. In 1898, however, the novelist Émile Zola published a newspaper article entitled *"J'accuse"* ("I Accuse") in which he contended that the army had consciously denied due process to Dreyfus and had plotted to suppress or forge evidence. Zola was convicted of libel and received a one-year prison sentence, which he avoided by fleeing to England.

Zola was only one of numerous liberals, radicals, and socialists who had begun to demand a new trial for Dreyfus. Although these forces of the political left had come to Dreyfus's support rather slowly, they soon realized that his cause could aid their own public image. They portrayed the conservative institutions of the nation as having denied Dreyfus the rights belonging to any citizen of the republic. They also claimed, and properly so, that Dreyfus had been singled out, so that the guilty persons, who were still in the army, could be protected. In August 1898, further evidence of forged material

came to light. The officer responsible for those forgeries committed suicide in jail, but a new military trial again convicted Dreyfus. The president of France immediately pardoned him, however, and eventually, in 1906, a civilian court set aside the results of both military trials.

The Dreyfus case divided France as no issue had done since the Paris Commune. By its conclusion, the conservatives were on the defensive. They had allowed themselves to persecute an innocent person and to manufacture false evidence against him to protect themselves from disclosure. They had also embraced violent anti-Semitism. On the political left, radicals, republicans, and socialists developed an informal alliance that outlived the fight over the Dreyfus case itself. These groups realized that republican institutions must be supported if the political left were to achieve its goals. Nonetheless, the political, religious, and racial divisions and suspicions growing out of the Dreyfus affair continued to divide the Third Republic until France's defeat by Germany in 1940.

The Habsburg Empire

After 1848 the Habsburg Empire was a problem both to itself and for the rest of Europe. An ungenerous critic remarked that a standing army of soldiers, a kneeling army of priests, and a crawling army of informers supported the empire. In the age of national states, liberal institutions, and industrialism, the Habsburg domains remained primarily dynastic, absolutist, and agrarian. The Habsburg response to the revolts of 1848–1849 had been the reassertion of absolutism. Francis Joseph, who became emperor in 1848 and ruled until 1916, was honest and hardworking, but unimaginative. He reacted to events but rarely commanded them.

During the 1850s, his ministers attempted to impose a centralized administration on the empire. The system amounted to a military and bureaucratic government dominated by German-speaking Austrians. The Vienna government abolished all internal tariffs in the empire. It divided Hungary, which had been so revolutionary in 1848, into military districts. The Roman Catholic church received control of education. National groups, such as the Croats and Slovaks, who had supported the empire against the Hungarians, received no rewards for their loyalty. Although this domestic system of neoabsolutism provoked resentment and opposition, it eventually floundered because of setbacks in Habsburg foreign affairs.

Austrian refusal to support Russia during the Crimean War meant that the new tsar would no longer help preserve Habsburg rule in Hungary as Nicholas I had done in 1849. An important

Political discourse in the Third French Republic was harsh. The cover of this anticlerical journal presents the French Roman Catholic Church as the enemy of the nation. A menacing figure symbolizing the Church holds the recently built Basilica of the Sacred Heart. [The Bettmann Archive]

external prop of Habsburg power for the past half-century thus disappeared. The Austrian defeat in 1859 at the hands of France and Piedmont and the subsequent loss of territory in Italy confirmed the necessity for a new domestic policy. For seven years the emperor, the civil servants, the aristocrats, and the politicians tried to construct a viable system of government.

Formation of the Dual Monarchy

In 1860 Francis Joseph issued the October Diploma, which created a federation among the states and provinces of the empire. There were

The coronation of Francis Joseph of Hungary in 1867 is depicted in this painting. The so-called Ausgleich, *or Compromise, of 1867 transformed the Habsburg Empire into a dual monarchy in which Austria and Hungary became almost separate states except for defense and foreign affairs. [Bildarchiv der Österreichischen Nationalbibliothek, Vienna]*

to be local diets dominated by the landed classes and a single imperial parliament. The Magyar nobility of Hungary, however, rejected the plan.

Consequently, in 1861, the emperor issued the February Patent, which set up an entirely different form of government. It established a bicameral imperial parliament, or *Reichsrat,* with an upper chamber appointed by the emperor and an indirectly elected lower chamber. Again the Magyars refused to cooperate in a system designed to give political dominance in the empire to German-speaking Austrians. The Magyars sent no delegates to the legislature. Nevertheless, for six years, the February Patent governed the empire, and it prevailed in Austria proper until World War I. Ministers were responsible to the emperor, not the *Reichsrat,* and civil liberties were not guaranteed. Armies

could be levied and taxes raised without parliamentary consent. When the *Reichsrat* was not in session, the emperor could simply rule by decree.

Meanwhile, negotiations continued secretly between the emperor and the Magyars. These produced no concrete result until the Prussian defeat of Austria in the summer of 1866 and the consequent exclusion of Austria from German affairs. The military disaster compelled Francis Joseph to come to terms with the Magyars. The subsequent *Ausgleich,* or Compromise, of 1867 transformed the Habsburg Empire into a dual monarchy, thereafter usually known as Austria-Hungary.

Francis Joseph was crowned king of Hungary in Budapest in 1867. Except for the common monarch, Austria and Hungary became almost wholly separate states. They shared ministers of foreign affairs, defense, and finance, but the other ministers were different for each state. There were also separate parliaments. Each year, sixty parliamentary delegates from each state met to discuss mutual interests. Every ten years, Austria and Hungary renegotiated their trade relationship. By this cumbersome machinery, unique in European history, the Magyars were reconciled to Habsburg rule. They had achieved the free hand they had long wanted in Hungary.

Unrest of Nationalities

The Compromise of 1867 had introduced two different principles of political legitimacy into

---

The Austrian Prime Minister Explains the Dual Monarchy

The multinational character of the Austrian Empire had long been a source of internal weakness and political discontent. After the defeat of Austria by Prussia in 1866, the Austrian government attempted to regain the loyalty of the Hungarians by making Hungary a separate kingdom within a dual monarchy, known thereafter as Austria-Hungary.

✦ *How does the Austrian prime minister define the problems of nationality within the empire? Why does he distinguish Hungary from the other national groups who seek independence or association with another nation? What are the principles he claims lie behind the establishment of the dual monarchy?*

The dangers which Austria has to face are of a twofold nature. The first is presented by the tendency of her liberal-minded German population to gravitate toward that larger portion of the German-speaking people . . . the second is the diversity of language and race in the empire. Of Austria's large Slav population, the Poles have a natural craving for independence after having enjoyed and heroically fought for it for centuries; while the other nationalities are likely at a moment of dangerous crisis to develop pro-Russian tendencies.

Now my object is to carry out a bloodless revolution—to show the various elements of this great empire that it is to the benefit of each of them to act in harmony with its neighbor. . . . But to this I have made one exception. Hungary is an ancient monarchy, more ancient as such than Austria proper. . . . I have endeavoured to give Hungary not a new position with regard to the Austrian empire, but to secure her in the one which she has occupied. The Emperor of Austria is King of Hungary; my idea was that he should revive in his person the Constitution of which he and his ancestors have been the heads. The leading principles of my plan are . . . the resuscitation of an old monarchy and an old Constitution; not the separation of one part of the empire from the other, but the drawing together of the two component parts by the recognition of their joint positions, the maintenance of their mutual obligations, their community in questions affecting the entire empire, and their proportional pecuniary responsibility for the liabilities of the whole State. It is no plan of separation that I have carried out: on the contrary, it is one of close union, not by the creation of a new power, but by the recognition of an old one. . . .

Memories of Friedrich Ferdinand Count von Beust, Vol. I, ed. by Baron Henry de Worms (London: Remington, 1887), pp. xx–xxvi.

MAP 23-3 NATIONALITIES WITHIN THE HABSBURG EMPIRE *The patchwork appearance reflects the unusual problem of the numerous ethnic groups that the Habsburgs could not, of course, meld into a modern national state. Only the Magyars were recognized in 1867, leaving nationalist Czechs, Slovaks, and the others chronically dissatisfied.*

the two sections of the Habsburg Empire. In Hungary, political loyalty was based on nationality because Hungary had been recognized as a distinct part of the monarchy on the basis of nationalism. In effect, Hungary was a Magyar nation under the Habsburg emperor. In the rest of the Habsburg domains, the principle of legitimacy meant dynastic loyalty to the emperor. Many of the other nationalities wished to achieve the same type of settlement that the Hungarians had won, or to govern themselves, or to unite with fellow nationals who lived outside the empire (see Map 23-3).

Many of those other national groups—including the Czechs, the Ruthenians, the Romanians,

and the Croatians—opposed the Compromise of 1867 that in effect had permitted the German-speaking Austrians and the Hungarian Magyars to dominate all other nationalities within the empire. The most vocal critics were the Czechs of Bohemia. They favored a policy of trialism, or triple monarchy, in which the Czechs would be given a position similar to that given the Hungarians. In 1871 Francis Joseph was willing to accept this concept. The Magyars, however, vetoed it lest they be forced to make similar concessions to their own subject nationalities. Furthermore, the Germans of Bohemia were afraid that the Czech language would be imposed on them and their children.

For more than twenty years, the Czechs were placated by generous patronage and posts in the bureaucracy. By the 1890s, however, Czech nationalism again became more strident. In 1897, Francis Joseph gave the Czechs and the Germans equality of language in various localities. Thereafter, the Germans in the Austrian *Reichsrat* opposed these measures by disrupting Parliament. The Czechs replied in kind. By the turn of the century, this obstructionism, which included the playing of musical instruments in the *Reichsrat*, had paralyzed parliamentary life. The emperor ruled by imperial décree through the bureaucracy. In 1907 Francis Joseph introduced universal male suffrage in Austria (but not in Hungary), but this action did not eliminate the chaos in the *Reichsrat*. In effect, by 1914 constitutionalism was a dead letter in Austria. It flourished in Hungary, but only because the Magyars relentlessly exercised political supremacy over all other competing national groups except Croatia, which was permitted considerable autonomy.

There is reason to believe that nationalism became stronger during the last quarter of the nineteenth century. It was then that language became the single most important factor in defining a nation. The expansion of education made this possible. In all countries where nationalistic groups prospered, their membership was dominated by intellectuals, students, and educated members of the middle class, all of whom were literate in the literary version of particular national languages. Furthermore, it was during these same years, as will be seen in Chapter 25, that racial thinking became important in Europe. Racial thought maintained there was a genetic basis for ethnic and cultural groups who had hitherto been generally defined by a common history and culture. Once language and race became the ways to define an ethnic or national group, the lines between such groups became much more sharply drawn.

The unrest of the various nationalities within the Habsburg Empire not only caused internal political difficulties, it also became a major source of political instability for all of central and eastern Europe. Each of the nationality problems normally had ramifications for both foreign and domestic policy. Both the Croats and the Poles wanted an independent state in

Major Dates in Late-Nineteenth-Century Habsburg Empire	
1848	Francis Joseph becomes emperor
1860	October Diploma
1861	February Patent
1866	Defeat by Prussia
1867	Compromise between emperor and Hungary establishing the Dual Monarchy
1897	Ordinances giving equality of language between Germans and Czechs in Austria
1907	Universal manhood suffrage introduced for Austria

union with their fellow nationals who lived outside the empire, and in the case of the Poles, with fellow nationals in the Russian empire. Other national groups, such as Ukrainians, Romanians, Italians, and Bosnians, saw themselves as potentially linked to Russia, Romania, Serbia, Italy, or to a yet-to-be established south Slavic or Yugoslav state. Many of these nationalities looked to Russia to protect their interests or influence the government in Vienna. The Romanians were also concerned about the Romanian minority in Hungary. Serbia sought to expand its borders to include Serbs who lived within Habsburg or Ottoman territory. Out of these Balkan tensions emerged much of the turmoil that would spark the First World War. Many of the same ethnic tensions account for the warfare in the former Yugoslavia.

The dominant German population of Austria proper was generally loyal to the emperor. A part of it, however, yearned to join the united German state being established by Bismarck. These nationalistic Austro-Germans often hated the non-German national groups of the empire, and many of them were anti-Semites. Such attitudes would influence the youth and young adulthood of Adolph Hitler.

For the next century of European and even world history, the significance of this nationalist unrest within the late-nineteenth-century Austrian empire and its neighbors can hardly be overestimated. These nationality problems touched all three of the great central and eastern European empires—the German, the Russian,

Lord Acton Condemns Nationalism

Lord Acton (1834–1902) was a major nineteenth-century English historian and commentator on contemporary religious and political events. In all his writings, he was deeply concerned with the character and preservation of liberty. His was one of the earliest voices to point to the political dangers of nationalism.

✦ *Why does Acton see the principle of nationality as dangerous to liberty? Why does he see nationalism as a threat to minority groups? Why does he see nationalism as a threat to democracy?*

The greatest adversary of the rights of nationality is the modern theory of nationality. By making the State and the nation commensurate with each other in theory, it reduces practically to a subject condition all other nationalities that may be within the boundary. It cannot admit them to an equality with the ruling nation which constitutes the State, because the State would then cease to be national, which would be a contradiction of the principle of its existence. According, therefore, to the degree of humanity and civilization in that dominant body which claims all the rights of the community, the inferior races are exterminated, or reduced to servitude, or outlawed, or put in a condition of dependence.

If we take the establishment of liberty for the realization of moral duties to be the end of civil society, we must conclude that those states are substantially the most perfect which, like the British and Austrian Empires, include various distinct nationalities without oppressing them. Those in which no mixture of races has occurred are imperfect; and those in which its effects have disappeared are decrepit. A State which is incompetent to satisfy different races condemns itself; a State which labors to neutralize, to absorb, or to expel them, destroys its own vitality; a State which does not include them is destitute of the chief basis of self-government. The theory of nationality, therefore, is a retrograde step in history. . . .

. . . [N]ationality does not aim either at liberty or prosperity, both of which it sacrifices to the imperative necessity of making the nation the mold and measure of the State. Its course will be marked with material as well as moral ruin, in order that a new invention may prevail over the works of God and the interests of mankind. There is no principle of change, no phrase of political speculation conceivable, more comprehensive, more subversive, or more arbitrary than this. It is a confutation of democracy, because it sets limits to the exercise of the popular will, and substitutes for it a higher principle.

John Emerich Edward Dalberg-Acton, First Baron Acton, Essays in the History of Liberty, *ed. by J. Rufus Fears (Indianapolis: Liberty Classics, 1985), pp. 431–433.*

and the Austrian. All had large Polish populations, and Russia had many minority groups. Each nationality regarded its own aspirations and discontents as more important than the larger good or even survival of the empires that they inhabited. The weakness of the Ottoman Empire allowed both Austria and Russia to compete in the Balkans for greater influence and thus further inflame nationalistic resentments.

Such nationalistic stirrings affected the fate of all three empires from the 1860s through the outbreak of World War I. The government of each of those empires would be overturned during the war, and the Austrian empire would disappear. Those same unresolved problems of central and eastern European nationalism would then lead directly to World War II. They continue to fester today.

Russia: Emancipation and Revolutionary Stirrings

Russia changed remarkably during the last half of the nineteenth century. The government both finally addressed the long-standing problem of serfdom and undertook a broad range of administrative reforms. During the same period, however, radical revolutionary groups began to organize. These groups tried to draw the peasants into revolutionary activity and assassinated major government officials, including the tsar. The government's response was a new era of repression following the years of reform.

Reforms of Alexander II

The defeat in the Crimean War and the humiliation of the Treaty of Paris compelled the Russian government to reconsider its domestic policies. Nicholas I had died in 1855 during the conflict. Because of extensive travel in Russia and an early introduction to government, his son Alexander II (r. 1855–1881) was familiar with the chief difficulties facing the nation. The debacle of the war had made reform both necessary and possible. Alexander II took advantage of this turn of events to institute the most extensive restructuring of Russian society and administration since Peter the Great. Like Peter, Alexander imposed his reforms from the top.

ABOLITION OF SERFDOM In every area of economic and public life, a profound cultural gap separated Russia from the rest of Europe. Nowhere was this more apparent than in the survival of serfdom. In Russia, the institution had changed very little since the eighteenth century, though every other nation on the Continent had abandoned it. Russian landowners still had a free hand with their serfs, and the serfs had little recourse against the landlords. In March 1856, at the conclusion of the Crimean War, Alexander II announced his intention to abolish serfdom. He had decided that only its abolition would permit Russia to organize its human and natural resources to maintain its status as a great power.

Serfdom had become economically inefficient. There was always the threat of revolt; the serfs forced into the army had performed poorly in the Crimean conflict. Moreover, nineteenth-century moral opinion condemned serfdom. Only Russia, Brazil, and certain portions of the United States among the Western nations still retained such forms of involuntary servitude. For five years, government commissions wrestled over how to implement the tsar's desire. Finally, in February 1861, against much opposition from the nobility and the landlords, Alexander II promulgated the long statute ending serfdom in Russia.

The actual emancipation statute proved to be a disappointment, however, because freedom was not accompanied by land. Serfs immediately received the personal right to marry without their landlord's permission as well as the rights to purchase and sell property freely, to engage in court actions, and to pursue trades. What they did not receive was free title to their land. They had to pay the landlords over a period of forty-nine years for allotments of land that were frequently too small to support them. They were also charged interest during this period. The serfs made the payments to the government, which had already reimbursed the landlords for their losses. The serfs would not receive title to the land until the debt was paid.

The procedures were so complicated and the results so limited that many serfs believed that real emancipation was still to come. The redemption payments led to almost unending difficulty. Poor harvests made it impossible for many peasants to keep up with the payments, and they fell increasingly behind in their debt. The situation was not remedied until 1906, when, during the widespread revolutionary unrest following the Japanese defeat of Russia in 1905, the government grudgingly completed the process of emancipation by canceling the remaining debts.

REFORM OF LOCAL GOVERNMENT AND THE JUDICIAL SYSTEM The abolition of serfdom required the reorganization of local government and the judicial system. The authority of village communes replaced that of the landlord over the peasant. The village elders settled family quarrels, imposed fines, issued internal passports, and collected taxes. Often, also, it was the village commune rather than individual peasants who owned the land. The nobility were permitted a larger role in local administration through a system of provincial and county *zemstvos*, or councils, organized in 1864. These

Life in Russian villages during the 1870s was very difficult. Tsar Alexander II abolished serfdom in 1861, but peasants were required to pay compensation to the government for 49 years and living standards remained dismal. This painting shows peasants waiting patiently outside a government office while officials inside take their time over lunch. [Bildarchiv Preussischer Kulturbesitz]

councils were to oversee local matters, such as bridge and road repair, education, and agricultural improvement. Because the councils received inadequate funds, however, local government never became vigorous.

The flagrant inequities and abuses of the pre-emancipation judicial system could not continue. In 1864 Alexander II promulgated a new statute on the judiciary. For the first time, western European legal principles were introduced into Russia. These included equality before the law, impartial hearings, uniform procedures, judicial independence, and trial by jury. The new system was far from perfect. The judges were not genuinely independent, and the tsar could increase as well as reduce sentences. Certain offenses, such as those involving the press, were not tried before a jury. Nonetheless, the new courts were both more efficient and less corrupt than the old system.

MILITARY REFORM The government also reformed the army. Russia possessed the largest military forced on the Continent, but it had floundered badly in the Crimean War. The usual period of service for a soldier was twenty-five years. Villages had to provide quotas of serfs to serve in the army. Often the recruiters simply appeared in the villages and seized serfs from their families. Once in the army, the recruits rarely saw their homes again. Life in the army was harsh, even by the brutal standards of most mid-century armies. In the 1860s, the army lowered the period of service to fifteen years and slightly relaxed discipline. In 1874 the enlistment period was lowered to six years of active duty, followed by nine years in the reserves. All males were subject to military service after the age of twenty.

REPRESSION IN POLAND Alexander's reforms became more measured shortly after the Polish Rebellion of 1863. As in 1830, Polish nationalists attempted to overthrow Russian dominance. Once again the Russian army suppressed the rebellion. Alexander II then moved to "russify" Poland. In 1864 he emancipated the Polish serfs to punish the politically restive Polish nobility. Russian law, language, and administration were imposed on all areas of Polish life. Henceforth, until the close of World War I, Poland was treated as merely another Russian province.

As the Polish suppression demonstrated, Alexander II was a reformer only within the limits of his own autocracy. His changes in Russian life failed to create new loyalty to or gratitude for the government among his subjects. The serfs felt that their emancipation had been inadequate. The nobles and the wealthier educated segments of Russian society resented the tsar's persistent refusal to allow them a meaningful role in government and policy making. Consequently, although Alexander II became known as the Tsar Liberator, he was never popular. He could be indecisive and closed-minded. These characteristics became more pronounced after 1866, when an attempt was made on his life. Thereafter Russia increasingly became a police state. This new repression fueled the activity of radical groups within Russia. Their actions, in turn, made the autocracy more reactionary.

Revolutionaries

The tsarist regime had long had its critics. One of the most prominent was Alexander Herzen (1812–1870), who lived in exile. From London, he published a newspaper called *The Bell*, in which he set forth reformist positions. The initial reforms of Alexander II had raised great hopes among Russian students and intellectuals, but they soon became discontented with the limited character of the reforms. Drawing on the ideas of Herzen and other radicals, these students formed a revolutionary movement known as *Populism*. They sought a social revolution based on the communal life of the Russian peasants. The chief radical society was called Land and Freedom.

In the early 1870s, hundreds of young Russians, including both men and women, took their revolutionary message into the countryside. They intended to live with the peasants, to gain their trust, and to teach them about the

Major Dates in Late-Nineteenth-Century Russia	
1855	Alexander II becomes tsar
1856	Defeat in Crimean War
1861	Serfdom abolished
1863	Suppression of Polish rebellion
1864	Reorganization of local government
1864	Reform of judicial system
1874	Military enlistment period lowered
1878	Attempted assassination of military governor of Saint Petersburg
1879	Land and Freedom splits
1881	The People's Will assassinates Alexander II
1881	Alexander III becomes tsar
1894	Nicholas II becomes tsar

peasant role in the coming revolution. The bewildered and distrustful peasants turned most of the youths over to the police. In the winter of 1877–1878, almost 200 students were tried. Most were acquitted or given light sentences, because they had been held for months in preventive detention and because the court believed that a display of mercy might lessen public sympathy for the young revolutionaries. The court even suggested that the tsar might wish to pardon those students given heavier sentences. The tsar refused and let it become known that he favored heavy penalties for all persons involved in revolutionary activity.

Thereafter the revolutionaries decided that the tsarist regime must be attacked directly. They adopted a policy of terrorism. In January 1878, Vera Zasulich (1849–1919) attempted to assassinate the military governor of Saint Petersburg. A jury acquitted her because the governor she had shot had a reputation for brutality. Some people also believed that Zasulich had a personal rather than a political grievance against her victim. Nonetheless, the verdict further encouraged the terrorists.

In 1879 Land and Freedom split into two groups. One advocated educating the peasants, and it soon dissolved. The other, known as The People's Will, was dedicated to the overthrow of the autocracy. Its members decided to assassinate the tsar himself. Several attempts failed, but on March 1, 1881, a bomb hurled by a

Tsar Alexander II (r. 1855–1881) was assassinated on March 1, 1881. The assassins first threw a bomb that wounded several Imperial guards. When the Tsar stopped his carriage to see to the wounded, the assassins threw a second bomb, killing him. [Bildarchiv Preussischer Kulturbesitz]

member of People's Will killed Alexander II. Four men and two women were sentenced to death for the deed. All of them had been willing to die for their cause. The emergence of such dedicated revolutionary opposition was as much a part of the reign of Alexander II as were his reforms. The limited character of those reforms convinced many Russians that the autocracy could never truly redirect Russian society.

The reign of Alexander III (r. 1881–1894) strengthened that pessimism. He possessed all the autocratic and repressive characteristics of his grandfather Nicholas I and none of the better qualities of his father. Some slight improvements were made in conditions in Russian factories, but Alexander III primarily sought to roll back his father's reforms. He favored the centralized bureaucracy over the *zemstvos*. He strengthened the secret police and increased press censorship. In effect, he confirmed all the evils that the revolutionaries saw as inherent in

autocratic government. His son, Nicholas II (r. 1894–1917), who became tsar in 1894, would discover that autocracy could not survive the pressures of the twentieth century.

Great Britain: Toward Democracy

While the continental nations became unified and struggled toward internal political restructuring, Great Britain continued to symbolize the confident liberal state. Britain was not without its difficulties and domestic conflicts, but it seemed able to deal with these through existing political institutions. The general prosperity of the third quarter of the century mitigated the social hostility of the 1840s. All classes shared a belief in competition and individualism. Even the leaders of trade unions during these years

The People's Will Issues a Revolutionary Manifesto

In the late 1870s, an extreme revolutionary movement appeared in Russia calling itself The People's Will. It advocated the overthrow of the tsarist government and the election of an Organizing Assembly to form a government based on popular representation. It directly embraced terrorism as a path toward its goal of the Russian people governing themselves. Members of this group assassinated Alexander II in 1881.

✦ Which of the group's seven demands might be associated with liberalism and which go beyond liberalism in their radical intent? Why does the group believe it must engage in terrorism as well as propaganda? Would there have been any reforms or steps toward reform that the Russian government might have taken that might have satisfied this group or dissuaded them from terrorist action?

Although we are ready to submit wholly to the popular will, we regard it as none the less our duty, as a party, to appear before the people with our program. . . . It is as follows:

1. Perpetual popular representation, . . . having full power to act in all national questions.

2. General local self-government, secured by the election of all officers, and the economic independence of the people.

3. The self-controlled village commune as the economic and administrative unit.

4. Ownership of the land by the people.

5. A system of measures having for their object the turning over to the laborers of all mining works and factories.

6. Complete freedom of conscience, speech, association, public meeting, and electioneering activity.

7. The substitution of a territorial militia for the army.

. . . .

In view of the stated aim of the party its operations may be classified as follows:

1. *Propaganda and agitation.* Our propaganda has for its object the popularization, in all social classes, of the idea of a political and popular revolution as a means of social reform, as well as popularization of the party's own program. Its essential features are criticism of the existing order of things, and a statement and explanation of revolutionary methods. The aim of agitation should be to incite the people to protest as generally as possible against the present state of affairs, to demand such reforms as are in harmony with the party's purposes, and, especially, to demand the summoning of an Organizing Assembly. . . .

2. *Destructive and terroristic activity.* Terroristic activity consists in the destruction of the most harmful persons in the Government, the protection of the party from spies, and the punishment of official lawlessness and violence in all the more prominent and important cases in which such lawlessness and violence are manifested. The aim of such activity is to break down the prestige of Governmental power, to furnish continuous proof of the possibility of carrying on a contest with the Government, to raise in that way the revolutionary spirit of the people and inspire belief in the practicability of revolution, and, finally, to form a body suited and accustomed to warfare.

Quoted in George Kennan, Siberia and the Exile System, *Vol. 2 (New York: The Century Co., 1891), pp. 495–499.*

asked mainly to receive more of the fruits of prosperity and to have their social respectability acknowledged. Parliament itself remained an institution through which new groups and interests were absorbed into the existing political processes. In short, the British did not have to create new liberal institutions and then learn how to live within them.

The Second Reform Act (1867)

By the early 1860s, most observers realized that the franchise would again have to be expanded. The prosperity and social respectability of the working class convinced many politicians that the workers deserved the vote. Organizations such as the Reform League, led by John Bright (1811–1889), were agitating for parliamentary action. In 1866 Lord Russell's Liberal ministry introduced a reform bill that was defeated by a coalition of traditional Conservatives and antidemocratic Liberals. Russell resigned, and the Conservative Lord Derby (1799–1869) replaced him. What then occurred surprised everyone.

The Conservative ministry, led in the House of Commons by Benjamin Disraeli (1804–1881), introduced its own reform bill in 1867. As the debate proceeded, Disraeli accepted one amendment after another and expanded the electorate well beyond the limits earlier proposed by the Liberals. When the final measure was passed, the number of voters had been increased from approximately 1,430,000 to 2,470,000. Britain had taken a major step toward democracy. Large numbers of male working-class voters had been admitted to the electorate.

Disraeli hoped that by sponsoring the measure, the Conservatives would receive the gratitude of the new voters. Because reform was inevitable, it was best for the Conservatives to enjoy the credit for it. Disraeli thought that eventually significant portions of the working class would support Conservative candidates who were responsive to social issues. He also thought that the growing suburban middle class would become more conservative. In the long run, his intuition proved correct. The Conservative Party has dominated British politics in the twentieth century.

The immediate election of 1868, however, dashed Disraeli's hopes. William Gladstone (1809–1898) became the new prime minister. Gladstone had begun political life in 1833 as a strong Tory, but over the next thirty-five years, he became steadily more liberal. He had supported Robert Peel, free trade, repeal of the Corn Laws, and efficient administration. As chancellor of the exchequer (finance minister) during the 1850s and early 1860s, he had lowered taxes and government expenditures. He had also championed Italian nationalism. Yet he had continued to oppose a new reform bill until the early 1860s. In 1866 he had been Russell's spokesman in the House of Commons for the unsuccessful liberal reform bill.

Gladstone's Great Ministry (1868–1874)

Gladstone's ministry of 1868–1874 witnessed the culmination of classical British liberalism. Those institutions that remained the preserve of the aristocracy and the Anglican church were opened to people from other classes and religious denominations. In 1870 competitive examinations for the civil service replaced patronage. In 1871 the purchase of officers' commissions in the army was abolished. The same year, Anglican religious requirements for the faculties of Oxford and Cambridge universities were removed. The Ballot Act of 1872 introduced voting by secret ballot.

The most momentous measure of Gladstone's first ministry was the Education Act of 1870. For the first time in British history, the government assumed the responsibility for establishing and running elementary schools. Previously, British education had been a task relegated to the religious denominations, which received small amounts of state support for the purpose. Henceforth, the government would establish schools where the efforts of religious denominations to establish them had proved inadequate.

All of these reforms were typically liberal. They sought to remove long-standing abuses without destroying existing institutions and to permit all able citizens to compete on the grounds of ability and merit. They tried to avoid the potential danger to a democratic state of an illiterate citizenry. These reforms also constituted a mode of state building, because they created new bonds of loyalty to the nation by abolishing many sources of discontent.

William Ewart Gladstone served in the British Parliament from the 1830s through the 1890s. Four times the Liberal Party Prime Minister, he was responsible for guiding major reforms through Parliament. [Bildarchiv Preussischer Kulturbesitz]

Disraeli in Office (1874–1880)

The liberal policy of creating popular support for the nation by extending political liberty and reforming abuses had its conservative counterpart in concern for social reform. Disraeli succeeded Gladstone as prime minister in 1874, when the election produced sharp divisions among Liberal Party voters over religion, education, and the sale of alcohol.

The two men had stood on different sides of most issues for over a quarter century. Whereas Gladstone looked to individualism, free trade, and competition to solve social problems, Disraeli believed in paternalistic legislation. Disraeli also believed in state action to protect the weak. In his view, such paternalistic legislation would alleviate class antagonisms.

Disraeli talked a better line than he produced. He had few specific programs or ideas. The significant social legislation of his ministry stemmed primarily from the efforts of his Home Secretary, Richard Cross (1823–1914). The

Public Health Act of 1875 consolidated previous sanitary legislation and reaffirmed the duty of the state to interfere with private property on matters of health and physical well-being. Through the Artisans Dwelling Act of 1875, the government became actively involved in providing housing for the working class. The same year, in an important symbolic gesture, the Conservative majority in Parliament gave new protection to British trade unions and allowed them to raise picket lines. The Gladstone ministry, although recognizing the legality of unions, had refused such protection.

The Irish Question

In 1880 a second Gladstone ministry took office when an agricultural depression and an unpopular foreign policy undermined the Conservative

Benjamin Disraeli served as British Prime Minister from 1874 to 1880. He is regarded as the founder of modern British conservatism because of his efforts to convince the Conservative Party to accept a democratic electorate, which he believed would vote conservative more often than not. [Bildarchiv Preussischer Kulturbesitz]

government. In 1884, with Conservative cooperation, a third reform act gave the vote to most male farm workers. The major issue of the decade, however, was Ireland. From the late 1860s onward, Irish nationalists had sought to achieve home rule for Ireland, by which they meant Irish control of local government.

During his first ministry, Gladstone had addressed the Irish question through two major pieces of legislation. In 1869 he had disestablished the Church of Ireland, the Irish branch of the Anglican church. Henceforth, Irish Roman Catholics would not pay taxes to support the hated Protestant church, to which few of the Irish belonged. Second, in 1870 the Liberal ministry sponsored a land act that provided compensation to those Irish tenants who were evicted and loans for those who wished to purchase their land. Throughout the 1870s, the Irish question continued to fester. Land remained the center of the agitation. Today Irish economic development seems more complicated and who owned the land seems less important than the methods of management and cultivation. Nevertheless, the organization of the Irish Land League in the late 1870s led to intense agitation and intimidation of landlords, who were often English. The leader of the Irish movement for a just land settlement and for home rule was Charles Stewart Parnell (1846–1891). In 1881 the second Gladstone ministry passed another Irish land act that strengthened tenant rights. It was accompanied, however, by a Coercion Act to restore law and order to Ireland.

By 1885 Parnell had organized eighty-five Irish members of the House of Commons into a tightly disciplined party that often voted as a bloc. They frequently disrupted Parliament to gain attention for the cause of home rule. They bargained with the two English political parties. In the election of 1885, the Irish Party emerged holding the balance of power between the English Liberals and Conservatives. Irish support could decide which party took office. In December 1885, Gladstone announced his support of home rule for Ireland. Parnell gave his votes to the formation of a Liberal ministry. The home rule issue then split the Liberal Party. In 1886 a group known as the Liberal Unionists joined with the Conservatives to defeat Gladstone's Home Rule Bill. Gladstone called for a new election, in which the Liberals were

defeated. They remained permanently divided, and Ireland remained firmly under English administration.

The new Conservative ministry of Lord Salisbury (1830–1903) attempted to reconcile the Irish to English government through public works and administrative reform. The policy, which was tied to further coercion, had only marginal success. In 1892 Gladstone returned to power. A second Home Rule Bill passed the House of Commons but was defeated in the House of Lords. There the Irish question stood until after the turn of the century. The Conservatives sponsored a land act in 1903 that carried out the final transfer of land to tenant ownership. Ireland became a country of small farms. In 1912 a Liberal ministry passed the third Home Rule Bill. Under the provisions of

---

Major Dates in Late-Nineteenth-Century Britain

1867	Second Reform Act
1868	Gladstone becomes prime minister
1869	Disestablishment of Church of Ireland
1870	Education Act and first Irish Land Act
1871	Purchase of army officers' commissions abolished
1871	Religious tests abolished at Oxford and Cambridge
1872	Ballot Act
1874	Disraeli becomes prime minister
1875	Public Health Act and Artisan Dwelling Act
1880	Beginning of Gladstone's second ministry
1881	Second Irish Land Act and Irish Coercion Act
1884	Third Reform Act
1885	Gladstone announces support of Irish home rule
1886	Home Rule Bill defeated and Lord Salisbury becomes the Conservative prime minister
1892	Gladstone begins his third ministry; second Irish Home Rule Bill defeated
1903	Third Irish Land Act
1912	Third Irish Home Rule Bill passed
1914	Provisions of Irish Home Rule Bill suspended because of the outbreak of World War I

William Gladstone Pleads for Irish Home Rule

Since 1800 Ireland had been governed as part of Great Britain, sending representatives to the British Parliament in Westminster. Throughout the century, there had been tension and violent conflict between the Irish and their English governors. Agitation for home rule whereby the Irish would directly control many of their own affairs reached a peak in the 1880s. In 1886 William Gladstone introduced a Home Rule Bill into Parliament. The evening when Parliament voted on the measure Gladstone made a long speech, part of which is quoted here, asking Parliament to reject the traditions of the past and to grant Ireland this measure of independence. That night the Home Rule Bill of 1886 went down to defeat, and the problem continues to vex British politics today.

◆ *Why did Gladstone support Irish home rule in 1886? How does he pose the issue as a matter of redeeming the reputation of England? How did the situation of nationalism that Gladstone confronted compare with that of the Austrian prime minister quoted earlier in this chapter?*

What is the case of Ireland at this moment? . . . Can anything stop a nation's demand, except its being proved to be immoderate and unsafe? But here are multitudes, and, I believe, millions upon millions, out-of-doors, who feel this demand to be neither immoderate nor unsafe. In our opinion, there is but one question before us about this demand. It is as to the time and circumstance of granting it. There is no question in our minds that it will be granted. . . .

. . . .

Ireland stands at your bar expectant, hopeful, almost suppliant. Her words are the words of truth and soberness. She asks a blessed oblivion of the past, and in that oblivion our interest is deeper than even hers. My right honourable Friend the Member [of Parliament] for East Edinburgh asks us tonight to abide by the traditions of which we are the heirs. What traditions? By the Irish traditions? Go into the length and breadth of the world, ransack the literature of all countries, find, if you can, a single voice, a single book, find, I would almost say, as much as a single newspaper article, unless the product of the [present] day, in which the conduct of England towards Ireland is anywhere treated except with profound and bitter condemnation. Are these the traditions by which we are exhorted to stand? No; they are a sad exception to the glory of our country. They are a broad and black blot upon the pages of its history; and what we want to do is to stand by the traditions of which we are the heirs in all matters except our relations with Ireland, and to make our relations with Ireland to conform to the other traditions of our country. So we treat our traditions—so we hail the demand of Ireland for what I call a blessed oblivion of the past. She also asks a boon [a favor] for the future; and that boon for the future, unless we are much mistaken, will be a boon to us in respect of honour, no less than a boon to her in respect of happiness, prosperity, and peace. Such . . . is her prayer. Think, I beseech you, think well, think wisely, think, not for the moment, but for the years that are to come, before you reject this Bill.

Quoted in Hans Kohn, ed., The Modern World: 1848 to the Present, *2nd ed. (New York: The Macmillan Company; London: Collier-Macmillan Limited, 1968), pp. 116, 118.*

the House of Lords Act of 1911, which curbed the power of that body, the bill had to pass the Commons three times over the Lords' veto to become law. The third passage occurred in the summer of 1914, but the implementation of the home rule provisions of the bill was suspended for the duration of World War I.

The Irish question affected British politics in a manner not unlike that of the Austrian nationalities problem. Normal British domestic issues could not be resolved because of the political divisions created by Ireland. The split of the Liberal Party proved especially harmful to the cause of further social and political reform. People who could agree about reform could not agree about Ireland, and the Irish problem seemed more important. Since the two traditional parties failed to deal with the social questions, by the turn of the century, a newly organized Labour Party began to fill the vacuum.

◆

Between 1850 and 1875, the major contours of the political systems that would dominate Europe until World War I had been drawn. Those systems and political arrangements solved, so far as such matters can be solved, many of the political questions and problems that had troubled Europeans during the first half of the nineteenth century. The concept of the nation-state had on the whole triumphed. Support for governments no longer stemmed from loyalty to dynasties but from various degrees of citizen participation. Moreover, the unity of nations was no longer based on dynastic links but on ethnic, cultural, linguistic, and historical bonds. The parliamentary governments of western Europe were different from the autocracies of eastern Europe, but both political systems had been compelled to recognize the force of nationalism and the larger role of citizens in political affairs. Only Russia failed to make such concessions, but the emancipation of serfs had partly been a concession to a mode of popular opinion.

The major sources of future discontent would arise from the demands of labor to enter the political processes and the still unsatisfied aspirations of subject nationalities. Those two areas of unrest would trouble Europe for the next forty years and would eventually undermine the political structures created during the third quarter of the nineteenth century.

Review Questions

1. Why was it so difficult to unify Italy? What groups were urging unification? Who was Camillo Cavour and how did he achieve what others failed to do? What were Garibaldi's contributions to Italian unification?

2. Who was Otto von Bismarck and why did he try to unify Germany? What attempts had preceded Bismarck's efforts and why did they fail? What was Bismarck's policy of unification and why did he succeed? What effect did the unification of Germany have on the rest of Europe?

3. Discuss the transformation in France from the Second Empire of Napoleon III to the establishment of the Third Republic. Why did the Second Empire fall and what problems faced the new republic? Why did the Paris Commune become a legend throughout Europe? What effect did the Dreyfus affair have on the politics of the Third Republic?

4. Describe the government changes in Austria after 1848. What unique problems did Austria have? Were they solved? Why was nationalism a more pressing problem for Austria than for any other nation?

5. What reforms were instituted by Tsar Alexander II in Russia? Were they effective in solving some of Russia's domestic problems? Can Alexander II be regarded as a "visionary" reformer? Why or why not?

6. How would you contrast the British Liberal and Conservative parties between 1860 and 1890? Who were the leaders of each? What problems did they face in those years and what different solutions did they favor? Specifically, how did British politicians handle the Irish Question? What are the parallels between England's relationship with Ireland and the nationality problem of the Austrian Empire?

Suggested Readings

M. Bentley, *Politics Without Democracy, 1815–1914* (1984). A well-informed survey of British development.

R. Blake, *Disraeli* (1967). The best biography.

J. Blum, *Lord and Peasant in Russia from the Ninth to the Nineteenth Century* (1961). A clear discussion of emancipation in the later chapters.

W. L. Burn, *The Age of Equipoise* (1964). A thoughtful and convincing discussion of Victorian social stability.

G. Chapman, *The Dreyfus Affair: A Reassessment* (1955). A detached treatment of a subject that still provokes strong feelings.

G. Craig, *Germany, 1866–1945* (1978). An excellent survey.

S. Edwards, *The Paris Commune of 1871* (1971). A useful examination of a complex subject.

S. Elwitt, *The Making of the Third Republic: Class and Politics in France, 1868–1884* (1975). An excellent introduction.

S. Elwitt, *The Third Republic Defended: Bourgeois Reform in France, 1880–1914* (1986). A study that continues the survey of the previously listed volume.

E. Hobsbawm, *The Age of Empire, 1875–1914* (1987). A stimulating survey that covers cultural as well as political developments.

I. V. Hull, *The Entourage of Kaiser Wilhelm II, 1888–1918* (1982). An important discussion of the scandals of the German court.

R. A. Kann, *The Multinational Empire*, 2 vols. (1950). The basic treatment of the nationality problem of Austria-Hungary.

G. Kitson Klark, *The Making of Victorian England* (1962). The best introduction.

R. R. Locke, *French Legitimists and the Politics of Moral Order in the Early Third Republic* (1974). An excellent study of the social and intellectual roots of monarchist support.

A. J. May, *The Habsburg Monarchy, 1867–1914* (1951). Narrates in considerable detail and with much sympathy the fate of the dual monarchy.

N. M. Naimark, *Terrorists and Social Democrats: The Russian Revolutionary Movement Under Alexander III* (1983). Useful discussion of a complicated subject.

C. C. O'Brien, *Parnell and His Party* (1957). An excellent treatment of the Irish question.

J. P. Parry, *Democracy and Religion: Gladstone and the Liberal Party, 1867–1876* (1987). An important study of the role of religious denominations in the British Liberal Party.

O. Pflanze, *Bismarck and the Development of Germany*, 3 vols. (1990). A major biography and history of Germany for the period.

A. Plessis, *The Rise and Fall of the Second Empire, 1852–1871* (1985). A useful survey of France under Napoleon III.

R. Shannon, *Gladstone: 1809–1865* (1982). Best coverage of his early career.

D. M. Smith, *The Making of Italy, 1796–1870* (1968). A narrative that incorporates the major documents.

D. M. Smith, *Cavour* (1984). An excellent biography.

A. J. P. Taylor, *The Habsburg Monarchy, 1809–1918* (1941). An opinionated but highly readable work.

J. M. Thomson, *Louis Napoleon and the Second Empire* (1954). A straightforward account.

R. Tombs, *The War Against Paris, 1871* (1981). Examines the role of the army in suppressing the Commune.

A. B. Ulam, *Russia's Failed Revolutionaries* (1981). A study of revolutionary societies and activities prior to the Revolution of 1917.

F. Venturi, *The Roots of Revolution* (trans., 1960). A major treatment of late-nineteenth-century revolutionary movements.

H. S. Watson, *The Russian Empire, 1801–1917* (1967). A far-ranging narrative.

H. U. Wehler, *The German Empire, 1871–1918* (1985). An important, controversial work.

J. Wertheimer, *Unwelcome Strangers: East European Jews in Imperial Germany* (1987). Examines the difficult position of Jews in Wilhelminian Germany.

R. Williams, *The World of Napoleon III*, rev. ed. (1965). Examines the cultural setting.

C. B. Woodham-Smith, *The Reason Why* (1953). A lively account of the Crimean War and the charge of the Light Brigade.

T. Zeldin, *France: 1848–1945*, 2 vols. (1973, 1977). Emphasizes the social developments.

R. E. Zelnick, *Labor and Society in Tsarist Russia: The Factory Workers of St. Petersburg, 1855–1870* (1971). An important volume that considers the early stages of the Russian industrial labor force in the era of serf emancipation.

Railways were an important part of late-nineteenth-century middle-class life. They helped promote the development of suburbs, allowing breadwinners to commute into the city to work, leaving their families at home. They also promoted travel to the vacation spots that were being developed across Europe during this era. [Bildarchiv Preussischer Kulturbesitz]

24

The Building of European Supremacy: Society and Politics to World War I

Key Topics in This Chapter

◆ The transformation of European life by the Second Industrial Revolution

◆ Urban sanitation, housing reform, and the redesign of cities

◆ The condition of women in late-nineteenth-century Europe and the rise of political feminism

◆ The development of labor politics and socialism in Europe to the outbreak of World War I

◆ Industrialization and political unrest in Russia

The growth of industrialism between 1860 and 1914 increased Europe's productive capacity to unprecedented and unparalleled levels. Newly *erected steel mills, railways, shipyards, and chemical plants reflected an expanding supply of capital goods in the second half of the nine-*

teenth century. By the first decade of the new century, the age of the automobile, the airplane, the bicycle, the refrigerated ship, the telephone, the radio, the typewriter, and the electric light bulb had dawned. The world's economies, based on the gold standard, became increasingly interdependent. European manufactured goods and financial capital flowed into markets all over the globe. In turn, Europeans imported foreign raw materials and foodstuffs. Within Europe itself, the countries toward the eastern part of the continent tended to import finished goods from the west and to export agricultural products.

During this half century, European political, economic, and social life assumed many of its current characteristics. Nation-states with large electorates, political parties, and centralized bureaucracies emerged. Business adopted large-scale corporate structures, and the labor force organized itself into trade unions. Increasing numbers of white-collar workers appeared. Urban life came to predominate throughout western Europe. Socialism became a major ingredient in the political life of all nations. The foundations of the welfare state and of vast military establishments were laid. Taxation increased accordingly.

Europe had also quietly become dependent on the resources and markets of the rest of the world. Changes in the weather conditions in Kansas, Argentina, or New Zealand might now affect the European economy. Before World War I, however, that dependence was concealed by Europe's industrial, military, and financial supremacy. Many Europeans assumed their supremacy to be natural and enduring, but the twentieth century would reveal it to have been temporary.

Population Trends and Migration

The proportion of Europeans in the world's total population was apparently greater around 1900—estimated at about 20 percent—than ever before or since. The number of Europeans had risen from approximately 266 million in 1850 to 401 million in 1900 and 447 million in 1910. Thereafter, birth and death rates declined

or stabilized in Europe and other developed regions, and population growth began to slow in those areas but not elsewhere. The result has been the demographic differential between the developed and undeveloped world—stable or slowly growing populations in developed countries and large, rapidly growing populations in undeveloped regions—that contributes to the world's present food and resource crisis.

Europe's peoples were on the move in the last half of the century as never before. The mid-century emancipation of peasants lessened the authority of landlords and made legal movement and migration easier. Railways, steamships, and better roads increased mobility. Cheap land and better wages accompanied economic development in Europe, North America, Latin America, and Australia, enticing people to move.

Europeans migrated away from their continent in record numbers. Between 1846 and 1932, more than 50 million left their homelands. The major areas to benefit from this movement were the United States, Canada, Australia, South Africa, Brazil, and Argentina. At mid-century most of the emigrants were from Great Britain (especially Ireland), Germany, and Scandinavia. After 1885 migration from southern and eastern Europe rose. This exodus helped to relieve the social and population pressures on the Continent. The outward movement of peoples in conjunction with Europe's economic and technological superiority contributed heavily to the Europeanization of the world. Not since the sixteenth century had European civilization had such an impact on other cultures.

The Second Industrial Revolution

During the third quarter of the nineteenth century, the gap that had long existed between British and continental economic development closed. The basic heavy industries of Belgium, France, and Germany underwent major expansion. In particular, the growth of all areas of German industry was stunning. German steel production surpassed that of Britain in 1893

European emigrants from eastern Europe wait to board a ship that will carry them to the United States. Between 1846 and 1932, more than 50 million Europeans emigrated to the United States, Canada, South America, Australia, and South Africa. [Bildarchiv Preussischer Kulturbesitz]

and had almost doubled Britain's by the outbreak of World War I. This emergence of an industrial Germany was *the* major fact of European economic and political life at the turn of the century.

New Industries

Initially the economic expansion of the third quarter of the century involved the spread of industries similar to those pioneered earlier in Great Britain. In particular, the expansion of railway systems on the Continent spurred economic growth. Thereafter, however, wholly new industries emerged. It is this latter development that is usually termed the *Second Industrial Revolution.* The first industrial revolution was associated with textiles, steam, and iron; by contrast, the second was associated with steel, chemicals, electricity, and oil.

In the 1850s, Henry Bessemer (1830–1898), an English engineer, discovered a new process, named after him, for manufacturing steel cheaply in large quantities. In 1860 Great Britain, Belgium, France, and Germany had produced 125,000 tons of steel. By 1913 the figure had risen to 32,020,000 tons.

The chemical industry also came of age during this period. The Solway process of alkali production replaced the older Leblanc process, allowing the recovery of more chemical by-products. The new process permitted increased production of sulfuric acid and laundry soap. New dyestuffs and plastics were also developed. Formal scientific research played an important role in this growth of the chemical industry, marking the beginning of a direct link between science and industrial development. As in so many other aspects of the Second Industrial

Electricity transformed industry and everyday life in Europe. This painting is of an early electric generating plant in France. [Bridgeman/Art Resource, N.Y.]

Revolution, Germany was a leader in forging this link, fostering scientific research and education.

The most significant change for industry and eventually for everyday life involved the application of electrical energy to production. Electricity was the most versatile and transportable source of power ever discovered. It could be delivered almost anywhere to run either large or small machinery, making factory location more flexible and factory construction more efficient. The first major public power plant was constructed in 1881 in Great Britain. Soon electric poles, lines, and generating stations dotted the European landscape. Homes began to use electric lights. Streetcar and subway systems were electrified.

The internal combustion engine was invented in 1886. When the German engineer Gottlieb Daimler (1834–1900) put it on four wheels and obtained a French patent in 1887, the automobile was born. France initially took the lead in auto manufacture, but for many years the car remained a novelty item that only the wealthy could afford. It was the American Henry Ford (1863–1947) who later made the automobile accessible to large numbers of people.

The automobile and new industrial and chemical uses for petroleum had, by the turn of the century, created the first significant demand for oil, and then as now Europe depended on imported supplies. The major oil companies were Standard Oil of the United States, British Shell Oil, and Royal Dutch Petroleum.

Economic Difficulties

Despite the multiplication of new industries, the second half of the nineteenth century was not a period of uninterrupted or smooth economic growth. Both industry and agriculture generally prospered from 1850 to 1873, but in the last quarter of the century economic advance was slower. Bad weather and foreign competition put grave pressures on European agriculture. Although these problems for agriculture lowered consumer food prices, they also put a drag on the economy. Many of the emigrants who left Europe during these years came from the countryside or from the least industrialized parts of Europe.

Several large banks failed in 1873, and the rate of capital investment slowed. Some industries then entered a two-decades-long period of stagnation that many contemporaries regarded as a depression. Overall, however, the general standard of living in the industrialized nations improved in the second half of the nineteenth century. Prices and wages, as well as profits, both fell, so real wages generally held firm, and in some countries even rose. Yet many workers still lived and labored in abysmal conditions. There were pockets of *unemployment* (a word that was coined during this period), and strikes and other forms of labor unrest were common. The economic difficulties fed the growth of trade unions and socialist political parties.

The new industries produced consumer goods, and expansion in consumer demand brought the economy out of stagnation by the end of the century. Lower food prices eventually allowed all classes to spend a marginally larger amount of their income on consumer goods. Urbanization naturally created larger markets. People living in cities simply saw more things they wanted to buy than they would have seen in the countryside. New forms of retailing and marketing appeared—department stores, chain stores, packaging techniques, mail-order cata-

---

Paris Department Stores Expand Their Business

The department store in Europe and the United States became a major institution of retailing in the last half of the nineteenth century. It was one of the reasons for the expansion in late-century consumer demand. This description, written by the Frenchman E. Levasseur in 1907, follows the growth of such stores in Paris and explains why they exerted such economic power. The reader will notice how many of their techniques of retailing are still used today.

◆ *Why should the various French governments have favored the growth of department stores? Where did these stores stand in the process of economic production and sales? Why was the volume of sales so important? What kinds of people might have benefitted from the jobs available in these stores?*

It was in the reign of Louis-Philippe [1830–1848] that department stores for fashion goods and dresses . . . began to be distinguished. The type was already one of the notable developments of the Second Empire; it became one of the most important ones of the Third Republic. These stores have increased in number and several of them have become extremely large. Combining in their different departments all articles of clothing, toilet articles, furniture and many other ranges of goods, it is their special object so to combine all commodities as to attract and satisfy customers who will find conveniently together an assortment of a mass of articles corresponding to all their various needs. They attract customers by permanent display, by free entry into the shops, by periodic exhibitions, by special sales, by fixed prices, and by their ability to deliver the goods purchased to customers' homes, in Paris and to the provinces. Turning themselves into direct intermediaries between the producer and the consumer, even producing sometimes some of their articles in their own workshops, buying at lowest prices because of

their large orders and because they are in a position to profit from bargains, working with large sums, and selling to most of their customers for cash only, they can transmit these benefits in lowered selling prices. They can even decide to sell at a loss, as an advertisement or to get rid of out-of-date fashions. . . .

The success of these department stores is only possible thanks to the volume of their business, and this volume needs considerable capital and a very large turnover. Now capital, having become abundant, is freely combined nowadays in large enterprises. . . . [T]he large urban agglomerations, the ease with which goods can be transported by the railways, the diffusion of some comforts to strata below the middle classes, have all favoured these developments. . . .

According to the tax records of 1891, these stores in Paris, numbering 12, employed 1,708 persons and rated their site values at 2,159,000 francs; the largest had then 542 employees. These same stores had, in 1901, 9,784 employees; one of them over 2,000 and another over 1,600; their site value was doubled.

Sidney Pollard and Colin Holmes, Documents of European Economic History, Vol. 3 *(London: Edward Arnold, 1972), pp. 95–96.*

Major Dates of the Second Industrial Revolution	
1856–1870	Passage of laws permitting joint stock companies: 1856, Britain; 1863, France; 1870, Prussia
1857	Bessemer process for making steel
1873	Beginning of major economic downturn
1876	Alexander Graham Bell invents the telephone
1879	Edison perfects the electric light bulb
1881	First electric power plant in Britain
1886	Daimler invents the internal combustion engine
1887	Daimler's first automobile
1895	Diesel engine invented
1895	Wireless telegraphy invented
1890s	Decade of first major impact of petroleum
1903	Wright brothers make first successful airplane flight
1909	Ford manufactures the Model T

logs, and advertising—simultaneously stimulating and feeding consumer demand. Overseas imperialism also opened new markets for European consumer goods.

The Middle Classes in Ascendancy

The sixty years before World War I were the age of the middle classes. The London Great Exhibition of 1851 held in the Crystal Palace had displayed the products and the new material life they had forged. Thereafter, the middle classes became the arbiter of consumer taste. After the revolutions of 1848, the middle classes ceased to be a revolutionary group. Once the question of social and property equality had been raised, large and small property owners across the Continent moved to protect what they possessed against demands from socialists and other working-class groups.

Social Distinctions Within the Middle Classes

The middle classes, never perfectly homogeneous, grew increasingly diverse. Their most prosperous members—the owners and managers of great businesses and banks—lived in splendor that rivaled and sometimes exceeded that of the aristocracy. Some, such as W. H. Smith (1825–1891), the owner of railway newsstands in England, were made members of the House of Lords. The Krupp family of Germany were pillars of the state and received visits from the German emperor and his court.

Only a few hundred families gained such wealth. Beneath them were the comfortable small entrepreneurs and professional people, whose incomes permitted private homes, large quantities of furniture, pianos, pictures, books, journals, education for their children, and vacations. Also in this group were the shopkeepers, schoolteachers, librarians, and others who had either a bit of property or a skill derived from education that provided respectable, nonmanual employment.

Finally, there was a wholly new element, white-collar workers, who formed the lower middle class or petty bourgeoisie. They included secretaries, retail clerks, and lower-level bureaucrats in business and government. They often had working-class origins and might even belong to unions, but they had middle-class aspirations and consciously sought to distance themselves from a lower-class lifestyle. They actively pursued educational opportunities and chances for even the slightest career advancement for themselves and more especially for their children. Many of them spent a considerable portion of their disposable income on consumer goods, such as stylish clothing and furniture, that were distinctively middle class in appearance.

Significant tensions and social anxieties marked relations among the various middle-class groups. Small shopkeepers resented the power of the great capitalists, with their department stores and mail-order catalogues. There is some evidence that the professions were becoming overcrowded. People who had only recently attained a middle-class lifestyle feared losing it in bad economic times. Nonetheless, the decades immediately before the First World War

The Paris Exhibition of 1889, like other exhibitions held during the second half of the nineteenth century, allowed Europeans to see the vast array of consumer goods that had become available to them. [Bildarchiv Preussischer Kulturbesitz]

saw the middle classes setting the values and goals for most of the society.

Late-Nineteenth-Century Urban Life

Europe became more urbanized than ever in the last half of the nineteenth century as migration to the cities continued. Between 1850 and 1911, urban dwellers rose from 25 to 44 percent of the population in France and from 30 to 60 percent of the population in Germany. Other western European countries experienced similar increases.

Growth of Major European Cities (FIGURES IN THOUSANDS)			
	1850	1880	1910
Berlin	419	1,122	2,071
Birmingham	233	437	840
Frankfurt	65	137	415
London	2,685	4,470	7,256
Madrid	281	398	600
Moscow	365	748	1,533
Paris	1,053	2,269	2,888
Rome	175	300	542
St. Petersburg	485	877	1,962
Vienna	444	1,104	2,031
Warsaw	160	339	872

The rural migrants to the cities were largely uprooted from traditional social ties. They often faced poor housing, social anonymity, and, because they rarely possessed the right kinds of skills, unemployment. People from different ethnic backgrounds found themselves in proximity to one another and had difficulty mixing socially. Competition for jobs generated new varieties of political and social discontent, such as the anti-Semitism directed at the thousands of Russian Jews who had migrated to western Europe. Indeed, much of the political anti-Semitism of the latter part of the century had its roots in the problems generated by urban migration.

The Redesign of Cities

The inward urban migration placed new social and economic demands on already strained city resources and gradually produced significant transformations in the patterns of urban living. National and municipal governments redesigned the central portions of many major European cities during the second half of the century. Previously, the central urban areas had been places where many people from all social classes both lived and worked. From the middle of the century onward, planners transformed these districts into areas where businesses, government offices, large retail stores, and theaters were located, but where fewer people resided. Commerce, trade, government, and leisure activities now dominated central cities.

THE NEW PARIS The most famous and extensive transformation of a major city occurred in Paris. Like so many other European cities, Paris had expanded from the Middle Ages onward with little or no design or planning. Great public buildings and squalid hovels stood near each other. The Seine River was little more than an open sewer. The streets were narrow, crooked, and crowded. It was impossible to cross easily from one part of the city to another either on foot or by carriage. In 1850 a fully correct map of the city did not even exist. Of more concern to the government of Napoleon III, the city's streets had for sixty years provided battlegrounds for urban insurrections that had on numerous occasions, most recently in 1848, toppled French governments.

Napoleon III personally determined that Paris must be redesigned. He appointed Georges Haussmann (1809–1891), who, as prefect of the Seine from 1853 to 1870, oversaw a vast urban reconstruction program. Whole districts were destroyed to open the way for the broad boulevards and streets that became the hallmark of modern Paris. Much, though by no means all, of the purpose of this street planning was political. The wide vistas were not only beautiful but also allowed for the quick deployment of troops to put down riots. The eradication of the many small streets and alleys removed areas where barricades could be and had been erected.

The project was also political in another sense. In addition to the new boulevards, parks such as the Bois de Boulogne and major public buildings such as the Paris Opera were also constructed or completed. These projects, along with the demolition and street building, created thousands of public jobs. Many other laborers found employment in the private construction that accompanied the public works.

Further rebuilding and redesign occurred under the Third Republic after the destruction that accompanied the suppression of the Commune. Many department stores, office complexes, and largely middle-class apartment buildings were constructed. By the late 1870s, mechanical trams were operating in Paris. After much debate, construction of a subway system (the "Métro") began in 1895, long after that of London (1863). New railway stations were also erected near the close of the century. This transport linked the refurbished central city to the suburbs.

In 1889 the Eiffel Tower was built, originally as a temporary structure for the international trade exposition of that year. Not all the new structures of Paris bespoke the impact of middle-class commerce and the reign of iron and steel, however. Between 1873 and 1914, the French Roman Catholic church oversaw the construction of the Basilica of the Sacred Heart high atop Montmartre as an act of national penance for

The Eiffel Tower, shown under construction in this painting, was to become a symbol of the newly redesigned Paris and its steel structure a symbol of French industrial strength. [Roger-Viollet]

the sins that had led to French defeat in the Franco-Prussian War. Those two landmarks—the Eiffel Tower and the Basilica of the Sacred Heart—visibly symbolized the social and political divisions between liberals and conservatives in the Third Republic.

DEVELOPMENT OF SUBURBS Commercial development, railway construction, and the clearing of slums displaced many city dwellers and raised urban land values and rents. Consequently, both the middle classes and the working class began to seek housing elsewhere. The middle classes looked for neighborhoods removed from urban congestion. The working class looked for affordable housing. The result, in virtually all countries, was the development of suburbs surrounding the city proper. These suburbs housed families whose breadwinner worked in the central city or in a factory located within the city limits. European suburbs, unlike those that developed in the United States, often consisted of apartment buildings or private houses built closely together with small lawns and gardens.

The expansion of railways with cheap workday fares and the introduction of mechanical and later electric tramways, as well as subways, allowed tens of thousands of workers from all classes to move daily between the city and the outlying suburbs. For hundreds of thousands of Europeans, home and work became more physically separated than ever before.

Urban Sanitation

The efforts of governments and of the increasingly conservative middle classes to maintain public order after 1848 led to a growing concern with the problems of public health and housing for the poor. A widespread feeling arose that only when the health and housing of the working class were improved would the middle-class health also be secure and the political order stable.

IMPACT OF CHOLERA These concerns first manifested themselves as a result of the great cholera epidemics of the 1830s and 1840s. Unlike many other common deadly diseases of the day that touched only the poor, cholera struck all classes, impelling the middle class to demand a solution. Before the development of the bacterial theory of disease late in the century, physicians and sanitary reformers believed that cholera and other diseases were spread through infection from miasmas in the air. These miasmas, the presence of which was marked by their foul odors, were believed to arise from filth. The way to get rid of the dangerous, foul-smelling air was to clean up the cities.

During the 1840s, many physicians and some government officials began to publicize the dangers posed by the unsanitary conditions associated with overcrowding in cities and with businesses such as basement slaughterhouses. In 1840 Louis René Villermé published his *Tableau de l'état physique et moral des ouvriers employés* (*Catalog of the Physical and Moral State of Workers*). In 1842 Edwin Chadwick's (1800–1890) *Report on the Sanitary Condition of the Labouring Population* shocked the English public. In Germany, Rudolf Virchow (1821–1902) published similar findings. These and various other private and public commission reports closely linked the issues of wretched living conditions and public health. They also demonstrated that sanitary reform would remove the dangers. These reports, incidentally, now provide some of the best information available about working-class living conditions in the middle of the nineteenth century.

NEW WATER AND SEWER SYSTEMS The proposed solution to the health hazard was cleanliness, to be achieved through new water and sewer systems. These facilities were constructed slowly, beginning usually in capital cities and then much later in provincial cities. Some major urban areas did not have good water systems until after the turn of the cen-tury. Nonetheless, the building of these systems was one of the major health and engineering achievements of the second half of the nineteenth century. The sewer system of Paris was a famous part of Haussmann's rebuilding program. In London, the construction of the Albert Embankment along the Thames involved not only large sewers discharging into the river but gas mains and water pipes as well; all were encased in thick walls of granite and concrete, one of the new building materials of the day. Wherever these sanitary facilities were installed, the mortality rate dropped considerably.

A French Physician Describes a Working-Class Slum in Lille Before the Public Health Movement

It is difficult to conceive of the world before the sanitation movement. The work of medical doctors frequently carried them into working-class areas of industrial cities rarely visited by other members of the middle class. Louis Villermé was such a French physician. He wrote extensive descriptions of the slums and the general living conditions of industrial workers. The passage here, published in 1840, describes a particularly notorious section of Lille, a major cotton-manufacturing town in northern France.

◆ *What does this physician find most disturbing about the scene he describes? How is his description possibly designed to call forth sympathy and concern from a middle-class reader? How might the conditions described have led the poor of France toward socialism or radical politics? How would addressing the problems described have led to a larger role for government?*

The poorest live in the cellars and attics. These cellars . . . open onto the streets or courtyards, and one enters them by a stairway which is very often at once the door and the window. . . . Commonly the height of the ceiling is six or six and a half feet at the highest point, and they are only ten to fourteen or fifteen feet wide.

It is in these somber and sad dwellings that a large number of workers eat, sleep, and even work. The light of day comes an hour later for them than for others, and the night an hour earlier.

Their furnishings normally consist, along with the tools of their profession, of a sort of cupboard or a plank on which to deposit food, a stove . . . a few pots, a little table, two or three poor chairs, and a dirty pallet of which the only pieces are a straw mattress and scraps of a blanket. . . .

In their obscure cellars, in their rooms, which one would take for cellars, the air is never renewed, it is infected; the walls are plastered with garbage. . . . If a bed exists, it is a few dirty, greasy planks; it is damp and putrescent straw; it is a coarse cloth whose color and fabric are hidden by a layer of grime; it is a blanket that resembles a sieve. . . . The furniture is dislocated, worm-eaten, covered with filth. Utensils are thrown in disorder all over the dwelling. The windows, always closed, are covered by paper and glass, but so black, so smoke-encrusted, that the light is unable to penetrate . . . everywhere are piles of garbage, of ashes, of debris from vegetables picked up from the streets, of rotten straw; of animal nests of all sorts; thus, the air is unbreathable. One is exhausted, in these hovels, by a stale, nauseating, somewhat piquante odor, odor of filth, odor of garbage. . . .

And the poor themselves, what are they like in the middle of such a slum? Their clothing is in shreds, without substance, consumed, covered, no less than their hair, which knows no comb, with dust from the workshops. And their skin? . . . It is painted, it is hidden, if you wish, by indistinguishable deposits of diverse exudations.

Louis René Villermé, Tableau de l'état physique et moral des ouvriers employés dans les manufactures de coton, de laine et de soie *(Paris, 1840), as quoted and trans. in William H. Sewell, Jr.,* Work and Revolution in France: The Language of Labor from the Old Regime to 1848 *(Cambridge, England: Cambridge University Press, 1980), p. 224.*

The vast sewer systems constructed during the nineteenth century to remove waste from cities were among the genuine wonders of the period. They were a source of public fascination and even a tourist attraction, as this illustration of a tour of the Paris sewers shows. [The Bettmann Archive]

EXPANDED GOVERNMENT INVOLVEMENT IN PUBLIC HEALTH This concern with public health led to an expansion of governmental power on various levels. In Britain the Public Health Act of 1848, in France the Melun Act of 1851, and various laws in the still-disunited German states, as well as later legislation, introduced new restraints on private life and enterprise. This legislation allowed medical officers and building inspectors to enter homes and other structures in the name of public health. Private property could be condemned for posing health hazards. Private land could be excavated for the construction of the sewers and water mains required to protect the public. New building regulations put restraints on the activities of private contractors.

Full acceptance at the close of the century of the bacterial theory of disease associated with the discoveries of Louis Pasteur (1822–1895) in France, Robert Koch (1843–1910) in Germany, and Joseph Lister (1827–1912) in Britain made cleanliness an even more prominent public concern. Throughout Europe, issues related to the maintenance of public health and the physical well-being of national populations repeatedly opened the way for new modes of government intervention in the lives of citizens.

Housing Reform and Middle-Class Values

The information about working-class living conditions brought to light by the sanitary reformers also led to heated debates over the housing problem. The wretched dwellings of the poor were themselves a cause of poor sanitation and thus became a newly perceived health hazard. Furthermore, middle-class reformers and bureaucrats found themselves shocked by the domestic arrangements of the poor, whose large families might live in a single room lacking all forms of personal privacy. A single toilet facility might serve a whole block of tenements. After the revolutions of 1848, the overcrowding in housing and the social discontent that it generated were also seen to pose a political danger.

Middle-class reformers thus turned to housing reform to solve the medical, moral, and

Major Dates Relating to Sanitation Reform	
1830s and 1840s	Cholera epidemics
1840	Villermé's *Catalog of the Physical and Moral State of Workers*
1842	Chadwick's *Report on the Sanitary Condition of the Labouring Population*
1848	British Public Health Act
1851	French Melun Act

Urban slums such as this one in Glasgow, Scotland, aroused the concern of sanitary and housing reformers. [Service Photographique des Musées Nationaux, Paris/Photo R.M.N.]

political dangers posed by slums. Proper, decent housing would foster a good home life, in turn leading to a healthy, moral, and politically stable population. As A. V. Huber, one of the early German housing reformers, declared:

Certainly it would not be too much to say that the home is the communal embodiment of family life. Thus the purity of the dwelling is almost as important for the family as is the cleanliness of the body for the individual. Good or bad housing is a question of life and death if ever there was one.[1]

Later advocates of housing reform, such as Jules Simon in France, saw good housing as leading to good family life and ultimately to

[1]*Quoted in Nicholas Bullock and James Read*, The Movement for Housing Reform in Germany and France, 1840–1914 *(Cambridge, England: Cambridge University Press, 1985), p. 42.*

strong patriotic feeling. It was widely believed that providing the poor and the working class with adequate, respectable, cheap housing would alleviate social and political discontent. It was also believed that the personal saving and investment required for owning a home would lead the working class to adopt the thrifty habits of the middle classes.

Private philanthropy made the first attack on the housing problem. Companies operating on low profit margins or making low-interest loans encouraged housing for the poor. Firms, such as the German Krupp armaments concern, seeking to ensure a contented, healthy, and stable workforce, constructed model housing projects and industrial communities.

By the mid-1880s, the migration into cities had made housing a political issue. Legislation in England in 1885 lowered the interest rates for the construction of cheap housing, and soon thereafter public authorities began public housing projects. In Germany, action on housing came later in the century through the initiative of local municipalities. In 1894 France made inexpensive credit available for constructing housing for the poor. None of these governments, however, adopted wide-scale housing experiments.

Nonetheless, by 1914 the housing problem had been fully recognized if not adequately addressed. The goal of housing reform across western Europe came to be to provide homes for the members of the working class that would allow them to enjoy a family life more or less like that of the middle class. Such a home would be in the form of a detached house or some kind of affordable city apartment with several rooms, a private entrance, and separate toilet facilities.

Varieties of Late-Nineteenth-Century Women's Experiences

Late-nineteenth-century women, like late-nineteenth-century men, led lives that reflected their social rank. Yet, within each rank, the experience of women was distinct from that of men. Women remained, generally speaking, in positions of economic dependence and legal inferiority, whatever their social class.

Social Disabilities Confronted by All Women

At the middle of the nineteenth century, virtually all European women faced social and legal disabilities in three areas: property rights, family law, and education. By the close of the century, there had been some improvement in each area.

WOMEN AND PROPERTY Until the last quarter of the century in most European countries, married women could not own property in their own names no matter what their social class. For all practical purposes, upon marriage women lost to their husbands' control any property they owned or that they might inherit or earn by their own labor. Their legal identities was subsumed in their husbands', and they had no independent standing before the law. The courts saw the theft of a woman's purse as a theft of her husband's property. Because European society was based on private property and wage earning, these disabilities put married women at a great disadvantage. They limited their freedom to work, to save, and to move from one location to another.

Reform of women's property rights came very slowly. By 1882 Great Britain had passed a Married Woman's Property Act that allowed married women to own property in their own right. In France, however, a married woman could not even open a savings account in her own name until 1895 and not until 1907 were married women granted possession of the wages they earned. In 1900 Germany allowed women to take jobs without their husbands' permission, but except for her wages, a German husband retained control of most of his wife's property. Similar laws prevailed elsewhere in Europe.

FAMILY LAW Virtually all European family law also worked to the disadvantage of women. Legal codes actually required wives to give obedience to their husbands. The Napoleonic Code and the remnants of Roman law still in effect made women legal minors throughout Europe. Divorce was difficult everywhere for most of the century. In England before 1857, divorce required an act of Parliament. Thereafter, divorce could be gained, with difficulty, through the Court of Matrimonial Causes. Most nations did not permit divorce by mutual consent. French law forbade divorce between 1816 and 1884.

Thereafter the chief recognized legal cause for divorce was cruelty and injury, which had to be proven in court. In Great Britain, adultery was the usual cause for divorce, but to gain a divorce a woman had to prove her husband's adultery plus other offenses, whereas a man only had to prove his wife's adultery. In Germany, only adultery or serious maltreatment were recognized as reasons for divorce. Across Europe, some version of the double standard prevailed whereby extramarital sexual relations of husbands were tolerated to a greater degree than those of wives. Everywhere, divorce required legal hearings and the presentation of legal proof, making the process expensive and all the more difficult for women who did not control their own property.

The authority of husbands also extended to children. A husband could take children away from their mother and give them to someone else for rearing. Only the husband, in most countries, could permit his daughter to marry. In some countries, he could virtually force his daughter to marry the man of his choice. In cases of divorce and separation, the husband normally assumed authority over children no matter how he had treated them previously.

The issues surrounding the sexual and reproductive rights of women that have been so widely debated recently could hardly be discussed in the nineteenth century. Until well into the twentieth century, both contraception and abortion were illegal. The law surrounding rape normally worked to the disadvantage of women. Wherever they turned with their problems—whether to physicians or lawyers—women confronted an official or legal world almost wholly populated and controlled by men.

EDUCATIONAL BARRIERS Throughout the nineteenth century, women had less access to education than men, and what was available to them was inferior to that available to men. Not surprisingly, the percentage of illiterate women exceeded that of men. Most women were educated only enough for the domestic careers they were expected to follow.

University and professional education remained reserved for men until at least the third quarter of the century. The University of Zurich first opened its doors to women in the 1860s. The University of London admitted

Women only gradually gained access to secondary and university education during the second half of the nineteenth century and the early twentieth century. Young women on their way to school, the subject of this 1880 English painting, would thus have been a new sight when it was painted. [Yale Center for British Art, Paul Mellon Collection]

women for degrees in 1878. Women's colleges were founded at Cambridge during the last quarter of the century. Women could take Oxford and Cambridge university examinations, but were not awarded degrees at Oxford until 1920 or at Cambridge until 1921. Women could not attend Sorbonne lectures until 1880. Just before the turn of the century, universities and medical schools in the Austrian Empire allowed women to matriculate, but Prussian universities did not admit women until after 1900. Russian women did not attend universities before 1914, but other institutions that awarded degrees were open to them. Italian universities proved themselves more open to both women students and women instructors than similar institutions elsewhere in Europe. In many countries, there were frequently more foreign than native women attending university classes. This was especially the case in Zurich, where many

Russian women studied for medical degrees. Many of the American women who founded or taught in the first women's colleges in the United States studied at European universities.

The absence of a system of private or public secondary education for women prevented most of them from gaining the qualifications they needed to enter a university whether or not the university prohibited them. Considerable evidence suggests that educated, professional men feared their professions would be overcrowded if they admitted women. Women who attended universities and medical schools, like the young Russian women who studied medicine at Zurich, were sometimes labeled political radicals.

By the turn of the century, men in the educated elites feared the challenge educated women posed to traditional gender roles in the home and workplace. Restricting their access to secondary and university education helped bar them from social and economic advancement. Women would benefit only marginally from the expansion of professional employment that occurred during the late nineteenth and early twentieth centuries. Some women did enter the professions, most particularly medicine, but their numbers remained few. Most nations refused to allow women to become lawyers until after World War I.

Schoolteaching at the elementary level, which had come to be seen as a female job because of its association with the nurturing of children, became a professional haven for women. Trained at institutions that were equivalent to normal schools, women schoolteachers were regarded as educated, but not as university educated. Secondary education remained largely the province of men.

The few women who pioneered in the professions and on government commissions and school boards or who dispersed birth control information faced grave social obstacles, personal humiliation, and often outright bigotry. These women and their male supporters were challenging that clear separation of life into male and female spheres that had emerged in middle-class European social life during the nineteenth century. Women themselves were often hesitant to support feminist causes or expanded opportunities for themselves because they had been so thoroughly acculturated into the recently stereotyped roles. Many women as well as men saw a real conflict between family responsibilities and feminism.

New Employment Patterns for Women

During the decades of the Second Industrial Revolution, two major developments affected the economic lives of women. The first was a significant expansion in the variety of jobs available outside the better-paying learned professions. The second was a significant withdrawal of married women from the workforce. These two seemingly contradictory developments require some explanation.

AVAILABILITY OF NEW JOBS The expansion of governmental bureaucracies, the emergence of corporations and other large-scale businesses, and the vast expansion of retail stores opened many new employment opportunities for

Women working in the London Central Telephone Exchange. The invention of the telephone opened new employment opportunities for women. [Mary Evans Picture Library]

women. The need for elementary school teachers, usually women, grew as governments adopted compulsory education laws. Technological inventions and innovations such as the typewriter and eventually the telephone exchange also fostered female employment. Women by the thousands became secretaries and clerks for governments and for private businesses. Still more thousands became shop assistants.

Although these jobs did open new and often somewhat better employment opportunities for women, they nonetheless required low-level skills and involved minimal training. They were occupied primarily by unmarried women or widows. Women were rarely to be found in more prominent positions.

Employers continued to pay women low wages, because they assumed, quite often knowing better, that a woman did not need to support herself independently but could expect additional financial support from her father or from her husband. Consequently, a woman who did need to support herself independently was almost always unable to find a job paying an adequate income—or a position that paid as well as one held by a man who was supporting himself independently.

WITHDRAWAL FROM THE LABOR FORCE Most of the women filling these new service positions were young and unmarried. Upon marriage, or certainly after the birth of her first child, a woman normally withdrew from the labor force. She either did not work or she worked at some occupation that could be pursued in the home. This pattern was not new, but it had become significantly more common by the end of the nineteenth century. The kinds of industrial occupations that women had filled in the middle of the nineteenth century, especially textile and garment making, were shrinking. There were thus fewer opportunities for employment in those industries for either married or unmarried women. Employers in offices and retail stores preferred young, unmarried women whose family responsibilities would not interfere with their work. The decline in the number of children being born also meant that fewer married women were needed to look after other women's children.

Although new opportunities opened to them in the late nineteenth century, many working-class women, like these women ironing in a laundry, remained in traditional occupations. As the wine bottle suggests, alcoholism was a problem for women as well as men engaged in tedious and boring work. The painting is by Edgar Degas (1834–1917). [Service Photographique des Musées Nationaux, Paris/Photo R.M.N.]

These German women are operating lathes in a metalworking plant. It was rare for women to have such skilled jobs. [The Bettmann Archive]

The real wages paid to male workers increased during this period, and so families had a somewhat reduced need for a second income. Also, thanks to improving health conditions, men lived longer than before, and so wives were less likely to be thrust into the workforce by an emergency. The smaller size of families also lowered the need for supplementary wages. Working children stayed longer at home and continued to contribute to the family's wage pool.

Finally, the cultural dominance of the middle class, with its generally idle wives, established a pattern of social expectations. The more prosperous a working-class family became, the less involved in employment its women were supposed to be. Indeed, the less income-producing work a wife did, the more prosperous and stable the family was considered.

Yet behind these generalities stands the enormous variety of social and economic experience late-nineteenth-century women actually encountered. As might be expected, the chief determinant of these individual experiences was social class.

Working-Class Women

Although the textile industry and garment making were much less dominant than earlier in the century, they continued to employ large numbers of women. The situation of women in the German clothing-making trades illustrates the kind of vulnerable economic situation that they could encounter as a result of their limited skills and the organization of the trade. The system of manufacturing mass-made clothes of uniform sizes in Germany was complex. It was designed to require minimal capital investment on the part of the manufacturers and to protect them from significant risk. A major manufacturer would arrange for the production of clothing through a putting-out system. He would purchase the material and then put it out for tailoring. The clothing was produced not in a factory but usually in numerous, independently owned, small sweatshops or by workers in their homes.

In Berlin in 1896, there were more than 80,000 garment workers, mostly women, who were so employed. When business was good and the demand strong, employment for these women was high. As the seasons shifted or business became poor, however, less and less work was put out, idling many of them. In effect, the workers who actually sewed the clothing carried much of the risk of the enterprise. Some women did work in factories, but they, too, were subject to layoffs. Furthermore, women in the clothing trade were nearly always in positions less skilled than those of the male tailors or the male middlemen who owned the workshops.

The expectation of separate social and economic spheres for men and women and the definition of women's chief work as pertaining to the home contributed mightily to the exploitation of women workers outside the home. Because their wages were regarded merely as supplementing their husbands', they became particularly vulnerable to the kind of economic exploitation that characterized the German putting-out system for clothing production and similar systems of clothing production elsewhere. Women were nearly always treated as casual workers everywhere in Europe.

Poverty and Prostitution

A major but little recognized social fact of most nineteenth-century cities was the presence of a surplus of working women who did not fit the stereotype of wife or daughter supplementing a family's income. There were almost always many more women seeking employment than there were jobs. The economic vulnerability of women and the consequent poverty many of them faced were among the chief causes of prostitution. In any major late-nineteenth-century European city, there were thousands of prostitutes.

Prostitution was, of course, not new. It had always been one way for very poor women to find some income. In the late nineteenth century, however, it was closely related to the difficulty encountered by very poor women who were trying to make their way in an overcrowded female labor force. On the Continent, prostitution was generally legalized and was subject to governmental and municipal regulations. Those regulations were, it should be noted, passed and enforced by male legislatures and councils and were enforced by male police and physicians. In Great Britain, prostitution received only minimal regulation.

Many myths and misunderstandings have surrounded the subject of prostitution. The most recent studies of the subject in England emphasize that most prostitutes were active on the streets for a very few years, generally from their late teens to about age twenty-five. They often were very poor women who had recently migrated from nearby rural areas. Others were born in the towns where they became prostitutes. Certain cities—those with large army garrisons or naval ports or those, like London, with large transient populations—attracted many prostitutes. There were far fewer prostitutes in manufacturing towns, where there were more opportunities for steady employment and where community life was more stable.

Women who became prostitutes usually came from families of unskilled workers and had minimal skills and education themselves. Many had been servants. They also often were from broken homes or were orphaned. Contrary to many sensational late-century newspaper accounts, there were few child prostitutes. Furthermore, rarely were women seduced into prostitution by middle-class employers or middle-class clients, although working-class women were always potentially subject to such pressure. The customers of poor working-class prostitutes were primarily working-class men.

Women of the Middle Class

A vast social gap separated poor working-class women from their middle-class counterparts. As their fathers' and husbands' incomes permitted, middle-class women participated in the vast expansion of consumerism and domestic comfort that marked the end of the nineteenth century and the early twentieth century. They filled their homes with manufactured items, including clothing, china, furniture, carpets, drapery, wallpaper, and prints. They enjoyed all the improvements of sanitation and electricity. They could command the services of numerous domestic servants. They moved into the fashionable new houses being constructed in the rapidly expanding suburbs.

THE CULT OF DOMESTICITY For the middle classes the distinction between work and family, defined by gender, had become complete and constituted the model for all other social groups. Middle-class women, if at all possible, did not work. More than any other women, they became limited to the roles of wife and mother.

As a result, they might enjoy great domestic luxury and comfort, but their lives, talents, ambitions, and opportunities for applying their intelligence were markedly circumscribed.

Middle-class women became, in large measure, the product of a particular understanding of social life. Home life was to be very different from the life of business and the marketplace. The home was to be a private place of refuge, a view set forth in scores of women's journals across Europe.

As studies of the lives of middle-class women in northern France have suggested, this image of the middle-class home and of the role of women in the home is quite different from the one that had existed earlier in the nineteenth century. During the first half of the century, the spouse of a middle-class husband might very well contribute directly to the business, handling accounts or correspondence. These women also frequently had little to do with rearing their children, leaving that task first to nurses and later to governesses. The reasons for the change over the course of the century are not certain, but it appears that men began to insist on doing business with other men. Magazines and books directed toward women began to praise motherhood, domesticity, religion, and charity as the proper work of women in accordance with the concept of separate spheres.

For middle-class French women, as well as for middle-class women elsewhere, the home came to be seen as the center of virtue, children, and the proper life. Marriages were usually arranged for

Family was central to the middle-class conception of a stable and respectable social life. This portrait of the Bellelli family is by Degas. Notice that the husband and father sits at his desk, suggesting his association with business and the world outside the home, whereas the wife and mother stands with their children, suggesting her domestic role. [Giraudon/Art Resource, N.Y.]

some kind of family economic benefit. Romantic marriage was viewed as a danger to social stability. Most middle-class women in northern France married by the age of twenty-one. Children were expected to follow very soon after marriage, and the first child was often born within the first year. The rearing and nurturing of her children was a woman's chief task. She would receive no experience or training for any role other than that of dutiful daughter, wife, and mother.

Within the home, a middle-class woman performed major roles. She was largely in charge of the household. She oversaw virtually all domestic management and child care. She was in charge of the home as a unit of consumption, which is why so much advertising was directed toward women. All this domestic activity, however, occurred within the limits of the approved middle-class lifestyle that set strict limits on a woman's initiative. In her conspicuous idleness, a woman symbolized first her father's and then her husband's worldly success.

RELIGIOUS AND CHARITABLE ACTIVITIES
The cult of domesticity in France and elsewhere assigned firm religious duties to women, which the Roman Catholic church strongly supported. Women were expected to attend Mass frequently and assure the religious instruction of their children. They were charged with observing meatless Fridays and with participating in religious observances. Prayer was a major part of their lives and daily rituals. They internalized those portions of the Christian religion that stressed meekness and passivity. In other countries as well, religion and religious activities became part of the expected work of women. For this reason, women were regarded by political liberals as especially susceptible to the influence of priests. This close association between religion and a strict domestic life for women was one of the reasons for later tension between feminism and religious authorities.

Another important role for middle-class women was the administration of charity. Women were judged especially qualified for this work because of their presumed innate spirituality and their capacity to instill domestic and personal discipline. Middle-class women were often in charge of clubs for poor youth, societies to protect poor young women, schools for infants, and societies for visiting the poor. Women were supposed to be particularly interested in the problems of poor women, their families, and their children. Quite often charity from middle-class women required the poor recipient to demonstrate good character. By the end of the century, middle-class women seeking to expand their spheres of activity became social workers for the Church, for private charities, or for the government. These vocations were a natural extension of the roles socially assigned to them.

SEXUALITY AND FAMILY SIZE The world of the middle-class wife and her family is now understood to have been much more complicated than was once thought. Neither they nor their families all conformed to the stereotypes. Recent studies have suggested that the middle classes of the nineteenth century enjoyed sexual relations within marriage far more than was once thought. Diaries, letters, and even early medical and sociological sex surveys indicate that sexual enjoyment rather than sexual repression was fundamental to middle-class marriages. Much of the inhibition about sexuality stemmed from the dangers of childbirth rather than from any dislike or disapproval of sex itself.

One of the major changes in this regard during the second half of the century was the acceptance of small family size among the middle classes. The fertility rate in France dropped throughout the nineteenth century. It began to fall in England steadily from the 1870s onward. During the last decades of the century, various new contraceptive devices became available, which middle-class couples used. One of the chief reasons for the apparently conscious decision of couples to limit family size was to maintain a relatively high level of material consumption. Children had become much more expensive to rear, and at the same time, more material comforts had become available. Fewer children probably meant more attention for each of them, possibly bringing mothers and their children emotionally closer.

The Rise of Political Feminism

As can be seen from the previous discussion, liberal society and its values neither automatically nor inevitably improved the lot of women.

The Virtues of a French Middle-Class Lady Praised

One of the chief social roles assigned to middle-class French women was that of charitable activity. This obituary of Mme Émile Delesalle from a Roman Catholic church paper of the late nineteenth century describes the work of this woman among the poor. It is a very revealing document because it clearly shows the class divisions that existed in the giving of charity. Also through the kinds of virtues it praises, it gave instruction to its women readers. Note the emphasis on home life, spirituality, and instruction of children in charitable acts.

✦ *What assumptions about the character of women allowed writers to see charity as a particularly good occupation for women? What middle-class attitudes toward the poor are displayed in this passage? How did the assignment of charity work to women lead to their being excluded from other kinds of work and the learned professions?*

The poor were the object of her affectionate interest, especially the shameful poor, the fallen people. She sought them out and helped them with perfect discretion which doubled the value of her benevolent interest. To those whom she could approach without fear of bruising their dignity, she brought, along with alms to assure their existence, consolation of the most serious sort—she raised their courage and their hopes. To others, each Sunday, she opened all the doors of her home, above all when her children were still young. In making them distribute these alms with her, she hoped to initiate them early into practices of charity.

In the last years of her life the St. Gabriel Orphanage gained her interest. Not only did she accomplish a great deal with her generosity, but she also took on the task of maintaining the clothes of her dear orphans in good order and in good repair. When she appeared in the courtyard of the establishment at recreation time, all her protégés surrounded her and lavished her with manifestations of their profound respect and affectionate gratitude.

Bonnie G. Smith, Ladies of the Leisure Class: The Bourgeois of Northern France in the Nineteenth Century. Princeton, NJ: Princeton University Press, 1981, pp. 147–148. Copyright © 1981 by Princeton University Press.

In particular, it did not give them the vote and access to political activity. Male liberals feared that granting the vote to women would benefit political conservatives, because women were thought to be unduly controlled by Roman Catholic priests. A similar apprehension existed about the alleged influence of the Anglican clergy over women in England. Consequently, anticlerical liberals often had difficulty working with feminists.

OBSTACLES TO ACHIEVING EQUALITY But women also were often reluctant to support feminist causes. Political issues relating to gender were only one of several priorities for many women. Some were very sensitive to their class and economic interests. Others subordinated feminist political issues to national unity and nationalistic patriotism. Still others would not support particular feminist organizations because of differences over tactics. The various social and tactical differences among women led quite often to sharp divisions within the feminists' own ranks. Except in England, it was often difficult for working-class and middle-class women to cooperate. Roman Catholic feminists were uncomfortable with radical secularist feminists. There were other disagreements about which goals for improvement in women's legal and social conditions were most important.

Although liberal society and law presented women with many obstacles, they also provided feminists with many of their intellectual and political tools. As early as 1792 in Britain, Mary Wollstonecraft (1759–1797), in *The Vindication of the Rights of Woman*, had applied the revolutionary doctrines of the rights of man to the predicament of the members of her own sex (see Chapter 18). John Stuart Mill (1806–1873), with his wife Harriet Taylor (1804–1858), had applied the logic of liberal freedom to the position of women in *The Subjection of Women* (1869). The arguments for utility and efficiency so dear to middle-class liberals could be used to expose the human and social waste implicit in the inferior role assigned to women.

Furthermore, the socialist criticism of capitalist society often, though by no means always, included a harsh indictment of the social and economic position to which women had been relegated. The earliest statements of feminism arose from critics of the existing order and were often associated with people who had unorthodox opinions about sexuality, family life, and property. This hardened resistance to the feminist message, especially on the Continent.

These difficulties prevented continental feminists from raising the kind of massive public support or mounting the large demonstrations that feminists in Great Britain and the United States could. Everywhere in Europe, however, including Britain, the feminist cause was badly divided over both goals and tactics.

VOTES FOR WOMEN IN BRITAIN Europe's most advanced women's movement was in Great Britain. There Millicent Fawcett (1847–1929) led the moderate National Union of Women's Suffrage Societies. She believed Parliament would grant women the vote only when convinced that they would be respectable and responsible in their political activity. In 1908 this organization could rally almost half a million women in London. Fawcett was the wife of a former Liberal Party cabinet minister and economist. Her tactics were those of English liberals.

Emmeline Pankhurst (1858–1928) led a different and much more radical branch of British feminists. Pankhurst's husband, who died near the close of the century, had been active in both labor and Irish nationalist politics. Irish nation-alists had developed numerous disruptive political tactics. Early labor politicians had also sometimes had confrontations with police over the right to hold meetings. In 1903 Pankhurst and her daughters, Christabel and Sylvia, founded the Women's Social and Political Union. For several years they and their followers, known derisively as suffragettes, lobbied publicly and privately for the extension of the vote to women. By 1910, having failed to move the government, they turned to the violent tactics of arson, window breaking, and sabotage of postal boxes. They marched en masse on Parliament. The Liberal government of Henry Asquith imprisoned many of the demonstrators and force-fed those who went on hunger strikes in jail. The government refused to extend the franchise. Only in 1918, and then as a result of their contribution to the war effort, did some British women receive the vote.

When British suffragettes went to prison, many of them went on hunger strikes. The response of the authorities was to force feed them by having physicians insert tubes down their throats through which liquid nourishment was pumped. Here Emmeline Pankhurst is undergoing this painful and humiliating experience. [Bildarchiv Preussischer Kulturbesitz]

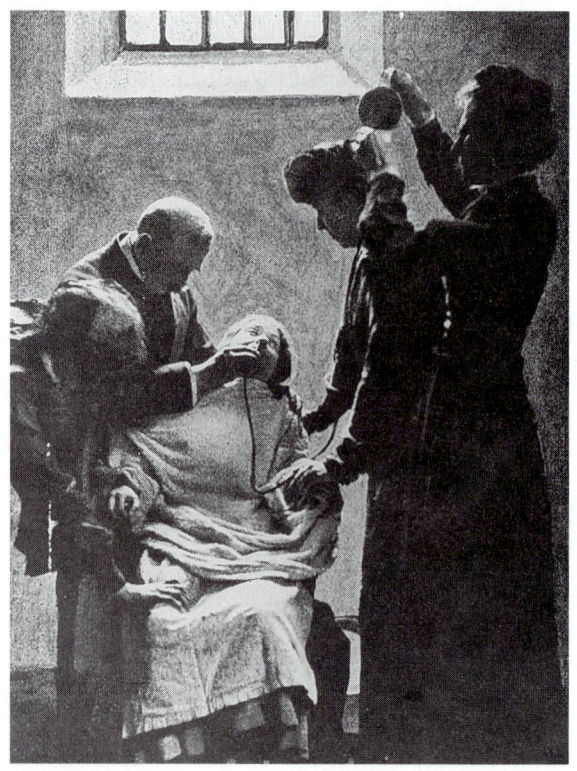

An English Feminist Defends
the Cause of the Female Franchise

Frances Power Cobby (1822–1904) wrote widely on many religious and social issues of the second half of the century. She had been a feminist since early adulthood. In this letter to a British feminist magazine in 1884, she explained why women should seek the vote.

◆ *What motives does Cobbe assign to the pursuit of the right to vote? Why does she emphasize the issue of "womanliness" as one that must not be allowed to undermine the cause of women? What is Cobbe's attitude toward violence? Why would later British advocates of votes for women turn to violent tactics?*

If I may presume to offer an old woman's counsel to the younger workers in our cause, it would be that they should adopt the point of view—that it is before all things our *duty* to obtain the franchise. If we undertake the work in this spirit, and with the object of using the power it confers, whenever we gain it, for the promotion of justice and mercy and the kingdom of God upon earth, we shall carry on all our agitation in a corresponding manner, firmly and bravely, and also calmly and with generous good temper. And when our opponents come to understand that this is the motive underlying our efforts, they, on their part, will cease to feel bitterly and scornfully toward us, even when they think we are altogether mistaken. . . .

The idea that the possession of political rights will destroy "womanliness," absurd as it may seem to us, is very deeply rooted in the minds of men; and when they oppose our demands, it is only just to give them credit for doing so on grounds which we should recognize as valid, *if their premises were true.* It is not so much that our opponents (at least the better part of them) despise women, as that they really prize what women now are in the home and in society so highly that they cannot bear to risk losing it by any serious change in their condition. These fears are futile and faithless, but there is nothing in them to affront us. To remove them, we must not use violent words, for every such violent word confirms their fears; but, on the contrary, show the world that while the revolutions wrought by men have been full of bitterness and rancor and stormy passions, if not of bloodshed, we women will at least strive to accomplish our great emancipation calmly and by persuasion and reason.

Letter to the Woman's Tribune, May 1, 1884, *quoted in Frances Power Cobbe,* Life of Frances Power Cobbe by Herself, Vol. 2 *(Boston: Houghton Mifflin, 1894), pp. 532–533.*

POLITICAL FEMINISM ON THE CONTINENT
The contrast of France and Germany shows how advanced the British women's movement was. In France, when Hubertine Auclert (1848–1914) began campaigning for the vote in the 1880s she stood virtually alone. During the 1890s, several women's organizations emerged. In 1901 the National Council of French Women (CNFF) was organized among upper-middle-class women, but it did not support the vote for women for several years. French Roman Catholic feminists such as Marie Mauguet (1844–1928) supported the franchise. Almost all French feminists, however, rejected any form of violence. They also were never able to organize mass rallies. The leaders of French feminism believed that the vote could be achieved through careful legalism. In 1919 the French Chamber of Deputies passed a bill granting the vote to women, but in 1922 the French Senate defeated the bill. It was not until after World War II that French women received the right to vote.

In Germany, feminist awareness and action was even more underdeveloped. German law actually forbade German women from political activity. Because no group in the German Empire enjoyed extensive political rights, women were not certain that they would benefit from demanding them. Any such demand would be regarded as subversive not only of the state but also of society.

In 1894 the Union of German Women's Organizations (BDFK) was founded. By 1902 it was supporting a call for the right to vote. But it was largely concerned with improving women's social conditions, their access to education, and their right to other protections. The group also worked to see women admitted to political or civic activity on the municipal level. Their work usually included education, child welfare, char-

ity, and public health. The German Social Democratic Party supported women's suffrage, but that socialist party was so disdained by the German authorities and German Roman Catholics that this support only served to make suffrage more suspect in their eyes. Women received the vote in Germany only in 1918, when the constitution of the Weimar Republic was promulgated after German defeat in war and revolution at home.

Throughout Europe in the years before World War I, women demanded rights widely and vocally. The tactics they used and the success they achieved, however, varied from country to country depending on political and class structures. Before World War I, only in Norway (1907) could women vote on national issues.

Major Dates in Late-Nineteenth-Century and Early-Twentieth-Century Women's History	
1857	Revised English divorce law
1865	University of Zurich admits women for degrees
1869	John Stuart Mill's *The Subjection of Women*
1878	University of London admits women as candidates for degrees
1882	English Married Woman's Property Act
1894	Union of German Women's Organizations founded
1901	National Council of French Women founded
1903	British Women's Social and Political Union founded
1907	Norway permits women to vote on national issues
1910	British suffragettes adopt radical tactics
1918	Vote extended to some British women
1918	Weimar constitution allows German women to vote
1920–1921	Oxford and Cambridge award degrees to women
1922	French Senate defeats bill extending vote to women
1928	Britain extends vote to women on same basis as men

Jewish Emancipation

The emancipation of European Jews from the narrow life of the ghetto into a world of equal or nearly equal citizenship and social status was a major accomplishment of political liberalism and had an enduring impact on European life. The process of emancipation, slow and never fully completed, began in the late eighteenth century and continued throughout the nineteenth. It moved at different paces in different countries.

Differing Degrees of Citizenship

In 1782 Joseph II, the Habsburg emperor, issued a decree that placed the Jews of his empire under more or less the same laws as Christians. In France, the National Assembly recognized Jews as French citizens in 1789. During the turmoil of the Napoleonic wars, Jewish communities in Italy and Germany were allowed to mix on a generally equal footing with the Christian population. These various steps toward political emancipation were always somewhat uncertain and were frequently limited or partially repealed with changes in rulers or governments. Certain freedoms were granted only to be partially withdrawn later. Even in countries that had advanced some political rights, Jews could not own land and could be subject to special discriminatory taxes. Nonetheless, during the first half of the century, European Jews in western

The era of Jewish emancipation allowed more freedom to European Jews and a wider recognition of their faith and culture. This painting by G. E. Opitz portrays the dedication of a new synagogue in Alsace in 1820. [Jewish Museum, N.Y./Art Resource, N.Y.]

Europe and to a much lesser extent in central and eastern Europe began to gain significant rights that brought them equal or more nearly equal citizenship.

In Russia, however, the traditional modes of prejudice and discrimination continued unabated until World War I. Jews were treated as aliens under Russian rule. The government undermined Jewish community life, limited publication of Jewish books, restricted areas where Jews might live, required internal passports from Jews, banned Jews from many forms of state service, and excluded Jews from many institutions of higher education. The police and others were allowed to conduct *pogroms*—organized riots—against Jewish neighborhoods and villages.

Broadened Opportunities

After the revolutions of 1848, European Jews saw a general improvement in their situation that lasted for several decades. In Germany, Italy, the Low Countries, and Scandinavia, Jews attained full rights of citizenship. After 1858 Jews in Great Britain could sit in Parliament. Austria-Hungary extended full legal rights to Jews in 1867. Indeed, from about 1850 to 1880, there was relatively little organized or overt prejudice toward Jews. They entered the professions and other occupations once closed to them.

They participated fully in the literary and cultural life of their nations. They were active in the arts and music. They became leaders in science and education. Jews intermarried freely with non-Jews as legal secular prohibitions against such marriages were repealed during the last quarter of the century.

Outside of Russia, Jewish political figures entered cabinets and served in the highest offices of the state. Politically, they often were aligned with liberal parties because these groups had championed equal rights. Later in the century, especially in eastern Europe, many Jews became associated with the socialist parties.

The prejudice that had been associated with Christian religious attitudes toward Jews seemed for a time to have dissipated, although it still appeared in Russia and other parts of eastern Europe. Hundreds of thousands of European Jews migrated from these regions to western Europe and the United States. Almost anywhere in Europe, Jews might encounter prejudice on a personal level. But in western Europe, including England, France, Italy, Germany, and the Low Countries, Jews felt fairly secure from the legalized persecution and discrimination that had so haunted them in the past.

That newfound security began to erode during the last two decades of the nineteenth century. Anti-Semitic voices began to be heard in the 1870s attributing the economic stagnation of the decade to Jewish bankers and financial interests. In the 1880s, organized anti-Semitism erupted in Germany as it did in France at the time of the Dreyfus Affair. As will be seen in the next chapter, these developments gave rise to the birth of Zionism, initially a minority movement within the Jewish community. Most Jewish leaders believed the attacks on Jewish life were merely temporary recurrences of older modes of prejudice; they felt their communities would remain safe under the liberal legal protections that had been extended over the course of the century. That analysis would be proved disastrously wrong during the second quarter of the twentieth century.

Labor, Socialism, and Politics to World War I

The late-century industrial expansion wrought further changes in the life of the labor force. In all industrializing continental countries, the numbers of the urban proletariat rose. The proportion of artisans and highly skilled workers declined, and for the first time factory wage earners predominated. The number of people engaged in the unskilled work associated with shipping, transportation, and building also grew considerably.

Workers still had to look to themselves to improve their lot. After 1848, however, European workers stopped rioting in the streets to voice their grievances. They also stopped trying to revive the paternal guilds and similar institutions of the past. After mid-century, workers turned to new institutions and ideologies. Chief among these were trade unions, democratic political parties, and socialism.

Trade Unionism

Trade unionism came of age as governments extended legal protections to unions during the second half of the century. Unions became fully legal in Great Britain in 1871 and were allowed to picket in 1875. In France, Napoleon III at first used troops against strikes, but as his political power waned, he allowed weak labor associations in 1868. The Third French Republic fully legalized unions in 1884. In Germany, unions were permitted to function with little disturbance after 1890. Union participation in the political process was at first marginal. As long as the representatives of the traditional governing classes looked after labor interests, members of the working class rarely sought office themselves.

Unions directed their mid-century organizational efforts toward skilled workers and the immediate improvement of wages and working conditions. By the close of the century, industrial unions for unskilled workers were being organized. With thousands of workers, these large unions met intense opposition from employers. They frequently had to engage in long strikes to convince employers to accept their demands. Europe suffered a rash of strikes in the prewar decade as unions sought to keep wages in line with inflation. Despite union advances, however, and the growth of union membership (in 1910 to approximately 3 million in Britain, 2 million in Germany, and 977,000 in France), most of Europe's labor force was never unionized in this period. What the unions did represent for workers was a new collective form of association for confronting economic difficulties and improving security.

Democracy and Political Parties

Except for Russia, all the major European states adopted broad-based, if not perfectly democratic, electoral systems in the late nineteenth century. Great Britain passed its second voting reform act in 1867 and its third in 1884. Bismarck brought universal manhood suffrage to the German Empire in 1871. The French Chamber of Deputies was democratically elected. Universal manhood suffrage was adopted in Switzerland in 1879, in Spain in 1890, in Belgium in 1893, in the Netherlands in 1896, and in Norway in 1898. Italy finally fell into line in 1912. The broadened franchise meant that politicians could no longer ignore workers and discontented groups could now voice their grievances and advocate their programs within the institutions of government rather than from the outside.

The advent of democracy brought organized mass political parties like those already in existence in the United States to Europe for the first time. In the liberal European states with narrow electoral bases, most voters had been people of property who knew what they had at stake in politics. Organization had been minimal. The expansion of the electorate brought into the political processes many people whose level of political consciousness, awareness, and interest was quite low. This electorate had to be organized and taught the nature of power and influence in the liberal democratic state.

The organized political party—with its workers, newspapers, offices, social life, and discipline—was the vehicle that mobilized the new voters. The largest single group in these mass electorates was the working class. The democratization of politics presented the socialists with opportunities and required the traditional ruling classes to vie with the socialists for the support of the new voters.

During these years, socialism as a political ideology and plan of action opposed nationalism. The problems of class were supposed to be transnational, and socialism was supposed to unite the working classes across national borders. European socialists, however, badly underestimated the emotional drawing power of nationalism. Many workers had both socialist and nationalist sympathies, which were rarely in conflict with each other. When the outbreak of war in 1914 did bring them into conflict, however, nationalist feelings prevailed.

The major question for late-century socialist parties throughout Europe was whether the improvement of the lot of the working class would come about through revolution or democratic reform. This question sharply divided all socialist parties and most especially those whose leadership adhered to the intellectual legacy of Karl Marx.

Karl Marx and the First International

Karl Marx himself made considerable accommodation to the new practical realities that developed during the third quarter of the century. Although he continued to predict the disintegration of capitalism, his practical, public political activity reflected a somewhat different approach.

In 1864 a group of British and French trade unionists founded the International Working Men's Association. Known as the First International, its membership encompassed a vast array of radical political types, including social-ists, anarchists, and Polish nationalists. In the inaugural address for the International, Marx supported and approved efforts by workers and trade unions to reform the conditions of labor within the existing political and economic processes. In his private writings he often criticized such reformist activity, but these writings were not made public until near the end of the century, and years after his death.

The violence involved in the rise and suppression of the Paris Commune (see Chapter 23), which Marx had declared a genuine proletarian uprising, cast a pall over socialism throughout Europe. British trade unionists, who in 1871 received legal protections, wanted no connection with the events in Paris. The French authorities used the uprising to suppress socialist activity. Under these pressures, the First International held its last European congress in 1873. It soon transferred its offices to the United States, where it was dissolved in 1876.

The short-lived First International had a disproportionately great impact on the future of European socialism. Throughout the late 1860s, the organization had gathered statistics, kept labor groups informed of mutual problems, provided a forum for the debate of socialist doctrine, and extravagantly proclaimed its own influence over contemporary events. From these debates and activities Marxism emerged as the single most important strand of socialism. Marx and his supporters defeated or drove out anarchists and advocates of other forms of socialism. The apparently scientific character of Marxism made it attractive—science was more influential than at any previous time in European history. German socialists, who were to establish the most powerful socialist party in Europe, were deeply impressed by Marx's thought and were the chief vehicle for preserving and developing it. The full development of German socialism also, however, involved the influence of non-Marxist socialists in Great Britain.

Great Britain: Fabianism and Early Welfare Programs

Neither Marxism nor any other form of socialism made significant progress in Great Britain, the most advanced industrial society of the day. There trade unions grew steadily, and their members normally supported Liberal Party candidates. The "new unionism" of the late 1880s and the 1890s organized the dock workers, the gas workers, and similar unskilled groups. In 1892 Keir Hardie became the first independent working man to be elected to Parliament, but the small socialist Independent Labour Party founded a year later remained ineffective. Until 1901 general political activity on the part of labor remained quite limited. In that year, however, the House of Lords, through the Taff Vale decision, removed the legal protection previously accorded union funds. The Trades Union Congress responded by launching the Labour Party. In the election of 1906, the fledgling party sent twenty-nine members to Parliament. Their goals as trade unionists, however, did not yet include socialism. In this same period, the British labor movement became more militant.

Beatrice and Sidney Webb, in a photograph from the late 1920s. These most influential British Fabian socialists wrote many books on governmental and economic matters, served on special parliamentary commissions, and agitated for the enactment of socialist policies. [UPI/Bettmann]

In scores of strikes before the war, workers fought for wages to meet the rising cost of living. The government took a larger role than ever before in mediating these strikes, which in 1911 and 1912 involved the railways, the docks, and the mines.

British socialism itself remained primarily the preserve of non-Marxist intellectuals. The Fabian Society, founded in 1884, was Britain's most influential socialist group. The society took its name from Q. Fabius Maximus, the Roman general whose tactics against Hannibal involved avoiding direct conflict that might lead to defeat. The name reflected the society's gradualist approach to major social reform. Its leading members were Sidney (1859–1947) and Beatrice (1858–1943) Webb, H. G. Wells (1866–1946), Graham Wallas (1858–1932), and George Bernard Shaw (1856–1950). Many Fabians were civil servants who believed that the problems of industry, the expansion of ownership, and the state direction of production could be achieved gradually, peacefully, and democratically. They sought to educate the country about the rational wisdom of socialism. They were particularly interested in modes of collective ownership on the municipal level, the so-called gas-and-water socialism.

The British government and the major political parties responded slowly to these various pressures. In 1903 Joseph Chamberlain (1836–1914) launched his unsuccessful tariff-reform campaign to match foreign tariffs and to finance social reform through higher import duties. The campaign badly split the Conservative Party. After 1906 the Liberal Party, led by Sir Henry Campbell-Bannerman (1836–1908) and after 1908 by Herbert Asquith (1852–1928), pursued a two-pronged policy. Fearful of losing seats in Parliament to the new Labour Party, they restored the former protection of the unions. Then, after 1909, with Chancellor of the Exchequer David Lloyd George (1863–1945) as its guiding light, the Liberal ministry undertook a broad program of social legislation. This included the establishment of labor exchanges, the regulation of the sweated labor trades, such as tailoring and lacemaking, and the National Insurance Act of 1911, which provided unemployment benefits and health care.

The financing of these programs brought the House of Commons into conflict with the Conservative-dominated House of Lords. The result was the Parliament Act of 1911, which allowed the Commons to override the legislative veto of the upper chamber. The new taxes and social programs meant that in Britain, the home of nineteenth-century liberalism, the state was taking on an expanded role in the life of its citizens. The early welfare legislation was only marginally satisfactory to labor, many of whose members still thought they could gain more from the direct action of strikes.

France: "Opportunism" Rejected

At the turn of the century, Jean Jaurès (1859–1914) and Jules Guesde (1845–1922) led the two major factions of French socialists. Jaurès believed that socialists should cooperate with middle-class Radical ministries to ensure the enactment of needed social legislation. Guesde opposed this policy, arguing that socialists could not, with integrity, support a bourgeois cabinet that they were theoretically dedicated to overthrow. The government's response to the Dreyfus affair brought the quarrel to a head. In 1899, seeking to unite all supporters of Dreyfus, Prime Minister René Waldeck-Rousseau (1846–1904) appointed the socialist Alexander Millerand (1859–1943) to the cabinet.

The Second International had been founded in 1889 in a new effort to unify the various national socialist parties and trade unions. By 1904 the Amsterdam Congress of the Second International debated the issue of "opportunism," as such cabinet participation by socialists was termed. The Amsterdam Congress condemned "opportunism" in France and ordered the French socialists to form a single party. Jaurès accepted the decision. Thereafter French socialists began to work together, and by 1914 the recently united Socialist Party had become the second largest group in the Chamber of Deputies. But Socialist Party members would not again serve in a French cabinet until the Popular Front Government of 1936.

The French labor movement, with deep roots in anarchism, was uninterested in either politics or socialism. French workers usually voted socialist, but the unions themselves, unlike those in Great Britain, avoided active political participation. The Confédération Générale du Travail, founded in 1895, regarded itself as a rival to the socialist parties. Its leaders sought to improve the workers' conditions through direct action. They embraced the doctrines of syndicalism, which had been most persuasively expounded by Georges Sorel (1847–1922) in *Reflections on Violence* (1908). This book enshrined the general strike as a device for generating worker unity and power. The strike tactic often conflicted with the socialist belief in aiding labor through state action. Strikes were common between 1905 and 1914, and the middle-class Radical ministry on more than one occasion used troops to suppress them.

Germany: Social Democrats and Revisionism

The negative judgment rendered by the Second International against French socialist participation in bourgeois ministries reflected a policy of permanent hostility to nonsocialist governments previously adopted by the German Social Democratic Party, or SPD. The organizational success of this party, more than any other single factor, kept Marxist socialism alive during the late nineteenth and early twentieth centuries.

The Social Democratic Party had been founded in 1875. Its origins lay in the labor agitation of Ferdinand Lasalle (1825–1864), who sought worker participation in German politics. Wilhelm Liebknecht (1826–1900) and August Bebel (1840–1913), who were Marxists and opposed reformist politics, soon joined the party. Thus from its founding the SPD was divided between those who advocated reform and those who advocated revolution.

BISMARCK'S REPRESSION OF THE SPD Twelve years of persecution under Bismarck forged the character of the SPD. The so-called Iron Chancellor believed that socialism would undermine German politics and society. He used an assassination attempt on William I in 1878, in which the socialists were not involved, to steer several antisocialist laws through the *Reichstag*. The measures suppressed the organization, meetings, newspapers, and other public activities of the SPD. Thereafter, to remain a socialist meant to remove oneself from the mainstream of respectable German life and possibly to lose one's job. The antisocialist legislation proved politically counterproductive. From the early 1880s onward, the SPD steadily polled more and more votes in elections to the *Reichstag.*

As simple repression failed to separate German workers from socialist loyalties, Bismarck undertook a program of social welfare legislation. In 1883 the German Empire adopted a health insurance measure. The next year saw the enactment of accident insurance legislation. Finally, in 1889 Bismarck sponsored a plan for old age and disability pensions. These programs, to which both workers and employers contributed, represented a paternalistic, conservative alternative to socialism. The state itself would organize a system of social security that did not require any change in the system of property holding or politics. Germany became the first major industrial nation to enjoy this kind of welfare program.

THE ERFURT PROGRAM After forcing Bismarck's resignation, Emperor William II (r. 1888–1918) allowed the antisocialist legislation to expire, hoping to build new political support among the working class. Even under the repressive laws, members of the SPD could sit in the *Reichstag.* With the repressive measures lifted, the party needed to decide what attitude to assume toward the German Empire.

The answer came in the Erfurt Program of 1891, formulated under the political guidance of Bebel and the ideological tutelage of Karl Kautsky (1854–1938). In good Marxist fashion, the program declared the imminent doom of capitalism and the necessity of socialist ownership of the means of production. The party intended to pursue these goals through legal political participation rather than by revolutionary activity. Kautsky argued that because capitalism by its very nature must collapse, the immediate task for socialists was to work for the improvement of workers' lives rather than for the revolution, which was inevitable. So, although in theory the SPD was vehemently hostile to the German Empire, in practice the party functioned within its institutions. The SPD members of the *Reichstag* maintained clear

political consciences by refusing to enter the cabinet (to which they were not invited anyway) and by refraining for many years from voting in favor of the military budget.

THE DEBATE OVER REVISIONISM The dilemma of the SPD, however, generated the most important challenge within the socialist movement to the orthodox Marxist analysis of capitalism and the socialist revolution. The author of this socialist heresy, Eduard Bernstein (1850–1932), had spent over a decade of his life in Great Britain and was familiar with the Fabians. Bernstein questioned whether Marx and his later orthodox followers, such as Kautsky, had been correct in their pessimistic appraisal of capitalism and the necessity of revolution. In *Evolutionary Socialism* (1899), Bernstein pointed to conditions that did not meet orthodox Marxists' expectations. The standard of living was on the rise in Europe. Ownership of capitalist industry was becoming more widespread through stockholding. The middle class was not falling into the ranks of the proletariat and was not identifying its problems with those of the workers. The inner contradictions of capitalism as expounded by Marx had simply not developed. Moreover, the extension of the franchise to the working class meant that parliamentary methods might achieve revolutionary social change. For Bernstein, social reform through democratic institutions replaced revolution as the path to a humane socialist society.

Bernstein's doctrines, known as *revisionism,* generated heated debate among German socialists, who finally condemned them. His critics argued that evolution toward social democracy might be possible in liberal, parliamentary Britain, but not in authoritarian, militaristic Germany, with its basically powerless *Reichstag.* Nonetheless, while still calling for revolution, the SPD pursued a course of action similar to that advocated by Bernstein. Its trade union members, prospering within the German economy, did not want revolution. Its grass-roots members wanted to consider themselves patriotic Germans as well as good socialists. Its leaders feared any actions that might renew the persecution that they had experienced under Bismarck.

Eduard Bernstein was a major theorist within the German SPD. In his Evolutionary Socialism *(1899), he set forth the ideas associated with revisionism, which was later rejected by the party. [The Bettmann Archive]*

Consequently, the SPD worked for electoral gains, membership expansion, and short-term political and social reform. It prospered and became one of the most important institutions of imperial Germany. Even some middle-class Germans voted for it as a way to oppose the illiberal institutions of the empire. And in August 1914, after long debate among themselves, the SPD members of the *Reichstag* abandoned their former practice and unanimously voted for the war credits that would finance Germany's participation in World War I.

Russia: Industrial Development and the Birth of Bolshevism

During the last decade of the nineteenth century, Russia entered the industrial age and confronted many of the problems that the more advanced nations of the Continent had experienced fifty or seventy-five years earlier. Unlike those other countries, Russia had to deal with major political discontent and economic development simultaneously. Russian socialism reflected that peculiar situation.

WITTE'S PROGRAM FOR INDUSTRIAL GROWTH Alexander III (r. 1881–1894) and, after him, Nicholas II (r. 1894–1917) were determined that Russia should become an industrial power. Only by doing so, they believed, could the country maintain its European military position and diplomatic role. It was Sergei Witte (1849–1915) who led Russia into the industrial age. After a career in railways and other private business, he was appointed finance minister in 1892. Witte, who pursued a policy of planned economic development, protective tariffs, high taxes, the gold standard, and efficiency, epitomized the nineteenth-century modernizer. He established strong financial relationships with the French money market, which led to later diplomatic cooperation between Russia and France.

Major Dates in the Development of Socialism	
1864	International Working Men's Association (the First International) founded
1875	German Social Democratic Party founded
1876	First International dissolved
1878	German antisocialist laws passed
1884	British Fabian Society founded
1889	Second International founded
1891	German antisocialist laws permitted to expire
1891	German Social Democratic Party's Erfurt Program
1895	French Confédération Générale du Travail founded
1899	Eduard Bernstein's *Evolutionary Socialism*
1902	Formation of the British Labour party
1902	Lenin's *What Is to Be Done?*
1903	Bolshevik–Menshevik split
1904	"Opportunism" debated at the Amsterdam Congress of the Second International

Eduard Bernstein Criticizes Orthodox Marxism

Eduard Bernstein was responsible for the emergence of "Revisionism" within the German Social Democratic Party. He was a dedicated socialist who believed that the Communist Manifesto *(1848) had not predicted the actual future of the European working classes. He believed there would be no sudden collapse or catastrophe in the capitalist system and that socialists should change their tactics to work to achieve political rights and pursue reform instead of revolution.*

◆ *According to Bernstein, what specific predictions in the* Communist Manifesto *failed to materialize? Why is the advance of democracy important to his argument? Why does he see the extension of political rights to German workers as so important?*

I set myself against the notion that we have to expect shortly a collapse of the bourgeois economy, and that social democracy should be induced by the prospect of such an imminent, great, social catastrophe to adapt its tactics to that assumption. . . .

The adherents of this theory of a catastrophe, base it especially on the conclusion of the *Communist Manifesto*. This is a mistake in every respect. . . .

Social conditions have not developed to such an acute opposition of things and classes as is depicted in the *Manifesto*. . . . The number of members of the possessing classes is to-day not smaller but larger. The enormous increase of social wealth is not accompanied by a decreasing number of large capitalists but by an increasing number of capitalists of all degrees. . . .

. . . .

In all advanced countries we see the privileges of the capitalist bourgeoisie yielding step by step to democratic organizations. . . . Factory legislation, the democratizing of local government, and the extension of its area of work, the freeing of trade unions and system of co-operative trading from legal restrictions, the consideration of standard conditions of labour in the work undertaken by public authorities—all these characterize this phase of the evolution.

. . . .

The conquest of political power by the working classes, the expropriation of capitalists, are not ends in themselves but only means for the accomplishment of certain aims and endeavours. As such they are demands in the program of social democracy. . . . Nothing can be said beforehand as to the circumstances of their accomplishment; we can only fight for their realization. But the conquest of political power necessitates the possession of political *rights*; and the most important problem of tactics which German social democracy has at the present time to solve, appears to me to be to devise the best ways for the extension of the political and economic rights of the German working classes.

Eduard Bernstein, Evolutionary Socialism: A Criticism and Affirmation 1899 *(New York: Schocken Books, 1961), pp. xxiv–xxvi, xxix–xxx.*

Witte favored heavy industries. Between 1890 and 1904, the Russian railway system grew from 30,596 to 59,616 kilometers. The 5,000-mile Trans-Siberian Railroad was almost completed. Coal output more than tripled during the same period. There was a vast increase in pig-iron production, from 928,000 tons in 1890 to 4,641,000 tons in 1913. During the same period, steel production rose from 378,000 to 4,918,000 tons. Textile manufacturing continued to expand and was still the single largest industry. The factory system began to be used more extensively throughout the country.

Industrialism brought considerable social discontent to Russia, as it had elsewhere. Landowners felt that foreign capitalists were earning too much of the profit. The peasants saw their grain exports and tax payments finance development that did not measurably improve their lives. A small but significant industrial proletariat emerged. At the turn of the century there were approximately three million factory workers in Russia. Their working and living conditions were poor by any standard. They enjoyed little state protection, and trade unions were illegal. In 1897 Witte did enact a measure providing for an 11 1/2-hour workday. But needless to say, discontent and strikes continued.

Similar social and economic problems arose in the countryside. Russian agriculture had not revived after the emancipation of the serfs in 1861. The peasants remained burdened with redemption payments, local taxes, excessive national taxes, and falling grain prices. Free peasants owned their land communally through the *mir*, or village. They farmed the land inefficiently through strip farming or the tilling of small plots. Many free peasants with too little land to support their families had to work on larger noble estates or for more prosperous peasant farmers known as *kulaks*. Between 1860 and 1914, the population of European Russia rose from approximately 50 million to approximately 103 million people. Land hunger and intense discontent spread among the peasants. Uprisings in the countryside were a frequent problem.

New political departures accompanied the economic development. The membership and intellectual roots of the Social Revolutionary Party, founded 1901, reached back to the Populists of the 1870s. The new party opposed industrialism and looked to the communal life of rural Russia as a model for the future. In 1903 the Constitutional Democratic Party, or Cadets, was formed. This liberal party drew its members from people who participated in the local councils called *zemstvos*. Modeling themselves on the liberal parties of western Europe, the Cadets wanted a parliamentary regime with responsible ministries, civil liberties, and economic progress.

LENIN'S EARLY THOUGHT AND CAREER
The situation of Russian socialists differed radically from that of socialists in other major European countries. Russia had no representative institutions and only a small working class. The compromises and accommodations achieved elsewhere were meaningless in Russia, where socialists believed that in both theory and practice they must be revolutionary. The repressive policies of the tsarist regime required the Russian Social Democratic Party, founded in 1898, to function in exile. The party members greatly admired the German Social Democratic Party and adopted its Marxist ideology.

The leading late-nineteenth-century Russian Marxist was Gregory Plekhanov (1857–1918), who wrote from exile in Switzerland. At the turn of the century, his chief disciple was Vladimir Ilyich Ulyanov (1870–1924), who later took the name of Lenin. The future leader of the Communist Revolution was the son of a high bureaucrat. His older brother, while a student in Saint Petersburg, had become involved in radical politics; arrested for participating in a plot against Alexander III, he was executed in 1887. In 1893 Lenin moved to Saint Petersburg, where he studied law. Soon he, too, was drawn to the revolutionary groups among the factory workers. He was arrested in 1895 and exiled to Siberia. In 1900, after his release, Lenin left Russia for the West. He spent most of the next seventeen years in Switzerland.

Once in Switzerland, Lenin became deeply involved in the organizational and policy disputes of the exiled Russian Social Democrats. They all considered themselves Marxists, but they differed about the meaning of a Marxist revolution for primarily rural Russia and about how to structure their own party. Unlike the backward-looking Social Revolutionaries, the Social Democrats were modernizers who favored further industrial development. The majority believed that Russia must develop a large proletariat before the revolution could come. This same majority hoped to build a mass political party like the German SPD.

Lenin dissented from both positions. In *What Is to Be Done?* (1902), he condemned any

A Russian Social Investigator Describes the Condition of Children in the Moscow Tailoring Trade

E. A. Oliunina was a young Russian woman who had been active among union organizers during the Revolution of 1905. Later, as a student at the Higher Women's Courses in Moscow, a school for women's postsecondary education, she began to investigate and to write about child garment workers. The clothes produced by these children might have ended up in Russian department stores that copied those in Paris, described in an earlier document in this chapter.

✦ *Why might the parents of these children have allowed them to work in these sweatshops? Why was alcoholism such a prevalent problem? Why does Oliunina regard schools as the solution to this problem?*

Children begin their apprenticeship between the ages of twelve and thirteen, although one can find some ten- and eleven-year-olds working in the shops. . . .

Apprenticeship is generally very hard on children. At the beginning, they suffer enormously, particularly from the physical strain of having to do work well beyond the capacity of their years. They have to live in an environment where the level of morality is very low. Scenes of drunkenness and debauchery induce the boys to smoke and drink at an early age.

For example, in one subcontracting shop that made men's clothes, a fourteen-year-old boy worked together with twelve adults. When I visited there at four o'clock one Tuesday afternoon, the workers were half-drunk. Some were lying under the benches, others in the hallway. The boy was as drunk as the rest of them and lay there with a daredevil look on his face, dressed only in a pair of longjohns and a dirty, tattered shirt. He had been taught to drink at the age of twelve and could now keep up with the adults.

"Blue Monday" is a custom in most subcontracting shops that manufacture men's clothes. The whole workshop gets drunk, and work comes to a standstill. The apprentices do nothing but hang around. Many of the workers live in the workshop, so the boys are constantly exposed to all sorts of conversations and scenes. In one shop employing five workers and three boys, "Blue Monday" was a regular ritual. Even the owner himself is prone to alcoholic binges. In these kinds of situations, young girls are in danger of being abused by the owner or his sons. . . .

In Russia, there have been no measures taken to improve the working conditions of apprentices. As I have tried to show, the situation in workshops in no way provides apprentices with adequate training in their trade. The young workers are there only to be exploited. Merely limiting the number of apprentices would not better their position, nor would it eradicate the influx of cheap labor. An incomparably more effective solution would be to replace apprenticeship with a professional educational system and well-established safeguards for child workers. However, the only real solution to the exploitation of unpaid child labor is to introduce a minimum wage for minors.

Quoted in Victoria E. Bonnell, The Russian Worker: Life and Labor Under the Tsarist Regime *(Berkeley: University of California Press, 1983), pp. 177, 180–181, 182–183.*

In this photograph taken in 1895, Lenin sits at the table among a group of other young Russian radicals from St. Petersburg. [The Bettmann Archive]

accommodations, such as those practiced by the German SPD. He also criticized trade unionism that settled for short-term gains rather than true revolutionary change for the working class. Lenin further rejected the concept of a mass democratic party composed of workers. He declared that revolutionary consciousness would not arise spontaneously from the working class. Rather, "people who make revolutionary activity their profession" must carry that consciousness to the workers.[2] Only a small, tightly organized, elite party could possess the proper dedication to revolution and prove able to resist penetration by police spies. The guiding principle of that party should be "the strictest secrecy, the strictest selection of members, and the training of professional revolutionaries."[3] Within the context of turn-of-the-century European socialist debates, Lenin thus rejected both Kautsky's view that revolution was inevitable and Bernstein's view that it would arrive democratically. Lenin substituted the small, professional, nondemocratic revolutionary party for Marx's proletariat as the instrument of revolutionary change.

[2]*Quoted in Albert Fried and Ronald Sanders, eds.,* Socialist Thought: A Documentary History *(Garden City, N.Y.: Anchor Doubleday, 1964), p. 459.*

[3]*Ibid., p. 468.*

In 1903, at the London Congress of the Russian Social Democratic Party, Lenin forced a split in the party ranks. During much of the congress, he and his followers lost many votes on various questions put before the body, but near the close they mustered a very slim majority. Thereafter Lenin's faction assumed the name *Bolsheviks,* meaning "majority," and the other, more moderate, democratic revolutionary faction came to be known as the *Mensheviks,* or "minority." There was, of course, a considerable public relations advantage to the name Bolshevik. (In 1912 the Bolsheviks organized separately.)

In 1905 Lenin complemented his organizational theory with a program for revolution in Russia. In *Two Tactics of Social Democracy in the Bourgeois-Democratic Revolution,* he urged the socialist revolution to unite the proletariat and the peasantry. Lenin grasped better than any other revolutionary the profound discontent in the Russian countryside. He believed that the tsarist government probably could not suppress an alliance of workers and peasants in rebellion.

Lenin's two principles—an elite party and a dual social revolution—guided later Bolshevik activity. The Bolsheviks ultimately seized power in November 1917, transforming the political landscape of the modern world. But they did so

Lenin Argues for the Necessity of a Secret and Elite Party of Professional Revolutionaries

Social democratic parties in western Europe had mass memberships and general-ly democratic structures of organization. In this passage from What Is to Be Done? *(1902), Lenin explained why the autocratic political conditions of Russia demanded a different kind of organization for the Russian Social Democratic Party. Lenin's ideas became the guiding principles of Bolshevik organization.*

◆ *What does Lenin mean by "professional revolutionaries"? Why are such revo-lutionaries especially needed in Russia? How does he reconcile his antidemo-cratic views to the goal of aiding the working class?*

I assert that it is far more difficult [for gov-ernment police] to unearth a dozen wise men than a hundred fools. This position I will defend, no matter how much you instigate the masses against me for my "anti-demo-cratic" views, etc. As I have stated repeatedly, by "wise men," in connection with organization, I mean *professional revolutionaries,* irrespec-tive of whether they have developed from among students or working men. I assert: (1) that no revolutionary movement can endure without a stable organization of leaders main-taining continuity; (2) that the broader the popular mass drawn spontaneously into the struggle, which forms the basis of the move-ment and participates in it, the more urgent the need for such an organization, and the more solid this organization must be . . . ; (3) that such an organization must consist chiefly of people professionally engaged in revolutionary activity; (4) that in an autocrat-ic state [such as Russia], the more we *confine* the membership of such an organization to people who are professionally engaged in rev-olutionary activity and who have been profes-sionally trained in the art of combating the political police, the more difficult will it be to unearth the organization; and (5) the *greater* will be the number of people from the work-ing class and from other social classes who will be able to join the movement and per-form active work in it. . . .

The only serious organization principle for the active workers of our movement should be the strictest secrecy, the strictest selection of members, and the training of professional revolutionaries.

Albert Fried and Ronald Sanders, eds., Socialist Thought: A Documentary History *(Garden City, N.Y.: Anchor Doubleday, 1964), pp. 460, 468.*

only after the turmoil of World War I had under-mined support for the tsar and only after other political forces had toppled the tsarist govern-ment earlier in 1917. Between the turn of the century and World War I, the government of Nicholas II confronted political upheaval more or less successfully.

THE REVOLUTION OF 1905 AND ITS AFTERMATH The quarrels among the exiled Russian socialists and Lenin's doctrines had no immediate influence on events in Russia. Industrialization proceeded and continued to stir resentment in many sectors. In 1903 Nicholas II dismissed Witte, hoping to quell the criticism. The next year Russia went to war against Japan, partly in hopes that the conflict would rally public opinion to the tsar. Instead, the Russians lost the war and the government faced an internal political crisis. The Japanese captured Port Arthur early in 1905. A few days later, on January 22, a priest named Father

On "Bloody Sunday," January 22, 1905, troops of Tsar Nicholas II fired on a peaceful procession of workers who sought to present a petition at the Winter Palace in St. Petersburg. After this event, there was little chance of reconciliation between the Tsarist government and the Russian working class. [Bildarchiv Preussischer Kulturbesitz]

Gapon led several hundred workers to present a petition to the tsar for the improvement of industrial conditions. As the petitioners approached the Winter Palace in Saint Petersburg, the tsar's troops opened fire. About 100 people were shot down in cold blood, and many more were wounded on what became known as Bloody Sunday.

During the next ten months, revolutionary disturbances spread throughout Russia. Sailors mutinied, peasant revolts erupted, and property was attacked. The uncle of Nicholas II was assassinated. Liberal leaders of the Constitutional Democratic Party from the *zemstvos* demanded political reform. Student strikes occurred in the universities. Social Revolutionaries and Social Democrats agitated among urban working groups. In early October 1905, strikes broke out in Saint Petersburg, and for all practical purposes, worker groups, called *soviets*, controlled the city. Nicholas II recalled Witte and issued the October Manifesto, which promised Russia constitutional government.

Early in 1906, Nicholas II announced the election of a representative body, the Duma, with two chambers. He reserved to himself, however, ministerial appointments, financial policy, military matters, and foreign affairs. The April elections returned a very radical group of representatives. The tsar then dismissed Witte and replaced him with P. A. Stolypin (1862–1911), who had little sympathy for parliamentary government. Stolypin persuaded Nicholas to dissolve the Duma. A second assembly was

Major Dates in Turn-of-the-Century Russian History	
1892	Witte appointed finance minister
1895	Lenin arrested and sent to Siberia
1897	Eleven-and-a-half-hour workday established
1898	Russian Social Democratic Party founded
1900	Lenin leaves Russia for western Europe
1901	Social Revolutionary Party founded
1903	Constitutional Democratic Party (Cadets) founded
1903	Bolshevik–Menshevik split
1903	Witte dismissed
1904	Russo-Japanese War begins
1905 (January)	Japan defeats Russia
1905 (January 22)	Revolution breaks out in Saint Petersburg after Bloody Sunday massacre
1905 (October 20)	General strike
1905 (October 26)	October Manifesto establishes constitutional government
1906 (May 10)	Meeting of first Duma
1906 (June)	Stolypin appointed prime minister
1906 (July 21)	Dissolution of first Duma
1906 (November)	Land redemption payments canceled for peasants
1907 (March 5–June 16)	Second Duma seated and dismissed
1907	Franchise changed and a third Duma elected, which sits until 1912
1911	Stolypin assassinated by a Social Revolutionary
1912	Fourth Duma elected
1914	World War I breaks

elected in February 1907. Again cooperation proved impossible, and the tsar dissolved that Duma in June. A third Duma, elected in late 1907 on the basis of a more conservative franchise, proved sufficiently pliable for the tsar and his minister. Thus, within two years of the 1905 Revolution, Nicholas II had recaptured much of the ground he had conceded.

Stolypin set about repressing rebellion, removing some causes of the revolt, and rallying property owners behind the tsarist regime. Early in 1907, special field courts-martial tried rebellious peasants, condemning almost 700 to death. Before undertaking this repression, the minister, in November 1906, had canceled any redemptive payments that the peasants still owed the government from the emancipation of the serfs in 1861. He took this step to encourage peasants to assume individual proprietorship of their landholdings and to abandon the communal system associated with the *mirs*. Stolypin believed that farmers would be more productive working for themselves. Combined with a program to instruct peasants in better farming methods, this policy did improve agricultural production. The very small peasant proprietors who sold their land increased the size of the industrial labor force.

The moderate liberals who sat in the Duma approved of the new land measures. They liked the idea of competition and individual property ownership. The Constitutional Democrats wanted a more genuinely parliamentary mode of government, but they compromised out of fear of new revolutionary disturbances. Hatred of Stolypin was still widespread, however, among the country's older conservative groups, and industrial workers remained antagonistic to the tsar. In 1911 Stolypin was assassinated by a Social Revolutionary, who may have been a police agent in the pay of conservatives. Nicholas II found no worthy successor. His government simply continued to muddle along.

Meanwhile, at court the monk Grigory Efimovich Rasputin (1871?–1916) came into ascendancy because of his alleged power to heal the tsar's hemophilic son, the heir to the throne. The undue influence of this strange, uncouth man, as well as continued social discontent and conservative resistance to any further liberal reforms, rendered the position and the policy of the tsar uncertain after 1911. Once again, as in 1904, he and his ministers thought that some bold move on the diplomatic front might bring the regime the broad popular support that it so desperately needed.

---------------◆---------------

The years from 1860 through 1914 saw the emergence of two apparently contradictory developments in European social life. On one hand, the lifestyle of the urban middle classes came to dominate, becoming the model to which much of society aspired. The characteristics of this lifestyle included a relatively small family living in its own house or large apartment, servants, and a wife who did not work. The middle classes in general benefitted from the many material comforts generated by the Second Industrial Revolution.

During the same period, the forces of socialism and labor unions assumed a new and major role in European political life. Their leaders demanded greater social justice and a fairer distribution of the vast quantities of consumer goods being produced in Europe. Some socialists sought in one way or another to work within existing political systems. Others—most particularly those in Russia—advocated revolution. The growth in wealth and the availability of new

goods and services magnified the injustices suffered by the poor and the contrast between them and the middle classes, contributing to the stridency of the demands of labor and the socialists. In Russia, the strains of the early stages of industrialization intensified social unrest. These strains, compounded by a humiliating defeat in a war against Japan, triggered the unsuccessful revolution of 1905.

The working class, however, was not alone in seeking change. Women, for the first time in European history, began in significant ways to demand a political role and to protest the gender inequalities embedded in law and family life. They were beginning to enter the professions in small numbers and were taking a significant role in the service economy, such as the new telephone companies. These changes, as much as the demands of socialists, would in time raise questions about the adequacy of the much admired late-nineteenth-century middle-class lifestyle.

Review Questions

1. How was European society transformed by the Second Industrial Revolution? What new industries developed and which do you think had the greatest impact in the twentieth cen-

Rasputin attracted the attention and support of many members of the court of Tsar Nicholas II. This photograph shows him surrounded by admirers. [The Mansell Collection]

tury? How do you account for European economic difficulties in the second half of the nineteenth century?

2. How would you describe living conditions in European cities during the late nineteenth century? Why were European cities redesigned during this period? In what ways were they redesigned? Why were housing and health key issues for urban reform? Be specific in your examples.

3. What was the status of European women in the second half of the nineteenth century? Why did they grow discontented with their lot? What factors led to change? To what extent had they improved their position by 1914? What tactics did they use in effecting change? Was the emancipation of women inevitable? How did women approach their situation differently from country to country?

4. What were the major characteristics of Jewish emancipation in the nineteenth century?

5. What was the status of the proletariat in 1860? Had it improved by 1914? What caused the growth in trade unions and organized mass political parties? Why were the debates over "opportunism" and "revisionism" important to the socialist parties?

6. Assess the value of industrialism for Russia. Were the tsars wise in attempting to modernize their country or would they have been better off leaving it as it was? How did Lenin's view of socialism differ from that of the socialists in western Europe?

Suggested Readings

J. ALBISETTI, *Schooling German Girls and Women: Secondary and Higher Education in the Nineteenth Century* (1988). Contains much information on the subject beyond Germany.

I. M. ARONSON, *Troubled Waters: The Origins of the 1881 Anti-Jewish Pogroms in Russia* (1990). The best discussion of this subject.

L. R. BERLANSTEIN, *The Working People of Paris, 1871–1914* (1985). Interesting and comprehensive.

D. BLACKBOURN and G. ELEY, *The Peculiarities of German History: Bourgeois Society and Politics in Nineteenth-Century Germany* (1985). An important and probing study.

N. BULLOCK and J. READ, *The Movement for Housing Reform in Germany and France, 1840–1914*

(1985). An important and wide-ranging study of the housing problem.

C. M. CIPOLLA, *The Economic History of World Population* (1962). A basic introduction.

R. J. EVANS and W. R. LEE, *The German Family: Essays on the Social History of the Family in Nineteenth- and Twentieth-Century Germany* (1981). Very useful.

P. GAY, *The Bourgeois Experience: Victoria to Freud, Vol. 1, Education of the Senses* (1984). *Vol. 2, The Tender Passion* (1986). A major study of middle-class sexuality.

P. GAY, *The Dilemma of Democratic Socialism: Eduard Bernstein's Challenge to Marx* (1952). A clear presentation of the problems raised by Bernstein's revisionism.

M. GIBSON, *Prostitution and the State in Italy, 1860–1915* (1986). An examination of state regulation of prostitution.

D. F. GOOD, *The Economic Rise of the Hapsburg Empire, 1750–1914* (1985). The best available study.

J. HARSIN, *Policing Prostitution in Nineteenth-Century Paris* (1985). A major study of this very significant subject in French social history.

S. C. HAUSE, *Women's Suffrage and Social Politics in the French Third Republic* (1984). A wide-ranging examination of the question.

P. HILDEN, *Working Women and Socialist Politics in France, 1880–1914* (1986). A study that traces both cooperation and tension between socialism and feminism in the French working class.

G. HIMMELFARB, *Poverty and Compassion: The Moral Imagination of the Late Victorians* (1991). The best examination of late Victorian social thought.

E. J. HOBSBAWM, *The Age of Capital* (1975). Explores the consolidation of middle-class life after 1850.

L. HOLCOMBE, *Wives and Property: Reform of the Married Women's Property Law in Nineteenth-Century England* (1983). The standard work on the subject.

S. S. HOLTON, *Feminism and Democracy: Women's Suffrage and Reform Politics in Britain, 1900–1918* (1986). An excellent treatment of the subject.

K. H. JARAUSCH, *Students, Society, and Politics in Imperial Germany: The Rise of Academic Illiberalism* (1982). The reaction of the academic community to the threat of socialism.

P. JOYCE, *Visions of the People: Industrial England and the Question of Class, 1848–1914* (1991). Based on important explorations of what actually occurred in the workplace.

S. KERN, *The Culture of Love: Victorians to Moderns* (1992). A major discussion of how Europeans have thought and behaved in regard to love, family, and sexuality.

S. Kern, *The Culture of Time and Space, 1880–1918* (1983). A lively discussion of the impact of the new technology.

K. Kolakowski, *Main Currents of Marxism: Its Rise, Growth, and Dissolution*, 3 vols. (1978). The relevant sections on the last years of the nineteenth century and the early years of the twentieth are especially good.

D. Landes, *The Unbound Prometheus: Technological Change and Industrial Development in Western Europe from 1750 to the Present* (1969). Includes excellent discussions of late-nineteenth-century development.

A. H. McBriar, *Fabian Socialism and English Politics, 1884–1918* (1962). The standard discussion.

W. O. McCagg, Jr., *A History of Habsburg Jews, 1670–1918* (1989). An excellent examination of the political and economic life of the Jews under Habsburg rule.

A. MacLaren, *Sexuality and Social Order: The Debate over the Fertility of Women and Workers in France, 1770–1920* (1983). Examines the debate over birth control in France.

G. L. Mosse, *German Jews Beyond Judaism* (1985). Sensitive essays exploring the relationship of Jews to German culture in the nineteenth and early twentieth centuries.

P. G. Nord, *Paris Shopkeepers and the Politics of Resentment* (1986). An examination of the political attitudes of Paris shopkeepers in the wake of the redesign of the city.

D. Olsen, *The City As a Work of Art: London, Paris, Vienna* (1986). A splendidly illustrated survey of nineteenth-century urban growth and design.

H. Pelling, *The Origins of the Labour Party, 1880–1900* (1965). Examines the sources of the party in the activities of British socialists and trade unionists.

M. Perrot, *Workers on Strike: France, 1871–1890* (1987). A major exploration of the social and cultural dimensions of strikes.

D. H. Pinkney, *Napoleon III and the Rebuilding of Paris* (1958). A classic study.

T. Richards, *The Commodity Culture of Victorian England: Advertising and Spectacle, 1851–1914* (1990). A study of how consumers were persuaded of their need for new commodities.

H. Rogger, *Jewish Policies and Right-Wing Politics in Imperial Russia* (1986). A very learned examination of Russian anti-Semitism.

H. Rogger, *Russia in the Age of Modernization and Revolution, 1881–1917* (1983). The best synthesis of the period.

M. L. Rozenblit, *The Jews of Vienna, 1867–1914: Assimilation and Identity* (1983). Covers the cultural, economic, and political life of Viennese Jews.

C. E. Schorske, *German Social Democracy, 1905–1917* (1955). A brilliant study of the difficulties of the Social Democrats under the empire.

J. Scott, *The Glassworkers of Carmaux: French Craftsmen and Political Action in a Nineteenth-Century City* (1974). A classic analysis of how highly skilled craftsmen confronted and were eventually defeated by the mechanization of their industry.

A. L. Shapiro, *Housing the Poor of Paris, 1850–1902* (1985). Examines what happened to working-class housing at the time of the remodeling of Paris.

B. G. Smith, *Ladies of the Leisure Class: The Bourgeoises of Northern France in the Nineteenth Century* (1981). Emphasizes the importance of the reproductive role of women.

R. A. Soloway, *Birth Control and the Population Question in England, 1877–1930* (1982). An important book that should be read with the MacLaren book.

N. Stone, *Europe Transformed* (1984). A sweeping survey that emphasizes the difficulties of late-nineteenth-century liberalism.

F. M. L. Thompson, *The Rise of Respectable Society: A Social History of Victorian Britain, 1830–1900* (1988). A major survey.

A. B. Ulam, *The Bolsheviks: The Intellectual and Political History of the Triumph of Communism in Russia* (1965). Early chapters discuss prewar developments and the formation of Lenin's doctrines.

A. M. Verner, *The Crisis of Russian Autocracy: Nicholas II and the 1905 Revolution* (1990). A major study of this crucial event.

J. R. Walkowitz, *Prostitution and Victorian Society: Women, Class, and the State* (1980). A work of great insight and sensitivity.

E. Weber, *Peasants into Frenchmen: The Modernization of Rural France, 1870–1914* (1976). An important and fascinating work on the transformation of French peasants into self-conscious citizens of the nation-state.

M. J. Wiener, *English Culture and the Decline of the Industrial Spirit, 1850–1980* (1981). The best study of the problem.

T. Zeldin, *France, 1848–1945*, 2 vols. (1973, 1977). Covers many areas of French social life.

Friedrich Nietzsche (1844–1900) was the most influential German philosopher of the late nineteenth century. His books, which challenged existing morality and values, have exerted a powerful influence on twentieth-century literature and philosophy. Detail from portrait by Kurt Stoeving, 1904. [Bildarchiv Preussischer Kulturbesitz]

The Birth of Modern European Thought

Key Topics in This Chapter
- The dominance of science in the thought of the second half of the nineteenth century
- The conflict of Church and state over education
- The effect of modernism, psychoanalysis, and the revolution in physics on intellectual life
- Racism and the resurgence of anti-Semitism
- Late-nineteenth- and early-twentieth-century developments in feminism

During the same period that the modern nation-state developed and the Second Industrial Revolution laid the foundations for the modern material lifestyle, the ideas and concepts that have marked European thought for much of the present century took shape. Like previous intellectual changes, these arose from earlier patterns of thought. The Enlightenment provided late-nineteenth-century Europeans with a heritage of rationalism, toleration, cosmopolitanism, and appreciation of science. Romanticism led them to value feelings, imagination, national identity, and the autonomy of the artistic experience.

By 1900 these strands of thought had become woven into a new fabric. Many of the traditional intellectual signposts were disappearing. The death of God had been proclaimed. Christianity had undergone the most severe attack in its his-

tory. The picture of the physical world that had prevailed since Newton had undergone major modification. The work of Darwin and Freud had challenged the special place that Western thinkers had assigned to humankind. Writers began to question the value long ascribed to rationality. The political and humanitarian ideals of liberalism and socialism gave way to new, aggressive nationalism. At the turn of the century, European intellectuals were more daring than ever before, but they were also probably less certain and less optimistic.

Many of the new ideas shaking Europe were not particularly sympathetic to the women's movement, but women could use the challenge to tradition for their own ends. Small groups of European feminists also began to challenge in new ways the idea of separate gender spheres.

The New Reading Public

The social context of intellectual life changed in the last half of the nineteenth century. For the first time in Europe, a mass reading public came into existence as more people than ever before became drawn into the world of print culture. In 1850 about half the population of western Europe and a much higher proportion of Russians were illiterate. Even those people who could technically read and write did so poorly. That situation changed during the next half century.

Advances in Primary Education

The literacy of the Continent improved steadily, as from the 1860s onward one government after another undertook state-financed education. Hungary provided elementary education in 1868; Britain, in 1870; Switzerland, in 1874; Italy, in 1877; and France, between 1878 and 1881. The already advanced education system of Prussia was extended in various ways throughout the German Empire after 1871. The attack on illiteracy proved most successful in Britain, France, Belgium, the Netherlands, Germany, and Scandinavia, where by 1900 approximately 85 percent or more of the people could read. Italy, Spain, Russia, Austria-Hungary, and the Balkans lagged well behind,

with illiteracy rates of between 30 and 60 percent.

The new primary education in the basic skills of reading and writing and elementary arithmetic reflected and generated social change. Both liberals and conservatives regarded such minimal training as necessary for orderly political behavior by the newly enfranchised voters. They also hoped that literacy might help the poor to help themselves and might create a better, more productive labor force. This side of the educational crusade embodied the Enlightenment rationalist faith that right knowledge would lead to right action.

Literacy and its extension, however, soon became forces in their own right. The schoolteaching profession grew rapidly in numbers and prestige and, as noted in the previous chapter, became a major area for the employment of women. Those people who learned to read the little they were taught could continue to read much more on their own. They soon discovered that much of the education that led to better jobs and political influence was still open only to those who could afford it. Having created systems of primary education, the major nations had to give further attention to secondary education by the time of World War I. In yet another generation, the question would become one of democratic university instruction.

Reading Material for the Mass Audience

The expanding literate population created a vast market for new reading material. There was a veritable explosion of printed matter of every variety. Advances in printing and paper technology lowered production costs. The number of newspapers, books, magazines, mail-order catalogues, and libraries grew rapidly. Cheap mass-circulation newspapers, such as *Le Petit Journal* of Paris and the *Daily Mail* and *Daily Express* of London, enjoyed their first heyday. Such newspapers carried advertising that alerted readers to the new consumer products made available through the Second Industrial Revolution. Other publishers produced newspapers with specialized political or religious viewpoints. The number of monthly and quarterly journals for families, women, and freethinking intellectuals increased. Probably more people with different

Public education became widespread in Europe during the second half of the nineteenth century and women came to dominate the profession of schoolteaching, especially at the elementary level. These English schoolchildren are going through morning drills in 1905. [The Bettmann Archive]

ideas could get into print in the late nineteenth century than ever before in European history. And more people could read their ideas than ever before.

Because many of the new readers were only marginally literate and still ignorant about many subjects, the books and journals catering to them often were mediocre. The cheap newspapers prospered on stories of sensational crimes and political scandal and on pages of advertising. Religious journals depended on denominational rivalry. A brisk market existed for pornography. Newspapers with editorials on the front page became major factors in the emerging mass politics. The news could be managed, but in central Europe more often by the government censor than by the publisher.

Social and artistic critics were correct in pointing to the low level of public taste. Nevertheless, the new education, the new readers, and the hundreds of new books and journals permitted a monumental popularization of knowledge that has become a hallmark of the contemporary world. The new literacy was the intellectual parallel of the railroad and the steamship. People could leave their original intellectual surroundings since literacy is not an end in itself, but it leads to other skills and the acquisition of other knowledge.

Science at Mid-Century

In about 1850 Voltaire would still have felt at home in a general discussion of scientific concepts. The basic Newtonian picture of physical nature that he had popularized still prevailed. Scientists continued to believe that nature operated as a vast machine according to mechanical principles. At mid-century, learned persons regarded the physical world as rational, mechanical, and dependable. Its laws could be ascertained objectively through experiment and observation. Scientific theory purportedly described physical nature as it really existed.

Auguste Comte, the founder of Positivism. Comte argued that all natural phenomena, including the workings of human society, could be explained scientifically in terms of empirically derived natural laws.
[Roger-Viollet]

Comte, Positivism, and the Prestige of Science

During the early nineteenth century, science had continued to establish itself as the model for all human knowledge. The French philosopher Auguste Comte (1798–1857), a late child of the Enlightenment and a one-time follower of Saint-Simon, developed a philosophy of human intellectual development that culminated in science. In *The Positive Philosophy* (1830–1842), Comte argued that human thought had developed in three stages. In the first, or theological, stage, physical nature was explained in terms of the action of divinities or spirits. In the second, or metaphysical, stage, abstract principles were regarded as the operative agencies of nature. In the final, or positive, stage, explanations of nature became matters of exact description of phenomena, without recourse to an unobservable operative principle.

Physical science had, in Comte's view, entered the positive stage, and similar thinking should penetrate other areas of analysis. In particular, Comte thought that positive laws of social behavior could be discovered in the same fashion as laws of physical nature. He is thus generally regarded as the father of sociology. Works like Comte's helped to convince learned Europeans that genuine knowledge in any area must resemble scientific knowledge.

From the middle of the nineteenth century onward, the links of science to the technology of the Second Industrial Revolution made the general European public aware of science and technology as never before. The British Fabian socialist Beatrice Webb (1858–1943) recalled this situation from her youth:

Who will deny that the men of science were the leading British intellectuals of that period; that it was they who stood out as men of genius with international reputations; that it was they who were the self-confident militants of the period; that it was they who were routing the theologians, confounding the mystics, imposing their theories on philosophers, their inventions on capitalists, and their discoveries on medical men; whilst they were at the same time snubbing the artists, ignoring the poets, and even casting doubts on the capacity of the politicians?[1]

Her remarks would have applied in virtually every industrialized nation in Europe. During the third quarter of the century, writers spoke of a religion of science that would explain all nature without resort to supernaturalism. Popularizers, such as Thomas Henry Huxley (1825–1895) in Britain and Ernst Haeckel (1834–1919) in Germany, wrote and lectured widely on scientific topics. They argued that science held the answer to the major questions of life. They worked for government support of scientific research and for inclusion of science in the schools and universities.

Darwin's Theory of Natural Selection

In 1859 Charles Darwin (1809–1882) published *The Origin of Species*, which carried the mechanical interpretation of physical nature

---

[1] *Beatrice Webb,* My Apprenticeship *(London: Longmans, Green, 1926), pp. 130–131.*

into the world of living things. The book proved to be one of the seminal works of Western thought and earned Darwin the honor of being regarded as the Newton of biology. Both Darwin and his book have been much misunderstood. He did not originate the concept of evolution, which had been discussed widely before he wrote. What he and Alfred Russel Wallace (1823–1913) did, working independently, was to formulate the principle of natural selection, which explained how species had changed or evolved over time. Earlier writers had believed that evolution might occur; Darwin and Wallace explained how it could occur.

Drawing on Malthus, the two scientists contended that more seeds and living organisms come into existence than can survive in their environment. Those organisms having some marginal advantage in the struggle for existence live long enough to propagate their kind. This principle of survival of the fittest Darwin called *natural selection*. The principle was naturalistic and mechanistic. Its operation required no guiding mind behind the development and change in organic nature. What neither Darwin nor anyone else in his day could explain was the origin of those chance variations that provided some living things with the marginal chance for survival. Only after 1900, when the work on heredity of the Austrian monk Gregor Mendel (1822–1884) received public attention, did the mystery of those variations begin to be unraveled.

Darwin's and Wallace's theory represented the triumph of naturalistic explanation, which removed the idea of purpose from organic nature. Eyes were not made for seeing according to the rational wisdom and purpose of God but had developed mechanistically over time. Thus, the theory of evolution through natural selection not only contradicted the biblical narrative of the Creation but also undermined the deistic argument for the existence of God from the design of the universe. Moreover, Darwin's work undermined the whole concept of fixity in nature or the universe at large. The world was a realm of flux and change. The idea that physical and organic nature might be constantly changing allowed people in the late nineteenth century to believe that society, values, customs, and beliefs should also change.

In two works of seminal importance, The Origin of Species *(1859) and* The Descent of Man *(1871), Charles Darwin enunciated the theory of evolution by natural selection and applied that theory to human beings. The result was a storm of controversy that affected not only biology but also religion, philosophy, sociology, and even politics. [Bildarchiv Preussischer Kulturbesitz]*

In 1871 Darwin carried his work a step further. In *The Descent of Man*, he applied the principle of evolution by natural selection to human beings. Darwin was hardly the first person to treat human beings as animals, but his arguments brought greater plausibility to that point of view. He contended that humankind's moral nature and religious sentiments, as well as its physical frame, had developed naturalistically largely in response to the requirements of survival. Neither the origin nor the character of humankind on earth, in Darwin's view, required the existence of a God for their explanation. Not since Copernicus had removed the earth from the center of the universe had the pride of Western human beings received so sharp a blow.

Darwin's theory of evolution by natural selection was controversial from the moment of the publication of *The Origin of Species*. It encountered criticism from both the religious and the scientific communities. By the end of the centu-

Darwin Defends a Mechanistic View of Nature

In the closing paragraphs of The Origin of Species *(1859), Charles Darwin contrasted the view of nature he championed with that of his opponents. He argued that an interpretation of organic nature based on mechanistic laws was actually nobler than an interpretation based on divine creation. In the second edition, however, Darwin, added the term Creator to these paragraphs.*

◆ *Why does Darwin believe a mechanistic creation suggests no less dignity than creation by God? How does the insertion of the term Creator change this passage? What is the grandeur that Darwin finds in his view of life?*

Authors of the highest eminence seem to be fully satisfied with the view that each species has been independently created. To my mind it accords better with what we know of the laws impressed on matter by the Creator, that the production and extinction of the past and present inhabitants of the world should have been due to secondary causes, like those determining the birth and death of the individual. When I view all beings not as special creations, but as the lineal descendants of some few beings which lived long before the first bed of the Cambrian [geological] system was deposited, they seem to me to become ennobled. . . .

It is interesting to contemplate a tangled bank, clothed with many plants of many kinds, with birds singing on the bushes, with various insects flitting about, and with worms crawling through the damp earth, and to reflect that these elaborately constructed forms, so different from each other, and dependent upon each other in so complex a manner, have all been produced by laws acting around us. These laws, taken in the largest sense, being Growth with Reproduction; Inheritance which is almost implied by reproduction; Variability from the indirect and direct action of the conditions of life, and from use and disuse: a Ratio of Increase so high as to lead to a Struggle for Life, and as a consequence to Natural Selection, entailing Divergence of Character and the Extinction of less-improved forms. Thus, from the war of nature, from famine and death, the most exalted object which we are capable of conceiving, namely the production of the higher animals, directly follows. There is grandeur in this view of life, with its several powers, having been originally breathed by the Creator into a few forms or into one; and that, whilst this planet has gone cycling on according to the fixed law of gravity, from so simple a beginning endless forms most beautiful and most wonderful have been, and are being evolved.

Charles Darwin, The Origin of Species and the Descent of Man *(New York: Modern Library, n.d.), pp. 373–374.*

ry, scientists widely accepted evolution, but not yet Darwin's mechanism of natural selection. The acceptance of the latter within the scientific community really dates from the 1920s and 1930s, when Darwin's theory was combined with the insights of modern genetics.

Science and Ethics

Darwin's ideas remained highly controversial. They were widely debated in popular and scientific journals. He changed some of them in the course of his writings. At issue, however, was not only the correctness of the theory and the place of humankind in nature but also the role of science and scientists in society.

One area in which science came to have a new significance was in social thought and ethics. Certain philosophers modeled theories of ethics on science. They applied the concept of the struggle for survival to human social relationships. The phrase "survival of the fittest" predated Darwin and reflected the competitive outlook of classical economics. Darwin's use of the phrase gave it the prestige associated with advanced science.

The most famous advocate of evolutionary ethics was Herbert Spencer (1820–1903), a British philosopher. Spencer, a strong individualist, believed that human society progressed through competition. If the weak received too much protection, the rest of humankind was the loser. In Spencer's work, struggle against one's fellow human beings became a kind of ethical imperative. The concept could be applied to justify the avoidance of aiding the poor and the working class or to justify the domination of colonial peoples or to advocate aggressive competition among nations. Evolutionary ethics and similar concepts, all of which are usually termed *social Darwinism*, often came close to saying that might makes right.

One of the chief opponents of such thinking was Thomas Henry Huxley, the great defender of Darwin. In 1893 Huxley declared that the physical cosmic process of evolution was at odds with the process of human ethical development. The struggle in nature held no ethical implications except to demonstrate how human beings should not behave.

Scientists and their admirers enjoyed a supreme confidence during the last half of the century. They genuinely believed that they had, for all intents and purposes, discovered all that might be discovered. The issues for science in the future would be the extension of acknowledged principles and the refinement of measurement. The turn of the century, however, held a much more brilliant and rapidly expanding horizon for science as a much more complicated picture of nature developed. Before examining those new departures, we must see how the cult of science affected religious thought and practice.

Christianity and the Church Under Siege

The nineteenth century was one of the most difficult periods in the history of the organized Christian churches. Many European intellectuals left the faith. The secular, liberal nation-states attacked the political and social influence of the Church. The expansion of population and the growth of cities challenged its organizational capacity to meet the modern age. Yet during all of this turmoil, the Protestant and Catholic churches still made considerable headway at the popular level.

Intellectual Skepticism

The intellectual attack on Christianity arose on the grounds of its historical credibility, its scientific accuracy, and its pronounced morality. The *philosophes* of the Enlightenment had delighted in pointing out contradictions in the Bible. The historical scholarship of the nineteenth century brought new issues to the fore.

HISTORY In 1835 David Friedrich Strauss (1808–1874) published *The Life of Jesus,* in which he questioned whether the Bible provided any genuine historical evidence about Jesus. Strauss contended that the story of Jesus was a myth that had arisen from the particular social and intellectual conditions of first-century Palestine. Jesus' character and life represented the aspirations of the people of that time and place rather than events that had actually occurred. Other authors also published skeptical lives of Jesus.

During the second half of the century, scholars such as Julius Wellhausen (1844–1918) in Germany, Ernst Renan (1823–1892) in France, and William Robertson Smith (1847–1894) in Great Britain contended that human authors had written and revised the books of the Bible with the problems of Jewish society and politics in mind. The Bible was not an inspired book but had, like the Homeric epics, been written by normal human beings in a primitive society. This questioning of the historical validity of the Bible caused more literate men and women to lose faith in Christianity than any other single cause.

SCIENCE The march of science also undermined Christianity. This blow was particularly cruel because many eighteenth-century writers had led Christians to believe that the scientific examination of nature provided a strong buttress for their faith. William Paley's (1743–1805) *Natural Theology* (1802) and books by numerous

T. H. Huxley Criticizes Evolutionary Ethics

T. H. Huxley (1825–1895) was a British scientist who had been among Darwin's strongest defenders. He was also an outspoken advocate for the advancement of science in the late nineteenth century. Huxley, however, became a major critic of social Darwinism, which attempted to deduce ethical principles from evolutionary processes involving struggle in nature. Huxley drew a strong distinction between the cosmic process of evolution and the social process of ethical development. He argued that human ethical progress occurred through combating the cosmic process. These passages are taken from Evolution and Ethics *(1893).*

✦ *What does Huxley mean by the "cosmic process"? Why does he equate "social progress" with the "ethical process"? In this passage, does Huxley present human society as part of nature or as something that may be separate from nature?*

Men in society are undoubtedly subject to the cosmic process. As among other animals, multiplication goes on without cessation, and involves severe competition for the means of support. The struggle for existence tends to eliminate those less fitted to adapt themselves to the circumstances of their existence. The strongest, the most self-assertive, tend to tread down the weaker. But the influence of the cosmic process on the evolution of society is the greater the more rudimentary its civilization. Social progress means a checking of the cosmic process at every step and the substitution for it of another, which may be called the ethical process; the end of which is not the survival of those who may happen to be the fittest, in respect of the whole of the conditions which obtain, but of those who are ethically the best.

As I have already urged, the practice of that which is ethically best—what we call goodness or virtue—involves a course of conduct which, in all respects, is opposed to that which leads to success in the cosmic struggle for existence. In place of ruthless self-assertion it demands self-restraint; in place of thrusting aside, or treading down, all competitors, it requires that the individual shall not merely respect, but shall help his fellows; its influence is directed, not so much to the survival of the fittest, as to the fitting of as many as possible to survive. It repudiates the gladiatorial theory of existence.

It is from neglect of these plain considerations that the fanatical individualism of our time attempts to apply the analogy of cosmic nature to society. . . .

Let us understand, once for all, that the ethical progress of society depends, not on imitating the cosmic process, still less in running away from it, but in combating it.

T. H. Huxley, Evolution and Ethics *(London: Macmillan & Co., 1894), as quoted in Franklin L. Baumer,* Main Currents of Western Thought: Readings in Western European Intellectual History from the Middle Ages to the Present, *3rd ed., rev. (New York: Alfred A. Knopf, 1970), pp. 561–562.*

scientists had enshrined this belief. The geology of Charles Lyell (1797–1875) suggested that the earth was much older than the biblical records contended. By looking to natural causes to explain floods, mountains, and valleys, Lyell removed the miraculous hand of God from the physical development of the earth. Darwin's theory cast doubt on the doctrine of the Creation. His ideas and those of other writers suggested that the moral nature of humankind could be explained without appeal to God. Finally, anthropologists, psychologists, and sociologists suggested that religion itself and religious sentiments were just one more set of natural phenomena.

MORALITY   Other intellectuals questioned the morality of Christianity. The old issue of immoral biblical stories was again raised. Much more important, the moral character of the Old Testament God came under fire. His cruelty and unpredictability did not fit well with the progressive, tolerant, rational values of liberals. They also wondered about the morality of the New Testament God, who would sacrifice for His own satisfaction the only perfect being ever to walk the earth. Many of the clergy began to ask themselves if they could honestly preach doctrines they felt to be immoral.

During the last quarter of the century, this moral attack on Christianity came from another direction. Writers like Friedrich Nietzsche (1844–1900) in Germany portrayed Christianity as a religion of sheep that glorified weakness rather than the strength life required. Christianity demanded a useless and debilitating sacrifice of the flesh and spirit rather than full-blooded heroic living and daring. Nietzsche once observed, "War and courage have accomplished more great things than love of neighbor."[2]

These widespread skeptical intellectual currents influenced only the upper levels of educated society directly. Yet they created a climate in which Christianity lost much of its intellectual respectability. Fewer educated people joined the clergy. More and more people found that they could lead their lives with little or no reference to Christianity. The secularism of everyday life proved as harmful to the faith as the direct attacks. This situation especially prevailed in the cities, which were growing faster than the capacity of the churches to meet the challenge. There was not even enough room in urban churches for potential worshipers to sit. Whole generations of the urban poor grew up with little or no experience of the Church as an institution or of Christianity as a religious faith.

Conflict of Church and State

The secular state of the nineteenth century clashed with both the Protestant and the Roman Catholic churches. Liberals generally disliked the dogma and the political privileges of the established churches. National states were often suspicious of the supranational character of the Roman Catholic church. The primary area of conflict between the state and the churches, however, was the expanding systems of educa-

[2]*Walter Kaufmann, ed. and trans.,* The Portable Nietzsche *(New York: Viking, 1967), p. 159.*

tion. Previously, most education in Europe had taken place in schools run by religious orders or denominations. The churches feared that future generations would emerge from the new state-financed schools without the rudiments of religious teaching. From 1870 through the turn of the century, religious education was heatedly debated in every major country.

GREAT BRITAIN In Great Britain, the Education Act of 1870 provided for the construction of state-supported schools run by elected school boards, whereas earlier the government had given small grants to religious schools. The new schools were to be built in areas where the religious denominations did not provide satisfactory education. There was rivalry not only between the Anglican church and the state but also between the Anglican church and the Nonconformist denominations, that is, those Protestant denominations that were not part of the Church of England. There was intense local hostility among all these groups. The churches of all denominations had to oppose improvements in education because these increased the costs of their own schools. In the Education Act of 1902, the government decided to provide state support for both religious and nonreligious schools but imposed the same educational standards on each.

FRANCE The British conflict was calm compared with that in France, which had a dual system of Catholic and public schools. Under the Falloux Law of 1850, the local priest provided religious education in the public schools. The conservative French Catholic church and the Third French Republic were hostile to each other. Between 1878 and 1886, the government passed a series of educational laws sponsored by Jules Ferry (1832–1893). The Ferry Laws replaced religious instruction in the public schools with civic training. Members of religious orders could no longer teach in the public schools, the number of which was to be expanded. After the Dreyfus affair, the French Catholic church again paid a price for its reactionary politics. The Radical government of Pierre Waldeck-Rousseau (1846–1904), drawn from pro-Dreyfus groups, suppressed the religious orders. In 1905 the Napoleonic Concordat was terminated, and Church and state were totally separated.

The conflict between Church and state disrupted German politics during the 1870s. In this contemporary cartoon Bismarck and Pope Pius IX seek to checkmate each other in a game of chess. [Bildarchiv Preussischer Kulturbesitz]

GERMANY AND THE *KULTURKAMPF* The most extreme example of Church–state conflict occurred in Germany during the 1870s. At unification, the German Catholic hierarchy had wanted freedom for the churches guaranteed in the constitution. Bismarck left the matter to the discretion of each federal state, but he soon felt that the activity of the Roman Catholic church and the Catholic Center Party threatened the political unity of the new German Empire. Through administrative orders in 1870 and 1871, Bismarck removed both Catholic and Protestant clergy from overseeing local education in Prussia and set education under state direction. This secularization of education represented the beginning of a concerted attack on the independence of the Catholic church in Germany.

The "May Laws" of 1873, which applied to Prussia but not to the entire German Empire, required priests to be educated in German schools and universities and to pass state-administered examinations. The state could veto the appointments of priests. The legislation abolished the disciplinary power of the pope and the Church over the clergy and transferred it to the state. When the bishops and many of the clergy refused to obey these laws, Bismarck used the police against them. In 1876 he had either arrested or driven from Prussia all the Catholic bishops.

In the end, Bismarck's *Kulturkampf* ("cultural struggle") against the Catholic church failed. Not for the first time, Christian martyrs aided resistance to persecution. By the end of the 1870s, the chancellor had abandoned his attack. He had gained state control of education and civil laws governing marriage only at the price of provoking long-term Catholic resentment against the German state. The *Kulturkampf* was probably the greatest blunder of Bismarck's career.

Areas of Religious Revival

The successful German Catholic resistance to the intrusions of the secular state illustrates the continuing vitality of Christianity during this period of intellectual and political hardship. In Great Britain, both the Anglican church and the Nonconformist denominations experienced considerable growth in membership and raised vast sums of money for new churches and schools. In Ireland, the 1870s saw a widespread Catholic devotional revival. In France after the defeat by Prussia, priests organized special pilgrimages by train to shrines for thousands of penitents who believed that France had been defeated because of their sins. The cult of the miracle of Lourdes grew during these years. There were efforts by churches of all denominations to give more attention to the urban poor.

In effect, the last half of the nineteenth century witnessed the final great effort to Christianize Europe. It was well organized, well led, and well financed. It failed not from want of effort but because the population of Europe had simply outstripped the resources of the churches. This persistent liveliness of the churches accounts in part for the intense hostility of its enemies.

The Roman Catholic Church and the Modern World

The most striking feature of Christian religious revival amidst turmoil and persecution was the resilience of the papacy. The brief hope for a liberal pontificate from Pope Pius IX (r. 1846–1878) vanished on the night in November 1848 when he fled the turmoil in Rome. In the 1860s, Pius IX, embittered by the process of Italian unification, launched a counteroffensive against liberalism in thought and deed. In 1864 he issued the *Syllabus of Errors,* which condemned all the major tenets of political liberalism and modern thought. He set the Roman Catholic church squarely against contemporary science, philosophy, and politics.

In 1869 the pope summoned the First Vatican Council. The next year, through the political manipulations of the pontiff and against much opposition from many bishops, the council promulgated the dogma of the infallibility of the pope when speaking officially on matters of faith and morals. No earlier pope had gone so far. The First Vatican Council ended in 1870, when Italian troops invaded Rome at the outbreak of the Franco-Prussian War.

Pius IX died in 1878 and was succeeded by Leo XIII (r. 1878–1903). The new pope, who was sixty-eight years old at the time of his election, sought to make accommodation with the modern age and to address the great social questions. He looked to the philosophical tradition of Thomas Aquinas (1225–1274) to reconcile the claims of faith and reason. Leo XIII's encyclicals of 1885 and 1890 permitted Catholics to participate in the politics of liberal states.

Leo's most important pronouncement on public issues was the encyclical *Rerum Novarum* (1891). In that document he defended private property, religious education, and religious control of the marriage laws; and he condemned socialism and Marxism. He also declared, however, that employers should treat their employees justly, pay them proper wages, and permit them to organize labor unions. He supported laws and regulations to protect the conditions of labor. The pope urged that modern society be organized according to corporate groups, including people from various classes, who might cooperate according to Christian principles. The corporate society, derivative of medieval social organization, was to be an alternative to both socialism and competitive capitalism. On the basis of Leo XIII's pronouncements, democratic Catholic parties and Catholic trade unions were founded throughout Europe.

Pius X, who reigned from 1903 to 1914 and who has been proclaimed a saint, hoped to resist the intrusions of modern thought and to restore traditional devotional life. Between 1903 and 1907, he condemned Catholic Modernism, a movement of modern biblical criticism within the Church, and in 1910 he required all priests to take an anti-Modernist oath. Pius X thus set the Church once more squarely against the intellectual currents of the day, and the struggle between Catholicism and modern thought continued. Although Pius X did not strongly support the social policy of Leo XIII, the Catholic church continued to permit its members to participate actively in social and political movements.

Toward a Twentieth-Century Frame of Mind

The last quarter of the nineteenth century and the first decade of the twentieth century constituted the crucible of modern Western and European thought. During this period, the kind of fundamental reassessment that Darwin's work had previously made necessary in biology and in understanding the place of human beings in nature became writ large in other areas of thinking. Philosophers, scientists, psychologists, and artists began to portray physical reality, human nature, and human society in ways different from those of the past. Their new concepts challenged the major presuppositions of mid-nineteenth-century science, rationalism, liberalism, and bourgeois morality.

Science: The Revolution in Physics

The changes in the scientific worldview originated within the scientific community itself. By the late 1870s, considerable discontent existed over the excessive realism of mid-century science. It was thought that many scientists believed that their mechanistic models, solid atoms, and absolute time and space actually described the real universe.

In 1883 Ernst Mach (1838–1916) published *The Science of Mechanics*, in which he urged that scientists consider their concepts descriptive not of the physical world but of the sensations experienced by the scientific observer. Scientists could describe only the sensations, not the physical world that underlay the sensations. In line with Mach, the French scientist and mathematician Henri Poincaré (1854–1912)

Leo XIII Considers the Social Question in European Politics

In his 1891 encyclical Rerum Novarum, *Pope Leo XIII addressed the social question in European politics, providing the Catholic church's answer to secular calls for social reforms. The pope denied the socialist claim that class conflict was the natural state of affairs. He urged employers to seek just and peaceful relations with workers.*

✦ *How does Leo XIII reject the concept of class conflict? What responsibilities does he assign to the rich and to the poor? Are these responsibilities equal? What kinds of social reform might emerge from these ideas?*

The great mistake that is made in the matter now under consideration is to possess oneself of the idea that class is naturally hostile to class; that rich and poor are intended by Nature to live at war with one another. So irrational and so false is this view that the exact contrary is the truth. . . . Each requires the other; capital cannot do without labour, nor labour without capital. Mutual agreement results in pleasantness and good order; perpetual conflict necessarily produces confusion and outrage. Now, in preventing such strife as this, and in making it impossible, the efficacy of Christianity is marvelous and manifold. . . . Religion teaches the labouring man and the workman to carry out honestly and well all equitable agreements freely made; never to injure capital, or to outrage the person of an employer; never to employ violence in representing his own cause, or to engage in riot or disorder; and to have nothing to do with men of evil principles, who work upon the people with artful promises and raise hopes which usually end in disaster and in repentance when too late.

Religion teaches the rich man and the employer that their work people are not their slaves; that they must respect in every man his dignity as a man and as a Christian; that labour is nothing to be ashamed of, if we listen to right reason and to Christian philosophy, but is an honourable employment, enabling a man to sustain his life in an upright and creditable way; and that it is shameful and inhuman to treat men like chattels to make money by, or to look upon them merely as so much muscle or physical power. Thus, again, Religion teaches that, as among the workman's concerns are Religion herself and things spiritual and mental, the employer is bound to see that he has time for the duties of piety; that he be not exposed to corrupting influences and dangerous occasions; and that he be not led away to neglect his home and family or to squander his wages. Then, again, the employer must never tax his work people beyond their strength, nor employ them in work unsuited to their sex or age. His great and principal obligation is to give every one that which is just.

As quoted in F. S. Nitti, Catholic Socialism, *trans. by Mary Mackintosh (London: S. Sonnenschein, 1895), p. 409.*

urged that the concepts and theories of scientists be regarded as hypothetical constructs of the human mind rather than as descriptions of the true state of nature. In 1911 Hans Vaihinger (1852–1933) suggested that the concepts of science be considered "as if" descriptions of the physical world. By World War I, few scientists believed any longer that they could portray the "truth" about physical reality. Rather, they saw themselves as recording the observations of instruments and as setting forth useful hypothetical or symbolic models of nature.

X RAYS AND RADIATION Discoveries in the laboratory paralleled the philosophical challenge to nineteenth-century science. With those discoveries, the comfortable world of supposedly "complete" nineteenth-century physics vanished forever. In December 1895, Wilhelm Roentgen (1845–1923) published a paper on his discovery of X rays, a form of energy that penetrated various opaque materials. Major steps in the exploration of radioactivity followed within months of the publication of his paper.

In 1896 Henri Becquerel (1852–1908), through a series of experiments building on Roentgen's work, discovered that uranium emitted a similar form of energy. The next year, J. J. Thomson (1856–1940), working in the Cavendish Laboratory of Cambridge University, formulated the theory of the electron. The interior world of the atom had become a new area for human exploration, which continues to this day. In 1902 Ernest Rutherford (1871–1937), who had been Thomson's assistant, explained the cause of radiation through the disintegration of the atoms of radioactive materials. Shortly thereafter, he speculated on the immense store of energy present in the atom.

THEORIES OF QUANTUM ENERGY, RELATIVITY, AND UNCERTAINTY The discovery of radioactivity and discontent with the existing mechanical models led to revolutionary theories in physics. In 1900 Max Planck (1858–1947) pioneered the articulation of the quantum theory of energy, according to which energy is a series of discrete quantities, or packets, rather than a continuous stream. In 1905 Albert Einstein (1879–1955) published his first epoch-making papers on relativity in which he contended that time and space exist not separately but rather as a combined continuum. Moreover,

Marie (1869–1934) and Pierre Curie (1859–1906) were two of the most important figures in the advance of physics and chemistry. Marie was born in Poland but worked in France for most of her life. She is credited with the discovery of radium, for which she was awarded the Nobel Prize in Chemistry in 1911. [Bildarchiv Preussischer Kulturbesitz]

the measurement of time and space depends on the observer as well as on the entities being measured.

In 1927 Werner Heisenberg (1901–1976) set forth the uncertainty principle, according to which the behavior of subatomic particles is a matter of statistical probability rather than of exactly determinable cause and effect. Much that only fifty years earlier had seemed certain and unquestionable about the physical universe had now become problematical.

The mathematical complexity of twentieth-century physics meant that, despite valiant efforts on the part of scientific writers, science would rarely again be successfully popularized. At the same time, through applied technology and further research in chemistry, physics and medicine, science affected daily living more than ever before in human history. Scientists from the late nineteenth century onward

The physicist Albert Einstein's theory of relativity, published in 1905, revolutionized fundamental concepts in physics. [Bildarchiv Preussischer Kulturbesitz]

became the most successful group of Western intellectuals in gaining the financial support of governments and private institutions for the pursuit of their research. They did so by relating the success of science to the economic progress, military security, and health of their various nations. In all those regards, science through pure research, medical knowledge, and technological change has affected modern life more significantly than any other intellectual activity.

Literature: Realism and Naturalism

Between 1850 and 1914, the moral certainties of learned and middle-class Europeans underwent changes no less radical than their concepts of the physical universe. The realist movement in literature portrayed the hypocrisy, the physical and psychic brutality, and the dullness that underlay bourgeois life and society. The realist

and naturalist writers brought scientific objectivity and observation to their work. By using the mid-century cult of science so vital to the middle class, they confronted readers with the harsh realities of life around them. Realism rejected the Romantic idealization of nature, the poor, love, and polite society. Realist novelists portrayed the dark, degraded, and dirty side of life almost, some people thought, for its own sake.

An earlier generation of writers, including Charles Dickens (1812–1870) and Honoré de Balzac (1799–1850), had portrayed the cruelty of industrial life and of a society based wholly on money. Other authors, such as George Eliot (born Mary Ann Evans, 1819–1880), had paid close attention to the details of the scenes and the characters portrayed. There had, however, always been room in their works for imagination, fancy, and artistry. They had felt a better moral world possible through Christian values or humane efforts or, for Eliot, through an appreciation of humanity arising from Auguste Comte's thought.

The major figures of late-century realism examined the dreary and unseemly side of life without being certain whether a better life was possible. In good Darwinian fashion, they regarded and portrayed human beings as animals, subject to the passions, the materialistic determinism, and the pressures of the environment like any other animals. Most of them, however, also saw society itself as perpetuating evil.

FLAUBERT AND ZOLA Critics have often considered Gustave Flaubert's (1821–1880) *Madame Bovary* (1857), with its story of colorless provincial life and a woman's hapless search for love in and outside of marriage, as the first genuinely realistic novel. It portrayed life without heroism, purpose, or even simple civility.

The author who turned realism into a movement was Émile Zola (1840–1902). He found artistic inspiration in Claude Bernard's (1813–1878) *An Introduction to the Study of Experimental Medicine* (1865). Zola argued that he could write an experimental novel in which he would observe and report the characters and their actions as the scientist might relate events within a laboratory experiment. He once declared, "I have simply done on living bodies

Émile Zola of France was the master of the realistic novel. [Bettmann Archive]

critics faulted his taste and middle-class moralists condemned his subject matter, Zola enjoyed a wide following in France and elsewhere. As noted in Chapter 23, he took a leading role in the public defense of Captain Dreyfus.

IBSEN AND SHAW   The Norwegian playwright Henrik Ibsen (1828–1906) carried realism into the dramatic presentation of domestic life. He sought to achieve new modes of social awareness and to strip away the illusory mask of middle-class morality. His most famous play is *A Doll's House* (1879). Its chief character, Nora, has a narrow-minded middle-class husband who cannot tolerate any independence of character or thought on her part. She finally confronts this situation, the play ending as she leaves him, slamming the door behind her. In *Ghosts* (1881), a respectable middle-class woman must deal with a son suffering from syphilis inherited from her husband. In *The Master Builder* (1892), an aging architect kills himself while trying to impress a young woman who perhaps loves him. Ibsen's works were extremely controversial. He had dared to attack sentimentality,

the work of analysis which surgeons perform on corpses."[3] He believed that absolute physical and psychological determinism ruled human events in the same manner as determinism prevailed in the physical world.

Between 1871 and 1893, Zola published twenty volumes of novels exploring subjects normally untouched by writers. In *L'Assommoir* (1877), he discussed the problem of alcoholism, and in *Nana* (1880), he followed the life of a prostitute. In other works, he considered the defeat of the French army in 1870 and the social strife arising from attempts to organize labor. Zola refused to turn his pen or his readers' thoughts away from the most ugly aspects of life. Nothing in his purview received the light of hope or the aura of romance. Although polite

Henrik Ibsen's plays challenged middle-class values in one area of life after another. He particularly questioned the values surrounding marriage and the family. [Bildarchiv Preussischer Kulturbesitz]

[3]Quoted in George J. Becker, *Documents of Modern Literary Realism* (Princeton, N.J.: Princeton University Press, 1963), p. 159.

the ideal of the female "angel of the house," and the cloak of respectability that hung so insecurely over the middle-class family.

One of Ibsen's greatest champions was the Irish writer George Bernard Shaw (1856–1950), who spent most of his life in England. During the late 1880s, Shaw vigorously defended Ibsen's work. He went on to make his own realistic onslaught against Romanticism and false respectability. In *Mrs. Warren's Profession* (1893), a play long censored in England, he explored prostitution. In *Arms and the Man* (1894) and *Man and Superman* (1903), he heaped scorn on the Romantic ideals of love and war, and in *Androcles and the Lion* (1913), he pilloried Christianity. Shaw added to the impact of his plays by writing long critical prefaces, in which he emphasized his social criticism.

These and many other realist writers believed it the duty of the artist to portray reality and the commonplace. In dissecting what they considered the "real" world, they helped to change the moral perception of the good life. They refused to let existing public opinion dictate what they wrote about or how they treated their subjects. By presenting their audiences with unmentionable subjects, they sought to remove the veneer of hypocrisy that had previously forbidden such discussion. They hoped to destroy social and moral illusions and to compel the public to face reality. That change in itself seemed good. Few of the realist writers who raised these problems posed solutions to them. They often left their readers unable to sustain old values and uncertain about where to find new ones.

Modernism

From the 1870s onward throughout Europe, a new multifaceted movement usually called *modernism* touched virtually all the arts. Like realism, modernism was critical of middle-class society and received morality. Modernism, however, whether in music, art, or literature, was not deeply concerned with social issues. What drove the modernists in every field was a concern for the aesthetic or the beautiful. The English essayist Walter Pater (1839–1903) set the tone of the movement when he declared in 1877 that art "constantly aspires to the condition of music."

Across the spectrum of the arts, modernists tried to break the received forms and to create new forms. To many contemporaries, the new forms seemed formless. Practitioners of the modern believed that each of the arts should and could influence the others. Painters gave their works musical titles, as did James Abbott McNeill Whistler (1834–1903) in "Nocturnes." Musicians combined material from many sources. In his at first notorious and then famous ballet, *The Rite of Spring* (1913), Igor Stravinsky (1882–1971) combined jazz rhythms, dissonance, and anthropological theory. Pablo Picasso (1881–1973) and other artists associated with cubism constructed paintings that involved viewing objects from a variety of angles at the same time and drew inspiration from primitive masks they saw in Paris anthropological museums. In England, practitioners of what was called the New Sculpture mixed various materials in richly sensuous statues. Other sculptors rejected traditional forms entirely. For all of these artists, the immediate aesthetic experience of a work of art, whatever its medium, dominated other concerns.

Among the chief proponents of modernism in England were the members of the Bloomsbury Group, including authors Virginia (1882–1941) and Leonard (1880–1969) Woolf, artists Vanessa Bell (1879–1961) and Duncan Grant (1885–1978), the historian and literary critic Lytton Strachey (1880–1932), and the economist John Maynard Keynes (1883–1946). These authors challenged what they regarded as the inherited values of their Victorian forebears. In *Eminent Victorians* (1918), Strachey used a series of biographical sketches less to write history than to heap contempt on his subjects. Grant and Bell looked to the modern artists on the Continent for their models. Keynes eventually challenged much of the structure of nineteenth-century economic theory. In both personal practice and theory, all in the Bloomsbury Group rejected what they regarded as the repressive sexual morality of their parents' generation.

No one charted these changing sensibilities with more care and eloquence than Virginia Woolf. Her novels, such as *Mrs. Dalloway* (1925) and *To the Lighthouse* (1927), portrayed individuals seeking to make their way in a world with most of the nineteenth-century social and moral certainties removed.

Virginia Woolf charted the changing sentiments of a world with most of the nineteenth-century social and moral certainties removed. In A Room of One's Own, *she also challenged some of the received notions of feminist thought, asking whether women writers should bring to their work any separate qualities they possessed as women, and concluding that men and women writers should strive to share each other's sensibilities. [Hulton/Deutsch Collection Limited]*

On the Continent, one of the major practitioners of modernism in literature was Marcel Proust (1871–1922). In his seven-volume novel *In Search of Time Past (A la Recherche du temps perdu,* published between 1913 and 1927), he adopted a stream-of-consciousness format that allowed him to explore his memories. He would concentrate on a single experience or object and then allow his mind to wander through all the thoughts and memories it evoked. In Germany, Thomas Mann (1875–1955), through a long series of novels, the most famous of which were

Buddenbrooks (1901) and *The Magic Mountain* (1924), explored both the social experience of middle-class Germans and how they dealt with the immediate intellectual heritage of the nineteenth century. In *Ulysses* (1922), James Joyce (1882–1941), who was born in Ireland but spent much of his life on the Continent, wholly transformed not only the novel, but also the structure of the paragraph. Joyce encountered enormous difficulty getting this novel published because of its challenging form and its frank sexuality.

Modernism in literature arose before World War I and flourished after the war, nourished by the turmoil and social dislocation it created. The war removed many of the old political structures and social expectations. After its appalling violence, readers found themselves much less shocked by upheavals in literary forms and the moral content of novels and poetry.

James Joyce transformed the novel and drew his readers into new modes of realism. [Bildarchiv Preussischer Kulturbesitz]

Dates of Major Works of Fiction	
1857	Flaubert, *Madame Bovary*
1877	Zola, *L'Assommoir*
1879	Ibsen, *A Doll's House*
1880	Zola, *Nana*
1881	Ibsen, *Ghosts*
1892	Ibsen, *The Master Builder*
1893	Shaw, *Mrs. Warren's Profession*
1894	Shaw, *Arms and the Man*
1901	Mann, *Buddenbrooks*
1903	Shaw, *Man and Superman*
1913	Shaw, *Androcles and the Lion*
	Proust, first volume of *In Search of Time Past*
1922	Joyce, *Ulysses*
1924	Mann, *The Magic Mountain*
1925	Woolf, *Mrs. Dalloway*
1927	Woolf, *To the Lighthouse*

Friedrich Nietzsche and the Revolt Against Reason

During the second half of the century, philosophers began to question the adequacy of rational thinking to address the human situation. No late-nineteenth-century writer better exemplified this new attitude than the German philosopher Friedrich Nietzsche (1844–1900), who had been educated as a classical philologist rather than as an academic philosopher. His books remained unpopular until late in his life, when his brilliance had deteriorated into an almost totally silent insanity. He was wholly at odds with the predominant values of the age. At one time or another, he attacked Christianity, democracy, nationalism, rationality, science, and progress. He sought less to change values than to probe the sources of values in the human mind and character. He wanted not only to tear away the masks of respectable life but also to explore how human beings made such masks.

His first important work was *The Birth of Tragedy* (1872), in which he urged that the nonrational aspects of human nature were as important and noble as the rational characteristics. Here and elsewhere, he insisted on the positive function of instinct and ecstasy in human life. To limit human activity to strictly rational behavior was to impoverish human life and experience. In this work, Nietzsche regarded Socrates as one of the major contributors to Western decadence because of the Greek philosopher's appeal for rationality in human affairs. In Nietzsche's view, the strength for the heroic life and the highest artistic achievement arose from sources beyond rationality.

In later works, such as the prose poem *Thus Spake Zarathustra* (1883), Nietzsche criticized democracy and Christianity. Both would lead only to the mediocrity of sheepish masses. He announced the death of God and proclaimed the coming of the Overman (*Übermensch*), who would embody heroism and greatness. This latter term was frequently interpreted as some mode of superman or super race, but such was not Nietzsche's intention. He was highly critical of contemporary racism and anti-Semitism. He sought a return to the heroism that he associated with Greek life in the Homeric age. He thought that the values of Christianity and of bourgeois morality prevented humankind from achieving life on a heroic level. Those moralities forbade too much of human nature from fulfilling and expressing itself.

Two of Nietzsche's most profound works are *Beyond Good and Evil* (1886) and *The Genealogy of Morals* (1887). Both are difficult books. Much of the former is written in brief, ambiguous aphorisms. Nietzsche sought to discover not what is good and what is evil but the social and psychological sources of the judgment of good and evil. He declared, "There are no moral phenomena at all, but only a moral interpretation of phenomena."[4] He dared to raise the question of whether morality itself was valuable: "We need a critique of moral values; the value of these values themselves must first be called in question."[5] In Nietzsche's view, morality was a human convention that had no independent existence apart from humankind. For Nietzsche, this discovery did not condemn morality but liberated human beings to create life-affirming instead of life-denying values. Christianity, utilitarianism, and middle-class respectability could, in good conscience, be abandoned. Human beings could, if they so willed, create a new moral order for themselves that would glorify

---

[4]*The Basic Writings of Nietzsche, ed. and trans. by Walter Kaufman (New York: The Modern Library, 1968), p. 275.*
[5]*Ibid., p. 456.*

pride, assertiveness, and strength rather than meekness, humility, and weakness.

In his appeal to feelings and emotions and in his questioning of the adequacy of rationalism, Nietzsche drew on the Romantic tradition. The kind of creative impulse that earlier Romantics had considered the gift of artists, Nietzsche saw as the burden of all human beings. The character of the human situation that this philosophy urged on its contemporaries was that of an ever-changing flux in which little or nothing but change itself was permanent. Human beings had to forge from their own inner will and determination the truth and values that were to exist in the world. Nietzsche's philosophy and that of other writers of the time questioned not only the rigid domestic and religious morality of the nineteenth century but also the values of toleration, cosmopolitanism, and benevolence that had been championed during the Enlightenment.

The Birth of Psychoanalysis

A determination to probe beneath surface or public appearances united the major figures of late-nineteenth-century science, art, and philosophy. They sought to discern the various undercurrents, tensions, and complexities that lay beneath the smooth, calm surfaces of hard atoms, respectable families, rationality, and social relationships. As a result of their theories and discoveries, articulate, educated Europeans could never again view the surface of life with smugness or complacency or even much confidence. No single intellectual development more clearly and stunningly exemplified this trend than the emergence of psychoanalysis through the work of Sigmund Freud (1856–1939).

DEVELOPMENT OF FREUD'S EARLY THEORIES Freud was born into an Austrian Jewish family that settled in Vienna. He originally planned to become a lawyer but soon moved to the study of physiology and then to medicine. In 1886 he opened his medical practice in Vienna, where he lived until driven out by the Nazis in 1938. Freud conducted all his research and writing from the base of his medical practice. His earliest medical interests had been psychic disorders, to which he sought to

Sigmund Freud forced a reconsideration of the role of rationality in human motivation. After Freud it was no longer possible to see reason as the sole determinant of behavior. [Bildarchiv Preussischer Kulturbesitz]

apply the critical method of science. In late 1885 he had studied for a few months in Paris with Jean-Martin Charcot (1825–1893), who used hypnosis to treat cases of hysteria. In Vienna, he collaborated with another physician, Josef Breuer (1842–1925), and in 1895 they published *Studies in Hysteria.*

In the mid-1890s, Freud changed the technique of his investigations. He abandoned hypnosis and allowed his patients to talk freely and spontaneously about themselves. Repeatedly, he found that they associated their particular neurotic symptoms with experiences related to earlier experiences, going back to childhood. He also noted that sexual matters were significant in his patients' problems. For a time, he thought that perhaps sexual incidents during childhood accounted for their illnesses.

By 1897, however, Freud had privately rejected this view. In its place he formulated a theory of infantile sexuality, according to which sexual drives and energy already exist in infants and do not simply emerge at puberty. For Freud, human beings were sexual creatures from birth through adulthood. He thus questioned in the most radical manner the concept of childhood innocence. He also portrayed the little-discussed or little-acknowledged matter of sexuality as one of the bases of mental order and disorder.

FREUD'S CONCERN WITH DREAMS During the same decade, Freud also examined the psychic phenomena of dreams. Romantic writers had taken dreams seriously, but few psychologists had examined them scientifically. As a rationalist, Freud believed that the seemingly irrational content of dreams must have a reasonable, scientific explanation. His research led him to reconsider the general nature of the human mind. He concluded that dreams allow unconscious wishes, desires, and drives that had been excluded from everyday conscious life and experience to enjoy freer play in the mind. "The dream," he wrote, "is the (disguised) fulfillment of a (suppressed, repressed) wish."[6] During the waking hours, the mind represses or censors those wishes, which are as important to the individual's psychological makeup as conscious thought. In fact, Freud argued, unconscious drives and desires contribute to conscious behavior. Freud developed these concepts and related them to his idea of infantile sexuality in his most important book, *The Interpretation of Dreams*, published in 1900.

FREUD'S LATER THOUGHT In later books and essays, Freud continued to maintain the significance of the human unconscious. He developed a new model of the internal organization of the mind. According to this model, the mind is an arena of struggle and conflict among three entities: the *id*, the *ego*, and the *superego*. The id consists of amoral, irrational, driving instincts for sexual gratification, aggression, and general physical and sensual pleasure. The superego embodies the external moral imperatives and expectations imposed on the personality by society and culture. The ego mediates

[6]The Basic Writings of Sigmund Freud, *trans. by A. A. Brill (New York: The Modern Library, 1938), p. 235.*

between the impulses of the id and the asceticism of the superego. The ego allows the personality to cope with the inner and outer demands of its existence. Consequently, everyday behavior displayed the activity of the personality as its inner drives were partially repressed through the ego's coping with the external moral expectations as interpreted by the superego.

It has been a grave misreading of Freud to see him as urging humankind to thrust off all repression. He believed that excessive repression could lead to mental disorder but that civilization and the survival of humankind required some repression of sexuality and aggression.

Freud's work revolutionized the understanding of human nature. As his views gained adherents just before and after World War I, new dimensions of human life became widely recognized. Human beings were seen as attaining rationality rather than merely exercising it. Civilization itself came to be regarded as a product of repressed or sublimated aggressions and sexual drive.

In his acknowledgment of the role of instinct, will, dreams, and sexuality, Freud reflected the Romantic tradition of the nineteenth century. In other respects, however, he was a son of the Enlightenment. Like the *philosophes*, he was a realist who wanted human beings to live free of fear and illusions by rationally understanding themselves and their world. He saw the personalities of human beings as being determined by finite physical and mental forces in a finite world. He was hostile to religion and spoke of it as an illusion. Freud, like the writers of the eighteenth century, wished to see civilization and humane behavior prevail. More fully than those predecessors, however, he understood the immense sacrifice of instinctual drives required for civilized behavior. He understood how many previously unsuspected obstacles lay in the way of rationality. Freud believed that the sacrifice and struggle were worthwhile, but he was pessimistic about the future of civilization in the West.

DIVISIONS IN THE PSYCHOANALYTIC MOVEMENT Freud's work marked the beginning of the psychoanalytic movement. By 1910 he had gathered around him a small but able group of disciples. Several of his early followers soon moved toward theories of which the master disapproved. The most important of these dissenters was Carl Jung (1875–1961), a Swiss whom for many years Freud regarded as his most distinguished and promising student. Before World War I, the two men had, however, come to a parting of the ways. Jung had begun to question the primacy of sexual drives in forming human personality and in contributing to mental disorder. He also put much less faith in the guiding light of reason.

Jung believed that the human subconscious contained inherited memories from previous generations. These collective memories, as well as the personal experience of an individual, constituted his or her soul. Jung regarded human beings in the twentieth century as alienated from these useful collective memories. In *Modern Man in Search of a Soul* (1933) and other works, Jung tended toward mysticism and saw positive values in religion. Freud was highly critical of most of Jung's work. If Freud's thought derived primarily from the Enlightenment, Jung's was more dependent on Romanticism.

By the 1920s, the psychoanalytic movement had become even more fragmented. Nonetheless, in its several varieties, it influenced not only psychology but also sociology, anthropology, religious studies, and literary theory. It has been one of the major tools of twentieth-century intellectuals in their efforts to understand themselves and their civilization. In recent years, psychoanalysis has confronted considerable criticism. Whether or not it survives as a model for understanding human behavior, however, there can be no question that it profoundly influenced the intellectual life of the twentieth century.

Retreat from Rationalism in Politics

Nineteenth-century liberals and socialists agreed that rational principles could guide society and politics. Rational analysis could discern the problems of society and prepare solutions. They generally felt that once given the vote, individuals would behave according to their rational political self-interest. Improvement of society and the human condition would be possible through education. By the close of the century, these views had come under attack in both theory and practice. Political scientists and soci-

Max Weber considered bureaucratization as the basic feature of modern social life. In contrast to Marx and Freud, Weber stressed the role of the individual and of rationality in human affairs. [Bildarchiv Preussischer Kulturbesitz]

ologists painted politics as frequently irrational. Racial theorists questioned whether rationality and education could affect human society at all.

WEBER During this period, however, one major social theorist was profoundly impressed by the role of reason in human society. The German sociologist Max Weber (1864–1920) regarded the emergence of rationalism throughout society as the major development of human history. Such rationalization displayed itself in both the development of scientific knowledge and the rise of bureaucratic organization.

Weber saw bureaucratization as the basic feature of modern social life. He used this view to oppose Marx's concept of the development of capitalism as the driving force in modern society. Bureaucratization involved the extreme division of labor as each individual began to fit himself or herself into a particular small role in much larger organizations. Furthermore, Weber believed that in modern society people derived their own self-images and sense of personal worth from their position in these organizations.

Weber also contended—again, in contrast to Marx—that noneconomic factors might account for major developments in human history. For example, in his best-known essay, *The Protestant Ethic and the Spirit of Capitalism* (1905), Weber traced much of the rational character of capitalist enterprise to the ascetic religious doctrines of Puritanism. The Puritans, in his opinion, had accumulated wealth and worked for worldly success less for its own sake than to assure themselves that they stood among the elect of God. The theory has generated both much historical research and critical debate from its publication to the present.

THEORISTS OF COLLECTIVE BEHAVIOR In his emphasis on the individual and on the dominant role of rationality, Weber differed from many contemporary social scientists, such as Gustave LeBon (1841–1931), Émile Durkheim (1858–1917), and Georges Sorel (1847–1922) in France, Vilfredo Pareto (1848–1923) in Italy, and Graham Wallas (1858–1932) in England. LeBon was a psychologist who explored the activity of crowds and mobs. He believed that in crowd situations rational behavior was abandoned. Sorel argued in *Reflections on Violence* (1908) that people did not pursue rationally perceived goals but were led to action by collectively shared ideals. Durkheim and Wallas became deeply interested in the necessity of shared values and activities in a society. These elements, rather than a logical analysis of the social situation, bound human beings together. Instinct, habit, and affections instead of reason directed human social behavior. Besides playing down the function of reason in society, all of these theorists emphasized the role of collective groups in politics rather than that of the individual formerly championed by liberals.

Racism

The same tendencies to question or even to deny the constructive activity of reason in human affairs and to sacrifice the individual to

Major Publication Dates of Nonfiction Works: The Nineteenth and Early Twentieth Centuries	
1830	Lyell's *Principles of Geology*
1830–1842	Comte's *The Positive Philosophy*
1835	Strauss's *The Life of Jesus*
1853–1854	Gobineau's *Essay on the Inequality of the Human Races*
1859	Darwin's *The Origin of Species*
1864	Pius IX's *Syllabus of Errors*
1865	Bernard's *An Introduction to the Study of Experimental Medicine*
1871	Darwin's *The Descent of Man*
1872	Nietzsche's *The Birth of Tragedy*
1883	Mach's *The Science of Mechanics* Nietzsche's *Thus Spake Zarathustra*
1891	Leo XIII's *Rerum Novarum*
1893	Huxley's *Evolution and Ethics*
1896	Herzl's *The Jewish State*
1899	Chamberlain's *The Foundations of the Nineteenth Century*
1900	Freud's *The Interpretation of Dreams* Key's *The Century of the Child*
1905	Weber's *The Protestant Ethic and the Spirit of Capitalism*
1908	Sorel's *Reflections of Violence*
1929	Woolf's *A Room of One's Own*

the group manifested themselves in theories of race. Racial thinking had long existed in Europe. Renaissance explorers had displayed considerable prejudice against nonwhite peoples. Since at least the eighteenth century, biologists and anthropologists had classified human beings according to the color of their skin, their language, and their stage of civilization. Late-eighteenth-century linguistic scholars had observed similarities between many of the European languages and Sanskrit. They then postulated the existence of an ancient race called the Aryans, who had spoken the original language from which the rest derived. During the Romantic period, writers had called the different cultures of Europe races.

The debates over slavery in the European colonies and the United States had given further opportunity for the development of racial

H. S. Chamberlain Exalts the Role of Race

Houston Stewart Chamberlain's Foundations of the Nineteenth Century *(1899) was one of the most influential works of the day to argue for the primary role of race in history. Chamberlain believed that most people in the world were racially mixed and that this mixture weakened those human characteristics most needed for physical and moral strength. As demonstrated in the passage here, he also believed that people assured of their racial purity could act with the most extreme self-confidence and arrogance. Chamberlain's views had a major influence on the Nazi Party in Germany and on others who wished to prove their alleged racial superiority for political purposes.*

✦ *What does Chamberlain mean by "race" in this passage? How, in his view, does race, as opposed to character or environment, determine human nature? How might a nationalist use these ideas?*

Nothing is so convincing as the consciousness of the possession of Race. The man who belongs to a distinct, pure race, never loses the sense of it. The guardian angel of his lineage is ever at his side, supporting him where he loses his foothold, warning him like the Socratic Daemon where he is in danger of going astray, compelling obedience, and forcing him to undertakings which, deeming them impossible, he would never have dared to attempt. Weak and erring like all that is human, a man of this stamp recognises himself, as others recognise him, by the sureness of his character, and by the fact that his actions are marked by a certain simple and peculiar greatness, which finds its explanation in his distinctly typical and super-personal qualities. Race lifts a man above himself; it endows him with extraordinary—I might almost say supernatural—powers, so entirely does it distinguish him from the individual who springs from the chaotic jumble of peoples drawn from all parts of the world: and should this man of pure origin be perchance gifted above his fellows, then the fact of Race strengthens and elevates him on every hand, and he becomes a genius towering over the rest of mankind, not because he has been thrown upon the earth like a flaming meteor by a freak of nature, but because he soars heavenward like some strong and stately tree, nourished by thousands and thousands of roots—no solitary individual, but the living sum of untold souls striving for the same goal.

Houston Stewart Chamberlain, Foundations of the Nineteenth Century, Vol. 1, *trans. by John Lees (London: John Lane, 1912), p. 269.*

theory. In the late nineteenth century, however, race emerged as a single dominant explanation of the history and the character of large groups of people.

GOBINEAU Count Arthur de Gobineau (1816–1882), a reactionary French diplomat, enunciated the first important theory of race as the major determinant of human history. In his four-volume *Essay on the Inequality of the Human Races* (1853–1854), Gobineau portrayed the troubles of Western civilization as being the result of the long degeneration of the original white Aryan race. He claimed it had unwisely intermarried with the inferior yellow and black races, thus diluting the qualities of greatness and ability that originally existed in its blood. Gobineau was deeply pessimistic because he saw no way to reverse the degeneration that had taken place.

Gobineau's essay remained little known for many years. In the meantime, a growing literature by anthropologists and explorers helped to spread racial thinking. In the wake of Darwin's theory, thinkers applied the concept of survival of the fittest to races and nations. The recognition of the animal nature of humankind made the racial idea all the more persuasive.

CHAMBERLAIN At the close of the century, Houston Stewart Chamberlain (1855–1927), an Englishman who settled in Germany, drew together these strands of racial thought into the two volumes of his *Foundations of the Nineteenth Century* (1899). He championed the concept of biological determinism through race, but he was somewhat more optimistic than Gobineau. Chamberlain believed that through genetics the human race could be improved and even that a superior race could be developed.

Chamberlain brought anti-Semitism to prominence in racial theory. He pointed to the Jews as the major enemy of European racial regeneration. Chamberlain's book and the works on which it drew aided the spread of anti-Semitism in European political life. Also in Germany, the writings of Paul de Lagarde (1827–1891) and Julius Langbehn (1851–1907) emphasized the supposed racial and cultural dangers posed by the Jews to traditional German national life.

LATE-CENTURY NATIONALISM Racial thinking was one part of a wider late-century movement toward more aggressive nationalism. Previously, nationalism had in general been a movement among European literary figures and liberals. The former had sought to develop what they regarded as the historically distinct qualities of particular national or ethnic literatures. The liberal nationalists had hoped to redraw the map of Europe to reflect ethnic boundaries. The drive for the unification of Italy and Germany had been major causes, as had been the liberation of Poland from foreign domination. The various national groups of the Habsburg Empire had also sought emancipation from Austrian domination.

From the 1870s onward, however, nationalism became a movement with mass support, well-financed organizations, and political parties. Nationalists often redefined nationality in terms of race and blood. The new nationalism opposed the internationalism of both liberalism and socialism. The ideal of nationality was used to overcome the pluralism of class, religion, and geography. The nation and its duties replaced religion in the lives of many secularized people. It sometimes became a secular religion in the hands of state schoolteachers, who were replacing the clergy as the instructors of youth. Nationalism of this aggressive racist variety would prove to be the most powerful ideology of the early twentieth century and would reemerge after the collapse of communism late in the century.

Anti-Semitism and the Birth of Zionism

Political and racial anti-Semitism, which have cast such dark shadows across the twentieth century, developed in part from this atmosphere of racial thought and the retreat from rationality in politics. Religious anti-Semitism dated from at least the Middle Ages. Since the French Revolution, West European Jews had gradually gained entry into the civil life of Britain, France, and Germany. Popular anti-Semitism, however, continued to exist as the Jewish community was identified with money and banking interests. During the last third of the century, as finance capitalism changed the economic structure of Europe, many non-Jewish Europeans pressured by the changes became hostile toward the Jewish community.

ANTI-SEMITIC POLITICS In Vienna, Mayor Karl Lueger (1844–1910) used anti-Semitism as a major attraction to his successful Christian Socialist Party. In Germany, the ultraconservative Lutheran chaplain Adolf Stoecker (1835–1909) revived anti-Semitism. The Dreyfus affair in France allowed a new flowering of hatred toward the Jews.

To this already ugly atmosphere, racial thought contributed the belief that no matter to what extent Jews assimilated themselves and their families into the culture of their country, their Jewishness—and thus their alleged danger to the society—would remain. According to racial thinkers, the problem of race was not in the character but in the blood of the Jew. An important Jewish response to this new, rabid outbreak of anti-Semitism was the launching in 1896 of the Zionist movement to found a sepa-

Herzl Calls for the Establishment of a Jewish State

In 1896 Theodor Herzl published his pamphlet The Jewish State. *Herzl had lived in France during the turmoil and anti-Semitism associated with the Dreyfus affair. He became convinced that only the establishment of a separate state for Jews would halt the various outbreaks of anti-Semitism that characterized late-nineteenth-century European political and cultural life. Following the publication of this pamphlet, Herzl began to organize the Zionist movement among Jews in both eastern and western Europe.*

◆ *Why does Herzl define what he calls the Jewish Question as a national question? What objections does he anticipate to the founding of a Jewish state? Why does he believe the founding of a Jewish state will be an effective move against anti-Semitism?*

The idea which I develop in this pamphlet is an age-old one: the establishment of a Jewish State.

The world resounds with outcries against the Jews, and this is what awakens the dormant idea.

. . . .

I believe I understand anti-Semitism, a highly complex movement. I view it from the standpoint of a Jew, but without hatred or fear. I think I can discern in it the elements of vulgar sport, of common economic rivalry, of inherited prejudice, of religious intolerance—but also of a supposed need for self-defense. To my mind, the Jewish Question is neither a social nor a religious one, even though it may assume these and other guises. It is a national question, and to solve it we must first of all establish it as an international political problem which will have to be settled by the civilized nations of the world in council.

We are a people, *one* people.

Everywhere we have sincerely endeavored to merge with the national communities surrounding us and to preserve only the faith of our fathers. We are not permitted to do so. . . .

. . . .

And will some people say that the venture is hopeless, because even if we obtain the land and the sovereignty only the poor people will go along? They are the very ones we need first! Only desperate men make good conquerors.

Will anybody say, Oh yes, if it were possible it would have been done by now?

It was not possible before. It is possible now. As recently as a hundred, even fifty years ago it would have been a dream. Today it is all real. The rich, who have an epicurean acquaintance with all technical advance, know very well what can be done with money. And this is how it will be: Precisely the poor and plain people, who have no idea of the power that man already exercises over the forces of Nature, will have the greatest faith in the new message. For they have never lost their hope of the Promised Land.

. . . .

Now, all this may seem to be a long-drawn-out affair. Even in the most favorable circumstances it might be many years before the founding of the State is under way. In the meantime, Jews will be ridiculed, offended, abused, whipped, plundered, and slain in a thousand different localities. But no; just as soon as we begin to implement the plan, anti-Semitism will immediately grind to a halt everywhere. . . .

Theodor Herzl, The Jewish State *(New York: The Herzl Press, 1970), pp. 27, 33, 109, as quoted in William W. Hallo, David B. Ruderman, and Michael Stanislawski, eds.,* Heritage: Civilization and the Jews Source Reader *(New York: Praeger, 1984), pp. 234–235.*

rate Jewish state. Its founder was the Austro-Hungarian Theodor Herzl (1860–1904).

HERZL'S RESPONSE The conviction in 1894 of Captain Dreyfus in France and the election of Karl Lueger in 1895 as mayor of Vienna, as well as personal experience of discrimination, deeply influenced Herzl. He became convinced that liberal politics and the institutions of the liberal state could not protect the Jews in Europe or ensure that they would be treated justly. In 1896 Herzl published *The Jewish State,* in which he called for the organization of a separate state in which all Jews might be assured of those rights and liberties that they should be enjoying in the liberal states of Europe. Furthermore, Herzl followed the tactics of late-century mass democratic politics by particularly directing his appeal to the economically poor Jews who lived in the ghettos of eastern Europe and the slums of western Europe. The original call to Zionism thus combined a rejection of the anti-Semitism of Europe and a desire to realize some of the ideals of both liberalism and socialism in a state outside Europe.

Theodor Herzl's visions of a Jewish state would eventually lead to the creation of Israel in 1948. [The Bettmann Archive/BBC Hulton]

Women and Modern Thought

The ideas that so shook Europe from the publication of *The Origin of Species* through the opening of World War I raised questions about much of the European intellectual legacy. Religion, science, art, and society came under new forms of criticism. Yet these new ideas and intellectual movements produced at best mixed results for women. Within the often radically new ways of thinking about the world, views of women and their roles in society often remained remarkably unchanged.

Antifeminism in Late-Century Thought

The influence of biology on the thinking of intellectuals during the late nineteenth century and their own interest in the nonrational side of human behavior led many of them to sustain what had become stereotyped views of women. The emphasis on biology, evolution, and reproduction led intellectuals to concen-

trate on women's mothering role. Their interest in the nonrational led them to reassert the traditional view that feeling and the nurturing instinct were basic to women's nature. Many late-century thinkers and writers of fiction also often displayed real fear and hostility toward women, portraying them as creatures susceptible to overwhelming and often destructive feelings and instincts. A genuinely misogynist strain emerged in late-century fiction and painting.

Much of the biological thought that challenged religious ideas and the received wisdom in science actually reinforced the traditional view of women as creatures weaker and less able than men. Darwin himself held such views of women, and he expressed them directly in his scientific writings. Medical thought of the late century similarly sustained these views. Whatever social changes were to be wrought through science, significant changes in the organization of the home and the relationship of men and women were not among them.

This conservative and hostile understanding of women manifested itself in several ways within the scientific community. In London in 1860, the Ethnological Society excluded women from its discussions on the grounds that the subject matter of the customs of primitive peoples was unfit for women and that women were amateurs whose presence would lower the level of the discussion. T. H. Huxley, the great defender of Darwin, took the lead in this exclusion as he had in a previous exclusion of women from meetings of the Geological Society. Male scientists also believed women should not discuss reproduction or other sexual matters. Huxley, in public lectures, claimed to have found scientific evidence of the inferiority of women to men. Karl Vogt (1817–1895), a leading German anthropologist, held similar views about the character of women. Darwin would repeat the ideas of both Huxley and Vogt in his *Descent of Man.* Late Victorian anthropologists tended likewise to assign women, as well as nonwhite races, an inferior place in the human family. Despite their otherwise conservative views on gender, however, both Darwin and Huxley supported the expansion of education for women.

The position of women in Freud's thought has always been controversial. Many of his earliest patients, upon whose histories he developed his theories, were women. Critics have claimed, nonetheless, that Freud portrayed women as incomplete human beings who might be inevitably destined to unhappy mental lives. He saw the natural destiny of women as motherhood, and their greatest fulfillment the rearing of sons. The first psychoanalysts were trained as medical doctors, and their views of women reflected contemporary medical education, which, like much of the rest of the scientific establishment, tended to portray women as inferior. Distinguished women psychoanalysts, such as Karen Horney (1885–1952) and Melanie Klein (1882–1960), would later sharply challenge Freud's views on women, and other writers would try to establish a psychoanalytic basis for feminism. Nonetheless, the psychoanalytic profession would remain dominated by men, as would nonpsychoanalytic academic psychology. Since psychology would increasingly influence child-rearing practices and domestic relations law in the twentieth century, it would, ironically, give men a large impact in the one area of social activity that had been dominated by women.

The social sciences of the late nineteenth and early twentieth centuries similarly reinforced traditional gender roles. Virtually all major theorists believed that women's role in reproduction and child rearing demanded a social position inferior to men. Auguste Comte, whose thought in this area owed much to Rousseau, portrayed women as biologically and intellectually inferior to men. Herbert Spencer, although an advocate for improving women's lot, thought they could never achieve genuine equality with men. Émile Durkheim portrayed women as essentially creatures of feeling and family rather than intellect. Max Weber favored improvements in the social condition of women but did not really support significant changes in their social roles or in their relationship to men. Virtually all of the early sociologists took a conservative view of marriage, the family, child rearing, and divorce.

New Directions in Feminism

The close of the century witnessed a revival of feminist thought in Europe that would grow as the twentieth century passed. The role of feminist writers during these years was difficult. Many women's organizations, as seen in the previous chapter, concentrated on achieving the vote for women, but feminist writers and activists raised other questions as well. Women became more clearly conscious of their problems as women in a variety of ways, confronting them not only by seeking the vote. Some organizations forged new ways of thinking about women, redefining their relationships to men and the larger society. Few of these groups were large, and their victories were rare. Nonetheless, they defined late in the last century and early in this one the issues that would become more fully and successfully explored after World War II.

SEXUAL MORALITY AND THE FAMILY In various nations, middle-class women began to challenge the double standard of sexual morality and the traditional male-dominated family. Often this challenge took the form of action relating to prostitution.

Between 1864 and 1886, English prostitutes were subject to the Contagious Diseases Acts. The police in certain cities with naval or military bases could require any woman identified as or suspected of being a prostitute to undergo immediate internal medical examination for venereal disease. Those found to have a disease could without legal recourse be confined for months to lock hospitals (women's hospitals for the treatment of venereal diseases). The law took no action against their male customers. Indeed, the purpose of the laws were to protect men, presumably sailors and soldiers, not the women themselves, from infection.

These laws angered English middle-class women who believed that the working conditions and the poverty imposed on so many working-class women were the true causes of prostitution. They framed the issue in the context of their own efforts to prove that women were as human and rational as men and thus properly subject to equal treatment. They saw poor women being made victims of the same kind of discrimination that prevented themselves from entering the universities and professions. The Contagious Diseases Acts assumed that women were inferior to men and treated them as less than human and less than rational creatures. The laws literally took women's bodies from their own control and put them under the control of male customers, medical men, and the police. They denied to poor women the freedoms that all men enjoyed in English society.

By 1869 the Ladies' National Association for the Repeal of the Contagious Diseases Acts, a distinctly middle-class organization led by Josephine Butler (1828–1906), began actively to oppose these laws. The group achieved the suspension of the acts in 1883 and their repeal in 1886. The issue of government and police regulation of prostitution roused similar movements in other nations, which adopted the English movement as a model. In Vienna during the 1890s, the General Austrian Women's Association, led by Auguste Ficke (1833–1916), combated the introduction of legally regulated prostitution, which would have put women under the control of police authorities. In Germany, women's groups divided between those who would have penalized prostitutes and those who saw them as victims of male society. By the turn of the century, the latter had come

to dominate, although tensions between the groups would remain for some time.

The feminist groups that demanded the abolition of laws that punished prostitutes without questioning the behavior of their customers were challenging the double standard and, by extension, the traditional relationship of men and women in marriage. In their view, marriage should be a free union of equals with men and women sharing responsibility for their children. In Germany, the Mothers' Protection League (*Bund für Mutterschutz*) contended that both married and unmarried mothers required the help of the state, including leaves for pregnancy and child care. This radical group emphasized the need to rethink all sexual morality. In Sweden, Ellen Key (1849–1926), in *The Century of the Child* (1900) and *The Renaissance of Motherhood* (1914), both widely read in Europe,

The Swedish feminist Ellen Key maintained that motherhood was so crucial to society that the support of mothers and children should be a government responsibility. [Hulton/Deutsch/Collection Limited]

maintained that motherhood was one of women's chief roles and was so crucial to society that the government, rather than husbands, should support mothers and their children.

Virtually all turn-of-the-century feminists in one way or another supported wider sexual freedom for women, often claiming that it would benefit society as well as improving women's lives. Many of the early advocates of contraception had also been influenced by social Darwinism. They hoped that limiting the number of children would allow a larger proportion of both healthy and intelligent children to survive. Such was the outlook of Marie Stopes (1880–1958), an Englishwoman with a doctorate in geology, who pioneered contraceptive clinics in the poor districts of London.

WOMEN DEFINING THEIR OWN LIVES For Josephine Butler and Auguste Ficke, as well as other Continental feminists, achieving legal and social equality for women would be one step toward transforming Europe from a male-dominated society to one in which both men and women could control their own destinies. Ficke wrote, "Our final goal is therefore not the acknowledgement of rights, but the elevation of our intellectual and moral level, *the development of our personality.*"[7] Increasingly, feminists would concentrate on freeing and developing women's personalities through better education and government financial support for women engaged in traditional social roles, whether or not they had gained the vote.

Some women also became active within socialist circles. There they argued that the socialist transformation of society should include major reforms for women. Socialist parties usually had all-male leadership. Most male socialist leaders by the close of the century, including Lenin and later Stalin, were intolerant of demands for changes in the family or greater sexual freedom for either men or women. Nonetheless, socialist writings began to include calls for improvements in the economic situation of women that were compatible with more advanced feminist ideals.

It was within literary circles, however, that feminist writers often most clearly articulated the problems that they now understood themselves to face. Distinguished women authors as authors were actually doing, on a more or less equal footing, something that men had always done, leading some to wonder whether simple equality was the main issue. Virginia Woolf's *A Room of One's Own* (1929) became one of the fundamental texts of twentieth-century feminist literature. In it, she meditated first on the difficulties that women of both brilliance and social standing encountered in being taken seriously as writers and intellectuals. She concluded that a woman who wished to write required both a room of her own, meaning a space not dominated by male institutions, and an adequate independent income. But Woolf was concerned with more than asserting the right of women to participate in intellectual life. Establishing a new stance for feminist writers, she asked whether women as writers must imitate men or should bring to their endeavors separate intellectual and psychological qualities that they possessed as women. As she had challenged some of the literary conventions of the traditional novel in her fiction, in *A Room of One's Own*, she challenged some of the received notions of feminist thought and concluded that male and female writers must actually be able to think as both men and women and share the sensibilities of each. In this sense, she sought to open the whole question of gender definition.

By World War I, feminism in Europe, fairly or not, had become associated in the popular imagination with challenges to traditional gender roles and sexual morality and with either socialism or political radicalism. So when extremely conservative political movements arose between the world wars, their leaders often emphasized traditional roles for women and traditional ideas about sexual morality. Lenin and Stalin would follow a similar path in the Soviet political experiment.

---◆---

By the opening of the twentieth century, European thought had achieved contours that seem familiar to us today. The study of science had led to virtually revolutionary changes in thinking about both biological and physical nature. Physicists had transformed the traditional views of matter and energy as they probed the mysteries of the atom. Research in evolutionary

---

[7]*Quoted in Harriet Anderson,* Utopian Feminism: Women's Movements in Fin-de-Siècle Vienna *(New Haven, Conn.: Yale University Press, 1992), p. 13.*

Virginia Woolf Urges Women to Write

In 1928 Virginia Woolf, the English novelist, delivered two papers at women's colleges at Cambridge University. Those papers provided the basis for A Room of One's Own, *published a year later. In this essay, Woolf discussed the difficulty a woman writer confronted in finding previous women authors as models. She also outlined many of the obstacles that women faced in achieving the education, the time, and the income that would allow them to write. At the close of her essay, she urged women to begin to write so that future women authors would have models. She then set forth an image of Shakespeare's sister who, lacking such models, had not written anything, but who through the collective efforts of women might in the future emerge as a great writer because she would have the literary models of the women Woolf addressed to follow and to imitate.*

♦ *How does Woolf's fiction of Shakespeare's sister establish a benchmark for women writers? What does Woolf mean by the common life through which women will need to work to become independent writers? Why does she emphasize the need for women to have both income and space if they are to become independent writers?*

A thousand pens are ready to suggest what you should do and what effect you will have. My own suggestion is a little fantastic, I admit; I prefer, therefore, to put it in the form of fiction.

I told you in the course of this paper that Shakespeare had a sister; but do not look for her in Sir Sidney Lee's life of the poet. She died young—alas, she never wrote a word. She lies buried where the omnibuses now stop, opposite the Elephant and Castle [a London intersection]. Now my belief is that this poet who never wrote a word and was buried at the cross-roads still lives. She lives in you and in me, and in many other women who are not here to-night, for they are washing up the dishes and putting the children to bed. But she lives; for great poets do not die; they are continuing presences; they need only the opportunity to walk among us in the flesh. This opportunity, as I think, it is now coming within your power to give her. For my belief is that if we live another century or so—I am talking of the common life which is the real life and not of the little separate lives which we live as individuals—and have five hundred [pounds income] a year each of us and rooms of our own; if we have the habit of freedom and the courage to write exactly what we think; if we escape a little from the common sitting-room and see human beings not always in their relation to each other but in relation to reality; and the sky, too, and the trees or whatever it may be in themselves; . . . if we face the fact, for it is a fact, that there is no arm to cling to, but that we go alone and that our relation is to the world of reality and not only to the world of men and women, then the opportunity will come and the dead poet who was Shakespeare's sister will put on the body which she has so often laid down. Drawing her life from the lives of the unknown who were her forerunners, as her brother did before her, she will be born. As for her coming without that preparation, without that effort on our part, without that determination that when she is born again she shall find it possible to live and write her poetry, that we cannot expect, for that would be impossible. But I maintain that she would come if we worked for her, and that so to work, even in poverty and obscurity, is worth while.

Virginia Woolf, A Room of One's Own *(London: The Hogarth Press, 1974), pp. 170–172.*

biology had revealed human beings as part of the natural order, not something distinct from it. In the minds of some writers, science was expected to provide human beings with a basis for new ethical knowledge and moral values. Christianity had experienced the strongest challenge in modern times. In part, this was a result of the strong new role for science, but also because of other intellectual changes arising from the study of history and philosophy and the goals of the politicians in secular national states.

Simultaneous with this struggle between religion and science, there arose a tendency among certain major nonreligious thinkers and writers to question the primacy of reason. Nietzsche and Freud in their different ways questioned whether human beings were primarily creatures of reason. Weber and other social and political theorists doubted that politics could be entirely rational. All these developments challenged the rational values associated with the Enlightenment. The racial theorists questioned whether mind and character were as important as alleged racial characteristics carried in the blood.

Racial thinking also allowed Europeans to believe that they were somehow inherently superior to other peoples and cultures in the world. Such racial thinking fostered anti-Semitism in Europe and discrimination against other ethnic minority groups. Similar racial attitudes also informed the thinking of virtually all the colonial administrators of the European imperial powers.

The feminists of the turn of the century, more than any of their predecessors, demanded a rethinking of gender roles. They urged equal treatment for women under the law, but no less important, they contended that the relationship of men and women within marriage and the family required rethinking. They set forth much of the feminist agenda for the twentieth century.

Review Questions

1. How would you account for the dominance of science in the thought of the second half of the nineteenth century? What were some of the major changes in scientific outlook between 1850 and 1914? Comment especial-ly on advances in physics. How would you define positivism? Describe Darwin and Wallace's theory of natural selection. What effect did it have on theories of ethics, on Christianity, and on European views of human nature?

2. How and why did Christianity come under attack in the late nineteenth century? Discuss the politics of Pius IX, Leo XIII, and Pius X. Why was Leo XIII regarded as a liberal pope? How do you account for the resilience of the papacy during this period of attack on the Church?

3. How had the social conditions of literature changed in the late nineteenth century? What was the significance of the explosion of literary matter? What was literary realism? How was it influenced by science? How did the realists undermine middle class morality? How did literary modernism differ from realism?

4. How did Nietzsche and Freud challenge traditional middle class and religious morality? Would you describe Freud more as a product of the Enlightenment or of Romanticism?

5. How do you account for the fear and hostility many late-nineteenth-century intellectuals displayed toward women? How did Freud view the position of women? What were some of the social and political issues affecting women in the late nineteenth and early twentieth centuries and how did reformers confront them? What new directions did feminism take?

6. What was the character of late-nineteenth-century racism? How did it become associated with anti-Semitism? What personal and contemporary political experiences led Herzl to develop the idea of Zionism?

Suggested Readings

J. L. ALTHOLZ, *The Churches in the Nineteenth Century* (1967). A useful overview.

H. ANDERSON, *Utopian Feminism: Women's Movements in Fin-de-Siècle Vienna* (1993). One of the best treatments of feminism on the Continent.

R. ARON, *Main Currents in Sociological Thought*, 2 vols. (1965, 1967). An introduction to the founders of the science.

S. AVINERI, *The Making of Modern Zionism: The Intellectual Origins of the Jewish State* (1981). An excellent introduction to the development of Zionist thought.

S. BARROWS, *Distorting Mirrors: Visions of the Crowd in Late Nineteenth-Century France* (1981). An imaginative examination of crowd psychology as it related to social tension in France.

F. L. BAUMER, *Modern European Thought: Continuity and Change in Ideas, 1600–1950* (1977). The best work on the subject for this period.

M. D. BIDDIS, *Father of Racist Ideology: The Social and Political Thought of Count Gobineau* (1970). Sets the subject in the more general context of nineteenth-century thought.

P. BOWLER, *The Eclipse of Darwinism: Anti-Darwinian Evolution Theories in the Decades Around 1900* (1983). A major study of the fate of Darwinian theory in the nineteenth-century scientific community.

P. BOWLER, *Evolution: The History of an Idea* (1989). An outstanding survey of the subject.

O. CHADWICK, *The Secularization of the European Mind in the Nineteenth Century* (1975). The best treatment available.

D. G. CHARLTON, *Positivist Thought in France During the Second Empire, 1852–1870* (1959), and *Secular Religions in France, 1815–1870* (1963). Two clear introductions to important subjects.

C. M. CIPOLLA, *Literacy and Development in the West* (1969). Traces the explosion of literacy in the past two centuries.

A. DANTO, *Nietzsche As Philosopher* (1965). A helpful and well-organized introduction.

A. DESMOND and J. MOORE, *Darwin* (1992). A brilliant biography.

R. J. EVANS, *The Feminist Movement in Germany, 1894–1933* (1976). Very good on the efforts to debate issues of the family and sexual morality.

P. GAY, *Freud: A Life for Our Time* (1988). The new standard biography.

C. C. GILLISPIE, *The Edge of Objectivity* (1960). One of the best one-volume treatments of modern scientific ideas.

H. S. HUGHES, *Consciousness and Society: The Reorientation of European Social Thought, 1890–1930* (1958). A wide-ranging discussion of the revolt against positivism.

C. JUNGNICKEL and R. MCCORMMACH, *Intellectual Mastery of Nature: Theoretical Physics from Ohm to Einstein*, 2 vols. (1986). A demanding but powerful exploration of the creation of modern physics.

J. KATZ, *From Prejudice to Destruction: Anti-Semitism, 1700–1933* (1980). An excellent and far-reaching analysis.

J. T. KLOPPENBERG, *Uncertain Victory: Social Democracy and Progressivism in European and American Thought* (1986). An extremely important comparative study.

T. A. KSELMAN, *Miracles and Prophesies in Nineteenth-Century France* (1983). A study of popular religion.

W. LACQUEUR, *A History of Zionism* (1989). The most extensive one-volume treatment.

B. LIGHTMAN, *The Origins of Agnosticism: Victorian Unbelief and the Limits of Knowledge* (1987). The best study of the subject.

W. J. MCGRATH, *Freud's Discovery of Psychoanalysis: The Politics of Hysteria* (1986). A study of the relationship of Freud's cultural and political background to his scientific thought.

J. MCMANNERS, *Church and State in France, 1870–1914* (1972). The standard treatment.

E. MAYR, *The Growth of Biological Thought: Diversity, Evolution, and Inheritance* (1982). A major survey by a scientist of note.

P. MEISEL, *The Myth of the Modern: A Study in British Literature and Criticism After 1850* (1987). A broad study.

T. MERZ, *A History of European Thought in the Nineteenth Century*, 4 vols. (1897–1914). Still a useful mine of information.

J. R. MOORE, *History, Humanity, and Evolution* (1989). A collection of major essays on evolution that touch upon science, religion, and the question of evolution and women.

J. MORRELL and A. THACKRAY, *Gentlemen of Science: Early Years of the British Association for the Advancement of Science* (1981). An important study that examines the role of science in early- and mid-nineteenth-century Britain.

G. L. MOSSE, *Toward the Final Solution: A History of European Racism* (1978). A sound introduction.

R. PASCAL, *From Naturalism to Expressionism: German Literature and Society, 1880–1918* (1973). A helpful survey.

H. W. PAUL, *From Knowledge to Power: The Rise of the Science Empire in France, 1860–1939* (1985). An extensive survey of both scientific thought and institutions in France.

L. POLIAKOV, *The Aryan Myth: A History of Racist and Nationalist Ideas in Europe* (1971). The best introduction to the problem.

P. G. J. PULZER, *The Rise of Political Anti-Semitism in Germany and Austria* (rev. 1989). A sound discussion of anti-Semitism in the world of central European politics.

C. E. SCHORSKE, *Fin de Siècle Vienna: Politics and Culture* (1980). Major essays on the explosively creative intellectual climate of Vienna.

F. STERN, *The Politics of Cultural Despair: A Study in the Rise of the German Ideology* (1965). An important examination of antimodern and anti-Semitic thought in imperial Germany.

F. M. TURNER, *Contesting Cultural Authority: Essays in Victorian Intellectual Life* (1993). Essays that deal with the relationship of science and religion and the problem of faith for intellectuals.

A. VIDLER, *The Church in an Age of Revolution* (1961). A sound account of the problems of Church and state in the nineteenth century.

J. P. VON ARX, *Progress and Pessimism: Religion, Politics, and History in Late Nineteenth Century Britain* (1985). A major study that casts much new light on the nineteenth-century view of progress.

C. WELCH, *Protestant Thought in the Nineteenth Century,* 2 vols. (1972, 1985). The most extensive recent study.

The German delegation signs the peace treaty ending the First World War in the Hall of Mirrors of the Palace of Versailles on June 28, 1919. This painting by Sir William Orpen, completed in 1921, now hangs in the Imperial War Museum in London. [Bildarchiv Preussischer Kulturbesitz]

26

Imperialism, Alliances, and War

Key Topics in This Chapter
◆ The economic, cultural, and strategic factors behind Europe's New Imperialism in the late nineteenth and early twentieth centuries
◆ The formation of alliances and the search for strategic advantage among Europe's major powers
◆ The origins and progress of World War I
◆ The Russian Revolution
◆ The peace treaties ending World War I

During the second half of the nineteenth century, and especially after 1870, Europe exercised unprecedented influence and control over the rest of the world. North and South America, as well as Australia and New Zealand, almost became part of the European world as great streams of European immigrants populated them. Until the nineteenth century, Asia (with the significant exception of India) and most of Africa had gone their own ways, having little contact with Europe. But in the latter part of that century, almost all of Africa was divided among a number of European nations. Europe also imposed its economic and political power across Asia. By the next century, European dominance had brought every part of the globe into a single world economy. Events in any corner of the world had significant effects thousands of miles away.

These developments might have been expected to lead to greater prosperity and good fortune. Instead, they helped to foster competition and hostility among the great powers of Europe and to bring on a terrible war that undermined Europe's strength and its influence in the world. The peace settlement, proclaimed as "a peace without victors," disillusioned idealists in the West. It treated Germany almost as harshly as Germany would have treated its foes if it had been victorious. Also, the new system failed to provide realistic and effective safeguards against a return to power of a vengeful Germany. The withdrawal of the United States into a disdainful isolation from world affairs destroyed the basis for keeping the peace on which the hopes of Britain and France relied. The frenzy for imperial expansion that seized Europeans in the late nineteenth century had done much to destroy Europe's peace and prosperity and its dominant place in the world.

Expansion of European Power and the New Imperialism

The explosive developments in nineteenth-century science, technology, industry, agriculture, transportation, communication, and military weapons provided the chief sources of European power. They made it possible for a few Europeans (or Americans) to impose their will on other peoples many times their number by force or the threat of force. Institutional as well as material advantages allowed westerners to have their way. The growth of national states that commanded the loyalty, service, and resources of their inhabitants to a degree previously unknown was a Western phenomenon. It permitted the European nations to deploy their resources more effectively than ever before.

The Europeans also possessed another, less tangible, weapon. They considered their civilization and way of life to be superior to all others. This gave them a self-confidence that was often

unpleasantly arrogant and fostered their expansionist mood.

The expansion of European influence was not anything new. Spain, Portugal, France, Holland, and Britain had controlled territories overseas for centuries, but by the mid-nineteenth century, only Great Britain still had extensive holdings. The first half of the century was generally hostile to colonial expansion. Even the British had been sobered by their loss of the American colonies. The French acquired Algeria and part of Indochina, and the British added territory to their holdings in Canada, India, Australia, and New Zealand. The dominant doctrine of free trade, however, opposed political interference in other lands as economically unprofitable.

Britain ruled the waves and had great commercial advantages as a result of being the first country to experience the Industrial Revolution. Therefore, the British were usually content to trade and invest overseas without annexations. Yet they were prepared to interfere forcefully if a "backward" country placed barriers in the way of their trade. Still, at mid-century, in Britain as elsewhere, most people opposed further political or military involvement overseas.

In the last third of the century, however, the European states swiftly spread their control over perhaps 10 million square miles and 150 million people—about one-fifth of the world's land area and one-tenth of its population. During this period, European expansion went forward with great speed and participation in it came to be regarded as necessary for a great power. The movement has been called the *New Imperialism*.

The New Imperialism

The word *imperialism* is now so loosely used that it has almost lost real meaning. It may be useful to offer a definition that might be widely accepted: "the policy of extending a nation's authority by territorial acquisition or by the establishment of economic and political hegemony over other nations."[1] That definition seems to apply equally well to ancient Egypt and Mesopotamia and to the European performance in the late nineteenth century. But there were

[1]American Heritage Dictionary of the English Language *(New York: Houghton Mifflin, 1969), p. 660.*

Queen Victoria (r. 1837–1901) works on state papers in 1893. Note the Indian attendant. The Queen was also Empress of India, which was by far the most important possession in the British Empire. [National Portrait Gallery, London]

new elements in the latter case. Previous imperialisms had taken the form either of seizing land and settling it with the conqueror's people or of establishing trading centers to exploit the resources of the dominated area. The New Imperialism did not completely abandon these devices, but it also introduced new ones.

The usual pattern of the New Imperialism was for a European nation to invest capital in a "backward" country, to develop its mines and agriculture, to build railroads, bridges, harbors, and telegraph systems, and to employ great numbers of natives in the process. They thereby transformed the local economy and culture. To safeguard its investments, the dominant European state would make favorable arrangements with the local government either by loaning the rulers money or by intimidating them.

If these arrangements proved inadequate, the dominant power would establish more direct political control. Sometimes this meant full annexation and direct rule as a colony, or it could be a protectorate status, whereby the local ruler became a figurehead controlled by the dominant European state and maintained by its military power. In other instances, the European state established "spheres of influence" in which it received special commercial and legal privileges without direct political involvement.

Motives for the New Imperialism: The Economic Interpretation

The predominant interpretation of the motives for the New Imperialism has been economic, in the form given by the English radical economist J. A. Hobson (1858–1928) and later adapted by Lenin. As Lenin put it, "Imperialism is the monopoly stage of capitalism,"[2] the last stage of a dying system. Competition inevitably eliminates inefficient capitalists and, therefore, leads to monopoly. Powerful industrial and financial capitalists soon run out of profitable areas of investment in their own countries and persuade their governments to gain colonies in "backward" countries. Here they can find higher profits from their investments, new markets for their products, and safe sources of raw materials.

Facts do not support this viewpoint, however. The European powers did invest considerable capital abroad, but not in a way that fit the model of Hobson and Lenin. Britain, for example, made heavier investments abroad before 1875 than during the next two decades. Only a small percentage of British and European investments overseas, moreover, went to their new

[2]*V. I. Lenin,* Imperialism, the Highest Stage of Capitalism *(New York: International Publishers, 1939), p. 88.*

colonies. Most capital went into other European countries or to older, well-established areas like the United States, Canada, Australia, and New Zealand. Even when investments were made in new areas, they were not necessarily put into colonies held by the investing country.

The facts are equally discouraging for those who emphasize the need for markets and raw materials. Colonies were not usually important markets for the great imperial nations, and all these states were forced to rely on areas that they did not control as sources of vital raw materials. It is not even clear that control of the new colonies was particularly profitable, though Britain, to be sure, benefitted greatly from its rule of India. It is also true that some European businessmen and politicians hoped that colonial expansion would cure the great depression of 1873–1896.

Nevertheless, as one of the leading students of the subject has said, "No one can determine whether the accounts of empire ultimately closed with a favorable cash balance."[3] That is true of the European imperial nations collectively, but it is certain that for some of them, like Italy and Germany, empire was a losing proposition. Some individuals and companies, of course, made great profits from particular colonial ventures, but such people were able to influence national policy only occasionally. Economic motives certainly played a part, but a full understanding of the New Imperialism requires a search for other motives.

Cultural, Religious, and Social Interpretations

Advocates of imperialism gave various justifications for it. Some argued that the advanced European nations had a duty to bring the benefits of their higher culture and superior civilization to more "backward" peoples. Religious groups demanded Western governments furnish political and even military support for Christian missionaries. Some politicians and diplomats supported imperialism as a tool of social policy. In Germany, for instance, some people suggested that imperial expansion would deflect public interest away from domestic politics and social

[3]D. K. Fieldhouse, The Colonial Empires (New York: Delacorte, 1966), p. 393.

reform. Yet Germany acquired few colonies, and such considerations played little if any role in its colonial policy.

In Britain, Joseph Chamberlain (1836–1914), the colonial secretary from 1895 to 1903, argued for the empire as a source of profit and economic security that would finance a great program of domestic reform and welfare. These arguments were not important as motives for British imperial expansion because they were made well after Britain had acquired most of its empire.

Another common and apparently plausible justification for imperialism was that colonies would attract a European country's surplus population. In fact, most European emigrants went to areas not controlled by their countries, chiefly to North and South America and Australia.

Strategic and Political Interpretations: The Scramble for Africa

Strategic and political considerations were more important in bringing on the New Imperialism. The scramble for Africa in the 1880s is one example (see Maps 26-1 and 26-2).

GREAT BRITAIN Britain was the only great power with extensive overseas holdings on the eve of the scramble. The completion of the Suez Canal in 1869 made Egypt vitally important to the British because it sat astride the shortest route to India. Under Disraeli, Britain purchased a major, but not a controlling, interest in the canal in 1875. When internal troubles threatened Egypt's stability in the 1880s, the British established control. Then, to protect Egypt, they advanced into the Sudan.

FRANCE AND SMALLER NATIONS France became involved in North Africa in 1830 by sending an expedition to attack the pirates in Algiers. The French gradually extended their control, and thousands of Europeans settled in the country. By the 1880s, France was in full control of Algeria. In 1882, to prevent Tunisia from falling into Italy's hands, France took over that country also. The French also annexed much of West Africa, the Congo, and the island of Madagascar.

Social Darwinism and Imperialism

One of the intellectual foundations of the New Imperialism was the doctrine of social Darwinism, a pseudoscientific application of Darwin's new ideas about biology to nations and races. It had a considerable influence on thought all around the world. In the following selection, an Englishman, Karl Pearson (1857–1936), attempts to connect concepts from evolutionary theory—the struggle for survival and the survival of the fittest—with the development of human societies.

✦ *How does the author connect Darwin's ideas with the concept of human progress? Is it reasonable to equate biological species with human societies, races, or nations? How do the author's ideas justify imperial expansion? What arguments can you make against the author's assertions?*

"History shows me one way, and one way only, in which a state of civilisation has been produced, namely, the struggle of race with race, and the survival of the physically and mentally fitter race."

"This dependence of progress on the survival of the fitter race, terribly black as it may seem to some of you, gives the struggle for existence its redeeming features; it is the fiery crucible out of which comes the finer metal. You may hope for a time when the sword shall be turned into the ploughshare, when American and German and English traders shall no longer compete in the markets of the world for raw materials, for their food supply, when the white man and the dark shall share the soil between them, and each till it as he lists. But, believe me, when that day comes mankind will no longer progress; there will be nothing to check the fertility of inferior stock; the relentless law of heredity will not be controlled and guided by natural selection. Man will stagnate . . ."

"The path of progress is strewn with the wreck of nations; traces are everywhere to be seen of the hecatombs of inferior races, and of victims who found not the narrow way to the greater perfection. Yet these dead peoples are, in very truth, the stepping stones on which mankind has arisen to the higher intellectual and deeper emotional life of today."

Karl Pearson, National Life from the Standpoint of Science, *2nd ed. (Cambridge, England: Cambridge University Press, 1907), pp. 21, 26–27, 64.*

Soon smaller states like Belgium, Portugal, Spain, and Italy were acquiring new African colonies or expanding old ones. By the 1890s, their intervention had compelled Britain to expand northward from the Cape of Good Hope into what is now Zimbabwe and Zambia. Britain may have had significant strategic reasons for protecting the Suez and Cape routes to India, but France and the other European nations did not. Their motives were political as well as economic, for they equated political status (Britain was the chief model) with the possession of colonies. They therefore sought colonies to buttress their own importance.

GERMANY Bismarck appears to have pursued an imperial policy, however briefly, from cold political motives. In 1884 and 1885, Germany declared protectorates over Southwest Africa (Namibia), Togoland, the Cameroons, and East Africa (Tanzania). None of these places was particularly valuable or of intrinsic strategic importance. Bismarck himself had no interest in overseas colonies and once compared them to fine furs worn by impoverished Polish nobles who had no shirts underneath. His concern lay in Germany's exposed position in Europe. On one occasion he said, "My map of Africa lies in Europe. Here is Russia, and there is France, and

MAP 26-1 IMPERIAL EXPANSION IN AFRICA TO 1880 *Until the 1880s, few European countries held colonies in Africa, mostly on its fringes.*

here in the middle are we. That is my map of Africa."[4] He acquired colonies chiefly to

improve Germany's diplomatic position in Europe. He hoped that colonial expansion would divert French hostility against Germany. Also, German colonies in Africa could be used as a subtle weapon with which to persuade the British to be reasonable.

[4]*Quoted by J. Remak*, The Origins of World War I, 1871–1914 *(New York: Holt, Rinehart & Winston, 1967), p.*

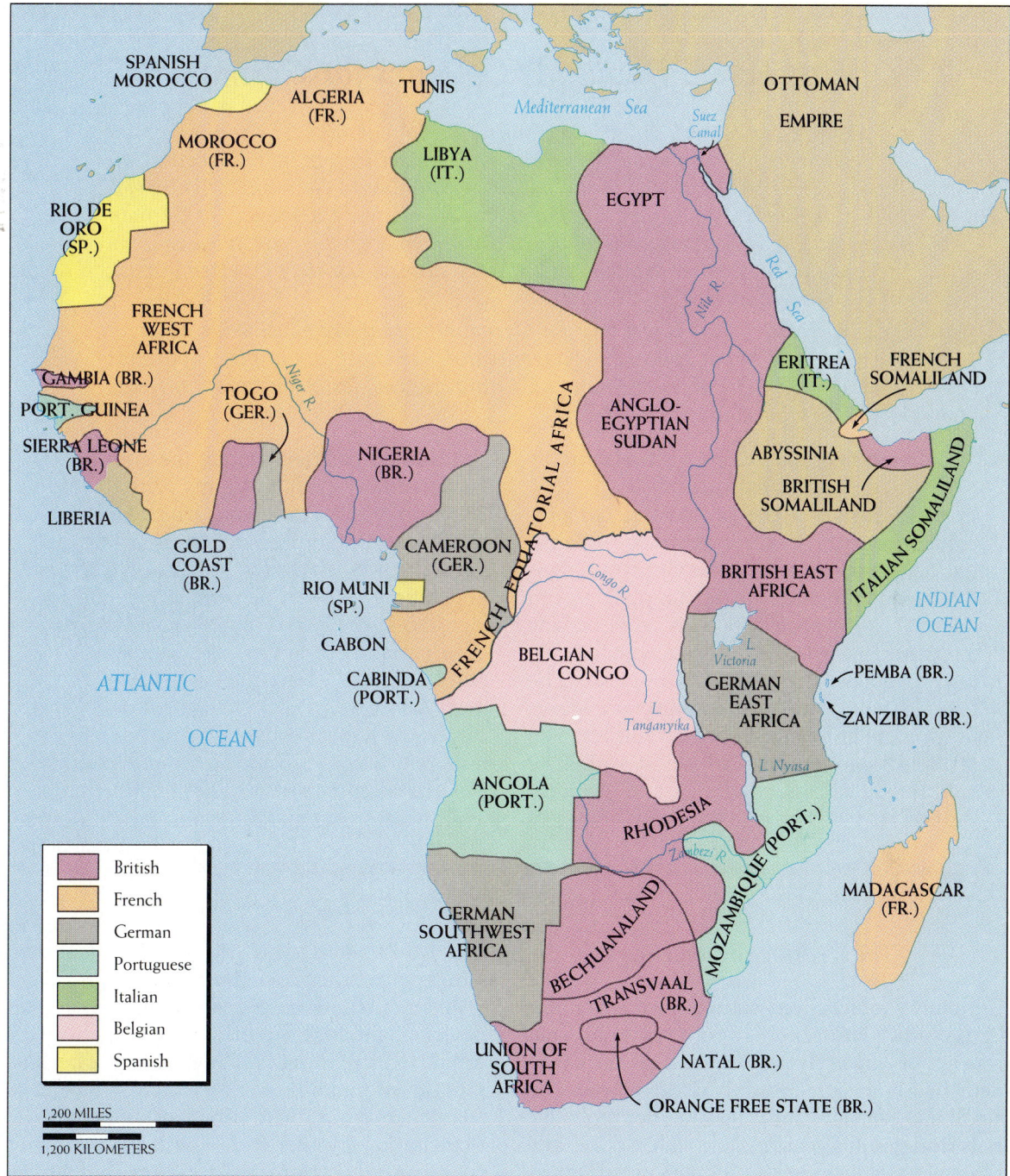

MAP 26-2 PARTITION OF AFRICA, 1880–1914 *Before 1880 the European presence in Africa was largely the remains of early exploration by old imperialists and did not penetrate the heart of the continent. By 1914 the occupying powers included most large European states; only Liberia and Abyssinia remained independent.*

Carl Peters Demands Colonies for Germany

Germany was a late arrival in the competition for colonies. The territories still available were neither profitable nor attractive for settlement by Europeans. Carl Peters (1856–1918) was one of the increasing number of Germans, who, nevertheless, were eager to acquire a colonial empire. He was the founder of German East Africa, now Tanzania. His arguments based on economic advantage and the prospects of German emigration proved to be absurd, but they provided a mask for less rational motives.

✦ *What reasons does Peters give for Germany to seek colonies? What assumptions does he make about their advantages? Are those assumptions correct? What do you think were the most important motives for colonization to Peters and those who supported his policy?*

Manifesto of the Society for German Colonization, April 1884

In the partition of the earth, as it has proceeded from the beginning of the fifteenth century up to our times, the German nation received nothing. All the remaining European culture-bearing peoples possess areas outside our continent where their languages and customs can take firm root and flourish. The moment that the German emigrant leaves the borders of the Reich behind him, he is a stranger sojourning on foreign soil. The German Reich, great in size and strength through its bloodily achieved unity, stands in the leading position among the continental European powers: her sons abroad must adapt themselves to nations which look upon us with either indifference or even hostility. For centuries the great stream of German emigration has been plunging down into foreign races where it is lost sight of. Germandom outside Europe has been undergoing a perpetual national decline.

This fact, so painful to national pride, also represents a great economic disadvantage for our *Volk*. Every year our Fatherland loses the capacity of approximately 200,000 Germans. The greatest amount of this capacity flows

The Irrational Element

Germany's annexations started a wild scramble by the other European powers to acquire what was left of Africa. By 1890 almost all the continent had been parceled out. Great powers and small had expanded into areas neither profitable nor strategic for reasons less calculating and rational than Bismarck's. "Empire in the modern period," D. K. Fieldhouse observed, "was the product of European power: its reward was power or the sense of power."[5]

Such motives were not new. They had been well understood by the Athenian spokesman at Melos in 416 B.C., whose words were reported by Thucydides: "Of the gods we believe and of men we know clearly that by a necessity of their nature where they have the power they rule."[6]

In Asia, the emergence of Japan as a great power frightened the other powers who were interested in China (see Map 26-3). The Russians were building a railroad across Siberia to Vladivostok and were afraid of any threat to Manchuria. Together with France and Germany, they applied diplomatic pressure that forced Japan out of the Liaotung Peninsula in northern China and its harbor, Port Arthur. All pressed feverishly for concessions in China. Fearing that China, its markets, and its investment opportunities would soon be closed to its citizens, the United States in 1899 proposed the Open Door Policy. This policy opposed foreign annexations

[5]*Fieldhouse, p. 393.*

[6]*Thucydides,* The Peloponnesian War, *5.105.2.*

directly into the camp of our economic competitors and increases the strength of our rivals. Germany's imports of products from tropical zones originate in foreign settlements whereby many millions of German capital are lost every year to alien nations. German exports are dependent upon the discretion of foreign tariff policies. Our industry lacks an absolutely safe market for its goods because our *Volk* lacks colonies of its own.

The alleviation of this national grievance requires taking practical steps and strong action.

In recognition of this point of view, a society has been organized in Berlin with the goal of mobilizing itself for such steps and such action. The Society for German Colonization aims to undertake on its own, in a resolute and sweeping manner, carefully chosen colonization projects and thereby supplement the ranks of organizations with similar tendencies.

Its particular tasks will be:

1. to provide necessary sums of capital for colonization;

2. to seek out and lay claim to suitable districts for colonization;

3. to direct German emigrants to these regions.

Imbued as we are with the conviction that it is no longer permissible to hesitate in energetically mobilizing ourselves for this great national task, we venture to come before the German *Volk* with a plea for active support of the endeavors of our Society! The German nation has proven time and again its willingness to make sacrifices for general patriotic undertakings: may she also bring her full energies to play in the solution of this great historical task.

Every German whose heart beats for the greatness and the honor of our nation is entreated to come to the side of our Society. What is at stake is compensation for centuries of deprivation: to prove to the world that, along with the splendor of the Reich, the German *Volk* has inherited the old German national spirit of its forefathers!

Carl Peters, Die Grundung von Deutsch-Ostafrika [The Foundation of German East Africa] *(Berlin, 1906), pp. 43–45, as trans. in Ralph A. Austen,* Modern Imperialism *(Lexington, Mass.: D. C. Heath, 1969), pp. 62–63.*

in China and allowed entrepreneurs of all nations to trade there on equal terms. The support of Britain helped win acceptance of the policy by all the powers except Russia.

The United States had only recently emerged as a force in international affairs. After freeing itself of British rule and consolidating its independence during the Napoleonic wars, the Americans had busied themselves with westward expansion on the North American continent until the end of the nineteenth century. The Monroe Doctrine of 1823 had, in effect, made the entire Western Hemisphere an American protectorate. Cuba's attempt to gain independence from Spain was the spark for the new United States involvement in international affairs. Sympathy for the Cuban cause, American investments on the island, the desire for Cuban sugar, and concern over the island's strategic importance in the Caribbean all helped persuade the Americans to fight Spain.

Victory in the Spanish–American War of 1898 brought the United States an informal protectorate over Cuba and the annexation of Puerto Rico and drove Spain completely out of the Western Hemisphere. The Americans forced Spain to sell the Philippine Islands and Guam, and Germany bought the other Spanish islands in the Pacific. The Americans and the Germans also divided Samoa between them. The remaining Pacific Islands were taken by France and Britain. Hawaii had been under American influence for some time and was annexed in 1898. This burst of activity after the Spanish War made the United States an imperial and Pacific power.

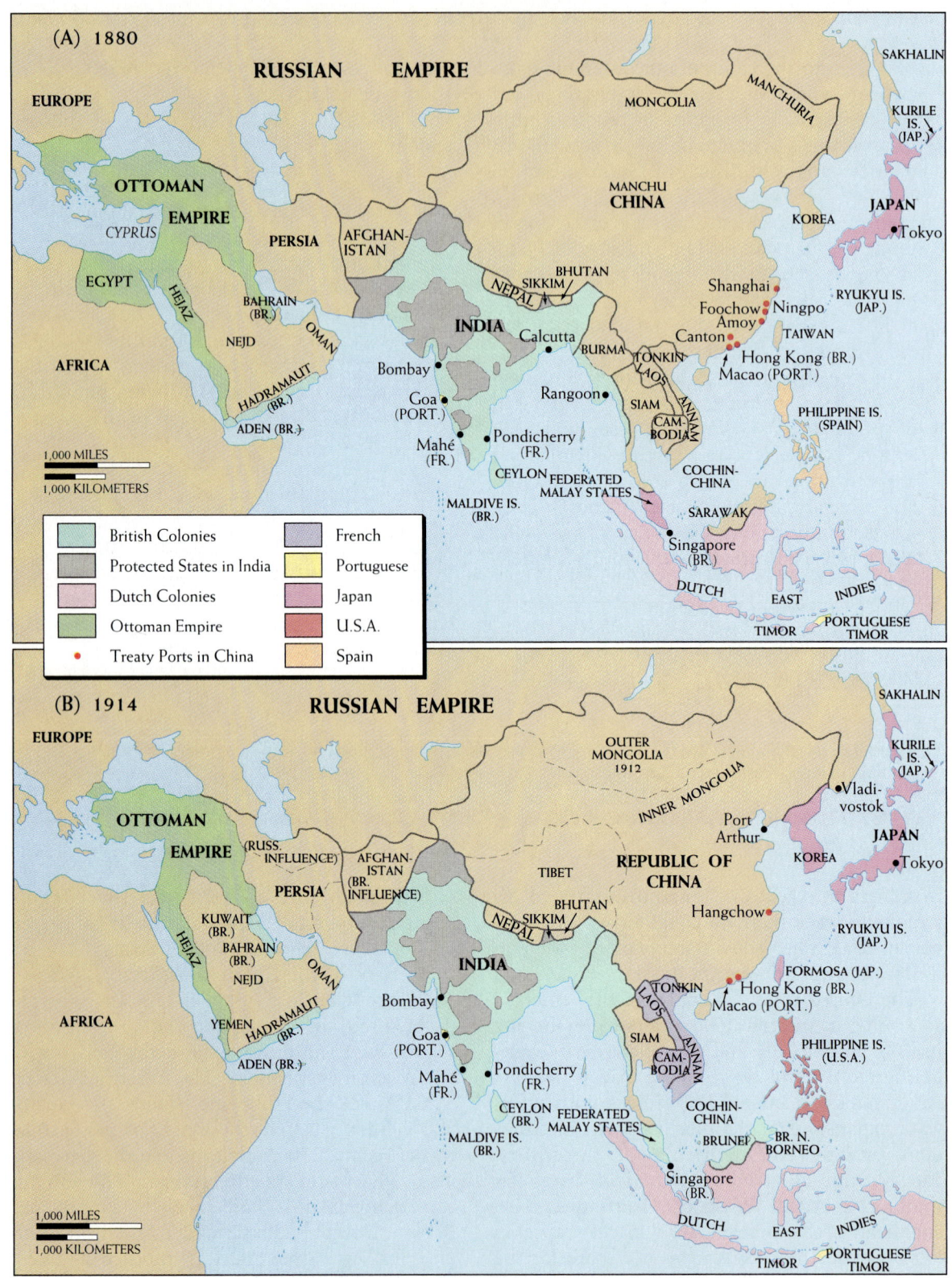

(A) 1880

RUSSIAN EMPIRE

EUROPE

OTTOMAN
EMPIRE
CYPRUS

EGYPT

AFRICA

HEJAZ

BAHRAIN
(BR.)

NEJD

OMAN

HADRAMAUT
(BR.)

ADEN (BR.)

PERSIA

AFGHAN-
ISTAN

BHUTAN
NEPAL SIKKIM

INDIA

Bombay

Goa
(PORT.)

Mahé
(FR.)

Pondicherry
(FR.)

CEYLON

MALDIVE IS.
(BR.)

Calcutta

BURMA

Rangoon

FEDERATED
MALAY STATES

MONGOLIA

MANCHURIA

MANCHU
CHINA

KOREA

Shanghai
Foochow Ningpo
Amoy
Canton

TONKIN
LAOS
SIAM
CAM-
BODIA

ANNAM

COCHIN-
CHINA

Singapore
(BR.)

DUTCH

SAKHALIN

KURILE
IS.
(JAP.)

JAPAN
Tokyo

RYUKYU IS.
(JAP.)

TAIWAN

Hong Kong (BR.)
Macao (PORT.)

PHILIPPINE IS.
(SPAIN)

SARAWAK

EAST INDIES

PORTUGUESE
TIMOR

1,000 MILES
1,000 KILOMETERS

	British Colonies		French
	Protected States in India		Portuguese
	Dutch Colonies		Japan
	Ottoman Empire		U.S.A.
•	Treaty Ports in China		Spain

(B) 1914

RUSSIAN EMPIRE

EUROPE

OTTOMAN
EMPIRE

(RUSS.
INFLUENCE)

PERSIA

AFGHAN-
ISTAN
(BR.
INFLUENCE)

AFRICA

HEJAZ

KUWAIT
(BR.)

BAHRAIN
(BR.)

NEJD

OMAN

HADRAMAUT
(BR.)

YEMEN

ADEN (BR.)

OUTER
MONGOLIA
1912

INNER MONGOLIA

TIBET

BHUTAN
NEPAL SIKKIM

INDIA

Bombay

Goa
(PORT.)

Mahé
(FR.)

Pondicherry
(FR.)

CEYLON
(BR.)

MALDIVE IS.
(BR.)

FEDERATED
MALAY STATES

REPUBLIC OF
CHINA

Port
Arthur

Hangchow

TONKIN
LAOS
SIAM
CAM-
BODIA

ANNAM

COCHIN-
CHINA

BRUNEI

Singapore
(BR.)

DUTCH

SAKHALIN

KURILE
IS.
(JAP.)

Vladi-
vostok

KOREA

JAPAN
Tokyo

RYUKYU IS.
(JAP.)

FORMOSA (JAP.)

Hong Kong (BR.)
Macao (PORT.)

PHILIPPINE IS.
(U.S.A.)

BR. N.
BORNEO

EAST INDIES

PORTUGUESE
TIMOR

1,000 MILES
1,000 KILOMETERS

MAP 26-3 ASIA 1880–1914 *As in Africa, the decades before World War I saw imperialism spread widely and rapidly in Asia. Two new powers, Japan and the United States,
joined the British, French, and Dutch in extending control both to islands and to the
mainland and in exploiting an enfeebled China.*

In the Spanish-American War of 1898, Spain was driven from the western hemisphere and Cuba came under U.S. influence. This lithograph shows the Ninth and Tenth Cavalry Regiments, composed of black Americans, engaged in the Battle of Quasimas, near Santiago, Cuba, on June 24, 1898. [The Granger Collection, New York]

Thus by the turn of the century, most of the world had come under the control of the industrialized West. The one remaining area of great vulnerability was the Ottoman Empire. Its fate, however, was closely tied up with European developments and must be treated in that context.

Emergence of the German Empire and the Alliance Systems (1873–1890)

Prussia's victories over Austria and France and its creation of a large, powerful German Empire in 1871 revolutionized European diplomacy. A vast new political unit had united the majority of Germans to form a nation of great and growing population, wealth, industrial capacity, and military power. Its sudden appearance created new problems and upset the balance of power that had been created at the Congress of Vienna. Britain and Russia retained their positions, though the latter had been weakened by the Crimean War.

Austria, however, had been severely weakened, and the forces of nationalism threatened it with disintegration. French power and prestige were badly damaged by the Franco-Prussian War and the German annexation of Alsace-Lorraine. The French were both afraid of their powerful new neighbor and resentful of their defeat and their loss of territory and France's traditional position as the dominant western European power.

Bismarck's Leadership (1873–1890)

Until 1890 Bismarck continued to guide German policy. He insisted after 1871 that Germany

Expansion of European Power and the New Imperialism	
1869	Suez Canal completed
1875	Britain gains control of Suez
1882	France controls Algeria and Tunisia
1880s	Britain establishes protectorate over Egypt
1884–1885	Germany establishes protectorate over Southwest Africa (Namibia), Togoland, the Cameroons, and East Africa (Tanganyika)
1898	Spanish–American War—United States acquires Puerto Rico, Philippines, and Guam; annexes Hawaiian Islands, establishes protectorate over Cuba
1899	United States proposes Open Door Policy in Far East

was a satisfied power and wanted no further territorial gains, and he meant it. He wanted to avoid a new war that might undo his achievement. He tried to assuage French resentment by friendly relations and by supporting French colonial aspirations. He also prepared for the worst. If France could not be conciliated, it must be isolated. Bismarck sought to prevent an alliance between France and any other European power—especially Austria or Russia—that would threaten Germany with a war on two fronts.

WAR IN THE BALKANS Bismarck's first move was to establish the Three Emperors' League in 1873. It brought together the three great conservative empires of Germany, Austria, and Russia. The league soon collapsed as a result of Austro-Russian rivalry in the Balkans that arose from the Russo-Turkish War that broke out in 1875. The tottering Ottoman Empire was held together chiefly because the European powers could not agree about how to partition it. Ottoman weakness encouraged Serbia and Montenegro to come to the aid of their fellow Slavs in Bosnia and Herzegovina when they revolted against Turkish rule. Soon the rebellion spread to Bulgaria.

Then Russia entered the fray and turned it into a major international crisis. The Russians hoped to pursue their traditional policy of expansion at Ottoman expense and especially to achieve their most cherished goal: control of Constantinople and the Dardanelles. Russian intervention also reflected the influence of the Pan-Slavic movement, which sought to unite all the Slavic peoples, even those under Austrian or Ottoman rule, under the protection of Holy Mother Russia.

The Ottoman Empire was weak and soon was forced to sue for peace. The Treaty of San Stefano of March 1878 was a Russian triumph. The Slavic states in the Balkans were freed of Ottoman rule, and Russia itself obtained territory and a large monetary indemnity. The terms of the settlement, however, alarmed the other great powers. Austria feared that the great Slavic victory and the powerful increase in Russian influence in the Balkans would threaten its own Balkan provinces. The British were alarmed both by the effect of the Russian victory on the European balance of power and by the possibility of Russian control of the Dardanelles, which

would make Russia a Mediterranean power and threaten Britain's control of the Suez Canal. Disraeli was determined to resist, and British public opinion supported him. A music-hall song that became popular gave the language a new word for superpatriotism: *jingoism.*

> We don't want to fight,
> But by jingo if we do,
> We've got the men,
> We've got the ships,
> We've got the money too!
> The Russians will not have Constantinople!

THE CONGRESS OF BERLIN Even before the Treaty of San Stefano, Disraeli sent a fleet to Constantinople. After the magnitude of Russia's appetite was known, Britain and Austria forced Russia to agree to an international conference at which the other great powers would review the provisions of San Stefano. The resulting Congress of Berlin met in June and July of 1878 under the presidency of Bismarck. The choice of site and presiding officer was a clear recognition of Germany's new importance and of Bismarck's claim that Germany wanted no new territory and sought to preserve the peace.

Bismarck referred to himself as an "honest broker," and the title was justified. He agreed to the congress simply because he wanted to avoid a war between Russia and Austria into which he feared Germany would be drawn with nothing to gain and much to lose. From the collapsing Ottoman Empire, he wanted nothing. "The Eastern Question," he said, "is not worth the healthy bones of a single Pomeranian musketeer."[7]

The decisions of the congress were a blow to Russian ambitions. Bulgaria, a Russian client, was reduced in size by two-thirds and was deprived of access to the Aegean Sea. Austria-Hungary was given Bosnia and Herzegovina to "occupy and administer," although those provinces remained formally under Ottoman rule. Britain received Cyprus, and France was encouraged to occupy Tunisia. These territories were compensation for the gains that Russia was permitted to keep. Germany asked for nothing but still earned Russian resentment. The Russians believed that they had saved Prussia in 1807 from complete dismemberment by Na-

---

[7]Quoted by Hajo Holborn, A History of Modern Germany, 1840–1945 (New York: Knopf, 1969), p. 239.

poleon and had expected a show of German gratitude. They were bitterly disappointed, and the Three Emperors' League was dead.

All of the Balkan states were also annoyed by the Berlin settlement. Romania wanted Bessarabia, which Russia kept; Bulgaria wanted a return to the borders of the Treaty of San Stefano; and Greece wanted a part of the Ottoman spoils. The major trouble spot, however, was in the south Slavic states of Serbia and Montenegro. They deeply resented the Austrian occupation of Bosnia and Herzegovina, as did many of the natives of those provinces. The south Slavic question, no less than the estrangement between Russia and Germany, was a threat to the peace of Europe.

GERMAN ALLIANCES WITH RUSSIA AND AUSTRIA For the moment Bismarck could ignore the Balkans, but he could not ignore the breach in his eastern alliance system. With Russia alienated, he concluded a secret treaty with Austria in 1879. The resulting Dual Alliance provided that Germany and Austria would come to each other's aid if either were attacked by Russia. If either were attacked by another country, each promised at least to maintain neutrality.

The treaty was for five years and was renewed regularly until 1918. As the anchor of German policy, it was criticized at the time, and some have considered it an error in retrospect. It appeared to tie German fortunes to those of the troubled Austro-Hungarian Empire and thus to borrow trouble for Germany. And, by isolating the Russians, it pushed them to seek alliances in the West.

Bismarck was fully aware of these dangers but discounted them with good reason. He never allowed the alliance to drag Germany into Austria's Balkan quarrels. As he put it, in any alliance there is a horse and a rider, and he meant Germany to be the rider. He made it clear to the Austrians that the alliance was purely defensive and that Germany would never be a party to an attack on Russia. "For us," he said, "Balkan questions can never be a motive for war."[8]

Bismarck believed that monarchical, reactionary Russia would not seek an alliance either with republican, revolutionary France or with increasingly democratic Britain. In fact, he expected the news of the Austro-German negotiations to frighten Russia into seeking closer relations with Germany, and he was right. Russian diplomats soon approached him, and by 1881 he had concluded a renewal of the Three Emperors' League on a firmer basis. The three powers promised to maintain friendly neutrality in case any of them was attacked by a fourth power. Other clauses included the right of Austria to annex Bosnia-Herzegovina whenever it wished and the support of all three powers for closing the Dardanelles to all nations in case of war.

The agreement allayed German fears of a Russian–French alliance and Russian fears of a combination of Austria and Britain against it, of Britain's fleet sailing into the Black Sea, and of a hostile combination of Germany and Austria. Most importantly, the agreement aimed to resolve the conflicts in the Balkans between Austria and Russia. Though it did not end such conflicts, it was a significant step toward peace.

THE TRIPLE ALLIANCE In 1882 Italy, ambitious for colonial expansion and annoyed by the French occupation of Tunisia, asked to join the Dual Alliance. The provisions of its entry were defensive and were directed against France. At this point, Bismarck's policy was a complete success. He was allied with three of the great powers and friendly with the other, Great Britain, which held aloof from all alliances. France was isolated and no threat. Bismarck's diplomacy was a great achievement, but an even greater challenge was to maintain this complicated system of secret alliances in the face of the continuing rivalries among Germany's allies. Despite another Balkan war that broke out in 1885 and that again estranged Austria and Russia, he succeeded.

Although the Three Emperors' League lapsed, the Triple Alliance (Germany, Austria, and Italy) was renewed for another five years. To restore German relations with Russia, Bismarck negotiated the Reinsurance Treaty of 1887, in which both powers promised to remain neutral if either was attacked. All seemed smooth, but a change in the German monarchy soon upset Bismarck's arrangements.

In 1888 William II (r. 1888–1918) came to the German throne. He was twenty-nine years

[8]Quoted by Remak, p. 14.

old, ambitious, and impetuous. He was imperious by temperament and believed that he ruled by divine right. He had suffered an injury at birth that left him with a withered left arm. He compensated for this disability with vigorous exercise, a military bearing and outlook, and an often embarrassingly bombastic rhetoric.

Like many Germans of his generation, William II was filled with a sense of Germany's destiny as the leading power of Europe. He wanted to achieve recognition of at least equality with Britain, the land of his mother and of his grandmother, Queen Victoria. To achieve a "place in the sun," he and his contemporaries wanted a navy and colonies like Britain's. These aims, of course, ran counter to Bismarck's limited continental policy. When William argued for a navy as a defense against a British landing in North Germany, Bismarck replied, "If the British should land on our soil, I should have them arrested." This was only one example of the great distance between the young emperor, or Kaiser, and his chancellor. In 1890 William

used a disagreement over domestic policy to dismiss Bismarck.

As long as Bismarck held power, Germany was secure, and there was peace among the great European powers. Although he made mistakes and was not always successful, there was much to admire in his understanding and management of international relations in the hard world of reality. He had a clear and limited idea of his nation's goals. He resisted pressures for further expansion with few and insignificant exceptions. He understood and used the full range of diplomatic weapons: appeasement and deterrence, threats and promises, secrecy and openness. He understood the needs and hopes of other countries and, where possible, tried to help them satisfy them or used them to his own advantage. His system of alliances created a stalemate in the Balkans and ensured German security.

During Bismarck's time, Germany was a force for European peace and was increasingly understood to be so. This position would not, of course, have been possible without its great military power. It also required, however, the leadership of a statesman who was willing and able to exercise restraint and who understood what his country needed and what was possible.

Bismarck and the young Kaiser William II meet in 1888. The two disagreed over many issues, and in 1890 William dismissed the aged chancellor. [German Information Center]

Forging of the Triple Entente (1890–1907)

FRANCO-RUSSIAN ALLIANCE Almost immediately after Bismarck's retirement, his system of alliances collapsed. His successor was General Leo von Caprivi (1831–1899), who had once asked, "What kind of jackass will dare to be Bismarck's successor?" Caprivi refused the Russian request to renew the Reinsurance Treaty, in part because he felt incompetent to continue Bismarck's complicated policy and in part because he wished to draw Germany closer to Britain. The results were unfortunate, as Britain remained aloof and Russia was alienated.

Even Bismarck had assumed that ideological differences would prevent a Franco-Russian alliance. Political isolation and the need for foreign capital, however, unexpectedly drove the Russians toward France. The French, who were even more isolated, were glad to encourage their investors to pour capital into Russia if it would help produce an alliance and security against

Germany. In 1894 a defensive Franco-Russian alliance against Germany was signed.

BRITAIN AND GERMANY   Britain now became the key to the international situation. Colonial rivalries pitted the British against the Russians in central Asia and against the French in Africa. Traditionally, Britain had also opposed Russian control of Constantinople and the Dardanelles and French control of the Low Countries. There was no reason to think that Britain would soon become friendly to its traditional rivals or abandon its accustomed friendliness toward the Germans.

Yet within a decade of William II's accession, Germany had become the enemy in British minds. Before the turn of the century, popular British thrillers about imaginary wars portrayed the French as the invader; after the turn of the century, the enemy was always Germany. This remarkable transformation has often been attributed to economic rivalry between Germany and Britain, in which Germany made vast strides to challenge and even overtake British production in various materials and markets. Certainly, Germany made such gains and many Britons resented them. Yet the problem was not a serious cause of hostility, and it waned during the first decade of the century. The real problem lay in the foreign and naval policies of the German emperor and his ministers.

William II admired Britain's colonial empire and mighty fleet. At first, Germany tried to win the British over to the Triple Alliance, but when Britain clung to its "splendid isolation," German policy changed. The idea was to demonstrate Germany's worth as an ally by withdrawing support and even making trouble for Britain. This odd manner of gaining an ally reflected the Kaiser's confused feelings toward Britain, which mixed dislike and jealousy with admiration. These feelings were shared by many Germans, especially in the intellectual community. Like William, they were eager for Germany to pursue a "world policy" rather than Bismarck's limited one that confined German interests to Europe. They, too, saw England as the barrier to German ambitions. Their influence in the schools, the universities, and the press guaranteed popular approval of actions and statements hostile to Britain.

The Germans began to exert pressure against Britain in Africa by barring British attempts to build a railroad from Capetown to Cairo. They also openly sympathized with the Boers of South Africa in their resistance to British expansion. In 1896 William insulted the British by sending a congratulatory telegram to Paul Kruger (1825–1904), president of the Transvaal, for repulsing a British raid "without having to appeal to friendly powers for assistance," i.e., Germany.

In 1898 William began to realize his dream of a German navy with the passage of a naval law providing for nineteen battleships. In 1900 a second law doubled that figure. The architect of the new navy was Admiral Alfred von Tirpitz (1849–1930), who openly proclaimed that Germany's naval policy was aimed at Britain. His "risk" theory argued that Germany could build a fleet strong enough, not to defeat the British, but to do enough damage to make the British navy inferior to that of other powers like France or the United States. The theory was, in fact, absurd because as Germany's fleet became menacing, the British would certainly build enough ships to maintain their advantage, and Britain had greater financial resources than Germany.

The naval policy, therefore, was doomed to failure. Its main achievements were to waste German resources and to begin a great naval race with Britain. Eventually, the threat posed by the German navy so antagonized and alarmed British opinion that the British abandoned their traditional attitudes and policies.

At first, however, Britain was not unduly concerned. The British were embarrassed by the general hostility of world opinion during the Boer War (1899–1902), in which their great empire crushed a rebellion by South African farmers, and their isolation no longer seemed so splendid. The Germans had acted with restraint during the war. Between 1898 and 1901, Joseph Chamberlain, the colonial secretary, made several attempts to conclude an alliance with Germany. The Germans, confident that a British alliance with France or Russia was impossible, refused and expected the British to make greater concessions in the future.

THE ENTENTE CORDIALE   The first breach in Britain's isolation came in 1902, when it concluded an alliance with Japan to defend British

Admiral Alfred von Tirpitz (1849–1930). Tirpitz was responsible for building the German navy into a force capable of challenging the Royal Navy of Great Britain, reflecting Kaiser William II's desire to increase Germany's prominence among the great powers of Europe. [Bildarchiv Preussischer Kulturbesitz]

interests in the Far East against Russia. Next, Britain abandoned its traditional antagonism toward France and in 1904 concluded a series of agreements with the French, collectively called the *Entente Cordiale.* It was not a formal treaty and had no military provisions, but it settled all outstanding colonial differences between the two nations. In particular, Britain gave France a free hand in Morocco in return for French recognition of British control over Egypt. The Entente Cordiale was a long step toward aligning the British with Germany's great potential enemy.

Britain's new relationship with France was surprising, but in 1904 hardly anyone believed that the British whale and the Russian bear would ever come together. The Russo-Japanese War of 1904–1905 made such a development seem even less likely because Britain was allied with Russia's enemy. But Britain had behaved with restraint, and the Russians were chastened

by their unexpected and humiliating defeat. The defeat also led to the Russian Revolution of 1905. Although the revolution was put down, it weakened Russia and reduced British apprehensions about Russian power. The British were also concerned that Russia might again drift into the German orbit.

THE FIRST MOROCCAN CRISIS At this point, Germany decided to test the new understanding between Britain and France and to press for colonial gains. In March 1905, Emperor William II landed at Tangier, made a speech in favor of Moroccan independence, and by implication asserted Germany's right to participate in Morocco's destiny. This was a challenge to France. Germany's chancellor, Prince Bernhard von Bülow (1849–1929), intended to show France how weak it was and how little support it could expect from Britain. He also hoped to gain significant colonial concessions.

The Germans demanded an international conference to show their power more dramatically. The conference met in 1906 at Algeciras in Spain. Austria sided with its German ally, but Spain, which also had claims in Morocco, Italy, and the United States voted with Britain and France. The Germans had overplayed their hand, receiving trivial concessions, and the French position in Morocco was confirmed. German bullying had, moreover, driven Britain and France closer together. In the face of the threat of a German attack on France, Sir Edward Grey (1862–1933), the British foreign secretary, without making a firm commitment, authorized conversations between the British and French general staffs. Their agreements became morally binding as the years passed. By 1914 French and British military and naval plans were so mutually dependent that the two countries were effectively, if not formally, allies.

BRITISH AGREEMENT WITH RUSSIA Britain's fear of Germany's growing naval power, its concern over German ambitions in the Near East (as represented by the German-sponsored plan to build a railroad from Berlin to Baghdad), and its closer relations with France made it desirable for Britain to become more friendly with France's ally, Russia. With French support, the British concluded an agreement with Russia in 1907 much like the Entente Cordiale with France. It settled Russo-British quarrels in central Asia and opened the door for wider cooperation. The Triple Entente, an informal, but powerful association of Britain, France, and Russia, was now ranged against the Triple Alliance. Italy was an unreliable ally, however, which meant that Germany and Austria-Hungary were encircled by two great land powers and Great Britain.

William II and his ministers had turned Bismarck's nightmare of the prospect of a two-front war with France and Russia into a reality. They had made it more horrible by adding Britain to their foes. The equilibrium that Bismarck had worked so hard to achieve was destroyed. Britain would no longer support Austria in restraining Russian ambitions in the Balkans. Germany, increasingly alarmed by a sense of being encircled, was less willing to restrain the Austrians for fear of alienating them, too. In the Dual Alliance of Germany and Austria, it had become less clear who was the horse and who the rider.

Bismarck's alliance system had been intended to maintain peace, but the new alliance increased the risk of war and made the Balkans a likely spot for it to break out. Bismarck's diplomacy had left France isolated and impotent; the new arrangement associated France with the two greatest powers in Europe besides Germany. The Germans could rely only on Austria, and Austria's troubles made it less likely to provide aid than to need it.

World War I

The Road to War (1908–1914)

The weak Ottoman Empire still controlled the central strip of the Balkan Peninsula running west from Constantinople to the Adriatic. North and south of it were the independent states of Romania, Serbia, and Greece, as well as Bulgaria, technically still part of the empire but legally autonomous and practically independent. The Austro-Hungarian Empire included Croatia and Slovenia and since 1878 had "occupied and administered" Bosnia and Herzegovina.

Except for the Greeks and the Romanians, most of the inhabitants of the Balkans spoke variants of the same Slavic language and felt a cultural and historical kinship with one another. For centuries they had been ruled by Austrians, Hungarians, or Turks, and the growing nationalism that characterized late-nineteenth-century Europe made many of them eager for independence. The more radical among them longed for a union of the south Slavic, or Yugoslav, peoples in a single nation. They looked to independent Serbia as the center of the new nation and hoped to detach all the Slavic provinces (especially Bosnia, which bordered on Serbia) from Austria. Serbia believed that its destiny was to unite the Slavs at the expense of Austria, as Piedmont had united the Italians and Prussia the Germans.

In 1908 a group of modernizing reformers called the *Young Turks* brought about a revolution in the Ottoman Empire. Their actions threatened to revive the life of the empire and to interfere with the plans of the European jackals preparing to pounce on the Ottoman corpse. These events brought on the first of a series of Balkan crises that would eventually lead to war.

THE BOSNIAN CRISIS In 1908 the Austrian and Russian governments decided to act quickly before Turkey became strong enough to resist. They struck a bargain in which Russia agreed to support the Austrian annexation of Bosnia and Herzegovina, in return for Austrian backing for opening the Dardanelles to Russian warships.

Austria, however, declared the annexation before the Russians could act. The British and French, eager for the favor of the Young Turks, refused to agree to the Russian demand for the opening of the Dardenelles. The Russians were humiliated and furious but too weak to do anything but protest. Their "little brothers," the Serbs, were frustrated and angered by the Austrian annexation of Bosnia, which they had hoped one day to annex themselves.

The Germans had not been warned in advance of Austria's plans and were unhappy because the action threatened their relations with Russia. Germany felt so dependent on the Dual Alliance, however, that it nevertheless assured Austria of its support. Austria had been given a free hand, and to some extent, German policy was being made in Vienna. It was a dangerous precedent. Also, the failure of Britain and France to support Russia strained the Triple Entente. This made it harder for them to oppose Russian interests in the future if they were to keep Russian friendship.

THE SECOND MOROCCAN CRISIS The second Moroccan crisis, in 1911, emphasized the French and British need for mutual support. When France sent an army to Morocco to put down a rebellion, Germany took the opportunity to "protect German interests" there as a means of extorting colonial concessions in the French Congo. To add force to their demands, the Germans sent the gunboat *Panther* to the Moroccan port of Agadir, allegedly to protect German citizens there. Once again, as in 1905, the Germans went too far. The *Panther's* visit to Agadir provoked a strong reaction in Britain. For some time Anglo-German relations had been growing worse, chiefly because of the intensification of the naval race. In 1907 Germany had built its first new dreadnought, a new type of battleship that Britain had launched in 1906. In 1908 Germany had passed still another naval law that accelerated the challenge to British naval supremacy.

These actions frightened and angered the British, because they threatened the security of the island kingdom and its empire. The German actions also forced Britain to increase taxes to pay for new armaments just when the Liberal government in Britain was launching its expensive program of social legislation. Negotiations failed to persuade William II and Tirpitz to slow down naval construction.

In this atmosphere, the British heard of the *Panther's* arrival in Morocco. They wrongly believed that the Germans meant to turn Agadir into a naval base on the Atlantic. The crisis passed when France yielded some insignificant bits of the Congo and Germany recognized the French protectorate over Morocco. The main result was to increase British fear and hostility and to draw Britain closer to France. Specific military plans were formulated for a British expeditionary force to defend France in case of German attack, and the British and French navies agreed to cooperate. Without any formal treaty, the German naval construction and the Agadir crisis had turned the Entente Cordiale into an alliance, de facto. If Germany attacked France, Britain must defend the French, for its own security was inextricably tied up with that of France.

WAR IN THE BALKANS The second Moroccan crisis also provoked another crisis in the Balkans. Italy sought to gain colonies and to take its place among the great powers. It wanted Libya, which though worth little before the discovery of oil in the 1950s was at least available. Italy feared that the recognition of the French protectorate in Morocco would encourage France also to move into Libya. So, in 1911, Italy attacked the Ottoman Empire to anticipate the French, defeated the faltering Turks, and forced Turkey to cede Libya and the Dodecanese Islands in the Aegean. The Italian victory demonstrated Turkish weakness and encouraged the Balkan states to try their luck. In 1912 Bulgaria, Greece, Montenegro, and Serbia jointly attacked the Ottoman Empire and won easily (see Map 26-4). After this First Balkan War, the victors fell out among themselves over the division of Macedonia, and in 1913 a Second Balkan War erupted. This time Turkey and Romania joined the other states against Bulgaria and stripped away much of what the Bulgarians had gained in 1878 and 1912.

After the First Balkan War, the alarmed Austrians were determined to limit Serbian gains and especially to prevent the Serbs from gaining a port on the Adriatic. This policy meant keeping Serbia out of Albania, but the Russians backed the Serbs, and tensions mounted. An international conference sponsored by Britain in early 1913 resolved the matter in Austria's favor and called for an independent kingdom of Albania. Austria, however, felt humiliated by the public airing of Serbian demands and the Serbs defied the powers and continued to occupy parts of Albania. Under Austrian pressure they eventually withdrew, but they returned to Albania in September 1913, after the Second Balkan War. Finally, in mid-October, Austria unilaterally issued an ultimatum, and Serbia again withdrew its forces from Albania.

During this crisis, many people in Austria had wanted an all-out attack on Serbia to remove its threat to the empire once and for all. Those demands had been resisted by Emperor Francis Joseph and the heir to the throne, Archduke Francis Ferdinand. At the same time, Pan-Slavic sentiment in Russia pressed Tsar Nicholas II to take a firm stand, but Russia once again let Austria have its way in its confrontation with Serbia. Throughout the crisis, Britain, France, Italy, and Germany restrained their

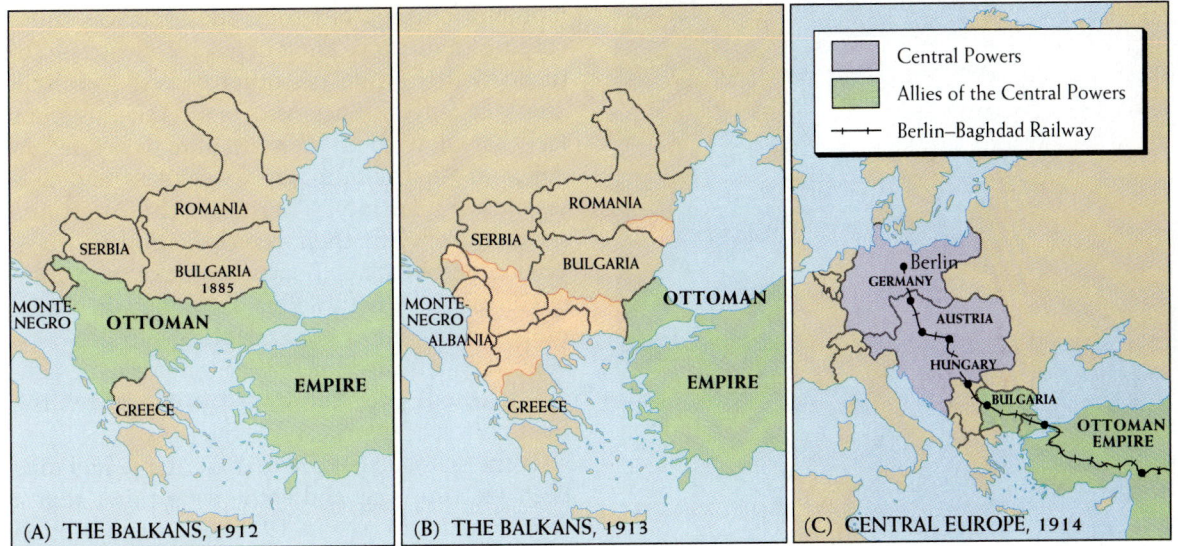

MAP 26-4 THE BALKANS, 1912–1913 *Two maps show the Balkans before (a) and after (b) the two Balkan wars; note the Ottoman retreat. In (c) we see the geographical relationship of the Central Powers and their Bulgarian and Turkish allies.*

allies, although each worried about seeming too reluctant to help its friends.

The lessons learned from this crisis of 1913 profoundly influenced behavior in the final crisis in 1914. The Russians had once again, as in 1908, been embarrassed by their passivity; and their allies were more reluctant to restrain them again. The Austrians were embarrassed by the results of accepting an international conference and were determined not to do it again. They had gotten better results from a threat of direct force; they and their German allies did not miss the lesson.

Sarajevo and the Outbreak of War (June–August 1914)

THE ASSASSINATION On June 28, 1914, a young Bosnian nationalist shot and killed Archduke Francis Ferdinand, heir to the Austrian throne, and his wife as they drove in an open car through the Bosnian capital of Sarajevo. The assassin was a member of a conspiracy hatched by a political terrorist society called *Union or Death*, better known as the *Black Hand*. The chief of intelligence of the Serbian army's general staff had helped plan and prepare the crime. Though his role was not actually known at the time, it was generally believed throughout Europe that Serbian officials were involved. The glee of the Serbian press after the assassination lent support to that belief.

The archduke was not popular in Austria, and his funeral evoked few signs of grief. He had been known to favor a form of federal government for Austria that would have raised the status of the Slavs in the empire. This position alienated the conservatives among the Habsburg officials and the Hungarians. It also alarmed radical Yugoslav nationalists, who feared that Habsburg reform might end their dream of an independent south Slav state.

GERMANY AND AUSTRIA'S RESPONSE News of the assassination produced outrage and condemnation everywhere in Europe except in Serbia. To those Austrians who had long favored an attack on Serbia as a solution to the empire's Slavic problem, the opportunity seemed irresistible. But it was never easy for the Dual Monarchy to make a decision. Conrad von Hötzendorf (1852–1925), chief of the Austrian general staff, urged an attack as he had often done before. Count Stefan Tisza (1861–1918), speaking for Hungary, resisted. Count Leopold von Berchtold (1863–1942), the Austro-Hungarian foreign minister, felt the need for strong action, but he knew that German support would be required in

ABOVE: The Austrian Archduke Franz Ferdinand and his wife in Sarajevo on June 28, 1914. Later in the day the royal couple were assassinated by young revolutionaries trained and supplied in Serbia, igniting the crisis that led to World War I. BELOW: Moments after the assassination the Austrian police captured one of the assassins. [Brown Brothers]

the likely event that Russia should decide to intervene to protect Serbia. He also knew that nothing could be done without Tisza's approval and that only German support could persuade the Hungarians to accept the policy of war. The question of peace or war against Serbia, therefore, had to be answered in Berlin.

William II and Chancellor Theobald von Bethmann-Hollweg (1856–1921) readily promised German support for an attack on Serbia. It has often been said that they gave the Austrians

a "blank check," but their message was more specific than that. They urged the Austrians to move swiftly while the other powers were still angry at Serbia. They also made the Austrians feel that they would view a failure to act as evidence of Austria-Hungary's weakness and uselessness as an ally. Therefore, the Austrians never wavered in their determination to make war on Serbia. They hoped, with the protection of Germany, to fight Serbia alone, but they were prepared to risk a general European conflict. The Germans also knew that they risked a general war, but they too hoped to "localize" the fight between Austria and Serbia.

Some scholars believe that Germany had long been plotting war, and some even think that a specific plan for war in 1914 was set in motion as early as 1912. The vast body of evidence on the crisis of 1914, however, gives little support to such notions. The German leaders plainly reacted to a crisis that they had not foreseen and just as plainly made decisions in response to events. The fundamental decision to support Austria, however, made war difficult if not impossible to avoid. That decision was made by the emperor and chancellor without significant consultation with either their military or diplomatic advisers.

William II appears to have reacted violently to the assassination. He was moved by his friendship for the archduke and by outrage at an attack on royalty. A different provocation would probably not have moved him so much. Bethmann-Hollweg was less emotional but under severe pressure. To resist the decision would have meant flatly opposing the emperor. The powerful military circles favored by William suspected the chancellor of being "soft." It would have been difficult for him to take a conciliatory position.

Moreover, Bethmann-Hollweg, like many other Germans, feared for the future. Russia was recovering its strength and would reach a military peak in 1917. The Triple Entente was growing closer and more powerful, and Germany's only reliable ally was Austria. The chancellor recognized the danger of supporting Austria, but he believed it to be even more dangerous to withhold that support. If Austria did not crush Serbia, it would soon collapse before the onslaught of Slavic nationalism defended by

Russia. If Germany did not defend its ally, the Austrians might look elsewhere for help. His policy was one of "calculated risk."

Unfortunately, the calculations proved to be incorrect. Bethmann-Hollweg hoped that the Austrians would strike swiftly and present the powers with a fait accompli while the outrage of the assassination was still fresh. And he felt that German support would deter Russian involvement. Failing that, he was prepared for a continental war against France and Russia. This policy depended on British neutrality; and the German chancellor convinced himself that the British could be persuaded to stand aloof.

The Austrians, however, were slow to act. They did not even deliver their deliberately unacceptable ultimatum to Serbia until July 24, when the general hostility toward Serbia had begun to subside. Serbia further embarrassed the Austrians by returning so soft and concilia-tory an answer that even the mercurial German emperor thought it removed all reason for war. But the Austrians were determined not to turn back. On July 28, they declared war on Serbia, even though the army would not be ready to attack until mid-August.

THE TRIPLE ENTENTE'S RESPONSE The Russians, previously so often forced to back off, responded angrily to the Austrian demands on Serbia. The most conservative elements of the Russian government opposed war, fearing that it would lead to revolution as it had in 1905. But nationalists, Pan-Slavs, and most of the politi-cally conscious classes in general demanded action. The government responded by ordering partial mobilization, against Austria only. This policy was militarily impossible, but its inten-tion was to put diplomatic pressure on Austria to refrain from attacking Serbia.

Mobilization of any kind, however, was a dangerous weapon because it was generally understood to be equivalent to an act of war. It was especially alarming to the German general staff. The possibility that the Russians might start mobilization before the Germans could move would upset the delicate timing of Germany's only battle plan, the Schlieffen Plan, which required an attack on France before the Russians were ready to act, and would put Germany in great danger. From this point on,

the general staff pressed for German mobiliza-tion and war. The pressure of military necessity soon became irresistible.

France and Britain were not eager for war. France's president and prime minister were on their way back from a visit to Russia when the crisis flared on July 24. The Austrians had, in fact, timed their ultimatum precisely so that these two men would be at sea when it was delivered to the Serbs. Had they been in Paris, they might have tried to restrain the Russians. The French ambassador to Russia gave the Russians the same assurances, however, that Germany had given its ally. The British worked hard to resolve the crisis by traditional means: a conference of the powers. Austria, still smarting from its humiliation after the London Confer-ence of 1913, would not hear of it. The Germans privately supported the Austrians but publicly took on a conciliatory tone in the hope of keep-ing the British neutral.

Soon, however, Bethmann-Hollweg came to realize what he should have known from the first. If Germany attacked France, Britain must fight. Until July 30, his public appeals to Austria for restraint were a sham. Thereafter, he sin-cerely tried to persuade the Austrians to negoti-ate and avoid a general war, but it was too late. The Austrians could not turn back without los-ing their own self-respect and the respect of the Germans.

On July 30, Austria ordered mobilization against Russia. Bethmann-Hollweg resisted the enormous pressure to mobilize, not because he had any further hope of avoiding war but because he wanted Russia to mobilize against Germany first and appear to be the aggressor. Only in that way could he win the support of the German nation for war, especially the paci-fist Social Democrats. His luck was good for a change. The news of Russian general mobiliza-tion came only minutes before Germany would have mobilized in any case. The Schlieffen Plan went into effect (see Map 26-5). The Germans occupied Luxembourg on August 1 and invaded Belgium, which resisted, on August 3. The inva-sion of Belgium violated the treaty of 1839 in which the British had joined the other powers in guaranteeing Belgian neutrality. This factor undermined the considerable sentiment in Britain for neutrality and united the nation

Austria's Ultimatum to Serbia

On the afternoon of July 23, 1914, Austria presented a list of demands to Serbia, giving the Serbs just forty-eight hours to reply. The Austrian ambassador was instructed to leave the country and break off relations if all the demands were not accepted without limitation by the specified time.

◆ *Which, if any, of the demands might Serbia or any country find insulting? What were the Austrians' intentions in making these demands and the manner in which they made them? Why did they act in this way? What problems did the ultimatum pose for the Serbs?*

The results brought out by the inquiry no longer permit the Imperial and Royal Government to maintain the attitude of patient tolerance which it has observed for years toward those agitations which center at Belgrade and are spread thence into the territories of the Monarchy. Instead, these results impose upon the Imperial and Royal Government the obligation to put an end to those intrigues, which constitute a standing menace to the peace of the Monarchy.

In order to attain this end, the Imperial and Royal Government finds itself compelled to demand that the Serbian Government give official assurance that it will condemn the propaganda directed against Austria-Hungary, that is to say, the whole body of the efforts whose ultimate object it is to separate from the Monarchy territories that belong to it; and that it will obligate itself to suppress with all the means at its command this criminal and terroristic propaganda.

In order to give these assurances a character of solemnity, the Royal Serbian Government will publish on the first page of its official organ of July 26/13, the following declaration:

The Royal Serbian Government condemns the propaganda directed against Austria-Hungary, that is to say, the whole body of the efforts whose ultimate object it is to separate from the Austro-Hungarian Monarchy territories that belong to it, and it most sincerely regrets the dreadful consequences of these criminal transactions.

The Royal Serbian Government regrets that Serbian officers and officials should have taken part in the above-mentioned propaganda and thus have endangered the friendly and neighborly relations, to the cultivation of which the Royal Government had most solemnly pledged itself by its declaration of March 31, 1909.

The Royal Government, which disapproves and repels every idea and every attempt to interfere in the destinies of the population of whatever portion of Austria-Hungary, regards it as its duty most expressly to call the attention of the officers, officials, and the whole population of the Kingdom to the fact that for the future it will proceed with the utmost rigor against any persons who shall become guilty of any such activities, activities to prevent and to suppress which, the Government will bend every effort.

This declaration shall be brought to the attention of the Royal army simultaneously by an order of the day from His Majesty the King, and by publication in the official organ of the army.

The Royal Serbian Government will furthermore pledge itself:

1. to suppress every publication which shall incite to hatred and contempt of the Monarchy, and the general tendency of which shall be directed against the territorial integrity of the latter;
2. to proceed at once to the dissolution of the *Narodna Odbrana,* to confiscate all of its means of propaganda, and in the same manner to proceed against the other unions and associations in Serbia which occupy themselves with propaganda against Austria-Hungary; the Royal Government will take such measures as are necessary to make sure that the dissolved associations may not continue their activities under other names or in other forms.
3. to eliminate without delay from public instruction in Serbia, everything, whether connected with the teaching corps or with the methods of teaching, that serves or may serve to nourish the propaganda against Austria-Hungary;
4. to remove from the military and administrative service in general all officers and officials who have been guilty of carrying on the propaganda against Austria-Hungary, whose names the Imperial and Royal Government reserves the right to make known to the Royal Government when communicating the material evidence now in its possession;
5. to agree to the cooperation in Serbia of the organs of the Imperial and Royal Government in the suppression of the subversive movement directed against the integrity of the Monarchy;
6. to institute a judicial inquiry against every participant in the conspiracy of the twenty-eighth of June who may be found in Serbian territory; the organs of the Imperial and Royal Government delegated for this purpose will take part in the proceedings held for this purpose;
7. to undertake with all haste the arrest of Major Voislav Tankositch and of one Milan Ciganovitch, a Serbian official, who have been compromised by the results of the inquiry;
8. by efficient measures to prevent the participation of Serbian authorities in the smuggling of weapons and explosives across the frontier; to dismiss from the service and to punish severely those members of the Frontier Service at Schabats and Losnitza who assisted the authors of the crime of Serajevo to cross the frontier;
9. to make explanations to the Imperial and Royal Government concerning the unjustifiable utterances of high Serbian functionaries in Serbia and abroad, who, without regard for their official position, have not hesitated to express themselves in a manner hostile toward Austria-Hungary since the assassination of the twenty-eighth of June;
10. to inform the Imperial and Royal Government without delay of the execution of the measures comprised in the foregoing points.

The Imperial and Royal Government awaits the reply of the Royal Government by Saturday, the twenty-fifth instant, at 6 P.M., at the latest.

A mémoire concerning the results of the inquiry at Serajevo, as far as they concern the functionaries referred to in Points 7 and 8, is appended to this note.

Walther Schüking and Max Montgelas, eds., Outbreak of the World War: German Documents Collected by Karl Kautsky, Supplement I *(New York: Carnegie Endowment for Peace, 1924), pp. 604–605.*

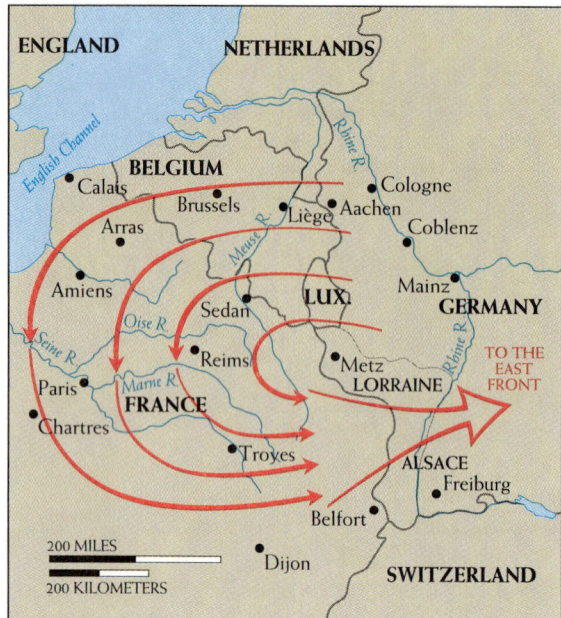

MAP 26-5 THE SCHLIEFFEN PLAN OF 1905 *Germany's grand strategy for quickly winning the war against France in 1914 is shown by the wheeling arrows on the map. The crushing blows at France were, in the original plan, to be followed by the release of troops for use against Russia on Germany's eastern front. The plan, however, was not adequately implemented, and the war on the Western Front became a long contest in place.*

against Germany. Germany then invaded France, and on August 4, Britain declared war on Germany.

The Great War had begun. As Sir Edward Grey, the British foreign secretary, put it, the lights were going out all over Europe. They would come on again, but Europe would never be the same.

Strategies and Stalemate: 1914–1917

Throughout Europe, jubilation greeted the outbreak of war. No general war had been fought since Napoleon, and few understood the horrors of modern warfare. The dominant memory was of Bismarck's swift and decisive campaigns, in which the costs and casualties were light and the rewards great. After the repeated crises of recent years and the fears and resentments they had created, war came as a release of tension. The popular press had increased public awareness of and interest in foreign affairs and had fanned the flames of patriotism. The prospect of

The Coming of World War I	
1871	The end of the Franco-Prussian War; creation of the German Empire; German annexation of Alsace-Lorraine
1873	The Three Emperors' League (Germany, Russia, and Austria-Hungary)
1875	The Russo-Turkish War
1878	The Congress of Berlin
1879	The Dual Alliance between Germany and Austria
1881	The Three Emperors' League is renewed
1882	Italy joins Germany and Austria in the Triple Alliance
1888	William II becomes the German emperor
1890	Bismarck is dismissed
1894	The Franco-Russian alliance
1898	Germany begins to build a battleship navy
1899–1902	Boer War
1902	The British alliance with Japan
1904	The Entente Cordiale between Britain and France
1904–1905	The Russo-Japanese War
1905	The first Moroccan crisis
1907	The British agreement with Russia
1908–1909	The Bosnian crisis
1911	The second Moroccan crisis
1911	Italy attacks Turkey
1912–1913	The First and Second Balkan Wars
1914	Outbreak of World War I

war moved even a rational man of science like Sigmund Freud to say, "My whole libido goes out to Austria-Hungary."[9]

Both sides expected to take the offensive, force a battle on favorable ground, and win a quick victory. The Triple Entente powers—or the Allies, as they called themselves—held superiority in numbers and financial resources as well as command of the sea (see Figure 26-1). Germany and Austria, the Central Powers, had the advantages of internal lines of communication and of having launched their attack first.

[9]*Quoted in Remak, p. 134.*

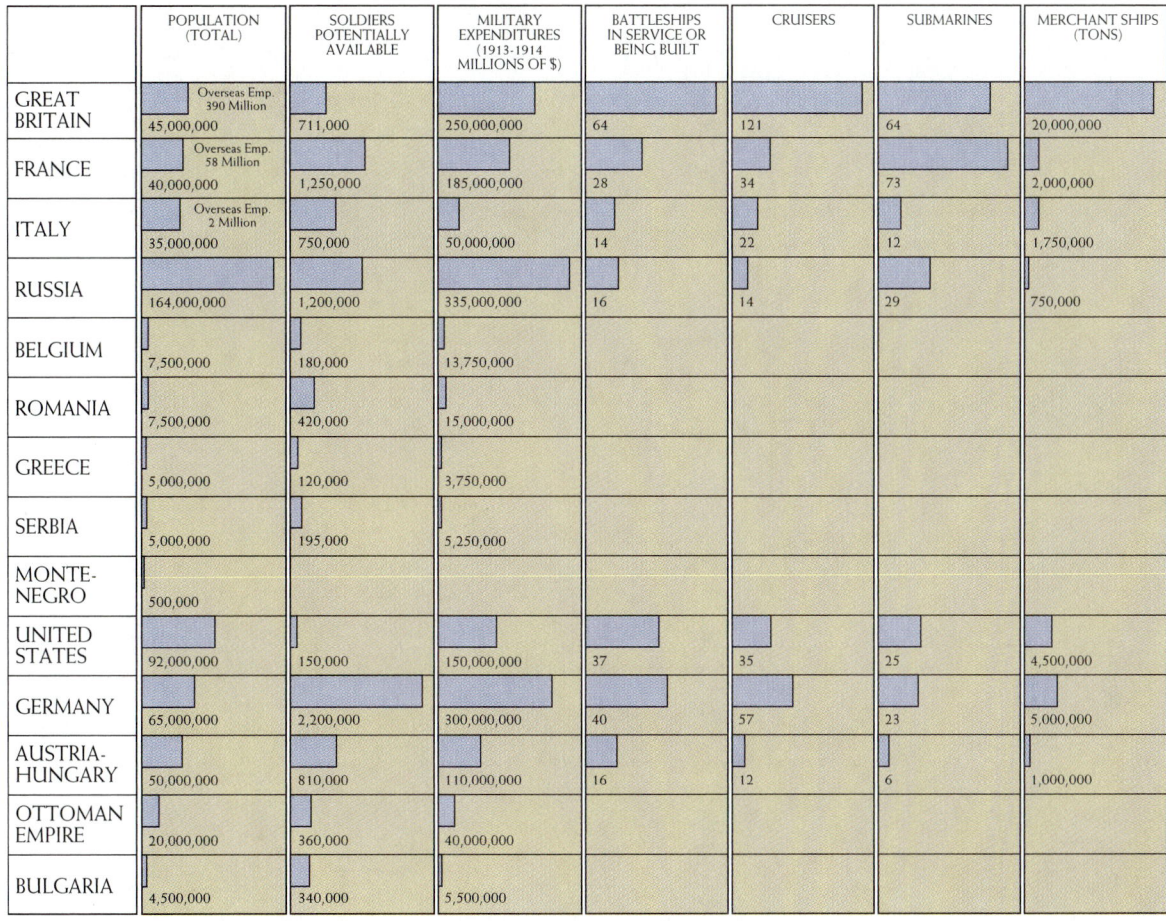

	POPULATION (TOTAL)	SOLDIERS POTENTIALLY AVAILABLE	MILITARY EXPENDITURES (1913-1914 MILLIONS OF $)	BATTLESHIPS IN SERVICE OR BEING BUILT	CRUISERS	SUBMARINES	MERCHANT SHIPS (TONS)
GREAT BRITAIN	Overseas Emp. 390 Million 45,000,000	711,000	250,000,000	64	121	64	20,000,000
FRANCE	Overseas Emp. 58 Million 40,000,000	1,250,000	185,000,000	28	34	73	2,000,000
ITALY	Overseas Emp. 2 Million 35,000,000	750,000	50,000,000	14	22	12	1,750,000
RUSSIA	164,000,000	1,200,000	335,000,000	16	14	29	750,000
BELGIUM	7,500,000	180,000	13,750,000				
ROMANIA	7,500,000	420,000	15,000,000				
GREECE	5,000,000	120,000	3,750,000				
SERBIA	5,000,000	195,000	5,250,000				
MONTE-NEGRO	500,000						
UNITED STATES	92,000,000	150,000	150,000,000	37	35	25	4,500,000
GERMANY	65,000,000	2,200,000	300,000,000	40	57	23	5,000,000
AUSTRIA-HUNGARY	50,000,000	810,000	110,000,000	16	12	6	1,000,000
OTTOMAN EMPIRE	20,000,000	360,000	40,000,000				
BULGARIA	4,500,000	340,000	5,500,000				

FIGURE 26-1 RELATIVE STRENGTHS OF THE COMBATANTS IN WORLD WAR I

After 1905 Germany's only war plan was the one developed by Count Alfred von Schlieffen (1833–1913), chief of the German general staff from 1891 to 1906 (see Map 26-5). It aimed at going around the French defenses by sweeping through Belgium to the Channel, then wheeling to the south and east to envelop the French and to crush them against the German fortresses in Lorraine. The secret of success lay in making the right wing of the advancing German army immensely strong and deliberately weakening the left opposite the French frontier. The weakness of the left was meant to draw the French into attacking the wrong place while the war was decided on the German right. As one keen military analyst has explained:

It would be like a revolving door—if a man pressed heavily on one side, the other side would spring round and strike him in the back. Here lay the real subtlety of the plan, not in the mere geographical detour.[10]

In the East, the Germans planned to stand on the defensive against Russia until France had been crushed, a task they thought would take only six weeks.

The apparent risk, besides the violation of Belgian neutrality and the consequent alienation of Britain, lay in weakening the German defenses against a direct attack across the frontier. The strength of German fortresses and the superior firepower of German howitzers made that risk more theoretical than real. The true danger was that the German striking force on the right through Belgium would not be powerful enough to make the swift progress vital to success.

[10]B. H. Liddell Hart, The Real War, 1914–1918 (Boston: Little, Brown, 1964; first published in 1930), p. 47.

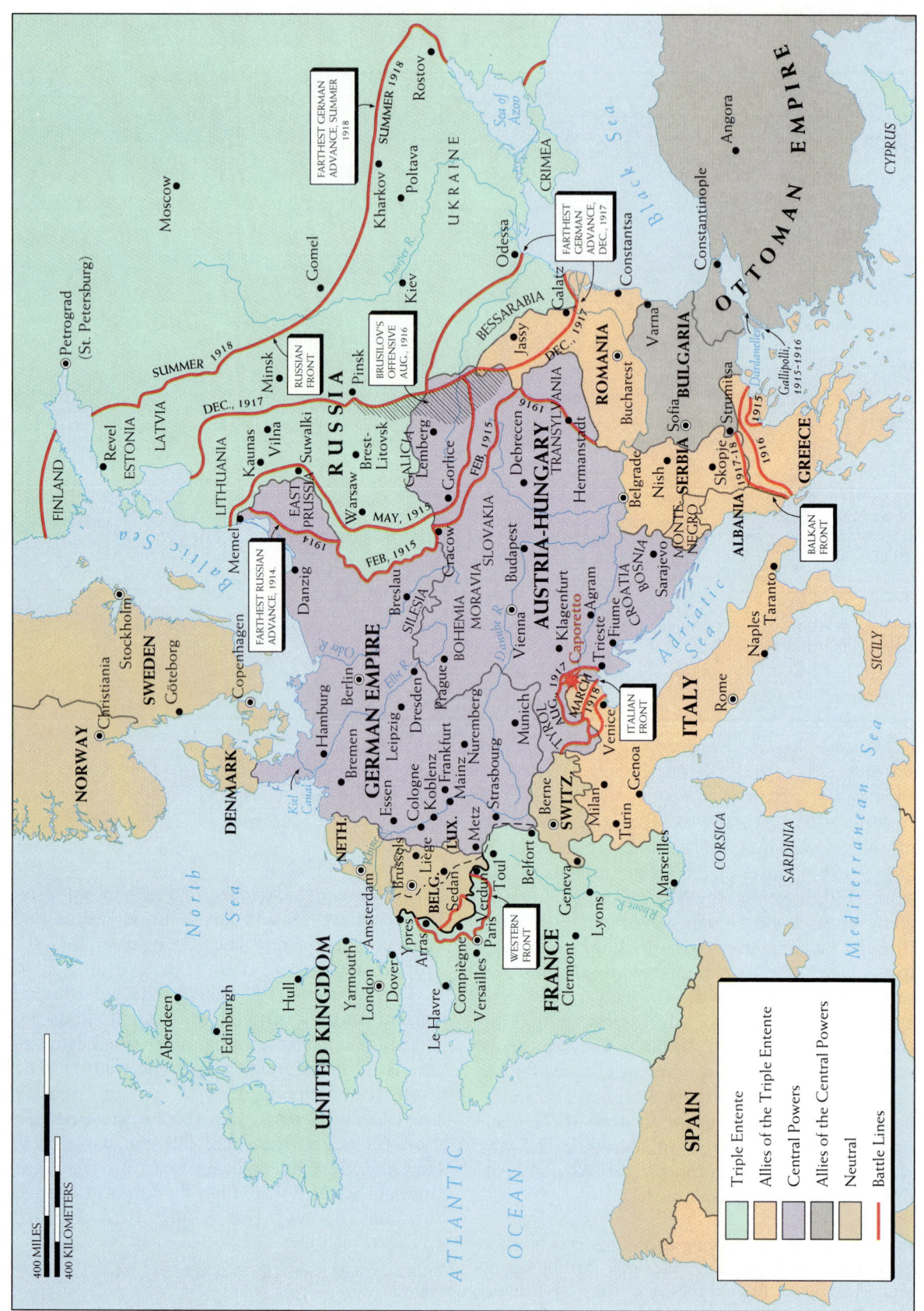

MAP 26-6 WORLD WAR I IN EUROPE *Despite the importance of military action in the Far East, in the Arab world, and at sea, the main theaters of activity in World War I were in*

Schlieffen is said to have died uttering the words, "It must come to a fight. Only make the right wing strong."

The execution of his plan, however, was left to Helmuth von Moltke (1848–1916), the nephew of Bismarck's most effective general. Despite Schlieffen's warning, Moltke (chief of staff 1906–1914) added divisions to the left wing and even weakened the Russian front for the same purpose. As a result of this hesitant strategy and of theoretical mistakes by German commanders in the field, the Schlieffen Plan failed by a narrow margin.

THE WAR IN THE WEST The French had also put their faith in the offensive, but with less reason than the Germans. They badly underestimated the numbers and effectiveness of the German reserves and overestimated the importance of the courage and spirit of their own troops. Courage and spirit, however, could not win against machine guns and heavy artillery. The French offensive on Germany's western frontier failed totally. This defeat probably was preferable to a partial success because it released troops for use against the main German army. As a result, the French and the British were able to stop the German advance on Paris at the Battle of the Marne in September 1914 (see Maps 26-6 and 26-7).

Thereafter, the nature of the war in the West became one of position instead of movement. Both sides dug in behind a wall of trenches protected by barbed wire that stretched from the North Sea to Switzerland. Strategically placed machine-gun nests made assaults difficult and dangerous. Both sides, nonetheless, attempted massive attacks preceded by artillery bombardments of unprecedented and horrible force and duration. Still the defense was always able to recover and to bring up reserves fast enough to prevent a breakthrough.

Sometimes assaults that cost hundreds of thousands of lives produced advances of only hundreds of yards. The introduction of poison gas to resolve the problem proved ineffective. In 1916 the British introduced the tank, which eventually proved to be the answer to the machine gun, but the Allied command was slow to understand this, and until the end of the war, defense was supreme. For three years after its

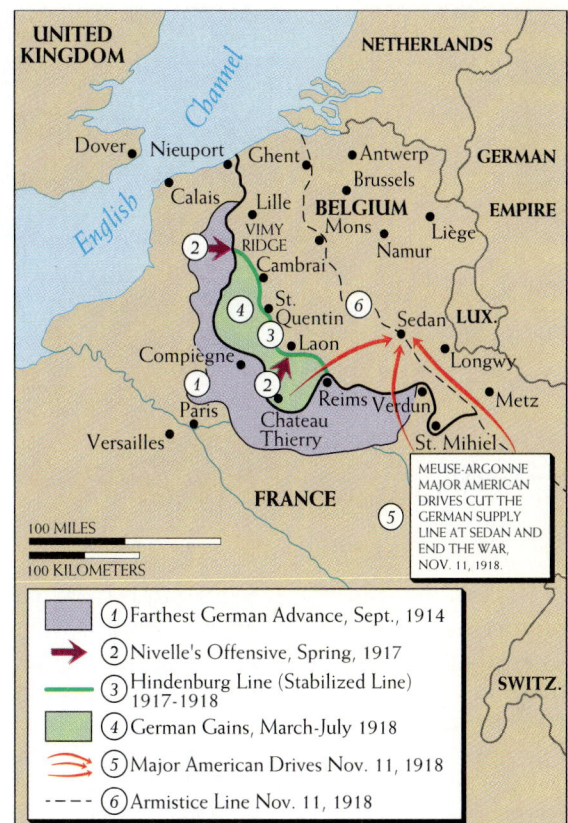

MAP 26-7 THE WESTERN FRONT 1914–1918 *This map shows the crucial Western Front in detail.*

establishment, the Western Front moved only a few miles in either direction.

THE WAR IN THE EAST In the East, the war began auspiciously for the Allies. The Russians advanced into Austrian territory and inflicted heavy casualties, but Russian incompetence and German energy soon reversed the situation. A junior German officer, Erich Ludendorff (1865–1937), under the command of the elderly General Paul von Hindenburg (1847–1934), destroyed or captured an entire Russian army at the Battle of Tannenberg and defeated another one at the Masurian Lakes. In 1915 the Central Powers pressed their advantage in the East and drove into the Baltic states and Russian Poland, inflicting more than two million casualties in a single year.

As the battle lines hardened, both sides sought new allies. Turkey (because of its hostility to Russia) and Bulgaria (the enemy of Serbia) joined the Central Powers.

German infantrymen eating in a trench on the Western Front. Trenches, defended by barbed wire and machine guns, gave the defense the advantage in World War I and prevented breakthroughs. [Bildarchiv Preussischer Kulturbesitz]

Both sides bid for Italian support with promises of the spoils of victory. Because what the Italians wanted most was held by Austria, the Allies could promise more. In a secret treaty of 1915, they agreed to deliver to Italy after victory most of *Italia Irredenta* (i.e., the South Tyrol, Trieste, and some of the Dalmatian Islands) plus new colonies in Africa and a share of the Turkish Empire. By the spring of 1915, Italy was engaging Austrian armies. The Italian campaign weakened Austria and divided some German troops, but the Italian alliance was generally a disappointment to the Allies and never produced significant results. Romania joined the Allies in 1916 but was quickly defeated and driven from the war.

In the Far East, Japan honored its alliance with Britain and entered the war. The Japanese quickly overran the German colonies in China and the Pacific and used the opportunity to improve their own position against China.

Both sides also appealed to nationalistic sentiment in areas held by the enemy. The Germans supported nationalist movements among the Irish, the Flemings in Belgium, and the Poles and the Ukrainians under Russian rule. They even tried to persuade the Turks to lead a Muslim uprising against the British in Egypt and India and the French in North Africa.

The Allies made the same appeals with greater success. They sponsored movements of national autonomy for the Czechs, the Slovaks, the south Slavs, and the Poles that were under Austrian rule. They also favored a movement of Arab independence from Turkey. Guided by Colonel T. E. Lawrence (1888–1935), this last scheme proved especially successful later in the war.

British tanks moving toward the battle of Cambrai in Flanders late in 1917. Tanks were impervious to machine-gun fire. Had they been used in great numbers they might have broken the stalemate in the West. [Bildarchiv Preussischer Kulturbesitz]

In 1915 the Allies undertook to break the deadlock on the Western Front by going around it. The idea came chiefly from Winston Churchill (1874–1965), first lord of the British admiralty. He proposed to attack the Dardanelles and capture Constantinople. This policy would knock Turkey from the war, bring help to the Balkan front, and ease communications with Russia. The plan was daring but promising and, in its original form, presented little risk. British naval superiority and the element of surprise would allow the forcing of the straits and the capture of Constantinople by purely naval action. Even if the scheme failed, the fleet could escape with little loss.

Success depended on timing, speed, and daring leadership, but all of these were lacking. The execution of the attack was inept and overly cautious. Troops were landed, and as Turkish resistance continued, the Allied commitment increased. Before the campaign was abandoned, the Allies lost almost 150,000 men and diverted three times that number from more useful occupations.

RETURN TO THE WEST Both sides turned back to the West in 1916. General Erich von Falkenhayn (1861–1922), who had succeeded Moltke in September 1914, sought success by an attack on the French stronghold of Verdun. His plan was not to take the fortress or to break through the French line but to inflict enormously heavy casualties on the French, who would have to defend Verdun against superior firepower from several directions. He, too, underestimated the superiority of the defense. The French were able to hold Verdun with comparatively few men and to inflict almost as many casualties as they suffered. The commander of Verdun, Henri Pétain (1856–1951), became a national hero, and "They shall not pass" became a slogan of national defiance.

The Allies tried to end the impasse by launching a major offensive along the River Somme in July. Aided by a Russian attack in the East that drew off some German strength and by an enormous artillery bombardment, they hoped at last to break through. Once again, the defense was superior. Enormous casualties on both sides brought no result. On all fronts, the losses were great and the results meager. The war on land dragged on with no end in sight.

THE WAR AT SEA As the war continued, control of the sea became more important. The British ignored the distinction between war supplies (which were contraband according to international law) and food or other peaceful cargo (which was not subject to seizure). They imposed a strict blockade meant to starve out the enemy, regardless of international law. The Germans responded with submarine warfare

The Allies promoted Arab efforts to secure independence from Turkey in an effort to remove Turkey from the war. Delegates to the peace conference of 1919 in Paris included British Colonel T. E. Lawrence, who helped lead the rebellion, and representatives from the Middle Eastern region. Prince Feisal, the third son of King Hussein, stands in the foreground of this picture; Colonel T. E. Lawrence is in the middle row, second from the right; and Brigadier General Nuri Pasha Said of Baghdad is second from the left. [The Bettmann Archive]

meant to destroy British shipping and to starve the British. They declared the waters around the British Isles a war zone, where even neutral ships would not be safe. Both policies were unwelcome to neutrals, and especially to the United States, which conducted extensive trade in the Atlantic. Yet the sinking of neutral ships by German submarines was both more dramatic and more offensive than the British blockade.

In May 1915, a German submarine torpedoed the British liner *Lusitania*. Among the 1,200 drowned were 118 Americans. President Woodrow Wilson (1856–1924) warned Germany that a repetition would have grave consequences; the Germans desisted for the time being rather than further anger the United States. This development gave the Allies a con-

siderable advantage. The German fleet that had cost so much money and had caused so much trouble played no significant part in the war. The only battle it fought was at Jutland in the spring of 1916. The battle resulted in a standoff and confirmed British domination of the surface of the sea.

AMERICA ENTERS THE WAR In December 1916, President Woodrow Wilson of the United States intervened to try to bring about a negotiated peace. Neither side, however, was willing to renounce war aims that its opponent found unacceptable. The war seemed likely to continue until one or both sides reached exhaustion.

Two events early in 1917 changed the situation radically. On February 1, the Germans announced the resumption of unrestricted submarine warfare, which led the United States to break off diplomatic relations. On April 6, the United States declared war on the Central Powers. One of the deterrents to an earlier American intervention had been the presence of autocratic tsarist Russia among the Allies. Wilson could conceive of the war only as an idealistic crusade "to make the world safe for democracy." That problem was resolved in March of 1917 by a revolution in Russia that overthrew the tsarist government.

Major Campaigns and Events of World War I	
August 1914	Germans attack in West
August–September 1914	First Battle of the Marne
September 1914	Battles of Tannenberg and the Masurian Lakes
April 1915	British land at Gallipoli, start of Dardanelles campaign
May 1915	Germans sink British ship *Lusitania*
February 1916	Germans attack Verdun
May–June 1916	Battle of Jutland
February 1917	Germans declare unrestricted submarine warfare
March 1917	Russian Revolution
April 1917	United States enters war
November 1917	Bolsheviks seize power
March 1918	Treaty of Brest-Litovsk
March 1918	German offensive in the West
November 1918	Armistice

The Russian Revolution

The March Revolution in Russia was neither planned nor led by any political faction. It was the result of the collapse of the monarchy's ability to govern. Although public opinion had strongly supported Russian entry into the war, the conflict put far too great demands on the resources of the country and the efficiency of the tsarist government.

Nicholas II was weak and incompetent and was suspected of being under the domination of his German wife and the insidious peasant faith healer Rasputin, who was assassinated by a group of Russian noblemen in 1916. Military and domestic failures produced massive casualties, widespread hunger, strikes by workers, and disorganization in the army. The peasant discontent that had plagued the countryside before 1914 did not subside during the conflict. In

1916 the tsar adjourned the Duma, Russian's parliament, and proceeded to rule alone. All political factions were discontented.

The Provisional Government

In early March 1917, strikes and worker demonstrations erupted in Petrograd, as Saint Petersburg had been renamed. The ill-disciplined troops in the city refused to fire on the demonstrators. The tsar abdicated on March 15. The government of Russia fell into the hands of members of the reconvened Duma, who soon formed a provisional government composed chiefly of Constitutional Democrats (Cadets) with Western sympathies.

At the same time, the various socialists, including both Social Revolutionaries and Social Democrats of the Menshevik wing, began to organize the workers into *soviets*, councils of workers and soldiers. Initially, they allowed the provisional government to function without actually supporting it. As relatively orthodox Marxists, the Mensheviks believed that a bourgeois stage of development must come to Russia before the revolution of the proletariat could be achieved. They were willing to work temporarily with the Constitutional Democrats in a liberal regime, but they became estranged when the Cadets failed to control the army or to purge "reactionaries" from the government.

In this climate, the provisional government decided to remain loyal to the existing Russian alliances and to continue the war against Germany. The provisional government thus accepted tsarist foreign policy and associated itself with the source of much domestic suffering and discontent. Its fate was sealed by the collapse of the last Russian offensive in the summer of 1917. Disillusionment with the war, shortages of food and other necessities at home, and the growing demand by the peasants for land reform undermined the government. This occurred even after its leadership had been taken over by the moderate socialist Alexander Kerensky (1881–1970). Moreover, discipline in the army had disintegrated.

Lenin and the Bolsheviks

Ever since April, the Bolshevik wing of the Social Democratic Party had been working against the provisional government. The Germans, in their most successful attempt at subversion, had rushed the brilliant Bolshevik leader V. I. Lenin in a sealed train from his exile in Switzerland across Germany to Petrograd. They hoped that he would cause trouble for the revolutionary government.

Lenin saw the opportunity to achieve the political alliance of workers and peasants that he had discussed before the war. In speech after

Petrograd Munitions workers demonstrating in 1917. [Ria-Novosti/Sovfoto]

The Outbreak of the Russian Revolution

The great Russian Revolution of 1917 started with a series of ill-organized demonstrations in Petrograd early in March. The nature of these actions and the incompetence of the government's response are described in the memoirs of Maurice Paléologue (1859–1944), the French ambassador.

✦ *What elements contributing to the success of the March Revolution emerge from this selection? Why might the army have been unreliable? Why did the two ambassadors think a new ministry should be appointed? What were the grievances of the revolutionaries? Why is there no discussion of the leaders of the revolution? What role did the emperor (tsar) play in these events?*

Monday, March 12, 1917

At half-past eight this morning, just as I finished dressing, I heard a strange and prolonged din which seemed to come from the Alexander Bridge. I looked out: there was no one on the bridge, which usually presents such a busy scene. But, almost immediately, a disorderly mob carrying red flags appeared at the end which is on the right bank of the Neva, and a regiment came towards it from the opposite side. It looked as if there would be a violent collision, but on the contrary the two bodies coalesced. The army was fraternizing with revolt.

Shortly afterwards, someone came to tell me that the Volhynian regiment of the Guard had mutinied during the night, killed its officers and was parading the city, calling on the people to take part in the revolution and trying to win over the troops who still remain loyal.

At ten o'clock there was a sharp burst of firing and flames could be seen rising somewhere on the Liteïny Prospekt which is quite close to the embassy. Then silence.

Accompanied by my military attaché, Lieutenant-Colonel Lavergne, I went out to see what was happening. Frightened inhabitants were scattering through the streets. There was indescribable confusion at the corner of the Liteïny. Soldiers were helping civilians to erect a barricade. Flames mounted from the Law Courts. The gates of the arsenal burst open with a crash. Suddenly the crack of machine-gun fire split the air: it was the regulars who had just taken up position near the Nevsky Prospekt. The revolutionar-

speech, he hammered away on the theme of peace, bread, and land. The Bolsheviks demanded that all political power go to the *soviets*, which they controlled. The failure of the summer offensive encouraged them to attempt a coup, but the effort was a failure. Lenin fled to Finland, and his chief collaborator, Leon Trotsky (1879–1940), was imprisoned.

The failure of a right-wing countercoup gave the Bolsheviks another chance. Trotsky, released from prison, led the powerful Petrograd *soviet.* Lenin returned in October, insisted to his doubting colleagues that the time was ripe to take power, and by the extraordinary force of his personality persuaded them to act. Trotsky organized the coup that took place on November 6 and that concluded with an armed assault on the provisional government. The Bolsheviks, almost as much to their own astonishment as to that of the rest of the world, had come to rule Russia.

The Communist Dictatorship

The victors moved to fulfill their promises and to assure their own security. The provisional government had decreed an election for late November to select a Constituent Assembly. The Social Revolutionaries won a large majority over the Bolsheviks. When the assembly gathered in January, it met for only a day before the Red Army, controlled by the Bolsheviks, dis-

ies replied. I had seen enough to have no doubt as to what was coming. Under a hail of bullets I returned to the embassy with Lavergne who had walked calmly and slowly to the hottest corner out of sheer bravado.

About half-past eleven I went to the Ministry for Foreign Affairs, picking up Buchanan [the British ambassador to Russia] on the way.

I told Pokrovski [the Russian foreign minister] everything I had just witnessed.

"So it's even more serious than I thought," he said.

But he preserved unruffled composure, flavoured with a touch of scepticism, when he told me of the steps on which the ministers had decided during the night:

"The sitting of the Duma has been prorogued to April and we have sent a telegram to the Emperor, begging him to return at once. With the exception of M. Protopopov [the Minister of the Interior, in charge of the police], my colleagues and I all thought that a dictatorship should be established without delay; it would be conferred upon some general whose prestige with the army is pretty high, General Russky for example."

I argued that, judging by what I saw this morning, the loyalty of the army was already too heavily shaken for our hopes of salvation to be based on the use of the "strong hand," and that the immediate appointment of a ministry inspiring confidence in the Duma seemed to me more essential than ever, as there is not a moment to lose. I reminded Pokrovski that in 1789, 1830, and 1848, three French dynasties were overthrown because they were too late in realizing the significance and strength of the movement against them. I added that in such a grave crisis the representative of allied France had a right to give the Imperial Government advice on a matter of internal politics.

Buchanan endorsed my opinion.

Pokrovski replied that he personally shared our views, but that the presence of Protopopov in the Council of Ministers paralyzed action of any kind.

I asked him:

"Is there no one who can open the Emperor's eyes to the real situation?"

He heaved a despairing sigh.

"The Emperor is blind!"

Deep grief was writ large on the face of the honest man and good citizen whose uprightness, patriotism and disinterestedness I can never sufficiently extol.

Maurice Paléologue, An Ambassador's Memoirs *(London: Doubleday & Company, Inc., Hutchinson Publishing Group Ltd., 1924), pp. 221–225. Reprinted by permission.*

persed it. All other political parties also ceased to function in any meaningful fashion. In November and January, the Bolshevik government issued decrees that nationalized the land and turned it over to its peasant proprietors. Factory workers were put in charge of their plants. Banks were taken from their owners and seized for the state, and the debt of the tsarist government was repudiated. Property of the Church reverted to the state.

The Bolshevik government also took Russia out of the war, which they believed benefitted only capitalism. They signed an armistice with Germany in December 1917. On March 3, 1918, they accepted the Treaty of Brest-Litovsk, by which Russia yielded Poland, the Baltic states, and the Ukraine. Some territory in the Transcaucasus region went to Turkey. The Bolsheviks also agreed to pay a heavy war indemnity.

These terms were a terribly high price to pay for peace, but Lenin had no choice. Russia was incapable of renewing the war effort, and the Bolsheviks needed time to impose their rule on a devastated and chaotic Russia. Moreover, Lenin believed that communist revolutions would soon occur across Europe as a result of the war and the Russian example.

Until 1921 the new Bolshevik government met major domestic resistance. A civil war erupted between the "Red" Russians supporting the revolution and the "White" Russians, who opposed it. In the summer of 1918, the Bolshe-

Lenin Establishes His Dictatorship

After the Bolshevik coup in October, elections for the Constituent Assembly were held in November. The results gave a majority to the Social Revolutionary Party and embarrassed the Bolsheviks. Using his control of the Red Army, Lenin closed the Constituent Assembly in January 1918, after it had met for only one day, and established the rule of a revolutionary elite and his own dictatorship. Here is the crucial Bolshevik decree.

✦ *What reasons does Lenin give for closing the legitimately elected Constituent Assembly? What other reasons might he have had? What were the Soviets? Did they have a legitimate claim to the monopoly of political power? Was the dissolution of the assembly a temporary or permanent measure? What defense can be made for the Bolsheviks' action? Is it enough to justify that action?*

The Constituent Assembly, elected on the basis of lists drawn up prior to the October Revolution, was an expression of the old relation of political forces which existed when power was held by the compromisers and the Cadets. When the people at the time voted for the candidates for the Socialist-Revolutionary Party, they were not in a position to choose between the Right Socialist-Revolutionaries, the supporters of the bourgeoisie, and the Left Socialist-Revolutionaries, the supporters of Socialism. Thus the Constituent Assembly, which was to have been the crown of the bourgeois parliamentary republic, could not but become an obstacle in the path of the October Revolution and the Soviet power.

The October Revolution, by giving the power to the Soviets, and through the Soviets to the toiling and exploited classes, aroused the desperate resistance of the exploiters, and in the crushing of this resistance it fully revealed itself as the beginning of the socialist revolution . . . the majority in the Constituent Assembly which met on January 5 was secured by the party of the Right Socialist-Revolutionaries, the party of Kerensky, Avksentyev and Chernov. Naturally, this party refused to discuss the absolutely clear, precise, and unambiguous proposal of the supreme organ of Soviet power, the Central Executive Committee of the Soviets, to recognize the program of the Soviet power, to recognize the "Declaration of Rights of the Toiling and Exploited People," to recognize the October Revolution and the Soviet power. . . .

The Right Socialist-Revolutionary and Menshevik parties are in fact waging outside the walls of the Constituent Assembly a most desperate struggle against the Soviet power. . . .

Accordingly, the Central Executive Committee resolves: The Constituent Assembly is hereby dissolved.

viks murdered the tsar and his family. Loyal army officers continued to fight the revolution and eventually received aid from the Allied armies. Under the leadership of Trotsky, however, the Red Army eventually overcame the domestic opposition. By 1921 Lenin and his supporters were in firm control.

The End of World War I

The collapse of Russia and the Treaty of Brest-Litovsk were the zenith of German success. The Germans controlled eastern Europe and its resources, especially food, and by 1918 they were free to concentrate their forces on the Western Front.

These developments would probably have been decisive had they not been balanced by American intervention. Still, American troops would not arrive in significant numbers for about a year, and both sides tried to win the war in 1917.

An Allied attempt to break through in the West failed disastrously. Losses were heavy and the French army mutinied. The Austrians, supported by the Germans, defeated the Italians at Caporetto and threatened to overrun Italy, until they were checked with the aid of Allied troops. The deadlock continued, but time was running out for the Central Powers.

Germany's Last Offensive

In March 1918, the Germans decided to gamble everything on one last offensive. (In this decision they were persuaded chiefly by Ludendorff, by then quartermaster-general, second-in-command to Hindenburg, but the real leader of the army.) The German army pushed forward and even reached the Marne again but got no farther. They had no more reserves, and the entire nation was exhausted. The Allies, on the other hand, were bolstered by the arrival of American troops in ever-increasing numbers. They were able to launch a counteroffensive that proved to be irresistible. As the Austrian fronts in the Balkans and Italy collapsed, the German high command knew that the end was imminent.

Ludendorff was determined that peace should be made before the German army could be thoroughly defeated in the field and that the responsibility for ending the war should fall on civilians. For some time, he had been the effective ruler of Germany under the aegis of the emperor. He now allowed a new government to be established on democratic principles and to seek peace immediately. The new government, under Prince Max of Baden, asked for peace on the basis of the Fourteen Points that President Wilson had declared as the American war aims. These were idealistic principles, including self-determination for nationalities, open diplomacy, freedom of the seas, disarmament, and establishment of a league of nations to keep the peace. Wilson insisted that he would deal only with a democratic German government, because he wanted to be sure that he was dealing with the German people and not merely their rulers.

German Republican Government Accepts Defeat

The disintegration of the German army forced William II to abdicate on November 9, 1918. The majority branch of the Social Democratic Party proclaimed a republic to prevent the establishment of a soviet government under the control of their radical, Leninist wing, which had earlier broken away as the Independent Socialist Party. Two days later, this republican, socialist-led government signed the armistice that ended the war by accepting German defeat. The German people were, in general, unaware that their army had been defeated in the field and was crumbling. No foreign soldier stood on German soil. Many Germans expected a negotiated and mild settlement. The real peace was quite different and embittered the Germans. Many of them came to believe that Germany had not been defeated but had been tricked by the enemy and betrayed—even stabbed in the back—by republicans and socialists at home.

The victors rejoiced, but they also had much to mourn. The casualties on all sides came to about ten million dead and twice as many wounded. The economic and financial resources of the European states were badly strained. The victorious Allies, formerly creditors to the world, became debtors to the new American colossus, itself barely touched by the calamities of war.

The old international order, moreover, was dead. Russia was ruled by a Bolshevik dictatorship that preached world revolution and the overthrow of capitalism everywhere. Germany was in chaos. Austria-Hungary had disintegrated into a half dozen small states competing for the remains of the ancient empire. These kinds of changes affected the colonial peoples ruled by the European powers, and overseas empires would never again be as secure as they had seemed before the war. Europe was no longer the center of the world, free to interfere when it wished or to ignore the rest of the world if it chose. Four years of horrible war had shattered its easy confidence in material and moral progress. The memory of that war lived on to

Women munitions workers in England. The first World War demanded more from the civilian populations than had previous wars, resulting in important social changes. The demands of the munitions industries and a shortage of men (so many of whom were in uniform) brought many women out of traditional roles at home and into factories and other war work. [Bettmann/Hulton]

shake the nerve of the victorious Western powers as they faced the new conditions of the postwar world.

The Settlement at Paris

The representatives of the victorious states gathered at Versailles and other Parisian suburbs in the first half of 1919. Wilson speaking for the United States, David Lloyd George (1863–1945) for Britain, Georges Clemenceau (1841–1929) for France, and Vittorio Emanuele Orlando (1860–1952) for Italy made up the Big Four. Japan also had an important part in the discussions. The diplomats who met in Paris had a far more difficult task than those who had sat at Vienna a century earlier. Both groups attempted to restore order to the world after long and costly wars. At the earlier conference, however, Metternich and his associates could confine their thoughts to Europe. France had acknowledged defeat and was willing to take part in and uphold the Vienna settlement. The diplomats at Vienna were not much affected by public opinion; and they could draw the new map of Europe along practical lines determined by the realities of power and softened by compromise.

Obstacles Faced by the Peacemakers

The negotiators at Paris in 1919 were less fortunate. They represented constitutional, generally democratic governments, and public opinion had become a mighty force. Though there were secret sessions, the conference often worked in the full glare of publicity. Nationalism had become almost a secular religion, and Europe's many ethnic groups could not be relied on to remain quiet while they were distributed on the map at the whim of the great powers. World War I, moreover, had been transformed by propaganda and especially by the intervention of Woodrow Wilson into a moral crusade to achieve a peace that would be just as well as secure. The Fourteen Points set forth the right of nationalities to self-determination as an absolute value; but in fact the map of Europe could not be drawn to match ethnic groups perfectly with their homelands. All these elements made compromise difficult.

Wilson's idealism, moreover, came into conflict with the more practical war aims of the victorious powers and with many of the secret treaties that had been made before and during the war. The British and French people had been told that Germany would be made to pay for the war. Russia had been promised control of Constantinople in return for recognition of the French claim to Alsace-Lorraine and British control of Egypt. Romania had been promised Transylvania at the expense of Hungary.

Some of the agreements contradicted others. Italy and Serbia had competing claims to the islands and shore of the Adriatic. During the war, the British had encouraged Arab hopes of an independent Arab state carved out of the Ottoman Empire. Those plans, however, contradicted the Balfour Declaration (1917), in which the British seemed to accept Zionist ideology and to promise the Jews a national home in Palestine. Both of these plans conflicted with an Anglo-French agreement to divide the Near East between themselves.

The continuing national goals of the victors presented further obstacles to an idealistic "peace without victors." France was painfully conscious of its numerical inferiority to Germany and of the low birth rate that would keep it inferior. So France was naturally eager to weaken Germany permanently and preserve

French superiority. Italy continued to seek the acquisition of *Italia Irredenta*; Britain continued to look to its imperial interests; Japan pursued its own advantage in Asia. And the United States insisted on freedom of the seas, which favored American commerce, and on its right to maintain the Monroe Doctrine.

Finally, the peacemakers of 1919 faced a world still in turmoil. The greatest immediate threat appeared to be the spread of Bolshevism. While Lenin and his colleagues were distracted by civil war, the Allies landed small armies at several places in Russia to help overthrow the Bolshevik regime. The revolution seemed likely to spread as communist governments were established in Bavaria and Hungary. Berlin also experienced a dangerous communist uprising led by the "Spartacus group." The Allies were sufficiently worried by these developments to support their suppression by right-wing military forces. They even allowed an army of German volunteers to operate against the Bolsheviks in the Baltic states.

Fear of the spread of communism affected the diplomats at Versailles, but it was far from dominant. The Germans played on such fears to get better terms, but the Allies, and especially the French, would not hear of it. Fear of Germany remained the chief concern for France. More traditional and more immediate interests governed the policies of the other Allies.

The Peace

The Paris settlement consisted of five separate treaties between the victors and the defeated powers. Formal sessions began on January 18, 1919, and the last treaty was signed on August 10, 1920 (see Map 26-8). Wilson arrived in Europe to unprecedented popular acclaim. Liberals and idealists expected a new kind of international order achieved in a new and better way, but they were soon disillusioned. "Open covenants openly arrived at" soon gave way to closed sessions in which Wilson, Clemenceau, and Lloyd George made arrangements that seemed cynical to outsiders.

The notion of "a peace without victors" became a mockery when the Soviet Union (as Russia was now called) and Germany were excluded from the peace conference. The Germans were simply presented with a treaty and compelled to accept it, fully justified in their complaint that the treaty had not been negotiated but dictated. The principle of national self-determination was violated many times, as was unavoidable. Still, the diplomats of the small nations were angered by their exclusion from decisions. The undeserved adulation accorded Wilson on his arrival gradually turned into equally undeserved scorn. He had not abandoned his ideals lightly but had merely given way to the irresistible force of reality.

THE LEAGUE OF NATIONS Wilson could make unpalatable concessions without abandoning his ideals because he put great faith in a new instrument for peace and justice, the League of Nations. Its covenant was an essential part of the peace treaty. The league was to be not an international government but a body of sovereign states who agreed to pursue common policies and to consult in the common interest, especially when war threatened. The members promised to submit differences among themselves to arbitration, an international court, or the League Council. Refusal to abide by the results would justify league actions in the form of economic sanctions and even military intervention. The league was unlikely to be effective, however, because it had no armed forces at its disposal. Furthermore, any action required the unanimous consent of its council, consisting permanently of Britain, France, Italy, the United States, and Japan, as well as four other states that had temporary seats. The Covenant of the League bound its members to "respect and preserve" the territorial integrity of all its members; this was generally seen as a device to ensure the security of the victorious powers. The exclusion from the League Assembly of Germany and the Soviet Union further undermined its claim to evenhandedness.

COLONIES Another provision of the covenant dealt with colonial areas. These were to be placed under the "tutelage" of one of the great powers under league supervision and encouraged to advance toward independence. This provision had no teeth, and little advance was made. Provisions for disarmament were equally ineffective. Members of the league remained fully sovereign and continued to pursue their own national interests. Only Wilson put much faith in its future ability to produce peace and

	Austria-Hungary, 1914
	Germany, 1914
	Areas lost by Germany in 1919
	Areas lost by Bulgaria
	Areas lost by Russia
	Areas lost by The Ottoman Empire

MAP 26-8 WORLD WAR I PEACE SETTLEMENT IN EUROPE AND THE MIDDLE EAST   *The map of central and eastern Europe, as well as that of the Middle East, underwent drastic revision after World War I. The enormous territorial losses suffered by Germany, Austria-Hungary, the Ottoman Empire, Bulgaria, and Russia were the other side of the coin represented by gains for France, Italy, Greece, and Romania and by the appearance, or reappearance, of at least eight new independent states from Finland in the north to Yugoslavia in the south. The mandate system for former Ottoman territories outside Turkey proper laid foundations for several new, mostly Arab, states in the Middle East.*

justice. To get the other states to agree to the league, he approved territorial settlements that violated his own principles.

GERMANY   In the West, the main territorial issue was the fate of Germany. Although a united Germany was less than fifty years old, no one seems to have thought of undoing Bismarck's work and dividing it into its component parts. The French would have liked to set the Rhineland up as a separate buffer state, but Lloyd George and Wilson would not permit it. Still, they could not ignore France's need for protection against a resurgent Germany. France received Alsace-Lorraine and the right to work the coal mines of the Saar for fifteen years. Germany west of the Rhine and fifty kilometers east of it was to be a demilitarized zone; Allied troops could stay on the west bank for fifteen years.

In addition to this physical barrier to a new German attack, the treaty provided that Britain and the United States would guarantee aid to France if it were attacked by Germany. Such an attack was made more unlikely by the permanent disarmament of Germany. Its army was limited to 100,000 men on long-term service, its fleet was reduced to a coastal defense force, and it was forbidden to have war planes, submarines, tanks, heavy artillery, or poison gas. As long as these provisions were observed, France would be safe.

THE EAST   The settlement in the East reflected the collapse of the great defeated empires that had ruled it for centuries. Germany lost part of Silesia, and East Prussia was cut off from the rest of Germany by a corridor carved out to give the revived state of Poland access to the sea. The Austro-Hungarian Empire disappeared entirely, giving way to five small successor states. Most of its German-speaking people were gathered in the Republic of Austria, cut off from the Germans of Bohemia and forbidden to unite with Germany.

The Magyars were left with the much-reduced kingdom of Hungary. The Czechs of Bohemia and Moravia joined with the Slovaks and Ruthenians to the east to form Czechoslovakia, and this new state included several million unhappy Germans plus Poles and Magyars. The southern Slavs were united in the kingdom of Serbs, Croats, and Slovenes, or Yugoslavia.

Italy gained Trentino and Trieste. Romania was enlarged by receiving Transylvania from Hungary and Bessarabia from Russia. Bulgaria lost territory to Greece, Romania, and Yugoslavia. Russia lost vast territories in the west. Finland, Estonia, Latvia, and Lithuania became independent states, and most of Poland was carved out of formerly Russian soil.

The old Ottoman Empire also disappeared. The new republic of Turkey was limited to little more than Constantinople and Asia Minor. The former Ottoman territories of Palestine and Iraq came under British control and Syria and Lebanon under French control as mandates of the League of Nations. Germany's former colonies in Africa were divided among Britain, France, Belgium, and South Africa. The German Pacific possessions went to Australia, New Zealand, and Japan.

In theory, the mandate system was meant to have the "advanced nations" govern the former colonies in the interests of the native peoples until the latter became ready to govern themselves. For this purpose they were divided into three categories—A, B, and C—in descending order of their readiness for independence. In practice, most mandated territories were treated as colonies by the powers under whose "tutelage" they came. Not even one Class A mandate had achieved full independence twenty years after the signing of the treaty. Colonialism was to remain a problem even after World War II.

REPARATIONS   Perhaps the most debated part of the peace settlement dealt with reparations for the damage done by Germany during the war. Before the armistice, the Germans promised to pay compensation "for all damages done to the civilian population of the Allies and their property." The Americans judged that the amount would be between $15 billion and $25 billion and that Germany would be able to pay that amount. France and Britain, however, worried about repaying their war debts to the United States, were eager to have Germany pay the full cost of the war, including pensions to survivors and dependents.

There was general agreement that Germany could not afford to pay such a huge sum, whatever it might be, and no sum was fixed at the conference. In the meantime, Germany was to pay $5 billion annually until 1921. At that time, a final figure would be set, which Germany would have to pay in thirty years. The French did not regret the outcome. Either Germany would pay and be bled into impotence, or Germany would refuse to pay and justify French intervention.

To justify these huge reparation payments, the Allies inserted the notorious Clause 231 into the treaty:

The Allied and Associated Governments affirm, and Germany accepts, the responsibility of Germany and her allies for causing all the loss and damage to which the Allied and Associated Governments and their nationals have been subjected as a consequence of the war imposed upon them by aggression of Germany and her allies.

The Germans, of course, did not believe that they were solely responsible for the war and bitterly resented the charge. They had lost territories containing badly needed natural resources. Yet they were presented with an astronomical and apparently unlimited reparations bill. To add insult to injury, they were required to admit to a war guilt that they did not feel.

Finally, to heap insult upon insult, they were required to accept the entire treaty as it was written by the victors, without any opportunity for negotiation. Germany's Prime Minister Philipp Scheidmann (1865–1939) spoke of the treaty as the imprisonment of the German people and asked, "What hand would not wither that binds itself and us in these fetters?" But there was no choice. The Social Democrats and the Catholic Center Party formed a new government, and their representatives signed the treaty. These parties formed the backbone of the Weimar government that ruled Germany until 1933. They never overcame the stigma of accepting the Treaty of Versailles.

Evaluation of the Peace

Few peace settlements have undergone more severe attacks than the one negotiated in Paris in 1919. It was natural that the defeated powers should object to it, but the peace soon came under bitter criticism in the victorious countries as well. Many of the French objected that the treaty tied French security to promises of aid from the unreliable Anglo-Saxon countries. In England and the United States, a wave of bitter criticism arose in liberal quarters because the treaty seemed to violate the idealistic and liberal aims that the Western leaders had professed.

It was not a peace without victors. It did not put an end to imperialism, but attempted to promote the national interests of the winning nations. It violated the principles of national self-determination by leaving significant pockets of minorities outside the borders of their national homelands.

THE ECONOMIC CONSEQUENCES OF THE PEACE   The most influential economic critic of the treaty was John Maynard Keynes (1883–1946), a brilliant British economist who took part in the peace conference. He resigned in disgust when he saw the direction it was taking and wrote a book called *The Economic Consequences of the Peace* (1920). It was a scathing attack, especially on reparations and the other economic aspects of the peace. It was also a skillful assault on the negotiators and particularly on Wilson, who was depicted as a fool and

John Maynard Keynes served on the British delegation to the Paris peace conference of 1919. His denunciation of the Versailles Treaty helped undermine Western willingness to uphold its terms. [Hulton-Deutsch Collection Limited]

a hypocrite. Keynes argued that the Treaty of Versailles was both immoral and unworkable. He called it a Carthaginian peace, referring to the utter destruction of Carthage by Rome after the Third Punic War. He argued that such a peace would bring economic ruin and war to Europe unless it were repudiated.

Keynes's argument had a great effect on the British, who were already suspicious of France and glad of an excuse to withdraw from continental affairs. The decent and respectable position came to be one that supported revision of the treaty in favor of Germany. Even more important was the book's influence in the United States. It fed the traditional American tendency toward isolationism and gave powerful weapons to Wilson's enemies. Wilson's own political mistakes helped prevent American ratification of the treaty. Thus, America was out of the League of Nations and not bound to defend France. Britain, therefore, was also free from its obligation to France. France was left to protect itself without adequate means to do so for long.

Many of the attacks on the Treaty of Versailles are unjustified. It was not a Carthaginian peace. Germany was neither dismembered nor ruined. Reparations could be and were scaled down. Until the great world depression of the 1930s, the Germans recovered a high level of prosperity. Complaints against the peace should also be measured against the peace that the victorious Germans had imposed on Russia at Brest-Litovsk and their plans for a European settlement in case of victory. Both were far more severe than anything enacted at Versailles. The attempt at achieving self-determination for nationalities was less than perfect, but it was the best effort Europe had ever made to do so.

Divisive New Boundaries and Tariff Walls The peace, nevertheless, was unsatisfactory in important ways. The elimination of the Austro-Hungarian Empire, however inevitable, created several serious problems. Economically it was disastrous, for it separated raw materials from manufacturing areas and producers from their markets by new boundaries and tariff walls. In hard times, this separation created friction and hostility that aggravated other quarrels also created by the peace treaties. Poland contained unhappy German and

Ukrainian minorities, and Czechoslovakia was a collection of nationalities that did not find it easy to live together as a nation. Disputes over territories in eastern Europe promoted further tension.

The peace was inadequate on another level, as well. It rested on a victory that Germany did not admit. The Germans believed that they had been cheated rather than defeated. And the high moral principles proclaimed by the Allies undercut the validity of the peace, for it plainly fell far short of those principles.

Failure to Accept Realities Finally, the great weakness of the peace was its failure to accept reality. Germany and Russia must inevitably play an important part in European affairs, yet they were excluded from the settlement and from the League of Nations. Given the many discontented parties, the peace was not self-enforcing; yet no satisfactory machinery for enforcing it was established. The League of Nations was never a serious force for this purpose. It was left to France, with no guarantee of support from Britain and no hope of help from the United States, to defend the new arrangements. Finland, the Baltic states, Poland, Romania, Czechoslovakia, and Yugoslavia were expected to be a barrier to the westward expansion of Russian communism and to help deter a revival of German power. Most of these states, however, would have to rely on France in case of danger, and France was simply not strong enough to protect them if Germany were to rearm.

The tragedy of the Treaty of Versailles was that it was neither conciliatory enough to remove the desire for change, even at the cost of war, nor harsh enough to make another war impossible. The only hope for a lasting peace was that Germany would remain disarmed while the more obnoxious clauses of the peace treaty were revised. Such a policy required continued attention to the problem, unity among the victors, and farsighted leadership; but none of these was consistently present during the next two decades.

———————— ◆ ————————

The outburst of European imperialism in the last part of the nineteenth century brought the Western countries into contact with almost all

the inhabited areas of the world. They intensified their activity in places where they had already been interested. The growth of industry, increased ease of transportation and communication, and the growth of a world economic system all brought previously remote and isolated places into the orbit of the West.

By the time of the outbreak of the war, European nations had divided Africa among themselves for exploitation in one way or another. The vast subcontinent of India had long been a British colony. The desirable parts of China were under European commercial control. Indochina was under French rule and the islands of the Pacific had been divided among the powers. Much of the Near East was under the nominal control of the Ottoman Empire, in its death throes and under European influence. The Monroe Doctrine made Latin America a protectorate of the United States. Japan, pushed out of its isolation, had itself become an imperial power at the expense of China and Korea.

But the world created by the New Imperialism did not last long. What began as yet another Balkan war involving the European powers became a general war that profoundly affected much of the rest of the world. As the terrible war of 1914–1918 dragged on, the real motives that had driven the European powers to fight gave way to public affirmations of the principles of nationalism and self-determination. The peoples under colonial rule took the public statements—and promises sometimes made to them in private—seriously and sought to win their independence and nationhood.

Mostly, they were disappointed by the peace settlement. The establishment of the League of Nations and the system of mandates in place of the previous system of open colonial rule changed little. The British Empire grew even larger as it inherited vast territories from the defeated German and the defunct Ottoman empires. The French retained and expanded their holdings in Africa, the Pacific, and the Near East. The Americans added to the islands they controlled in the Pacific. Japanese imperial ambitions were rewarded at the expense of China.

A glance at the new map of the world could give the impression that the old imperial nations, especially Britain and France, were more powerful than ever, but that impression would be superficial and misleading. The great western European powers had paid an enormous price in lives, money, and will for their victory in the war. Colonial peoples pressed for the rights that were proclaimed as universal by the West but denied to their colonies; and some influential minorities in the countries that ruled them sympathized with colonial aspirations for independence. Tension between colonies and their ruling nations was a cause of serious instability in the world created by the Paris treaties of 1919.

Review Questions

1. To what areas of the world did Europe extend its power after 1870? How and why did European attitudes toward imperialism change after 1870? What features differentiate the New Imperialism from previous imperialistic movements? What features did they have in common?

2. What role in the world did Bismarck envisage for the new Germany after 1871? How successful was he in carrying out his vision? What was Bismarck's attitude toward colonies? Was he wise to tie Germany to Austria-Hungary?

3. Why and in what stages did Britain abandon its policy of "splendid isolation" at the turn of the century? Were the policies it pursued instead wise ones, or should Britain have followed a different course?

4. How did developments in the Balkans lead to the outbreak of World War I? What was the role of Serbia? Of Austria? Of Russia? What was the aim of German policy in July 1914? Did Germany want a general war?

5. Why did Germany lose World War I? Could Germany have won, or was victory never a possibility? Assess the settlement of Versailles. What were its benefits to Europe, and what were its drawbacks? Was the settlement too harsh or too conciliatory? Could it have secured lasting peace in Europe? How might it have been improved?

6. Why was Lenin successful in establishing Bolshevik rule in Russia? What role did Trotsky play? Was it wise policy for Lenin to take Russia out of the War?

Suggested Readings

L. ALBERTINI, *The Origins of the War of 1914,* 3 vols. (1952, 1957). Discursive but invaluable.

M. BALFOUR, *The Kaiser and His Times* (1972). A fine biography of William II.

V. R. BERGHAHN, *Germany and the Approach of War in 1914* (1973). A work similar in spirit to Fischer's 1967 book but stressing the importance of Germany's naval program.

R. BOSWORTH, *Italy and the Approach of the First World War* (1983). A fine analysis of Italian policy.

L. CECIL, *Wilhelm II Prince and Emperor 1859–1900* (1989). The first part of a projected two-volume history of the Kaiser.

S. B. FAY, *The Origins of the World War,* 2 vols. (1928). The best and most influential of the revisionist accounts.

M. FERRO, *The Great War, 1914–1918* (1973). A solid account of the course of World War I.

D. K. FIELDHOUSE, *The Colonial Experience: A Comparative Study from the Eighteenth Century* (1966). An excellent recent study.

F. FISCHER, *Germany's Aims in the First World War* (1967). An influential interpretation that stirred an enormous controversy by emphasizing Germany's role in bringing on the war.

F. FISCHER, *War of Illusions* (1975). A long and diffuse book that tries to connect German responsibility for the war with internal social, economic, and political developments.

I. GEISS, *July 1914* (1967). A valuable collection of documents by a student of Fritz Fischer. The emphasis is on German documents and responsibility.

O. J. HALE, *The Great Illusion 1900–1914* (1971). A fine survey of the period, especially good on public opinion.

M. B. HAYNE, *The French Foreign Office and the Origins of the First World War* (1993). An examination of the work of the influence on French policy of the professionals in the foreign service.

J. N. HORNE, *Labour at War: France and Britain, 1914–1918* (1991). An examination of a major issue on the home fronts.

J. JOLL, *The Origins of the First World War* (1984). A brief but thoughtful analysis.

P. KENNEDY, *The Rise of the Anglo-German Antagonism 1860–1914* (1980). An unusual and thorough analysis of the political, economic, and cultural roots of important diplomatic developments.

J. M. KEYNES, *The Economic Consequences of the Peace* (1920). The famous and influential attack on the Versailles treaty.

V. G. KIERNAN, *European Empires from Conquest to Collapse 1815–1960* (1981). A study of the course of modern European imperialism.

L. LAFORE, *The Long Fuse* (1965). A readable account of the origins of World War I that focuses on the problem of Austria-Hungary.

W. L. LANGER, *The Diplomacy of Imperialism* (1935). A continuation of the study listed next for the years 1890–1902.

W. L. LANGER, *European Alliances and Alignments,* 2nd ed. (1966). A splendid diplomatic history of the years 1871–1890.

D. C. B. LIEVEN, *Russia and the Origins of the First World War* (1983). A good account of the forces that shaped Russian policy.

E. MANTOUX, *The Carthaginian Peace* (1952). A vigorous attack on Keynes's view.

W. J. MOMMSEN, *Theories of Imperialism* (1980). A study of the debate on the meaning of imperialism.

J. STEINBERG, *Yesterday's Deterrent* (1965). An excellent study of Germany's naval policy and its consequences.

Z. STEINER, *Britain and the Origins of the First World War* (1977). A perceptive and informed account of the way British foreign policy was made before the war.

A. J. P. TAYLOR, *The Struggle for Mastery in Europe, 1848–1918* (1954). Clever but controversial.

L. C. F. TURNER, *Origins of the First World War* (1970). Especially good on the significance of Russia and its military plans.

S. R. WILLIAMSON, JR., *Austria-Hungary and the Origins of the First World War* (1991). A valuable new study of a complex subject.

Anxiety over the spread of the Bolshevik Revolution was a fundamental factor of European politics during the 1920s. Images like this Soviet portrait of Lenin as a heroic revolutionary conjured fears among people in the rest of Europe of a political force determined to overturn their social, political, and economic institutions. [Bildarchiv Preussischer Kulturbesitz]

27

Political Experiments of the 1920s

Key Topics in This Chapter
◆ Economic and political disorder in the aftermath of World War I
◆ The Soviet Union's far-reaching political and social experiment
◆ Mussolini and the Fascist seizure of power in Italy
◆ French determination to enforce the Versailles treaty
◆ First Labour government and general strike in Britain
◆ The development of authoritarian governments in all the successor states to the Austrian Empire except Czechoslovakia
◆ Reparations, inflation, political turmoil, and the rise of Nazism in the German Weimar Republic

Experimentation in politics and the pursuit of normality in economic life marked the decade following the conclusion of the Paris peace settlement, also known throughout the period as the Versailles settlement. These treaties, as examined in the last chapter, established a bold new experiment in European diplomatic relations. The Paris settlement instituted the League of Nations and imposed economic and military arrangements that fostered friction among all the powers and deep resentment in Germany. In the Soviet Union, the Bolsheviks, after seizing control of the government in 1917 and then winning the civil war, proceeded to reorganize every aspect of life in Russia. In Italy, the political turmoil and social strains of the postwar era resulted in the emergence of the authoritarian movement known as fascism. In Great Britain, the Labour Party came to power for the first time, and most of Ireland became an independent nation. Through war and revolution the Habsburg Empire collapsed, and its peoples formed several small successor states, only one of which became a successful democracy. Germany, after suffering a humiliating military defeat, jettisoned the imperial monarchy and set out on the experiment of the Weimar Republic, which encountered numerous determined and violent opponents.

Many of these political experiments failed, and the economic and social normality so many Europeans sought proved elusive. By the close of the 1920s, the political path had been paved for the nightmares of brutally authoritarian governments and international aggression that were to mark the 1930s and 1940s. Yet many of the people who had survived the Great War had hoped and worked for a better outcome. Authoritarianism and aggression were not the inescapable destiny of Europe. They emerged from the failure to secure alternative modes of democratic political life and stable international relations and from the inability to achieve long-term economic prosperity.

Political and Economic Factors After the Paris Settlement

New Governments

In 1919 experimental political regimes studded the map of Europe. From Ireland to Russia, new governments were seeking to gain the active support of their citizens and to solve the grievous economic problems caused by the war. In the Soviet Union, the Bolsheviks regarded themselves as forging a new kind of civilization, one built on achieving communism. To that end, they constructed a vast authoritarian state apparatus.

The situation was different elsewhere on the Continent. In many, though not all, countries, the turn to liberal democracy resulted in the right to vote being given to women and previously disenfranchised males. For the first time in European history, the governments handling diplomatic and economic matters were responsible to mass electorates. Even where the authoritarian, military empires of Germany and Austria-Hungary had previously held sway, democratically elected parliamentary governments took form. Their goals were substantially more modest and less utopian than those of the Bolsheviks. Yet to pursue parliamentary politics where it had never been meaningfully practiced proved no simple task. The Wilsonian vision of democratic, self-determined nations foundered on the harsh realities of economics, aggressive nationalism, and revived political conservatism. Too often, nations that had been given democratic, parliamentary government lacked both the will and the political skill to make the new system work. Moreover, in many of the new democracies, important sectors of the citizenry believed that parliamentary politics was inherently corrupt or unequal to great nationalistic enterprises. Economics and politics had become more intimately connected than ever before. The economic and social anxieties of the electorate as well as nationalistic ambitions could and eventually did overcome political scruples.

Demands for Revision of the Paris Settlement

The Paris peace treaties themselves became domestic political issues. Usually the objections arose from nationalistic concerns and resentments. Germany had been humiliated. The arrangements for reparations led to endless haggling over payments. Various national groups in the successor states of eastern Europe also felt that they had been treated unjustly or been denied self-determination. There were demands for further border adjustments. On the other side, the victorious powers, and especially France, often believed that the provisions of the treaty were not being adequately enforced. So, throughout the 1920s, calls either to revise or to enforce the Paris treaties contributed to domestic political turmoil across the Continent. Many political figures were willing to fish in these troubled international waters for a large catch of domestic votes.

Postwar Economic Problems

Along with the move toward political experimentation and the demands for revision of the new international order, there existed a widespread desire to return to the economic prosperity of the prewar years. After 1918, however, it was impossible to restore in the economic realm what American President Warren Harding (1865–1923) would shortly term "normalcy." During the Great War, Europeans had turned the vast military and industrial power that they had created during the previous century against themselves and their civilization. What had been "normal" in economic and social life during the previous half century could not be reestablished.

More than 750,000 British soldiers had perished. The combat deaths for France and Germany were 1,385,000 and 1,808,000, respectively. Russia had lost no fewer than 1,700,000 troops. Hundreds of thousands more from other nations had also been killed. Still more millions had been wounded. These casualties represented not only the waste of human life and talent but also the loss of producers and consumers.

Another casualty of the conflict was the financial dominance and independence of Europe. At the opening of hostilities, Europe had been the financial and credit center of the world. At the close of the fighting, European states were deep in debt to each other and to the United States. The Bolsheviks had repudiated the debt of the tsarist government, much of which was owed to French creditors. Other nations could not pursue this revolutionary course. The Paris settlement had imposed heavy financial obligations on Germany and its allies. The United States refused to ask reparations from Germany but demanded repayment of war debts from its own allies.

On one hand, the reparation and debt structure meant that no nation was fully in control of its own economic life. On the other hand, the absence of international economic cooperation meant that more than ever individual nations felt compelled to pursue or to try to pursue selfish, nationalistic economic aims. It was perhaps the worst of all possible international economic worlds.

The market and trade conditions that had prevailed before 1914 had also changed radically. In addition to the unprecedented loss of human life, much of Europe's transport facilities, mines, and industry had been damaged or destroyed. Russia all but withdrew from the European economic order. The political reconstruction of eastern and central Europe into a multitude of small states broke up the trade region formerly encompassed by Germany and Austria-Hungary. Most of those new states had weak economies hardly capable of competing in modern economic life. The new political boundaries separated raw materials from the factories using them. Railway systems on which finished and unfinished products traveled might now lie under the control of two or more nations. Political and economic nationalism went together. Nations raised new customs barriers where before there had been none.

International trade also followed novel patterns. The United States became less dependent on European production and was now a major competitor. During the war, the belligerents had been forced to sell many of their investments on other continents to finance the conflict. As a consequence, European dominance over the world economy weakened. Slow postwar economic growth or even the decline of economic activity within colonies or former colonies lowered the international demand for European goods. The United States and Japan began to penetrate markets in Latin America and Asia that European producers and traders had previously dominated.

New Roles for Government and Labor

Throughout Europe, the war had given labor new prominence. In every country, the unions had actively supported the war effort. They had ensured labor peace for wartime production. In turn, their members had received better wages, and their leaders had been admitted to high political councils. This wartime cooperation of unions and labor leaders with the various national governments destroyed the internationalism of the prewar labor movement. It also, however, meant that henceforth government could not ignore the demands of labor. After the war, many wages were lowered, but rarely to prewar levels. European workers intended to receive their just share of the fruits of their labor. Collective bargaining and union recognition brought on by the war were also there to stay. This improvement in both the status and the effective influence of labor was one of the most significant social and political changes to flow from World War I.

The social condition of workers seemed to be improving while that of the middle class seemed to be stagnating or declining. Throughout the 1920s, people from the various segments of the middle class remained suspicious of the new role of labor and of socialist political parties. This suspicion and fear of potential loss of property by the middle classes led them to seek to perpetuate the status quo and to fend off further social and economic advances by the working classes. Thus, the European middle classes, once the vanguard of the liberal revolution, became a generally conservative political force in the 1920s. Their conservatism deepened as fear of Bolshevism spread across the Continent.

The Beginning of the Soviet Experiment

The consolidation of the Bolshevik Revolution in Russia established the most extensive and durable of all the twentieth-century authoritarian governments that came to power in the political turmoil of World War I and its aftermath. The Communist Party of the Soviet Union retained power from 1917 until the end of 1991, and its presence influenced the political history of Europe during this century as did no other single factor. The Communist Party was neither a mass party nor a nationalistic one. Its early membership rarely exceeded 1 percent of the Russian population. For several years after 1917, it faced widespread domestic opposition, and the Communist leaders long felt that their hold on the country was insecure. Yet the Communists also regarded their government and their revolution not as local events in a national history but as epoch-making events in the history of the world and the development of humanity. Communism was an exportable commodity that could disrupt the political life of other nations, and throughout the history of the Soviet Union, its leaders sought to export its ideology and doctrines. Fear of communism and determination to stop its spread became one of the leading political forces in western Europe and the United States for most of the rest of the century.

War Communism

Within the Soviet Union, the Red Army under the organizational direction of Leon Trotsky (1879–1940) eventually suppressed internal and foreign military opposition to the new government. The White Russian armies, which fought the Red Army for several years, could not adequately organize themselves, and Allied help was inadequate to defeat the Bolsheviks. The existence of a military threat allowed the Bolsheviks rapidly to pursue authoritarian policies. Within months of the revolution, a new secret police, known as the *Cheka*, appeared.

During the civil war in the Soviet Union hunger and starvation haunted the countryside. Here a group of malnourished children posed for a photograph. [Bildarchiv Preussischer Kulturbesitz]

Throughout the civil war, Lenin had declared that the Bolshevik Party, as the vanguard of the revolution, was imposing the dictatorship of the proletariat. Political and economic administration became highly centralized. All major decisions flowed from the top in a nondemocratic manner. Under the economic policy of "War Communism," the revolutionary government confiscated and then operated the banks, the transport system, and heavy industry. The state also seized grain from the peasants to feed the army and the workers in the cities. The fact of the civil war permitted the Bolsheviks to suppress resistance to this economic policy.

"War Communism" aided the victory of the Red Army. The revolution had survived and triumphed. The policy, however, generated domestic opposition to the Bolsheviks, who in 1920 numbered only about 600,000 members. The alliance of workers and peasants forged by the slogan of "Peace, Bread, and Land" had begun to come apart at the seams. Many Russians were no longer willing to make the sacrifices demanded by the central party bureaucrats. In 1920 and 1921, large strikes occurred in many factories. Discontented peasants resisted the requisition of grain as they had since 1918. In March 1921, the Baltic fleet mutinied at Kronstadt. The Red Army crushed the rebellion with grave loss of life.

Each of these incidents suggested that the proletariat itself was opposing the dictatorship of the proletariat as embodied in the Communist Party. Also, by late 1920 it had become clear that revolution was not going to erupt across the rest of Europe. For the time being, the Soviet Union would be a vast island of revolutionary socialism in the worldwide sea of capitalism.

The New Economic Policy

Under these difficult conditions, Lenin made a crucial strategic retreat. In March 1921, following the Kronstadt mutiny and in the face of continuing peasant resistance to the requisition of grain needed to feed the urban population, he outlined the New Economic Policy, normally called NEP. Apart from what he termed "the commanding heights" of banking, heavy industry, transportation, and international commerce, the government would tolerate private economic

After the Bolshevik Revolution there were many shortages in the cities of the new Soviet Union. This painting shows citizens buying and selling goods in a Moscow street market in the early 1920s. [Bildarchiv Preussischer Kulturbesitz]

enterprise. In particular, peasants could farm for profit. They would pay taxes like other citizens, but they could sell their surplus grain on the open market. The New Economic Policy was in line with Lenin's earlier conviction that the Russian peasantry held the key to the success of the revolution.

After 1921 the countryside did become more stable, and a more secure food supply seemed assured for the cities. Similar free enterprise flourished within light industry and domestic retail trade. The implementation of the New Economic Policy, however, was not fully successful, because there were virtually no consumer goods for the peasants to purchase with the money they received for their grain. Yet by 1927 industrial production had reached its 1913 level. The revolution seemed to have transformed Russia into a land of small, if frequently discontented, family farmers and owners of small, private shops and businesses.

Trotsky Urges the Use of Terror

Leon Trotsky led the Red Army to its victory in the civil war that followed the Bolshevik Revolution in 1918. He later became a major opponent and victim of Stalin. In this discussion of 1920, he explains how terror and intimidation must be used to achieve Communist revolution. He contends that capitalist society itself came to power through the use of force and that only force will allow the working class to establish its dominance. He argues there is no real moral argument against the use of terror and violence. In particular, he directs his remarks toward liberals who thought social change could be achieved by parliamentary means and against the German Marxist socialists, the Kautskians, who had argued that historical forces would bring about the revolution of the working class without the use of violence. These words of Trotsky help explain the fear of Bolshevism that swept across much of Europe immediately after World War I, a fear right-wing politicians manipulated during the 1920s and 1930s.

◆ *How does Trotsky's justification of terror compare with that associated with the Reign of Terror during the French Revolution? How might the circumstances of the Russian Civil War have led Trotsky to these views? Do you agree that the Communist terror advocated by Trotsky differed from the repressive police policies of the tsars?*

The problem of revolution, as of war, consists in breaking the will of the foe, forcing him to capitulate and to accept the conditions of the conqueror. The will, of course, is a fact of the physical world, but in contradistinction to a meeting, a dispute, or a congress, the revolution carries out its object by means of the employment of material resources—though to a lesser degree than war. The bourgeoisie itself conquered power by means of revolts, and consolidated it by the civil war. In the peace period, it retains power by means of a system of repression. As long as class society, founded on the most deep-rooted antago-

Stalin Versus Trotsky

The New Economic Policy had caused sharp disputes within the Politburo, the highest governing committee of the Communist Party. Some members considered the partial return to capitalism a betrayal of Marxist principles. These frictions increased when Lenin's firm hand disappeared. In 1922 he suffered a stroke and never again dominated party affairs. In 1924 Lenin died.

The resulting power vacuum led to an intense struggle for the leadership of the party. Two factions emerged. One was led by Leon Trotsky; the other by Joseph Stalin (1879–1953), who had become general secretary of the party in 1922. Shortly before his death, Lenin had criticized both men but was especially harsh toward Stalin. Stalin's power base, however, lay with the party membership and in the day-to-day management of party affairs. Consequently, he was able to withstand the posthumous strictures of Lenin.

The issue between the two factions was power within the party, but the struggle was fought out over the question of Russia's path toward industrialization and the future of the communist revolutionary movement. Trotsky, speaking for what became known as the left wing, urged rapid industrialization financed through the expropriation of farm production. Agriculture should be collectivized, and the peasants should be made to pay for industrialization. Trotsky further argued that the revolution in Russia could succeed only if new revolutions took place elsewhere. Russia needed the skills and wealth of other nations to build its

nisms, continues to exist, repression remains a necessary means of breaking the will of the opposing side.

Even if, in one country or another, the dictatorship of the proletariat grew up within the external framework of democracy, this would by no means avert the civil war. The question as to who is to rule the country, i.e., of the life or death of the bourgeoisie, will be decided on either side, not by references to the paragraphs of the constitution, but by the employment of all forms of violence. . . .

The question of the form of repression, or of its degree, of course, is not one of "principle." It is a question of expediency. . . .

. . . Terror can be very efficient against a reactionary class which does not want to leave the scene of operations. *Intimidation* is a powerful weapon of policy, both internationally and internally. A victorious war, generally speaking, destroys only an insignificant part of the conquered army, intimidating the remainder and breaking their will. The revolution works in the same way: it kills individ-uals, and intimidates thousands. In this sense, the Red Terror is not distinguishable from the armed insurrection, the direct continuation of which it represents. The State terror of a revolutionary class can be condemned "morally" only by a man who, as a principle, rejects (in words) every form of violence whatsoever—consequently, every war and every rising. For this one has to be merely and simply a hypocritical Quaker.

"But, in that case, in what do your tactics differ from the tactics of Tsarism?", we are asked by the high priests of Liberalism and Kautskianism.

You do not understand this, holy men? We shall explain to you. The terror of Tsarism was directed against the proletariat. The gendarmerie of Tsarism throttled the workers who were fighting for the Socialist order. Our Extraordinary Commissions shoot landlords, capitalists, and generals who are striving to restore the capitalist order. Do you grasp this—distinction? Yes? For us Communists it is quite sufficient.

Leon Trotsky, Terrorism and Communism *(1920; English trans.,* Dictatorship vs. Democracy: A Reply to Karl Kautsky, *New York: Workers' Party of America, 1922), pp. 54, 57–59, as quoted in Robert V. Daniels,* A Documentary History of Communism, *rev. ed., Vol. 1 (Hanover, N.H., and London: University Press of New England, 1984), pp. 121–122.*

The leadership of the Communist Party gathered for this picture at the Party Congress in 1919. Lenin is third from left in the second row and Stalin, next to him, is second from left. [Bildarchiv Preussischer Kulturbesitz]

A Communist Woman Demands
a New Family Life

While Lenin sought to consolidate the Bolshevik revolution against internal and external enemies, there existed within the young Soviet Union a vast utopian impulse to change and reform virtually every social institution that had existed before the revolution or that was associated in the Communists' minds with capitalist society. Alexandra Kollontai (1872–1952) was a spokesperson of the extreme political left within the early Soviet Union. In Communist circles, there had been much speculation on how the end of bourgeois society might change the structure of the family and the position of women. In this passage written in 1920, Kollontai states one of the most idealistic visions of this change. During the years immediately after the revolution, extreme rumors circulated in both Europe and America about sexual and family experimentation in the Soviet Union. Statements such as this fostered such rumors. Kollontai herself later became a supporter of Stalin and a Soviet diplomat.

◆ *Why did Kollontai see the restructuring of the family as essential to the establishment of a new kind of Communist society? Would these changes make people loyal to that society? What changes in society does the kind of economic independence she seeks for women presuppose? What kind of childhood might the children of this society expect to experience when they are the children of the state rather than of specific parents?*

There is no escaping the fact: the old type of family has seen its day. It is not the fault of the Communist State, it is the result of the changed conditions of life. *The family is ceasing to be a necessity of the State,* as it was in the past; on the contrary, it is worse than useless, since it needlessly holds back the female workers from more productive and far more serious work. . . . But on the ruins of the former family we shall soon see a new form rising which will involve altogether different relations between men and women,

---

own economy. As Trotsky's influence within the party waned, he also demanded that party members be permitted to criticize the policies of the government and the party. Trotsky was, however, a latecomer to the advocacy of open discussion. When he had controlled the Red Army, he had been an unflinching disciplinarian.

A faction known as the right wing opposed Trotsky. Its chief ideological voice was that of Nikolai Bukharin (1888–1938), the editor of *Pravda* (*Truth*), the official party paper. Stalin was the major political manipulator of this group. In the mid-1920s, in the face of uncertain economic recovery, this faction pressed for the continuation of Lenin's NEP and for relatively slow industrialization. At the time, this position represented an economic policy based largely on decentralized economic planning and the tolerance of modest free enterprise and small landholdings. Stalin emerged as the victor in these intraparty rivalries.

Stalin had been born in 1879 into a poor family. Unlike the other early Bolshevik leaders, he had not spent a long period of exile in western Europe and was much less intellectual and internationalist in his outlook. He was also much more brutal. As Commissar of Nationalities, Stalin's handling of various recalcitrant national groups within Russia after the revolution had shocked even Lenin, though not enough for Lenin to dismiss him. As the Party General Secretary, a post that party intellectuals disdained as merely clerical, Stalin amassed power through his command of bureaucratic

and which will be *a union of affection and comradeship, a union of two equal members of the Communist society, both of them free, both of them independent, both of them workers.* No more domestic "servitude" of women. No more inequality within the family. No more fear on the part of the woman lest she remain without support or aid with little ones in her arms if her husband should desert her. The woman in the Communist city no longer depends on her husband but on her work. It is not her husband but her robust arms which will support her. There will be no more anxiety as to the fate of her children. The State of the Workers will assume responsibly for these. Marriage will be purified of all its material elements, of all money calculations, which constitute a hideous blemish on family life in our days. . . .

The woman who is called upon to struggle in the great cause of the liberation of the workers—such a woman should know that in the new State there will be no more room for such petty divisions as were formerly understood: "These are my own children, to them I owe all my maternal solicitude, all my affection; those are your children, my neighbour's children; I am not concerned with them. I have enough to do with my own." Henceforth the worker-mother, who is conscious of her social function, will rise to a point where she no longer differentiates between *yours* and *mine;* she must remember that there are henceforth only *our* children, those of the Communist State, the common possession of all the workers.

The Worker's State has need of a new form of relation between the sexes. The narrow and exclusive affection of the mother for her own children must expand until it embraces all the children of the great proletarian family. In place of the indissoluble marriage based on the servitude of woman, we shall see rise the free union, fortified by the love and mutual respect of the two members of the Workers' State, equal in their rights and in their obligations. In place of the individual and egotistic family there will arise a great universal family of workers, in which all the workers, men and women, will be, above all, workers, comrades.

Alexandra Kollontai, Communism and the Family, *as reprinted in Rudolf Schlesinger, ed. and trans.,* The Family in the USSR *(London: Routledge and Kegan Paul, 1949), pp. 67–69.*

and administrative methods. He was neither a brilliant writer nor an effective public speaker. He did, however, master the crucial, if dull, details of party structure, including admission to the party and promotion within it. That mastery meant that he had the support of the lower levels of the party apparatus when he clashed with other leaders.

In the mid-1920s, Stalin expediently supported Bukharin's position on economic development. In 1924 he also enunciated, in opposition to Trotsky, the doctrine of "socialism in one country." He urged that socialism could be achieved in Russia alone. Russian success did not depend on the fate of revolutions elsewhere. Stalin thus nationalized the previously international scope of the Marxist revolution. He cunningly used his control over the Central Committee of the Communist Party to edge out Trotsky and his supporters.

By 1927 Trotsky had been removed from all his offices, expelled from the party, and exiled to Siberia. In 1929 he was forced out of Russia and eventually moved to Mexico, where he was murdered in 1940, presumably by one of Stalin's agents. With Trotsky defeated, Stalin was firmly in control of the Soviet state. It remained to be seen where he would take it and what "socialism in one country" would mean in practice.

The Third International

The success of the revolution in Russia and the outlook of its leaders divided socialist parties and socialist movements in the rest of Europe. As already noted, the early leaders of the Bolshevik Revolution believed they were beginning a new era of history and that their revolution would spread. Even after Stalin's declaration of "socialism in one country," the Soviet Union worked to expand communism.

In 1919 the Soviet Communists founded the Third International of the European socialist movement, better known as the Comintern. The Comintern wished to make the Bolshevik model of socialism, as developed by Lenin, the rule for all socialist parties outside the Soviet Union. In 1920, a year after its inception, the Comintern imposed its Twenty-one Conditions on any other socialist party that wished to join it. The conditions included acknowledgment of leadership from Moscow, rejection of reformist or revisionist socialism, and repudiation of previous socialist leaders. In effect, the Comintern sought to destroy all democratic socialism.

The decision whether to accept these conditions split every major European socialist party. As a result, separate Communist and social democratic parties emerged in many countries. The Communist parties modeled themselves after the Soviet party, and Moscow dictated their policies. The social democratic parties attempted to pursue both social reform and liberal parliamentary politics. Throughout the 1920s and early 1930s, the Communists and social democrats fought each other more intensely than they fought either capitalism or conservative political parties. Their fierce conflict was one of the fundamental features of the interwar European political landscape.

These policies of the Comintern directly and importantly affected the rise of the Fascists and the Nazis in western Europe. It is difficult to exaggerate the fears that Soviet political rhetoric and Communist party activity roused throughout Europe during the 1920s and 1930s. These fears, often exaggerated, were repeatedly manipulated by conservative and right-wing political groups. The presence of separate Communist parties in western Europe meant that right-wing politicians always had a convenient target that they could justly accuse of seeking to overthrow the existing government and to impose Soviet-style political and economic experiments in their respective nations. Furthermore, right-

wing politicians continued to accuse the democratic socialist parties of supporting policies that might facilitate a Communist takeover. The division of the European political left also meant that right-wing political movements rarely had to confront a united left-wing opposition.

The Fascist Experiment in Italy

Italy witnessed the first authoritarian political experiment in western Europe that arose in part from fears of the spread of Bolshevism. From the Italian Fascist movement of Benito Mussolini (1883–1945) came the general term *fascist*, frequently used to describe a number of right-wing dictatorships that arose across Europe between the wars.

Both historians and political scientists disagree about the exact meaning of *fascism* as a political term. Most scholars agree, however, that the government regimes regarded as fascist were antidemocratic, anti-Marxist, antiparliamentary, and frequently anti-Semitic. These governments claimed to hold back the spread of Bolshevism, which because of Soviet rhetoric and the activity of domestic Communist parties seemed at the time a real threat. They sought to make the world safe for the middle class, small businesses, owners of moderate amounts of property, and small farmers. The fascist regimes rejected the political inheritance of the French Revolution and of nineteenth-century liberalism. Fascist movements were invariably nationalistic in response to the feared international expansion of communism.

Fascists believed that normal parliamentary politics and parties sacrificed national honor and greatness to petty disputes. They wanted to overcome the class conflict of Marxism and the party conflict of liberalism by consolidating the various groups and classes within the nation for great national purposes. As Mussolini declared in 1931, "The fascist conception of the state is all-embracing, and outside of the state no human or spiritual values can exist, let alone be desirable."[1] The fascist governments were usually single-party dictatorships characterized by terrorism and police surveillance. These fascist

[1] *Quoted in Denis Mack Smith,* Italy: A Modern History *(Ann Arbor: University of Michigan Press, 1959), p. 412.*

The Third International Issues Conditions of Membership

After the Russian Revolution, the Russian Communist Party organized the Third Communist International. Any Communist party outside the Soviet Union was required to accept these twenty-one conditions, adopted in 1920, to join the International. In effect, this program demanded that all such parties adopt a distinctly revolutionary program. They also needed to cease operating as legal parties within their various countries. By this means, the Soviet Union sought to achieve leadership of the socialist movement throughout Europe. The non-Russian socialist parties quickly split into social democratic parties that remained independent of Moscow and Communist parties that adopted the policy imposed by the Russian Communist Party.

◆ What are the major forms of revolutionary agitation that these conditions assume? Why was the Russian Communist Party willing to forgo all alliances with other socialist parties that would not declare and rename themselves Communist? How could this document and the organization it established be used by conservative and right-wing political groups elsewhere in Europe?

1. The daily propaganda and agitation must bear a truly communist character and correspond to the program and all the decisions of the Third International. All the organs of the press that are in the hands of the party must be edited by reliable communists who have proved their loyalty to the cause of the proletarian revolution. . . .

. . . .

4. The obligation to spread communist ideas includes the particular necessity of persistent, systematic propaganda in the army. . . .

5. It is necessary to carry on systematic and steady agitation in the rural districts. . . .

. . . .

14. Every party that desires to belong to the Communist International must give every possible support to the Soviet Republics in their struggle against all counterrevolutionary forces. . . .

. . . .

16. All decisions of the congresses of the Communist International . . . are binding on all parties affiliated to the Communist International. . . .

17. In connection with all this, all parties desiring to join the Communist International must change their names. Every party that wishes to join the Communist International must bear the name: Communist party of such-and-such country. This question as to name is not merely a formal one, but a political one of great importance. The Communist International has declared a decisive war against the entire bourgeois world and all the yellow social democratic parties. Every rank-and-file worker must clearly understand the difference between the communist parties and the old official "social democratic" or "socialist" parties which have betrayed the cause of the working class.

18. Members of the party who reject the conditions and thesis of the Communist International, on principle, must be expelled from the party.

Helmut Gruber, ed., International Communism in the Era of Lenin: A Documentary History (Garden City, N.Y.: Doubleday, 1972), pp. 241–246.

dictatorships, in contrast to the Communist Party of the Soviet Union, were rooted in the base of mass political parties.

The Rise of Mussolini

The Italian *Fasci di Combattimento* ("Bands of Combat") was founded in 1919 in Milan. Its members came largely from Italian war veterans who felt that the Paris conference had cheated Italy of the hard-won fruits of victory. They especially resented Italy's failure to gain Fiume (now Rijeka) on the northeast coast of the Adriatic Sea. They also feared the spread of socialism and the effects of inflation.

Their leader, Benito Mussolini, had been born the son of a blacksmith. He had worked as a schoolteacher and a day laborer before becoming active in Italian socialist politics. By 1912 he had become editor of the socialist newspaper *Avanti* (meaning "forward"). In 1914 Mussolini broke with the socialists and supported Italian entry into the war on the side of the Allies. His interventionist position lost him the editorship of *Avanti*. He then established his own paper, *Il Popolo d'Italia* (*The People of Italy*). Later he served in the army and was wounded. In 1919, although of some prewar political stature, Mussolini was simply one of many Italian politicians, and his *Fasci* organization was just one more small political group in a country full of them. As a politician, Mussolini was an opportunist par excellence. He could change his ideas and principles to suit every new occasion. Action for him was always more important than thought or rational justification. His one real goal was political survival.

POSTWAR ITALIAN POLITICAL TURMOIL Postwar Italian politics was a muddle. During the conflict, the Italian Parliament had virtually ceased to function, and it allowed ministers to rule by decree. Many Italians, however, were already dissatisfied with the parliamentary system. Italian nationalists—not just Mussolini's followers—felt that Italy had not been treated as a great power at the peace conference and had not received the territories it deserved.

The main spokesman for this discontent was the extreme nationalist writer Gabriele D'Annunzio (1863–1938). In 1919 he seized Fiume with a force of patriotic Italians. He was eventually driven out, but D'Annunzio had shown how a nongovernmental military force could be put to political use. Moreover, the use of force against D'Annunzio embarrassed the Italian government and made it appear less patriotic than the ultranationalists.

Between 1919 and 1921, Italy also experienced considerable internal social turmoil. Many industrial strikes occurred, and workers occupied factories. Peasants seized uncultivated land from large estates. Parliamentary and constitutional government seemed incapable of dealing with this unrest. The Socialist Party had captured a plurality of seats in the Chamber of Deputies in the 1919 election. The sharp division between socialists and Communists had not yet emerged, and so the Socialist Party included many people who were soon to become Communists. A new Catholic Popular Party had also done well in the election. Both appealed to the working and agrarian classes. Neither party, however, would cooperate with the other; parliamentary deadlock resulted. Under these conditions, many Italians honestly and still others conveniently believed that the social upheaval and political paralysis would lead to a Communist revolution.

EARLY FASCIST ORGANIZATION Initially, Mussolini was uncertain of the direction of the political winds. He first supported the factory occupations and land seizures. Never one to be concerned with consistency, however, he soon reversed himself. He had discovered that many upper-class and middle-class Italians, pressured by inflation and fearing the loss of their property, had no sympathy for the workers or the peasants. They wanted order rather than some vague social justice that might harm their own interests.

Consequently, Mussolini and his Fascists took direct action in the face of the government inaction. They formed local squads of terrorists who disrupted Socialist Party meetings, beat up Socialist leaders, and intimidated Socialist supporters. They attacked strikers and farm workers and protected strikebreakers. Conservative land and factory owners were grateful. The officers and institutions of the law simply ignored the crimes of the Fascist squads. By early 1922 the Fascists had turned to intimidation through arson, beatings, and murder against local officials in cities such as Ferrara, Ravenna, and Milan. They controlled the local government in much of northern Italy.

MARCH ON ROME In the election of 1921, Italian voters sent Mussolini and thirty-four of his followers to the Chamber of Deputies. Their importance grew as the local Fascists gained more direct power. The movement now had hundreds of thousands of supporters. In October 1922, the Fascists, dressed in their characteristic black shirts, began a march on Rome. King Victor Emmanuel III (r. 1900–1946), because of both personal and political concerns, refused to sign a decree that would have authorized the army to stop the marchers. Probably no other single decision so ensured a Fascist seizure of power. The cabinet resigned in protest. On October 29, the monarch telegraphed Mussolini in Milan and asked him to become prime minister. The next day, Mussolini arrived in Rome by sleeping car and greeted his followers as head of the government when they entered the city.

Technically, Mussolini had come into office by legal means. The monarch had the constitutional authority to appoint the prime minister. Mussolini, however, had no majority or even near majority in the Chamber of Deputies. Behind the legal facade of his coming to power lay months of terrorist disruption and intimidation and the threat of the Fascist march itself. The non-Fascist politicians, whose ineptitude had prepared the way for Mussolini, believed that his ministry, like others since 1919, would be brief. They did not comprehend that he was not a traditional Italian politician.

The Fascists in Power

Mussolini had not really expected to be appointed prime minister. He moved cautiously to shore up his support and to consolidate his power. His success was the result of the impotence of his rivals, his own effective use of his office, his power over the masses, and his sheer ruthlessness. On November 23, 1922, the king and Parliament granted Mussolini dictatorial authority for one year to bring order to local and regional government. Wherever possible, Mussolini appointed Fascists to office.

REPRESSION OF OPPOSITION Late in 1924, under Mussolini's guidance, Parliament changed the election law. Previously, parties had been represented in the Chamber of Deputies in proportion to the popular vote cast for them. According to the new election law, the party that gained the largest popular vote (if at least 25 percent) received two-thirds of the seats in the chamber. Coalition government, with all its compromises and hesitant policies, would no longer be necessary. In the election of 1924, the Fascists won a great victory and complete control of the Chamber of Deputies. They used that majority to end legitimate parliamentary life. A

Mussolini poses with supporters the day after the Black Shirt March on Rome intimidated the King of Italy into making him Prime Minister. [Bildarchiv Preussischer Kulturbesitz]

Mussolini Heaps Contempt on Political Liberalism

The political tactics of the Italian Fascists wholly disregarded the liberal belief in the rule of law and the consent of the governed. In 1923 Mussolini explained why the Fascists so hated and repudiated these liberal principles. Note his emphasis on the idea of the twentieth century as a new historical epoch requiring a new kind of politics and his undisguised praise of force in politics.

◆ *Who would be some nineteenth-century liberal political leaders included in Mussolini's attack? Why might Mussolini's audience have been receptive to these views? What events or developments within liberal states allowed Mussolini to portray liberalism as so corrupt and powerless?*

Liberalism is not the last word, nor does it represent the definitive formula on the subject of the art of government. . . . Liberalism is the product and the technique of the 19th century. . . . It does not follow that the Liberal scheme of government, good for the 19th century, for a century, that is, dominated by two such phenomena as the growth of capitalism and the strengthening of the sentiment of nationalism, should be adapted to the 20th century, which announces itself already with characteristics sufficiently different from those that marked the preceding century. . . .

I challenge Liberal gentlemen to tell if ever in history there has been a government that was based solely on popular consent and that renounced all use of force whatsoever. A government so constructed there has never been and never will be. Consent is an ever-changing thing like the shifting sand on the sea coast. It can never be permanent: It can never be complete. . . . If it be accepted as an axiom that any system of government whatever creates malcontents, how are you going to prevent this discontent from overflowing and constituting a menace to the stability of the State? You will prevent it by force. By the assembling of the greatest force possible. By the inexorable use of this force whenever it is necessary. Take away from any government whatsoever force—and by force is meant physical, armed force—and leave it only its immortal principles, and that government will be at the mercy of the first organized group that decides to overthrow it. Fascism now throws these lifeless theories out to rot. . . . The truth evident now to all who are not warped by [liberal] dogmatism is that men have tired of liberty. They have made an orgy of it. Liberty is today no longer the chaste and austere virgin for whom the generations of the first half of the last century fought and died. For the gallant, restless and bitter youth who face the dawn of a new history there are other words that exercise a far greater fascination, and those words are: order, hierarchy, discipline. . . .

Know then, once and for all, that Fascism knows no idols and worships no fetishes. It has already stepped over, and if it be necessary it will turn tranquilly and step again over, the more or less putrescent corpse of the Goddess of Liberty.

Benito Mussolini, "Force and Consent" (1923), as trans. in Jonathan F. Scott and Alexander Baltzly, eds., Readings in European History Since 1814 (New York: F. S. Crofts, 1931), pp. 680–682.

series of laws passed in 1925 and 1926 permitted Mussolini, in effect, to rule by decree. In 1926 all other political parties were dissolved. By the close of that year, Mussolini had transformed Italy into a single-party dictatorial state.

Their growing dominance over the government had not, however, diverted the Fascists from their course of violence and terror. Fascists were put in charge of the police force, and the terrorist squads became a government militia.

In late 1924 their thugs murdered Giacomo Matteotti (1885–1924), a leading non-Communist socialist leader and member of Parliament. He had persistently criticized Mussolini and had exposed the criminality of the Fascist movement. In protest against the murder, most opposition deputies withdrew from the Chamber of Deputies. That tactic gave Mussolini an even freer hand. The deputies were refused readmission.

PARALLEL STRUCTURE OF PARTY AND GOVERNMENT The parallel organizations of the party and the government sustained support for the regime. For every government institution, there was a corresponding party organization. The Fascist Party thus dominated the political structure at every level. When all other political parties were outlawed, the citizens had to look to the Fascists in their community for political favors. They also knew the high price of opposition. By the late 1920s, the Grand Council of the party, which Mussolini controlled, had become an organ of the state. It decided who would stand for election to the Chamber of Deputies and on which policies the chamber would vote.

The party used propaganda to great effect. A cult of personality surrounded Mussolini. His skills in oratory and his general intelligence allowed him to hold his own with both large crowds and prominent individuals, foreign as well as Italian. Many respectable Italians tolerated and even admired Mussolini because they believed that he had saved them from Bolshevism. Those who did have the courage to oppose him were usually driven into exile, and some, like Matteotti, were murdered.

ACCORD WITH THE VATICAN Mussolini made one important domestic departure that brought him significant political dividends. Through the Lateran Accord of February 1929, the Roman Catholic church and the Italian state made peace with each other. Ever since the armies of Italian unification had seized papal lands in the 1860s, the Church had been hostile to the state. The popes had remained secluded in the Vatican after 1870. The agreement of 1929 recognized the pope as the temporal ruler of Vatican City. The Italian government agreed to pay an indemnity to the papacy for the territory it had confiscated. The state also recognized Catholicism as the religion of the nation, exempted Church property from taxes, and allowed Church law to govern marriage. The Lateran Accord brought further respectability to Mussolini's authoritarian regime.

Joyless Victors

France and Great Britain, with the aid of the United States, had won the war. France became the strongest military power on the Continent. Britain had escaped with almost no physical damage. Both nations, however, had lost vast

With the Lateran Accord of February 11, 1929, Mussolini made peace with the Roman Catholic Church, gaining respectability for his regime. Cardinal Gasparri, sitting on Mussolini's right, signed the agreement for the Vatican. [Archive Photos]

numbers of young men in the conflict. Their economies were weakened, their overseas investments and power much diminished. Compared with events in Russia and Italy, the interwar political development of the two major democracies seems rather tame. Neither experienced a revolution or a shift to authoritarian government. Yet this surface calm was largely illusory. Both France and Britain were troubled democracies. To neither did victory in war bring the good life in peace.

France: The Search for Security

At the close of World War I, as after Waterloo, the revolution of 1848, and the defeat of 1871, the French voters elected a doggedly conservative Chamber of Deputies. The preponderance of military officers in blue uniforms among its members led to the nickname of the "Blue Horizon Chamber." The overwhelmingly conservative character of the chamber was registered in 1920 when it defeated Georges Clemenceau's bid for the presidency. The crucial factor had been, of all things, the alleged leniency of the Paris treaties and Clemenceau's failure to establish a separate Rhineland state. The deputies wanted to achieve future security against Germany and Russian communism. They intended to make as few concessions to domestic social reform as possible. The 1920s were marked by frequent changes of ministries and drift in domestic policy. The political turnstile remained ever active. Between the end of the war and January 1933, France was governed by no fewer than twenty-seven different cabinets.

NEW ALLIANCES During the first five years after the conclusion of the Paris settlement, France accepted its role as the leading European power. The French plan was to enforce strictly the clauses of the treaty that were meant to keep Germany weak and also to build a system of eastern alliances to replace the prewar alliance with Russia. In 1920 and 1921, three eastern states that had much to lose from revision of the Versailles treaty—Czechoslovakia, Romania, and Yugoslavia—formed the Little Entente. Before long, France made military alliances with these states and with Poland. A border dispute

with Czechoslovakia prevented the Poles from joining the Little Entente, but Poland's independence depended on the maintenance of the Paris settlement.

This new system of eastern pacts was the best France could do, but it was far weaker than the old Franco-Russian alliance. Even combined, the new states were no match for the former power of tsarist Russia, and they were neither united nor reliable. Poland and Romania were more concerned about Russia than about Germany, and the main target of the Little Entente was Hungary. If one of these states was threatened by a resurgent Germany, it could not rely on the others to come to its aid.

The formation of this new alliance system heightened the sense of danger and isolation felt by the two excluded powers, Germany and the Soviet Union. In 1922, while the European states were holding an economic conference at Genoa, the Russians and the Germans met at nearby Rapallo and signed a treaty of their own. It established diplomatic and economic relations that proved useful to each of them. Although the treaty contained no secret political or military clauses, other governments suspected that such arrangements did exist. And it is now known that the Germans did help train the Russian army, and their own army got valuable experience in the use of tanks and planes in the Soviet Union. Rapallo confirmed the French in their belief that Germany would not live up to the terms of the Versailles treaty and helped move them to strong action.

QUEST FOR REPARATIONS In early 1923 the Allies, and France in particular, declared Germany to be in technical default of its reparations payments. Raymond Poincaré (1860–1934), France's powerfully nationalistic prime minister, decided to teach the Germans a lesson and to force them to comply. On January 11, 1923, to ensure receipt of the hard-won reparations, the French government ordered its troops to occupy Germany's borderland Ruhr mining and manufacturing district. In response, the German government ordered passive resistance. This policy amounted to calling a general strike in the largest industrial region of Germany. Confronted with this tactic, Poincaré sent French civilians to run the German mines and railroads. France prevailed.

The French invasion of the German Ruhr began a crisis that brought strikes and rampant inflation in Germany. Here French troops have commandeered a German locomotive during one of the strikes. [UPI/Bettmann Newsphotos]

The Germans paid, but France's victory was costly. The English were alienated by the French heavy-handedness and took no part in the occupation. They became more suspicious of France and more sympathetic to Germany. The cost of the Ruhr occupation, moreover, vastly increased French as well as German inflation and hurt the French economy. The Ruhr invasion demonstrated how the uncertainties surrounding the Versailles system could harm even the nations whom it was intended to benefit.

In 1924 Poincaré's conservative ministry gave way to a coalition of leftist parties, the so-called *Cartel des Gauches,* led by Edouard Herriot (1872–1957). The new cabinet recognized the Soviet Union and adopted a more conciliatory policy toward Germany. This policy was the work of Aristide Briand (1862–1932), who was foreign minister for the remainder of the decade. He championed the League of Nations and tried to persuade France that its military power did not give it unlimited influence in the foreign affairs of Europe.

Under the leftist coalition, a mild inflation also occurred. It had begun under the conservatives but picked up intensity in 1925. When the value of the franc fell sharply on the international money market in 1926, Poincaré returned to office as head of a national government of several parties. The value of the franc recovered somewhat, and inflation cooled. For the rest of the 1920s, the conservatives remained in power, and France enjoyed a general prosperity that lasted until 1931, longer than in any other nation.

Great Britain: Economic Confusion

World War I profoundly changed British politics if not the political system. In 1918 Parliament expanded the electorate to include all men aged twenty-one and women aged thirty. (In 1928 the age for women voters was also lowered to twenty-one.) The prewar structure of parties and leadership also shifted. A coalition cabinet of Liberal, Conservative, and Labour ministers had directed the war effort. The wartime ministerial participation of the Labour Party helped dispel its radical image. For the Liberal Party, however, the conflict brought further division.

Until 1916 Liberal Prime Minister Herbert Asquith (1852–1928) had presided over the cabinet. As disagreements over war management developed, he was ousted by fellow Liberal David Lloyd George (1863–1945). The party split sharply between followers of the two men. In 1918, against the wishes of both the Labour Party and the Asquith Liberals, Lloyd George decided to maintain the coalition through the tasks of the peace conference and the domestic reconstruction. In December 1918, the wartime coalition, now minus its Labour members, won a stunning victory at the polls. Lloyd George, however, could thereafter remain prime minister only as long as his dominant Conservative partners wished to keep him.

During the election campaign, there had been much talk about creating "a land fit for heroes to live in." It did not happen. Except for the three years immediately after the war, the British economy was depressed throughout the 1920s. There was no genuine postwar recovery. Unemployment never dipped below 10 percent and often hovered near 11 percent. There were never fewer than a million workers unemployed. Government insurance programs to cover unemployed workers, widows, and orphans were expanded. There was no similar meaningful expansion in the number of jobs available. From 1922 onward, accepting the "dole" with little expectation of future employment became a wretched and degrading way of life for scores of thousands of poor British families.

THE FIRST LABOUR GOVERNMENT   In October 1922, the Conservatives replaced Lloyd George with Andrew Bonar Law (1858–1923), one of their own. A Liberal would never again be prime minister. Stanley Baldwin (1867–1947) soon replaced Law, who had fallen victim to throat cancer. Baldwin decided to attempt to cure Britain's economic plight by abandoning free trade and imposing protective tariffs. The voters rejected that policy in 1923. In the election, the Conservative Party lost its majority in the House of Commons, but only votes from both Liberal and Labour party members could provide an alternative majority.

Labour had elected the second largest group of members to the Commons. Consequently, in December 1923, King George V (r. 1910–1936) asked Ramsay MacDonald (1866–1937) to form the first Labour ministry in British history. The Liberal Party did not serve in the cabinet but provided the necessary votes in the House of Commons to give Labour a working majority.

The Labour Party was socialistic in its platform, but democratic and distinctly nonrevolutionary. The party had expanded beyond its early trade-union base. MacDonald himself had opposed World War I and for a time had also broken with the party. His own version of socialism owed little, if anything, to Marx. His program consisted of plans for extensive social reform rather than for the nationalization or public seizure of industry. A sensitive politician, if not a great leader, MacDonald understood that the most important task facing his govern-

ment was proving to the nation that the Labour Party was both respectable and responsible. His nine months in office achieved that goal, if little else of major importance. The establishment of Labour as a viable governing party signaled the permanent demise of the Liberal Party. It has continued to exist, but the bulk of its voters have drifted into either the Conservative or the Labour ranks.

THE GENERAL STRIKE OF 1926   The Labour government fell in the autumn of 1924 over charges of inadequate prosecution of a Communist writer. Stanley Baldwin returned to office, where he remained until 1929. The stagnant economy remained uppermost in the public mind. Business and political leaders continued to believe that all would be well if they could restore the prewar conditions of trade. A major element in these conditions had been the gold standard as the basis for international trade. In 1925 the Conservative government returned to the gold standard, abandoned during the war, in hopes of recreating the former monetary stability. The government, however, set the conversion rate for the pound too high against other currencies and thus, in effect, raised the price of British goods to foreign customers.

To make their products competitive on the world market, British management attempted to lower prices by cutting wages. The coal industry was the sector most directly affected by the wage cuts. It was inefficient and poorly managed and had been in trouble since the end of the war.

Labor relations in the coal industry long had been unruly. In 1926, after cuts in wages and a breakdown in negotiations, the coal miners went on strike. Soon thereafter, in May 1926, sympathetic workers in other industries engaged in a general strike lasting nine days. There was much tension but little violence. In the end, the miners and the other unions capitulated. With such high levels of unemployment, organized labor was in a weak position. After the general strike, the Baldwin government attempted to reconcile labor primarily through new housing and reforms in the poor laws. Despite the economic difficulties of these years, the actual standard of living of most British workers, including those receiving government insurance payments, actually improved.

Stanley Baldwin was the Conservative Party Prime Minister during the general strike of 1926. His solid, calm appearance suggested to many voters the qualities most needed in their government. [UPI/Bettmann]

EMPIRE   World War I also modified Britain's imperial position. The aid given by the dominions, such as Canada and Australia, demonstrated a new independence on their part. Empire was a two-way proposition. The idea of self-determination as applied to Europe filtered into imperial relationships. In India, the Congress Party, led by Mohandas Gandhi (1869–1948), was beginning to attract widespread support. The British started to talk more about eventual self-government for India.

Moreover, during the 1920s the government of India achieved the right to impose tariffs to protect its own industry rather than for the advantage of British manufacturers. British textile producers no longer had totally free access to the vast Indian market.

IRELAND   A new chapter was written in the unhappy relations between Britain and Ireland during and after the war. In 1914 the Irish Home Rule Bill had passed Parliament, but its implementation was postponed until after the war. As the war dragged on, Irish nationalists determined to wait no longer. On Easter Monday in April 1916, a nationalist uprising occurred in Dublin. It was the only rebellion of a national group to occur against any government engaged in the war. The British suppressed it in less than a week but then made a grave tactical blunder. They executed the Irish nationalist leaders who had been responsible for the uprising. Overnight those rebels became national martyrs. Leadership of the nationalist cause quickly shifted from the Irish Party in Parliament to the extremist Sinn Fein ("Ourselves Alone") movement.

In the election of 1918, the Sinn Fein Party won all but four of the Irish parliamentary seats outside Ulster. They refused to go to the Parliament at Westminster. Instead they constituted themselves into a Dail Eireann, or Irish Parliament. On January 21, 1919, they declared Irish independence. The military wing of Sinn Fein became the Irish Republican Army (IRA).

Eamon De Valera inspects troops of the Irish Republican Army during the Irish Civil War. [Archive Photos]

The first president was Eamon De Valera (1882–1975), who had been born in the United States. What amounted to a guerrilla war broke out between the IRA and the British army supported by auxiliaries known as the Black and Tans. There was intense bitterness and hatred on both sides.

In late 1921, the two governments began secret negotiations. In the treaty concluded in December 1921, the Irish Free State took its place beside the earlier dominions in the British Commonwealth: Canada, Australia, New Zealand, and South Africa. The six counties of Ulster, or Northern Ireland, were permitted to remain part of what was now called the United Kingdom of Great Britain and Northern Ireland, with provisions for home rule. No sooner had the treaty been signed than a new civil war broke out between Irish moderates and diehards. The moderates supported the treaty; the diehards wanted to abolish the oath to the British monarch and establish a totally independent republic. The second civil war continued until 1923. De Valera, who supported the diehards, resigned the presidency and organized resistance to the treaty. In 1932 he was again elected president. The next year, the Dail Eireann abolished the oath of allegiance to the monarch.

During World War II, the Irish Free State remained neutral. In 1949 it declared itself the wholly independent republic of Eire.

Trials of the Successor States in Eastern Europe

Only the barest outline can be given of the dreary political story of the successor states of eastern Europe. They were termed the *successor states* because they succeeded all or portions of the overturned German, Austrian-Hungarian, and Russian empires. Their story is significant because except for Austria after 1956 the interwar era provided those lands with their only modern experience of political independence before the revolutions of 1989 toppled their Communist regimes.

It had been an article of faith among nineteenth-century liberals sympathetic to nationalism that only good could flow from the demise of Austria-Hungary, the restoration of Poland, and the establishment of nation-states throughout eastern Europe. These new states were to embody the principle of national self-determination and to provide a buffer against the westward spread of Bolshevism. They were, however, in trouble from the beginning.

Both France and Great Britain had long experience in liberal democratic government. Their primary challenges during the 1920s lay in responding to economic pressures and allowing new groups, such as the Labour Party, to share political power. In Germany, Poland, Austria, Czechoslovakia, and the other successor states, the challenge for the 1920s was to make new parliamentary governments function in a satisfactory and stable manner. Before the war, the elected parliaments of both Germany and Austria-Hungary had not exercised genuine political power. The question after the war became whether those groups that had previous-

Major Political Events of the 1920s	
1919 (August)	Constitution of the Weimar Republic promulgated
1920	Kapp Putsch in Berlin
1921 (March)	Kronstadt mutiny leads Lenin to initiate his New Economic Policy
1921 (December)	Treaty between Great Britain and the Irish Free State
1922 (April)	Treaty of Rapallo between Germany and the Soviet Union
1922 (October)	Fascist march on Rome leads to Mussolini's assumption of power
1923 (January)	France invades the Ruhr
1923 (November)	Hitler's Beer Hall Putsch
1923 (December)	First Labour government in Britain
1924	Death of Lenin
1925	Locarno Agreements
1926	General strike in Britain
1928	Kellogg–Briand Pact
1929 (January)	Trotsky expelled from the Soviet Union
1929 (February)	Lateran Accord between the Vatican and the Italian state

ly sat powerless in parliaments could assume both power and responsibility. Another question was how long conservative political groups and institutions, such as the armies, would tolerate or cooperate with the liberal experiments.

Economic and Ethnic Pressures

All the new states faced immense postwar economic difficulties. None of them possessed the kind of strong economy that nation-states such as France and Germany had developed in the nineteenth century. Indeed, political independence disrupted the previous economic relationships that each of them had developed as part of one of the prewar empires. None of the new states was financially independent; except for Czechoslovakia, all of them depended on foreign loans to finance economic development. Nationalistic antagonisms often prevented these states from trading with each other, and as a consequence, most became highly dependent upon trade with Germany. The successor states of eastern Europe were poor and overwhelmingly rural nations in an industrialized world. The depression hit them especially hard, because they had to import finished goods for which they paid with agricultural exports whose value was falling sharply.

Finally, throughout eastern Europe the collapse of the old German, Russian, and Austrian empires allowed various ethnic groups—large and small—to pursue nationalistic goals unchecked by any great power or central political authority. The major social and political groups in these countries were generally unwilling to make compromises lest they undermine their nationalist identity and independence. Each state included minority groups who wanted to be independent or to become part of a different nation in the region. Again except for Czechoslovakia, all of these states succumbed to some form of domestic authoritarian government.

It is important to recognize these interwar economic difficulties and nationalistic pressures because many of them seem to be reemerging in the region in the 1990s. Indeed, to a considerable extent, the breakup of Yugoslavia and Czechoslovakia, the present turmoil in the former Soviet Union, and the efforts at political reorganization in the rest of the areas dominated by the Soviet Union constitute one more attempt by the peoples of eastern Europe to achieve political and economic stability in the wake of the upheaval in that region caused by the events surrounding World War I.

Poland: Democracy to Military Rule

The nation whose postwar fortunes probably most disappointed liberal Europeans was Poland. For more than 100 years, the country had, as a result of the late-eighteenth-century partitions, been erased from the map. Restoration of an independent Poland had been one of Woodrow Wilson's Fourteen Points. When the country was finally reconstructed in 1919, nationalism proved an insufficient bond to overcome political disagreements stemming from class differences, diverse economic interests, and regionalism. The new Poland had been constructed from portions governed by Germany, Russia, and Austria for over a century. Each of those regions of partitioned Poland had different administrative systems and laws, different economies, and different degrees of experience with electoral institutions. A vast number of small political parties bedeviled the new Polish Parliament. The constitution assigned too little power to the executive. In 1926 Marshal Josef Pilsudski (1857–1935) carried out a military coup. Thereafter he ruled in effect personally until his death, when the government passed into the hands of a group of his military followers.

Czechoslovakia: Successful Democratic Experiment

Only one central European successor state escaped the fate of self-imposed authoritarian government. Czechoslovakia possessed a strong industrial base, a substantial middle class, and a tradition of liberal values. During the war, Czechs and Slovaks had cooperated to aid the Allies. They had learned to work together and to trust each other. After the war, the new government had broken up large estates in favor of small peasant holdings. In the person of Thomas Masaryk (1850–1937), the nation possessed a gifted leader of immense integrity and fairness. The country had a real chance of becoming a viable modern nation-state.

Marshal Josef Pilsudski took control of Poland after a military coup in 1926 and ruled the country until his death in 1935. [The Bettmann Archive]

high political and economic price. In Hungary during 1919, Bela Kun (1885–1937), a Communist, established a short-lived Hungarian Soviet Republic, which received support from the socialists as well. The Allies authorized an invasion by Romanian troops to remove the Communist danger. The Hungarian landowners then established Admiral Miklós Horthy (1858–1957) as regent, a position he held until 1944. After the collapse of the Kun government, thousands of Hungarians were either executed or imprisoned. It was in part in reaction to Kun's cooperation with socialists that Lenin ordered the Comintern to reject such cooperation in the future. Kun himself was later murdered by Stalin in purges of the late 1930s.

There was also deep resentment in Hungary over the territory it had lost in the Paris settlement. The largely agrarian Hungarian economy suffered from a general stagnation. During the 1920s, the effective ruler of Hungary was Count Stephen Bethlen (1874–1947). He presided over

Thomas Masaryk was the first president of the Czechoslovak Republic, which was the only successful democratic state in eastern Europe during the interwar period. [Bildarchiv Preussischer Kulturbesitz]

Czechoslovakia encountered discontent among its smaller national groups, including the German population of the Sudetenland, which the Paris settlement had placed within Czech borders. The parliamentary regime might have been able to deal with this problem, but extreme German nationalists in the Sudetenland looked to Hitler for aid. For his part, the German dictator wished to expand into eastern Europe. In 1938, at Munich, the great powers first divided liberal Czechoslovakia to appease Hitler's aggressive instincts and then watched passively as he occupied the country.

Hungary: Turmoil and Authoritarianism

Hungary was one of the defeated powers of the First World War. In that defeat it achieved its long-desired separation from Austria, but at a

a government that was parliamentary in form but aristocratic in character. In 1932 he was succeeded by General Julius Gömbös (1886–1936), who pursued anti-Semitic policies and rigged elections. No matter how the popular vote turned out, the Gömbös party controlled Parliament. After his death in 1936, anti-Semitism lingered in Hungarian politics.

Austria: Political Confusion and Nazi Conquest

The situation in Austria was little better. A quarter of the eight million Austrians lived in Vienna. Viable economic life was almost impossible, and the Paris settlement forbade union with Germany. Throughout the 1920s, the leftist Social Democrats and the conservative Christian Socialists contended for power. Both groups employed small armies to terrorize their opponents and to impress their followers.

In 1933 the Christian Socialist Engelbert Dollfuss (1892–1934) became chancellor. He tried to steer a course between the Austrian Social Democrats and the German Nazis, who had surfaced in Austria. In 1934 he outlawed all political parties except the Christian Socialists, the agrarians, and the paramilitary groups, which composed his own Fatherland Front. He used troops against the Social Democrats, but was shot later that year during an unsuccessful Nazi coup. His successor, Kurt von Schuschnigg (1897–1977) presided over Austria until Hitler annexed it in 1938.

Southeastern Europe: Royal Dictatorships

In southeastern Europe, revision of the arrangements in the Paris settlement was less of an issue. Parliamentary government floundered there nevertheless. Yugoslavia had been founded by the Corfu Agreement of 1917 and was known as the Kingdom of the Serbs, Croats, and Slovenes until 1929. Throughout the interwar period, the Serbs dominated the government and were opposed by the Croats. The two groups clashed violently, but the Serbs had the advantage of having had an independent state with an army prior to World War I, whereas the Croats and Slovenes had been part of the Austro-Hungarian Empire. The Croats generally were Roman Catholic, better educated, and accustomed to reasonably incorrupt government administration. The Serbs were Orthodox, somewhat less well educated, and considered to be corrupt administrators by the Croats. Furthermore, though each group predominated in certain areas of the country, each national group had isolated enclaves in other parts of the nation. Bosnia-Herzegovina, in addition to Serbs and Croats, had a significant Muslim population. The Slovenes, Muslims, and other small national groups often played the Serbs and the Croats off against each other. All of the political parties except the small Communist Party represented a particular ethnic group rather than the nation of Yugoslavia. The violent clash of nationalities eventually led to a royal dictatorship in 1929 under King Alexander I (r. 1921–1934), himself a Serb. He outlawed political parties and jailed popular politicians. Alexander was assassinated in 1934, but the authoritarian government continued under a regency for his son.

Other royal dictatorships were imposed elsewhere in the Balkans: in Romania by King Carol II (r. 1930–1940), and in Bulgaria by King Boris III (r. 1918–1943). They regarded their own illiberal regimes as preventing the seizure of power by more extreme antiparliamentary movements and as quieting the discontent of the varied nationalities within their borders. In Greece, the parliamentary monarchy floundered amidst military coups and calls for a republic. In 1936 General John Metaxas (1871–1941) instituted a dictatorship that for the time being ended parliamentary life in Greece.

The fate of the eastern European successor states disappointed those who had hoped that political liberty would result from the dissolution of the Habsburg Empire and from the restoration of an independent Poland. By the early 1930s, in most of those states, the authoritarianism of the Habsburgs had been replaced by that of other rulers. Meanwhile, Germany conducted the most momentous democratic experiment between the wars. There, after a century of frustration and disappointment, Germans had constructed a liberal state. It was in Germany that parliamentary democracy and its future in Western civilization faced its major trial.

The Corfu Pact Brings Yugoslavia into Existence

The Corfu Pact was arranged in 1917 by representatives of the Serbs, Croats, and Slovenes. Its contents are relevant to the 1920s because they illustrate the kinds of problems that Yugoslavia would have to address as an independent state. Throughtout the agreement, there is a tension between the desire to establish an independent state and a desire to maintain the autonomy of the national groups that entered into the agreement. Serbia was the strongest of the units because it was already an independent nation before the war. The Croats and Slovenes had been administered by Hungary within the Austro-Hungarian Empire. It is important to note that this pact said nothing about the fate of Bosnia-Herzegovina, which included a population of Serbs, Croats, and Muslims and which would become part of the new Yugoslavian state.

✦ *Why do you think the authors of this pact placed so much emphasis on cultural and political symbols of their national groups? From reading this pact, what seems to have been the basis for unity? What particular kinds of political problems might have been anticipated as arising in the new state simply from reading its founding pact?*

The authorized representatives of the Serbs, Croats, and Slovenes, in declaring that it is the desire of our people to free itself from every foreign yoke and to constitute itself a free, national, and independent State, a desire based on the principle that every nation has the right to decide upon its own destiny, are agreed in judging that this state should be founded on the following modern and democratic principles:

1. The State of the Serbs, Croats, and Slovenes, who are also known as the Southern Slavs or Jugoslavs, will be a free and independent kingdom, with indivisible territory and unity of allegiance. It will be a constitutional, democratic, and Parliamentary Monarchy under the Karageorgevitch Dynasty, which has always shared the ideas and the feelings of the nation, placing liberty and the national will above all else.

2. This State will be named "The Kingdom of the Serbs, Croats, and Slovenes." . . .

3. The State will have a single coat-of-arms, a single flag, and a single crown. These emblems will be composed of the present existing emblems. The unity of the State will be symbolized by the coat-of-arms and the flag of the Kingdom.

5. The three national designations—Serbs, Croats, and Slovenes—are equal before the law throughout the territory of the Kingdom, and every one may use them freely upon all occasions of public life and in dealing with the authorities.

6. The two alphabets, the Cyrillic and the Latin, also rank equally and every one may use them freely throughout the territory of the Kingdom. . . .

7 All recognized religions may be freely and publicly exercised. The Orthodox, Roman Catholic, and Musulman (*sic*) faiths, which are those chiefly professed by our nation, shall rank equally and enjoy rights with regard to the State.

In consideration of these principles the legislature will take special care to safeguard religious concord in conformity with the spirit and tradition of our whole nation.

11. All citizens throughout the territory of the Kingdom shall be equal and enjoy the same rights with regard to the State and before the Law.

Alfred J. Bannan and Achilles Edelenyi, eds., Documentary History of Eastern Europe *(New York: Twayne Publishers, Inc., 1970), pp. 259–260.*

The Weimar Republic in Germany

The German Weimar Republic was born amidst the defeat of the imperial army, the revolution of 1918 against the Hohenzollerns, and the hopes of German Liberals and Social Democrats. Its name derived from the city of Weimar, in which its constitution was written and promulgated in August 1919. While the constitution was being debated, the republic, headed by the Social Democrats, accepted the humiliating terms of the Versailles treaty, that part of the Paris settlement that applied to Germany. Although it had signed only under the threat of an Allied invasion, the republic was nevertheless permanently associated with the national disgrace and the economic burdens of the treaty.

Throughout the 1920s, the government of the republic was required to fulfill the economic and military provisions imposed by the Paris settlement. It became all too easy for German nationalists and military figures whose policies had brought on the tragedy and defeat of the war to blame the young republic and the socialists for the military defeat and its grievous social and political results. In Germany, more than in other countries, all political groups shared the desire to revise the treaty, though they differed about the means. Some wished to oppose its provisions whenever good tactical opportunities arose; others simply assumed a position of total opposition to the treaty. Because of those revisionist desires, there were different degrees of loyalty among Germans to the political arrangements of the Weimar Constitution, which many of them associated with the Paris settlement.

Constitutional Flaws

The Weimar Constitution was in many respects a highly enlightened document. It guaranteed civil liberties and provided for direct election, by universal suffrage, of the *Reichstag* and the president. It also contained, however, certain crucial structural flaws that eventually allowed its liberal institutions to be overthrown. It provided for proportional representation for all elections. This system made it relatively easy for small parties to gain seats in the *Reichstag*. Ministers were technically responsible to the *Reichstag*, but the president appointed and removed the chancellor. Perhaps most important, Article 48 allowed the president, in an emergency, to rule by decree. The constitution thus permitted a temporary presidential dictatorship.

Lack of Broad Popular Support

Beyond the burden of the Paris settlement and these potential constitutional pitfalls, the Weimar Republic did not command the sympathy or loyalty of many Germans. No social revolution had accompanied the new political structure. Many important political figures favored a constitutional monarchy. The schoolteachers, civil servants, and judges of the republic were generally the same people who had served the Kaiser and the empire. Before the war, they had distrusted or even hated the Social Democratic Party, which figured so prominently in the establishment and the politics of the republic.

The officer corps was also deeply suspicious of the government and profoundly resentful of the military provisions of the peace settlement. Its leaders and other nationalistic Germans perpetuated the myth that the German army had surrendered on foreign soil only because it had been stabbed in the back by civilians at home. Thus, many Germans in significant social and political positions wanted both to revise the peace treaty and to modify the system of government. The early years of the republic only reinforced those sentiments.

Major and minor humiliations as well as considerable economic instability impinged on the new government. In March 1920, the right-wing Kapp Putsch, or armed insurrection, erupted in Berlin. Led by a conservative civil servant and supported by army officers, the attempted coup failed. But the putsch collapsed only after the government had fled the city and German workers had carried out a general strike. In the same month, strikes took place in the Ruhr. The government sent in troops. Such extremism from both the left and the right would haunt the republic for all its days.

In May 1921, the Allies presented a reparations bill for 132 billion gold marks. The German republican government accepted this preposterous demand only after new Allied threats of occupation. Throughout the early

1920s, there were numerous assassinations or attempted assassinations of important republican leaders. Violence marked the first five years of the republic.

Invasion of the Ruhr and Inflation

Inflation brought on the major crisis of this period. Borrowing to finance the war and the continued postwar deficit spending generated an immense rise in prices. Consequently, the value of the German currency fell. By early 1921 the German mark traded against the American dollar at a ratio of 64 to 1, compared with a ratio of 4.2 to 1 in 1914. German bankers contended that the mark could not be stabilized until the reparations issue had been solved. In the meantime, the printing presses kept pouring forth paper money, used to redeem government bonds as they fell due.

The French invasion of the Ruhr in January 1923 and the German response of economic passive resistance produced cataclysmic inflation. The Weimar government subsidized the Ruhr labor force, who had laid down their tools. Unemployment soon spread from the Ruhr to other parts of the country, creating a new drain on the treasury and also reducing tax revenues. The printing presses by this point had difficulty providing enough paper currency to keep up with the daily rise in prices. In November 1923, an American dollar was worth more than 800 million German marks. Money was literally not worth the paper it was printed on. Stores were unwilling to exchange goods for the worthless currency, and farmers withheld produce from the market.

The social and economic consequences of the great inflation of 1923 were disastrous for many Germans. Middle-class savings, pensions, and insurance policies were wiped out, as were investments in government bonds. Simultaneously, debts and mortgages could be paid off. Speculators in land, real estate, and industry made great fortunes. Union contracts generally allowed workers to keep up with rising prices. Farmers who supplied food to the cities did well, as did food stores whose proprietors benefitted from the barter that took place. The inflation thus was not a disaster to everyone. To the middle class and the lower middle class, however, the inflation was another trauma coming hard on the heels of the military defeat and the peace treaty. Only when the social and economic upheaval of these months is grasped can the later German desire for order and security at almost any cost be comprehended.

Hitler's Early Career

Late in 1923 Adolf Hitler (1889–1945) made his first major appearance on the German political scene. In 1889 he had been born the son of a minor Austrian customs official. By 1907 he had gone to Vienna, where his hopes of becoming an artist were soon dashed. He lived off money sent by his widowed mother and later off his Austrian orphan's allowance. He also painted postcards for further income and worked as a day laborer. In Vienna, he became acquainted

In 1923 Germany suffered from cataclysmic inflation. Paper money became worthless and children used packets of it as building blocks. [Bettmann/Hulton]

with Mayor Karl Lueger's (1844–1910) Christian Social Party, which prospered on an anti-Semitic ideology.

Hitler also absorbed the rabid German nationalism and extreme anti-Semitism that flourished in Vienna. He came to hate Marxism, which he associated with Jews. During World War I, Hitler fought in the German army and was wounded; he was promoted to the rank of corporal and awarded the Iron Cross for bravery. The war gave him his first sense of purpose.

After the conflict, Hitler settled in Munich. There he became associated with a small nationalistic, anti-Semitic political party that in 1920 adopted the name of National Socialist German Workers Party, better known simply as the Nazis. The same year, the group began to parade under a red and white banner with a black swastika. It issued a platform, or program, of Twenty-five Points. These called for the repudiation of the Versailles treaty, the unification of Austria and Germany, the exclusion of Jews from German citizenship, agrarian reform, the prohibition of land speculation, the confiscation of war profits, state administration of the giant cartels, and the replacement of department stores with small retail shops.

Originally, the Nazis had called for a broad program of nationalization of industry in an attempt to compete directly with the Marxist political parties for the vote of the workers. As the tactic failed, the Nazis redefined the meaning of the word *socialist* in their name, so that it suggested a *nationalistic* outlook. In 1922 Hitler said:

Whoever is prepared to make the national cause his own to such an extent that he knows no higher ideal than the welfare of his nation; whoever has understood our great national anthem, *Deutschland, Deutschland, Über Alles* ["Germany, Germany, Over All"], to mean that nothing in the wide world surpasses in his eyes this Germany, people and land, land and people—that man is a Socialist.[2]

This definition, of course, had nothing to do with traditional German socialism. The "socialism" that Hitler and the Nazis had in mind was not state ownership of the means of production but the subordination of all economic enterprise to the welfare of the nation. It often implied

[2]Quoted in Alan Bullock, Hitler: A Study in Tyranny, rev. ed. (New York: Harper & Row, 1962), p. 76.

In this painting, which reflects the mood of social and political disillusionment that prevailed in much of Europe in the 1920s, George Grosz satirized conservative and right-wing groups in Weimar Germany, including the army, the courts, the newspapers, and the Nazi Party. [Bildarchiv Preussischer Kulturbesitz]

protection for small economic enterprise. Increasingly, the Nazis discovered that their party appealed to virtually any economic group that was experiencing pressure and instability. They often tailored their messages to the particular local problems confronting these groups in different parts of Germany. The Nazis especially found considerable support among war veterans who faced economic and social displacement in Weimar society.

Soon after the promulgation of the Twenty-

Hitler Denounces the Versailles Treaty

One of the chief complaints of the National Socialist movement was the unfairness of the Versailles treaty of 1919. Virtually all German public figures, including leaders of the Weimar Republic, hoped to see that settlement revised. Hitler and his followers made denunciation of the treaty their single most uncompromising declaration. In this speech of April 17, 1923, Hitler explained how the treaty had undermined the German nation.

✦ *How might the French invasion of the Ruhr and the resulting inflation have made this speech particularly effective? To what extent was Hitler's condemnation of the control imposed on Germany by the Versailles treaty correct? How does Hitler oppose his young Nazi movement to the young Weimar Republic? Why does the one appear a strong and the other a weak supporter of German national goals?*

With the armistice begins the humiliation of Germany. If the Republic on the day of its foundation had appealed to the country: "Germans, stand together! Up and resist the foe! The Fatherland, the Republic expects of you that you fight to your last breath," then millions who are now the enemies of the Republic would be fanatical Republicans. Today they are the foes of the Republic not because it is a Republic but because this Republic was founded at the moment when Germany was humiliated, because it so discredited the new flag that men's eyes must turn regretfully towards the old flag.

It was no Treaty of Peace which was signed, but a betrayal of Peace.

The Treaty was signed which demanded from Germany that she should perform what was for ever impossible of performance. But that was not the worst; after all that was only a question of material values. This was not the end: Commissions of Control were formed! For the first time in the history of the modern world there were planted on a State agents of foreign Powers to act as Hangmen, and German soldiers were set to serve the foreigner. And if one of these Commissions was "insulted," a company of the German army had to defile before the French flag. We no longer feel the humiliation of such an act; but the outside world says, "What a people of curs!"

So long as this Treaty stands there can be no resurrection of the German people: no social reform of any kind is possible! The Treaty was made in order to bring 20 million Germans to their deaths and to ruin the German nation. But those who made the Treaty cannot set it aside. At its foundation our Movement formulated three demands:

1. Setting aside of the Peace Treaty.
2. Unification of all Germans.
3. Land and soil to feed our nation.

Our Movement could formulate these demands, since it was not our Movement which caused the War, it has not made the Republic, it did not sign the Peace Treaty.

There is thus one thing which is the first task of this Movement: it desires to make the German once more National, that his Fatherland shall stand for him above everything else. It desires to teach our people to understand afresh the truth of the old saying: He who will not be a hammer must be an anvil. An anvil are we today, and that anvil will be beaten until out of the anvil we fashion once more a hammer, a German sword!

Norman H. Baynes, ed., The Speeches of Adolph Hitler, April 1922–1939 *(Oxford, England: Oxford University Press, 1942).*

five Points, the storm troopers, or SA (*Sturmabteilung*), were organized under the leadership of Captain Ernst Roehm (1887–1934). It was a paramilitary organization that initially provided its members with food and uniforms and eventually paid them as well. In the mid-1920s, the SA adopted its infamous brown-shirted uniform. The storm troopers were the chief Nazi instrument for terror and intimidation before the party came into control of the government. They were a law unto themselves. They attacked socialists and communists. The organization was a means of preserving military discipline and values outside the small army permitted by the Paris settlement. The existence of such a private party army was a sign of the potential for violence in the Weimar Republic. It also represented widespread contempt for the law and the institutions of the republic. In response to the Nazi forces, both the Social Democrat and the Communist parties also organized paramilitary organizations, but in neither size nor discipline could they rival the Nazis. These paramilitary forces greatly weakened the Weimar Republic.

The social and economic turmoil following the French occupation of the Ruhr and the German inflation provided the fledgling Nazi Party with an opportunity for direct action against the Weimar Republic, which seemed incapable of giving Germany military or economic security. Because of his immense oratorical skills and organizational abilities, Hitler personally dominated the Nazi Party.

On November 9, 1923, Hitler and a band of followers, accompanied by General Ludendorff, attempted an unsuccessful putsch at a beer hall in Munich. When the local authorities crushed the uprising, sixteen Nazis were killed. Hitler and Ludendorff were arrested and tried for treason. The general was acquitted. Hitler employed the trial to make himself into a national figure. In his defense, he condemned the republic, the Versailles treaty, the Jews, and the weakened condition of his adopted country. He was convicted and sentenced to five years in prison. He actually spent only a few months in jail before being paroled. During this time, he dictated *Mein Kampf* (*My Struggle*). Another result of the brief imprisonment was his decision to seize political power by legal methods.

During a Nazi Party rally in Nuremberg in 1927, Adolf Hitler stops his motorcade to receive the applause of the surrounding crowd. In the late 1920s the Nazi movement was only one of many bringing strife to the Weimer Republic. [Bildarchiv Preussischer Kulturbesitz]

The Stresemann Years

Elsewhere, the officials of the republic were trying to repair the damage from the inflation. Gustav Stresemann (1878–1929) was primarily responsible for the reconstruction of the republic and for giving it a sense of self-confidence. As chancellor from August to November 1923, Stresemann abandoned the policy of passive resistance in the Ruhr. The country simply could not afford it. Then, with the aid of the banker Hjalmar Schacht (1877–1970), he introduced a new German currency. The rate of exchange was one trillion of the old German marks for one new Rentenmark.

Stresemann also moved against challenges from both the left and the right. He supported the crushing of both Hitler's abortive putsch and smaller Communist disturbances. In late November 1923, he resigned as chancellor and became foreign minister, a post that he held until his death in 1929. He continued to exer-

Ernst Roehm Demands a Return to German Military Values

Ernst Roehm (1887–1934) was the early Nazi leader who headed the SA (Sturmabteilung, storm troopers). He had fought in the First World War and saw himself primarily as a soldier. In this passage from his autobiography, he emphasizes a soldier's understanding of German nationalism and how National Socialism could contribute to German renewal. Roehm himself was executed in 1934 along with other SA officers when Hitler consolidated his personal power at their expense.

◆ *Why would this speech have appealed to the tens of thousands of German World War I veterans? Why does Roehm oppose nationalistic and military values to those of peace and prosperity? Why are "politicians" such a convenient target for his attack?*

I am a believer in plain talk and have not hid my heart like a skeleton in the closet.

I must write without fear, with defiance—just as it comes from my soul. . . .

Soldierly comradeship, cemented with blood, can perhaps temporarily relax, but it can never be torn out of the heart, it cannot be exterminated.

Still, all of Germany has not been awakened yet—despite National Socialism. My words shall be a trumpet call to those who are still asleep.

I am not appealing to the hustling and sneaky trader who has made accursed gold his God, but to the warrior who is struggling in the battle of life, who wants to win freedom and with it the kingdom of heaven.

I approve of whatever serves the purpose of German Freedom. I oppose whatever runs counter to it. Europe, aye, the whole world, may go down in flames—what concern is it of ours? Germany must live and be free.

One may call me a bigoted fool—I can't help that. I am opposed to sport in its present form and to its effects. Moreover, I consider it a definite national danger. We cannot rebuild the Fatherland with champions and artificially nurtured "big guns of sport." Only the most careful development which provides physical strength and capability, with spiritual elasticity and ethical backbone, can be of use to the Volk community. . . .

The Germans have forgotten how to hate.

Virile hate has been replaced by feminine lamentation. But he who is unable to hate cannot live either. Fanatical love and hate—their fires kindle flames of freedom.

Passionlessness, matter-of-factness, objectivity, are impersonality, are sophistry.

Only passion gives knowledge, creates wisdom.

"Peace and order" is the battle cry of people living on pensions. In the last analysis you cannot govern a state on the basis of the needs of pensioners. . . .

"Irresponsible dreamers" for years and years have called upon the people to rise up against enslavement and oppression. The "responsible politicians" of the new Germany in these same years have sold Germany lock, stock, and barrel. . . .

From time immemorial Germany was not suited to "diplomacy" and "politics." The sword has always determined the greatness of its history. . . .

Only the soldier could lead his people and Fatherland out of wretchedness and shame to freedom and honor.

Ernst Roehm, Die Geschichte eines Hochverraters *(Munich: Verlang Frz. Eher Nachf.,* 1928), pp. 365–367 *(7th ed.,* 1934), as quoted in George L. Mosse, Nazi Culture: Intellectual, Cultural, and Social Life in the Third Reich *(New York: Grosset & Dunlap,* 1966), pp. 101–103.

cise considerable influence over the affairs of the republic.

In 1924 the Weimar Republic and the Allies agreed to a new system of reparation payments. The Dawes Plan, submitted by the American banker Charles Dawes, lowered the annual payments and allowed them to vary according to the fortunes of the German economy. The last French troops left the Ruhr in 1925 (see Map 27-1).

The same year, Friedrich Ebert (1871–1925), the Social Democratic president of the republic, died. Field Marshal Paul von Hindenburg (1847–1934), a military hero and a conservative monarchist, was elected as his successor. He governed in strict accordance with the constitution, but his election suggested that German politics had become more conservative. It looked as if conservative Germans had become reconciled to the republic. This conservatism was in line with the prosperity of the later 1920s. The new political and economic stability meant that foreign capital flowed into Germany, and employment rose smartly. In the steel and chemical industries, large combines spread. The prosperity helped to broaden acceptance of and appreciation for the republic.

In foreign affairs, Stresemann was conciliatory. He fulfilled the provisions of the Paris settlement, even as he attempted to revise it by diplomacy. He was willing to accept the settlement in the West but was a determined, if sometimes secret, revisionist in the East. He aimed to recover German-speaking territories lost to Poland and Czechoslovakia and possibly to unite with Austria, chiefly by diplomatic means. The first step, however, was to achieve respectability and economic recovery. That goal required a policy of accommodation and "Fulfillment," for the moment at least.

Locarno

These developments gave rise to the Locarno Agreements of October 1925. The spirit of conciliation led foreign secretary Austen Chamberlain (1863–1937) for Britain and Aristide Briand for France to accept Stresemann's proposal for a fresh start. France and Germany both accepted the western frontier established at Paris as legitimate. Britain and

Italy agreed to intervene against whichever side violated the frontier or if Germany sent troops into the demilitarized Rhineland. Significantly, no such agreement was reached about Germany's eastern frontier. The Germans

MAP 27-1 GERMANY'S WESTERN FRONTIER *The French–Belgian–German border area between the two world wars was sensitive. Despite efforts to restrain tensions, there were persistent difficulties related to the Ruhr, Rhineland, Saar, and Eupen-Malmédy regions that required strong defenses.*

Occupied by the Allies and the United States to 1923

Eupen and Malmédy, to Belgium by Plebiscite, 1920

Saar Basin under the League of Nations, to Germany by Plebiscite, 1935

Demilitarized Areas, a 30 mile-wide strip along the east bank of the Rhine

The Locarno Agreements, signed in October of 1925, brought a new, if temporary, spirit of conciliation and hope to Europe. [Bildarchiv Preussischer Kulturbesitz]

signed treaties of arbitration with Poland and Czechoslovakia, however, and France strengthened its ties with the Little Entente. France supported German membership in the League of Nations and agreed to withdraw its occupation troops from the Rhineland in 1930, five years earlier than specified at Paris.

Locarno pleased everyone. Germany was pleased to have achieved respectability and a guarantee against another Ruhr occupation, as well as the possibility of revision in the east. Britain was pleased to be allowed to play a more evenhanded role. Italy was glad to be recognized as a great power. The French were happy, too, because the Germans voluntarily accepted the permanence of their western frontier, also guaranteed by Britain and Italy, while France maintained its allies in the east.

The Locarno Agreements brought a new spirit of hope to Europe. Germany's entry into the League of Nations was greeted with enthusiasm. Chamberlain and Dawes received the Nobel Peace Prize in 1925, and Briand and Stresemann were awarded it in 1926. The spirit of Locarno was carried even further when the leading European states, Japan, and the United States signed the Kellogg–Briand Pact in 1928, renouncing "war as an instrument of national policy."

The joy and optimism were not justified. France had merely recognized its inability to coerce Germany without help. Britain had shown its unwillingness to uphold the Paris settlement in the east. Austen Chamberlain declared that no British government would ever "risk the bones of a British grenadier" for the Polish corridor. Germany remained unreconciled to the eastern settlement. It continued its clandestine military connections with the Soviet Union, which had begun with the Treaty of

Rapallo, and planned to continue to press for revision of the Paris settlement.

In both France and Germany, moreover, the conciliatory politicians represented only a part of the nation. In Germany, especially, most people continued to reject Versailles and regarded Locarno as only an extension of it. When the Dawes Plan ran out in 1929, it was replaced by the Young Plan. Named after the American businessman Owen D. Young (1874–1962), who devised it on behalf of the Allies, this plan lowered the reparation payments, put a limit on how long they must be made, and removed Germany entirely from outside supervision and control. The intensity of the outcry in Germany against the continuation of any reparations showed how far the Germans were from accepting their situation.

Despite these problems, major war was by no means inevitable. Europe, aided by American loans, was returning to prosperity. German leaders like Stresemann would certainly have continued to press for change, but they would certainly not have resorted to force, much less to a general war. Continued prosperity and diplomatic success might have won the loyalty of the German people for the Weimar Republic and moderate revisionism. But the Great Depression of the 1930s brought new forces to power.

◆

At the close of the 1920s, Europe appeared finally to have emerged from the difficulties of the World War I era. The Soviet Union, regarded in the West as a communist menace, was isolated by the other powers and had withdrawn into its own internal power struggles. Elsewhere, the initial resentments over the peace settlement seemed to have abated. The major powers were cooperating. Democracy was still functioning in Germany. The Labour Party was about to form its second ministry in Britain. France had settled into a less assertive international role. Mussolini's Fascism seemed to have little relevance to the rest of the Continent. The successor states had not fulfilled the democratic hopes of the Paris conference, but their troubles were their own.

The European economy seemed finally to be on an even keel. The frightening inflation of the

One effect of the Locarno Agreements was to allow Germany to become a member of the League of Nations. In this picture Gustav Stresemann, as Germany's Foreign Minister, addresses the League on behalf of Germany's newly seated delegation. [The Bettmann Archive]

early years of the decade was over, and unemployment had eased. American capital was flowing into the Continent. The reparation payments had been systematized by the Young Plan. Yet both this economic and political stability proved illusory and temporary. What brought them to an end was the deepest economic depression in the modern history of the West. As the governments and electorates responded to the economic collapse, the search for liberty gave way in more than one instance to a search for security. The political experiments of the 1920s gave way to the political tragedies of the 1930s.

Review Questions

1. How did the Bolshevik Revolution pose a challenge to the rest of Europe? Why did Lenin institute the New Economic Policy? Was it successful? Could the Russian Revolution have succeeded without Lenin? How did Lenin's policies lead to divisions among western socialist parties?

2. Discuss the rise of Joseph Stalin. How did he overcome the opposition of Trotsky and establish himself as head of the Soviet state?

3. Define Fascism. How and why did the Fascists succeed in obtaining power in Italy? What tactics did they use? To whom did they appeal? To what extent does Mussolini deserve the credit for his success? Was there a difference between the right-wing Fascist dictatorship of Mussolini and the left-wing Communist dictatorship of Stalin?

4. Why were Britain and France "joyless victors" after World War II? What weakness did each have? How did World War I change British politics? Discuss the decline and fall of the Liberal Party. How successful was the general strike of 1926? By what stages did Ireland win its independence?

5. Discuss France's foreign policy problems after the Versailles treaty. By what means could it best obtain security? Was the invasion of the Ruhr wise? Should France have signed the Locarno pact?

6. Why did all but one of the successor states in eastern and central Europe fail to establish viable democracies?

7. Could the Weimar Republic have taken root in Germany, or was its failure inevitable? Between 1919 and 1929, what were the republic's greatest strengths and weaknesses? To what extent did its fate depend on personalities, rather than on underlying trends? Why did the Versailles Treaty loom so large in domestic German politics?

Suggested Readings

I. BANAC, *The National Question in Yugoslavia: Origins, History, Politics* (1984). An outstanding treatment of the reorganization of eastern European political life.

R. BESSEL, *Political Violence and the Rise of Nazism: The Storm Troopers in Eastern Germany, 1925–1934* (1984). A study of the uses of violence by the Nazis.

K. D. BRACHER, *The German Dictatorship* (1970). A comprehensive treatment of both the origins and the functioning of the Nazi movement and government.

A. BULLOCK, *Hitler: A Study in Tyranny*, rev. ed. (1964). The best biography of Hitler.

E. H. CARR, *A History of Soviet Russia*, 14 vols. (1950–1978). An extensive study by a historian sympathetic to the Soviet policies of the time.

S. F. COHEN, *Bukharin and the Bolshevik Revolution: A Political Biography, 1888–1938* (1973). An interesting examination of Stalin's chief opponent on the Communist right.

I. DEUTSCHER, *The Prophet Armed* (1954), *The Prophet Unarmed* (1959), and *The Prophet Outcast* (1963). A major biography of Trotsky.

O. FIGES, *Peasant Russia, Civil War: The Volga Countryside in Revolution (1917–1921)* (1989). An important study of the Russian Civil War in a single district.

L. FISCHER, *The Life of Lenin* (1964). A sound biography by an American journalist.

P. FUSSELL, *The Great War and Modern Memory* (1975). A brilliant account of the literature arising from World War I during the 1920s.

P. GAY, *Weimar Culture: The Outsider as Insider* (1968). A sensitive analysis of the intellectual life of Weimar.

H. J. GORDON, *Hitler and the Beer Hall Putsch* (1972). An excellent account of the event and the political situation in the early Weimar Republic.

N. GREENE, *From Versailles to Vichy: The Third Republic, 1919–1940* (1970). A useful introduction to a difficult subject.

H. GRUBER, *International Communism in the Era of Lenin: A Documentary History* (1967). An excellent collection of difficult-to-find documents.

H. GRUBER, *Red Vienna: Experiment in Working-Class Culture, 1919–1934* (1991). A discussion of social democratic policies in Vienna after the fall of the Habsburgs.

J. HELD (ED.), *The Columbia History of Eastern Europe in the Twentieth Century* (1992). Individual essays on each of the nations.

B. JELAVICH, *History of the Balkans*, Vol. 2 (1983). The standard work.

L. JONES, *German Liberalism and the Dissolution of the Weimar Party System, 1918–1933* (1988). A major study of the parties that failed during the experiment of the Weimar Republic.

P. KENEZ, *The Birth of the Propaganda State: Soviet Methods of Mass Mobilization, 1917–1929* (1985). An examination of how the Communist government inculcated popular support.

B. KENT, *The Spoils of War: The Politics, Economics, and Diplomacy of Reparations, 1918–1932* (1993). A comprehensive account of the intricacies of the reparations problem of the 1920s.

B. LINCOLN, *Red Victory: A History of the Russian Civil War* (1989). An excellent narrative account.

A. LYTTLETON, *Seizure of Power* (1973). A good narrative of the Italian Fascist rise to power.

M. McAuley, *Bread and Justice: State and Society in Petrograd, 1917–1922* (1991). A study that examines the impact of the Russian Revolution and Leninist policies on a major Russian city.

C. S. Maier, *Recasting Bourgeois Europe: Stabilization in France, Germany, and Italy in the Decade After World War I* (1975). An important interpretation written from a comparative standpoint.

A. Marwick, *The Deluge: British Society and the First World War* (1965). Full of insights into both major and more subtle minor social changes.

E. Nolte, *Three Faces of Fascism* (1963). An important, influential, and difficult work on France, Italy, and Germany.

R. Pipes, *The Formation of the Soviet Union*, 2nd ed. (1964). A study of internal policy with emphasis on Soviet minorities.

J. F. Pollard, *The Vatican and Italian Fascism 1929–32: A Study in Conflict* (1985). Provides the background to the Lateran pacts.

J. Rothschild, *East Central Europe Between the Two World Wars* (1974). A detailed and authoritative survey.

S. A. Schuker, *The End of French Predominance in Europe: The Financial Crisis of 1924 and the Adoption of the Dawes Plan* (1976). An excellent study of a complicated issue.

H. Seton-Watson, *Eastern Europe Between the Wars, 1918–1941* (1946). Somewhat dated, but still a useful work.

D. P. Silverman, *Reconstructing Europe After the Great War* (1982). Examines the difficulties faced by the major powers.

D. M. Smith, *Italy: A Modern History*, rev. ed. (1969). Good chapters on the Fascists and Mussolini.

D. M. Smith, *Italy and Its Monarchy* (1989). A major treatment of an important neglected subject.

R. J. Sontag, *A Broken World, 1919–1939* (1971). An exceptionally thoughtful and well-organized survey.

M. Steinberg, *Sabers and Brownshirts: The German Students' Path to National Socialism, 1918–1935* (1977). An interesting study of the recruitment of young Germans.

A. J. P. Taylor, *English History, 1914–1945* (1965). Lively and opinionated.

M. Tractenberg, *Reparations in World Politics: France and European Economic Diplomacy, 1916–1923* (1980). Points to the special role of reparations in French calculations.

R. Tucker, *Stalin as Revolutionary, 1879–1929: A Study in History and Personality* (1973). A useful and readable account of Stalin's rise to power.

N. Tumarkin, *Lenin Lives: The Lenin Cult in Soviet Russia* (1983). An interesting work on the uses of Lenin's reputation after his death.

E. G. Walters, *The Other Europe: Eastern Europe to 1945* (1988). An excellent introduction to the problems in the region.

T. Wilson, *The Downfall of the Liberal Party, 1914–1935* (1966). A close examination of the surprising demise of a political party in Britain.

E. Wiskemann, *Fascism in Italy: Its Development and Influence* (1969). A comprehensive treatment.

R. Wohl, *The Generation of 1914* (1979). An important work that explores the effect of the war on political and social thought.

In Hitler's Germany and Mussolini's Italy Europe witnessed the emergence of new and troubling forms of authoritarian government. This picture is from a German postcard that commemorated Mussolini's visit to Berlin in 1937. [Bildarchiv Preussischer Kulturbesitz]

28

Europe and the Great Depression of the 1930s

> **Key Topics in This Chapter**
> ◆ Financial collapse and depression in Europe
> ◆ The emergence of the National Government in Great Britain and the Popular Front in France in response to the political pressures caused by the depression
> ◆ The Nazi seizure of power in Germany, the establishment there of a police state, and the imposition of racial laws
> ◆ Planned industrialism, agricultural collectivization, and purges in the Soviet Communist Party and army under Stalin

In Europe, unlike in the United States, the 1920s had not been "roaring." Economically, it had been a decade of insecurity, of a search for elusive stability, of a short-lived upswing, followed by collapse in finance and production. The Great Depression that began in 1929 was the most severe downturn ever experienced by the capitalist economies. The high unemployment, low production levels, financial instability, and shrinking trade arrived and would not depart. Capitalist business and political leaders despaired over the failure of the market mechanism to save them. Marxists and indeed many other observers thought that the final downfall of capitalism was at hand.

European voters looked for new ways out of the doldrums, and politicians sought escapes from the pressures that the depression had *brought on them. One result of the fight for economic security was the establishment of the Nazi dictatorship in Germany. Another was the piecemeal construction of what has since become known as* the mixed economy; *that is, governments became directly involved in economic decisions alongside business and labor. In both cases, most of the political and economic guidelines of nineteenth-century liberalism were abandoned for good. Two other casualties of these years were decency and civility in political life.*

Toward the Great Depression

Three factors combined to bring about the intense severity and the extended length of the Great Depression. First, there was a financial crisis that stemmed directly from the war and the peace settlement. Second, a crisis arose in the production and distribution of goods in the world market. These two problems became intertwined in 1929 and, so far as Europe was concerned, reached the breaking point in 1931. Finally, both of these difficulties became worse because neither the major western European nations nor the United States offered strong economic leadership or acted responsibly. Without cooperation or leadership in the Atlantic economic community, the economic collapse in finance and production simply lingered and deepened.

The Financial Tailspin

Most European nations emerged from World War I with inflated currencies. Immediately after the armistice, the unleashed demand for consumer and industrial goods drove up prices. The price and wage increases generally subsided after 1921. Yet the problem of maintaining the value of their national currencies still haunted political leaders—and was intensified after the German financial disaster of 1923. The frightening German example of uncontrolled inflation helped explain the later refusal of most governments to run budget deficits when the depression struck. They feared inflation as a source of social instability and political turmoil the way that European governments since World War II have feared unemployment.

REPARATIONS AND WAR DEBTS Reparation payments and international war-debt settlement further complicated the picture. Here France and the United States were the stumbling blocks. France had twice paid reparations as a defeated nation, once after 1815 and again after 1871. As a victor, it now intended both to receive reparations and to finance its postwar recovery through them. The 1923 invasion of the Ruhr demonstrated French determination on this question.

The United States was no less determined to be repaid for the wartime loans it had made to its allies. Moreover, the European Allies owed various debts to each other. It soon became apparent that German reparations were to provide the means by which other European nations intended to repay all these debts. Most of the money that the Allies collected from each other eventually went to the United States.

In 1922 Great Britain announced that it would insist on payment for its own loans only to the extent that the United States required payments from Britain. The American government, however, would not relent. The reparations and the war debts made normal business, capital investment, and international trade difficult and expensive for the European nations. Governments exercised various controls over credit, trade, and currency. Currency speculation drew funds away from capital investment in productive enterprise. The monetary problems reinforced the general tendency toward high tariff policies. If a nation imported too many goods from abroad, it might have difficulty meeting those costs and the expenses of debt or reparation payments. The financial and money muddle thus discouraged trade and production and, in consequence, hurt employment.

AMERICAN INVESTMENTS In 1924 the Dawes Plan reorganized the administration and transfer of reparations, which procedures in turn smoothed the debt repayments to the United States. Thereafter, private American capital flowed into Europe and especially into Germany. Much of this money, which provided the basis for Europe's brief prosperity after 1925, was in the form of short-term loans.

In 1928 this lending began to contract as American money was withdrawn from European

Crowds gathered on Wall Street in New York on October 29, 1929, the day the stock market crashed. The Depression in the United States dried up American capital previously available for investment in Europe. [Brown Brothers]

investments into the booming New York stock market. In the Wall Street crash of October 1929—the result of virtually unregulated financial speculation—huge amounts of money were lost. United States banks had made large loans to customers, who then invested the money in the stock market. When stock prices collapsed, the customers could not repay the banks. Consequently, within the United States all kinds of credit that had been available shrank severely or disappeared, and many banks failed. Thereafter, little American capital was available for investment in Europe. Furthermore, loans already made to Europeans were not renewed, as American banks strove to cover domestic shortages.

THE END OF REPARATIONS When the credit to Europe began to run out, a major financial crisis struck the continent. In May 1931, the *Kreditanstalt*, a major bank in Vienna, collapsed. It was a primary lending institution for much of central and eastern Europe. The German banking system came under severe pressure and was saved only through government guarantees. It became clear, however, that in this crisis Germany would be unable to make its next reparation payment as stipulated in the 1929 Young Plan. As the German difficulties mounted, American President Herbert Hoover (1874–1964) announced in June 1931 a one-year moratorium on all payments of international debts.

Major Dates of the Economic Crisis	
1923	German inflation following French invasion of Ruhr
1924	Dawes Plan on reparations
1929 (June)	Young Plan on reparations
1929 (October)	Wall Street crash
1931 (May)	Collapse of *Kreditanstalt* in Vienna
1931 (June)	Hoover announces moratorium on reparations
1932	Lausanne Conference ends reparations

The Hoover moratorium was a prelude to the end of reparations. Hoover's action was a sharp blow to the French economy, for which the flow of reparations had continued to be important. The French agreed to the moratorium most reluctantly but really had little alternative because the German economy had all but collapsed. The Lausanne Conference in the summer of 1932 in effect ended the era of reparations. The next year, the debts owed to the United States were settled either through small token payments or simply through default. Nevertheless, the financial politics of the 1920s had done its damage.

Problems in Agricultural Commodities

In addition to the dramatic financial turmoil and collapse, a less dramatic, but equally fundamental, downturn occurred in production and trade. The 1920s saw the market demand for European goods shrink relative to the Continent's capacity to produce goods. This meant idle factories and fewer jobs. Part of this problem originated within Europe, and part outside. In both instances, the difficulty arose from agriculture. Better methods of farming, improved strains of wheat, expanded tillage, and more extensive transport facilities all over the globe vastly increased the world supply of grain. World wheat prices fell to record lows. This development was, of course, initially good for consumers. The collapse in grain prices, however, meant lower incomes for European farmers and especially for those of central and eastern Europe.

Also, higher industrial wages raised the cost of the industrial goods used by farmers or peasants. The farmers could not purchase those products. Moreover, farmers began to have difficulty paying off their mortgages and normal annual operational debts. They normally borrowed money to plant their fields, expecting to pay the debt when the crops were sold. The fall in commodity prices made it difficult for the farmers to repay those debts.

These farm problems became especially pressing in eastern Europe. Immediately after the war, the new governments there had undertaken land-reform programs. The democratic franchise in the successor states had opened the way for considerable redistribution of tillable soil. In Romania and Czechoslovakia, large amounts of land changed hands. This occurred to a lesser extent in Hungary and Poland.

These new small farms, however, proved to be inefficient, and the farmers who worked them were unable to earn sufficient incomes. Protective tariffs often prevented the export of grain among European countries. The credit and cost squeeze on eastern European farmers and on their counterparts in Germany played a major role in their disillusionment with liberal politics. For example, farmers in Germany were a major source of political support for the Nazis.

Outside Europe, similar problems affected other producers of agricultural commodities. The prices that they received for their products plummeted. Government-held reserves of agricultural commodities accumulated to record levels. This glut involved the supplies of wheat, sugar, coffee, rubber, wool, and lard. The people who produced these goods in underdeveloped nations in Asia, Africa, and Latin America could no longer make enough money to buy finished goods from industrial Europe. As world credit collapsed, the economic position of these commodity producers worsened. Commodity production had simply outstripped world demand.

The collapse in the agricultural prices and the financial turmoil resulted in stagnation and depression for European industry. European coal, iron, and textiles had depended largely on international markets. Unemployment spread from these industries to those producing fin-

The League of Nations Reports the Collapse of European Agriculture

A crisis in agriculture was as much a cause of the Great Depression as was the turmoil in the financial community. The League of Nations reported in 1931 how, in part, the desperate situation in agriculture had developed.

◆ *How did the fall in agricultural prices affect the likelihood of immediate future production? How did the crisis in farm prices affect other sectors of the European economy? What was the relationship between farm prices outside Europe to the prices in Europe and to the demand for European industrial goods around the world?*

It is the lowness of prices that constitutes the agricultural crisis. It is becoming difficult to sell products, and in many cases prices have reached a level at which they are scarcely, if at all, sufficient to cover the cost of production.

The reason for the crisis and for its continuance is to be found in the fact that agricultural prices are low in comparison with the expenditure which the farmer must meet. . . . Agricultural products cost a lot to produce and then fetch very little in the market. In spite of the great technical progress achieved, operating costs remain implacably higher than selling prices, farmers obtain no longer a fair return on their labour or on their capital. Frequently the returns of agricultural undertakings are not enough to cover the necessary outlay for the purchase of the material or products necessary for continued operation or for the payment of wages and taxes and so forth.

This disproportion between the income and expenditure of agricultural undertakings . . . appears to constitute the dominant and decisive element of the prevailing agricultural depression.

Until 1929, prices were low as compared with prices of industrial products, but were above pre-war prices. The predominating tendency to a fall which was observed was not altogether general nor was it abnormally rapid. The general character of the price movement completely changed in 1930. A fall, sometimes catastrophic, spread with extreme violence to almost all agricultural produce. It was so rapid that at the end of the year, whilst some products reached the pre-war level of prices, others fell as low as one-quarter or one-half below the 1913 level. . . . Farmers throughout the world have suffered from it.

League of Nations, Economic Committee, The Agricultural Crisis, Vol. 1 (1931), pp. 7–8, as reprinted in S. B. Clough, T. Moodie, and C. G. Moodie, Economic History of Europe: The Twentieth Century (New York: Harper & Row, 1968), pp. 216–217.

---

ished consumer goods. The persistent unemployment in Great Britain and to a lesser extent in Germany during the 1920s had already meant "soft" domestic markets in those countries. The policies of reduced government spending with which the governments confronted the depression further weakened domestic demand. By the early 1930s, the Great Depression was growing on itself.

Depression and Government Policy

The Great Depression did not mean absolute economic decline. Nor did it mean that everyone was out of a job. People with work always well outnumbered those without work. New economic sectors such as production of automobiles, radios, synthetics, and the service industries around them did develop. But the economic downturn made people extremely anxious. People in nearly all walks of life feared that their own economic security and lifestyle would suffer next. The depression also frustrated social and economic expectations. People with jobs frequently improved their standard of living or were promoted much more slowly than might have been the case under sound economic conditions. They were working, but in their own eyes they seemed to be going nowhere. Their anxieties created a major source of social discontent.

The governments of the late 1920s and the early 1930s were not well fitted in either structure or ideology to confront these problems. The Keynesian theory of governments' spending the economy out of depression was not yet available. John Maynard Keynes's (1883–1946) *General Theory of Employment, Interest, and Money* was not published until 1936. Before Keynes, orthodox economic policy called for cuts in government spending to prevent inflation. Eventually, the market mechanism was supposed to bring the economy back to prosperity.

Nonetheless, the length and severity of the depression, plus direct political pressure from the new mass electorates, led governments across Europe to interfere with the economy as never before. Government participation in economic life was not new. One need only recall the mercantilistic policies of the seventeenth and eighteenth centuries and the government encouragement of railway building in the nineteenth century. From the early 1930s onward, however, government involvement increased rapidly. Private economic enterprise became subject to new trade, labor, and currency regulations. The political goals of restoring employment and providing for defense established new state-related economic priorities. As in the past, state intervention generally increased as one moved from west to east across the Continent. These new economic policies usually also involved further political experimentation.

Confronting the Great Depression in the Democracies

The Great Depression ended the business-as-usual attitude that had marked the political life of Great Britain and France during the late 1920s. In Britain, the emergency led to a new coalition government and the abandonment of economic policies considered sacred for a century. The economic stagnation in France proved to be the occasion for a bold political and economic program sponsored by the parties of the left. The relative success of the British venture gave the nation new confidence in the democratic processes; the new departures in France created social and political hostilities that undermined faith in republican institutions.

Great Britain: The National Government

In 1929 a second minority Labour government, headed by Ramsay MacDonald, took office. As the number of British unemployed rose to more than 2.5 million workers in 1931, the ministry became divided over what to do. MacDonald believed that the budget should be slashed, government salaries reduced, and unemployment benefits cut. This was a bleak program for a Labour government. MacDonald's strong desire to make the Labour Party respectable led him to reject more radical programs. Many of the cabinet ministries resisted MacDonald's proposals. They refused to take income away from the poor and the unemployed. The prime minister requested the resignations of his entire cabinet and arranged for a meeting with King George V.

Everyone assumed that the entire Labour ministry was about to leave office. To the surprise of his party and the nation, MacDonald, however, did not resign. At the urging of the king and probably of his own ambition, MacDonald formed a coalition ministry, called the *National Government*, composed of Labour, Conservative, and Liberal ministers. The bulk of the Labour Party believed that their leader had sold them out. In the election of 1931, the National Government received a comfortable majority. After the election, however, MacDonald, who remained prime minister until 1935, was little more than a tool of the Conservatives. They held a majority in their own right in the House of Commons, but the appearance of a coalition was useful for imposing unpleasant programs.

The National Government took three decisive steps to attack the depression. First, to balance the budget, it raised taxes, cut insurance benefits to the unemployed and the elderly, and lowered government salaries. Its leaders argued that the fall in prices that had taken place meant that those reductions did not appreciably cut real income. Second, in September 1931, Britain went off the gold standard. The value of the British pound on the international money market fell by about 30 percent. This move somewhat stimulated exports. Third, in 1932 Parliament passed the Import Duties Bill, which placed a 10 percent *ad valorem* tariff (a tax levied in proportion to the value of each imported good) on all imports except those from the empire. In the context of previous British policy, these steps were extraordinary. Gold and free trade, the hallmarks of almost a century of British commercial policy, were abandoned.

The policies of the National Government produced significant results. Great Britain avoided the banking crisis that hit other countries. By 1934 industrial production had expanded beyond the level for 1929. Britain was the first nation to restore that level of production. Of course, the mediocre British industrial performance of the 1920s made the British task easier. The government also encouraged lower interest rates. This, in turn, led to the largest private housing boom in British history. Industries related to housing and the furnishing of homes prospered.

Those people who were employed generally improved their standard of living. Nonetheless, the hard core of unemployment remained. In 1937 the number of jobless had fallen to just below 1.5 million. That same year, when George Orwell (1903–1950) described the laboring districts of Britain in *The Road to Wigan Pier*, the poverty and the idle days without work of the people he met dominated his picture.

George Orwell Observes a Woman in the Slums

Although Great Britain was beginning to emerge from the Great Depression by the late 1930s, much poverty and human degradation remained. This scene, described in 1937 by the social critic and novelist George Orwell (1903–1950), captures a glimpse of the sadness and hopelessness that many British citizens experienced every day of their lives.

✦ *How does Orwell's descriptive language evoke sympathy for the woman he portrays? What economic conditions led to such poverty? What class attitudes does Orwell begin to explore in this passage?*

The train bore me away, through the monstrous scenery of slag-heaps, chimneys, piled scrap-iron, foul canals, paths of cindery mud crisscrossed by the prints of clogs. . . . As we moved slowly through the outskirts of the town we passed row after row of little grey slum houses running at right angles to the embankment. At the back of one of the houses a young woman was kneeling on the stones, poking a stick up the leaden waste-pipe which ran from the sink inside, and which I suppose was blocked. I had time to see everything about her—her sacking apron, her clumsy clogs, her arms reddened by the cold. . . . She had a round pale face, the usual exhausted face of the slum girl who is twenty-five and looks forty, thanks to miscarriages and drudgery; and it wore, for the second in which I saw it, the most desolate, hopeless expression I have ever seen. It struck me then that we are mistaken when we say that "It isn't the same for them as it would be for us," and that people bred in the slums can imagine nothing but the slums. For what I saw in her face was not the ignorant suffering of an animal. She knew well enough what was happening to her—understood as well as I did how dreadful a destiny it was to be kneeling there in the bitter cold, on the slimy stones of a slum backyard, poking a stick up a foul drain-pipe.

George Orwell, The Road to Wigan Pier *(New York: Berkley Medallion Books, 1967; originally printed in 1937), p. 29.*

Britain had entered the depression with a stagnant economy and left the era with a stagnant economy. Yet the British political system was not fundamentally challenged. There were demonstrations by the unemployed, but social insurance, though hardly generous, did support them. To the employed citizens of the country, the National Government seemed to pursue a policy that avoided the extreme wings of both the Labour and the Conservative parties. When MacDonald retired in 1935, Stanley Baldwin again took office. He was succeeded in 1937 by Neville Chamberlain (1869–1940). The new prime minister is today known for the disastrous Munich agreement, but when he took office, he was considered one of the more progressive thinkers on social issues in the Conservative Party.

One movement in Britain did flirt with the extreme right-wing politics of the Continent. In 1932 Sir Oswald Mosley (1896–1980) founded the British Union of Fascists. He had held a minor position in the second Labour government and was disappointed by its feeble attack on unemployment. Mosley urged a program of direct action through a new corporate structure for the economy. His group wore black shirts and attempted to hold mass meetings. Even at the height of his popularity, he gained only a few thousand adherents. Thereafter his anti-Semitism began to alienate supporters, and by the close of the decade, he was little more than a political oddity.

France: The Popular Front

The timing of the Great Depression in France was the reverse of that in Britain. It came later and lasted longer. Only in 1931 did the economic slide begin to affect the French economy. Even then, unemployment did not become a major problem. Rarely were more than half a million French workers without jobs. In one industry after another, however, wages were lowered. The government raised tariffs to protect French goods and especially French agriculture. Ever since that time, French farmers have enjoyed unusual protection by the government. These measures helped maintain the home market but did little to overcome industrial stagnation. Relations between labor and management were tense.

The first political fallout of the depression was the election of another Radical coalition government in 1932. Fearful of contributing to inflation as they had after 1924, the Radicals pursued a generally deflationary policy. In the same year that the new ministry took office, reparation payments upon which the French economy depended had stopped. As the economic crisis tightened, normal parliamentary and political life became difficult and confused.

RIGHT-WING VIOLENCE Outside the Chamber of Deputies, politics grew ugly. Various right-wing groups with authoritarian tendencies became active. These leagues included the *Action Française*, founded before World War I in the wake of the Dreyfus affair, and the *Croix de Feu* ("Cross of Fire"), composed of army veterans. These and similar groups had a total of more than two million members. Some of them wanted a monarchy; others favored what would have amounted to military rule. They were hostile to parliamentary government, socialism, and communism. They wanted what they regarded as the greater good and glory of France to be set above the petty machinations of political parties. They thus resembled the Fascists and the Nazis.

The activities and propaganda of these leagues weakened loyalty to republican government and made French political life more bitter and vindictive. They also led to an incident of extraordinary havoc that produced important long-range political consequences.

The incident grew out of the Stavisky affair, the last of those curious scandals that punctuated the political fortunes of the Third Republic. Serge Stavisky (d. 1934) was a small-time gangster who appears to have had good connections within the government. In 1933 he became involved in a fraudulent bond scheme. When finally tracked down by the police, he committed suicide in January 1934. The official handling of the matter suggested a political cover-up. It was alleged that people in high places wished to halt the investigation. To the right wing in France, the Stavisky incident symbolized all the seaminess, immorality, and corruption of republican politics.

On February 6, 1934, a large demonstration of the right-wing leagues took place in Paris. The exact purpose and circumstances of the rally remain uncertain, but the crowd did attempt to march on the Chamber of Deputies. Violence erupted between right and left political groups and between them and the police. Fourteen demonstrators were killed; scores of others were injured. It was the largest disturbance in Paris since the Commune of 1871.

In the wake of the night of February 6, the Radical ministry of Edouard Daladier (1884–1970) resigned and was replaced by a national coalition government composed of all living former premiers. The Chamber of Deputies permitted the ministry to deal with economic matters by decree. The major result of the right-wing demonstrations, however, was a political self-reassessment by the parties of the left. Radicals, Socialists, and Communists began to realize that a right-wing coup might be possible in France.

EMERGENCE OF SOCIALIST–COMMUNIST COOPERATION Between 1934 and 1936, the French left began to make peace within its own ranks. This was not easy. French Socialists, led by Léon Blum (1872–1950), had been the major target of the French Communists since the split over joining the Comintern in 1920. Only Stalin's fear of Hitler as a danger to the Soviet Union made this new cooperation possible.

Despite deep suspicions on all sides, the Popular Front of all left-wing parties had been established by July 1935. Its purpose was to preserve the republic and press for social reform.

The election of 1936 gave the Popular Front a majority in the Chamber of Deputies. The Socialists were the largest single party for the first time in French history. They organized the cabinet as they had long promised they would do when they constituted the majority party of a coalition. Léon Blum assumed the premiership on June 5, 1936. From the early 1920s, this Jewish intellectual and humanitarian had opposed the Communist version of socialism. Cast as the successor to Jean Jaurès (1859–1914), who had been assassinated in 1914, Blum pursued socialism in the context of democratic, parliamentary government.

BLUM'S GOVERNMENT During May 1936, before the Popular Front came to power, strikes had begun to spread throughout French industry. Immediately after assuming office on June 6, the Blum government faced further spontaneous work stoppages involving over half a million workers who had occupied factories in sit-down strikes. These were the most extensive labor disturbances in the history of the Third Republic. They aroused new fears in the conser-

During a Bastille Day rally for the French Popular Front government in July, 1936, crowds carried a large portrait of Premier Léon Blum through the streets of Paris. [UPI/Bettmann]

vative business community, already frightened by the election of the Popular Front.

Blum acted swiftly to bring together representatives of labor and management. On June 8, he announced the conclusion of an accord that reorganized labor–management relations in France. Wages were immediately raised between 7 and 15 percent, depending on the job involved. Employers were required to recognize unions and to bargain collectively with them. Workers were given annual, paid two-week vacations. The forty-hour week was established throughout French industry. Blum hoped to overcome labor hostility to French society, to

French Management and Labor Reach an Agreement

When the Popular Front government came to power in France in 1936, it immediately faced widespread strikes. Premier Léon Blum called together the representatives of labor and management. The result of these negotiations was an accord that gave the unions more secure rights, raised wages, and ended the strikes.

♦ Why did the election of the Popular Front government make this agreement possible? What guarantees do union members receive in this agreement? Which elements of this agreement seem to favor the workers economically and which politically?

The delegates of the General Confederation of French Production (CGPF) and the General Confederation of Labour (CGT) have met under the chairmanship of the Premier (Léon Blum) and have concluded the following agreement, after arbitration by the Premier:

1. The employer delegation agrees to the immediate conclusion of collective agreements.

2. These agreements must include, in particular, articles 3, ...

3. All citizens being required to abide by law, the employers recognize the freedom of opinion of workers and their right to freely join and belong to trade unions.

In their decisions on hiring, organization or assignment of work, disciplinary measures or dismissals, employers agree not to take into consideration the fact of membership or nonmembership in a union. . . .

The exercise of trade union rights must not give rise to acts contrary to law.

4. The wages actually paid to all workers as of 25 May 1936 will be raised, as of the resumption of work, by a decreasing percentage ranging from 15 per cent for the lowest rates down to 7 per cent for the highest rates. In no case must the total increase in any establishment exceed 12 per cent. . . .

The negotiations, which are to be launched at once, for the determination by collective agreement of minimum wages by regions and by occupations must take up, in particular, the necessary revision of abnormally low wages. . . .

. . . .

6. The employer delegation promises that there will be no sanctions for strike activities.

7. The CGT delegation will ask the workers on strike to return to work as soon as the managements of establishments have accepted this general agreement and as soon as negotiations for its application have begun between the managements and the personnel of the establishments.

As cited in V. R. Lorwin, The French Labour Movement *(Cambridge, Mass.: Harvard University Press, 1954), pp. 313–315.*

establish a foundation for justice in labor–management relations, and to increase the domestic consumer demand of the nation.

Blum followed his labor policy with other bold departures. He raised the salaries of civil servants and instituted a program of public works. Government loans were extended to small industry. Spending on armaments was increased, and some armament industries were nationalized. A National Wheat Board was set up to manage the production and sale of grain. Initially, Blum had promised to resist devaluation of the franc. By the autumn of 1936, however, international monetary pressure forced him to devalue. He did so again in the spring of 1937. The devaluations came too late to help French exports.

These moves enraged the conservative banking and business community. In March 1937, they brought enough influence to bear on the ministry to cause Blum to halt the program of reform. It was not taken up again. Blum's Popular Front colleagues considered the pause in reform an unnecessary compromise. In June 1937, Blum resigned. The Popular Front ministry itself held on until April 1938, when it was replaced by a Radical ministry under Daladier. Not until 1939 did French industrial production reach the level of 1929.

By the close of the 1930s, citizens from all walks of life had begun to wonder if the republic was worth preserving. The left remained divided. Businesspeople found the republic inefficient and too much subject to socialist pressures. The right wing hated the republic in principle. When the time came in 1940 to defend the republic, too many French citizens were not sure that it was worth defending.

Germany: The Nazi Seizure of Power

The most remarkable political event caused by the uncertainty and turmoil of the Great Depression was the coming to power of the National Socialists (Nazis) in Germany. By the late 1920s, the Nazis were a major presence in the Weimar Republic, but were not yet real contenders for political dominance. The financial

Depression Years in Great Britain and France	
1929	Second Labour government comes to power in Britain with Ramsay MacDonald as prime minister
1931	Formation of National Government in Britain
1931	British government goes off the gold standard
1932	Oswald Mosley founds British Union of Fascists
1933–1934	Stavisky affair in France
1934 (February 6)	Right-wing riots in Paris
1935	Stanley Baldwin becomes British prime minister
1936 (June 5)	Popular Front government in France under Blum
1936 (June 8)	Labor accord in France
1937	Neville Chamberlain becomes British prime minister
1938	Popular Front replaced by Radical ministry in France

crisis, economic stress, and social anxiety associated with the onset of the depression rapidly changed that situation. All the fragility of the Weimar Constitution stood exposed, and the path opened for the most momentous and far-reaching event of the decade, the Nazi seizure of power.

Depression and Political Deadlock

The outflow of foreign, especially American, capital from Germany beginning in 1928 undermined the economic prosperity of the Weimar Republic. The resulting economic crisis brought parliamentary government to an end. In 1928 a coalition of center parties and the Social Democrats governed. All went reasonably well until the depression struck. Then the coalition partners disagreed sharply on economic policy. The Social Democrats refused to reduce social and unemployment insurance. The more conservative parties, remembering the inflation of 1923, insisted on a balanced budget. The coalition dissolved in March 1930.

To resolve the parliamentary deadlock in the *Reichstag*, President von Hindenburg appointed Heinrich Brüning (1885–1970) as chancellor. Lacking a majority in the *Reichstag*, Brüning governed through emergency presidential decrees as authorized by Article 48 of the constitution. The party divisions in the *Reichstag* prevented parliament from overriding the decrees. The Weimar Republic was thus transformed into an authoritarian regime.

German unemployment rose from 2,258,000 in March 1930 to more than 6,000,000 in March 1932. There had been persistent unemployment during the 1920s, but nothing of such magnitude or duration. The economic downturn and the parliamentary deadlock worked to the advantage of the more extreme political parties. In the election of 1928, the Nazis had won only 12 seats in the *Reichstag*, and the Communists had won 54 seats. After the election of 1930, the Nazis held 107 seats and the Communists 77.

For the Nazis, politics meant the capture of power by terror and intimidation as well as by legal elections. All decency and civility in political life vanished. Thousands of unemployed joined the storm troopers (SA), which had 100,000 members in 1930 and almost one million in 1933. The SA freely and viciously attacked Communists and Social Democrats, who also went on fighting each other. The Nazis held mass rallies that resembled religious revivals. They gained powerful supporters and sympathizers in business, military, and newspaper circles. Some intellectuals were also sympathetic. The Nazis transformed this new enthusiasm born of economic despair and nationalistic frustration into impressive electoral results.

Hitler Comes to Power

For two years Brüning governed with the confidence of his president, von Hindenburg. The economy did not improve, however, and the political situation deteriorated. In 1932 the eighty-three-year-old president stood for reelection. Hitler ran against him and forced a runoff. The Nazi leader got 30.1 percent of the first vote, and 36.8 percent in the runoff. Although Hindenburg remained in office, the results of the poll convinced him that Brüning no longer

commanded sufficient confidence from conservative German voters.

On May 30, 1932, Hindenburg dismissed Brüning and the next day appointed Franz von Papen (1878–1969) as chancellor. The new chancellor was one of a small group of extremely conservative advisers on whom the aged Hindenburg had become increasingly dependent. Others included the president's son and several military figures. With the continued paralysis in the *Reichstag*, their influence over the president virtually amounted to control of the government. Thus, only a handful of people made the crucial decisions of the next several months.

Papen and the circle around the president wanted to find some way to draw the Nazis into cooperation with them without giving any effective power to Hitler. The government needed the mass popular support that only the Nazis seemed able to generate. The Hindenburg circle decided to convince Hitler that the Nazis could not come to power on their own. Papen removed the ban on Nazi meetings that Brüning had imposed. Furthermore, he called a *Reichstag* election for July 1932. The Nazis won 230 seats and polled 37.2 percent of the vote. As the price for his entry into the cabinet, Hitler demanded appointment as chancellor. Hindenburg refused. The government called another election in November, partly to wear down the Nazis' financial resources, which it did. The Nazis lost 34 seats, and their popular vote dipped to 33.1 percent. The advisers around Hindenburg still refused to appoint Hitler to office.

In November 1932, Papen resigned, and the next month General Kurt von Schleicher (1882–1934) became chancellor. Fear of civil war between the left and the right mounted. Schleicher tried to build a broad-based coalition of conservative groups and trade unionists. The prospect of such a coalition, including groups from the political left, frightened the Hindenburg circle even more than the prospect of Hitler. They did not trust Schleicher's motives, which have never been clear. Consequently, they persuaded Hindenburg to appoint Hitler as chancellor. To control Hitler and to see that he did little mischief, the Hindenburg circle appointed Papen as vice-chancellor and named other traditional conservatives to the cabinet.

Hitler's mastery of the techniques of mass politics and propaganda—including huge staged rallies like this one in 1938—was an important factor in his rise to power. [Bildarchiv Preussischer Kulturbesitz]

On January 30, 1933, Adolf Hitler became the chancellor of Germany.

Hitler had come into office by legal means. All the proper legal forms and procedures had been observed. This was important, for it permitted the civil service, the courts, and the other agencies of the government to support him in good conscience. He had forged a rigidly disciplined party structure and had mastered the techniques of mass politics and propaganda. He understood how to touch the raw social and political nerves of the electorate. His support appears to have come from across the social spectrum and not simply from the lower middle class, as was once thought to be the case. Pockets of resistance appeared among Roman Catholic voters in the country and small towns. Otherwise, support for Hitler was particularly strong among groups such as farmers, war veterans, and the young, who had especially suffered from the insecurity of the 1920s and the depression of the early 1930s. Hitler promised them security against communists and socialists, effective government in place of the petty politics of the other parties, and an uncompromising nationalist vision of a strong, restored Germany.

German big business once received much of the credit for the rise of Hitler. There is little evidence, however, that business contributions made any crucial difference to the Nazis' success or failure. Hitler's supporters were frequently suspicious of business and giant capitalism. They wanted a simpler world and one in which small property would be safe from both socialism and large-scale capitalist consolidation. These people looked to Hitler and the Nazis rather than to the Social Democrats because the latter, though concerned with social issues, never appeared sufficiently nationalistic.

The Nazis won out over other conservative nationalistic parties because, unlike those conservatives, the Nazis did address the problem of social insecurities.

Hitler's Consolidation of Power

Once in office, Hitler moved with almost lightning speed to consolidate his control. This process had three facets: the capture of full legal authority, the crushing of alternative political groups, and the purging of rivals within the Nazi Party itself.

On February 27, 1933, a mentally ill Dutch Communist set fire to the *Reichstag* building in Berlin. The Nazis quickly claimed that the fire proved the existence of an immediate Communist threat against the government. To the public, it was plausible that the Communists might attempt some action against the state now that the Nazis were in power. Under Article 48, Hitler issued an Emergency Decree suspending civil liberties and proceeded to arrest Communists or alleged Communists. This decree was not revoked for as long as Hitler ruled Germany.

In early March, another *Reichstag* election took place. The Nazis still received only 43.9 percent of the vote and won 288 seats. The arrest and removal of all Communist deputies, however, and the political fear aroused by the fire enabled Hitler to control the *Reichstag*. On March 23, 1933, the *Reichstag* passed an Enabling Act that permitted Hitler to rule by decree. Thereafter there were no legal limits on his exercise of power. The Weimar Constitution was never formally repealed or amended. It had simply been supplanted by the February Emergency Decree and the March Enabling Act.

Perhaps better than anyone else, Hitler understood that he and his party had not inevitably come to power. In a series of complex moves, Hitler outlawed or undermined any German institution that might have served as a rallying point for opposition. In early May 1933, the Nazi Party, rather than any government agency, seized the offices, banks, and newspapers of the free trade unions and arrested their leaders. In late June and early July, all other German political parties were outlawed. By July 14, 1933, the National Socialists were the only legal party in Germany. During the same months, the Nazis moved against the governments of the individual federal states in Germany. By the close of 1933, all major institutions of potential opposition had been eliminated.

The final element in Hitler's consolidation of power involved the Nazi Party itself. By late 1933 the SA, or storm troopers, consisted of approximately one million active members and a larger number of reserves. The commander of this party army was Ernst Roehm (1887–1934), a possible rival to Hitler himself. The German army officer corps, on whom Hitler depended to rebuild the national army, were jealous of the SA leadership. So, to protect his own position and to shore up support with the regular army, on June 30, 1934, Hitler personally ordered the

The Reichstag *fire in 1933 provided Hitler an excuse to consolidate his power. [Bildarchiv Preussischer Kulturbesitz]*

Josef Goebbels Explains How to Use Radio for Political Propaganda

Radio produced a communications revolution during the interwar years. It also created an entirely new industry while many other areas of the economy stagnated. Radio, as popular at that time as television is today, also became an important political instrument. Most of the early radio stations were government owned and controlled. Political leaders could address their nations as they never could before. Communication became instant and could enter every home with a radio. Radio, unlike newspapers, did not depend upon the literacy of its audience. Shortly after coming into power, Josef Goebbels (1897–1945), who was in charge of Nazi propaganda, discussed the role of radio in the new Nazi order. Note how he urges his listeners, who were broadcasters, never to be boring. All radio broadcasting had to be interesting to audiences so they would be receptive to its political messages.

✦ *Why does Goebbels emphasize the Nazi monopoly on broadcasting? What new attitudes did Goebbels want radio to bring to its audience? What advantages did radio have over newspapers as a propaganda device?*

We make no bones about the fact that the radio belongs to us and to no one else. And we will place the radio in the service of our ideology [*Idee*] and [. . .] no other ideology will find expression here. . . . The radio must subordinate itself to the goals which the Government of the national revolution has set itself. The Government will give the necessary instructions. . . .

I consider radio to be the most modern and the most crucial instrument that exists for influencing the masses. I also believe—one should not say that out loud—that radio will in the end replace the press. . . .

First, principle: At all costs avoid being boring. I put that before *everything*. . . . So do not think that you have the task of creating the correct attitudes, of indulging in patriotism, of blasting out military music and declaiming patriotic verse—no, that is not what this new orientation is all about. Rather you must help to bring forth a nationalist art and culture which is truly appropriate to the pace of modern life and to the mood of the times. The correct attitudes must be conveyed but that does not mean they must be boring. And simply because you have the task of taking part in this national enterprise you do not have *carte blanche* to be boring. You must use your imagination, an imagination which is based on sure foundations and which employs all means and methods to bring to the ears of the masses the new attitude in a way which is modern, up to date, interesting, and appealing; interesting, instructive but not schoolmasterish. Radio must never go down with the proverbial disease—the intention is clear and it puts you off.

I am placing a major responsibility in your hands for you have in your hands the most modern instrument in existence for influencing the masses. By means of this instrument you are the creators of public opinion. If you carry this out well we shall win over the people and if you do it badly in the end the people will once more desert us. . . .

J. Noakes and G. Pridham, eds., Nazism 1919–1945, *Vol. 2,* State, Economy and Society 1933–39, A Documentary Reader, *Exeter Studies in History, No. 8 (Exeter: University of Exeter, 1984), p. 386.*

Joseph Goebbels (1897–1945) was in charge of Nazi propaganda. [Bildarchiv Preussischer Kulturbesitz]

Germany and stood second only to Hitler in power and influence.

The police character of the Nazi regime was all-pervasive, but the people who most consistently experienced the terror of the police state were the German Jews. Anti-Semitism had been a key plank of the Nazi program. It was anti-Semitism based on biological racial theories stemming from late-nineteenth-century thought rather than from religious discrimination. Before World War II, the Nazi attack on the Jews went through three stages of increasing intensity. First, in 1933, shortly after assuming power, the Nazis excluded Jews from the civil service. They also tried to enforce boycotts of Jewish shops and businesses, but these won little public support.

Second, in 1935, a series of measures known as the Nuremberg Laws robbed German Jews of their citizenship. All persons with at least three Jewish grandparents were defined as Jews. The professions and the major occupations were closed to them. Marriage and sexual intercourse between Jews and non-Jews were prohibited.

Soon after seizing power, the Nazi government began harassing German Jewish businesses. Non-Jewish German citizens were urged not to buy merchandise from shops owned by Jews. [Bildarchiv Preussischer Kulturbesitz]

murder of key SA officers, including Roehm. Between June 30 and July 2, more than 100 persons were killed, including former chancellor General Kurt von Schleicher and his wife. The German army, the only institution that might have prevented the murders, did nothing.

A month later, on August 2, 1934, President Hindenburg died. Thereafter Hitler combined the offices of chancellor and president. He was now the sole ruler of Germany and of the Nazi Party.

The Police State and Anti-Semitism

Terror and intimidation had been major factors in the Nazi march to office. As Hitler consolidated his power, he oversaw the organization of a police state. The chief vehicle of police surveillance was the SS (*Schutzstaffel*, protective force), or security units, commanded by Heinrich Himmler (1900–1945). This group had originated in the mid-1920s as a bodyguard for Hitler and had become a more elite paramilitary organization than the much larger SA. In 1933 there were approximately 52,000 members of the SS. It was the instrument that carried out the blood purges of the party in 1934. By 1936 Himmler had become head of all police matters in

The Nazis Pass Their Racial Legislation

Anti-Semitism was a fundamental tenet of the Nazi Party and became a major policy of the Nazi government. This comprehensive legislation of September 15, 1935, carried anti-Semitism into all areas of public life and into some of the most personal areas of private life as well. It was characteristically titled the Law for the Protection of German Blood and Honor. Hardly any aspect of Nazi thought and action shocked the non-German world as much as this policy toward the Jews.

✦ *How would this legislation have affected the normal daily interaction between Jews and non-Jews in Germany? Why are there specific prohibitions against mixed marriages and sexual relations between Jews and non-Jews? How does this legislation separate German Jews from the symbols of German national life?*

Imbued with the knowledge that the purity of German blood is the necessary prerequisite for the existence of the German nation, and inspired by an inflexible will to maintain the existence of the German nation for all future times, the Reichstag has unanimously adopted the following law, which is now enacted:

Article I: (1) Any marriages between Jews and citizens of German or kindred blood are herewith forbidden. Marriages entered into despite this law are invalid, even if they are arranged abroad as a means of circumventing this law.

(2) Annulment proceedings for marriages may be initiated only by the Public Prosecutor.

Article II: Extramarital relations between Jews and citizens of German or kindred blood are herewith forbidden.

Article III: Jews are forbidden to employ as servants to their households female subjects of German or kindred blood who are under the age of forty-five years.

Article IV: (1) Jews are prohibited from displaying the Reich and national flag and from showing the national colors.

(2) However, they may display the Jewish colors. The exercise of this right is under state protection.

Article V: (1) Anyone who acts contrary to the prohibition noted in Article I renders himself liable to penal servitude.

(2) The man who acts contrary to the prohibition of Article II will be punished by sentence to either a jail or penitentiary.

(3) Anyone who acts contrary to the provisions of Articles III or IV will be punished with a jail sentence up to a year and with a fine, or with one of these penalties.

Article VI: The Reich Minister of Interior, in conjunction with the Deputy to the Führer and the Reich Minister of Justice, will issue the required legal and administrative decrees for the implementation and amplification of this law.

Article VII: This law shall go into effect on the day following its promulgation, with the exception of Article III, which shall go into effect on January 1, 1936.

Louis L. Snyder, ed. and trans., Documents of German History *(New Brunswick, N.J.: Rutgers University Press, 1958), pp. 427–428.*

Legal exclusion and humiliation of the Jews became the order of the day.

Then the persecution of the Jews increased again in 1938. Business careers were forbidden to them. In November 1938, under orders from the Nazi Party, thousands of Jewish stores and synagogues were burned or otherwise destroyed on what became known as *Kristallnacht*. The Jewish community itself was required to pay for the damage because the government confiscated the insurance money. In many other ways, large and petty, German Jews were harassed. This persecution allowed the Nazis to inculcate the rest of the population with the concept of a

In early November, 1938, the Nazi authorities in Germany increased their persecution of Jews. On what has come to be called Kristallnacht, *Nazis destroyed Jewish businesses and burned synagogues.* [Bildarchiv Preussischer Kulturbesitz]

master race of pure German "Aryans" and also to display their own contempt for civil liberties.

Finally, after the war broke out, Hitler decided in 1941 and 1942 to destroy the Jews in Europe. More than six million Jews, mostly from eastern European nations, died as a result of that staggering decision, unprecedented in its scope and implementation.

Nazi Economic Policy

Besides consolidating power and pursuing anti-Semitic policies, Hitler still had to confront the Great Depression. German unemployment had helped propel him to power. The Nazis attacked this problem with a success that astonished and frightened Europe. By 1936, while the rest of the European economy remained stagnant, the specter of unemployment and other difficulties associated with the Great Depression no longer haunted Germany.

As far as the economic crisis was concerned, Hitler had become the most effective political leader in Europe. This success was a most important source of the internal strength and support for his tyrannical regime. The Nazi success against the Great Depression gave the regime considerable contemporary credibility. Behind the direction of both business and labor stood the Nazi terror and police. The Nazi eco-

nomic experiment proved that by sacrificing all political and civil liberty, destroying a free trade-union movement, preventing the private exercise of capital, and ignoring consumer satisfaction, full employment to prepare for war and aggression could be achieved.

Nazi economic policies maintained private property and private capitalism, but subordinated all significant economic enterprise and decisions about prices and investment to the goals of the state. Hitler reversed the deflationary policy of the cabinets that had preceded him. He instituted a massive program of public works and spending. Many of these projects related directly or indirectly to rearmament. The government sponsored canal building, land

Major Dates in the Nazi Seizure of Power	
1928	National Socialists win 12 seats in the *Reichstag*
1930	National Socialists win 107 seats in the *Reichstag*
1930	Brüning appointed Chancellor
1932 (April 10)	Hindenburg defeats Hitler for presidency
1932 (May 31)	Von Papen replaces Brüning
1932 (July 31)	National Socialists win 230 seats in the *Reichstag*
1932 (November 6)	Indecisive *Reichstag* election; National Socialists lose 34 seats
1932 (November 17)	Von Papen resigns
1932 (December 2)	Von Schleicher appointed Chancellor
1933 (January 28)	Von Schleicher resigns
1933 (January 30)	Hitler appointed Chancellor
1933 (February 27)	*Reichstag* fire
1933 (March 5)	National Socialists win 288 seats in the *Reichstag*
1933 (March 23)	Enabling Act passed
1933 (July 14)	National Socialists declared the only legal party
1934 (June 30)	Murder of SA leadership
1934 (August 2)	Death of von Hindenburg
1935	Passage of Nuremberg Laws
1938 (November 9)	Night of attack on Jewish businesses and synagogues (*Kristallnacht*)

reclamation, and the construction of a large highway system with clear military uses. The government returned some unemployed workers to farms if they had originally come from there. Other laborers were not permitted to change jobs.

In 1935 renunciation of the military provisions of the Versailles treaty led to open rearmament and expansion of the army with little opposition, as will be explained in Chapter 29. These measures essentially restored full employment. In 1936 Hitler instructed Hermann Göring (1893–1946), who had headed the air force since 1933, to undertake a Four-Year Plan to prepare the army and the economy for war. The government determined that Germany must be economically self-sufficient. Armaments received top priority. This economic program satisfied both the yearning for social and economic security and the desire for national fulfillment.

With the crushing of the trade unions in 1933, strikes became illegal. There was no genuine collective bargaining. The government handled labor disputes through compulsory arbitration. It also required workers and employers to participate in the Labor Front, an organization intended to demonstrate that class conflict had ended. The Labor Front sponsored a "Strength Through Joy" program that provided vacations and other forms of recreation for the labor force.

The Volkswagen, which first appeared in 1938, was intended to provide inexpensive transportation for German workers. This advertisement declares that saving five marks a week is all it takes to buy one. [Bildarchiv Preussischer Kulturbesitz]

Women in Nazi Germany

Hitler and other Nazis thought there were naturally separate social spheres for men and women. Men belonged in the world of action, women in the home. The two spheres should not mix. Women who sought to liberate themselves and to adopt roles traditionally followed by men in public life were considered symptoms of cultural decline. Respect for women should arise from their function as wives and mothers.

These attitudes stood in direct conflict with many of the social changes that German women, like women elsewhere in Europe, had experienced during the first three decades of the twentieth century. German women had become much more active and assertive. More of them worked in factories or were independently employed, and they had begun to enter the professions. Under the Weimar Constitution, they voted. Throughout the Weimar period, there was also a lively discussion of issues surrounding women's emancipation. The Nazis saw many of these developments as signs of cultural weakness. They urged a much more traditional role for women in their new society. Nazi writers portrayed women as wives and mothers first and foremost.

The Nazis' point of view brought them the support of women of a conservative outlook and women who were following traditional roles as housewives, confirming the choices these women had made about the direction of their lives. In a period of high unemployment, the Nazi attitude also appealed to many men because it discouraged women from competing with men in the workplace. Such competition had begun during World War I and was regarded

Hitler Rejects the Emancipation of Women

According to Nazi ideology, women's place was in the home producing and rearing children and supporting their husbands. In this speech, Hitler urges this view of the role of women. He uses anti-Semitism to discredit those writers who had urged the emancipation of women from their traditional roles and occupations. Hitler returns here to the "separate spheres" concept of the relationship of men and women. His traditional view of women was directed against contrary views that were associated with the Soviet experiment during the interwar years. This Nazi outlook on women and the family should be contrasted with the view set forth by the young Bolshevik Alexandra Kollontai in the document in Chapter 27. Ironically, once World War II began, the Nazi leadership demanded that women leave the home and work in factories to support the war effort.

✦ *What are the social tasks Hitler assigns to women? Why does he associate the emancipation of women with Jews and intellectuals? How does he attempt to subordinate the lives of women to the supremacy of the state?*

The slogan "Emancipation of women" was invented by Jewish intellectuals and its content was formed by the same spirit. In the really good times of German life the German woman had no need to emancipate herself. She possessed exactly what nature had necessarily given her to administer and preserve; just as the man in his good times had no need to fear that he would be ousted from his position in relation to the woman. . . .

If the man's world is said to be the State, his struggle, his readiness to devote his powers to the service of the community, then it may perhaps be said that the woman's is a smaller world. For her world is her husband, her family, her children, and her home. But what would become of the greater world if there were no one to tend and care for the smaller one? How could the greater world survive if there were no one to make the cares of the smaller world the content of their lives? No, the greater world is built on the foundation of this smaller world. This great world cannot survive if the smaller world is

by many Nazis as an indication of the social confusion that had followed the German defeat.

The Nazi discussion of the role of women was also deeply rooted in the racism of Nazi ideology. Nazi writers argued that the superiority of the pure German race depended on the purity of the blood of each and every individual. It was the special task of German women in their role as mothers to preserve racial purity. Hitler particularly championed this view of women. They were to breed strong sons and daughters for the German nation. Nazi journalists often compared the role of women in childbirth to that of men in battle. Each served the state in particular social and gender roles. In both cases, the good of the nation was more important than that of the individual.

Most Nazis who discussed the role of women relegated them to the home. They also attacked feminist outlooks. They wanted women to bear many children. They believed the declining German birth rate was the result of emancipated women having spurned their natural and proper role as mothers. The Nazis established special medals for women who bore large families. They also sponsored schools that taught women how to care for and rear children.

The Nazis also intended women to be educators of the young. In that role, women were the special protectors of German cultural values. Through cooking, dress, music, and stories, mothers were to instill a love for the nation in their children. As consumers for the home, women were to support German-owned shops,

not stable. Providence has entrusted to the wo-man the cares of that world which is her very own, and only on the basis of this smaller world can the man's world be formed and built up. The two worlds are not antagonistic. They complement each other, they belong together just as man and woman belong together.

We do not consider it correct for the woman to interfere in the world of the man, in his main sphere. We consider it natural if these two worlds remain distinct. To the one belongs the strength of feeling, the strength of the soul. To the other belongs the strength of vision, of toughness, of decision, and of the willingness to act. In the one case this strength demands the willingness of the woman to risk her life to preserve this important cell and to multiply it, and in the other case it demands from the man the readiness to safeguard life.

The sacrifices which the man makes in the struggle of his nation, the woman makes in the preservation of that nation in individual cases. What the man gives in courage on the battle field, the woman gives in eternal self-sacrifice, in eternal pain and suffering. Every child that a woman brings into the world is a battle, a battle waged for the existence of her people. . . .

So our women's movement is for us not something which inscribes on its banner as its programme the fight against men, but something which has as its programme the common fight together with men. For the new National Socialist national community acquires a firm basis precisely because we have gained the trust of millions of women as fanatical fellow-combatants, women who have fought for the common life in the service of the common task of preserving life. . . .

Whereas previously the programmes of the liberal, intellectualist women's movements contained many points, the programme of our National Socialist Women's movement has in reality but one single point, and that point is the child, that tiny creature which must be born and grow strong and which alone gives meaning to the whole life-struggle.

J. Noakes and G. Pridham, eds., Nazism, 1919–1945, Vol. 2, State, Economy and Society, 1933–39: A Documentary Reader, Exeter Studies in History No. 8 (Exeter: University of Exeter, 1984), pp. 449–450.

Young women among an enthusiastic crowd extend the Nazi salute at a party rally in 1938. Nazi ideology encouraged women to favor traditional domestic roles over employment in the workplace and to bear many children. The onset of the war, however, forced the government to recruit women workers. [Bildarchiv Preussischer Kulturbesitz]

to buy German-produced goods, and to boycott Jewish merchants.

Nazi ideology permitted women to be employed, but work was regarded as secondary to their being wives and mothers living in the home. The Nazis recognized that in the midst of the depression many women would need to work, but the party urged them to pursue employment that was natural to their character as women. These tasks included agricultural labor, teaching, nursing, social service, and domestic service. The Nazis seem to have achieved female political support because the party assigned to women roles in which most German women actually found themselves. Despite some variation throughout the decade, however, in 1939, 37 percent of German women were employed, the same as in 1928. Thereafter, the war effort forced the government to recruit women into the German workforce.

A few Nazi feminists hoped that women could achieve new standing in the Nazi order. They appealed to ancient German history to prove that German men and women had once been equal. They also contended that only by allowing a broader role to women could Nazi society actually attain major achievements. They argued that if sons were not reared to respect their mothers, then those mothers could not carry out their role as educators of children for the nation. It would appear that most of these Nazi feminists were professional women who hoped both to support the party and to maintain their position in German society. They had only minimal influence on the policies of the party and none on the major leaders.

Italy: Fascist Economics

The Fascists had promised to stabilize Italian social and economic life. Discipline was a substitute for economic policy and creativity. During the 1920s, Mussolini undertook vast public works, such as draining the Pontine Marshes near Rome for settlement. The government subsidized the shipping industry and introduced protective tariffs. Mussolini desperately sought to make Italy self-sufficient. He embarked on the "battle of wheat" to prevent foreign grain from appearing in products on Italian tables. Wheat farming in Italy expanded

Mussolini was determined to make Italy a self-sufficient food producer. In July 1938, he stood on a threshing platform at a farm rally, stripped to the waist in the hot sun, to declare that Italy would never turn to other nations for grain. [Archive Photos]

enormously. These policies, however, did not keep the Great Depression from affecting Italy. Production, exports, and wages fell. Even the increased wheat production backfired. So much poor marginal land that was expensive to cultivate came into production that the domestic price of wheat, and thus of much other food, actually rose.

Syndicates

Both before and during the depression, the Fascists sought to steer an economic course between socialism and a liberal laissez-faire system. Their policy was known as *corporatism*. It was a planned economy linked to the private ownership of capital and to government arbitration of labor disputes. Major industries were first organized into *syndicates* representing labor and management. The two groups negotiated labor settlements within this framework and submitted differences to compulsory government arbitration. The Fascists contended that class conflict would be avoided if both labor and management looked to the greater goal of productivity for the nation.

Whether this arrangement favored workers or managers is still in dispute. From the mid-1920s, however, Italian labor unions lost the right to strike and to pursue independent economic goals. In that respect, management clearly profited.

Corporations

After 1930 these industrial syndicates were further organized into entities called *corporations*. These bodies included all industries relating to a major area of production, such as agriculture or metallurgy, from raw materials through finished products and distribution. Twenty-two such corporations were established to encompass the whole economy. In 1938 Mussolini abolished the Italian Chamber of Deputies and replaced it with a Chamber of Corporations.

This vast organizational framework did not increase production; instead, bureaucracy and corruption proliferated. The corporate state allowed the government to direct much of the nation's economic life without a formal change in ownership. Consumers and owners could no longer determine what was to be produced. The Fascist government gained further direct economic power through the Institute for Industrial Reconstruction, which extended loans to businesses in financial difficulty. The loans, in effect, established partial state ownership.

How corporatism might have affected the Italian economy in the long run is unknown. In 1935 Italy invaded Ethiopia, and economic life was put on a formal wartime footing. The League of Nations imposed economic sanctions, urging member nations to refrain from purchasing Italian goods. The sanctions had little effect. Thereafter taxes rose. During 1935 the government imposed a forced loan on the citizenry by requiring property owners to purchase bonds. Wages continued to be depressed. As international tensions increased during the late 1930s, the Italian state assumed more and more direction over the economy. The order that Fascism brought to Italy had not proved to be the order of prosperity. It had brought economic dislocation and a falling standard of living.

The Soviet Union: Central Economic Planning and Party Purges

While the capitalist economies of western Europe floundered in the doldrums of the Great Depression, the Soviet Union began a tremendous industrial advance. Like similar eras of past Russian economic progress, the direction and impetus came from the top. Stalin far exceeded his tsarist predecessors in the intensity of state coercion and terror he brought to the task. Russia achieved its stunning economic growth during the 1930s only at the cost of literally millions of human lives and the degradation of still other millions. Stalin's economic policy clearly proved that his earlier rivalry with Trotsky had been a political power struggle rather than one over substantial ideological differences.

The Decision for Rapid Industrialization

Through 1927 Lenin's New Economic Policy (NEP), as championed by Bukharin with Stalin's support, had charted the course of Soviet economic development. The government permitted private ownership and enterprise to flourish in the countryside to ensure an adequate food supply for the workers in the cities. Though the industrial production level of 1913 had been achieved by 1927, industrial growth had slowed. During 1927 the Party Congress decided to push for rapid industrialization. This policy, which began in 1928, marked a sharp departure from NEP.

The industrial achievement of the Soviet Union between 1928 and World War II is one of the most striking accomplishments of the twentieth century. The Russian economy grew more rapidly than that of any other nation in the Western world during any similar time period.

By even the conservative estimates of Western observers, Soviet industrial production rose approximately 400 percent between 1928 and

An enormous propaganda effort accompanied the Soviet Five-Year Plans. This poster proclaims, "For the betterment of the Soviet people we are building an electricity plant." [Bildarchiv Preussischer Kulturbesitz]

1940. The production of iron, steel, coal, electrical power, tractors, combines, railway cars, and other heavy machinery was emphasized. Few consumer goods were produced. The labor for this development was supplied internally. Capital was raised from the export of grain even at the cost of internal shortages. The technology was generally borrowed from already industrialized nations. This paralleled the manner in which the tsarist government had pursued industrialization in the late nineteenth century.

Unlike the tsarist drive toward an industrial economy, however, Stalin's organizational vehicle for industrialization was a series of Five-Year Plans starting in 1928. The State Planning Commission, or Gosplan, oversaw the program. It set goals for production and organized the economy to meet them. The task of coordinating all facets of production was immensely difficult and complicated. Deliveries of materials from mines or factories had to be assured before the next unit could carry out its part of the plan. There was many a slip between the cup and the lip. The troubles in the countryside were harmful. The government and Communist Party undertook a vast program of propaganda to sell the Five-Year Plans to the Russian people and to elicit cooperation. The industrial labor force, however, soon became subject to the same regimentation that was being imposed on the peasants.

By the close of the 1930s, the results of the three Five-Year Plans were truly impressive and probably allowed the Soviet Union to survive the German invasion. Industries that had never before existed in Russia now challenged and in some cases, such as tractor production, surpassed their counterparts in the rest of the world. Large, new industrial cities had been built and populated by hundreds of thousands of people. The social and human cost of this effort had, however, been astounding.

The Collectivization of Agriculture

The decision to industrialize rapidly brought enormous consequences for Soviet agriculture. Under NEP, a few farmers, the *kulaks*, had become prosperous. They probably numbered less than 5 percent of the rural population. They and other farmers were discontented with their situation, because there were few consumer goods to purchase with the cash they received for their crops. They had frequently withheld grain from the market in the 1920s and did so again during 1928 and 1929. Food shortages then occurred in the cities, and the government worried about potential unrest.

During these troubled months, Stalin came to a momentous decision. Agriculture must be collectivized to produce enough grain for food and export, to achieve control over the farm sector of the economy, and to free peasant labor for the factories in the expanding industrial sector. The implementation of this program of collectivization, which basically embraced Trotsky's earlier economic position, unleashed a second Russian revolution and unprecedented violence in the countryside.

In 1929 Stalin ordered party agents into the countryside to confiscate any hoarded wheat. The *kulaks* were blamed for the grain shortages. As part of the general plan to erase the private ownership of land and to collectivize farming, the government decided to eliminate the *kulaks* as a class. The definition of a *kulak*, however, soon embraced anyone who opposed Stalin's policy. Peasants and farmers of all levels of wealth resisted collectivization. The stubborn peasants were determined to keep their land.

Russian farmers attend a rally to celebrate the arrival of new tractors at their collective farm. [Bildarchiv Preussischer Kulturbesitz]

They sabotaged collectivization by slaughtering more than 100 million horses and cattle between 1929 and 1933. The situation in the countryside amounted to open warfare. Peasant resistance caused Stalin to call a brief halt to the process in March 1930. He justified the slowdown on the grounds of "dizziness from success."

Soon thereafter the drive to collectivize the farms was renewed with vehemence, and the costs remained very high. As many as ten million peasants were killed, and millions of others were dragged off to collective farms or labor camps. Initially, because of the turmoil on the land, agricultural production fell. There was famine in 1932 and 1933. Milk and meat remained scarce because of the livestock slaughter. Yet Stalin persevered. The uprooted peasants were moved to thousand-acre collective farms. The state provided the machinery for these

units through machine-tractor stations. The state monopoly in heavy farm machines was a powerful weapon.

Collectivization changed Russian farming dramatically. In 1928 approximately 98 percent of Russian farmland consisted of small peasant holdings. Ten years later, despite all opposition, more than 90 percent of the land had been collectivized, and the quantity of farm produce directly handled by the government had risen by 40 percent. Those shifts in control meant that the government now controlled the food supply. The farmers and peasants could no longer determine whether there would be stability or unrest in the cities. Stalin and the Communist Party had won the battle of the wheat fields, but they had not solved the problem of producing enough grain. That difficulty would plague the Soviet Union until its collapse in 1991 and remains a

Stalin Calls for the Liquidation of the Kulaks as a Class

The core of Stalin's agricultural policy undertaken in the late 1920s and early 1930s was the eradication of private farms and their replacement with large collective farms. The greatest obstacle to this policy was the kulaks, peasants who owned substantial farms. In this remarkable speech of 1929, Stalin first explains why small peasant farming must be replaced with collective farms to achieve an adequate food supply for the cities and the industrial sector of the population. He then calls for the liquidation of the kulaks as a class. As might be expected, the kulaks resisted collectivization by destroying crops and farm animals. In turn, Communist Party agents killed millions of peasants to achieve collectivization.

◆ What were the goals of the collectivization of farms in the Soviet Union? How did the kulaks stand in the way of collectivization? How does Stalin dehumanize the kulaks as people by discussing them entirely as a class and as part of the capitalistic system?

Can we advance our socialized industry at an accelerated rate as long as we have an agricultural base, such as is provided by small-peasant farming, which is incapable of expanded reproduction, and which, in addition, is the predominant force in our national economy? No, we cannot. . . .

What, then, is the solution? The solution lies in enlarging the agricultural units, in making agriculture capable of accumulation, of expanded reproduction, and in thus transforming the agricultural bases of our national economy.

. . . [T]he *socialist* way [to enlarge farming units], which is to introduce collective farms and state farms in agriculture, the way which leads to the amalgamation of the small-peasant farms into large collective farms, employing machinery and scientific methods of farming, and capable of developing further, for such agricultural enterprises can achieve expanded reproduction. . . .

---

problem for the new Commonwealth of Independent States.

Foreign Reactions and Repercussions

Many foreign contemporaries looked at the Soviet economic experiment naïvely. While the capitalist world lay in the throes of the Great Depression, the Soviet economy had grown at a pace never realized in the West. The American writer Lincoln Steffens (1866–1936) reported after a trip to Russia, "I have seen the future and it works." Beatrice and Sidney Webb, the British Fabian Socialists, spoke of "a new civilization" in the Soviet Union. These and similar observers ignored the shortages in consumer goods and the poor housing. More important,

they had little idea of the social cost of the Soviet achievement. Millions of human beings had been killed and millions more uprooted. The total picture of suffering and human loss during those years will probably never be known; however, the deprivation and sacrifice of Soviet citizens far exceeded anything described by Marx and Engels in relation to nineteenth-century industrialization in western Europe.

The internal difficulties caused by collectivization and industrialization led Stalin to make an important shift in foreign policy. In 1934 he began to fear that the nation might be left isolated against future aggression by Nazi Germany. The Soviet Union was not yet strong enough to withstand such an attack. So that year he ordered the Comintern to permit

The characteristic feature in the work of our Party during the past year is that we, as a Party, as the Soviet power,

(a) have developed an offensive along the whole front against the capitalist elements in the countryside;

(b) that this offensive, as you know, has brought about and is bringing about very palpable, *positive* results.

What does this mean? It means that we have passed from the policy of *restricting* the exploiting proclivities of the kulaks to the policy of *eliminating* the kulaks as a class. . . .

Until recently the Party adhered to the policy of *restricting* the exploiting proclivities of the kulaks. . . .

. . . Could we have undertaken such an offensive against the kulaks five year or three years ago? Could we then have counted on success in such an offensive? No, we could not. That would have been the most dangerous adventurism. It would have been playing a very dangerous game at offensive. We would certainly have failed, and our failure would have strengthened the position of the kulaks.

Why? Because we still lacked a wide network of state and collective farms in the rural districts which could be used as strongholds in a determined offensive against the kulaks. Because at that time we were not yet able to *substitute* for the capitalist production of the kulaks the socialist production of the collective farms and state farms. . . .

. . . Now we are able to carry on a determined offensive against the kulaks, to break their resistance, to eliminate them as a class and substitute for their output the output of the collective farms and state farms. Now, the kulaks are being expropriated by the masses of poor and middle peasants themselves, by the masses who are putting solid collectivization into practice. Now, the expropriation of the kulaks in the regions of solid collectivization is no longer just an administrative measure. Now, the expropriation of the kulaks is an integral part of the formation and development of the collective farms. Consequently it is now ridiculous and foolish to discourse on the expropriation of the kulaks. You do not lament the loss of the hair of one who has been beheaded.

Stalin, "Problems of Agrarian Policy in the USSR," Speech at a conference of Marxist students of the agrarian question, December 27, 1929, in Problems of Leninism, *pp. 391–393, 408–409, 411–412, as quoted in Robert V. Daniels,* A Documentary History of Communism, *rev. ed. (Hanover, N.H., and London: University Press of New England, 1984), pp. 224–227.*

Communist parties in other countries to cooperate with non-Communist parties against Nazism and Fascism. This reversed the Comintern policy established by Lenin as part of the Twenty-one Conditions in 1919. The new Stalinist policy allowed the formation of the Popular Front Government in France.

The Purges

Stalin's decisions to industrialize rapidly, to move against the peasants, and to reverse the Comintern policy aroused internal political opposition. They were all departures from the policies of Lenin. In 1929 Stalin forced Bukharin, the fervent supporter of NEP and his own former ally, off the Politburo. Little detailed information is known about further opposition, but it seems to have existed among lower-level party followers of Bukharin and other opponents of rapid industrialization. In 1933 Stalin began to fear that he might lose control over the party apparatus and that effective rivals to his power might emerge. These fears were probably produced as much by his own paranoia as by real plots. Nevertheless, they resulted in the Great Purges, one of the most mysterious and horrendous political events of the twentieth century. The purges were not understood at the time and have not been fully comprehended either inside or outside the former Soviet Union to the present day.

On December 1, 1934, Sergei Kirov (1888–1934), the popular party chief of Leningrad (for-

Collective farmers bringing grain to a shipment center. Note that horse-drawn wagons are the only form of transport in this picture; there are no trucks or tractors. [Bildarchiv Preussischer Kulturbesitz]

merly and now again Saint Petersburg) and a member of the Politburo, was assassinated. In the wake of the shooting, thousands of people were arrested, and still more were expelled from the party and sent to labor camps. At the time, it was believed that Kirov had been murdered by opponents of the regime. Direct or indirect complicity in the crime became the normal accusation against the persons whom Stalin attacked. It is now almost certain that Stalin himself authorized Kirov's assassination because he was afraid of the Leningrad leader.

The purges after Kirov's death were just the beginning of a larger process. Between 1936 and 1938, a series of spectacular show trials were held in Moscow. Previous high Soviet leaders, including former members of the Politburo,

publicly confessed to political crimes. They were convicted and executed. It is still not certain why they made their palpably false confessions. Other leaders and lower-level party members were tried in private and shot. Hundreds of thousands of people received no trial at all. The purges touched persons in all areas of party life. No one can explain why some were executed, others sent to labor camps, and still others left unmolested.

After the civilian party members had been purged, the prosecutors turned against the army. Important officers, including heroes of the civil war, were shot. Within the party itself, hundreds of thousands of members were expelled, and applicants for membership were removed from the rolls. The exact numbers of executions, imprisonments, and expulsions are unknown but certainly ran into the millions.

The trials and purges astonished Western observers. Nothing like it had been seen before. Political murders and executions were not new, but the absurd confessions were novel. The scale of the political turmoil was also unprecedented. The Russians themselves did not believe or comprehend what was occurring. No national emergency or crisis existed. There were only accusations of sympathy for Trotsky, of complicity in Kirov's murder, of plots against the long-dead Lenin, or of other nameless crimes.

If a rational explanation is to be sought, it probably lies in Stalin's fears for his own power. In effect, the purges created a new party structure absolutely subservient and loyal to him.

The "old Bolsheviks" of the October Revolution were among his earliest targets. They and others active in the first years of the revolution knew how far Stalin had moved from Lenin's policies. New, younger members replaced the party members executed or expelled. The newcomers had little knowledge of old Russia or of the ideals of the original Bolsheviks. They had not been loyal to Lenin, to Trotsky, or to any other Soviet leader except Stalin himself.

◆

By the middle of the 1930s, dictators of the right and the left had established themselves across much of Europe. Political tyranny was hardly new to Europe, but several factors combined to give these rulers unique characteristics. They

By the mid 1930s Stalin's purges had eliminated many leaders and other members from the Soviet Communist Party. This photograph of a meeting of a party congress in 1936 shows a number of the surviving leaders with Stalin, who sits fourth from the right on the front row. To his left is Vyacheslav Molotov, long-time foreign minister. The first person on the left in the front row is Nikita Khrushchev, who headed the Soviet Union in the late 1950s and early 1960s. [ITAR-TASS/SOVFOTO]

Major Dates in Soviet History During the Five-Year Plans and Purges	
1927	Decision to move toward rapid industrialization
1928	First Five-Year Plan begun
1929	Beginning of collectivization of agriculture
1929	Expulsion of Bukharin from Politburo affirms Stalin's central position
1930	Call of Stalin for moderation in his policy of agricultural collectivization because of "dizziness from success"
1934	Assassination of Kirov
1936	Major purge trials begin

drew their immediate support from well-organized political parties. Except for the Bolsheviks, these were mass parties. The roots of support for the dictators lay in nationalism, the social and economic frustration of the Great Depression, and political ideologies that promised to transform the social and political order. As long as the new rulers seemed successful, they did not lack support. Many citizens believed that these leaders had ended the pettiness of everyday politics.

After coming to power, the dictators possessed a practical monopoly over mass communications. Through armies, police forces, and party discipline, they also monopolized terror and coercive power. They could propagandize large populations and compel people to obey them and their followers. Finally, as a result of the Second Industrial Revolution, they commanded a vast amount of technology and a capacity for immense destruction. Earlier rulers in Europe may have shared the ruthless ambitions of Hitler, Mussolini, and Stalin, but they had lacked the ready implements of physical force to impose their wills.

Mass political support, the monopoly of police and military power, and technological capacity meant that the dictators of the 1930s held more extensive sway over their nations than any other group of rulers who had ever governed on the Continent. Soon the issue would become whether they would be able to maintain peace among themselves and with their democratic neighbors.

Review Questions

1. Explain the causes of the Depression of the 1930s. Why was it more severe and longer-lasting than previous depressions? Could it have been avoided?

2. Compare the relative success of Britain's National Government and France's Popular Front in dealing with their respective economic problems. How would you account for the differences? Why did France's Third Republic have so few supporters?

3. How did the Depression affect Germany? Discuss Hitler's rise to power between 1929 and 1934. Was his dictatorship inevitable? Was his seizure of power due more to personalities than to impersonal forces?

4. Discuss Hitler's economic policies. Why were they successful? Compare and contrast his economic policies with those used in Britain, Italy, and France. Why were some nations more successful than others in addressing the Depression?

5. What were the characteristics of a "police state"? How necessary is terror and intimidation in the consolidation of an authoritarian regime? How did Hitler, Mussolini, and Stalin use terror to achieve their goals?

6. Why did Stalin decide that Russia had to industrialize rapidly? Why did this require the collectivization of agriculture? What obstacles stood in the way of collectivization, and how did Stalin overcome them? What were the causes of the purges in the Soviet Union? What groups became the special targets of the purges?

Suggested Readings

W. S. ALLEN, *The Nazi Seizure of Power: The Experience of a Single German Town, 1930–1935,* rev. ed. (1984). A classic treatment of Nazism in a microcosmic setting.

K. E. BAILES, *Technology and Society Under Lenin and Stalin: Origins of the Soviet Technical Intelligentsia, 1917–1941* (1978). An important study of the people who actually put the programs of modernization into place.

N. BRANSON and M. HEINEMANN, *Britain in the Nineteen Thirties* (1971). Primarily considers the social and economic problems of the day.

J. Colton, *Léon Blum: Humanist in Politics* (1966). One of the best biographies of any twentieth-century political figure.

R. Conquest, *The Great Terror: Stalin's Purges of the Thirties* (1968). Remains the most useful treatment of the subject to date.

R. Conquest, *The Harvest of Sorrow: Soviet Collectivization and the Terror-Famine* (1986). A study of how Stalin used starvation against his own people.

G. Craig, *Germany, 1866–1945* (1978). An important survey.

R. W. Davies, *The Socialist Offensive: The Collectivization of Soviet Agriculture, 1929–1930* (1980). Examines the crucial years when Stalin moved against the *kulaks*.

I. Deutscher, *Stalin: A Political Biography*, 2nd ed. (1967). The best biography in English.

B. Eichengreen, *Golden Fetters: The Gold Standard and the Great Depression, 1919–1939* (1992). A remarkable study of the role of the gold standard in the economic policies of the interwar years.

R. Gellately, *The Gestapo and German Society: Enforcing Racial Policy, 1933–1945* (1990). A discussion of how the police state supported Nazi racial policies.

R. F. Hamilton, *Who Voted for Hitler?* (1982). An important examination of voting patterns.

E. C. Helmreich, *The German Churches Under Hitler: Background, Struggle, and Epilogue* (1979). A useful study.

J. Jackson, *The Politics of Depression in France, 1932–1936* (1985). A detailed examination of the political struggles prior to the Popular Front.

J. Jackson, *The Popular Front in France: Defending Democracy, 1934–1938* (1988). An extensive recent treatment.

H. James, *The German Slump: Politics and Economics, 1914–1936* (1986). A difficult but informative examination of the German experience of the Great Depression.

C. Kindleberger, *The World in Depression, 1929–1939* (1973). An account by a leading economist whose analysis is comprehensible to the layperson.

D. Landes, *The Unbound Prometheus: Technological Change and Industrial Development in Western Europe from 1750 to the Present* (1969). Includes an excellent analysis of both the Great Depression and the few areas of economic growth at the time.

E. Mendelsohn, *The Jews of East Central Europe Between the World Wars* (1983). An excellent survey of the subject.

I. Mueller, *Hitler's Justice: The Courts of the Third Reich* (1991). An account of how German courts cooperated with the Nazis.

D. J. K. Peukert, *Inside Nazi Germany: Conformity, Opposition, and Racism in Everyday Life* (1987). An excellent discussion of life under Nazi rule.

R. Proctor, *Racial Hygiene: Medicine Under the Nazis* (1988). An exploration of how medical science contributed to racism.

L. J. Rupp, *Mobilizing Women for War: German and American Propaganda, 1939–1945* (1978). Although concentrating on a later period, it includes an excellent discussion of general Nazi attitudes toward women.

D. Schoenbaum, *Hitler's Social Revolution: Class and Status in Nazi Germany* (1966). A fascinating analysis of Hitler's appeal to various social classes.

D. M. Smith, *Mussolini's Roman Empire* (1976). A general description of the Fascist regime in Italy.

W. D. Smith, *The Ideological Origins of Nazi Imperialism* (1986). A study that links Nazi expansionist thought to earlier German foreign policy.

A. Solzhenitsyn, *The Gulag Archipelago*, 3 vols. (1974–1979). A major examination of the labor camps under Stalin by one of the most important contemporary writers.

J. Stephenson, *The Nazi Organization of Women* (1981). Examines the attitude and policies of the Nazis toward women.

H. A. Turner, Jr., *German Big Business and the Rise of Hitler* (1985). An important major study of the subject.

L. Yahil, *The Holocaust: The Fate of the European Jewry, 1932–1945* (1990). A major recent study of this fundamental subject in twentieth-century history.

Reference should also be made to the works cited in Chapters 27 and 29.

Global Conflict, Cold War, and New Directions

THE PEOPLE OF Europe and the United States regarded the great conflict of 1914-1918 as a world war, but by far the largest part of the fighting and suffering was confined to the European continent. The second great political and military upheaval of the twentieth century, the war of 1939-1945, was truly global in scope and even more devastating than the first. Heavy fighting took place in Africa and Asia as well as in Europe. The people of every inhabited continent were involved. Battle casualties were many, and the assault on civilians was unprecedented. Massive aerial bombardment of cities began with the German attack on Britain in 1940 and concluded with the use of the new and terrifying atomic weapons against Japan in 1945. The cost of World War II in life and property was even greater than that of World War I.

After World War II, the hopes of many for peace and stability rested with a new international organization, the United Nations. Unlike the League of Nations, which the United States had never joined, the new organization included all the victorious powers and came to include almost all the nations of the world. Its success, however, depended on cooperation among the great powers, which grew elusive as the war drew to an end.

The coalition of victors had been threatened from the start by differences between the political and economic systems of the Soviet Union and the Western nations and their mutual suspicion. The Western powers' insistence on free, democratic elections in the liberated states of eastern Europe was incompatible with the Soviet Union's desire to secure control over the areas on its western border. Disputes over Poland, the Balkan states, and Germany led to a division of Germany and of all Europe into East and West. Thus began a period of competition and sometimes open hostility called the *Cold War*. The division hardened with the formation of the North Atlantic Treaty Organization (NATO) in 1949 and the Warsaw Pact in 1955. From that time through the mid-1980s, the former allies faced each other across what Winston Churchill called an "Iron Curtain" with ever-increasing collections of deadly weapons and with continuing tension, occasionally relaxed by hopes for cooperation.

The Cold War quickly spread to Asia, where the Communist Party under Mao Tse-tung gained control of China and allied itself with the Soviet Union. They supported the Communist regime in North Korea against South Korea, which was in turn supported by the United States and its allies. Later, the same alignment influenced the emerging conflict in Vietnam. By the 1960s, however, a split between the Chinese and the Russians became apparent and international relations became even more complex. During the 1970s, the sharp exchanges of the Cold War gave way to a period of hesitant cooperation under the American policy known as *détente*. Negotiation replaced confrontation between the United States and the Soviet Union.

Throughout the postwar era, the influence of the United States touched Europe as never before. The NATO alliance, trade relations, and an enormous annual wave of tourists brought Americans into a series of close relationships with Europeans. At the same time, the nations of western Europe began to forge new economic links among themselves through the establishment of the European Economic Community, founded in 1957. By the opening of the 1990s, the members of the Community looked forward to unprecedented economic cooperation and unhindered movement of peoples and goods across their borders.

From the late 1940s through the mid-1980s, the peoples of the Soviet bloc, including the Soviet Union and its eastern European neighbors, had lived under authoritarian political systems dominated by Communist parties. Their economies were centrally controlled. In 1956 in Poland and Hungary and in 1968 in Czechoslovakia, the Soviet Union had demonstrated either politically or militarily its determination to dominate and control its eastern European satellites. The activities of the Solidarity trade union movement in Poland began to challenge that dominance. The imposition of martial law in Poland in 1981 suppressed that challenge for a time. Then, in 1985, Mikhail Gorbachev began to lead the Soviet Union in new directions, instituting policies of economic and political liberalization. The year 1989 saw popular uprisings throughout eastern Europe against the political domination of the Communist Party and the Soviet Union. In the wake of these revolutions, Germany became reunited. In 1991, after an unsuccessful attempt by conservative forces to turn back reform, the Communist government of the Soviet Union collapsed and the nation broke up into its constituent republics, loosely federated in the Commonwealth of Independent States. With these events, a fundamentally new era in European history began. ◆

1939–1960	*1939* World War II begins
	1941 Japan attacks Pearl Harbor, U.S. enters war
	1942 Battle of Stalingrad
	1944 Normandy invasion
	1945 Yalta Conference; Germany surrenders; atomic bombs dropped on Japan; Japan surrenders; United Nations founded
	1946 Churchill gives Iron Curtain speech
	1947 Truman Doctrine
	1948 Communist takeover in Czechoslovakia and Hungary; state of Israel proclaimed
	1948–1949 Berlin blockade
	1949 NATO founded; East and West Germany emerge as separate states
	1950–1953 Korean Conflict
	1953 Death of Stalin
	1954 French defeat at Dien Bien Phu
	1955 Warsaw Pact founded
	1956 Khrushchev denounces Stalin; Polish Communist Party crisis; Suez crisis; Soviet invasion of Hungary
1960–1980	*1960* Khruschev aborts Geneva summit
	1961 Berlin Wall erected
	1962 Cuban Missle Crisis
	1963 Test Ban Treaty
	1963–1973 Major U.S. involvement in Vietnam
	1964–1982 Brezhnev era in Soviet Union
	1967 Six Days' War between Israel and Arab states
	1968 Soviet invasion of Czechoslovakia
	1973 Yom Kippur War between Israel and Egypt
	1975 Helsinki Accords
	1978 Camp David Accords; Solidarity founded in Poland
	1979–1988 Soviet troops in Afghanistan
1980–1993	*1981–1983* Martial law in Poland
	1982 Israel invades Lebanon
	1985 Gorbachev comes to power in the Soviet Union
	1987 Major U.S.–Soviet arms limitation treaty; Palestinian *intifada* begins on West Bank
	1989 Revolutions sweep across eastern Europe
	1990 German reunification; Yugoslavia breaks up
	1991 Persian Gulf War; Civil war in former Yugoslavia; August coup in Moscow; Gorbachev resigns; Soviet Union dissolved
	1992 Ascendancy of Yeltsin in Russia
	1993 Israel and PLO recognize one another

Society and Economy	Religion and Culture
1945–1951 Attlee ministry establishes the Welfare State in Great Britain	*1940* Koestler, *Darkness at Noon*
	1942 Lewis, *The Screwtape Letters*
	1943 Sartre, *Being and Nothingness*
1947 Marshall Plan to rebuild Europe instituted	*1947* Camus, *The Plague*; Gramsci, *Letters from Prison*
1949 Europe divided into eastern and western blocs	*1949* de Beauvoir, *The Second Sex*; Crossman, *The God That Failed*
1950s and 1960s Increase in agricultural production	
1957 European Economic Community founded	*1958* Pasternak forbidden to accept Nobel Prize for *Dr. Zhivago*; John XXIII becomes Pope
1960s Rapid growth of student population in universities; migration of workers from eastern and southern to northern and western Europe; migration of non-European workers to northern and western Europe	*1960s* The Beatles take world by storm
	1962–1965 Second Vatican Council
	1963 Solzhenitsyn, *One Day in the Life of Ivan Denisovich*; Robinson, *Honest to God*
	1968 Student rebellion in Paris
1972 Club of Rome founded	
1973–1974 Arab oil embargo	*1974* Solzhenitsyn expelled from Soviet Union
	1978 John Paul II becomes Pope
1980s and 1990s Internal migration from eastern to western Europe; racial and ethnic tensions in western Europe	*1980s* Growth of environmental groups
	1990s Expanding influence of Roman Catholic Church in independent eastern Europe
1986 Chernobyl nuclear disaster	
1990s Changes in eastern Europe and Soviet Union open way for economic growth and new trade relations across Europe	

A member of the Royal Observation Corps watches for German planes on England's south coast during World War II. [The Hulton-Deutsch Collection Limited]

29

World War II

Key Topics in This Chapter
◆ The origins of World War II
◆ The course of the war
◆ Racism and the Holocaust
◆ The impact of the war on the people of Europe
◆ Relationships among the victorious allies and the preparations for peace

---

The more idealistic survivors of the First World War, especially in the United States and Great Britain, thought of it as "the war to end all wars" and a war "to make the world safe for democracy." Only thus could they justify the horrible slaughter, expense, and upheaval of that terrible conflict. How appalled they would have been had they known that only twenty years after the peace treaties a second great war would break out that would be more terribly global than the first. In this war, the democracies would be fighting for their lives against militaristic, nationalistic, authoritarian, and totalitarian states in Europe and Asia, and they would be allied with the Communist Soviet Union in the struggle. The defeat of the militarists and dictators would not bring the peace they longed for, but a Cold War. In this Cold War, the European states would become powers of the second class, subordinate to the two new superpowers, partially or fully non-European: the Soviet Union and the United States.

Again the Road to War (1933–1939)

World War I and the Versailles treaty themselves had only a marginal relationship to the world depression of the 1930s. In Germany, however, where the reparations settlement had contributed to the vast inflation of 1923, economic and social discontent focused on the Versailles settlement as the cause of all ills. Throughout the late 1920s, Adolf Hitler and the Nazi Party had denounced Versailles as the source of all Germany's trouble. The economic woes of the early 1930s seemed to bear them out. Nationalism and attention to the social question, along with party discipline, had been the sources of Nazi success. They continued to influence Hitler's foreign policy after he became chancellor in January 1933. Moreover, the Nazi destruction of the Weimar Constitution and of political opposition meant that Hitler himself totally dominated German foreign policy. Consequently, it is important to know what his goals were and how he planned to achieve them.

Hitler's Goals

From the first expression of his goals in a book written in jail, *Mein Kampf* (*My Struggle*), to his last days in the underground bunker in Berlin where he killed himself, Hitler's racial theories and goals were at the center of his thought. He meant to go far beyond Germany's 1914 boundaries, which were the limit of the vision of his predecessors. He meant to bring the entire German people (*Volk*), understood as a racial group, together into a single nation.

The new Germany would include all the Germanic parts of the old Habsburg Empire, including Austria. This virile and growing nation would need more space to live (*Lebensraum*), which would be taken from the Slavs, a lesser race, fit only for servitude. The new Germany would be purified by the removal of the Jews, another inferior race in Nazi theory. The plans required the conquest of Poland and Ukraine as the primary areas for the settlement of Germans and for the provision of badly needed food. Neither *Mein Kampf* nor later statements of policy were blueprints for action. Hitler was a brilliant improviser who exploited opportunities as they arose. He never lost sight of his goal, however, which would almost certainly require a major war.

GERMANY REARMS When Hitler came to power, Germany was far too weak to permit a direct approach toward reaching his aims. The first problem he set out to resolve was to shake off the fetters of Versailles and to make Germany a formidable military power. In October 1933, Germany withdrew from an international disarmament conference and also from the League of Nations. Hitler argued that because the other powers had not disarmed as they had promised, it was wrong to keep Germany helpless. These acts alarmed the French but were merely symbolic. In January 1934, Germany signed a nonaggression pact with Poland that was of greater concern to France, for it undermined France's chief means of containing the Germans. At last, in March 1935, Hitler formally renounced the disarmament provisions of the Versailles treaty with the formation of a German air force, and soon he reinstated conscription, which aimed at an army of half a million men.

THE LEAGUE OF NATIONS FAILS His path was made easier by growing evidence that the League of Nations could not keep the peace and that collective security was a myth. In September 1931, Japan occupied Manchuria, provoking an appeal to the League of Nations by China. The league responded by sending out a commission under a British diplomat, the earl of Lytton (1876–1951). The Lytton Report condemned the Japanese for resorting to force, but the powers were unwilling to impose sanctions. Japan withdrew from the league and kept control of Manchuria.

When Hitler announced his decision to rearm Germany, the league formally condemned that action, but it took no steps to prevent Germany's rearming. France and Britain opposed German rearmament, but they felt unable to object forcefully because they had not carried out their own promises to disarm. Instead, they met with Mussolini in June 1935 to form the so-called Stresa Front, promising to use force to maintain the status quo in Europe. This show of unity by the three powers was short-lived, however. Britain, desperate to maintain superiority at sea, violated the spirit of the

Hitler Describes His Goals in Foreign Policy

From his early career, Hitler had certain long-term general views and goals. They were set forth in his Mein Kampf (My Struggle), *which appeared in 1925, and included consolidation of the German* Volk *(people), more land for the Germans, and contempt for such "races" as Slavs and Jews. Here are some of Hitler's views on land.*

◆ *What is the basic principle on which Hitler's policy is founded? How does he justify his plans for expansion? What reasons does he give for hostility to France and Russia? What is the basis for Hitler's claim of a right of every man to own farmland? Was that a practical goal for Germany in the 1930s? Was there any way for Hitler to achieve his goals without a major war?*

The National Socialist movement must strive to eliminate the disproportion between our population and our area—viewing this latter as a source of food as well as a basis for power politics—between our historical past and the hopelessness of our present impotence. . . .

. . . .

The demand for restoration of the frontiers of 1914 is a political absurdity of such proportions and consequences as to make it seem a crime. Quite aside from the fact that the Reich's frontiers in 1914 were anything but logical. For in reality they were neither complete in the sense of embracing the people of German nationality, nor sensible with regard to geomilitary expediency. . . .

As opposed to this, we National Socialists must hold unflinchingly to our aim in foreign policy, namely, to secure for the German people the land and soil to which they are entitled on this earth. . . .

. . . The soil on which some day German generations of peasants can beget powerful sons will sanction the investment of the sons of today, and will some day acquit the responsible statesmen of blood-guilt and sacrifice of the people, even if they are persecuted by their contemporaries. . . .

Much as all of us today recognize the necessity of a reckoning with France, it would remain ineffectual in the long run if it represented the whole of our aim in foreign policy. It can and will achieve meaning only if it offers the rear cover for an enlargement of our people's living space in Europe. . . .

If we speak of soil in Europe today, we can primarily have in mind only *Russia* and her vassal border states. . . .

. . . See to it that the strength of our nation is founded, not on colonies, but on the soil of our European homeland. Never regard the Reich as secure unless for centuries to come it can give every scion of our people his own parcel of soil. Never forget that the most sacred right on this earth is a man's right to have earth to till with his own hands, and the most sacred sacrifice the blood that a man sheds for this earth.

Adolf Hitler, Mein Kampf, *trans. by Ralph Manheim (Boston: Houghton, Mifflin, 1943), pp. 646, 649, 652, 653, 656.*

Stresa accords and sacrificed French security needs to make a separate naval agreement with Hitler. This pact allowed him to rebuild the German fleet to 35 percent of the British navy. Italy's expansionist ambitions in Africa soon brought it into conflict with the Western powers. Hitler had taken a major step toward his goal without provoking serious opposition.

Italy Attacks Ethiopia

The Italian attack on Ethiopia made the impotence of the League of Nations and the timidity of the Allies even clearer. Using a border incident as an excuse, Mussolini attacked Ethiopia in October 1935. His purpose was to avenge a humiliating defeat that the Italians had suffered in 1896, to begin the restoration of Roman imperial glory, and, perhaps, to distract Italian public opinion from domestic problems.

France and Britain were eager to appease Mussolini in order to offset the growing power of Germany. They were prepared to allow him the substance of conquest if he would only maintain Ethiopia's formal independence. For Mussolini, however, the form was more important than the substance. His attack outraged opinion in the West, and the French and British governments were forced at least to appear to resist.

The League of Nations condemned Italian aggression and, for the first time, voted economic sanctions. It imposed an arms embargo that limited loans and credits to and imports from Italy. Britain and France were afraid of alienating Mussolini, however, and so they refused to embargo oil, the one economic sanction that could have prevented Italian victory. Even more important, the British fleet allowed Italian troops and munitions to use the Suez Canal. The results of this wavering policy were disastrous. The League of Nations and collective security were totally discredited, and Mussolini was alienated as well. He now turned to Germany, and by November 1, 1936, he could speak publicly of a Rome–Berlin "Axis."

Remilitarization of the Rhineland

No less important a result of the Ethiopian affair was its effect on Hitler's evaluation of the strength and determination of the Western powers. On March 7, 1936, he took his greatest risk yet, sending a small armed force into the demilitarized Rhineland. This was a breach not only of the Versailles treaty but of the Locarno Agreements of 1925 as well—agreements Germany had made voluntarily. It also removed a crucial element of French security. France and Britain had every right to resist; and the French especially had a claim to retain the only element of security left to them after the failure of the Allies to guarantee France's defense. Yet neither power did anything but register a feeble protest with the League of Nations. British opinion would not permit support for France, and the French would not act alone. They were paralyzed by internal division and by military doctrine that concentrated on defense and shunned

the offensive. Both countries were further weakened by a growing pacifism.

In retrospect, the Allies lost a great opportunity in the Rhineland to stop Hitler before he became a serious menace. The failure of his gamble, taken against the advice of his generals, might have led to his overthrow; at the least, it would have made German expansion to the east dangerous if not impossible. Nor is there much reason to doubt that the French army could easily have routed the tiny German force in the Rhineland. As the German General Alfred Jodl (1890–1946) said some years later, "The French covering army would have blown us to bits."[1]

A Germany that was rapidly rearming and had a defensible western frontier presented a completely new problem to the Western powers. Their response was the policy of "appeasement." It was based on the assumption that Germany had real grievances and that Hitler's goals were limited and ultimately acceptable. They believed that the correct policy was to negotiate and make concessions before a crisis could lead to war.

Behind this approach was the general horror of another war. Memories of the losses in the last war were still vivid, and the prospect of aerial bombardment made the thought of a new war even more terrifying. A firmer policy, moreover, would have required rapid rearmament. British leaders especially were reluctant to pursue this path because of the expense and the widespread belief that the arms race had been a major cause of the last war. As Germany armed, the French huddled behind their newly constructed defensive wall, the Maginot Line, and the British hoped for the best.

The Spanish Civil War

The new European alignment that found the Western democracies on one side and the Fascist states on the other was made clearer by the Spanish Civil War, which broke out in July 1936 (see Map 29-1). In 1931 the monarchy collapsed, and Spain became a democratic republic. The new government followed a program of moderate reform that antagonized landowners, the Catholic church, nationalists, and conservatives without satisfying the

[1]Quoted in W. L. Shirer, The Collapse of the Third Republic (New York: Simon & Schuster, 1969), p. 281.

MAP 29-1   THE SPANISH CIVIL WAR, 1936–1939   *The purple area on the map shows the large portion of Spain quickly overrun by Franco's insurgent armies during the first year of the war. In the following two years, progress came more slowly for the fascists as the war became a kind of international rehearsal for the coming World War II. Madrid's fall to Franco in the spring of 1939 had been preceded by that of Barcelona a few weeks earlier.*

demands of peasants, workers, Catalan separatists, or radicals. Elections in February 1936 brought to power a Spanish Popular Front government ranging from republicans of the left to Communists and anarchists. The losers, especially the Falangists, the Spanish fascists, would not accept defeat at the polls. In July, General Francisco Franco (1892–1975) led an army from Spanish Morocco against the republic.

Thus began a civil war that lasted almost three years, cost hundreds of thousands of lives, and provided a training ground for World War II. Germany and Italy supported Franco with troops, airplanes, and supplies. The Soviet Union sent equipment and advisers to the republicans. Liberals and leftists from Europe and America volunteered to fight in the republican ranks against fascism.

General Francisco Franco led an uprising against the duly elected government of Spain in 1936, producing a bloody civil war. Here he marches through the city of Burgos, in northern Spain. [Mary Evans Picture Library]

The civil war, fought on blatantly ideological lines, profoundly affected world politics. It brought Germany and Italy closer together, leading to the Rome–Berlin Axis Pact in 1936. Japan joined the Axis powers that year in the Anti-Comintern Pact, ostensibly directed against international communism but really a new and powerful diplomatic alliance. Western Europe, especially France, had a great interest in preventing Spain from falling into the hands of a fascist regime closely allied with Germany and Italy. Appeasement reigned, however. Although international law permitted the sale of weapons and munitions to the legitimate republican government, France and Britain forbade the export of war materials to either side, and the United States passed new neutrality legislation to the same end. When Barcelona fell to Franco early in 1939, the fascists had won effective control of Spain.

Austria and Czechoslovakia

Hitler made good use of his new friendship with Mussolini. He had always planned to annex his native Austria. In 1934 the Nazi Party in Austria assassinated the prime minister and tried to seize power. Mussolini had not yet allied with Hitler and was suspicious of German intentions. He quickly moved an army to the Austrian border, thus preventing German intervention and causing the coup to fail.

In 1938 the new diplomatic situation encouraged Hitler to try again. He perhaps hoped to achieve his goal by propaganda, bullying, and threats, but the Austrian Chancellor Kurt Schuschnigg (1897–1977) refused to be intimidated. Schuschnigg announced a plebiscite for March 13, in which the Austrian people themselves could decide whether to unite with Germany. To forestall the plebiscite, Hitler sent his army into Austria on March 12. To his great relief, Mussolini did not object, and Hitler rode to Vienna amid the cheers of his Austrian sympathizers.

The *Anschluss,* or union of Germany and Austria, was another clear violation of Versailles. The treaty, however, was now a dead letter, and the West remained passive. The *Anschluss* had great strategic significance, however, because Germany now surrounded Czechoslovakia, one of the bulwarks of French security, on three sides.

In fact, the very existence of Czechoslovakia was an affront to Hitler. It was democratic and pro-Western; it had been created partly as a check on Germany and was allied both to France and to the Soviet Union. It also contained about 3.5 million Germans who lived in the Sudetenland near the German border. These Germans had belonged to the dominant nationality group in the old Austro-Hungarian Empire and resented their new minority position. Supported by Hitler and led by Konrad Henlein

(1898–1945), the chief Nazi in Czechoslovakia, they made ever-increasing demands for privileges and autonomy within the Czech state. The Czechs made many concessions, but Hitler did not really want to improve the lot of the Sudeten Germans. He wanted to destroy Czechoslovakia. He told Henlein, "We must always demand so much that we can never be satisfied."[2]

As pressure mounted, the Czechs grew nervous. In May 1938, they received false rumors of an imminent attack by Germany and mobilized their army. The French, British, and Russians all warned that they would support the Czechs. Hitler, who had not planned an attack at that time, was forced to publicly deny any designs on Czechoslovakia. The public humiliation infuriated him, and he planned a military attack on the Czechs. The affair stiffened Czech resistance, but it frightened the French and British. The French, as had become the rule, deferred to British leadership. The British prime minister was Neville Chamberlain (1869–1940), a man thoroughly committed to the policy of appeasement. He was determined not to allow Britain to go to war again. He pressed the Czechs to make further concessions to Germany, but no concession was enough.

[2]Quoted in Alan Bullock, Hitler, A Study in Tyranny (New York: Harper & Row, 1962), p. 443.

On September 12, 1938, Hitler made a provocative speech at the Nuremberg Nazi Party rally. His rhetoric led to rioting in the Sudetenland, and the Czechs declared martial law. German intervention seemed imminent. Chamberlain, aged sixty-nine, had never flown before, but between September 15 and September 29, he made three flights to Germany in an attempt to appease Hitler at Czech expense and thus to avoid war. At Hitler's mountain retreat, Berchtesgaden, on September 15, Chamberlain accepted the separation of the Sudetenland from Czechoslovakia. And he and the French premier, Edouard Daladier (1884–1970), forced the Czechs to agree by threatening to abandon them if they did not. A week later, Chamberlain flew yet again to Germany only to find that Hitler had raised his demands. He wanted cession of the Sudetenland in three days and immediate occupation by the German army.

Munich

Chamberlain returned to England, and France and Britain prepared for war. At Chamberlain's request and at the last moment, Mussolini proposed a conference of Germany, Italy, France, and Britain. It met on September 29 at Munich. Hitler received almost everything he had demanded (see Map 29-2). The Sudetenland, the key to Czech security, became part of Germany, thus depriving the Czechs of any chance of self-

On September 29–30, 1938, Hitler met with the leaders of Britain and France at Munich to decide the fate of Czechoslovakia. The Allied leaders abandoned the small democratic nation in a vain attempt to appease Hitler and avoid war. Hitler sits in the center of the picture. To his right is British Prime Minister Neville Chamberlain. [Ullstein Bilderdienst]

MAP 29-2 PARTITIONS OF CZECHOSLOVAKIA AND POLAND, 1938–1939 *The immediate background of World War II is found in the complex international drama unfolding on Germany's eastern frontier in 1938 and 1939. Germany's expansion inevitably meant the victimization of Austria, Czechoslovakia, and Poland. With the failure of the Western powers' appeasement policy and the signing of a German–Soviet pact, the stage for the war was set.*

defense. In return, Hitler agreed to spare the rest of Czechoslovakia. He promised, "I have no more territorial demands to make in Europe." Chamberlain returned to England with the Munich agreement and told a cheering crowd that he had brought "peace with honour. I believe it is peace for our time."

Even in the short run, the appeasement of Hitler at Munich was a failure. Czechoslovakia did not survive. Soon Poland and Hungary tore more territory from it, and the Slovaks demanded a state of their own. Finally, on March 15, 1939, Hitler broke his promise and occupied Prague, putting an end to the Czech state and to illusions that his only goal was to restore Germans to the Reich. Defenders of the appeasers have argued that their policy was justified because it bought valuable time in which

the West could prepare for war. But that argument was not made by the appeasers themselves, who thought that they were achieving peace, nor does the evidence support it.

If the French and the British had been willing to attack Germany from the west while the Czechs fought in their own defense, their efforts might have been successful. High officers in the German army were opposed to Hitler's risky policies and might have overthrown him. Even failing such developments, a war begun in October 1938 would have forced Hitler to fight without the friendly neutrality and material assistance of the Soviet Union—and without the resources of eastern Europe that became available to him as a result of appeasement and Soviet cooperation. If, moreover, the West ever had a chance of concluding an alliance with the

Churchill's Response to Munich

In the parliamentary debate that followed the Munich conference at the end of September 1938, Winston Churchill was one of the few critics of what had been accomplished. In the selections from his speech that follow, he expresses his concerns.

✦ *What was decided at Munich? Why were the representatives of Czechoslovakia not at the meeting? Why did Chamberlain think the meeting was successful? Munich was the high point of the policy called* appeasement. *How would its advocates defend this policy? Churchill was a leading opponent of appeasement. What are his objections to it?*

I will begin by saying what everybody would like to ignore or forget but which must nevertheless be stated, namely, that we have sustained a total and unmitigated defeat, and that France has suffered even more than we have.

. . . .

We really must not waste time after all this long Debate upon the difference between the positions reached at Berchtesgaden, at Godesberg and at Munich. They can be very simply epitomized if the House will permit me to vary the metaphor. One pound was demanded at the pistol's point. When it was given, £2 were demanded at the pistol's point. Finally, the dictator consented to take £1 17s. 6d. and the rest in promises of good will for the future.

. . . .

All is over. Silent, mournful, abandoned, broken, Czechoslovakia recedes into the darkness. She has suffered in every respect by her association with the Western democracies and with the League of Nations, of which she has always been an obedient servant.

. . . .

We have been reduced in those five years from a position of security so overwhelming and so unchallengeable that we never cared to think about it. We have been reduced from a position where the very word "war" was considered one which could be used only by persons qualifying for a lunatic asylum. We have been reduced from a position of safety and power—power to do good, power to be gener-

ous to a beaten foe, power to make terms with Germany, power to give her proper redress for her grievances, power to stop her arming if we chose, power to take any step in strength or mercy or justice which we thought right—reduced in five years from a position safe and unchallenged to where we stand now.

. . . .

The responsibility must rest with those who have had the undisputed control of our political affairs. They neither prevented Germany from rearming, nor did they rearm ourselves in time. They quarreled with Italy without saving Ethiopia. They exploited and discredited the vast institution of the League of Nations and they neglected to make alliances and combinations which might have repaired previous errors, and thus they left us in the hour of trial without adequate national defense or effective international security.

. . . .

We are in the presence of a disaster of the first magnitude which has befallen Great Britain and France. Do not let us blind ourselves to that. It must now be accepted that all the countries of Central and Eastern Europe will make the best terms they can with the triumphant Nazi power. The system of alliances in Central Europe upon which France has relied for her safety has been swept away, and I can see no means by which it can be reconstituted. The road down the Danube Valley to the Black Sea, the road which leads as far as Turkey, has been opened.

Winston S. Churchill, Blood, Sweat, and Tears *(New York: G. P. Putnam's Sons, 1941), pp. 55–56, 58, 60–61.*

Soviet Union against Hitler, the exclusion of the Russians from Munich and the appeasement policy helped destroy it. Munich remains an example of shortsighted policy that helped bring on war in disadvantageous circumstances because of the very fear of war and the failure to prepare for it.

Hitler's occupation of Prague discredited appeasement in the eyes of the British people. In the summer of 1939, a Gallup Poll showed that three-quarters of the British public believed it worth a war to stop Hitler. Though Chamberlain himself had not lost all faith in his policy, he felt he had to respond to public opinion, and he responded to excess.

Poland was the next target of German expansion. In the spring of 1939, the Germans put pressure on Poland to restore the formerly German city of Danzig and to allow a railroad and a highway through the Polish Corridor to connect East Prussia with the rest of Germany. When the Poles would not yield, the usual propaganda campaign began, and the pressure mounted. On March 31, Chamberlain announced a Franco-British guarantee of Polish independence. Hitler appears to have expected to fight a war with Poland but not with the Western allies, for he did not take their guarantee seriously. He had come to hold their leaders in contempt. He knew that both countries were unprepared for war and that large segments of their populations were opposed to fighting for Poland.

Moreover, France and Britain had no means of getting effective help to the Poles. The French, still dominated by the defensive mentality of the Maginot Line, had no intention of attacking Germany. The only way to defend Poland was to bring Russia into the alliance against Hitler, but a Russian alliance posed many problems. Each side was profoundly suspicious of the other. The French and the British were hostile to communism; and since Stalin's purge of the Red Army, they were skeptical of the military value of a Russian alliance. Besides, the Russians could not help Poland without being given the right to enter Poland and Romania. Both nations, suspicious of Russian intentions, and with good reason, refused to grant these rights. As a result, Western negotiations for an alliance with Russia made little progress.

The Nazi–Soviet Pact

The Russians had at least equally good reason to hesitate. They resented being left out of the Munich agreement. They were annoyed by the low priority that the West gave to negotiations with Russia compared with the urgency with which they dealt with Hitler. They feared, quite rightly, that the Western powers meant them to bear the burden of the war against Germany. As a result, they opened negotiations with Hitler, and on August 23, 1939, the world was shocked to learn of a Nazi–Soviet nonaggression pact.

Its secret provisions, which were easily guessed and soon carried out, divided Poland between the two powers and allowed Russia to occupy the Baltic states and to take Bessarabia from Romania. The most bitter ideological enemies had become allies. Communist parties in the West changed their line overnight from the ardent advocacy of resistance to Hitler to a policy of peace and quiet. Ideology gave way to political and military reality. The West offered the Russians immediate danger without much prospect of gain. Hitler offered Stalin short-term gain without immediate danger. There could be little doubt about Stalin's decision.

The Nazi–Soviet pact sealed the fate of Poland, and the Franco-British commitment guaranteed a general war. On September 1, 1939, the Germans invaded Poland. Two days later, Britain and France declared war on Germany. World War II had begun.

World War II (1939–1945)

World War II has a better claim to its name than its predecessor, for it was truly global. Fighting took place in Europe and Asia, the Atlantic and the Pacific oceans, the Northern and Southern hemispheres. The demand for the fullest exploitation of material and human resources for increased production, the use of blockades, and the intensive bombing of civilian targets made the war of 1939 even more "total"—that is, comprehensive and intense—than that of 1914.

The German Conquest of Europe

The German attack on Poland produced swift success. The new style of "lightning warfare," or

The Coming of World War II

1919 (June)	The Versailles treaty
1923 (January)	France occupies the Ruhr
1925 (October)	The Locarno Agreements
1931 (Spring)	Onset of the Great Depression in Europe
1931 (September)	Japan occupies Manchuria
1933 (January)	Hitler comes to power
(October)	Germany withdraws from the League of Nations
1935 (March)	Hitler renounces disarmament, starts an air force, and begins conscription
(October)	Mussolini attacks Ethiopia
1936 (March)	Germany reoccupies and remilitarizes the Rhineland
(July)	Outbreak of the Spanish Civil War
(October)	Formation of the Rome–Berlin Axis
1938 (March)	*Anschluss* with Austria
(September)	The Munich Conference and partition of Czechoslovakia
1939 (March)	Hitler occupies Prague; France and Great Britain guarantee Polish independence
(August)	The Nazi–Soviet pact
(September 1)	Germany invades Poland
(September 3)	Britain and France declare war on Germany

Blitzkrieg, employed fast-moving, massed armored columns supported by airpower. The Poles had no tanks and few planes, and their defense soon collapsed. The speed of the German victory astonished the Russians, who hastened to collect their share of the booty before Hitler could deprive them of it.

On September 17, Russia invaded Poland from the east, dividing the country with the Germans. Stalin then forced the encircled Baltic countries to allow the Red Army to occupy them. By 1940 Estonia, Latvia, and Lithuania had become puppet republics within the USSR (Union of Soviet Socialist Republics, or the Soviet Union). In June 1940, the Russians forced Romania to cede Bessarabia. In November 1940, the Russians invaded Finland, but the Finns resisted fiercely for six months. Although they were finally worn down and compelled to yield territory and bases to Russia, the Finns remained independent. Russian expansionism and the poor performance of the Red Army in Finland may well have encouraged Hitler to invade the Soviet Union in June 1941, just twenty-two months after the 1939 treaty.

Until the spring of 1940, the Western Front was quiet. The French remained behind the Maginot Line while Hitler and Stalin swallowed Poland and the Baltic states. Britain hastily rearmed, and the British navy blockaded Germany. Cynics in the West called it the phony war, or *"Sitzkrieg,"* but Hitler shattered the stillness in the spring of 1940. In April, without warning and with swift success, the Germans invaded Denmark and Norway. Hitler's northern front was secure, and he now had both air and naval bases closer to Britain. A month later, a combined land and air attack struck Belgium, the Netherlands, and Luxembourg. German airpower and armored divisions were irresistible. The Dutch surrendered in a few days; the Belgians, though aided by the French and the British, gave up less than two weeks later.

The British and French armies in Belgium were forced to flee to the English Channel to seek escape on the beaches of Dunkirk. The heroic efforts of hundreds of Britons manning small boats saved more than 200,000 British and 100,000 French soldiers. Casualties, however, were high and valuable equipment was abandoned.

The Maginot Line ran from Switzerland to the Belgian frontier. Until 1936 the French had expected the Belgians to continue the fortifications along their German border. After Hitler remilitarized the Rhineland without opposition, the Belgians lost faith in their French alliance and proclaimed their neutrality, leaving the Maginot Line exposed on its left flank. Hitler's swift advance through Belgium therefore circumvented France's main line of defense.

The French army, poorly and hesitantly led by aged generals who did not understand how to use tanks and planes, collapsed. Mussolini, eager to claim the spoils of victory when it was clearly safe to do so, invaded southern France on

German troops stage a victory parade past the Arc de Triomphe in Paris in June, 1940. [Bildarchiv Preussischer Kulturbesitz]

Churchill had been an early and forceful critic of Hitler, the Nazis, and the policy of appeasement. He was a descendant and biographer of the duke of Marlborough (1650–1722), who had fought to prevent the domination of Europe by Louis XIV in the eighteenth century. Churchill's sense of history, his feeling for British greatness, and his hatred of tyranny and love of freedom made him reject any thought of compromise with Hitler. His skill as a speaker and a writer enabled him to inspire the British people with his own courage and determination and to undertake what seemed a hopeless fight. Hitler and his allies, including the Soviet Union, controlled all of Europe. Japan was having its way in Asia. The United States was neutral, dominated by isolationist sentiment, and determined to avoid involvement outside the Western Hemisphere.

One of Churchill's greatest achievements was establishing a close relationship with the American President Franklin D. Roosevelt (1882–1945). Roosevelt found ways to help the British despite strong political opposition. In 1940 and 1941, before the United States was at war, America sent military supplies, traded badly needed warships for leases on British naval bases, and even convoyed ships across the Atlantic to help the British survive.

June 10. Less than a week later, the new French government, under the ancient hero of Verdun, Marshal Henri Philippe Pétain (1856–1951), asked for an armistice. In two months Hitler had accomplished what Germany had failed to achieve in four years of bitter fighting in the previous war.

The Battle of Britain

The fall of France left Britain isolated, and Hitler expected the British to come to terms. He was prepared to allow Britain to retain its empire in return for a free hand for Germany on the Continent. The British had never been willing to accept such an arrangement and had fought the long and difficult war against Napoleon to prevent the domination of the Continent by a single power. If there was any chance that the British would consider such terms, it disappeared when Winston Churchill (1874–1965) replaced Chamberlain as prime minister in May of 1940.

The close cooperation between Prime Minister Winston Churchill of Britain and President Franklin Roosevelt of the United States greatly helped to assure the effective cooperation of their two countries in World War II.

As weeks passed and Britain remained defiant, Hitler was forced to contemplate an invasion, and that required control of the air. The first strikes by the German air force (*Luftwaffe*), directed against the airfields and fighter planes in southeastern England, began in August 1940. If these attacks had continued, Germany might soon have gained control of the air and, with it, the chance of a successful invasion.

In early September, however, seeking revenge for some British bombing raids on German cities, the *Luftwaffe* switched its main attacks to London. For two months, London was bombed every night. Much of the city was destroyed and about 15,000 people were killed. The theories of victory through airpower alone, however, proved false. Casualties were much less than expected, and morale was not shattered. In fact, the bombings united the British people and made them more resolute.

The Royal Air Force (RAF) inflicted heavy losses on the *Luftwaffe*. Aided by the newly developed radar and an excellent system of communications, the British Spitfire and Hurricane fighter planes destroyed more than twice as many enemy planes as were lost by the RAF. Hitler had lost the Battle of Britain in the air and was forced to abandon his plans for invasion.

The German Attack on Russia

The defeat of Russia and the conquest of the Ukraine to provide *Lebensraum* ("living space") for the German people had always been a major goal for Hitler. Even before the assault on Britain, he had informed his staff of his intention to attack Russia as soon as conditions were favorable. In December 1940, even while the bombing of England continued, he ordered his generals to prepare for an invasion of Russia by May 15, 1941 (see Map 29-3). He apparently thought that a *Blitzkrieg* victory in the East would also destroy any further British hope of resistance.

Operation Barbarossa, the code name for the invasion of Russia, was aimed at destroying Russia before winter could set in. Success depended in part on an early start, but here Hitler's Italian alliance proved costly. Mussolini was jealous of Hitler's success and annoyed by the treatment he had received from the German dictator. His invasion of France was a fiasco even though the main French forces were being simultaneously crushed by the Germans. Hitler did not allow Mussolini to annex French territory in Europe or North Africa. Mussolini instead launched an attack against the British in Egypt and drove them back some sixty miles. Encouraged by this success, he also invaded Greece from his base in Albania (which he had seized in 1939). His purpose was revealed by his remark to his son-in-law, Count Ciano: "Hitler always faces me with a *fait accompli*. This time I am going to pay him back in his own coin. He will find out in the newspapers that I have occupied Greece."[3]

[3]*Quoted in Gordon Wright,* The Ordeal of Total War, 1939–1945 *(New York: Harper & Row, 1968), pp. 35–36.*

Mussolini inspecting Italian troops at the Florence train station in October 1940 as he awaits a visit from Hitler. Mussolini's military reverses in North Africa and the Balkans would divert German resources in 1941 and delay the beginning of Hitler's planned invasion of Russia. [Popperfoto]

MAP 29-3 AXIS EUROPE, 1941   *On the eve of the German invasion of the Soviet Union, the Germany–Italy Axis bestrode most of western Europe by annexation, occupation, or alliance—from Norway and Finland in the north to Greece in the south and from Poland to France. Britain, the Soviets, a number of insurgent groups, and, finally, America had before them the long struggle of conquering this Axis "fortress Europe."*

In North Africa, however, the British counterattacked and drove the Italians back into Libya. The Greeks themselves pushed into Albania. In March 1941, the British sent help to the Greeks, and Hitler was forced to divert his attention to the Balkans and Africa. General Erwin Rommel

(1891–1944), later to earn the title "The Desert Fox," went to Africa and soon drove the British out of Libya and back into Egypt. In the Balkans, the German army swiftly occupied Yugoslavia and crushed Greek resistance. The price, however, was a delay of six weeks. The diversion caused by Mussolini's vanity proved to be costly the following winter in the Russian campaign.

Operation Barbarossa was launched against Russia on June 22, 1941, and it almost succeeded. Despite their deep suspicion of Germany (and the excuse later offered by apologists for the Soviet Union that the Nazi–Soviet pact was meant to give Russia time to prepare), the Russians were taken quite by surprise. Stalin appears to have panicked. He had not fortified his frontier, nor did he order his troops to withdraw when attacked. In the first two days, 2,000 Russian planes were destroyed on the ground. By November, Hitler had gone further into Russia than Napoleon. The German army stood at the gates of Leningrad, on the outskirts of Moscow, and on the Don River. Of the 4.5 million troops with which the Russians had begun the fighting, they had lost 2.5 million; of their 15,000 tanks, only 700 were left. Moscow was in panic, and a German victory seemed imminent.

Yet the Germans could not deliver the final blow. In August, they delayed their advance while Hitler decided strategy. The German general staff wanted to drive directly for Moscow and take it before winter. This plan probably would have brought victory. Unlike in Napoleon's time, Moscow was the hub of the Russian system of transportation. Hitler, however, diverted a significant part of his forces to the south. By the time he was ready to return to the offensive near Moscow, it was too late. Winter devastated the German army, neither dressed nor equipped to face it.

Given precious time, Stalin restored order and built defenses for the city. Even more important, troops arrived from Siberia, where they had been placed to check a possible Japanese attack. In November and December, the Russians counterattacked. The *Blitzkrieg* had turned into a war of attrition, and the Germans began to have nightmares of Napoleon's retreat.

Hitler's Plans for Europe

Hitler often spoke of the "new order" that he meant to impose after he had established his Third Reich (Empire) throughout Europe. The first two German empires were those of Charlemagne in the ninth century and Bismarck in the nineteenth. Hitler predicted that his own would last for a thousand years. If his organization of Germany before the war is a proper guide, he had no single plan of government but relied frequently on intuition and pragmatism. His organization of conquered Europe had the same patchwork characteristics. Some conquered territory was annexed to Germany; some was not annexed but administered directly by German officials; other lands were nominally autonomous but were ruled by puppet governments.

Hitler's regime was probably unmatched in history for carefully planned terror and inhumanity. His plan of giving *Lebensraum* to the Germans was to be accomplished at the expense of people he deemed inferior. Hitler established colonies of Germans in parts of Poland, driving the local people from their land and employing them as cheap labor. He had similar plans on an even greater scale for Russia. The Russians would be driven eastward to central Asia and Siberia; they would be kept in check by frontier colonies of German war veterans. European Russia would be settled by Germans.

Hitler's long-range plans included germanization as well as colonization. In lands inhabited by people racially akin to the Germans, like the Scandinavian countries, the Netherlands, and Switzerland, the natives would be absorbed into the German nation. Such peoples would be reeducated and purged of dissenting elements, but there would be little or no colonization. He even had plans, only slightly realized, of adopting selected people from the lesser races into the master race. One of these plans involved bringing half a million Ukrainian girls into Germany as servants and finding German husbands for them; about 15,000 were actually sent to Germany.

In the economic sphere, Hitler regarded the conquered lands merely as a source of plunder. From eastern Europe, he removed everything useful, including entire industries. In Russia and Poland, the Germans simply confiscated the land. In the West, the conquered countries were forced to support the occupying army at a rate several times above the real cost. The Germans used the profits to buy up everything useful and desirable, stripping the conquered peoples of most necessities. The Nazis were frank about their policies. One of Hitler's high officials said, "Whether nations live in prosperity or starve to

These are some of the dead at the Nordhausen concentration camp, which was liberated by the American army in April 1945. The Nazis set up their first concentration camps in Germany in 1933 to hold opponents of their regime. After the conquest of Poland, new camps were established there as part of the "final solution," the extermination of the Jews. About six million Jews were murdered in these camps. Even in those camps not dedicated to extermination—in which political prisoners and "undesirables" such as Gypsies, homosexuals, and Jehovah's Witnesses were held—conditions were brutal in the extreme, and tens of thousands died. The crimes of the Nazi regime have no precedent in human history. [National Archives]

death interests me only insofar as we need them as slaves for our culture."[4]

Racism and the Holocaust

The most horrible aspect of the Nazi rule in Europe arose not from military or economic necessity but from the inhumanity and brutality inherent in Hitler's racial doctrines. He considered the Slavs *Untermenschen,* subhuman creatures like beasts who need not be thought of or treated as people. In parts of Poland, the upper and professional classes were entirely removed—either jailed, deported, or killed. Schools and churches were closed; marriage was controlled by the Nazis to keep down the Polish birth rate; and harsh living conditions were imposed.

In Russia, things were even worse. Hitler spoke of his Russian campaign as a war of extermination. Heinrich Himmler, head of Hitler's elite SS guard, planned to eliminate thirty million Slavs to make room for the Germans; he formed extermination squads for the purpose. The number of Russian prisoners of war and deported civilian workers who died under Nazi rule may have reached six million.

[4]*Quoted in Wright, p. 117.*

Hitler had special plans for the Jews. He meant to make all Europe *Judenrein* ("free of Jews"). For a time he thought of sending them to the island of Madagascar. Later he arrived at the "final solution of the Jewish problem": extermination. The Nazis built extermination camps in Germany and Poland and used the latest technology to achieve the most efficient means of killing millions of men, women, and children simply because they were Jews. Before the war was over, perhaps six million Jews had died in what has come to be called the *Holocaust.* Only about a million remained alive, those mostly in pitiable condition.

World War II was unmatched in modern times in cruelty. When Stalin's armies conquered Poland and entered Germany, they raped, pillaged, and deported millions to the East. The British and American bombing of Germany killed thousands of civilians, and the dropping of atomic bombs on Japan inflicted terrible harm on civilian populations. The bombings, however, were thought of as acts of war that would help defeat the enemy. Stalin's atrocities were not widely known in the West at the time or even today.

The victorious Western allies were shocked by what they saw when they came on the Nazi extermination camps and their pitiful survivors.

Little wonder that they were convinced that the effort of resistance to the Nazis and all the pain it had cost were well worth it.

Japan and America's Entry into the War

The American government was very pro-British. The various forms of assistance that Roosevelt gave Britain would have justified a German declaration of war. Hitler, however, held back. The U.S. government might not have overcome isolationist sentiment and entered the war in the Atlantic if war had not been thrust on America in the Pacific.

Since the Japanese conquest of Manchuria in 1931, American policy toward Japan had been suspicious and unfriendly. The outbreak of the war in Europe emboldened the Japanese to accelerate their drive to dominate Asia. They allied themselves with Germany and Italy, made a treaty of neutrality with the Soviet Union, and penetrated Indochina at the expense of defeated France. They also continued their war in China and planned to gain control of Malaya and the East Indies at the expense of beleaguered Britain and the conquered Netherlands. The only barrier to Japanese expansion was the United States.

The Americans had temporized, unwilling to cut off vital supplies of oil and other materials for fear of provoking a Japanese attack on Southeast Asia and Dutch East Indies. The Japanese occupation of Indochina in July 1941 changed that policy, which had already begun to stiffen.

The successful Japanese attack on the American base at Pearl Harbor in Hawaii on December 7, 1941, together with simultaneous attacks on other Pacific bases, brought the United States into war against the Axis powers. This picture shows the battleships U.S.S. West Virginia and U.S.S. Tennessee in flames as a small boat rescues a man from the water. [U.S. Army Photograph]

Mass Extermination at Belsen

Hitler's calculated plan to wipe out Europe's Jews, along with millions of other people he considered undesirable for racial and other reasons, was not widely known during the war. Care was taken to keep the mass murders secret. Even when news of them leaked out, many were reluctant to believe what they heard, and participants in the crimes were naturally not eager to talk about them. Kurt Gerstein, a colonel in the SS, was part of the apparatus of extermination. Unlike most people involved and at great risk to himself, however, he tried to tell the world what was taking place. The following is an account of what he saw at the death camp at Belsen in 1942.

✦ *Who participated in the murder of the victims described here? Why did the guards lie to the victims about their fate? Why were all their personal belongings, even their hair, collected? History is full of the brutal treatment of people by those who have power over them. What was different about the Nazis' treatment of their victims? What was the basis of their choice of victims? How did the rest of the world react to these atrocities? Was a different reaction possible and warranted?*

A train arrived from Lemberg [Lvov]. There were forty-five cars containing 6,700 people, 1,450 of whom were already dead. Through the gratings on the windows, children could be seen peering out, terribly pale and frightened, their eyes filled with mortal dread . . . The train entered the station, and two hundred Ukrainians wrenched open the doors and drove the people out of the carriages with their leather whips. Instructions came through a large loudspeaker telling them to remove all their clothing, artificial limbs, glasses, etc. They were to hand over all objects of value at the counter. . . . Shoes were to be carefully tied together, for otherwise no one would ever again have been able to find shoes belonging to each other in a pile that was a good eighty feet high. Then the women and girls were sent to the barber who, with two or three strokes of his scissors, cut off all their hair and dropped it into potato sacks. "That's for some special purpose or other on U-Boats, for packing or something like that," I was told by an SS-Unterscharführer. . . .

Then the column moved off. Headed by an extremely pretty young girl, they walked along the avenue, all naked, men, women, and children, with artificial limbs removed. I myself was stationed up on the ramp between the [gas] chambers with Captain Wirth.

Mothers with babies at their breasts came

The United States froze Japanese assets and cut off oil supplies; the British and Dutch did the same. Japanese plans for expansion could not continue without the conquest of the Indonesian oil fields and Malayan rubber and tin.

In October, a war faction led by General Hideki Tojo (1885–1948) took power in Japan and decided to risk a war rather than yield. On Sunday morning, December 7, 1941, while Japanese representatives were discussing a settlement in Washington, Japan launched an air attack on Pearl Harbor, Hawaii, the chief American naval base in the Pacific. The technique was similar to the one Japan had used against the Russian fleet at Port Arthur in 1904, and it caught the Americans equally by surprise. Much of the American fleet and many airplanes were destroyed; the American capacity to wage war in the Pacific was negated for the time being. The next day, the United States and Britain declared war on Japan. Three days later, Germany and Italy declared war on the United States.

up, hesitated, and entered the chambers of death. At the corner stood a burly SS man with a priest-like voice. "Nothing at all is going to happen to you!" he told the poor wretches. "All you have to do when you get into the chambers is to breathe in deeply. That stretches the lungs. Inhaling is necessary to prevent disease and epidemics." When asked what would be done with them, he replied: "Well, of course, the men will have to work building houses and roads, but the women won't need to work. They can do housework or help in the kitchen, but only if they want to." For some of these poor creatures, this was a small ray of hope that was enough to make them walk the few steps to the chambers without resistance. Most of them knew what was going on. The smell told them what their fate was to be. They went up the small flight of steps and saw everything. Mothers with their babies clasped to their breasts, small children, adults, men, women, all naked; they hesitated, but they entered the chambers of death, thrust forward by the others behind them or by the leather whips of the SS [protective force]. Most went in without a word. . . . Many were saying prayers. I prayed with them. I pressed myself into a corner and cried aloud to my God and theirs. How gladly I should have gone into the chambers with them; how gladly I should have died with them. Then they would have found an SS officer in uniform in their gas chambers; they would have believed it was an accident and the story would have been buried and forgotten. But I could not do that yet. First, I had to make known what I had seen here. The chambers were filling up. Fill them up well—that was Captain Wirth's order. The people were treading on each other's feet. There were 700–800 of them in an area of 270 square feet, in 1,590 cubic feet of space. The SS crushed them together as tightly as they possibly could. The doors closed. Meanwhile, the rest waited out in the open, all naked. "It's done exactly the same way in winter," I was told. "But they may catch their death!" I said. "That's what they're here for," an SS man said. . . . The Diesel exhaust gases were intended to kill those unfortunates. But the engine was not working. . . . The people in the gas chambers waited, in vain. I heard them weeping, sobbing. . . . After 2 hours and 49 minutes, measured by my stop watch, the Diesel started. Up to that moment, men and women had been shut up alive in those four chambers, four times 750 people in four times 1,590 cubic feet of space. Another twenty-five minutes dragged by. Many of those inside were already dead. They could be seen through the small window when the electric light went on for a moment and lit up the inside of the chamber. After twenty-eight minutes, few were left alive. At the end of thirty-two minutes, all were dead.

From Saul Friedlaender, Pius XII and the Third Reich: A Documentation *(New York: Alfred A. Knopf, 1966), pp. 126–128.*

The Tide Turns

The potential power of the United States was enormous, but America was ill prepared for war. Though conscription had been introduced in 1940, the army was tiny, inexperienced, and poorly supplied. American industry was not ready for war. The Japanese swiftly captured Guam, Wake Island, and the Philippine Islands. Also, they attacked Hong Kong, Malaya, Burma, and the Dutch East Indies. By the spring of 1942, they controlled these places and the Southwest Pacific as far as New Guinea. They were poised for an attack on Australia, and it seemed that nothing could stop them.

In 1942 the Germans also advanced deeper into Russia and almost reached the Caspian Sea in their drive for Russia's oil fields. In Africa, too, Axis fortunes were high. Rommel drove the British back into Egypt toward the Suez Canal until he was stopped at El Alamein, only seventy miles from Alexandria. Relations between the democracies and their Soviet ally were not close.

Russian soldiers, in their heroic defense of Stalingrad, dug trenches from building to building in the city. The German defeat at Stalingrad in February 1943 marked the turning point of the Russian campaign. Thereafter the Russians advanced inexorably westward. [Archive Photos]

German submarine warfare was threatening British supplies. The Allies were being thrown back on every front, and the future looked bleak.

The first good news for the Allied cause in the Pacific came in the spring of 1942. A naval battle in the Coral Sea sank many Japanese ships and gave security to Australia. A month later, the United States defeated the Japanese in a fierce air and naval battle off Midway Island; they thus blunted the chance of another assault on Hawaii and did enough damage to halt the Japanese advance. Soon American Marines landed on Guadalcanal in the Solomon Islands and began to reverse the momentum of the war. The war in the Pacific was far from over, but the check to Japan allowed the Allies to concentrate their efforts first in Europe.

More than twenty nations located all over the world were opposed to the Axis powers. The main combatants, however, were Great Britain, the Soviet Union, and the United States. The two Western democracies cooperated to an unprecedented degree, but suspicion between them and the Soviet Union continued. The Russians accepted all the aid they could get. Nevertheless, they did not trust their allies, complained of inadequate help, and demanded that the democracies open a "second front" on the mainland of Europe.

In 1942 American preparation and production were inadequate for an invasion of Europe. German submarines made the Atlantic unsafe for crossing by the vast numbers of troops needed for an invasion. Not until 1944 were conditions right for the invasion, but in the meantime other developments forecast the doom of the Axis.

ALLIED LANDINGS IN AFRICA, SICILY, AND ITALY In November 1942, an Allied force landed in French North Africa (see Map 29-4). Even before that landing, British Field Marshal Bernard Montgomery (1887–1976), after stopping Rommel at El Alamein, had begun a drive to the west. Now, the American General Dwight D. Eisenhower (1890–1969) had pushed eastward through Morocco and Algeria. The two armies caught the German army between them in Tunisia and crushed it. The Allies now controlled the Mediterranean and could attack southern Europe.

In July and August 1943, the Allies took Sicily. Mussolini was driven from power, but the Germans occupied Italy. The Allies landed in Italy, and Marshal Pietro Badoglio (1871–1956), the leader of the new Italian government, went over to their side, declaring war on Germany. Churchill had spoken of Italy as the "soft under-

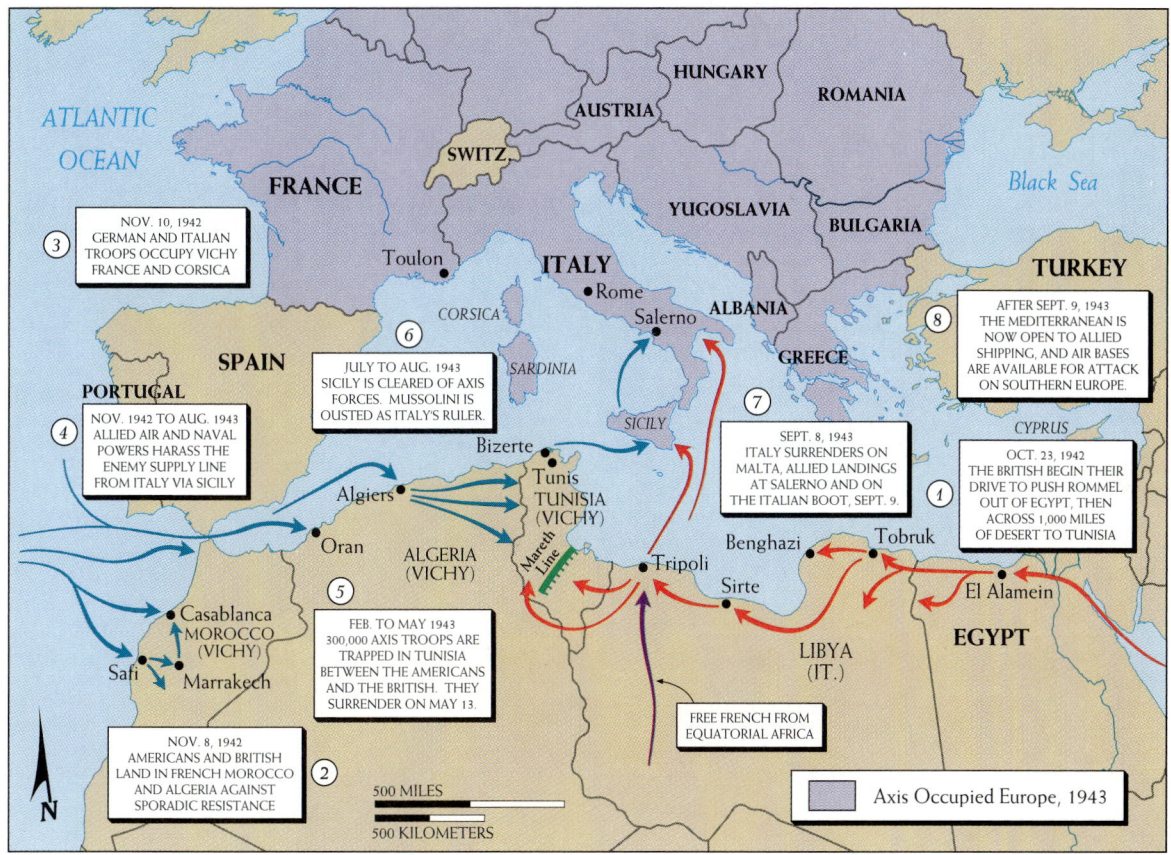

MAP 29-4 NORTH AFRICAN CAMPAIGNS, 1942–1945 *Control of North Africa would give the Allies access to Europe from the south. The map illustrates this theater of the war from Morocco to Egypt and the Suez Canal.*

belly" of the Axis, but the Germans there resisted fiercely. Still the need to defend Italy diverted the Germans' energy and resources and left them vulnerable on other fronts.

BATTLE OF STALINGRAD The Russian campaign became especially demanding. In the summer of 1942, the Germans resumed the offensive on all fronts but were unable to get far except in the south (see Map 29-5). Their goal was the oil fields near the Caspian Sea. Stalingrad on the Volga was a key point on the flank of the German army in the south. Hitler was determined to take the city and Stalin to hold it. The Battle of Stalingrad raged for months with unexampled ferocity. The Russians lost more men in this one battle than the Americans lost in combat during the entire war, but their heroic defense prevailed. Because Hitler again overruled his generals and would

not allow a retreat, an entire German army was lost at Stalingrad.

Stalingrad marked the turning point of the Russian campaign. Thereafter, the Americans provided material help. Even more important, increased production from their own industry, which had been moved to or built up in the safety of the central and eastern regions of the USSR, allowed the Russians to gain and keep the offensive. As the Germans' resources dwindled, the Russians inexorably advanced westward.

STRATEGIC BOMBING In 1943 the Allies also gained ground in production and logistics. The industrial might of the United States began to come into full force, and new technology and tactics greatly reduced the submarine menace.

In the same year, the American and British air forces began a series of massive bombardments of Germany by night and day. The Ameri-

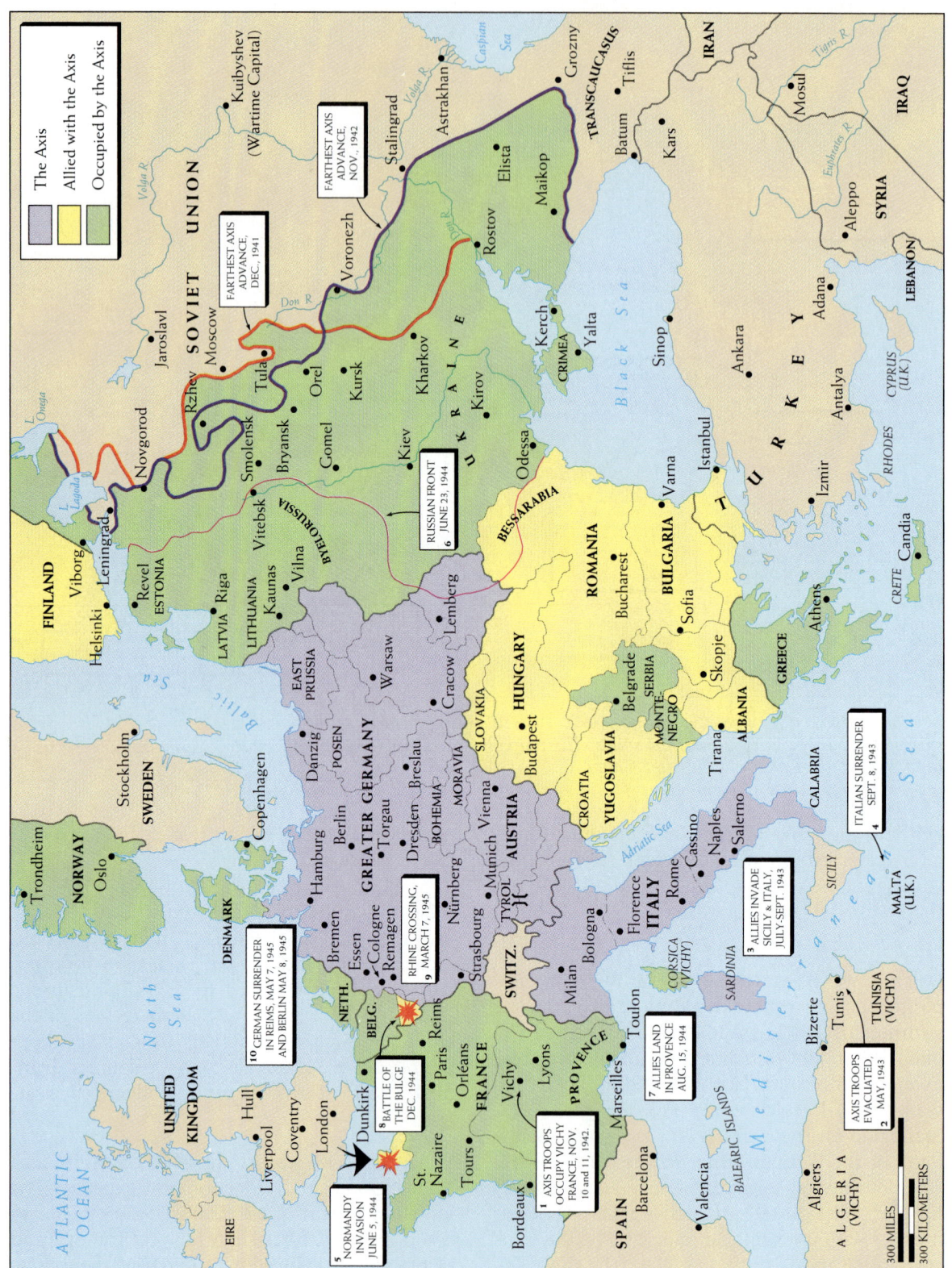

MAP 29-5 DEFEAT OF THE AXIS IN EUROPE, 1942–1945 *Here we see some major steps in the progress toward Allied victory against Axis Europe. From the south through Italy, the*

Allied troops landed in Normandy on D-Day, June 6, 1944. This photograph, taken two days later, shows long lines of men and equipment moving inland from the beach to reinforce the troops leading the invasion. [Archive Photos]

cans were more committed to the theory of "precision bombing" of military and industrial targets vital to the enemy war effort, and so they flew the day missions. The British considered precision bombing impossible and therefore useless. They preferred indiscriminate "area bombing" aimed to destroy the morale of the German people; this kind of bombing could be done at night. Neither kind of bombing had much effect on the war until 1944, when the Americans introduced long-range fighters that could protect the bombers and allow accurate missions by day.

By 1945 the Allies had virtually cleared the skies of German planes and could bomb at will. Concentrated attacks on industrial targets, especially communications centers and oil refineries, did extensive damage and helped to shorten the war. Terror bombing continued, too, with no useful result. The bombardment of Dresden in February 1945 was especially savage and destructive. It was much debated within the British government and has raised moral questions since. Whatever else it accomplished, the aerial war over Germany did take a heavy toll of the German air force and diverted vital German resources away from other military purposes.

The Defeat of Nazi Germany

On June 6, 1944 ("D-Day"), American, British, and Canadian troops landed in force on the coast of Normandy. The "second front" was opened. General Dwight D. Eisenhower, the commander of the Allied armies, faced a difficult problem. The European coast was heavily

In April 1945, Americans invaded the heavily armed and fortified Japanese island of Okinawa, less than four hundred miles from the Japanese home islands. Japanese resistance was strong, and the fighting was unbelievably fierce. In this picture, American Marines move forward in heavy fighting. [Bildarchiv Preussischer Kulturbesitz]

fortified. Amphibious assaults, moreover, are especially vulnerable to changes of wind and weather. Success depended on meticulous planning, advance preparation by heavy bombing, and feints to mask the point of attack. The German defense was strong, but the Allies were able to establish a beachhead and then to break out of it. In mid-August, the Allies landed in southern France to put more pressure on the enemy. By the beginning of September, France had been liberated.

THE BATTLE OF THE BULGE All went smoothly until December, when the Germans launched a counterattack in Belgium through the Ardennes Forest. Because the Germans were able to push forward into the Allied line, this was called the Battle of the Bulge. Although the Allies suffered heavy losses, the Bulge was the last gasp for the Germans in the West. The Allies soon recovered their momentum and pushed eastward. They crossed the Rhine in March of 1945, and German resistance rapidly crumbled. This time there could be no doubt that the Germans had lost the war on the battlefield.

THE CAPTURE OF BERLIN In the East, the Russians swept forward no less swiftly despite fierce German resistance. By March 1945, they were near Berlin. Because the Allies insisted on unconditional surrender, the Germans fought on until May. Hitler and his intimates committed suicide in an underground bunker in Berlin on May 1, 1945. The Russians occupied Berlin by agreement with their Western allies. The Third Reich had lasted a dozen years instead of the thousand predicted by Hitler.

Fall of the Japanese Empire

The war in Europe ended on May 8, 1945, and by then victory over Japan was also in sight. The original Japanese attack on the United States had been a calculated risk against the odds. Japan was inherently weaker than the United States. The longer the war lasted, the more American superiority in industrial production and population counted.

AMERICANS RECAPTURE THE PACIFIC ISLANDS In 1943 the American forces, still small in number, began a campaign of "island hopping." They did not try to recapture every Pacific island held by the Japanese but selected major bases and strategic sites along the enemy supply line (see Map 29-6). Starting from the Solomon Islands, they moved northeast toward Japan itself. By June 1944, they had reached the

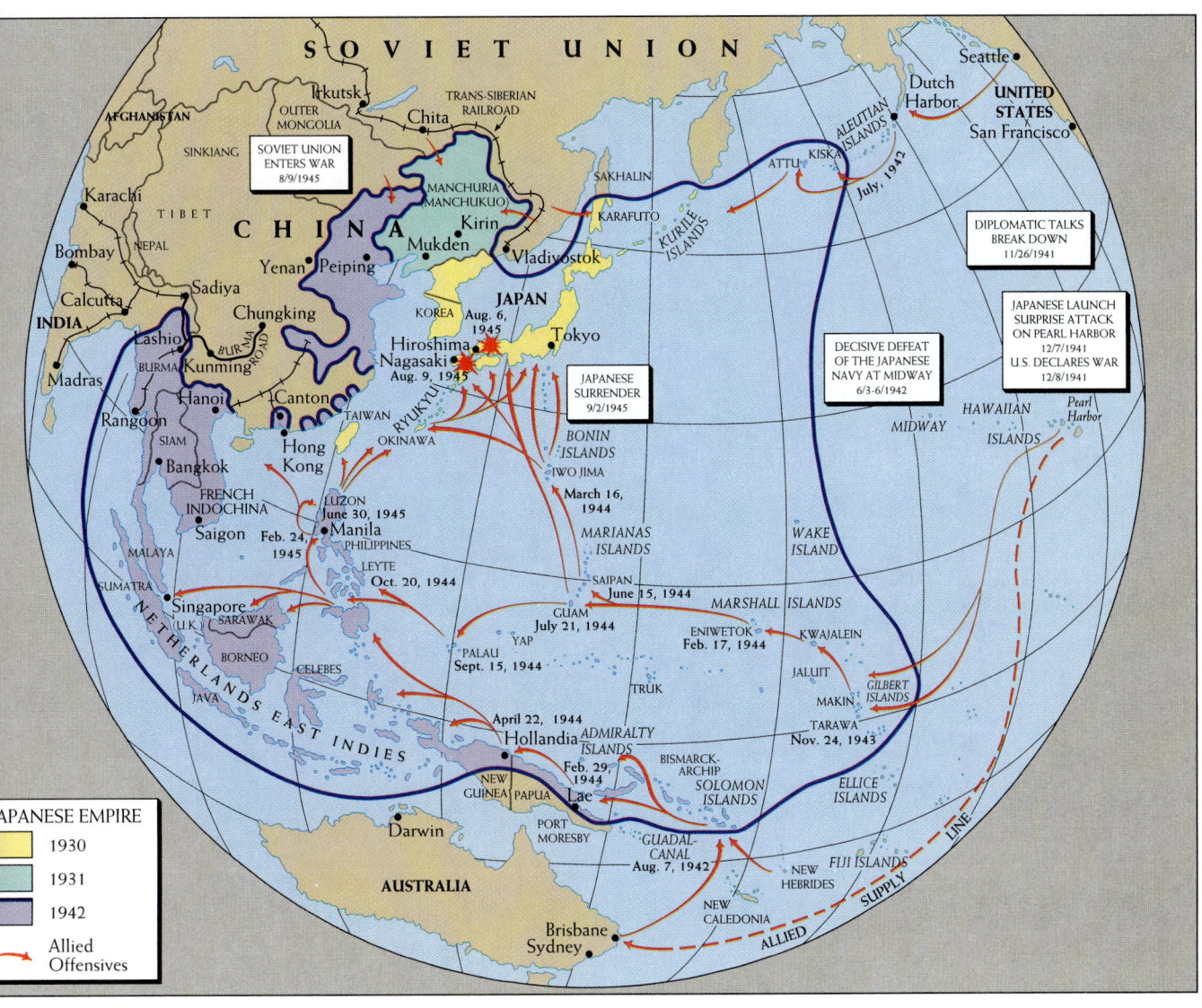

MAP 29-6 WORLD WAR II IN THE PACIFIC *As in Europe, the Pacific war involved Allied recapture of areas that had been quickly taken earlier by the enemy. The enormous area represented by the map shows the initial expansion of Japanese holdings to cover half the Pacific and its islands, as well as huge sections of eastern Asia, and the long struggle to push the Japanese back to their homeland and defeat them by the summer of 1945.*

Mariana Islands, usable as bases for bombing the Japanese in the Philippines, China, and Japan itself.

In October of the same year, the Americans recaptured most of the Philippines and drove the Japanese fleet back into its home waters. In 1945 Iwo Jima and Okinawa fell, despite a determined Japanese resistance that included *kamikaze* attacks, suicide missions in which specially trained pilots deliberately flew their explosive-filled planes into American warships.

From these new bases, closer to Japan, the American bombers launched a terrible wave of bombings that destroyed Japanese industry and disabled the Japanese navy. Still the Japanese government, dominated by a military clique, refused to surrender.

Confronted with Japan's determination, the Americans made plans for a frontal assault on the Japanese homeland. They calculated it might cost a million American casualties and even greater losses for the Japanese. At this

The Allied campaign of aerial bombardment did terrible damage to German cities. This photograph shows the devastation it delivered to the city of Cologne on the Rhine. [UPI/Bettmann]

point, science and technology presented the Americans with another choice.

THE ATOMIC BOMB Since early in the war, a secret program had been in progress. Its staff, made up in significant part of exiles from Hitler's Europe, was working to use atomic energy for military purposes. On August 6, 1945, an American plane dropped an atomic bomb on the Japanese city of Hiroshima. The city was destroyed, and more than 70,000 of its 200,000 residents were killed. Two days later, the Soviet Union declared war on Japan and invaded Manchuria. The next day, a second atomic bomb fell, this time on Nagasaki. Even then, the Japanese cabinet was prepared to resist further, to face an invasion rather than give up.

The unprecedented intervention of Emperor Hirohito (r. 1926–1989) finally forced the government to surrender on August 14. Even then they made the condition that Japan could keep its emperor. Although the Allies had continued to insist on unconditional surrender, President Harry S. Truman (1884–1972), who had come to office on April 12, 1945, on the death of Franklin D. Roosevelt, accepted the condition. Peace was formally signed aboard the U.S.S. *Missouri* in Tokyo Bay on September 2, 1945.

Revulsion and horror at the only use of atomic bombs as well as hindsight arising from the Cold War have made the decision to use the bomb against Japanese cities controversial. Some have suggested that the bombings were unnecessary to win the war and that their main purpose was to frighten the Russians into a more cooperative attitude after the war. Others have emphasized the bureaucratic, almost automatic nature of the decision, once it had been decided to develop the bomb. To the decision makers and their contemporaries, however, matters were simpler. The bomb was a way to end the war swiftly and save American lives. The decision to use it was conscious, not automatic, and required no ulterior motive.

The Cost of War

World War II was the most terrible war in history. Military deaths are estimated at some fifteen million, and at least as many civilians were killed. If deaths linked indirectly to the war, from disease, hunger, and other causes, are included, the number of victims might reach as high as forty million. Most of Europe and significant parts of Asia were devastated. Yet the end of so terrible a war brought little opportunity for relaxation. The dawn of the atomic age and the dramatic end it brought to the war made people conscious that another major war might extinguish humanity. Everything depended on concluding a stable peace, but even as the fighting ended, conflicts among the victors made the prospects of a lasting peace doubtful.

The Domestic Fronts

World War II represented an effort at total war by all the belligerents. Never in European or world history had so many men and women and so many resources been devoted to military effort. One result was the carnage that occurred on the battlefields, at sea, and in the air. Another was an unprecedented organization of civilians on the various home fronts. Each domestic effort and experience was different, but few escaped the impact of the conflict. Everywhere there were shortages, propaganda campaigns, and new political developments.

Germany: From Apparent Victory to Defeat

Hitler had expected to defeat all his enemies by a series of rapid strokes, *Blitzkrieg*. Such campaigns would have required little change in Germany's society and economy. During the first two years of the war, in fact, Hitler demanded few important sacrifices from the German people. Spending on domestic projects continued, and food was plentiful; the economy as a whole was not on a full wartime footing. The failure to quickly overwhelm the Soviet Union changed everything. Food could no longer be imported from the East in needed quantities, Germany had to mobilize for total war, and the government demanded major sacrifices from the people.

A great expansion of the army and of military production began in 1942. As Minister for Armaments and Munitions, Albert Speer (1905–1981) directed the economy, and Germany met its military needs instead of making consumer goods. The government sought the cooperation of major German business enterprises to aid the growth of wartime production. Between 1942 and late 1944, the output of military products tripled; as the war went on, more men were drafted from industry into the army, and military production suffered.

As the manufacture of armaments replaced the production of consumer goods, shortages of everyday products became serious. Prices and wages were controlled, but the standard of living of German workers fell. Burdensome food rationing began in April 1942, and shortages were severe until the Nazi government seized more food from the occupied regions of Europe. To preserve their own home front, the Nazis passed on the suffering to their defeated neighbors.

By 1943 there were also serious labor shortages. The Nazis required German teenagers and retired men to work in the factories, and increasing numbers of women joined them. To achieve total mobilization, the Germans closed retail businesses, raised the age of women eligible for compulsory service, shifted non-German domestic workers to wartime industry, moved artists and entertainers into military service, closed theaters, and reduced such basic public services as mail and railways. Finally, the Nazis compelled thousands of people from conquered lands to do forced labor in Germany.

Hitler assigned women a special place in the war effort. The celebration of motherhood continued, with an emphasis on women who were the mothers of important military figures. Films portrayed ordinary women who became especially brave and patriotic during the war and remained faithful to their husbands who were at the front. Women were thereby shown as mothers and wives who sent their sons and husbands off to war. The government pictured other wartime activities of women as the natural fulfillment of their maternal roles. As air raid wardens, they protected their families; as factory workers in munitions plants, they aided their sons on the front lines. Women working on farms were providing for their soldier sons and husbands; as housewives, they were helping to win the war by conserving food and managing their households frugally. Finally, by their faithful chastity, German women were protecting racial purity. They were not to marry or to engage in sexual relations with men who were not Germans.

The war years also saw an intensification of political propaganda on the domestic front beyond what occurred in other countries. Hitler and other Germans genuinely believed that weak domestic support had led to Germany's defeat in World War I; they were determined that this situation would not happen again. Nazi propaganda blamed the outbreak of the war on the British and the Jews and its prolongation on the policies of Germany's opponents. It also stressed the power of Germany and the inferiority of its foes.

Propaganda Minister Josef Goebbels (1897–1945) used both radio and films to boost the Nazi cause. Movies of the collapse of Poland, Belgium, Holland, and France were shown in Germany to demonstrate German military might. Throughout the conquered territories, the Nazis used the same mass media to frighten inhabitants about the possible consequences of an Allied victory. Later in the war, the ministry broadcast exaggerated claims of Nazi victories. As the German armies were checked on the battlefield, especially in Russia, propaganda became a substitute for victory. To stiffen German resolve, propaganda now aimed to frighten Germans about the consequences of defeat.

After May 1943, when the Allies began their major bombing offensive over Germany, the German people had much to fear. One German city after another was devastated, but German morale was not undermined. The bombing may even have increased German resistance by seeming to confirm the regime's propaganda about the ruthlessness of Germany's opponents.

World War II increased the power of the Nazi Party in Germany. Every area of the economy and society came under the direct influence or control of the party. The Nazis were determined that they, rather than the traditionally honored

German officer corps, would profit from the new authority that the war effort was giving to the central government. Throughout the war years, there was virtually no serious opposition to Hitler or his ministers. In 1944 a small group of army officers attempted to assassinate Hitler; the effort failed, and there were few indications of significant popular support for this act.

The war brought great changes to Germany, but what transformed the country was the experience of vast physical destruction, invasion, and occupation. Hitler and the Nazis had brought Germany to such a complete and disastrous defeat that only a new kind of state with new political structures could emerge.

France: Defeat, Collaboration, and Resistance

The terms of the armistice, signed June 22, 1940, allowed the Germans to occupy more than half of France, including the Atlantic and English Channel coasts. To prevent the French from continuing the fight from North Africa, and even more to prevent them from turning their fleet over to Britain, Hitler left southern France unoccupied until November 1942. Marshal Pétain set up a dictatorial regime at the resort city of Vichy and followed a policy of close collaboration with the Germans in hopes of preserving as much autonomy as possible.

Some of the collaborators believed that the Germans were sure to win the war and wanted to be on the victorious side. A few sympathized with the ideas and plans of the Nazis. Many conservatives regarded the French defeat as a judgment on what they saw as the corrupt, secularized, liberal ways of the Third Republic. Most of the French were not active collaborators but were helpless and demoralized by defeat and the evidence of German power.

Many conservatives and extreme rightists saw in the Vichy government a way to reshape the French national character and to halt the decadence they associated with political and religious liberalism. The Roman Catholic clergy, who had lost power and influence under the Third Republic, gained status under Vichy. The Church supported Pétain, and his government restored religious instruction in the state schools and increased financial support for

Catholic schools. Vichy adopted the Church's views on the importance of family and spiritual values. The government forbade divorce during the first three years of marriage and made subsequent divorce difficult; large families were encouraged and subsidized.

The Vichy regime also encouraged an intense, chauvinistic nationalism. It exploited the long-standing prejudice against foreigners working in France and fostered resentment even against French men and women who were not regarded as genuinely French. The chief victims were French Jews. Anti-Semitism was not new in France, as the Dreyfus affair had demonstrated. Even before Germany undertook Hitler's "final solution" in 1942, the French had begun to remove Jews from positions of influence in government, education, and publishing. In 1941 the Germans began to intern Jews living in occupied France; soon they carried out assassinations and imposed large fines collectively on the Jews of the occupied zone. In the spring of 1942, they began to deport Jews from France, ultimately more than 60,000, to the extermination camps of eastern Europe. The Vichy government had no part in these decisions, but it made no protest, and its own anti-Semitic policies made the whole process easier to carry out.

A few French, most notably General Charles de Gaulle (1890–1969), fled to Britain after the defeat of France. There they organized the French National Committee of Liberation, or "Free French." Until the end of 1942, the Vichy government controlled French North Africa and the navy, but the Free French began operating in central Africa. From London, they broadcast hope and defiance to their compatriots in France.

Serious internal resistance to the German occupiers and to the Vichy government, however, began to develop only late in 1942. The Germans tried to force young people in occupied France to work in German factories; some of them joined the Resistance, but the number of all the resisters was small. Many were deterred by fear of harsh punishment by the Germans. Some disliked the violence inevitably connected with resistance to a powerful ruthless nation. So long as it appeared the Germans would win the war, moreover, resistance seemed imprudent and futile. For these reasons, the organized resistance never attracted vast numbers of followers; well under 5 percent of the adult French population appears to have been involved.

By early 1944, the tide of battle had shifted. The Allies seemed sure to win, and the Vichy government would clearly not survive; only then did a large-scale active resistance assert itself. General de Gaulle spoke confidently for Free France from his base in London and urged the French people to resist their conquerors and the German lackeys in the Vichy government. Within France, resistance groups joined forces to plan for a better day. From Algiers on August 9, 1944, the Committee of National Liberation declared the authority of Vichy illegitimate. Soon French soldiers joined in the liberation of Paris and established a government for Free France. On October 21, 1945, France voted to end the Third Republic and adopted a new constitution as the basis of the Fourth Republic. The French people had experienced defeat, disgrace, deprivation, and suffering in the war. Hostility and bitter quarrels over who had done what during the occupation and under Vichy divided them for decades.

Great Britain: Organization for Victory

On May 22, 1940, the British Parliament gave the government emergency powers. Together with others already in effect, this measure allowed the government to institute compulsory military service, food rationing, and various controls over the economy.

To deal with the crisis facing them, all British political parties joined in a national government under Winston Churchill. Churchill and the British war cabinet moved as quickly as possible to mobilize the nation. Perhaps the most pressing immediate need was the production of airplanes to fight the Germans in the Battle of Britain. This effort was led by Lord Beaverbrook (1879–1964), one of Britain's most important newspaper publishers. The demand for more planes and other armaments inspired a massive campaign to reclaim scrap metal. Wrought-iron fences, kitchen pots and pans, and every conceivable kind of scrap metal were collected for the war effort. This was only one successful example of the many ways the civilian population was enthusiastically engaged in the struggle.

By the end of 1941, British production had already surpassed Germany's. To meet the heavy demands on the labor force, factory hours were extended, and many women were brought into the workforce. Unemployment disappeared, and the working classes had more money to spend than they had enjoyed for many years. To avoid inflation caused by increased demand for an inadequate supply of consumer goods, savings were encouraged, and taxes were raised to absorb the excess purchasing power.

The "blitz" air attacks of the winter and spring of 1940–1941 were the most immediate and dramatic experience of the war for the British people themselves. The German air raids killed thousands of people and left many others homeless. Once the bombing began, many families removed their children to the countryside. Ironically, the rescue effort improved the standard of living of many of the children, for the government paid for their food and medication. Gas masks were issued to thousands of city dwellers, who were frequently compelled to take shelter from the bombs in the London subways.

After the spring of 1941, Hitler needed most of his air force on the Russian front, but the bombing of Britain continued, killing more than 30,000 people by the end of the war. Terrible as it was, this toll was much smaller than the number of Germans killed by Allied bombing in the war. In England, as in Germany, however, the bombing, far from breaking the people's spirit, may well have made them more determined.

The British made many sacrifices. Transportation facilities were strained simply from carrying enough coal for domestic heating and for running factories. Food and clothing for civilians were scarce, and the government adopted strict rationing to achieve a fair distribution. Every scrap of land was farmed, increasing the productive portion by almost four million acres. Gasoline was scarce, and so private vehicles almost vanished.

The British established their own propaganda machine to influence the Continent. The British Broadcasting Company (BBC) sent programs to every country in Europe in the local language to encourage resistance against the Nazis. At home, the government used the radio to unify the nation. Soldiers at the front heard the same programs as their families at home. The most famous program, second only to

Winston Churchill walks through the rubble-strewn streets of London after the city had experienced a night of German bombing. Despite many casualties and widespread devastation, the German bombing of London did not break British morale or prevent the city from functioning. [UPI/Bettmann Newsphotos]

Churchill's speeches, was *It's That Man Again*, a humorous broadcast filled with imaginary figures that the entire nation came to treasure.

Strangely, for the broad mass of the population, the standard of living improved during the war. The general health of the nation also improved for reasons that are still not clear. These improvements should not be exaggerated, but they did occur, and many connected them with the active involvement of the government in the economy and in the lives of the citizens. This wartime experience may have contributed to the Labour Party's victory in 1945; many feared that a return to Conservative Party rule would also mean a return to the economic problems and unemployment of the 1930s.

The Soviet Union: "The Great Patriotic War"

The war against Germany came as a great surprise to Stalin and the Soviet Union. The German attack violated the 1939 pact with Hitler and put the government of the Soviet Union on the defensive militarily and politically. It showed the failure of Stalin's foreign policy and the ineptness of his preparation for war. He claimed that the pact had given the nation an extra year and a half to prepare for war, but this was clearly a lame and implausible excuse in light of the ease of Germany's early victories. Within days, German troops occupied much of the western Soviet Union. The Communist government feared that Soviet citizens who had been conquered by the Germans, many of them not ethnic Russians, might welcome the conquerors as liberators; these Soviet citizens had been harshly oppressed by the Stalinist regime.

No nation suffered greater loss of life or more extensive physical destruction during World War II than the Soviet Union. Perhaps as many as sixteen million people were killed, and vast numbers of Soviet troops were taken prisoner. Hundreds of cities and towns and well over half of the industrial and transportation facilities of the country were devastated. From 1942 thousands of Soviet prisoners worked in German factories as forced labor. The Germans also served their own war effort with grain, mineral resources, and oil confiscated from the Soviet Union.

Stalin conducted the war as virtual chief of the armed forces, and the State Committee for Defense provided strong central coordination. In the decade before the war, Stalin had already made the Soviet Union a highly centralized state; he had tried to manage the entire economy from Moscow through the Five-Year Plans, the collectivization of agriculture, and the purges. The country was thus already on what amounted to a wartime footing long before the conflict erupted. When the war began, millions of citizens entered the army, but the army itself did not grow in influence at the expense of the state and the Communist Party, that is, of Stalin. He was suspicious of the generals, though he had presumably eliminated officers of doubtful loyalty in the purges of the late 1930s. As the war continued, however, the army gained

some degree of independence, and eventually the generals were no longer subservient to party commissars. The army thus gained some freedom of action. It was, however, still sharply limited by the power of Stalin and by the nature of Soviet government and society.

Soviet propaganda was different from that of other nations. Because the Soviet government distrusted the loyalty of its citizens, it confiscated radios to prevent the people from listening to German or British propaganda. In cities, the government broadcast to the people over loudspeakers in place of radios. During the war, Soviet propaganda emphasized Russian patriotism rather than traditional Marxist themes that stressed class conflict. The struggle against the Germans was called "The Great Patriotic War."

Great Russian novels of the past were republished; more than half a million copies of Tolstoy's *War and Peace* were printed during the siege of Leningrad (Saint Petersburg). Other authors wrote straightforward propaganda fostering hatred of the Germans. Serge Eisenstein (1898–1948), the great filmmaker, produced a vast epic entitled *Ivan the Terrible*, which glorified this brutal tsar of the Russian past. Musicians, such as Dimitri Shostakovich (1906–1975), produced scores that sought to contribute to the struggle and evoke heroic emotions. The most important of these was Shostakovich's *Seventh Symphony*, also known as the *Leningrad Symphony*.

The pressure of war led Stalin to make peace with the Russian Orthodox church, allowing Church leaders to enter the Kremlin. Stalin hoped that this new policy would give him more support at home and permit the Soviet Union to be viewed more favorably in eastern Europe, where the Orthodox church predominated.

Within occupied portions of the western Soviet Union, an active resistance movement arose against the Germans. The swiftness of the German invasion had stranded thousands of Soviet troops behind German lines. Many were shipped to Germany as prisoners of war, but others escaped and carried on guerrilla resistance warfare behind enemy lines. Stalin supported partisan forces in lands held by the enemy for two reasons. He wanted to cause as much difficulty as possible for the Germans, and Soviet-sponsored resistance reminded the peasants in the conquered regions that the Soviet government, with its policies of collectivization, had not disappeared. Stalin feared that the peasants' hatred of the Communist government might lead them to collaborate with the invaders. When the Soviet army moved westward toward the end of the war, it incorporated the partisans into the regular army.

As its armies reclaimed the occupied areas and then moved across eastern and central Europe, the Soviet Union established itself as a world power second only to the United States. Stalin had entered the war a reluctant belligerent, but he emerged a major victor. In that respect, the war and the extraordinary patriotic effort and sacrifice it generated consolidated the power of Stalin and the party more effectively than the political and social policies of the previous decade.

Preparations for Peace

The split between the Soviet Union and its wartime allies should cause no surprise. As the self-proclaimed center of world communism, the Soviet Union was openly dedicated to the overthrow of the capitalist nations. This message, however, was muted when the occasion demanded. On the other side, the Western allies were no less open about their hostility to communism and its chief purveyor, the Soviet Union. Although they had been friendly to the early stages of the Russian Revolution, they had intervened to try to overthrow the Bolshevik regime during the Russian Civil War. The United States did not grant formal recognition to the Union of Soviet Socialist Republics until 1933. The Western powers' exclusion of the Soviets from the Munich conference and Stalin's pact with Hitler did nothing to improve relations between them during the war.

Nonetheless, the need to cooperate against a common enemy and strenuous propaganda efforts helped improve Western feeling toward the Soviet ally. Still, Stalin remained suspicious and critical of the Western war effort, and Churchill was determined to contain the Soviet advance into Europe. Roosevelt perhaps had been more hopeful that the Allies could continue to work together after the war, but even he

was losing faith by 1945. Differences in historical development and ideology, as well as traditional conflicts over political power and influence, soon dashed hopes of a mutually satisfactory peace settlement and continued cooperation to uphold it.

The Atlantic Charter

In August 1941, even before the Americans were at war, Roosevelt and Churchill had met on a ship off Newfoundland and agreed to the Atlantic Charter. This broad set of principles in the spirit of Wilson's Fourteen Points provided a theoretical basis for the peace they sought. When Russia and the United States joined Britain in the war, the three powers entered a purely military alliance in January 1942, leaving all political questions aside. The first political conference was the meeting of foreign ministers in Moscow in October 1943. The ministers reaffirmed earlier agreements to fight on until the

Major Campaigns and Events of World War II	
September 1939	Germany and the Soviet Union invade Poland
November 1939	The Soviet Union invades Finland
April 1940	Germany invades Denmark and Norway
May 1940	Germany invades Belgium, the Nether-lands, Luxembourg, and France
June 1940	Fall of France
August 1940	Battle of Britain begins
June 1941	Germany invades the Soviet Union
July 1941	Japan takes Indochina
December 1941	Japan attacks Pearl Harbor; United States enters war against Axis Powers
June 1942	Battle of Midway
November 1942	Battle of Stalingrad begins
July–August 1943	Allies take Sicily, land in Italy
June 1944	Allies land in Normandy
May 1945	Germany surrenders
August 1945	Atomic bombs dropped on Hiroshima and Nagasaki
September 1945	Japan formally surrenders

enemy surrendered unconditionally and to continue cooperating after the war in a united-nations organization.

Tehran: Agreement on a Second Front

The first meeting of the leaders of the Big Three (as the USSR, Britain, and the United States were known) took place at Tehran, the capital of Iran, in 1943. Western promises to open a second front in France the next summer (1944) and Stalin's agreement to join in the war against Japan when Germany was defeated created an atmosphere of goodwill in which to discuss a postwar settlement. Stalin wanted to retain what he had gained in his pact with Hitler and to dismember Germany. Roosevelt and Churchill were conciliatory, but they made no firm commitments.

The most important decision was the one that chose Europe's west coast as the main point of attack instead of the Mediterranean. That meant, in retrospect, that Soviet forces would occupy eastern Europe and control its destiny. At Tehran in 1943, the Western allies did not foresee this clearly, for the Russians were still fighting deep within their own frontiers, and military considerations were still paramount.

CHURCHILL AND STALIN By 1944 the situation was different. In August, Soviet armies were before Warsaw, which had revolted against the Germans in expectation of liberation. But the Russians halted, allowing the Polish rebels to be annihilated while they turned south into the Balkans. They gained control of Romania and Hungary, advances that centuries of expansionist tsars had only dreamed of achieving. Alarmed by these developments, Churchill went to Moscow and met with Stalin in October. They agreed to share power in the Balkans on the basis of Soviet predominance in Romania and Bulgaria, Western predominance in Greece, and equality of influence in Yugoslavia and Hungary. These agreements were not enforceable without American approval, and the Americans were known to be hostile to such un-Wilsonian devices as "spheres of influence."

GERMANY The three powers easily agreed on Germany—its disarmament, denazification, and division into four zones of occupation by France and the Big Three. Churchill, however, began to balk at Stalin's demand for $20 billion in reparations as well as forced labor from all the zones, with Russia to get half of everything. These matters were left to fester and cause dissension in the future.

EASTERN EUROPE The settlement of eastern Europe was an equally thorny problem. Everyone agreed that the Soviet Union deserved to have friendly neighboring governments, but the West insisted that they also be autonomous and democratic. The Western leaders, especially Churchill, were not eager to see eastern Europe fall under Russian domination. They were also, especially Roosevelt, committed to democracy and self-determination.

Stalin, however, knew that independent, freely elected governments in Poland and Romania could not be counted on to be friendly to Russia. He had already established a puppet government in Poland in competition with the Polish government-in-exile in London. Under pressure from the Western leaders, however, he agreed to reorganize this government and include some Poles friendly to the West in it. He also signed a Declaration on Liberated Europe promising self-determination and free democratic elections. Stalin may have been eager to avoid conflict before the war with Germany was over. He was always afraid that the Allies would make a separate peace with Germany and betray him. And he probably thought it worth endorsing some hollow principles as the price of continued harmony. In any case, he wasted little time violating these agreements.

Yalta

The next meeting of the Big Three was at Yalta in the Crimea in February 1945. The Western armies had not yet crossed the Rhine, but the Soviet army was within a hundred miles of Berlin (see Map 29-7). The war with Japan continued, and no atomic explosion had yet taken place. Roosevelt, faced with a prospective invasion of Japan and heavy losses, was eager to bring the Russians into the Pacific war as soon as possible. As a true Wilsonian, he also suspected Churchill's determination to maintain the British Empire and Britain's colonial advantages. The Americans thought that Churchill's plan to set up British spheres of influence in Europe would encourage the Russians to do the same and lead to friction and war. To encourage Russian participation in the war against Japan, Roosevelt and Churchill made extensive concessions to Russia of Sakhalin and the Kurile islands, in Korea, and in Manchuria.

Again in the tradition of Wilson, Roosevelt laid great stress on a united-nations organization: "Through the United Nations, he hoped to achieve a self-enforcing peace settlement that would not require American troops, as well as an open world without spheres of influence in which American enterprise could work freely."[5] Soviet agreement on these points seemed well worth concessions elsewhere.

Potsdam

The Big Three met for the last time in the Berlin suburb of Potsdam in July 1945. Much had changed since the last conference. Germany had been defeated, and news of the successful experimental explosion of an atomic weapon reached the American president during the meetings. The cast of characters was also different. President Truman replaced the deceased Roosevelt, and Clement Attlee (1883–1967), leader of the Labour Party that had defeated Churchill's Conservatives in a general election, replaced Churchill as Britain's spokesman during the conference. Previous agreements were reaffirmed, but progress on undecided questions was slow.

Russia's western frontier was moved far into what had been Poland and included most of German East Prussia. In compensation, Poland was allowed "temporary administration" over the rest of East Prussia and Germany east of the Oder–Neisse river line, a condition that became permanent. In effect, Poland was moved about a hundred miles west, at the expense of Germany, to accommodate the Soviet Union. The Allies agreed that Germany would be divided into occupation zones until the final peace treaty was signed. Germany remained divided until 1990.

A Council of Foreign Ministers was established to draft peace treaties for Germany's allies. Growing disagreements made the job difficult, and Italy, Romania, Hungary, Bulgaria,

[5]Robert O. Paxton, Europe in the Twentieth Century (New York: Harcourt Brace Jovanovich, 1975), p. 487.

MAP 29-7 YALTA TO THE SURRENDER *"The Big Three"—Roosevelt, Churchill, Stalin—met at Yalta in the Crimea in February of 1945. At the meeting, concessions were made to Stalin concerning the settlement of eastern Europe because Roosevelt was eager to bring the Russians into the Pacific war as soon as possible. This map shows the positions held by the victors when Germany surrendered.*

and Finland did not sign treaties until February 1947. The Russians were dissatisfied with the treaty that the United States made with Japan in 1951 and signed their own agreements with the Japanese in 1956. These disagreements were foreshadowed at Potsdam.

◆

The second great war of the twentieth century (1939–1945) grew out of the unsatisfactory resolution of the first. In retrospect, the two wars appear to some people to be one continuous conflict, a kind of twentieth-century "Thirty

This photograph shows the "Big Three" at Potsdam. By the summer of 1945, only Stalin remained of the original leaders of the major Allies. Roosevelt and Churchill had been replaced by Harry Truman and Clement Atlee. [UPI/Bettmann]

Years' War," with the two main periods of fighting separated by an uneasy truce. To others, that point of view oversimplifies and distorts the situation by implying that the second war was the inevitable result of the first and its inadequate peace treaties. The latter opinion seems more sound, for, whatever the flaws of the treaties of Paris, the world suffered an even more terrible war than the first because of failures of judgment and will on the part of the victorious democratic powers.

The United States, which had become the wealthiest and potentially the strongest nation in the world, disarmed almost entirely and withdrew into a shortsighted and foolish isolation. Therefore, it could play no important part in restraining the angry and ambitious dictators who brought on the war. Britain and France refused to face the threat posed by the Axis powers until the most deadly war in history was required to put it down. If the victorious democracies had remained strong, responsible, and realistic, they could easily have remedied whatever injustices or mistakes arose from the treaties without endangering the peace.

The second war itself was so plainly a world war that little need be said to indicate its global character. There is good reason to think that if the Japanese occupation of Manchuria in 1931 was not technically a part of that war, it was a significant precursor. Moreover, there was Italy's attack on the African nation of Ethiopia in 1935; the Italian, German, and Soviet interventions in the Spanish Civil War (1936–1939); and Japan's attack on China in 1937. These acts revealed that aggressive forces were on the march around the globe and that the defenders of the world order lacked the will to stop them. The formation of the Axis among Germany, Italy, and Japan guaranteed that when the war came it would be fought around the world.

There was fighting and suffering in Asia, Africa, the Pacific islands, and Europe; and men and women from all the inhabited continents

Negotiations Among the Allies	
August 1941	Churchill and Roosevelt meet off Newfoundland to sign Atlantic Charter
October 1943	American, British, and Soviet foreign ministers meet in Moscow
November 1943	Churchill, Roosevelt, and Stalin meet at Tehran
October 1944	Churchill meets with Stalin in Moscow
February 1945	Churchill, Roosevelt, and Stalin meet at Yalta
July 1945	Attlee, Stalin, and Truman meet at Potsdam

took part in it. The use of atomic weapons brought the frightful struggle to a close. Still, what are called conventional weapons did almost all the damage; their level of destructiveness threatened the survival of civilization, even without the use of atomic or nuclear devices.

This war ended not with unsatisfactory peace treaties but with no treaty at all in the European arena, where the war had begun. The world quickly split into two unfriendly camps: the western led by the United States, and the eastern led by the Soviet Union. This division, among other things, hastened the liberation of former colonial territories. The bargaining power of the new nations that emerged from them was temporarily increased as the two rival superpowers tried to gain their friendship or allegiance. It has become customary to refer to these nations as "the Third World," with the former Soviet Union and the United States and their respective allies being the first two. The passage of time has shown that the differences among Third World nations are so great as to make the term all but meaningless.

The surprising treatment received by the defeated powers of the second war was also largely the result of the emergence of the Cold War. Instead of holding them back, the Western powers installed democratic governments in Italy, West Germany, and Japan, took them into the Western alliances designed to contain communism, and helped them recover economically. Japan and Germany are now among the richest nations in the world, and Italy is more prosperous than it has ever been.

By the last decade of the twentieth century, Japan had become one of the greatest industrial, commercial, and financial powers in the world and a major investor in the American economy. Its manufacturers have offered stiff competition to their counterparts in the United States and western Europe, provoking concern and calls for protective tariffs.

Germany, divided between East and West by the war, never ceased to hope for eventual unification. The startling events of 1989, in which the Soviet Union gave up its hold over eastern Europe, made unification suddenly possible, and it occurred in 1990. One result has been to open again a question that lay behind the two great wars of the twentieth century, the place of a unified Germany in Europe.

Review Questions

1. What were Hitler's foreign policy aims? Was he bent on conquest in the east and dominance in the west, or did he simply want to return Germany to its 1914 boundaries?
2. Why did Britain and France adopt a policy of appeasement in the 1930s? What were its main features? Did the appeasers buy the West valuable time to prepare for war by their actions at Munich in 1938?
3. How was Hitler able to defeat France so easily in 1940? Why was the air war against Britain a failure? Why did Hitler invade Russia? Why did the invasion ultimately fail? Could it have succeeded?
4. Why did Japan attack the United States at Pearl Harbor? What was the significance of American intervention in the war? Why did the United States drop atomic bombs on Japan? Did President Truman make the right decision when he ordered the bombs used?
5. What impact did World War II have on the civilian population of Europe? How did experiences on the domestic front of Great Britain differ from those of Germany and France? What impact did "The Great Patriotic War" have on the people of the Soviet Union? Did participation in World War II solidify Stalin's hold on power?
6. What was Hitler's "final solution" to the Jewish problem? Why did Hitler want to eliminate Slavs as well? Some historians have looked at the twentieth century and have seen a period of great destruction as well as of great progress. Is this truly a "century of Holocaust"? Discuss the ramifications of these questions.

Suggested Readings

A. ADAMTHWAITE, *France and the Coming of the Second World War, 1936–1939* (1977). A careful account making good use of the newly opened French archives.

J. ADLER, *The Jews of Paris and the Final Solution: Communal Response and Internal Conflicts, 1940–1944* (1987). Written by a former member of the French resistance.

E. R. BECK, *Under the Bombs: The German Home Front, 1942–1945* (1986). An interesting examination of a generally unstudied subject.

A. Bullock, *Hitler: A Study in Tyranny*, rev. ed. (1964). A brilliant biography.

W. S. Churchill, *The Second World War*, 6 vols. (1948–1954). The memoirs of the great British leader.

H. Feis, *From Trust to Terror: The Onset of the Cold War, 1945–1950* (1970). The best general account.

H. W. Gatzke, *Stresemann and the Rearmament of Germany* (1954). An important monograph.

M. Gilbert, *The Holocaust: A History of the Jews of Europe During the Second World War* (1985). The best and most comprehensive treatment.

M. Gilbert and R. Gott, *The Appeasers*, rev. ed. (1963). A revealing study of British policy in the 1930s.

M. Harrison, *Soviet Planning in Peace and War, 1938–1945* (1985). An examination of the Soviet wartime economy.

J. Keegan, *The Second World War* (1990). A lively and penetrating account by a master military historian.

M. Knox, *Mussolini Unleashed* (1982). An outstanding study of Fascist Italy's policy and strategy in World War II.

G. Kolko, *The Politics of War* (1968). An interesting example of the revisionist school that finds the causes of the Cold War in economic considerations and emphasizes American responsibility.

W. L. Langer and S. E. Gleason, *The Challenge of Isolation* (1952). American foreign policy in the 1930s.

D. C. Large (Ed.), *Contending with Hitler: Varieties of German Resistance in the Third Reich* (1992). Essays that examine the efforts of resistance to Hitler and their limits.

B. H. Liddell Hart, *History of the Second World War*, 2 vols. (1971). A good military history.

S. Marks, *The Illusion of Peace* (1976). A good discussion of European international relations in the 1920s and early 1930s.

V. Mastny, *Russia's Road to the Cold War* (1979). Written by an expert on the Soviet Union and eastern Europe.

W. Murray, *The Change in the European Balance of Power 1938–1939* (1984). A brilliant study of the relationship between strategy, foreign policy, economics, and domestic politics in the years before the war.

N. Rich, *Hitler's War Aims*, 2 vols. (1973–1974). The best study of the subject in English.

M. Sherwin, *A World Destroyed: The Atomic Bomb and the Grand Alliance* (1975). An analysis of the role of the atomic bomb in the years surrounding the end of World War II.

R. J. Sontag, *A Broken World 1919–1939* (1971). An excellent survey.

A. J. P. Taylor, *The Origins of the Second World War* (1966). A lively, controversial, even perverse study.

H. Thomas, *The Spanish Civil War*, 3rd ed. (1986). The best account in English.

C. Thorne, *The Approach of War 1938–1939* (1967). A careful analysis of diplomacy.

P. Wandycz, *The Twilight of French Eastern Alliances, 1926–1936* (1988). A well-documented account of the diplomacy of central and eastern Europe in a crucial period.

G. Wright, *The Ordeal of Total War 1939–1945* (1968). An excellent survey.

United States armed forces patrol in Vietnam. At the war's peak, more than 500,000 American troops were stationed in South Vietnam. The United States struggled in Vietnam for more than a decade, seriously threatening its commitment to Western Europe. [C. Simonpietri/SYGMA]

Europe and the Soviet–American Rivalry

Key Topics in This Chapter
- The origins of the Cold War and the division of Europe into eastern and western blocs following World War II
- The American domestic scene
- The Soviet Union and the Cold War through the Khrushchev and Brezhnev eras
- Political and economic developments in western Europe during the Cold War
- Decolonization and the conflicts in Korea and Vietnam
- The Arab–Israeli conflict

From the end of World War II in 1945 until the collapse of the Soviet Union and its subject regimes in the late 1980s, the Soviet Union and the United States—two nuclear-armed superpowers—confronted each other in a simmering conflict known as the Cold War. While it lasted, this conflict dominated global politics and threatened the peace of Europe, which stood at its center, divided between the U.S.-dominated NATO (North Atlantic Treaty Organization) and the Soviet-dominated Warsaw Pact.

Undertaking an active role in Europe and the rest of the world was a major shift in policy for the United States, reflecting its leaders' awareness of the dangers to which the country had been exposed when it retreated from the world scene after World War I. Moving to oppose what it regarded as the expansion of Soviet power and Communist influence across the globe, the United States assumed a position of military, political, and economic leadership. This policy of active leadership prompted the Marshall Plan, the formation of NATO, and military intervention in Korea and Vietnam.

The Communist government of the Soviet Union, established in 1917 and consolidated under Stalin's dictatorship, underwent many changes and attempts at redirection after World War II. The turmoil of the First World War had allowed the Soviet Union to come into existence; the turmoil of the Second World War permitted it to establish hegemony over eastern Europe. From the late 1940s through the 1980s, the Soviet Union tried to retain dominance in eastern Europe and to challenge the United States around the globe.

The Soviet Union pursued two not always compatible foreign policy goals. One was to lead the international Communist movement, dedicated to the overthrow of capitalism throughout the world. The other was to secure its own national interests, which sometimes put it at odds with Communist movements elsewhere. Eventually, harsh rivalries emerged between the Soviet Union and other Communist nations, most notably the People's Republic of China. The leaders of the Soviet Union, meanwhile, failed to build lasting support for their goals, either internally or in their eastern European dependencies. Nonetheless, the Soviet Union maintained its position as a superpower and its

Cold War antagonism to the United States through the opening years of the 1980s.

As the nations of Europe retreated from empire, the rivalry between the two superpowers expanded into a contest for dominance in the postcolonial world. Superpower intervention aggravated local conflicts on every continent. Southeast Asia in particular developed into a battleground. In its efforts to limit Communism, the United States became embroiled in bitter wars in Korea and Vietnam. The struggle between Israel and the Arab nations was likewise an arena of superpower conflict.

The Emergence of the Cold War

The tense relationship between the United States and the Soviet Union started in the closing months of World War II. Some scholars attribute the hardening of the atmosphere between the two countries to Harry Truman's assumption of the presidency in April 1945, after the death of the more sympathetic Franklin Roosevelt, and to the American possession of an effective atomic bomb. Evidence suggests, however, that Truman was trying to carry Roosevelt's policies forward and that Roosevelt himself had become distressed by Soviet actions in eastern Europe. Nor did Truman use the atomic bomb to try to keep Russia out of the Pacific. On the contrary, he worked hard to ensure Russian intervention against Japan at the end of the war. In part, the new coldness among the Allies arose from the mutual feeling that each had violated previous agreements. The Russians were plainly asserting permanent control of Poland and Romania under puppet Communist governments. The United States, on the other hand, was taking a harder line on the extent of German reparations to the Soviet Union.

The Lines Drawn and the Iron Curtain

In retrospect, however, it is unlikely that friendlier styles on either side could have avoided a split that rested on basic differences of ideology and interest. The Soviet Union's attempt to extend its control westward into central Europe and the Balkans and southward into the Middle

East was a continuation of the policy of tsarist Russia. It had been Britain's traditional role to try to restrain Russian expansion into these areas, and it was not surprising that the United States should inherit that task as Britain's power waned.

The Americans made no attempt to roll back Soviet power where it existed (see Map 30-1). At the time, American military forces were the greatest in their history, American industrial power was unmatched in the world, and atomic weapons were an American monopoly. In less than a year from the war's end, Americans reduced their forces in Europe from 3.5 million to half a million. The speed of the withdrawal reflected pressure to "get the boys home" but was also fully in accord with America's peace-time plans and goals. Those goals included support for self-determination, autonomy, and democracy in the political sphere; and free trade, freedom of the seas, no barriers to investment, and the Open Door in the economic sphere. They reflected American principles and they served American interests well. As the strongest, richest nation in the world—the one with the greatest industrial plant and the strongest currency—the United States would benefit handsomely if an international order based on such goals were established.

American hostility to colonial empires created tensions with France and Britain, but these were minor. The main conflict was with the Soviet Union. From the Soviet perspective, extending the borders of the USSR and dominating the formerly independent states of eastern Europe would provide needed security and would be a proper compensation for the fearful losses the Soviet people had endured in the war. The Soviets could thus see American resistance to their expansion as a threat to their security and their legitimate aims. American objections over Poland and other states could be seen as attempts to undermine regimes friendly to Russia and to encircle the Soviet Union with hostile neighbors. This point of view might also be seen to justify Russian attempts to overthrow regimes friendly to the United States in western Europe and elsewhere.

The growth in France and Italy of large, popular Communist parties plainly taking orders from Moscow led the Americans to believe that Stalin was engaged in a worldwide plot to destroy capitalism and democracy by subversion. Without reliable evidence about Stalin's

MAP 30-1 TERRITORIAL CHANGES AFTER WORLD WAR II
The map pictures the shifts in territory following the defeat of the Axis. No treaty of peace formally ended the war with Germany.

Churchill Invents the Iron Curtain

In 1946 Winston Churchill chose an American audience (at Westminster College in Fulton, Missouri) for the speech that contributed the expression "Iron Curtain" to the language. More important, it defined the existence of what came to be known as the Cold War between the Communist and the democratic camps.

◆ *Why do you think Churchill chose to deliver this address to an American audience? What events and concerns arising at the end of World War II and in the months immediately following had led Churchill to these conclusions? Would Churchill's description have been more accurate had he delivered this speech five years later? Why or why not?*

A shadow has fallen upon the scenes so lately lighted by the Allied victory. Nobody knows what Soviet Russia and its Communist international organization intends to do in the immediate future, or what are the limits, if any, to their expansive and proselytizing tendencies. . . .

From Stettin in the Baltic to Trieste in the Adriatic, an iron curtain has descended across the Continent. Behind that line lie all the capitals of the ancient states of central and eastern Europe. Warsaw, Berlin, Prague, Vienna, Budapest, Belgrade, Bucharest and Sofia; all these famous cities and the populations around them lie in the Soviet sphere and all are subject in one form or another, not only to Soviet influence but to a very high and increasing measure of control from Moscow. Athens alone, with its immortal glories, is free to decide its future at an election under British, American, and French observation. The Russian-dominated Polish government has been encouraged to make enormous and wrongful inroads upon Germany, and mass expulsions of millions of Germans on a scale grievous and undreamed of are now taking place. The Communist parties, which were very small in all these eastern states of Europe, have been raised to preeminence and power far beyond their numbers and are seeking everywhere to obtain totalitarian control. Police governments are prevailing in nearly every case, and so far except in Czechoslovakia, there is no true democracy. . . .

. . . I do not believe that Soviet Russia desires war. What they desire is the fruits of war and the indefinite expansion of their power and doctrines. . . .

. . . If the western democracies stand together in strict adherence to the principles of the United Nations Charter, their influence for furthering these principles will be immense and no one is likely to molest them. If, however, they become divided or falter in their duty, and if these all-important years are allowed to slip away, then indeed catastrophe may overwhelm us all.

"Winston Churchill's Speech at Fulton," in Vital Speeches of the Day, Vol. 12 *(New York: City News Publishing),* March 15, 1946, pp. 331–332.

intentions, it is impossible to be certain if these suspicions were justified, but most people in the West certainly thought them plausible. Rivalry between the Soviet Union and the United States dominated international relations for the next three decades. In the flawed world of reality, it is hard to see how it could have been otherwise.

The important question then was whether the conflict would take a diplomatic or a military form.

Evidence of the new mood of hostility among the former allies was not long in coming. In February 1946, both Stalin and his foreign minister, Vyacheslav Molotov (1890–1986), gave public speeches in which they spoke of the Western democracies as enemies. A month later, Churchill gave a speech in Fulton, Missouri, in which he viewed Russian actions in eastern Europe with alarm. He spoke of an Iron Curtain that had descended on Europe, dividing a free and democratic West from an East under totalitarian rule. He warned against Communist subversion and urged Western unity and strength as a response to the new menace. In this atmosphere, difficulties grew.

Early Frustrations of the United Nations

Toward the end of the war, one of Roosevelt's major goals had been the formation of the United Nations. He hoped this new international body would provide a forum for negotiation and consultation among the nations of the world and would have sufficient military muscle to intervene against aggression. By committing itself to this organization and providing it a home, the United States, in contrast to its inward retreat following World War I, signaled its readiness to accept the responsibilities of a world power.

The United States had taken the leading role in devising the organization of the United Nations, formally founded in February 1945. It was organized around two governing bodies: a large General Assembly in which all member nations sat and a smaller Security Council. The Security Council soon emerged as the dominant body. It had five permanent members—Great Britain, France, China, the Soviet Union, and the United States—and two temporary members drawn from among the U.N.'s other member states. Each of the five permanent members— the major allied powers of World War II—had the right to veto any measure brought to the Security Council.

By the late 1940s, hopes that the United Nations would resolve the world's major conflicts had been disappointed. Like the League of Nations, it was (and is) dependent on voluntary contributions of money and troops. The U.N. Charter, moreover, forbids interference in the internal affairs of nations, and many of the problems of the late 1940s were internal in nature. Finally, during the late 1940s and throughout the 1950s, the Soviet Union repeatedly used its veto in the Security Council, frustrating the ability of the United Nations to resolve problems.

The attempt to deal with the problem of atomic energy was an early victim of the Cold War and the paralysis of the United Nations. The Americans put forward a plan to place the manufacture and control of atomic weapons under international control, but the Russians balked at proposed requirements for on-site inspection and for limits on veto power in the United Nations. The plan fell through. The United States continued to develop its own atomic weapons in secrecy, and the Russians did the same. By 1949, with the help of information obtained by Soviet spies in Britain and the United States, the Soviet Union had exploded its own atomic bomb, and the race for nuclear weapons was on.

Containment in American Foreign Policy

The resistance of westerners to what they increasingly perceived as Soviet intransigence and Communist plans for subversion and expansion took clearer form in 1947.

THE TRUMAN DOCTRINE Since 1944, civil war had been raging in Greece between the royalist government restored by Britain and insurgents supported by the Communist countries, chiefly Yugoslavia. In 1947 Britain informed the United States that it was financially no longer able to support the Greeks. On March 12, President Truman asked Congress for legislation that would provide funds to support Greece and also Turkey, then under Soviet pressure to yield control of the Dardanelles, and Congress complied. In his speech to Congress that gave these actions much broader significance, the president set forth what came to be called the Truman Doctrine. He advocated a policy of support for "free people who are resisting attempted subjugation by armed minorities or by outside pressures," by implication anywhere in the world.

THE MARSHALL PLAN American aid to Greece and Turkey took the form of military equipment and advisers. For western Europe, where postwar poverty and hunger fueled the menacing growth of Communist parties, the Americans devised the European Recovery

The Truman Doctrine Declared

In 1947 the British informed the United States that they could no longer support the Greeks in their fight against a Communist insurrection supported from the outside. On March 12 of that year, President Truman asked Congress for legislation in support of both Greece and Turkey, which was also in danger. The principle behind that request, which became known as the Truman Doctrine, appears in the following selections from Truman's speech to the Congress.

✦ *How does Truman relate the goals of the Second World War to the emerging Cold War with the Soviet Union? What are the qualities that Truman associates with free governments and how were those absent in the Soviet Union and the nations of eastern Europe under its domination? How does this speech establish guidelines that might be applied to U.S. policy in parts of the world beyond Greece?*

One of the primary objectives of the foreign policy of the United States is the creation of conditions in which we and other nations will be able to work out a way of life free from coercion. This was a fundamental issue in the war with Germany and Japan. Our victory was won over countries which sought to impose their will, and their way of life, upon other nations.

To insure the peaceful development of nations, free from coercion, the United States has taken a leading part in establishing the United Nations. The United Nations is designed to make possible lasting freedom and independence for all its members. We shall not realize our objectives, however, unless we are willing to help free peoples to maintain their free institutions and their national integrity against aggressive movements that seek to impose upon them totalitarian regimes. . . .

At the present moment in world history nearly every nation must choose between alternative ways of life. The choice is too often not a free one.

One way of life is based upon the will of the majority, and is distinguished by free institutions, representative government, free elections, guaranties of individual liberty, freedom of speech and religion, and freedom from political oppression.

The second way of life is based upon the will of a minority forcibly imposed upon the majority. It relies upon terror and oppression, a controlled press and radio, fixed elections, and the suppression of personal freedoms.

I believe that it must be the policy of the United States to support free peoples who are resisting attempted subjugation by armed minorities or by outside pressures.

I believe that we must assist free peoples to work out their own destinies in their own way.

I believe that our help should be primarily through economic and financial aid, which is essential to economic stability and orderly political processes.

Senate Committee on Foreign Relations, A Decade of American Foreign Policy: Basic Documents 1941–1949 (1950), *pp. 1235–1237.*

Program. Named the Marshall Plan after George C. Marshall (1880–1959), the secretary of state who introduced it, this program provided broad economic aid to European states on condition only that they work together for their mutual benefit. The Soviet Union and its satellites were invited to participate. Finland and Czechoslovakia were willing to do so, and Poland and Hungary showed interest. The Soviets, however, fearing that American economic aid would attract many satellites out of their orbit, forbade them to take part.

The Marshall Plan was a great success in restoring prosperity to western Europe and in setting the stage for Europe's unprecedented postwar economic growth. It also led to the waning of Communist strength in the West and to the establishment there of solid democratic regimes.

Soviet Assertion of Domination of Eastern Europe

From the Western viewpoint, this policy of "containment" was a new and successful response to the Soviet and Communist challenge. The Soviet Union viewed the matter differently. The Soviet determination to control eastern Europe had in their eyes historical as well as ideological roots. Western European powers had invaded the lands of the Soviet Union once in the nineteenth century (under Napoleon) and already twice in the twentieth. For its part, tsarist Russia had governed Poland for over a century and intervened at the request of the Austrian Empire to put down the Hungarian revolution in 1848. Russia's interests in the lands around the Black Sea were long-standing. Given this history and the Soviet Union's extraordinary losses in World War II, it is not surprising that Soviet leaders would seek to use their eastern European satellites as a buffer against future invasions.

To Stalin, containment may have looked like a renewed attempt by the West to isolate and encircle the USSR. His answer was to put an end to all multiparty governments behind the Iron Curtain and to replace them with thoroughly Communist regimes completely under his control. He also called a meeting of all Communist parties around the world at Warsaw in the autumn of 1947. There they organized the Communist Information Bureau (Cominform), a revival of the old Comintern, dedicated to spreading revolutionary communism throughout the world. The era of the popular front was officially over. Communist leaders in the West who favored friendship, collaboration, and reform were replaced by hard-liners who attempted to sabotage the new structures.

In February 1948, Stalin gave a dramatic and brutal display of his new policy in Prague. The Communists expelled the democratic members of what had been a coalition government and

President Harry Truman greets Secretary of State George Marshall returning from Europe. Truman and Marshall were the architects of American foreign policy during the early years of the Cold War. (Archive Photos)

murdered Jan Masaryk (1886–1948), the foreign minister and son of the founder of Czechoslovakia, Thomas Masaryk. President Eduard Benes (1884–1948) was also forced to resign, and Czechoslovakia was brought fully under Soviet rule.

During the late 1940s, the Soviet Union moved to dominate the other subject governments in eastern Europe. It required them to impose Stalinist policies, including one-party political systems, close military cooperation with the Soviet Union, collectivization of agriculture, Communist Party domination of universities and other institutions of education, and attacks on the Church. Longtime Communist Party officials were purged and subjected to show trials like those that had taken place in Moscow during the late 1930s. The catalyst for this harsh tightening probably was the success of Marshal Tito (1892–1980), the leader of Communist Yugoslavia, in freeing his country from Soviet domination. Stalin feared other eastern European states might follow the Yugoslav example and moved to prevent them from doing so.

The Postwar Division of Germany

These Soviet actions, especially those in Czechoslovakia, increased American determination to go ahead with its own arrangements in Germany.

The Church and the Communist Party Clash over Education in Hungary

Throughout eastern Europe, the Roman Catholic church became one of the strongest opponents of the postwar Communist Party governments. It raised issues relating to Church schools, free worship, participation in Church-sponsored organizations, and the erection of new Church buildings. One of the harshest clashes took place in Hungary. Following are two statements that illustrate the opposing positions of the Church and the Party. Cardinal Mindszenty (1892–1975) was later imprisoned and became one of the most well-known political prisoners in eastern Europe.

◆ *How does Mindszenty relate the position of Church-supported schools to the nature and rights of parenthood? How does he compare the actions of the Communist Party to those of Hitler? How does the Minister of Public Worship set party members against the Church? How does he attempt to place loyalty to the party above private beliefs? What does the Communist Party fear from religious education and participation in religious activities on the part of its members or their children?*

Statement of Josef Cardinal Mindszenty, May 20, 1946

The right of the Church to schools is entirely in concord with the right of parents to educate their children. What is incumbent upon the parents in all questions of natural life is incumbent upon the Church with regard to the supernatural life. Parents are prior to the state, and their rights were always and still are, acknowledged by the Church. The prerogative of parents to educate their children cannot be disputed by the state, since it is the parents who give life to the child. They feed the child and clothe it. The child's life is, as it were, the continuation of theirs. Hence it is their right to demand that their children are educated according to their faith and their religious outlook.

DISAGREEMENTS OVER GERMANY During the war, the Allies had never decided how to treat Germany after its defeat. At first they all agreed it should be dismembered, but differed on how. By the time of Yalta, Churchill had come to fear Russian control of eastern and central Europe and began to oppose dismemberment.

The Allies also differed on economic policy. The Russians proceeded swiftly to dismantle German industry in the Eastern Zone, but the Americans acted differently in the Western Zone (see Map 30-2). They concluded that following the Soviet policy would require the United States to support Germany economically for the foreseeable future. It would also cause political chaos and open the way for communism. They preferred, therefore, to try to make Germany self-sufficient, and this meant restoring rather than destroying its industrial capacity. To the Soviets, the restoration of a powerful industrial Germany, even in the Western Zone only, was frightening and unacceptable. The same difference of approach hampered agreement on reparations. The Soviets claimed the right to the industrial equipment in all the zones, and the Americans resisted their demands.

BERLIN BLOCKADE Disagreement over Germany produced the most heated of postwar debates. When the Western powers agreed to go forward with a separate constitution for the western sectors of Germany in February 1948, the Soviets walked out of the joint Allied Control Commission. In the summer of that year, the Western powers issued a new currency

It is their right to withhold their children from schools where their religious convictions are not only disregarded but even made the object of contempt and ridicule. It was this parental right which German parents felt was violated when the Hitler government deprived them of their denominational schools. The children came home from the new schools like little heathens, who smiled derisively or laughed at the prayers of their parents.

You Hungarian parents will likewise feel a violation of your fundamental rights if your children can no longer attend the Catholic schools solely because the dictatorial State closes down our schools by a brutal edict or renders their work impossible.

Statement of the Hungarian Communist Minister of Public Worship, June 7, 1950
We must start a vast work of enlightenment, and in the first place explain to our party colleagues and also to all workers that any father who sends his child to religion classes, places it in the hands of the enemy and entrusts his soul and thinking to the enemies of peace and imperialistic warmongers.

A part of our working people believes that participation of children in religious instruction is a private matter which has nothing to do with the political conviction of their parents. They are wrong. To send children to a reactionary pastor for religious instruction, is a political movement against the People's Democracy, whether intentional or not. . . .

In carrying out the basic principles, religion within the party is no private matter, but we must make a difference between plain party members and party officials, and must not in any case make party membership dependent on the fact whether our party members are religious. In the first place, we must expect from our party officials, our leading men, that they do not send their children to religious instruction courses, do not take part in religious ceremonies and train their wives in the spirit of communistic conception.

Also, we must patiently endeavor to enlighten our members, and ensure through training and propaganda that they realize; "In going to Church, taking part in processions, sending our children to religious instruction, we unconsciously further the efforts of clerical reaction."

Colman J. Barry, ed., Readings in Church History *(Westminster, Md.: The Newman Press, 1965), pp. 496-498.*

---

in their zone. Berlin, though well within the Soviet zone, was governed by all four powers. The Soviets feared the new currency, which was circulating in Berlin at better rates than their own. They chose to seal the city off by closing all railroads and highways to West Germany. Their purpose was to drive the Western powers out of Berlin.

The Western allies responded to the Berlin blockade with an airlift of supplies to the city that lasted almost a year. In May 1949, the Russians were forced to back down and to open access to Berlin. The incident, however, was decisive. It increased tensions and suspicions between the opponents and hastened the separation of Germany into two states. West Germany formally became the German Federal Republic in September 1949, and the eastern region

became the German Democratic Republic a month later. Ironically, Germany had been dismembered in a way no one had planned or expected. The two Germanies and the divided city of Berlin, isolated within East Germany, would remain central fixtures in the geopolitics of the Cold War.

NATO and the Warsaw Pact

Meanwhile, the nations of western Europe had been coming closer together. The Marshall Plan encouraged international cooperation. In March 1948, Belgium, the Netherlands, Luxembourg, France, and Britain signed the Treaty of Brussels, providing for cooperation in economic and military matters. In April 1949, these nations joined with Italy, Denmark, Norway, Portugal,

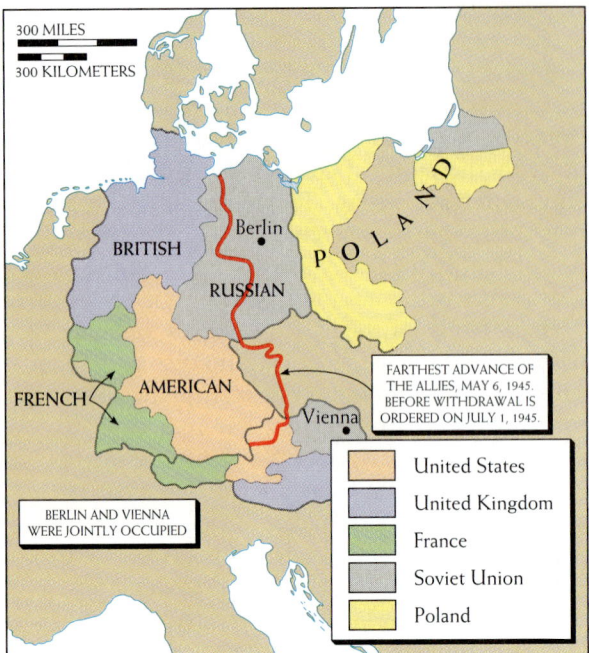

MAP 30-2 OCCUPIED GERMANY AND AUSTRIA *At the war's end, defeated Germany, including Austria, was occupied by the victorious Allies in the several zones shown here. Austria, by prompt agreement, was reestablished as an independent, neutral state, no longer occupied. The German zones hardened into an "East" Germany (the former Soviet zone) and a "West" Germany (the former British, French, and American zones). Berlin, within the Soviet zone, was similarly divided.*

The Allied airlift in action during the Berlin blockade. Every day for almost a year Western planes supplied the city until Stalin lifted the blockade in May 1949. [Bildarchiv Preussischer Kulturbesitz]

and Iceland to sign a treaty with Canada and the United States that formed the North Atlantic Treaty Organization (NATO). NATO committed its members to mutual assistance in case any of them was attacked. For the first time in history, the United States was committed to defend allies outside the Western Hemisphere. The NATO treaty formed the West into a bloc. A few years later, West Germany, Greece, and Turkey joined the alliance.

A series of bilateral treaties providing for close ties and mutual assistance in case of attack governed Soviet relations with the states of eastern Europe. In 1949 these states formed the Council of Mutual Assistance (COMECON) to integrate their economies. Unlike the NATO states, the eastern alliance system was under direct Soviet domination through local Communist parties controlled from Moscow and overawed by the presence of the Red Army. The Warsaw Pact of May 1955, which included Albania, Bulgaria, Czechoslovakia, East Germany, Hungary, Poland, Romania, and the Soviet Union, merely gave formal recognition to the system that existed. Europe was divided into two unfriendly blocs. The Cold War had taken firm shape in Europe (see Map 30-3).

The Korean Conflict

While early stages of the Cold War took place in Europe, the United States found itself confronting armed aggression in Asia. As part of a U.N. police action, it intervened militarily in Korea, following the same principle of containment that informed its actions in Europe.

Between 1910 and 1945, Japan, as an Asian colonial power, occupied and exploited Korea. By the close of World War II, the Japanese had been driven out. Under the direction of the United States, Japan was politically reconstructed as a democracy. The United States then committed itself, as a cornerstone of its postwar policy, to maintain a democratic Japan.

The Japanese empire, however, still had to be dealt with. The United States and the Soviet Union presided over the division of Korea into two parts with the thirty-eighth parallel of latitude as the line of separation. It was expected that the country would eventually be reunited. By 1948, however, two separate states had been organized: the Democratic People's Republic of

MAP 30-3 MAJOR EUROPEAN ALLIANCE SYSTEMS *The North Atlantic Treaty Organization, which includes both Canada and the United States, stretches as far east as Turkey. By contrast, the Warsaw Pact nations were the contiguous Communist states of eastern Europe, with the Soviet Union, of course, as the dominant member.*

Korea under Kim Il Sung in the North and the Republic of Korea under Syngman Rhee (1875–1965) in the South. The former was supported by the Soviet Union and the latter by the United States.

Numerous border clashes occurred between the two states. In late June 1950, forces from North Korea invaded across the thirty-eighth parallel (see Map 30-4). The United States intervened and was soon supported by a United Nations mandate. Great Britain, Turkey, and Australia sent token forces. The troops were commanded by General Douglas MacArthur (1880–1964). The Korean police action was technically a United Nations venture to halt aggression. (It had been made possible by a boycott by the Soviet ambassador to the United Nations at the time of the key vote.) For the

United States, the point of the Korean conflict was to contain the spread and to halt the aggression of communism.

General MacArthur's forces initially repelled the North Koreans. He then pushed them almost to Manchuria. Late in 1950, however, the Chinese, responding to the pressure against their border, sent troops to support North Korea. The American forces had to retreat. The U.S. policymakers believed that the Chinese, who since 1949 had been under the Communist government of Mao Tse-tung (1893–1976), were simply the puppets of the Soviet Union. American policymakers conceived of the Communist world as a single unit directed from Moscow. The movement of forces into South Korea was, in their view, simply another example of Communist pressure against a non-

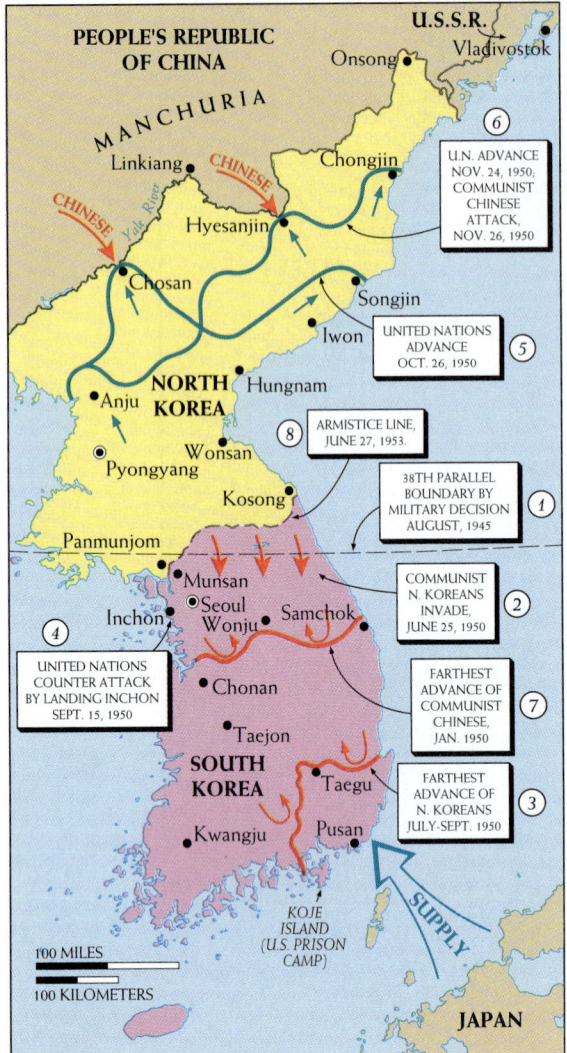

MAP 30-4 KOREA, 1950–1953 *The North Korean invasion of South Korea in 1950 and the bitter three-year war to repulse the invasion and stabilize a firm boundary near the thirty-eighth parallel are outlined here. The war was a dramatic application of the American policy of "containment" of communism.*

Communist state similar to that previously confronted in Europe. Today it is clear there was much tension between Moscow and the People's Republic of China, but those difficulties were little known or appreciated at the time.

For more than two years the war bogged down. Eventually, a border near the thirty-eighth parallel was restored. The war lasted until June 16, 1953, when an armistice was signed.

In Korea, limited military action had halted and contained the military advance of a Com-

munist nation. The lessons of the Cold War learned in Europe appeared to have been successfully applied to Asia. The American government was confirmed in its faith in a policy of containment. The Korean conflict transformed the Cold War into a global encounter and rivalry.

The formation of NATO and the Korean conflict capped the first round of the Cold War. Stalin's death in 1953 and the armistice in Korea the same year fostered hopes that international tensions might ease. In early 1955 Soviet occupation forces left Austria after that nation agreed to neutral status. Later that year the leaders of France, Great Britain, the Soviet Union, and the United States held a summit conference at Geneva. Nuclear weapons and the future of divided Germany were the chief items on the agenda. The hopefulness inspired by this gathering of leaders to discuss so many grave issues was dubbed "the spirit of Geneva." Despite public displays of friendliness, however, the meeting produced few substantial agreements on major problems. The spirit of Geneva proved short-lived, and the rivalry and polemics of the Cold War soon resumed.

The American Domestic Scene Since World War II

A full understanding of the American response to the Cold War and its role in Europe and elsewhere requires a look at U.S. domestic history since World War II. Three major themes have characterized the postwar American experience: an opposition to the spread of communism, an expansion of civil rights to African-Americans and other minorities at home, and a determination to achieve continuing economic growth. Virtually all major postwar political debates and social divisions have arisen from one or more of these issues.

The Truman and Eisenhower Administrations

President Harry Truman's foreign policy, as we have seen, was directed against Communist expansion in Europe and East Asia. Domestically, the Truman administration pursued

Major Dates of Early Cold War Confrontation	
1945	Yalta Conference
1945	Founding of the United Nations
1946	Churchill's Iron Curtain speech
1947	(March) Truman Doctrine regarding Greece and Turkey
1947	(June) Announcement of Marshall Plan
1948	Communist takeover in Czechoslovakia
1948	Communist takeover in Hungary
1948–1949	Berlin blockade
1949	NATO founded
1949	East and West Germany emerge as separate states
1950–1953	Korean conflict
1955	Warsaw Pact founded

what may be regarded as a continuation of Roosevelt's New Deal policies. Conservative Republicans, however, provided stiff opposition to his initiatives. The major achievement of those Republicans was the passage of the Taft–Hartley Act in 1947, which placed limits on various forms of labor union activity.

Truman won the 1948 election against great odds. In a set of policies he termed the Fair Deal, he sought to use the federal government to extend economic security. He was frustrated in these efforts, however, by a wave of fear that the country faced a domestic Communist menace. Senator Joseph McCarthy of Wisconsin (1908–1957) led a campaign against this perceived danger, ferreting out suspected alleged Communists among the ranks of American citizens and within government agencies. Scores of prominent Americans came under public scrutiny, their patriotism and loyalty questioned. This anticommunism, a frustration with the war in Korea, and perhaps the natural weariness of the electorate after twenty years of Democratic Party government led to the election of war hero Dwight D. Eisenhower (1890–1969) in 1952.

In retrospect, the Eisenhower years now seem a period of calm after the war years of the 1940s and before the turmoil of the 1960s. Eisenhower, personally popular, brought the Korean War to a conclusion. During his presidency, the country was generally prosperous. Homebuilding increased dramatically, and the vast interstate highway system was initiated. The president was deliberately less activist than either Roosevelt or Truman had been.

Beneath the apparent quiet of the Eisenhower years, however, stirred several forces that would lead to disruptions in the 1960s. One of these flowed from the injustices of segregation and racial inequality. Another flowed from the long-term implications of some of the major foreign policy commitments the Eisenhower administration made in its effort to oppose the advance of communism. One of those commitments led to American involvement in Vietnam; indeed, that involvement began under Eisenhower.

Civil Rights

On May 17, 1954, the United States Supreme Court, in the decision of *Brown* v. *Board of Education of Topeka,* declared unconstitutional the segregation of black and white schoolchildren. A year later, the Court ordered the desegregation of schools with "all deliberate speed." For the next ten years, the struggle over school integration and civil rights for black Americans stirred the nation. Various southern states tried to resist school desegregation. In 1957, when hostile crowds and the governor of Arkansas physically blocked the entrance of black students to an all-white high school in Little Rock, Eisenhower reluctantly sent troops into the city to integrate the schools. Resistance to desegregation continued in various forms in other southern states.

While the battle raged over the schools, an awakened civil rights movement among American blacks began to protest segregation in other areas of national life. In 1955 Reverend Martin Luther King, Jr. (1929–1968) organized a boycott in Montgomery, Alabama, to protest segregation on buses. The Montgomery bus boycott marked the beginning of the use of civil disobedience to fight racial discrimination in the United States. Drawing upon the ideas of Henry David Thoreau and the experience of Gandhi in India, the leaders of the civil rights movement went to jail rather than obey laws they believed to be unjust. In 1963 the march on Washington by tens of thousands of supporters of civil rights legislation gave dramatic testimony to the

The Reverend Martin Luther King, Jr., was the foremost civil rights leader in the United States from the 1950s until his assassination in 1968. He organized many thousands of African-Americans in a movement of nonviolent resistance to segregation. [Woodfin Camp & Associates]

growth and moral force of the movement. The next two years witnessed the passage of landmark legislation—the Civil Rights Act of 1964, which desegregated public accommodations, and the Voting Rights Act of 1965, which cleared the way for large numbers of African-Americans to vote. The results of that legislation as well as of continuing protests in areas of housing and job discrimination brought black citizens nearer to the mainstream of American life than ever before.

Much, however, remained to be done. In 1967 many people were killed in race riots that broke out in several American cities. Those riots, followed by the assassination of Martin Luther King, Jr. in 1968, which provoked additional riots, greatly weakened the civil rights movement. Despite new efforts to fight discrim-

ination, the movement suffered from lack of a major national leader. In the late 1980s, Jesse Jackson (b. 1941) rose to prominence, actively contesting the Democratic Party nomination for the presidency in 1984 and 1988. Jackson raised new issues of racial equality and promoted drives that led to the registration of many new black voters. There has, however, been little follow-up to this campaign.

The problems of race relations continue to plague the social life of the United States. Although African-Americans have made much progress toward access to education and to public office, especially in urban areas, they continue to lag behind other Americans economically and in their prospects for good health. Furthermore, as other groups, particularly Hispanic-Americans, began to enter the political process in the 1980s and to raise issues on behalf of their own communities, the issues surrounding racial relations in the nation became more complicated. In 1992 one of the most destructive riots in American history—triggered by the acquittal of police officers who had been videotaped beating an African-American they were arresting—devastated parts of Los Angeles, bringing to the fore continuing problems with race relations in the United States. The presidential campaign of 1992 was conspicuous for the absence of a discussion of minority issues.

New Social Programs

The civil rights movement in the late 1950s and early 1960s was the cutting edge of a new advance of political liberalism. In 1960 John F. Kennedy (1917–1963) narrowly won the presidential election. Pursuing a domestic agenda he called the New Frontier, he presented himself as setting the country moving again after the years of Eisenhower calm. One of his goals was to enable the U.S. space program to put a man on the moon. He also tried, unsuccessfully, to expand government-sponsored health care under the Social Security program.

On civil rights, Kennedy reacted more than he led. The shock of his assassination in 1963, however, enabled his successor, Lyndon Johnson (1908–1973), to carry out activist policies. Johnson pushed the Civil Rights Act of 1964 through Congress, which in the same year also passed a tax cut. Johnson then set forth a bold domestic program known as the War on Poverty, which established major federal programs to create jobs and provide job training. New entitlements were added to the Social Security program, including Medicare, which helps provide medical services for the elderly. Johnson's drive for what he termed the Great Society closed the era of major federal government initiatives that had begun under Franklin Roosevelt. The liberal impulse remained alive in American politics, but by the late 1960s the electorate had begun to favor a much more conservative stance.

The Vietnam War and Domestic Turmoil

Johnson's activist domestic vision was quickly overshadowed by issues surrounding U.S. involvement in Vietnam (discussed more fully later in the chapter). By 1965 Johnson had decided to send tens of thousands of Americans to Vietnam. This policy led to the longest of American wars. At home, the war and, in particular, the draft, provoked serious dissent, dividing the country more than any conflict since the American Civil War. The overwhelming majority of young American men who were drafted entered the armed forces, but many, especially college and university students, resisted. Large-scale protests involving civil disobedience, often patterned after those of the civil rights movement, erupted on campuses throughout the country. In some cases, units of the National Guard were sent to restore calm. At Kent State University in Ohio in 1970, the National Guard killed four protesters.

The national unrest led Lyndon Johnson to decide not to seek reelection in 1968. Richard Nixon (b. 1913) led the Republicans to victory, beginning an era in American politics dominated by conservative policies. Nixon campaigned on a platform of law and order. He also stressed the experience his tenure as vice president under Eisenhower gave him in foreign policy. Perhaps the most important foreign policy action of his administration was to establish diplomatic relations between the United States and the People's Republic of China for the first time in a quarter century. Initially, Nixon's policies toward Vietnam were no more successful than those of Johnson. Half the casualties in the war occurred under his administration. Nonetheless, he concluded the war in 1973.

Very soon thereafter, however, the Watergate scandal began to erode his administration.

The Watergate Scandal

On the surface, the Watergate scandal involved only the burglary of the Democratic Party national headquarters by White House operatives in 1972. It raised deeper issues, however, involving the extent of presidential authority and the right of the government to intrude into the personal lives of citizens. In 1973 Congress established a committee to investigate the scandal. Testimony before that committee revealed that President Nixon had recorded many conversations in the White House. The special prosecutor appointed to investigate the charges finally gained access to the tapes in the summer of 1974 through a legal struggle that reached the Supreme Court. In the meantime, the Judiciary Committee of the House of Representatives voted three articles of impeachment against Nixon. Shortly thereafter, certain of the newly released tapes revealed that Nixon had ordered federal agencies to try to cover up White House participation in the burglary. After this revelation Nixon resigned, the only president in American history to do so.

Economic Growth and Changing Fiscal Policy

The Watergate scandal shook public confidence in the government. It also proved a remarkable distraction from the major problems facing the country, such as inflation, which had resulted from funding the war in Vietnam while expanding federal domestic expenditures. The subsequent administrations of Gerald Ford (1974–1977, b. 1913) and Jimmy Carter (1977–1981, b. 1924) battled inflation and high interest rates without significant success. The Carter administration became bogged down in a crisis in November 1979 when Iranian protesters took more than forty Americans hostage in Tehran and held them for more than a year.

In 1980 Ronald Reagan (b. 1911) was elected president by a large majority; he was reelected four years later. Reagan was the first fully ideological conservative to be elected in the postwar era. His goals were relatively straightforward. In foreign policy, he took a tough line toward the

President Ronald Reagan (left) and President Mikhail Gorbachev (right). Their policies brought about the surprising end of the Cold War. Reagan's defense spending placed enormous pressures on the economy of the Soviet Union. Gorbachev responded by attempting to reform the Soviet system. [SYGMA]

Soviet Union and vastly increased defense spending. He also had concluded a major missile reduction treaty with the Soviet Union by the end of his second term. In domestic policy, Reagan sought to reduce the role of the federal government in American life. The chief vehicle to this end was a major tax cut and reform of the tax system. The consequence of the defense spending and the tax policy was the accumulation of the largest fiscal deficit in American history. Inflation, however, came under control and the economy experienced its longest peacetime expansion.

The straightforward conservatism of the Reagan administration proved offensive to many groups of Americans who had traditionally supported a liberal political and social agenda. They regarded Reagan's policies as hostile to minori-

ties and women. There were several scandals during his presidency that implicated, directly or indirectly, several high administration officials. The most important of these involved the sale of arms to Iran in exchange for the promised release of American hostages being held in Lebanon. Despite these difficulties, Reagan left office as probably the most popular and successful of the post–World War II American presidents.

In 1988 Vice President George Bush (b. 1924) was elected to succeed Reagan. He was immediately confronted by the major changes that Mikhail Gorbachev (b. 1931) was carrying out in the Soviet Union and the extraordinary transformations occurring in eastern Europe (see Chapter 31). Bush worked to keep the NATO alliance strong and close to the United States though observers had begun to question its utility. In 1989 he sent troops into Panama to oust the Panamanian dictator, Manuel Noriega (b. 1938). In the fall of 1990, in response to the invasion of Kuwait by Iraq, he initiated the largest mobilization of American troops since the Vietnam War. Using the United Nations, he forged a broad worldwide coalition against Iraq's aggression. In early 1991 the coalition launched Operation Desert Storm and forced Iraq out of Kuwait.

The victory in the Persian Gulf War was the high point of the Bush presidency. Thereafter, he stumbled in the face of the serious economic problems facing the nation. The campaign of 1992 saw a major third-party effort headed by Ross Perot (b. 1930) of Texas. It was, however, the Democratic nominee, Governor William Clinton (b. 1946) of Arkansas, who won the election. In the first year of his presidency, Clinton has attacked a broad range of domestic problems. Perhaps his boldest initiatives have been in the area of health care reform.

The Khrushchev Era in the Soviet Union

The Last Years of Stalin

Many Russians had hoped that the end of World War II would signal a lessening of Stalinism. No other nation had suffered greater losses or more deprivation than the Soviet Union. Its people expected some immediate reward for their sacrifice and heroism. They desired a reduction in the scope of the police state and a redirection of the economy away from heavy industry to consumer products. They were disappointed. Stalin did little or nothing to modify the character of the regime he had created. The police remained ever-present. The cult of personality expanded, and the central bureaucracy continued to grow. Heavy industry was still favored over production for consumers. Agriculture continued to be troubled. Stalin's personal authority over the party and the nation remained unchallenged. The Cold War stance of the United States simply served to confirm Stalin in his ways.

By late 1952 and early 1953, Stalin appeared ready to unloose a new series of purges. In January 1953, a group of Jewish physicians was arrested and charged with plotting the deaths of important leaders. Claims of an extensive conspiracy appeared in the press. All these developments were similar to the events preceding the purges of the 1930s, which had been directed against both Communist Party members and the military. Then, quite suddenly, in the midst of this new furor, on March 6, 1953, Stalin died. The circumstances surrounding his death are unclear.

For a time, no single leader replaced Stalin. Rather the Presidium (the renamed Politburo) pursued a policy of collective leadership. Gradually, however, power and influence began to devolve on Nikita Khrushchev (1894–1971), who in 1953 had been named party secretary. Three years later, Khrushchev himself became premier. His rise ended collective leadership, but he was never to enjoy the extraordinary powers of Stalin.

Khrushchev's Domestic Policies

During the 1930s and 1940s, Stalin had placed his mark and control on virtually every aspect of Soviet politics, life, and culture. With his death in 1953, the Soviet system had to deal with his legacy. The Khrushchev era, which lasted until the autumn of 1964, witnessed a marked retreat from Stalinism, though not from authoritarianism. Indeed, Stalin's rule had been so repressive that it left considerable room for his successors to relax their grip while still maintaining tyranny. Politically, the demise of Stalinism meant that shifts in leadership and party structure would occur by means other than purges.

In retrospect, Khrushchev's attempts at reform show some similarities to Gorbachev's later *perestroika* policies of the 1980s (discussed in Chapter 31). Both promised relief from the most repressive aspects of the Soviet state. From the time Khrushchev was removed from power in 1964 until Gorbachev's rise, however, the leaders of the Soviet Union, while avoiding the excesses of Stalinism, returned to repressive authoritarianism.

INTELLECTUAL LIFE Under Khrushchev, intellectuals were somewhat more free to express their opinions. This so-called thaw in the cultural life of the country was closely related to the premier's interest in the opinions of experts on problems of industry and agriculture. He often went outside the usual bureaucratic channels in search of information and new ideas. Novels such as Aleksandr Solzhenitsyn's (b. 1918) *One Day in the Life of Ivan Denisovich* (1963) could be published. Boris Pasternak (1890–1960), the author of *Dr. Zhivago* (1957), however, was not permitted to accept the Nobel Prize for Literature in 1958. The intellectual liberalization of Soviet life during this period should not be overestimated. It was favorable only in comparison with what had preceded it and with the decline in freedom of expression after Khrushchev's fall.

ECONOMIC EXPERIMENTS Khrushchev's economic policy also differed somewhat from Stalin's. By 1953 the economy had recovered from the strains and destruction of the war, but consumer goods and housing remained in short supply and maintaining adequate supplies of food continued to be a problem. Khrushchev favored efforts to meet the demand for consumer goods. He also made some moves to decentralize economic planning and execution. During the late 1950s, he often boasted that Soviet production of consumer goods would overtake that of the West. Steel, oil, and electric-power production continued to grow, but the consumer sector improved only marginally.

Khrushchev, however, was trying to move the country in too many directions at once. The Soviet Union's ambitious space program put the first artificial satellite—Sputnik—in orbit in

1957. This program, however, and the ever-growing defense budget made great demands on the nation's productive resources.

Khrushchev strongly redirected Stalin's agricultural policy. He recognized that in spite of the collectivization of the 1930s the Soviet Union had not produced an agricultural system capable of feeding its own people. He removed many of the most restrictive regulations on private cultivation. The machine tractor stations were abandoned. Existing collective farms were further amalgamated. The government undertook an extensive "virgin lands" program to increase the land available for wheat cultivation by hundreds of thousands of acres. The initial effect of this program was to increase grain production to new records. Inappropriate farming techniques, however, caused soil erosion on the newly farmed lands within a few years, reducing yields. The agricultural problem simply continued to grow, forcing the Soviet Union to import vast quantities of grain from the United States and other countries. These American grain exports were an important facet of the policy of détente that marked relations between the Soviet Union and the United States for much of the 1970s (discussed later in this chapter).

THE SECRET SPEECH OF 1956 In an extraordinary departure from expected practice, Khrushchev delivered a direct attack on the policies of the Stalin years. In February 1956, at the Twentieth Congress of the Communist Party, Khrushchev made a secret speech (later published outside the Soviet Union) in which he denounced Stalin and his crimes against socialist justice during the purges of the 1930s. The speech caused shock and consternation in party circles, but it also opened the way for genuine, if limited, internal criticism of the Soviet government and for many of the changes in intellectual and economic life already discussed. Gradually, the strongest supporters of Stalinist policies were removed from the Presidium. By 1958 all Stalin's former supporters were gone, but none had been executed.

Khrushchev's speech had repercussions well beyond the borders of the Soviet Union. Communist leaders in eastern Europe took it as a signal that they could govern with greater leeway than before. Khrushchev's attack on Stalin, they believed, would allow them to retreat, not from Communism certainly, but from the Stalinist policies that had been required of them since the late 1940s. The result was a series of crises that made 1956 one of the key years in the Cold War.

The Crises of 1956

During 1956, Britain and France intervened ineffectively in the Middle East and the Soviet Union confronted crises in Poland and Hungary. These events confirmed the new post–World War II power relationships.

SUEZ In July, President Gamal Abdel Nasser (1918–1970) of Egypt nationalized the Suez Canal, until then controlled by British and French interests. Great Britain and France feared this action could threaten their access to Persian Gulf oil supplies. In October 1956, war broke out between Egypt, then receiving arms from the Soviet Union, and the eight-year-old state of Israel, closely tied to the West. (The formation of Israel and the Arab–Israeli conflict are discussed later in the chapter.) Britain and France seized the opportunity to intervene. They justified their actions as a way to separate the combatants, but their real motive was to regain control of the canal. Although a military success—Israel seized the Sinai, and Britain and France landed troops in the canal zone—the operation ended in a humiliating diplomatic defeat. The United States refused to support the Anglo-French action. The Soviet Union protested in the most severe terms. The Anglo-French forces had to be withdrawn, and control of the canal remained with Egypt. Israeli forces withdrew from the Sinai and the Gaza Strip in 1957.

The Suez intervention proved that without the support of the United States the nations of western Europe could no longer use military force to impose their will on the rest of the world. Also, the United States and the Soviet Union showed that they would restrain their allies from undertaking actions that might result in a wider conflict.

POLAND The autumn of 1956 also saw important developments in eastern Europe. These demonstrated the limitations on independent action among the Soviet-bloc nations. When the prime minister of Poland died, the Polish Communist Party leaders refused to accept as his

Khrushchev Denounces the Crimes of Stalin: The Secret Speech

In 1956 Khrushchev denounced Stalin in a secret speech to the Party Congress. The New York Times published a text of that speech smuggled from Russia.

◆ *What are the specific actions on the part of Stalin that Khrushchev denounced? Why does Khrushchev pay so much attention to Stalin's creation of the concept of an "enemy of the people"? Why does Khrushchev draw a distinction between the actions of Stalin and those of Lenin?*

Stalin acted not through persuasion, explanation, and patient cooperation with people, but by imposing his concepts and demanding absolute submission to his opinion. Whoever opposed this concept or tried to prove his viewpoint and the correctness of his position was doomed to removal from the leading collective [group] and to subsequent moral and physical annihilation. . . .

Stalin originated the concept of "enemy of the people." This term automatically rendered it unnecessary that the ideological errors of a man or men engaged in a controversy be proved; this term made possible the usage of the most cruel repression violating all norms of revolutionary legality, against anyone who in any way disagreed with Stalin, against those who were only suspected of hostile intent, against those who had bad reputations.

This concept "enemy of the people" actually eliminated the possibility of any kind of ideological fight or the making of one's views known on this or that issue, even those of a practical character. In the main, and in actuality, the only proof of guilt used, against all norms of current legal science, was the "confession" of the accused himself; and, as a subsequent probing proved, "confessions" were acquired through physical pressures against the accused. . . .

Lenin used severe methods only in the most necessary cases, when the exploiting classes were still in existence and were vigorously opposing the revolution, when the struggle for survival was decidedly assuming the sharpest forms, even including civil war.

Stalin, on the other hand, used extreme methods and mass repressions at a time when the revolution was already victorious, when the Soviet State was strengthened, when the exploiting classes were already liquidated and Socialist relations were rooted solidly in all phases of national economy, when our party was politically consolidated and had strengthened itself both numerically and ideologically. It is clear that here Stalin showed in a whole series of cases his intolerance, his brutality and his abuse of power. Instead of proving his political correctness and mobilizing the masses, he often chose the path of repression and physical annihilation, not only against actual enemies, but also against individuals who had not committed any crimes against the party and the Soviet Government. . . .

The New York Times, June 5, 1956, *pp. 13–16.*

successor the person designated by Moscow. Considerable tension developed. The Soviet leaders even visited Warsaw to make their opinions known. In the end, Wladyslaw Gomulka (1905–1982) emerged as the new Communist leader of Poland. He was the choice of the Polish Communists and he also proved acceptable to the Soviets because he promised continued economic and military cooperation and most particularly continued Polish membership in the Warsaw Pact. Within those limits, he moved to halt the collectivization of Polish agriculture and

The Suez Canal was repaired in 1957 after the Egyptians had sunk ships to block the canal during the Anglo-French-Israeli invasion in 1956. [Archive Photos]

to improve the relationship between the Communist government and the Polish Roman Catholic church. This settlement more or less allowed the Polish Communist Party to settle its own affairs, leading another eastern European country to seek similar autonomy.

UPRISING IN HUNGARY In late October, as the Polish problem was nearing resolution, Hungarians in Budapest demonstrated in sympathy for the Polish people. Hungary's Communist government moved to stop the demonstrations, and street fighting erupted. The Hungarian Communist Party then installed a new government headed by former premier Imre Nagy (1896–1958).

Nagy, although a Communist, sought greater independence for Hungary. He demanded more than had Gomulka in Poland and appealed to non-Communist groups in Hungary for support. He wanted Soviet troops withdrawn and ultimately for Hungary to become a neutral state. He even went so far as to call for Hungarian withdrawal from the Warsaw Pact. These demands were wholly unacceptable to the Soviet Union. In early November, Soviet troops invaded the country, deposed Nagy (who was later executed), and imposed Janos Kadar (1912–1989) as premier.

The Polish and Hungarian disturbances had several results. They did not end pressure for more independence in eastern Europe, but they showed the limits of the Soviet Union's tolerance for independence within its bloc in the wake of Khrushchev's criticisms of Stalinism. They also demonstrated that the countries of eastern Europe would not be permitted to imitate Austrian neutrality. It should also be noted that the Suez intervention had provided an international diversion permitting the Soviet Union freer action within its sphere of influence. Finally, the failure of the United States to take any action in the Hungarian uprising demonstrated the hollowness of American domestic political rhetoric about liberating the captive nations of eastern Europe.

Collapse of the 1960 Paris Summit Conference

The events of 1956 brought to a close the era of fully autonomous action by the European nation-states. In different ways and to differing degrees, the two superpowers had demonstrated this new political reality to their allies. After 1956 the Soviet Union began to talk about "peaceful coexistence" with the United States.

With the 1957 launch of Sputnik into space, the Soviet Union appeared to have achieved enormous technological superiority over the West. In 1958 negotiations began between the two countries for limitations on the testing of nuclear weapons. The same year, however, the Soviet Union announced that the status of West Berlin must be changed and the Allied occupation forces must be withdrawn. The demand was refused. In 1959 tensions relaxed sufficiently for several Western leaders to visit Moscow and for Soviet Premier Khrushchev to tour the United States. A summit meeting was scheduled for May 1960, and U.S. President Eisenhower was to go to Moscow.

The Paris Summit Conference of 1960 proved anything but a repetition of the friendly days of the 1955 meeting in Geneva. Just before the gathering, the Soviet Union shot down an American U-2 aircraft that was flying reconnaissance over Soviet territory. Khrushchev demanded an apology from Eisenhower for this air surveillance. Eisenhower accepted full responsibility for the surveillance policy but refused to issue any apology. Khrushchev then refused to take part in the summit conference, just as the participants arrived in the French capital. The conference was thus aborted, and Eisenhower's proposed trip to the Soviet Union never took place.

The Soviets did not scuttle the summit meeting on the eve of its opening simply because of the American spy flights. They had long been aware of these flights and had other reasons for protesting them when they did. First, they had not wanted to protest until they had shot down a plane, which they had not been able to do, because they feared their military technology would seem weak despite Sputnik. Second, Khrushchev had hoped that the leaders of Britain, France, and the United States would be sufficiently divided over the future of Germany that they would not present a united front at the summit. When these divisions failed to develop, the conference was of little use to him. Third and most important, by 1960 the Communist world itself had split between the Soviets and the Chinese. The latter were portraying the Russians as lacking sufficient revolutionary zeal. Destroying the summit was, in part, a way to prove the Soviet Union's hard-line attitude toward the capitalist world.

President John Kennedy of the United States and Premier Nikita Khrushchev of the Soviet Union meet in Vienna in 1961. The discussions were very difficult, leaving both leaders with feelings of mutual distrust. [Sovfoto/Eastfoto]

Khrushchev's Clashes with John Kennedy

The abortive Paris conference opened the most difficult period of the Cold War. In 1961 the new U.S. president, John F. Kennedy, and Premier Khrushchev met in Vienna. The conference was inconclusive, but the American president left wondering if the two nations could avoid war.

THE BERLIN WALL   Throughout 1961 thousands of refugees from East Germany were crossing the border into West Berlin. This outflow was a political embarrassment to East Germany and detrimental to its economy. It was one indication to the Soviet Union of its inability to control events in eastern Europe.

In August 1961, the East Germans, with the support of the Soviet Union, took decisive action. They erected a concrete wall along the border between East and West Berlin, shutting the two parts of the city off from each other. Crossing from one part to the other was possible only at designated checkpoints for people with

The Berlin wall, erected in August 1961, came to symbolize the tensions of the Cold War era. [Bildarchiv Preussischer Kulturbesitz]

proper papers. The United States protested and sent Vice President Lyndon Johnson to Berlin to reassure its citizens, but the wall remained until the collapse of East Germany in 1989, becoming a major symbol of the Cold War era. The wall halted the flow of refugees and brought the United States' commitment to West Germany into doubt.

THE CUBAN MISSILE CRISIS   The most dangerous days of the Cold War occurred during the Cuban missile crisis of 1962. Cuba, less than 100 miles from the United States, became a Communist state and a Soviet ally after Fidel Castro's (b. 1926) successful revolution in 1957. When the Soviet Union began to place nuclear missiles on the island, the American government blockaded Cuba, halted the shipment of new missiles, and demanded the removal of

existing installations. After a tense week, with Washington and Moscow exchanging threats and other messages, the Soviets backed down and the crisis ended. The incident undermined Khrushchev's credibility in the ruling circles of the Soviet Union and caused other non-European Communist regimes to question the Soviet Union's commitment to their security and survival. One result was to increase the influence of the People's Republic of China in Communist circles. The backdown over Cuba also convinced Soviet military leaders of the need to strengthen their forces so that in any future confrontation their forces would be as strong as or stronger than those of the United States.

If the Cuban missile crisis had led to war, missiles could have been launched over Europe or from European bases into the Soviet Union.

The crisis thus threatened Europe directly, but it was the last major Cold War confrontation to do so. Thereafter, the American–Soviet rivalry shifted to the war in Vietnam and the Arab–Israeli conflict in the Near East. In 1963 the United States and the Soviet Union concluded a Nuclear Test Ban Treaty. This agreement marked the beginning of a lessening in the tensions between them. The German problem subsided somewhat in the late 1960s as West Germany, under Premier Willy Brandt (1913–1992), moved to improve its relations with the Soviet Union and eastern Europe. By 1964 many Russian leaders and people lower in the party had concluded that Khrushchev had tried to do too much too soon and had done it too poorly. On October 16, 1964, after defeat in the Central Committee of the Communist Party, Khrushchev resigned.

The Brezhnev Era in the Soviet Union

Khrushchev was replaced by Alexei Kosygin (1904–1980) as premier and Leonid Brezhnev (1906–1982) as party secretary. Brezhnev eventually emerged as the dominant figure. In 1977 the constitution of the Soviet Union was changed to combine the offices of president and party secretary. Brezhnev became president, and thus head of the state as well as of the party. He held more personal power than any Soviet leader since Stalin.

Invasion of Czechoslovakia

The events in Poland and Hungary of 1956 demonstrated the refusal of the Soviet Union to tolerate significant independence in its eastern

In the summer of 1968, Soviet tanks rolled into Czechoslovakia, ending that country's experiment in liberalized Communism. This picture shows defiant, flag-waving Czechs on a truck rolling past a Soviet tank in the immediate aftermath of the invasion. [Archive Photos]

The Warsaw Pact Justifies the Invasion of Czechoslovakia

In 1968 the Soviet Union and its Warsaw Pact allies invaded Czechoslovakia to halt the political liberalization being carried out by that portion of the Czech Communist Party led by Alexander Dubcek. Their intention was to place other, less liberal Communists into power. This invasion provided the occasion for the declaration of the Brezhnev Doctrine, according to which the Warsaw Pact members had the right to interfere in the internal affairs of their Communist neighbors.

✦ *On what grounds does the Soviet Union justify its invasion of Czechoslovakia? Why does this justification appeal to the possibility of the Czechs' involvement with foreign enemies? What limits does this justification place on political experimentation in eastern European nations dominated by the Soviet Union? How could the principles of this justification be applied to other nations under Soviet control?*

Tass [the Soviet Government news agency] is authorized to state that [Communist] party and Government leaders of the Czechoslovak Socialist Republic have asked the Soviet Union and other allied states to render the fraternal Czechoslovak people urgent assistance, including assistance with armed forces. This request was brought about by the threat that has arisen to the socialist system existing in Czechoslovakia and to the statehood established by the Constitution—the threat emanating from the counterrevolutionary forces that have entered into a collusion with foreign forces hostile to socialism.

The events in Czechoslovakia and around her were repeatedly the subject of exchanges of views between leaders of fraternal socialist countries, including the leaders of Czechoslovakia. These countries are unanimous in that the support, consolidation and defense of the people's socialist gains is a common internationalist duty of all the socialist states. . . .

The Soviet Government and the Governments of the allied countries—the People's Republic of Bulgaria, the Hungarian People's Republic, the German Democratic Republic, the Polish People's Republic—proceeding from the principles of inseparable friendship and cooperation and in accordance with the existing contractual commitments, have decided to meet the above-mentioned request for rendering necessary help to the fraternal Czechoslovak people.

The decision is fully in accord with the right of states to individual and collective self-defense envisaged in treaties of alliance concluded between the fraternal socialist countries. This decision is also in line with vital interests of our countries in safeguarding European peace against forces of militarism, aggression and revenge, which have more than once plunged the peoples of Europe into wars.

Soviet armed units, together with armed units of the above-mentioned allied countries, entered the territory of Czechoslovakia on Aug. 21 [1968]. They will be immediately withdrawn from the Czechoslovak Socialist Republic as soon as the obtaining threat to the gains of socialism in Czechoslovakia, the threat to the security of the socialist countries, is eliminated and lawful authorities find that further presence of these armed units there is no longer necessary.

The actions which are being taken are not directed against any state and in no measure infringe state interests of anybody. They serve the purpose of peace and have been prompted by concern for its consolidation.

The New York Times, December 5, 1989, *p. A15.*

European neighbors. In 1968, during what became known as the *Prague Spring,* the government of Czechoslovakia, under Alexander Dubcek (1921–1992), began to experiment with a more liberal communism. Dubcek expanded freedom of discussion and other intellectual rights at a time when they were being suppressed in Russia. In the summer of 1968, the Soviet government sent troops into Czechoslovakia and installed Communist leaders more to its own liking.

At the time of the invasion, Soviet Party Chairman Brezhnev, in what came to be termed the Brezhnev Doctrine, declared the right of the Soviet Union to interfere in the domestic politics of other Communist countries. No further direct intervention occurred after 1968. Yet the invasion of Czechoslovakia had profound effects throughout the Communist world. It made clear that any political experimentation involving greater liberalization could trigger Soviet military repression.

Dissidents

Under Brezhnev, the Soviet government also became markedly more repressive at home, suggesting a return to Stalinist policies. Intellectual freedoms were curtailed, and intellectuals were given little direct access to the government leadership. In 1974 the government expelled novelist Aleksandr Solzhenitsyn. The government also began to harass Jewish citizens, creating bureaucratic obstacles for those who wanted to emigrate to Israel.

The internal repression gave rise to a dissident movement. Certain Soviet citizens dared to criticize the regime in public and to carry out small demonstrations against the government. They accused the government of violating the human rights provision of the 1975 Helsinki Accords (described in the next section). The dissidents included several prominent citizens, such as the Nobel Prize-winning physicist Andrei Sakharov (1921–1989). The response of the Soviet government was further repression.

Foreign Policy and Relations with the United States

Soviet foreign policy under Brezhnev combined attempts to reach an accommodation with the United States with continued efforts to expand Soviet influence and maintain Soviet leadership of the Communist movement.

THE UNITED STATES AND DÉTENTE Although the Soviet Union sided with North Vietnam in its war with the United States, its support was restrained. Under President Richard Nixon (1969–1974), the United States began a policy of détente with the Soviet Union and the two countries concluded agreements on trade and mutual reduction of strategic arms. Despite these agreements, Soviet spending on defense, and particularly on its navy, continued to grow, damaging the consumer sectors of the economy.

During Gerald Ford's presidency (1974–1977), the United States and the Soviet Union both signed the Helsinki Accords, recognizing the Soviet sphere of influence in eastern Europe. The signers of the accords, including the Soviet Union, also committed themselves to recognize and protect the human rights of their citizens. President Jimmy Carter (1977–1981), a strong advocate of human rights, sought to induce the Soviet Union to comply with this commitment, cooling relations between the two countries. Relations hardened further when the Soviet Union invaded Afghanistan in 1979.

INVASION OF AFGHANISTAN Although the Soviet Union already had a presence in Afghanistan, the Brezhnev government, for reasons that remain unclear, felt it had to send in troops to ensure its influence in central Asia. The invasion brought a sharp response from the United States. The Senate refused to ratify a second Strategic Arms Limitation agreement that President Carter had signed in 1979. The United States also embargoed grain shipments to the Soviet Union and boycotted the 1980 Olympic Games in Moscow. As its forces bogged down in Afghanistan, the invasion grew increasingly unpopular within the Soviet Union.

RELATIONS WITH THE REAGAN ADMINISTRATION Brezhnev died in 1982, early in the administration of President Ronald Reagan (1981–1989) in the United States. Under Reagan, the United States relaxed its grain embargo and placed less emphasis on human rights. At the same time, however, Reagan intensified Cold War rhetoric. More important,

Afghan rebels with a captured Soviet armored vehicle in January of 1980 near Afghanistan's border with Pakistan. The Soviet invasion of Afghanistan in 1979 met with fierce resistance and sparked a sharp response from the United States, which halted sales of wheat to the Soviet Union and boycotted the Olympic Games held in Moscow in 1980. [C. Spengler/SYGMA]

Communism and Solidarity in Poland

Events in Poland in the late 1970s—a time when the Soviet government was becoming increasingly rigidified—challenged both the authority of the Polish Communist Party and the influence of the Soviet Union.

After 1956 the Polish Communist Party, led by Wladyslaw Gomulka (1905–1982), made peace with the Roman Catholic church, halted land collectivization, established trade with the West, and participated in cultural exchange programs with non-Communist nations. Poland was plagued, however, by chronic economic mismanagement and persistent shortages of food and consumer goods. In 1970 food shortages led to a series of strikes, the most famous of which occurred in the shipyards of Gdansk. In December 1970, the Polish authorities broke the strike at the cost of a number of workers' lives. These events led to the departure of Gomulka. His successor was Edward Gierek (b. 1913).

In the decade after 1970, the Polish economy made very little progress. Food and other consumer goods remained in short supply. In early July 1980, the Polish government raised meat prices. The result was hundreds of protest strikes across the country. On August 14, workers occupied the Lenin shipyard at Gdansk. The strike soon spread to other shipyards, transport facilities, and factories connected with the shipbuilding industry. The most important leader to emerge from among the strikers was Lech Walesa (b. 1944). He and the other strike leaders refused to negotiate with the government through any of the traditionally government-controlled unions. The Gdansk strike ended on August 31 after the government promised the workers the right to organize an independent union. The agreement with the government guaranteed both the new union—called Solidarity—and the Polish Roman Catholic church the right of access to the news media, including television.

Less than a week later, on September 6, Gierek was dismissed as the head of the Polish Communist Party. He was replaced by Stanislaw Kania (b. 1927). Later in September, the Polish courts recognized Solidarity as an independent union, and the state-controlled radio for the first time in thirty years broadcast a Roman Catholic Mass.

he also increased U.S. military spending, slowed arms limitation negotiations, successfully deployed a major new missile system in Europe, and proposed the Strategic Defense Initiative (dubbed *Star Wars* by the press), involving a high-technology defense in space against nuclear attack. The Star Wars proposal, although very controversial in the United States, was a major issue in later arms control negotiations between the Soviet Union and the United States. Combined with the Reagan defense spending, Star Wars forced the Soviet Union to increase defense spending when it could ill afford to do so, contributing to the economic problems that helped bring about its collapse (see Chapter 31).

The summer of 1981 saw events that were no less remarkable occurring within the Polish Communist Party itself. For the first time in any European Communist state, secret elections for the party congress were permitted with real choices among the candidates. Poland remained a nation governed by a single party, but for the time being, real debate was permitted within the party congress.

This extraordinary Polish experiment came to a rapid close in late 1981. General Wojciech Jaruzelski (b. 1923) became head of the party, and the army moved into the center of Polish events. In December 1981, martial law was declared. The government moved against Solidarity and arrested several of its leaders. The Polish military leaders succeeded for the time being with this political repression. They proved unsuccessful, however, in addressing Poland's major economic problems. Martial law would continue in effect until late in the 1980s.

By the time of Brezhnev's death in 1982, the entire Soviet system had grown rigid and seemed hardly capable of meeting the needs of its people or pursuing a successful foreign policy. Until the middle of the 1980s, however, no observers expected rapid change in the Soviet Union or its satellites. The nations of eastern Europe were expected to continue with one-party governments, their aspirations for self-determination smothered, and only limited possibilities for independent political action. What had lasted forty years, it was assumed, would endure into the future. No one anticipated the vast changes that were imminent.

Western European Political Developments During the Cold War

During the Cold War, the nations of western Europe achieved unprecedented economic prosperity and maintained liberal democratic governments. All of them confronted the problems associated with maintaining economic growth and with decolonization. France, in addition, faced a difficult path to long-term political stability.

After the war, except for Portugal and Spain, which remained dictatorships until the mid-1970s, the nations of western Europe followed the path of liberal democracy. Their leaders realized, however, that the prewar democratic political structures had been insufficient to ensure peace, stability, material prosperity, and domestic liberty for their peoples. It had become clear that democracy required a social and economic base as well as a political structure. Most Europeans came to feel it was the duty of government to assure economic prosperity and social security. Success at doing so, they believed, would stave off the kind of turmoil that had brought on tyranny and war and could lead to communism.

Christian Democratic Parties

Except for the British Labour Party, the vehicles of the new postwar politics were not, as might have been expected, the democratic socialist parties. On the whole, those parties did not

---

Major Dates in Soviet History 1945–1985

1953	Death of Stalin
1955	Austria established as a neutral state
1955	Geneva Summit
1956	(February) Khrushchev's Secret Speech denouncing Stalin
	(Autumn) Polish crisis
	(October) Suez crisis
	(October) Hungarian uprising
1957	Sputnik launched
1959	Khrushchev visit to the United States
1960	Failed Paris Summit
1961	Soviet Union erects Berlin Wall
1962	Cuban missile crisis
1963	Test Ban Treaty between Soviet Union and the United States
1964	Khrushchev falls from power
1968	Soviet invasion of Czechoslovakia
1972	Strategic Arms Limitation Treaty
1974	Solzhenitsyn expelled
1975	Helsinki Accords
1979	Soviet invasion of Afghanistan
1980	U.S. Olympic Games boycott
1981	Martial law declared in Poland in response to Solidarity

prosper after the onset of the Cold War. They stood opposed by both Communists and groups more conservative than themselves. Rather, the new policies were introduced by various Christian Democratic parties, usually leading coalition governments.

These parties were a major new feature of postwar politics. They were largely Roman Catholic in leadership and membership. Catholic parties had previously existed in Europe. From the late nineteenth century through the 1930s, however, they had been very conservative and had protected the social, political, and educational interests of the Church. They had traditionally opposed communism but proposed few positive programs of their own. The postwar Christian Democratic parties of Germany, France, and Italy, however, were progressive. They accepted democracy and advocated social reform. They welcomed non-Catholic members. Democracy, social reform, economic growth, and anticommunism were their hallmarks.

The events of the war years largely determined the political leadership of the postwar decade. On the Continent, those groups and parties, including Communist parties, that had been active in the resistance against Nazism and Fascism held an initial advantage. After 1947, however, in a policy quite naturally favored by the United States, Communists were systematically excluded from all western European governments.

The most immediate postwar domestic problems included not only those created by the physical damage of the conflict but often also those that had existed in 1939. The war, however, although it may not have ended those prewar difficulties, opened new opportunities for solving them.

Margaret Thatcher, Britain's first woman prime minister, took office in 1979. She moved against trade unions and promoted a more nearly free-market economy. (Peter Marlow/SYGMA)

Economic Concerns

Within western Europe, with the exception of France, the economy dominated all other political issues from the end of World War II onward. The most remarkable success story of those years was what became known as the "economic miracle" of West Germany. That nation, under both Christian Democratic and Social Democratic ministries, achieved unprecedented levels of prosperity. In Great Britain, the Labour ministry of Clement Attlee, which governed from 1945 to 1950, introduced the welfare state and nationalized several major industries. The British economy never achieved the dynamism that both the Conservative and the Labour Party sought. From the 1960s through the 1970s, clashes between unions and business became commonplace. When Margaret Thatcher (b. 1925), the first woman prime minister of Great Britain, took office in 1979, she moved strongly against the unions and pressed for a more nearly free market economy.

Search for Stability in France

For almost a quarter century after the end of World War II, France experienced persistent political instability. Many of its problems arose from its postcolonial struggles in Indochina (discussed later) and Algeria.

Shortly after the war, French citizens ratified a constitution that established the Fourth Republic. Charles de Gaulle, who had led the forces of Free France during the war, grew disgusted with the politicians of the new Republic and left government. He returned to power in 1958 during the turmoil and unrest that accompanied France's war in Algeria. He imposed a new constitution establishing the Fifth French Republic and led a strategic retreat from Algeria that culminated in Algerian independence in 1962.

For ten years de Gaulle led France according to his own priorities. Those included hostility to the United States and Great Britain, maintenance of an independent French nuclear capacity, and a tense relationship with NATO. In May 1968, however, he faced a domestic upheaval that nearly toppled his government. The troubles began among student groups in Paris but quickly spread. Hundreds of thousands of workers went on strike. After assuring himself the support of the army, de Gaulle made a brief tele-

Charles de Gaulle returned to power as President of France in 1958 during the turmoil of the war in Algeria. He extricated France from Algeria, imposed the constitution that established the Fifth Republic, and for ten years led France on a determinedly independent course. [Bildarchiv Preussischer Kulturbesitz]

vision speech to rally his followers. Soon they, too, came into the streets to demonstrate in support of de Gaulle and stability. The strikes ended and police moved against the student groups. The government, to prevent more unrest, quickly moved to improve the wages and benefits of workers. The events of May 1968 revealed the fragility of the Fifth Republic, but they also showed that the many citizens who had benefitted from France's postwar economic progress had enough stake in the status quo to fear and prevent disruption.

In 1969 President de Gaulle resigned after some minor constitutional changes he had proposed were rejected in a referendum. French political life became remarkably stable thereafter. In contrast to de Gaulle, his various successors, most importantly Valéry Giscard d'Estaing (b. 1926), a Gaullist, and François Mitterand (b. 1916), a Socialist, have strongly supported European unification. Mixed electoral results have required the various French political parties to learn to cooperate and accommodate themselves to each other.

Toward Western European Unification

The internal political changes of the western European nations may in the long run prove less important than the unprecedented steps those nations have taken in the past thirty-five years toward cooperation and unity.

The moves toward unification have related primarily to economic integration. They arose originally from American encouragement in response to the Soviet domination of eastern Europe and from the western European states' own sense that they lacked effective political power. The process of economic integration has not been steady, nor is it near completion. The collapse of the Soviet Union and the emergence of new free governments in eastern Europe have further complicated the already difficult process.

Postwar Cooperation

The movement toward unity could have occurred in at least three ways: politically, militarily, or economically. The economic path was taken largely because the other paths were blocked. In 1949, ten European states organized the Council of Europe, which meets in Strasbourg, France. Its organization involved foreign ministers and a Consultative Assembly elected by the parliaments of the participants. The Council of Europe was and continues to be only an advisory body. Some had hoped that the council might become a parliament of Europe, but during the early 1950s none of the major states was willing to surrender any sovereignty to the newly organized body. The initial failure of the council to foster significant political cooperation ruled out for the time being the political or parliamentary routes to unification.

Between 1950 and 1954, there was some interest in a more thorough integration of the military forces of NATO. When the Korean War broke out, the United States began to urge the rearmament of West Germany. The German forces would provide western Europe with further protection against possible Soviet aggression while the United States was involved in Korea. France, however, continued to fear a German army. In 1951 the French government suggested the creation of a European Defense Community that would constitute a supranational military organization. This organization would have required a permanent British commitment of forces to the Continent to help France, in effect, counter any future German threat. The proposal was considered for some time, but in 1954 the French Parliament itself vetoed it. In 1955 West Germany was permitted to rearm and to enter NATO. Supranational military organization had not been achieved.

Economic cooperation, unlike military and political cooperation, involved little or no immediate loss of sovereignty. Furthermore, it brought material benefits to all the states involved, increasing popular support for their governments.

The Marshall Plan of the United States created the Organization for European Economic Cooperation (OEEC). This vehicle was set up to require common planning and cooperation among the participating countries and to discourage a return to the prewar economic nationalism. The OEEC and NATO, as well as other economic organizations tied to the Marshall Plan, gave the countries involved new experience in working with each other and demon-

strated the productivity and efficiency that resulted from cooperative action.

Among European leaders and civil servants, the opinion was widespread that only through the abandonment of economic nationalism could the newly organized democratic states avoid the economic turmoil that had proved such fertile ground for dictatorship. Economic cooperation carried the possibility of greater efficiency, prosperity, and employment. The leading proponents of this viewpoint were Robert Schuman (1886–1963), the foreign minister of France; Konrad Adenauer (1876–1967), the chancellor of the Federal Republic of Germany; Alcide De Gasperi (1881–1954), the prime minister of Italy; and Paul-Henri Spaak (1899–1972), the prime minister of Belgium. Among major civil servants and bureaucrats, Jean Monnet (1885–1981) of France was the leading representative.

In 1950 Schuman proposed that coal and steel production in western Europe be organized on an integrated, cooperative basis. The next year, France, West Germany, Italy, and the "Benelux" countries (Belgium, the Netherlands, and Luxembourg) organized the European Coal and Steel Community. Its activity was limited to a single sector of the economy, but that sector affected almost all other industrial production. An agency called the *High Authority* administered the plan. The authority was genuinely supranational, and its members could not be removed during their appointed terms. The Coal and Steel Community prospered. By 1955, coal production had grown by 23 percent. Iron and steel production was up by almost 150 percent. The community both benefitted from and contributed to the immense growth of material production in western Europe during this period. Its success reduced the suspicions of government and business groups about coordination and economic integration.

The European Economic Community

It took more than the prosperity of the European Coal and Steel Community to draw European leaders toward further unity. The unsuccessful Suez intervention and the resulting diplomatic isolation of France and Britain persuaded many Europeans that only through unified action could they exert any significant

The European Economic Community Is Established

The 1957 Treaty of Rome identified the major goals of the European Economic Community (Common Market) for the original six members.

◆ *How might the achievement of the goals of this treaty aid the internal political stability of the nations who entered into it? How might this economic community be seen as creating still another organization that would confront potential communist pressures in Europe? What areas of cooperation outlined here seem to favor free market activity and which might lead to greater government or community involvement in the economies of the nations signing the treaty?*

Article 2: It shall be the aim of the Community, by establishing a Common Market and progressively approximating the economic policies of Member States, to promote throughout the Community a harmonious development of economic activities, a continuous and balanced expansion, an increased stability, an accelerated raising of the standard of living and closer relations between its Member States.

Article 3: For the purposes set out in the preceding Article, the activities of the Community shall include, under the conditions and with the timing provided for in this Treaty:

(a) the elimination, as between Member States, of customs duties and of quantitative restrictions in regard to the importation and exportation of goods, as well as of all other measures with equivalent effect;

(b) the establishment of a common customs tariff and a common commercial policy towards third countries;

(c) the abolition, as between Member States, of the obstacles to the free movement of persons, services and capital;

(d) the inauguration of a common agricultural policy;

(e) the inauguration of a common transport policy;

(f) the establishment of a system ensuring that competition shall not be distorted in the Common Market;

(g) the application of procedures which shall make it possible to co-ordinate the economic policies of Member States and to remedy disequilibria in their balances of payments;

(h) the approximation of their respective municipal law to the extent necessary for the functioning of the Common Market;

(i) the creation of a European Social Fund in order to improve the possibilities of employment for workers and to contribute to the raising of their standard of living;

(j) the establishment of a European Investment Bank intended to facilitate the economic expansion of the Community through the creation of new resources; and

(k) the association of overseas countries and territories with the Community with a view to increasing trade and to pursuing jointly their effort towards economic and social development.

Treaty Establishing the European Economic Community (Brussels: Secretariat of the Interim Committee for the Common Market and Euratom, 1957), pp. 17–18.

influence on the two superpowers or control their own destinies. So, in 1957, through the Treaty of Rome, the six members of the Coal and Steel Community agreed to form a new organization: the European Economic Community (EEC). The members of the *Common Market*, as the EEC soon came to be called, envisioned more than a free-trade union. They sought to achieve the eventual elimination of tariffs, a free flow of capital and labor, and similar wage and social benefits in all the participating countries. The chief institutions of the EEC were a Council of Foreign Ministers and a High Commission composed of technocrats. The former came to be the dominant body.

The Common Market achieved a stunning degree of success during its early years. By 1968 all tariffs among the six members had been abolished well ahead of schedule. Trade and labor migration among the members grew steadily. Moreover, nonmember states began to copy the community and later to seek membership. In 1959 Britain, Denmark, Norway, Sweden, Switzerland, Austria, and Portugal formed the European Free Trade Area. By 1961, however, Great Britain had decided to seek Common Market membership. Twice, in 1963 and 1967, British membership was vetoed by President de Gaulle of France. He felt that Britain was too closely tied to the United States to support the EEC wholeheartedly.

The French veto of British membership demonstrated the major difficulty facing the Common Market during the 1960s. The Council of Ministers, representing the individual national interests of member states, came to have more influence than the High Commission. Political as well as economic factors increasingly entered into decision making. France particularly was unwilling to compromise on any matter that it regarded as pertaining to its sovereignty. On more than one occasion, President de Gaulle demanded enactment of his own policies and refused French participation under any other conditions. This attitude caused major problems over agricultural policy.

Despite the French actions, the Common Market survived and continued to prosper. In 1973 Great Britain, Ireland, and Denmark became members. Discussions continued on further steps toward integration, including proposals for a common currency. Throughout the late 1970s, however, and into the 1980s, there was a loss of momentum. Norway and Sweden, with relatively strong economies, declined to join. Although in 1982 Spain, Portugal, and Greece applied for membership and were eventually admitted, sharp disagreements and a sense of stagnation within the Community continued.

After this decade of disagreement and loss of direction, the leaders of the Community reached an important decision in early 1988. They targeted the year 1992 for achieving a virtual free-trade zone throughout the Community, entailing the elimination of the remaining trade barriers and other restrictive trade policies. In 1991 the leaders of the Community signed the Treaty of Maastricht, which made a series of specific proposals leading to a unified currency and to a strong central bank. This treaty was submitted to referendums in several European states. It initially failed to be adopted in Denmark and only narrowly passed in France and Great Britain. Elsewhere in Europe, it has also encountered organized opposition and probably never will be implemented as originally written. Part of the opposition has arisen from nationalistic concerns and part from the economic pressures arising from the current European recession.

The troubles of the Maastricht treaty illustrate a new and important phase in the process of achieving European unity. Until recently, the process has been carried out primarily by political leaders and by bureaucrats in the individual governments and the Community High Commission in Brussels. As the prospect of unity has become stronger, however, the people of Europe have begun to raise issues that relate to the democratic nature of the emerging political entity they are being asked to join. They are clearly for some kind of close cooperation and perhaps union, but they are unwilling to see it defined only by politicians and bureaucrats. They wish to see a wider European market, but they want that market to be genuinely free and not overregulated. Finally, the European Community has had to deal recently with the question of how it should relate to the host of newly independent states in eastern Europe.

European Retreat from Empire

The first two decades of the Cold War took place against the backdrop of the breakup of the great European empires. At the onset of World War II, many of the nations of Europe were still imperial powers. Great Britain, France, Russia, the

The move to achieve economic unity within Europe by eliminating all internal trade barriers and restrictive trade policies has encountered organized resistance. These French farmers are demonstrating against EEC policies. [Gamma-Liaison]

Netherlands, Belgium, Italy, and Portugal governed millions of non-Europeans. One of the most striking and significant postwar developments has been the decolonization of these imperial holdings and the consequent emergence of the so-called Third World political bloc (see Map 30-5). The one exception to this decolonization movement was the vast Asiatic empire of the Soviet Union that had been established by the tsars.

The Effects of World War II

Decolonization since 1945 has been a direct result of both the war itself and the rise of indigenous nationalist movements within the European colonial world. World War II drew the military forces of the colonial powers back to Europe. The Japanese conquests of Asia helped force the European powers from that area. After the military and political dislocations of the war came the postwar economic collapse, which left the colonial powers unable to afford to maintain their positions abroad.

The war aims of the Allies undermined colonialism. It was difficult to fight against tyranny in Europe while maintaining colonial dominance abroad. Moreover, the postwar policy of the United States generally opposed the continuation of European empires. Within the colonies, nationalist movements of varying strength had arisen. These movements were often led by gifted people who had been educated in Europe. They used the values and political ideologies they had learned in Europe to develop effective critiques of the colonial situation. Such leadership, as well as the frequently blatant injustice imposed on colonial peoples, helped make the nationalist movements effective.

DECOLONIZATON

Before 1950
1950-1959
1960-1969
After 1970

PACIFIC OCEAN

PHILIPPINES 1946

VIETNAM 1954

MALAYSIA 1963

INDONESIA 1950

SINGAPORE 1965

LAOS 1954

CAMBODIA 1953

BURMA 1948

SRI LANKA 1948

A S I A

E. PAKISTAN 1947
BANGLADESH 1973

INDIA 1947

PAKISTAN 1947

MALDIVES 1965

I N D I A N   O C E A N

KUWAIT 1961

UNITED ARAB EMIRATES 1971

OMAN 1977

BAHRAIN 1971

QATAR 1971

YEMEN 1967

SOUTH YEMEN 1967

MAURITIUS 1968

CYPRUS 1959

ERITREA

DJIBOUTI 1977

ETHIOPIA

SOMALIA 1960

MADAGASCAR 1960

EGYPT

SUDAN 1956

KENYA 1963

MALAWI 1964

SWAZILAND 1968

EUROPE

MALTA 1964

LIBYA 1951

CHAD 1960

CENTRAL AFRICAN REP.

UGANDA 1962

BURUNDI 1962

TANZANIA 1961

ZAMBIA 1964

MOZAMBIQUE 1974

ZIMBABWE 1971

LESOTHO 1965

TUNISIA 1956

A F R I C A

RWANDA 1962

ZAIRE 1960

BOTSWANA 1966

SOUTH AFRICA

MOROCCO 1956

ALGERIA 1962

NIGER 1960

CAMEROON 1960

CONGO 1960

ANGOLA 1976

NAMIBIA

MAURITANIA 1960

SENEGAL

MALI 1959

UPPER VOLTA 1960

NIGERIA 1960

GABON 1960

EQ. GUINEA 1968

GAMBIA 1965

GUINEA-BISS. 1974

GUINEA 1958

SIERRA LEONE 1961

LIBERIA

IVORY COAST 1960

GHANA 1957

TOGO 1960

DAHOMEY 1960

ATLANTIC OCEAN

MAP 30-5   DECOLONIZATION SINCE WORLD WAR II   *The Western powers' rapid retreat from imperialism after World War II is graphically shown on this outline map covering*

Major Areas of Colonial Withdrawal

There was a wide variety in decolonization. Some cases proceeded systematically; in others, the European powers simply beat a hasty retreat. In 1947 Britain left India, which, as a result of internal disputes, including religious differences, broke into two states, India and Pakistan. In 1948 Burma and Sri Lanka (formerly Ceylon) became independent. During the 1950s, the British tried to prepare colonies for self-government. Ghana (formerly the Gold Coast) and Nigeria—which became self-governing in 1957 and 1960, respectively—were the major examples of planned decolonization. In other areas, such as Malta and Cyprus, the British withdrawal occurred under the pressure of militant nationalist movements.

The smaller colonial powers had much less choice. The Dutch were forced from their East Indies possessions, which became independent as Indonesia, in 1950. In 1960 the Belgian Congo, now Zaire, became independent in the midst of great turmoil. For a considerable time, as will be seen, France tried to maintain its position in Southeast Asia but met defeat in 1954. It was similarly driven from North Africa. President de Gaulle carried out a policy of referendums on independence within the remaining French colonial possessions. By the late 1960s, only Portugal remained a traditional colonial power. Following a revolution in Portugal in 1974, its African colonies of Mozambique and Angola were finally liberated in 1974 and 1975 respectively.

Today in the various republics of the former Soviet Union, non-Europeans are seeking to establish their own political independence separate from the political control of Moscow. It is too early to say what will be the outcome of the various separatist movements in those republics.

France, the United States, and Vietnam

The problem of decolonization was one of the factors that helped to transfer the Cold War rivalry that had developed in Europe to other continents. French decolonization in particular became an integral part of the Cold War and led directly to the long military involvement of the United States in the Southeast Asian country of Vietnam.

Resistance to French Colonial Rule

During the years of the Korean conflict, another war was being fought in Asia between France and the Viet Minh nationalist movement in Indochina. France, in its push for empire, had occupied this territory (which contained Laos, Cambodia, and Vietnam) between 1857 and 1883. France had administered the area and had invested heavily in it, but the economy of Indochina remained overwhelmingly agrarian. During World War I, tens of thousands of Indochinese troops supported France. The French also educated many people from the colony. Neither the military aid the Indochinese provided France nor their Western education, however, prevented the French colonial rulers from discriminating against their subjects.

HO CHI MINH'S LEADERSHIP By 1930, Ho Chi Minh (1892–1969) had organized a movement against French colonial rule into the Indochinese Communist Party. Ho had traveled throughout the world and had held jobs in several places in Europe before World War I. He and other Indochinese had lobbied at the Versailles Conference in 1919 to have the principle of self-determination applied to their country. In 1920 he was part of the wing of the French Socialist Party that formed the French Communist Party. In 1923 he was sent to Moscow. By 1925 he had formed the Vietnam Revolutionary Youth. After organizing the Indochinese Communist Party, he traveled in Asia and spent considerable time in the Soviet Union. Throughout the 1930s, however, the French succeeded in suppressing most activities by the Communist Party in their colony.

World War II provided new opportunities for Ho Chi Minh and other nationalists. When Japan invaded, it found the pro-Vichy French colonial administration ready to collaborate. Thus, action against the Japanese thereafter meshed quite neatly with action against the French. It was during these wartime actions that Ho Chi Minh established his position as a major nationalist leader. He was a Communist to be sure, but he was first and foremost a

Ho Chi Minh (1892–1969), center, and advisors meet during the war against the French in 1954. [Black Star]

nationalist. Most important, he had achieved his position in Vietnam during the war without the support of the Chinese Communist movement.

In September 1945, Ho Chi Minh declared the independence of Vietnam under the Viet Minh, a coalition of nationalists soon dominated by the Communists. There was considerable internal Vietnamese resistance to this claim of political control. The opposition arose from religious groups and non-Communist nationalists. After the war, the French immediately took advantage of these divisions to set up a government favorable to their own interests. The United States, in line with its wartime anticolonialist position, urged the French to make some kind of accommodation with Ho Chi Minh.

In 1946 France and the Viet Minh reached an armistice. It was short-lived; in 1947 fullfledged war broke out. The next year, the French established a friendly Vietnamese government under Bao Dai (b. 1911). It was to be independent within a loose union with France. This arrangement would have meant very limited independence and was clearly unacceptable to both the Viet Minh and most other nationalists.

Until 1949 the United States had showed minimal concern about the Indochina War. The defeat of Chiang Kai-shek (1887–1975), however, and the establishment of the Communist People's Republic of China in 1949 dramatically changed its outlook. The United States now saw the French colonial war against Ho Chi Minh as an integral part of the Cold War conflict. The French government, hoping for U.S. support, worked to maintain that point of view. Early in 1950 the United States recognized the Bao Dai government. At about the same time, the Soviet Union and the People's Republic of China recognized the government of Ho Chi Minh. Indochina was thus transformed from a colonial battleground into an area of Cold War confrontation.

FRENCH DEFEAT AT DIEN BIEN PHU In May 1950, the United States announced that it would supply financial aid to the French war effort. Between that time and 1954, more than $4 billion flowed from the United States to France. Despite this aid, the French position deteriorated. In the spring of 1954, the French army was overrun by the Viet Minh forces at the Battle of Dien Bien Phu. Psychologically and militarily, the French could not muster new energy for the war. Campaigning on a promise to conclude the conflict, Pierre Mendès-France (1907–1982) was elected premier in Paris. At this point, the U.S. government was badly divided, but it decided against military intervention.

The Geneva Settlement and Its Aftermath

During the late spring and the early summer of 1954, a conference was held at Geneva to settle the Indochina conflict. It proved a most unsatisfactory gathering. To one degree or another, all the major powers were involved in the proceedings, but they did not sign the agreements. Technically, the agreements were between the armed forces of France and those of the Viet Minh. The precedents for such arrangements were the surrender of the German army in 1945 and the Korean armistice of 1953.

NORTH AND SOUTH VIETNAM   The Geneva conference provided for the division of Vietnam at the seventeenth parallel of latitude. This was to be a temporary border. By 1956 elections were to be held to reunify the country. North of the parallel, centered in Hanoi, the Viet Minh were in charge; below it, centered in Saigon, the French were in charge. The prospect of elections meant that theoretically both groups could function politically in the territory of the other. In effect, the conference attempted to transform a military conflict into a political one.

The United States was less than happy about the results of the Geneva discussions. Its first major response came in September 1954, with the formation of the Southeast Asia Treaty Organization (SEATO). This collective security agreement in some respects paralleled the European NATO alliance. It did not, however, involve the integration of military forces achieved in NATO, nor did it include all the major states of the region. Its membership consisted of the United States, Great Britain, France, Australia, New Zealand, Thailand, Pakistan, and the Philippines.

By 1955 American policymakers had begun to think about the Indochina region, and more especially Vietnam, largely in terms of the Korean example. The U.S. government assumed that the government being established in North Vietnam was, like the government of North Korea, basically a Communist puppet state. The same year, French troops began to withdraw from the South. As they left, the various Vietnamese political groups began to fight for power.

THE UNITED STATES AND THE DIEM GOVERNMENT   The United States stepped into this turmoil with military and economic aid. Among the Vietnamese politicians, it chose to support Ngo Dinh Diem (1901–1963). He was a strong non-Communist nationalist who had not collaborated with the French. The Americans hoped that he would become a leader around whom a non-Communist Vietnamese nationalist movement might rally. Because the United States had publicly and deeply committed to the French, however, any government it supported would be, and was, viewed with suspicion by Vietnamese nationalists. In October 1955, Diem established a Republic of Vietnam in the territory for which the Geneva conference had made France responsible. By 1956 the United States was training troops and government officials, paying salaries, and providing military equipment.

In the meantime, Diem announced that he and his newly established government were not bound by the Geneva agreements and that elections would not be held in 1956. The American government, which had not signed the Geneva documents, supported his position. Diem undertook an anti-Communist campaign, attacking many citizens who had earlier resisted the French. This was the beginning of a program of political repression that characterized his regime and those that followed.

There was a long series of ordinances that gave Diem's government extraordinary power over its citizens. Diem alienated the peasants by restoring rents to landlords and generally strengthening large landowners. He abolished elected village councils and replaced them with his own officials, who had often come from the North. In fact, Diem's major base of political support lay with the more than one million Vietnamese who had migrated to the South after 1954.

By 1960 Diem's policy had created considerable internal resistance in South Vietnam. In that year, the National Liberation Front was founded, with the goals of overthrowing Diem, unifying the country, reforming the economy, and ousting the Americans. It was anticolonial, nationalist, and Communist. Its military arm was called the Viet Cong. Sometime in the late 1950s, the government of North Vietnam began to aid the insurgent forces of the South (see Map

MAP 30-6 VIETNAM AND ITS NEIGHBORS *This map identifies important locations in the long and complex struggle centered in Vietnam.*

The U.S. Involvement

The Eisenhower and early Kennedy administrations in the United States continued to support Diem while demanding reforms in his government. The American military presence grew from somewhat more than 600 people in early 1961 to more than 16,000 troops in late 1963. The political situation in Vietnam became increasingly unstable. On November 1, 1963, Diem was overthrown and murdered in an army coup. The United States was deeply involved in this plot. Its officials hoped that if the Diem regime were eliminated, the path would be opened to establish a new government in South Vietnam capable of generating popular support. Thereafter, the political goal of the United States was to find a leader who could fill this need. It finally settled on Nguyen Van Thieu (b. 1923), who governed South Vietnam from 1966 to 1975.

President Kennedy was assassinated on November 22, 1963. His successor, Lyndon Johnson, continued and vastly expanded the commitment to South Vietnam. In August 1964, after an attack on an American ship in the Gulf of Tonkin, the first bombing of North Vietnam was authorized. In February 1965, major bombing attacks began that continued, with only brief pauses, until the early weeks of 1973. The land war grew in extent, with more than 500,000 Americans stationed in South Vietnam.

In 1969 President Richard Nixon began a policy of gradual withdrawal from Vietnam called *Vietnamization.* Drawn-out peace negotiations had begun in Paris in the spring of 1968. In January 1973, a cease-fire was finally arranged. The troops of the United States were pulled back, and prisoners of war held in North Vietnam were returned. Thereafter, violations of the cease-fire occurred on both sides. In early 1975 an evacuation of South Vietnamese troops from the northern part of their country turned into a complete rout as they were attacked by the troops of North Vietnam. On April 30, 1975, Saigon fell to the troops of the Viet Cong and North Vietnam. The Second Indochina War had ended.

The Second Indochina War was, in effect, a continuation of the first war, which the French had lost. The United States saw the conflict as part of the Cold War and as a repetition of Korea. Aggression from the North had to be

30-6). The Viet Cong and their supporters carried out a program of widespread terrorism and political disruption. They imposed an informal government through much of the countryside. Many peasants voluntarily supported them; others supported them from fear of reprisals.

In addition to the Communist opposition, Diem faced mounting criticism from non-Communist citizens. The Buddhists agitated against the Roman Catholic president. The army was less than satisfied with him. Diem's response to all these pressures was further repression and dependence on an ever-smaller group of advisers.

halted. There was also hope that the military power of the United States might buy time so that a strong nationalist, non-Communist regime could be established in South Vietnam.

The war grew out of a power vacuum left by decolonization. It produced a major impact on all the Western world. For a decade after the Cuban missile crisis, the attention of the United States was largely diverted from Europe. American prestige suffered, and the American commitment to western Europe came into question. Moreover, the American policy in Southeast Asia made many Europeans wonder about the basic wisdom of the American government. Many young Europeans—and not a few Americans—born after World War II came to regard the United States not as a protector of liberty but as an ambitious, aggressive, and cruel power trying to keep colonialism alive after the end of the colonial era.

The Arab–Israeli Conflict

A final arena for East–West confrontation during the decades following World War II was the Arab–Israeli conflict (see Map 30-7). Like Southeast Asia, Palestine before World War II was governed by a European power, in this case Great Britain. The events in this area represent in one respect another example of the turmoil that has resulted from the retreat of a colonial power. Furthermore, this dispute has directly involved Europe because many of the citizens of Israel are immigrants from Europe and because Europe, like the United States, is highly dependent on oil from Arab countries.

British Balfour Declaration

The modern state of Israel was the achievement of the world Zionist movement founded in 1897 by Theodore Herzl and later led by Chaim Weizmann (1874–1952). The British Balfour Declaration of 1917 had favored establishing a national home for the Jewish people in Palestine. Between the wars, thousands of Jews, mainly from Europe, immigrated to the area, then governed by Great Britain under a mandate of the League of Nations. During the interwar

Major Dates in the Vietnam Conflict	
1945	Ho Chi Minh proclaims Vietnamese independence from French rule
1947–1954	War between France and Vietnam
1950	U.S. financial aid to France
1954	French defeat at Dien Bien Phu
1954	Geneva Conference on Southeast Asia
1954	Southeast Asia Treaty Organization founded
1955	Diem establishes Republic of Vietnam in the South
1960	Foundation of National Liberation Front to overthrow the Diem government
1961	Six hundred American troops and advisers in Vietnam
1963	Diem overthrown and assassinated
1964	Gulf of Tonkin Resolution
1965	Major U.S. troop commitment
1969	Nixon announces policy of Vietnamization
1973	Cease-fire announced
1975	Saigon falls to North Vietnamese troops

period, the *Yishuv,* or Jewish community in Palestine, developed its own political parties, press, labor unions, and educational system. There were many conflicts with the Arabs already living in Palestine, who considered the Jewish settlers intruders. The British rather unsuccessfully tried to mediate those clashes.

This situation might have prevailed longer in Palestine except for the outbreak of World War II and the attempt by Hitler to exterminate the Jewish population of Europe. The Nazi persecution united Jews throughout the world behind the Zionist ideal of a Jewish state in Palestine. Also, the knowledge of Nazi atrocities touched the conscience of the United States and other Western powers. It seemed morally right that something be done for Jewish refugees from Nazi concentration camps.

In 1947 the British turned over to the United Nations the whole problem of the relationship of Arabs and Jews in Palestine. That same year, the United Nations passed a resolution calling for a division of the territory into a Jewish state

MAP 30-7 ISRAEL AND ITS NEIGHBORS *Israel's occupied territories include lands that were previously part of Syria, Jordan, or Egypt. The future of those lands, their inhabitants, and the refugees who left Israel and its territories lies at the heart of the region's unresolved problems.*

The Birth of the State of Israel

In May 1948, the Yishuv declared the independence of a new Jewish state called Israel. The United States, through President Truman, almost immediately recognized the new nation, whose first prime minister was David Ben-Gurion (1886–1973). During 1948 and 1949, Israel fought its war of independence against the Arabs. In that war, Israel expanded its borders beyond the limits originally set forth by the United Nations. By 1949 Israel had, through force of arms, secured its existence and peace. It had not, however, secured diplomatic recognition by its Arab neighbors—Egypt, Jordan, Syria, Lebanon, and Saudi Arabia, to name those closest. The peace amounted to little more than an armed truce.

Then in 1952 a group of Egyptian army officers seized power in Egypt. Their leader was Gamal Abdel Nasser. He established himself as a dictator and, more important, as a spokesman for militant Arab nationalism. His policy was marked by hatred of all the old imperial powers. In 1956 Nasser nationalized the Suez Canal. That same year, as noted previously, Great Britain and France responded to Nasser's action by attacking the canal. Israel joined with France and Britain. This alliance helped Israel fend off certain Arab guerrilla attacks but associated Israel with the former imperial powers. After 1956 a United Nations peacekeeping force separated the armies of Israel and Egypt. The bases of the U.N. force were located in Egypt. Still there was no official Arab recognition of the existence of Israel.

The 1967 Six Days' War

An uneasy peace continued until 1967. Meanwhile, the Soviet Union increased its influence in Egypt and the United States increased its influence in Israel. Both great powers supplied weapons to their friends in the area. In 1967 President Nasser calculated, mistakenly, that the Arab nations could defeat Israel, by then nearly two decades old. He began to mass troops in the Sinai Peninsula, and he attempted to close the Gulf of Aqaba to Israeli shipping. He also demanded the withdrawal of the U.N. peacekeeping force. Diplomatic activity failed to

and an Arab state. The Arabs in Palestine and the surrounding area resisted the United Nations resolution. Not unnaturally, they resented the influx of new settlers. Many Palestinian Arabs were displaced and themselves became refugees.

stem the crisis and the Arab attempt to isolate Israel.

On June 5, 1967, the armed forces of Israel, under the direction of Defense Minister Moshe Dayan (1915–1981), attacked Egyptian airfields rather than endure additional provocation by Egypt. Almost immediately, Syria and Jordan entered the war on the side of Egypt. Yet, by June 11, the Six Days' War was over, and Israel had won a stunning victory. The military forces of Egypt lay in shambles. Moreover, Israel had occupied the entire Egyptian Sinai Peninsula, as well as the West Bank region along the Jordan River that had been part of the state of Jordan. This victory marked the height of Israeli power and prestige.

Egyptian Policy Under Anwar el-Sadat

In 1970 President Nasser died. He was succeeded by Anwar el-Sadat (1918–1981). Sadat had first to shore up his support at home. The existing tensions between Israel and the defeated Egypt, of course, continued, and the Soviet Union still poured weapons into Egypt. Sadat, however, deeply distrusted the Russians and in 1972 ordered them to leave Egypt.

Sadat and his advisers also felt that only another war with Israel could return to Egypt the lands lost in 1967. In October 1973, on the Jewish holy day of Yom Kippur, the military forces of Egypt and Syria launched an attack across the Suez Canal into Israeli-held territory. The invasion came as a complete surprise to the Israelis. Initially, the Egyptian forces made considerable headway. Then the Israeli army thrust back the invasion. In November 1973, a truce was signed between the forces in the Sinai. Although Israel had been successful in repelling the Egyptians, the cost in troops and prestige was very high.

The Yom Kippur War added a major new element to the Middle East problem. In the fall of 1973, when the war broke out, the major Arab oil-producing states shut off the flow of oil to the United States and Europe. This dramatic move was an attempt to force the Western powers to use their influence to moderate the policy of Israel. The threat of the loss of oil was particularly frightening to Europeans, whose industry depends on it. At that time (prior to the develop-

ment of the North Sea oil fields), Western Europe depended almost entirely on Middle Eastern oil.

In November 1977, President Sadat of Egypt, in a dramatic personal gesture, flew to Israel. He addressed the Israeli Parliament and held discussions with Prime Minister Menachem Begin (1913–1992), although the two states were still technically at war. In effect, for the first time the head of a major Arab state recognized the existence of Israel. Previously, all contacts had taken place through either the United Nations or other third parties.

The Camp David Accords and the PLO

The Sadat initiative, roundly condemned in many Arab quarters, resulted in direct conversations. The most important occurred at Camp David in the United States with President Carter as moderator. The Camp David Accords of September 1978 have provided one framework for continuing negotiations on Middle East questions. Since 1978 numerous meetings have occurred between Egyptian and Israeli officials.

Until 1986 no other Arab states joined these talks. The major stumbling block to an agreement has been the Palestine refugee problem. The Palestine Liberation Organization (PLO) was then and remains the major representative for the refugees. The PLO demanded a separate Palestinian state; the government of Israel steadily refused to recognize the PLO. Israel also believed that virtually any independent Palestinian state would be a threat to its own independence and ultimate survival.

In early 1981 Prime Minister Begin's coalition was reelected, but in October of that year President Sadat was assassinated by Muslim extremists. The death of the Egyptian president cast doubt on the long-range stability of the Camp David process. Further strains appeared in late December 1981, when the Israeli Parliament suddenly annexed the Golan Heights while the attention of most of the Western world was on the crisis in Poland.

Lebanon and the Intifada

In 1982 Israeli troops invaded Lebanon in an effort to destroy PLO bases and to disperse the PLO leadership. They were largely successful. At

Beginning in the late 1980s, in a movement known as the intifada, *Palestinian youths on the West Bank began active resistance to Israeli occupation. [Contact Press Images]*

the same time, however, the fragile Lebanese state, long racked by civil war, virtually collapsed. For a few months in 1983, the United States stationed Marines in Lebanon. After a terrorist bombing killed more than 300 troops, the Marines were withdrawn. In 1985 Israeli troops withdrew. Syrian troops remain and battle with the various Lebanese factions and their armies. Various radical Arab factions have held British, French, and American citizens as hostages to attempt to put pressure on their governments. Lebanon has remained a center of political and social disorder.

In 1983 Begin, who was in ill health, resigned as prime minister of Israel. He was succeeded by a series of coalition governments. One of the most important developments in the region has been the *intifada*, the Arab uprising against

Israeli rule that began in 1987 on the West Bank. This area was conquered in the 1967 war, but it has neither been annexed to Israel nor made independent. The Israelis have responded to the political and social unrest and the frequent local revolts on the West Bank since 1987 with increasing and often deadly force. Their actions have generated intense controversy in Israel and the world community.

A series of events beginning in 1988 that led to unexpected and complicated diplomatic developments can only be summarized here. Late in 1988 the PLO, led by Yasir Arafat (b. 1929), publicly stated that Israel had a right to exist and that it would henceforth refrain from terrorist activity. Earlier that year, the PLO had declared the existence of a Palestinian state in the West Bank and Gaza.

In 1990 Iraq invaded Kuwait. In the months thereafter, the United States organized a worldwide coalition to drive Iraq from Kuwait. That coalition included the Soviet Union, all the major European powers, Japan, Israel, Saudi Arabia, and other Arab States. Among the Arabs, only Jordan and the PLO supported Iraq. During a brief war in 1991, the coalition drove Iraq from Kuwait. The result was viewed not only as a defeat for Iraq but as a defeat for the entire radical Arab cause. Thereafter Saudi Arabia and other wealthy Arab states either decreased or ended their financial support of the PLO. The full details of those arrangements are still not fully public. By the end of 1991, the PLO found itself increasingly isolated within the Arab world.

During the early 1990s, the United States also sponsored peace talks in the Middle East. By early 1993 the Israeli government decided to permit meetings between the PLO and Israelis. Several months of secret negotiations followed, sponsored by Norway. In September 1993, Israel and the PLO signed a formal agreement recognizing each other and agreeing to Palestinian self-government in Gaza and the city of Jericho. The agreement came as a general surprise to the entire world community. Signed in Washington, D.C., on September 14, 1993, it left most details to further negotiation. It has, nonetheless, transformed the diplomatic situation in the Middle East. Israel and various of the Arab states have since moved toward formal

In 1993 the leaders of Israel and the Palestine Liberation Organization signed a peace accord in Washington, D.C. From left to right are Prime Minister Yitzhak Rabin of Israel, President Bill Clinton of the United States, PLO Chairman Yasir Arafat, and Warren Christopher, United States Secretary of State. [SYGMA]

diplomatic recognition. Radical groups among both the Israelis and the Palestinians have opposed the agreement and carried out terrorist action to disrupt its implementation.

◆

The quarter century following the conclusion of World War II saw the relative decline of European power. The United States and the Soviet Union emerged as two economic and military superpowers. They confronted each other across the globe at one crisis point after another in a long-lasting conflict called the Cold War. In Europe, the point of confrontation was often the divided city of Berlin. The United States voiced concern about eastern Europe but was never willing to exert significant influence in that region.

There were, however, other pressure points throughout the world. In Asia, the United States twice intervened. First, it led the United Nations police action in Korea. Second, it became involved in the long war over the political future of Vietnam. The revolution in Cuba and the establishment there of a Communist government provided another point of tension, which in 1962 provoked the Cuban missile crisis, the most dangerous confrontation of the postwar era. In the Middle East, both the Soviet Union and the United States became involved in the Arab–Israeli conflict.

Following almost two decades of tension and crises, the United States and the Soviet Union entered upon two decades of negotiation that culminated in a significant arms reduction treaty. The Cold War ended in the late 1980s as major structural and policy changes shook the Soviet Union and led eventually to its collapse.

In the midst of this superpower rivalry, western Europe achieved new levels of economic *prosperity and political stability. Its nations established the European Economic Community and have moved steadily, if with difficulty, toward economic cooperation.*

Review Questions

1. How did Europe come to be dominated by the United States and the Soviet Union after 1945? Trace the stages of the Cold War. Why were 1956 and 1962 particularly crucial years?

2. How would you define the policy of "containment"? Give some specific examples of how this policy was instituted by the United States throughout the world from 1945 to 1982.

3. How did Khrushchev's policies and reforms change the Soviet state after the repression of Stalin? Why did many people inside and outside the Soviet Union regard Khrushchev as reckless?

4. After World War II, Europe "achieved unprecedented economic prosperity and main-

tained liberal democratic governments." How did western Europe move toward political unity? How important was the Marshall Plan to western Europe's political and economic success? To what extent were the domestic policies of Charles de Gaulle important for maintaining political stability in France?

5. Trace the process of European decolonization. Why did the nations of Europe give up their empires? Was the retreat orderly? How did the United States become involved in Vietnam? What was the effect of the Vietnam War on Europe?

6. Discuss the origin of problems that led to Arab-Israeli conflict in the Middle East after 1948. Why are the Camp David Accords historically important? What are the most recent peace initiatives in the region?

Suggested Readings

K. L. BAKER, R. J. DALTON, and K. HILDEBRANDT (Eds.), *Germany Transformed: Political Culture and the New Politics* (1981). Useful essays on the functioning of the political structures of West Germany.

C. D. BLACK and G. DUFFY (Eds.), *International Arms Control Issues and Agreements* (1985). Useful essays on arms issues as they stood at the close of the Cold War.

E. BOTTOME, *The Balance of Terror: Nuclear Weapons and the Illusion of Security, 1945–1985* (1986). An examination of the role of nuclear weapons in the Cold War climate.

R. V. DANIELS, *Year of the Heroic Guerilla: World Revolution and Counterrevolution in 1968* (1989). A worldwide examination of the events of that year.

A. W. DEPORTE, *Europe Between the Superpowers: The Enduring Balance* (1979). This remains a significant study.

R. EMERSON, *From Empire to Nation: The Rise to Self-assertion of Asian and African Peoples* (1960). An important discussion of the origins of decolonization.

B. B. FALL, *The Two Vietnams: A Political and Military Analysis*, rev. ed. (1967). A discussion by a journalist who spent many years on the scene.

H. FEIS, *From Trust to Terror: The Onset of the Cold War, 1945–1950* (1970). The best general account.

D. HOLLOWAY, *The Soviet Union and the Arms Race* (1985). Excellent treatment of internal Soviet decision making.

P. Jenkins, *Mrs. Thatcher's Revolution: The Ending of the Socialist Era* (1988). The best work on the subject.

W. W. Kulski, *DeGaulle and the World: The Foreign Policy of the Fifth Republic* (1968). A straightforward treatment of de Gaulle's drive toward French and European autonomy.

R. F. Leslie, *The History of Poland Since 1863* (1981). An excellent collection of essays that provide the background for later events in Poland.

F. Lewis, *Europe: Road to Unity* (1992). A discussion of contemporary Europe by a thoughtful journalist.

L. Martin (Ed.), *Strategic Thought in the Nuclear Age* (1979). A collection of useful essays on an issue that lay at the core of the American relationship to western Europe.

L. P. Morris, *Eastern Europe Since 1945* (1984). Concentrates on the political and economic organization of the Soviet-dominated states.

J. Rothchild, *Return to Diversity: A Political History of East Central Europe Since World War II* (1989). A clear, well-organized introduction.

L. Schapiro, *The Communist Party of the Soviet Union* (1960). A classic analysis of the most important institution of Soviet Russia.

Z. Schiff and E. Ya'ari, *Intifada: The Palestinian Uprising—Israel's Third Front* (1990). An analysis of recent developments.

H. Simonian, *The Privileged Partnership: Franco-German Relations in the European Community (1969–1984)* (1985). An important examination of the dominant role of France and Germany in the EEC.

J. Steele, *Soviet Power: The Kremlin's Foreign Policy—Brezhnev to Andropov* (1983). A broad survey.

A. Ulam, *Expansion and Coexistence: The History of Soviet Foreign Policy, 1917–1967* (1968). A major treatment.

A. Ulam, *The Communists: The Story of Power and Lost Illusions: 1948–1991* (1992). The best account to date of the days of Communist strength and collapse.

M. Walker, *The Cold War and the Making of the Modern World* (1994). A major new survey.

The opening of the Berlin Wall in November, 1989, more than any other event, symbolized the collapse of the Communist governments in Eastern Europe. [R. Bossu/SYGMA]

Toward a New Europe and the Twenty-first Century

Key Topics in This Chapter
- Unprecedented prosperity and the expansion of the consumer society in western Europe
- Demographic trends, migrations, and growing ethnic tensions
- Intellectual and social movements since World War II
- Perestroika and glasnost in the Soviet Union
- The collapse of communism in eastern Europe and the Soviet Union
- The civil war in Yugoslavia

The second half of the twentieth century has witnessed remarkable social and intellectual changes in European life. One of the most important of these, the formation of the European Economic Community, was discussed in the previous chapter. Other important trans-formations, overshadowed by the Soviet–American rivalry, occurred quietly and with little notice.

Western Europe experienced unprecedented economic growth. Much of western Europe and even the popular culture of eastern Europe became "Americanized." Consumers enjoyed more goods and services than ever before. A second agricultural revolution made Europe still more urban, with fewer people living on the land. The role of women in the workplace and in society at large became more important than during any previous era of history. A distinct youth culture blossomed, affecting both political and intellectual life. The Roman Catholic church reformed itself more radically than at any time since the Council of Trent in the sixteenth century. Secular intellectuals found themselves compelled to wrestle with the problems posed by communism. And science was making remarkable advances in virtually every area of research. The effects of technology and industrialism, however, created growing concern for the environment in Europe and the United States.

The last decades of the twentieth century saw an astonishing and largely unexpected political transformation that will bring still further social and economic change. The Communist governments of the Soviet Union and its eastern European subject states collapsed in a manner and with a rapidity that amazed the entire world. As a result, Germany again became united, the nations of eastern Europe became independent, civil war rages in Yugoslavia, and the Soviet Union has been replaced by a Commonwealth of Independent States. A new Europe is now emerging in a period of flux and redirection that in recent history can only be compared with the period immediately after World War I or World War II.

European Society in the Second Half of the Twentieth Century

The sharp division of Europe into a democratic West and Communist East for most of the second half of the twentieth century makes generalizations about social and economic developments difficult. Prosperity in the West contrasted with the conditions of consumer goods shortages in the Eastern economies, which were managed for the benefit of the Soviet Union. Most of the developments discussed in this chapter have taken place in western Europe.

The "Americanization" of Europe

During the past half century, the United States has exerted enormous influence on Europe and most especially western Europe. After the war, the U.S. government, through the Marshall Plan, rebuilt the western European economies. The United States was the leader of the NATO alliance. Over the decades, hundreds of thousands of American military personnel have been stationed in Europe. Thousands of American students have studied in Europe, and millions of American tourists have flocked there.

The term *Americanization*, which has appeared in European publications, refers in part to this economic and military influence, but it also refers to concerns about cultural loss. Many Europeans feel that American popular entertainment and economic enterprises threaten to extinguish some of the unique qualities of their various nations and regions. American banks and other financial institutions as well as law firms often have European branches. Large American corporations such as the McDonald's fast-food chain have established a presence in European cities from Dublin to Moscow. American liquor companies and distilleries now sell their goods in Europe. Styles of clothing, such as blue jeans, first popular in America, are now equally popular in Europe. Shopping centers, first pioneered in America, and supermarkets are displacing neighborhood shopping areas. American television programs and movies are readily available. Perhaps most impressive is the manner in which American rock music has come to dominate much of the European popular cultural scene. As a result, Americans and Europeans look up to the same movie stars and popular entertainers.

Furthermore, as Europe moves toward greater economic cooperation, English seems to be emerging as the most common language of business and even of some academic fields. And it is American influence, not British, that lies behind this trend.

This Americanization is, of course, relative. The United States is not the only economic power impinging on Europe. Asian nations, particularly Japan, also have enormous presence. In Europe, as in the United States, the electronic merchandise that fills many stores today is

Many American fast-food and retail chains are now appearing in East Europe as well as West Europe. This Pizza Hut is in Moscow. [Wolfgang Kaehl]

important political results. Throughout the Soviet Union and the nations it dominated in eastern Europe, economic planning overwhelmingly favored capital investment and military production. Those nations produced inadequate food for their people and a very low level of consumer goods. Long lines for food and nonfood staples such as shoes and clothing were not uncommon. Automobiles were a luxury; housing was inadequate. The quality of all consumer goods was low.

By contrast, the last fifty years has seen a steady increase in the availability of consumer goods elsewhere in Europe. By the early 1950s, western Europeans enjoyed an excellent food supply that has only improved over the years. The variety of fresh foods and vegetables available to western consumers has increased, as has the variety of frozen foods. And in a sign of the strength of western Europe's consumer economy, if not the healthfulness of its diet, the number of fast food outlets has also expanded markedly.

Western Europe has enjoyed a similarly great expansion of virtually all other kinds of consumer goods and services. The number of automobiles increased and they became widely accessible. The number of people owning refrigerators, washing machines, electric ranges, televisions, and now microwaves, video cassette recorders, computers, compact disc players, and other small electronic consumer items has grown rapidly. A wide variety of everyday clothing became available, from woolen goods to blue jeans and sneakers. Like their American counterparts, western Europeans now have a whole gamut of products, such as disposable diapers, to help them raise their children. They take foreign vacations year round, prompting the expansion of ski resorts in the Alpine countries and beach resorts on the Mediterranean.

This vast expansion of consumerism, which, as noted in Chapter 16, began in the eighteenth century, became a defining characteristic of western Europe in the late twentieth century. It stood in marked contrast to the consumer shortages in eastern Europe. Yet through even the limited number of radios, televisions, movies, and videos available to them, people in the East grew increasingly aware of the discrepancy between their lifestyle and that of the West.

often manufactured in Japan or elsewhere in Asia. Nonetheless, the infiltration of American values, products, and popular culture has been a major feature of European social life during the past half century. Europeans have frequently regretted or criticized this development, but it has become a major fact of European social life.

A Consumer Society

Although European economies have been under pressure in the early 1990s, most of the last half century has witnessed an extraordinary expansion in the consumer sector. This expansion was limited almost entirely to Europe outside the Soviet bloc.

The consumer orientation of the western European economy emerged as one of the most important characteristics differentiating it from eastern Europe. Those differences produced

They saw Western consumerism clearly linked to democratic governments, free societies, and economic policies that favored the free market and only limited government planning. Thus the expansion of consumerism in the West, deplored by many commentators and Christian moralists, helped generate the discontent that brought down the Communist governments of eastern Europe and the Soviet Union.

Population Changes

The wars of the twentieth century, from Ireland to the Soviet Union, killed millions of people in Europe. Yet despite these losses—in combat, from the slaughter of civilians, and from the hunger and deprivation associated with war—Europe's population has grown over the course of the century. Growth rates have varied over time and from country to country, but the overall increase has been substantial. Between 1913 and 1985, the population is estimated to have grown by more than 44 percent.[1] Yet it is important to note that population growth elsewhere in the world has outpaced that of Europe. Whereas in the first decade of the century Europeans accounted for approximately 20 percent of the world's population, today they account for only about 11 percent. This shift in population has changed Europe's place in the world and accounts in part for the growing pressure on natural resources from non-European and non-Western regions.

The largest European population expansion in history took place during the twenty years after World War II. During that period, there were no wars to decimate the population, and Europe experienced a material prosperity, especially in the West, that it had not known previously in its history. Europeans today live more closely together than in earlier eras. Population density rose from 66 people per square kilometer in 1920 to 101 in 1985. The most densely populated regions are the Netherlands, Belgium, England, western Germany, and Italy.

The chief factors behind this remarkable population growth are increased life expectancy and a reduced infant mortality rate, both a result of medical advances and improved living standards. In effect, a greater percentage of European children survive infancy than before and then go on to live longer lives than their predecessors. Despite regional variations and a persistently longer life expectancy for women than men, life expectancy has now increased almost uniformly across Europe.

Equally striking has been the decline in Europe's birthrate over the course of the century. Birth control information and contraceptives became widely available from the 1920s on. Although a "baby boom" did occur in the decade and a half following World War II, it was closely associated with the prosperity of those years. The European birthrate reached a peak in 1964 and has declined since then to much lower levels. The advent of the birth control pill during the 1960s contributed directly to this trend. Possibly also contributing to it was the legalization of abortion in many western European countries. Abortion was generally already legal in eastern Europe and the Soviet Union.

Effective and widely available contraception has combined with changing social attitudes to reduce the size of the European family significantly. Around the turn of the century, families with five or more children were not uncommon. Near the close of the century, the two-child family has become the norm. Evidence suggests that average family size is becoming still smaller in the 1990s.

Modern European Household Structures

Despite the media attention devoted to unconventional lifestyles, the half century following World War II has actually seen an increase in the number of married people in Europe. Before then, a significant number of women remained unmarried all their lives, but many fewer do so now. Women are also marrying at a younger age than before, particularly in eastern and southern Europe. Overall, more people in the last half century have married, and have married at an earlier age, than in all of previous European history.

At the same time, many of the traditional ideas and expectations surrounding marriage have changed. Family size is smaller. The incidence of divorce has increased over the course of

[1]The information on population and most of the other statistical information in this chapter is taken from Gerold Ambrosius and William H. Hubbard, A Social and Economic History of Twentieth-Century Europe (Cambridge, Mass.: Harvard University Press, 1989).

the century. Divorce laws have eased throughout Europe, although not until after 1980 in the nations of southern Europe, where the Roman Catholic church is influential.

In the Scandinavian countries, there has been an increase in the number of children born out of wedlock. Quite often the couple having the children live together, but are not married. Such arrangements and the possibility of single motherhood have been made economically possible by government-sponsored programs directed toward the care of children. Despite the attention such arrangements have received, they have not become the norm anywhere in Europe.

The Movement of Peoples

Many people have migrated from, to, and within Europe during the past half century.

EXTERNAL MIGRATION   In the decade and a half after 1945, approximately a half million Europeans each year settled elsewhere in the world. This was the largest outward migration since the 1920s, when the rate had been approximately 700,000 persons annually. A major difference between this post–World War II emigration and that of the second half of the nineteenth century was that the earlier migrants had mostly been from rural areas whereas the later migrants often included educated city dwellers.

Decolonization in the postwar period contributed to an inward flow of European colonials from overseas. The most dramatic example of this phenomenon was the more than one million French colonials who moved to France after the end of the Algerian War. British citizens returned from various parts of the British Empire; Dutch came back to the Netherlands from Indonesia; and Portuguese returned from Mozambique and Angola.

Decolonization also provoked a migration of non-European inhabitants of the former colonies to Europe. Great Britain, for example, received thousands of immigrants from India

Immigration has heightened ethnic and racial tensions throughout Europe. In 1983 major riots erupted in the south of London among immigrants to England from the West Indies. [Stuart Franklin/SYGMA]

and Pakistan as well as from some of its former African colonies. France received many immigrants from its former colonies in Indochina and the Arab world. This influx has been a source of social tension and conflict. In Great Britain, for example, racial tension was high during the 1980s, with angry clashes between the police and non-European immigrants. France has had similar difficulties, which have contributed to the emergence there of the National Front, an extreme right-wing group led by Jean-Marie LePen. This group has drawn strength from the racial and ethnic tensions that have developed as a tight job market provokes resentment among some working-class voters toward North African immigrants.

INTERNAL MIGRATION   World War II and its aftermath created a vast refugee problem. Millions of people were displaced from their homes. Many cities in Germany and in central and eastern Europe had been bombed or overrun by invading armies. Hundreds of thousands of foreign workers had been moved into Germany to contribute to the war effort. There were thousands of prisoners of war. Some of these people were returned to their homeland willingly; others, unwillingly. Changes in borders after the war also caused many people to move or be moved. For example, Poland, Czechoslovakia, and Hungary removed millions of ethnic Germans from their territories and sent them to Germany. Hundreds of thousands of Poles were transferred within Poland's new borders and out of territory taken over by the Soviet Union. Before the construction of the Berlin Wall in 1961, an estimated three million East Germans migrated to West Germany.

Once the Cold War set in, Soviet domination made it impossible for eastern Europeans to migrate to other parts of Europe, whether for political or economic reasons. As a result, until the collapse of the Soviet empire, most internal migration in Europe after the immediate postwar years occurred outside the Communist bloc.

The major motivation for internal migration from the late 1950s onward was economic opportunity. The prosperous nations of northern and western Europe had jobs that paid good wages and provided excellent benefits, often financed in part by the governments. Thus, there was a flow of workers from the poorer countries of Turkey, Greece, Yugoslavia, Italy, Spain, and Portugal into the wealthier countries of France, West Germany, Switzerland, and the Benelux nations. The establishment of the European Economic Community in 1957 made this movement of labor much easier.

The migration of workers into northern Europe grew to substantial proportions after 1960. Several hundred thousand workers would enter France and Germany each year. Virtually all these migrants settled in cities. The migrants usually were welcomed in the host countries during years of prosperity. When, however, European economies began to slow in the mid-1980s, these guest workers, as they were sometimes called, met increasing resentment. In Germany during the early 1990s, they were the targets of hostile assaults.

In the late 1980s, politics again became a major factor in European migration. The pressure of thousands of refugees seeking to escape from eastern Europe to the West contributed to the collapse of the Communist governments of eastern Europe in 1988 and 1989. Since 1989 people from all regions of eastern Europe have migrated to western European nations. The civil war in the former Yugoslavia has also created many refugees. Europe has been in recession, however, and the new migrants are generating tension, resentment, and strife. Several nations have taken legal and administrative steps to restrict migration.

URBAN EXPANSION   Since at least the eighteenth century, European populations have shifted from the countryside toward cities. This trend has become even more pronounced in the last half century. Today, except for Albania, at least one-third of the population of every European nation lives in large cities. In western Europe, city dwellers are approximately 75 percent of the population.

In nations that were already heavily urbanized, the process has continued, although at a slower rate. In other nations, such as those surrounding the Mediterranean and in eastern Europe, the process since World War II has been much more rapid.

The general effect of this urban growth has been to increase the size of cities that were already large. London, Paris, Rome, Athens, and Istanbul have, for example, experienced contin-

Youthful right-wing rioters clashed with police and threw firebombs in Rostock, Germany in August, 1992. Much of the violence was directed against foreign workers. [Reuters/Bettmann]

ued growth. The capital cities of Austria, Denmark, Finland, Greece, and Hungary embrace as much as 20 percent of their national populations. In Mediterranean Europe, the growth of metropolitan areas has been almost uncontrolled, putting enormous pressure on city services such as water, electricity, sanitation, and police, as well as housing and medical facilities. Similarly, urban growth in eastern and Mediterranean Europe has often been accompanied by serious pollution.

A Second Agricultural Revolution

Never in history has so much food in so many varieties been available in Europe; however, never have fewer Europeans been involved in agriculture—approximately 10 percent. This development is, of course, the reverse process of the growth of cities. Agriculture remains, however, a major element in the European economy and one that has experienced major changes in the past half century.

The years of the Great Depression and World War II saw a steep drop in agricultural production in Europe. The farm sector was naturally among the hardest hit as the worldwide commodities crisis spread. The two decades after the war, however, saw a remarkable recovery and increase in production and productivity. European farming became more mechanized. New kinds of fertilizers were introduced, and better methods were developed to control diseases that afflicted crops. Although not without problems—in the Netherlands, for example, the use of fertilizers has raised growing environmental concerns—these changes have roughly doubled European agricultural production. The result has been nothing less than a second agricultural revolution.

The agricultural policies of the European Economic Community sought to foster medium-sized farms. The Communist governments of eastern Europe sought to create large collective farms. Agricultural policies in eastern Europe were mostly ineffective, but collectivization did increase the amount of land tilled. Across Europe, the amount of land under cultivation expanded until the 1970s.

One result of changes in landholding has been the disappearance of the peasant in western Europe. In France, for example, there are now virtually no peasants, whereas before World War II they still constituted most of the farming population.

The Welfare State

The Great Depression, the rise of authoritarian states, and the experience of World War II, which saw larger groups of people involved in a war effort than ever before, led to a marked change in thinking about social welfare in Europe. The result was the emergence of the modern European welfare state.

The forces that created the welfare state are complex and differed from country to country. Before World War II, except in Scandinavia, there were two basic models for social legislation: the German and the British. Bismarck had introduced some forms of social insurance in Germany during the 1880s. His purpose was to undermine the influence of the German Social Democratic Party. In effect, he had the imperial German government provide workers with social insurance and thus some sense of social security while denying them significant political participation. In early-twentieth-century Great Britain, where all classes had access to the political system, social insurance was targeted toward the very poor. According to both approaches, workers should be insured against the risks arising from disease, injury on the job, and old age. Although various legislative efforts had been made to address unemployment, it was assumed to be only a short-term problem and often one that workers brought on themselves. People higher up in the social structure were assumed to be able to look out for themselves and not to need help.

After World War II, the concept emerged that social insurance against predictable risks was a right and should be universally available to all citizens. This concept had been most famously set forth in Great Britain by William B. Beveridge (1879–1963) in 1942. Paradoxically, making coverage universal, as Beveridge recommended,

was attractive to conservatives as well as socialists. If medical care, old age pensions, and other benefits were available to all, they would not be seen as a device for redistributing income from one portion of the population to another.

The first European nation to begin the creation of a welfare state was Great Britain during the Labour Party ministry of Clement Attlee (1883–1967). The most important element of this early legislation was the creation of the National Health Service. Similar health care legislation was not adopted in France and Germany until the 1970s because the governments of those countries initially refused to consider making coverage universal.

The spread of welfare legislation (including various forms of unemployment insurance) within western Europe was closely related to the Cold War as well as to domestic political and economic policy. The Communist states were promising their people enormous social security as well as full employment. The capitalists states came to believe that they must respond in their own way by producing similar security for their people. In point of fact, the social security of the Communist states was often more a matter of rhetoric than reality.

The systems of government-furnished services now found across Europe in varying forms are beginning to encounter resistance. The payment systems on which they are based assume a growing population. As the proportion of the population consuming the services of the welfare state—the sick, the injured, and the elderly—increases relative to the able-bodied employed population that pays for them, the costs of those services rise. The significant leveling off of population growth in Europe thus places the benefits of the welfare state in some peril.

New Patterns in the Work and Expectations of Women

The decades since World War II have witnessed striking changes in the work patterns and the social expectations of women. In all social ranks, women have begun to assume larger economic and political roles. Women have entered the learned professions and are filling more major managerial positions than ever before in European history.

More Married Women in the Workforce

One of the patterns firmly established at the turn of the century has reversed itself. The number of married women in the workforce has sharply risen. Both middle-class and working-class married women have sought jobs outside the home. Because of the rather low birthrate in the 1930s, there were not many young single women to be employed in the years just after the war. Married women entered the job market to replace them. Some factories changed their work shifts to accommodate the needs of married women. Consumer conveniences and improvements in health care also made it easier for married women to enter the workforce by reducing somewhat the demands of child care on their time.

In the twentieth century, children have no longer been expected to make substantial contributions to family income. They now spend large amounts of their time in compulsory schools. When families need more income than one worker can provide, both parents will work, bringing many married women with children into the workforce. Such financial necessity led many married women back to work. Consid-

erable evidence also suggests that married women began to work to escape the boredom of housework and to find company among other female workers.

New Work Patterns

In the late twentieth century, the work pattern of European women has displayed much more continuity than it had in the nineteenth century. Single women enter the workforce after their schooling and continue to work after marriage. They might withdraw from the workforce to care for young children but return when the children begin school. Several factors created this new pattern, but women's increasing life expectancy is one of the most important.

When married women died relatively young, child rearing filled a large proportion of their lives. The lengthening life span has meant that child rearing occupies a much smaller proportion of women's lives. Consequently, women throughout the Western world have new concerns about how they will spend those years when they are not involved with rearing children. The age at which women have decided to bear children has risen. Women have tended to bear children in their early twenties in eastern Europe and in their late twenties in western Europe. In urban areas, childbearing is later and the birthrate lower than elsewhere.

In Europe, as in the United States, women have gained access to new roles and opportunities. Geraldine Bridgewater was the first woman to hold a seat on the London Stock Exchange. [Gamma-Liaison]

Many women have begun to choose to limit sharply the number of children they bear or to forgo childbearing and child rearing altogether. Both men and women continue to expect to marry. But the new careers open to women and the desire of couples to maintain as high a standard of living as possible has contributed to the declining birthrate mentioned earlier in the chapter.

Women in the New Eastern Europe

Many paradoxes surround the situation of women in eastern Europe now that it is no longer governed by Communists. Under communism, women generally enjoyed social equality as well as a broad spectrum of government-financed benefits. A significant proportion (normally well over 50 percent) of women worked in these societies both because they could and because it was expected of them. There were, however, no significant women's movements since they, like all independent associations, were regarded with suspicion.

The new governments of the region are free, but have so far shown little concern toward women's issues. The economic difficulties faced by the new governments may endanger the funding of various health and welfare programs that benefit women and children. For example, it is uncertain that a free market economy will allow eastern European women the extensive maternity benefits to which they were previously entitled. Moreover, the high proportion of women in the workforce could leave them more vulnerable than men to the region's economic troubles. Women may well find themselves being laid off before men and hired into new jobs later than men.

Transformations in Knowledge and Culture

The realms of knowledge and culture have rapidly transformed themselves in the twentieth century. Institutions of higher education have reached out to an increasingly large and diverse student body, making knowledge more widely available than ever before. Also, intellectual movements, such as existentialism, have challenged many traditional intellectual attitudes. Concerns about the environment have also brought new issues to the fore. Throughout this ferment, representatives of the Christian faith have tried to keep the message of their religion relevant.

Communism and Western Europe

Throughout this century, western Europe has had organized Communist parties as well as groups of intellectuals sympathetic to communism. The relationship of these groups to the western European political experience must be seen in a context that goes back to the Bolshevik victory itself. That event in 1917 cast all pre–World War I European socialism into disarray. The western European socialist movement rapidly divided into independent democratic socialist parties and Soviet-dominated Communist parties that followed the directions of the Third International. Throughout the 1920s and 1930s, those two groups fought against each other with only rare moments of cooperation, as during the French Popular Front in 1936. European left-wing intellectuals divided between those who supported socialism and those who supported communism. The results of those divisions and debates have continued to influence western European political life through the 1990s.

THE INTELLECTUALS During the 1930s, as liberal democracies floundered during the Great Depression and as right-wing regimes spread across the Continent, communism appeared to many people at the time as a vehicle for protecting humane and even liberal values. Throughout Europe, students in the universities were often affiliated with the Communist Party. They and older intellectuals visited the Soviet Union and praised Stalin's achievements. Some of these writers did not know of Stalin's terror; others simply closed their eyes to it, somehow believing that humane ends might come from inhuman methods; still others actually defended Stalinist terror. During the late 1920s and the 1930s, communism became for some Europeans little less than a substitute religion. One group of former Communists, writing after

George Orwell (1903–1950), shown here with his son, was an English writer of socialist sympathies who wrote major works opposing Stalin and Communist authoritarianism. [Bildarchiv Preussischer Kulturbesitz]

World War II, described their attraction and later disillusionment with communism in a book entitled *The God That Failed* (1949).

Four events proved crucial to the disillusionment of the intellectuals. These were the great public purge trials of 1936 and later, the Spanish Civil War (1936–1939), the Nazi–Soviet pact of 1939, and the Soviet invasion of Hungary in 1956. Arthur Koestler's (1905–1983) novel *Darkness at Noon* (1940) recorded a former Communist's view of the purges. George Orwell, who had never been a Communist but who had sympathized, presented his disappointment

with Stalin's policy in Spain in *Homage to Catalonia* (1938). The Nazi–Soviet pact destroyed the image of Stalin as an opponent of Fascism. Other intellectuals, such as the French philosopher Jean-Paul Sartre, continued to put faith in the Soviet Union through the war, but the Hungarian Revolution cooled his ardor. The later invasion of Czechoslovakia simply confirmed a general disillusionment with Soviet policies on the part of even left-wing western European intellectuals.

Yet disillusionment with the Soviet Union or with Stalin did not in all cases mean disillusionment with Marxism or with radical socialist criticism of European society. Some writers and social critics looked to the establishment of alternative Communist governments based on non-Soviet models. During the decade after World War II, Yugoslavia provided the example of such a different path. Beginning in the late 1950s, radical students and a few intellectuals looked for inspiration to the Chinese Revolution. Other groups hoped for the development of a European Marxist system. Among the more important contributors to this non-Soviet tradition was the Italian Communist Antonio Gramsci (1891–1937) and his work *Letters from Prison* (published posthumously in 1947). The thought of such non-Soviet Communists became very important to western European Communist parties, such as that of Italy, which hoped to gain office democratically.

Another way to accommodate Marxism within mid-twentieth-century European thought was to redefine the basic message of Marx himself. During the 1930s, a considerable body of previously unprinted essays by Marx was published. These books and articles, written before the *Communist Manifesto* of 1848, are quite abstract and philosophical. They make the "young Marx" appear to belong more nearly to the humanist than to the revolutionary tradition of European thought. Since World War II, these works, including *Philosophic Manuscripts of 1844* and *German Ideology*, have been widely read. Today many people are more familiar with them than with the *Manifesto* or *Capital*. They have allowed some people to consider themselves sympathetic to Marxism without also seeing themselves as revolutionaries or supporters of the Soviet Union. With the collapse of the

Communist governments of eastern Europe and the Soviet Union, it is now unclear what influence Marxism will continue to have on European intellectual life in the future.

THE RISE AND FALL OF EUROCOMMUNISM During the 1970s and early 1980s, a form of Marxism known as Eurocommunism appeared to be developing in western Europe. This new Marxist alternative tried to accommodate western European Communist parties to the political realities of their positions in successfully functioning liberal democracies. The chief architect of this strategy was Enrico Berlinguer (1922–1984), the leader of the Italian Communist Party, which was the largest and best organized in western Europe. The strategy was carried farther in Italy than in any other state.

During the mid-1970s, weariness with the corruption of the Christian Democratic Party, which had governed Italy since shortly after World War II, allowed the Italian Communist Party to make significant political gains. They won many municipal elections and then, in 1976, won more than 35 percent of the popular vote for the Chamber of Deputies. They were, however, refused a place in the cabinet. In an effort to gain entry into this real arena of government, Berlinguer at that point set forth a policy that became known as the Historic Compromise.

Berlinguer's policy represented a major break not only with the previous stand of the Italian Communist Party but also with the Moscow-dominated Communist movement. With the "historic compromise," Berlinguer announced the willingness of the Italian Communist Party to enter a coalition government with the Christian Democrats and non-Communist parties. Thus, the Italian Communists in effect renounced revolution as the path to political power. They also agreed to participate in a government that they would not dominate or control. The Italian Communist Party also promised that as a partner in the coalition or as the governing party, should it be elected, it would govern constitutionally and would respect individuals' civil liberties. It also urged continued Italian participation in NATO and criticized the crackdown on Solidarity in Poland.

The "historic compromise" was never put to the test in Italy. There is little evidence voters believed the Communists would keep their word once in power. The Italian Communists reached their electoral peak in the early 1980s. Berlinguer died in 1984 and no strong successor emerged. The importance of Eurocommunism may have been overestimated at the time. Yet it marked still another development in the evolution of the Communist movement in the West and in its attempts to separate itself from the Soviet model.

Western European Communist parties found their position entirely transformed during the second half of the 1980s. Radical reform began in the Soviet Union, Communist governments collapsed in eastern Europe, and western electorates became more conservative. In the wake of these developments, western Europe's Communist parties reorganized themselves and, often with great irony considering the struggles of the 1930s, dropped the term "Communist" and relabeled themselves as some form of "socialist" party.

Existentialism

The intellectual movement that perhaps best captured the predicament and mood of mid-twentieth-century European culture was existentialism. Like the modern Western mind in general, existentialism, which has been termed the philosophy of Europe in the twentieth century, was badly divided; most of the philosophers associated with it disagreed with each other on major issues. The movement represented in part a continuation of the revolt against reason that began in the nineteenth century.

ROOTS IN NIETZSCHE AND KIERKEGAARD Friedrich Nietzsche, discussed in Chapter 25, was one of the major forerunners of existentialism. Another was the Danish writer Søren Kierkegaard (1813–1855), who wrote during the second quarter of the nineteenth century but received little attention until after World War I. Kierkegaard was a rebel against both the Hegelian philosophy and the Lutheran Christianity he encountered in Denmark. In works such as *Fear and Trembling* (1843), *Either/Or* (1843), and *Concluding Unscientific Postscript* (1846), he maintained that the truth of Christianity could not be contained in creeds, doctrines, and church organizations. It could be grasped only in the living experience of those who faced extreme human situations.

Kierkegaard also criticized Hegelian philosophy and, by implication, all modes of academic rational philosophy. Its failure, he felt, was the attempt to contain all of life and human experience within abstract categories. Kierkegaard spurned this faith in the power of mere reason. "The conclusions of passion," he once declared, "are the only reliable ones."[2]

The intellectual and ethical crisis of World War I brought Kierkegaard's thought to the fore and also created new interest in Nietzsche's critique of reason. The war led many people to doubt whether human beings were actually in control of their own destiny. Its destructiveness challenged faith in human rationality and improvement. Indeed, the war's most terrible weapons were the products of rational technology. The pride in rational human achievement that had characterized much nineteenth-century European civilization lay in ruins. The sunny faith in rational human development and advancement had not withstood the extreme experiences of war.

QUESTIONING OF RATIONALISM Existentialist thought came to thrive in this climate and received further support from the trauma of World War II. The major existential writers included the Germans Martin Heidegger (1889–1976) and Karl Jaspers (1883–1969) and the French Jean-Paul Sartre (1905–1980) and Albert Camus (1913–1960). Their books are often very difficult and in some cases simply obscure. Although they frequently disagreed with each other, they all, in one way or another, questioned the primacy of reason and scientific understanding as ways of coming to grips with the human situation. Heidegger went so far as to argue, "Thinking only begins at the point where we have come to know that Reason, glorified for centuries, is the most obstinate adversary of thinking."[3]

The tradition of the Enlightenment suggested that analysis, or the separation of human expe-

Jean-Paul Sartre (1905–1980) and Simone de Beauvoir (1908–1986) were two leading mid-century French intellectuals. His was a major voice in the existentialist movement, and she wrote extensively on the social position, experience, and psychology of women. [Bildarchiv Preussischer Kulturbesitz]

rience into its component parts, was the proper path to understanding. Existential writers rejected this approach. They argued that the human condition was greater than the sum of its parts and must be grasped as a whole.

The Romantic writers of the early nineteenth century had also questioned the primacy of reason, but they did so in a much less radical manner than the existentialists. The Romantics emphasized the imagination and intuition, but the existentialists dwelled primarily on the extremes of human experience. Death, dread, fear, and anxiety provided their themes. The titles of their works illustrate their sense of foreboding and alienation: *Being and Time* (1927) by Heidegger; *Nausea* (1938) and *Being and Nothingness* (1943) by Sartre; *The Stranger* (1942) and *The Plague* (1947) by Camus. The touchstone of philosophic truth became the experience of the individual under extreme conditions.

According to the existentialists, human beings are compelled to formulate their own ethical values and cannot depend on ethical guidance from traditional religion, rational philosophy, intuition, or social customs. The

[2]*Quoted in Walter Kaufman, ed.,* Existentialism from Dostoevsky to Sartre *(Cleveland: The World Publishing Company, 1962), p. 18.*

[3]*Quoted in William Barrett,* Irrational Man *(Garden City, N.Y.: Doubleday, 1962), p. 20.*

Sartre Discusses the Character of His Existentialism

Jean-Paul Sartre, dramatist, novelist, and philosopher, was the most important French existentialist. In the first paragraph of this 1946 statement, Sartre assert- ed that all human beings must experience a sense of anguish or the most extreme anxiety when undertaking a major commitment. That anguish arises because consciously or unconsciously they are deciding whether all human beings should make the same decision. In the second paragraph, Sartre argued that the existence or nonexistence of God would make no difference in human affairs. What humankind must do is to discover the character of its own situation by itself.

◆ *How might the experiences of Fascism in Europe and the fall of France to the Nazis have led Sartre to emphasize the need of human beings to choose? Why does Sartre believe existentialism must necessarily be related to atheism? Why did Sartre regard existentialism as optimistic?*

The existentialist frankly states that man is in anguish. His meaning is as follows—When a man commits himself to anything, fully realiz- ing that he is not only choosing what he will be, but is thereby at the same time a legislator deciding for the whole of mankind—in such a moment a man cannot escape from the sense of complete and profound responsibility. There are many, indeed, who show no such anxiety. But we affirm that they are merely disguising their anguish or are in flight from it. Certainly, many people think that in what they are doing they commit no one but themselves to any- thing: and if you ask them, "What would hap- pen if everyone did so?" they shrug their shoulders and reply, "Everyone does not do so." But in truth, one ought always to ask one- self what would happen if everyone did as one is doing; nor can one escape from that disturb- ing thought except by a kind of self-deception. The man who lies in self-excuse, by saying "Everyone will not do it" must be ill at ease in his conscience, for the act of lying implies the universal value which it denies. By its very dis- guise his anguish reveals itself.

Existentialism is nothing else but an attempt to draw the full conclusions from a consistently atheistic position. Its intention is not in the least that of plunging men into despair. And if by despair one means—as the Christians do—any attitude of unbelief, the despair of the existentialist is something dif- ferent. Existentialism is not atheist in the sense that it would exhaust itself in demon- stration of the nonexistence of God. It declares, rather, that even if God existed that would make no difference from its point of view. Not that we believe God does exist, but we think that the real problem is not that of His existence; what man needs is to find himself again and to understand that noth- ing can save him from himself, not even a valid proof of the existence of God. In this sense existentialism is optimistic. It is a doc- trine of action, and it is only by self-decep- tion, by confusing their own despair with ours that Christians can describe us as with- out hope.

Jean-Paul Sartre, Existentialism and Humanism, *trans. by Philip Mairet (London: Methuen), in Walter Kaufman, ed.,* Existentialism from Dostoevsky to Sartre *(New York: Meridian Books, 1956), pp. 292, 310–311.*

opportunity and need to define values endow humans with a dreadful freedom.

The existentialists largely were protesting against a world in which reason, technology, and politics produced only war and genocide. Their thought reflected the uncertainty of social institutions and ethical values in the era of the two world wars. Since the 1950s, however, their works and ideas have found their way into university curriculums around the world, making them objects of study if not the source of intellectual ferment they had been. They will probably continue to be subjects of philosophy and literature classes, but it is unlikely that they will again achieve their former popularity.

An attraction to communism and existentialism was very much a characteristic of European intellectuals before and just after World War II. The 1960s, with the turmoil over Vietnam and the youth rebellion, brought other intellectual and social factors to the fore. Even before the collapse of communism, these had begun to redirect European intellectual interests.

Expansion of the University Population and Student Rebellion

As rapid changes in communications technology have vastly expanded access to information, increasing numbers of Europeans have received some form of university education. At the turn of the century, no more than a few thousand people were enrolled in universities in any major European country. By the 1980s that figure had risen to hundreds of thousands, though university education is still less common in Europe than in the United States. Higher education is now available to people from a variety of social and economic backgrounds and, for the first time, readily available to women.

This expanding population of university-educated people is closely related to a surge of intense self-criticism among Europeans. Millions of citizens have acquired the critical intellectual skills and familiarity with critical writers that in previous centuries were usually the preserve of small literate elites. Television has given critical voices an even wider audience. Indeed, in Great Britain, the Open University uses television to provide university training to thousands of people.

Previously known only to a privileged few, the "student experience"—leaving home and settling for several years in a community composed primarily of late adolescents—has come to be widely shared. Since World War II, it has become a major feature of European society.

The expanding student population in Europe and elsewhere required an increase also in the number of university teachers. As a result, there have been more scientists, historians, economists, literary critics, and other professional intellectuals during the last seventy-five years than in all previous human history. Not since the early years of the Reformation have university intellectuals exerted such widespread influence. The major intellectual developments of the seventeenth, eighteenth, and nineteenth centuries took place primarily outside the university. In the twentieth century, the university has become the most likely home for the intellectual. And the symbol of success for a writer in almost any field has been the inclusion of his or her work in the university curriculum.

One of the most striking and unexpected results of this rising population of students and intellectuals was the student rebellion of the 1960s. This development is still not well understood. Student uprisings began in the early 1960s in the United States and assumed major proportions as opposition grew to the war in Vietnam. The student rebellion then spread into Europe and other parts of the world. It was almost always associated with a radical political critique of the United States, although in eastern Europe some resentment was directed toward the Soviet Union. The movement was generally antimilitarist. In addition to their political concerns, students questioned middle-class values, traditional sexual mores, and traditional family life.

The student movement reached its high point in 1968. That year, students in the United States participated in demonstrations against U.S. involvement in Vietnam. The same year, students at the Sorbonne in Paris instigated a serious challenge to the government of Charles de Gaulle. Students were also in the forefront of the liberal socialist experiment in Czechoslovakia during 1968. These protests ultimately failed to redirect in an immediate manner the policies of the governments at which they were

The Russian rock group "Dynamic" performs in Moscow in 1987. Rock music has been a hallmark of European and American culture since the 1960s. In the 1970s and 1980s rock music and its lyrics emerged as a major vehicle for cultural and political criticism in Eastern Europe and the Soviet Union. [ITAR-TASS/SOVFOTO]

directed. The United States remained in Vietnam for several more years. De Gaulle's government survived the challenge of May 1968. The Soviets suppressed the Czech experiment.

By the early 1970s, the era of student rebellion seemed to have passed. Students remained active in European movements against nuclear weapons and particularly against the placement of American nuclear weapons in Germany and elsewhere in Europe. From the middle of the 1970s, however, although often maintaining a radical political stance, they generally abandoned the kind of disruptive protests that marked the 1960s.

Students and Popular Music

Nothing has so characterized both student and youth culture in the second half of the twentieth century as rock music, which first emerged in the 1950s. Now part of the fabric of contemporary European life, rock music abounds on radio and television. The lyrics of the Beatles, the British rock group that became wildly popular on both sides of the Atlantic in the 1960s, may be by now the most widely dispersed poetry in the history of the world. Rock had a universality that appealed across national and cultural borders. It did as much to create a more uniform

European culture as advertising or the economic freedom provided by the European Economic Community.

Rock music became part of a continuing critique of contemporary society. Many lyrics emphasized the need for love, the anguish of isolation, a desire for sexual liberation, and hopes for community and peace. During the 1960s, rock music in the West was an integral feature of the antiwar movement and a vehicle for expressing discontent with the older generation. In the 1970s and 1980s, it emerged as a major vehicle for cultural and political criticism in eastern Europe and the Soviet Union. Rock stars came to symbolize daring and even heroism. Their music emphasized subjectivity and individualism. Lyrics directly criticized Communist governments, as in this example from "Get Out of Control," sung at a rock concert in Leningrad in 1986:

We were watched from the days of kindergarten.
Some nice men and kind women
Beat us up. They chose the most painful places
And treated us like animals on the farm.
So we grew up like a disciplined herd.
We sing what they want and live how they want
And we look at them downside up, as if we're trapped.

We just watch how they hit us
Get out of control!
Get out of control!
And sing what you want
And not just what is allowed
We have a right to yell![4]

This song later became popular throughout eastern Europe. Sentiments like these were common in popular songs and undoubtedly contributed to the dramatic changes that swept through the region.

Environmentalism

Consumer goods were in short supply after World War II, creating a demand that fueled postwar economic reconstruction and growth into the 1950s and 1960s. There was little room for public debate in this period about the ethics of economic expansion and efficiency and their effects on the environment. Concerns about the environment began to emerge in the 1970s, and by the 1980s had developed real political clout. Environmental groups gained public and political prominence. Among the most important of these were the Club of Rome, founded in 1972, and the German Greens. The Greens formed a political party in 1979 that immediately became an electoral force.

Several developments lay behind this new concern about dangers to the environment. The Arab oil embargo of 1973–1974 pressed home to Europeans that natural resources are limited and that they were dependent for many of them on foreign supplies. By the 1970s, the environmental consequences of three decades of economic expansion were becoming increasingly apparent. Fish were dying in the Thames River in England. Industrial pollution was destroying the rivers of Germany and France. Acid rain had begun to kill trees throughout Germany. Finally, long-standing apprehensions about nuclear weapons merged with concerns about their environmental effects to strengthen antinuclear groups and generate opposition to the placement of nuclear weapons in Europe.

[4]Quoted in Artemy Troitsky, Back in the USSR: The True Story of Rock in Russia (Boston: Faber & Faber, 1987), p. 127, as cited in Sabrina P. Ramet, Social Currents in Eastern Europe: The Sources and Meaning of the Great Transformation (Durham, N.C.: Duke University Press, 1991), p. 239.

The German Green movement originated among the radical student groups of the late 1960s. It shared with them an anticapitalist point of view, holding business responsible for pollution. The Greens and other European environmental groups also assumed a strong antinuclear position. Unlike the students of the 1960s, the Greens avoided violence and mass demonstrations. Rather, they sought to enter the electoral process directly. They succeeded in electing a few representatives to the West German Parliament as well as to local offices.

The 1986 disaster at the Chernobyl nuclear reactor in the Soviet Union heightened concern about environmental issues and raised questions that no European government could ignore. The Soviet government had to confront deaths and injuries at the site and had to relocate tens of thousands of people. Clouds of radioactive fallout spread westward across Europe. Environmentalists had always contended that their issues transcended national borders. The Chernobyl fire proved them right.

In the wake of Chernobyl, virtually all European governments, east and west, have begun to respond to environmental concerns. Some observers believe the environment may become a major political issue across the Continent. In western Europe, environmental groups command a significant share of votes. Economic and political integration opens the possibility of transnational cooperation on environmental matters. As the European Economic Community solidifies, the Community and its member nations will likely move to impose environmental regulations on business and industry. The nations of eastern Europe face the daunting task of cleaning up vast areas polluted by industrial development during the Communist era and devising policies that combine environmental protection with economic growth.

Developments in Feminism

Since World War II, European feminism, although less highly organized than American feminism, has set forth a new agenda. The most widely read postwar work on women's issues was undoubtedly Simone de Beauvoir's (1908–1986) The Second Sex, published in 1949. In that work, de Beauvoir tried to explore

World Leaders Point to the Problems of the Environment

In 1989 leaders of the major industrialized nations, including the United States, Japan, Canada, the United Kingdom, France, Germany, and Italy, gathered in Paris for an annual summit meeting. In this statement, they addressed themselves to the problem of preserving and cleaning up the environment.

◆ *What evidence is cited for a world environmental crisis? Why does the crisis require international cooperation? How did the signers of this statement see environmental issues related to economic issues?*

There is growing awareness throughout the world of the necessity to preserve better the global ecological balance. This includes serious threats to the atmosphere, which could lead to future climate changes. We note with great concern the growing pollution of air, lakes, rivers, oceans and seas; acid rain; dangerous substances; and the rapid desertification and deforestation. . . .

Decisive action is urgently needed to understand and protect the Earth's ecological balance. We will work together to achieve the common goals of preserving a healthy and balanced global environment in order to meet shared economic and social objectives. . . .

We urge all countries to give further impetus to scientific research on environmental issues, to develop necessary technologies and to make clear evaluations of the economic costs and benefits. . . .

In this connection, we ask all countries to combine their efforts in order to improve observation and monitoring on a global scale. . . .

We believe that international cooperation also needs to be enhanced in the field of technology and technology transfer in order to reduce pollution. . . .

We believe that industry has a crucial role in preventing pollution at the source, in waste minimization, in energy conservation, and in the design and marketing of cost-effective clean technologies. The agricultural sector must also contribute to tackling problems such as water pollution, soil erosion and desertification. . . .

Environmental protection is integral to issues such as trade, development, energy, transport, agriculture and economic planning. Therefore, environmental considerations must be taken into account in economic decision-making.

The New York Times, July 17, 1989, p. A7.

---

the difference it had made in her life to be a woman rather than a man. She was very much a part of the French intellectual establishment and thus wrote from a privileged position. Over the years, however, she and other European women came to argue that within European culture women experienced distinct social and economic disadvantages. They pointed out the legal inequalities to which women were subject, such as laws relating to divorce and the family, and the social problems that were particular to them, such as spousal abuse.

In contrast to earlier feminism, recent feminism has been less a political movement pressing for specific rights than a social movement offering a broader critique of European culture. More radical European feminists have asserted that their society, as presently organized, inherently represses women. They have been equally critical of all political parties—from conservative to socialist—that avoid a full airing of women's issues. Several new feminist publications appeared during the 1970s, many of which are still publishing. These include *Courage,*

Environmental activists on a research tour of Russia's Lake Baikal in part of an effort to save the lake. European governments, both east and west, have increasingly had to confront environmental issues. [Boyd Norton]

Emma—Magazine by Women for Women, and *Spare Rib.* A statement in *Spare Rib,* an English magazine, captures the spirit of these publications:

Spare Rib aims to reflect women's lives in all their diverse situations so that they can recognize themselves in its pages. This is done by making the magazine a vehicle for their writing and their images. Most of all, *Spare Rib* aims to bring women together and support them in taking control of their lives.[5]

This emphasis on women controlling their own lives may be the most important element of recent feminism. Whereas in the past feminists sought and in significant measure gained legal and civil equality with men, they have now turned their attention to the pursuit of personal independence and issues that are particular to women.

[5]*Quoted in Bonnie S. Anderson and Judith P. Zinsser,* A History of Their Own: Women in Europe from Prehistory to the Present, *Vol. 2 (New York: Harper Perennial, 1988), p. 412.*

The women's movement and the environmental movement have come to play a significant, new role in European politics and culture. The collapse of communism in eastern Europe has raised questions about socialism and challenged the credibility of the cultural criticism it has generated. Feminist and environmental groups now provide the continuing critique of society that had been the role of socialist parties. In this sense, feminism is an important manifestation of the critical tradition that has long been part of Western culture.

The Christian Heritage

In most ways, Christianity has continued to be as hard-pressed during the twentieth century as it had been in the late nineteenth. Material prosperity, political ideologies, environmentalism, gender politics, and simple indifference to religion have replaced religious faith as the dominant factor in many people's lives. Despite the loss of much of their popular support and former legal privileges, however, the European Christian churches still exercise considerable social and political influence. In Germany, the churches were one of the few major institutions not wholly subdued by the Nazis. Lutheran clergymen, such as Martin Niemöller and Dietrich Bonhoeffer (1906–1945), were leaders of the opposition to Hitler. After the war, in Poland and elsewhere in eastern Europe, the Roman Catholic church actively opposed the influence of communism.

In western Europe, religious affiliation provided much of the initial basis for the Christian Democratic parties. Across Europe, the churches have raised critical questions about colonialism, nuclear weapons, human rights, and other moral issues. Consequently, even in this most secular of all ages, Christian churches have influenced many issues of state and society.

Neo-Orthodoxy

Liberal theologians of the nineteenth century often softened the concept of sin and portrayed human nature as not very far removed from the divine. The horror of World War I destroyed that optimistic faith, leaving many Europeans feeling that evil had stalked the continent.

The most important Christian response to this experience appeared in the theology of Karl Barth (1886–1968). In 1919 this Swiss pastor published *A Commentary on the Epistle to the Romans*, which reemphasized the transcendence of God and the dependence of humankind on the divine. Barth portrayed God as wholly other than, and different from, humankind. In a sense, Barth was returning to the Reformation theology of Luther, but the work of Kierkegaard had profoundly influenced his reading of the reformer. Barth, like the Danish writer, regarded the lived experience of men and women as the best testimony to the truth of his theology. Those extreme moments of life described by Kierkegaard provided the basis for a real knowledge of humankind's need for God.

This view challenged outright much nineteenth-century writing about human nature. Barth's theology, which came to be known as neo-orthodoxy, proved very influential throughout the West in the wake of new disasters and suffering.

Liberal Theology

Neo-orthodoxy did not, however, sweep away liberal theology, which had a strong advocate in Paul Tillich (1886–1965). This German-American theologian tended to regard religion as a human rather than a divine phenomenon. Whereas Barth saw God as dwelling outside humankind, Tillich believed that evidence of the divine had to be sought in human nature and human culture.

Other liberal theologians, such as Rudolf Bultmann (1884–1976), continued to work on the problems of naturalism and supernaturalism that had troubled earlier writers. Bultmann's major writing took place before World War II but was popularized thereafter in Anglican Bishop John Robinson's *Honest To God* (1963). Another liberal Christian writer from Britain, C. S. Lewis (1878–1963), attracted millions of readers during and after World War II. This layman and scholar of medieval literature often expressed his thoughts on theology in the form of letters and short stories. His most famous work is *The Screwtape Letters* (1942). In recent years, however, there have been few major Protestant voices in European religious thought.

Roman Catholic Reform

Among Christian denominations, the most significant postwar changes have been in the Roman Catholic church. Pope John XXIII (r. 1958–1963) initiated these changes, the most extensive in Catholicism for more than a century and, some would say, since the Council of Trent in the sixteenth century. In 1959 Pope John summoned the twenty-first ecumenical council (the first had been called by the emperor Constantine in the fourth century), which came to be called Vatican II. The council finished its work in 1965 under John's successor, Pope Paul VI (r. 1963–1978). Among many changes in Catholic liturgy, the council ended the practice of celebrating the Mass in Latin, requiring it instead to be recited in the vernacular. It also permitted freer relations with other Christian denominations and gave more power to bishops. In recognition of the growing importance to the Church of the world outside Europe and North America, Pope Paul also appointed several cardinals from nations of the former colonial world,

Pope John Paul II Discusses International Social Justice

Pope John Paul II issued his encyclical The Social Concerns of the Church *in 1988. In the passages given here, he attempted to set concerns for justice among developed and developing nations into the larger context of Christian moral theology.*

♦ *How does the pope relate the fate of poorest nations to the international system of trade and finance? What evidence is there that the pope did not favor radical social action on the part of Roman Catholic clergy? How does this encyclical illustrate the pope's concerns for non-European parts of the world?*

The Church's social doctrine is not a "third way" between liberal capitalism and Marxist collectivism, nor even a possible alternative to other solutions less radically opposed to one another: rather, it constitutes a category of its own. Nor is it an ideology, but rather the accurate formulation of the results of a careful reflection on the complex realities of human existence, in society and in the international order, in the light of faith and of the Church's tradition. Its main aim is to interpret these realities, determining their conformity with or divergence from the lines of the Gospel teaching on man and his vocation, a vocation which is at once earthly and transcendent; its aim is thus to guide Christian behavior. It therefore belongs to the field, not of ideology, but of theology and particularly moral theology.

The international trade system today frequently discriminates against the products of the young industries of the developing countries and discourages the producers of raw materials. There exists, too, a kind of international division of labor, whereby the low-cost products of certain countries which lack effective labor laws or which are too weak to apply them are sold in other parts of the world at considerable profit for the companies engaged in this form of production, which knows not frontiers. . . .

. . . [H]umanity today is in a new and more difficult phase of its genuine development. It needs a greater degree of international ordering, at the service of the societies, economies and cultures of the whole world.

It is desirable, for example, that nations of the same geographical area should establish forms of cooperation which will make them less dependent on more powerful producers; they should open their frontiers to the products of the area; they should examine how their products might complement one another; they should combine in order to set up those services which each one separately is incapable of providing; they should extend cooperation to the monetary and financial sector.

The Church well knows that no temporal achievement is to be identified with the Kingdom of God, but that all such achievements simply reflect and in a sense anticipate the glory of the Kingdom, the Kingdom which we await at the end of history, when the Lord will come again. But that expectation can never be an excuse for lack of concern for people in their concrete personal situations and in their social, national, and international life, since the former is conditioned by the latter, especially today.

The New York Times, February 20, 1988, p. 4.

Pope John Paul II, elected in 1978, is the first non-Italian pope since 1522. He has reasserted traditional Roman Catholic practices and values while also emphasizing the Church's commitment to social justice. [Gamma-Liaison]

has encouraged the expansion of the Church in the non-Western world, stressing the need for social justice but limiting the political activity of priests.

Finally, he took a firm and important stand against communism and directly contributed to the spirit of freedom in eastern Europe that brought an end to the Communist regimes. As a cardinal in Poland he had clashed with Poland's Communist government. After his election, he visited Poland, lending support to the activities of the Solidarity movement. There is no question that his Polish origins helped make him an important factor in the popular resistance to eastern Europe's Communist governments that developed during the 1980s. In this respect, his actions, both public and private, opened a new chapter in the relationship between Church and state in modern Europe.

The Collapse of European Communism

The events of the past decade in eastern Europe and the former Soviet Union are among the most important of this century. They occurred rapidly and quite unexpectedly. They will influence not only the political future of Europe but also its economic and social life. In 1980 most observers believed that the Soviet Union would remain a major military power and dominate eastern Europe indefinitely. Although internal forces had long been undermining Soviet authority, what brought those forces to a head and began the dramatic collapse of the Soviet empire was the accession to power of Mikhail S. Gorbachev (b. 1931).

Gorbachev Redirects the Soviet Union

Brezhnev died in 1982. Both of his immediate successors, Yuri Andropov (1914–1984) and Constantin Chernenko (1911–1985), died after holding office for very short periods. In 1985 Mikhail S. Gorbachev came to power. In what proved to be the last great attempt to reform the Soviet system and eliminate its repressive Stalinist heritage, he immediately set about making the most remarkable changes that the Soviet Union had witnessed since the 1920s.

transforming the Church into a truly world body.

In contrast to these liberal changes, however, Pope Paul and his successors have firmly upheld the celibacy of priests, maintained the Church's prohibition on contraception, and opposed moves to open the priesthood to women. The Church's unyielding stand on clerical celibacy has caused many men to leave the priesthood and many men and women to leave religious orders. The prohibition on contraception has caused resentment among the laity.

The current pope, John Paul II, was elected in 1978 after the death of John Paul I, whose reign lasted only 34 days. John Paul II, the former Karol Wojtyla, archbishop of Cracow in Poland, was the youngest pope to be elected in more than a century. He has pursued a three-pronged policy. First, he has maintained a traditional policy in doctrinal matters, stressing the authority of the papacy and attempting to limit doctrinal and liturgical experimentation. Second, he

This attempt ultimately failed. The reforms Gorbachev initiated unloosed forces that within seven years had forced him to retire and ended both Communist rule and the Soviet Union as it had existed since the Bolshevik Revolution of 1917. The backdrop for these events was the stagnation of the Soviet economy, the lost war in Afghanistan, and the absence of open political life.

By the early 1980s, the Soviet Union stood in a paradoxical situation. Militarily, it was stronger than it had ever been. After the Soviet backdown during the Cuban missile crisis, the Soviet government had embarked on an extensive and successful military buildup. The diversion of resources to the military, however, had left the nonmilitary side of the economy stagnant and neglected. The country's overall rate of economic growth declined. Progress in all but military technology slowed. Shortages in all kinds of consumer goods were extensive. Both absenteeism at work and alcoholism among the populace were high.

When Ronald Reagan began the military buildup in the United States in the 1980s (discussed in Chapter 30), the leaders of the Soviet Union felt challenged to respond in kind. It appears, however, that they simply could not afford to do so.

Gorbachev had been known in his earlier administrative career for impatience with the inefficiencies of the Soviet system. He believed that only drastic change could restore the Soviet Union's political and economic health. Russian and Soviet history are replete with figures who sought to impose reform from above, and Gorbachev assumed a role in that tradition. It should be noted, however, that he never repudiated socialism or much of the intellectual framework of Soviet communism. He hoped to rejuvenate the original Bolshevik vision, which he believed had been undermined by corruption and political terror. Unlike other strong leaders in the Russian tradition, Gorbachev quickly unleashed political and social forces far beyond his control and was ultimately overwhelmed by them.

ECONOMIC PERESTROIKA Initially, Gorbachev and his supporters moved to challenge the way the party and bureaucracy had traditionally managed the Soviet government and economy. Under the policy of *perestroika,* or restructuring, they proposed major economic and political reforms. A target of this effort was the various centralized economic ministries, which were considerably reduced in size. A larger role was allowed for private enterprise on the local level. By early 1990, in a clear abandonment of traditional Marxist ideology, Gorbachev had begun to advocate private ownership of property. Throughout 1990 he and his advisers considered policies to liberalize the economy and move it rapidly toward a free market.

During these same years, Gorbachev confronted troubling labor discontent. A major strike by miners occurred in July 1989 in Siberia. Gorbachev had to settle their grievances quickly because the economy desperately needed their output. He promised them better wages and wider political liberties.

Within the Soviet context, Gorbachev's approach was genuinely radical. It challenged centralized planning and centralized Communist Party control. He and his supporters were also exceedingly critical of the corruption and inefficiencies in the economy and the party bureaucracy. The results of their policies, however, were not what they hoped. They did implement many organizational changes, but for all intents the Soviet economy, instead of growing, experienced stagnation and even decline. Shortages of food, consumer goods, and housing became chronic. Old-fashioned Communists blamed these results on the abandonment of centralized planning. Democratic critics blamed overly slow reform and urged a more rapid move to a free market economy.

The failure of Gorbachev's economic policies affected his political policies. To some extent, he pursued bold political reform because of the absence of economic progress.

GLASNOST Gorbachev allowed, within the Soviet context, an extraordinarily broad public discussion and criticism of Soviet history and Soviet Communist Party policy. This development was termed *glasnost,* or openness. Certain Communist figures from the 1920s such as Bukharin, who had been purged by Stalin, once again received official public recognition for their positive contributions to Soviet history.

Within factories, workers were permitted to criticize party officials and the economic plans of the party and the government. Censorship was relaxed and free expression encouraged. Dissidents were released from prison. In the summer of 1988, Gorbachev presided over a party congress that witnessed very full debates.

At the same time, national minorities voiced increasing demands for political autonomy. Throughout its history, the Soviet Union had remained a vast empire of diverse peoples and nationalities. Some of those groups had been conquered under the tsars; others, such as the Baltic states, had been incorporated into the Soviet Union under Stalin. Glasnost quickly brought to the fore the discontents of all such peoples, no matter how or when they had been incorporated into the Soviet state. Gorbachev proved particularly inept in addressing these ethnic complaints.

POLITICAL PERESTROIKA Gorbachev soon moved from glasnost to perestroika in the political arena. In 1988 a new constitution was adopted, permitting openly contested elections. After real political campaigning, a new experience for the Soviet Union, the Congress of People's Deputies was elected in 1989. One of the new members of the Congress was Andrei Sakharov (1921–1989), the dissident physicist who had been persecuted under Brezhnev. Lively debate took place in the Supreme Soviet when it met. This body formally elected Gorbachev as president in 1989.

During that same year, in a series of events closely related to developments in the Soviet Union, Soviet domination and Communist rule in eastern Europe came to an abrupt end.

1989: Year of Revolution in Eastern Europe

As seen in Chapter 30, the Soviet Union maintained tight control over eastern Europe throughout the Cold War era. Twice it intervened with military forces to halt political experiments: in Hungary in 1956 and in Czechoslovakia in 1968. At the time of the 1968 invasion, Soviet Party Chairman Brezhnev, in what came to be termed the Brezhnev Doctrine, declared the right of the Soviet Union to intervene in the domestic politics of other Communist countries. After 1968 the Soviet Union did not again send troops into an eastern European country. In 1981, however, Poland's Communist government itself imposed martial law to suppress the Solidarity trade union movement and prevent Soviet military intervention. The Polish government may have acted in order to forestall Soviet intervention. This self-imposed martial law marked, in effect, the third use of military force to prevent reform in a Soviet-dominated eastern European nation. Until Gorbachev began his radical changes in the Soviet Union, reform seemed unlikely anywhere in eastern Europe.

SOLIDARITY REEMERGES IN POLAND During the mid-1980s, Poland's government relaxed martial law, although Jaruzelski remained in control. By 1984 several leaders of Solidarity had been released from prison, and in defiance of the conditions of their release, began again to work for free trade unions and democratic government. An active underground press developed, and several new dissenting political organizations emerged. Poland's economy continued to deteriorate, demonstrating there, as elsewhere, the inability of Communist governments to deliver economic growth and prosperity.

During 1987 the government released the last of its Solidarity prisoners in a sweeping amnesty. In 1988 new strikes occurred that even the leaders of Solidarity had not anticipated. This time, the Communist government was unable to reimpose control. After consultations between the government and Solidarity, the union was legalized. Lech Walesa again came into the public spotlight, now as a kind of mediator between the government and the more independent elements of the trade union movement he had founded.

Jaruzelski began some political reforms with the tacit consent of the Soviet Union. He repealed martial law and promised free elections to a parliament with increased powers. When elections were held, in 1989, the Communists lost overwhelmingly to Solidarity candidates. Late in the summer, Jaruzelski, unable to find a Communist who could forge a majority coalition in Parliament, turned to Solidarity. On August 24, 1989, after negotiating with Lech

Andrei Sakharov Criticizes the Limits of Perestroika

Throughout the 1970s and early 1980s, Andrei Sakharov was one of the foremost Soviet dissidents. A noted physicist, he was placed under arrest and exiled from Moscow. With the Gorbachev reforms, however, he was allowed to enter Soviet political life. Before his death in 1989, he was an outspoken member of the Congress of People's Deputies, which met in Moscow. At the close of the Congress, he was permitted to deliver a speech criticizing the progress or lack thereof that he thought had occurred. He was not, however, permitted to deliver all his remarks; these were later printed in the United States. He criticized the large powers that the Congress reserved for Gorbachev and urged the Congress to assert greater authority on its own. He also paid special attention to the possibility of ethnic strife in the Soviet Union.

✦ *Why, according to Sakharov, had the Soviet government lost credibility? Why did Sakharov believe much of the difficulty confronting the Soviet Union stemmed from the years under Stalin? How did Sakharov's image of reform differ from Gorbachev's?*

We are in the throes of spreading economic catastrophe and a tragic worsening of interethnic relations; one aspect of the powerful and dangerous processes at work has been the general crisis of confidence in the nation's leadership. If we simply float with the current, hoping that things will gradually get better in the distant future, then the accumulating tensions could explode, with dire consequences to our society.

Comrade deputies, at this moment in history, an enormous responsibility has fallen to you. Political decisions are needed in order to strengthen the local Soviet organs and resolve our economic, social, ecological, and ethnic problems. If the Congress of People's Deputies cannot take power into its hands, then there is not the slightest hope that the soviets of Union Republics [the local governments of the separate Soviet Republics] regions, districts, and villages will do so. But without strong local soviets, it won't be possible to implement land reform or any agrarian policy other than nonsensical attempts to resuscitate uneconomic collective farms.

Without a strong Congress and strong and independent soviets, it won't be possible to overcome the dictates of the bureaucracy, to work out and implement new laws on commercial enterprises, to fight against ecological folly.

. . . .

We have inherited from Stalinism a constitutional structure that bears the stamp of imperial thinking and the imperial policy of "divide and rule." The smaller Union Republics and the autonomous national subdivisions, which are administratively subordinated to the Union Republics, are victims of this legacy. For decades they have been subjected to national oppression. Now these problems have come to the surface in dramatic fashion. But to an equal extent the more numerous ethnic groups have also suffered, and that includes the Russian people who have had to bear the main burden of imperial ambitions and the consequences of adventurism and dogmatism in foreign and domestic policy.

Andrei Sakharov, "A Speech to the People's Congress," The New York Review of Books, *August 17, 1989, p. 25.*

Why Historical Truth Became Important to Dissidents in Eastern Europe

G. M. Tamás is a leader of an opposition party in present-day Hungary. In this passage, he explores how eastern European and Soviet dissidents used the rights guaranteed in the Helsinki Accords of 1975 to document the repression of the Communist regimes. He contends that telling these truths and bearing witness helped both to spread information and to embarrass the Communist governments by showing how they violated what they had signed.

✦ *How did the right to free expression become so closely related to the telling of historical truth? What does Tamás mean by the right to historical truth? What was the importance of the Helsinki Accords in creating it? Why did the dissidents believe more strongly in the value of the rights guaranteed in the Helsinki Accords than did some people in the West?*

The first, most important human right for dissident intellectuals was the right to freedom of expression. But freedom of expression meant a licence to tell the truth, especially the truth about the Communist system, the truth about the martyrdom of East European peoples under the Gulag regime. The moral attitude which emerged from this simple idea of uncensored truth-telling was that of *bearing witness:* so the chief genre of dissident writing is neither philosophical treatise nor poetry, but *testimony.* Martyrs are . . . witnesses. The eloquence of their martyrdom, where the whole community was martyred, created a new symbolic community: the community of those who suffered and lived to tell and were ready to suffer again for the right to tell.

Walesa, Jaruzelski named Tadeusz Mazowiecki (b. 1927) the first non-Communist prime minister of Poland since 1945. The appointment was made with the express approval of Gorbachev.

THE SOVIET STANCE TOWARD REVOLUTIONARY DEVELOPMENTS The establishment in August 1989 of a Solidarity government in Poland had been the result of almost a decade of struggle. Within a few months of that event, however, Communist Party governments had fallen throughout Soviet-dominated eastern Europe. Except in Romania, the transitions were relatively peaceful.

None of these revolutions could have taken place without the refusal of the Soviet Union to intervene militarily as it had done in 1956 and 1968. As events unfolded, it became clear that Gorbachev would not come to the aid of the old-line Communist governments and party leaderships in eastern Europe. In October 1989, he formally renounced the Brezhnev Doctrine. For the first time since the end of World War II, the people of eastern Europe could shape their own political destiny without the almost certain military intervention of the Soviet Union. Once they realized the Soviets would stand back, thousands of ordinary citizens took to the streets to denounce Communist Party domination and to assert their desire for democracy.

The generally peaceful character of most of these revolutions was not inevitable. It may, in part, have resulted from the shock with which much of the world responded to the violent repression of prodemocracy protesters in Beijing's Tiananmen Square by the People's Republic of China in the late spring of 1989. The Communist Party officials of eastern Europe and the Soviet Union clearly decided at

The irresistible force of this surge of testimony was lethal, because in spite of denial, a sometimes almost psychotic refusal to know, everyone half-consciously knew that it was true. . . .

In the struggle for the right to historical truth, for the right to bear witness (where history and morals, strangely, become one), dissidents were harassed, persecuted and punished. They continued to document these new abuses—one of the chief tasks of the dissident movement was to write its own chronicle, a testimony this time on the fate of the witnesses themselves. They did not at first demand the usual fundamental human rights: their emphasis was on the Word. They did not set up political parties or organize conspiracies. They wanted to expose unspeakable, even unimaginable crimes and show the continuity of the Great Terror through the servility and mendacity of their present. The rulers were told that the communiqués they had signed guaranteed the right to free speech, peaceful assembly and the like. "Why, therefore, cannot people say what they believe to be the truth?" . . .

In the West, little of this passion for historico-moral truth was understood. But the West's shaky faith in the universality of its basic principles (human and civil rights) was challenged by the East European dissidence: people putting themselves at risk for the pious and dull commonplaces of the Helsinki accords. The unasked-for support for Western constitutional principles by trustworthy people, made so by their willingness to suffer for those principles, gave a new distinction to a certain idea of natural right; the dissidents' behaviour forced the ideas of the American Revolution on to the political agenda after two hundred years. There was a universalist discourse common to both systems, and the debate conducted within it was won by the West and its allies, the dissidents. No *Realpolitik* could ever have won that controversy.

G. M. Tamás, *"The Legacy of Dissent: How Civil Society Has Been Seduced by the Cult of Privacy,"* The Times Literary Supplement, *May 14, 1993, p. 15.*

some point in 1989 that they could not risk offending world opinion with a similar attack on democratic demonstrators.

HUNGARY MOVES TOWARD INDEPENDENCE Of the eastern European nations, Hungary had for some time shown the greatest national economic independence of the Soviet Union. The Hungarian government had emphasized the production of food and consumer goods. It had also permitted a small stock exchange. During the early months of 1989, as events unfolded in Poland, the Hungarian Communist government began to take other independent actions. In January its parliament passed legislation to permit independent political parties. Soon thereafter the government opened the Hungarian border with Austria and permitted free travel between the two nations, opening the first breach in the Iron Curtain. One immediate result was the movement of thousands of East Germans into Austria through Hungary. From Austria, they proceeded into West Germany.

Not long thereafter, various political changes occurred in Hungary. In May, Premier Janos Kadar, who had been installed after the Soviet intervention in 1956, was voted from office by the Parliament. Hungarians demonstrated their determination to validate this change when thousands of people gave an honorary burial to the body of Hungarian Premier Imre Nagy, who had been executed in 1958. The Hungarian Communist Party changed its name to the Socialist Party and permitted the emergence of other opposition political parties. In October, Hungary promised free elections. By 1990 a coalition of democratic parties controlled the parliament and governed the country.

THE BREACH OF THE BERLIN WALL AND GERMAN REUNIFICATION No part of Europe had so come to symbolize the tensions of the Cold War as the divided Germanies. The Berlin Wall had been erected in 1961 to halt the out-flow of East Germans to the West. In the autumn of 1989, as tens of thousands of East Germans moved into West Germany through Hungary and then Austria, popular demonstrations erupted in many German cities. The most important demonstrations occurred in Leipzig. The streets filled with people demanding democracy and an end to Communist Party rule.

Adding to the pressure of the popular demonstrations, Gorbachev told the leaders of the East German Communist Party that the Soviet Union would no longer support them. With startling swiftness, the Communist leaders of the East German government, including Premier Erich Honecker (b. 1912), resigned, making way for a younger generation of Communist Party leaders. These new leaders, who remained in office for only a matter of weeks, promised political and economic reform. They convinced few East Germans, however, and the emigration to the West continued. In November 1989, in one of the most emotional moments in European history since 1945, the government of East Germany ordered the opening of the Berlin Wall. That week, tens of thousands of East Berliners crossed into West Berlin to celebrate, to visit families, and to shop with money provided by the West German government. Shortly thereafter, free travel began between East and West Germany (see Map 31-1).

Further political change occurred in East Germany. For all intents, the Communist Party had become thoroughly discredited. Enormous corruption among party officials was exposed. The East German Communist Party changed its name and claimed that henceforth it would be a social democratic party. Free elections in 1990 brought into the East German Parliament a conservative majority that sought rapid unification with West Germany.

The revolution in East Germany, more than those elsewhere in Europe, had broad ramifications for international relations. Within days of the first dramatic events in East Germany, the issue of the reunification of the Germanies confronted West Germany and the other Western nations. Helmut Kohl (b. 1930), the Chancellor of West Germany, proposed a tentative plan for reunification. Late in 1989 the ministers of the European Economic Community accepted in principle the unification of Germany. By February 1990, some form of reunification had become a foregone conclusion, accepted by the United States, the Soviet Union, Great Britain, and France.

In the closing months of 1989 and the opening weeks of 1990, it became clear that the citizens of the two Germanies were determined to reunify. With the collapse of Communist Party government in East Germany, there was no longer a viable distinction between the two Germanies. With the Communists in confusion, the forces of national self-determination came to the fore. The rapidity of German reunification, however, was to sow the seeds of new problems.

THE VELVET REVOLUTION IN CZECHOSLOVAKIA The hard-line wing of the Czechoslovak Communist Party had been restored to power by the Soviet invasion of 1968. This wing of the party then removed the Communist leaders of the 1968 Prague Spring from public life and retained virtually unquestioned authority for twenty years. Any opponents could find themselves imprisoned for their activities.

Late in 1989, in a series of events dubbed "the velvet revolution," Communist rule in Czechoslovakia quickly unraveled. In November 1989, under popular pressure from street demonstrations and well-organized political opposition, the Communist Party began to retreat from office. The patterns were similar to those occurring elsewhere. The old leadership resigned, and younger Communists replaced them. The changes they offered were inadequate.

The popular new Czech leader who led the forces against the party was Vaclav Havel (b. 1936), a playwright of international standing who had been frequently imprisoned by the government. Havel and the group he represented, which called itself Civic Forum, negotiated a series of changes with the government. These included an end to the political dominance of the Communist Party (which had been written into the constitution), inclusion of non-Communists in the government, elimination of tra-

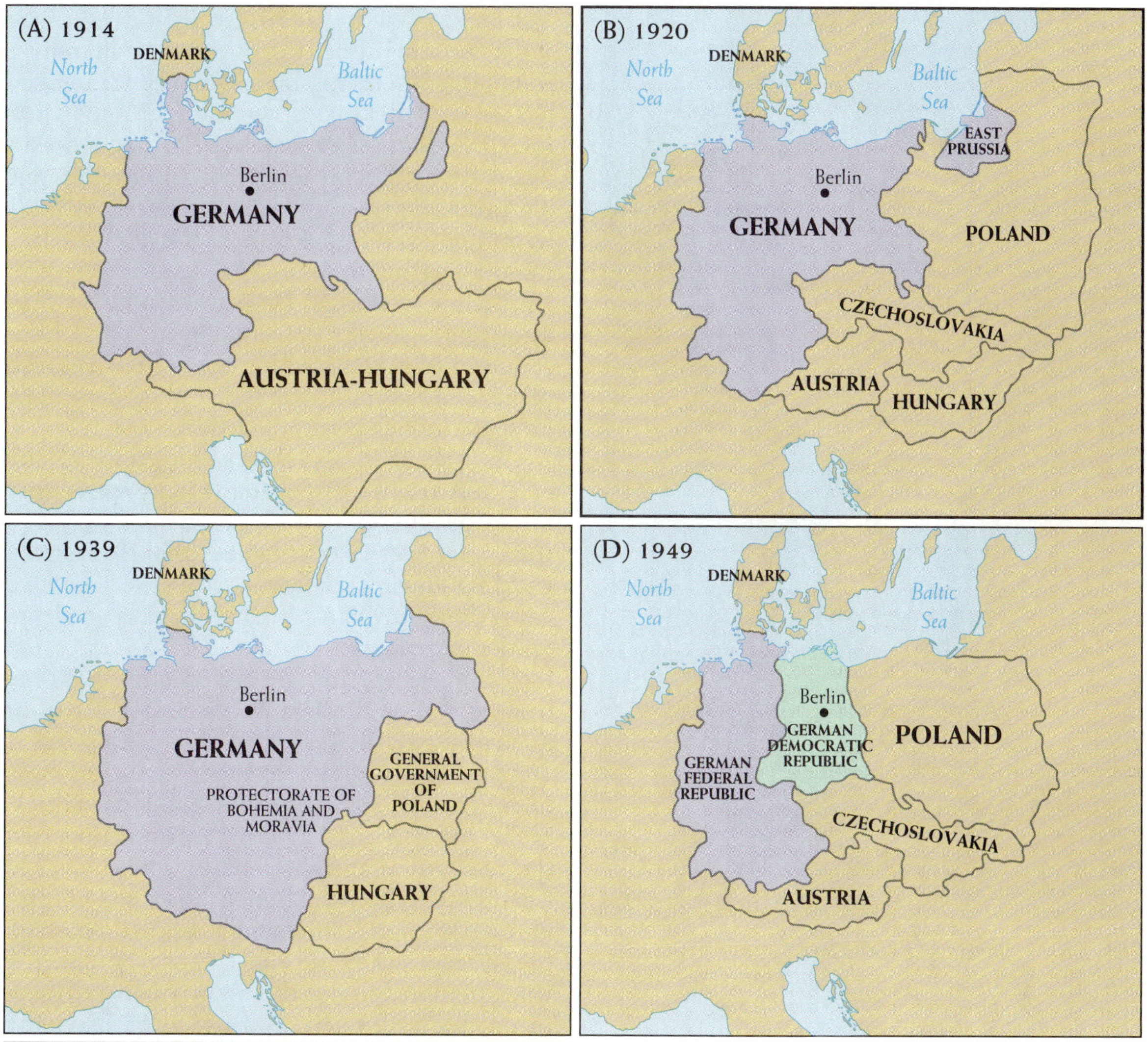

(A) 1914

DENMARK

North Sea

Baltic Sea

Berlin

GERMANY

AUSTRIA-HUNGARY

(B) 1920

DENMARK

North Sea

Baltic Sea

EAST PRUSSIA

Berlin

GERMANY

POLAND

CZECHOSLOVAKIA

AUSTRIA

HUNGARY

(C) 1939

DENMARK

North Sea

Baltic Sea

Berlin

GERMANY

PROTECTORATE OF BOHEMIA AND MORAVIA

GENERAL GOVERNMENT OF POLAND

HUNGARY

(D) 1949

DENMARK

North Sea

Baltic Sea

Berlin

GERMAN DEMOCRATIC REPUBLIC

GERMAN FEDERAL REPUBLIC

POLAND

CZECHOSLOVAKIA

AUSTRIA

(E) 1990

DENMARK

North Sea

Baltic Sea

Berlin

GERMANY

POLAND

CZECHOSLOVAKIA

AUSTRIA

MAP 31-1 THE BORDERS OF GERMANY IN THE TWENTIETH CENTURY *Map A shows the borders of Imperial Germany at the outbreak of World War I. Map B shows Germany after the Versailles peace settlement. Map C shows the borders of Germany after Hitler's invasion of the Rhineland, the Anschluss with Austria, the Munich Pact, the invasion of Czechoslovakia, and the invasion of Poland. Map D illustrates the division of Germany into the German Federal Republic (West Germany) and the German Democratic Republic (East Germany) in the aftermath of World War II. Map E illustrates the borders of Germany after reunification in 1990.*

President Vaclav Havel of the Czech Republic led the revolution that overthrew the Communist government of his nation and has since become a powerful advocate of political democracy and moderation in eastern Europe. [Gamma-Liaison]

ditional Marxist education, removal of travel restrictions, and relaxation of censorship.

Early in December, the tottering Communist government admitted that the invasion of 1968 had been a mistake. The Soviet Union and other Warsaw Pact states did likewise. Shortly thereafter, Civic Forum succeeded in forcing the resignation of Gustav Husak (b. 1913), who had been president of Czechoslovakia since 1968, and in guaranteeing a free election for his successor. On December 28, 1989, Alexander Dubček returned to public office as chairman of the Parliament. The next day, Havel was elected president.

VIOLENT REVOLUTION IN ROMANIA The most violent upheaval of 1989 occurred in Romania, where President Nicolae Ceauşescu (1918–1989) had governed without opposition for almost a quarter century. Romania was a one-party state with total centralized economic planning. Ceauşescu, who had been at odds with the Soviet government for some time, maintained his Stalinist regime in the face of Gorbachev's reforms. He was supported by an army and a smaller security force loyal to himself. He had also placed his closest relatives into major political positions where they personally profited through corrupt practices.

On December 15, troubles erupted in the city of Timisoara in western Romania. The security forces sought to arrest a clergyman who had tried to protect the rights of ethnic Hungarians within Romania's borders. Over the next two days, the Romanian security forces opened fire on demonstrators in Timisoara. Casualties ran into at least the hundreds and quite possibly higher. A few days later, demonstrators in Bucharest publicly shouted against Ceauşescu at a major rally, and by December 22 the city was in full revolt. Fighting, with many casualties, broke out between the army, which supported the revolution, and the security forces loyal to Ceauşescu. The revolutionaries gained control of the television station and broadcast reports of the spreading revolution. Ceauşescu and his wife attempted to flee the country but were captured, secretly tried, and executed by firing squad on December 25. With his death, the shooting between the army and security forces ended. The provisional government in Bucharest announced that the first free elections since the end of World War II would take place in the spring of 1990. During the early months there were many demonstrations, both for and against the new government. Political turmoil continued for some time.

The Collapse of the Soviet Union

Gorbachev clearly believed, as shown by his behavior toward eastern Europe in 1989, that the Soviet Union could no longer afford to support Communist governments in that region or intervene to uphold their authority. He was beginning to advance a similar view of the

Major Events in the Revolutions of 1989

January 11	Independent parties permitted in Hungary	November 19	Czechoslovak opposition groups organize into Civic Forum and demand resignation of Communist leaders responsible for 1968 invasion
April 5	Solidarity legalized in Poland and free elections accepted by government		
May 2	Hungary dismantles barriers along its borders	November 24	Czechoslovak Communist leadership resigns
May 8	Janos Kadar removed from office in Hungary	December 1	New Czechoslovak Communist leaders denounce 1968 invasion; Soviet Union and Warsaw Pact express regret over 1968 invasion
May 17	Polish government recognizes Roman Catholic church		
June 4	Solidarity victory in Polish parliamentary elections		
July 25	Solidarity asked to join coalition government	December 3	Czechoslovak government announces ministry with non-Communist members
August 24	Solidarity member appointed premier in Poland	December 16–17	Massacre of civilians in Timisoara, Romania
October 18	Erich Honecker removed from office in East Germany	December 22	Ceauşescu government overthrown in Romania with many casualties
October 23	Hungary proclaims itself a republic		
October 25	Gorbachev renounces Brezhnev Doctrine	December 25	Announcement of Ceauşescu's execution
November 9	Berlin Wall opened; Zhivkov removed as leader in Bulgaria	December 28	Alexander Dubček elected chairman of Czechoslovak Parliament
November 17	Large antigovernment demonstration in Czechoslovakia crushed by police	December 29	Vaclav Havel elected president of Czechoslovakia

nature of the authority of the Communist Party within the Soviet Union.

RENUNCIATION OF COMMUNIST POLITICAL MONOPOLY During this period, Gorbachev tried to establish a new political structure with a strong presidency, eventually to be filled by election in the Supreme Soviet. He was also trying to build a political base outside the Soviet Communist Party. In early 1990 he formally proposed to the Central Committee of the Soviet Communist Party that the party abandon its monopoly of power. After intense debate, the Committee adopted his proposal, abandoning the Leninist position that only a single elite party could act as the vanguard of the revolution and forge a new Soviet society. Gorbachev seems not to have wanted wholly to abandon communism and most assuredly not socialism, but

he did want to open the political process to genuine competition. He was determined, however, that the Soviet Union should remain a single strong state with a powerful central government.

NEW POLITICAL FORCES By this time, however, Gorbachev was not the only player in the Soviet Union's new political scene. He soon found himself, more than in the past, reacting to events rather than controlling them. In 1990 he experienced a sharp drop in popularity from which he never recovered.

Gorbachev confronted challenges from three major political forces by 1990. One consisted of those groups—considered conservative in the Soviet context—whose members wanted to maintain the influence of the Communist Party and the Soviet army. They were deeply disturbed by the country's economic stagnation and politi-

Gorbachev Proposes the Soviet Communist Party Abandon Its Monopoly of Power

On February 5, 1990, President Mikhail Gorbachev proposed to the Central Committee of the Soviet Communist Party that the Party abandon its position as the single legal party as provided in Article 6 of the Soviet Constitution. His proposal followed similar actions by several of the Communist parties of eastern Europe. From the time of Lenin through Brezhnev, the Soviet Communist Party portrayed itself as the sole vanguard of the revolution. Gorbachev argued that it should abandon that special role and compete for political power with other political parties. Within two years, the party was no longer in power.

◆ *Why did Gorbachev argue that the Soviet Communist Party must reform itself? To what extent did Gorbachev in this speech actually abandon traditional Communist Party goals? How did he think the Soviet Communist Party could function in a pluralistic political system?*

The main thing that now worries Communists and all citizens of the country is the fate of perestroika, the fate of the country and the role of the Soviet Communist Party at the current, probably most crucial, stage of revolutionary transformation.

. . . .

[It is important to understand] . . . that the party will only be able to fulfill the mission of political vanguard if it drastically restructures itself, masters the art of political work in the present conditions and succeeds in cooperating with forces committed to perestroika.

The crux of the party's renewal is the need to get rid of everything that tied it to the authoritarian-bureaucratic system, a system that left its mark not only on methods of

---

cal and social turmoil. They still appeared to control significant groups in the economy and society. During late 1990 and early 1991, Gorbachev, who himself seems to have been disturbed by the nation's turmoil, began to appoint members of these factions to key positions in the government. In other words, Gorbachev seemed to be making a strategic retreat. He apparently believed that only these more conservative forces would give him the support he needed.

Gorbachev made this calculation because he was now facing opposition from members of a second group, those who wanted much more extensive and rapid change. Their leading spokesman was Boris Yeltsin (b. 1931). He and those supporting him wanted to move quickly to a market economy and a more democratic government. Like Gorbachev, Yeltsin had come up through the ranks of the Communist Party and then become disillusioned with its policies.

Throughout the late 1980s, he had been critical of Gorbachev. In 1990 he was elected president of the Russian Republic, the largest and most important of the Soviet Union's constituent republics. In the new political climate, that position gave him a firm political base from which to challenge Gorbachev's authority and increase his own.

The third force that came into play from 1989 onward was regional unrest in some of the republics of the Soviet Union. These republics had experienced considerable discontent in the past, but it had been repressed by military or Communist Party action. Initially, the greatest unrest came from the three Baltic republics of Estonia, Latvia, and Lithuania. These had been independent republics until the eve of the Second World War. In accord with secret arrangements in the Soviet-German nonaggression pact of 1939, they had been turned over to the Soviet Union. That prewar pact with Nazi

work and inter-relationships within the party, but also on ideology, ways of thinking and notions of socialism.

The [newly proposed] platform says: our ideal is a humane, democratic socialism, expressing the interests of the working class and all working people; and relying on the great legacy of Marx, Engels and Lenin, the Soviet Communist Party is creatively, developing socialist ideals to match present-day realities and with due account for the entire experience of the 20th century.

The platform states clearly what we should abandon. We should abandon the ideological dogmatism that became ingrained during past decades, outdated stereotypes in domestic policy and outmoded views on the world revolutionary process and world development as a whole.

We should abandon everything that led to the isolation of socialist countries from the mainstream of world civilization. We should abandon the understanding of progress as a permanent confrontation with a socially different world. . . .

The party's renewal presupposes a fundamental change in its relations with state and economic bodies and the abandonment of the practice of commanding them and substituting for their functions.

The party in a renewing of society can exist and play its role as vanguard only as a democratically recognized force. This means that its status should not be imposed through constitutional endorsement.

The Soviet Communist Party, it goes without saying, intends to struggle for the status of the ruling party. But it will do so strictly within the framework of the democratic process by giving up any legal and political advantages, offering its program and defending it in discussions, cooperating with other social and political forces, always working amidst the masses, living by their interests and their needs.

The New York Times, February 6, 1990, p. A16.

Germany provided the only legal basis for the Soviet Union's continued control over them.

During 1989 and 1990, the parliaments of the Baltic republics tried in various ways to increase their independence from the Soviet Union, and Lithuania actually declared independence. Discontent also arose in the Soviet Islamic republics in central Asia. Riots broke out in Azerbaijan and Tajikistan. Throughout 1990 and 1991, Gorbachev sought to negotiate new constitutional arrangements between the republics and the central government. His failure in this effort may in time be seen as the most important reason for the rapid collapse of the Soviet Union.

THE AUGUST 1991 COUP The turning point in all of these events came in August 1991, when the conservative forces that Gorbachev had brought into the government attempted a coup. Armed forces occupied Moscow, and Gorbachev himself was placed under house arrest while on vacation in the Crimea. The forces of political and economic reaction—led by people who, at the time, were associated with Gorbachev—had at last attempted to seize control. The day of the coup, Boris Yeltsin climbed on a tank in front of the Russian Parliament building to denounce the coup and ask for the help of the world in maintaining the Soviet Union's movement toward democracy.

Within two days, the coup collapsed. Gorbachev returned to Moscow, but in humiliation, having been victimized by the groups to whom he had turned for support. One of the largest public demonstrations in all Russian history, perhaps the largest, celebrated the failure of the coup in Moscow. From that point on, Yeltsin steadily became the dominant political figure in the nation. In the months immediately after the coup, the Communist Party, compromised by its

Lithuanians demonstrate for independence in 1990. As the Gorbachev reform era came to a close, the various republics of the former Soviet Union began to demand independence. [Lehtikuva Oy/Woodfin Camp & Associates]

participation in the coup, totally collapsed as a political force. The constitutional arrangements between the central government and the individual republics were revised. On December 25, 1991, the Soviet Union ceased to exist, Gorbachev left office, and the Commonwealth of Independent States came into being.

CRUSHING THE RUSSIAN PARLIAMENT Boris Yeltsin emerged as the strongest leader within the new Commonwealth. As president of Russia, he was the head of the largest and most powerful of the new states. His popularity was high both in Russia and in the Commonwealth in 1992, but by 1993, he faced serious economic and political problems. Opposition to Yeltsin personally and to his policies of economic and political reform grew in the Russian Parliament. The members of this parliament were mostly former Communists who wanted to slow or halt

the movement toward reform. Relations between the president and the parliament reached an impasse, crippling the government. In September 1993, Yeltsin suspended Parliament, which responded by deposing him. Parliament's leaders tried to provoke popular uprisings against Yeltsin in Moscow. The military, however, backed Yeltsin, and he eventually surrounded the Parliament building with troops and tanks. On October 4, 1993, after pro-Parliament rioters rampaged through Moscow, Yeltsin ordered the tanks to attack the Parliament building, crushing the revolt.

These actions temporarily consolidated Yeltsin's position and authority. All the major Western powers, deeply concerned by the turmoil in Russia, supported him. In December 1993, Russians voted for a new Parliament and approved a new constitution. The constitution strictly limits parliamentary authority and gives

After the failed coup in August, 1991, Boris Yeltsin soon displaced Mikhail Gorbachev as leader of the new Commonwealth of Independent States. Here they appeared jointly before the parliament of the collapsing Soviet Union. [Gamma]

In October, 1993, President Boris Yeltsin ordered the military to bombard the Russian Parliament building. More than a hundred people were killed. [SYGMA]

the president strong powers. Russia's future, however, re-mains insecure. The crushing of Parliament left Yeltsin far more dependent than before on the military. And the country's continuing economic problems breed unrest. In the December elections, for example, radical nationalists who are openly intolerant of non-Russian ethnic groups and who advocate rebuilding Russia's empire made an uncomfortably strong showing, nearly capturing more seats in the new Parliament than supporters of Yeltsin. The most outspoken of these nationalist leaders and the one most likely to challenge Yeltsin was Vladimir V. Zhirinovsky.

When the newly elected Russian Parliament gathered early in 1994, tension between it and Yelstin immediately developed. Nationalists and former Communists cooperated to force Yeltsin to moderate his reformist, market-oriented economic program. Futhermore, early in 1994 the Parliament granted amnesty both to the parliamentary leaders imprisoned after the attack on the parliament building the previous October and to the leaders of the 1991 coup against Gorbachev. It is clear that futher political and policy turmoil will continue, as will the general struggle between Yeltsin and Parliament. This conflict over political authority may be played out along constitutional lines during the election for President of Russia in 1996, but in the last several years in Russia events have often moved so rapidly and in directions so unexpected that it is unwise to attempt any confident predictions.

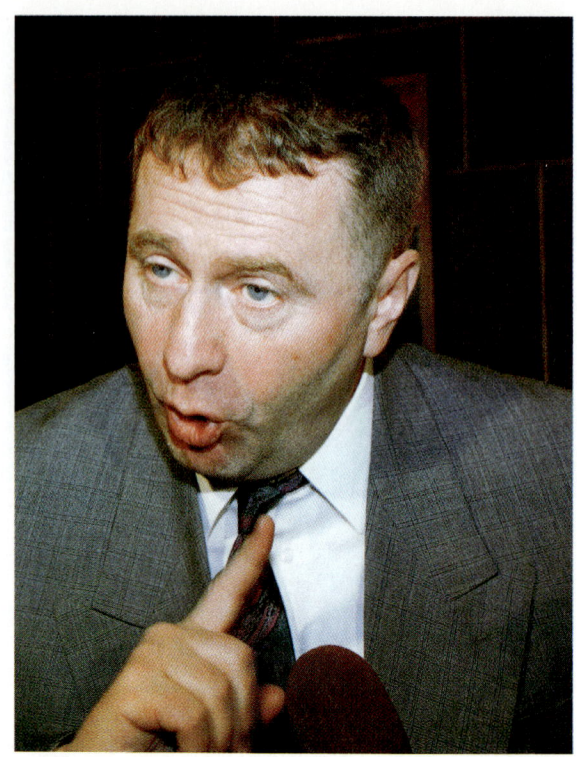

Vladimir Zhirinovsky emerged as the leading advocate of extreme nationalism during the Russian parliamentary elections of December, 1993. [Reuters/ Bettmann]

The Future of the Commonwealth of Independent States

The Commonwealth of Independent States is a loosely organized federation of eleven of the fifteen former Soviet Republics, of which Russia is the largest and most powerful (see Map 31-2). What will eventually develop within this new commonwealth is uncertain, and the rapid changes of recent years makes prediction both difficult and foolhardy. Several issues, however, should be noted.

First, very real differences and disagreements exist among these states. The status of the federation is thus quite shaky. Many republics include ethnic minorities that are sometimes the dominant group in other republics. Persecution of these minorities is thus a source of conflict both within and between republics. As conflicts arise, the parties involved may seek military aid from other republics. Russia has already used these conflicts to play groups off against each other to gain influence within the commonwealth. Ethnic Russians themselves form a significant minority in many republics, including the independent Baltic states. Associated as they are with the former Soviet rulers, they have often been badly treated. It is uncertain how long the Russian Republic will tolerate this situation. The treatment of these ethnic Russian minorities, in other words, could provide Russia with a pretext for leaving troops in the Baltic states or even reasserting control over the territories of what had been the Soviet (and tsarist) empire.

Second, the economy of the commonwealth as a whole as well as of each of the individual republics remains weak. All the consumer

MAP 31-2 THE COMMONWEALTH OF INDEPENDENT STATES *In December 1991, the Soviet Union broke up into its fifteen constituent republics. Eleven of these are now loosely joined in the Commonwealth of Independent States. Not in the CIS are Estonia, Latvia, Lithuania, and Georgia.*

shortages that existed before 1991 still exist. It is uncertain what level of economic aid Western countries will be willing to supply to help the democratic experiment survive.

Third, certain conservative institutions remain. The secret police still exists and is largely subject to its own direction. The former Soviet army also still exists, although it is under much strain as the various republics vie for control of its weapons and attempt to claim the allegiance of troops on their soil.

Fourth, the general situation is volatile; the present leaders could quickly become unpopular and new ones come to the fore. The important question is whether subsequent leaders will support democracy or favor some new kind of authoritarian government.

Finally, many common political terms—"liberal" and "conservative," for example—have special meanings when used in the context of Russia and the Commonwealth of Independent States that bear little relationship to their meaning in Western politics. In fact, almost all the major political figures within the commonwealth are former Communists. Much of the political conflict there is thus a struggle among these former Communists to retain power and office in a new political framework.

The Collapse of Yugoslavia and Civil War

The Communist government of Yugoslavia had long been distinct from those of the other eastern bloc nations dominated by the Soviet Union. The country's leader, Marshal Tito, had acted independently of Stalin in the late 1940s. Thereafter, Yugoslavia pursued a foreign policy that was independent of the Soviet Union. After Tito's death in 1980, Yugoslavia began a decade of growing instability that has culminated in a major civil war.

Yugoslavia was created after World War I. Its borders included six major national groups—Serbs, Croats, Slovenes, Montenegrins, Macedonians, and Bosnians (Muslims)—among whom there have been ethnic disputes for centuries (see Map 31-3). The Croats and Slovenes are Roman Catholic and use the Latin alphabet. The Serbs, Montenegrins, and Macedonians are Eastern Orthodox and use the Cyrillic alphabet. The Bosnians are Islamic. Most members of each group reside in a region with which they are associated historically—Serbia, Croatia, Slovenia, Montenegro, Macedonia, and Bosnia-Herzegovina—and these regions constituted individual republics within Yugoslavia. Many Serbs, however, live in areas outside Serbia proper.

Tito succeeded in muting these ethnic differences by encouraging a cult of personality around himself and by a complex arrangement of political power sharing. In addition to the central government, each state had its own government. After Tito's death, Yugoslavia encountered serious economic difficulties that undermined the authority of the central government. Because the presidency rotated among the leaders of the six republics, however, no strong leader could emerge to deal with the country's problems.

In the late 1980s, the old ethnic differences came to the fore again in Yugoslav politics. Nationalist leaders—most notably Slobodan

MAP 31-3 THE ETHNIC COMPOSITION OF BOSNIA-HERZEGOVINA, CROATIA, AND SERBIA IN THE FORMER YUGOSLAVIA *The rapid changes in eastern Europe during the close of the 1980s has brought to the fore various long-standing ethnic tensions in the former Yugoslavia. This map shows national and ethnic borders and major ethnic enclaves within areas generally dominated by a single ethnic group.* [Source: CIA]

Milošević (b. 1941) in Serbia and Franjo Tudjman (b. 1922) in Croatia—gained increasing authority. The Serbs contended that Serbia did not exercise sufficient influence in Yugoslavia and that Serbs living in Yugoslavia but outside Serbia encountered systematic discrimination, especially from Croats. The Croats and Slovenes believed they could prosper economically if a market economy were pursued more rapidly. Ethnic tension and violence soon resulted. During the summer of 1990, in the wake of the changes in the former Soviet bloc nations, Slovenia and Croatia declared independence from the central Yugoslav government. Within a year, their independence was recognized by several European nations, including, most importantly, Germany. Recognition from the full European community soon followed.

From this point on, violence escalated steadily. Serbia—concerned about Serbs living in Croatia and about the loss of lands and resources there—was determined to maintain a unitary Yugoslav state that it would dominate. Croatia was equally determined to secure independence. Croatian Serbs demanded safeguards against discrimination and violence, providing the Serbian army with a pretext to move against Croatia. By June 1991, full-fledged war had erupted between the two republics. Serbia accused Croatia of reviving Fascism, while Croatia accused Serbia of maintaining a Stalinist regime. At its core, however, the conflict is ethnic and as such highlights the potential for violent ethnic conflict within the former Soviet Union.

The conflict took a new turn in 1992 as Croatian and Serbian forces determined to divide Bosnia-Herzegovina. The Muslims in Bosnia—who had lived alongside Serbs and Croats in the region for generations—soon became crushed between the opposing forces. The Serbs in particular, pursuing a policy called "ethnic cleansing," a euphemism redolent of some of the worst horrors of World War II, have killed or forcibly moved large numbers of Bosnian Muslims.

More than any other single event, the unremitting bombardment of Sarajevo, the capital of Bosnia-Herzegovina, brought the violence of the Yugoslav civil war to the attention of the world. In long negotiations the United Nations attempted unsuccessfully to mediate the conflict and imposed sanctions, which had little influence. Early in 1994, however, a shell expoded in the marketplace in Sarajevo, killing dozens of people. Thereafter, NATO issued an ultimatum threatening to bomb Serbian military positions if the Serbs did not withdraw their artillery from around Sarajevo. The ultimatum, and the military actions taken to enforce it—the first such

An elderly parishioner walks through the ruins of St. Mary's Roman Catholic Church in Sarajevo. The church was destroyed by Serb shelling in May, 1992. [Reuters/Bettmann]

Vaclav Havel Ponders the Future of Europe

In October 1993, Vaclav Havel, the president of the Czech Republic, gave an address in which he outlined many of the problems confronting Europe in the wake of the collapse of communism. The setting of the speech was the General Assembly of the Council of Europe, and so his general theme was European unity. In particular, he discussed what he regarded as the danger of resurgent ethnic nationalism. Elsewhere in the speech, he observed that twice in this century nationalism had caused major wars in Europe. He was seeking to convince European leaders and nationalist groups to think differently about their interests in the future and to create a European rather than a particular national ethos.

♦ *What are the values around which Havel believes European nations might integrate and unify themselves? How does he portray special interests as undermining cooperation? What are the special dangers that he associates with the appearance of new forms of nationalism?*

All of us—whether from the west, the east, the south, or the north of Europe—can agree that the common basis of any effort to integrate Europe is the wealth of values and ideas we share. Among them are respect for the uniqueness and the freedom for each human being, the principles of a democratic and pluralistic political system, a market economy, and a civic society with the rule of law. All of us respect the principle of unity in diversity and share a determination to foster creative cooperation between the different nations and ethnic, religious, and cultural groups— and the different spheres of civilization—that exist in Europe. . . .

Despite general agreement on the values upon which European integration should stand, this process today, . . . has encountered a number of obstacles. . . .

There are many reasons for this state of affairs, but I feel strongly that they all have one thing in common: the erroneous belief that the great European task before us is a purely technical, a purely administrative, or a

---

actions in NATO history—were successful. Serb forces did withdraw from the city. At the time of this writing, the civil war continues, but hopes for a negotiated settlement remain. If there is such a settlement, United Nations or NATO forces may well be required to enforce it.

Problems in the Wake of the Collapse of Communism

The collapse of communism in eastern Europe and the Soviet Union has presented Europe with new problems and new opportunities. The opportunities include the possibility of establishing democratic governments and market economies throughout the region. They also include the restoration of civil liberties in countries where they have not been known for over half a century. If the countries of the former Soviet bloc reorganize their economies successfully, their citizens may come to enjoy the kinds of consumer goods—and the standard of living they make possible—that have been available in western Europe for decades. Realizing these opportunities, however, is unlikely to be a rapid process and will require enormous patience. Such patience may be in short supply. Already by the winter of 1993–1994, there were indications that eastern Europeans have tired of the difficulties they face in transforming their economies. In Poland, for example, elections have brought many former

purely systematic matter. . . .

To put it more succinctly: Europe today lacks an ethos; it lacks imagination, it lacks generosity, it lacks the ability to see beyond the horizon of its own particular interests, be they partisan or otherwise. . . . Europe does not appear to have achieved a genuine and profound sense of responsibility for itself as a whole, and thus for the future of all those who live in it. . . .

The former Yugoslavia is the first great testing ground for Europe in the era that was initiated by the end of the cold war. . . .

Another one consists in how we deal with the temptation to open the back gate to the demons of nationalist collectivism with an apparently innocent emphasis on minority rights and on the right of minorities to self determination. At first sight, this emphasis would seem harmless and beyond reproach. But one real consequence could be new unrest and tension, because demands for self-determination inevitably lead to questioning the integrity of the individual states and the inviolability of their present borders, and even the validity of all postwar treaties. Attempts of this kind are dangerous chiefly because they look not to the future, but to the past, for they call in question the very principle of civil society and the indivisible rights of the individual, as well as the certainty that only democracy, individual rights and freedoms, and the civil principle can guarantee the genuinely full development of even that aspect of one's identity represented by membership in a nationality. . . .

If various Western states cannot rid themselves of their desire for a dominant position in their own sphere of interests, if they don't stop trying to outwit history by reducing the idea of Europe to a noble backdrop against which they continue to defend their own petty concerns, and if the post-Communist states do not make radical efforts to exorcise the ghosts their newly won freedom has let loose, then Europe will only with great difficulty be able to respond to the challenge of the present and fulfill the opportunities that lie before it.

Vaclav Havel, Address to the General Assembly of the Council of Europe, October 9, 1993, New York Review of Books, *November 18, 1993, p. 3.*

Communists back into political prominence. In Poland and elsewhere, the old Communist parties have disappeared, but their members and leaders remain active within the new political institutions.

The problems in the new political and economic situation are enormous. Unemployment is widespread throughout the former Soviet Union and eastern Europe. The plants and factories that the Communist governments built are obsolete. Many also are so polluting that they have left the former Communist nations with some of the worst environmental problems in the world. These nations also now recognize that, by the standards of western Europe, they are very poor. As a result, hundreds of thousands of people are migrating from eastern to western Europe looking for work. In western countries such as Germany, however, eastern European migrants, like those from elsewhere in the world, have encountered resentment, opposition, and physical violence. Responding to these ethnic tensions, western countries have taken steps to restrict immigration.

The nations of western Europe, facing considerable public resentment over the costs already incurred from the collapse of communism, are hesitant to send economic aid to the East. This is especially true in Germany, where the costs of unification have been very high. Many citizens of the former West Germany are angry about the state aid that has been directed to the former East Germany. Other parts of Europe, most notably Great Britain, are also experiencing an economic downturn and believe they lack the resources to aid the eastern Europeans. Western Europeans are also grappling with another issue—how should the former Communist economies relate to the European Economic Community? Many eastern Europeans want rapid economic integration, but western European leaders fear eastern Europe's economic difficulties could threaten prosperity in the West.

The political challenges of the collapse of communism are no less great than the economic. Civil war rages in Yugoslavia. Ethnic violence has already erupted in the former Soviet Union, where nuclear weapons are still available. The Czechs and the Slovaks, unable to establish a stable, unified state, divided Czechoslovakia into two separate nations in 1993. The liberty made possible by the end of the Communist governments has thus far tended to be used in pursuit of ethnic goals, leading almost inevitably to domestic political turmoil. Except for Romania, Bulgaria, and Greece, all of the nations between Germany and the Commonwealth of Independent States have existed as distinct political units within more or less their present borders only since World War I, although many of the national groups in them enjoyed some form of political autonomy decades or centuries earlier. Moreover, between World War I and 1989, all of them found themselves under either Fascist or Communist government at one time or another. After World War II, West Germany and Austria developed strong democratic institutions, but elsewhere this did not happen. The key question is whether democratic governments can survive in the midst of the resulting disorder, economic stagnation, and competing ethnic claims or whether they will succumb to some form of illiberal alternative.

The collapse of European communism has broader implications. It has almost certainly closed an era in the development of European socialism that began with the adoption of Marxist thought by German socialists in the 1870s. From that time, Marxism dominated European socialist thought. The Bolshevik victory in the Russian Revolution seemed to validate it, and the policies of Lenin and Stalin sought to extend it in Europe and elsewhere.

Now the Soviet Union and the Communist governments of eastern Europe—heirs to the Bolshevik Revolution—lie in ruins, the economies they built in collapse. As a result, Marxist socialism has been discredited, and socialism in general may find itself on the defensive. Other groups, as we have seen—feminists and environmentalists, for example—are now providing the kind of social criticism that had previously flowed from socialism. To play a role in the new era taking shape in Europe, socialists must come to grips with the benefits of markets, economic decentralization, and political democracy.

On another front, the collapse of European communism has profoundly altered international relations within Europe. The demise of the Warsaw Pact has raised concerns about the role of NATO. The primary function of this alliance had been to deter a Soviet attack on western Europe. As that danger recedes, maintaining the alliance becomes more difficult. Many argue that NATO should be kept as an instrument to preserve international order. Its failure to play an effective role in ending the Yugoslav civil war, however, raises doubts that it could counter the kinds of problems Europe may face in the future. Much debate has centered on the possible admission of some eastern European nations, once members of the Warsaw Pact, into NATO. Poland, the Czech Republic, and Hungary would like membership in NATO to protect themselves from possible future Russian aggression and to integrate themselves more fully into the west European economy. NATO leaders, concerned about appearing to isolate Russia, have hesitated to comply with the requests of these states. As of early 1994, NATO had offered them a form of association but not full membership.

⸻◆⸻

Although recent transformations in Europe have been rapid and stunning, they are securely embedded in the context of Western civilization. The concern for constitutional government has again come to the fore. The Church has played a major role in the revolutionary changes in eastern Europe. The Western penchant for critical self-examination survived in Soviet-dominated

Europe, at first secretly in intellectual circles, then emerging publicly in the political debates that followed the revolutions of 1989.

The desire of eastern Europeans to share in the prosperity of western Europe has been key to recent events. It would, however, be a mistake to explain the collapse of European communism only in terms of economic stagnation and consumer dissatisfaction. For more than forty years, the citizens of eastern Europe were denied the broad array of civil liberties that are almost taken for granted in western Europe and the United States. Lacking religious freedom, a free press, the right to free speech, the possibility of free assembly, and the security of law and judicial procedure, they lived under the shadow of police surveillance and arbitrary arrest. Individuals could not travel freely, workers could not organize independent unions, and even the most harmless associations, like hobby clubs, singing groups, and jazz ensembles, raised political suspicion. Communist Party governments jailed writers who voiced opposition and party officials who advocated reform. They repressed religious expression and imposed martial law when threatened with rebellion.

When the people of eastern Europe took to the streets in the summer and autumn of 1989, when Romanian students fell before the bullets of government troops, when citizens of Moscow resisted the August Coup, they carried banners and shouted slogans demanding democracy, fundamental political liberties, and human rights. This desire for constitutional government and respect for human dignity are part of the Western heritage, however much they have been denied or compromised over the centuries in different parts of the West.

Twice in the first half of the twentieth century, nationalism in Europe contributed to the outbreak of worldwide conflict. In the second half of the century, militant nationalism appeared remarkably to have disappeared as a significant force in European politics. In eastern Europe, the long years of Soviet domination suppressed nationalism and ethnic conflict. Recently, however, they have reemerged, unleashed by the collapse of communism. Europe once again faces the challenge of containing this threatening force and the ethnic strife that accompanies it. It is simply too early to predict whether the civil war in Yugoslavia will be replicated elsewhere, or whether it will be seen as a warning of the dangers of nationalism and ethnic rivalry.

Before the end of World War II, class conflict had also characterized much of European society. The recent prosperity in western Europe, however, has brought changes in the region's economic structure and reduced class strife. Many serious social problems nonetheless persist. Unemployment and the social strains of economic dislocation have not disappeared. Homeless people walk the streets of Europe as they do in the United States. The presence of workers from Pakistan, India, Turkey, and North Africa has heightened racial and ethnic tensions. And nobody can predict the political turmoil that might result from another serious worldwide economic downturn. The kind of class conflict that marked Europe's past, however, is clearly less evident than it was.

Indeed, the development of technology may come to be seen as a more important historical force in this century than was class struggle. For some observers, technology is only an enemy and a threat to the environment. Yet science has touched in a positive manner the lives of more people than might have been imagined even fifty years ago. And it will be from scientific understanding that the problems of the environment and resource shortages will be resolved. Rationalism has never been more a factor in everyday life, despite the continuing concern of some intellectuals over its limitations.

These persistent features of European life—concern for constitutionalism, tension between Church and state, pursuit of science and rationalism, and a penchant for self-criticism—have not ensured that its civilization, as well as the results flowing from it, will be morally good. Rather they have meant that Western civilization has possessed in itself the possibility of correcting and redirecting itself and of raising questions about what are the good life and the good society. The possibility of asking those questions is necessary before the desired improvement and reform can be attained. Perhaps the chief carriers of Western culture today are those who within its midst most criticize it and demand that it justify itself.

Review Questions

1. In what specific ways has Europe been "Americanized" in the second half of the twentieth century? How do you account for the trend toward a consumer society in the West? What population changes and migration patterns have marked the period since World War II and how have they affected Europe's economy and society?

2. How have women's social and economic roles changed in the second half of the twentieth century? What tensions and difficulties have new work patterns created for women? What changes and problems have women faced amidst the political instability in eastern Europe?

3. Discuss the changes in the pursuit and diffusion of knowledge in the twentieth century. What has been the effect of the communications revolution? Of the boom of universities? Has Western intellectual life become more unified or less so? Why?

4. Discuss the contributions of Nietzsche and Kierkegaard to existentialism. What does Sartre mean when he says that existentialism is a philosophy of anguish and despair? How is existentialism a response to the various crises of the twentieth century?

5. Trace the collapse of communism in eastern Europe and the Soviet Union. How important was Gorbachev in transforming the political and economic atmosphere of the Soviet Union? Why did he fail? Compare and contrast the revolutions of 1989 with the revolutions of 1848.

6. How did Marshal Tito maintain political stability in Yugoslavia after 1945? Why have vio-lence and civil war steadily escalated there in the 1990s? What are some of the problems and opportunities that the collapse of communism has presented to Europe?

Suggested Readings

G. AMBROSIUS and W. H. HUBBARD, *A Social and Economic History of Twentieth-Century Europe* (1989). The best one-volume treatment of the subject.

B. S. ANDERSON and J. P. ZINSSER, *A History of Their Own: Women in Europe from Prehistory to the Present*, Vol. 2 (1988). A broad-ranging survey.

T. G. ASH, *The Uses of Adversity* (1989). Important essays on central European culture and politics prior to the events of 1989.

T. G. ASH, *The Magic Lantern: The Revolution of '89 Witnessed in Warsaw, Budapest, Berlin and Prague* (1990). Essays by a longtime observer of central Europe.

P. BALDWIN, *The Politics of Social Solidarity: Class Bases of the European Welfare State 1875–1975* (1990). An excellent analysis of the political forces that allowed the welfare state to come into being.

I. BANAC (Ed.), *Eastern Europe in Revolution* (1992). Excellent articles on the events of 1989 and afterward.

J. H. BILLINGTON, *Russia Transformed: Breakthrough to Hope, Moscow, August, 1991* (1992). A thoughtful essay on the attempted coup.

E. BRAMWELL, *Ecology in the 20th Century: A History* (1989). Traces the environmental movement to its late-nineteenth-century origins.

W. M. BRINTON and A. RINZLER (Eds.), *Without Force or Lies: Voices from the Revolutions of Central Europe, 1989–90* (1990). Selections by major spokesmen for political change and reform.

R. CROSSMAN (Ed.), *The God That Failed* (1949). Essays by former Communist intellectuals.

P. DESAI, *Perestroika in Perspective: The Design and Dilemmas of Soviet Reform* (1989). A thoughtful essay on Gorbachev's reforms.

A. N. DRAGNICH, *Serbs and Croats: The Struggle in Yugoslavia* (1992). An introduction to the historical roots of the current struggle.

J. EISEN (Ed.), *The Glasnost Reader* (1990). An anthology of selections on political change in the Soviet Union.

M. ELLMAN and V. KONTOROVICH, *The Disintegration of the Soviet Economic System* (1992). An overview of the economic strains that the Soviet Union experienced during the 1980s.

M. I. GOLDMAN, *Gorbachev's Challenge: Economic Reform in the Age of High Technology* (1988). Emphasizes the economic goals of Gorbachev's program.

B. GWERTZMAN and M. T. KAUFMAN (Eds.), *The Collapse of Communism* (1991). A collection of contemporary news accounts.

B. GWERTZMAN and M. T. KAUFMAN (Eds.), *The Decline and Fall of the Soviet Empire* (1992). Another collection of contemporary news accounts.

W. F. HANRIEDER, *Germany, America, and Europe: Forty Years of German Foreign Policy* (1989). A major survey.

M. J. Hogan (Ed.), *The End of the Cold War: Its Meaning and Implications* (1992). A collection of essays by contributors from a wide political spectrum.

H. S. Hughes, *Sophisticated Rebels: The Political Culture of European Dissent, 1968–1987* (1988). A series of thoughtful essays on recent cultural critics.

W. G. Hyland, *The Cold War Is Over* (1990). Discussion of the end of Cold War tensions from the point of view of the United States.

T. Judt, *Past Imperfect: French Intellectuals, 1944–1956* (1992). An important study on French intellectuals and communism.

R. G. Kaiser, *Why Gorbachev Happened* (1992). A useful overview.

W. Laqueur, *Soviet Realities: Culture and Politics from Stalin to Gorbachev* (1990). Essays on developments in Soviet intellectual life.

C. Lemke and G. Marks (Eds.), *The Crisis of Socialism in Europe* (1992). Essay on the difficulties now confronted by socialism.

R. Maltby (Ed.), *Passing Parade: A History of Popular Culture in the Twentieth Century* (1989). A collection of essays on a topic just beginning to receive scholarly attention.

R. Medvedev and C. Chiesa, *Time of Change: An Insider's View of Russia's Transformation* (1989). An effort to explain recent changes through analysis of Soviet society and political structures.

Z. A. Medvedev, *Gorbachev* (1986). The best available biography for his early career.

P. H. Merkl, *German Unification in the European Context* (1993). The first major essay on the impact of German unity.

G. Montefiore, *Philosophy in France Today* (1983). A good introduction to one of the major centers of contemporary thought.

J. Morrison, *Boris Yeltsin* (1992). A useful biography.

B. Nahaylo and V. Swoboda, *Soviet Disunion: A History of the Nationalities Problem in the USSR* (1990). A discussion of one of the major areas of political difficulty today.

D. Oberdorfer, *The Turn: How the Cold War Came to an End: The United States and the Soviet Union 1983–1990* (1992). A major narrative by a Washington journalist.

M. Poster, *Existential Marxism in Postwar France* (1975). An excellent and clear work.

S. P. Ramet, *Social Currents in Eastern Europe: The Sources and Meaning of the Great Transformation* (1991). A broad survey of eastern European social life and popular culture on the eve of the revolutions of 1989.

S. P. Ramet (Ed.), *The Religious Policy in the Soviet Union* (1993). Essays on an important subject that has often received little attention.

D. Remnick, *Lenin's Tomb: The Last Days of the Soviet Empire* (1993). An excellent account by an American journalist working in the Soviet Union.

G. Ross, *Workers and Communists in France: From Popular Front to Eurocommunism* (1982). A useful survey.

J. Rothschild, *Return to Diversity: A Political History of East Central Europe Since World War II* (1989). A clear, well-organized introduction.

J. Ruscoe, *The Italian Communist Party, 1976–1981: On the Threshold of Government* (1982). Examines the party at the height of its influence.

H. A. Turner, *Germany from Partition to Reunification* (1992). The best brief introduction.

Index

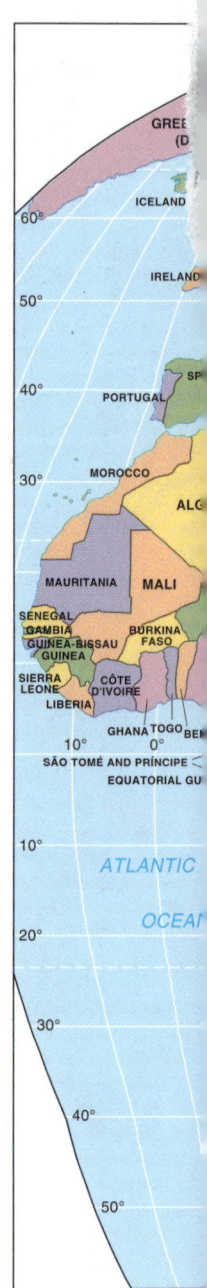

ARCTIC OCEAN

80°

70°

RUSSIA

UNITED
STATES
(ALASKA)

GREENLAND
(DEN)

70°

ICELAND

60°

60°

C A N A D A

50°

50°

ATLANTIC

40°

UNITED STATES

40°

30°

OCEAN

30°

Tropic of Cancer

BAHAMAS

U.S.
(HAWAII)

PACIFIC

20°

MEXICO

CUBA

DOMINICAN REP.

PUERTO RICO (U.S.)

20°

JAMAICA

HAITI

ANTIGUA & BARBUDA

OCEAN

BELIZE
HONDURAS

ST. CHRISTOPHER-
NEVIS

DOMINICA

ST. LUCIA

GUATEMALA
EL SALVADOR

NICARAGUA

ST. VINCENT
GRENADA

BARBADOS

COSTA RICA

TRINIDAD AND TOBAGO

10°

VENEZUELA

GUYANA

10°

PANAMA

SURINAM

COLOMBIA

FR. GUIANA

Equator

40°

140°

130°

120°

110°

100°

90°

0°

ECUADOR

B R A Z I L

10°

10°

10°

PERU

10°

20°

20°

20°

BOLIVIA

20°

Tropic of Capricorn

PARAGUAY

PITCAIRN
(UK)

30°

30°

30°

URUGUAY

30°

CHILE

ARGENTINA

40°

40°

40°

40°

50°

50°

50°

FALKLAND IS.
(UK)

S. GEORGIA
(UK)

50°

60°

IRELAND

50°

40°

PORTUGAL

SP

40°

30°

MOROCCO

ALG

30°

MAURITANIA

MALI

SENEGAL

GAMBIA

BURKINA
FASO

GUINEA-BISSAU
GUINEA

SIERRA
LEONE

CÔTE
D'IVOIRE

LIBERIA

GHANA TOGO

10°

SÃO TOMÉ AND PRÍNCIPE

0°

EQUATORIAL GU

10°

ATLANTIC

20°

OCEAN

20°

30°

30°

40°

40°

50°